Complete Peerage

OF

ENGLAND, SCOTLAND, IRELAND, GREAT BRITAIN

AND

THE UNITED KINGDOM

EXTANT, EXTINCT, OR DORMANT;

ALPHABETICALLY ARRANGED AND

EDITED BY

G. E. C.

VOLUME V.

L to M.

LONDON:
GEORGE BELL & SONS, YORK STREET, COVENT GARDEN.
EXETER: WILLIAM POLLARD & Co., NORTH STREET.
1893.

CONTENTS.

PEERAGES FROM **L to M** INCLUSIVE.

viz:—

L.

LADYKIRK.

See "MARJORIBANKS OF LADYKIRK, co. Berwick," Barony (*Marjoribanks*), *cr.* 12, and *ex.* 19 June 1873.

LAGEHAM.

See "ST. JOHN DE LAGEHAM" [co. Surrey], Barony (*St. John*), *cr.* 1299; *dormant* since 1349.

LAHORE.

See "HARDINGE OF LAHORE AND KING'S NEWTON, co. Derby," Viscountcy (*Hardinge*), *cr.* 1846.

LAKE OF DELHI AND LASWARY AND ASTON CLINTON, co. Buckingham.

Barony. I. 1804.
Viscountcy. I. 1807.

1. GERALD LAKE, of Aston Clinton, Bucks, 1st s.[a] of Lancelot Charles LAKE, of Flambards, in Harrow on the Hill, Midx., by Letitia, da. of John GUMLEY, of Isleworth, was *b.* 27 July 1744; entered the Army (1st Life Guards), 9 May 1759, in which he became Major Gen. in 1790; Lieut. Gen. in 1797, and finally General, 29 April 1802. He was also Col. of the 53d Foot, 1794; of the 73d Foot, 1797, and of the 80th in 1800. He was M.P. for Aylesbury, 1790—1802, as also for Armagh [I.] 1800. In 1797 he was in command of the north of Ireland, during the rebellion, and defeated a French force which there landed in Aug. 1798. From Aug. 1800 to July 1805 he was COMMANDER IN CHIEF in India during the Mahratta war which, in conjunction with Sir Arthur Wellesley (afterwards Duke of Wellington) he brought to a successful close, after the battles of Delhi, Assaye, and Laswary, 11 and 23 Sep. and 1 Nov. 1803. He consequently received the thanks of Parl. and was *cr.*, 13 Sep. 1804,[b] BARON LAKE OF DELHI AND LASWARY[c] AND ASTON CLINTON, co. Buckingham, and (three years later), 4 Nov. 1807, VISCOUNT LAKE OF DELHI AND LASWARY[c] AND ASTON CLINTON, co. Buckingham. He *m.*, 3 July 1770, Elizabeth, da. of Edward BARKER, of St. Juliaus, Herts, sometime Consul at Tripoli. She, who was *b.* 17 Aug. 1751, *d.* 20 July 1798, and was *bur.* at Aston Clinton. He (being an inveterate gambler) *d.* a poor man, in Lower Brook street, 20 Feb. 1808, aged 64, and was *bur.* 5 March at Aston Clinton. Will pr. 1808.

II. 1808. *2.* FRANCIS GERARD (LAKE), VISCOUNT LAKE OF DELHI, &c., s. and h. *b.* 31 March 1772, and *bap.* at Curzon Street, Chapel; entered the Army 1790, in which eventually (1821) he became Lieut. Gen., being sometime (1798) Lieut. Col. of the 1st Foot Guards, and subsequently (1808) of the

---

(a) The second son, Warwick Lake, Commissioner of the Stamp office, and Gent. of the Privy Chamber, *d.* unm., 31 Jan. 1821, aged 76, and was *bur.* at Kensington.

(b) It is somewhat remarkable that, tho' he had served with distinction upwards of 40 years in the Army, he was never knighted.

(c) See vol. i, p. 79, note "a," *sub* "Amherst," as to titles referring to some victory gained by the grantee.

60th Foot; *suc. to the peerage*, and to a pension of £2,000 a year, 20 Feb. 1808; was a Lord of the Bedchamber, 1813, and again 1820 to 1830. He *m.* firstly 1 Jan. 1800, at St. Geo. Han. sq., Priscilla, widow of Sir Bellingham GRAHAM, 6th Bart, sister of Charles, 1st EARL WHITWORTH, da. of Sir Charles WHITWORTH, of Leybourne, co. Kent, by Martha, da. of Richard SHELLEY. She *d.* 8 May 1833 at Bath, in her 75th year and was *bur.* at Norton Conyers, co. York. Will pr. June 1833. He *m.* secondly 12 Aug. 1833 at "Crawley's Hotel," Albemarle Street, Piccadilly, Anne, 2nd da. of Admiral Sir Richard ONSLOW, 1st Bart, by Anne, da. of Matthew MITCHELL. He *d.* s.p., 12 May 1836, aged 64, at Crawley's Hotel afsd., and was *bur.* at Aston Clinton. Will pr. June 1836. His widow *m.* 14 Sep. 1837, at Dover (as his second wife) Henry GRITTON, of Woolwich, Lieut. Royal Marines, and *d.* 4 April 1853, at Brussels.

III. 1836, to 1848. *3.* WARWICK (LAKE), VISCOUNT LAKE OF DELHI, &c., yst. and only surv. br. and h.,(a) *b.* 9 Nov. 1783; was post-captain in the Navy, but dismissed (for cruelty) in 1810; Lieut. 7th Foot, 1815; Royal Agent for Van Diemen's Land, 1832; *suc. to the peerage* and to a pension of £2,000 a year, 12 May 1836. He *m.* 28 Nov. 1815, at Lewisham, co. Kent, Elizabeth Duncan, only da. James Beveridge DUNCAN, of Damside and Marlefield, co. Perth, by Isabel da. and coheir of Thomas MARSHALL, sometime Provost of Perth. He *d.* s.p.m.s.(b) 24 June 1848, aged 64, in Park Street, Grosvenor Square, when *all his honours* became *extinct*. Will pr. Aug. 1848. His widow who was *b.* at Blackheath, May 1791, and *bap.* at St. Andrews Undershaft, London, became sole heir to her brother, James Beveridge Duncan, and *d.* 16 Oct. 1865, aged 74.

LAKE SUNDERLIN.

See "SUNDERLIN OF LAKE SUNDERLIN, co. Westmeath," Barony, [I], (*Malone*) *cr.* 1785; *ex.* 1816.

LAMBART OF CAVAN.

See "CAVAN," (or "Lambart of Cavan") Barony [I] (*Lambart*), *cr.* 1618.

LAMBTON and LAMBTON CASTLE.

See "DURHAM OF THE CITY OF DURHAM AND OF LAMBTON CASTLE, co. Durham," Barony (*Lambton*), *cr.* 1828.

i.e. "LAMBTON" Viscountcy (*Lambton*) *cr.* 1833, with the EARLDOM OF DURHAM, which see.

LAMINGTON.

Barony. I. 1880. *1.* ALEXANDER-DUNDAS-ROSS COCHRANE-WISHART-BAILLIE, s. and h. of Admiral Sir Thomas John COCHRANE,(c) G.C.B. (who *d.* 19 Oct. 1872, aged 83), by his first wife, Matilda (who took the name of *Ross-Wishart* and *d.* 4 Sep. 1819), da. of Lieut. Gen. Sir Charles LOCKHART-ROSS, 7th Bart. [S.], which Matilda was only child of his first wife, Maria Theresa, COUNTESS LOCKHART-WISHART in the Holy Roman Empire; was *b.* 24 Nov. 1816; ed. at Eton and at Trin. Coll., Cambridge; B.A., 1837; M.P. for

(a) The other brother, Lieut. Col. the Hon. George Augustus Frederick Lake, *b.* 21 Feb. 1781 *d.* unm. He was severely wounded (by the side of his father) at Laswary, 1 Nov. 1803, and was slain at Vimiera in Portugal, 17 Aug. 1808.

(b) He left two daughters and coheirs of whom the eldest was unm. but the youngest, Elizabeth Georgiana, *b.* 19 March 1821, *m.* 3 Aug. 1866, John Austin GLOAG, who *d.* 1883.

(c) He was s. and h. of Admiral the Hon. Sir Alexander Forrester Inglis Cochrane, G.C.B. (who *d.* 29 June 1832, aged 73), 6th s. of Thomas, 8th Earl of Dundonald [S.]

Bridport, 1841-52; for Lanarkshire, Feb. to April 1857; for Honiton, 1859-68, and for the Isle of Wight, 1870 to 1880, when (having been in the House of Commons for 40 years) he was *cr.*, 3 May 1880, BARON LAMINGTON of Lamington, co. Lanark. He was a Knight of the Redeemer of Greece. He *m.*, 4 Dec. 1844, Annabella Mary Elizabeth, 1st da. of Andrew Robert DRUMMOND, of Cadlands, co. Southampton, by Elizabeth Frederica, da. of John Henry (MANNERS), 5th DUKE OF RUTLAND. He *d.* at 26 Wilton crescent, 15 Feb. 1890, aged 73.(a) His widow, who was *b.* 4 April 1824, living 1892.

II. 1890. 2. CHARLES WALLACE ALEXANDER NAPIER ROSS (COCHRANE-BAILLIE), BARON LAMINGTON, only s. and h., *b.* 31 July 1860; ed. at Eton and at Ch. Ch., Oxford; B.A., 1831; Assistant Private Sec. to the Prime Minister (Salisbury), 1885-86; M.P. for North St. Pancras, 1886, till on 15 Feb. 1890, he *suc. to the peerage.*

Family Estates.—These, in 1883, consisted of 10,833 acres in Lanarkshire and 1,750 in Haddingtonshire, besides 125 (worth £680 a year) in Hampshire. *Total* 12,708 acres, worth £10,463 a year exclusive of £1,388 for minerals. *Principal Residences.* Lamington, near Biggar, co. Lanark, and Quarr Abbey, near Ryde, Isle of Wight.

LANARK.

i.e., "LANARK" ["Lanerick"] Earldom [S.] (*Hamilton*), *cr.* 1639; *ex.* (apparently) 1651. See "HAMILTON" Dukedom [S.], *cr.* 1643, under the 2d Duke.

LANCASTER, or DE LANCASTRE.

Barony by Writ. I. 1299, to 1334. JOHN DE LANCASTER or LANCASTRE, of Rydal, co. Westmorland, s. and h. of Roger DE LANCASTER,(b) of Rydal afsd., by Philippa, 1st da. and coheir of Hugh DE BOLEBEC, of Northumberland; *suc.* his father in 1291; served in the French and Scotch wars and was sum. to Parl. as a Baron (LORD DE LANCASTRE) by writs from 29 Dec. (1299), 28 Ed. I., to 12 Dec. (1309), 3 Ed. II.(c) His name as "*Joh's. de Lancastr,' Dns. de Grisdale,*" is affixed to the letter of the Barons to the Pope in 1301.(d) He *d.* s.p. 1334 when *the Barony became extinct.* His widow, Annora, *d.* 1338.(e)

Barony by Writ. I. 1299. 1. HENRY PLANTAGENET, *styled* "OF LANCASTER," 2d. s. of Edmund, EARL OF LANCASTER, who was yr. s. of King Henry III, was *b.* about 1281, and sum. to Parl. (v.p.) as a Baron (LORD DE LANCASTRE) by writ 6 Feb. (1298/9), 27 Ed. I. addressed "*Henrico de Lancastre, nepoti Regis,*" and by other writs directed "*Henrico de Lancastre,*" from that year, to 26 Dec. (1323), 17 Ed. II. On 29

(a) He was well known in society and is the "*Buckhurst*" in Disraeli's novel of "*Coningsby,*" being ("in the forties") one of the young England party. His very interesting reminiscences (of that period) entitled "*In the days of the Dandies*" were being pub. in Blackwood's Magazine at the time of his death.

(b) This Roger (who *d.* 1291) was bastard brother of William de Lancaster, feudal Lord of Kendal (*d.* about 1246) who was s. and h. of Gilbert Fitz Roger Fitz Reinfred, by Helewise, da. and h. of William de Lancaster, s. and h. of William de Tailbois, feudal Lord of Kendal, who assumed the name of "Lancaster."

(c) He was also sum. 26 Jan. (1296/7), 25 Ed. I. See vol. i, p. 111, note "b," *sub* "AP ADAM," as to this writ not constituting a regular writ of summons to Parl.

(d) See account thereof in "*Nicolas,*" pp. 761-809.

(e) See "*Coll. Top. et Gen.,*" vii, p. 265. It appears that on *her* death one "John Lancaster, of Holgill, was found to be one of her heirs *virtute doni.*" The heir of the Baron (according to Dugdale) was Richard, son of Richard de Plaiz, aged 12 years at his death.

March 1324, he was restored in blood and on 10 May 1324 was *cr.* EARL OF LEICESTER. In 1327 he was restored to the family honours (forfeited in 1322 by his eldest br.) becoming thus EARL OF LANCASTER and sitting, as such, in Parl. See fuller particulars under that dignity, *cr.* 1267, *sub.* the 3d. Earl. He *d.* 22 Sep. 1345.

II. 1335, to 1362. *2.* HENRY (PLANTAGENET), LORD DE LANCASTRE, s. and h. afs., *b.* about 1299, was v.p. sum. to Parl. as above, 3 Feb. (1334/5) 9 Ed. III, and was (also v.p.), *cr.*, 16 March 1337, EARL OF DERBY. He was, after his succession to his Father's honours, *cr.* EARL OF LINCOLN, 20 Aug. 1349 and, on 6 March 1351/2, was *cr.* DUKE OF LANCASTER. See fuller particulars under that dignity. He *d.* s.p.m., 13 March 1361/2, when (the rest of his honours becoming presumably extinct) the Barony of Lancastre fell into abeyance between his two daughters and coheirs.(a)

* * * * *

III. 1362? *3.* BLANCHE, DUCHESS OF LANCASTER, possibly *suo jure* COUNTESS OF DERBY (see that dignity), da. and coheir, became *suo jure* BARONESS DE LANCASTRE, on the death (1362?) s.p. of her elder and only sister, Maud, DUCHESS OF BAVARIA. She was 1st wife of John (PLANTAGANET), DUKE OF LANCASTER (4th s. of King Edw. III), whom she *m.* 19 May 1359, at the age of 12 years. See fuller particulars under that dignity, *cr.* 1362. She *d.* 1369.

IV. 1369. to 1399. *4.* HENRY (PLANTAGENET), LORD DE LANCASTRE and possibly (as early in 1369) EARL OF DERBY, s. and h. *b.* about 1366. On 3 Sep. (1385), 9 Ric. II, he was sum. to parl. *as* EARL OF DERBY. On 29 Sep. 1397, he was *cr.* DUKE OF HEREFORD and, on his fathers death, 3 Feb. 1398/9, he became DUKE OF LANCASTER. See fuller particulars under that dignity. On 29 Sep. 1399, he *suc.* to the throne as **Henry IV**, when *all his honours* became *merged* in the Crown.

LANCASTER [county of.]

[ROGER OF POITOU, 3d s. of Roger, EARL OF SHREWSBURY (the "*Comes Rogerus*"(b) of the Domesday survey), *b.* about 1060, having built the Castle of Lancaster and founded the priory there, is sometimes said to have been (about 1094?) *cr.* EARL OF LANCASTER. He, who *m.* before July 1094, Almodis, da. and h. of Audebert II., COUNT OF LA MARCHE, in Poitou, is generally known as COUNT OF LA MARCHE. He was banished from England about 1102.]

[JOHN (PLANTAGENET), EARL OF GLOUCESTER, 6th and yst. s. of **King Henry II.**, *b.* 24 Dec. 1166, is often considered to have been EARL OF CORNWALL and sometimes EARL OF LANCASTER.(c) He was *deprived* of his honours in 1194 but *restored* in 1195. He ascended the throne, as **King John**, 6 April 1199, when *all his honours merged* in the Crown. See fuller particulars under the EARLDOM OF GLOUCESTER].

(a) These were (1) Maud, 22 years old at her Fathers' Death in 1361/2, *m.* William Count of Holland and Zealand, Duke of Bavaria, and *d.* s.p. about 1362. (2) Blanche, *m.* John (Plantagenet), Duke of Lancaster, as in the text.

(b) See vol. i, p. 188, *sub* "Arundel," as to this Roger, who, from his tenure of the Castle of Arundel, is sometimes considered as Earl of Arundel.

(c) See vol. iii, p. 66, note "a," as to the Earldoms supposed to have been conferred on (Prince) John by his brother King Richard I.

Earldom. I. 1267, or 1276. 1. EDMUND PLANTAGENET, *styled* "CROUCHBACK" [" *Gibbosus* "], 4th and yst. but 2d surv. s. of **King Henry III.**, by Eleanor, da. and coheir of Raymond Berenger, COUNT OF PROVENCE, was *b.* 16 Jan. 1245/6,(a) in London, and was, in his 8th year, invested by the Pope's legate, 18 Oct. 1254, as *King of Sicily*, a kingdom of which he never obtained possession. He was *cr.*, 26 Oct. 1265, EARL OF LEICESTER and Seneschal or *High Steward of England* (on the forfeiture of Simon de Montfort) which dignities with all the (other) honours of Simon (the late Earl), were confirmed to him by a charter of Ed. I. in 1274.(b) Having, also, on the final forfeiture of Robert Ferrers, late Earl of Derby, been granted 12 July 1266, his vast estates, which included the honour of Derby, he is accordingly sometimes spoken of as EARL OF DERBY. See vol. iii, p. 67, *sub* "Derby," as to this theory. Finally, 30 June 1267, he had a charter of the honour,(c) county, castle, and town of Lancaster to him and the heirs of his body, in which charter, however, "he is *not* styled EARL OF LANCASTER tho' probably he was [so] *cr.* at the same time by the girding of the sword, being sum. to Parl. as *Earl of Lancaster* from 12 Dec. (5 Ed. I.), 1276"(d) In right of his second wife (whom he *m.* in or before 1276) he was styled COUNT OF CHAMPAGNE AND BRIE in France. He was joint Ambassador to France in 1279; served in the Scotch, Welsh, and French wars; and had lic. in 1292 to castellate his house called "The Savoy"(e) in Westminster. He *m.* firstly 6 April 1269 (or 8 April 1270), Avelina, who may be considered *suo jure* COUNTESS OF ALBEMARLE (see that dignity.) She made proof of her age in 1273 but *d.* s.p. 1274 and was *bur.* in Westm. Abbey. *Inq.* 12 March 1274/5. He *m.* secondly, in or before 1276, Blanche,(f) Dow. QUEEN OF NAVARRE, da. of Robert, COUNT OF ARTOIS (s. of LOUIS VIII, KING OF FRANCE), by Matilda, da. of Henry, DUKE OF BRABANT. He *d.* 5 June 1296, in his 50th year, at Bayonne (while besieging Bourdeaux), and was *bur.* in Westm. Abbey. His widow *d.* 2 May 1302.

II. 1296, to 1322. 2. THOMAS (PLANTAGENET, *styled* "OF LANCASTER"),(g) EARL OF LANCASTER and EARL OF LEICESTER *High Steward of England*, s. and h., by second wife, *b.* about 1278; *suc. to the peerage*, 5 June 1296, having livery of his lands 8 Sep. 1298. He was constantly engaged in the Scotch Wars, and was bearer of the "*curtana*" (sword) at the coron. of Ed. II., 25 Feb. 1308. He is styled on one of his seals,(h) 12 Feb. 1301, "Earl of

(a) There was a tradition that this Edmund was *older* than his brother King Edward I. (who in point of fact was six and a half years his senior, having been *b.* 17 June 1239), but that he was *postponed* to his said brother on account of his deformity. On this pretext John "of Gaunt," Duke of Lancaster, moved in Parl. (1395-96), 19 Ric. II., that his own son Henry (afterwards King Henry IV.) who was, in right of his mother, *heir of line* to the said *Edmund* "might be adjudged heir to the Kingdom of England." (See "*Sandford*," Book iv, p. 252), a motion which treated the then King and his predecessors, the three Edwards, as usurpers.

(b) See "Courthope," *sub* "Leicester."

(c) "The honor of Lancaster at that time extended into the counties of Lancaster, Norfolk, Suffolk, Lincoln, Nottingham, Leicester, Derby, York, Rutland and Stafford"—"within these possessions the Earls, and subsequently the Dukes, of Lancaster, enjoyed, by grants from the Crown, certain *Jura Regalia* and such high prerogative rights as were communicable to a subject." [30th Report of the D.K. of the Pub. Records (1869), p. iv.]

(d) See "Courthope," *sub* "Lancaster."

(e) This remains as part of the estates of the Duchy of Lancaster to the present period.

(f) Vincent (in his eagerness to contradict Brooke), "against the authority of Reuanerus, Heninges, Albitius, Favianus, and others would prove this Queen of Navarre's name to be *Elianor*, only depending upon the authority of *one* record for the same; but with the current of so many authors I have seen above half a dozen records that plainly prove her name to be *Blanch* and not Elianor." [*Sandford.*]

(g) His *surname* was that of the title of his father's *peerage* as was not unusual at that period; so also the sons of the Earls of Arundel were styled "Arundel," &c.

(h) In the circumscription on *another* seal engraved in "Sandford" there is no mention of "Derby" (or "Ferrers"), the words being "*Sigillum Thome Comitis Lancastrie et Leicestrie, Seneschalli Anglie.*"

Lancaster, Leicester and *Ferrers*" which last must be taken as equivalent to EARL OF DERBY. Having *m.* on or before 28 Oct. 1294, Alice, then aged 11, who may in (1312) be considered as *suo jure* COUNTESS OF LINCOLN AND SALISBURY, being only surv. da. and h. of Henry (DE LACY), EARL OF LINCOLN (who *d.* 5 Feb. 1311/2), by his first wife Margaret (who may be considered as *suo jure* COUNTESS OF SALISBURY, and who *d.* 22 Nov. 1310). he may, in or after 1312, be considered as EARL OF LINCOLN AND SALISBURY, and he did homage for these (his wife's) possessions in 1312. Having taken a prominent part with the Barons against the King's favourites, he was taken prisoner at Broughbridge, 16 March 1321/2, and beheaded on the 22d. at his Castle of Pontfract, when, having been attainted, *all his honours* became *forfeited.* He *d.* s.p. aged about 44 and was *bur.* at Pontefract.(a) His widow *m.* before 1326 Eubulus (LE STRANGE), LORD LE STRANGE (so sum., from 8 Dec. 1326 to 1 April 1335), who is sometimes, in her right, *styled* EARL OF LINCOLN, and who *d.* s.p. 1335, and was *bur.* in Berling Abbey. She *m.* thirdly, early in 1336, Hugh (DE FRENE), LORD FRENE (so sum. 29 Nov. 1336), who is sometimes, in her right, *styled* EARL OF LINCOLN, and who *d.* s.p. Dec. 1336 at Perth. The Countess herself, who was *b.* 1283, *d.* s.p. 2 Oct. 1348, and was *bur.* at Berling Abbey afsd.

* * * * *

III. 1327. *3.* HENRY PLANTAGENET, styled "OF LANCASTER,"(b) next br. and h., *b.* about 1281; was sum. to Parl. (v.p.) as a Baron (LORD DE LANCASTRE) by writ 6 Feb. (1298/9), 27 Ed. I., addressed "*Henrico de Lancastre, nepoti Regis,*" and by other writs directed "*Henrico de Lancastre*" from that year to 26 Dec. (1323), 17 Ed. II. He was one of the Barons whose signature as "*Henr. de Lancastr., Dnus. de Muneme*" [*i.e.*, Monmouth], appears on the letter of the Barons to the Pope in 1301.(c) He was bearer of the Rod with the Dove at the Coronation, 25 Feb. 1308, of Edward II. Having been restored in blood on 29 March he was on 10 May 1321, *cr.* EARL OF LEICESTER and was sum. to Parl. 4 Aug. following, and subsequently, as "*Henry de Lancaster, Earl of Leicester.*" He was in the Scotch wars and (like his brother) took an active part against King Edward II. whom he sometime (at his Castles of Monmouth, Ledbury, and Kenilworth), kept in custody. On the accession of Edward III., he was appointed his Guardian, and when, by Act of Parl. 7 March 1326/7 (1 Ed. III.), the attainder of his br., Earl Thomas, was reversed, he became EARL OF LANCASTER [1267], EARL OF LEICESTER [1265], and *High Steward of England.* Some additional *Jura Regalia* were granted to him in 1342.(d) He became blind in 1329. He *m.* in 1298 Maud, da. and h. of Sir Patrick CHAWORTH, of Kidwelly, by Isabel, da. of William (BEAUCHAMP), EARL OF WARWICK. He *d.* 22 Sep. 1345, aged about 64, and was *bur.* in great state at Leicester. Will pr. 15 Feb. 1345/6, at Lincoln. His widow was living (38 Ed. III.), 1364.

IV. 1345. Dukedom. I. 1351, to 1361. *1* and *4.* HENRY (PLANTAGENET, *styled* "OF LANCASTER,"(b) also "OF GROSMONT," as also "TORTCOL" [*Wry-neck*]), EARL OF LANCASTER,(e) LEICESTER, DERBY, &c., *High Steward of England*, only s. and h., *b.* about 1300 at Grosmont, co. Monmouth. He was sum. v.p. to Parl. 3 Feb. (1334/5), 9 Ed. III., in his father's Barony as LORD DE LANCASTRE and was (also v.p.) *cr.* 16 March 1336/7, EARL OF DERBY "to hold to him and his heirs."(f) He distinguished himself greatly in the wars with France. He was v.p. elected K.G. (as *Earl of Derby*) in 1344, being one of the 25 original Knights(g) of

---

(a) There is a very full account of his capture in *Dugdale* as also of his merits (and demerits) "many miracles" being "reported to have been afterwards wrought in the place where his corpse was buried."

(b) See p. 5, note "g."

(c) See "*Nicolas*," pp. 761—809, for a full account thereof.

(d) See 30th Rep. of the D.K. of the Pub. Records, p. iv.

(e) See p. 7, note "d."

(f) See vol. iv, p. 42, note "c," *sub* "Gloucester," for a list of the creations made at that date.

(g) See a list of these in vol. i, p. 276, note "a," *sub* "Beauchamp."

that most noble Order. He *suc.* his father 22 Sep. 1345, as EARL OF LANCASTER AND LEICESTER and *High Steward of England*. He was also *Lord of Bergerac* (1 June 1347), *and of Beaufort* in France. In 1349 he "surrendered his grant *in tail* to the King, because, as it was alleged, the *Jura Regalia* granted to his father in 1342 were of a magnitude so great that they appeared to the King and his council to be *ad maximum dampnum et nimiam exhæredationem Regis*." He, however, "was permitted to hold those royal rights during his life-time, as appears by the Charter granted to him on the 25 Sept. 1349, the terms of which are precisely the same as in the surrendered charter, except that the former was *in tail* and the present for *life* only."(a) He was cr. 20 Aug. 1349, EARL OF LINCOLN,(b) and, finally, on 6 March 1350/1, was *cr.* DUKE OF LANCASTER with Palatine jurisdiction(c) for life within the county of Lancaster. He is said to have been *cr.* by King David II. [S.] EARL OF MORAY [S.] He *m.* before 1338 Isabel, da. of Henry (DE BEAUMONT), 1st LORD BEAUMONT (sometime EARL OF BUCHAN [S.]), by Alice, 1st da. and coheir of Sir Alexander COMYN, niece and heir of line to John, EARL OF BUCHAN [S.] He *d.* s.p.m. (of the plague) 13 March 1360/1. and was *bur.* (with his father) at Leicester. At his death *the Dukedom became extinct* and the other *honours* may, most probably, be considered to have *reverted to the Crown*, tho' in right of his da. (and eventually sole heir) his son in law (see next below) her husband claimed the four Earldoms of Lancaster, Derby, Lincoln, and Leicester. The Duke's will, in which he styles himself "*Duke of Lancaster*,(d) *Earl of Derby, Lincoln, and Leicester, Steward of England,*

(a) See 30th Rep. of the D.K. of the Pub. Records (1869) p. iv, where it is added that "this decision may have arisen from the fact that the Earl had no male issue, and there might be great inconvenience in allowing these royal rights to be enjoyed by the husbands of his daughters."

(b) "The words of this Charter are peculiar and show very plainly in what manner the grant of the annuity for the third penny carried with it the title of EARL OF LINCOLN. The words are, 'Nos sibi nomen Comitis Lincoln adicimus volentes et concedentes q'd nedum ip's set heredes sui imp'petuum h'eant et teneant nomen illud. Et ne d'c'm nomen nudum penitus dicatr et inutile, dedimus et concessimus et hac carta n'ra confirmavimus p'fato Comiti sub no'ie Comitis Lincoln viginti libras p'cipiend' sibi et heredibus suis p'tercio denario dci. comitatus.'" [*Courthope.*]

(c) This was the *second* Dukedom conferred in England that of CORNWALL (granted to the King's eldest son in 1337) being the first. The *Palatinate* jurisdiction of the DUKEDOM of Lancaster "was in the EARLDOM of Lancaster altho' now to be administered under the higher *personal dignity of Duke*," the patent of the Dukedom giving the grantee "Palatinate jurisdiction similar to that of Chester within the said *county* of Lancaster." Both Dukedoms (Cornwall and Lancaster) were *cr.* in Parl. "by girding." The patent of the Dukedom of Lancaster "contains no words of limitation whatever, being *prefato Henrico nomen Ducis Lancast. imponimus et ipsum de nomine Ducis dicti loci per cincturam gladii p'sentialiter investimus*; the next clause gives him a Chancery within the said COUNTY *ad totam vitam suam*, so that this dignity may be considered to have been a life estate." [*Courthope* "on dignities," pp. lxii-lxiii.] Thus the *Duchy* of Lancaster, of which the muniments [presented by Queen Victoria to the nation] are *private* (tho' concerning the *entire* jurisdiction of its vast dominion) *includes* the *Palatinate*, as *one* of its members. The muniments of the Palatinate, however, are *public*, tho' purely *local*, and remain in the county to which they refer. See 30th Report of the D.K. of the Pub. Records. It is also there remarked "that the *county* of Lancaster *became* a *palatinate* in [1351] 25 Ed. III. in the person of Henry, 1st Duke of Lancaster; it, however, *ceased* to be a *palatinate* on his death, in 1361, and continued extinguished for 16 [*sic*] years. In 1377 [*sic*, but *query* if not 1364], however, King Edward III. *revived* it in the person of his son, John of Gaunt. That illustrious prince had thus conferred upon him *Jura Regalia* within the county Palatine, co-extensive with those exercised by the King of England in counties *not Palatinate*. From that time to the present, the Palatinate of Lancaster has always been dealt with and described as being a parcel or member of the greater regality—the Duchy of Lancaster, under which comprehensive denomination the county palatine is included."

(d) *The Barony* of Lancaster when its owner was *Earl* of the same place, as also the *Earldom* of Lancaster when he was *Duke* of the *same place* are (according apparently to the ancient custom in such cases) omitted. See vol. iv, p. 143, note "c" (*circa finem*), *sub* "Hamilton," as to this practise in Scottish titles.

Lord of Brigerak and Beaufort," is dat. at Leicester Castle 15 and pr. at Leicester 30 March and in London 9 May 1361.[a] His wife survived him.

Earldom. V. 1361.
Dukedom. II. 1362.

1 and *5*. JOHN PLANTAGENET, *styled* "of Gaunt," 4th but 3d. surv. s. of **King Edward III.**, by Philippa, da. of William, COUNT OF HOLLAND AND HAINAULT, was *b.* 24 June 1340, at Ghent [*Gaunt*] in Flanders, and was, in his infancy, *cr.*, 20 Sep. 1342, EARL OF RICHMOND, a dignity which (30 years later) he resigned to the King, his Father, 25 June 1372.[b] Having *m.* 19 May 1359, Blanche da. and eventually (10 April 1362), sole heir to Henry (PLANTAGENET), DUKE OF LANCASTER abovenamed, he in her right obtained, firstly [1361] the moiety and finally [1362] the entirety of the great possessions of her father becoming (possibly) thus [in 1361], EARL OF LANCASTER,[c] DERBY[d] and LINCOLN,[e] and [in 1362], EARL OF LEICESTER[f] and *High Steward of England*, no less than 4 Earldoms in addition to his own Earldom of Richmond. It is certain that these 4 were in several official documents allowed to him.[g] **K.G.**, 1361, being, 13 Nov. 1362, *cr.* DUKE OE LANCASTER.[c] In right of his second marriage in 1372 (shortly after her Father's death), with Constance, da. and heir of line of Pedro, King of Castile and Leon, he assumed the style of KING OF CASTILE AND LEON[h] in 1372, which however, in 1388, he relinquished in favour of his son in law. He was thrice (1369, 1370, and 1373), in chief command in France, but neither there nor in his expedition (1386) for the conquest of Castile was he much distinguished. He was, however, on

---

(a) Nichols's "*Royal Wills.*"

(b) Patent 46 Ed. III., m. 25.

(c) "In the notice of his creation to the Dukedom of Lancaster in the Rolls of Parliament, he is styled Earl of Lancaster, a dignity to which he could only have succeeded in right of his wife, under the Charter of 30 June 1267." [*Courthope*]. "The *Jura Regalia*, however, which were attached to the earldom," and which had become, in 1361, vested in the Crown, "remained there until 1364, in which year King Edward III. granted them to his son John of Gaunt and Blanche his wife (who had inherited her sister Maude's portion, and had become sole heir of her father Henry, Duke of Lancaster) in nearly the same terms as in the before-mentioned charters severally granted in [1342 and 1349] 16 and 23 Ed. III. In the recital of the charter [of 1364] 38 Ed. III. to John of Gaunt and Blanche his wife, it is, however, distinctly stated that the surrender by Earl Henry in 1349, and the cancellation of the charter granted in 1342, were invalid acts, because they were in disherison of the heirs of the Earl's body issuing according to the custom of the realm, and could not be cancelled, but in vigour ought to remain. King Richard II., in the 20th year of his reign [1396-97] granted a further extension of those rights and settled them in perpetuity on the Dukes of Lancaster."

(d) It does not appear, however, that the title of *Earl of Derby* was at this time considered as attendant on the possessions of the Ferrers family, which had been inherited by the Lady Blanche of Lancaster, but this Earldom was undoubtedly one of four (Richmond, Derby, Lincoln and Leicester) used by her husband, when Duke of Lancaster. See Vol. iii, p. 68, note "a," *sub.* "Derby."

(e) The estates of the de Lacy family, Earls of Lincoln, appear to have been part of the heritage of the Lady Blanche, whose husband styled himself *Earl of Lincoln*. See note "d" next above.

(f) The Castle and honor of Leicester (on which, however, remarks Courthope "it does not appear that at this time, the title of *Earl of Leicester* was considered as attendant) was allotted to the Lady Maud, the elder coheir, but on her death s.p., 10 April 1362, devolved on the Lady Blanche her only sister, whose husband styled himself Earl of Leicester. See note "d" next above.

(g) "Johan Fitz du Roy Dengleterre, Duc de Guyene et de Lancastre, *conte de Derby, de Nicol.* [the most usual terme for *Lincolne*, in all ancient French records and evidences] *et Leycestre*, Seneschall Dengleterre, a toux, &c. This is out of his owne deed." See "*Vincent*," pp. 298 and 321. This deed was after his resignation of the Earldom of Richmond.

(h) He was sum. to Parl. 6 Oct. (1372), 46 Ed. III, by writ directed, "carissimo filio nostro Johanni, *Regi Castellæ et Legionis*, duci Lancastriæ, &c" and so also on subsequent occasions.

2 March (1389/90), 13 Ric. II., *cr. Duke of Aquitaine in Normandy* by imposition of the cap of estate, &c. He *m.* firstly (as above stated) 19 May 1359, Blanche ("*of Lancaster*"), 2d and yst. da. (who on 9 May 1361, became coheir and on 10 April 1362, by her sister's death, *sole* heir) of Henry (PLANTAGENET), DUKE OF LANCASTER, by Isabel, his wife, both abovenamed. She *d.* 1369 and was *bur.* in St. Paul's, London. M.I. He *m.* secondly, about June 1372, at Bordeaux, Constance, 1st surv. da. and heir of line of Pedro (the cruel) KING OF CASTILE AND LEON (1350-69), by his 2d or 3d wife, Maria PADILLA. She, who was *b.* 1354, *d.* s.p.m.(a) June 1394 and was *bur.* in the Collegiate Church of St. Mary, Leicester. He *m.* thirdly, 13 Jan. 1396/7, at Lincoln, Katharine, widow of Sir Hugh SWINFORD (who *d.* 1372), da. and coheir of Sir Payne ROELT (a native of Hainault), Guienne King of Arms. He *d.* at Ely Palace, Holborn, 3 Feb. 1398/9, aged 58, and was *bur.* in St. Paul's, London. M.I. Will dat. 3 Feb. 1397.(b) His widow who was *b.* before 1356 and who for some 25 years or upwards before their marriage (in the lifetime apparently(c) of each of their respective Consorts) had fulfilled the post of Mistress to the Duke himself and of Governess to his children, *d.* 10 May 1403, and was *bur.* in Lincoln Cathedral. M.I.

Dukedom. III. Earldom(d). VI. — 1399, Feb. to Sep.

2 and *6*. HENRY (PLANTAGENET, *styled* "OF BOLINGBROKE"), DUKE OF LANCASTER,(d) DUKE OF HEREFORD, EARL OF DERBY, EARL OF LINCOLN and EARL OF LEICESTER, *High Steward of England*, also DUKE OF AQUITAINE in Normandy, s. and h., being only son by first wife, Blanche "of Lancaster," *b.* 1367, at Bolingbroke, co. Lincoln; *styled* EARL OF DERBY; K.G., 23 April 1377; Bearer of the Principal Sword at the Coronation of Richard II., 16 July 1377; sum. to Parl. as EARL OF DERBY, 3 Sep. (1385), 9 Ric. II. He *m.* as his first wife) between 27 July 1380, and 6 March 1381, at Rochford,(e) Mary, 2d. and yst. da. and coheir (1373), of Humphrey (DE BOHUN), EARL OF HEREFORD, ESSEX AND NORTHAMPTON, by Joan, da. of Richard (FITZALAN), EARL OF ARUNDEL. She *d.* (as *Countess of Derby*), 1394, and was *bur.* in Canterbury Cathedral. In consequence of this match (by which he is sometimes considered as *Earl of Hereford and Northampton*), he was (some 3 years after his said wife's death), *cr.* 29 Sep. 1397, DUKE OF HEREFORD. He was, however, shortly afterwards, banished from the Kingdom, but having on 3 Feb. 1398/9, *suc.* his father, as *Duke of Lancaster*, &c., he returned to England and was 30 Sep. 1399, elected King thereof as **Henry IV**; when *all his honours merged in the Crown*.(f)

(a) Her only child, Katharine, *m.* in 1397, her cousin Henry, afterwards (1390-1406), Henry III, King of Castile and Leon, who was s. and h. of John, King of Castile, &c. (1379-90), the s. and h. of Henry II., King of Castile, &c., the bastard br. of Pedro the cruel, who was maternal grandfather of the said Katharine. On their posterity these Kingdoms were settled and accordingly devolved, passing in 1504 to Charles, afterwards Charles V., Emperor of Germany, the great great grandson and heir of line of Henry III., by the said Katharine of Lancaster.

(b) See Nichols's, "*Royal Wills*."

(c) Their eldest son John (Beaufort), Earl of Somerset (great grandfather to King Henry VII. *ex parte maternâ*), who was a Knight in 1391 (while his *younger* br. Henry was a Bishop in 1397), was probably born before 1372, the date of the death of his mother's *husband*, Sir Hugh Swinford; indeed Richard III., expressly says of him that he was "*in double advoutrow* [i.e. adultery], *gotten*." The character of the mother may be inferred from the fact that the legitimacy of her son, Thomas Swinford (*undoubtedly* born during her coverture) was questioned and had to be declared by letters patent, 5 Oct. 1411, before he could inherit as her heir. An interesting account of the Swinford family and of the issue of Katharine Roelt, both by Sir Hugh Swinford and by John of Gaunt, and the respective legitimation of each such issue is in the "*Excerpta Historica*" (1831), pp. 152-159.

(d) See p. 7, note "d."

(e) See "*N. and Q*," 7th s., vi, p. 73.

(f) One of his first acts, as King, "was to grant in Parl. a charter, in which the lands and possessions of the Duchy of Lancaster were declared to be a *separate inheritance* distinct from the lands and possessions of the Crown. The *prerogatives of the*

Dukedom. IV. 1399, to 1413. HENRY PLANTAGENET, *styled* "OF MONMOUTH," s. and h. ap. of **King Henry IV.**, by his first wife Mary abovenamed, was *b.* 16 Sep. 1386, at Monmouth, and was *cr.* in Parl. 13 Oct. 1399, **Prince of Wales**, DUKE OF CORNWALL([a]) and EARL OF CHESTER being, by charter of the same date, invested with the said Principality and Dukedom together with the counties of Chester and Flint "sibi et heredibus suis Regibus Angliæ." On 10 Nov. 1399, he was declared DUKE OF LANCASTER([b]) in parl. as also DUKE OF AQUITAINE in France and that he should bear the titles of "Prince of Wales, Duke of Aquitaine, Lancaster([c]) and Cornwall, and Earl of Chester." He ascended the throne, 21 March 1412/3, as **Henry V.**, when *all his honours merged in the Crown.*([d])

LANDAFF, see LLANDAFF.

LANERTON.

Barony. I. 1874, to 1880. *1.* THE HON. EDWARD GRANVILLE GEORGE HOWARD, 4th s. of George, 6th EARL OF CARLISLE, by Georgiana, 1st sister and coheir of William Spencer, 6th Duke, and da. of William (CAVENDISH), 5th DUKE OF DEVONSHIRE, was *b.* 23 Dec. 1809; entered the Royal Navy, attaining finally (1870) the rank of Admiral, but retired on the reserved half pay list before 1874; M.P. for Morpeth, 1833—1837 and 1840—1852, and was on 8 Jan. 1874, *cr.* BARON LANERTON of Lanerton, co. Cumberland. He *m.*, 16 Aug. 1842, Diana, only surv. da. and h. of the

---

King were annexed to all the possessions so separated, but . . the ordering of all matters connected therewith was vested in an establishment called the Chancellor and Council of the Duchy." [30th report of the D.K. of the Public Records.]

([a]) See Vol. ii, p. 365 notes, "d" and "e," *sub.* "Cornwall."

([b]) The Dukedom of Lancaster has never been again conferred, tho' in a case where the grantee is in direct succession to the Crown (as was the case of Prince Albert Victor of Wales, and again of Prince George of Wales, each of them successively heir apparent of the Prince of Wales), it would seem a very appropriate title. See Vol. ii, p. 375 note "a" *sub.* "Cornwall," for a list of "royal" titles.

With respect to the vast estates of the Duchy of Lancaster, Mr. Courthope has the following note. "The Duchy of Lancaster was, by an act in the first year of King Edward IV., vested in the said king and his heirs to hold as a separate inheritance, but annexed to the Crown; Henry VII., by a similar act [1 Hen. VII.] vested the same in himself, reversing the attainder of Henry VI., under which Edward IV. had acted; Henry VII. probably claimed the property rather as King, in right of the Crown, than as heir to King Henry VI."

There is a popular notion that the Crown, as *owner* of the estates of the Duchy, is thereby "*Duke* of Lancaster" founded probably on the untenable notion of its being a "*territorial*" Dukedom. The Crown is also owner of the Honour of Clare, yet nobody considers it to be thereby (territorial), Duke of Clarence. The case of "Cornwall" is, of course, quite different, *that* Dukedom, being regulated by the limitation of its creation (in Parl.) 17 March 1337, and by subsequent Acts of Parl.

([c]) Henry V., by a statutory charter granted in Parl. (1414) in his 2d year annexed the inheritance of the house of Bohun (which he had derived from his mother) to that of the Duchy of Lancaster, so that to that inheritance there thus became attached all the *Jura Regalia* belonging to the Duchy. See 30th Report of the D.K. of the Pub. Records, where it is added that "from the reign of Henry V., the Sovereigns of this realm have enjoyed the splendid inheritance of the Duchy of Lancaster, as well out of as within the county palatine, as an estate with Sovereign prerogatives, entirely distinct and separate from the Crown of England."

([d]) In the case of "Ryves and Ryves *v.* the Attorney General" tried in 1866 under the Legitimacy Declaration Act, being that of the daughter and grandson of the *soi-disant* Princess Olive of Cumberland (which Olive was stated to have been the legitimate da. of *H.R.H.* Henry Frederick, Duke of Cumberland; see vol. ii, p. 441, note "d," *circa finem*), the following instrument was set up, "GEORGE R. We hereby are pleased to create Olive of Cumberland, DUCHESS OF LANCASTER,

Hon. George PONSONBY, of Woolbeding, Sussex (4th s. of William Brabazon, 1st BARON PONSONBY OF IMOKILLY), by his 2d wife, Diana Juliana Margaretta, da. of the Hon. Edward BOUVERIE. He d. s.p. 8 Oct. 1880, aged 70, at 29 Grosvenor square, when his *peerage* became *extinct*. His widow living at Woolbeding 1892.

LANESBOROUGH.

i.e., "CLIFFORD OF LANESBOROUGH, co. York," Barony (*Boyle*), *cr.* 1644, with the EARLDOM OF BURLINGTON, which see; *ex.* 1753.

Viscountcy [I.] I. 1676. 1. SIR GEORGE LANE, Bart., of Tulske, co. Roscommon, s. and h. of Sir Richard LANE, Bart. (so *cr.* 11 Feb. 1660/1), by his first wife, Mabell, da. and h. of Gerald FITZ GERALD, of Clonbolg and Rathaman, *suc.* his father 5 Oct. 1668; was Sec. of War, Clerk of the Star Chamber, Keeper of the Records, P.C., and Sec. of State for Ireland, and was *cr.*, 31 July 1676, VISCOUNT LANESBOROUGH, co. Longford [I.] He *m.* firstly, 21 March 1644, Dorcas, da. of Sir Anthony BRABAZON, of Tallaghstown, co. Louth (br. to William, 1st EARL OF MEATH [I.]), by Margaret, da. of Christopher HOVENDEN, of Chisnor, Oxon. She *d.* 18 July 1671, and was *bur.* at St. Catharine's, Dublin. He *m.* secondly, 11 Dec. 1673, at St. Giles in the fields, Frances, da. of Richard (SACKVILLE), 5th EARL OF DORSET, by Frances, da. of Lionel (CRANFIELD), 1st EARL OF MIDDLESEX. He *d.* 11 Dec. 1683, and was *bur.* at Lanesborough. Will dat. 10 July 1683, enrolled on Close Rolls. His widow *d.* about 1722. Will pr. 1722.

II. 1683, to 1724. 2. JAMES (LANE), VISCOUNT LANESBOROUGH [I.], also a Baronet [1661], s. and h. by first wife, *b.* 7 Dec. 1646, or 7 Jan. 1649. He *m.*, 15 May 1676, at Fulham Chapel, Midx., Mary, da. of the Hon. Sir Charles COMPTON (2d s. of Spencer, 2d EARL OF NORTHAMPTON), by Mary, da. of Sir Hatton FERMOR. He *d.* s.p. at Lanesborough House,[a] Hyde Park corner, 2, and was *bur.* 11 Aug. 1724, aged 78, at St. James, Westm., when the *peerage* became *extinct*.[b] Will dat. 15 Oct. 1722, pr. 13 Aug. 1724. His widow *d.* 24 May and was *bur.* 1 June 1738, at St. James' afsd., aged 93. Her will dat. 5 Aug. 1735, pr. 27 May 1738.

III. 1728. 1. BRINSLEY (BUTLER), BARON OF NEWTOWN-BUTLER, co. Fermanagh [I.], 2d s. of Francis BUTLER, of Belturbet, co. Cavan, by Judith, da. of the Rt. Hon. Sir Theophilus JONES, of Osberstown, co. Meath; was Gent. Usher of the Black Rod [I.], 1711; Lieut. and sometime (May to Aug. 1714) Col. of the Battle-axe Guards [I.]; M.P. for Kells, 1703-13, and for Belturbet, 1713-23; *suc.* his eldest br. 11 March 1723, in the *Barony of Newtown-Butler* [I.] under the spec. rem. in the creation (21 Oct. 1715) of that dignity, taking his seat 7 Sep. 1725; P.C. [I.] to Geo. I. in 1726 as also to Geo. II. by whom he was *cr.*, 12 Aug. 1728, VISCOUNT LANESBOROUGH,[c] of co. Longford [I.], taking his seat 27 Oct. 1731. He *m.* about 1700, Catharine posthumous da. and coheir of Nevill POOLEY, of

---

and to grant our Royal authority for Olive, our said niece, to bear and use *the title and arms of Lancaster* should she be in existence at the period of our Royal demise. Given at our Palace at St. James's May 17th, 1773. CHATHAM. J. DUNNING." See "*Annual Register*" for 1866 (pp. 227-259) for an interesting account of this curious trial.

(a) Converted into an infirmary about 1740, being the site of St. George's Hospital.

(b) His only sister was mother, by her husband, Henry Fox, of three sons (1) George Lane-Fox, *cr.* Baron Bingley 1762, *d.* s.p.s. 1772; (2) James Fox who inherited the Surrey estates and *d.* s.p. 1773, and (3) Sackville Fox, ancestor of the family of Lane-Fox, of Bramham Park, co. York, and of the Lords Conyers.

(c) It does not appear that this family was in any way connected with the previous Viscounts Lanesborough.

Dublin, Counsellor-at-law, by Mary, da. of Sir Humphrey JERVAIS, sometime (1681-82) Lord Mayor of Dublin. He d. in Dublin 6 March 1735, and was bur. the 7th at St. Ann's, Dublin. Will dat. 4 Dec. 1734, pr. at Dublin. His widow (by whom he had 23 children) was bap. 10 Nov. 1676, and d. in Dawson street, Dublin, Dec. 1759.

IV. 1735. — Earldom [I.] I. 1756.

1 and *2*. HUMPHREY (BUTLER), VISCOUNT LANESBOROUGH, &c. [I.], s. and h., b. about 1700; was M.P. for Belturbet, 1725-35; Sheriff of co. Cavan, 1727, and of co. Westmeath, 1728; sometime Capt. of the Battle-axe Guards; *suc. to the peerage* [I.], 6, taking his seat 23 March 1735; P.C. [I.], 1749; Gov. of co. Cavan, 1756; Bencher of King's Inns, 1756, and was, 20 July 1756, *cr.* EARL OF LANESBOROUGH [I.], taking his seat 11 Oct. 1757, and being Speaker of the House of Lords [I.], 14 March 1760, during the Chancellor's illness. He *m.* May 1726, Mary, da. and h. of Richard BERRY, of Wardenstown, co. Westmeath. She *d.* 19 Dec. 1761. He *d.* 11 April 1768, at St. Stephen's Green, Dublin.

Earldom [I.] II. Viscountcy [I.] V. — 1768.

2 and *3*. BRINSLEY (BUTLER), EARL OF LANESBOROUGH, VISCOUNT LANESBOROUGH, &c. [I], only s. and h. *b.* 4 March 1728; Joint Clerk of the Pipe, 1749; M.P., for co. Cavan, 1751-68; *styled* LORD NEWTOWN-BUTLER, 1756-68; a Commissioner of the revenue, 1760; *suc. to the peerage* [I], 11 April, and took his seat 11 May 1768. He *m.* 26 June 1754, Jane, sister and h. of George (2d Earl), and only da. of Robert (ROCHFORT), 1st EARL OF BELVIDERE [I], by his 2d wife, Mary, da. of Richard (MOLESWORTH), 3d VISCOUNT MOLESWORTH [I]. He *d.* 24 Jan. 1779. aged 50. His widow, who was *b.* 30 Oct. 1737, *m.* John KING (who *d.* Aug. 1823, at Florence) and *d.* Feb. 1828.

Earldom [I.] III. Viscountcy [I.] VI. — 1779.

3 and *6*. ROBERT HERBERT (BUTLER), EARL OF LANESBOROUGH, &c. [I.], s. and h., *b.* 1 Aug. 1759; *styled* LORD NEWTOWN-BUTLER, 1768, till he *suc. to the peerage* [I.], 24 Jan. 1779: took his seat 8 Aug. 1780. He *m.* (Lic. 17 Jan. 1781), Elizabeth, 1st da. of the Rt. Hon. David LATOUCHE, of Dublin, by Elizabeth d. of the Rt. Rev. George MARLAY, Bishop of Dromore. She *d.* in London ("of a putrid fever"), 23 Sep. 1788, and was *bur.* 13 Oct. He *d.* 17 April 1806, aged 66.

Earldom [I.] IV. Viscountcy [I.] VII. — 1806.

4 and *7*. BRINSLEY (BUTLER), EARL OF LANESBOROUGH, &c. [I.], s. and h., *b.* 22 Oct. 1783; *styled* LORD NEWTOWN-BUTLER, till he *suc. to the peerage* [I.], 17 April 1806. He *d.* unm. 13 June 1847, aged 63, at Brislington, Somerset. Will pr. Aug. 1847.

Earldom [I.] V. Viscountcy [I.] VIII. — 1847.

5 and *8*. GEORGE JOHN DANVERS (BUTLER-DANVERS), EARL OF LANESBOROUGH, &c. [I.], cousin and h. male, being s. and h. of the Hon. Augustus Richard BUTLER-DANVERS, by his first wife, Mary, da. and h. of Sir John DANVERS, 2d Bart., of Swithland, co. Leicester, which Augustus (who took by royal lic., 14 Sep. 1796, the name of *Danvers* before that of *Butler*, and who *d.* 26 April 1820, aged 54), was next br. of the 3d Earl. He was *b.* 6 Dec. 1794 in London, *suc. to the peerage* [I.], 13 June 1847; REP. PEER [I.], 1849-66. He *m.* firstly, 29 Aug. 1815, Frances Arabella, 3d da. of Stephen Francis William FREMANTLE, Col. in the Army, by Albinia, da. of Sir St. John JEFFREYS, Bart. She *d.* 5 Oct. 1850, at Lanesborough Lodge, co. Cavan. He *m.* secondly, 24 Nov. 1851, at St. Geo. Han. sq., Frederica Emma, widow of Sir Richard HUNTER, yst. da. of Charles BISHOP, Procurator Gen. to Geo. III. He *d.* s.p. 7 July 1866, in his 72d year, at 8 Great Stanhope street, Park lane. His widow *d.* 3 Oct. 1870, aged 62, at Swithland Hall, co. Leicester.

Earldom [I.] VI. Viscountcy [I.] IX. } 1866. 6 and 9. JOHN VANSITTART DANVERS (BUTLER-DANVERS), EARL OF LANESBOROUGH [1756], VISCOUNT LANESBOROUGH [1728], and BARON OF NEWTOWN-BUTLER [1715], in the peerage of Ireland, nephew and h., being s. and h. of Capt. the Hon. Charles Augustus DANVERS-BUTLER, by Letitia Rudyerd Ross, yst. da. of John William FREESE, Col. Madras Artillery, which Charles Augustus was yr. br. (of the half blood) to the 5th Earl, his mother being (*not* the abovenamed heiress of the *Danvers* family from whom, consequently, he had *no descent* but) his father's *second* wife, Eliza Bisarre, da. of Humphrey STURT. He was *b.* 18 April 1839; ed. at Rugby school; was a Lieut. R.N. 1860, retiring 1866 and being a retired Capt. 1881. *He suc. to the peerage* [I.], 7 July 1866; REP. PEER [I.], 1870; Lord Lieut. of co. Cavan. He *m.*, 21 June 1864, Anne Elizabeth, only child of the Rev. John Dixon CLARK, of Belford Hall, Northumberland, by Anne, 2d da. of Addison FENWICK, of Pallion and Bishopwearmouth.

[CHARLES-JOHN-BRINSLEY BUTLER-DANVERS, *styled* LORD NEWTOWN-BUTLER, 1st s. and h. ap., *b.* 12 Dec. 1865, at Devonport; ed. at Eton; Lieut. Coldstream Guards. He *m.*, 31 Jan. 1891, at St. Peter's, Eaton square, Dorothea Gladys, 1st da. of Major Gen. Sir Henry TOMBS, K.C.B., by Georgina Janet, da. of Admiral Sir James STIRLING.]

Family Estates.—These, in 1883, consisted of 7,946 acres in co. Cavan, 6,606 acres in co. Fermanagh, besides 1,845 acres (worth £5,840 a year) in co. Leicester. *Total* 16,397 *acres, worth* £17,419 *a year. Principal Residences.* Swithland Hall, near Loughborough, co. Leicester, and Lanesborough Lodge, near Belturbet, co. Cavan.

LANGAR.

See "HOWE OF LANGAR, co. Nottingham," Viscountcy (*Howe*), *cr.* 1782; *ex* 1799.

See "HOWE OF LANGAR, co. Nottingham," Barony (*Howe*), *cr.* 1788.

LANGDALE.

Barony. I. 1836, to 1851. HENRY BICKERSTETH, 3d s. of Henry B., a medical practitioner, of Kirkby Lonsdale, by Elizabeth, da. of John BATTY, of the same place, Farmer, was *b.* there 18 June 1783; ed. at the Free Grammar school there; entered into, but relinquished, his father's business; became a scholar of Caius Coll., Cambridge, Oct. 1802, being, however, long absent from ill health and travelling as medical attendant to the Earl of Oxford, 1803-05; B.A., Senior Wrangler and Senior Smith's prizeman in Jan. 1808; M.A., 1811, being Fellow of his College; Barrister (Inner Temple), 1811; King's Counsel, 1827; P.C. and Master of the Rolls, 16, and 19 Jan. 1836, being *cr.*, 23 Jan. 1836, BARON LANGDALE of Langdale, co. Westmorland. He was chief of the three Commissioners of the Great Seal from 19 June to 15 July 1850. He resigned office (after 15 years service) 28 March 1851,(*) less than three weeks before his death. He *m.*, 17 Aug. 1835, at St. Mary's, Paddington, Jane Elizabeth, 1st da. of Edward (HARLEY), 5th EARL OF OXFORD AND EARL MORTIMER, by Jane Elizabeth, da. of the Rev. James SCOTT. He *d.* s.p.m. 18 April 1851, in his 68th year, at Tunbridge Wells, and was *bur.* the 24th in the Temple church, London, when the *peerage* became *extinct*. Will pr. May 1851. His widow, who was *b.* 9 March 1796, became on 19 Jan. 1853, coheir to her brother, Alfred, 6th and last Earl of Oxford and Earl Mortimer, when she took by Royal lic. 14 March 1853, the name of *Harley* in lieu of that of *Bickersteth*. She *d.* 1 Sep. 1872, aged 76, at Innspruck in Germany.

(*) A friend and disciple of Jeremy Bentham, he was an early and zealous advocate for law reform, tho' his labours, as far as reform of the Court of Chancery was concerned, fell far short of his intentions, but as regards the custody of the public records they have "justly gained for him the title of *Father of Record Reform.*" [Foss's "Judges."] His "*Memoirs*," written by Sir Thomas Duffus Hardy, were pub. in 1852.

LANGDALE OF HOLME.

Barony. I. 1658. *1.* SIR MARMADUKE LANGDALE, of Holme in Spaldingmore in the East Riding of co. York, only s. and h. of Peter L., of Pighill, near Beverley, by Anne, da. of Michael WHARTON, of Beverley afsd., was *knighted* at Whitehall, 5 Feb. 1627/8, and distinguished himself greatly in many actions, during the civil wars, on the part of the King,(a) was taken prisoner at Preston but, having escaped abroad, was by the exiled King,(b) by patent dat. at Bruges 4 Feb. (10 Car. II.) 1657/8, *cr.* BARON LANGDALE OF HOLME, in Spaldingmore, co. York. He *m.* Lenox, da. of Sir John RHODES, of Barlborough, co. Derby, by his third wife, Catharine, da. of Marmaduke CONSTABLE, of Holderness. He *d.* at Holme 5 Aug. 1661, and was *bur.* at Santon, co. York.

II. 1661. *2.* MARMADUKE (LANGDALE), BARON LANGDALE OF HOLME, s. and h. *suc. to the peerage*, 5 Aug 1661; was Gov. of Hull to James II., on whose deposition he was made prisoner. He *m.* Elizabeth, da. of the Hon. Thomas SAVAGE, of Beeston, Cheshire (2d s. of Thomas, 1st VISCOUNT SAVAGE), by Elizabeth, da. and coheir of William WHITMORE, of Leighton, co. Chester. He *d.* 1703, and was *bur.* at Santon. Will pr. March 1703.

III. 1703. *3.* MARMADUKE (LANGDALE), BARON LANGDALE OF HOLME, s. and h. He *m.* Frances, da. of Richard DRAYCOTT, of Painesley, co. York. He *d.* 12 Dec. 1718, and was *bur.* at Santon.

IV. 1718. *4.* MARMADUKE (LANGDALE), BARON LANGDALE OF HOLME, s. and h. He *m.* Elizabeth, da. of William (WIDDRINGTON), 3d BARON WIDDRINGTON OF BLANKNEY, by Alathea, da. and h. of Charles (FAIRFAX), 5th VISCOUNT FAIRFAX OF EMLEY [I]. She *d.* in Golden Square, Midx., 7 Jan. 1765, and was *bur.* at Santon. He *d.* 8 Jan. 1771. Will pr. Feb. 1771.

V. 1771, to 1778. *5.* MARMADUKE (LANGDALE), BARON LANGDALE OF HOLME, only s. and h. He *m.* Constantia, da. of Sir John SMYTHE, 3d Bart., of Eshe, by Constantia, da. of George BLOUNT, of Sodington. He *d.*, s.p. m.s.,(c) 5 April 1778, when the *peerage* became *extinct.* He was *bur.* at St. Pancras, Midx. Will pr. 1778. His widow *d.* about 1792, and was *bur.* at St. Pancras afsd.. Her will pr. Dec. 1792.

(a) He is said to have lost no less than £160,000 in the King's service.

(b) This was one of the 18 peerages made by Charles II. in exile, previous to 1660 the year of his restoration. These creations were as follows:—

SEVEN ENGLISH PEERAGES, *viz.* (1) WOTTON, Barony (*Kirckhoven*), *cr.* 31 Aug. 1650; *ex.* 1684; (2) ROCHESTER, Earldom (*Wilmot*, Viscount Wilmot), *cr.* 13 Dec. 1652; *ex.* 1681; (3) LANGDALE OF HOLME, Barony (*Langdale*), *cr.* 4 Feb. 1657/8; *ex.* 1777; (4) CROFTS OF SAXHAM, Barony (*Crofts*), *cr.* 18 May 1658; *ex.* 1677; (5) BERKELEY OF STRATTON, Barony (*Berkeley*), *cr.* 19 May 1658; *ex.* 1773; (6) GLOUCESTER, Dukedom, with the Earldom of CAMBRIDGE (*Stuart*), *cr.* 10 May 1659; *ex.* 1660; and (7) MORDAUNT OF AVALON, Viscountcy, with the Barony of MORDAUNT OF RYEGATE, (*Mordaunt*), *cr.* 10 July 1659; *ex.* (with the Earldoms of Peterborough and Monmouth) 1814.

SEVEN SCOTCH PEERAGES, *viz.* (1) DUFFUS, Barony (*Sutherland*), *cr.* 8 Dec. 1650; *forfeited* 1715; *restored* 1826; *dormant* 1827; (2) COLVILL OF OCHILTREE (*Colvill*), *cr.* 4 Jan. 1651; *dormant* 1728; (3) BALCARRES, Earldom, with the Barony of LINDSAY AND BALNEIL (*Lindsay*), *cr.* 9 Jan. 1651; (4) ROLLO OF DUNCRUB, Barony (*Rollo*). *cr.* 10 Jan. 1651; (5) KINGSTON, Viscountcy (*Seton*), *cr.* 6 Feb. 1651; *forfeited*, 1715; (6) ORMOND, Earldom, with the Barony of BOTHWELL AND HARTSIDE (*Douglas*), *cr.* 3 April 1651; *exchanged* in 1661 for the Earldom of Forfar and Barony of Wandale and Hartside; *ex.* or *dorm.* 1715; and (7) RUTHVEN OF FREELAND (*Ruthven*), *cr.* 1651.

FOUR IRISH PEERAGES, *viz.* (1) TARA, Viscountcy (*Preston*), *cr.* 2 July 1650; *ex.* 1674; (2) INCHIQUIN, Earldom, with the Barony of O'BRIEN OF BURREN, co. Clare, *cr.* 21 Oct. 1654; *ex.* (with the Marquessate of Thomond) 1855; (3) CLANCARTY, Earldom (*Macearty*), *cr.* 27 Nov. 1658; *attainted* 1691, and (4) ULSTER, Earldom (*Stuart*), *cr.* 10 May 1659; *merged* in the Crown 1685.

(c) Of his three daughters and coheirs (1) Elizabeth, *m.* Robert Butler, of Ballyragget; (2) Mary, *m.* 15 June 1775, Charles Philip (Stourton), Baron Stourton, and

LANGFORD OF LANGFORD LODGE.

Viscountcy [I.] I. 1766. 1. ELIZABETH-ORMSBY ROWLEY, wife of the Rt. Hon. Hercules Langford ROWLEY, of Summerhill, co. Meath, da. and h. of Clotworthy UPTON, of Castle Upton, co. Antrim, by Jane da. (whose issue became heir) to John ORMSBY, of Ballvenoge, co. Limerick, was b. 1713, and having m. her said husband, 31 Aug. 1732, was cr. 19 Feb. 1766, BARONESS SUMMERHILL, co Meath, and VISCOUNTESS LANGFORD of LANGFORD LODGE, co. Antrim [I.], with rem. (as to those dignities) to the heirs male of her body by her said husband. She d. at Summerhill, Dec. 1791. Her husband, who was s. and h. of Hercules ROWLEY, by Frances, da. of Arthur UPTON, of Castle Upton (which Hercules was s. and h. of Sir John ROWLEY, by Mary, 1st da. and coheir of Sir Hercules LANGFORD, Bart. [I], of Kilmackedrett, and of Summerhill afsd.), suc. his father in 1742: was M.P. for co. Londonderry, 1743, and for co. Meath 1761, till his death; P.C. [I], &c. He d. 25 March 1794.

II. 1791, to 1792? 2. HERCULES (ROWLEY), VISCOUNT LANGFORD OF LANGFORD LODGE, and BARON SUMMERHILL [I.], 1st and only surv. s. and h., b. 29 Oct. 1737; suc. his mother in the peerage [I.] Dec. 1791. He d. soon afterwards unm. when the peerage became extinct.

LANGFORD OF SUMMERHILL.

Barony [I.] I. 1800. 1. THE HON. CLOTWORTHY ROWLEY, *formerly* TAYLOUR, 4th s. of Thomas (TAYLOUR), 1st EARL OF BECTIVE [I.], by Jane, 1st da. of the Rt. Hon. Hercules Langford ROWLEY, and Elizabeth Ormsby, *suo jure* VISCOUNTESS LANGFORD [I.], b. 31 Oct. 1763; M.P. for Trim, 1791-95, and for co. Meath, 1795-97, having m. in 1794 his cousin, Frances, only da. and h. of the Hon. Clotworthy ROWLEY, by Elizabeth, da. of William CROSBIE, of co. Kerry (which Clotworthy was 2d s. of the *suo jure* VISCOUNTESS LANGFORD [I.] above named) assumed the name of *Rowley* in lieu of that of *Taylour* and was cr., 31 July 1800,(a) BARON LANGFORD OF SUMMERHILL, co. Meath [I.] He d. 13 Sep. 1825, aged 62. Will pr. Oct. 1825. His widow d. 30 April 1860, aged 85, at 47 Berkeley square.

II. 1825. 2. HERCULES LANGFORD (ROWLEY), BARON LANGFORD OF SUMMERHILL [I.], s. and h., b. 1795; suc. to the peerage [I.], 13 Sep. 1825. He m. in 1818 Louisa Augusta, da. of William RHODES. He d. 3 June 1839, aged 44. Will pr. Oct. 1840. His widow m. April 1840, George Edward GUSTARD and d. 27 Feb. 1874, aged 80, at Westfield House, Brighton.

III. 1839. 3. CLOTWORTHY WELLINGTON WILLIAM ROBERT (ROWLEY), BARON LANGFORD OF SUMMERHILL [I.], b. 24 July 1824, in Paris; suc. to the peerage [I.], 3 June 1839; sometime (1844-46) Lieut. in the 7th Foot. He m., 28 July 1846, at Celbridge, co Kildare, Louisa Augusta, 1st da. of Col. Edward Michael CONOLLY, of Castletown, co. Kildare, by Catharine Jane, da. of Chambré Brabazon PONSONBY-BARKER. She, who was b. 12 June 1822, d. 4 Nov. 1853, at Balbriggan, being accidentally drowned. He d. 19 July 1854, in his 30th year at Castletown, near Dublin.

IV. 1854. 4. HERCULES EDWARD (ROWLEY), BARON LANGFORD OF SUMMERHILL [I.], s. and h., b. 1 June 1848; suc. to the peerage [I.], 19 July 1854; ed. at Eton; sometime (1867-70) Lieut. Gren. Guards; REP. PEER [I.], 1884; State Steward to the Viceroy [I.] He m., 11 July 1889, at Agher, co

---

had a yr. son, Charles, who in 1815, took the name of *Langdale* in lieu of Stourton, under the will of Philip Langdale, of Houghton, co. York. (3) Apollonia, Baroness Clifford of Chudleigh, d. s.p., 31 Dec. 1815, aged 60.

(a) He was one of the 16 Barons cr. that day, being one of the 26 new members added to the Irish House of Lords in that one year. See vol. iv, p. 205, note "c," *sub* "Henniker."

Meath, Georgina Mary, 6th da. of Sir Richard SUTTON, 4th Bart., by his second wife, Harriet Anne, da. of William Fitzwilliam BURTON, of Burton Hall, co. Carlow.

Family Estates.—These, in 1883, consisted of 3,855 acres in co. Limerick, 3,659 in co. Dublin, and 2,231 in co. Meath. *Total* 9,745 acres, worth £9,281 a year. *Principal Residence.* Summerhill House, co. Meath.

LANGLEY.

i.e., "RADCLYFFE AND LANGLEY, co. Cumberland," Viscountcy (*Radclyffe*), *cr.* 1688, with the EARLDOM OF DERWENTWATER, which see; *attainted* 1716.

LANGPORT.

i.e., "BOTETOURT OF LANGPORT, co. Somerset," Barony (*Berkeley*), *cr.* 1664, with the EARLDOM OF FALMOUTH, which see; *ex.* 1665.

LANHYDROCK.

See "ROBARTES OF LANHYDROCK AND OF TRURO, co. Cornwall," Barony (*Robartes*), *cr.* 1869.

LANSDOWN.(a)

i.e., "GRANVILLE OF LANSDOWN," Viscountcy (*Granville*), *cr.* 1661, with the EARLDOM OF BATH, which see; *ex.* 1711.

LANSDOWN OF BIDDEFORD.

Barony.
I. 1712, to 1735.

GEORGE GRANVILLE, 2d (but in 1706, 1st surv.) s. of Bernard GRANVILLE, Groom of the Bedchamber, by Anne, da. and h. of Cuthbert MORLEY, of Hornby, co. York (which Bernard was yr. br. to John, EARL OF BATH, VISCOUNT GRANVILLE OF LANSDOWN, &c.), was *b.* 1667: ed. in France and at Trin. Coll., Cambridge; M.A., 1679; was Capt. of a Ship and Gov. of Deal Castle; was M.P. for Fowey, 1702, and for Cornwall, 1710; Sec. of War, Sep. 1710, and was *cr.* 1 Jan. 1711/2,(b) BARON LANSDOWN OF BIDDEFORD, co. Devon; P.C., and Comptroller of the Household, 1712;(c) Treasurer of the Household, 1713, to 11 Oct. 1714, when he was removed therefrom and imprisoned as a suspected person, in the Tower of London, 26 Sep. 1715, to 8 Feb. 1717. He was restored to his seat in Parl., but soon afterwards went abroad for many years. He appears to have been in 1721 *cr.* a Duke [DUKE OF LANSDOWN ?] by the titular King James III.(d) He *m.* 1711, Mary, widow of Thomas THYNNE, da. of Edward (VILLIERS), 1st EARL OF JERSEY, by Barbara, da. of William CHIFFINCH. She *d.* 17 Jan. 1734/5. He *d.* s.p.m. (two weeks later) 30 Jan. 1734/5, in Hanover square, when the *peerage became extinct.*(e) Both are *bur.* at St. Clement Danes. His admon. 6 May 1737, is full of genealogical information.

(a) At *Lansdown*, near Bath, the parliamentary army under Sir William Waller, was defeated by the gallant Sir Bevill Granville (who was there slain) 5 July 1643, the place-name of his victory being accordingly selected as a title of peerage by his descendants.

(b) "*Horâ primâ post meridiem.*" See vol. 1, p. 269, note "d," *sub.* "Bathurst," as to the twelve Peers (of whom this grantee was one) *cr.* in 5 days to secure a majority in the House of Lords.

(c) Of him when "turned of 40 years," it is thus said in Macky's "*Characters.*" "He is a Gentleman of tolerable good sense, with an undaunted assurance; very hot for his party and partial; jolly, and of a fair complexion, middle stature, inclining to fat."

(d) See vol. i, p. 59, note "b," *sub* "Albemarle," for a list of the JACOBITE PEERAGES conferred 1689 to 1760.

(e) He was a poet and the author of several plays as also of other works. He is the "*Alcander*" of the "Autobiography of Mrs. Delany," who was his niece.

LANSDOWNE.

Marquessate. I. 1784. 1. WILLIAM (PETTY), EARL OF SHELBURNE [1753], VISCOUNT FITZMAURICE [1751], AND BARON DUNKERON [1751], in the peerage of Ireland, also LORD WYCOMBE, BARON OF CHIPPING WYCOMBE [1760], in the peerage of Great Britain, s. and h. of John (PETTY, formerly FITZMAURICE), EARL OF SHELBURNE, &c., by Mary, da of William FITZMAURICE, of Gallane, co. Kerry, was *b.* 2 and *bap.* 13 May 1737; *styled* VISCOUNT FITZMAURICE, 1753-61; mat. at Oxford (Ch. Ch.), 11 March 1755; entered the Army, 1757, in which he finally (1783) became General; was M.P. for Chipping Wycombe, May 1760 to 10 May 1761, when *he suc. to the peerage*; P.C., 1763; President of the Board of Trade and a Cabinet Minister, April to Sep. 1763; took his seat in the Irish House of Lords, 25 April 1764; Sec. of State for the south, 1766-68; Foreign Sec., March 1782; K.G., 19 April 1782,(a) being inst., 9 May 1801; First Lord of the Treasury (PRIME MINISTER), 13 July 1782, to 24 Feb. 1783,(b) and was *cr.*, 6 Dec. 1784, VISCOUNT CALNE AND CALSTON, co. Wilts, EARL WYCOMBE OF CHEPPING WYCOMBE, and MARQUESS OF LANSDOWNE,(c) co. Somerset. He *m.* firstly, 3 Feb. 1765, at the Chapel Royal, St. James', Sophia, da. of John (CARTERET), EARL GRANVILLE, by his second wife, Sophia, da. of Thomas (FERMOR), EARL OF POMFRET. She, who was *b.* 26 Aug. 1745, *d.* 5 Jan. 1771, aged 25, and was *bur.* at Bowood. He *m.* secondly, 19 July 1779, at St. George's, Bloomsbury, Louisa, da. of John (FITZPATRICK), 1st EARL OF UPPER OSSORY [I.], by Evelyn, da. of John (LEVESON-GOWER), 1st EARL GOWER. She, who was *b.* 1755, *d.* 7 Aug. 1789. He *d.* 7 May 1805, aged 68, at his house(d) in Berkeley square and was *bur.* at High Wycombe. Will pr. 1805.(e)

II. 1805. 2. JOHN HENRY (PETTY), MARQUESS OF LANSDOWNE, &c., also EARL OF SHELBURNE, &c. [I.], s. and h., being 1st, but only surv. s. by first wife; *b.* 6 Dec. 1765; *styled* VISCOUNT FITZMAURICE, till 1784, and *styled* EARL OF WYCOMBE, 1784-1805; *cr.* M.A. of Oxford (Ch. Ch.), 12 July 1785; M.P. for Chipping Wycombe, 1786-1805; *suc. to the peerage*, 7 May 1805. He *m.* 27 May 1805, by spec. lic. at the house of Messrs. Le Neufville and Taverner, 23 Mount

(a) Of the four unappropriated Garters at the time of Lord North's resignation the new Ministers allowed one to Prince William Henry and reserved three for themselves and never (said the Prince of Wales) did three men receive the Order in so dissimilar and characteristic a manner. "The Duke of Devonshire advanced up to the Sovereign with his phlematic cold, awkward air, like a clown; Lord Shelburne came forward, bowing on every side, smiling and fawning like a courtier; the Duke of Richmond presented himself easy, unembarrassed and with dignity, like a gentleman." [Wraxall's "*Memoirs*."]

(b) It was generally supposed that when the "Coalition Ministry" (Lord North and Fox) was displaced by William Pitt in Dec. 1783 that he would have held a leading place in the next administration. His *past* services were, indeed, rewarded with a Marquessate, but he thenceforth retired from public affairs. He was, tho' he "wanted no external quality requisite to captivate or conciliate mankind," suspected "of systematic duplicity and insincerity," being given "the epithet of *Malagrida* from the name of a Portuguese Jesuit well known in the modern history of that kingdom." [Wraxall's "*Memoirs*."]

(c) This title appears to have been selected by the grantee because his *first* wife (then deceased) Lady Sophia Carteret was granddaughter of. Grace, *suo jure* Countess Granville, da. of John, 1st Earl of Bath, Viscount Granville of Lansdown. &c., and granddaughter of Sir Bevill Granville, the hero of the battle of Lansdown. See p. 16, note "a." The descent, however, of any Marquess of Lansdowne from the Granville family applies only to the 2d Peer, and that too during the short space (1805-09) of under five years.

(d) Lansdowne (formerly Shelburne) House, forming the whole of the south side of Berkeley square, was purchased (from the Marquess of Bute) by the 1st Marquess of Lansdowne (when Earl of Shelburne) in 1765 for £22,000 in an unfinished state, being about £3,000 less than the building of it had already cost.

(e) His entailed estates in England and Ireland amounted to more than £35,000 a year, "but £10,000 per annum and nearly £100,000 in specie are willed to his son Lord Henry Petty." [*Ann. Reg.*, 1805.]

Street, St. Geo. Han. sq., Maria Arabella, widow of Sir Duke GIFFORD, of Castle Jordan, co. Meath, da. of the Rev. Hinton MADDOX. He *d.* s.p., 15 Nov. 1809, in his 44th year, at his house(a) in Berkeley Square, and was *bur.* (by his own request), at Paddington, Midx. His Will pr. 1809. His widow *d.* 24 April 1833, at Wycombe Lodge, Kensington. Will pr. June 1833.

III. 1809. 3. HENRY (PETTY, *afterwards*, 1818, PETTY-FITZMAURICE), MARQUESS OF LANSDOWNE, &c., also EARL OF SHELBURNE, &c. [I.], br. and h., being 3th s. (1st by *second* wife) of the 1st Marquess; *b.* 2 July 1780, at Shelburne House,(a) Berkeley Square; ed. (as Lord Henry Petty), at Westm. School, at Edinburgh, and at Trin. Coll., Cambridge; M.A., 1801; was M.P., for Calne, 1802-06; for the Univ. of Cambridge, 1806-07, and for Camelford, 1807-09; P.C., 1806; Chancellor of the Exchequer, Feb. 1806 to March 1807; *suc. to the peerage*, 15 Nov. 1809; F.R.S., 1811; *cr.* LL.D. of Cambridge, 1 July 1811. By the death of his cousin to whom he was heir male, he became, 4 July 1818, EARL OF KERRY [1722], VISCOUNT CLANMAURICE [1722], and BARON KERRY AND LIXNAW [1223 ?] in the peerage of Ireland, whereupon he reassumed his patronymic of *Fitz Maurice*, after the surname of *Petty*. He was High Constable for Ireland, 19 July 1821, at the coronation of George IV. Cabinet Minister, May 1827, being Home Sec. July 1827 to Jan. 1828; LORD PRESIDENT OF THE COUNCIL, Nov. 1830 to Nov. 1834, April 1835 to Sep. 1841, and (thirdly), July 1846 to Feb. 1852, being still in the Cabinet tho' without office, Feb. 1855 to Feb. 1858; Lord Lieut. of Wilts, 1829; Lord Rector of the Univ. of Glasgow, 1827-31, K.G., 5 Feb. 1836. He *m.* 30 March 1808, Louisa Emma, 5th da. of Henry Thomas (FOX-STRANGWAYS), 2d EARL OF ILCHESTER, by his first wife Mary Theresa, da. of Standish GRADY. She, who was *b.* 27 June 1785, *d.* at Bowood Park, 3 March 1851. He *d.* 31 Jan. 1863, aged 82, at Bowood. Personalty sworn under £350,000.

[WILLIAM THOMAS PETTY-FITZMAURICE, *styled* EARL OF WYCOMBE, 1811-18, and *styled* EARL OF KERRY from 1818, 1st s. and h. ap., *b.* 30 March 1811, at Lansdowne House,(a) Berkeley square; M.P. for Calne, 1832-36. He *m.*, 18 March 1834, at Viscount Dungannon's house, Cavendish square, Marylebone, Augusta Lavinia Priscilla, 2d da. of John William (PONSONBY), 4th EARL OF BESSBOROUGH [I.] He *d.* s.p. and v.p., 21 Aug. 1836, aged 25. His widow, who was *b.* 11 May 1814, *m.* 2 April 1845, at All Souls', Marylebone, the Hon. Charles Alexander GORE, and was living 1892.]

IV. 1863. 4. HENRY (PETTY-FITZMAURICE), MARQUESS OF LANSDOWNE, &c., also EARL OF KERRY, EARL OF SHELBURNE, &c. [I.], 2d but only surv. s. and h., *b.* 7 Jan. 1816, at Lansdowne House afsd.; ed. at Westm. school and at Trin. Coll., Cambridge; *styled* EARL OF SHELBURNE from Aug. 1836 to Jan. 1863; M.P. for Calne, 1837-56; one of the Lords of the Treasury, 1847-48, and for many years Chairman of the Great Western Railway; Under Sec. for Foreign Affairs, 1856-58, was sum. v.p. in his father's Barony as LORD WYCOMBE by writ 14 July 1856; *suc. to the Marquessate*, &c., 31 Jan. 1863. K.G., 10 Oct. 1864. He *m.* firstly, 18 Aug. 1840, at Wilton, Wilts, Georgiana, da. of George Augustus (HERBERT), 11th EARL OF PEMBROKE, by his second wife, Catherine, da. of Simon, COUNT WORONZOW, of Russia. She, who was *b.* 3 Aug. 1817, at Wilton, *d.* 28 Feb. 1841 (as Countess of Shelburne) at Wilton afsd. and was *bur.* at Bowood. He *m.* secondly, 1 Nov. 1843, at Vienna, the Hon. Emily Jane Mercer ELPHINSTONE-DE-FLAHAULT, 1st da. of Margaret, *suo jure* BARONESS NAIRNE [S.], BARONESS KEITH OF STONEHAVEN MARISHAL [I.], and BARONESS KEITH OF BANHEATH [U.K.], by Auguste Charles Joseph, COUNT DE FLAHAULT DE LA BILLARDRIE. He *d.* 5 July 1866, aged 50, at Lansdowne house afsd., and was *bur.* at Bowood. His widow, who was *b.* 16 May 1819, *suc.* her mother 11 May 1867, as BARONESS NAIRNE [S.] and was living 1892.

V. 1866. 5. HENRY CHARLES KEITH (PETTY-FITZMAURICE), MARQUESS OF LANSDOWNE [1784], EARL OF WYCOMBE [1784], VISCOUNT CALNE AND CALSTON [1784], and LORD WYCOMBE, BARON OF CHEPPING WYCOMBE

(a) *Vide* p. 17, note "d."

[1760], also EARL OF KERRY [1722], EARL OF SHELBURNE [1753], VISCOUNT CLANMAURICE [1722], VISCOUNT FITZMAURICE [1751], BARON KERRY AND LIXNAW [1223 ?] and BARON DUNKERRON [1751], in the peerage of Ireland, s. and h., b. 14 Jan. 1845, being known as VISCOUNT CLANMAURICE (when his father was *styled* Earl of Shelburne) till 1863; ed. at Eton and at Balliol Coll., Oxford; *styled* EARL OF KERRY from 1863 till he *suc. to the peerage*, 5 July 1866; a Lord of the Treasury, 1868-72; Under Sec. for War, 1872-74; Under Sec. for India, April to July 1880; Gov. GEN. OF CANADA, 1883-88; G.C.M.G., 1884; VICEROY OF INDIA, 1888; *cr.* D.C.L. of Oxford, 1888.(a) He *m.*, 8 Nov. 1869, at Westm. Abbey, Maud Evelyn, 7th and yst. da. of James (HAMILTON), 1st DUKE OF ABERCORN [I.], by Louisa Jane, 2d da. of John (RUSSELL), 6th DUKE OF BEDFORD. She, who was b. 17 Dec. 1850, is C.I.

[HENRY-WILLIAM-EDMOND PETTY-FITZMAURICE, *styled* EARL OF KERRY, 1st s. and h. ap., b. 14 Jan. 1872; ed. at Eton.]

Family Estates.—These, in 1883, consisted of about 11,000 acres in England (worth about £21,000 a year), about 122,000 acres in Ireland (worth about £32,000 a year), and about 10,000 acres in Scotland (worth about £9,000 a year) which last belonged to the Dowager Marchioness. The amount in detail, is 11,145 acres in Wilts and four in Hants; also 94,983 acres in co. Kerry, 12,995 in co. Meath, 8,980 in Queen's county, 2,132 in co. Dublin, 1,642 in co. Limerick, and 617 in King's county; also 9,070 acres in Perthshire, and 1,348 in Kinrossshire. *Total* (in the three kingdoms) 142,916 acres, worth £62,025 a year.

The Marquess of Lansdowne is one of the 28 noblemen who in 1883 possessed above 100.000 acres in the United Kingdom and stands 14th in order of acreage and 16th in order of income. See a list of these vol. ii, p. 51, note "a," *sub* "Buccleuch."

LANSLADRON.

Barony by Writ.

I. 1299, to 1306.

SERLO DE LANSLADRON was sum. to Parl. as a Baron [LORD LANSLADRON] by five several writs from 24 Dec. (1299), 28 Ed. I., to 3 Nov. (1306), 34 Ed. I.(b) He had issue (besides a da., Miranda), Henry Lansladron, father of Sir Odo Lansladron, who was father of William Lansladron, who *d.* s.p. when the male issue of the Baron, none of whom were ever sum. to Parl., became *extinct*.(c)

LANTHONY.

i.e., "BUTLER OF LANTHONY, co. Monmouth," Barony (*Butler*), *cr.* 1660 with the EARLDOM OF BRECKNOCK. See "ORMONDE" Dukedom, *cr.* 1682; *forfeited* 1715.

---

i.e., "BUTLER OF LANTHONY, co. Monmouth," Barony (*Butler*), *cr.* 1801; see "ORMONDE" Marquessate [I.], *cr.* 1816; *ex.* 1820.

LA POER or POER see "POWER."

(a) He was one of "*the three great disappointments*" (as they were more playfully than seriously called by Lord Houghton) the other two being the Earl of Pembroke and (tho' it seems hardly applicable) the Earl of Rosebery [S.]

(b) Camden remarks that he was sum. to Parl. *when the wise and good were* [so summoned] *and* [when] *their posterity* [was] *omitted if incapable or deficient in knowledge.*

(c) The posterity of his great aunt, Miranda (only da. of Serlo, Lord Lansladron) was his heir. She *m.* John Goveley, of Goveley, co. Cornwall, by whom she had an only da. and h., Rose, who *m.* Sir Otes de Trerice, of Trerice (living 17 Ed. II.), and had a s. and h., Michael de Trerise (living 15 Ed. III.), whose only da. and h., Alice, *m.* firstly Sir Ralph Arundel, of Kenvelhelves, and secondly Sir John Arundel, of Lanherne, being mother, by her 1st husband, of Nicholas Arundel, of Trerice and Goveley, ancestor of the Barons Arundel, of Trerice, in which family the representation of Lansladron vests.

LARGS.

See "KELVIN OF LARGS, co. Ayr," Barony (*Thomson*), *cr.* 1892.

LASCELLES or LASCELLS.

Barony by Writ.
I. 1295, to 1297?

ROGER DE LASCELLES, of co. York, was, with about 60 others, sum. 8 June (1294), 22 Ed. I., to attend the King wherever he might be([a]) and had summons to Parl. as a Baron [LORD LASCELLES] by writs 23 June, 30 Sep., and 2 Nov. (1295), 23 Ed. I., to 26 Aug. (1296), 24 Ed. I. He *m.* Isabel, da. and h. of Thomas FITZ THOMAS. He *d.* s.p.m. about 1297 when the *Barony* fell into abeyance.([b]) His widow *d.* 28 May 1326.

---

i.e., "LASCELLES," Viscountcy (*Lascelles*), *cr.* 1812, with the EARLDOM OF HAREWOOD, which see.

LASWARY.

See "LAKE OF DELHI AND LASWARY AND ASTON-CLINTON, co. Buckingham," Barony (*Lake*), *cr.* 1804; Viscountcy *cr.* 1807; both *ex.* 1848.

LATHOM.

Earldom.
I. 1880.

1. EDWARD (BOOTLE-WILBRAHAM), BARON SKELMERSDALE, s. and h. of the Hon. Richard BOOTLE-WILBRAHAM (by Jessy, 3d da. of Sir Richard BROOKE, 6th Bart. of Norton), which Richard was 1st s. and h. ap. of Edward, 1st BARON SKELMERSDALE (so *cr.* 30 Jan. 1828), but *d.* v.p. 5 May 1844, aged 42, was *b.* 12 Dec. 1837, at Blythe, co. Lancaster; ed. at Eton and at Ch. Ch., Oxford; *suc.* his grandfather, 3 April 1853, *in the peerage* of Skelmersdale; was a Lord in Waiting, 1866-68; Capt. of the Yeomen, of the Guard, 1874-80; P.C., 1874, and was *cr.*, 3 May 1880, EARL OF LATHOM, co. Lancaster; Lord Chamberlain of the Household, June 1885 to Feb. 1886, and again Aug. 1886 to Aug. 1892. He *m.*, 16 Aug. 1860, Alice, 2d da. of George (VILLIERS), 4th EARL OF CLARENDON, by Katharine, da. of James Walter (GRIMSTON), 1st EARL OF VERULAM. She was *b.* 17 Sep. 1841.

[EDWARD-GEORGE BOOTLE-WILBRAHAM, *styled* LORD SKELMERSDALE, 1st s. and h. ap., *b.* 26 Oct. 1864, in Grosvenor Crescent; Capt. Royal Horse Guards. He *m.* 15 Aug. 1889, at Britford, Wilts, Wilma, da. of William (PLEYDELL-BOUVERIE) 5th EARL OF RADNOR, by Helen Matilda, da. of the Rev. Henry CHAPLIN, of Ryhall, Rutland. She was *b.* 16 Sep. 1869.]

Family Estates.—These, in 1883, consisted of 7,213 acres in Lancashire, worth £21,869 a year (acreage said to be understated, rental somewhat overstated.) *Principal Residence.* Lathom House, near Ormskirk, Lancashire.

LATIMER([c]) or LE LATIMER.

Barony by Writ.
I. 1299.

1. THOMAS LATIMER,([d]) of Braybrooke, co. Northampton, s. and h. of John Latimer,([e]) by Christian, youngest of the two daughters and coheirs of John LEDET *alias* BRAYBROOKE, of Braybrooke, Warden, and Corby, co. Northampton, by Ermentrude DE L'ISLE; *suc.* his father (1283), 11 Ed. I., being then aged 12 years and *suc.* his mother in 1292; had summons to the meeting at Carlisle (1296), 25 Ed. I., where he is placed among the "*Barones*," and was sum. to Parl. as a Baron

---

([a]) See vol. i, p. 259, note "c," as to this writ not constituting a regular writ of summons to Parl.

([b]) The coheirs were his four daughters of whom (1) Matilda *m.* firstly Robert de Hilton, of Swine (by whom she had issue) and secondly Sir Robert Tilliol (2) Theophania *m.* Ralph Fitz Randolph (3) Johanna *m.* (as first wife) Thomas de Culwen, and (4) Avicia *m.* Sir Robert Constable, of Halsham, and had issue.

([c], [d], [e]) *Vide* notes "c," "d," "e," on page 21.

(LORD LATIMER) from 29 Dec. (1299), 28 Ed. I., to 16 June (1311), 4 Ed. II. He attended the Coronation of Edward II, and served in the Scotch and French wars.(f) He m. Lora, da. of Henry (Hastings), Lord Hastings,(d) and is said(g) to have been twice married. He died (apparently) as late as (1334), 8 Ed. III., but was never sum. to Parl.(h) after the writ of 1311 nor was any of his issue(i) so summoned.

LATIMER or LE LATIMER.

Barony by writ. I. 1299.

1. William Latimer, of Corby, co. Northampton, and (about 1298) of Danby, co. York, *styled* "The Rich," s. and h. of William Le Latimer, of Billinges, co. York, was Sheriff of Yorkshire, 1254-60(j), and again 1267-69: Eschaetor Gen. north of Trent, 1259. He, having m. in or after 1257 Alice, eldest of the two daughters and coheirs(k) of John Ledet, *alias* Braybrooke, of Braybrooke, Warden, and Corby, co. Northampton (by Ermentrude de Lisle), acquired with her the lordship of Corby afsd. He appears to have taken the side of the King (Henry III.) in his contests witth the Barons. He served in the Holy land in 1270 and in the Welsh and Scotch wars and was sum. to Parl. as a Baron (LORD

(c) "A corruption of the Anglo-Norman *Latinier*, a speaker of *Latin*, or, more loosely, an *interpreter*, the term *Latin* having formerly been applied, as Halliwell observes, to languages in general. The noble families of this surname are descended according to the peerages from Wrenock, the son of Meirric, who held certain lands on the Welsh border, under the Anglo-Norman kings by the service of being *Latimer* or interpreter between the Welsh and the English." [Lower's "*Patron. Britannica.*"] On the other hand Mr. Beltz ["*Knights of the Garter*," p. 146, note 2], writes, "The name sometimes written *Le* Latimer (*latus mari*) but more commonly *De* Latimer (*de lato mari*) was doubtless Norman."

(d) See pedigree and account of "Latimer and Nevill, Barons Latimer," &c., by William Loftie Rutton in the "Bucks. Arch. Soc.," vol. vi, pp. 48-71.

(e) This John was br. to William Latimer, sum. as Lord Latimer 29 Dec. 1299, each of the brothers marrying sisters, coheirs of Braybrooke and Corby, co. Northampton.

(f) In (1324-25), 18 Ed. II., when in the expedition into Gascony he is called "Thomas Le Latimer, *Bochard*."

(g) Bridge's "*Northamptonshire*," vol. ii, p. 11.

(h) See p. 19, note "b," *sub* "Lansladron."

(i) His issue continued till 1410 in the male line. Sir Warine Latimer, Knight Banneret, his s. and h. by the first wife, was 30 at his father's death. He m. Catharine, sister to John De-la-Warr, and *d.* 13 Aug. (1349), 23 Ed. III. His widow *d.* (1361), 35 Ed. III. He left four sons, all successively of Braybrook, *viz.* (1) John Latimer, s. and h., aged 15 at his father's death, who *d.* a minor and unm. and was suc. by his br., (2) Warine Latimer, who also *d.* a minor and unm. before 1361 and was *suc.* by his br., (3) Sir Thomas Latimer, aged 20, and a minor in 1361. He was one of the Lollards. His will as "*of Braybroke, a fals Knyght to God*" is dat. 13 Sep. 1401, and pr. 21 May 1402. He *d.* s.p. leaving Ann, his widow, who *d.* 1402, and was *suc.* by his br., (4) Edward Latimer (called, like his grandfather, *Bochard*), who also *d.* s.p. (1410-11), 12 Hen. IV., leaving a widow, Margaret (who m. Nicholas Merbury) on whose death, John Griffin, his great nephew and heir, succeeded. This John was s. and h. of Richard, who was s. and h. of Thomas Griffin, by Elizabeth (or Catharine) sister of the said Edward Latimer. John Griffin *d.* s.p. (1443-44), 22 Hen. VI., and the representation of the Latimer family passed eventually as well as their estates to Sir Nicholas Griffin, K.B., great grandson of his br., Nicholas Griffin. This Sir Nicholas, who *d.* 1509, had two sons, *viz.* (1) Thomas, and (2) Edward. The *second* son, Sir Edward Griffin, was Attorney Gen. to Queen Mary, and his posterity eventually inherited the Braybrooke estates, his great grandson, Edward, being *cr.* in 1688 Baron Griffin of Braybrooke. Sir Thomas Griffin, the eldest son, *d.* s.p.m.s. 1569, leaving, however, a grandaughter and heir, Mary (da. and h. of Sir Rice Griffin), who *m.* Thomas Markham, of Ollerton, Notts, and left a numerous issue among whom the representative of this Barony of Latimer is to be found.

(j) *Query* whether the earlier dates may not relate to his *Father*.

(k) Christian, the other da. and coheir, *m.* John Latimer, and was mother of Thomas Latimer, of Braybrooke, sum. (also in 1299) to Parl. as Lord Latimer.

LATIMER) by writs directed "*Willielmo Le Latimer, Seniori*"(a) from 29 Dec. (1299), 28 Ed. I., to 22 Jan. (1304/5), 33 Ed. I.(b) His name as *Willielmus Le Latimer, Dominus de Corby,*" is affixed to the Barons letter to the Pope in 1301.(c) He *d.* 1305. His widow *d.* 1316.

II. 1299, and 1305. *1 and 2.* WILLIAM (LATIMER), LORD LATIMER, s. and h.,(d) who had in his father's lifetime, some 10 or 11 months *before* his father's summons, been himself sum. to Parl. as a Baron 6 Feb. (1298/9), 27 Ed. I.(e) This writ and subsequent writs down to 22 Jan. (1304/5), 33 Ed. I., were directed "*Willielmo Le Latimer, Juniori,*" but from that date to 3 Dec. (1327), 20 Ed. II., to "*Willielmo Le Latimer.*" He was Gov. of Rockingham Castle, 1307; fought at Bannockburn, 1314; was one of the confederate nobles in 1320 but fought against them at Boroughbridge in 1322; Gov. of York, 1327. Having *m.* in or before 1298 Lucy, da. and h. of Robert DE THWENG, of Danby,(f) co. York, he acquired that estate which was thenceforth the principal one of his race. From her, however, he was divorced by sentence of the Pope(g) pronounced at York. He *m.* secondly in 1314 Sybil, widow of William DE HUNTINGFIELD. He *d.* 1327 and was *bur.* at Guisborough priory.

III. 1327. *3.* WILLIAM (LATIMER), LORD LATIMER, s. and h. by 1st wife, *b.* about 1300, being 26 years at the death of his father. He was sum. to Parl. as a Baron from 6 Aug. (1327), 1 Ed. III., to 1 April (1335), 9 Ed. III. He (and his wife) received from the King a grant of the manor of Iselhampsted (afterwards called Latimers), Bucks. He *m.* Elizabeth, da. of John (DE BOTETOURT), 1st LORD BOTETOURT, by Matilda, da. of Thomas FITZ-OTHO. He *d.* 1335 aged 34. His widow *m.* in or before 1337 Robert DE UFFORD, who was s. and h. ap. of William, 1st EARL OF SUFFOLK, which Robert was sum. to Parl. in 1342 as LORD UFFORD but *d.* v.p. and s.p. before 1369.

IV. 1335. *4.* WILLIAM (LATIMER), LORD LATIMER, s. and h., aged six years at the death of his father. He was sum. to Parl. as a Baron(h) from 24 Feb. (1367/8), 42 Ed. III., to 20 Oct. (1379), 3 Ric. II.; was in the expedition to Gascony, 1359; Gov. of Becherelle in Britanny, 1360; Capt. Gen. to the Duke of Britanny, 1361, distinguishing himself greatly in 1364 by defeating at Doveroy a French army of 3,600 with only 1,600 men. K.G., 1361. Warden, north of Trent, 1368; Steward of the Household, 1369; Gov. of St. Sauveur in Normandy, 1370; Chamberlain of the Household, 1376, but was deprived of all his offices shortly afterwards tho' restored by the new King, Richard II., in 1377. He *m.* Elizabeth said to have been a da. of Edmund (FITZALAN), EARL OF ARUNDEL.(i) He *d.* s.p.m. 28 May 1381, and was *bur.* at Guisborough priory. Will dat. 10 July 1377, pr. 30 May 1381. His widow *d.* 11 March 1384. Will pr. April 1384 at Lincoln.

(a) This was to distinguish him from his son, William, who had been sum. to Parl. some nine months before him.

(b) His name occurs in the Rolls of Parl. before the record of writs of summons commenced.

(c) See full account thereof in "*Nicolas,*" pp. 761—809.

(d) His br., Sir John Latimer, acquired the estate of Duntish, co. Dorset, by marriage, where for five generations this family remained in the male line.

(e) The precedency, therefore, of this Barony is above that which he inherited from his father.

(f) The manor of Danby (some 12 miles west of Whitby) was about 1298 granted, or rather confirmed, by the King to William Latimer, the elder, "with rem. to William Latimer, his son, and Lucia, his wife, and to the right heirs of Lucia."

(g) She appears to have been incontinent, leaving, in 1303-04, her husband's house at Brunne and living with Nicholas de Meinill. She subsequently *m.* Robert de Everingham and finally Bartholomew de Fancourt and *d.* in 1347, being *bur.* (with her ancestors) at Guisborough priory.

(h) There is proof in the Rolls of Parl. of his sitting.

(i) In Beltz's "*Knights of the Garter,*" p. 148, is a note to the effect that it is so stated in a ped. by Vincent, No. 5, p. 33, but adds the writer "*we have not seen upon what authority.*"

V. 1381. *5*. ELIZABETH, *suo jure* BARONESS LATIMER, da. and h., aged 24 years at her father's death and then (second) wife to John (NEVILL), LORD NEVILL DE RABY, who *d.* 17 Oct. 1388, and was *bur.* at Durham. She *m.* secondly (as his third wife) Robert (WILLOUGHBY), LORD WILLOUGHBY DE ERESBY, by whom (who surviving her a year *d.* 9 Aug. 1396), she had no issue. She *d.* 5 Nov. 1395, and was *bur.* at Guisborough priory.

VI. 1395. *6*. JOHN (NEVILL), LORD LATIMER, s. and h. of his mother (by her first husband) being 12 years old at her death. He proved his full age in 1404 and was sum. to Parl.[a] as a Baron (*Lord Latimer*) from 25 Aug. (1404), 5 Hen. IV., to 27 Nov. (1430), 9 Hen. VI. He was *knighted* by King Henry VI. at Leicester on Whitsunday 1426. He *m.* Maud, widow of Richard (PLANTAGENET), EARL OF CAMBRIDGE (*executed* 5 Aug. 1415), da. of Thomas (CLIFFORD), LORD DE CLIFFORD, by Elizabeth, da. of Thomas (DE ROOS), LORD ROOS. Having no issue he settled the greater parts of his estates (tho' derived *ex parte maternâ*) on his br. of the his half blood (*ex parte paternâ*) Ralph, 1st EARL OF WESTMORLAND, to the exclusion of sister (of the whole blood) and heir. He *d.* s.p. Dec. 1430. His widow *d.* Aug. 1446.

VII. 1430. *7*. SIR JOHN WILLOUGHBY, *de jure* LORD LATIMER, but who never assumed that title, nephew and h., being only s. and h. of Sir Thomas Willoughby,[b] by Elizabeth, sister (the only sister who had issue) of the late Lord Latimer. He was *b.* about 1400, being aged 30 at his uncle's death[c] and was living 1435. He *m.* Joan, da. and h. of (—) WELBY.

VIII. 1450? *8*. SIR JOHN WILLOUGHBY, *de jure* LORD LATIMER, but who never assumed that title, only s. and h. He was *knighted*, 3 May 1471, by King Ed. IV., at Grafton, co. Glouc. He *m.* Anne, da. and coheir of Sir Edmund CHENEY, of Brooke, co. Wilts, and of Ottery, co. Devon, by Alice, da. of Sir Humphrey STAFFORD, of Southwicke, Wilts.

IX. 1480? *9*. SIR ROBERT WILLOUGHBY, *de jure* LORD LATIMER, but who never assumed that title, s. and h. He was, however, sum. to Parl. as a Baron, LORD WILLOUGHBY DE BROOKE by writ 12 Aug. 1492. He claimed the *Barony of Latimer* as against Richard (Nevill), the 2d Lord Latimer, of the creation of 1432,[d] but compounded the matter with the said Lord, from whom he received a regrant of several of the Latimer estates, including that of Iselhampsted Latimers, Bucks. He *d.* Dec. 1502.

See fuller account under "WILLOUGHBY DE BROOKE," Barony cr. 1492, *sub* the first Lord.

(a) There is proof in the rolls of Parl. of his sitting.

(b) He was 3d s. of Robert, 1st Lord Willoughby de Eresby (who *m.* for his 3d wife Elizabeth, *suo jure* Baroness Latimer abovenamed), by his *first* wife, Alice, da. of Sir William Skipwith. See Tabular pedigree on p., 24 note "b."

(c) Dugdale (vol. i, p. 312, *sub* "Nevill"), who states this John to be the Baron's "next heir, then 30 years of age," but in Collins' "*Precedents*" (p. 15) it is stated that "the Lord John Latymer's two sisters were both *living* at his death," it being added that, this "being true, the Lord Brooke had no colour of title" to the Barony of Latimer. This statement is apparently on the principle that all Baronies when once in abeyance *merge* in the Crown, and consequently that no *subsequent* extinction of coheirs can give the right of inheritance thereto to the (then) sole heir without a regrant from the Crown. It is certain that of the two sisters, Margaret, *d.* unm. and that the Lord Brooke, at the time of his claim, was great grandson and representative of Elizabeth, the other sister.

(d) He appears, however, not so much to have claimed the *old* Barony of Latimer [1299] as heir general of the first Lord as to have *disputed the right* of Richard (Nevill), Lord Latimer, to the title of Latimer. He, however, "perceiving his error, was contented to renounce his claim to that style, having one [*i.e.*, a peerage dignity] of his own" after having been "informed by a Herald that Sir George Nevill, grandfather to Richard, was *cr.* [1432] Lord Latymer *by a new title*, and therefore [that title] lineally descended *by* [should be "*to*"] Richard, son of Henry, son of the said George, and that the Lord Brooke had made a wrong claim which should have claimed his style from William Latymer first created Earl [should be "*Baron Latimer*"], of Danby, the head manor of the Barony which [manor] was also descended to Richard, Lord Latymer." [Collins' "*Precedents*," p. 15.]

X. 1502, to 1521. *10.* ROBERT (WILLOUGHBY), LORD WILLOUGHBY DE BROOKE, and *de jure* LORD LATIMER, but who never assumed the latter title, only s. and h. He *d.* s.p.m.s. 10 Nov. 1621, when the *Baronies* vested in him *fell into abeyance* between his two grandaughters and coheirs,(a) the right to the Barony of Latimer continuing henceforth vested in those who (by the cessation of such abeyance) became subsequently entitled to the Barony of Willoughby de Brooke, which see. } See fuller account under "WILLOUGHBY DE BROOKE" Barony *cr.* 1492, *sub* the second Lord.

LATIMER (*cr. by Henry VI.*)

Barony by writ.

I. 1432. *1.* SIR GEORGE NEVILL, 5th s. of Ralph, 1st EARL OF WESTMORLAND (who *d.* 21 Oct. 1425), being his 3d s. by his 2d wife, the Lady Jane BEAUFORT, legitimated da. of John (PLANTAGENET, "*of Gaunt*") DUKE OF LANCASTER, having, in Dec. 1430, on the death of his paternal uncle (of the half(b) blood) John (NEVILL), LORD

(a) These were the children of his only s. and h. ap., Edward Willoughby (who *d.* v.p.), by Margaret, da. of Richard (Nevill), 2d Lord Latimer (of the creation of 1432) the marriage between whom had been part of the compromise of the conflicting claim of each family to the Latimer dignities. Of these two coheirs Blanche, Lady Dawtrey, *d.* s.p. when the right to the Barony of Willoughby de Brooke passed to her sister or to her issue. This was Elizabeth, wife of Sir Fulke Greville, who had two children, *viz.* (1) Fulke Greville, who was *cr.* Baron Brooke, of Beauchamps Court, co. Warwick, in 1621 (with a spec. rem. in favour of his male cousins), and who *d.* unm. 30 Sep. 1628, in his 75th year, (2) Elizabeth, wife of Sir Richard Verney. To her grandson and heir, Richard Verney, the Barony of Willoughby de Brooke was allowed (3 Feb. 1696), and in his issue it still continues. See Tabular pedigree in note "b." next below.

(b) Sir George had *no descent from the Latimer family*, the heiress of which was mother to his said *uncle*, while the mother of his *father* was (his grandfather's first wife, Maud Percy. The following pedigree shews the connection of the *two* (separate) *Baronies of Latimer* [1299 and 1432], those entitled to the old Barony of 1299 being marked with an asterisk*

Maud Percy, 1st wife. = John (Nevill), Lord Nevill de Raby, *d.* 1388. = *Elizabeth, *suo jure* BARONESS LATIMER; *d.* 1395. = Robert (Willoughby), Lord Willoughby de Eresby, *d.* 1396. = Alice Skipwith, 1st wife.

Ralph, *cr.* Earl of Westmorland, 1397, *d.* 1425. =
*John (Nevill), LORD LATIMER, s. and h. of his mother, *d.* s.p. 1430.
Margaret *d.* unm.
Elizabeth = Sir Thomas Willoughby 3d son.

George Nevill, 5th son, *cr.* LORD LATIMER 1432; *d.* 1469. =
*Sir John Willoughby *b.* about 1400. =

Sir Henry Nevill = *alias* Latimer *d.* v.p. 1469.
*Sir John Willoughby *knighted* 1471. =

*Robert, *cr.* Lord Willoughby de Brooke, 1492; *d.* 1502. =

Richard (Nevill), 2d LORD LATIMER, *d.* 1530. =
*Robert, Lord Willoughby de Brooke, *d.* s.p.m.s. 1521. =

John (Nevill), 3d LORD LATIMER, *d.* 1542. =
Margaret. = Edward Willoughby, only s. and h. ap., *d.* v.p.

John (Nevill), 4th LORD LATIMER, *d.* 1577, s.p.m. =
Sir Fulke Greville, *d.* 1559. = *Elizabeth ancestress of the Lords Willoughby de Brooke.
Ann d. unm.
Blanche, m. Sir Francis Dawtrey and *d.* s.p.

LATIMER, *suc.* to a great portion of the estates formerly held by the family of Latimer; was sum. to Parl.(a) as a Baron (LORD LATIMER) by writs directed "*Georgio Latymer, Chev.*," from 25 Feb. (1431/2), 10 Hen. VI., to 7 Sep. (1469), 9 Ed. IV. He was in command against the Scots in 1435, but is said to have become an idiot in or before 1460 (b) He *m.* Elizabeth, da. (whose issue became coheir) of Richard (BEAUCHAMP), 5th EARL OF WARWICK, by his first wife, Elizabeth, da. and h. of Thomas (BERKELEY), LORD BERKELEY. He *d.* 30 Dec. 1469. *Inq. post mortem* 9 Ed. IV. His widow, who was *b.* 16 Sep. 1415, at Hanley, co. Worcester, and who inherited (from her mother) Stowe, Kislingbury, &c., co. Northampton, made her will 22 Sep. 1480.(c)

II. 1469. *2.* RICHARD (NEVILL), LORD LATIMER, grandson and h., being s. and h. of Sir Henry NEVILL, *alias* LATIMER,(d) by Joan, da. of John (BOURCHIER), LORD BERNERS, which Sir Henry *d.* a few months before his father, 14 July 1469, being slain at the battle of Edgcott and *bur.* in the Beauchamp chapel, Warwick. He was aged one year in 1469 at the death of his grandfather. He was sum. to Parl. as a Baron from 12 Aug. (1492), 7 Hen. VII., to 3 Nov. (1529), 21 Hen. VIII., by writs directed "*Ricardo Nevill de Latimer, Chivalier.*" His title as "*Lord Latimer*" was disputed by Robert (Willoughby), Lord Willoughby de Brooke, the heir to the old [1299] Barony of Latimer.(e) He was in 1487 in command against the insurgents at the battle of Stoke as also in 1496 and in 1513 (at Flodden) against the Scots. He was one of those who signed the letter to the Pope in favour of the King's divorce being granted. He *m.* about 1490 Anne, da. of Sir Humphrey STAFFORD, of Grafton, co. Worcester and Blatherwyck, co. Northampton. He *d.* 1530 at Snape Castle(f) and was *bur.* (as was his wife) at Well, co. York.

III. 1530. *3.* JOHN (NEVILL), LORD LATIMER, s. and h., *b.* 1493, was sum. to Parl. as a Baron by writs directed "*Johanni Nevill de Latimer, Chivalier,*" from 5 Jan. (1533/4), 25 Hen. VIII., to 16 Jan. (1541/2), 33 Hen. VIII. He was *knighted* before 1518. Being a zealous supporter of the old faith he took part in the rising called "*the Pilgrimage of Grace,*" and was one of the three nobles deputed to treat with the King's forces.(g) He was, however, pardoned. He *m.* firstly, 20 July 1518, in the chapel of Snape manor, Elizabeth, da. of Sir Richard MUSGRAVE, of Hartland, co. Westmorland. She *d.* s.p. He *m.* secondly Dorothy, sister and coheir of John, 14th EARL OF OXFORD, da. of Sir George VERE, by Margaret, da. and h. of Sir William STAFFORD. She *d.* 1526-27 and was *bur.* at Well afsd. He *m.* thirdly Katharine, widow of Edward (BURGH), LORD BURGH (or BOROUGH DE GAYNESBORO), who *d.* 1528-29, da. of Sir Thomas PARR, of Kendal, by Matilda, da. and coheir of Sir Thomas GREEN, of Green's Norton, co. Northampton. He was *bur.* at St. Paul's Cathedral, London, 1543. Will dat. 12 Sep. 1542, pr. 15 March 1542/3. His widow, who was *b.* about 1513, *m.* (within a few months) 12 July 1543, at Hampton Court (as his 6th and last wife) **King Henry VIII.**, who *d.* 28 Jan. 1546/7, aged 55. She *m.* fourthly (a few weeks after the King's death) Thomas (SEYMOUR), BARON SEYMOUR OF SUDELEY (maternal uncle to King Edward VI.) who was *beheaded* 20 March 1548/9. She (the Queen Dowager) *d.* s.p.s. 5 Sep. 1548, in her 36th year, and was *bur.* in Sudeley chapel, co. Glouc. Will dat. 5 Sep. 1548, pr. 1548-49.

(a) There is proof in the Rolls of Parl. of his sitting.

(b) It must, however, be observed that he continued to be sum. to Parl. till the time of his death.

(c) See this curious will in "*Test. Vet.,*" as also in Baker's "*Northamptonshire,*" vol. i, p. 442, where is a good pedigree of these Lords.

(d) He is spoken of as "my natural born son, Harrie *Latimer,*" in his mother's will.

(e) See p. 23, note "d."

(f) Snape Castle (built probably by the first Lord Latimer of this creation) was the chief residence of *this* line of Barons, as Danby had been of the *earlier* line. It was but nine miles from Middleham, the ancient seat of the Nevill race. It passed by inheritance in 1577 to the Cecil family with whom it remained till sold about 1810 by the Marquess of Exeter.

(g) The four noblemen concerned in this (Ask's) rebellion were the Lords Scrope, Lumley, Darcy, and Latimer.

IV. 1543, to 1577. 4. JOHN (NEVILL), LORD LATIMER, only s. and h. by second wife; was sum. to Parl. as a Baron by writs directed "*Johanni Nevill de Latimer, Chivaler*," from 14 June (1543), 35 Hen. VIII., to 6 Jan. (1580/1), 23 Eliz.(a) He, in 1550, sold the manor and hundred of Corby,(b) co. Northampton. He m. Lucy, 2d da. of Henry (SOMERSET), 2d EARL OF WORCESTER, by Elizabeth, da. of Sir Anthony BROWNE. He d. s.p.m. 22 April 1577, when the *Barony of Latimer* (cr. in 1432) *fell into abeyance* between his four daughters and coheirs.(c) He was *bur.* at Well afsd. Monument there.(d) *Inq. post mortem* 19 Eliz. Admon. 1 May 1577. His widow d. 23 April 1581/2, and was *bur.* at Hackney, co. Midx. Monument there. Her will pr. 1583.

The title (tho' one in fee) was [erroneously] assumed by the heir *male* for some 70 years as under.

V. 1577. *5.* RICHARD NEVILL, of Penwyn, and Wyke Snpie, co. Worcester, cousin and heir *male* (but not heir *general*), being only s. and h. of William N., of Penwyn afsd., by Elizabeth, da. of Sir Giles GREVILLE, which William was yr. br. of John, the 3d Lord. He [wrongfully] assumed(e) the title of LORD LATIMER on the death of his cousin abovenamed in 1577. He m. Barbara, da. of (—) ARDEN, of Park Hall, co. Warwick. He d. 1590. Admon. 17 Sep. 1590, to his son, "*Edmund Nevill, Lord Latimer.*"

VI. 1590, to *1640?* *6.* EDMUND NEVILL, only s. and h., who assumed the title of LORD LATIMER on his father's death, b. before 1555; an officer in the Spanish army before 1577; a prisoner in the tower of London for 14 years. By the death, 16 Nov. 1601, of his cousin, Charles (NEVILL), 6th EARL OF WESTMORLAND (*attainted* 1571) he would have been entitled (had it not been forfeited) to that title but was never able to obtain the repeal of its attainder. He m. firstly Jane MARTIONIS, DAME DE COLOMBE, of Hainault. He m. secondly, before 1580, Jane, da. of Richard SMYTHE. He was living 1638 but d. s.p.m.s.(f) at Brussels about 1640 and was *bur.* at East Ham, Essex.(g) Admon. 13 July 1646. His widow is said to have d. in 1647.

(a) This appears to have been three years or so after his death.

(b) This had been the inheritance of the family (thro' descent from Braybrooke, Ledet, and Latimer), since the time of King John.

(c) These were (1) Katharine, aged 31, in 1577, who inherited Burton Latimer, co. Northampton, &c. She, by her first husband Henry (Percy), 8th Earl of Northumberland, was represented till 1865 by the Earls and Dukes of that name (whom see) who were thence [tho' erroneously being only coheirs and *not sole* heirs] often held to be LORDS LATIMER, (2) Dorothy, aged 29, who inherited Snape Castle, co. York, also Church Brampton, co. Northampton, &c. She m. Thomas (Cecil), 1st Earl of Exeter, and was represented by her s. and h., William, the 2d Earl, on whose death s.p.m. in 1640 such representation (tho' not the estates) devolved on his daughters and coheirs, (3) Lucy, who was first wife of Sir William Cornwallis, of Brome, co. Suffolk (ancestor by second wife of the Earls Cornwallis) and who d. 1577 the same year as her father, leaving four daughters among whose issue is her representation, (4) Elizabeth who inherited Danby, co. York, also Stowe and Kislingbury, co. Northampton, &c. She by her first husband, Sir John Danvers, had three sons and seven daughters of whom Sir Charles Danvers, the eldest, d. s.p. in 1601; Henry Danvers, the second, was cr. in 1603 Baron Danvers of Dantsey, and in 1626 Earl of Danby, but d. unm. 1644, while Sir John Danvers, the third son (one of the Regicides) d. 1655, leaving two daughters and coheirs, both of whom left issue, among which the representation of this coheir is to be found. See pedigree in Baker's "*Northamptonshire*," vol. ii, p. 444, and Banks' "*Bar. Ang. Conc.*," vol. i, p. 278.

(d) This is engraved in Drummond's "Noble British Families." The inscription commences "Here lyeth buried Sir John Neveil, Knight, *laste Lord Lattimor*," &c.

(e) So also his cousin, Sir Edward Nevill, claimed the Barony of Abergavenny in 1598, not only as being seized of that castle, but as being heir *male* of the last Lord, and consequently "the more eligible person."

(f) He appears to have had two sons each named Ralph and five daughters of whom 'Dame Dorothy Hill alias Nevill" [who had m. Arthur Hill] consented, 13 July 1646, to the admon. of her father being granted to Thomas Ferrour, his kinsman.

(g) There was issue *male* existing long after the 17th century from the 1st Lord

LATIMER OF DANBY.

i.e., "LATIMER OF DANBY, co. York," Viscountcy (*Osborne*); *cr.* 1673. See "LEEDS" Dukedom, *cr.* 1694.

LAUDERDALE(a) and LAUDERDALE OF THIRLESTANE.

Viscountcy [S.] I. 1616.
Earldom [S.] I. 1624.

1. JOHN (MAITLAND), LORD MAITLAND OF THIRLESTANE, co. Berwick [S.], only s. and h. of John, 1st LORD MAITLAND OF THIRLESTANE [S.] (so *cr.* 18 May 1590), by Jean, only da. and h. of James (FLEMING), 4th LORD FLEMING [S.]; *suc. to the peerage* [S.] on the death of his father, 3 Oct. 1595, and was *cr.*, 2 April 1616, VISCOUNT OF LAUDERDALE(a) [S.] with rem. to his heirs male and successors in the Lordship of Thirlestane; was a Lord of Session [S.], 1618 to 1626, and an extraordinary Lord thereof, 1626 to 1628. He was *cr.*, 14 March 1624, EARL OF LAUDERDALE,(a) VISCOUNT MAITLAND, LORD THIRLESTANE AND BOLTOUN [S.], with rem. to heirs male bearing name and arms of Maitland. He was President of the Parl. [S.] 1644 to his death. He *m.* before 18 June 1610, Isabel, da. of Alexander (SETON), 1st EARL OF DUNFERMLINE [S.], by his first wife, Lilias, da. of Patrick (DRUMMOND), 3d LORD DRUMMOND [S.] She (by whom he had 15 children of which but three sons and one da. survived him) was *b.* 1 Aug. 1594, and *d.* 2 Nov. 1638, in her 45th year, being *bur.* at Haddington. He *d.* 18 Jan. 1645, and was *bur.* at Haddington afsd.

II. 1645.
Dukedom [S.] I. 1672, to 1682.

2 and 1. JOHN (MAITLAND), EARL OF LAUDERDALE, &c. [S.], 1st surv. s. and h., *b.* 24 May 1616, at Leithington, and (probably) *styled* VISCOUNT MAITLAND from 1624 to 1645; joined the Covenanters and was in 1643 a Commissioner from the Church [S.] to the Assembly of Divines at Westminster, and in 1644 (and again in 1647) from the estates [S.] to the King. *He suc. to the peerage* [S.], 18 Jan. 1645; joined Charles II. in Holland and accompanied him in 1650 to Scotland; was taken prisoner at the battle of Worcester in 1651 and detained nine years in the Tower of London, being excepted out of Cromwell's "act of Grace" in 1654. After the Restoration, however, he became Gent. of the Bedchamber, 1660; Sec. of State [S.], 1661-82; High Commissioner to the Parl. [S.], 1669-74, as also to the Convention [S.], 1678; President of the Council [S.], 1672-81, &c., holding in fact the whole power and patronage in Scotland for 18 years, 1662—1680; Gov. of Edinburgh Castle, &c. He was, in 1670, one of five Ministers for Foreign Affairs who formed the unpopular "*Cabal*."(b) Having no male issue he obtained, after resignation, a new grant, 16 Sep. 1667, of his dignities in favour (after his death) of his only da., Mary,(c) with, however, a power of redemption which he subsequently in 1675 exercised, leaving thereby the limitation to heirs *male*, as originally granted, unaltered. He was *cr.*, 1 May 1672, DUKE OF LAUDERDALE and MARQUESS OF MARCH(d)

Latimer of this creation. That from Thomas Nevill, of Pigotts Ardley, co. Essex (who *d.* 1550 and who was next yr. br. to William N. abovenamed and to John, the 3d Lord Latimer), ancestor of the Nevills, of Halstead, in that county, is said to have existed for eight generations in Drummond's "*Noble British Families.*"

(a) Lauderdale is a district of Berwickshire.

(b) See account thereof in vol. i, p. 131, note "c," *sub* "Arlington."

(c) "For several years subsequently she continued the *fiar* and heir apparent to the honours," and it seems to have been owing to her stepmother, the Duchess of Lauderdale, that the Duke ousted her therefrom. See "Riddell," pp. 215--216. She was the only child of the Duke (by his 1st wife), and *m.* John Hay, *styled* Lord Hay, of Yester, who *suc.* in 1697 as 2d Marquess of Tweeddale [S.]

(d) This title was chosen to mark his descent from the Earls of *March* or Dunbar [S.], thro' Elizabeth, sister of Earl George (by whom that Earldom was forfeited in 1435) and da. of Earl Patrick. This lady *m.* his lineal ancestor, John Maitland, of Thirlestane, who *d.* about 1395. See a note as to the title of March, under "Lennox," Dukedom [S.], the 3d Duke of Lennox [S.] having, in 1619, been *cr.* Earl of March [E.]

[S.] with rem. to the heirs male of his body. He was el. K.G., 18 April, and inst. 3 June 1672. Shortly afterwards he was made a Peer of England, being *cr.*, 25 June 1674, BARON PETERSHAM and EARL OF GUILDFORD, both co. Surrey; LL.D. (Cambridge), 11 Oct. 1676; Commissioner to the Convention of the Estates [S.], 1678-80; P.C. [E.], 1679. In 1680, however, his credit declined, and he was shortly afterwards deprived of all his offices. He *m.* firstly Anne, sister and coheir (1633) of James, 2d EARL OF HOME [S.], 2d and yst. da. of Alexander (HOME), 1st EARL OF HOME [S.], by his second wife, Mary, da. of Edward (SUTTON *alias* DUDLEY), 9th LORD DUDLEY. She *d.* at Paris about 1671. He *m.* secondly, 17 March 1671/2, at Petersham, Surrey (Lic. Vic. Gen.), Elizabeth, *suo jure* COUNTESS OF DYSART [S.], widow of Sir Lionel TOLLEMACHE, 3d Bart., 1st da. and h. of line of William (MURRAY), 1st EARL OF DYSART [S.], by Catharine BRUCE, his wife. He *d.* s.p.m. at Tunbridge Wells 24 Aug. 1682, in his 67th year, and was *bur.* at Haddington,(a) when *his English titles* as also the *Dukedom of Lauderdale* and the *Marquessate of March* [S.] became *extinct.* M.I. Will pr. Jan. 1683. His widow, by whom he had no issue, was *bur.* 16 June 1698, at Petersham. Her will pr. 28 Oct. 1698.

Earldom, &c. [S.] III. 1682. *3.* CHARLES (MAITLAND), EARL OF LAUDERDALE, &c. [S.], br. and h. male, being 3d and yst. s. of the 1st Earl; was M.P. for Midlothian, 1669-72; a Lord of Session, 1670; Treasurer Depute, 1672, and Gen. of the Mint [S.] He *suc. to the peerage* [S.], 24 Aug. 1682.(b) He *m.*, 18 Nov. 1652, at Hatton, co. Edinburgh, Elizabeth, 2d da. and coheir(c) of Richard LAUDER, of Hatton afsd., and of Overgogar, Norton, &c., with whom he acquired those estates. He *d.* 9 June 1691.

IV. 1691. *4.* RICHARD (MAITLAND), EARL OF LAUDERDALE, &c. [S.], s. and h., *b.* 20 June 1653; P.C., 1678; Joint Gen. of the Mint [S.]; Lord Justice Gen. [S.], 1681-84; *styled* VISCOUNT MAITLAND from 1682 till he *suc. to the peerage* [S.] in June 1691. After the Revolution he being a Roman(d) Catholic accompanied King James II. in 1689 to St. Germain and was outlawed by the Court of Justiciary [S.], 23 June 1694. He *m.* Anne, 2d da. of Archibald (CAMPBELL), 9th EARL OF ARGYLL [S.], by his first wife, Mary, da. of James (STEWART), EARL OF MORAY [S.] He *d.* s.p. in Paris 1695.(e) His widow *m.* Charles (STEWART), EARL OF MORAY [S.], (who *d.* s.p. 7 Oct. 1735), and *d.* 18 Sep. 1734, in her 76th year.

V. 1695. *5.* JOHN (MAITLAND *sometime* LAUDER), EARL OF LAUDERDALE, &c. [S.], br. and h., *b.* about 1655; a member of Faculty of Advocates, 1680. He was *cr.*, 18 Nov. 1680, *a Baronet* [S.]; M.P. for Midlothian, 1685-86 and 1689-96; was a Lord of Session [S.], 1689, by the style of *Lord Ravelrig*, holding that office till his death; Col. of the Edinburgh Militia; *suc. to the peerage* [S.] in 1695, taking his seat 8 Sep. 1696, and supporting the treaty of Union. He *m.* about 1680 Margaret, only da. and h. of Alexander (CUNNINGHAM), 10th EARL OF GLENCAIRN [S.], by Nicola, da. of Sir James STEWART. He *d.* 30 Aug. 1710, aged about 55.(f) His widow *d.* 12 May 1742, aged about 80, at Hawthornden.

(a) Bishop Burnet says of him "he was very big; his hair red, hanging oddly about him; his tongue was too big for his mouth."

(b) He is often said to have been *cr.* a Baronet [S], 12 May 1672, but this creation (made to heirs male whatsoever) apparently applies to *Richard* Maitland (the elder), of Pitrichie, co. Aberdeen.

(c) Jean, her elder sister, *m.* Sir Thomas Elphinstone, of Calder Hall, but Elizabeth seems to have inherited the family estates.

(d) He was author of a translation of Virgil. He is facetiously called (Fountainhall Diary, 215), "All *Roman* but the nose."

(e) Admon. 22 Jan. 1703/4, of the goods of "Richard, Lord Maitland," granted to James Gray, Esq., principal creditor.

(f) In Macky's "*Characters*" [1707 ?] it is said of him that "he is a gentleman that means well to his country but comes far short of his predecessors who for three or four generations were Chancellors and Secretaries of State. He is a well bred man, handsome in his person, fair complexioned, and towards 50 years old."

[JAMES MAITLAND, *styled* VISCOUNT MAITLAND, 1st s. and h. ap., *b.* about 1680; *m.* (contract dat. 31 Aug. 1702), Jean, 1st da. of John (GORDON), EARL OF SUTHERLAND [S.] He *d.* v.p. and s.p.m.(a) 1709. His widow *d.* at Edinburgh 11 Feb. 1747, aged 67.]

VI. 1710. 6. CHARLES (MAITLAND), EARL OF LAUDERDALE, &c. [S.], 2d but 1st surv. s. and h. male; *b.* about 1688; *styled* VISCOUNT MAITLAND from 1709 till he *suc. to the peerage* [S.] on 30 Aug. 1710; an officer in 1715 at the battle of Sheriffmuir; Lord Lieut. and Sheriff of Midlothian; Master of the Mint [S.]; REP. PEER [S.], 1741-44. He *m.* about 1711 Elizabeth, 1st da. of James (OGILVY), 4th EARL OF FINDLATER [S.], sometime High Chancellor [S.], by Anne, da. of Sir William DUNBAR, Bart. [S.] He *d.* at Hatton, 15 July 1744, in his 56th year. Fun. entry in Lyon office. Will pr. 1745.(b) His widow *d.* at Bath 24 Sep. 1778.

VII. 1744. 7. JAMES (MAITLAND), EARL OF LAUDERDALE, &c. [S.], s. and h., *b.* 23 Jan. 1718; *styled* VISCOUNT MAITLAND till he *suc. to the peerage* [S.], 15 July 1744. Having served in the Army from 1740, he became Lieut. Col. in 1745 but resigned in 1765. REP. PEER [S.], 1747-89; a Lord of Police, 1766-82. He *m.*, 24 April 1749, at Merton, co. Surrey (she being then in her 15th year) Mary, da. and h. (or coheir) of Sir Thomas LOMBE,(c) Alderman (and 1727-28 Sheriff) of London, by Elizabeth, da. of John TURNER, of Heden in Kingston, co. Kent. She *d.* at Hatton, 20 July 1789, aged 55. He *d.* there 17 Aug. 1789, aged 71. Will pr. 1789.

[VALDAVE CHARLES LAUDER MAITLAND, *styled* VISCOUNT MAITLAND, 1st s. and h. ap., *b.* 14 Dec. 1752; *d.* young and v.p. 5 Sep. 1754, at Hatton.]

VIII. 1789. 8 and 1. JAMES (MAITLAND), EARL OF LAUDERDALE, &c. [S.], 2d but 1st surv. s. and h., *b.* 26 Jan. 1759, at Hatton; *styled* VISCOUNT MAITLAND till 1789, being (as such) ed. at the Univs. of Edinburgh, Glasgow, and Paris; Member of the Faculty of Advocates, 1780; M.P. for Newport, co. Cornwall, 1780-84, and for Malmesbury, 1784-89 (being an ardent "*Jacobin*," and calling himself "*Citizen Maitland*") till he *suc. to the peerage* [S.], 17 Aug. 1789. REP. PEER [S.] 1790.(d) On the dissolution of the Pitt Ministry he obtained a peerage [U.K.], being *cr.*, 22 Feb. 1806, BARON LAUDERDALE OF THIRLESTANE, co. Berwick. He was Joint Commissioner to France, 1 Aug. 1806; P.C., 1806, and for a short time (1806-07) Keeper of the Great Seal [S.] K.T. (1821?) He *m.*, 15 Aug. 1782, at Walthamstow, Essex, Eleanor, da. and h. of Anthony TODD, Sec. of the Gen. Post Office, by Ann, da. and h. of Christopher ROBINSON, of Appleby, Westmorland. He *d.* 15 Sep. 1839, aged 80, at Thirlestane Castle (e) Will pr. Oct. 1839. His widow *d.* there 16 Sep. 1856, aged 94. Will pr. Oct. 1856. Both were *bur.* at Haddington.

Barony [U.K.]
I. 1806.

(a) His only da. and h., Jean, was the *heir of line* to the Earls of Glencairn. See vol. iv, p. 33, note "a," *sub* "Glencairn."

(b) "A nobleman of the sweetest disposition and finest accomplishments." [Wood's "*Douglas.*"]

(c) He *d.* 3 Jan. 1738/9, at his house in St. Olave's Jury, London, worth £120,000, having been the discoverer of the best method of silk-manufacture in 1719, for which, when in 1732 the patent expired, he received £14,000 from Parl.

(d) He obtained £1,000 (in full of his claim for £8,000) for the regality of Thirlestane and the bailiary of Lauderdale under the act for abolishing heritable jurisdictions.

(e) "This nobleman was throughout most of his life an impetuous advocate of popular opinions. He was the friend of Brissot, the dupe of Bonaparte, and finally died the opponent of Lord Grey's Reform Government." [Note by Dr. Doran in Wraxall's "*Memoirs*," edit. 1884, vol. ii, p. 78.] It appears from the obituary notice of him in the "*Annual Register*" of 1839 that his political views "underwent a complete change" about 1820, and that, 10 years later, at the date of Reform Bill, "he may be considered as the main spring and mover of the high Tory party among the Scotch peerage."

Earldom, &c. [S.] IX. Barony [U.K.] II. 1839. *9 and 2.* JAMES (MAITLAND), EARL OF LAUDERDALE, &c. [S.], also BARON LAUDERDALE OF THIRLESTANE [U.K.], s. and h., *b.* 12 Feb. 1784, in Wimpole street, Marylebone; *styled* VISCOUNT MAITLAND, 1789—1839; ed. at the Univ. of Edinburgh; M.P. for Camelford, 1806-07; for Richmond, 1818-20, and for Appleby, 1826-32; *suc. to the peerage* [S. and U.K.], 15 Sep. 1839; Lord Lieut. of Berwickshire. He *d.* unm. 22 Aug. 1860, aged 76, at Thirlestane Castle.

Earldom, &c. [S.] X. Barony [U.K.] III. 1860. *10 and 3.* ANTHONY (MAITLAND), EARL OF LAUDERDALE, &c. [S.], also BARON LAUDERDALE OF THIRLESTANE [U.K.], br. and h., *b.* 10 June 1785, at Walthamstow, Essex; entered the Royal Navy and was severely wounded in the attack on the Boulogne flotilla in Aug. 1801, becoming finally, 1862, Admiral of the Red; K.C.M.G., 1820; M.P. for Haddington Burghs, 1813-18, and for Berwickshire, 1826-32; *suc. to the peerage* [S. and U.K.], 22 Aug. 1860; G.C.B., 1862. He *d.* unm. 22 March 1863, at Thirlestane Castle, aged 77, when the *Barony of Lauderdale of Thirlestane* [U.K.] became *extinct*.

Earldom [S.] XI. 1863. *11*, THOMAS (MAITLAND), EARL OF LAUDERDALE, &c. [S.], cousin and h., being only s. and h. of Gen. the Hon. William Mordaunt MAITLAND, by his first wife, Mary, widow of John TRAVERS, da. of the Rev. Richard ORPEN, of Killowen, co. Kerry, which William (who *d.* 1841), was br. to the 8th and yst. s. of the 7th Earl. He was *b.* 3 Feb. 1803, at Frankfort, co. Cork; entered the Royal Navy; was in command on the coast of Spain during the civil war of 1836-37, being then made a Knight of the Spanish order of Charles III.; C.B., 1841; *knighted*, 1843; Commander of the Fleet in the Pacific, 1860-65, becoming finally, 1868, Admiral R.N. He *suc. to the peerage* [S.], 22 March 1863; K.C.B., 1865; Naval Aide-de-Camp to the Queen, 1866-73. REP. PEER [S.], 1867-78; G.C.B., 1873. He *m.* in 1828, Amelia, 3d da. of William YOUNG, of Rio de Janeiro. He *d.* s.p.m.s.(a) 1 Sep. 1878, aged 75, at Thirlestane Castle. His widow *d.* 18 Feb. 1890, at Cannes in France.

XII. 1878. *12.* CHARLES (BARCLAY-MAITLAND), EARL OF LAUDERDALE, &c. [S.], cousin and h. male, being only s. and h. of the Rev. Charles BARCLAY-MAITLAND, Rector of Little Longford, Wilts, by Anne, da. of Thomas KNOTT, of Stockland, which Charles last mentioned (who *d.* Dec. 1844) was s. of Charles MAITLAND-BARCLAY, of Tillycoultry, s. of the Hon. Charles MAITLAND, afterwards MAITLAND-BARCLAY (by his first wife, Isabel BARCLAY, the heiress of Towie, who *d.* 23 Oct. 1761), which last named Charles (who *d.* 28 Nov. 1795), was next br. to the 7th and 2d son to Charles, the 6th Earl. He was *b.* 29 Sep. 1822, and *suc. to the peerage* [S.], 1 Sep. 1878. He *d.* unm. 13 Aug. 1884, in his 62d year, having been struck by lightning on Braidshaw Rigg moor, near Lauder.

XIII. 1884. *13.* FREDERICK HENRY (MAITLAND), EARL OF LAUDERDALE [1624], VISCOUNT OF LAUDERDALE [1616], VISCOUNT MAITLAND [1624], LORD MAITLAND OF THIRLESTANE [1590], and LORD THIRLESTANE AND BOLTOUN [1624], in the peerage of Scotland, also a Baronet [1680. S.], and heritable Standard Bearer [S.], cousin and h. male, being s. and h. of Frederick Colthurst MAITLAND, Major Gen. in the Indian army, by Anna Dering, da. of Stephen WILLIAMS, which Frederick (who *d.* 3 Aug. 1876), was s. of Patrick MAITLAND, of

(a) Mary Jane, his only surv. child and h., *m.* 7 Jan. 1868, Reginald (Brabazon), 13th Earl of Meath [I.], and had issue.

Kilmaron Castle, co. Fife, sometime a Banker at Calcutta (d. 29 Jan. 1821), son(a) of Col. the Hon. Richard MAITLAND (d. 13 July 1772, aged 48), who was 4th s. of Charles, the 6th Earl. He was b. 16 Dec. 1840; entered the 8th Hussars, 1861; Lieut. 1866; Capt. 1873; Major in the Bengal Staff Corps, 1881, retiring as Lieut.-Col.; was sometime Political agent in central India; suc. to the peerage [S.], 13 Aug. 1884, his claim being established, July 1885. REP PEER [S.], 1889; Lord Lieut. of Berwickshire. He m. firstly, 28 Nov. 1864, Charlotte Sarah, da. of B.W.A. SLEIGH, Lieut.-Col. of the 77th Reg. She was living 1877. He m. secondly, 16 Oct. 1883, at James', Paddington, Ada Twyford, 4th da. of the Rev. Henry Trail SIMPSON, Rector of Swindon, co. Gloucester and formerly Rector of Adel, co. York.

[FREDERICK COLIN MAITLAND, *styled* VISCOUNT MAITLAND, s. and h. ap. by 1st wife, b. 12 April 1868; Lieut. Scots Guards, 1889. He m. 16 April 1890, at St. Peter's Eaton square, Gwendoline Lucy, yst. da. of the Rt. Hon. Sir Edward VAUGHAN-WILLIAMS, one of the Justices of the Common Pleas (1846-65) by Jane Margaret, da. of the Rev. Walter BAGOT, of Pype Hall, co. Stafford.]

Family Estates.—These, in 1883, consisted of 24,681 acres in Berwickshire; 756 in Roxburghshire and 75 (worth £482 a year) in Haddingshire. *Total* 25,512 acres, worth 17,318 a year. *Principal Residence.* Thirlestane Castle, near Lauder, Berwickshire.

LAUDERDALE OF THIRLESTANE.

i.e., "LAUDERDALE OF THIRLESTANE, co. Berwick," Barony (*Maitland*), cr. 1806; ex. 1863; see "LAUDERDALE" Earldom [S.], cr. 1624, sub. the 8th, 9th and 10th Earls.

LAUGHTON.

See "PELHAM OF LAUGHTON, co. Sussex," Barony (*Pelham*), cr. 1706; ex. (with the *Dukedom of Newcastle-upon-Tyne*, the *Marquessate and Earldom of Clare*, &c.), 1768.

LAUNCESTON.

i.e., "LAUNCESTON, co. Cornwall," Viscountcy. (*H.R.H. Prince* Frederick-Lewis), cr. 1726 with the DUKEDOM OF EDINBURGH, which see; *merged* in the Crown, 1760.

LAVINGTON.

Barony [I.]
I. 1793, to 1807.

RALPH PAYNE, only surv. s. and h. of Ralph PAYNE of St. Christophers, Ch. Judge of the said island, by his first wife, Alice, da. of Francis CARLISLE, of Antigua, was b. 19 March 1739 in the parish of St. George Basseterre in St. Christopher afsd.; was M.P. for Shaftesbury, 1768; for Camelford, 1774; for Plympton, 1780, and for Woodstock, 1795; was installed K.B., 15 June 1772, being when he died, the *Senior Knight* of that order; Gov. of the Leeward islands (for the first time) 1774-75, and, again, 1801-07 till his death; Clerk of the Board of Green cloth, 1775, till that office was abolished. He was cr. 1 Oct. 1795, BARON LAVINGTON of Lavington [I.], P.C., 1801. He m. 1 Sep. 1767, at St. Geo. Han. sq., Frances Lambertina Christiana Charlotte Harriet Theresa KOLBEL, da. of Henry (sometimes called "Frederick Maximilian") BARON KOLBEL, of the Holy Roman Empire; a Gen. in the Imperial service, sister of Rudolph, Baron Kolbel. He d. s.p.

(a) The legitimacy by the Scotch [and Canon] law, of this Patrick was established by the decision of the Committee for privileges in 1885. His father, Col. Richard m. (Patrick's mother), Mary McAdam at New York, on 11 July 1772 (2 days before his death) having had 3 sons then alive by her (of which Patrick was the second) and leaving her "big with child." See vol. ii, p. 17, note "c" for a somewhat similar case in the succession to the Earldom of Breadalbane [S.], confirmed by the House of Lords, 27 May 1864.

1 Aug. 1807, aged 68, when the *Barony of Lavington* [I.], became *extinct*. Will pr. 1808.(a) His widow, who was *b.* at Dresden and who is said to have been in the *suite* of Queen Charlotte, *d.* at Hampton Court Palace, 2 May 1830, at a great age. Will pr. July 1830, and March 1840.

LA WARD, see DE LA WARD.

LA WARR, see DE LA WARR.

LAWRENCE OF THE PUNJAUB(b) AND OF GRATELY.

I. 1869. *1.* "The Rt. Hon. SIR JOHN LAIRD LAWRENCE, Bart., G.C.B., G.C.S.I., lately Her Majesty's Viceroy and Governor General of India," was *cr.* 3 April 1869, BARON LAWRENCE OF THE PUNJAUB(b) AND OF GRATELY, co. SOUTHAMPTON. He was 5th s.(c) of Lieut.-Col. Alexander LAWRENCE, Gov. of Upton Castle, co. Kent, by Letitia, da. of the Rev. George KNOX, Rector of Strabane, co. Antrim. He was *b.* 4 March 1811 and *bap.* at Richmond, co. York; ed. at Haileybury College, 1827; entered the Bengal Civil service, 1828; assistant to the Chief Commissioner at Delhi, 1831; Magistrate and Collector of Delhi, 1836; settlement officer at Ettawah, 1838; Commissioner of the Sutlej, 1848, and of the Punjaub, 1852-58; K.C.B., 1856; G.C.B., 1857; *cr. a Baronet* 16 Aug. 1858,(d) having aided considerably in quelling the Sepoy mutiny of 1857; for which he received the thanks of Parl. and (from the East Indian company) a pension of £2000; Lieut.-Gov. of the Punjaub, 1859; P.C., 1859; Member of the Supreme Council, 1858-63; K.S.I., 1861; G.C.S.I., 1866; GOVERNOR GENERAL OF INDIA, Dec. 1863 to Sep. 1868, being, on his resignation, *raised to the peerage*, in 1869, as before stated. He *m.* 26 Aug. 1841, at Culdoff, co. Donegal, Harriette Katharine, da. of the Rev. Richard HAMILTON, Rector of Culdoff, by Katharine, da. of Edward TIPPING, of Bellinge Park, co. Louth. He *d.* 27 June 1879, in his 69th year at No. 23, Queen's Gate Gardens, Hyde Park, and was *bur.* in Westm. Abbey. His widow, who was C.I., was living 1892.

II. 1879. *2.* JOHN HAMILTON (LAWRENCE), BARON LAWRENCE OF THE PUNJAUB AND OF GRATELY, s. and h., *b.* 1 Oct. 1846, and *bap.* at Simla in India; ed. at Trin. Coll., Cambridge; B.A., 1869; Barrister (Linc. Inn), 1872; *suc. to the peerage*, 27 June 1879. He *m.* 22 Aug. 1872, Mary Caroline Douglas, only child of Richard CAMPBELL, of Auchinbreck, co. Argyll, by Anne Glassford, da. of Archibald DOUGLAS, of Glenfinnart in that county.

Family Estates.—These, in 1883, were under 2000 acres.

(a) Wraxall in his "*Memoirs*" (vol. iii, p. 411. Edit. 1884), says of him, with whom he was "well acquainted," that he "always appeared to be a good natured, pleasing, well bred man," but that "he was reported not always to treat his wife with kindness." He then narrates how that Sheridan being asked to write an epitaph for this lady's favourite monkey (named "Ned") for whose death she was in great distress, wrote—

"Alas! poor Ned
My monkey's dead!
I had rather, by half,
It had been Sir Ralph."

At Payne's house in Grafton street the leaders of the opposition frequently met, among whom was Erskine, who being one day indisposed is said to have replied to her ladyship, who had kindly enquired after his health.

"Tis true I am ill, but I cannot complain;
For he never knew *Pleasure* who never knew *Payne*."

(b) See vol. i, p. 29, note "a," *sub* "Amherst" as to titles referring to some achievement of the grantee.

(c) The 4th son was Gen. Sir Henry Montgomery Lawrence, K.C.B., who, when Chief Commissioner of Oude, was mortally wounded at the heroic defence of Lucknow and *d.* 4 July 1857, aged 51, his son being *cr. a Baronet* 10 Aug. 1858, in commemoration thereof.

(d) *i.e.*, 6 days after his nephew had been so created. See note "c" next above.

LAXTON.

See "Everingham de Laxton, *alias* Lexinton, Notts," Barony (*Everingham*) *cr.* 1309; in *abeyance* 1372.

LA ZOUCHE or DE LA ZOUCHE, see Zouche.

LEA.

See "Herbert of Lea, co. Wilts," Barony (*Herbert*), *cr.* 1861.

LE BLOUNT, see Blount.

LE BRUN, see Brun.

LECAGH.

i.e., "Feilding of Lecagh, co. Tipperary," Barony [I.] (*Feilding*), *cr.* with the Viscountcy of Callan [I.] 1622; see "Desmond" Earldom [I.] *cr.* (in reversion), 1622.

LECALE.

i.e., "Lecale,"(a) Viscountcy [I.] (*Cromwell*), *cr.* 1624; see "Ardglass," Earldom [I.], *cr.* 1645; *ex.* 1687.

LECALE OF ARDGLASS.

Barony [I.]
I. 1800, to 1810.

Lord Charles-James Fitzgerald, 3d but 2d surv. s. of James, 1st Duke of Leinster [I.], by Emilia, da. of Charles (Lennox), 2nd Duke of Richmond, was *b.* 30 June 1756; entered the Royal Navy, becoming eventually (1799), Rear Admiral; M.P. for co. Kildare, 1776-90; for Cavan, 1790-97, and for Ardfert, 1798-1800, in which year, on 27 Dec. 1800(b) he was *cr.* BARON LECALE(a) OF ARDGLASS, co. Down [I.] He was Muster Master Gen. [I.] and Gov of Kilmainham Castle; M.P. for Arundel, 1807. He *m.* 18 July 1808(c) at his house in Clarges street, St. Geo. Han. sq., Julia, widow of Thomas Carton, of Maidstown, co. Dublin. He *d.* s.p. 18 Feb. 1810 when the *peerage* became *extinct*. Will pr. 1810. His widow *d.* 6 May 1844, aged 65, at Courtlands, Devon. Will pr. July 1844.

LECHMERE OF EVESHAM.

Barony.
I. 1721, to 1727.

Nicholas Lechmere, 2d son of Edmund L. of Hanley Castle, co. Worcester, by Lucy, da. of Sir Anthony Hungerford, of Farley, co. Somerset (which Edmund was s. and h. of Sir Nicholas Lechmere, Baron of the Exchequer), was *b.* 1675; Barrister at law (Middle Temple); M.P. for Appleby, 1708; for Cockermouth, 1710, 1713 and 1715, and for Tewkesbury, 1717: Solicitor Gen. 1714-15; Chancellor of the Duchy of Lancaster, 1717, till his death in 1727; P.C., 1718; Attorney Gen., 1718-20. He was *cr.* 4 Sep. 1721, BARON LECHMERE OF EVESHAM, co. Worcester. He *m.* Elizabeth, 1st da. of Charles (Howard), 3d Earl of Carlisle, by Anne, da. of Arthur (Capell), 1st Earl of Essex. He *d.* s.p., aged 52, of apoplexy, at Camden House, 18 June 1727, when the *peerage* became *extinct*. He was *bur.* at Hanley Castle. Admon. 18 May, 1728 and 9 June 1739.(d) His

---

(a) Lecale is a Barony on the east coast of co. Down, containing the parishes of Ardglass, Down, &c.

(b) See vol. i, p. 166, note "a" for a list of the commoners raised on that date to the peerage [I.]

(c) He is said to have been a *widower* at that date.

(d) He was one of the managers of the trial of Dr. Sacheverell, and, being a good speaker, was much courted by the Whigs. He was (says the "*Historical Register*"

widow m. 25 Oct. 1723 (or 3 Feb. 1728/9), Sir Thomas Robinson, Bart. (so cr. 10 March 1730), of Rokeby Park, co. York (who d. s.p. 1777), and d. at Bath 10 April 1739. Her admon. 8 March 1739 to her said husband.

LECONFIELD.

Barony. I. 1859. 1. George Wyndham, of Petworth, co. Sussex, eldest of the 3 illegit. sons,(a) of George O'Brien (Wyndham), 3d Earl of Egremont(b) (who d. unm. 11 Nov. 1837, in his 86th year) by (—) da. of the Rev. (—) Iliff (one of the Masters of Westm. School) was b. 5 June 1787 at Marylebone, Midx.: entered the army (27th foot), becoming Colonel in 1830, and having, in 1837, suc. to Petworth, Leconfield, and other of the estates of Wyndham family, was cr. 14 April 1859, BARON LECONFIELD of Leconfield in the east riding of co. York. He m. 25 April 1815, Mary Fanny, da. of the Rev. William Blunt, of Crabbett, Sussex. She d. suddenly, 23 May 1863, at 4 Grosvenor place. He d. 18 March 1869, in his 82d year at Petworth. Will pr. 1869, under £250,000.

II. 1869. 2. Henry (Wyndham), Baron Leconfield, s. and h., b. 31 July 1830, at Brighton; ed. at Eton; matric. at Oxford (Ch. Ch.), 15 June 1848; sometime, 1849-67, an officer in the 1st Life Guards; M.P. for West Sussex, 1854, till he suc. to the peerage, 18 March 1869. He m. 15 July 1867, Constance Evelyn, sister of Archibald Philip, 5th Earl of Rosebery [S.], 2nd and yst. da. of Archibald Primrose, styled Lord Dalmeny, by Catherine Lucy Wilhelmina, da. of Philip Henry (Stanhope), 4th Earl Stanhope. She was b. 1 May 1846.

Family Estates. These, in 1883, consisted of about 66,000 acres in England and about 44,000 in Ireland, viz., 30,221 acres in Sussex; 24,733 in Yorkshire and 11,147 in Cumberland, besides 37,292 in co. Clare; 6,269 in co. Limerick and 273 in co. Tipperary. Total 109,935 acres, worth £88,112 a year. *Principal Residence.* Petworth House, Sussex.

Lord Leconfield is one of the 28 Noblemen, who, in 1883, possessed above 100,000 acres in the United Kingdom and stands 24th in order of acreage tho' 10th in order of income. See a list of these, vol. ii, p. 51, note "a," *sub* "Buccleuch."

LE DESPENCER, see Despencer.

LEE.

i.e., "Baring of Lee, co. Kent," Viscountcy (*Baring*), *cr.* 1876 with the Earldom of Northbrook, which see.

LEEDS.

Dukedom. I. 1694. 1. Sir Thomas Osborne, Bart., of Kiveton, co. York, 2nd but 1st surv.(c) s. and h. of Sir Edward Osborne, Bart. (so cr. 13 July 1620), by his second wife, Ann, 2d da. of Thomas Walmesley, of Dunkenhalg, co. Lancaster, was b. 1631; suc. his father, as second Baronet, 9 Sep. 1647; High Sheriff of Yorkshire, 1661; Joint Com. of Public Accounts, 1667; Joint Treasurer of the Navy, 1668; Treasurer of the Navy, 1671,

for 1727), "of great parts and learning and particularly consummate in the laws of England and parliamentary proceedings, a bold and strenuous stickler, in the worst of times, for the Protestant succession, but of a haughty and assuming temper, which made him oppose any measures he did not like, and which for some years past had rendered him obnoxious to those very ministers with whom he agreed in principle."

(a) See vol. iii, p. 248, note "c," *sub* "Egremont" for an account of these children

(b) The Earldom became extinct on the death of the 4th Earl in 1845.

(c) Edward Osborne, the 1st s. and h. ap. (only s. of his mother) d. v.p. unm., being killed 31 Oct. 1638, by a fall of a chimney-stack at York manor house.

and was *cr.* 2 Feb. 1672/3, VISCOUNT OSEBURNE [*i.e.*, OSBORNE] OF DUNBLANE [S.], which dignity he surrendered in Aug. 1673 (in which month he obtained an English Viscountcy) in favour of his second son, Peregrine Osborne, afterwards 2d Duke of Leeds. P.C., 1673; LORD TREASURER, June 1673 to March 1678/9, being *cr.* 15 Aug. 1673, BARON OSBORNE OF KIVETON AND VISCOUNT LATIMER(a) OF DANBY,(b) co. York, and, on 27 June 1674, EARL OF DANBY,(b) co. York. He was Lord Lieut. of the West Riding, 1674 79; P.C. [S.], 1674; *el.* K.G., 24 March 1676/7, and inst. 19 April 1677. In 1679 being accused (by the House of Commons) of high treason he was sent prisoner to the Tower of London for five years, whence he was released (with "the Popish Lords") in 1684. He now took an active part in bringing about the Revolution(c) and was rewarded accordingly. P.C., 1689; LORD PRESIDENT of the Council, 1689-95, being *cr.*, 9 April 1689, MARQUESS OF CARMARTHEN,(d) and five years later,(e) 4 May 1694, DUKE(f) OF LEEDS. He had in 1690 been subjected to an attempt of reviving the impeachment of 1679, and an action was actually commenced in 1695 against him for receiving bribes. He was LORD HIGH STEWARD 3 Feb. 1693, for the trial of Lord Mohun; Lord Lieut. of the West Riding, 1689, of the East Riding, 1691-99; *cr.* D.C.L. of Oxford, 9 Nov. 1695; Ch. Justice in Eyre, North of Trent, 1711. He *m.* before 1655, Bridget, 2d da. of Montagu (BERTIE), 2d EARL OF LINDSEY, by his first wife, Martha, sister of Charles, 1st VISCOUNT CULLEN [I.], da. of Sir William COKAYNE, of Rushton, co. Northampton, sometime (1618-19) Lord Mayor of London. She, who was *bap.* 6 June 1629, at St. Peter-le-Poor, London, *d.* 7 Jan. 1704, and was *bur.* at Kiveton. M.I. He *d.* 26 July 1712, in his 81st year, at Easton Neston, co. Northampton.(g) Will pr. April 1713.

(a) This ancient title he selected inasmuch as his mother was *descended* from (tho' in no way a representative of) the former Lords Latimer; Elizabeth, 4th da. and coheir of John, Lord (Nevill) Latimer (who *d.* 1577) having had by her husband, Sir John Danvers, besides three sons (by whose issue she is represented) seven daughters, one of whom Elizabeth *m.* Thomas Walmesley by whom she had besides a son and heir, Sir Thomas Walmesley (thro' whose issue this Elizabeth is now represented by the Lords Petre) two daughters, one of whom, Anne, by her second husband, Sir Edward Osborne, was (as stated in the text) mother of the grantee.

(b) Danby (in Cleveland), the ancient inheritance of the Latimer family, passed, thro' the family of Nevill, Lords Latimer, to the family of Danvers in 1577 on the partition of the estates among the coheirs. It had, however, been sold by Sir Henry Danvers to five freeholders of the district, by whom, in 1656, it was sold to John Dawnay, of Cowick, in whose posterity (Viscounts Down [I.]) it still remains. It was never possessed by the grantee or even by his mother's family, the Walmesleys, who derived no estates or representation (thro' the match with Danvers) from the families of Danvers, Nevill, or Latimer.

(c) He, as were his two sons, Edward Osborne *styled* Viscount Latimer, and Peregrine (Osborne), Viscount Dunblane [S.], was one of those in arms for the Revolution. See vol. i, p. 28, note "b," *sub* "Abingdon," for a list of these. He, indeed, was one of seven who signed the *invitation* to the Prince of Orange in June 1688 (the month in which the Prince of Wales was born) to come over to rescue the country from the rule of its native Sovereigns. These seven were (1) *the Earl* [afterwards, 1694, Duke] *of Devonshire* (2) *the Earl of Danby*, afterwards, 1694, Duke of Leeds (3) *the Earl* [afterwards, 1694, Duke] *of Shrewsbury* (4) *Viscount Lumley* [I.], afterwards, 1690, Earl of Scarbrough (5) *the Bishop* (Compton) *of London* (6) *Henry Sidney*, afterwards, 1694, Earl of Romney (7) *Edward Russell*, afterwards, 1697, Earl of Orford. It will be seen that these seven were not unrewarded by the grateful Dutchman when he was enthroned as King of England.

(d) It does not appear that he had any estate or interest in that county. See vol. iii, p. 69, note "d" [*circa finem*], *sub* "Derby."

(e) "To colour the dismissing him from business with the increase of title." [*Burnet.*]

(f) He was 6th of the nine Dukes (2d in a batch of five) *cr.* by William III. See vol. ii, p. 274, note "a," *sub* "Clare." The title that was supposed would have been given him was "*Pontefract*," but this probably was abandoned as the *Barony of Pontefract* was at that time vested in George (Fitzroy), Duke of Northumberland.

(g) This is what Macky says of him in his "*Characters*," "was of a good family in Yorkshire and brought to Court by the late Duke of Buckinghamshire. He with

[EDWARD OSBORNE, *styled* (1674-89) VISCOUNT LATIMER, *b.* about 1655; a Gent. of the Bedchamber to Charles II. He with his father and yr. brother was in 1688 (a few months before his death) in arms to support the Revolution.(a) He *m.* Elizabeth, da. of Simon BENNET, of Beachampton, Bucks. She, who was *bap.* 27 March 1659, at Beachampton, *d.* (v.p.) 1 and was *bur.* 5 May 1680, in Westm. Abbey. He *d.* s.p s. and v.p. Jan. 1688/9.]

II. 1712. 2. PEREGRINE (OSBORNE), DUKE OF LEEDS, &c., also VISCOUNT DUNBLANE [S.], 3d and yst. but only surv. s. and h., *b.* 1659. He was on 5 Dec. 1674, confirmed as VISCOUNT DUNBLANE [S.] a dignity conferred (as "VISCOUNT OSBURNE, OF DUNBLANE" [S.]), on his father, 2 Feb. 1672/3, but surrendered in his favour in Aug. 1673 as above mentioned. He was M.P. for Berwick-on-Tweed, 1677-79, and for York, 1689-90. He with his father and elder br. was in 1688 in arms to support the Revolution.(a) From 1689 to 1694 he was *styled* EARL OF DANBY and from 1694 to 1712 he was *styled* MARQUESS OF CARMARTHEN, being also sum. v.p. in his father's Barony as LORD OSBORNE OF KIVETON by writ 13 March 1690, directed "*Peregrine Osborne, Kiveton, Chl'r.*" He was Capt, R.N. in 1690, becoming finally, 1703, Vice Admiral of the Red, and was, in 1690, Col. of the City of London Dragoons as also of the 1st Marines.(b) He *suc. to the Dukedom*, &c., 26 July 1712, and was Lord Lieut. of the East Riding, 1713-14. He *m.*, 25 April 1682, at St. Marylebone, Bridget, only da. and h. of Sir Thomas HYDE, 2d Bart., of Albury, Herts, by Mary, da. of John WHITCHURCH, of Walton, Bucks. He *d.* 25 June 1729, in his 71st year, and was *bur.* 4 July at Aldbury. His widow *d.* 8 and was *bur.* 16 March 1733/4, at Aldbury. Will pr. 1734.

[WILLIAM HENRY OSBORNE, 1st s. and h. ap., *b.* 31 July and *bap.* 12 Sep. 1690, at North Mims, Herts, usually known as VISCOUNT LATIMER till 1694 and as EARL OF DANBY from 1694 till his death. He *d.* v.p. and unm. (of the small pox) at Utrecht 16 and was *bur.* 20 Aug. 1711, as "*Earl of Danby*" at St. Margaret's, Westm.]

III. 1729. 3. PEREGRINE HYDE (OSBORNE), DUKE OF LEEDS, &c., also VISCOUNT DUNBLANE [S], 2d and yst. but only surv. s. and h., *b.* 11 Nov. and *bap.* 10 Dec. 1691, at North Mims afsd. From 1711 to 1712 he was usually known as EARL OF DANBY and from 1712 to 1729 was *styled* MARQUESS OF CARMARTHEN and was sum. v.p. in his father's Barony as LORD OSBORNE OF KIVETON by writ 29 Jan. 1712, directed "*Peregrine Hyde Osborne de Kiveton, Chevalier.*" He

---

Lords Shaftesbury and Clifford were the advisers and carriers on of that scandalous part of King Charles' reign the shutting up of the Exchequer. He was made Lord Treasurer, Earl of Danby, and had the Garter. He was impeached in the House of Commons by the present Earl of Montagu, then Ambassador in France, not only for being a pensioner of France himself, but [for] advising and bargaining for a pension for the King, and was, on this impeachment, sent to the Tower where he lay many years. At the Revolution he declared for King William, was taken into favour by that Prince, made a Duke and President of the Council, but the people's suspicions of his being in the French interest, his taking a bribe of £6,000 to pass the East India charter with some other reasons, threw him out of all. He is a gentleman of admirable natural parts, great knowledge and experience in the affairs of his own country, but *of no reputation with any party*. Since the Queen's accession he hath not been regarded, tho' he took his place at the Council board. He hath been very handsome and is near 70 years old."

(a) See vol. i, p. 28, note "b," *sub* "Abingdon," for a list of those "in arms" in 1688 for the Prince of Orange.

(b) Macky says of him in his "*Characters*" when he was "Marquis of Carmarthen, Vice Admiral," and towards 50 years old. "He is of low stature but very well shaped and strong made tho' thin; fair complexioned; is very rakish and extravagant in his manner of living, otherwise he had risen quicker; he is strong and active with abundance of fire and does not want wit; he is bold enough to undertake any thing and understands all the parts of a sailor well. He contrived to build a ship called *the Royal Transport* which proves so good a sailor that it shews his knowledge of that part of navigation also."

suc. to the Dukedom, &c., 25 June 1729. He *m.* firstly, 16 Dec. 1712 (mar. lic. London on 13th, each aged 21), Elizabeth, da. of Robert (HARLEY), 1st EARL OF OXFORD, by his first wife, Elizabeth, da. of Thomas FOLEY. She *d.* in childbed 20 Nov. 1713, aged 25, and was *bur.* at Kiveton. M.I. He *m.* secondly, 17 Sep. 1719, Anne, 3d da. of Charles (SEYMOUR), 6th DUKE OF SOMERSET, by his first wife, Elizabeth, da. and h. of Jocelyn (PERCY), EARL OF NORTHUMBERLAND. She *d.* s.p.s. 27 Nov. 1722. He *m.* thirdly, 9 April 1725, at St. Anne's, Soho, Juliana, da. and coheir of Roger HELE, of Halewell, Devon. He *d.* 9 April 1731, in his 40th year. Will pr. Dec. 1731. His widow *m.*, 7 Oct. 1732, Charles (COLYEAR), 2d EARL OF PORTMORE [S.], who *d.* 5 July 1785. She *d.* 20 Nov. 1794, aged 89.(a) Will pr. Feb. 1795.

IV. 1731. 4. THOMAS (OSBORNE), DUKE OF LEEDS, &c., also VISCOUNT DUNBLANE [S.], 1st and only surv. s. and h., by first wife, *b.* 6 Nov. 1713, usually known as EARL OF DANBY till 1729 when he was styled MARQUESS OF CARMARTHEN till he *suc. to the peerage*, 9 April 1731; ed. at Westm. and at Ch. Ch., Oxford; mat., 6 July 1731; *cr.* D.C.L., 9 April 1738; F.R.S., 1739; a Lord of the Bedchamber, 1748; Ch. Justice in Eyre, south of Trent, 1748-56; el. K.G., 22 June 1749, and inst., 12 July 1750; Cofferer of the Household, 1756-61; P.C., 1757; Ch. Justice in Eyre, north of Trent, 1761-74. He *m.*, 26 June 1740, at St. Martins in the fields, Mary, 2d and yst. da. and coheir (whose issue became sole heir) of Francis (GODOLPHIN), 2d EARL OF GODOLPHIN, by Henrietta, *suo jure* DUCHESS OF MARLBOROUGH, 1st da. and coheir of (the famous) John (CHURCHILL), 1st DUKE OF MARLBOROUGH.(b) She *d.* 3 Aug. 1764, aged 41, and was *bur.* the 12th at Harthill, co. York. Will pr. 1764. He *d.* 23 March 1789, in St. James square, aged 75, and was *bur.* at Harthill. Will pr. April 1789.

[THOMAS OSBORNE, *styled* MARQUESS OF CARMARTHEN, s. and h. ap., *b.* 5 Oct. 1747, and *bap.* 28th at St. James' Westm., *d.* v.p. (of the small pox) 15 Aug. 1761, and was *bur.* 23d at Harthill, aged 13.]

V. 1789. 5. FRANCIS GODOLPHIN (OSBORNE), DUKE OF LEEDS, &c., also VISCOUNT DUNBLANE [S.], yst. but only surv. s. and h., *b.* and *bap.* 29 Jan. 1750/1, at St. James' Westm., *styled* MARQUESS OF CARMARTHEN, 1761-89; ed. at Westm. and at Ch. Ch., Oxford; mat., 11 June 1767; *cr.* M.A., 30 March 1769, and D.C.L., 7 July 1773; F.R.S., 1773; M.P. for Eye, 1774, and for Helston, 1774-75, being sum. v.p. in his father's Barony as LORD OSBORNE OF KIVETON by writ dat. 15 May 1776; a Lord of the Bedchamber, 1776-77; Lord Chamberlain to the Queen Consort, 1777-80; P.C., 1777; Lord Lieut. of the East Riding of co. York, 1778-80, and again 1782; Ambassador to Paris, 10 Feb. to 9 April

(a) At the Coronation of George III. in 1761, she being then wife of the Earl of Portmore [S.] claimed to walk as "Dowager Duchess of Leeds," by which designation she always styled herself. This claim was (of course) refused tho' she received summons to walk thereat as Countess of Portmore. See Cruise's "*Dignities*," 2d edit., 1823, p. 90, where is quoted the saying of Lord Coke, "If a Duchess by marriage afterwards marries a Baron she remains a Duchess and does not lose her name, because her husband is Noble," a saying which subverts the old rule of "that which is gained by marriage may be lost by marriage. *Eodem modo quod quid constituitur, dissolvitur.*" See also vol. iii, p. 153, note "b," for a similar claim by a Dowager Duchess of Dorset.

"The Duchess of Leeds" (says Sir N. Wraxall in his "*Posthumous memoirs*") exhibited in my time a melancholy example of human decrepitude, frightful in her person, wholly deprived of one eye, and sinking under infirmities. When young she had been a friend of the celebrated Lady Vane and is mentioned in the memoirs of that extraordinary woman, pub. by Smollett in his novel of *Peregrine Pickle*. She outlived her first husband more than 63 years. Her jointure amounted to £3,000 per annum and she consequently drew from the Leeds estate the incredible sum of £190,000 during her widowhood."

(b) The heir of line of the great Duke of Marlborough is consequently among her descendants, as the present Duke of M. derives his descent from Ann, wife of Charles (Spencer), Earl of Sunderland, *second* da. and coheir of the great Duke.

1783; Foreign Sec. of State, 1783-91; *suc. to the Dukedom*, &c., 23 March 1789; el. K.G., 15 Dec. 1790, but never installed. He *m.* firstly, 29 Nov. 1773, at Holdernesse House, Hertford street, St. Geo. Han. sq. (spec. lic., he being 22 and she 19) Amelia (who in 1778 became), *suo jure* Baroness Conyers, only surv. child of Robert (Darcy), 8th Earl of Holdernesse (Lord Conyers, &c.), by Mary, da. of Francis Doublet. She, who was *b.* 12 Oct. and *bap.* 11 Nov. 1754, having eloped from her husband 13 Dec. 1778, was *divorced* by Act of Parl. in May 1779.(a) He *m.* secondly, 11 Oct. 1788, at Hanwell, co. Midx., Catharine, da. of Thomas Anguish, one of the Masters in Chancery. He *d.* 31 Jan. 1799,(b) aged 48. Will pr. March 1799. His widow, who was *b.* 21 Jan. 1764, and who became Mistress of the Robes to Adelaide, the Queen Consort, *d.* 8 Oct. 1837, in Grosvenor street.(c) Will pr. Oct. 1837.

VI. 1799. 6. George William Frederick (Osborne), Duke of Leeds, &c., also Viscount Dunblane [S.], s. and h., by first wife, *b.* 21 July 1775, in Grosvenor square, *bap.* 15 Aug. at St. Geo. Han. sq., the King (*George III.*) being one of his sponsors; usually known as Earl of Danby till 1789 when he was *styled* Marquess of Carmarthen till 1799; *suc.* as Lord Conyers on the death of his mother, 26 Jan. 1784, to which Barony he was declared to be entitled by the House of Lords, 27 April 1798, and was accordingly sum. *as Lord Conyers* May 1798. He *suc. to the Dukedom*, &c., 31 Jan. 1799, and in July following sold the manor and estate of North Mims; Lord Lieut. of North Riding, co. York, 1802; P.C., 1827; Master of the Horse, 1827-30. K.G., 10 May 1827. He *m.*, 17 Aug. 1797, Charlotte, da. of George (Townshend), 1st Marquess Townshend, by his second wife, Anne, da. of Sir William Montgomery, 1st Bart., of Magbiehill. He *d.* 10 July 1838, in his 63d year, in London. Will pr. Nov. 1838. She, who was *b.* 16 March 1776, and *bap.* at St. Marylebone, *d.* 30 July 1856, aged 81, at Hornby Castle.

VII. 1838. 7. Francis Godolphin D'Arcy (Osborne, *afterwards* D'Arcy-Osborne), Duke of Leeds, &c., also Viscount Dunblane [S.], 1st but only surv s. and h., *b.* 21 May 1798, in London, baptism reg. at Hornby, *styled* Marquess of Carmarthen, 1799—1838; mat. at Oxford (Ch. Ch.), 4 May 1815; sometime, 1817-28, in the Army, retiring as Capt. 2d Life Guards; M.P. for Helston, 1826-30; was sum. v.p. in his father's Barony as Lord Osborne of Kiveton(d) by writ dat. 2 July 1838, but *suc. to the Dukedom*, &c (a few days later) 10 July 1838; took the name of *D'Arcy* before that of *Osborne* by Royal lic. 6 Aug. 1849. He *m.*, 24 April 1828, at Chelsea, Louisa Catherine, widow of Sir Felton Elwell Bathurst-Hervey, Bart., da. of Richard Caton, of Maryland, by (—), da. of Charles Carroll, of Carrollstown, in Maryland. He *d.* s.p. (of diphtheria) at the Clarendon hotel, St. Geo. Han. sq., 4 May 1859, aged 60. At his death the *Barony of Conyers* [*cr.* 1509] devolved on his nephew (*ex parte sororis*) and heir general (see that dignity) but the other honours devolved as below. His widow *d.* 8 April 1874, in her 83d year, at the Roman Catholic convent at St. Leonards on Sea.

VIII. 1859. 8. George Godolphin (Osborne), Duke of Leeds, &c., also Viscount Dunblane [S.], cousin and h. male, being s. and h. of Francis Godolphin (Osborne), 1st Baron Godolphin of Farnham Royal (so *cr.* 14 May 1832), by Elizabeth Charlotte, da. of William (Eden), 1st Baron Auckland, which Francis (sometime Lord Francis Godolphin Osborne) was 2d s. of the 5th Duke by his first wife. He was *b.* 16 July 1802, at Gogmagog hills in Stapleford, co.

(a) She *m.* (a few days afterwards) 9 June 1779, John Byron, who *d.* 10 April 1786, aged 63, and who was father (by a second wife) of Lord Byron, the Poet. She *d.* in London "of a consumption" 27 Jan. and was *bur.* 11 Feb. 1784, in her 30th year, at Hornby, co. York.

(b) "After a short illness of erysipelas in his side which turned to a mortification." [*Annual Reg.* 1799.] According to Sir N. Wraxall (*Hist. Mem.*, ii, p. 186), he was "highly accomplished, of the most pleasing manners, and of very elegant deportment."

(c) In the obituary notice of her husband [*Annual Reg.* 1799] it is said that she "chiefly attracted the attention of his Grace by her peculiar taste and skill in music."

(d) It seems curious that he was not sum. in the (more ancient) Barony of Conyers which had been allowed (in 1798) to his father.

Cambridge; matric. at Oxford (Ch. Ch.), 27 Nov. 1819; *suc.* his father, 15 Feb. 1850, as BARON GODOLPHIN OF FARNHAM ROYAL, and *suc.* his cousin, nine years later, 4 May 1859, *in the Dukedom, &c.* He *m.*, 21 Oct. 1824, Harriet Emma Arundel STEWART, spinster. She (Lady Godolphin) *d.* 28 Oct. 1852, aged 52, at Gogmagog Hills, co. Cambridge. He *d.* 8 Aug. 1872, in his 71st year, at Gogmagog Hills.

IX. 1872. 9. GEORGE GODOLPHIN (OSBORNE), DUKE OF LEEDS [1694], MARQUESS OF CARMARTHEN [1689], EARL OF DANBY [1674], VISCOUNT LATIMER OF DANBY [1673], BARON OSBORNE OF KIVETON [1673], and BARON GODOLPHIN OF FARNHAM ROYAL [1832], also VISCOUNT DUNBLANE [S., 1675], and a Baronet [1620], s. and h., *b.* 11 Aug. 1828, in Paris: *styled* MARQUESS OF CARMARTHEN from 1859 till he *suc. to the peerage* 8 Aug. 1872. He *m.*, 16 Jan. 1861, Frances Georgiana, sister and coheir [1867] of Henry Peter (PITT-RIVERS), 5th BARON RIVERS OF SUDELEY CASTLE, 2d da. of George, 4th Baron, by Susan Georgiana, da. of Granville (LEVESON-GOWER), 1st EARL GRANVILLE. She, who was *b.* 26 Dec. 1836, was sometime Lady of the Bedchamber to the Princess of Wales.

[GEORGE FREDERICK OSBORNE, usually called EARL OF DANBY, 1st s. and h. ap., *b.* 4 and *d.* 6 Nov. 1861, in his grandfather's lifetime.]

[GEORGE GODOLPHIN OSBORNE, 2d but 1st surv. s. and h. ap., *b.* 18 Sep. 1862, usually known as EARL OF DANBY till 1872 but since that date *styled* MARQUESS OF CARMARTHEN; M.P. for Brixton, 1887; Ass. Sec. to Sec. of State for the Colonies, 1887-88. He *m.*, 13 Feb 1884, at St. Paul's, Knightsbridge, Katharine Frances, 2d da. of George Frederick D'Arcy (LAMBTON), 2d EARL OF DURHAM, by Beatrix Frances, da. of James (HAMILTON), 1st DUKE OF ABERCORN [I.] She was *b.* 5 Sep. 1862.]

Family Estates.—These, in 1883, consisted of 14,772 acres in the North and West Ridings of Yorkshire (worth £21,470 a year); 5,911 in Cornwall; 3,117 in Bucks; 436 in Cambridgeshire, and one acre (worth £650 a year) in Middlesex. *Total* 24,237 acres, worth £33,381 a year. *Principal Residences.* Hornby Castle,(a) near Bedale, co. York, and Gogmagog Hill, co. Cambridge.

LEES COURT.

i.e., "SONDES OF LEES COURT, co. Kent," Viscountcy (*Sondes, afterwards De Duras*), *cr.* 1676, with the EARLDOM OF FEVERSHAM, which see; *ex.* 1709.

---

i.e., "SONDES OF LEES COURT, co. Kent," Viscountcy (*Watson*), *cr.* 1714, with the EARLDOM OF ROCKINGHAM, which see; *ex.* 1746.

See "SONDES OF LEES COURT, co. Kent," Barony (*Watson, formerly Monson*), *cr.* 1760, and Earldom (*Milles, formerly Watson*), *cr.* 1880.

LEIBURN, see LEYBURN.

LEICESTER [county of.]

[EDGAR, son of Algar, the Saxon Earl of Mercia [Leicester] and grandson, by the far famed Godiva, of Leofric, Earl of Mercia, "was restored to the honours of his father, Algar, by William the Conqueror, and was consequently" [as stated by

---

(a) Hornby Castle (erected by William, Lord Conyers, 1509-24), descended thro' the families of Conyers and Darcy to that of Osborne in 1784, in the male line of which family it remains, tho' the representation of the Lords Conyers departed therefrom in 1859 to the heir *general.*

Mr. Planché] "the first EARL OF LEICESTER under the Norman dynasty."(a) He is not, however, generally included among those considered to have been entitled to such Earldom. He *d.* 1071.]

Earldom. I. 1107? ROBERT DE BEAUMONT,(b) otherwise BELMONT, or DE BELLOMONT,(c) s. of Roger DE BEAUMONT, SEIGNEUR DE PONTAUDEMER, by Adelina, sister of Hugh, and da. of Waleran, each of them COMTE DE MEULAN,(d) was *b.* about 1046; accompanied the Conqueror in his invasion of England, and tho' very young distinguished himself greatly at the battle of Hastings(e) in 1066, receiving soon afterwards 90 Lordships (in Warwickshire, Leicestershire, &c.), as a reward. On the death of his mother in 1081 he (being heir to her br., Hugh), was acknowledged as COMTE DE MEULAN or MELLENT, and did homage accordingly to the King of France, sitting in 1082 as a Peer of France in a Parl. at Poissy. He was also Seigneur de Beaumont, Pontaudemer, Brionne, &c., in Normandy, and was in command, 28 Sep. 1106, of the English army which established the King's rule there. He was rewarded by Henry I. about 1107 with a grant(f) of the county of Leicester (including the Wardenship of the Castle and the Royal desmesnes within and about the city) and is generally considered (tho' perhaps erroneously) to have become EARL OF LEICESTER.(g) His first wife is said to

(a) See an article by J. R. Planché "On the genealogy and armorial ensigns of the Anglo-Norman Earls of Leicester," read at the Leicester Congress, 1862, and printed in the "*Collectanea Archæologica*" (4to., 1871), vol. ii, pp. 31-41. This, which corrects "the contradictions and discrepancies which abound" in the account of these Earls, by John Nichols, in his "*Leicestershire*," has been mainly followed in the article in the text. See also Planché's "*Conqueror and his Companions*," sub "*Beaumont*."

(b) See articles on "Beaumont, Robert de, Count of Meulan," and on his son and grandson (Earls of Leicester) in the "*Nat. Biogr.*" by Mr. J. Horace Round, who, however, does *not* attribute the Earldom of Leicester to the first mentioned Robert.

(c) He was br. to Henry, Seigneur de Neufbourg, *cr.* Earl of Warwick by William II.

(d) "Meulan or Meulent [is not, as is often said, in Normandy, but] is a town and Comté on the Seine, between St. Germain-en-Laye and Vernon; both town and Comté are divided by that river into two portions, the one in the Vexin français, the other in the pays de Pincerais." *Ex inform.*, G. W. Watson.

(e) The Beaumont who in the "*Roman de Rou*" is described as being present at the battle of Hastings was *Roger* Beaumont, *i.e.*,

"Rogier li Veil, cil de Belmont
Assalt Engleis el primier front."

The name, however, in the MS. of Wace (in the Brit. Mus.) is "*Robert*," and in spite of the assertion of Wace to the contrary, it seems that *Roger* de Beaumont remained in Normandy at that date as President of the Council. Mr. Planché conjectures that the epithet "li Veil," tho' not appropriate to the then age of young Robert, stands for "de Vielles," inasmuch as Humphrey *de Vielles* (s. of Thorold de Pontaudemer) was father of Roger and grandfather of Robert de Beaumont.

(f) The story of this grant is thus told by Ordericus Vitalis, who after stating that the town of Leicester had then four masters, *viz.* (1) the King (2) the Bishop of Lincoln (3) "Earl Simon" [*i.e.*, Simon (de Saint Liz), Earl of Northampton], and (4) "Ivo, son of Hugh" [*i.e.*, of Hugh de Grentmesnil], relates how that the said Ivo, being in disgrace at Court, pledged his share (apparently by far the largest one) to the Count of Meulan who never restored the same (as had been promised) to the said Ivo's son and heir, and who subsequently, by favour of the King, contrived to get the *whole* of Leicester into his own hands.

(g) In no charter apparently is he called Earl of *Leicester*. As "Robertus, Comes *Mellenti*," he with Elizabeth, his wife, and their sons, Waleran, Robert, and Hugh, confirms the grant of Roger de Beaumont, his father, to the Church of St. Mary at Bec in Pontaudemer. (Registres de la Chambre des Comptes—La Roque, Histoire de Harcourt, preuves, pp. 1,835, 1,619, and suppl.) *Ex inform.* G. W. Watson, who adds, however, that "in an inspeximus by one of the Edwards his charter is quoted as calling himself Count of Mellent and Leicester, which double title appears very suspicious." Mr. J. Horace Round in the "*Nat. Biogr.*" (*sub* "*Beaumont*"), says of him that tho' "distinctly stated by Orderic to have been *cr.* Earl of Leicester ('inde

have been[a] Godechilde, da. of Ralph (sometimes, tho' erroneously, called Roger), SEIGNEUR DE TORNI ET CONCHES. From her (if indeed she ever was *m.* to him) he was separated before 1096.[b] He is also said (tho' probably in error) to have *m.* Emma, a da. of Roger DE BRETEUIL.[c] He unquestionably *m.* in or shortly before April 1096 Isabella[d] or Elizabeth (mother of all his children), da. of Hugh the Great, COMTE DE VERMANDOIS (son of Henry I., King of France), by Adelheid, da. of Herbert, also COMTE DE VERMANDOIS. He *d.* 5 June 1118, and was *bur.* (with his father) in the Abbey of Preaux. His widow or repudiated wife (for it is doubtful which she was) *m.* William (DE WARENNE), 2d EARL OF SURREY (with whom she had intrigued in her husband's lifetime) who *d.* 11 May 1138. She herself *d.* 1131 aged probably about 50.

II. 1118. 2. ROBERT (DE BEAUMONT), EARL OF LEICESTER, called "*Le Goczen*"[e] and "*Le Bossu*" (Crook-back), 2d son[f] but heir to his father's English estates and dignities, was *b.* 1104, being twin with Waleran his elder br.; was *knighted* by Henry I. in 1122. As *Earl of Leicester* he was one of the five Earls[g] who witnessed the charter to Salisbury granted at the Northampton Council, 8 Sep. 1131. He was present at the King's death in 1135. He *m.*, in or after 1120[h] Amicia, da. of Ralph DE GAEL[i] or DE

Consul in Anglia factus') of this the Lords' committee 'found no evidence' (*3d Rep. on the dignity of a Peer*, p. 133), nor does he seem to have been so styled tho' he possessed the *tertius denarius* and tho' that dignity devolved upon his son."

(a) By Orderious Vitalis.

(b) In that year, when still under 17, she *m.* Baldwin de Boulogne, afterwards King of Jerusalem, and *d.* at Marash in Syria in 1097. A Godelbreda who was living 1110 as wife of Robert de Neufbourg (nephew of the 1st Earl of Leicester) is sometimes confused with her. *Ex inform.* G. W. Watson.

(c) See vol. iv, p. 211, note "d," as to the issue of this Roger.

(d) A dispensation was obtained from the Pope (the parties being within the prohibited degrees) on condition that Count Hugh should join the Crusade, and the marriage was celebrated before his departure thereto, which took place in April 1096. The Earl was third cousin to his bride's mother, as appears from a statement (which was held good) of Ivo of Chartres who forbade the marriage:—"dicunt enim" says he in an epistle to the Clerks of Meulent and all in the Archdeacoury of the Pincerais, "quia Gualterius albus genuit matrem Gualeranni Comitis, qui genuit matrem Roberti Comitis, item supradictus Gualterius genuit Radulphum, patrem alterius Radulphi, qui genuit Vermandensem Comitissam, ex quâ nata est uxor Comitis Hugonis, cujus filiam nunc ducere vult Mellentinus Comes. Si autem prædicta genealogia ita sibi cohæret, legitimum esse non poterit conjugium, sed incestum contubernium, nec filios poterunt habere legitimos, sed spurios." *Ex. inform.* G. W. Watson.

(e) "*Gotzen*" in La Roque, but "*Goczen*" in Delisle, who adds that Ducange gives *gossum* in the sense of *bosse*.

(f) The eldest son, Waleran, *b.* 1104, who *suc.* to his father's French territory as Comte de Meulan, *m.* Agnes, da. of Amauri III., Count of Evreux, and *d.* April 1166, aged 61, at Preaux. The third son, Hugh, was in 1138 *cr.* Earl of Bedford. Of the two daughters (1) Isabel, *m.* Simon (Saint Liz), Earl of Huntingdon and Northampton, while (2) Hawise, *m.* William (Fitz Robert), Earl of Gloucester.

(g) The five Earls were Robert of Gloucester, William of Warenne, Randulf of Chester, Robert of Leicester, and Roger of Warwick. There were 46 witnesses in all, there being (besides these Earls and some 22 Prelates, &c.), 19 Barons. See full account thereof in Round's "*Geoff. de Mandeville*," p. 265.

(h) This Amicia was affianced to Richard (illegit. son of King Henry I.) who perished in Nov. 1120 in the wreck of the White ship. (Ord. Vit., xii, 25.)

(i) "The statement in Dugdale that he *m.* Ita or Amicia, da. of Ralph, Earl of Norfolk, was followed by English genealogists till Mr. Planché (*Conqueror and his Companions*," ii, p. 14), adopted the account by Orderic, *viz.*, that Amicia was da. of Ralph, Seigneur de Montfort and de Gael, in Britanny, son of Ralph, Earl of Norfolk. Mr. Planché, however, seems not to have noticed that Dugdale was merely following the Continuator of William of Jumièges: 'Emma [filia Willelmi, Comitis Herefordi] juncta est Rodulpho de Waiet, genere Britoni, qui fuit Comes Norwicensis, sed quia contra fidelitatem Willelmi Regis Senioris munitionem Norwich, aliquando tenere attentavit, expulsus et extorris de regno Angliæ, cum uxore sua Hierusalem perrexit, relinquens unam filiam, nomine Ittam, quæ procedenti tempore nupsit Roberto,

MONTFORT([a]) in Britanny, son, by Emma, da. of William (FITZ OSBORN), EARL OF HEREFORD, of Ralph (DE GAEL), sometime EARL OF NORFOLK. In consequence of this alliance [his wife's grandmother, the above mentioned Emma, being sister of William de Breteuil (who *d.* 1102) as also of Roger (DE BRETEUIL), EARL OF HEREFORD, who incurred forfeiture in 1074] he became Seigneur of Breteuil, &c., in Normandy; was *cr.* about 1138 (by King Stephen) EARL OF HEREFORD (which Earldom, however, he held but for a short time) and not improbably obtained the post of *Steward of England.*([b]) He subsequently took the part of Henry (afterwards Henry II.) against King Stephen and was a witness to the compromise between them in 1153. From that date till his death he is said to have become a "Canon regular"([c]) in Leicester Abbey but this seems incredible as from 1155 he was Chief Justiciar, and was Vice Regent of the Kingdom, 1158–1163, as also 1165–67.([d]) He *d.* 5 April 1168, and was *bur.* in Leicester Abbey. His wife or widow *d.* 1 Sep. (in what year is uncertain) in the convent at Nuneaton.

III. 1168? ROBERT (DE BEAUMONT), EARL OF LEICESTER, Seigneur of Breteuil and Pacy in Normandy, *Steward of England* called "*Blanchemains*" (White hands),([e]) *s.* and h. By charter, dat. at Bristol, from Henry, Duke of Normandy (afterwards King Henry II.), he as "Robert, *son* of the

---

Comiti Legrecestriæ, filio Roberti, Comitis Mellenti, unde factum est ut Lire, Glos., Britollium et plurimam partem terræ, quam Willelmus filius Osberni, avus uxoris suæ, idem Comes haberet; genuit autem ex eâ unum filium et plures filias.' Earl Ralph, of Norfolk, was married, as is well known, in 1074, so that Orderic's version is more likely chronologically; further he is extremely circumstantial. There is, moreover, a charter of Robert III. (*aux Blanches-Mains*) which decides the matter in Orderic's favour. In it he positively calls William Fitz Osbern his *atavus* [great-great-grandfather] and as if to show the word is not used at random he further specifies Hugh de Grentemesnil (the founder of St. Evroult) as being the *proavus* [great-grandfather] of his wife, Petronilla." *Ex inform.* G. W. Watson. The issue of Earl Ralph (or Raoul) of Norfolk by Emma, his wife, was, according to the version adopted by Planché, "two surviving sons one of whom, Raoul the second, was the father of Amicia, Countess of Leicester."

([a]) "From the fact that the family of De Gael were Lords of Montfort-sur-Rille, Ralph de Gael is sometimes called Ralph de Montfort by contemporary writers." [Planché.] "*Sur-Rille*" should, however, be omitted, as the De Gaels were Lords of Montfort near Rennes, *in Britanny*, while "Montfort-sur-Rile" is in *Normandy*.

([b]) The important office of Steward of England is said to have been held by William (Fitz Osborne), Earl of Hereford, who undoubtedly was Steward of Normandy. It is, also, generally (tho' apparently without any conclusive evidence) considered to have been *attached* to the Barony of Hinckley, co. Leicester, and, with it to have been brought into the Beaumont family from that of Grentmesnil by the marriage of the 3d Earl of Leicester with Pernelle, but, says Mr. Planché, "Mr. Nichols has shewn that the honour of Hinckley and *the consequent Stewardship of England* were *previously* [to this match] in the family of De Beaumont, having come to them, he says, in the same manner as the Lordship of Breteuil, or, may we not suggest, as the Earldom of Hereford, for William Fitz Osborne held that high office [*i.e.*, the Stewardship] in the time of the Conqueror." The Stewardship of England and Normandy was included in a grant of Henry, Duke of Normandy (afterwards King Henry II.), to Robert, son of Robert, Earl of Leicester, which somewhat militates against the Hinckley theory.

([c]) "The Canons regular were perhaps the least ascetic of the *monastic* orders." See full description of these in Cutts's "*Middle Ages*," pp. 18-21.

([d]) "The Monks' genealogy says that Earl Robert 'de consensu Amiciæ, uxoris suæ, sumpsit in Abbatia ista [de Pratis Leicestriæ] habitum nostræ religionis, vivens juste et sancte quindecim annos et amplius; ipsa quoque Amicia uxor sua, Sanctimonialis apud Eton est effecta.' This statement that Earl Robert was a monk at Leicester from 1153 must be received with some reservations, for we know that he was Chief Justice of all England in 1155, and in that capacity acted as Viceroy during the absences of King Henry from England in 1158-62 and 1165-67." *Ex inform.* G. W. Watson. See also p. 43, note "b."

([e]) Doubtless "as it has been shrewdly suggested from the effects of a fearful malady with which another of his family [his son, William de Breteuil, the *leper*], appears to have been afflicted."

Earl of Leicester," had a grant (v.p.) of all the land his father had in England,(a) of Breteuil and of Pacy, and of the Stewardship of England and Normandy. It is open to conjecture that, *possibly*, he was, by this charter *recognised* (v.p.) as Earl of Leicester and consequently that *he* (and not his father who is said to have been a monk since 1153) was the Justiciar of England,(b) 1153—1168. In 1173 he espoused the side of Prince Henry against King Henry II., by whom he was taken prisoner (his castle of Breteuil being burnt and the town of Leicester nearly destroyed) and not released till Jan. 1177 when he was restored in blood and honours. He was again arrested in April 1183 but was restored before 25 Dec. 1186, when he performed his office of "*Dapifer.*" He was bearer of the third sword at the first Coronation (3 Sep. 1189), of Richard I. He *m.* in 1168 Pernell or Petronilla, heiress of the powerful family of GRENTMESNIL, said to be da. of Hugh de GRENTMESNIL,(c) and with her acquired vast estates.(d) She was living in 1179 and, possibly, in 1190,(e) at which date he departed on the Crusade during which he *d.* (on the voyage) 31 Aug. 1190, and was *bur.* at Durazzo (Dyrrachium) in Albania.

(a) "Totam terram Rodberti Comitis patris sui de Anglia, sicut Comes Rodbertus de Mellend, avus suus * * tenuit; insuper reddidi et concessi Britolium, cum toto honore, &c., sicut Willelmus de Britolio * * tenuit. * * Praeterea dedi et concessi in feudo et hereditate Pasci cum toto honore et totam terram quam Willelmus de Pasci in Anglia et in Normannia tenuit in feudo de me et de quocumque eam tenuisset, et Dapiferatum Anglie et Normannie." (Original sealed at the Trésor de Chartes, *Conches et Breteuil*, No. 1, Carton J, 219. Printed by M. Delisle, Cartulaire Normand, p. 2.) With reference to Pacy we read in R. du Mont (sub an. 1153) "Mortuo Willelmo de Paceio absque liberis redditum est castrum Pacii Roberto, filio Comitis Legecestriae, quia pertinebat ad honorem Britolii, unde ille erat legitimus haeres ex parte matris suae." *Ex inform.* G. W. Watson.

(b) It is to be observed that Stapleton says that *Dapifer* or *Seneschallus Normanniae* was the usual title of the Chief Justiciar of Normandy and was a dignity held by William Fitz Osbern, son of Osbern Dapifer. Now the *Dapiferatus Anglie et Normannie* was granted to this Earl in his father's lifetime (see note "a" next above), from which fact (if taken by itself) it would seem thereby likely that *he* (and not his father) was the Chief Justiciar of England 1155—1168 (see p. 42, note "d"), but there are, writes Mr. G. W. Watson, "powerful objections to this theory. In the first place the Justiciar is uniformly described as *Earl* of Leicester. Now we read in the Convention between Henry II. and the Count of Flanders (Hearne's Lib. Nig. I, p. 34), among the sureties of the King of England '*Robertus, filius Comitis Leircestre, pro c. marc.*' This Convention is of date 1163 and it is out of the question that the *filius* is meant for *Robertus fil. Petronillae*; in other words Robert Blanchmains was *filius Comitis* and not *Comes* in 1163. Other charters there are of 1155 and 1160 to which Robert, *son* of the Earl of Leicester, is witness, and the former contains also Robert, *Earl* of Leicester, as witness (see Eyton, pp. 11, 49.) This seems to me to prove that Robert, the son, was *not* Robert, the Viceroy."

(c) Her father's name is thus given in the genealogy by the monks of St. Mary at Leicester, but Mr. Planché (who says that at this date no "Hugh de Grentesmil" appears elsewhere) expressly states that "the *parentage* of Pernelle has not been exactly ascertained." See, however, p. 41, note "h," where Hugh de Grentemesnil (the founder of St. Evroult) is spoken of as being her great grandfather. This would make her father to be (Hugh) the s. and h. of that Ivo who was cheated out of his inheritance of Leicester by Robert, Count of Meulan. See p. 40, note "f." The above genealogy (*Monast.*, edit. 1830, vi, 467), also attributes (2) to this lady the heirship of the honour of Hinckley; is, also, responsible (3) for Earl Robert being a monk 15 years before his death, and makes (4) Amicia de Beaumont to be the *mother* of Earl Simon who was slain at Evesham. This last statement we *know* to be wrong so that not improbably the other three may be wrong also.

(d) Doubtless (among others) the Grentmesnil fiefs in Normandy, for the Leicestershire estates had already passed (at all events *in pledge*) to the Beaumont family. See p. 40, note "f."

(e) She attested a charter (undated) to the monks of Lire shortly before the Earl, her husband, set forth on his journey to Jerusalem. He was, however, on *two* pilgrimages there; one in 1179 (Annals of Waverley) and the other in 1190. *Ex inform.* G. W. Watson.

(f) "Robertus, Comes Leicestriae, Anandiae, sancti Egidii obiit languore praeventus in mare mediterraneo, et apud Duraz, Graeciae urbem, sepultus est." (Chron. de Mailros, Fell's Collect., I, p. 178.) *Ex inform.* G. W. Watson.

IV. 1190, to 1204. 4. ROBERT (DE BEAUMONT), EARL OF LEICESTER, Seigneur of Breteuil and Pacy in Normandy, *Steward of England*, called (from his mother's name) *Fitz Pernell*, 2d son(a) but h. to his father's dignities, being invested with the Earldom, 1 Feb. 1191, at Messina. He was Commander of the English forces at Rouen, 1193, but was taken prisoner, 15 June 1194, and not released till after 15 Jan. 1195/6, when his castle of Pacy was ceded to France. He acted as Steward at the Coronation of King John, 27 May 1199. He *m.* Lauretta, da. of William DE BRAOSE.(b) He *d.* s.p. 6 Jan. 1204,(c) and was *bur.* in Leicester Abbey, when the *Earldom of Leicester lapsed to the Crown*. His widow became a recluse at Hackington but was dead before 1208.(d)

V. 1207, to 1218. 1. SIMON DE MONTFORT,(e) younger son of Simon, COUNT OF EVREUX in Normandy, by Amicia,(f) sister and coheir(g) of Robert (DE BEAUMONT), EARL OF LEICESTER, next abovenamed, was *b.* probably about 1170;(h) *suc.* his father in or before 1181

(a) His elder br., William de Breteuil, was a leper, and, as such, even if he survived his father, would have been passed over in the succession. He was probably dead before Jan. 1195/6. At all events he does not appear to be among those who ratified the Earl's cession of Pacy at that date. These were (1) the King (2) Roger, Bishop of St. Andrew's (3) Amicia, Countess of Montfort (the said Roger and Amicia being brother and sister of the said Earl) and (4) Simon "Dominus Montisfortis," who speaks of the said Earl as "Avunculus meus." See La Roque, Maison de Harcourt, preuves, pp. 126, 127, &c. *Ex. inform.* G. W. Watson.

(b) It seems doubtful which William de Braose is indicated, and this Lauretta is not mentioned in the elaborate account of that family in "*the Genealogist*" (O. S., vols. iv and v), while that given by Dugdale is inaccurate. She is usually called the da. of William de Braose who *m.* Matilda de St. Valery, but perhaps was his sister. *Ex. inform.* G. W. Watson.

(c) The date of his death, according to Doyle's "*Official Baronage*," was 20 Oct. 1206, but 1204 is given in the Annals of Waverley (Gale ii, 168), and the correctness of this date is certain, for in 1204 his sister, as "*Amicia, Countess of Leicester*," ceded to the King of France her castle of Breteuil and *all that her brother had possessed* over sea. See La Roque (as in note "a" next above), p. 2174.

(d) In that year Philip, King of France, confirms to the monks of Lire all that "Laureta, *quondam* Comitissa Leycestrie," had given. *Ex inform.* G. W. Watson.

(e) The account of the De Montfort family as given in the (admirable) "life of Simon de Montfort," by G. W. Prothero (1877), has been followed here. The name was "from a stronghold still known as Montfort L'Amauri" half way between Paris and Evreux; situated in "the Mantois," in Ile-de-France. By the marriage of Simon I. (who *d.* 1087) with Agnes, da. of Richard and sister and heir (1118) of William, Counts of Evreux, that important territory came in 1104 (on the death of Simon II.) to his son Amauri (*d.* 1137), whose s. and h. Simon III. surrendered it (retaining, however, the title) in 1159 to King Henry II. and *d.* 1181. His *eldest son*, Amauri, *d.* about 1193, leaving an only s. and h., Amauri, Earl of Gloucester (*jure matris*) and Count of Evreux, who *d.* s.p. in or before Nov. 1213, while the *second* son, Simon IV., who took the de Montfort estates, was Count of Montfort and Earl of Leicester (so cr. in 1207) as in the text. Of Simon's children, Simon V., a younger son, was the 2d Earl of Leicester (of that house), while the elder son Amauri, Count of Montfort (*d.* 1241), was *suc.* by his son John (*d.* 1249), whose da. and heir Beatrice (*d.* 1312) was, by Robert, Count of Dreux, mother of Yolande, who, by Arthur, Count of Brittany, carried the estates into that family in which "they remained until the union of Brittany with the Crown of France completed the absorption of the once princely domains of Montfort into the royal treasury."

(f) Courthope (following the old version) makes the first Earl of Leicester the *husband* and not the son of Amicia (the heiress), and gives the following note, "Pierre [*sic*] Anselme, in his 'Histoire des Connestables de France,' vol. i. p. 314, makes this same Simon de Montfort to be the *son*, and not the *husband*, of Amicia de Beaumont. There is an entry on the Close Rolls, 1206-07, which would seem to support the account so given, whilst the charter above referred to [*i.e.*, the confirmation of the Earldom in

in the territory of Montfort L'Amauri (tho' not in that of Evreux) whence he became COUNT OF MONTFORT in the Mantois. He appears to have been at once recognised in England as the successor of Robert, his maternal uncle, being in Aug. 1206 spoken of[i] and being on 10 March 1207, *confirmed* (by King John) as EARL OF LEICESTER (with the third penny of that county) and as *Steward of England*. His connexion with England was, however, little more than nominal, and "it is very doubtful whether he ever set foot" there, anyhow, "in the very same year (Rot. Lit. Claus. 27 Dec. 1207), we find that the King deprived him of his possessions." He was as "*Comte de Montfort*" well known in the Crusades as also in 1209 as "*the Scourge of the Albigenses*" against whom he was the leader. In Dec. 1212 he styles himself "Comte de Leicester et de Montfort, Vicomte de Béziers et de Carcassonne, Seigneur D'Albi et de Rodez." About 1215 he was restored to his English estates, his nephew, Randolph, Earl of Chester, being made *Custos* of the fief of the Earldom of Leicester. He obtained the Comté of Toulouse by letter from the Pope, 2 April 1215, and made himself master of the Duchy of Narbonne, being, after doing homage for them, invested by the King of France, 3 April 1216, as COUNT OF TOULOUSE and DUKE OF NARBONNE. He *m.* in or before 1190 Alice, da. of Bouchard V. (or IV.), SIRE DE MONTMORENCY, D'ESCOUEN, DE CONFLANS-SAINTE HONORINE, ET D'ATTICHY, by Laurence, da. of Baldwin IV., COUNT OF HAINAULT. He was slain at the siege of Toulouse, 27 June 1218, and was *bur.* in the Priory church of Hautesbruyeres, near Montfort, his funeral having been magnificently celebrated at Carcassonne. His widow *d.* 22 Feb. 1221, and was *bur.* with him.

* * * * *

[Amauri de Montfort, COUNT OF MONTFORT, s. and h., styled himself EARL OF LEICESTER, tho' never acknowledged as such. He, however, resigned all claim thereto to Simon, his younger brother, tho' probably not till June 1232 or even later. He became a Constable of France and *d.* on his return from a crusade in 1241 leaving issue.[k]]

VI. 1230 to 1265. 2. SIMON (DE MONTFORT), EARL OF LEICESTER, yst. s. of Earl Simon abovenamed, was *b.* probably between 1195 and 1205, is said to have been confirmed as EARL OF LEICESTER and *Steward of England*, 2 (or 6) Feb. (1229/30) 14 Hen. III.[l] and was certainly, in 1232, confirmed in all the land held by his father in England. He acted as Sewer at the Coronation of the Queen Consort, 20 Jan. 1236, and 3 years later obtained the King's sister in marriage. A history of his career from that time would be that of the nation. After serving the King faithfully in Gascony and elsewhere, he incurred the royal displeasure; took lead in the great revolution of 1258; was in command at the battle of Lewes, 14 May 1264, taking the King and his eldest son Edward, Earl of Chester, captive, and summoning a Parl. in the King's name, 24 Dec.

1207] would lead to a different conclusion. Dugdale and all other English genealogists give the same version as in the text." There can, however, be no doubt (in spite of "Dugdale and all other English genealogists") that Pere Anselme is right. Among other proofs, Simon, Count of Montfort, by deed dat. Jan. 1195 (printed in the *Cartulaire Normand*, p. 278) speaks of Robert Earl of Leicester as "*his dear uncle.*" See also page 44, note "a," for another charter, in which he is also called "uncle" by the said Simon.

(g) She had a younger sister, Margaret, wife of Saher (de Quincy), 1st Earl of Winchester. This Margaret *d.* in 1235.

(h) The marriage of his parents was "not later than 1173" says Dr. Pauli, but Mr. Prothero (see page 44, note "e") adds that "it could not well have been later than 1160."

(i) Amicia, his mother, is spoken of as "Comitissa, mater *Comitis Leicestriæ*," in the close rolls of 28 Aug. 1206, while in those of the previous year the lady is called "Amicia, Comitissa de Montford."

(k) See Prothero's "*Simon de Montfort*" as on page 44, note "e."

(l) The patent-roll (14 Hen. III., pt. 2, m. 6) states that the lands were at that time in the hands of Ranulph, Earl of Chester and Lincoln, who held them "of our lease, by our charter."

1264. By letters patent 24 Dec. 1264 and 20 May 1265, he was *cr.*, by the captive King, EARL OF CHESTER, which Earldom some 8 months afterwards (on his death and attainder) came back again to the young Prince Edward abovenamed. He was defeated and slain (together with his eldest son, Henry) at the battle of Evesham, 4 Aug. 1265. when, having been attainted, all his *honours* became *forfeited.*(a) He *m.* 7 Jan. 1238/9 in the King's private chapel at Westminster the Lady Eleanor PLANTAGENET, 2d da. of John, King of England by Isabella, da. and h. of Aimar, COUNT OF ANGOULEME. She who was *b.* 1215 had been betrothed, 23 April 1224, to William (MARSHAL) EARL OF PEMBROKE, who (some 25 years older than herself) *d.* s.p. 24 April 1231, when, tho' only 16, she took a vow of chastity, which vow gave considerable scandal to her subsequent marriage. She *d.* 13 April 1275, aged about 60 at the convent of Montargis in France.

VII. 1265. *1.* EDMUND PLANTAGENET, yst. s. of King Henry III., *b.* 16 Jan. 1245/6, was *cr.* 26 Oct. 1265, EARL OF LEICESTER and *Steward of England*, which dignities were confirmed to him by a charter of Ed. I., dated 1274. He was *cr.* EARL OF LANCASTER, 30 June 1267. He *d.* 5 June 1296.

VIII. 1296, to 1322. *2.* THOMAS (PLANTAGENET), EARL OF LANCASTER, EARL OF LEICESTER, &c., s. and h., *b.* about 1278; *beheaded* 22 March 1321/2, when, having been attainted, *all his honours were forfeited.*

* * * * *

IX. 1324, and 1327. *3.* HENRY PLANTAGENET, next br. and h., *cr.* 10 May 1324, EARL OF LEICESTER. His brother's attainder being reversed by Act of Parl. 7 March 1326/7, he became EARL OF LANCASTER, EARL OF LEICESTER, &c., by inheritance. He *d.* 22 Sep. 1345.

X. 1345. *4.* HENRY (PLANTAGENET), EARL OF LANCASTER, EARL OF LEICESTER, &c., only s. and h., *b.* about 1300. He was *cr.* 6 March 1350/1, DUKE OF LANCASTER, a dignity which became extinct on his death s.p.m. 13 March 1360/1, while *the Earldoms of Lancaster, Leicester*, &c. may be considered to have *reverted to the Crown.*

See fuller account under "Lancaster" Earldom, *cr.* 1267; *cr.* 1361.

XI. 1361. WILLIAM, COUNT OF HAINAULT, HOLLAND, ZEALAND AND FRIESLAND, 2d s. of Louis of Bavaria, EMPEROR OF GERMANY by Margaret sister of William, COUNT OF HAINAULT. &c. (who *d.* s.p. legit. 1345), was *b.* about 1327; *suc.* in Jan. 1349, as Count of Holland, &c., and in Feb. 1356, as Count of Hainault, He, having *m.* Nov. 1344, Maud widow of Ralph STAFFORD, 1st da. and coheir of Henry (PLANTAGENET), DUKE OF LANCASTER [by Isabel da. of Henry (DE BEAUMONT), 1st LORD BEAUMONT] obtained in her right (on her father's death) the *Earldom of Leicester* (b), and was styled EARL OF HAINAULT AND LEICESTER, 10 Oct. 1361 (c). She, however, *d.* s.p. 10 April 1362. He *d.* April 1389.

(a) Of his five sons, Henry was slain in 1265; Simon, who continued the resistance to the King for a year longer, *d.* in 1273; Guy, Count of Nola, *d.* 1288, leaving daughters, *viz.* (1) Anastasia (*suo jure*) Countess of Nola, who *m.*, 8 June 1293, Raimondo Orsini, and was ancestress of the Counts of Nola (2) Thomasse who *m.* Pietro Vico, Prefect of Rome; Amauri (in Holy Orders about 1273), *d.* as a soldier in Italy, and Richard who is said to have *d.* in France. The only da., Eleanor, *m.* in Oct. 1278, Llewelyn, Prince of Wales, and *d.* in child birth, June 1282 [1281 ?] leaving a da., Gwendolen, a nun at Sempringham who *d.* in 1337.

(b) See p. 8, note "f," *sub* "LANCASTER" Dukedom.

(c) Doyle's "*Official Baronage*," the reference therein given being "*Pat. 3, m. 19.*"

XII. *1362.* *1.* JOHN (PLANTAGENET, *styled* "of Gaunt)," 4th s. of **King Edward III**, having m. 19 May 1359, Blanche, 2d and yst. da. and coheir of Henry (PLANTAGENET), DUKE OF LANCASTER, by Isabel, his wife, both abovenamed, obtained in her right, firstly [1361] the *moiety* and finally (on the death of her sister, Maud, COUNTESS OF HAINAULT, abovenamed) in 1362, the *whole* of the possessions of her father, becoming (possibly) thus (in 1361) EARL OF LANCASTER, DERBY AND LINCOLN and (in 1362) EARL OF LEICESTER,(a) and *High Steward of England*. He was, 13 Nov. 1362, *cr.* DUKE OF LANCASTER. He *d.* 3 Feb. 1398/9, aged 58.

XIII. *1399,* *Feb.* *to* *Sep.* *2.* HENRY (PLANTAGENET, *styled* "of Bolingbroke), DUKE OF LANCASTER, DUKE OF HEREFORD, EARL OF DERBY, EARL OF LINCOLN, and EARL OF LEICESTER, *High Steward of England*, &c., s. and h., *b.* 1367; elected King as **Henry IV**. 30 Sep. 1399, when *all his honours merged in the Crown.*

See fuller account under "LANCASTER" Dukedom, cr. 1362; *merged* 1399.

XI. 1564, to 1588. LORD ROBERT DUDLEY, 5th s. of John (DUDLEY), DUKE OF NORTHUMBERLAND (so *cr.* 1551) by Jane, da. of Sir Edward GUILFORD, was *b.* 24 June 1532 (or 1533) and, having been *Knighted*, *m.* 4 June 1549 (when about 18) at Sheen Palace, Surrey, in the King's presence,(b) Amy, the only legit. child of Sir John ROBSART, of Siderstern, Norfolk, by Elizabeth, widow of Roger APPLEGARD, of Stansfield, co. Norfolk, da. of John SCOTT, of Camberwell, Surrey. She, who was *b.* at Stansfield about 1532, *d.* s.p. 8 Sep. 1560, being found dead at the foot of the staircase in Cumnor place, Berks. She was *bur.* the 22d, in great state at St. Mary's, Oxford, M.I. Her death(c) was generally supposed to have been contrived by her husband to allow of his marriage with Queen Elizabeth, whom there is "no doubt at all that on her succession she contemplated marrying."(d) He had in 1551 been Gent. of the Privy Chamber and, 1552-53, Master of the Buckhounds to King Edward VI; was M.P. for Norfolk. *circ.* 1549-52 and 1553, but taking part (with his Father) in proclaiming Lady Jane Grey as Queen, was committed to the Tower in July 1553, attainted and sentenced to death 22 Jan. 1553/4, but was pardoned 13 Oct. 1554 and restored in blood 7 March 1557/8. He was Master of the Horse, from Jan. 1558/9 to Dec. 1587; el. **K.G.**, 24 April and inst. 3 June 1559; M.A., Cambridge, 10 Aug. 1564; P.C.; and having been suggested as a husband to Mary, Queen of Scots was, on 28 Sep. 1564,(e) *cr.* BARON OF DENBIGH and, on the day following, EARL OF LEICESTER.(f) He was Chancellor of Oxford Univ. 1564, and was made *Knight of St. Michael* of France, 24 Jan. 1566; Lieut of the order of the Garter, June 1572 and April 1584. From 9 to 27 July 1575

(a) The following note (slightly altered from one by Nicolas) is given by Courthope; "It is to be observed that at the Coronation of Richard II., John of Gaunt, King of Castile and Leon, claimed as *Earl of Leicester* the High Stewardship of England; as *Duke of Lancaster* to bear the chief sword called Curtana; and as *Earl of Lincoln* to be carver at the King's table, all of which claims appear to have been allowed. *Vide* Red Book of the Exchequer."

(b) Sir Walter Scott, in his "*Kenilworth*," falsifies history by representing this as a *secret* marriage. Froude in his "*Elizabeth*" (vol. i, p. 86), remarks that "it had been a love match of a doubtful kind" [tho' he does not indicate what was the doubt] and that it was spoken of by Cecil as "*nuptiæ carnales.*"

(c) "In 1584 the story adopted by Sir Walter Scott (in '*Kenilworth*') was first published in a libel on Dudley usually known as '*Leicester's commonwealth.*' There Anthony Forster and Sir Richard Verney were said to have flung Lady Amy downstairs, but none of the statements in this libel deserves credit. In spite of the suspicious circumstances of the death nothing can be historically proved against Dudley. The theory of suicide has most in its favour." [*Nat. Biography.*]

(d) *Nat. Biogr.*

(e) 28 Sep., 6 Eliz., *i.e.*, 1564, tho' generally (in error) called 1563.

(f) His connection with Leicestershire is not clear. Lands in *ten* other counties had been granted him in 1563; see p. 48, note "a."

he sumptuously entertained the Queen at Kenilworth,(a) at an expense of about £60,000: was Lord Steward of the Household, 1584-88. In Oct. 1585 he was given the command of the English forces to aid the States General, and was, in Feb. 1586 proclaimed Governor of the United provinces, but was finally recalled in Nov. 1587. In Oct. 1586 he was one of the Commissioners to try the Queen of Scots. He was also Lord Lieut. of Warwickshire (1559), Berks (1560 ?), Worcestershire (1569-70) Essex, Herts and Midx. (all in 1585) and of Leicestershire and Rutland (1587). About 1571 he *m.* privately at a house in Cannon Row, and again (2 years later) in May 1573 (two days before the birth of their son) (b) at Esher, Surrey, in the presence of many witnesses,(c) Douglas, widow of John (SHEFFIELD), 2d BARON SHEFFIELD OF BUTTERWICKE, da. of William (HOWARD), 1st BARON HOWARD OF EFFINGHAM, by his second wife, Margaret, da. of Sir Thomas GAMAGE. In 1577 or 1578 (before Sep. 1578) this lady *m.* Edward STAFFORD, of Grafton, co. Northampton, while the Earl himself *m.*, 21 Sep. 1578.(d) at Wanstead, co. Essex, Lettice, widow of Walter (DEVEREUX), 1st EARL OF ESSEX, sister of William, 1st EARL OF BANBURY, 1st da. of Sir Francis KNOLLYS, K.G., by Catharine, da. of William CARY, and Mary, his wife, who was sister to Ann BOLEYN, Consort to **Henry VIII.** The Earl *d.* s.p. legit.(e) 4 Sep. 1588, aged about 56 (not without suspicion of poison) at his house at Cornbury, Oxon, and was *bur.* at the cost of £4,000 in the Beauchamp chapel at Warwick. Will dat. at Middleburg 1 Aug. 1587, pr. 1589. At his death *all his honours became extinct.* His widow, who was *b.* in the time of Henry VIII., and *d.* in that of Charles I., *m.* (within a year of his death) before Aug. 1589, Sir Christopher BLOUNT, one of the late Earl's Gentlemen of the Horse, who was executed for high treason 18 March 1600/1, on Tower Hill. She *d.* 25 Dec. 1634, aged about 95, at Drayton Basset, and was *bur.* (with her second husband) at Warwick. M.I. Will dat. 15 Oct. 1622, pr. 17 Jan. 1634/5.

(a) "In 1563 he received from the Crown the manor and lordship and castle of *Kenilworth*, the lordship and castle of *Denbigh* and lands in Lancashire, Surrey, Rutland, Denbigh, Carmarthen, York, Cardigan, and Brecknock. The manors of Caldicote and Pelynge, Beds, with many other parcels of land, followed in the next year, and in 1566 sixteen other estates in different parts of England and Wales were assigned him." [*Nat. Biogr.*]

(b) "Of whose legitimacy there can be little doubt." [*Nat. Biogr.* in an able article by S. L. Lee, *sub* Dudley, Earl of Leicester.] This son was the well known Sir Robert Dudley who styled himself DUKE OF NORTHUMBERLAND [see under that title] and whose widow, Alice, was *cr.* in 1644 DUCHESS DUDLEY. His male issue became, in all probability, *extinct* in 1728.

(c) This is the account of these marriages according to her own statement. It appears, however, to have obtained little credit in the Star Chamber, probably on account of her re-marriage (which shortly preceded that of the Earl on 21 Sep. 1578), in spite of her explanation of this having been [which indeed was not improbably the fact] "to secure her life, having had some ill potions given her." It is to be remarked that it was not till 1604 that the Act passed "*To restrain all persons from marriage until their former wives and former husbands be dead,*" whereby such offence is made felony and punishable by death. The re-marriage, therefore, of each of these two parties in or about 1578 was not felony, and is, therefore, no *positive* proof against their marriage in 1573.

(d) See vol. iii., p. 205, note "c," as to the suspicion of their having been previously over-familiar. A previous (private) marriage between them in 1576 is alluded to by Camden in his "*Annals.*" See note "g," next below.

(e) The illegitimacy of his son Robert (see, however, note "b" next above) is here assumed, who it is certain (at all events) did not succeed to his Father's Earldom.

(f) "Dudley combined in himself the worst qualities of both sexes; without courage; without talent; without virtue." [Froude's "*Elizabeth*," vol. i., p. 86.] The following epitaph was written on him by Ben Jonson:—

"Heere lyes a valiaunt warrior who never drew a sword,
Heere lyes a noble courtier who never kept his word,
Here lies the Earle of Leicester who governed the Estates
Whom the earth could never, living, love, and the just heaven now hates."

(g) An interesting and accurate account of this lady by "Edward Levien, M.A., F.S.A.," is in the "*Collectanea Archæologia*" (4to), vol. ii, pp. 42-54.

[ROBERT DUDLEY, *styled* LORD DENBIGH, s. and h. ap. by Lettice, his last wife, *d.* v.p., an infant, 19 July 1584, at Wanstead, and was *bur.* in the Beauchamp chapel, Warwick. M.I.]

XII. 1618. *1.* SIR ROBERT SYDNEY(a) of Penshurst, co. Kent, 2d,(b) but eventually 1st surv. s. and h. male of Sir Henry SYDNEY, K.G., by Mary, 1st sister of Robert, late EARL OF LEICESTER, da. of John (DUDLEY), DUKE OF NORTHUMBERLAND, was *bap.* 28 Nov. 1563; mat. at Oxford (Ch. Ch.) about 1574; M.P. for Glamorganshire, 1584-85 and 1593, for Kent, 1597-98, served in the wars in the Netherlands and Brabant; *knighted* (by the Earl of Leicester) 7 Oct. 1586; *cr.* M.A. of Oxford, 11 April 1588.(c) Gov. of Flushing, 1588-1616; *cr.* 13 May 1603, BARON SYDNEY OF PENSHURST, co. Kent (being at that date Chamberlain to the Queen (Consort) and was *cr.* 4 May 1605, VISCOUNT L'ISLE.(d) He was el. K.G., 26 May and inst. 7 July 1616, being, finally, *cr.* 2 Aug. 1618,(e) EARL OF LEICESTER. He *m.* firstly, 23 Sep. 1584, at St. Donats, co. Glamorgan, Barbara da. and h. of John GAMAGE. of Coity. She *d.* May 1621. He *m.* secondly, Sarah, widow of Sir Thomas SMYTHE. of Bidborough, co. Kent, da. and h. of William BLOUNT. He *d.* at Penshurst, 13 July 1626, aged 63. Admon. 23 June 1627. His widow *d.* about 1656. Her will pr. 1656.

XIII. 1626. *2.* ROBERT (SYDNEY), EARL OF LEICESTER, &c., 3d, but 1st surv. s. and h.(f) *b.* 1 Dec. 1595 in London; mat. (with his elder br., William) at Oxford (Ch. Ch.) 27 Feb. 1606/7; K.B., 3 June 1610; M.P. for Wilton, 1614; for Kent, 1621-22, and for Monmouthshire, 1624 and 1625 having been *styled* VISCOUNT L'ISLE, since 1618, till he *suc. to the Earldom* 13 July 1626; P.C., 1630, and again 1660; Ambassador to Denmark, July to Nov. 1632, to Holstein, 1632, and to Paris, 1636-41; Chief Governor of Ireland as Lord Lieut., and Gen. of the Army there, 1641-43. Lord Lieut. of Kent (on the nom. of the Parl.) 1642 and several times in that year Speaker of the House of Lords. He *m.* about Jan. 1615, Dorothy, da. of Henry (PERCY), 9th EARL OF NORTHUMBERLAND, by Dorothy, da. of Walter (DEVEREUX), 1st EARL OF ESSEX. She, who was *bap.* at Petworth, Sussex, 20 Aug. 1598, *d.* 19 Aug. 1650. He *d.* 2 Nov. 1677, aged 81. Will pr. 1677.

XIV. 1677. *3.* PHILIP (SYDNEY), EARL OF LEICESTER, &c., s. and h., *b.* Jan. 1619; *styled* VISCOUNT L'ISLE, 1626-77, was M.P. for Yarmouth, March to April 1640 and Nov. 1640-48, for Kent, 1658 and for co. Louth [I.] 1642-44, and was a zealous republican. Chief Gov. of Ireland, as Lord Lieut., for the Parl., and Commander-in-Chief of the forces there, 1646-47; Councillor of State, 1649, being President of that Council, Feb. to March 1652; Councillor to the "Lord Protector" Dec. 1653, with a salary of £1000 being in Dec. 1657 (under the designation of "*Lord Viscount Lisle*") one of the (62) members of Cromwell's

(a) An elaborate ped. of Sidney (with many coats of arms beautifully engraved) is in the "*Mis. Gen. et Her.*" (1st series), vol. ii, pp. 160, &c.

(b) The eldest son was the celebrated Sir Philip Sydney, who *d.* s.p.m., 16 Oct. 1586, of wounds received at the battle of Zutphen.

(c) The following persons "*purpureo habitu, more Academico, induti*" were created M.A. in convocation at Oxford, on 11 April 1588; CLINTON, Dominus, son of the Earl of Lincoln; NORRIS Dominus John, President of Munster; SIDNEY, Dominus Robert [afterwards, 1618, Earl of Leicester]; NORRIS, Dominus Henry [Lord Norris de Rycote, 1572-97] CAREW, Magister Robert; BUTLER, Dominus Philip; GREVELL [*i.e.*, GREVILLE] Magister Fouke [*cr.* Baron Brooke, 1621] and DARSEY [*i.e.*, DARCY], Magister Francis." See Clark's "Reg. of the Univ. of Oxford" 1571-1622. Vol. ii. part i, p. 234.

(d) The Viscountcy and Barony of L'Isle had been previously enjoyed by his maternal ancestors, the Barony becoming extinct in 1589 on the death of his mother's brother, Ambrose (Dudley), Earl of Warwick, the last heir male of that family.

(e) See vol. iii, p. 113, note "e," as to the nicknames of the grantees of the four Earldoms *cr.* that day.

(f) The second son was the well known Algernon Sydney, executed 7 Sep. 1683, and the 4th and yst. s., Henry Sydney, was *cr.* Earl of Romney in 1694.

"*House of Lords*."(a) He *suc. to the* (legitimate) *Peerage* (as Earl of Leicester) 2 Nov. 1677. He *m.* 9 May 1645. Catharine, da. of William (Cecil), 2d EARL OF SALISBURY, by Catharine, da. of Thomas (HOWARD), EARL OF SUFFOLK. She *d.* 18 Aug. 1652. He *d.* 6 March 1697/8. Will pr. 1698.

XV. 1698. 4. ROBERT (SYDNEY), EARL OF LEICESTER, &c., s. and h., *b.* 1649, *styled* VISCOUNT L'ISLE, 1677-98. He was sum. to Parl. v p. in his fathers Barony as BARON SYDNEY OF PENSHURST(b) by writ 11 July 1689, addressed "*Roberto Sydney de Penshurst, Chev.*" He *suc. to the Earldom* 6 March 1697/8. He *m.* in 1672, Elizabeth, da. of John (EGERTON), 2d EARL OF BRIDGWATER, by Elizabeth, da. of William (CAVENDISH), 1st DUKE OF NEWCASTLE. He *d.* 11 Nov. 1702, aged 53 and was *bur.* at Penhurst. M.I. Will pr. Dec. 1702. His widow, who was *b.* 24 Aug. 1653, *d.* 1709 and was *bur.* at Penshurst. Will pr. March 1710.

XVI. 1702. 5. PHILIP (SYDNEY), EARL OF LEICESTER, &c., s. and h., *b.* 8 July 1676; M P. for co. Kent, 1695-98; *styled* VISCOUNT L'ISLE, 1698 till he *suc. to the peerage*, 11 Nov. 1702. He *m.* 17 Dec. 1700 at St. Giles in the fields, Midx., Anne. da. and coheir of Sir Robert REEVES, of Thwates, co. Suffolk. He *d.* s.p.s. 24 July 1705 aged 29. Will pr. Aug. 1705.

XVII. 1705. 6. JOHN (SYDNEY), EARL OF LEICESTER, &c., br. and h., *b.* 14 Feb. 1680; Lieut.-Col. 1st Foot Guards, 1702-05; M.P. for Brackley, 1705; *suc. to the peerage* 24 July 1705; Cupbearer at the Coronation, 20 Oct. 1714; one of the Lords of the Bedchamber 1717; Warden of the Cinque Ports, &c., 1717; Lord Lieut. of Kent, 1724; K.B. 27 May 1725; Capt. of the Yeomen of the Guard, 1725-31; Constable of the Tower of London, &c., 1731 and P.C., 1731. He *d.* unm. 27 Sep, 1737, aged 57. Will pr. 1737.

XVIII. 1736 to 1743. 7. JOCELYN (SYDNEY), EARL OF LEICESTER [1618], VISCOUNT L'ISLE [1605] and BARON SYDNEY OF PENSHURST [1603], br. and h., *b.* 1682 at "St. Jones," Midx.; Matric. at Oxford (Univ. Coll) 28 June 1710, aged 18; Chief Porter of the Tower of London, 1734-37. *Suc. to the peerage*, 27 Sep. 1737. He *m.* Feb. 1717, Elizabeth, da. and h. of Lewis THOMAS, of co. Glamorgan by Emmett, his wife. He *d.* s p. legit.(c) 7 July 1743, aged about 61, when *all his honours* became *extinct*(d). Will pr. 1746. His widow *d.* 14 Nov. 1747. Admon. 10 Feb. 1747/8(e).

(a) See a list of these Lords with some notice of each, vol. ii, p. 84, note "c," *sub* "BURNELL."

(b) "The Barony of Sydney was claimed, in May 1782, by Elizabeth, widow of William Perry, Esq., and da. and eventually sole heir of Thomas Sydney, next br. of Josceline, last Earl of Leicester and Baron Sydney, under the presumption that Robert Sydney (the Petitioner's grandfather), the s. and h. apparent of Philip XIV. 3rd Earl of Leicester, having been summoned to Parl. v.p, in his father's Barony, a Barony IN FEE was thereby created; but the House of Lords resolved, 17 June 1782, 'That Robert Sydney, commonly called Viscount L'Isle, the Petitioner's grandfather, under whom she derives her claim, acquired no new Barony, but being the eldest son of his father, the Earl of Leicester, was summoned into his father's Barony in tail male—therefore the Petitioner has no right in consequence of her grandfather's summons and sitting.'" [*Courthope.*]

(c) "It appears, however, by the Plea Rolls (No. 441 and No. 442) enrolled in the treasury of the Court of Common Pleas in Easter term, 21 Geo. III., that John Sydney, of Yalding, in this county [*Qy.*, Kent?] claiming to be the only son of the said Jocelyn [Earl of Leicester] was permitted to sue out a writ of right as the *8th Earl of Leicester.*" See Berry's "*Sussex*," p. 299, where it is stated that this John, who was *b.* 29 Sep. 1738, *m.* Elizabeth, da. of Rev. John Apsley, D.D., and *d.* 15 Dec, 1812. Of his numerous issue (eight daughters and six sons) the eldest son, Paul Algernon Sidney, *b.* 17 April 1774; is there stated to have had issue and to have claimed "to be the *9th Earl of Leicester*, and his case is referred by his Majesty to the Attorney General who has not yet (1830) made his report on the claim."

"By a trial at bar on a writ of right, at Westm, 11 Feb. 1782 for Penshurst place, park and premises in co. Kent, it appeared that Jocelyn, Earl of Leicester, never was divorced from his wife, and that she had a child, *John Sydney*, the demandant at the trial afsd. which John, therefore, *in the eye of the law*, was to be considered a

XIX. 1744, to 1759. THOMAS COKE, of Holkham, co. Norfolk, s. and h. of Edward COKE, of the same, by Carey, da. of Sir John NEWTON, 3d Bart. of Barrs Court, was *b.* about 1695: *suc.* his father, 18 April 1707; was M.P. for Norfolk, 1722 and 1727-28; K.B., 27 May 1725, was *cr.* 28 May 1728, BARON LOVEL OF MINSTER LOVEL, co. Oxford and was *cr.* 9 May 1744, VISCOUNT COKE OF HOLKHAM, co. Norfolk, and EARL OF LEICESTER, being at various dates (1733 to 1759) either joint or sole Postmaster General; F.R.S., &c. He *m.* 2 July 1718, Margaret, 3d da. and coheir of Thomas (TUFTON), 6th EARL OF THANET, by Catharine, da. and coheir of Henry (CAVENDISH) DUKE OF NEWCASTLE. He *d.* s.p.s.,(f) 20 April 1759, aged about 65, when *all his honours* became *extinct*. Will pr. June 1759. His widow, who was *b.* 16 June 1700, had become before his death, *suo jure*, BARONESS DE CLIFFORD, the abeyance of that Barony (*cr.* 1299), being terminated in her favour by patent, 3 Aug. 1734. She *d.* 28 Feb. 1775, aged 74, at Holkham, afsd., when that Barony fell again into abeyance. Will pr, March 1775.

[EDWARD COKE, *styled* VISCOUNT COKE (1744-53), only s. and h. ap., *b.* about 1720; mat. at Oxford (Ch. Ch.), 12 June 1735; M.P. for Norfolk, 1741-47, and for Harwich, 1747-53. He *m.* in 1747, Mary, 5th & yst. da. and coheir of John (CAMPBELL), 2d DUKE OF ARGYLL [S.], and DUKE OF GREENWICH. He *d.* v.p., and s.p. in London, 31 Aug. and was *bur.* 7 Sep. 1753, at Charlton, co. Kent. His widow *d.* 30 Sep. 1811. Will pr. 1811.]

XX. 1784. *1.* GEORGE (TOWNSHEND), LORD DE FERRERS and LORD COMPTON, having *suc.* his mother in these Baronies, 14 Sep. 1770, and having been sum. to Parl. as Lord Ferrers, by writ 25 April 1774, was cr. 18 May 1784(g) EARL OF LEICESTER(h) (*i.e.*, "Earl of the County of Leicester") in the lifetime of his father, George, then VISCOUNT TOWNSHEND OF RAYNHAM, but subsequently (*cr.* 31 Oct. 1787) MARQUESS TOWNSHEND OF RAYNHAM. He *suc* his Father, 14 Sep. 1807, as 2d Marquess Townshend of Raynham. He *d.* 27 July 1811, aged 56.

XXI. 1811, to 1855. *2.* GEORGE FERRARS (TOWNSHEND), MARQUESS TOWNSHEND OF RAYNHAM [1787], EARL OF LEICESTER [1784], VISCOUNT TOWNSHEND OF RAYNHAM [1682], LORD DE FERRERS [1299], LORD COMPTON [1572] and BARON TOWNSHEND OF LYNN REGIS [1661], s. and h., *b.* 13 Dec. 1778; *styled* LORD FERRERS, 1784-1807, and *styled* EARL OF LEICESTER from 1807 till he *suc. to the Marquessate of Townshend*, 27 July 1811. He *d.* s.p. 31 Dec. 1855, aged 77, when the *Earldom of Leicester* became *extinct*.

See fuller particulars under "TOWNSHEND" Marquessate, cr. 1787.

---

legitimate person and as such, well entitled to the inheritance of the *honours* of the family. But with respect to the inheritance of the *estates* demanded by him he failed to establish a better right than the tenant in possession. This (according to the statement at the trial) arose from his averment that his father, Earl Jocelyn, was possessed thereof *in fee* and not as tenant for life, which was the fact, as opened by the tenant; and further contended, that even had he been possessed thereof in fee then by his will the Earl had given them away to a third party. The event of this trial going to admit the legitimacy of the demandant embraces an important question as to the absolute extinction of the *honours*." [*Banks.*]

(d) "See note "c" next above, as to the claim to the Earldom of Leicester, &c., and see p. 50, note "b" as to the claim to a Barony of Sydney supposed to have been *cr.* by writ in 1639.

(e) It was granted to her sister, Mary, wife of Charles Morgan, her mother, Emmett Dorset, widow, the next of kin, having renounced. No notice is taken of her (infant) son, John Sydney (*b.* 1783, *d.* 1812), mentioned in note "c" next above.

(f) The estates, after the death of his widow, devolved on his sister's son, Wenman Roberts, who took the name of Coke, and who was father of Thomas William Coke, *cr.* in 1837, EARL OF LEICESTER OF HOLKHAM.

(g) See vol. iii, p. 335, note "c" as to his designation in that patent.

(h) In "Collins" (vol. ii, p. 482), is a tabular pedigree shewing his descent, in two ways, from the old Earls of Leicester of the house of Beaumont, *viz.* (1) thro' the

LEICESTER OF HOLKHAM.

I. 1837. *1.* THOMAS WILLIAM COKE, of Holkham, co. Norfolk, s. and h. of Wenman ROBERTS, afterwards COKE, of Longford, co. Derby and of Holkham afsd. by Elizabeth, da. of George DENTON, formerly CHAMBERLAYNE, of Hillesden, Bucks, which Wenman was s. and h. of Philip ROBERTS, Major in the 2d Horse Guards, by Anne, sister of Thomas (COKE), EARL OF LEICESTER (*cr.* 1744 but *d.* s.p.s. 1759) was *b.* 6 and *bap.* 16 May 1754 at St. James, Westm., *suc.* his Father, 11 April 1776; was M.P. for Norfolk 1776-84, 1790-1806, and 1807-1832, having, 1806-07, sat for Derbyshire. He "gloried in the reputation of being the first Commoner of England,"(a) tho' after 6 years' retirement from public life, he, at the mature age of 83, was *cr.* 12 Aug. 1837, VISCOUNT COKE and EARL OF LEICESTER OF HOLKHAM,(b) co. Norfolk. He *m.* firstly 5 Oct. 1775 at Sherborne, Jane, sister of James, 1st BARON SHERBORNE, yst. da. of James Lennox DUTTON, formerly NAPER, of Loughcrew, co. Meath, by his second wife Jane, da. of Christopher BOND. She *d.* s.p.m. 2 June 1800, and was *bur.* at Tittleshall, Norfolk. He *m.* secondly 26 Feb. 1822,(c) in St. James' square, Westminster, Anne Amelia, 3d da. of William Charles (KEPPEL), 3d EARL OF ALBEMARLE, by his first wife Elizabeth, da. of Edward (SOUTHWELL), LORD DE CLIFFORD. He *d.* at Longford Hall, co. Derby, 30 June 1842, and was *bur.* at Tittleshall, aged 88.(d) Will pr. 26 Oct. 1842. His widow, who was *b.* 16 June 1803 *m.* 25 June 1843, at St. Geo. Han. sq., the Rt. Hon. Edward ELLICE (who *d.* 20 Sep. 1863) and *d.* 22 July 1844, aged 41, at Longford Hall.

II. 1842. *2.* THOMAS WILLIAM (COKE), EARL OF LEICESTER OF HOLKHAM, &c., s. and h., by second wife, *b.* 26 Dec. 1822, at Holkham; ed. at Eton and Winchester; *styled* VISCOUNT COKE from 1837 till he *suc. to the peerage,* 30 June 1842; Lord Lieut. of Norfolk, 1846; Privy Seal to the

---

families of Compton, Shirley, Ferrers (of Tamworth and Groby), De Quincy and Beaumont and (2) thro' the families of Compton, Shirley, Ferrers (of Chartley, Lords Ferrers), De Quincy, and Beaumont, of which last line (Lords Ferrers, 1299—1646, and again since 1677) he was a representative. See also vol. iii, p. 334, note "a," *sub* "Ferrers," where the double descent from William (Ferrers), Earl of Derby, who m. Lady Margaret de Quincy is set forth.

(a) *Annual Register* for 1842, where it is added that he was "throughout his political career, a zealous whig," opposing "the war against revolutionary France and the general policy of Pitt." He was anyhow "*the first commoner*" who obtained a peerage from the Queen, the Earldom of Innes, conferred on the Duke of Roxburghe [S.], having been granted one day previously.

(b) The title conferred in 1744 on his Father's maternal uncle was "Viscount *Coke of Holkham,* co. Norfolk, and *Earl of Leicester.*" On the strength of this Earldom having been enjoyed for some 15 years by one of his collateral relatives (as above), Mr. Coke, tho' the Earldom of Leicester was then *actually in existence,* being vested (as it had been for above half a century) in a *totally distinct family,* actually prevailed on the Melbourne Ministry to grant him a sort of sham duplicate thereof, *viz.*, *Leicester of Holkham,* so as to *appear to be* (what, for 15 years, 1744-59, his said relative really was) an *Earl of Leicester.*—Oh ! shade of Simon de Montfort, what a burlesque on your great Earldom of the county of Leicester ! Perhaps, however, your ghost, as also those of Warwick (the King maker) and other holders of far famed dignities will shortly behold, among the *modern-antiques* of the 19th century, such creations as *Westmorland of Wormwood Scrubs, Pembroke of Putney, Norfolk of Norwood, Huntingdon of Highgate,* and *Dorset of Didlington* (which last, like Holkham, is a small village in Norfolk) and perhaps even (unless indeed royal titles are to be exempt) an Earldom of *Chester of Camberwell* and a Dukedom of *Cornwall of Clapham Rise.* It is evident that the precedent of 1 Victoria (1837) allows of the creation of such dignities, notwithstanding that the Earldom of the county, whose designation they adopt as the first word of the peerage title, is still in existence.

(c) He had been more than 21 years a widower, and was then nearly 70 ; the young lady who was 50 years his junior, being under 19, as she "was not *born* for 3 years after his first wife's *death* and was seven years younger than his grandaughter, the Countess of Rosebery." The marriage was "it is said in consequence of dissatisfaction with his nephew and heir presumptive." [*Ann. Register,* 1842.]

(d) In his youth, he was, at Rome, known as "the handsome Englishman."

Prince of Wales, 1870; K.G., 30 June 1873. He *m.* firstly, 20 April 1843, at Cardington, Beds, Juliana, da. of Samuel Charles WHITBREAD, by his first wife, Juliana, da. of Henry Otway (BRAND), LORD DACRE. She *d.* (of bronchitis) 21 April 1870, aged 44, at Holkham. He *m.* secondly, 26 Aug. 1875, at Latimers, Bucks, Georgiana Caroline, 1st da. of William George (CAVENDISH), 2d BARON CHESHAM, by Henrietta Frances, da. of the Rt. Hon. William Saunders Sebright LASCELLES. She was *b.* 4 Feb. 1852.

[THOMAS WILLIAM COKE, *styled* VISCOUNT COKE, 1st s. and h. ap. by first wife, *b.* 20 July 1848; ed. at Harrow; an officer in the Scots Guards, 1868, serving in the Egyptian campaign, 1882, and in the Suakim expedition, 1885; Major, 1888. He *m.*, 26 Aug. 1879, at All Saints, Ennismore Gardens, Alice, 2d da. of Luke (WHITE), 2d BARON ANNALY, by Emily, da. of James STUART. She was *b.* 29 Sep. 1855.]

Family Estates.—These, in 1883, consisted of 44,090 acres in Norfolk, worth £59,578 a year. *Principal Residence*. Holkham Park, near Wells, Norfolk.

LEIGH OF STONELEIGH.

Barony. I. 1643.

1. SIR THOMAS LEIGH, Bart., of Stoneleigh, co. Warwick, s. and h. of Sir John Leigh, by his first wife, Ursula, da. and h. of Sir Christopher HODDESDON, of Leighton, Beds, which Sir John (who *d.* v.p.) was s. and h. ap. of Sir Thomas Leigh, Bart. (so *cr.* 29 June 1611), was *b.* 1595; *suc.* his said grandfather in the *Baronetcy*, 1 Feb. 1625/6; M.P. for the county of Warwick, 1628/29; entertained the King (when the gates of Coventry were shut against him) at Stoneleigh and was *cr.* by pat. dat 1 July 1643, at Oxford, BARON LEIGH OF STONELEIGH,(a) co. Warwick. He was a great sufferer in the Royal cause, his composition amounting to £4,895. He *m.* about 1615, Mary, da. and coheir of Sir Thomas EGERTON (s. and h. ap. of Thomas, 1st VISCOUNT BRACKLEY and BARON ELLESMERE), by Elizabeth, da. of Thomas VENABLES, of Kinderton. She was *bur.* 21 March 1669, at Stoneleigh. He was *bur.* there 24 Feb. 1671/2, aged 76. Will (as "Thomas, Lord Leigh, Baron of *Stoneleigh*(a)"), dat. 6 Jan. 1671, pr. 6 April 1672.

II. 1672. *2.* THOMAS (LEIGH), BARON LEIGH OF STONELEIGH, grandson and h., being only s. and h. of the Hon. Sir Thomas LEIGH (M.P. for co. Stafford, 1661-62), by his second wife, Jane, da. of Patrick (FITZ MAURICE), BARON OF KERRY AND LIXNAW [I.], which Sir Thomas was s. and h. ap. of the late Peer but *d.* v.p. in April 1662 aged 46. He was *bap.* 17 June 1652, at Hamstall Ridware, co. Stafford; *suc. to the peerage*, Feb. 1671/2, on the death of his grandfather, taking his seat, 26 Jan. 1673/4. He was aged 31 at the Her. Visit. of Warwickshire, 1683. He *m.* firstly Elizabeth, da. of Richard BROWN, of Shingleton in Chart, co. Kent. She *d.* s.p. in or before 1679. He *m.* secondly, 23 Oct. 1679, at Rockingham, co. Northampton, Eleanor, 1st da. of Edward (WATSON), 2d BARON ROCKINGHAM, by Ann, da. of Thomas (WENTWORTH), 1st EARL OF STRAFFORD. She, who was *b.* 26 Feb. 1658/9, at Rockingham, *d.* 23 July 1705, and was *bur.* at Stoneleigh. He was *bur.* there 16 Nov. 1710, aged 58. Will dat. 26 Oct. to 5 Nov. 1710, pr. 16 March 1710/1.

III. 1710. *3.* EDWARD (LEIGH), BARON LEIGH OF STONELEIGH, 2d but 1st surv. s. and h. by second wife, *b.* 13 Jan. and *bap.* 8 Feb. 1684, at Stoneleigh; *suc. to the peerage*, 16 Nov. 1710, and took his seat, 13 March 1710/1. He *m.* about 1707 Mary, da. and h. of Thomas HOLBECH, of Fillongley, co. Warwick, by Elizabeth, da. and h. of Bernard PAULET. He *d.* at Stoneleigh 9 March 1737/8, aged 53, and was *bur.* there. Will dat. 26 July 1737, pr. 7 April 1738. His widow *d.* 6 Sep. 1743, and was *bur.* at Stoneleigh. Her admon. (as "of Guys Cliffe, co. Warwick"), 25 Oct. 1743, and 22 May 1753.

(a) "*Stoneley*" is, however, the spelling in the docquet (the patent was never enrolled) and this (apparently) was the usual way in which the name of the parish was then spelt.

IV. 1738. 4. THOMAS (LEIGH), BARON LEIGH OF STONELEIGH, 2d but only surv. s. and h., *bap.* 29 April 1713, at Stoneleigh; *suc. to the peerage*, 9 March 1737/8, taking his seat, 29 March 1739. He *m.* firstly, about 1736, Maria Rebecca, sister of William, 5th BARON CRAVEN OF HAMPSTED MARSHALL, da. of John CRAVEN, of Whitley, co. Warwick, by Maria Rebecca, da. of Henry GREEN, of Wykin in Coventry. She was *bur.* 9 Dec. 1746, at Stoneleigh. He *m.* secondly, in Dec. 1747, Catharine, da. of his maternal uncle, Rowland BERKELEY, formerly GREEN, of Cotheridge, co. Worcester, by Mary, da. and coheir of George BOHUN, of Coundon, co. Warwick. He *d.* 30 Nov. and was *bur.* 9 Dec. 1749, aged 36, at Stoneleigh. Will dat. 28 June 1748, to 2 Nov. 1749, pr. 7 April 1750.

V. 1749, to 1786. 5. EDWARD (LEIGH), BARON LEIGH OF STONELEIGH [1643], and a Baronet [1611], 3d but only surv. s. and h. by 1st wife, *b.* 1 March 1742, and *bap.* at Stoneleigh; *suc. to the peerage*, 30 Nov. 1749, taking his seat 15 March 1764. He was found a lunatic, 7 Aug. 1774. He *d.* unm. 4 June 1786, aged 44, when *all his honours* became *extinct.*(a) Will dat. 11 May 1767, pr. 22 July 1786.(b)

VI. 1839. 1. CHANDOS LEIGH, of Stoneleigh Abbey, co. Warwick and of Adlestrop, co. Gloucester, s. and h. of James Henry LEIGH, of Adlestrop afsd., by Julia Judith, da. of Thomas (TWISLETON), LORD SAY AND SELE. He was *b.* 27 June and *bap.* 22 July 1791, at St. Marylebone; mat. at Oxford (Ch.

(a) The title was claimed by George Leigh, as the 7th Baron, in 1813. He was br. and h. of John Leigh, who *d.* unm. 24 July 1860, aged 50, and who was s. and h. of James Leigh, of Blackrod, co. Lancaster, who *d.* 22 May 1788, aged 58, all three being alleged to have been (since 1786) *de jure* Barons Leigh of Stoneleigh. The said James was 1st s. of Robert Leigh (*d.* 1785, aged 73), who was 1st s. of James Leigh (*d.* 1709, aged 29), who was 1st surv. s. of Roger Leigh (*d.* 1702), all three being of Haigh, co. Lancaster. The said Roger last mentioned was alleged to have been a son (by a first wife, whose maiden name was Cotton), of the Hon. Christopher Leigh (*bur.* at Stoneleigh 16 Sep. 1672), the 4th son of the 1st Baron. It appears, however, that the true descent of the claimant's great great grandfather, Roger Leigh, of Haigh (who *d.* 1702) was that (instead of being the son of the Hon. Christopher Leigh) he was the son of Robert Leigh, of Haigh (by Jane *bur.* at Wigan in 1674), which Robert was s. of (another) Roger Leigh, also of Haigh, who *d.* before 1625. See "*The Leigh Peerage*," &c., two vols., 8vo., pub. by Causton [1832?] In this curious work there is allusion to a monumental inscription said to have existed in Stoneleigh church to this Christopher and to have been removed in 1811, it being stated that Christopher's (*alleged*) first marriage and the issue thereof was thereon recorded. It appears also (see *Annual Register* for 1848, *Chronicle*, p. 62), that a mob on behalf of George Leigh attempted to seize Stoneleigh Abbey, on the plea that it belonged to him, and that in May 1848 Lord Leigh (it's owner) was actually charged with the murder of some of these rioters.

(b) By his will he devised his estates in favour of his sisters and their issue with a rem. (which took effect on the death of the Hon. Mary Leigh, 2 July 1806), "unto the first and nearest of my kindred being male and of my name and blood" that was then living. Under this devise James Henry Leigh, of Adlestrop (father of Chandos Leigh, who in 1839 was raised to the peerage of Leigh of Stoneleigh) became entitled in 1806. He (who *d.* 1823, aged 58), was s. and h. of James L. (*d.* 1774, aged 50), who was s. and h. of William L. (*d.* 1757, aged 66), who was s. and h. of Theophilus L. (*d.* 1725), who was 4th s. of William L. (*d.* 1690, aged 86), all four being of Adlesthorp afsd. The last named William L. was s. and h. of William L., of Longborough, co. Warwick (*d.* 1632, aged 46), who was 1st s. of Rowland L. of the same (living 1596) which Rowland was eldest br. of Sir Thomas Leigh, of Stoneleigh, *cr.* a Baronet in 1611, who was father of Thomas, the 1st Baron Leigh of Stoneleigh.

Ch.). 8 June 1810;(a) suc. his father in the Leigh estates, 27 Oct. 1823,(b) and was cr., 11 May 1839, BARON LEIGH OF STONELEIGH, co. Warwick, taking his seat on the 13th. He m., 8 June 1819, at St. Marylebone, Margarette, da. of the Rev. William Shippen WILLES,(c) of Astrop house, co. Northampton, by Margaret, da. of John WILLIAMS, of Panthowell, co. Carmarthen. He d. 27 Sep. 1850, aged 59, at Bonn on the Rhine and was bur. 8 Oct. at Stoneleigh. Will pr. Nov. 1850. His widow d. 5 Feb. 1860, at 30 Portman square, and was bur. at Stoneleigh.

VII. 1850. 2. WILLIAM HENRY (LEIGH), BARON LEIGH OF STONELEIGH [1839], s. and h., b. 17 Jan. 1824, and bap. at Adlestrop, co. Gloucester; ed. at Cambridge (Trin. Coll.); LL.D.; suc. to the peerage, 27 April 1850, taking his seat, 7 Feb. 1851; Lord Lieut. of Warwickshire, 1856. He m., 22 Aug. 1848, at St. Geo. Han. sq., Caroline Amelia, 5th da. of Richard (GROSVENOR), 2d MARQUESS OF WESTMINSTER, by Elizabeth Mary, da. of George Granville (LEVESON-GOWER), 1st DUKE OF SUTHERLAND. She was b. 14 June and bap. 28 July 1828, at Eccleston, co. Chester.

Family Estates.—These, in 1883, consisted of 14 891 acres in Warwickshire; 2,850 in Staffordshire; 2,232 in Gloucestershire; 1,198 in Cheshire, and 294 in Leicestershire. *Total* 20,965 acres, worth £32,018 a year. *Principal Residences.* Stoneleigh Abbey, near Kenilworth, co. Warwick, and Adlestrop House, co. Gloucester.

LEIGHLIN.

See "BRERETON OF LEIGHLIN, co. Carlow," Barony [I.] (*Brereton*), *cr.* 1624; *ex.* 1722.

LEIGHTON-BROMSWOLD.

See "CLIFTON OF LEIGHTON-BROMSWOLD" [co. Huntingdon], Barony (*Clifton*), *cr.* 1608.

---

i.e., "STUART OF LEIGHTON-BROMSWOLD, co. Huntingdon," Barony (*Stuart*), *cr.* 1619, with the EARLDOM OF MARCH. See "LENNOX" Dukedom [S.], *cr.* 1581, *sub* the third Duke.

LEINSTER (d)

[See vol. i, p. ix, for some remarks on the Kingdom of Leinster and its subsequent division.]

i.e., "LEINSTER" Earldom [I.] (*Cholmondeley*), *cr.* 3 March 1645/6; see "CHOLMONDELEY OF KELLS" Viscountcy [I.], *cr.* 1628; both honours *ex.* 1659.

(a) He was "early distinguished by his elegant scholarship;" was the author of *The island of Love* [1812] and other poems and was "among those young men of ability and distinction to whom Holland House offered its brilliant attractions." These early promises, however (inasmuch as he never held any office and was never in Parl.) seem hardly to merit the peerage granted to him by the "liberal" Ministry of Lord Melbourne.

(b) See p. 54, note "b."

(c) He was son of Edward Willes, a Justice of the King's Bench, 1768-87, who was 2d son of Sir John Willes, Lord Ch. Justice of the Common Pleas, 1737-61.

(d) See vol iv, p. 321, note "c." *sub* "Ireland," as to a creation by the Pope's nuncio to Ireland, 1572-85, of Sir Thomas Stukeley as *Marquess of Leinster*, &c.,.

Dukedom [I.] I. 1691, to 1719. LORD MEINHARDT SCHOMBERG (Comte de Schomberg), 2d s. of Frederic, the famous DUKE OF SCHOMBERG (so *cr.* 1689) was *cr.* 3 March 1691, BARON TARA [" *Baron of Tarragh* "], EARL OF BANGOR, and DUKE OF LEINSTER [I.] By the death of his brother 17 Oct. 1693, he *suc.* to his father's peerage as DUKE OF SCHOMBERG. He *d.* s.p.m. 16 July 1719, when *all his honours* became *extinct.* See fuller account under " SCHOMBERG " Dukedom, *cr.* 1689, *sub* the 3d and last Duke.

---

i.e., " LEINSTER " Earldom for life [I.] (KIELMANSEGGE), *cr.* 11 Sep. 1721 ; see " DARLINGTON " Earldom for life, *cr.* 1722 ; both honours *ex.* 1725.

Dukedom [I.] II. 1766. *1.* JAMES (FITZ GERALD), EARL OF KILDARE and BARON OF OFFALY [I.], 3d but 1st surv. s. and h. of Robert, 19th EARL OF KILDARE, &c. [I.], by Mary, 1st da. of William (O'BRIEN), 3d EARL OF INCHIQUIN [I.], was *b.* 29 May 1722, being *styled* LORD OFFALY till 1744 ; M.P. for Athy (when under age), 1741-44, until, on 20 Feb. 1744,(a) he *suc. to the peerage* [I.] as 20th Earl of Kildare ; P.C. [I.], 1745 ; was *cr.*, 21 Feb. 1746/7,(b) VISCOUNT LEINSTER OF TAPLOW,(c) co. Buckingham [G.B.] From 1749 to 1755 he was one of the leaders of the popular party [I.], being 1756-57 one of the Lords Justices Vice Regents [I.] ; Master Gen. of the Ordnance [I.] and Col. of the Royal Irish Artillery, 1760-66 ; Major Gen., 1761 ; Lieut. Gen., 1770 ; Gov. of co. Kildare, 1761. He was *cr.*, 3 March 1761,(d) EARL OF OFFALY and MARQUESS OF KILDARE [I.] (taking his seat 10 Dec. 1761), and was *cr.*, 26 Nov. 1766, DUKE OF LEINSTER [I.], taking his seat 27 Jan. 1768. He *m.*, 7 Feb. 1746/7,(e) at her father's house, in Whitehall place, St. Margarets' Westm., Amelia Mary, 2d surv. da. of Charles (LENNOX), 2d DUKE OF RICHMOND, by Sarah, da. and coheir of William (CADOGAN), EARL CADOGAN. By her he had no less than nine sons(f) and eight daughters. He *d.* 19 Nov. 1773, aged 51, at Leinster House, Dublin, and was *bur.* at Christ Church in that city. His widow, who was *b.* 6 Oct. 1731, and *bap.* at St. Geo. Han. sq., and who was a godaughter of King George II., *m.* in 1774 William OGILVIE, who *d.* at Ardglass, co. Down, 18 Nov. 1832, aged 92. She *d.* in Grosvenor sq. 27 March 1814, aged 82, and was *bur.* in Chichester cathedral.

[GEORGE FITZ GERALD, *styled* LORD OFFALY, and (since 1761) EARL OF OFFALY, 1st s. and h. ap., *b.* 15 Jan. 1747/8 ; was godson to King George II. ; ed. at Eton. He *d.* unm. and under age at Richmond House, Whitehall, 26 Sep. 1765, and was *bur.* at St. Martins in the fields.]

(a) He was at that date the only male representative of the Kildare branch of the Geraldines.

(b) This was on the occasion of his marriage, as to which Horace Walpole remarks (23 Feb. 1747), that the bride's parents " have not given her a shilling but the King endows her by making Lord Kildare a Viscount *sterling*."

(c) Taplow, however, did not belong to him but to his maternal uncle, the 4th Earl of Inchiquin [I.]

(d) The letter (24 Feb. 1761), from the Duke of Bedford announcing to him this elevation contained also a promise that he should " be created a Duke whenever " the King " shall think proper to make one of that degree either in England or Ireland exclusive of any of his own family." This event occurred in Oct. 1766 when Hugh (Percy formerly Smithson), Earl of Northumberland [1749], was *cr.* Duke of Northumberland, and the Marquess received his Dukedom accordingly, becoming thus the *premier Duke* as well as the *premier Earl* and *Marquess* in Ireland.

(e) See as to this marriage note " b " next above.

(f) Of these sons one was *cr.* in 1800 Baron Lecale [I.], another (by his wife, the *suo jure* Baroness De Ros), was ancestor of the Lords de Ros, while the 5th son, Lord Edward Fitz Gerald, was attainted of high treason in 1798. One of the daughters (the wife of J. J. Strutt) was in 1821 *cr.* Baroness Rayleigh.

II. 1773. 2. William Robert (Fitz Gerald), Duke of Leinster, &c. [I.], also Viscount Leinster of Taplow [G.B.], 2d but 1st surv. s. and h., *b.* 13 March 1748/9, in Arlington place, Piccadilly; *styled* Earl of Offaly, 1765-66, and Marquess of Kildare, 1766-73; ed. at Eton and at Cambridge; sometime (1765) Cornet of Horse; M.P. for city of Dublin, 1767-71; Sheriff of co. Kildare, 1772; *suc. to the peerage*, 19 Nov. 1773; Gov. of co. Kildare, 1773; P.C. [I.], 1777; Col. of the 1st Reg. of Dublin Volunteers, 1777; K.P., 5 Feb. 1783, being one of the Founders(a) of that Order; Master of the Rolls [I.], 1788 89, and Clerk of the Crown and Hanaper [I.], 1795-97; was a cordial supporter of the Union.(b) He *m.*, 7 Nov. 1775, Emilia Olivia, da. and h. of St. George (Usher St. George), Baron St. George of Hatley St George [I.], by Elizabeth, da. and h. of Christopher Dominick, of Dublin. She *d.* 23 June 1798, at Thomas' Hotel, Berkeley sq., and was *bur.* at Taplow, Bucks. He *d.* 20 Oct. 1804, aged 55, at Carton House, co. Kildare, and was *bur.* in Kildare Abbey.

[George Fitz Gerald, *styled* Marquess of Kildare, s. and h. ap., *b.* 20 June 1783, at Carton afsd., King George III. being his sponsor. He *d.* an infant 10 Feb. 1784.]

III. 1804. 3. Augustus Frederick (Fitz Gerald), Duke of Leinster, &c. [I.], also Viscount Leinster of Taplow [G.B.], 2d but 1st surv. s. and h., *b.* 21 Aug. 1791, at Carton afsd., being godson to George, Prince of Wales, afterwards George IV.; *styled* Marquess of Kildare till he *suc. to the peerage*, 20 Oct. 1804; ed. at Eton; mat. at Oxford (Ch. Ch.), 18 Oct. 1810; P.C. [I. and E.], 1831; Lord Lieut. of co. Kildare, 1831; Lord High Constable [I.] for Coronation of William IV., 8 Sep. 1831, and of Queen Victoria, 28 June 1838;(c) Grand Master of the Freemasons in Ireland. He *m.*, 16 June 1818, Charlotte Augusta, 3d and yst. da. of Charles (Stanhope), 3d Earl of Harrington, by Jane, da. and coheir of Sir John Fleming, Bart. She, who was *b.* 15 Feb. 1793, *d.* 15 Feb. 1859, at Carton afsd. He *d.* 10 Oct. 1874, aged 83, at Carton afsd., and was *bur.* at Maynooth.

IV. 1874. 4. Charles William (Fitz Gerald), Duke of Leinster, &c. [I.], also Viscount Leinster of Taplow [G.B.], *b.* 30 March 1819, in Dublin, *styled* Marquess of Kildare till 1874; mat. at Oxford (Ch. Ch.), 19 Oct. 1837; B.A., 1840; M.A., 1852; a Commissioner of Nat. Educ. [I.], 1841; High Sheriff for co. Kildare, 1843; M.P. for co. Kildare, 1847-52; Chancellor of the Queen's Univ. of Ireland, 1870; was *cr.* v.p., 3 May 1870, BARON KILDARE of Kildare, co. Kildare [U.K.], but, four years later, *suc.*, 10 Oct. 1874, *to his father's peerages* [I. and G.B.]; P.C. [I.], 1879. He *m.*, 13 Oct. 1847, Caroline, 3d da. of George Granville (Sutherland-Leveson-Gower), 2d Duke of Sutherland, by Harriet Elizabeth Georgiana, da. of George (Howard), 6th Earl of Carlisle. He *d.* 10 Feb. 1887, aged 67, at Carton afsd.(d) Will resealed in London 25 April 1887 above £61,000. His widow, who was *b.* 15 April 1827, *d.* (a few months after him) 13 May 1887, aged 60, at Kilkea Castle, co. Kildare.

(a) See vol. i, p. 136, note "d," *sub* "Arran," for a list of these Founders.

(b) He received for compensation for the loss of his borough influence, £15,000 for Kildare, £13,000 for Athy, and £1,200 for Enniskillen.

(c) His part therein is thus alluded to in Barham's inimitable "Ingoldsby Legends," *sub* "Mr. Barney Maguire's account of the Coronation."

"Och! the Coronation!—What celebration
For emulation—can with it compare;
When to West-minster—the Royal Spinster
And the *Duke of Leinster*—all in order did repair!"

(d) See vol. iii, p. 358, note "a," *sub* "Fitz Gerald," for some notice of his work (when Marquess of Kildare) entitled "*The Earls of Kildare*" and the "*Addenda*" thereto.

V. 1887. 5. GERALD (FITZ GERALD), DUKE OF LEINSTER [1766], MARQUESS OF KILDARE [1761], EARL OF KILDARE [1316], EARL OF OFFALY [1761], and BARON OF OFFALY [*restored* 1554] in the peerage of Ireland, in which kingdom he is *premier Duke, Marquess, and Earl*, also VISCOUNT LEINSTER OF TAPLOW [1747], and BARON KILDARE [1870], s. and h., *b.* 16 Aug. 1851, in Dublin; known as EARL OF OFFALY till 1874 when he was *styled* MARQUESS OF KILDARE till, on 10 Feb. 1887, he *suc. to the peerage.* He *m.*, 17 Jan. 1884, at St Paul's, Knightsbridge, Hermione Wilhelmina, 1st da. of William Ernest (DUNCOMBE), 1st EARL OF FEVERSHAM, by Mabel Violet, 2d da. of the Rt. Hon. Sir James Robert George GRAHAM, 2d Bart., of Netherby, G.C.B. She was *b.* 30 March 1864.

[MAURICE FITZ GERALD, *styled* MARQUESS OF KILDARE, s. and h. ap., *b.* 1 March 1887, at Kilkea Castle afsd.]

Family Estates.—These, in 1883, consisted of 71,977 acres in co. Kildare and of 1,123 in co. Meath. *Total* 73,100 acres worth £55,877 a year. *Principal Residences.* Carton (near Maynooth) and Kilkea Castle (near Mageney) both in co. Kildare.

LEINSTER OF TAPLOW.

i.e., "LEINSTER OF TAPLOW, co. Buckingham," Viscountcy (*Fitz Gerald*), *cr.* 1747; see "LEINSTER" Dukedom [I.], *cr.* 1766.

LEITRIM.

Barony [I.] I. 1583. 1. JOHN DE BURGH, or BURKE, of Meelick Castle, co. Galway, yst. s. of Ulick, 1st EARL OF CLANRICARDE [I.], by his 3d wife, Maria LYNCH, disputed unsuccessfully the legitimacy of his elder br. (of the half blood) the 2d Earl, which, however, was established in (1580), 22 Eliz.(a) He, however, was recognised, 7 Sep. 1582, as next in rem. to that Earldom, failing his said brother and his issue male, and, having been granted the castle of Leitrim, was *cr.*, 30 April 1583,(b) BARON LEITRIM ["Baron of Leitrim"], co. Clanricarde in Connaught [I]. He *m.* Joanna, da. of Sir William O'CARROLL. He *d.* a few months after his creation, being murdered, 11 Nov. 1583.

II. 1583, to 1600? 2. JOHN (DE BURGH, or BURKE), BARON LEITRIM [I.], s. and h. He is said to have been taken in rebellion [1600?] and beheaded, when his *honours*, after the attainder, which doubtless followed, would be *forfeited*.(c)

LEITRIM and LEITRIM OF MANOR HAMILTON.

Barony [I.] I. 1783. Viscountcy [I.] I. 1793. Earldom [I.] I. 1795. 1. ROBERT CLEMENTS, of Killadoon, co. Kildare, s. and h. of the Rt. Hon. Nathaniel CLEMENTS, Dep. Vice Treasurer and Teller of the Exchequer [I.], by Hannah, da. of the Very Rev. William GORE, Dean of Down, was *b.* 25 Nov. and *bap.* 18 Dec. 1732; M.P. for co. Donegal, 1765-68; for Carrick, 1768-76, and for co. Donegal [again], 1776-83, and was *cr.*, 11 Oct. 1783,(d) BARON LEITRIM OF MANOR HAMILTON, co. Leitrim [I.], taking his seat 16 Oct. following. He was subsequently *cr.*, 20 Dec. 1793, VISCOUNT LEITRIM [I.] and on 6 Oct. 1795, EARL OF LEITRIM [I.]; was Gov. of co.

(a) See vol. ii, p. 257, note "b," *sub* "Clanricarde."

(b) This is the date assigned to the patent in Burke's "*extinct peerage*" [1883] but it appears that no patent was inrolled. The Queen's letters are dated 14 March and the "*fiant*" 30 April [1583], 25 Eliz. *Ex. inform.* J. B. Burke, Ulster King of Arms.

(c) He had two brothers of whom (1) Redmond assumed the title of BARON LEITRIM [I.] and was a distinguished Captain among the Connaught rebels. He was living in Spain as a fugitive in 1615; (2) William, living 4 Sep. 1603, when, by the King's letters, he was granted a pension.

(d) One of the nine *Irish* Baronies made by the Fox Ministry at a time when the King refused to make any additions to the peerage of *Great Britain*. See vol. iii, p. 44, note "d," *sub* "Delaval."

Donegal and Ranger of Phœnix Park, co. Dublin, and was REP. PEER [I.], 1801-04, being one of the original 28 so elected at the time of the Union. He m., 31 May 1765, Elizabeth, 1st da. of Clotworthy (SKEFFINGTON), 1st EARL OF MASSEREENE [I.], by his second wife, Elizabeth, da. of Henry EYRE. He d. 27 July 1804, aged 71, in Grosvenor square, and was *bur.* at St. Michans Dublin. Will pr. 1804. His widow *d.* 29 May 1817, in Grosvenor square afsd. Will pr. 1818.

II. 1804. *2.* NATHANIEL (CLEMENTS), EARL OF LEITRIM, &c. [I.], *b.* 9 May 1768, in Dublin; *styled* VISCOUNT CLEMENTS, 1795—1804; was M.P. for Carrick, 1790-97, and for co. Leitrim, 1798—1804; *suc. to the peerage* [I.], 27 July 1804; Lord Lieut. of co. Leitrim. He was *cr.*, 20 June 1831, BARON CLEMENTS OF KILMACRENAN, co. Donegal [U.K.]; K.P., 8 April 1834. He *m.* about 1804, Mary, 1st da. and coheir of William BERMINGHAM, of Ross Hill, co. Galway, by (—), da. and coheir of Thomas RUTLEDGE, of Bushfield, co. Mayo. She *d.* 5 Feb. 1840. He *d.* 31 Dec. 1854, aged 86, at Killadoon afsd. Will pr. June 1855.

[ROBERT BERMINGHAM CLEMENTS, *styled* VISCOUNT CLEMENTS, 1st s. and h. ap., *b.* May 1805; M.P. for co. Leitrim, 1826-30, and 1832-39. He *d.* unm. and v.p. 24 Jan. 1839, aged 33.]

III. 1854. *3.* WILLIAM SYDNEY (CLEMENTS), EARL OF LEITRIM, &c. [I.], also BARON CLEMENTS OF KILMACRENAN, 2d but 1st surv. s. and h., *b.* 1806; *styled* VISCOUNT CLEMENTS, 1839-54; M.P. for co. Leitrim, 1839-47; was sometime in 52d Foot, retiring from the Army as Lieut. Col. in 1855: Col. of the Leitrim Militia, 1843; *suc. to the peerage*, 31 Dec. 1854. He *d.* unm. 2 April 1878, aged 72, being murdered (with his clerk and his coachman) at Cratlaghwood, near Milford, co. Donegal.

IV. 1878. *4.* ROBERT BERMINGHAM (CLEMENTS), EARL OF LEITRIM, &c. [I.], also BARON CLEMENTS OF KILMACRENAN, nephew and h., being only s. and h. of the Rev. the Hon. Francis Nathaniel CLEMENTS, Vicar of Norton and Canon of Durham, by his first wife, Charlotte, da. of the Rev. Gilbert KING, of Longfield, co. Tyrone; *b.* 5 March 1847; sometime an officer in the Royal Navy; *suc. to the peerage*, 2 April 1878. He *m.*, 2 Sep. 1873, Winifred, 5th da. of Thomas William (COKE), 2d EARL OF LEICESTER OF HOLKHAM, by his first wife, Juliana, da. of Samuel Charles WHITBREAD. He *d.* at 40 Portman square, 5 April 1892, aged 45, and was *bur.* at Mulroy, co. Donegal. Personalty sworn at £130,694, including £17,529 in Ireland and £5,189 in Scotland. His widow, who was *b.* 12 Jan. 1851, living 1892.

V. 1892. *5.* CHARLES (CLEMENTS), EARL OF LEITRIM [1795], VISCOUNT LEITRIM [1793], and BARON LEITRIM OF MANOR HAMILTON [1783], in the peerage of Ireland, also BARON CLEMENTS OF KILMACRENAN [1831], 1st s. and h., *b.* 23 June 1879, at 37 Upper Grosvenor street; *styled* VISCOUNT CLEMENTS till he *suc. to the peerage*, 5 April 1892.

Family Estates.—These, in 1883, consisted of 54.352 acres in co. Donegal and of 2,500 in co. Leitrim. *Total* 56,852 acres, worth £11,006 a year. *Principal Residence.* Mulroy, near Milford, co. Donegal.

LEIX.

[As to the honour of Leix or Ossory, one of the five divisions made in 1245 of the great honour of Leinster, see vol. i, p. x, *sub* "Irish Peerage, &c., before the 16th century."]

i.e., "SYDNEY OF LEIX" ["Baron Stradbally"], Queen's county, Barony [I.] (*Cosby*), *cr.* 1768; *ex.* 1774.

LEMPSTER, see LEOMINSTER.

LENNOX [or LEVENACH].

Earldom [S.] I. 1180? to 1184? 1. DAVID OF SCOTLAND, br. of King WILLIAM THE LION [S.] was cr. by that Monarch, EARL OF GARIOCH [S.] and having obtained, probably at the same time, the district of Levenach or Lennox,(a) consisting "of the northern part of the old Cumbrian Kingdom (nearly represented by the county of Dumbarton") is generally considered EARL OF LENNOX [S.] In 1184, he received, by the resignation of his said brother, an English Earldom, becoming thus EARL OF HUNTINGDON AND CAMBRIDGE, "and it is probable that, on that occasion, he resigned the Earldom of Lennox in favour of the Head of its Gaelic population."(b)

II. 1184? 1. ALWYN (*styled* MAC ARKYLL), son of Arkyll, a Celt, from whom he inherited tracts of lands, now part of Dumbartonshire and Stirlingshire, appears to have been as early as (and not improbably before) 1193 cr. EARL OF LENNOX [S.]

III. 1200? 2. ALWYN, EARL OF LENNOX [S.], s. and h. He, being a minor at his father's death, was a ward to David of Scotland, Earl of Huntingdon, sometimes Earl of Lennox [S.], abovenamed. He m. Eva, da. of Gilchrist, EARL OF MENTEITH [S.] He d. about 1224.

IV. 1224? 3. MALDWIN, EARL OF LENNOX(c) [S.], s. and h., who, under that title, made a grant in 1225, of the island of Clarinis in Loch Lomond. In 1237 he was one of the guarantors of the truce between England and Scotland. He surrendered his Earldom and all his possessions to the King, who, retaining the castle of Dumbarton and the territory of Morach,(d) regranted the rest to him and his heirs in 1238. He m. Beatrix, or Elizabeth, da. of Walter STEWARD, High Steward [S.], by Beatrix, da. of Gilchrist, EARL OF ANGUS [S.] He, who was a great benefactor to the Church, was living 1250.

V. 1260? 4. MALCOLM, EARL OF LENNOX [S.], grandson and h., being s. and h. of Malcolm, who was s. and h. ap. of the late Earl, but who d. v.p. in 1248. He was one of the nobles, who, on 5 Feb. 1283/4, acknowledged the right of Margaret of Norway, in the succession to the throne [S.] He d. between July 1290 and 1292.

VI. 1291? 5. MALCOLM, EARL OF LENNOX [S.], s. and h. *suc.* his father (before 1292) being then a nominee on the part of Bruce in his claim to the Crown [S.] He invaded Cumberland, 1296, but swore fealty to England in that year. In 1306 he was one of Bruce's principal supporters, and obtained from him, when King, the hereditary shrievalty of co. Clackmannan, &c. In 1320 he was one of the signatories of the letter to the Pope asserting Scotland's independency. He d. 19 July 1333, being slain at the battle of Halidon Hill against the English.

VII. 1333. 6. DONALD, EARL OF LENNOX [S.], s. and h. He was one of the nobles bound for the ransom of David II. [S.], in 1357, and was present at the coronation of Robert II. [S.] 16 March 1371. He d. s.p.m.(e) 1373.

(a) There is at the British Museum a "*Cartularium comitatus de Levenax*" as also a copy of one of the most valuable of the many genealogical works of Sir William Fraser, K.C.B., viz: "*The Lennox,*" 2 vols., 4to., privately printed 1874.

(b) Skenes "*Celtic Scotland*" (1880), vol. iii, p. 69-70.

(c) "Lennox" appears (for the first time) among "the Seven Earls of Scotland" (in the place, probably, of "Fife") in 1237, but was omitted (when "Fife" re-appeared) in 1244. Lennox, however, re-appeared among them, in 1297, being the last time these Earls are mentioned *as* "the Seven." See remarks under "Angus." Vol. i, pp. 88-90.

(d) "Quæ ex consensu et bonâ voluntate ipsius *Maldovini comitis*, in manu nostrâ retinuimus." Chartul. of Lennox as quoted in Wood's Douglas peerage.

(e) The representation of this family in the *male* line devolved in 1373 on the family of Macfarlane, of Arrochar, descended from Gilchrist, yr. br. of Maldwin, 3d Earl of Lennox, being 4th son of Alwyn, the 2d Earl.

VIII. 1373. 7. Margaret, *suo jure* COUNTESS OF LENNOX [S.], da. and h. She *m.*, about 1350, Walter DE FASLANE, of Faslane, s. of Alan de F., of the same. By a charter "which in one place terms Walter de Faslane *Dominus de Levenax* [and] in another holds him to be *Comes de Levenax*,"(a) the King in 1384 bestowed on him "the right of summoning to weapon—shawings, or musters."(a) He and his wife resigned the Earldom before 1385 in favour of their eldest son as below.

IX. 1385. 8. DUNCAN, EARL OF LENNOX [S.], 1st s. and h.,(b) by reason of his parent's resignation. He, who was *b.* about 1350, was in 1385 confirmed by the King in the Earldom, which, having no legit. male issue, he resigned and obtained a new grant thereof, 8 Nov. 1392, with rem. to himself and the heirs male of his body whom failing, to Isabel, his da., and her husband, Murdoch STEWART, and the survivor of them and the heirs of their bodies, with rem. to his own right heirs. This entail was renewed in 1411. He *d.* s.p.m. legit.(c) 25 May 1425, aged about 80, being beheaded on the Castle Hill of Stirling (with his son in law, the said Murdoch, then Duke of Albany [S.], and others) for (presumably) high treason.(d) It is probable that Ellen, Countess of Lennox, living in 1434,(e) was his widow.

X. 1425, to 1459. 9. Isabel, *suo jure* COUNTESS OF LENNOX [S.], 1st da. and heir of line, who also by reason of the regrant of the Earldom in 1392 (above mentioned) was entitled to that dignity.(f) She *m.* (settl. 17 Feb. 1391/2), Murdoch (STEWART), 2d DUKE OF ALBANY [S.], who (together with her father) was beheaded 25 May 1425. She was kept a prisoner from that date and was living (as "*Duchess of Albany* and *Countess of Lennox*," 18 May 1451, but *d.* s.p.s.(g) at Inchmurrin Castle, Loch Lomond, in 1458 or 1459.

* * * * * *

[From the date of the death of the Countess Isabel till 1473 (when the Earldom was assumed by the family of Stuart of Darnley) no one appears to have borne the title; it was not assumed by her bastard grandson, Andrew (Stewart), Lord Avandale [S.], to whom, on 4 May 1471, the whole "*comitatus*" of Lennox had been granted *for life* and who lived till 1487 or 1488. The heir general of Earl

(a) Wood's "Douglas' peerage."

(b) The second son was named Alexander, and it was by virtue of "an alleged service in 1765" and of a pretended [but "utterly unsupported"] male descent" from him that Alexander Lennox, by petition (referred to the Lords 15 March 1769), claimed the Earldom as heir male (collateral) of Duncan, Earl of Lennox (eldest br. of the claimant's said ancestor) "falsely and unblushingly" setting forth "that the regulating charter was simply to Earl Duncan's *heirs male whatsoever*," whereas "the ultimate substitution" was "to the Earl's *heirs whatsoever*." [" *Riddell*," p. 651.]

(c) Donald Lennox, one of his bastard sons, was ancestor in the male line of William Lennox, of Woodhead, who at a peerage election [S.] in 1768 opposed the claim of Alexander Lennox to the Earldom (see note "b" next above) as being "preferable heir male."

(d) "What the crimes were for which he [the Regent Albany] and his aged father in law were put to death are unknown, no record existing to throw light on the subject—the charter of Robert III. preserved the Earldom. It does not appear of much moment which of the victims suffered first; if the Regent, then the succession to the Lennox title never opened to him, and the moment the breath passed from the body of the Earl the *comitatus, jure sanguinis*, vested in his da., Isabella, by force of the Royal Charter." See "Earldom of Lennox," No. 6, in Maidment's "*Collectanea Genealogica*, 1883.

(e) See "*Riddell*," p. 652, note "i."

(f) It appears to be owing to this regrant that the Earldom was not forfeited by the treason of the late holder. See note "d" next above.

(g) The two daughters (*if* indeed they ever existed) assigned to her in Wood's "*Douglas*" and in Fraser's "*Lennox*" must have *d.* s.p. either before her or certainly before the succession opened to the issue of her younger sisters. Her four sons all *d.* before her, without *legitimate* issue, tho' one left several bastard sons.

Duncan was (after the death of his eldest da. the said Countess) the heir of the body of one or other of his two other daughters, Elizabeth and Margaret, *according* to their seniority, but it remains uncertain, *which* of the two was the senior. Of these two ladies (1) Elizabeth *m.* about 1392, Sir John Stuart of Darnley, co Renfrew (slain at Orleans, 12 Feb. 1428/9) and *d.* Nov. 1429, leaving a s. and h., Sir Alan Stuart, of Darnley (slain 1439) whose s. and h., John, Lord Darnley [S.], assumed this Earldom in 1473, and was recognised as Earl of Lennox in 1488, as mentioned below. The other sister (2) Margaret, who *m.* before 25 July 1392, Robert Menteth, of Rusky and was living, 18 May 1451 (more than twenty years later than Elizabeth) was mother of Sir Murdoch Menteth, of Rusky (*d.* before 1456) who (besides a son Patrick, who *d.* young and unm.) had two daughters of whom, the youngest, Elizabeth, *m.* John Napier, of Merchistoun and had seizin of the 4th part of the Earldom of Lennox, 16 Nov. 1473. Agnes Menteth, the 1st da. and heir of line, *m.* about 1460, Sir John Haldane of Gleneagles, who claimed the Earldom of Lennox, *jure uxoris*, in right of her as the heir of line of her grandmother the said Margaret (Menteth *neé* Lennox) therein stated to have been *older* than her sister, Elizabeth (Stuart *neé* Lennox) abovenamed. He, his said wife and their son, James Haldane, obtained in 1475, a writ of error as against a service of 23 July 1473, under which Lord Darnley, the heir of Elizabeth, had been served heir, to half the property and to the principal messuage of the Earldom and had accordingly assumed the title. Dame Agnes Haldane, *neé* Menteth, *d.* about 1477, and in Oct. 1488, Lord Darnley (the rival claimant) sat in Parl. [S.], as *Earl of Lennox*. Sir James Haldane, however, son and heir of the said Agnes, was on 21 and 24 May 1490, served heir of Duncan, Earl of Lennox (his said mother's great grandfather), and was "infeoffed in the fourth part of the Earldom, which belonged to him in property," when "he entered a formal protest that his not then claiming and insisting on his right to the said superiority of the whole Earldom should be no prejudice to him in future time of his *right* to the said superiority or his being hold *the principal of the said Earldom*, as it was known he descended from the *eldest* sister." In Sep. 1491, a submission was entered into whereby the Haldanes([a]) agreed to give up their quarter of the *property* of the Earldom to Lord Darnley, who "should resign to Sir James all the right of the superiority and tenendry of the said Earldom" which division was carried out in 1493. Notwithstanding these proceedings the title (assumed in 1473) was, since 1488, enjoyed by the family of Stuart as below, and appears never to have been seriously disputed by the family of Haldane.}

XI. 1473, or 1488. *10* or *1.* Sir John Stewart, or Stuart, of Darnley (or Dernely) co. Renfrew, s. and h of Sir Alan S. of the same, by Catharine, da. of Sir William Seton, of Seton, which Alan was s. and h. of Sir John Stewart, or Stuart of Darnley afsd. by Elizabeth, one of the three daughters and coheirs of Duncan, Earl of Lennox [S.] abovenamed; *suc.* his father in 1439, and was *cr.* a Lord of Parl. [S.], by the title of LORD DERNELEY or DARNLEY [S.], between 17 July 1460 and 20 July 1461 ([b]) most probably at the Coronation of James III. [S.], who *suc.* to the throne, 3 Aug. 1460. He was served heir, 23 July 1473 to his great grandfather, Duncan, Earl of Lennox [S], abovenamed, in half of that Earldom and in the principal messuage thereof, whereupon he assumed the title of EARL OF LENNOX [S.], sitting in Parl. as such 20 Nov. 1475, and being so recognised in Royal letters. This service, however, was reduced, 12 June 1475, the Earldom of Lennox being claimed by the Haldane family as representatives of Margaret, da. of Earl Duncan, she being stated to have been *older* than her sister, Elizabeth, the grandmother of Lord

---

([a]) "A memorial relative to the ancient Earls of Lennox," relating to the claim of the Haldane family to the succession thereto, was prepared by Alexander Wedderburn, afterwards Earl of Rosslyn, and shews an intimate acquaintance with the feudal law of Scotland. See "Maidment's "*Coll. Gen.*"

([b]) The Askoun Chronicle says that he was made a Lord of Parl. [S.] at the "same time as Earl of Erroll was beltit." *i.e.*, June 1452 [*ex. inform.* M. J. Shaw-Stewart]. He, however, had two charters of the Barony of Torbolton in Ayrshire, one, 17 July 1460, to him as "Sir John Stewart of Derneley," and the other 20 July 1461, to him as "John, Lord Derneley."

Darnley. He accordingly reverted to his former designation, as Lord Darnley; was Warden of the West borders, 1481, and was one of the Lords who seized King James III. [S.] at Lauder in 1482, from whom, however, he received pardon, continuing in attendance on him. In Oct. 1488 (the 1st Parl. of James IV. [S.]) he again sat as EARL OF LENNOX [S.] which appears henceforth(a) to have been allowed to him and his issue. The custody of Dumbarton Castle was given to him and his eldest son, 20 Oct. 1488, but they next year rebelled against the King, were defeated at Tillymoss and were forfeited in June 1489, tho' the sentence was annulled, 5 Feb. 1489/90. He *m.* (indre. 15 May 1438), Margaret, 1st da. of Alexander (MONTGOMERY), 1st LORD MONTGOMERY [S.], by Margaret, da. of Sir Thomas BOYD, of Kilmarnock. He *d.* between 8 July and 11 Sep. 1495.

XII. 1495. *11* or *2.* MATTHEW (STUART), EARL OF LENNOX, and LORD DARNLEY [S.], s. and h. He, on 5 May 1488 (being then called "Master of Derneley") had safe conduct to go into England and was with his father in his rebellion, 1488-90. He *m.* before 11 Sep. 1495, Elizabeth, da. of James (HAMILTON), 1st LORD HAMILTON [S.], by THE LADY MARY STEWART (widow of Thomas [BOYD], Earl of Arran [S.]), da. of **King James II.** [S.] He *d.* 9 Sep. 1513, being slain at the battle of Flodden(b) where he was in command of the right wing.

[WILLIAM STUART, MASTER OF LENNOX, s. and h. ap. He *m.* Margaret, da. of William (GRAHAM), 1st EARL OF MONTROSE [S.], and *d.* s.p. and v.p. in or before 1513. His widow *m.* Sir John SOMERVILLE, of Cambusnethan.]

XIII. 1513. *12* or *3.* JOHN (STUART), EARL OF LENNOX and LORD DARNLEY [S.], 2d but only surv. s. and h. He was one of the Lords of the regency, 1524, during the minority of King James V. [S.], whose rescue from the hands of the Douglas family he endeavoured to effect but was defeated, 4 Sep. 1526, at Linlithgow, taken prisoner and murdered in cold blood. He *m.* Anne, da. of John (STEWART), EARL OF ATHOLE [S.] (uterine br. of **King James II.** [S.], by his second wife, Eleanor, da. of William (SINCLAIR), 1st EARL OF CAITHNESS [S.] He *d.* 4 Sep. 1526, as afsd.

(a) Andrew (Stewart), Lord Avandale [S.], who held a life grant of the *comitatus* of Lennox (as above stated) had died shortly before.

(b) The following notice of the effect of the battle of Flodden, 9 Sep. 1513, on the Scotch nobles was compiled by one of them who was well versed in their history, *viz.*, the Earl of Caithness, who *d.* 20 Jan. 1891, aged 63.—"The battle of Flodden made sad havoc amongst the holders of peerages at that date, although none of the peerages themselves became extinct. There were at that time 21 Earls and 29 [30 ?] Barons or Lords of Parliament. Of the former [*i.e., the 21 Earls*], *ten* perished on the field of battle, *viz.* (1) Crawford (2) Erroll (3) Caithness (4) Argyll (5) Athole (6) Rothes (7) Lennox (8) Bothwell (9) Montrose and (10) Cassilis. *Eleven* either escaped or were not present, *viz.* (1) Sutherland (2) Angus (3) Menteith (4) Huntly (5) Marischal (6) Morton (7) Buchan (8) Glencairn (9) Moray (10) Arran and (11) Eglinton. *Two eldest sons of Earls* were killed, *viz.*, the Masters (1) of Angus and (2) of Marischal. Of *the* [abovenamed] *Barons* there were [also *ten*] slain [*viz.*] the Lords (1) Seton (2) Maxwell (3) Borthwick (4) Erskine (5) Hay of Yester (6) Sinclair (7) Sempill (8) Herries (9) Ross of Hawkhead and (10) Elphinstone. Those who escaped or who were not present were [*nineteen, viz.*], the Lords (1) Somerville (2) Forbes (3) Saltoun (4) Gray (5) Lindsay of Byres (6) Lyle (7) Cathcart (8) Glamis (9) Fleming (10) Livingstone (11) Oliphant (12) Lovat (13) Home (14) Carlyle (15) Ruthven (16) Drummond (17) Crichton (18) Ogilvie and (19) Evandale. [*Four eldest sons of Barons, viz.*], the Masters of (1) Cathcart (2) Oliphant (3) Lovat and (4) Ruthven were also slain." From this list it appears that out of *fifty Peers* no less than *twenty* were slain, which twenty, alphabetically arranged, are as under, *viz* (1) Argyll (2) Athole (3) Bothwell (4) Borthwick (5) Caithness (6) Cassilis (7) Crawford (8) Elphinstone (9) Erroll (10) Erskine (11) Hay of Yester (12) Herries (13 Lennox (14) Maxwell (15) Montrose (16) Ross of Hawkhead (17) Rothes (18) Sempill (19) Seton and (20) Sinclair, besides *six eldest sons of Peers, viz.*, the masters of (1) Angus (2) Cathcart (3) Lovat (4) Marischal (5) Oliphant and (6) Ruthven. If, however (as seems to have been the case) Thomas Stewart the holder of the Barony of Innermeath in 1513 was a *Lord of Parl.*, he must be added to the above list, making the total number, 51 out of which 21 were slain.

XIV. 1526. *13 or 4.* MATTHEW (STUART), EARL OF LENNOX and LORD DARNLEY [S.], s. and h., served, when young, under the French crown, in the Italian war. He was, in 1543, a great promoter of the English interest at the Court [S.], and incurred forfeiture 1 Oct. 1545, which was rescinded in Dec. 1564, during which period he resided in England, receiving from Henry VIII., a grant of the manor of Temple Newsam, co. York. He was elected REGENT [S.], 11 July 1570, on behalf of (his grandson) the infant King, but was taken prisoner by the party of Queen Mary [S.], and mortally wounded, 4 Sep. 1571, at Stirling, where he was *bur.* He *m.* about 1544, Margaret, da. of Archibald (DOUGLAS), EARL OF ANGUS [S.], by his second wife THE LADY MARGARET TUDOR, **Queen Dow. of Scotland**, da. of **King Henry VII.** She *d.* 9 March 1577, aged 61, at Hackney, co. Midx., and was *bur.* in Westm. Abbey. M.I. Will pr. 1578.

[HENRY STUART, *styled* LORD DARNLEY, 1st s. and h. ap., *b.* 1545, at Temple Newsam afsd.; *cr.* LORD ARDMANNOCH and EARL OF ROSS [S.], 15 May 1565 and DUKE OF ALBANY [S.], 20 July following. On 29 July 1565, he *m.* Mary, **Queen of Scotland**, at Holyrood chapel, having been proclaimed **King of Scotland**, the day previous. He *d.* (from an explosion of gunpowder) at Kirk O' Field, 10 Feb. 1566/7, aged 21 and was *bur.* in Holyrood chapel. The abdication of the Queen, his widow, 24 July 1567, and her execution 10 Feb. 1586/7, at Fotheringay Castle are matters of national history.]

XV. 1571. *14 or 5.* **James VI., King of Scotland**, grandson and h., being only s. and h. of Henry STUART, *styled* LORD DARNLEY, &c. by **Queen Mary** [S.], his wife both abovenamed, *b.* as DUKE OF ROTHESAY, &c. [S.], 19 June 1566, at Edinburgh Castle, *suc.* his father, 10 Feb. 1566/7 as DUKE OF ALBANY, &c. [S.], became 24 July 1567, by the abdication of the Queen, his mother, **King of Scotland**, and *suc.* his paternal grandfather (the abovenamed Matthew), 4 Sep. 1571, as EARL OF LENNOX and LORD DARNLEY [S.], *which honours*, accordingly, as soon as they were thus inherited, merged in the Crown.

XVI. 1572, to 1576. CHARLES STUART, paternal uncle to **King James VI.** [S.], being 2d and yst. but only surv. s. (tho' not heir) to Matthew (STUART), EARL OF LENNOX [S.], and Margaret, his wife, both abovenamed. He was *b.* about 1556 and was *cr.*, 18 April 1572, EARL OF LENNOX and LORD DARNLEY [S.], with rem. to his heirs male, and had, by four charters of the same date, the lands of that Earldom settled on him in like manner. He *m.*, in 1574, Elizabeth, sister of William, 1st EARL OF DEVONSHIRE, da. of Sir William CAVENDISH, K.B., by his third wife, the well known Elizabeth (afterwards COUNTESS OF SHREWSBURY), da. of John HARDWICK, of Hardwick, co. Derby. He *d.* s.p.m.(a) in London in 1576, in his 21st year, and was *bur.* in Westm. Abbey when *all his honours* became *extinct.*

XVII. 1578, to 1580. ROBERT STUART, Bishop of Caithness, paternal grand uncle to **King James VI.** [S.], being 2d s. of John, 3d EARL OF LENNOX [S.] (of the Stuart family), by Anne, his wife, both abovenamed, *b.* about 1515; was in Holy Orders, being sometime Provost of Dumbarton; elected Bishop of Caithness in 1543 but deprived of that post the same year for rebellion; restored 1563 and, taking the part of the Reformation, had a gift of the priory of St. Andrew's. He was *cr.*, 16 June 1578, EARL OF LENNOX and LORD DARNLEY [S.], with rem. to the heirs male of his body, but resigning the said dignities, within two years thereof, was *cr.*, 5 March 1579/80, EARL OF MARCH and LORD OF DUNBAR [S.], titles which were confirmed by Royal charter

(a) The career of his only da. and h., the Lady Arabella Stuart, and her secret marriage with William Seymour, afterwards (1621) Earl of Hertford, and finally (1660) Duke of Somerset, is well known. She *d.* a lunatic in the Tower of London and was *bur.* 27 Sep. 1615, in Westm. Abbey, aged about 38.

5 Oct. 1582. He m. before 1579 Elizabeth, widow of Hugh (FRASER), 6th LORD LOVAT [S.] (who d. Jan. 1576/7), 1st da. of John (STEWART), 4th EARL OF ATHOLE [S.], by his first wife, Elizabeth, da. of George (GORDON), 4th EARL OF HUNTLY [S.] She obtained in or before 1581 a divorce(a) from him for impotency.(b) He d. s.p. 29 March 1586, in his 70th year, at St. Andrew's, when *all his honours became extinct.*

XVIII. 1580. Dukedom [S.] I. 1581. 1. ESME(c) STUART, 6th Seigneur D'Aubigny(d) in France, only s. and h. of John STUART, 5th Seigneur D'Aubigny, by Anne, yst. da. and coheir of Francois, SEIGNEUR DE LA QUEULLE (which John was br. to Robert, EARL OF LENNOX, and afterwards EARL OF MARCH [S.] next above mentioned), was b. about 1542; *suc.* his father in the Seigneurie of Aubigny, 31 May 1567. At the invitation of his cousin, King James VI. [S.], he came over to Scotland, 8 Sep. 1569, and received a grant of the rich Abbey of Arbroath and the custody of the Castle of Dumbarton. He was cr. on 5 March 1579/80, EARL OF LENNOX, LORD DARNLEY, AUBIGNY, AND DALKEITH [S.], with rem. to the heirs male of his body, which failing, the dignity to return to the King. He was, 17 months later, on 5 Aug. 1581, cr. DUKE OF LENNOX, EARL OF DARNLEY, LORD AUBIGNY, DALKEITH, TORBOLTOUN, AND ABERDOUR [S.](e) with, probably, the same rem.(f) having been, 15 Oct. 1580, made heritable GREAT CHAMBERLAIN [S.] He appears, however, to have been secretly in the interest of restoring the King's mother, Mary Queen of Scots, to the throne, and after "*the raid of Ruthven,*" 23 Aug. 1582, the King issued orders for his quitting Scotland. He m. in 1572 (his

---

(a) She m., 6 July 1581, James (Stewart), Earl of Arran [S.] (*attainted* in Nov. 1585) and d. April 1596.

(b) He had, however, an illegit. da., Margaret, who m. Robert Algeo, of Easter Walkinshaw, co. Renfrew. [Craufurd's Peerage, p. 292.]

(c) Esme or Aymé.

(d) See (as to this branch of the family) an accurate and interesting little work, privately printed in 1891 (pp. 130) entitled "Some account of the Stuarts of Aubigny in France [1422–1672], by Lady Elizabeth Cust." The seigneurie of Aubigny in Berry was granted by King Charles VII., of France, to Sir John Stuart, of Darnley (constable of the Scottish army in France) 26 March 1423, and confirmed by Parl. 30 July 1425. He had distinguished himself in the victory over the English at Baugé, 21 March 1420/1, soon after which he entered permanently into the service of France and was slain near Orleans 1429. His second son, John Stuart, *suc.* him as 2d Seigneur D'Aubigny and d. 1482, being *suc.* by his son, Bernard Stuart, 3d Seigneur D'Aubigny, who d. s.p.m. in 1508. On his death the Seigneurie was established to his cousin and son in law, Robert Stuart, 4th s. of John, 1st Lord Darnley afterwards Earl of Lennox, which John was s. and h. of Sir Alan Stuart, s. and h. of the 1st Seigneur D'Aubigny. This Robert, the 4th Seigneur, d. s.p. 1543, when the Seigneurie was established to his great nephew, John Stuart, yst. s. of John, and br. of Matthew and Robert, all Earls of Lennox, which John, the 5th Seigneur, who d. 1567, was father of Esme, the 6th Seigneur, cr. Duke of Lennox, as in the text, who was the last of these Seigneurs that resided permanently in France.

(e) According to Douglas (vol. ii, p. 671) the Baronies granted were "Aubigny, Torboltoun and Dalkeith," but there is no reference given to the "*Mag. Sig.*" or any other authority. In Lady Eliz. Cust's "*Stuarts of Aubigny*" it is stated that his titles were proclaimed as "Duick of Lenox, Erle Dernlie, Lord Obignnie, Dalkeith, Torboltoun, *Aberdowre*, Knyght of Cruickstoun, Great Chamberlain of Scotland." Andrew Stuart (pp. 258 and 260) also mentions *Aberdour.*

(f) The original grant of the *Dukedom* of Lennox is not to be found. If it was to heirs *general*, the Earls of Darnley [I.] would be entitled thereto, and it was, indeed, claimed in 1829 by the 4th Earl, as *heir of line*, which undoubtedly he was. His petition was referred to the Lords, but no further proceedings were taken thereon. See p. 67, note "d."

mother's fourth cousin), Katharine,[a] 9th child of Guillaume DE BALSAC, SEIGNEUR D'ENTRAGUES (slain 1555), by Louise, da. of Jean, SEIGNEUR D'HUMIERES. He *d.* at Paris of a fever, 26 May 1583, aged about 40, and was *bur.* at Aubigny. His widow distinguished herself in defending the town of Aubigny, Jan. 1590/1, during the wars of the League and, having survived her husband nearly 50 years, *d.* about 1631 or 1632, being living, tho' in "great years and weakness," 3 Dec. 1630.[b]

Dukedom [S.] II. Earldom [S.] XIX. } 1583.

2. LUDOVIC (STUART) DUKE OF LENNOX, &c. Heritable Great Chamberlain [S.], s. and h., *b.* 29 Sep. 1574; *suc.* to the peerage [S.] 26 May 1583, but not to the Seigneurie of Aubigny in France. He returned to Scotland about 1584 and was in high favour at Court. President of the Privy Council [S.] 1589; Joint Lieut. of Scotland, Nov. 1589 to May 1590; Chamberlain of the Household [S.] 1590; High Admiral [S.] 1591. Had a grant of the disestablished religious house of St. Andrew's in 1593.[c] Ambassador [S.] to England, 1601. He attended the King to England, on his accession, as James I., to that throne in 1603, and was there naturalised 18 July 1603; Gent. of the Bedchamber and P.C., 1603; el. K.G., 25 June and inst. 9 July 1603; was *cr.* M.A., of Oxford, on the occasion of the King's visit there, 30 Aug. 1605;[d] Ambassador to Paris, 1604-1605, and again, 1613; High Commissioner to the Scotch Parl. 1608. He was *cr.* on 6 Oct. 1613, BARON OF SETRINGTON, co. York, and EARL OF RICHMOND, and on 17 May 1623, EARL OF NEWCASTLE-UPON-TYNE and DUKE OF RICHMOND. He was Deputy Earl Marshal, 1614; Steward of the Household, 1615-24; Lord Lieut. of Kent, 1620, and Joint Commissioner of the Great Seal, May to July 1621. He *m.* firstly, Sophia, 3d da. of William (RUTHVEN), 1st EARL OF GOWRIE [S.], by Dorothea, da. of Henry (STEWART), 2d LORD METHVEN [S.] She *d.* before June 1590. He *m.* secondly, Jane, widow of the Hon. Robert MONTGOMERIE (who *d.* Aug. 1596), sister of Hugh, 1st LORD CAMPBELL OF LOUDOUN [S.], da. of Sir Matthew CAMPBELL, of Loudoun, by Isabel, da. of Sir John DRUMMOND. He *m.* thirdly, June 1621, Frances, Dow. COUNTESS OF HERTFORD (relict of Henry PRANELL, of London), da. of Thomas (HOWARD), 1st VISCOUNT HOWARD OF BINDON, by his third wife, Mabel, da. of Nicholas BURTON. He *d.* s.p.s. legit. 16 Feb. 1623/4, in his 50th year at St. Andrew's Holborn and was *bur.* the 17th in Westm. Abbey, when the *Dukedom and Earldom of Richmond*, the *Earldom of Newcastle-upon-Tyne* and the *Barony of Setrington* became *extinct*, but the Scotch dignities devolved on his br. and h. Admon. 13 March 1623/4. His widow *d.* s.p., at Exeter house, Strand, 8, and was *bur.* 12 Oct. 1639, in Westm. Abbey, aged 63. Funeral cert. in Public Record office. Will dat. 28 July and pr. 31 Oct. 1639.

Dukedom [S.] III. Earldom [S.] XX. } 1623/4.

3. ESME (STUART), DUKE OF LENNOX, &c. [S.], also EARL OF MARCH, &c., br. and h., *b.* 1579, ed. at the Univ. of Bourges; *suc.* his father (tho' the second son), 26 May 1583, as 7th Seigneur D'Aubigny, and did homage for the same to Henry IV., King of France, 8 April 1600; naturalised in England, 24 May 1603; High Steward of Grafton, &c., 1609; Gent. of the Bedchamber; Joint Lord Lieut. of co. Huntingdon, 1619, &c. Having *m.* in or before 1609, Katharine, who on the death of her father in Oct. 1615, became (*de jure*) *suo jure* BARONESS CLIFTON OF LEIGHTON BROMSWOLD (see that dignity), he was *cr.* 7 June 1619, BARON STUART OF LEIGHTON BROMSWOLD, co. Huntingdon,

---

(a) She and her husband were both descended from the French Armagnacs and Bourbons and the Italian Viscontis, Scaligers and Dorias. See tabular pedigree in Lady Elis. Cust's "*Stuarts of Aubigny*," as on p. 65, note "d."

(b) See p. 65, note "d."

(c) See vol. iv, p. 247, note "a," *sub* "Holyrood house" for a list of some of these grants.

(d) See vol. iii, p. 236, note "a," *sub* "Effingham," for the names of those so created.

and EARL OF MARCH.(a) He, on 16 Feb. 1623/4, *suc. to the Scotch Dukedom*; el. K.G.,(b) 22 April 1624, but *d.* of the spotted fever at Kirkby, co. Northampton, soon afterwards, 30 July and was *bur.* 6 August 1624. in Westm. Abbey. His widow *m.* in or before 1632, James (HAMILTON), 2d EARL OF ABERCORN [S.], and had Royal lic. 28 Nov. 1632, to retain her title and rank as *Duchess of Lennox*, notwithstanding such marriage. The Earl survived her till about 1670, but she *d.* in Scotland, and was *bur.* "without ceremonie," 17 Sep. 1637. aged about 45. Her will, signed "Kath. Lenox," dat. 12 Aug. 1637, pr. 15 Jan. 1638/9.

Dukedom [S.] IV. Earldom [S.] XXI. — 1624.

4. JAMES (STUART), DUKE OF LENNOX, &c. [S.], also EARL OF MARCH, &c. [E.], s. and h.,(c) *b.* 6 April 1612, *suc. to the peerage*, 30 July 1624. He was *cr.* 8 Aug. 1641, DUKE OF RICHMOND, with a spec. rem. failing his issue male to that of his brothers. He *d.* 30 March 1655.

Dukedom [S.] V. Earldom [S.] XXII. — 1655.

5. ESME (STUART), DUKE OF RICHMOND, &c., also DUKE OF LENNOX, &c. [S.], only s. and h.,(c) *b.* 2 Nov. 1649, *suc.* to the peerage, 20 March 1655, and *d.* unm. 10 Aug. 1660.

Dukedom [S.] VI. Earldom [S.] XXIII. — 1660, to 1672.

6. CHARLES (STUART), DUKE OF RICHMOND [1641], &c. [E.], also DUKE OF LENNOX, [1581], EARL OF LENNOX [1580], EARL OF DARNLEY [1581], LORD DARNLEY, AUBIGNY AND DALKEITH [1580], and LORD AUBIGNY, DALKEITH, TORBOLTOUN AND ABERDOUR [1581], in the peerage of Scotland,(c) Seigneur D'Aubigny, cousin and h. male, being s. and h. of Lord George STUART, 9th Seigneur D'Aubigny, br. of James, 4th Duke of Lennox [S.], abovenamed. He was *b.* 7 March 1640, and was *cr.* 10 Dec. 1645, BARON STUART OF NEWBURY, co. Berks, and EARL OF LICHFIELD, co. Stafford. He *suc.* to the two Dukedoms [E. and S.], 10 Aug. 1660. He *d.* s.p.s., 12 Dec. 1672, when *all his honours*, save the Barony of Clifton of Leighton Bromswold (see that dignity) became *extinct* or *merged* in the Crown.(d)

See fuller particulars under "RICHMOND" Dukedom, cr. 1641; ex. 1672.

(a) His great-uncle, Robert (Stuart), Earl of Lennox [S.], had, on resigning that peerage, been in 1580 *cr. Earl of March* and Lord of Dunbar *in the peerage of Scotland* which dignities became extinct on his death in 1586 but the *Earldom of March* conferred in 1619 on Lord Esme Stuart was unquestionably an *English peerage.* Curiously enough eight months *before* its extinction (12 Dec. 1672), the *Marquessate of March in the peerage of Scotland* was (1 May 1672), conferred on the family of Maitland, who were descended from that of Dunbar, the ancient *Earls of March* or Dunbar [S.]

(b) He was elected in the room of his brother and this is said to be the first instance of any Knight of that Order succeeding to the place vacant therein by his immediate predecessor in the *peerage.*

(c) The style attributed to the 4th and 5th Dukes of Lennox in Doyle's "Official Peerage," *sub* "Richmond," is "Duke of Richmond and Lennox, Earl of March, and Darnley, *Viscount of Torbolton and Methven*, Baron Stuart of Leighton Bromswold, Lord Darnley, Settrington, St. Andrew's and Aubigny," but in that attributed to the 6th and last Duke the Viscountcies of "*Torbolton and Methven*" [Qy. whence derived ?] are omitted.

(d) It is said that King Charles II. was served his heir. See p. 65, note "f," as to the claim to the *Dukedom.*

Dukedom [S.] VII. 1672. I. CHARLES LENNOX,(a) illegit. s. of King Charles II., b. 29 July 1672, was on 9 Aug. 1675 (when three years old) cr. DUKE OF RICHMOND, EARL OF MARCH, and BARON OF SETRINGTON, all co. York [E.], and a month later on 9 Sep. 1675, was cr. DUKE OF LENNOX, EARL OF DARNLEY, and LORD OF TORBOLTOUN(b) [S.] See "RICHMOND" Dukedom, cr. 1672.

LEOMINSTER [or LEMPSTER.]

Barony. I. 1692. I. SIR WILLIAM FERMOR, 2d Bart., of Easton Neston, co. Northampton, 2d but 1st surv. s. and h. of Sir William FERMOR, Bart. (so cr. 6 Sep. 1641), by Mary, da. of Hugh PERRY, Alderman and sometime (1632) Sheriff of London, was b. 3 and bap. 18 Aug. 1648, at Easton Neston, suc. his father (who had greatly distinguished himself in the Royal cause) in the Baronetcy and estates, 14 May 1661; rebuilt the family mansion with great magnificence and was cr., 12 April 1692, BARON LEOMINSTER, co. Hereford.(c) He m. firstly in London, 21 Dec. 1671 (Lic. Vic. Gen.) Jane, da. of Andrew BARKER, of Fairford, co. Glouc., by Elizabeth, da. of William ROBINSON, of Cheshunt, Herts. She d. s.p.m. 10 and was bur. 12 Aug. 1673, at Easton Neston. He m. secondly, June 1682, Catharine, 1st da. of John (POULETT), 3d BARON POULETT OF HINTON ST. GEORGE, by his first wife, Essex, da. of Alexander POPHAM. She also d. s.p.m. He m. thirdly, 5 March 1691/2 (Lic. Vic. Gen.), Sophia,(d) widow of Donough O'BRIEN, styled LORD O'BRIEN, 6th da. of Thomas (OSBORNE), 1st DUKE OF LEEDS, by Bridget, da. of Montagu (BERTIE), 2d EARL OF LINDSEY.(e) He d. 7 and was bur. 15 Dec. 1711, aged 63, at Easton Neston. Will pr. Jan. 1711/2. His widow d. 8 and was bur. 17 Dec. 1746, at Easton Neston. Will pr. 1746.

II. 1711. 2. THOMAS (FERMOR), BARON LEOMINSTER, s. and h., by third wife, b. 23 March 1697; cr. 27 Dec. 1721, EARL OF POMFRET or PONTEFRACT, co. York. See that title which together with the *Barony of Leominster* became *extinct* 8 June 1867.

LE POER, LA POER or POER, see "POWER."

LEPPINGTON.

i.e., "CAREY OF LEPPINGTON, co. York," Barony (*Carey*), cr. 1622; see "MONMOUTH" Earldom, cr. 1626; both dignities ex. 1661.

LESLIE.

i.e., "LESLIE" or "LESLIE OF LEVEN," Barony [S.] (*Leslie*), cr. 1445; regranted in 1663 as "LESLIE AND BALLINBREICH"; see "ROTHES" Earldom [S.], cr. before 1458.

(a) The King, as head of the house of Stuart, represented Sir John Stuart, of Darnley, afterwards (1488-95) EARL OF LENNOX [S.], who claimed to be the representative of the Lennox family, Earls of Lennox [S.], which name of *Lennox* His Majesty accordingly bestowed on his bastard son, Charles, named in the text, at or before his elevation to the peerage. The child had, apparently, previously been known as "*Fitzroy*." See vol. ii, p. 285, note "d," *sub* "Cleveland."

(b) "Baron *Methuen* [Methven?] of Torbolton in Scotland" according to Doyle's "Official Peerage."

(c) His peerage appears to have been owing to the influence of the father of his third wife. See note "e" next below.

(d) She was second cousin to her husband, both being great grandchildren of Sir William Cokayne, of Rushton, co. Northampton, whose second da., Anne, m. Sir Hatton Fermor, the bridegroom's grandfather, and whose third da., Martha, m. the said Earl of Lindsey, the bride's grandfather.

(e) The Duke "gave with her £10,000 and Sir William will be made an English Baron." [Luttrell's "*Diary*."]

i.e., "LESLIE" Earldom [S.] (*Leslie*), *cr.* 1680, with the DUKEDOM OF ROTHES [S.], which see; *ex.* 1681.

LETRIM, see LEITRIM.

LEVENAX, see LENNOX.

LEVEN.(a)

Earldom [S.] I. 1641. *1.* ALEXANDER LESLIE, of Balgonie, co. Fife, s. of George L., of the same, Commander of Blair Castle, by his second wife(b) was *b.* about 1580, served in Holland against the Imperialists, and afterwards, with great distinction, in the service of Sweden (1628-30) under Gustavus Adolphus, by whom he was made Field Marshal. In 1639, he returned to Scotland, was in command of the Covenanters' army, for whom he took the castle of Edinburgh. In 1640 (28 Aug.) he defeated the Royalist army at Newburn, taking possession of Newcastle, &c. He was one of the Commissioners to treat with the King at Ripon, by whom he was *cr.* on 11 (sealed 20th) Oct. 1641, LORD BALGONIE and EARL OF LEVEN(c) [S.], with rem. to the heirs male of his body. He took his seat in Parl. 6 Nov. following.(d) In 1642 he was Gen. of the Scotch forces in Ireland, whence he joined the Parl. forces with 21,000 men, contributing greatly to their victory, 2 July 1644, at Marston Moor. In 1647 he was Lord General of Scotland. After the execution of Charles I., he appears to have favoured the Royal cause, serving as a volunteer in 1650, at the battle of Dunbar. He was taken at Dundee by the Government, 28 Aug. 1651, imprisoned in the tower of London, whence he was released, at the intercession of Christina, Queen of Sweden, returning to Scotland in May 1654. He *m.*, about 1610, Agnes, da. of David RENTON, of Billie, co. Berwick. She *d.* at Inchmartin(e) 26 June, and was *bur.* 23 July 1651, at Markinch.(f) He *d.* at Balgonie 4 and was *bur.* 19 April 1661, at Markinch, aged above 80.

[ALEXANDER LESLIE, *styled* LORD BALGONIE, 2d but only surv. s. and h. ap. was a Col. in the Army and accompanied his father in 1642 to Ireland. He *m.* in 1636, Margaret, da. of John (LESLIE), EARL OF ROTHES [S]. He *d.* v.p. soon after 12 Jan. 1644, the date of his will. His widow *m.* (contract 25 July 1646), Francis (SCOTT), 2d EARL OF BUCCLEUCH [S.], who *d.* 25 Nov. 1651 in his 25th year. She *m.* thirdly, 13 Jan. 1652/3, at Sheriffhall (as his 3d wife), David (WEMYSS), 2 EARL OF WEMYSS [S.], who *d.* June 1679, and *d.* (his widow) 1688.](g)

II. 1661. *2.* ALEXANDER (LESLIE), EARL OF LEVEN, &c. [S.], grandson and h., being only s. of Alexander Leslie, *styled* Lord Balgonie and Margaret, his wife, both abovenamed. He was *styled* LORD BALGONIE

(a) "The Melvilles, Earls of Melville, and the Leslies, Earls of Leven" (3 vols. 4to, 1890) is one of the many magnificent and elaborate works of Sir William Fraser, K.C.B., LL.D.

(b) This Lady had previously given birth to the said Alexander, who by her subsequent marriage became legitimate. She was, according to a contemporary journal, "a wench in Rannoch."

(c) The title was taken from a little river, near his lands in Fife, called Leven. The Barony of Balgonie, co. Fife was purchased by him in 1636.

(d) The Earl of Callendar claimed precedency of him, his *warrant* being dated five days earlier, tho' the completion of his patent was not till after that of Leven.

(e) Inchmartin, in the Carse of Gowrie, was purchased by him from the Ogilvies in 1650 and called Inchleslie till 1720, when it was re-acquired by the Ogilvie family.

(f) According to Wood's "Douglas" he *m.* secondly Dame Francis Pakington, da. of Sir John Ferrers. A marriage is recorded at St. Antholin's, London, 29 Dec. 1626 of "Mr. *Robert* Leasly, Gent., and the Lady Fraunces Packington," which probably gave rise to this statement which appears to be quite unfounded.

(g) By her three husbands she was mother of one Earl [Leven] and three *suo jure* Countesses, viz., two of Buccleuch and one of Wemyss [S.]

from his father's death (1644 ?) till he *suc. to the peerage* [S.], 4 April 1661. He *m.*, 30 Dec. 1656, at Naworth Castle, Margaret, sister to Charles, 1st EARL OF CARLISLE, 5th da. of Sir William HOWARD, of Corby, by Mary, da. of William (EURE), BARON EURE OF WOTTON. Having no male issue, he, on 12 Feb. 1663, covenanted to resign his honours in favour of the heirs male, whom failing to the heirs female (without division) of his body, with rem. to the second son of John, Earl of Rothes,([a]) and the heirs male of his body with rem. to the second son of (his sister) Catharine, by George, Lord Melville, and the heirs male of his body with rem. to the second son of (his mother) Margaret by (her then husband) David, Earl of Wemyss, in like manner, with rem. to his own heirs male whatever, whom failing to his heirs and assignees whatsoever. He *d.* s.p.m. of a high fever at Balgonie, 15 July and was *bur.* 3 Aug. 1664, at Markinch, before a charter and precept could be past of the above, but it was confirmed under the great seal 7 Sep. 1665. His widow *d.* at Edinburgh 30 Sep. and was *bur.* 3 Oct. 1664, at Markinch.

III. 1664. *3.* Margaret, *suo jure* COUNTESS OF LEVEN, &c. [S.], 1st da. and heir of line, *suc. her father in that dignity*, 15 July 1664.([b]) She *m.* early in 1674 (as his first wife) the Hon. Francis MONTGOMERY, of Giffen, co. Ayr, and *d.* a few months later s.p. and under age 6 Nov. 1674.

IV. 1674, to 1676. *4.* Catharine, *suo jure* COUNTESS OF LEVEN and BARONESS OF BALGONIE [S.], yst. and only surv. sister and heir; was served *heir in the said Earldom* and Barony([c]) 22 May 1675. She was *b.* 1663 or 1664 and *d.* unm. 21 Jan. 1676.

[Until the death of the Duke (formerly Earl) of Rothes [S.] on whose *second son* (tho' none such was in existence) the Earldom of Leven was next entailed that dignity remained suspended. The Duke, however, died s.p.m. 27 July 1681, when the succession opened as under.]

V. 1681. *5.* DAVID (LESLIE, *formerly* MELVILLE), EARL OF LEVEN AND LORD BALGONIE [S.], *second* son of George (MELVILLE), 1st EARL OF MELVILLE [S.], by Catharine, only sister of Alexander (LESLIE), 2d EARL OF LEVEN, abovenamed, was, *as such second son*, heir to the *Earldom of Leven*, &c., the issue of the said Earl of Leven, and no such issue of the Duke of Rothes as was in remainder thereto being in existence having failed.([b]) He was *b.* 5 May 1660, and *bap.* the 11th at Monimal; was Col. of a regiment of foot which he brought over to England in 1688 with the Prince of Orange, by whom (when King), he was made P.C., Col. of the 25th Regiment, and Gov. of Edinburgh Castle in 1689, in which year (17 July) he distinguished himself at the battle of Killicrankie, as also in the campaign in Flanders in 1692. He, on the death of, his cousin, the Countess Catherine, 21 Jan. 1676, assumed *the peerage* [S.] *of Leven*, &c., but was not recognised till the death s.p. of the Duke of Rothes [S.], 27 Feb. 1681, some of whose (possible) issue had prior right thereto.([b]) He was Major Gen. in 1703 and Commander in Chief in 1706 of the forces in Scotland; was a Commissioner for the Union, being REP. PEER [S.], (one of the original ones) in 1707, and again in 1708. He *suc.* his father (his eldest br. having previously in 1698, *d.* s.p.) 20 May 1707 as EARL OF MELVILLE [1690], VISCOUNT OF KIRKALDY [1690], LORD MELVILLE OF MONYMAILL [1616] and LORD RAITH, MONYMAILL AND BALWEARIE [1690] in the peerage of Scotland. He was dismissed from all his offices in 1712. He *m.* (contract 3 Sep. 1691) Anne, da of David (WEMYSS), LORD BURNTISLAND [S.], by Margaret, *suo jure*, COUNTESS OF WEMYSS [S.] She, who was *b.* 18 Oct. 1675, *d.* at Edinburgh Castle, 9 Jan. 1702. He *d.* 6 and was *bur.* 12 June 1728 in his 68th year, at Markinch.

[GEORGE LESLIE, *styled* LORD BALGONIE, s. and h. ap., *b.* Jan. 1695, was sometime Capt. in the 3rd Foot Guards, but retired in 1716. He *m.* Aug.

([a]) This Earl, afterwards (1667) Duke, of Rothes [S.] *d.* s.p.m. in 1681 so that this remainder came to an end after that date.

([b]) According to the covenant of resignation of the dignities, 12 Feb. 1663, confirmed under the great seal 7 Sep. 1665.

([c]) He and his father, Lord Melville were two out of the six persons whom James II. intended to except from his act of indemnity.

1716, his cousin, Margaret, da. of David (CARNEGIE), 4th EARL OF NORTHESK [S.], by Margaret, sister of Anne, Countess of Leven abovenamed. He *d.* v.p., 20 Aug. 1721, aged 26. His wife who was *b.* 6 Dec. 1697, *d.* 7 July 1722.]

VI. 1728. *6.* DAVID (LESLIE), EARL OF LEVEN, EARL OF MELVILLE &c. [S.], grandson and h., being only s. and h. of George LESLIE-MELVILLE, *styled* LORD BALGONIE and Margaret his wife, both abovenamed. He was *b.* probably in Milne's Square, Edinburgh, 17 Dec. 1717, being *styled* LORD BALGONIE till he *suc. to the peerage* [S.], May 1728. He *d.* unm. in his 12th year, June 1729.

VII. 1729. *7.* ALEXANDER (LESLIE), EARL OF LEVEN, EARL OF MELVILLE, &c. [S.], uncle and h., being 2d s. of David, EARL OF LEVEN, &c., the 5th holder of that dignity. He was *b.* about 1699, was sometime an Ensign in the 3d Foot Guards, but was admitted to the Faculty of Advocates, 1719; *suc. to the peerage* [S.], June 1729; one of the Lords of Session [S.], 1734: High Commissioner to the gen. assembly of the church [S.], 1741-53. REP. PEER [S.], 1747, to April 1754, and one of the Lords of Police, 1754. He *m.* firstly, 22 Feb. 1721, Mary, 1st da. of the Hon. John ERSKINE, of Carnock (3d s. of David, 2d LORD CARDROSS [S.]), by his second wife, Anna, da. and coheir of William DUNDAS, of Kincavel. She *d.* 12 July 1723. He *m.* secondly, 10 March 1726, Elizabeth, da. of David MONYPENNY, of Pitmilly, co. Fife. He *d.* suddenly, at Balcarres, 2 and was *bur.* from Melville, 7 Sep. 1754. Fun. entry in Lyon office. His widow *d.* at Edinburgh, 15 March 1783, in her 84th year.

VIII. 1754. *8.* DAVID (LESLIE), EARL OF LEVEN, EARL OF MELVILLE, &c. [S.], s. and h., by first wife, *b.* 4 March 1722; *styled* LORD BALGONIE from 1729 till he *suc. to the peerage* [S.], 2 Sep. 1754; ed. at the Univ. of Cambridge; was sometime (1744) Capt. in the 16th Foot; Grand Master of the Freemasons [S.], 1759-61; one of the Lords of Police [S.], 1773-82, and High Commissioner to the gen. assembly of the church [S.], 1783—1801. He *m.*, 29 July 1747, at Edinburgh, Willielmina, posthumous da. of William NISBET (who *d.* Oct. 1794), of Dirleton, co. Haddington, She *d.* at Melville House, co. Fife (after her "golden wedding") 10 May 1798, aged 74. He *d.* at Edinburgh, 9 June 1802, aged 80, and was *bur.* from Balgonie, at Markinch.

IX. 1802. *9.* ALEXANDER (LESLIE, afterwards [1805] LESLIE-MELVILLE), EARL OF LEVEN, EARL OF MELVILLE, &c. [S.], s. and h., *b.* 7 Nov. 1749, *styled* LORD BALGONIE from 1754 till he *suc. to the peerage* [S.], 9 June 1802; Comptroller of the Customs [S.], 1786. REP. PEER [S.], 1806. He *m.*, 12 Aug. 1784, at Clapham, Surrey, Jane, da. of John THORNTON, Merchant of London, by Lucy, da. of Samuel WATSON, and Margaret, da. of Sir Charles HOGHTON, 4th Bart. She *d.* 13 Feb. 1818. He *d.* 22 Feb. 1820, at Melville House, co. Fife, aged 70.

X. 1820. *10.* DAVID (LESLIE-MELVILLE), EARL OF LEVEN, EARL OF MELVILLE, &c. [S.], s. and h., *b.* in Spring Gardens, Midx., 22 June 1785, *styled* LORD BALGONIE from 1802 till he *suc. to the peerage* [S.], 22 Feb. 1820; was in the Royal Navy, distinguishing himself when in command at the bay of Rosas in Oct. 1809; Rear Admiral, 1846; Vice Admiral, 1858; REP. PEER [S.], 1831-60. He *m.*, 21 June 1824, Elizabeth Anne, da. of Sir Archibald CAMPBELL, 2d Bart., of Succoth, by Elizabeth, da. of John BALFOUR, of Balbirnie. He *d.* s.p.m.s. 8 Oct. 1860, aged 75. of apoplexy, at Melville House afsd., and was *bur.* at Monimail.(a) His widow *d.* there 8 Nov. 1863, and was *bur.* at Monimail.

[ALEXANDER LESLIE-MELVILLE, *styled* LORD BALGONIE, 1st s. and h. ap., *b.* 19 Nov. 1831, at Melville House afsd.; ed. at Eton; entered the Army, 1850, serving in the Crimean war: Capt. Grenadier Guards, 1854; Knight of the Legion of Honour of France, serving in the Crimean war. He *d.* unm. and v.p. 29 Aug. 1857, aged 25. at (his uncle's house) Roehampton House, Surrey, and was *bur.* at Monimail. M.I. there and in the Guards chapel, Wellington barracks, London.]

(a) He was *suc.* in the Lordship of Monimail and the lands known as the estate of Melville by his 1st da. and heir of line, Elizabeth Jane, wife of Thomas-Robert-Brooke Cartwright, afterwards Leslie-Melville-Cartwright.

XI. 1860. *11.* JOHN THORNTON (LESLIE-MELVILLE), EARL OF LEVEN, EARL OF MELVILLE, &c. [S.], br. and h. male, *b.* 18 Dec. 1786; Dep. Paymaster to the Forces in the Peninsula, 1809; an orig. partner in the Banking house of Williams, Deacon, Labouchere, Thornton, and Co., London; *suc. to the peerage* [S.], 8 Oct. 1860; REP. PEER [S.], 1865-76. He *m.* firstly, 15 Sep. 1812, at St. James, Westm., Harriet, da. of Samuel THORNTON, of Albury Park, Surrey (br. to Jane, Countess of Leven abovenamed), by Elizabeth, da. of Robert MILNES, of Wakefield. She *d.* 26 July 1832. He *m.* secondly, 23 April 1834, Sophia, 4th da. of Henry THORNTON, of Battersea, Surrey (another br. to Jane, Countess of Leven abovenamed), by Anne, da. of Joseph SYKES, of West Ella, co. York. He *d.* 16 Sep. 1876, in his 90th year, at Glenferness, co. Nairn, and was *bur.* at Brompton cemetery. His widow *d.* at Roehampton House afsd., 28 June 1887, and was *bur.* with him. Will pr. 12 Dec. 1887, over £57,000.

XII. 1876. *12.* ALEXANDER (LESLIE-MELVILLE), EARL OF LEVEN, EARL OF MELVILLE, &c. [S.], s. and h., by first wife, *b.* 11 Jan. 1817; ed. at Eton and at Trin. Coll., Cambridge; *styled* VISCOUNT KIRKCALDIE from 1860 till he *suc. to the peerage* [S.], 16 Sep. 1876; was a partner in the London banking house of "Williams, Deacon, and Co."; REP. PEER [S.], 1880-89. He *d.* unm. at Glenferness afsd. 22 Oct. 1889 (from the effects of a carriage accident on the 16th) aged 72. Personalty sworn at £525,000.

XIII. 1889. *13.* RONALD RUTHVEN (LESLIE-MELVILLE), EARL OF LEVEN [1641], EARL OF MELVILLE [1690], VISCOUNT KIRKCALDIE [1690], LORD MELVILLE OF MONYMAILL [1616], LORD BALGONIE [1641], and LORD RAITH, MONYMAILL, AND BALWEARIE [1690], in the peerage of Scotland, br. (of the half blood) and h., being s. of the penultimate Earl, by his second wife. He was *b.* 19 Dec. 1835; ed. at Eton and at Ch. Ch., Oxford; B.A., 1858; M.A., 1865; is a partner in the banking house of "Melville, Evans, and Co."; *suc. to the peerage* [S.], 22 Oct. 1889. He *m.*, 7 May 1885, Emma Selina, 1st da. of William Henry Berkeley (PORTMAN), 1st VISCOUNT PORTMAN, by Mary Selina Charlotte, da. of William Charles WENTWORTH-FITZWILLIAM, *styled* VISCOUNT MILTON. She was *b.* 5 April 1863.

[JOHN DAVID LESLIE MELVILLE, *styled* LORD BALGONIE, 1st s. and h. ap., *b.* 5 April 1886, at Portman house, London.]

Family Estates.—These, in 1883, consisted of 7,805 acres in Nairnshire and 1,019 in Fifeshire. *Total* 8,824 acres, worth £3,078 a year. *Principal Residences.* Glenferness, near Dunphail, Nairnshire (purchased in 1869); Hallhill, co. Fife (one of the ancient estates of the Melville family), and Roehampton House, Surrey.

LEVESON OF STONE.

i.e., "LEVESON OF STONE, co. Stafford," Barony (*Leveson-Gower*), *cr.* 1833, with the EARLDOM OF GRANVILLE, which see.

LEWES.

i.e., "LEWES, co. Sussex," Earldom (*Nevill*), *cr.* 1876, with the MARQUESSATE OF ABERGAVENNY, which see.

LEWISHAM.

i.e., "LEWISHAM, co. Kent," Viscountcy (*Legge*), *cr.* 1711, with the EARLDOM OF DARTMOUTH, which see.

LEYR MARNEY.

See "MARNEY OF LEYR MARNEY, co. Essex," Barony (*Marney*), *cr.* 1523; *ex.* 1525.

LEXINGTON, alias LAXTON.

See "EVERINGHAM DE LAXTON, *alias* LEXINGTON, Notts," Barony (*Everingham*), *cr.* 1309; *in abeyance* 1372.

LEXINTON OF ARAM.

Barony. I. 1645. *1.* ROBERT SUTTON, of Aram, or Averham, Notts, s. and h. of Sir William Sutton, of the same (14 years old in 1575), by Susan, da. of Thomas CONY, of Basingthorpe, co. Lincoln, was M.P. for Notts, 1624-25, April to May 1640, and from Nov. 1640 till disabled in 1644. He, being a zealous Royalist and having contributed largely to the garrisoning of the town of Newark-upon-Trent, was *cr.*, 21 Nov. 1645, BARON LEXINTON(a) OF ARAM, co. Nottingham. He *m.* firstly, 14 April 1616, Elizabeth, sister of John, 8th EARL OF RUTLAND, da. of Sir George MANNERS, of Haddon, co. Derby, by Grace, da. of Sir Henry PIERREPONT. She *d.* s.p. He *m.* secondly Anne, widow of Sir Thomas BROWNE, Bart., da. of Sir Guy PALMES, of Lindley, co. York, by Anne, da. of Sir Edward STAFFORD. She was *bur.* at Aram. He *m.* thirdly, 21 Feb. 1660/1, at St. James, Clerkenwell, Mary, da. of Sir Anthony ST. LEGER. He *d.* 13 Oct. 1668, and was *bur.* at Aram. Will dat. 26 Feb. 1665, to 7 Oct. 1668, pr. 7 and 14 July 1669, and 25 April 1673. The will of his widow dat. 8 July was pr. 13 Dec. 1669.

II. 1668 to 1723. *2.* ROBERT (SUTTON), BARON LEXINTON OF ARAM, only s. and h. by third wife. He was Gent. of the Horse to the Princess Anne of Denmark and subsequently Gent. of the Bedchamber to the King; was Envoy from King William III. to the court of Vienna and Ambassador from Queen Anne to that of Spain for the treaty of Ryswick. He *m.* (Lic. Fac. office 24 Sep. 1691, he about 25 and she about 18, to marry at Coulston) Margaret, da. and h. of Sir Giles HUNGERFORD, of Coulston, Wilts, and Margaret, his wife. She, whose fortune was said to be £30,000,(b) *d.* in or before 1712. Admon. 2 June 1712. He *d.* s.p.m.s. 19 Sep. 1723,(c) when the *Barony* became *extinct.*(d)

LEY.

i.e., "LEY of Ley, co. Devon," Barony (*Ley*), *cr.* 1625; see "MARLBOROUGH" Earldom, *cr.* 1626; *ex.* 1679.

LEYBURN.

Barony by Writ. I. 1299, to 1310. *1.* WILLIAM DE LEYBURN, of Leyburn, co. Kent, s. and h. of Roger L., of the same, Sheriff of Cumberland, by his 1st wife, Eleanor, 1st da. and coheir of Stephen DE TURNHAM, of Turnham, Kent, *suc.* his father in 1271, accompanied Edward I. in the expedition to Wales, 1281; Constable of Pevensey Castle, 1294; Admiral of the Fleet, &c. He was sum. to Parl. as a Baron (LORD LEYBURN), 6 Feb. (1298/9), 27 Ed. I., as also (posthumously) 16 June (1311), 4 Ed. II. He was one of the Barons who in 1301 subscribed the letter to the Pope,(e) therein styling himself "*Willielmus, Dominus de Leyburn.*" He *m.* Juliana, da. and h. of Sir Ralph DE SANDWICH, Constable of Dover Castle, who brought to him the manors of Dane Court, Westgate, and Preston, Kent. He *d.* s.p.m.s. before 12 March

(a) Lexinton, now called Laxton, Notts, was anciently held by a family of that name, of whom the last was Henry de Lexinton, Bishop of Lincoln, on whose death in 1258 his nephews, William de Markham (son of Cicely, his elder sister), and Robert de Sutton, then aged 40 (s. and h. of Robert de Sutton, by Alice, his yr. sister), were found his heirs. From this Robert the grantee descended.

(b) Luttrell's "*Diary.*"

(c) Bishop Burnet's character of him when about 40 with Dean Swift's additions thereto (printed in *italics*) is as under—"He is of good understanding and very capable to be in the Ministry; a well-bred gentleman and an agreeable companion—*a very moderate degree of understanding.*"

(d) Bridget, his only surv. da. and h., *m.* in 1717, John (Manners), 3d Duke of Rutland, and was ancestress thro' her youngest son, Lord George Manners-Sutton, (who eventually inherited the Sutton estates) of the family of Manners-Sutton, of Kelham, Notts, and of the Viscounts Canterbury and the Barons Manners of Foston.

(e) See full account thereof in "*Nicolas,*" pp. 761—809.

(1309/10), 3 Ed. II., when the writ was issued for his *Inq. p. mortem* taken at Elmham, Kent, April 1310. His wife survived him. Her *Inq. post mortem* taken (1327), 1 Ed. III.

On his death the representation of any Barony in fee which he may have enjoyed devolved on his grandaughter and h., Juliana, then aged six years, da. and h. of Thomas Leyburn, his 1st s. and h. ap., who *d.* v.p. 1307. On the death of her great grandson, John (de Hastings), Earl of Pembroke, in 1391, her issue became extinct and the representation passed to the descendants of Idonea (her aunt) only da. of William Leyburn (the Baron) who *m.* Geoffrey de Say, and was ancestress of the Lords Say.

LEYBURN [of Ellesmere.]

Barony by Writ.

I. 1337, to 1384.

JOHN DE LEYBURN, of Ellesmere, Salop, s. and h. of Sir Simon L., of Berwick, in that co., by Lucy, da. of Roger and sister of John LE STRANGE, of Ellesmere, afsd., was found h. to his father and aged 14 in 1309, and h. to his uncle, John Le Strange, in 1330; M.P. for Salop, 1322, in which year he was involved in the insurrection of the Earl of Lancaster. He served in the Gascon and the Scotch wars; was sum. to Parl. as a Baron (LORD LEYBURN) 21 June (1337), 11 Ed. III., to 14 Feb. (1348), 22 Ed. III. He *m.* after 1322 Beatrix, widow of Peter CORBET, of Caus, da. of John BEAUCHAMP, of Somerset. She *d.* s.p. in his lifetime. He *d.* s.p. in 1384 when his *peerage* became *extinct*. *Inq. p. mortem* at Exeter, 19 Nov. 1348.

LIBBERTON.

The BARONY OF LIBBERTON [S.] is sometimes said to have been conferred, 18 Sep. 1628, on Sir Robert Dalzell, but the proper designation of the peerage granted appears to have been DALZELL. See "CARNWATH" Earldom [S.], *cr.* 1639.

LICHFIELD.

[LORD BERNARD STUART, yst. s. of Esmé, 3d DUKE OF LENNOX [S.], *b.* about 1623, *knighted* 18 April 1642, having greatly distinguished himself in the Royal cause at Newbury and again near the city of Lichfield, was, before 15 June 1645, *designated* BARON STUART OF NEWBURY, Berks, and EARL OF LICHFIELD, but *d.* unm. before any warrant to that effect past the seals, being slain 26 Sep. 1645,(a) at the battle of Rowton heath, near Chester, tho' his burial at Christ Church cathedral, Oxford (probably misdated) is not recorded till 11 March 1645/6.]

Earldom.

I. 1645, to 1672.

1. CHARLES STUART, 11th Seigneur D'Aubigny, only s. and h. of Lord George STUART, 10th Seigneur D'Aubigny, who was br. to Lord Bernard Stuart said to have been *cr.* EARL OF LICHFIELD as above stated, was *b.* 7 March 1640, and was on 10 Dec. 1645, *cr.* BARON STUART OF NEWBURY, Berks, and EARL OF LICHFIELD.(b) On 14 Aug. 1660, he *suc.* as DUKE OF RICHMOND, &c. He *d.* s.p. in Dec. 1672 when that Dukedom, &c., together with the *Earldom of Lichfield* and the *Barony of Stuart of Newbury* became *extinct*. See "RICHMOND" Dukedom, *cr.* 1641, *ex.* 1672, *sub* the 3d Duke.

(a) See "*The Loyalists Bloody Roll*" (vol. i, p. 194, note "c"), in which he is called "Earl of Lichfield."

(b) These titles, conferred on a child of five years old, were those that had been intended for his said uncle, Lord Bernard Stuart, had he so long lived.

II. 1674. 2. SIR EDWARD HENRY LEE, Bart. [1611], of Quarrendon, Bucks, and of Ditchley, Oxon, s. and h. of Sir Francis Henry LEE, 4th Bart., by Elizabeth, da. and h. of Thomas (POPE), 2d EARL OF DOWNE [I.], was b. about 1656; suc. his father in the Baronetcy, Nov. 1667, and having m. (at her age of 12) 6 Feb. 1676/7, the Lady Charlotte FITZROY (to whom he had been affianced in or before 1674), illegit. da. of King Charles II., by Barbara, suo jure DUCHESS OF CLEVELAND, was by the King, his father-in-law, cr., 5 June 1674, BARON OF SPELSBURY, Oxon, VISCOUNT QUARENDON, Bucks, and EARL OF THE CITY OF LICHFIELD, co. Stafford. He was Gent. of the Bedchamber, 1683-88; Lord Lieut. of Oxon, 1687-88, and Col. of the 1st Foot Guards, Nov. to Dec 1688, but retired from office at the Revolution.(a) He d. 14 July 1716, aged 54, at Greenwich, and was bur. at Spelsbury. M.I. Admon. 3 Aug. 1716. His widow, who was b. 5 Sep. 1664, and who was famous for her beauty, d. 17 Feb. 1717/8, and was bur. at Spelsbury, aged 55. M.I. Will pr. March 1718.(b)

[CHARLES LEE, styled VISCOUNT QUARENDON, 1st s. and h. ap., b. at Windsor Castle, 6 May 1680, King Charles II. and Prince Rupert being his sponsors. He d. v.p., aged 22 weeks, and was bur. 13 Oct. 1680, in the vault of the St. John family at Battersea, Surrey.]

[EDWARD HENRY LEE, styled VISCOUNT QUARENDON, 2d but 1st surv. s. and h. ap., b. at Windsor, 6 June 1681; Col. of the Royal Reg. of Guards. He d. v.p. and unm. 1713.]

III. 1716. 2. GEORGE HENRY (LEE), EARL OF LICHFIELD, &c., 6th but 1st surv. s. and h., b. in St. James' Park, 12 March 1689/90; styled VISCOUNT QUARENTON from 1713 till he suc. to the peerage, 14 July 1716; Custos Brevium in the Court of Common Pleas; cr. D.C.L. of Oxford, 19 Aug. 1732. He m.(c) Frances, da. of Sir John HALES, 4th Bart., of Woodchurch, co. Kent, by his first wife, Helen, da. of Sir Richard BEALING. He d. 15 Feb. 1742/3, and was bur. at Spelsbury. Will pr. 1743. His widow d. 25 Feb. 1769, aged 71, and was bur. at St. Pancras, Midx. M.I.

IV. 1743. 3. GEORGE HENRY (LEE), EARL OF LICHFIELD, &c., s. and h., b. 21 May 1718, being styled VISCOUNT QUARENTON till 1743; mat. at Oxford (St. John's Coll.), 1 Jan. 1735/6; cr. M.A., 14 Feb. 1737; M.P. for Oxon, 1740-43; suc. to the peerage, 15 Feb. 1742/3; cr. D.C.L. of Oxford, 25 Aug. 1743, and again (by diploma) 27 Sep. 1762; Custos Brevium in the Court of Common Pleas; High Steward of the Univ. of Oxford, 1760; Lord of the Bedchamber, 1760; Capt. of the Gen. Pensioners, 1762; P.C., 1762; Chancellor of the Univ. of Oxford, 1762. He m., Jan. 1744/5, at the chapel in Queen square, Bath, Dinah, da. and coheir of Sir Thomas FRANKLAND, 3d Bart., of Thirkleby, co. York, one of the Lords of the Admiralty, by his first wife, Dinah, da. and h. of Francis TOPHAM, of Agelthorpe, co. York. He d. s.p. 17 Sep. 1772, aged 54,(d) and was bur at Spelsbury. Will dat. 21 Feb. 1769, to 5 Sep. 1772, pr. 15 Oct. 1772. His widow d. 8 Jan. 1779, aged 60. Will dat. 14 March 1778, pr. 15 Jan. 1779.

(a) "A man of honour; never could take the oaths to King William; hath good sense; is not yet come to Queen Anne's court; 50 years old." [Macky's "Characters."]

(b) She had no less than 18 sons and five daughters, of all of whom the births and baptisms are given in "Sandford."

(c) The date of this marriage is not known and it was "for some cause or another kept secret for some time." See "Her. and Gen.," vol. iii, where are a series of articles on this family by "F. G. L."

(d) His eldest sister, Charlotte, became eventually the heiress of the estates of the family of Lee, at Ditchley, Oxon, and elsewhere. She, who was wife of Henry (Dillon), 11th Viscount Dillon of Costello Gallen [I.], d. 11 June 1794, being ancestress of the succeeding Viscounts Dillon, who have taken the surname of Lee after that of Dillon.

V. 1772, to 1776. 4. ROBERT (LEE), EARL OF LICHFIELD, VISCOUNT QUARENTON, and BARON OF SPELSBURY [1674], also a *Baronet* [1611], uncle and h. male, being 13th and yst. s. of the 1st Earl. He was *b.* 3 July 1706, in St. James' street, Westm.; M.P. for city of Oxford, 1754, and 1761-68, residing at Lee's Place, near Chelbury, Oxon.; *suc. to the peerage*, 19 Sep. 1772; *Custos Brevium* in the Court of Common Pleas. He *m.*, 29 May 1745, at St. Paul's Cathedral, London, Catharine, da. of Sir John STONEHOUSE, Bart., of Radley, Berks, by his second wife, Penelope, da. of Sir Robert DASHWOOD, Bart. He *d. s.p.* at Ditchley, 4 Nov. 1776, aged 71, when *all his peerage dignities* and possibly *the Baronetcy also* became *extinct*. He was *bur.* at Spelsbury. His will pr. 1776. His widow *d.* 8 March 1784. Will pr. March 1784.

VI. 1831. 1. THOMAS WILLIAM (ANSON), VISCOUNT ANSON OF SHUGBOROUGH AND ORGREAVE, co. Stafford, and BARON SOBERTON of Soberton, co. Southampton, s. and h. of Thomas, the 1st Viscount and Baron (so *cr.* 17 Feb. 1806), by Margaret, da. of Thomas William (COKE), 1st EARL OF LEICESTER OF HOLKHAM, was *b.* 20 Oct. 1795, at Shugborough, and *bap.* at Colwich, co. Stafford; M.P. for Yarmouth, 1818, till he *suc.*, on his father's death, 31 July 1818, *to the peerage* as Viscount Anson; Lieut. Col. of the Staffordshire Yeomanry, 1819; Master of the Buckhounds, 1830-34; P.C., 1830, being *cr.*, 15 Sep. 1831,(a) EARL OF LICHFIELD, co. Stafford; Postmaster General, 1835-41. He *m.*, 11 Feb. 1819, at St. James, Westm., Louisa Barbara Catherine (then a minor), yst. da. of Nathaniel PHILLIPS, of Slebech Hall, co. Pembroke, by Mary Dorothy, his wife. He *d.* 18 March 1854, aged 58, at 2 Great Stanhope street. Will pr. Aug. 1854. His widow, who for nearly 40 years was well known as one of the leaders of fashion,(b) *d.* 20 Aug. 1879, at 28 Hill street, Berkeley square.

VII. 1854. 2. THOMAS GEORGE (ANSON), EARL OF LICHFIELD, &c., s. and h., *b.* 15 Aug. 1825; *styled* VISCOUNT ANSON, 1831-54; Précis writer at the Foreign office, 1846-47; M.P. for Lichfield, 1847, and 1852-54; *suc. to the peerage*, 18 March 1854; Lord Lieut. of Staffordshire, 1863-71. He *m.*, 10 April 1855, Harriet Georgiana Louisa, 1st da. of James (HAMILTON), 1st DUKE OF ABERCORN [I.], by Louisa Jane, da. of John (RUSSELL), 6th DUKE OF BEDFORD. He *d.* 7 Jan. 1892, aged 66, in Granville Place, Portman square, and was *bur.* (from Shugborough) at Great Haywood, co. Stafford. Probate duty (net) £98,059. His widow, who was *b.* 6 July 1834, living 1892.

VIII. 1892. 3. THOMAS FRANCIS (ANSON), EARL OF LICHFIELD [1831], VISCOUNT ANSON OF SHUGBOROUGH AND ORGREAVE, and BARON SOBERTON [1806], s. and h., *b.* 31 Jan. 1856; *styled* VISCOUNT ANSON till he *suc. to the peerage*, 7 Jan. 1892; ed. at Harrow and at Trin. Coll., Cambridge. He *m.*, 5 Nov. 1878, his cousin, Mildred, da. of Thomas William (COKE), 2d EARL OF LEICESTER OF HOLKHAM, by his first wife, Juliana, da. of Samuel Charles WHITBREAD. She was *b.* 24 Jan, 1854.

Family Estates.—These, in 1883, consisted of 21,433 acres in Staffordshire and 97 in Suffolk worth £42,042 a year, but these "Figures [are] absurd and unaccountable" according to Lord Lichfield's letter to Mr. Bateman, author of "*The Great Landowners*," edit. 1883. *Principal Residence.* Shugborough Park, co. Stafford.

LIDDESDALE.

The well known Lordship of Liddesdale was, apparently, never a peerage dignity. Sir William DOUGLAS, however, who was *cr.* in 1341 EARL OF ATHOLE [S.], having resigned that Earldom, made an entail of his lands of Liddesdale in 1351, under the style of "*Dominus Vallis de Lydel.*"

(a) This was one of the Coronation Peerages of King William IV. for a list of which see vol. ii, p. 312, note "a," *sub* "Clonourry."

(b) See vol. iv, p. 414, note "c," *sub* "Kinnoul."

LIDDELL.

There is in possession of the Graham family at Netherby a "Patent, in Latin, granting to Richard (Graham), Viscount Preston, in Scotland, the title of BARON LIDDELL,(a) co. Cumberland. There is no date attached to it and it was never sealed." [Appendix to 6th Report of the Hist. MSS., p. 321.]

LIDIARD, see LYDIARD.

LIFFORD or LIFFER.

See "FITZWILLIAM OF LIFFER, *alias* LIFFORD, co. Down," Barony [I.] (*Fitzwilliam*), *cr.* 1620.

FREDERIC CHARLES DE ROYE DE LA ROCHEFOUCAULD,(b) COUNT DE ROYE, &c., s. of Francis, COUNT DE ROUCY, by Julienne Catherine DE LA TOUR, da. of Henry, DUKE DE BOUILLON, was *b.* 1633; became a Lieut. Gen. in the French army in 1676, but, owing to his religion being Protestant, joined the Danish service where he became Grand Marshal, receiving also the Danish Order of the Elephant. He *m.*, 8 June 1656, his cousin, Elizabeth DE DURFORT, sister of Louis (DE DURAS), 2d EARL OF FEVERSHAM, da. of Guy Aldonce, MARQUIS DE DURAS, by Elizabeth, sister of Julienne Catherine abovenamed. In 1687 he settled in England where his wife had, the year before, been made a Lady in Waiting to the Queen Consort, and in 1687 he is presumed to have been made an Irish Peer(c,) as BARON LIFFORD or possibly EARL OF LIFFORD [I.] He *d.* at Bath 9 June 1690, aged 57, and was *bur.* in the Abbey church. M.I. His widow *d.* in London, 14 Jan. 1715, aged 82.

FREDERIC WILLIAM DE ROYE DE LA ROCHEFOUCAULT, 4th s. of the above, *b.* 1666, originally styled COUNT DE CHAMPAGNE-MOUTON, but afterwards COUNT DE MARTHON, or MARTON; was made a Guidon in the Horse Guards in 1687 by King James II, but attended King William III. in Ireland throughout the Irish war and was present at the battle of the Boyne. He was Col. of a Refugee regiment, 1693, till it was disbanded after the peace of Ryswick. He was (with his sisters) naturalised by letters patent, 20 Sep. 1694, and, apparently, was by King William

(a) The name of the *English* Barony conferred on Viscount Preston [S.] by James II. appears to have been "ESK, co. Cumberland," in right of which he claimed his writ on 11 Nov. 1689, which was, however, refused. See vol. i, p. 59, note "b," *sub* "Albemarle," as to this and other "*Jacobite Peerages*." The territorial Barony of Liddell (so called from the river *Liddell* which joins the *Esk*) had been purchased by the grantee's grandfather.

(b) A good account of this family (which has been here followed) is in a valuable work entitled the "*Protestant exiles from France in the reign of Louis XIV.*," by the Rev. David C. A. Agnew, 2 vols., 4to., 2d edit., 1871.

(c) "The reason why the Comte de Roye *is made an Irish Baron* was that his lady might with the less difficulty, it is supposed, wait on the Queen's Majesty and have the honour to be *saluted* by her which otherwise she could not have pretended to." See a letter, dat. London 23 July 1687, in the Ellis correspondence, as quoted in Agnew's "*Protestant Exiles*" where it is added that "altho' no patent of nobility was ever given to Comte de Roye under the Great Seal of Ireland yet there is evidence for the fact that he received the King's letter *to be the Earl of Lifford*, and that he bore that title for life, as was usual in similar cases when some obstacle prevented the Royal grant from passing under the Great Seal." His Earldom is acknowledged in his epitaph in Bath Abbey which commences "Fredericus de Roye de la Rochefoucault, Comes de Roye, de Rouci et Liffort," &c.

cr.(a) EARL OF LIFFORD [I.] in July 1698 tho' no patent appears to have been enrolled. He d. unm. in the parish of St. Geo. Han. sq., 24 Feb., and was bur. 2 March 1748/9, at St. James, Westm. M.I. Will dat. 3 Nov. 1746, to 24 May 1748, pr. 25 Feb. 1748/9, by William Elliott, the residuary legatee.

See "MEXBOROUGH OF LIFFORD, co. Donegal," Earldom [I.] (*Savile*), cr. 1766.

Barony [I.] I. 1768.
Viscountcy [I.] I. 1781.

1. JAMES HEWITT, s. of William H., mercer and draper, sometime (1744) Mayor of Coventry, was b. there 1709; served his articles for becoming an Attorney, but was called to the Bar (Mid. Temple) in Nov. 1742; became Serjeant, 1755, and King's Serjeant in 1759; M.P. for Coventry, 1761 66; one of the Justices of the King's Bench, Nov. 1766, to Jan. 1768; LORD CHANCELLOR OF IRELAND, 9 Jan. 1768, retaining that post till his death 22 years afterwards.(b) He was accordingly cr., 9 Jan. 1768, BARON LIFFORD of Lifford, co. Donegal [I.], taking his seat the 27th (as Speaker of the House) and was subsequently cr., 4 Jan. 1781, VISCOUNT LIFFORD, co. Donegal [I.], taking his seat 9 Oct. following. He m. firstly, before 1750 (—), da. of the Ven. Rice WILLIAMS, D.D., of Stapleford Abbots, Essex, Archdeacon of Carmarthen and Preb. of Worcester. She d. 1765. He m. secondly Ambrosia da. of the Rev. Charles BAYLEY, of Navestock, Essex. He d. in Dublin, 28 April 1789, aged 80, and was bur. in Christ Church cathedral there. M.I. Will pr. 1789. His widow d. in Warwickshire, March 1807. Will pr. 1807.

II. 1789. 2. JAMES (HEWITT), VISCOUNT LIFFORD, &c. [I.], s. and h., by first wife, b. 27 Oct. 1750; ed. at Trin. Coll., Dublin; B.A., 1776 (*ad eundem*, Oxford); M.A. and LL.D., 1778; in Holy Orders; Dean of Armagh, 1796—1830; *suc. to the peerage* [I.], 28 April 1789. He m. firstly, 25 July 1776, Henrietta Judith, 1st da. of Arthur (POMEROY), 1st VISCOUNT HARBERTON [I.], by Mary, da. and h. of Henry COLLEY. She, who was b. 18 June 1754, d. s.p. 22 April 1778. He m. secondly, 23 Dec. 1781, Alicia, 1st da. of the Ven. John OLIVER, D.D., Archdeacon of Ardagh, by Elizabeth, da. of the Rt. Rev. John RYDER, Archbishop of Armagh. He d. 15 April 1830, aged 79, at Ranfurly House, co Down. His widow d. 15 March 1845, at Astley's Court, near Coventry, co. Warwick. Will pr. Nov. 1845.

III. 1830. 3. JAMES (HEWITT), VISCOUNT LIFFORD, &c. [I.], s. and h., by second wife, b. 29 Aug. 1783; mat. at Oxford (Ch. Ch.), 22 Oct. 1801; B.A., 1804; Student of the Inner Temple, 1805; Resident Comiss. of Excise for Scotland; *suc. to the peerage* [I.], 15 April 1830. He m., 15 April 1809, Mary Anne, da. of Cornwallis (MAUDE), 1st VISCOUNT HAWARDEN [I.], by his third wife, Anne Isabella, da. of Thomas MONCK. He d. 22 April 1855, in his 72d year, at Brighton.(c) Will pr. May 1855. His widow d. 3 Jan. 1877, in her 92d year, at Torquay.

IV. 1855. 4. JAMES (HEWITT), VISCOUNT LIFFORD, &c. [I.], s. and h., b. 31 March 1811, in Merrion square, Dublin; mat. at Oxford (Ch. Ch.), 4 March 1830; B.A., 1833; *suc. to the peerage* [I.], 22 April 1855; REP.

(a) "Luttrell notes, under date 19 July 1698, 'Count Marton, son of the late Count de Roy, and Col. of a Reg. of French Refugees, will be made *Earl of Lifford* in Ireland;' Beatson informs us (*Polit. Index*, vol. iii, p. 156, edit 1806), that a King's letter was granted to cr. him Earl of Lifford but no patent passed the seals, tho' "he was styled *Earl of Lifford* during his life. It is also acknowledged on his monument (where it is expressly said that "*he was made Earl of Lifford in Ireland*") in the entry of his burial, in his will, &c.

(b) "Longer than any of his predecessors from the time of Edward I." See "Nat. Biogr." where it is added that he had "amassed a considerable fortune, the emoluments of the office in his time being estimated at £12,000 per annum."

(c) He was author of a work entitled "Ireland and the Irish church."

PEER [I.], 1856-87. He m. firstly, 9 July 1835, Mary, 1st da. of Archibald (ACHESON), 2d EARL OF GOSFORD [I.], by Mary, da. of Robert SPARROW. She, who was b. 27 June 1809, d. 13 March 1850, at Monellan House, co. Donegal. He m. secondly, 9 Dec. 1851, Lydia Lucy, widow of Charles Purdon COOTE, da. of the Rev. John Digby WINGFIELD-DIGBY, Vicar of Coleshill, co. Warwick, by Anne Eliza, da. of Sir John Wyldbore SMITH, 2d Bart., of Sydling, Dorset. He d. 20 Nov. 1887, aged 76 (after a long illness) at Meen Glas and was bur. at Monellane, co. Donegal. His widow living 1892.

V. 1887. *5.* JAMES WILFRID (HEWITT), VISCOUNT LIFFORD [1781], and BARON LIFFORD [1768], in the peerage of Ireland, s. and h., by first wife, b. 12 Oct. 1837; sometime, 1856-65, an officer in the Army, retiring as Lieut.; *suc. to the peerage* [I.], 20 Nov. 1887. He m., 4 July 1867, at Lillington, co. Warwick, Annie Frances, 1st da. of Sir Arthur HODGSON, K.C.M.G., of Clopton, co. Warwick, by Eliza, da. of Sir James DOWLING, Ch. Justice of New South Wales.

Family Estates.—These, in 1883, appear to have been under 2,000 acres. *Principal Residence.* Meen Glas, near Stranorlar, co. Donegal.

LIGONIER, LIGONIER OF ENNISKILLEN, LIGONIER OF CLONMELL, and LIGONIER OF RIPLEY.

Viscountcy [I.] I. 1757, to 1782. I. 1762. Barony [G.B.] I. 1763, to 1782. Earldom [G.B.] I. 1766, to 1782.

1. Field Marshal the Rt. Hon. SIR JOHN LOUIS LIGONIER,[a] K.B., 2d s. of Louis DE LIGONNIER,[b] Seigneur de Monteuquet, in Languedoc, by Louise, da. of (—) DE POUNSET, was b. 7 Nov. 1680, at Castres in Languedoc, came over to England in 1697; was naturalised about 1702; entered the army and greatly distinguished himself therein; was Lieut. Col. of Horse, 1706; took part in *all* the battles fought under Marlborough; was Gent. of the Privy Chamber (to George I.), 1721; Aide-de-Camp to King George II. in 1729 by whom he is said to have been *cr.* a Knight Banneret at the battle of Dettingen, 16 June 1743; K.B., 12 July 1743; Commander in Chief in Flanders, 1746; P.C., 1749; M.P. for Bath, 1754 and 1762-63; Commander in Chief in Great Britain, 1757-66; FIELD MARSHAL, 30 Nov. 1757, and was (at the age of 77) *cr.*, 31 Dec. 1757, VISCOUNT LIGONIER OF ENNISKILLEN, co. Fermanagh [I.] Having no issue, he was, five years later, *cr.*, 20 May 1762, VISCOUNT LIGONIER OF CLONMELL [I.], with a *spec. rem.*, failing heirs male of his body, to Lieut. Col. Edward LIGONIER, Capt. in the 1st Foot Guards. Shortly afterwards he was *cr.*, 27 April 1763, a Peer of Great Britain, as LORD LIGONIER, BARON OF RIPLEY, co. Surrey, and having resigned, in Aug. 1766, the office of Commander in Chief, was (finally) *cr.*, 10 Sep. 1766, EARL LIGONIER.[c] He was Col. of several regiments, *i.e.*, of the 7th Horse in 1720, of the 2d Horse in 1749, of the Horse Guards, 1753, and of the 1st Foot Guards, 1757. He d. unm.[d] in his 90th year, 28 April 1770, and was *bur.* at Cobham, Surrey, when the *Earldom and Barony* [G.B.] as also the *Viscountcy* [I.], *cr.* in 1757, became *extinct.* M.I. at Westm. Abbey. Will dat. 17 Jan. 1769, pr. 2 May 1770.

(a) A very valuable pedigree of this family, compiled by Henry Wagner, F.S.A. (correcting numerous errors in which all previous ones had fallen) is in Howard's "*Misc. Gen. et Her.*," N.S., vol. iv, p. 219. See also Agnew's "*Protestant Exiles*" as on p. 77, note "b," *sub* "Lifford."

(b) The name appears to have been so spelt in France.

(c) No territorial designation being added.

(d) He left an illegit. da. (*Query* if not by "Penelope Miller, of Southwark, Spinster," an annuitant under his will) Penelope, who m. Arthur Graham, Lieut. Col. of the 1st Foot Guards and had issue.

Viscountcy [I.] II. 1770. Earldom [I.] I. 1776, to 1782.

2 and 1. EDWARD (LIGONIER), VISCOUNT LIGONIER OF CLONMELL [I.], illegit. son of Francis Augustus LIGONIER,(a) Col. of the 13th Dragoons (br. of John, EARL LIGONIER, above named), by Anne FREEMAN, widow, da. of (—) MURRAY. He was *b.* 1740; served, under Prince Ferdinand of Brunswick, in the "seven years war" during five campaigns, and bore the dispatch announcing the victory of Minden, 1 Aug. 1759, becoming, on the 15th, Capt. in the 1st Foot Guards (Lieut. Col. in the Army), was Aide-de-Camp to the King, 1763, becoming finally in 1777 Lieut. Gen. in the Army, and in 1771 Col. of the 9th Foot. He *suc. to the peerage* [I.] as Viscount, on the death, 28 April 1770, of his uncle, Earl Ligonier [G.B.] abovenamed, and was *cr.*, 19 July 1776, EARL LIGONIER OF CLONMELL [I.] He was invested at St. James, 17 Dec 1781, as K.B., but *d.* before installation. He *m.* firstly, 16 Dec. 1766, at the British Embassy at Paris, Penelope, da. of George (PITT), 1st BARON RIVERS, by Penelope, da. of Sir Henry ATKINS, Bart., of Clapham. She, who was *b.* 23 Feb. 1749, was *divorced* by act of Parl., 7 Nov. 1771.(b) He *m.* secondly, 14 Dec. 1773, Mary, 3d da. of Robert (HENLEY), 1st EARL OF NORTHINGTON, by Jane, da. of Sir John HUBAND. He *d.* s.p., 14 June 1782, aged 42, when *all his honours became extinct.* Will pr. July 1782. His widow *m.*, 2 Feb. 1788 (by spec. lic. in South Audley square) at St. Geo. Han. sq., Thomas (NOEL), 2d VISCOUNT WENTWORTH, who *d.* 17 April 1815, aged 69. She *d.* s.p. 29 June 1814.

LILFORD.

Barony. I. 1797.

1. THOMAS POWYS, of Lilford, co. Northampton, s. and h. of Thomas POWYS, of the same, by Henrietta, da. of Thomas SPENCER, Serjeant of the House of Commons, was *b.* 4 May 1743, *suc.* his father, 2 April 1767; was M.P. for Northamptonshire, 1774-97, distinguishing himself for his numerous and apposite speeches, and was, 26 Oct. 1797, *cr.* BARON LILFORD of Lilford, co. Northampton. He *m.*, 31 March 1772, Mary, sister of Sir Horace MANN, 2d Bart., da. of Galfridus MANN, of Boughton Malherbe, Kent, by Sarah, da. of John GREGORY, of London. He *d.* 26 Jan. 1800, in Albemarle street, aged 56. Will pr. April 1800.(c) His widow *d.* Jan. 1823. Will pr. 1823.

II. 1800.

2. THOMAS (POWYS), BARON LILFORD, s. and h., *b.* 8 April 1775; ed. at St. John's Coll., Cambridge; B.A., 1797; M.A., 1802. He *suc. to the peerage*, 25 Jan. 1800. He *m.*, 5 Dec. 1797, Anna Maria, 1st da. and coheir of Robert Vernon ATHERTON, of Atherton Hall, co. Lancaster, by Henrietta Maria, da. and coheir of Peter LEGH, of Lyme, co. Chester. She *d.* 11 Aug. 1820, in Grosvenor place. He *d.* there 4 July 1825, aged 50. Will pr. Dec. 1825.

(a) He came to England in 1710 and entered the Army, distinguishing himself greatly when Lieut. Col. of the 8th Light Dragoons, at Dettingen; was Col. of the 48th Foot in April 1745 and of the 13th Light Dragoons in Sep. following, at the head of *both* of which he fought at Falkirk, 17 Jan. 1746, but *d.* 25th following. M.I. in Westm. Abbey

(b) The cause was her adultery in May 1771 with Vittorio Amadeo, the well known Count Alfieri, with whom the Viscount accordingly fought a duel in the Green Park. The date of *May* (not Dec.) 1766 is assigned to their marriage in the act of Parl. of 1771. A beautiful portrait of her by Gainsborough is in the Nat. Portrait Gallery, the catalogue of which calls her erroneously "*Countess*" instead of "*Viscountess*." She subsequently resided at Lightcliffe, in Yorkshire, and *m.* in 1784 (when Alfieri's attentions to her had ceased) a Capt. Smith by whom she had issue.

(c) Sir N. Wraxall ("*Memoirs*," vol. ii, p. 217, edit. 1884), writes of him under 8 March 1782 (when his speech, imputing "want of foresight and ability" to the Ministry, "was calculated to produce the deepest impression") that "he was indeed a man of great Parliamentary talents and of distinguished integrity, tho' by no means unaccompanied with deep ambition. From 1782 till 1797, during 15 years, he seems under successive Administrations, *never for an instant to have lost sight of the Peerage* to which he ultimately attained."

III. 1825. 3. THOMAS ATHERTON (POWYS), BARON LILFORD, s. and h., b. 2 Dec. 1801; ed. at Eton and at Christ Church, Oxford; B.A. and 2d Class in Classics, 1824; *suc. to the peerage*, 4 July 1825; was a Lord in Waiting till Sep. 1841. He m., 24 May 1830, Mary Elizabeth, da. of (who on 18 Dec. 1859, became sole heir to) Henry Richard (FOX), BARON HOLLAND, by Elizabeth, da. and h. of Richard VASSALL, of Jamaica. He d. 15 March 1861, aged 59, at Lilford Park. His widow, who was b. 19 Feb. 1806, living 1892.

IV. 1861. 4. THOMAS LYTTLETON (POWYS), BARON LILFORD, s. and h., b. 18 March 1833; ed. at Harrow; mat. at Oxford (Ch. Ch.), 12 June 1851; *suc. to the peerage*. 15 March 1861. He m. firstly, 14 June 1859, Emma Elizabeth, yst. da. of Robert William BRANDLING, of Low Gosforth, Northumberland, by Mary, da. of Thomas JAQUES, of Leeds. She d. 9 July 1884, at Brook Lodge, Ascot, Berks. He m. secondly, 21 July 1885, at Hawthorne Hill, Bracknell, Berks, Clementina, 1st da. and coheir of Ker BAILLIE-HAMILTON, C.B., Governor of Newfoundland, by Emma, da. of Charles BLAIR. She was b. 1839.

Family Estates.—These, in 1883, consisted of 7,998 acres in Northamptonshire, 7,552 in Lancashire, and four in Huntingdonshire. *Total* 15,554 acres, worth £26,398 a year. *Principal Residences*. Lilford Hall, near Oundle, co. Northampton, and Bewsey Hall, co. Lancaster.

LILE or L'ISLE, see LYLE.

LIMERICK.

[See vol. i, p. xi, as to the grant in 1179 of the honour or Lordship of LIMERICK to Philip de Braose.]

See "GRANDISON OF LIMERICK, co. Leitrim" (*St. John* afterwards *Villiers*), *cr.* 1621.

See "ESMOND OF LIMERICK," Barony [I.] (*Esmond*), *cr.* 1622; *ex.* 1646.

---

i.e., "LIMERICK," Barony [I.] (*Palmer*), *cr.* in 1661 with the EARLDOM OF CASTLEMAINE [I.], which see; *ex.* 1705.

Earldom [I.] I. 1686. 1. SIR WILLIAM DUNGAN, or DONGAN, 2d s.(a) of Sir John Dungan, 2d Bart. [I.], of Castletown, co. Kildare, by Mary, da. of Sir William TALBOT, 1st Bart. [I.], of Carton, b. about 1630; distinguished himself in the military service and was cr., 14 Feb. 1661/2, VISCOUNT DUNGAN OF CLANE,(b) co. Kildare [I.], with a *spec. rem.* failing heirs male of his body, to his brothers, Robert, Michael, and Thomas Dungan, being subsequently, 2 Jan. 1685/6, cr.(c) EARL OF LIMERICK [I.], with a like spec. rem. to his brother, Col. Thomas Dungan, rem. to his cousin [*consobrinus*] John Dungan. He was Col. of a Reg. of Dragoons in the service of King James II. in Ireland in 1688, in whose cause he appears to have suffered greatly. He m. when abroad, probably about 1660, a Spanish lady, named Euphemia, da. of (—.) She brought him £30,000 as a portion. After the defeat at the Boyne (1 July 1690) he

(a) The eldest son, Sir Walter Dongan, 2d Bart., was in 1646 one of the confederate Catholics of Kilkenny. He d. s.p. but at what date is unknown.

(b) His name as "Viscount Dungan of Clare" appears among the Roman Catholics who prayed the Royal protection in 1663. See vol. ii, p. 149, note "d," *sub* "Carlingford."

(c) He was one of the five persons on whom a hereditary Irish peerage was conferred during the reign of James II. See vol. iv, p. 9, note "c," *sub* "Galway."

retired to France and was (with his wife) *attainded* in 1691 whereby, it is presumed, *all his honours* were *forfeited*.(a) He d. s.p.m.s.(b) in France, Dec. 1698. His widow was living 1700.

[WALTER DUNGAN, *styled* LORD DUNGAN, only s. and h. ap., *b.* abroad but subsequently naturalised; was M.P. for Naas in the Parl. of King James II.; was in command of a Reg. of Dragoons for that King, at the battle of the Boyne, 1 July 1690, and was there slain v.p. and unm.]

II. 1698, to 1715. 2. THOMAS (DUNGAN), EARL OF LIMERICK, &c. [I.], yr. br. of the above Earl, and on whom this Earldom and the Viscountcy of Dungan of Clane were entailed under the spec. rem. in their respective creations, was *b.* 1654 and appears, notwithstanding the attainder of 1691, to have assumed in 1698 and been generally allowed the peerage [I.] He was for some time Col. of an Irish Regiment in the service of King Louis XIV. of France but was subsequently (for King Charles II. of England) Lieut. Gov. of Tangier and Gov. of New York. He claimed, under a deed of 1684, to be entitled to the whole of his late brother's estate. He *m.* Mary, da. of (—.) He *d.* s.p., 14 Dec. 1715, aged 81, *bur.* at St. Pancras, Midx. M.I. Will pr. Dec. 1718. At his death the *Viscountcy of Dungan of Clane* [I.] and apparently(c) the *Earldom of Limerick* [I.] (both of which seem (tho' possibly, not legally) to have been previously *forfeited* by the attainder of 1691) became *extinct*. His widow *d.* 9 Nov. 1720.

Viscountcy [I.] I. 1719. 1. JAMES HAMILTON, of Tollymore, co. Down, was *cr.*, 13 May 1719, BARON CLANEBOYE, co. Down, and VISCOUNT OF THE CITY OF LIMERICK [I.] He was *cr.*, 24 Nov. 1756, EARL OF CLANBRASSILL, co. Armagh [I.] He *d.* 17 March 1758.

II. 1758, to 1798. 2. JAMES (HAMILTON), EARL OF CLANBRASSILL [1756], VISCOUNT LIMERICK, and BARON CLANEBOYE [1719], in the peerage of Ireland, only s. and h., *b.* 13 Aug. 1729, *styled* VISCOUNT LIMERICK from 1756 till he *suc. to the peerage* [I.], 17 March 1758; *d.* s.p. 6 Feb. 1798, when *all his honours* became *extinct*.

For fuller particulars see "CLANBRASSILL," Earldom [I.], *cr.* 1756; *ex.* 1798.

---

i.e., "FITZGIBBON OF LIMERICK, co. Limerick," Viscountcy [I.] (*Fitzgibbon*), *cr.* 1793; see "CLARE" Earldom [I.], *cr.* 1795; both dignities *ex.* 1798.

Viscountcy [I.] III. 1800. Earldom [I.] III. 1803. 1. EDMOND HENRY (PERY), BARON GLENTWORTH OF MALLOW [I.], only s. and h. of the Rt. Rev. William Cecil PERY, Bishop of Limerick (1784-94) who was *cr.*, 2 June 1790, BARON GLENTWORTH OF MALLOW [I.], by his first wife, Jane, da. of John Minchin WALCOTT, of Creagh, was *b.* 8 Jan. 1758; M.P. for the city of Limerick, 1786-94, being a zealous supporter of the English Government;(d) *suc. to the peerage* [I.] on the death of the Bishop of Limerick, his father, 4 July 1794; Keeper of the Signet and Privy Seal

(a) His estates of nearly 30,000 acres were forfeited to the King who granted them to his Dutch favourite, the Earl of Athlone [I.], to whom they were confirmed by act of Parl. in 1698.

(b) Ursula his da. (who was *b.* abroad and subsequently naturalised) *m.* Lucas (Dillon), Viscount Dillon [I.], and *d.* s.p. and v.p. before 1681.

(c) John Dungan, a cousin of the grantee, was named as in rem. to the Earldom of Limerick in the grant thereof in 1686. It is presumed he *d.* s.p. before 1715.

(d) In Sir Jonah Barrington's "*Historic memoirs*" (vol. ii, p. 122, note), he is spoken of as "occasionally an active member [of Parl.], *always crafty*, sometimes

[I.], 1795; Clerk of the Crown and Hanaper [I.], 1797;(a) P.C. [I.]; was cr., 29 Dec. 1800, VISCOUNT LIMERICK of the city of Limerick [I.]; Rep. Peer [I.] (one of the 28 originally elected) 1801-44; cr., 22 Jan. 1803, EARL OF LIMERICK [I.], and cr. a Peer of the United Kingdom,(b) 11 Aug. 1815, as BARON FOXFORD OF STACKPOLE COURT, co. Clare. He m., 29 Jan. 1783, Mary Alice, only da. and h. of Henry Ormsby, of Cloghan, co. Mayo, by Mary, sister and h. of Sir Henry Hartstonge, Bart. [I.], of Bruff, co. Limerick. He d. 7 Dec. 1844, in his 87th year, at Southill Park, near Bracknell, Berks, and was bur. in Limerick cathedral.(c) Will dat. 29 July 1840, pr. 12 Feb. 1845. His widow d. 13 June 1850, aged 87, in Mansfield street, Marylebone, and was bur. with him. Will dat. 16 June 1848, pr. 21 Oct. 1850.

[Henry Hartstonge Pery, *styled* (since 1803) Lord Glentworth, s. and h. ap., *b.* 26 May 1789. He *m.*, 11 May 1808, Annabella Tenison, 2d da. of Tenison Edwards, of Old Court, co. Wicklow, by Charity, da. of John Barrington, of Queen's county. He *d.* v.p. 7 Aug. 1834, aged 45, at Killaloe.(d) His widow *d.* at 79 Chester square, 17 Sep. 1868, aged 77.]

[Edmond Henry Pery, *styled* (since 1834) Viscount(e) Glentworth, grandson and h. ap., being s. and h. of H. H. Pery, *styled* Lord Glentworth, and Annabella, his wife, both abovenamed. He was *b.* 3 March 1809. He *m.*, 8 Oct. 1836, Eve Maria, 2d da. of Henry Villebois, of Marham House, co. Norfolk. He *d.* s.p., ten months before his grandfather, 16 Feb. 1844, in Manchester square, aged 35. Will pr. March 1844. His widow *m.* 29 Dec. 1847, at St. John's, Paddington, Hugh Smith Baillie, of Redcastle, Rossshire, Col. Royal Horse Guards, and was living 1892.]

IV. 1844. 2. William Tenison (Pery), Earl of Limerick, &c [I.], also Baron Foxford of Stackpole Court, grandson and h., being 2d but 1st surv. s. and h. of H. H. Pery, *styled* Lord Glentworth, and Annabella, his wife, both abovenamed. He was *b.* 19 Oct. 1812, at Limerick House, in Limerick; was sometime a Magistrate and Superintendant of Agriculture in Norfolk Island, New South Wales; *styled* Lord Glentworth from 16 Feb. to 7 Dec. 1844, when *he suc.* his grandfather *in the peerage*. He *m.* firstly, 16 April 1838, Susanna, da. of William Sheaffe, Surveyor of the excise at Mallow, in Ireland (br. of Sir Roger Hale Sheaffe, Bart., so cr. 1813), by Mary, da. of (—) Wright. She,

impetuous and frequently efficient. He was prouder than he had a right to be and bore no similitude to his illustrious uncle [Edmond Sexton Pery, Speaker of the Irish House of Commons, 1771 to 1785, who, in 1785, was cr. a Peer [I.] as Viscount Pery of Newtown Pery]; he had a sharp, quick, active intellect; he generally guessed right in his politics and if he chanced to be wrong he expertly patched up the failure of his judgment by his skill and perseverance. Lord Limerick took a leading part in 1799 against that Constitution which his uncle and benefactor had so nobly helped to establish."

(a) On the abolition of which office he received a pension of £846 for his life.

(b) So that for 29 years, *i.e.*, from 1815 to his death, he sat in the House of Lords in two capacities, the Irish Rep. Peers being [unlike those of Scotland] elected *for life*.

(c) His strong Tory politics and absenteeism had rendered him so unpopular in his native city that it was with great difficulty his body was safely conveyed over the bridge to its burial, a large mob endeavouring to throw it over into the river.

(d) The "*Annual Reg.*" for 1834 speaks of him as "a clever but imprudent young nobleman, gifted by nature with great talents," who "fell a victim to a career of reckless indulgence" and who spent "the greatest part of his time, after he became of age, in prison."

(e) The designation of "*Viscount*" in combination with "*Glentworth*," (which is a "*Barony*,") is an anomalous and absurd assumption. It was, however, undoubtedly used by the grandson (and possibly by the son and other descendants) of the 1st Earl, who in his will speaks of his grandson as "commonly called Lord *Viscount* Glentworth." On this principle we ought to have an *Earl* of Mandeville and an *Earl* of Castlereagh as the eldest sons of the Duke of Manchester and the Marquess of Londonderry respectively, each of these noblemen having *an* Earldom (tho' not one of the name above indicated) vested in them. See vol. i, p. 316, note "b" (*sub* "Belmore"), for some remarks on courtesy titles.

who was *b.* 27 Dec. 1802, *d.* 21 Aug. 1841. He *m.* secondly, 6 April 1842, in Norfolk Island, Margaret Jane, da. of Nicholas HORSLEY, of Durham, Capt. 96th Foot. In Feb. 1863 she was judicially separated from him by decree of the Court of Divorce. He *d.* of bronchitis, 5 Jan. 1866, aged 53, at Norwood, Surrey, and was *bur.* in Limerick cathedral. His widow *d.* 25 Nov. 1875, aged 47, at 55 Upper Brook street.

V. 1866. 3. WILLIAM HALE JOHN CHARLES (PERY), EARL OF LIMERICK [1803], VISCOUNT LIMERICK [1800], and BARON GLENTWORTH OF MALLOW [1790], in the peerage of Ireland, also BARON FOXFORD OF STACKPOLE COURT [1815], s. and h., being only child by the first wife; *b.* 17 Jan. 1840, in Norfolk Island, *styled* LORD GLENTWORTH, 1844-66; sometime, 1858-62, Ensign in the Rifle Brigade; *suc. to the peerage,* 5 Jan. 1866; a Lord in Waiting, 1886-89; Aide de Camp to the Queen, 1887; Capt. of the Yeomen of the Guard, 1889; Conservative "whip" in the House of Lords; K.P., 1892. He *m.* firstly, 28 Aug. 1862, his cousin, Caroline Maria, da. of the Rev. Henry GRAY, Vicar of Almondsbury, co. Gloucester (son of Robert GRAY, Bishop of Bristol), by Emilie Caroline, sister of the 2d EARL OF LIMERICK [I.], da. of Henry Harstonge PERY, *styled* LORD GLENTWORTH abovenamed. She *d.* 24 Jan. 1877, at 36 Queen's Gate terrace, South Kensington. He *m.* secondly, 20 Oct. 1877, Isabella, da. of the Chevalier James DE COLQUHOUN.

[WILLIAM-HENRY-EDMOND-DE-VERE-SHEAFFE PERY, *styled* (since 1863) LORD GLENTWORTH, s. and h. ap., being only son by first wife, *b.* 16 Sep. 1863; ed. at Eton; sometime (1884) Lieut. in the Rifle Brigade. He *m.*, 23 July 1890, at St. Mary's, Cadogan street, Pimlico, May Imelda, da. of J. Burke IRWIN, of the Priory, Limerick.]

Family Estates.—These, in 1883, consisted of 4,083 acres in co. Limerick, 1,550 in co. Clare, and 76 in co. Cork. *Total* 5,709 acres, worth £14,986 a year, inclusive of the rental of nearly 3,000 acres let on long leases and returned in the lessees' names. *Principal Residence.* Dromore Castle, near Pallaskenry, co. Limerick.

See "GOUGH OF GOOJERAT in the Punjaub AND OF THE CITY OF LIMERICK," Viscountcy (*Gough*), *cr.* 1849.

LIMINGTON see LYMINGTON.

LINCHLADE.

See "CORBET OF LINCHLADE, co. Buckingham," Viscountcy (*Corbet, neé Monson*), *cr.* for life 1679; *ex.* 1682.

LINCOLN (county of.)

[*Remarks.*—No Earldom has, probably, received more attention than that of Lincoln,(a) but (notwithstanding this) none, apparently, is more obscure.(b)

(a) The word "*Nicole*" is "the most usual term for *Lincoln* in all ancient French records and evidences." [*Vincent*, p. 321.]

(b) Mr. Courthope states *sub* "LINCOLN" that "the late Francis Townsend, Esq., Windsor Herald, bestowed considerable pains upon the elucidation of the early history of the Earls of Lincoln, and the result of his labour, much of which has been incorporated into this article, will be found in the *Excerpta* from his collections by Sir Charles Young, Garter, printed in the *Coll. Top. et Gen.* [vol. viii, pp. 155—158.] An elaborate article on the same subject will be found in the first vol. [1846] of the *Top. and Gen.*" As to that article (which, tho' full of information, is in some points not altogether satisfactory) the writer thereof acknowledges "his obligations to Thomas Stapleton, Esq., F.S.A., for the most valuable of its materials." It's author was most probably Mr. John Gough Nichols, the accomplished Editor of the work itself. That gentleman certainly contributed, in 1848, a paper on the "*Earldom of Lincoln*" to the proceedings of the "*Archæological Institute,*" pp. 253—279. Lastly, in the "*Genealogist,*"

Nicolas, following "Vincent," makes William de Romare to be the *first* Earl of Lincoln, and this version (as there appears to be no really valid authority for the existence of any previous ones) has been followed in the text below. Courthope, however, in his edition of Nicolas' work, introduces one of the Earls of Chester as an Earl of Lincoln as follows, "Randle de Meschines, 3d Earl of Chester, possessed *the Earldom of Lincoln*(a) in right of his wife, Lucy,(b) da. and h. of Ivo de Tailleboys (by Lucy, sister and h. of Morcar, the Saxon Earl of Northumberland *and Lincoln*), widow of Robert de Romara; *d.* 1128," but this statement appears to be based on an error.(c) It has also been argued that the allusion to the rights of a "*Comes*" in the Domesday survey of Lincoln implies the existence at that time of an Earl *of Lincoln*, but this apparently (to judge from other causes) is a groundless assumption.

Passing over, however, any supposed right either of (1) the above named Randle, Earl of Chester, or of (2) Morcar, the Saxon Earl of Northumberland to be Earls of Lincoln, there remains the remarkable fact that William (de Albini), 1st Earl of Arundel (the husband, in 1138, of the Queen Dowager Adelicia) appears (possibly by mistake but yet) in *two* distinct documents as an *Earl of Lincoln*.(d)

Earldom. I. 1140? to 1155? — *I.* WILLIAM DE ROUMARE, of Bolingbroke, co. Lincoln, Seigneur de Roumare(e) in Normandy, s. of Roger FITZ-GEROLD Seigneur de Roumare, by Lucy, heiress of Spalding, co. Lincoln (generally considered(f) to have been da., but sometimes called the widow, of Ivo DE TAILLEBOIS), was *b.* about 1095; Gov. of Neufmarché in Normandy, supporting at first the authority of the King of Eng-

N.S. (vols. v to ix), 1888-92, are various very elaborate articles by "R. E. G. Kirk," and (chiefly as comments thereon) by Mr. J. Horace Round (to whom the Editor is in this article especially indebted) entitled "*The Family of Lincoln,*" "*The Countess Lucy, singular or plural,*" "*Adeliza the Viscountess,*" &c.

(a) "In a catalogue of tenants of land co. Linc., made previous to his succession to the Earldom of Chester, the words 'Comes Linc.,' are twice placed over his name. Cotton MS. Claud., C. v. f. 8, 9, quoted in *Coll. Top. et Gen.*" [*Courthope.*] These words, however, are a subsequent addition (as is shewn by Mr. Greenstreet's published facsimile of the MS.) and, therefore, of no authority.

(b) This Lucy is a great "*crux*" in the genealogy of these Earls. Mr. Round remarks that "she has been sometimes represented as the *widow* of Ivo Tailbois and sometimes as his *daughter* by *another Lucy* there being thus *two* not one. The latest writer on the subject, Mr. R. E. G. Kirk (see p. 84, note "b") considers there was only *one* and that she married thrice and was the daughter of "Thorold the Sheriff."

(c) "In spite of the network of speculation that has been spun about this Earldom [of Lincoln] we have no ground in the contemporary evidence or records for asserting that Randulf [Earl of Chester 1129—1153] or his father before him, held or even professed to hold the Earldom of Lincoln." See Round's "*Adeliza the Viscountess*" in "*the Genealogist,*" vol. viii, pp. 148—150.

(d) "That he held this title is a fact so utterly unsuspected and indeed so incredible that Mr. Eyton, finding him so styled in a cartulary of Lewes Priory, dismissed the title without hesitation as an obvious error of the scribe. [Hist. of Shropshire, ii, 273.] But I have identified in the Public Record office the actual charter from which the scribe worked and the same style is there employed. Even so, error is possible; but the evidence does not stand alone. In a cartulary of Reading [*Harl. MS.* 1708, fo. 97], we find William confirming, as *Earl of Lincoln*, a grant from the Queen, his wife, and here again the orig. charter is there [*Add. Cart.*, 19,586], to prove that the cartulary is right. The early history of the Earldom of Lincoln is already difficult enough without this additional complication, of which I do not attempt to offer any solution." See Round's "*Geoffrey de Mandeville,*" p. 324.

(e) "Roumare, the place from which the name of this family was derived, is a vill not far distant from Rouen and gives name to the forest of Roumare." [*Top. and Gen.*, i, 17.]

(f) Her parentage and even her individuality whether "*Singular or Plural*" is a matter of great difficulty and has been much discussed. See note "b" next above. She m., after Roger Fitz-Gerold's death, Randolph, Earl of Chester [1121-29], by whom she was mother of Randolph ("de Gernon"), Earl of Chester [1129-53] sometimes reputed to have been Earl of Lincoln. See note "c," next above.

land there in the rebellion of 1118, but subsequently taking a leading part on the other side. He was, however, reconciled to King Henry I, in 1128, and was made, by King Stephen, in 1135, one of the Lords Marchers, and in 1138 joint Justiciar of Normandy, being, shortly afterwards (1140 ?) cr. EARL OF LINCOLN,(a) probably

(a) A complete list of the Earldoms conferred by King Stephen (*nine*, all of which were conferred in the short space of three years, 1138-41), is given in Appendix D. (entitled "*The 'fiscal' Earls*") to Mr. J. Horace Round's "*Geoffrey de Mandeville, a study of the anarchy*," a truly wonderful work, of the greatest learning and acumen, which effectually disposes of many delusions which hang over Stephen's troublous reign. Among others (1) is the term "*Fiscal*," as applied to the Earls of Stephen's creation under the [erroneous] impression that they were provided for "by pensions on the *Exchequer*," whereas "the term *fiscus* was used, at the time, in the sense of *Crown demesne*" and "no such beings as *fiscal Earls* ever existed;" another such delusion (2) is that "to abolish the *fiscal* Earldoms [*i.e.*, the Earldoms of Stephen's creation] was among the first of Henry's reforms," whereas not "a single man who enjoyed Comital rank at the death of Stephen can be shewn to have lost that rank under Henry II." Another delusion and one that, in an account of the Peerage, is more especially noteworthy is (3) "a most extraordinary" one. It is "based on the radically false assumption of the *poverty* of Stephen's Earls," whence it is assumed that they were "*taken from the ranks*," whereas "they belonged, in the main, to that class of magnates from whom, both before and after his time, the Earls were usually drawn." The names Albini, Aumâle, Beaumont, Bigod, Clare [2], Ferrers, Mandeville, and Roumare (being those of King Stephen's *Earls*) "are those of the noblest and wealthiest houses in the *Baronage* of Stephen's realm."

To the nine Earldoms, created by Stephen himself, should be added six created by the Empress Maud, in or shortly after 1141 "the titles conferred by the rival competitors to the Crown," being "chosen from those portions of the Realm in which their strength respectively lay. Nor do they seem to have encroached upon the sphere of one another by assigning to the same county rival Earls," while also the Earls themselves (as had previously been the case in the Earldoms of Buckingham, Chester, Gloucester, Huntingdon, Leicester, Northampton, and Warwick, these seven being with Surrey, which was an exception to this rule, the eight *existing* Earldoms at the accession of King Stephen) "took their title wherever possible from the counties in which lay their chief territorial strength," or, if that county was already disposed of, from "the *nearest* county remaining vacant at that time." "It may have been observed" [adds Mr. Round] that I assume throughout that each Earl is the *Earl of a County*. It would not be possible here to discuss the point in detail, so I will merely give it as my own conviction that while Comital Rank was at this period so far a personal dignity that men spoke of *Earl Hugh*, *Earl Gilbert* or *Earl Geoffrey*, yet that an Earl, *without a County*, was a conception that had not yet entered into the minds of men."

THE 15 EARLDOMS CREATED DURING THE REIGN OF STEPHEN.—

(9 by the King himself and 6 by the Empress Maud, the latter being denoted by an* asterisk), are, when arranged alphabetically (from the list given by Mr. Round) as under.

[ALBEMARLE, see YORK.]

1. ARUNDEL, or CHICHESTER, or SUSSEX (William *de Albini*) before Xmas, 1141.
2. BEDFORD (Hugh DE BEAUMONT), 1138? ["The dignity together with the fief itself lost in 1141"].

[CAMBRIDGE. "A shadowy Earldom of Cambridge, known to us only from an Inspeximus, *temp.* Edward III, need not be considered here."]

[CHICHESTER, see ARUNDEL.]

3. *CORNWALL (Reginald *Fitz Roy*), 1141 ?
4. DERBY (Robert *de Ferrers*), 1138.
5. *DEVON (Baldwin *de Redvers*) before June 1141.
6. *DORSET, or SOMERSET (William *de Mohun*) before June 1141. [This Earldom does not occur subsequent to 1142].
7. ESSEX (Geoffrey *de Mandeville*), 1140.
8. *HEREFORD (Miles *of Gloucester*), July 1141.
9. HERTFORD (Gilbert *de Clare*) before Xmas 1141.

[KENT. This Earldom often attributed to William *of Ypres*, being considered to have been one of Stephen's creations, was never so conferred neither did the said William ever receive an English Earldom.]

before Christmas 1140,([a]) at which date he (and the Earl of Chester([b]) his br. of the half blood) rebelled against the King. He *m.*, about 1128, Hawise,([c]) sister of Baldwin, EARL OF DEVON, da. of Richard DE REDVERS, by Adeliza, da. of William PEVEREL, of Nottingham. She joined with him (as did their son) in the foundation of the

10. LINCOLN (William *de Roumare*) 1139—1140 ? ; and again (Gilbert *de Gant*) 1147-8.
11. NORFOLK (Hugh *Bigod*) before Feb. 1141.
12. *OXFORD (Aubrey *de Vere*) 1142.
13. PEMBROKE (Gilbert *de Clare*) 1138.
14. *SALISBURY or WILTSHIRE (Patrick *of Salisbury*) in or before 1149.

[SOMERSET, see DEVON.]
[SUSSEX, see ARUNDEL.]
[WILTSHIRE, see SALISBURY.]
[WORCESTER. "A doubtful Earldom of Worcestershire, bestowed on the Count of Meulan, need not be considered here."]

15. YORK (William *of Aumâle*) 1138 [" William of Aumâle, sometimes but rarely during the reign of Stephen styled himself *Earl of York*. He did not under Henry II, lose his *Comital rank*. Aumale (Albemarle) is notoriously a difficult title, as one of those of which the bearer enjoyed Comital rank, tho' *whether* as a *Norman Count* or an *English Earl* it is, at first, difficult to decide. Eventually, of course, the dignity became an English Earldom."]

The whole of the Earldoms (23 in number) that existed at this early period (1135—1154) can be ascertained, if to the above (15) creations be added the (8) Earldoms in existence at the *accession* of King Stephen. It may be noted that at that date (1) *the Earldom of Northumberland* can hardly be considered as existing as an independent English Earldom ; at all events any right to the same was held (together with the Earldom of Huntingdon) by the Royal family of Scotland during the first nine decads of the 12th century ; and that (2) the *Earldom of Richmond* was not, as yet, allowed to the *Counts* of Britanny, tho' they were the holders of the (vast) honour of Richmond. The Earldoms in actual existence in 1135 were apparently eight, being, with the names of the families of their respective holders, as under.

1. BUCKINGHAM (*Giffard.*)
2. CHESTER (*de Gernon.*)
3. GLOUCESTER (*Fitzroy.*)
4. HUNTINGDON (*the Royal house of Scotland.*)
5. LEICESTER (*de Beaumont.*)
6. NORTHAMPTON (*St. Liz.*)
7. SURREY (*Warenne.*)
8. WARWICK (*de Newburgh.*)

([a]) They are then spoken of by Ordericus as " The Earl of Chester and William de Roumare " but immediately afterwards as " the *two* Earls." This illustrates (writes Mr. Round) the carelessness of the Chroniclers and how unsafe it is to trust any of them (more especially Ordericus) in such matters.

([b]) To this Earl of Chester (Randolph "*de Gernon*," who *d.* 16 Dec. 1153), King Stephen granted the Castle and city of Lincoln, perhaps after the pacification of 1151, and he has been sometimes considered as having been Earl of Lincoln conjointly with his said brother. Thus, Mr. Courthope (somewhat obscurely) speaks of Randolph's "*share of the Earldom*" of Lincoln, as follows ; "Altho' William de Romara enjoyed the title of Earl of Lincoln and is so styled as late as 1153, it is not the less certain that Randle de Gernons [*i.e.*, the Earl of Chester], who is said to have made over his share of the Earldom [of Lincoln] to his niece, Rohais, continued to hold a large portion of the honours or rather the profits of the Earldom, and was in possession of them long after that event, probably thro' the deprivation of Gilbert de Gant, her husband." But, writes Mr. Round, " there is no foundation for the statement that he is *said to have made over his share of the Earldom to his niece*, which was an interpolation by Mr. Nichols, based on his own peculiar hypothesis of *shares* in the Earldom."

([c]) See the various " Errors of Dugdale and the Genealogists " as to this Lady, in the " *Top. and Gen.*" Vol. i, p. 23, where her parentage is given as (in the text, *viz.*), " sister to Baldwin, 1st Earl of Devon, da. of Richard de Redvers, Lord of Tiverton in Devon," &c., but see also (*per contra*) Planché's " *Earls of Devon* " *Coll. Arch.*, vol. i 4to), refuting Mr. Stapleton's arguments that Baldwin (and not his father, Richard), was the *first* Earl of Devon.

Abbey of Revesby about 1143. He was living in 1153, when he granted a charter to the Abbey of St. Ouen, at Rouen. He became a monk shortly before his death. He *d.* 5 Aug. [1155?], but in what year is unknown and was *bur.* in Revesby Abbey.

[WILLIAM DE ROUMARE, s. and h. ap. *b.* about 1130. He *m.* Agnes, da. of Stephen (DE BLOIS), EARL OF ALBEMARLE. He *d.* v.p. 1151, being possibly slain in the defence of his father's Castle of Neufmarché, against the French, which took place in that year. His widow *m.* Peter DE BRUCE, who *d.* 1211].

[WILLIAM DE ROUMARE, grandson and h. being s. and h. of William de Roumare and Agnes his wife both abovenamed. He was *b.* about 1150, and, probably owing to his infancy when he suc. his grandfather, never obtained recognition as EARL OF LINCOLN, tho' he appears to have been sometimes so styled.(a) He however possessed large estates, *viz.* 57 Knights fees in Lindsey and in Wiltshire and 14 in the Roumois in Normandy. He *m.* firstly Alicia. He *m.* secondly Philippa,(b) da. of John, COUNT OF ALENCON. He, who was living 1197-98, *d.* s.p. shortly before Oct. 1198, and was *bur.* at Revesby. His widow *m.* William MALET, of Graville in Normandy, and *m.* thirdly, in or before 1215, William DE PREAUX, but *d.* before 1223, which was the date of her last husband's death.]

II. 1147? to 1156. *1.* GILBERT DE GAND,(c) of Folkingham, co. Lincoln, s. and h. of Walter DE GAND of the same, by Maud, da. of Stephen, COUNT OF BRITANNY, *suc.* his father in his vast estates, 1138-39, and having been (together with the King) taken prisoner at the battle of Lincoln in 1141, by the Earl of Chester was compelled by him to marry his niece.(d) This Lady was Rohesia, sister of Roger, EARL OF HERTFORD, da. of Richard Fitz-Gilbert, *styled* DE CLARE, by Adeliza, or Christiana,(e) sister of the said Randolph, EARL OF CHESTER and sister (of the half blood *ex parte materna*) of William (DE ROUMARE), EARL OF LINCOLN abovenamed. He was, not long afterwards, about 1147 or 1148, *cr.*, by King Stephen, EARL OF LINCOLN, and that too in the lifetime of his wife's said uncle, the existing Earl.(f) He was founder of Rufford Priory, Notts. He *d.* s.p.m.,(g) 1156(h) and was *bur.* at Bridlington. His widow *m.* Robert STEWARD, *i.e.* "Robertus dapifer Willielmi de Percy."

(a) "To a charter of John, Earl of Mortain, to the Metrop. church of Rouen, his attestation appears among the Earls as *Earl William de Roumara* and before that of Geoffrey Fitz Piers, Earl of Essex. This shews that his hereditary *rank* at least was partially acknowledged, and in the several inquisitions respecting his lands in Lincolnshire during the reign of John the title of *Earl* is likewise given him." [*Top. and Gen.*, vol. i, p. 26.] Mr. Round points out that as the creation of the Earldom of Essex was in 1199 its holder could not (as Earl of Essex) have been a fellow witness with one who *d.* before Oct. 1198, and that as Geoffrey Fitz Piers was not Earl of Essex in Richard's reign (to which the charter belongs) the precedence proves nothing.

(b) Her mother was Beatrix, da. of Elias D'Anjou, Count of Maine, by Philippa, da. of Rotrou, Count of Perche, and his first wife, Matilda (drowned in the White ship, 1120) illegit. da. of King Henry I.

(c) See a good pedigree of this family in Baker's "*Northamptonshire*," vol. i, p. 440, where, however, Gilbert is stated to have been "Earl of Lincoln *jure uxoris*," the said wife being there stated to have been "Hawise, da. and heir [*sic*] of William de Romara, Earl of Lincoln." See also Mr. Chester Waters' "*Survey of Lindsey*" as to their great possessions in that district.

(d) "Walter's son and heir, Gilbert, was a great match in his youth, and when he was taken prisoner at the battle of Lincoln, in 1141, was only released from captivity on condition of his marrying Rohese de Clare, who was the niece of the Earls of Chester and Lincoln." (Chester Waters' *Survey of Lindsey*, p. 13.)

(e) See *Coll. Top. et Gen.*, vol. i, p. 388, where "Christiana," wife of Richard Fitz Gilbert, is witness to a deed said to have been made in 1154.

(f) The *fact* seems undoubted but it is a strange and perhaps unique case, there appearing to have been no *forfeiture* of the Earldom by the previous holder.

(g) Alice, his only da. and h., *m.* Simon (Saint Liz), Earl of Huntingdon, who *d.* s.p. 1184 "which Simon had with her all her heritage as the words of the charter import, whereby it seems that he was also *Earle of Lyncolne*." [Milles' "*Cat. of Honour*," 1610, p. 912.] Such, however, does not appear to have been the case.

(h) "*Chronicon Normanniæ*" as quoted by Eyton.

[After the death of these two Earls at one time *joint Earls*, tho' both of them left issue (the issue *male* of the former existing till or after 1198) the *Earldom of Lincoln* appears to have *lapsed to the Crown* for some 60 years. It was however conferred in 1216 by Louis, the Dauphlin of France, when invading England on GILBERT DE GANT(a) who accordingly styled himself EARL OF LINCOLN. He was nephew and heir of the late Earl, being s. and h. of Robert DE GANT (br. of the said Earl) by his second wife, Gundreda, da. of Hugh DE GURNAY, which Gilbert received in London from the said Prince the "sword of the county of Lincoln."(b) He was defeated by the Royal forces at Lincoln, 19 May 1217, and kept as a prisoner by his cousin the Earl of Chester, till his death(c) in (1241-42), 26 Hen. III].

III. 1217, to 1232. *1.* Randolph, *styled* "*de Blondeville*," EARL OF CHESTER, to which dignity he had *suc.* in 1181 on the death of his father, Hugh, Earl of Chester [1153—1181], who was s. and h. of Randolph, Earl of Chester [1129 - 1153], yr. br. of the half blood, *ex parte maternâ* of William (DE ROUMARE), EARL OF LINCOLN abovenamed, was (soon after the defeat of the rebels at Lincoln, in which he had borne a prominent part), *cr.* by the young King Henry III., 23 May 1217, EARL OF LINCOLN, an Earldom to which he appears to have laid some hereditary claim.(d) He, shortly before his death, transferred his interest therein(e) as far as such right belonged to him, to Hawise de Quincy one of his sisters and coheirs expectant "*ut inde Comitissa existat.*" He *d.* s.p., 28 Oct. 1232, aged above 60, when *all his honours lapsed to the Crown.*

See fuller account under "CHESTER," Earldom, 1181 to 1232.

(a) It is curious that Brooke, uncontradicted by Vincent, makes this Gilbert to be grandson of the first Earl Gilbert "by his son, Gilbert, who was disinherited by King Henry II." Mr. Townsend follows this version, while Dugdale (on this occasion more accurate, apparently, than Vincent) gives the pedigree as in the text.

(b) Roger of Wendover.

(c) His grandson and heir, Gilbert de Gant, was sum. to Parl. as a Baron, 1295, but *d.* s.p. 1298.

(d) "Earl Ranulph's hereditary claim to the Earldom of Lincoln was immediately admitted, for by writ on the 23d of May, the Sheriff was commanded 'quod habere facias dilecto et fideli nostro Ranulpho, Comiti Cestriæ, *tertium denarium de Comitatu Lincolniæ*, qui eum contingit jure hæreditario ex parte Ranulphi Comitis, patris sui.' [*Rot. Claus.*, 1 Hen. III., m. 17.] The word '*patris*' occurs in this record, but his *father's* name was Hugh. It was probably his *grandfather*, Ranulph, that was referred to. A further injunction to the like effect was directed to the same officer from Worcester on the 15th March following 'Rex Vicecomiti Linc.,' salutem; Precipimus tibi quod habere facias dilecto et fideli nostro Ranulpho, Comiti Cestriæ et Lincolniæ tercium denarium de denariis quí pervenient de placitis comitatus Lincolniæ, *percipiendum nomine Comitis Lincolniæ* donec inquisierimus quantum predecessores sui *Comites quondam Lincolniæ* inde percipere consueverunt nomine Comitis Lincolniæ,' &c. [*Ibid*, 2 Hen. III., m. 9.]" See "*Top and Gen.*," vol. i, p. 313.

(e) This remarkable charter is witnessed (*inter alios*) by Richard Marshal, Earl of Pembroke, and must, therefore, be subsequent to August 1231 if not later still. It is printed in the *Coll. Top. et Gen.*, vol. vii, p. 130, in the *Top. and Gen.*, vol. i, p. 313, &c. In it the Earl grants to his dearest sister, Hawise de Queney, "Comitatum Lincolniæ scilicet quantum ad me pertinuit, *ut inde Comitissa existat.*" Mr. J. Horace Round suggests that what he really made over was the *tertius denarius* of the county, adding that "at that time belting was essential to an Earl, and no *woman* would be made a Countess in her own right tho' her husband might be made an Earl as in the Warwick cases, tho,' of course, all this is very imperfectly known to us and probably the system was constantly undergoing changes." Brooke, after stating that all dignities are derived from the Sovereign, considers it to be "idle and altogether untrue that this gift of Randoll to his sister could make her a Countess," but is (as usual) contradicted by Vincent, who, after quoting the charter, adds "that the King did no way disallow of it," but it should be noted that tho' the King granted the Earldom of Lincoln to John de Lacy *with the consent of his mother, the said Hawise*, he in no way recognised her title thereto as Countess. See p. 90 note "a."

[HAWISE, *suo jure* (according to some) COUNTESS OF LINCOLN (tho' never so recognised(a) by the Crown), 4th sister and coheir of Earl Randolph (to whom her brother the abovenamed EARL OF CHESTER and LINCOLN resigned his interest in the Earldom of Lincoln as above mentioned) inherited, at the partition of his estates, all his lands in the provinces of Lindsey and Holland, co. Lincoln, of which the Castle of Bolingbroke was the *caput*. Within a month of her said brother's death the King at her request *cr.* her son in law, John de Lacy (as mentioned below) EARL OF LINCOLN. She *m.* Robert DE QUINCY, s. and h. ap. of Sayer, 1st EARL OF WINCHESTER, which Robert, however, on his father's death in 1219 never *suc.* to that Earldom. The date of her death has not been ascertained.]

IV. 1232. *1.* JOHN DE LACY, s. and h. of Roger DE LACY, of Pontefract, co. York, and of Halton, co. Chester, Hereditary Constable of Chester, *suc.* his father in his vast estates and hereditary office, 1 Oct. 1211, and was in 1215 one of the 25 Barons appointed to enforce the observance of *Magna Charta*. He *m.* firstly Alice, da. of Gilbert DE L'AIGLE, which lady appears to have *d.* s.p. or s.p.m. He, certainly, *m.* secondly at some date before 1232 Margaret, only da. and h. of Robert DE QUINCY, by Hawise, sometimes considered as *suo jure* COUNTESS OF LINCOLN (tho' not recognised(a) as such by the King) abovenamed, and was (owing to such alliance) by charter dat. 22 Nov. 1232, *cr.* EARL OF LINCOLN with a rem.(b) to his heirs by Margaret, his said wife. He was Constable of Whitchurch Castle, 1233; of Chester and Beeston Castle, 1237, and Sheriff of co. Chester, 1237 and 1240. He *d.* 22 July 1240. His widow *m.* about 6 Jan. 1243, Walter (MARSHALL), 5th EARL OF PEMBROKE, who *d.* s.p. 24 Nov. 1245.

V. 1240. *2.* EDMUND (DE LACY), EARL OF LINCOLN, s. and h., by the second wife, was a minor and in the King's custody in 1246 and appears never to have been formally invested(c) with the Earldom.(d) He was Page [" *Valettus* "] to the King in 1251. He *m.* in May 1247 Alicia,(e) 1st da of Manfred III., MARQUIS OF SALUZZO in Italy, by Eleanora, da. of Philip, COUNT OF SAVOY. He *d.* 21 July 1257. His widow is styled "Alesia, late Countess of Lincoln," in Letters close of 12 July 1311.

(a) It is to be observed that the grant of the Earldom does not recognise Hawise as having become by her brother's gift *Countess* of Lincoln, tho' doubtless (by that gift) she was in possession of the revenue of the *Comitatus*. This grant is as follows :— "Rex, ad instanciam Hawisiæ de Quency, dedit et concessit Johanni de Lascy, Constabulario Cestriæ, illas xx libras, quas R. quondam Comes Cestriæ et Lincolniæ recepit pro tertio denario Comitatus Lincolniæ et quas predictus Comes in vitâ suâ dedit prædictæ Hawisiæ, sorori suæ, habendas et tenendas *nomine Comitis Lincolniæ* de Rege et heredibus suis, ipsi Johanni et hæredibus suis, qui exibunt de Margareta uxore sua, filia prædictæ Hawisiæ, imperpetuum. In cujus, &c. Teste Rege, apud Northampton 22° die Novembris."

(b) The Earldom of Kent had on 11 Feb. 1226/7 (five years previously) been entailed on Hubert de Burgh with rem. to his heirs by Margaret of Scotland, his wife. These probably are the earliest instances of such entails.

(c) He is spoken of in 1246 as one "qui, si vixerit, Comes erit Lincolniæ," when the King promises to marry him to one of the grandaughters of the Count of Savoy. [*Coll. Top. et Gen.*, vol. vi, p. 148.]

(d) "Dugdale says he never used the title of Earl of Lincoln nor was it attributed to him in any grant although he enjoyed the *tertium denarium* of the county ; but in this statement Dugdale is in error, for even in the record referred to by him, and relating to Henry de Laci, his son, this Edmund is expressly described as 'Edmundus de Lacy, pater ejusdem Henrici, quondam *Comites Lincolniæ*,' and in the patent of safe conduct to the King and Queen of Scotland, dat. 5 Sep. 1255, he is called 'Edmundum de Lacy, Comitem de Lincoln.'" [Courthope,] Mr. Round states that "Letters close of 6 Oct. 1310, order the payment to Henry, Earl of Lincoln, of this *tertius denarius* which his grandfather and father, 'Earls of Lincoln,' and he, had received till the death of Edward I. but which had been detained from him since."

(e) Dugdale calls her "an outlandish lady from the parts of Savoy, brought over purposely for him by Peter de Savoy, uncle to the Queen, which occasioned much discontent amongst the nobles of England."

VI. 1257. 3. HENRY (DE LACY), EARL OF LINCOLN, s. and h., b. about 1250, being *knighted* and invested with the Earldom, 13 Oct. 1272. He was one of the greatest nobles of his time and was distinguished in the wars with Wales, Scotland,(a) and France, to which last country he was several times sent as Envoy. He was bearer of the sword at the Coronation of Ed. II., 25 Feb. 1308, and was Guardian OF THE REALM, 1 Sep. 1310, during the King's absence in Scotland. He m. firstly (marriage contract 22 Dec. 1256), Margaret, generally considered as *suo jure* COUNTESS OF SALISBURY, she being da. and h. of William DE LONGESPEE, the 3d EARL OF SALISBURY(b) of that race, by Matilda, da. and h. of Walter (CLIFFORD), LORD DE CLIFFORD.(c) She d. 22 Nov. 1310. He m. secondly Joan, da. of William (MARTIN), LORD MARTIN, by Eleanor, da. of William DE MOHUN. He d. s.p.m. at his house called "Lincoln's Inn" near Chancery lane, London, 5 Feb. 1310/1, and was *bur.* in St. Paul's cathedral. His widow, who in 1326 became coheir to her brother, m. Nicholas (AUDLEY), 1st LORD AUDLEY, who d. 1317.

[EDMUND DE LACY, s. and h. ap., d. young and v.p., being drowned in a well at Denbigh Castle.]

VII. 1311, to 1348. 4. ALICE, *suo jure* COUNTESS OF LINCOLN, and [probably] COUNTESS OF SALISBURY, only surv. da. and h., b. about 1283, m. on or before 28 Oct. 1294 (at her age of 11) THOMAS (PLANTAGENET), EARL OF LANCASTER and EARL OF LEICESTER, who *suc.* his father, Edmund (yr. son of King Henry III.) in those dignities, 5 June 1296, and who, *jure uxoris*, may be considered as EARL OF LINCOLN and perhaps also EARL OF SALISBURY, and who received the £20 a year "*pro tertio denario* in com. Lincoln" in 1312, which had belonged to his wife's father. He d. s.p., being *beheaded* at the castle of Pontefract, 22 March 1321/2, aged about 44, when, having been attainted, *all his honours* were *forfeited*. (See fuller account of him under "LANCASTER" Earldom.) The King seized on all the lands of the Countess' inheritance "till she had made a regular conveyance of them to him, which she did by deed 26 June [1322], 15 Ed. II., and acknowledged such surrender in Chancery, 11 July [1322], 16 Ed. II. On 29 Sep. following(d) he restored to her *for life* the annuity of £20 which her father had received in lieu of the third penny of the county of Lincoln.

The *suo jure* Countess who had in 1317 during her coverture been forcibly carried away from Earl Thomas, her then husband,(e) m. before 1326 EUBULUS LE STRANGE who

(a) At the siege of Carlaverock, 1300, he is styled "Henri le bon Conte de Nichole."

(b) This William (who d. s.p.m. in 1256) was s. and h. of another William, Earl of Salisbury (who d. 1250), *neither* of them having been actually invested with that Earldom, tho' *both* of them were generally considered to have been entitled thereto. The last named William was s. and h. of William de Longespee [d. 1226] who had received the Earldom of Salisbury from King Richard I. on his marriage with Ela, da. and h. of a former William, Earl of Salisbury, who d. s.p.m. in 1196. This Ela, by some considered as *suo jure* Countess of Salisbury, and who unquestionably was "the original heiress of the Earldom of Salisbury, died an aged woman in 1261, her great granddaughter and her affianced husband [the Earl of Lincoln] being then minors." See "*The Earldom of Salisbury*" by J. G. Nichols.

(c) One would have expected that (according to the custom of the period) he would *jure uxoris* have styled himself EARL OF SALISBURY; indeed Dugdale says that he "had thereupon the Earldom of Salisbury," but Mr. Townsend in his notes thereon (*Coll. Top. et Gen.*, vol. vi, p. 149), says, "I think it will appear that this Henry de Lacy never enjoyed that honour. He is not called so in any writ of summons, but his *daughter* is called COUNTESS OF LINCOLN AND SARUM, 15 Ed. II. [*Fine.*, No. i, 145."]

(d) *Coll. Top. et Gen.*, vol. vi, p. 151.

(e) It appears that "a person of very low stature, lame, and hunchbacked, called Richard de St. Martin, challenged her for his wife, confidently affirming that he had carnally known her before she was married to the Earl, which she denied not, whereupon he grew so bold to *make claim to the Earldoms of Lincoln and Salisbury* in her right, the news whereof being brought to the Pope he sent two Cardinals to make peace between the King and his Barons and especially with this Earl Thomas." [Dugdale.] Sandford, speaking of this lady's "four husbands," adds, "if we may call that match of her's with Richard de St. Martin, in the lifetime of her first husband, a marriage, for, indeed, she was of very light behaviour, which was no small stain to her good name."

was sum. from 8 Dec. 1326, to 1 April 1335, as LORD LE STRANGE and who is sometimes in her right considered to have been EARL OF LINCOLN([a]) and perhaps also EARL OF SALISBURY. He *d.* s.p., 10 Sep. 1335, and was *bur.* in Berling Abbey.

The *suo jure* Countess *m.* lastly, early in 1336, HUGH DE FRENE, who (a few months later) on 29 Nov. 1336, was sum. to Parl. as LORD DE FRENE. He, who is also (tho' erroneously) sometimes considered to have been *jure uxoris* EARL OF LINCOLN, *d.* s.p. (a month later), Dec. 1336, at Perth. The Countess herself *d.* s.p.([b]) 2 Oct. 1348, aged about 65, and was *bur.* at Berling Abbey afsd., when the *Earldom of Lincoln lapsed to the Crown.* Her *inq. post mortem* (at Bolingbroke) 15 Oct. 1348.

VIII. 1349. *1.* HENRY (PLANTAGENET), EARL OF LANCASTER, LEICESTER, and DERBY, s. and h. of Henry, EARL OF LANCASTER and LEICESTER (who was brother of Thomas, EARL OF LANCASTER, &c., *jure uxoris* EARL OF LINCOLN, as above mentioned) obtained on the death of the Countess Alice (his uncle's widow) the inheritance([c]) of the ancient Earls of Lincoln and was *cr.*, 20 Aug. 1349,([d]) EARL OF LINCOLN. He was *cr.*, 6 March 1350/1, DUKE OF LANCASTER. He *d.* s.p.m., 13 March 1360/1, aged about 60, when the *Dukedom* became *extinct*, while the *other honours* may most probably be considered to have *reverted to the Crown*, tho' in right of his da. and coheir (eventually, 1362, sole heir) his son in law (see next below) her husband, claimed the four *Earldoms of Lancaster, Derby, Lincoln, and Leicester.*

IX. 1362. *2.* JOHN (PLANTAGENET, *styled* "of Gaunt"), EARL OF RICHMOND, 4th but 3d surv. s. of King Edward III., having *m.*, 19 May 1359, Blanche, da. and eventually (10 April 1362), sole heir of Henry (Plantagenet), Duke of Lancaster, Earl of Lincoln, &c., abovenamed, became (possibly) in her right EARL OF LANCASTER, DERBY, LINCOLN,([e]) and LEICESTER, which Earldoms were in several official documents allowed to him. He was *cr.*, 13 Nov. 1362, DUKE OF LANCASTER. He *d.* 3 Feb. 1398/9, aged 58.

X. 1399, Feb. to Sep. *3.* HENRY (PLANTAGENET, *styled* "of Bolingbroke"), DUKE OF LANCASTER, DUKE OF HEREFORD, EARL OF DERBY, EARL OF LINCOLN, and EARL OF LEICESTER, also Duke of Aquitaine in France, s. and h., *b.* 1367 at Bolingbroke; sum. to Parl. v.p. as EARL OF DERBY, 3 Sep. 1385, and *cr.* DUKE OF HEREFORD, 29 Sep. 1397. He *suc.* his father, 3 Feb. 1398/9, as Duke of Lancaster, &c., and was on 30 Sep. 1399, elected King of England, as Henry IV., when *all his honours merged in the Crown.*

See fuller account under "Lancaster" Dukedom, *cr.* 1351 and 1362.

([a]) The mandamus in (1325-26), 19 Ed. II., to pay all arrears of the £20 annuity granted in lieu of the third penny of the county of Lincoln "to the said Ebulo, or Alice, has given a colour to some to call him *Earl of Lincoln* [Vinc., 215, 320], and he is so styled in a deed of his nephew and heir, Roger Lestrange [1339], 13 Ed. III., but it is certain," writes Mr. Townsend, "that he never enjoyed that honour, for I find him regularly sum. to Parl. by the name of Ebulo Lestrange only and ranked amongst the Barons."

([b]) "The Earldom of Lincoln according to the grant which settled it on John de Lacy and his heirs by Margaret de Quincy, his wife, ought to have fallen among the issue of her cousins, Eleanor, Margaret, and Elizabeth de Clare, grandaughters of her aunt, Maud, Countess of Gloucester, the only sister of her father, Henry, Earl of Lincoln." *Coll. Top. et Gen.*, vol. viii, p. 155. It was, however, (as Mr. Round remarks) diverted in favour of the Royal family just as the Earldom of Norfolk was diverted, by the surrender of Earl Roger Bigod, in 1302.

([c]) The Castle of Lincoln, the Castle, manor and honour of Bolingbroke, &c., co. Lincoln, parcel of the manor of Halton in Cheshire, &c.

([d]) See p. 7, note "b," *sub* "Lancaster," for the words of this charter.

([e]) See p. 8, note "g," *sub* "*Lancaster*," as to his being in his own deed termed "*Comte de Nicol*" the French term for "*Lincoln*." See p. 84, note "a."

XI. 1467, to 1487. JOHN DE LA POLE, 1st s. and h. ap. of John (DE LA POLE), DUKE OF SUFFOLK, by the Lady Elizabeth PLANTAGENET, sister of King Edward IV., b. about 1464; was (when about three years old) cr. (v.p.) 13 March 1467, EARL OF LINCOLN. He was K.B., 18 April 1475; bearer of the orb at the Coronation, 7 July 1483, of King Richard III.;(a) President of the Council of the North, 1483, and Chief Gov. of Ireland, as Lord Lieut., 1484-85. He was declared by the said King Richard, his uncle, to be *next heir*, failing the issue of the King's body, *to the Crown*. He *m.* Margaret, da. of Thomas (FITZALAN), EARL OF ARUNDEL, by Margaret, da. of Richard (WYDVILLE), EARL RIVERS. He is said(b) to have *m.* secondly (—), da. and h. of Sir John GOLAFRE. Being a staunch Yorkist he took a conspicuous part in the various risings against King Henry VII. and was slain at the battle of Stoke, 16 June 1487. He *d.* v.p. and s.p. when the *Earldom* became *extinct*.

XII. 1525, to 1540? HENRY BRANDON, 1st s. and h. ap. of Charles (BRANDON), DUKE OF SUFFOLK, by the Lady Mary TUDOR, QUEEN DOW. OF FRANCE, sister of King Henry VIII. and da. of King Henry VII., was *b.* 1516 and was (when about nine years old) *cr.* (v.p.), 18 June 1525,(c) EARL OF LINCOLN. He was living 1538 but *d.* unm. and v.p. before 14 Aug. 1545, when the *Earldom* became *extinct*.

XIII. 1572. *1.* Edward (CLINTON), LORD CLINTON, only s. and h. of Thomas, 8th LORD CLINTON, by Mary, illegit. da. of Sir Edward POYNINGS, K.G., was *b.* 1512; *suc. to the peerage* on the death of his father, 7 Aug. 1517, and was sum. to Parl. 27 April (1536), 28 Hen. VIII., by writ(d) directed "*Edwardo Clinton, Chevalier.*" He was in attendance on the King (whose mistress he had, about this date, married) in 1532 at Boulogne and Calais; was one of 12 Peers who were chief mourners at the funeral of King Henry VIII.; was in the expedition to Scotland where he was *knighted* (by the Duke of Somerset), 11 May 1544; Chief Capt. of Boulogne, 1548, till its surrender, 25 April 1550; LORD HIGH ADMIRAL, 1550-54 and again Feb. 1557/8 till his death; P.C. and Gent. of the Privy Chamber, 1550; el. K.G., 24 April and inst., 30 June 1551; Lord Lieut. co. Lincoln, 1552; Constable of the Tower,(e) 7 to 19 July 1553. He made his peace with Queen MARY, taking her part against Wyatt's rebellion; was Commissioner(f) for the investiture with the Garter of Emanuel Philibert, Duke of Savoy, which took place 6 Nov. 1554 (in the camp) at Auxy; P.C. to Queen Mary, 1557, and to Queen Eliz., 1558; attended the Queen to Cambridge and was *cr.*, 10 Aug. 1564, M.A. In 1569 he was in command of the army that quelled the great rebellion in the North and subsequently took command of the fleet in the North sea, being for these services *cr.*, 4 May 1572,(g) EARL OF LINCOLN; Lieut. of the Order of the Garter, 1570, and

(a) See vol. iii, p. 8, note "c," *sub* "Dacre," for a list of the Nobles present at that Coronation.

(b) Doyle's "*Official Baronage.*"

(c) He was one of the six noblemen who were so *cr.* at the date that Henry Fitzroy, the King's illegit. son, was *cr.* Duke of Richmond. See vol. ii, p. 438, note "c," *sub* "Cumberland."

(d) See vol. ii, p. 305, *sub* "Clinton," concerning the precedency of the Barony of Clinton as decided in 1558.

(e) This important stronghold was probably committed to him the day after the death of King Edward VI. that he might hold the same for Lady Jane Grey, he being one of the 26 Peers (for a list of whom see vol. iii, p. 70, note "f," *sub* "Derby"), who had signed the letters patent of 16 June 1553, settling the Crown upon her.

(f) See vol. ii, p. 192, note "a," *sub* "Cathcart," for a list of these special Garter missions.

(g) "In the memorial of the investiture of Edward, Lord Clinton and Say, as Earl of Lincoln, 4 May 1572, preserved among *the State Papers (Domestic)* the new Earl is styled Lord Clinton *and Say*, and the Heralds declared his style as *Sir Edward Fynes, Conte de Lincoln, Seigneur Clinton et Say.*" [*Ex. inform.* J. Horace Round.] See also vol. iii, p. 284, note "d," *sub* "Essex," as to the account of his investiture.

again 1578; Ambassador to Paris in Aug. 1572 for the marriage of the French King's sister to the King of Navarre. In 1572 he was one of the Peers for the trial of the Duke of Norfolk. He m. firstly about 1531 (when he would have been about 19) Elizabeth, widow of Gilbert (TALBOYS), LORD TALBOYS (who d. 15 April 1530), 1st da. of Sir John BLOUNT, of Kinlet, Salop, by Catherine, da. and h. of Sir Hugh PERSHALL, of Knightley, co. Stafford. She had as early as 1519(a) been mistress to King Henry VIII. By her, the date of whose death is unknown, he had three daughters. He m. secondly, about 1540, but certainly before 1548(b) Ursula, da. of William (STOURTON), 6th BARON STOURTON, by his first wife, Elizabeth, sister of John, DUKE OF NORTHUMBERLAND, da. of Edmund DUDLEY, alias SUTTON. She d. 4 Sep. 1551, in Lincolnshire.(c) He m. thirdly before Jan. 1552/3(c) Elizabeth,(d) widow of Sir Anthony BROWNE, yst. da. of Gerald (FITZ GERALD), 9th EARL OF KILDARE [I.], by his second wife, Elizabeth, da. of Thomas (GREY), MARQUESS OF DORSET. He d. 16 Jan. 1584/5, aged 72, and was bur. in St. George's chapel, Windsor. M.I. Will dat. 11 July 1584, pr. 19 May 1585.(e) His widow, who was b. at Maynooth, co. Dublin, about 1528, d. March 1589, and was bur. at St. George's chapel afsd. Will dat. 15 April, pr. 13 May 1589.

XIV. 1585. 2. HENRY (CLINTON), EARL OF LINCOLN and LORD CLINTON, s. and h., by second wife, b. about 1540; K.B., 29 Sep. 1553, being one of the 15 Knights made at the Coronation of Queen Mary; M.P. for Launceston, 1559, and for Lincolnshire, 1571; styled LORD CLINTON, 1572-85; suc. to the peerage, 16 Jan. 1584/5; was one of the noblemen(f) for the trial of Mary, Queen of Scots, at Fotheringay in Oct. 1586 and for that of the Earl of Arundel in 1589 and for the Earl of Essex in 1601; Ambassador to the Landgrave of Hesse, 1596.(g) He m. firstly, Feb. 1557, Catharine, 1st da. of Francis (HASTINGS), 2d EARL OF HUNTINGDON, by Catharine, da. and coheir of Henry (POLE), LORD MONTAGU. She was b. 11 and bap. 20 Aug. 1542, at Ickenham, Midx. He m. secondly, after 1579, Elizabeth, widow of the Hon. William NORREYS, da. of Sir Richard MORRISON, of Cashiobury in Watford, Herts, by Bridget, da. of John (HUSSEY), LORD HUSSEY. She d. Whitmonday 1611. He d. 29 Sep. 1616. Admon. 25 Oct. 1616, and 3 Feb. 1618/9.

XV. 1616. 3. THOMAS (CLINTON, alias FIENNES), EARL OF LINCOLN and LORD CLINTON, s. and h., b. about 1568 in Lincolnshire; mat. at Oxford (Ch. Ch.), 22 June 1582, and then aged 14; styled LORD CLINTON, 1585—1616; M.A., Oxford, 11 April 1588(h); M.P. for Great Grimsby, 1601-04, and for Lincolnshire, 1604-10; was sum. to Parl. v.p., 2 June 1610, in his father's Barony as LORD

(a) Her son (Henry Fitzroy, Duke of Richmond), by that King, was b. 1519 and d. unm. 1536 in his 17th year. She herself was probably 10 years, or so, senior to Lord Clinton, but as her father (who d. 1524 in his 40th year) was b. 1483, she is hardly likely to have been born before 1502, in which case she was a mother at 17, a very likely age for the young King's paramour. "An history of the beautiful Elizabeth Blount, Mistress to Henry VIII., written by the (well known) Rev. Mark Noble is printed in Marshall's "Genealogist," vol. ii, pp. 19 and 44.

(b) See her father's will.

(c) Machyn's diary.

(d) This lady called "the fair Geraldine" was the object of the poems of Henry Howard, Earl of Surrey.

(e) "That he must have been a man of remarkable tact is abundantly proved by his having maintained himself in a foremost position in the State under the very different circumstances of the four reigns of Henry, Edward, Mary, and Elizabeth, and by his having been the confidential friend of such very different men as Somerset, Northumberland, and Burghley." [Nat. Biog. in an able article by Professor J. K. Laughton.]

(f) See vol. iii, p. 72, note "a," sub "Derby," for their names.

(g) His proceedings there were arraigned "in most bitter terms" and his conduct among the gentry in Lincolnshire was that of "a great tyrant," in fact "his behaviour appears to have been strongly tinctured with insanity." [Lodge's "Illustrations," vol. iii, p. 107, and Brydges' "Peers, temp. James I."]

(h) See p. 49, note "c," sub "Leicester."

CLINTON DE SAY(a) and placed accordingly. He *suc. to the Earldom of Lincoln*, 29 Sep. 1616. He *m.* Elizabeth, da. and coheir of Sir Henry KNEVITT, of Charlton, Wilts, by Elizabeth, da. and h. of Sir James STUMPE, of Malmesbury, Wilts,(b) He *d.* at his Castle at Tattershall, co. Lincoln, 15 Jan. 1618/9, aged 50, and was *bur.* at Tattershall. Will dat. 11 Jan. 1618/9, pr. 18 Oct. 1619. His widow, who was an authoress, long survived him.

XVI. 1619. 4. THEOPHILUS (CLINTON, *alias* FIENNES), EARL OF LINCOLN and LORD CLINTON, 3d but 1st surv. s. and h., *b.* about 1600, being 19 years old at his father's death, *styled* LORD CLINTON, 1616-19; K.B., 4 Nov. 1616; *suc. to the peerage*, 11 Jan. 1618/9; Col. of an English Reg. in Germany for the assistance of the Elector Palatine, 1624; Col. of a Reg. of Foot, 1642, and Commissioner to the Scotch army, 1645, for the Parl.; Speaker of the House of Lords, 1 Aug. 1647; assisted as Carver at the Coronation of Charles II., 23 April 1661. He *m.* firstly Bridget, da. of William (FIENNES), 1st VISCOUNT SAY AND SELE, by Elizabeth, da. of John TEMPLE, of Stow, Bucks. He *m.* secondly his cousin, Elizabeth, widow of Sir Robert STANLEY (*d.* 1632), da. of Sir Arthur GORGES, of Chelsea, by Elizabeth, da. of Henry (CLINTON), 2d EARL OF LINCOLN. He *d.* in London 22 May 1667, aged about 67.(c) His widow was *bur.* 5 May 1675, at Chelsea. Admon. 2 July 1675, to her son, Sir Charles STANLEY, K.B.

[EDWARD CLINTON, *alias* FIENNES, *styled* LORD CLINTON, 1st s. and h. ap. by first wife; was M.P. for Callington, 1646, till secluded in 1648. He *m.* Anne, 1st da. of John (HOLLES), 2d EARL OF CLARE, and *d.* v.p. at Covent Garden, Midx. Admon. 21 April 1657. His widow *m.* Charles BATES, who survived her. She *d.* at St. Giles in the fields, Oct. and was *bur.* Nov. 1707 "in a Presbiterian meeting house yard."(d) Admon. 5 Dec. 1707, to her said husband.]

XVII. 1667. 5. EDWARD (CLINTON, *alias* FIENNES), EARL OF LINCOLN and LORD CLINTON, grandson and h., being only s. and h. of Edward CLINTON, alias FIENNES, *styled* LORD CLINTON, and Anne, his wife, both abovenamed; *b.* about 1650; *styled* LORD CLINTON, 1657-67; *cr.* K.B., 23 April 1661, at the Coronation of Charles II.; *suc. to the peerage*, 21 May 1667. He *m.* after 1670 Jeanne,(e) da. of Pierre DE GULIBRÉ, Lord of Verun in France. She *d.* 25 and was *bur.* 1 Sep. 1688, at Westm. Abbey. He *d.* s.p., 25 Nov. 1692, at his house in Bloomsbury square, when the *Barony of Clinton* fell into abeyance between (the heirs *general*) his aunts and coheirs or their issue.(f) He is said to have been *bur.* privately

(a) Lords Journals. In his father's will he is spoken of as my son and h. ap. "the Rt. Hon. Sir Theophilus *Fines*, K.B., Lord Clinton and Saye." See vol. ii, p. 306, note "a," as to this description of "Saye." The family of *Fiennes* was (as was that of Clinton) a coheir of the Barony of Say and the great great grandmother of the 1st Earl was a da. (but not h. or coheir) of Richard (*Fiennes*), Lord Dacre, but there seems no apparent reason why the name of "Fiennes" was substituted for "Clinton." The surname of the second Earl when made a K.B. in 1553 was "Sir Henry *Clinton*," but that of the 4th Earl when, in 1661, he was so made (by his courtesy title) as "Lord Clinton," is not given.

(b) See "*Coll. Top. et Gen.*," vol. vii, p. 83.

(c) In Sir Joseph Williamson's "Lincolnshire families, temp. Charles II." (*Her. and Gen.*, vol. ii, p. 116), the Earls of Lincoln are thus noticed; "calle themselves Fiennes, *alias* Clinton, tho' really they are Barons Clinton, of ye eldest, in England.' At Tattershall Castle, on Lindsey coast; at Sempringham, in Kesteven; ye first was ye L. Cromwell's in H. VI. and in likelyhood purchased by Clinton, ye last a monastery and dissolved; about £3,000 per ann. or better."

(d) Peter Le Neve's "*obituary*."

(e) "A Frenchwoman, niece to Sir William St. Ravi (of Monpelier), Ranger of Woodstock Park, *temp. Regis Car. I.*" [Dugdale's MS. "additions," *Coll. Top. et Gen.*, vol. i, p. 217]

(f) See tabular pedigree in vol. ii, p. 306, note "c," *sub* "Clinton."

on the 28th at Westm. Abbey.[a] Will (in which he leaves all his estates to "*Sir Francis Clinton*" his successor in the Earldom) dat. 6 Nov. 1684, to Dec. 1690, pr. 20 Dec. 1692.

XVIII. 1692. *6.* FRANCIS (CLINTON), EARL OF LINCOLN,[b] cousin and h. male, being only s. and h. of Francis CLINTON, of Stourton Parva, co. Lincoln, by Priscilla, da. of John HILL, which Francis was 3d s. of the Hon. Sir Edward CLINTON, 2d s. (by first wife) of Henry, 2d EARL OF LINCOLN. He was *b.* about 1635; *knighted*, 14 May 1661; was Gent. of the Privy Chamber, 1669, and *suc. to the peerage*, 25 Nov. 1692. He *m.* firstly Elizabeth, da. of Sir William KILLIGREW, Vice Chamberlain to Catharine, the Queen Consort, by Mary, da. of John HILL, of Honiley, co. Warwick. She, who was dresser to the said Queen, *d.* s.p.s. and was *bur.* 11 Dec. 1677 (as Lady Clinton) in Westm. Abbey. He *m.* secondly about 1683 Susan, da. of Anthony PENYSTONE, a yr. s. of Sir Thomas P., of Cornwell, Oxon. He *d.* 4 Sep. 1693, within a year of his succession to the peerage, aged 58. Will dat. 25 Aug., pr. 29 Dec. 1693. His widow *d.* 23 Sep. 1720.

XIX. 1693. *7.* HENRY (CLINTON), EARL OF LINCOLN, 2d but 1st surv. s. and h., being 1st s. by second wife, *b.* 1684; *styled* LORD CLINTON, 1692-93; *suc. to the peerage*, 4 Sep. 1693; Lord of the Bedchamber, to George, Prince of Denmark, 1708; Master of the Horse to the Prince of Wales, 1714; Lord of the Bedchamber (to the King), 1714; Bearer of the second Crown at the Coronations (20 Oct. 1714, and 11 Oct. 1727), of George I. and George II.; Joint Paymaster Gen. of the Forces, 1715-20; P.C., 1715; el. K.G., 27 March, and inst., 25 April 1721; Constable of the Tower, &c., 1722-25; Cofferer of the Household, 1725; Lord Lieut. of Cambridgeshire, March to Sep. 1728. He *m.*, 16 May 1717, Lucy, sister of Thomas (HOLLES, *formerly* PELHAM), DUKE OF NEWCASTLE-UPON-TYNE [1715], and DUKE OF NEWCASTLE-UNDER-LYNE [1756], da. of Thomas (PELHAM), 1st BARON PELHAM OF LAUGHTON, by Grace, sister of John (HOLLES), DUKE OF NEWCASTLE [1694], &c. He *d.* 7 Sep. 1728, in his 44th year. Admon. 31 Oct. 1728, and 5 May 1748. His widow *d.* 20 July 1736, at Weybridge, co. Surrey. Admon. 1788.

XX. 1728. *8.* GEORGE (CLINTON), EARL OF LINCOLN, s. and h., *b.* 15 Jan. 1718, King George I. being his godfather; styled LORD CLINTON till he *suc. to the peerage*, 7 Sep. 1728. He *d.* unm. 30 April 1730, in his 13th year.

XXI. 1730. *9.* HENRY (CLINTON), EARL OF LINCOLN, br. and h., *b.* 24 April 1720, *suc. to the peerage*, 30 April 1730. Having *m.*, 16 Oct. 1744, Catharine, 1st da. and coheir of the Rt. Hon. Henry PELHAM, br. to Thomas, DUKE OF NEWCASTLE-UPON-TYNE and DUKE OF NEWCASTLE-UNDER-LYNE abovenamed, he, on the death of his Grace, 17 Nov. 1768, *suc.* him as DUKE OF NEWCASTLE-UNDER-LYNE under the *spec. rem.* in the creation (1756) of that title, which see.

(a) Col. Chester in his "*Westm. Abbey Registers*" states, however, that "there is no record of it in any of the Abbey Registers."

(b) The Earldom of Lincoln, to which in 1768 the Dukedom of Newcastle-under-Lyne became joined, is an instance of a peerage title of the highest grade held without a Barony. The following (not reckoning Viscountcies of which there are several) are some of the instances of titles so held. *Viz.* (1) the anomalous Earldom of Devon since 1553 (2) the Earldom of Derby from 1594 to 1628 and again from 1702 to 1834 (3) the Earldom of Shrewsbury from 1616 to 1856 (4) the Earldom of Lincoln since 1692, together with, since 1768, the Dukedom of Newcastle-under-Lyne (5) the Earldom of Huntingdon since 1789 (6) the Earldom of Lindsey since 1809 and (7) the Earldom of Berkeley since 1810.

LINDORES.

Barony [S.] *1.* The Hon. Sir Patrick Leslie, of Pitcairly, 2d s.
I. 1600? of Andrew, 4th Earl of Rothes [S.], by his first wife, Grisel, da. of Sir James Hamilton, of Finnart, was Gent. of the Bedchamber to King James VI. [S.], was, before 1581, Commendator of the Abbey of Lindores, co. Elgin, and is supposed(a) to have been *cr.*, by Royal charter, 31 March, ratified by Parl. 15 Nov. 1600,(b) a Lord of Parl.(c) as LORD LINDORES [S.] (probably on the resignation of his eldest son and subsequent heir *whom see*) with rem. to his heirs male whatever. An act of Parl. in 1600 speaks of him as "Patrick, now *Lord of Lundoris*,(d) sumtyme Commendator of the Abbacie of Lundores." He *m.* Jean, da. of Robert (Stewart), Earl of Orkney [S.] (illegit. s. of King James V. [S.]), by Janet, da. of Gilbert (Kennedy), 3d Earl of Cassillis [S.] He *d.* between 1606 and 1609. His widow *m.* as his third wife Robert (Melville), 1st Lord Melville of Monymaill [S.], who *d.* Dec. 1621, aged 94. She was living 1642.

II. 1608? *2.* Patrick (Leslie), Lord Lindores [S.], s. and h. To him was granted v.p. a charter, 31 March 1600,(e) erecting the Abbacy of Lindores (which had been resigned to him by his father) "into the *temporal Lordship*(d) *of Lindores* with the title, rank, and vote of a Lord of Parl." [S.] to him and his heirs male whatsoever. It is presumed that he must have resigned this dignity some few months later in favour of his father as above mentioned, at all events in an act of Parl. dat. 15 Nov. following, ratifying this grant, he is mentioned as (merely) "Patrick Leslie, of Pitcarelie," while his father in an act of 1606 is mentioned as "now Lord of Lindoris." He *suc.* his father before 9 April 1609, and *d.* unm. Aug. 1649.(e)

III. 1649. *3.* James (Leslie), Lord Lindores [S.], s. and h. He *m.* firstly Mary, da. of Patrick (Gray), Lord Gray [S.], by his second wife, Mary, da. of Robert (Stewart), Earl of Orkney [S.], abovenamed. He *m.* secondly (—), da. of (—) Clerburn, of Yorkshire. He *d.* about 1660.

IV. 1660? *4.* John (Leslie), Lord Lindores [S.], only s. and h. by first wife, *suc. his father* before 20 July 1667. He *m.* firstly Marion, widow of James (Elphinstone), 1st Lord Coupar [S.] (who *d.* Jan. 1669, aged 82), da. of James (Ogilvy), 2d Earl of Airlie [S.], by his first wife, Helen, da. of George (Ogilvy), 1st Lord Banff [S.] He *m.* secondly, 6 Sep. 1695, at Cramond, Jean, widow of Sir Hugh Macculloch, da. of (—) Gibson. He *d.* 1706. His widow *d.* 1712.

V. 1706. *5.* David (Leslie), Lord Lindores [S.], only s. and h. by first wife. He *m.* Margaret, widow of Sir Archibald Stewart,

---

(a) "*Riddell*," p. 778.
(b) The date and the limitation of the peerage is so given (as granted to Patrick, the Commendator), in the *first* edit. of Douglas' peerage.
(c) The House of Lords in the case of the Barony of Lindores 1790-93 "from the striking circumstance of Patrick, *the son*, being only a Commoner and Master of Lindores long *after* the charter [whereby he was *cr.* Lord Lindores] 1600 (which never appears to have been acted upon in respect to the dignity) presumed in favour of a later more valid grant, tho' unknown, probably upon resignation, *to the father*, and (according to their adopted rule) solely to the heirs male of his body.". [*Riddell*, p. 778.] It is to be observed that in the "decreet of ranking" in 1606 this Barony is placed between that of Roxburgh *cr.* about 1599 and of Loudoun *cr.* 1601 which tallies with its taking the rank of the charter of 31 March 1600.
(d) This was one of the patrimonies of religious houses which were *together with a peerage* secured to Laics. See vol. iv, p. 247, note "a," *sub* "Holyroodhouse," and p. 408, note "b," *sub* "Kinloss," for a list of some of these.
(e) He "was never married but had above 67 basse children, sons and daughters." [Balfour's "*Annals*" iii, 423.]

of Burray, da. of Sir Archibald STEWART, of Dunearn. He *d.* s.p. July 1719.(a) His widow *d.* Oct. following. On his death the issue male of the grantee of this peerage became extinct. The title, however, on the presumption of it having been conferred to heirs male *whatsoever*, was assumed as under.

VI. 1719. 6. ALEXANDER (LESLIE), LORD LINDORES [S.], cousin and h. male, being s. and h. of John LESLIE, of Quarter, in Burntisland, by (—), da. of (—) SPITTAL, of Leuchart, which John (who *d.* 29 July 1706), was s. and h. of Andrew LESLIE, of Quarter afsd. (*d.* before 30 Nov. 1679), who was 2d s. of the Hon. Sir John LESLIE, of Newton (slain 1 Sep. 1651), 5th s. of Andrew, 4th EARL OF ROTHES [S.] abovenamed, and yr. br. (tho' of the half blood) to Patrick, 1st LORD LINDORES [S.], the 2d s. of the said Earl. He was an officer in the army in 1734 and eventually (1761) Major General; Col. of the 77th Foot, 1758; Col. of the 41st Foot, 1764. He voted (1736-65) at the elections of Scotch Peers.(b) He *m.* Jean, da. of Colin CAMPBELL, Commissioner of the Customs, 2d s. of Sir Colin CAMPBELL, 1st Bart. [S.], of Aberuchill. He was *bur.* in Chelsea College 3 Sep. 1765. His widow living Aug. 1784. Will pr. May 1790.

VII. 1765. 7. JAMES FRANCIS (LESLIE), LORD LINDORES [S.], only s. and h.; Capt. in the Marine force, 1757. He voted at the elections, 1767-74, of Scotch Peers.(b) He *d.* unm. 30 June and was *bur.* 4 July 1775, at Hackney, Midx. Admon. 3 Aug. 1784, to a creditor.

VIII. 1775, to 1813. 8. JOHN (LESLIE), LORD LINDORES [S.], cousin and h. male, being s. and h. of John LESLIE, of Lumquhat (*d.* 1771-74), only s. and h. of John LESLIE, of the same (*d.* before 8 Nov. 1728), s. of Capt. John LESLIE, of the same (living Oct. 1706), s. of James LESLIE, of the same (*d.* 1705), 3d s. of the Hon. Sir John LESLIE, of Newton (ancestor of the 6th Lord), who was yr. br. (tho' of the half blood) to Patrick, 1st Lord Lindores, both being sons of Andrew, 4th EARL OF ROTHES [S.] He was *b.* 1750; was an officer in the 26th Foot in 1774 and became eventually Lieut. General in the army. He voted at the election of Scotch Peers in 1780, 1784, without protest, but at the general election in 1790 his votes were disallowed.(c) He *m.*, 22 March 1789, in Mr. Mansell's house, South Audley street, St. Geo. Han. sq., Jane, yst. da. and coheir of Sir Thomas REEVE, of Hendens, in Bray, Berks. He *d.* s.p.m. May 1813 in his 64th year, being said to have been "the last male heir of the noble family of Leslie."(d) Since his death the *Barony of Lindores* has remained *unclaimed*. Will pr. 1813. His widow *d.* 11 Nov. 1837, aged 77, at Gey's house, near Maidenhead, Berks. Will pr. Dec. 1837.

(a) By deed 18 Dec. 1718, he settled the Lindores estate on his second cousin, Jean, 1st da. and h. of line of David (Leslie), 2d Lord Newark [S.], who was s. and h. of David, 1st Lord Newark, yr. br. of James, Lord Lindores, the settlors' grandfather. She was served heir accordingly, 20 Aug. 1736, and executed in April 1738 with consent of her husband, Sir Alexander Anstruther, a disposition of the estate in favour of Alexander (Leslie), Lord Lindores, the heir male.

(b) "Alexander [Lord Lindores] constantly voted at elections of Rep. Peers without protest or question. He *d.* 1765 and was *suc.* by his only son, Francis John, who voted at the elections of Rep. Peers in 1767, 1771, and 1774, without protest or question." [*Hewlett*, p. 65.]

(c) The House on 6 June 1793, resolved that "the votes *given by the Lord Lindores* at the said election [1790] were not good." Mr. Hewlett remarks that "there is no known report of the judgment given against the votes of Lord Lindores, nor are the grounds on which it proceeded known. It was, however, merely a decision against the votes given by Lord Lindores on that election and *not a decision against any claim* made by him *to the dignity* and it is to be observed that the wording of the resolution is very different from cases in which the dignity is impugned, *e.g.*, in that of Belhaven where the words run that "the votes given by the person *who voted under the title* of Lord Belhaven were not good;" so also in the case of Newark and of others.

(d) Annual Register for 1813.

LINDSAY, and LINDSAY OF THE BYRES.

A *Barony of Lindsay* [S.], of a very ancient date, was allowed, 11 Aug. 1848, together with the *Earldom of Crawford* [S.] The date of this Earldom is 1398 and that date, or any earlier one may probably be considered as being also that of the Barony; certainly David, the 3d Earl, was in 1443 designated "Earl of Crawford and *Lord the Lyndissay*" and the title of Lord Lindsay has been "ever since borne by the Earls of Crawford;" whom see.

Barony [S.] I. 1445. 1. Sir John Lindsay, of the Byres, co. Haddington, was s. and h. of Sir William(a) Lindsay, of the same, by Christiana, da. of Sir William Keith, Mareschal of Scotland, which William Lindsay was s. and h. of Sir William Lindsay, also of the Byres, a yr. s. of Sir David Lindsay, of Crawford, the grandfather of David, 1st Earl of Crawford [S.] He was one of the hostages for the ransom of King James I. [S.] in 1424; was P.C. to King James II. [S.], and (having witnessed a charter in 1431 as "*Dominus de Byres*") was styled in a Royal charter of confirmation, 22 Feb. 1445, LORD LINDSAY OF THE BYRES [S.], having safe conduct into England (under that designation) 5 July 1451, and sitting in Parl. 19 Oct. 1456, 6 March 1457/8, and 1464;(b) Justiciary [S.] North of Forth, 1457, and a Lord of Session, 6 March 1457/8. He is said to have m. (—), da. of Sir Robert Stewart, of Lorn. He *d.* 6 Feb. 1482.

II. 1482. 2. David (Lindsay), Lord Lindsay of the Byres [S.], s. and h., one of the Lords of Council [S.] He sat in Parl. 10 Oct. 1487; was one of the chief adherents to King James III. [S.] in the battle of Sauchieburn,(c) 11 June 1488 (where he was slain) for which adherence he was summoned to answer by the new King but escaped judgment. He m. Janet, da and h. of Walter Ramsay, of Carnock and Pitcruvie. He *d.* s.p. 1490.

III. 1490. 3. John (Lindsay), Lord Lindsay of the Byres [S.], br. and h., being so found 30 Jan. 1490; called "*John out-with-the-sword.*" He m. Mariot, da. of Sir William Baillie, of Lamington. He *d.* s.p.m. after 25 Dec. 1496, and probably before 5 Nov. 1497. His widow m. Robert Douglas, of Lochleven.

IV. 1497. 4. Patrick (Lindsay), Lord Lindsay of the Byres [S.], br. and, according to the enfeoffment of the late Lord,(d) heir, 5 Nov. 1497. He was sometime an advocate or "forespekar."(e) He sat in Parl. 1505 and 1526. He accompanied the King in 1513 in his fatal expedition to England (of

(a) It is highly probable that William (and not his son, John), should be considered the *first* Baron. The precedence of the Barony of Lindsay at the ranking of 1606 is in favour thereof (see note "b" below) inasmuch as this William (equally as his descendants) was in possession (*jure matris*) of the Barony of Abercorn. Besides this, he is styled "*William, Lord Lindsay*" (a designation implying more than mere territorial Lordship) when alluded to (as the founder of a Chaplaincy) in the conveyance of the estate of Byres, on its alienation in 1609, and he is also *recognised* as Lord Lindsay in two Royal charters (6 and 29 June 1609), confirming that seal. *Ex. inform.* W. A. Lindsay.

(b) In the decreet of ranking, 5 March 1606, "Lord Lindesay" is placed above all the Barons, next under the "Earl of Dunbar" and above "Lord Forbes," the creation of which Barony was before 12 July 1442. This is said to have been in respect to the *Barony of Abercorn*; Christiana, da. of Sir William Mure, *of Abercorn*, having m. Sir William Lindsay (the first) of Byres, and being mother of Sir William Lindsay, the father of John, Lord Lindsay of Byres, abovenamed.

(c) He it was who presented the King with "the great grey horse" on which he rode at that battle. He is said to have brought thereto no less than 3,000 foot and 1,000 horse.

(d) His elder br., George Lindsay, was living 26 Oct. 1498.

(e) As such he pleaded for his brother, the 2d Lord, when on his trial in 1488 for having assisted the late King at Sauchieburn.

which he greatly disapproved) and was present at the battle of Flodden, being one of the few Scotch nobles who survived that defeat.(a) He was one of the four Lords appointed by Parl., 1 Dec. 1513, to be of the council to the Queen Dowager [S.] He had a grant of the Sheriffdom of Fife in July 1525. He *m.* Isabella, da. of (—) PITCAIRN, of Foethan. He *d.* 1526, and was *bur.* at St Andrew's.

V. 1526. 5. JOHN (LINDSAY), LORD LINDSAY OF THE BYRES [S.], grandson and h., being s. and h. of Sir John LINDSAY, of Pitcruvy, Master of Lindsay, by Elizabeth, 1st da. of Sir Robert LUNDIE, Treasurer of Scotland (1497—1502), which Sir John was s. and h. ap. of the late Lord, and tho' living in July 1525 *d.* v.p. soon afterwards. He sat in Parl. 10 Dec. 1540; was an extraordinary Lord of Session [S.] in 1541; was present at the death of King James V. was one of the nobles to whose charge the infant Queen Mary was committed in 1542, and was in command at Ancrum-Muir, 1544. P.C. [S.], 25 June 1545. It was chiefly thro' him that in 1559 a mediation was effected between the Lords of the Congregation (Protestants) of which he was one, and the Dowager Queen, the Regent. He was confirmed in his hereditary office of Justiciary of St. Andrews.(b) He *m.* Helen, 2d da. of John (STEWART), 2d EARL OF ATHOLE [S.], by Mary, da. of Archibald (CAMPBELL), 2d EARL OF ARGYLL [S.] He *d.* at a good age before 13 March 1562/3. His widow *m.* Thomas MONCUR, and *d.* May 1577. Will pr. 11 May 1577, confirmed 10 May 1580.

VI. 1563. 6. PATRICK (LINDSAY), LORD LINDSAY OF THE BYRES [S.], who before his succession to the peerage [S.] had as "Master of Lindsay" taken a lead among the Reformers, being one of the first of the nobles who joined that cause. He was P.C. [S.], 15 May 1565; sat in Parl., 1567; was chief among those who took part in the murder of Rizzio, the Queen's favourite, and who obtained from the Queen [S.] at Lochleven, 24 July 1567, her resignation of the Crown to her son, James VI. [S.], and the nomination of the Earl of Moray [S.] as Regent. He also contributed to the Queen's final defeat, 2 May 1568, at the battle of Longsyde. Many years later in 1582 he was one of the nobles concerned in seizing the person of King James VI. [S.] at "the raid of Ruthven." He *m.* Euphemia,(c) 1st da. of Sir Robert DOUGLAS, of Lochleven, by Margaret, da. of John (ERSKINE) EARL OF MAR [S.], mother (by King James V. [S.]), of the Regent, Earl of Moray [S.], abovenamed. She *d.* intestate June 1580. Admon. 13 Nov. 1591, at Edinburgh. He *d.* at Struthers, co. Fife, 11 Dec. 1589. Will pr. at Edinburgh, 13 Nov. 1591.

VII. 1591. 7. JAMES (LINDSAY), LORD LINDSAY OF THE BYRES [S.], only s. and h. He *m.* before 16 Feb. 1573/4, Euphemia, 1st da. of Andrew (LESLIE), 4th EARL OF ROTHES [S.], by his first wife, Grizel, da. of Sir James HAMILTON, of Finnart. He *d.* 5 Nov. 1601. His wife survived him.

VIII. 1601. 8. JOHN (LINDSAY), LORD LINDSAY OF THE BYRES [S.], s. and h., served heir to his father, 13 April 1602; P.C. [S.], 7 June 1605. He *m.* (contract 4 July 1599, at Dalkeith), Anne, sister of Laurence, 5th LORD OLIPHANT [S.], da. of Laurence OLIPHANT, Master of Oliphant, by Christian, 2d da. of William (DOUGLAS), 2d EARL OF MORTON [S.] He *d.* s.p.m.(d) 5 Nov. 1609.(e)

IX. 1609. 9. ROBERT (LINDSAY), LORD LINDSAY OF THE BYRES [S.], br. and h. male, served heir [male] to his father, 8 Dec. 1609. P.C. [S.], 1610. He *m.* contract 26 June 1610, Christian, 1st da. of Thomas

(a) See p. 63, note "b," *sub* "Lennox," for a list of the nobles [S.] there present.

(b) The office was retained in the family till the passing of the Heritable Jurisdictions Act in 1748.

(c) She was one of the seven beautiful sisters known as "the seven fair porches of Lochleven."

(d) Anne, his only da. and h., *m.* Alexander (Falconer), 2d Lord Falconer of Halkertoun [S.], and had issue.

(e) The estate of Byres was sold in 1609 (according to his contract, carried out by his successor), to Sir Thomas Hamilton, *cr.* 1613, Lord Binning and *Byres*, and subsequently Earl of Haddington [S.]

(HAMILTON), 1st EARL OF HADDINGTON [S.], by his first wife, Margaret, da. of James BORTHWICK, of Newbyres. He *d.* at Bath, 9 July 1616. His widow *m.* contract 9 Dec. 1617 (as second wife) Robert (BOYD), 5th LORD BOYD [S.], who *d.* Aug. 1628, aged 33.

X. 1616.
Earldom [S.]
I. 1633.

10 and *1*. JOHN (LINDSAY), LORD LINDSAY OF THE BYRES [S.], only s. and h., *b.* about 1598; *suc.* his father in the peerage [S.], 9 July 1616; was *cr.*, 8 May 1633, EARL OF LINDSAY and LORD PARBROATH [S.], to him and his heirs male bearing the name and arms of Lindsay; *suc.*, probably in 1652 but certainly before 1663, as EARL OF CRAWFORD [S.] (under a regrant of that Earldom on 15 Jan. 1642), since which date he styled himself (as did also his five immediate successors) "*Earl of Crawford-Lindsay.*" He *d.* 1676—1678 in his 81st year.

Earldom [S.] II.
Barony [S.] XI.
1678?

2 and *11*. WILLIAM (LINDSAY), EARL OF CRAWFORD, and EARL OF LINDSAY (or *Earl of Crawford-Lindsay*), &c. [S.], s. and h., *b.* April 1644, and *d.* 6 March 1698.

Earldom [S.] III.
Barony [S.] XII.
1698.

3 and *12*. JOHN (LINDSAY), EARL OF CRAWFORD, and EARL OF LINDSAY (or *Earl of Crawford-Lindsay*), &c. [S.], s. and h. He *d.* Dec. 1713.

Earldom [S.] IV.
Barony [S.] XIII.
1713.

4 and *13*. JOHN (LINDSAY), EARL OF CRAWFORD, and EARL OF LINDSAY (or *Earl of Crawford-Lindsay*), &c. [S.], s. and h., *b.* 4 Oct. 1702; *d.* 25 Dec. 1749.

Earldom [S.] V.
Barony [S.] XIV.
1749.

5 and *14*. GEORGE (LINDSAY-CRAWFORD), EARL OF CRAWFORD, and EARL OF LINDSAY (or *Earl of Crawford-Lindsay*), VISCOUNT GARNOCK, &c. [S.], cousin and h. male, being 2d but only surv. s. of Patrick, 2d VISCOUNT GARNOCK [S.], who was s. and h. of John LINDSAY, *cr.* in 1703, VISCOUNT OF GARNOCK, LORD KILBIRNY AND DRUMRY [S.], with rem. to his heirs male, which John, 1st Viscount Garnock, was s. and h. of the Hon. Patrick CRAWFORD, formerly LINDSAY, 2d s. of John, 17th EARL OF CRAWFORD, and 1st EARL OF LINDSAY [S.], abovenamed. He was *b.* about 1723; *suc.* his br., the 3d VISCOUNT GARNOCK [S.], in that dignity, 22 Sep. 1738, and *suc.* his cousin abovenamed in the Earldoms of Crawford and Lindsay, &c. [S.], 25 Dec. 1749. He *d.* 11 Aug. 1781.

Earldom [S.] VI.
Barony [S.] XV.
1781.

6 and *15*. GEORGE (LINDSAY-CRAWFORD), EARL OF CRAWFORD, and EARL OF LINDSAY (or *Earl of Crawford-Lindsay*), VISCOUNT GARNOCK, LORD LINDSAY OF THE BYRES, LORD PARBROATH, and LORD KILBIRNY AND DRUMRY [S.], s. and h., *b.* 31 Jan. 1758, *d.* unm. 30 Jan. 1808, aged 50. By his death the issue male of John, 17th Earl of Crawford, and 1st Earl of Lindsay, became extinct, when the right to the *Earldom of Crawford* devolved on (the Earl of Balcarres [S.]) the heir male of the body of the 1st Earl of Crawford (see that dignity *sub* the 23d Earl) but the right to the Earldom of Lindsay and the inferior titles devolved on the heir male collateral of the 1st Earl of Lindsay as below.

See fuller account under "CRAWFORD" Earldom [S.], *cr.* 1398, *sub* the 17th to the 22d Earls.

[Earldom [S.] VII. Barony [S.] XVI.] [1808.]

7 and 16. DAVID LINDSAY, *de jure*[a] EARL OF LINDSAY, &c. [S.], cousin and h. male, being only s. and h. of John LINDSAY (living 1760 and said[b] to have been "a common soldier"), 3d s. of John Lindsay, of Kirkforthar, who was s. and h. of David L. (*m.* 1669), s. and h. of David L. (*m.* 1631), s. and h. of David L. (*m.* 1609 but *d.* v.p.), s. and h. ap. of Patrick L. (*m.* 1584), s. and h. of John L., s. and h. of David L. (*d.* 1592 at a great age) all of Kirkforthar afsd., the said David being yr. br. of John, 5th LORD LINDSAY OF THE BYRES [S.], great grandfather of John, *cr.* in 1633 EARL OF LINDSAY [S.] He, who was a Sergeant in the army, was 23 Aug. 1808, served heir male[b] of the family of Lindsay of Kirkforther, but *d.* s.p. and was *bur.* 5 May 1809, in the Canongate churchyard at Edinburgh.

[Earldom [S.] VIII. Barony [S.] XVII.] [1809.]

8 and 17. SIR PATRICK LINDSAY, K.C.B., &c., *de jure*[a] EARL OF LINDSAY, &c. [S.], cousin and h. male, being only s. and h. of John LINDSAY, Lieut. Col. 83d Foot, by Margaret Maria, 2d da. of Charles Halket CRAIGIE, of Hallhill and Dunbarnie, which John (*m.* 1776) was yr. br. of Patrick Lindsay, of Eaglescairnie, in East Lothian (who *d.* s.p.m. 18 Oct. 1801, in his 83d year), both being sons of Patrick L., sometime M.P. and Provost of Edinburgh (*d.* 1753), who was only surv. s. of the Rev. Patrick L., Rector of the Grammar School at St. Andrews, who was s. of Patrick L., of that city (living 1646), who was s. of James L., yr. br. of David, and 2d s. of Patrick Lindsay, of Kirkforthar abovenamed, which Patrick was s. and h. of John L., s. and h. of David L. (*d.* 1592 at a great age) the yr. br. of John, 5th LORD LINDSAY OF THE BYRES [S.], as aforestated. He was *b.* 24 Feb. 1778, and served in the army no less than 44 years; distinguished himself at the reduction of Coorg in India, becoming finally, 10 Jan. 1837, Major-General. K.C.H., 1834; K.C.B., 19 July 1838. He *d.* s.p. 14 July 1839, and was *bur.* at Inveresk. Will dat. 26 March 1837, pr. April 1839.

[Earldom [S.] IX. Barony [S.] XVIII.] [1839.]

9 and 18. SIR HENRY BETHUNE, Bart., *de jure*[a] EARL OF LINDSAY, &c. [S.], cousin and h. male, being s. and h. of Martin Eccles Lindsay BETHUNE, Major in the army, by Margaret Augusta, da. of (—) TOVEY, Gen. in the army, which Martin (who *d.* v.p. 1813) was s. and h. ap. of Henry BETHUNE, formerly LINDSAY, of Kilconquhar, co. Fife (who *d.* 1819, aged 83, having assumed the name of *Bethune* on inheriting the estate of Kilconquhar under an entail of his maternal uncle, David Bethune), the said Henry being s. of George LINDSAY, of Wormistoun, co. Fife (by Margaret BETHUNE, his wife), which George (who *d.* 1764) was s. and h. of John Lindsay (*d.* 1715) who was s. and h. of Patrick Lindsay (a prisoner, *ex parte Regis*, at the battle of Worcester 1651), s. and h. of John Lindsay (living 1647), s. and h. of Patrick Lindsay, all being of Wormistoun afsd., which Patrick (who *d.* about 1625 at a great age) was s. and h. of John L., of Cupar, co. Fife, who was 2d s. of William Lindsay, of Pictstoun (living 1539), who was 2d s. of Patrick, 4th LORD LINDSAY OF THE BYRES [S.] He was *b.* 12 April 1787; entered the service of the East India Company; was sent from Madras to Persia (when a Major) to assist the Crown Prince (Abbas Mirza) in organising his artillery and was subsequently accredited as Agent to the Court of Persia, where he was greatly distinguished. He was *cr. a Baronet* (as "of Kilconquhar, co. Fife"), 7 March 1836. He *m.*, 9 July 1822, at St. James' Westm., Coutts, da. of John TROTTER, of Dyrham Park, Herts (br. of Sir Coutts TROTTER, 1st Bart.), by Felicité, da. of Samuel

(a) According to the decision of the House of Lords, in consequence whereof the Earldom of Lindsay, &c., was, 5 April 1878, confirmed to Sir John Trotter Bethune.

(b) "Riddell," p. 618, note 2, where his death from brain fever in 1809 and other curious particulars about him are related; it being added that "what is singular, John Lindsay, *the soldier*, his father, was actually younger brother of Capt. George Lindsay, of Kirkforther (son of John Lindsay, of Kirkforther), and in 1760 had been served tutor of law to his daughters. So ended the line of Kirkforther."

Swinton, Capt. R.N. He d. 19 Feb. 1851, in his 64th year, at Teheran in Persia, and was bur. in the churchyard of the Armenians there. Admon. Aug. 1851. His widow (who was a minor in 1822) d. 31 Dec. 1877, at 13 Prince's Gardens, Kensington.

Earldom [S.] X. Barony [S.] XIX. [1851, and] 1878.

10 and *19*. Sir John Trotter Bethune, Bart., s. and h., who on his father's death, 19 Feb. 1851, *suc. to the Baronetcy*, becoming also *de jure*(a) Earl of Lindsay, &c. [S.] He became subsequently, by the decision in his favour of the House of Lords, 5 April 1878, *de facto*, Earl of Lindsay [1633], Viscount Garnock [1703], Lord Lindsay of the Byres [1445], Lord Parbroath [1633], and Lord Kilbirny and Drumry [1703], in the peerage of Scotland. He was b. 3 Jan. 1827, at Kilconquhar; sometime Lieut. 91st Highlanders; Rep. Peer [S.] since 10 June 1885. He m., 18 July 1858, Jeanne Eudoxie Marie, da. of Jacques Victor Duval, of Bordeaux, in France.

Family Estates.—These, in 1883, consisted of 2,205 acres in Fifeshire, worth £5,548 a year. *Principal Residence*. Kilconquhar House, co. Fife.

LINDSAY AND BALNEIL.

i.e., "Lindsay and Balneil," Barony [S.] (*Lindsay*), *cr.* 1651 with the Earldom of Balcarres [S.], which see.

LINDSAY OF BALCARRES.

i.e., "Lindsay of Balcarres," Barony [S.] (*Lindsay*), *cr.* 1633; see under "Balcarres."

LINDSEY.

Earldom. I. 1626.

1. Robert (Bertie), Lord Willoughby of Eresby, s. and h. of Peregrine, Lord Willoughby of Eresby, by Mary, aunt of the *whole* blood of Henry, 18th Earl of Oxford (who d. s.p. in May 1625 leaving as his coheirs three sisters of the *half* blood), only da. of John (de Vere), 16th Earl of Oxford, was b. 17 Dec. 1582;(b) ed. at Cambridge; accompanied (his godfather), Robert, Earl of Essex, in the expedition to Cadiz in 1596, serving also in Denmark and Norway as well as in the United Provinces where in 1624 he was Col. of an English Regiment of Foot. K.B., 5 Jan. 1604/5. Having, in 1625, on the death of his cousin, Henry, Earl of Oxford, abovenamed, laid claim to that Earldom and to the other dignities vested in his maternal ancestors, he obtained judgment in his favour so far as concerned their hereditary office of *Great Chamberlain*,(c) and took his seat, 13 April 1627, above all other Barons in virtue of being possessed of that dignity. On 22 Nov. 1626, he was *cr.* EARL OF LINDSEY, co. Lincoln, it being recited in the patent that the office of Great Chamberlain was in the earliest times enjoyed by none under the dignity of an Earl; Lord Lieut. of Lincolnshire, 1629; elected K.G., 18 April, and inst. 5 Oct. 1630; *Lord High Constable* for two special occasions, 1631 and 1634, Admiral (*Custos Maris*) and Capt. Gen. at Sea, 1635; Governor of Berwick, 1639; a Commissioner of Regency, Aug. to Nov. 1641; Col. of

(a) See p. 102, note "a."

(b) Born in 1572, according to Lloyd's "*Memoirs*," but the inscription on his monument gives his death as "Anno ætatis 60, Christi 1642," and his father, who was born at Wesel in Oct. 1555, was probably unmarried as late as 1574. See Lady Georgiana Bertie's "*Five generations of a loyal house*."

(c) See vol. i, p. 207, note "d," *sub* "Aveland," for an account of the office of Great Chamberlain.

the Foot Guards, 1642, and, on the breaking out of the civil war, General of the King's forces. He m., about 1605, Elizabeth, da. of Edward (MONTAGU), 1st BARON MONTAGU OF BROUGHTON, by his 1st wife, Elizabeth. da. and h. of Sir John JEFFERIES, of Shillingley, Sussex, Lord Ch. Baron of the Exchequer. He d. a prisoner in Warwick Castle, 23 Oct. 1642, aged 60, of wounds received that morning at the battle of Edge Hill (where he was in command) and was bur. at Edenham, co. Lincoln.(a) M.I. Admon. 2 May 1643. His widow d. 30 Nov. 1654, and was bur. at Weekley, co. Northampton. Will pr. 1655.

II. 1642. 2. MONTAGU (BERTIE), EARL OF LINDSEY AND LORD WILLOUGHBY DE ERESBY, *Lord Great Chamberlain*, s. and h.; b. shortly before 1608; ed. at Sidney Sussex Coll., Cambridge; K.B. 4 Nov. 1616. M.P. for Lincoln, 1624-25, and for Stamford, 1625-26; *styled* LORD WILLOUGHBY, 1626-42, being also sum. to Parl. v.p. in that Barony (vested in his father) 31 Oct. 1640 as LORD WILLOUGHBY DE ERESBY; Gent. of the Privy Chamber 1634; *suc. as Earl of Lindsey* in Oct. 1642. He was Capt. of the King's Guards, and, as such, was taken prisoner with his father at Edgehill in 1642, but soon released; was wounded at the battle of Naseby, &c., P.C. and Gent. of the Bedchamber, 1643-49; Joint Commissioner at Newport, Sept. 1648(b), being a most faithful adherent to Charles I., whose funeral, at Windsor, he attended. During the usurpation he compounded, at £300 a year, for his estates. P.C. and Lord-Lieutenant of co. Lincoln 1660. Elected K.G. 1 and inst. 15 April 1661, officiating as Great Chamberlain at the Coronation of Charles II. He m. firstly, 18 April 1627, at St. Peter le Poor, London, Martha, Dow. COUNTESS OF HOLDERNESSE, sister of Charles, 1st VISCOUNT CULLEN [I.] da. of Sir William COKAYNE of Rushton, co. Northampton (sometime Lord Mayor of London), by Mary, da. of Richard MORRIS, of St. Leonards, Eastcheap, London. She who was *bap.* 26 May 1605, at St. Peters afsd., *d.* July 1641 and was *bur.* at Edenham. M.I. He m. secondly, in or after 1646, Bridget, widow of the Hon. Edward SACKVILLE (who d. 1646) da. and h. of Edward WRAY, Groom of the Bedchamber, by Elizabeth, da. and h. of Francis (NORREYS), EARL OF BERKSHIRE and LORD NORREYS(c). She who was *b.* 12 May and *bap.* 15 June 1627, at Hackney, Midx., was *bur.* (with her mother) 24 March 1656/7, in Westm. Abbey. He d. at Campden House, Kensington, 25 July 1666, aged 58, and was *bur.* at Edenham. Will pr. 1666.

III. 1666. 3. ROBERT (BERTIE), EARL OF LINDSEY, AND LORD WILLOUGHBY DE ERESBY, *Lord Great Chamberlain*, s. and h. by first wife; *b.* about 1630; *styled* LORD WILLOUGHBY, from 1642 till he *suc. to the peerage* in 1666; M.P. for Boston, 1661-66; P.C. 1666, 1682, and 1689; Gent. of the Bedchamber, 1673; Lord Lieut. of co. Lincoln, 1689-1700. He m. firstly (pub. of banns 19 Nov. to 3 Dec., 1654, at St. Margaret's, Westm.) Mary, widow of the Hon. George BERKELEY, da. and coheir of John MASSINGBERD, of London, Treasurer of the East India company, by Cecilia, da. of Thomas PELLIT, also of London, merchant. She *d.* s.p.m. He m. secondly Elizabeth, da. of Philip (WHARTON), 4th Lord WHARTON, by his wife Elizabeth, da. of Sir Rowland WANDESFORD. He m. thirdly Elizabeth, widow of Sir Francis Henry LEE, Bart., of Ditchley, da. and h. of Thomas (POPE), 2nd EARL OF DOWNE, [I], by Lucy, da. of John DUTTON, of Sherborne. He *d.* 8 May 1701(d). Will pr. Feb. 1701. His widow *d.* 1 July 1719. Will pr. 1719.

(a) See vol. i, p. 194, note "c," in "The Loyalists Bloody Roll." His character, a very noble one, is fully given by Clarendon.

(b) "He was one of the Quadrumvirate that had been so eminently distinguished for their unparelled loyalty to the late King by offering their lives as his councillors; a brave, experienced soldier, &c." Echard's History.

(c) James Bertie, their eldest son, became, in right of his mother, Lord Norreys, and in 1682 was *cr.* Earl of Abingdon.

(d) "Estate £5,000 at Grimsthorp, from ye heir general of ye house of Willoughby," See Williamson's "Lincolnshire families temp. Charles II." in "*Her and Gen.*," Vol. II., p. 116.

IV. 1701. Marquessate. I. 1706. 4 and 1. ROBERT (BERTIE), EARL OF LINDSEY, and LORD WILLOUGHBY DE ERESBY, *Lord Great Chamberlain*, s. and h. by second wife, *b.* 30 Oct. 1660; *styled* LORD WILLOUGHBY DE ERESBY from 1666 to 1701, and was sum. to Parl. v.p. in that Barony (vested in his father) 21 April 1690; *suc. to the Earldom of Lindsey* in 1701; was *cr.*, 21 Dec. 1706, MARQUESS OF LINDSEY, and was *cr.* on 26 July 1715, DUKE OF ANCASTER AND KESTEVEN. He *d.* 26 July 1723.

Marquessate. II. Earldom. V. 1723. 2 and 5. PEREGRINE (BERTIE), DUKE OF ANCASTER AND KESTEVEN, MARQUESS OF LINDSEY, EARL OF LINDSEY, and LORD WILLOUGHBY DE ERESBY, *Lord Great Chamberlain*, 1st surv. s. and h., *b.* 29 April 1686; *styled* MARQUESS OF LINDSEY from 1715 till he *suc. to the peerage* in 1723; *d.* 1 Jan. 1741/2.

Marquessate. III. Earldom. VI. 1742. 3 and 6. PEREGRINE (BERTIE), DUKE OF ANCASTER AND KESTEVEN, MARQUESS OF LINDSEY, EARL OF LINDSEY, and LORD WILLOUGHBY DE ERESBY, *Lord Great Chamberlain*, s. and h., *b.* 1714; *styled* MARQUESS OF LINDSEY from 1723 till he *suc. to the peerage* in 1742; *d.* 12 Aug. 1778.

[PEREGRINE THOMAS BERTIE, *styled* MARQUESS OF LINDSEY, s. and h. ap., *b.* 21 May 1755; *d.* young and v.p. 12 Dec. 1758.]

Marquessate. IV. Earldom. VII. 1778. 4 and 7. ROBERT (BERTIE), DUKE OF ANCASTER AND KESTEVEN, MARQUESS OF LINDSEY, EARL OF LINDSEY, and LORD WILLOUGHBY DE ERESBY, *Lord Great Chamberlain*, only surv. s. and h., *b.* 17 Oct. 1756; *styled* MARQUESS OF LINDSEY from 1758 till he *suc. to the peerage* in 1778. He *d.* unm. in his 23d year, 8 July 1779, when the office of Great Chamberlain(a) and the *Barony of Willoughby de Eresby* fell into *abeyance* between the heirs general his two sisters and coheirs. See that dignity.

Marquessate. V. Earldom. VIII. 1779. 5 and 8. BROWNLOW (BERTIE), DUKE OF ANCASTER AND KESTEVEN, MARQUESS OF LINDSEY, and EARL OF LINDSEY, uncle and h. male, *b.* 1 May 1729. He *d.* s.p.m., 8 Feb. 1809, when the issue male of the grantee of the Dukedom and Marquessate and of all his brothers (who had been included in the remainder of those honours) having failed, the *Dukedom of Ancaster and Kesteven* and the *Marquessate of Lindsey* became *extinct*.

See fuller particulars under "ANCASTER," Dukedom, *cr.* 1715; *ex.* 1809.

Earldom. IX. 1809. 9. ALBEMARLE (BERTIE), EARL OF LINDSEY, cousin and h. male, being only surv. s. & h. of Peregrine BERTIE, Barrister-at-law, by Elizabeth, da. of Edward PAYNE, of Tottenham Wick, Wilts, which Peregrine (who *d.* 1779, aged 70) was 2nd s. of Charles B. of Uffington, co. Lincoln, (*d.* 1730, aged 52), who was only s. and h. of the Hon. Charles B., of Uffington, afsd. (*d.* 1711, aged 76), who was 5th s. of Montagu, the 2nd Earl, being his yst. s. by Martha (formerly Martha COKAYNE) his 1st wife(b) abovenamed. He was *b.* 17 Sep. 1744. Entered the Army 1762, becoming finally,

(a) See vol. i, p. 207, note "d," *sub* "AVELAND," as to this office.

(b) In right of this descent it appears that, on the death of his distant cousin, Borlase (Cokayne), 6th Viscount Cullen [I.], who *d.* unm. 11 Aug. 1810, he became entitled to that peerage [I.] according to the limitation in the *docquet* of the patent (11 Aug. 1642), by which it was created. See "CULLEN" Viscountcy [I.] *cr.* 1642.

in 1808, General. Col. of the 9th Foot 1794, of the 77th Foot 1804, and of the 89th Foot 1808. M.P. for Stamford 1801-09; *suc. to the peerage* 8 Feb 1809; Gov. of Blackness Castle 1814; Gov. of Charlemont Fort 1818. He *m.* firstly, 7 May 1794, Eliza Maria, widow of Thomas SCROPE, of Coleby, co. Lincoln, da. of William CLAY, of Burridge Hill, Notts. She *d.* s.p. July 1806. He *m.* secondly, 18 Nov. 1809, Charlotte Susanna Elizabeth, da. of Charles Peter LAYARD, D.D., Dean of Bristol, by Elizabeth, da. of Joseph WARD. He *d.* 18 Sep. 1818, at Uffington aforesaid, aged 74. Will pr. 1818. His widow *m.*, 14 April 1821, at St. Geo., Han.-sq., Rev. Peter William PEGUS, who *d.* 21 April 1860. She *d.* 28 Nov. 1858, at Uffington House, aged 78.

X. 1818. *10.* GEORGE AUGUSTUS FREDERICK ALBEMARLE (BERTIE), EARL OF LINDSEY, s. and h. by second wife; *b.* 4 Nov. 1814, at Uffington, King George IV. and *H.R.H.* Frederick, Duke of York, being his sponsors; styled LORD BERTIE, till he *suc. to the peerage* in 1818. He *d.*, unm., 21 March 1877, aged 62, at Uffington House aforesaid.

XI. 1877. *11.* MONTAGU PEREGRINE (BERTIE), EARL OF LINDSEY, only br. and h., *b.* 25 Dec., 1815; ed. at Eton; sometime (1839) Captain Grenadier Guards; *suc. to the peerage*, 1877. He *m.* 30 May 1854, at St. Geo., Han.-sq., Felicia Elizabeth, da. of Rev. John EARLE WELBY, Rector of Hareston, co. Leicester, by Felicia Eliza, da. of Rev. George Hole, of Chumleigh and North Tawton, Devon.

[MONTAGU PEREGRINE ALBEMARLE BERTIE, *styled* LORD BERTIE, only s. & h. *b.* 3 Sep. 1861; ed. at Eton and at Mag. Coll., Cambridge; Aide-de-camp to the Gov. of New South Wales, 1885-86. He *m.* 12 February 1890, at Sydney, in that colony, Millicent Emma, 1st da. of F. H. Cox, of Craig Crook, St. Leonard's, Sydney.]

Family Estates.—These, in 1883, consisted of 4,790 acres in Lincolnshire, worth £9,286 a year. *Principal Residence.*—Uffington(a) House, near Stamford, co. Lincoln.

LINE, see LYNE.

LINEDOCH, see LYNEDOCH.

LINGEN.

Barony. I. 1885. SIR RALPH-ROBERT-WHEELER LINGEN, K.C.B., permanent Secretary to the Treasury, was *cr.* 3 July 1885,(b) BARON LINGEN of Lingen, co. Hereford. He was only s. of Thomas LINGEN, of Birmingham, by Ann Palmer, da. of Robert WHEELER, of the same town, was *b.* at St. Martins, Birmingham, 19 Feb. 1819; ed. at Bridgnorth school; mat. at Oxford (Trin. Coll.) 22 May 1837; Scholar thereof, 1837-41; Ireland scholar, 1838; Hertford scholar, 1839; 1st class (classics) 1840; B.A. 1841; Fellow of Balliol Coll. 1841-50; Latin essay. 1843; Assistant Master at Rugby School 1843; Eldon scholar 1846; M.A. 1846; Barrister (Linc. Inn) 1847; Ch. Sec. to the Educational Committee of the P.C. 1849-69; C.B. 1869; Permanent Sec. to the Treasury 1870-85; K.C.B. 31 May 1879; *cr.* D.C.L. (Oxford), 22 June 1881; being *raised to the peerage* 3 July 1885, as abovementioned. Hon. Fellow of Trin. Coll., Oxford, 1886; an Alderman of the London County Council. He *m.* 4 Dec. 1852, Emma, 4th da. of Robert HUTTON, of Putney Park, Surrey, sometime M.P. for Dublin.

(a) Uffington was purchased in 1674 by the Hon. Charles Bertie, from George, 2nd Duke of Buckingham.

(b) See vol. iv., p. 235, note "a" *sub.* "Hobhouse" as to this batch of a dozen Baronies *cr.* in June and July 1885.

LINLITHGOW,

Earldom. [S.] I. 1600. 1. ALEXANDER (LIVINGSTON), 7th LORD LIVINGSTON [S.] s. and h. of William, 6th LORD LIVINGSTON [S.], by Agnes, da. of Malcolm (FLEMING), 3rd LORD FLEMING [S.], *suc. to the peerage* [S] on the the death of his Father, before 24 Dec. 1580, and having *m.* before 1582, Eleanor, da. of Andrew (HAY) 8th EARL OF ERROLL [S], by his first wife, Jean, sister and heir of line of William (HAY), 6th EARL OF ERROLL [S.] appears, with his wife, to have had the charge of bringing up the children of the King [S] and consequently was rewarded with several grants of offices and lands and was *cr.*(a) 15 Nov. 1600 (or, according to Sir James Balfour, 25 Dec. 1600, at the baptism of Prince Charles) EARL OF LINLITHGOW, LORD LIVINGSTON AND CALENDAR [S,] He and his wife were both living 2 April 1622, but he *d*, at Calendar and was *bur.* at Falkirk 5 Feb. 1622/3. Fun. entry in Lyon office.

[JOHN LIVINGSTON, *styled* LORD LIVINGSTON, from 1600 till his death; s. and h. ap. He *d.* unm. and v,p. before 18 Feb. 1614, when his br. was served his heir.]

II. 1623. 2. ALEXANDER (LIVINGSTON), EARL OF LINLITHGOW, &c. [S.], 2d(b) but 1st surv. s. and h.; was made an extraordinary Lord of Session [S.], 13 Jan. 1610; *styled* LORD LIVINGSTON since the death (1614?) of his elder brother till he *suc. to the peerage* [S.] in 1623; Hereditary Constable of Linlithgow palace. He *m.* firstly Elisabeth, 2d da. of George (GORDON), 1st MARQUESS OF HUNTLY [S.], by his first wife, Henrietta, da. of Esme (STUART), DUKE OF LENNOX [S.] She *d.* in childbed at Edinburgh, July 1616. He *m.* secondly Mary, 1st da. of William (DOUGLAS), 10th EARL OF ANGUS [S.], by Elisabeth, da. of Laurence (OLIPHANT), 4th LORD OLIPHANT [S.] He was living 15 Dec. 1642, but was dead at the time of the Restoration in 1660.

III. 1650? 3. GEORGE (LIVINGSTON), EARL OF LINLITHGOW, &c. [S.], s. and h., *b.* July 1616; *styled* LORD LIVINGSTON from 1623 till he *suc. to the peerage* [S.] between 1642 and 1660; was Col. of the Horse Guards; suffered much for the Royal cause; was P.C. [S.], 1661; resigned his command in the army, 1681; Justice General [S.], 1681-88; was implicated in Montgomery's plot to restore the House of Stuart. He *m.*, 30 July 1650, Elizabeth, Dow. COUNTESS OF KINGHORN [S.], da. of Patrick (MAULE), 1st EARL OF PANMURE [S.], by his first wife, Frances, da. of Sir Edward STANHOPE. She *d.* Oct. 1659 at Castle Huntly. He *d.* 1 Feb. 1690, aged 74.

IV. 1690. 4. GEORGE (LIVINGSTON), EARL OF LINLITHGOW, &c. [S.], s. and h., *styled* LORD LIVINGSTON till he *suc. to the peerage* [S.] in 1690; P.C. [S.], 1692, and a Commissioner of the Treasury. He *m.* Henrietta, da. of Alexander (SUTHERLAND), 1st LORD DUFFUS [S.], by his third wife, Margaret, da. of James (STEWART), EARL OF MORAY [S.] He *d.* s.p. 7 Aug. 1695.(c)

(a) The patent was never enrolled and its contents are nowhere recorded. It is therefore presumed to have been to heirs male of the body of the grantee.

(b) The third son, James, was *cr.* Earl of Calendar [S.] in 1641 with spec. limitations. The 4th Earl of Calendar succeeded in 1695 to the Earldom of Linlithgow as mentioned in the text.

(c) It appears that either this Earl or his successor *m.* (as his last wife) one Agnes Wauchope who was dead in 1712. Mr. R. R. Stodart, late "Lyon Depute," states in May 1884 as follows, "There is a service 1712 of John Scott to his grandmother, *Agnes Wauchope, Countess of Linlithgow.* Andrew Wauchope, of Niddrie, had a da., Agnes, *b.* 13 April 1677, who was alive, *married*, and resident at Silvercraigs, near Glasgow, 1711, the husband's name not stated. Her aunt, Anna, da. of Sir John Wauchope, of Niddry, *m.* 1668 Francis Scott, of Gorrenberrie. Anna, often spelt Annas, might be made Agnes by mistake."

V. 1695, to 1716. 5. JAMES (LIVINGSTON), EARL OF LINLITHGOW [1600], EARL OF CALENDAR [1641], LORD LIVINGSTON [1458 ?], LORD LIVINGSTON AND CALENDAR [1600], and LORD LIVINGSTON OF ALMOND [1633 and 1641], in the peerage of Scotland, nephew and heir, being only s. and h. of Alexander, 3d EARL OF CALENDAR [S.], by Anne, da. of James (GRAHAM), 2d MARQUESS OF MONTROSE [S.], which Alexander (who *suc.* to the Earldom of Calendar in Aug. 1685) was yr. br. to George, 4th Earl of Linlithgow. He was *styled* LORD LIVINGSTON OF ALMOND from 1685 till he *suc.* his father in Dec. 1692 as *Earl of Calendar*, &c. [S.] He *suc.* (three years afterwards) in Aug. 1695 his uncle (Earl George abovenamed) as *Earl of Linlithgow*, &c. [S.] REP. PEER [S.], 13 Jan. 1712/3, and 12 Nov. 1713. He *m.* Margaret, yr. sister of Mary, *suo jure*, COUNTESS OF ERROLL [S.] both being daughters of John (HAY), 12th EARL OF ERROLL [S.] by Anne, da. of James (DRUMMOND), 3d EARL OF PERTH [S.] Having joined in the rising in 1715 on behalf of the house of Stuart he was attainted, 17 Feb. 1715/6, of high treason, whereby (his estate of £1,206 a year and) all *his honours* became *forfeited*. He *d.* s.p.m.s.(a) at Rome, 25 April 1723, when the *issue male of the 1st Earl* became *extinct*.

[JAMES LIVINGSTON, *styled* LORD LIVINGSTON, only s. and h. ap. *d.* v.p. and unm. 30 April 1715.]

LINN, see LYNN REGIS.

LINTON.

i.e., "LINTON AND CABERSTON," Barony [S.] (*Stewart*) *cr.* 1633 with the EARLDOM OF TRAQUAIR [S.], which see; *dormant* or *ex.* 1861.

LINTRATHEN.

i.e., "OGILVY OF ALITH AND LINTRATHEN, co. Forfar." Barony [S.] (*Ogilvy*) *cr.* 1639 with the EARLDOM OF AIRLIE [S.], which see.

LION, see LYON.

LIONS, see LYONS.

LISBURNE.

Viscounty [I.] I. 1685, to 1690. ADAM LOFTUS, of Rathfarnam, co. Dublin, s. and h. of Sir Arthur LOFTUS, of the same, Provost Marshal of the province of Ulster, by Dorothy, da. of Richard (BOYLE), 1st EARL OF CORK [I.] was *cr.* 29 January 1685, BARON OF RATHFARNAM, co. Dublin, and VISCOUNT LISBURNE [I.] He *m.* Lucy da. and coheir of George (BRYDGES), 6th BARON CHANDOS OF SUDELEY, by his second wife, Jane, da. of John (SAVAGE), EARL RIVERS. He *d.* s.p.m.(b) being slain at the siege of Limerick 1690, when in command of a regiment for King William III. Will pr. Oct. 1691.

(a) Lady Anne Livingston, his da. and h., *m.* 15 June 1724 William (Boyd), 4th Earl of Kilmarnock [S.] who was beheaded in 1746, by whom she was mother of James Boyd who in 1758 (by the death of his mother's maternal aunt, Mary, *suo jure* Countess of Erroll [S.], abovenamed) became Earl of Erroll [S].

(b) Lucy, his da. and h. *m.* Thomas (Wharton), 1st Marquess of Wharton, and was mother of Philip, Duke of Wharton, who sold the Rathfarnam estates to William Conolly for £62,000.

II. 1695. *1.* JOHN VAUGHAN, of Crosswood, (Trawscoed) co. Cardigan, s. and h. of Edward VAUGHAN,(a) of the same, one of the Lords of the Admiralty, by Letitia, da. of Sir William HOOKER, was *b.* about 1670; *suc.* his father in 1683, and having *m.* 18 Aug. 1692, at St. Giles in the fields; (Lic. Fac.), Mallet, sister and coheir (1681) of Charles, 3d Earl of Rochester, 3d da. of John WILMOT), 2d EARL OF ROCHESTER (the well known favourite of Charles II.) by Elizabeth, da. and h. of John MALET, of Enmore, Somerset, was *cr.* BARON OF FETHARD ("Fethers") co. Tipperary and VISCOUNT LISBURNE co. Antrim [I.] He was M.P. for Cardiganshire in several Parls., and in 1714 was Lord Lieut. thereof. She, who was *b.* about 1675, *d.* 1716. He was *bur.* 5 April 1721 at Greenwich. Will pr. 1721.

III. 1721. *2.* JOHN (VAUGHAN), VISCOUNT LISBURNE, &c. [I.] s. and h., *b.* about 1695; *suc. to the peerage* [I.] in 1721; Lord Lieut. of Cardiganshire, 1721; M.P. for that county, 1727-34. He was refused his seat in the House of Lords [I.] by reason of the patent not being enrolled, whereupon he petitioned the said house, 29 March 1736, for his writ, but no resolution thereon was passed. He *m.* firstly, at her father's house in Essex street, Strand (—) da. of Sir John BENNET, Serjeant at Law. She *d.* s.p. 31 July 1723. He *m.* secondly, 1725, Dorothy, da. of Richard HILL, of Henblas, co. Montgomery. He *d.* s.p.m. 15 Jan. 1741 at (Trawscoed) Crosswood. His widow *d.* 20 Nov. 1790.

IV. 1741. *3.* WILMOT (VAUGHAN), VISCOUNT LISBURNE, &c. [I.], br. and h. male; Lord Lieut. of Cardiganshire, 1744-60. He *m.* in 1727 Elizabeth 1st da. of Thomas WATSON, of Berwick-upon-Tweed and Grindon Ridge, co. Durham. He *d.* at (Trawscoed) Crosswood, 19 January 1766.

V. 1766. Earldom [I.] 1. 1776. *4.* and *1.* WILMOT (VAUGHAN), VISCOUNT LISBURNE, &c. [I.], s. and h., *b.* about 1730; was M.P. for Cardiganshire 1755-61, for Berwick-upon-Tweed, 1765-68, and for Cardiganshire (again) 1768-91. Lord Lieut. of Cardiganshire 1760; *suc. to the peerage* [I.] Jan. 1766: a Lord of Trade 1768 and a Lord of the Admiralty 1770-82. He *m.* firstly, 3 July 1754, at St. Geo. Han. sq., Elizabeth, sister and (in 1734) h. to Washington Nightingale, being only da. of Joseph Gascoigne NIGHTINGALE, of Mamhead, Devon, and of Enfield, Midx., by Elizabeth, da. and coheir of Washington (SHIRLEY) 2d EARL FERRERS. She *d.* 19 and was *bur.* 24 May 1755 at Enfield. He *m.* secondly 19 April 1763, Dorothy, 1st da. of John SHAFTO, of Whitworth, co. Durham, by Mary, da. and h. of Thomas JACKSON, of Nunnington, co. York. He *d.* 6 Jan. 1800 aged about 70. Will pr. March 1800. His widow *d.* 12 Sep. 1805.

Earldom [I.] II. Viscountcy [I.] VI. 1800. *2* and *5.* WILMOT (VAUGHAN), EARL OF LISBURNE, &c. [I.], s. and h. by first wife, *b.* 9 May 1755; *styled* LORD VAUGHAN from 1766 till he *suc. to the peerage* [I.] in 1800. He *d.* unm., 6 May 1820, in his 65th year, near Stamford, co. Lincoln.(b) Admon. Dec. 1820.

Earldom [I.] III. Viscountcy [I.] VII. 1820. *3* and *6.* JOHN (VAUGHAN), EARL OF LISBURNE, &c. [I.], br. (of the half blood) and h., being s. of the 1st Earl by his second wife; *b.* 3 March 1769; a Col. in the army; M.P. for Cardigan, 1796—1818; *suc. to the peerage* [I.], 6 May 1820. He *m.*, 2 Aug. 1798, Lucy, sister (whose issue in 1835 became coheir) to William, EARL OF DEVON, da. of William (COURTENAY), 2d VISCOUNT COURTENAY OF POWDERHAM CASTLE (*de jure* EARL OF DEVON), by Frances, da. of Thomas CLACK. She, who was *b.* 13 June 1770, *d.* in Paris, 27 Jan. 1821, aged 51. He *d.* 18 May 1831, aged 62. Will pr. July 1831.

(a) His father, Sir John Vaughan, was Chief Justice of the Court of Common Pleas 1668-74, and was *bur.* in the Temple Church, London, near the grave of the learned Selden, to whom he was executor.

(b) His estates "near £18,000 a year" devolved on his half brother.

Earldom [I.] IV. Viscountcy [I.] VIII.	1831.	4 and 7. ERNEST AUGUSTUS (VAUGHAN), EARL OF LISBURNE, &c. [I.], 2d but 1st surv. s. and h., *b.* 30 Oct. 1800; *styled* LORD VAUGHAN from 1820 till he *suc. to the peerage* [I.] in May 1831; Sheriff 1851, and M.P., for Cardiganshire, 1854-59. He *m.* firstly, 27 Aug. 1835, at St. James', Piccadilly, his

cousin, Mary, 2d da. of Sir Lawrence PALK, 2d Bart., by his second wife, Dorothy Elizabeth, da. of Wilmot (VAUGHAN), 1st EARL OF LISBURNE [I.], abovenamed. She *d.* 23 July 1851, aged 52, at Enfield, Midx. He *m.* secondly, 5 April 1853, at Alverstoke church, Elizabeth Augusta Harriet (sometime Maid of Honour to Queen Adelaide), da. of Henry Hugh MITCHELL, Col. in the army, by Harriet Isabella Elizabeth, da. of Henry (SOMERSET), 5th DUKE OF BEAUFORT. He *d.* 8 Nov. 1873, aged 73, at Crosswood. His widow *d.* s.p.s. 13 Dec. 1883, at Mornington, Cowes, Isle of Wight. Will pr. 7 Jan. 1884, above £4,000.

Earldom [I.] V. Viscountcy [I. IX.	1873.	5 and 8. ERNEST AUGUSTUS MALET (VAUGHAN), EARL OF LISBURNE, &c. [I.], s. and h., *b.* 26 June 1836, in Great Stanhope street; *styled* LORD VAUGHAN till he *suc. to the peerage* [I.] in Nov. 1873; ed. at Eton and at Ch. Ch., Oxford. He *m.* firstly, 24 June 1858, at St. Peter's, Eaton square, Laura

Gertrude, 3d. da. of Edwin BURNABY, of Baggrave Hall, co. Leicester, by Anne Caroline, da. of Thomas SALISBURY, of Marshfield House, co. York. She *d.* (as "*Lady Vaughan*"), 29 March 1865, at Birch Grove near Aberystwith. He *m.* secondly, 15 May 1878, at Huntley, co. Gloucester. Alice Dalton, 1st da. of Edmund PROBYN, of Huntley manor, by Sophia, da. of Richard DALTON, of Knaith, co. Lincoln. He *d.* 31 March 1888 aged 51 at the Victoria Hotel, St. Leonards-on-Sea. His widow *m.* (as second wife) 25 Sep. 1889, at Christ Church, Down street, William Archer (AMHERST), 3d EARL AMHERST and was living 1892.

Earldom [I.] VI. Viscounty [I.] X.	1888.	6. and 9. ARTHUR HENRY GEORGE (VAUGHAN), EARL OF LISBURNE [1776] VISCOUNT LISBURNE and BARON OF FETHARD [1695] in the peerage of Ireland, only s. and h., *b.* 30 July 1862, *styled* LORD VAUGHAN, from 1873 till he *suc. to the peerage* [I.] in March 1888. High Sheriff of Cardiganshire

1889. He *m.* 24 Oct 1888 at St. Andrews, Evelyn (sister to his step-mother) 2d da. of Edmund PROBYN, by Sophia, da. of Richard DALTON abovenamed.

Family estates. These, in 1883, consisted of 42,720 acres in co. Cardigan; 40 in co. Carmarthen and 1 (worth £20 a year) in Midx. *Total* 42,761 acres, worth £13,676 a year. *Principle Residence*, Crosswood near Aberystwith co. Cardigan.

LISGAR OF LISGAR AND BAILLIEBOROUGH.

Barony. I. 1870. to 1876	"The Rt. Hon. SIR JOHN YOUNG, Bart., G.C.B., G.C.M.G., Governor Gen. of the Dominion of Canada, and Commander-in-Chief in and over the island of Prince Edward" was *cr.* 26 Oct. 1870, BARON LISGAR OF LISGAR AND BAILLIEBOROUGH, co. Cavan. He was a. and h. of Sir William YOUNG, Bart. (so *cr.* 28 Aug.

1821) of Baillieborough Castle, co. Cavan, a director of the East India Company, by Lucy, da. of Lieut.-Col. Charles FREDERICK, and was *b.* 31 Aug. 1807; ed. at Eton and at Corpus Christi College, Oxford; B.A., 1829; Barrister (Linc. Inn), 1834; M.P. for co. Cavan, 1831-55; a Lord of the Treasury, 1841-44; Sec. to the Treasury, 1844-46; *suc.* his father *as a Baronet*, 10 March 1848; Ch. Sec. to the Viceroy of Ireland, 1852-55; P.C. [G.B. and I.], 1852; Lord High Commissioner of the Ionian Islands, 1855-59; G.C.M.G., 1855; K.C.B, 1859; Gov. of New South Wales, 1860-67; G.C.B., 1868; Gov. of Canada, 1868-72, being, in 1870, *raised to the peerage* as above stated; Lord Lieut. of co. Cavan, 1871. He *m.*, 8 April 1835, Adelaide

Annabella, da. of Edward Tuite DALTON, by Olivia, da. of Sir Edward STEVENSON, of Dublin, Mus. Doc. He d. s.p. 6 Oct, 1876 aged 69, at Lisgar House, Baillieborough, co. Cavan, when *the Barony* became *extinct*, but the Baronetcy devolved on his nephew. His widow m. 3 Aug. 1878 (her late husbands Principal Secretary) Sir Francis Charles Fortescue TURVILLE, K.C.M.G., of Bosworth Hall, co. Leicester, who d. 20 Dec. 1889, aged 58. She was living 1892.

Family Estates.—Those of the late Lord Lisgar appear in 1883 to have consisted of 8,924 acres in co. Cavan, worth £7,007 a year.

LISLE, or LISLE OF THE ISLE OF WIGHT.

Barony by writ.

I. 1299.

1. JOHN DE LISLE, of Wodeton, [Watton] in the Isle of Wight, s. and h. of William DE LISLE, was made Gov. of Carisbrooke Castle, in 1267, and had, with about 60 other persons, summons, 8 June 1294,(a) to attend the King to advise on the affairs of the realm. He distinguished himself in the wars with France and Scotland and was sum. to Parl. as a Baron (LORD LISLE) by writ directed "*Johi de Insula*" 29 Dec. (1299) 28 Ed. I., and subsequently.(b) He was one of the Barons whose signature (as "*Joh'es de Lisle, D'n's de Wodeton*") is to the letter to the Pope in 1301.(c) He d. about 1303-04; *Esch* 32 Ed. I.

II. 1304.

2. JOHN (DE LISLE), Lord LISLE, s. and h. aged 23 in (1303-04) 32 Ed. I., when he had livery of his lands as "John, s. and h. of John s. of William de Insula." K.B. (with Prince Edward, &c.) 1306; served in the wars with Scotland, and was sum. to Parl. by writs from 22 Jan. (1304/5) 33 Ed. I to 29 Dec. (1311) 5 Ed. II., directed (for the most part) "*Johi de Insula de Insula Vectis,*" in which last named writ he is placed among the "*Barones.*" A writ dated 29 July (1314) 8 Edit. II.(d) may, possibly, also apply to him. He was in (1317-18) 11 Ed. II. one of the commissioners to treat with Scotland, but, says Dugdale, "farther I cannot say of him." He may not impossibly be the "John de L'Isle, of Gatcombe" on whose death an inquisition was holden, 24 Nov. 1337, John being found to be his son and heir.(e)

(a) See vol. i., p. 259, note "c" *sub* "Basset de Sapcote," as to this not constituting a regular writ of summons to Parl.

(b) Dugdale and almost evey other authority attribute all the writs to John (who in the text above is considered as) the 2nd Lord. As this John was but 23 in 1304 it is unlikely he should have been sum. to Parl. in 1299; and it was the opinion of Courthope, Banks, &c. that the earlier writs refer to the father, who appears to have been alive till about 1303. Had these writs referred to the son, the word "*junior*" would probably have been inserted.

(c) See "Nicolas" pp. 761-809 for a full account of this letter.

(d) This writ directed "*Johi Insula-de Wyth,*" probably applies to John de Lisle, a Baron of the exchequer, who had been sum. (among the King's Justices and Council) from 23 Ed. I.

(e) According to a pedigree (full of dates and other information) in Baker's "*Northamptonshire*" (vol. i., p. 706) this Lord Lisle, who was of Wodeton afsd., of Chute, Wilts and of Walton, co. Northampton, m Petronilla and d. (1331) 5 Ed. III., leaving (1) *Sir Bartholomew de Lisle*, then aged 23, his s. and h., who m. Elizabeth and d. Aug. (1345) 19 Ed. III., leaving (2) *Sir John de Lisle*, aged 9, his s. and h., who m. Matilda (who d. 1388 having held Walton in dower) and d. (1371) 45 Ed. III., leaving (3) *Sir John de Lisle*, then aged 3 (aged 22 in 1388), his s. and h., who d. 1 Feb. (1407/8) 9 Hen. IV, leaving (4) *John de Lisle*, his s. and h., who d. seized of Wodeton and of Chute (having apparently alienated the estate of Walton) in (1429) 7 Hen. VI., leaving (5) *John de Lisle*,, his s. and h., then age 22. This pedigree seems more reliable than a very different one given in Banks's "*Bar. Angl.*" vol. i., p. 282, which makes a Walter de Insula to be br. and h. of John, the Baron *temp.* Ed. II., stating that the said John (the Baron) d. s.p. (1357) 31 Ed. III. According to that pedigree Eleanor, sister and h. of Sir John Lisle, of Wodeton, (7th in descent from the said Walter) m. John Kingston, of Kingston, of Berks, and was mother of (besides 2 sons who d. s.p.) Mary, who m. Sir Thomas Lisle and d. s.p, (1528-29) 20 Hen. VIII.

LISLE, or LISLE DE ROUGEMONT.

Barony by writ. I. 1311. 1. ROBERT DE LISLE,(a) of Rougemont and Cameldon Beds, only s. and h. of Warine DE LISLE(b) of the same, by Margaret, or Alice, d. and h. of Sir Robert DE MUCEGROS, *suc.* his father in (1298) 26 Ed. I., being then aged 6 years. In (1309-10) 3 Ed. II., he claimed, with success, the estate of Harewood, co. York, &c. as heir of Isabella, Dow. Countess of Albemarle (who had *d. s.p.* in 1293) grandaughter of Baldwin de Ripariis, by Margaret da. and heir of Warine Fitzgerold(c) of Harewood afsd. He was in the expedition to Flanders in 1539 and was sum. to Parl.(d) as a Baron (LORD LISLE) by writs from 19 Dec. (1311) 5 Ed. II. to 25 Feb. (1341/2) 16 Ed. III. directed either "*Roberto de Insula*" or "*Roberto del Isle.*" He *m.* Margaret, sometimes said to be da. of (—) PEVERELL. She *d.* before him. He (having taken religious orders a few months previously) *d.* 4 Jan. 1342/3 and was *bur.* at Grey Friars, London.

II. 1343. 2. JOHN (DE LISLE), LORD LISLE, or LORD LISLE DE ROUGEMONT, son, or more probably grandson(e) and h., aged 24 in 1343 when he *suc.* his predecessor; had (seven years previously) been granted the manor of Harewood to enable him to serve in the wars in which he, afterwards, was greatly distinguished; K.G., 1344, being one of the Founders(f) of that Order, receiving 28 Aug. 1346 (after the battle of Cressy) £200 a year to support the degree of a *Banneret.* He was sum. to Parl. (as LORD LISLE DE ROUGEMONT) from 25 Nov. (1350), 24 Ed. III., to 5 March (1353/4), 28 Ed. III., by writs directed "*Johanni de Insula de Rubeo Monte.*" He *m.* Maud. He *d.* (of wounds received in a foray in Gascony) 14 Oct. 1356.

III. 1356, to 1399? 3. ROBERT (DE LISLE), LORD LISLE DE ROUGEMONT, s. and h., aged 22(g) at his father's death in 1356. He was sum. to Parl. by writs 15 Dec. (1357), 31 Ed. III., and 20 Nov. (1360), 34 Ed. III., directed "*Roberto de Insula de Rubeo Monte,*" but never afterwards nor any of his posterity. In 1364 he settled Harewood on his sister, Elizabeth, and her husband, William DE ALDEBURGH, and in 1368 "he gave to the King 86 Knight's fees in divers counties of England,"(h) which transactions raise the inference that at

---

(a) This family are said to derive their name from the *isle* of Ely.

(b) This Warine was s. and h. of Sir Robert de L'Isle, of Rougemont, elder br. of Sir Gerard de L'Isle, of Mundford, co. Norfolk (who was grandfather of Gerard, 1st Lord Lisle of Kingston Lisle) both being sons of Robert de L'Isle, of Rougemont and Mundford afsd., by Alice, da. and h. of Henry Fitzgerold, Chamberlain to King Henry II., through which lady a considerable inheritance came into the Lisle family. See a good pedigree of this branch of the de L'Isle family and its connections in Baker's "*Northamptonshire,*" vol. i., pp. 619 and 443.

(c) This Warine was elder br. of Henry Fitzgerold, whose da. and h. Alice was (by Robert de L'Isle) greatgrandmother of the claimant, see note "b" next above.

(d) There is proof in the rolls of Parl. of his sitting.

(e) Robert, the 1st Lord Lisle, appears to have settled the manors of Rampton, Cottenham, &c., on "Alice, da. of Robert de Lisle," and others for life with rem. to "*John, son of Robert de Lisle*" and his heirs. Among the burials at Grey Friars is that of "*Dnus Robert de Lyle, fil. et hær. p'fati Dni,*" by which it may be conjectured that this Robert was the *eldest* son of the first Lord. He, however, must have *d.* v.p. probably leaving a s. and h. the said John (the remainder man in the settlement) who would thus be heir at law of his grandfather.

(f) See vol. i, p. 276, note "a," *sub* "Beauchamp," for a list of these.

(g) Esch., 30 Ed. III., No. 40; but "it is remarkable that the officers of the Prince of Wales, of whom the deceased had held the manor of Heyford Waryn in chief, considered the heir to be still a minor." [Beltz's "*Garter.*"]

(h) *Claus., 42 Ed III., m. 6, in dorso,* as quoted in Beltz's "Garter."

his death, said to be 1399, he had no legitimate issue.(a) If so any right to the Barony would be vested in the heirs of the body of his said sister, Elizabeth (who *d.* about 1377), by her husband, William, LORD ALDEBURGH. See that dignity *cr.* 1371.

LISLE [of Kingston Lisle].

Barony by Writ. I. 1357. *1.* SIR GERARD DE LISLE, of Kingston Lisle, in Sparsholt, Berks, and of Stowe, co. Northampton, s. and h. of Sir Warine de Lisle,(b) of the same, by Alice, da. of Henry (DE TYES), LORD TYES, and heir (1321) to her br., Henry, LORD TYES; *suc.* his father (who was hanged at Pomfret), March 1321/2; was aged 22 (1327), 1 Ed. III. when he was restored to his father's lands; served in the Scotch and French wars, and was sum. to Parl. as a Baron (LORD LISLE) by writ directed "*Gerardo de Insula*," 15 Dec. (1357), 31 Ed. III., but never afterwards. He *m.* firstly Alianora who was living 1333. He *m.* secondly, before Nov. 1354, Elizabeth, widow of Hugh ST. JOHN, of Basing, who *d.* 1337. He *m.* thirdly Ann. He *d.* 9 June 1360. *Esch.*, 34 Ed. III. His widow held Kislingbury, co. Northampton, in dower.

II. 1360. *2.* WARINE (DE LISLE), LORD LISLE, s. and h. by first wife, aged 27 at his father's death in 1360. He was greatly distinguished in the French wars and was made a Knight Banneret. He was sum. to Parl. from 6 April (1369), 43 Ed. III., to 24 March (1381/2), 5 Ric. II., by writs directed "*Warino de Insula*."(c) He *m.* firstly Margaret, da. and coheir of Sir William PIPARD, of Wingrave, Bucks. She was living 1376. He *m.* secondly Joan. He *d.* s.p.m.s.(d) 28 June 1382. *Esch.*, 6 Ric. II. His widow held Stowe, co. Northampton, in dower.

III. 1382. *3.* MARGARET (*de jure*) *suo jure* BARONESS LISLE, da. and h., *b.* about 1360, being aged 22 in 1382 and aged 30 in 1391; *m.* Nov. 1367 at Wingrave afsd. (but, being then aged but seven, remained apart for four years) Thomas (DE BERKELEY), LORD BERKELEY, who, in her right, appears to have

---

(a) "The inference raised by the transactions of 1364 and 1368 is that Robert, Lord Lisle, had not legit. issue. According, however, to a pedigree copied in the Visit. Book of Somersetshire, 1623, he had a son, Sir William Lisle, seated at Waterpery, Oxon, from whom a lineal descent is given down to George Lisle, of Compton Darvill, in the former county. Should the filiation of Sir William to the last Peer not be susceptible of proof the representation would be vested in the heirs of the body of Elizabeth Aldeburgh; for the brothers John [Lisle] and Sir William Lisle, of Cameldon, are asserted to have left no issue." Beltz's "*Garter*," p. 44. In the ped. in Baker's "Northamptonshire" (vol. i, p. 620), Robert, Lord Lisle, as also his son, William de Lisle, and his brother, Sir William Lisle, are all three stated to be living (1394), 17 Ric. II.

(b) This Warine was s. and h. of Sir Gerard de Lisle, of Stowe afsd. and of Mundford, co. Norfolk (*d.* about 1287), who was yr. br. of Sir Robert de Lisle, of Rougemont, Beds (see p. 112, note "b"), ancestor of the Lords Lisle de Rougemont.

(c) No local description whatever is given, thus falsifying the statement that the summons to Parl. was "by reason of the Lordship and manor of Kingston Lisle" as was recited in the patent creating the Barony of "Lisle of Kingston Lisle" in 1444. The following is the note on the subject of this summons by Sir N. Harris Nicolas slightly altered by Courthope, "The cause of Gerard de L'Isle having been sum. to Parl. in 1357 probably arose from his having inherited from his mother, Alice, sister and heir of Henry, Baron Tyes, *a right to the Barony of Tyes*; for although the last Baron Tyes was probably attainted in 1321 his heir, together with those of the other adherents of the Earl of Lancaster, was fully restored to his honours and possessions 1 Edw. III., and, as it has been satisfactorily established, that the *tenure* of the manor of Kingston L'Isle did not constitute a right to a writ of summons to Parliament, it is highly probable that the said Gerard was summoned *jure matris* notwithstanding that no mention of the Barony of Tyes is to be found in the writs directed to him."

(d) Gerard de Lisle, his only s. and h. ap., had *m.* in 1373 Ann, da. of Michael (Delapore), Earl of Suffolk, and *d.* v.p. and s.p.

been styled LORD LISLE,(a) after her father's death, from whom she inherited very considerable estates. She *d.* 20 March 1391/2, and he *d.* s.p.m., 13 July 1417, in his 65th year, both being *bur.* at Wotton under Edge, co. Glouc. See fuller particulars under "BERKELEY" Barony, *cr.* 1295, *sub* the 5th Lord.

IV. 1392, to 1420? 4. ELIZABETH (*de jure*), *suo jure* BARONESS LISLE, da. and h., aged 30 at her father's death in 1417 and then wife of Richard (BEAUCHAMP), EARL OF WARWICK, whom she *m.* (as his first wife) before May 1399, who *d.* 30 April 1439, leaving (by a second wife) male issue. See fuller particulars under "WARWICK" Earldom. She was living 1417 but *d.* s.p.m. before Nov. 1423 and was *bur.* in Kingswood Abbey, Wilts, when the *Barony* fell into *abeyance* between her three daughters and coheirs.(b)

Barony. I. 1444. Viscountcy. I. 1451. 1. Sir JOHN TALBOT, 4th s. of John (TALBOT), 1st EARL OF SHREWSBURY, being s. and h. of his *second* wife, Margaret, da. of Richard (BEAUCHAMP), 12th EARL OF WARWICK, which Margaret was 1st da. and coheir of that Earl's *first* wife, Elizabeth, *suo jure* BARONESS LISLE, abovenamed, was *b.* about 1423, and, having been *knighted*, was *cr.*, 26 July (1444), 22 Hen. VI., LORD AND BARON OF LISLE ("*Dominum et Baronem de Lisle*") with rem. to his heirs *being Lords of the manor of Kingston Lisle*, Berks,(c) it being recited in this charter (one of the most extraordinary on record) as a fact(d) that the grantee's ancestor "Warine de

---

(a) His da., the Countess of Warwick, is called on her monument "filia et hæres Thomæ, nuper *Dni* de Berkeley et de *Lisle*." See vol. i, p. 329, note "b," *sub* "Berkeley."

(b) See vol. i, p. 329, note "c," *sub* "Berkeley," as to these three ladies, *viz.* (1) Margaret, Countess of Shrewsbury (2) Eleanor, Baroness de Roos, and (3) Elizabeth, Baroness Latimer. In 1824 the coheirs to the *Barony of Lisle* [*cr.* 1357] are set forth in the case presented to the House of Lords on behalf of Sir John Shelley Sydney, Bart. (who petitioned for the determination of the abeyance in his favour) as under—(I) "Sir John Shelley Sydney, Bart., as sole heir of the body of Margaret, Countess of Shrewsbury, above mentioned (II) George, Earl of Essex, Sir Henry Hunloke, Bart., and Charlotte, Baroness de Ros, as coheirs of the body of Eleanor, wife of Thomas, Lord Roos (III) Hugh, Duke of Northumberland, Winchcomb Henry Howard Hartley, Esq., James Knightley, Esq., Grey Jermyn Grove, Esq., George William Villiers, Esq., Montague, Earl of Abingdon, Sir Francis Burdett, Bart., William Fermor, Esq., and John, Lord Rollo, as coheirs of the body of Elizabeth, Lady Latimer. These individuals were, also, it is presumed, coheirs of the body [*sic*] of the *Barony of Berkeley* under the writ of summons to Thomas de Berkeley, 23 June (23 Edw. I.), 1295, being coheirs of the body of the said Thomas de Berkeley." [Courthope.] The petition was, however, without success, for "in 1826 the House of Lords resolved that there did not appear sufficient ground to advise His Majesty to allow the claim of the Petitioner. The claimant's case was considered to have failed for want of proof that either of his ancestors had ever taken their seats and sat in Parl. a fact necessary to be established by the Records of Parl. in order to give a dignity *of inheritance* to a writ of summons." See a pamphlet on "*Barons by tenure*" by Sir C. G. Young, Garter. The claimant's only son, however, received (as a consolation) a peerage in 1835, *viz.*, the Barony of DE L'ISLE AND DUDLEY OF PENSHURST. His descent from Gerard, 1st Lord Lisle (1357), was thro' the families of Shelley, Perry, Sydney, Dudley, Grey, Talbot, Beauchamp, Berkeley, and De Lisle. See vol. iii, p. 53, note "a," under "De L'Isle" &c., Barony, *cr.* 1835.

(c) See vol. ii, p. 14, note "b," *sub* "Breadalbane," for a curious proviso (of like nature) in the creation of that Earldom [S.] in 1681 *viz.*, that in the event of the non-possession of the estate of Glenurchy certain of the dignities created should cease.

(d) This assertion, says Nicolas, is "satisfactorily proved, by the Lords' Committee on the Dignity of a Peer of the Realm in their Third Report, to have been entirely without foundation, for not only had the said manor never been held *in capite* of the Crown, but a period of above sixty years had elapsed (*viz.*, from 23 Edw. I. to 31 Edw. III.), after writs of summons were generally issued, before the family of L'Isle,

L'Isle and his ancestors, by reason of the lordship and manor of Kingston L'Isle, had from time whereof the memory of man was not to the contrary,(a) the name and dignity of Baron and Lord L'Isle, and by that name had seat in Parliament, &c., as other Barons of the Realm had."(b) The patent (which tho' *in fact* it created a *new* Barony with a new limitation, was apparently *meant* to terminate the *abeyance* of the *old* Barony *cr.* by the writ of 1357) contained also a clause that the grantee should have the precedency(c) held by "the said Warine or any other person heretofore having the afsd. Barony." He was accordingly sum. to Parl. from 13 Jan. (1444/5), 23 Hen. VI., to 5 Sep. (1450), 29 Hen. VI., by writs directed "*Johanni Talbot de Lisle, Militi.*" He was subsequently *cr.*, 30 Oct. 1451, VISCOUNT LISLE, with the usual rem. to the heirs male of his body. P.C., 1453; Capt. of an Armada for Aquitaine, March 1453. He *m.* Joan, widow of Richard STAFFORD, da. and coheir of Sir Thomas CHEDDER, of Chedder, co. Somerset. He was slain (with his father) 20 July 1453, at the battle of Chatillon. His widow *d.* 15 July 1464.

II. 1453, to 1470. 2. THOMAS (TALBOT), VISCOUNT LISLE [1451], and (being Lord of the manor of Kingston Lisle) BARON LISLE [1444], only s. and h., *b.* 1443; *suc. to the peerage.* 1453; K.B., 3 May 1465. He *m.* Sep. 1466 Margaret, yst. da. of William (HERBERT), 1st EARL OF PEMBROKE, by Anne, sister of Walter, LORD FERRERS, da. of Sir Walter DEVEREUX. He *d.* s.p., 20 March 1469/70, being slain in a skirmish (at Nibley, co. Gloucester), with the Berkeley family, from whom he claimed certain lands in right of his grandmother, Margaret, Countess of Shrewsbury, abovenamed. His widow, however, came to terms with the Berkeleys, 6 Oct. 1472, and *m.* shortly afterwards Sir Henry BODRUGAN, of Bodrugan, co. Cornwall, who was convicted of treason 9 Nov. 1487, but escaped abroad, and *d.* before 1503. She predeceased him. On the death of the Viscount in 1470 the *Viscountcy of Lisle* became *extinct* while the *Barony of Lisle* fell into *abeyance.*(d)

* * * * * * *

---

tenants of the manor of Kingston L'Isle, were ever sum. to Parl. Many arguments might be adduced to support the conclusion stated [in note "d" next below] relative to this dignity, but they are rendered useless, even if the limits of this work permitted their insertion, by the statement of the case in the Report of the Lords' Committee just cited, p. 191, *et seq.*, and by the opinion of the great legal authorities [therein] referred to. It is, therefore, sufficient to remark that this singular creation probably arose from the powerful influence possessed by the Earl of Shrewsbury in a reign when more anomalies connected with dignities are to be found than under any preceding or subsequent monarch."

(a) A similar recital "*entirely without foundation*" is in the judgment of 1433, confirming the petition of John Fitz Alan for the Earldom of Arundel, wherein it is recited "that Richard Fitz Alan was seized of the Castle, Honour, and Lordship [of Arundel] in fee [and] that *by reason of his possession* thereof he was, without other reason or creation, EARL OF ARUNDEL, &c." The fallacy of this statement has been ably exposed by Mr. J. Horace Round in his "*Geoffrey de Mandeville*" (pp. 316—325), who shews conclusively that the assertion that William de Albini (ancestor of the said Richard) became Earl of Arundel (1135-39) "in virtue of his possession of Arundel Castle is *pure assumption* and nothing else," and that, in fact, as to this Earldom "there is nothing to distinguish it in its origin from the other Earldoms of the day."

(b) A copy of each of the patents which create the Barony of Lisle in 1444 and in 1457 is in Nicolas's "*Report on the claim to the Barony of L'Isle*" (1829), pp. 32-37. Both of these Baronies are among the 16 which were *cr.* by patent before the 16th century, for a list of which see vol. iii, p. 31, note "e," *sub* "Daubeny."

(c) See vol. i, p. 229, note "a," *sub* "Banbury," as to the prerogative of the Crown as to the precedency of Peers.

(d) The coheirs were his two sisters of whom (1) Margaret, wife of Sir George Vere, *d.* s.p. within five years afterwards when (2) Elizabeth, the survivor, inherited the Barony. Sir Harris Nicolas makes the following observations on this subject. "It is a very doubtful point into what state the Barony then [*i.e.*, on the death of the 2d Viscount in 1470] fell, and upon a question so abstruse, and which has been the subject of so much discussion, the Editor scarcely feels himself justified in hazarding an opinion. In the Third Report of the Lords' Committee on the Dignity of a Peer of the Realm

Barony.
III. 1475,
Viscountcy.
III. 1483.

3 and *1.* Elizabeth, *suo jure* BARONESS LISLE, only surv. da., became by the death s.p. in or before 1475 of her only sister (Margaret, wife of Sir George VERE) sole heir to her father, and, as such was (being also in possession of the manor of Kingston Lisle) *entitled* to the *Barony of Lisle* under the terms of its creation in 1444. She *m.* SIR EDWARD GREY, 2d s. of Edward (GREY), LORD FERRERS DE GROBY by Elizabeth, *suo jure* BARONESS FERRERS DE GROBY. He was, accordingly *cr.* by patent[a] 14 March 1474/5, LORD AND BARON OF LISLE ("*Dominum et Baronem de Lisle*") with rem. to his heirs by the said Elizabeth, his wife, being possessed of the manor of Kingston Lisle[b] with a clause (as in the patent of 1444) of the ancient precedency.[c] About eight years subsequently, having distinguished himself in the wars with France, he was, *cr.* 28 June 1483, VISCOUNT LISLE with the usual limitation to heirs male of his body, but "with place and precedence of Thomas Talbot, late Viscount Lisle."[d] He was bearer of the Rod with the Dove at the Coronation of Richard III., 7 July 1483.[e] His wife the *suo jure* Baroness *d.* 8 Sep. 1487, and was *bur.* at Astley, co. Warwick. He *m.* secondly, Jane, widow of Sir Robert DROPE, Lord Mayor of London (1474-75), who *d.* 21 Jan. 1487. He *d.* 17 July 1492 and was *bur.* at Astley afsd. Will pr. 26 Aug. 1492. His widow was *bur.* (with her first husband) at St. Michael's, Cornhill. Will dat. 8 Aug 1499, pr. 21 May 1500.

Viscountcy.
IV. 1492,
to
1504.
Barony.
IV. 1492.

2 and *4.* JOHN (GREY), VISCOUNT LISLE [1483], and BARON LISLE [1444 and 1475], only s. and h., *b.* 1481; *suc.* to the Viscountcy, &c., 17 July 1492, having, possibly, been entitled *jure matris* to the Barony [1444] since her death in 1487; K.B., 18 Feb. 1503. He *m.* Muriel, da. of Thomas (HOWARD), 2d DUKE OF NORFOLK, by his first wife, Elizabeth, da. and h. of Sir Frederick TILNEY. He *d.* s.p.m. 9 Sep. (20 Hen. VII.), 1504, when the *Viscountcy of Lisle* again became *extinct.* Will dat. 6 Sep. 1504. His widow *m.* Sir Thomas KNYVETT, K.B., of Buckenham, Norfolk, who *d.* between 15 Aug. and 13 Dec. 1512. She was *bur.* in the Friar's church at Greenwich 1512. Will dat. 13 Dec. 1512, pr. 12 Jan. 1512/3.

[p. 191, et seq.], the case is most ably stated, and to it he refers in support of the following conclusions; 1st, that the patent to John Talbot in 1444 did not (though evidently intended so to do) affect the Barony created by the writ to Gerard de L'Isle [1357], 31 Ed. III., and which consequently still remained in abeyance, but created a *new* Barony, descendible according to the provisions of the patent; and 2ndly, with respect to the extremely difficult question, 'In whom is that Barony now vested?' it is to be observed that, according to the high authority of Lord Chief Justice Coke [*Co. Litt.*, 27], and of Justice Blackstone [*Commentaries*, vol. ii, p. 109], John Talbot and his heirs, under the patent, had *only a base or qualified fee* in that dignity, and 'that the instant he or his heirs quitted the seigniory of this manor the dignity was at an end.' On the death of Thomas, 2d Viscount, in 1469, s.p., his two sisters became his heirs, *viz.*, Margaret, the wife of Sir George Vere, Knt., and Elizabeth, hereafter mentioned, when it is presumed that the Barony of L'Isle became *suspended*; for although the said Elizabeth was possessed of the manor she was not *sole* heir of John Talbot, her father, and consequently had not the two constituent qualifications necessary to entitle her to the dignity. On the death of her sister, Lady Vere, however, s.p., she appears to have become legally seised of the Barony as is recited in the patent of 14 Mar. (15 Edw. IV.) 1475, granted to her husband, Edward Grey."

(a) See p. 115, note "b" next above.

(b) The patent was in effect the same as that of 1444, but contained recitals of the devolution of the manor of Kingston Lisle, from Warine de Lisle to Elizabeth Grey, after the death of her sister, Margaret de Vere, and how that the said Warine "et omnes Antecessores sui, *ratione dominii et manerii prædictorum*, nomen et dignitatem Baronis et Domini de Lisle, a tempore, quo memoria hominum non existit, optinuerunt et habuerunt."

(c) See p. 115, note "c."

(d) See "Creations, 1483-1646" in ap. 47th Rep. D. K. Pub. Records. As to the precedency hereby granted, see p. 115, note "c."

(e) See a list of the 45 Peers there present in vol. iii, p. 8, note "c," *sub* "Dacre."

V. 1504. Viscountcy. V. 1513, to 1523.

5 and 1. ELIZABETH, *suo jure* BARONESS LISLE [1444 and 1475], da. and h., and as such (being also in possession of the manor of Kingston Lisle) entitled to this Barony; aged eight weeks in 1504. She was betrothed to SIR CHARLES BRANDON, K.G., who accordingly(a) was *cr.*, 15 May 1513, VISCOUNT LISLE with rem. "to the heirs male of the body of Elizabeth Grey, VISCOUNTESS(b) LISLE, by the said Charles begotten." The marriage not taking place, he, on 20 April (14 Hen. VIII.), 1523, *surrendered the patent of the Viscountcy of Lisle,*(c) having previously been *cr.* DUKE OF SUFFOLK (see that title *cr.* 1514, *ex.* 1551.) The *suo jure* Baroness *m.* (as his first wife) after 1 June 1515, Henry (COURTENAY), EARL OF DEVON (*cr.* in 1525 MARQUESS OF EXETER), who was beheaded 9 Jan. 1538/9, aged 40. She, however, *d.* s.p. and under age between 31 March and 12 May 1519,(d) when the *Barony of Lisle* fell into *abeyance.*(e)

* * * * * * *

Barony. VI. 1519, to 1540? Viscountcy. VI. 1523, to 1542.

6 and 1. ELIZABETH, *suo jure* BARONESS LISLE [1444 and 1475], aunt and eventually sole heir, who as heir to the grantees [1444 and 1475] of that Barony (being in possession(f) of the manor of Kingston Lisle) was entitled to that Barony. She *m.* firstly, about 1495, Edmund DUDLEY (the well known Minister of Henry VII.) who was beheaded on Tower hill, 28 August (2 Hen. VIII.), 1510. She *m.* secondly, 12 Nov. 1511, ARTHUR PLANTAGENET, illegit. son of King Edward IV. He was *b.* about 1470. His mother's name is unknown; by some said to be the "Lady Elizabeth LUCY," by others the notorious Jane SHORE, and by others one Elizabeth WAITE, he himself being at first known as "*Arthur Waite.*" He appears to have been unnoticed till the accession of (his

(a) Compare the creation in 1477 of Richard (Plantagenet), Duke of York, as Duke of Norfolk, &c., on his betrothal to Ann, the da. and h. of John (Mowbray), Duke of Norfolk.

(b) "Ad tunc Vicecomitissæ Lysle," but the word Viscountess is apparently a mistake for Baroness. The patent is printed in Nicolas's "Report on the claim to the Barony of L'Isle," p. 409.

(c) The following note is on the margin of the inrollment of this patent. "The inrollment of these letters patent is vacated because that the within written Charles, now Duke of Suffolk, on the 20 April [1523], 14 Hen. VIII., surrendered into the hands of the said Lord the King his letters patent afsd. freely of his own accord and absolutely to be cancelled. Therefore the inrollment is cancelled and made void." *Pat. Rolls,* 15 Hen. VIII., part i, m. 12.

(d) See F. M. Nichols' "*Lawford Hall*" (p. 376) where the dates of all the former possessors thereof are most carefully elaborated.

(e) The coheirs were her aunts, the daughters of Edward (Grey), 1st Viscount Lisle, *viz.* (1) Anne, living 20 Hen. VII., as the wife of Sir John Willoughby, of Wollaton, Notts, but who *d.* s.p. before 1523 (2) Elizabeth, the survivor, who inherited the Barony as in the text. Muriel, another da., who was first wife of Henry (Stafford), Earl of Wiltshire [1510], had *d.* s.p. before her niece.

(f) "*Vide* 'Case of the Barony of L'Isle 1790,' drawn up by the Hon. Hume Campbell setting forth the claim of Abraham Atkins, Esq., to the said dignity as tenant of the manor of Kingston Lisle and consequently assignee of John Talbot, 1st Viscount L'Isle. It appears that this case escaped the notice of the Lords' Committee; for their Report states that '*they had not discovered* whether the manor belonged to the three coheirs of Elizabeth Grey or to any of them or to whom it then belonged,' p. 209. And again, 'No person seised of the manor has ever, as far as the Committee have been informed, pretended to be entitled to the dignity of Baron de L'Isle by virtue of such seisin,' p. 210. The latter of these statements is contradicted by the case just cited, which not only contains the information relative to the descent of the manor of Kingston L'Isle here given, but was compiled in favour of a claimant who had no other pretensions whatever than the tenure of the manor in question, and, as such tenant, assignee of John Talbot, to whom the singular patent was granted by Henry VI. After Sir John Dudley sold the said manor to Mr. Hyde it descended in

ineal cousin), Henry VIII., by whom he was *knighted*, 14 Oct. 1513; Sheriff of Hants, 1513-14, and was, in consequence of his abovenamed marriage, *cr.*, 25 April 1523 (after the resignation of the dignity on the 20th inst. by the Duke of Suffolk) VISCOUNT LISLE with rem. to the heirs male of [*Qy.* ? his body, by] the body of Elizabeth, his wife,(a) the heiress of the Lisle family, being invested(b) the 27th following; K.G., 23 April 1524; Vice Admiral of England, 1525; First Commissioner to Francis I., King of France, with the Garter, who was invested at Paris, 10 Nov. 1527; Gov. of Calais, 1533-40; Pantler at the Coronation of Anne Boleyn, 1 June 1533; P.C., 1540. Being suspected of a design of betraying Calais to the French, he was imprisoned in the Tower from April 1540 till his death there 3 March 1541/2, which was said to be caused by joy at the King having ordered his release on being convinced of his innocence. He was *bur.* there. His wife, Elizabeth, the *suo jure* Baroness, who was living 27 March 1538, *d.* before him, probably about 1540, and on her death (her son and heir ap. having sold his reversion in the manor of Kingston Lisle) the *Barony of Kingston Lisle* became (under the peculiar limitations of its creation in 1444 and

---

succession to John Hyde, Esq., who died seised thereof in May 1745, and his widow in the following year sold the same to Abraham Atkins, of Clapham, in Surrey, Esq., the possessor when the case was printed in 1790." [Nicolas.] This claim was printed for private use only and it does not appear that Mr. Atkins pursued the subject by any formal claim [addressed] to the Crown. See Sir C. G. Young's pamphlet on "*Barons by tenure.*"

(a) The limitation intended is not very clear when the circumstances of the case are considered. John Dudley was, at the date thereof, the eldest son and heir male *apparent* of the said Elizabeth and became on her death (about 1540) her (*actual*) heir. The remainder of the creation of "Arthur Plantagenet, Knt.," to the Viscountcy of L'Isle as set out in (that most useful and valuable work compiled by Mr. R. Douglas Trimmer) the "*Creations of Peers and Baronets*" (ap. to 47th Report of D. K. Pub. Records) is "*Limitation to the heirs male of the body of Elizabeth, his wife*, sister and heir of John Grey, late Viscount L'Isle." If this be the true rendering of the patent, not only would Sir Arthur's creation be almost tantamount to a life peerage, but most certainly on his death (he died without male issue in 1542) the said John Dudley would, as heir male of the body of the said Elizabeth, his mother, have inherited the Viscountcy of Lisle under the creation of 1523. So far, however, was that from being the case that on 12 March 1542/3, he, under the name of "John Dudley" [only] is created [*de novo*] "Viscount L'Isle" with the usual rem. to heirs male of his body. Mr. Trimmer, with his usual courtesy, re-investigated the matter and (27 Oct. 1892), writes as follows, "I have referred to the Patent Roll [No. 642] for 15 Hen. VIII. and the words of the patent of creation appear to bear out the statement in my inventory as to the limitation of succession to the title in question and are as follows, '*Hend. et tenend. eandem statum* [&c., &c.], *prefato Arthuro et hered. masculis de corpore Elizabetha uxoris ejus, sororis et hered. Johis. Grey, nuper Vicecomitis Lysle, procreatis sive procreandis, Volentes et per presentes concedentes pro nobis hered. et successoribus nostris, quod prefatus Arthurus et hered. masculi predictæ Elizabethæ, nomen* [&c., &c.], *predict. successive gerant et habeant et eorum quilibet gerat et habeat et per nomen Vicecomitis Lysle successive vocitentur et nuncupentur et eorum quilibet vocitetur et nuncupetur. Quodque idem Arthurus et hered. masculi predictæ Elizabethæ successive Vicecomit. Lysle in omnibus teneantur.*'" The Editor of this work, not being satisfied (considering the position of the parties) as to what should be the correct construction of the above, submitted the matter to one most competent to judge thereon (Mr. J. Horace Round) who replied thereto as under, "On full consideration I am of opinion that tho' the patent of 1523 if strictly construed and if taken apart from the relevant facts *would* limit the dignity to the heirs male of the body of Elizabeth (on the analogy of patents granted to males) yet that, bearing in mind all the *facts* of the case, one must read it as (clumsily) expressing a limitation to the heirs male of the *body of Arthur, by his wife, Elizabeth*, the object evidently being to exclude his heirs by any *other* wife. We must, therefore, read '*prefato Arthuro et heredibus masculis* [*suis*] *de corpore Elizabethæ, uxoris ejus.*'"

(b) Viscount Lisle and the Lords Berkeley, Sandys, and Vaux, were invested 27 April 1523, at Bridewell Palace.

1475) *extinguished*. The Viscount is sometimes said to have *m.* secondly Honor, widow of Sir John Bassett, da. of (—) Granville. He *d.* s.p.m.([a]) as afsd. when the *Viscountcy of Lisle* [1523] is generally considered to have become *extinct*.([b])

Viscountcy. VII. 1543, to 1553. John Dudley, s. and h. of Elizabeth, *suo jure* Baroness Lisle, by Edmond Dudley, her first husband, both abovenamed, was *b.* 1502, sold in his mother's lifetime, 27 March 1538 (to William Hyde) his reversion on the estate of Kingston Lisle, whereby when, on her death, he became heir to the grantees of the Barony of Lisle [1444 and 1475] he failed to comply with the condition of the grants thereof and consequently to be entitled thereto.([c]) Shortly after the death of his step father (the last mentioned Viscount Lisle) he was *cr.*, 12 March 1542/3, VISCOUNT LISLE; K.G., 23 April 1543; *cr.*, 16 Feb. 1546/7, EARL OF WARWICK, and on 11 Oct. 1551, DUKE OF NORTHUMBERLAND. *Beheaded* 22 Aug. 1553, when, having been attainted, *all his honours* became *forfeited*. See fuller particulars under "Northumberland" Dukedom, *cr.* 1551, *forfeited* 1553.

Barony. I. 1561, to 1590. Lord Ambrose Dudley, 4th but 1st surv. son of John, Duke of Northumberland, Earl of Warwick, and Viscount Lisle, next abovenamed, *b.* about 1528; was restored in blood, 7 March 1557/8, and was *cr.*, 25 Dec. 1561, BARON LISLE (with the usual rem.) and on the next day (with an extended rem.) EARL OF WARWICK. He *d.* s.p., 21 Feb. 1589/90, when *all his honours* became *extinct*. See fuller particulars under "Warwick" Earldom, *cr.* 1561, *ex.* 1590.

Viscountcy. VIII. 1605. 1. Robert (Sydney), 1st Baron Sydney of Penshurst, 2d but 1st surv. s. and h. male of Sir Henry Sydney, K.G., thrice Lord Deputy of Ireland, by Mary, sister (whose issue([d]) became heir) of Ambrose (Dudley), Earl of Warwick and Baron Lisle, da. of John (Dudley), Duke of Northumberland, &c., and Viscount Lisle, both next above described, was *cr.*, 4 May 1605, VISCOUNT LISLE, and on 2 Aug. 1618, EARL OF LEICESTER. See "Leicester" Earldom, *cr.* 1618, *extinct* (together with the *Viscountcy of Lisle* and the Barony of Sydney of Penshurst) on death of the 7th Earl 1743.

LISLE, see De Lisle and Dudley of Penshurst.([e])

([a]) He had three daughters, who, tho' coheirs of their father [a bastard] in no way represented their mother nor (of course) the families of Beauchamp and Teyes from whom she descended; yet because George Monck, the famous General, was a descendant (not even a representative) of one of these Ladies he was *cr.* (*inter alia*) Baron *Beauchamp* and *Teyes* and (not improbably for the same reason) Duke of *Albemarle*. See vol. i, p. 58, note "a," *sub* "Albemarle."

([b]) See p. 118, note "a."

([c]) "For" (says Nicolas) "according to Coke and Blackstone the two requisite constituents of the title to the said dignity then became and have ever since continued divided, whence it is concluded, on those high authorities, that the Barony is *extinct*. How far the dignity would be *revived*, in the barely possible contingency of the two qualifications of tenant of the said manor and lordship, and sole heir of the body of John Talbot, being again united in one person, it is not now necessary to inquire." See p. 117, note "f," as to the claim in 1790 of Mr. Atkins, as tenant of the manor of Kingston Lisle, to the Barony of Lisle.

([d]) This assumes the illegitimacy of Sir Robert Dudley, the son of the well known Earl of Leicester.

([e]) The grantee of this mixed title (conferred in 1835) was thro' the families of Shelley, Perry, Sydney, Dudley, Grey, Talbot, Beauchamp, Berkeley, and L'Isle, a coheir of the Barony of Lisle, cr. by the writ of 1357, for the determination of the *abeyance* of which his father had petitioned in 1824. See vol. iii, p. 153, note "a," *sub* "De Lisle."

LISLE OF MOUNTNORTH.

Barony [I.] I. 1758. 1. JOHN LYSAGHT, of Mountnorth, co. Cork, s. and h of Nicholas LYSAGHT, of the same (Col. of a troop of horse in King William's regiment at the battle of the Boyne), by Grace, yst. da. of Col. Thomas HOLMES, of Kilmallock, was admitted to the Middle Temple, 19 April 1721; was M.P. for Charleville, 1721-58, and was cr., 18 Sep. 1758, BARON LISLE OF MOUNTNORTH, co. Cork [I.], taking his seat 16 Oct. 1759. He m. firstly, 17 Dec. 1725, Catharine, 3d da. and coheir of Joseph DEANE, of Crumlin, co. Dublin, Ch. Baron of the Exchequer [I.], by Margaret, sister of Henry, 1st EARL OF SHANNON [I.], da. of the Hon. Henry BOYLE, of Castle Martyr, co. Cork. She d. 5 July 1743. He m. secondly, in 1746, Elizabeth, da. of Edward MOORE, of Mooresfort, co. Tipperary. He d. 15 July 1781. His widow d. s.p.m. Nov. 1788.

II. 1781. 2. JOHN (LYSAGHT), BARON LISLE OF MOUNTNORTH [I.], s. and h. by first wife; was M.P. for Castlemartyr, 1758-60, and for co. Cork, 1765-68. He m. in 1778 Mary Anne, da. of George CONNOR, of Ballybracken, co. Cork. He d. 9 Jan. 1798. His widow d. 19 Oct. 1815.

III. 1798. 3. JOHN (LYSAGHT), BARON LISLE OF MOUNTNORTH [I.], s. and h., b. 6 Aug. 1781. He m., 14 Sep. 1809, at 229 Piccadilly, St. James' Westm., Sarah, da. of William GIBB, of Inverness. He d. s.p., 26 Nov. 1834, in Hants, aged 53. Will pr. Dec. 1834. His widow d. at Millbrook cottage, Southampton, 20 Sep. 1857, aged 95. Her will pr. Dec. 1857.

IV. 1834. 4. GEORGE (LYSAGHT), BARON LISLE OF MOUNTNORTH [I.], br. and h., b. 6 June 1783. He m. firstly, 11 Oct. 1810, Elizabeth, 1st da. of Samuel KNIGHT, of Milton, co. Cambridge. She d. 12 April 1815. He m. secondly, 14 Oct. 1816, Elizabeth Anne, 2d da. of John Davy FOULKES, of Tiverton, Devon. She, who was b. 1790, d. 1 Nov. 1825. He m. thirdly, 16 Aug. 1836, Elizabeth, 3d da. of John CHURCH, of Bedford Place, Bloomsbury, Midx. She d. at Exeter 8 April 1855. He d. 7 July 1868, aged 85, at Kenton, near Exeter.

V. 1868. 5. JOHN ARTHUR (LYSAGHT), BARON LISLE OF MOUNTNORTH [I.], s. and h. by first wife; b. 12 Oct. 1811, at Pilton (near Barnstaple), Devon. He m., 6 March 1837, at Antony, co. Cornwall, Henrietta Anne, sister of his step mother, 5th da. of John CHURCH, abovenamed. She d. April 1860.

Family Estates.—These, in 1883, were under 2,000 acres.

LISMORE OF SHANBALLY and LISMORE OF SHANBALLY CASTLE.

Barony [I.] I. 1785. 1. CORNELIUS O'CALLAGHAN, of Shanbally, co. Tipperary, 1st s. and h. of Thomas O'CALLAGHAN, of the same, by his first wife, Sarah, da. of John DAVIS, of Carrickfergus, co. Antrim, by Anne, da. of William (CAULFEILD), 2d VISCOUNT CHARLEMONT [I.], was b. 7 Jan. 1740/1; M.P. for Fethard (in four Parls.) 1761 to 1785, when, on 27 June 1785, he was cr. BARON LISMORE OF SHANBALLY, co. Tipperary [I.], taking his seat on the 30th. He m., 13 Dec. 1774, Frances, sister of William, 1st BARON PONSONBY OF IMOKILLY, 2d da. of the Rt. Hon. John PONSONBY (2d s. of Brabazon, 1st EARL OF BESSBOROUGH [I.]), by Elizabeth, da. of William (CAVENDISH), 3d DUKE OF DEVONSHIRE. He d. 12 July 1797, aged 56. Will pr. April 1798. His widow, who was b. 18 Feb. 1757, d. 25 May 1827.

II. 1797. Viscountcy [I.] I. 1806. Barony [U.K.] I. 1838. — 2 and 1. CORNELIUS (O'CALLAGHAN), BARON LISMORE OF SHANBALLY [I.], s. and h., b. 2 Oct. 1775; suc. to the peerage [I.], 12 July 1797; was cr., 30 May 1806, VISCOUNT LISMORE OF SHANBALLY, co. Tipperary [I.]; P.C. [I.], 1835; was cr., 6 July 1838,(a) BARON LISMORE OF SHANBALLY CASTLE, co. Tipperary [U.K.]; Lord Lieut. of Tipperary, 1851. He m., 11 Aug. 1808, Eleanor, sister of Walter, 1st MARQUESS OF ORMONDE [I.], yst. da. of John (BUTLER), EARL OF ORMONDE AND OSSORY [I.], by Frances Susanna Anne, da. and h. of John (WANDESFORD), EARL WANDESFORD [I.] She, who was b. in 1788, was divorced by act of Parl. 1826 (b) He d. 30 May 1857, aged 83, at Shanbally Castle.

Viscountcy [I.] and Barony [U.K.] II. Barony [I.] III. 1857. — 2 and 3. GEORGE PONSONBY (O'CALLAGHAN), VISCOUNT LISMORE OF SHANBALLY [1806], and BARON LISMORE OF SHANBALLY [1785], in the peerage of Ireland, also BARON LISMORE OF SHANBALLY CASTLE [1838], 3d but only surv. s. and h.,(c) b. 16 March 1815; sometime an officer in the 17th Lancers; suc. to the peerage, 30 May 1857; Lord Lieut. of co. Tipperary, 1857-85; Hon. Col. 4th Batt. Royal Irish Militia. He m., 25 July 1839, Mary, 2d da. of John George NORBURY.

Family Estates.—These, in 1883, consisted of 34,945 acres in co. Tipperary, 6,067 in co. Cork, and 1,194 in co. Limerick. *Total* 42,206 acres, worth £16,354 a year. *Principal Residence*. Shanbally Castle, near Clogheen, co. Tipperary.

LISNASKEA.

i.e., "FERMANAGH OF LISNASKEA, co. Fermanagh," Barony (*Crichton*), cr. 1876; see "ERNE" Earldom [I.], cr. 1789, under the 3d holder thereof.

LISSANOURE.

i.e., "MACARTNEY OF LISSANOURE, co. Antrim," Barony [I.] (*Macartney*), cr. 1776; see "MACARTNEY" Earldom [I.], cr. 1794; ex. 1806.

LISSON EARL.

i.e., "EARLSFORT OF LISSON EARL, co. Tipperary," Barony [I.] (*Scott*), cr. 1784; see "CLONMELL" Earldom [I.], cr. 1793.

LISTOWEL, and ENNISMORE AND LISTOWEL.

Viscountcy [I.] I. 1816. Earldom [I.] I. 1822. — 1. WILLIAM HARE, of Ennismore, co. Kerry, 1st s. of Richard HARE,(e) of the same, by Margaret, or Catherine, da. of Samuel MAYLOR, was b. Sep. 1751; M.P. for Cork, 1796-97 and for Athy, 1798—1800, and was cr., 30 July 1800,(f) BARON ENNISMORE, co. Kerry [I.], and subsequently, 22 Jan. 1816, VISCOUNT ENNISMORE AND LISTOWEL [I.], and finally, 5 Feb. 1822, EARL OF LISTOWEL [I.] He m., 30 May 1772, Mary, da. of Henry

(a) This was one of the Coronation Peerages of Queen Victoria for a list of which see vol. ii, p. 145, note "b," *sub* "Carew."

(b) She d. at Sorrento, near Naples, 27 Sep. 1859, aged 71.

(c) Of his elder brothers (1) the Hon. Cornelius O'Callaghan, 12th Lancers, d. unm. in London, 16 Aug. 1849, aged 40, and (2) the Hon. William Frederick O'Callaghan, Capt. 44th Foot, d. unm. in India in 1836.

(d) His eldest and only surv. son, the Hon. George Cornelius Gerald O'Callaghan, b. 3 Nov. 1846, m. 24 Dec. 1874, at Umballa, in India, Rosina, widow of Edward Charles Follett, and d. s.p. and v.p. in March 1885.

(e) See "*Her. and Gen.*," vol. ii, pp. 473—487, for some astute remarks on "Hare of Stow Bardolph and *the ancestry of Lord Listowel*" by "G. H. D."

(f) One of the 26 peerages [I.] conferred that year. See list thereof in vol. i, p. 166, note "a," *sub* "Ashtown."

WRIXON, of Ballygiblin, co. Cork, by Anna, da. of William MANSFIELD. She *d.* 5 and was *bur.* 11 Aug. 1810 (as "*Baroness Ennismore*") aged 59, in Westm. Abbey. He *m.*, secondly, 5 March 1812, Anne, 2d da. of John LATHAM, of Meldrum, co. Tipperary. He *d.* at Kingston House, Knightsbridge, 13, and was *bur.* 24 July 1837, aged 87, at Westm. Abbey afsd. Will pr. Aug. 1837. His widow *d.* s.p., 2 Oct. 1859, aged 81, at 39 Eaton square.

[RICHARD HARE, *styled* VISCOUNT ENNISMORE (since 1822), 1st s. and h. ap. by first wife. *b.* 20 March 1773; M.P. for Athy, 1798—1800, and for co. Cork, 1812-27. He *m.*, 10 June 1797, Catherine Bridget, 1st da. of Robert (DILLON), 1st BARON CLONBROCK [I.] He *d.* v.p., 24 Sep. 1827, aged 54. His widow, who was *b.* 11 Dec. 1776, *d.* 13 Oct. 1828.]

II. 1837. 2. WILLIAM (HARE), EARL OF LISTOWEL, &c. [I.], grandson and h., being s. and h. of Richard Hare, *styled* VISCOUNT ENNISMORE, by Catharine Bridget, his wife, both abovenamed; *b.* 22 Sep. 1801, at Bally-Ellis, near Mallow; M.P. for co. Kerry, 1826-30; styled VISCOUNT ENNISMORE after his father's death in 1827 till he *suc. to the peerage* [I.] in 1837; Vice Admiral of Munster, 1838; M.P. for St. Albans, Feb. 1841 to July 1847; one of the Lords in Waiting, 1838-41, and 1853-56. K.P., 29 April 1839. He *m.*, 23 July 1831, at Felbrigg Hall, Norfolk, Maria Augusta, widow of George Thomas WYNDHAM, of Cromer, da. of Vice Admiral William WINDHAM, formerly LUKIN, of Felbrigg Hall afsd., by Anne, sister of Peter Isaac, 1st BARON RENDLESHAM [I.], da. of Peter THELLUSSON, of Broadsworth, co. York. He *d.* 4 Feb. 1856, aged 54, at Morrison's Hotel, Dublin. Will pr. June 1856. His widow *d.* 31 Oct. 1871, aged 67, at Convamore, co. Cork. Will pr. under £30,000.

III. 1856. 3. WILLIAM (HARE), EARL OF LISTOWEL [1822], VISCOUNT ENNISMORE AND LISTOWEL [1816], and BARON ENNISMORE [1800], in the peerage of Ireland; s. and h., *b.* 29 May 1833, at Convamore afsd.; *styled* VISCOUNT ENNISMORE, 1837-56; Lieut. Scots Fusileer Guards, 1852-56, being severely wounded at the battle of the Alma; *suc. to the peerage* [I.], 4 Feb. 1856; was *cr.*, 8 Dec. 1869, BARON HARE OF CONVAMORE, co. Cork [U.K.] K.P., 20 Feb. 1873; a Lord in Waiting, May to Sep. 1880, He *m.*, 31 Aug. 1865, at St. Geo. Han. sq., Ernestine Mary, yst. da. of Ernest Augustus Charles (BRUCE), 3d MARQUESS OF AILESBURY, by Louisa Elizabeth, 2d da. of John (HORSLEY-BERESFORD), 2d BARON DECIES [I.] She was *b.* 15 March 1847.

[RICHARD GLANVILLE HARE, *styled* VISCOUNT ENNISMORE, s. and h. ap., *b.* 12 Sep. 1866; ed. at Eton and at Ch. Ch., Oxford; sometime Lieut. 1st Life Guards.]

Family Estates.—These, in 1883, consisted of 30,000 acres in co. Kerry and 5,541 in co. Cork. *Total* 35,541 acres, worth £19,500 a year. *Principal Residence.* Convamore, near Mallow, co. Cork.

LITTLETON, see LYTTELTON.

LITTLE EASTON.

See "MAYNARD OF LITTLE EASTON, co. Essex," Barony (*Maynard*), *cr.* 1628; *ex.* 1775.

LITTLE HAMPDEN.

See "HAMPDEN of Great and Little Hampden, co. Buckingham," Viscountcy (*Trevor*), *cr.* 1776; *ex.* 1824.

LITTON, see LYTTON.

see LYTTON.

LIVEDEN, see LYVEDEN.

LIVERPOOL.

Earldom. I. 1796. 1. CHARLES JENKINSON, 1st son of Charles JENKINSON, Col. of the Horse Guards (3d s. of Sir Robert JENKINSON, 2d Bart.), by Amarantha, da. of Wolfran CORNEWALL, Capt. R.N., was b. 16 May 1729,(a) at Winchester; ed. at Charterhouse and at Univ. Coll., Oxford; mat., 14 March 1745/6, and then aged 16; B.A., 1749; M.A., 1752, being cr. D.C.L., 7 July 1773. He was M.P. for Cockermouth, 1761-66; for Appleby, 1767-72; for Harwich, 1772-74; for Hastings, 1774-80, and for Saltash, 1780-86. Having been Private Secretary (1756-58) to Lord Holderness, and again (1760-61) to Lord Bute, he was Under Sec. for the South, 1761-62; Treasurer of the Ordnance, 1762; Joint Sec. to the Treasury, 1763 to 1765, being the leader of the "King's friends" in the House of Commons. Under the Grafton Ministry he was a Lord of the Admiralty, 1766-67; a Lord of the Treasury, 1767-73; Joint Vice Treasurer [I.], 1772-75; P.C., 1773; Clerk of the Pells [I.], 1775, and Sec. at War,(b) 1778-82, at the close of the war with America, taking subsequently a prominent part in framing the commercial treaties that arose after the peace. In 1784 he was made a Lord of Trade. He was cr., 21 Aug. 1786, BARON HAWKESBURY of Hawkesbury, co. Gloucester, and was President of the Board of Trade from Aug. 1786 to June 1804, and Chancellor of the Duchy of Lancaster from Sep. 1786 to Nov. 1803. He suc. his cousin, Sir Banks Jenkinson, the 6th Bart., on 22 July 1789, in the *Baronetcy* (cr. 18 May 1661), and family estates as also in the office of Collector of the Inland Customs. He was cr., 1 June 1796, EARL OF LIVERPOOL.(c) He m. firstly, Feb. 1769, at St. Marylebone, Amelia, da. of William WATTS, Gov. of Fort William, and President of the Council at Bengal. She d. 7 and was bur. 12 July 1770, aged 19, at Hawkesbury. M.I. He m. secondly, 22 June 1782, at her house in Hertford street, St. Geo. Han. sq., Catherine, widow of Sir Charles COPE, Bart., 5th and yst. da. of Sir Cecil BISSHOPP, Bart., by Anne, da. of Hugh (BOSCAWEN), 2d VISCOUNT FALMOUTH. He d. in Hertford street, Mayfair, 17 Dec. 1808, in his 80th year, and was bur. at Hawkesbury. M.I. Will pr. 1809.(d) His widow, who was b. 30 Nov. 1744, d. 1 Oct. 1827, and was bur. the 10th at Buxted, aged 82. Will pr. Oct. 1827.

II. 1808. 2. ROBERT BANKS (JENKINSON), EARL OF LIVERPOOL, &c., 1st s. and h. by first wife, b. 7 June 1770, at St. Margaret's, Westm.; ed. at Charterhouse and at Ch. Ch., Oxford; mat. 27 April 1787; cr. M.A., 19 May 1790; M.P. for Rye, 1790—1803; a Commissioner for the affairs of India, 1793-99; *styled* LORD HAWKESBURY, 1796—1808; P.C., 1799; Master of the Mint, 1799—1801, with a seat in the Cabinet. He was sum. v.p. by writ, 15 Nov. 1803, in his father's Barony as BARON HAWKESBURY; Home Secretary, 1804-06, and again 1807-09, being (under Pitt's Administration) Leader in the House of Lords; Lord Warden of the Cinque Ports, 1806-27; *suc. to the Earldom*, 17 Dec. 1808; War Secretary, 1809-12, and, finally, First Lord of the Treasury (PRIME

(a) See his M.I. as in "*Gloucestershire Notes and Queries*," vol. v, p. 254. The usually received account is that he was b. 26 April and bap. 16 May 1727.

(b) "The Secretary at War constituted an object of universal consideration and attracted all eyes towards him. * * Throughout Lord North's administration, 1770-82, his intercourse with the King and even his influence over the Royal mind were assumed to be constant," &c. See Wraxall's "*Hist. Memoirs*" (vol. i, pp. 415—420, edit. 1884), where is an admirable summary of his character. He was popularly nicknamed "*The King's Secret Adviser.*"

(c) At the request of the Municipality of Liverpool he by Royal lic., 23 July 1796, was permitted to bear the arms thereof as an augmentation (on a chief) to his paternal coat.

(d) His "*Collection of Treaties, 1648—1783*" is well known and his (extremely clever) "*Coins of the Realm*" first issued in 1805, was reprinted by the Bank of England in 1880.

MINISTER) 9 June 1812, to 30 April 1827.(a) K.G., 9 June 1814, on the occasion of the visit of the allied Sovereigns to London; cr. LL.D. of Cambridge, 1826. He m. firstly, 25 March 1795, Theodosia Louisa, 3d da. of Frederick Augustus (HARVEY), 4th EARL OF BRISTOL, by Elizabeth, da. of Sir Jermyn DAVERS, Bart. She d. 12 June 1821, at Fife House, Whitehall, and was bur. at Hawkesbury. He m. secondly, 24 Sep. 1822, Mary, 6th da. of Charles CHESTER, formerly BAGOT, by Catherine, da. of the Hon. Heneage LEGGE. He d. s.p., 4 Dec. 1828, aged 58, at Fife house afsd., having, as far back as 17 Feb. 1827, had a stroke of paralysis. He was bur. at Hawkesbury. Will pr. Feb. 1829. His widow d. 18 Oct. 1846, aged 69, and was bur. at Kingston on Thames. Will pr. Nov. 1846.

III. 1828, to 1851. 3. CHARLES CECIL COPE (JENKINSON), EARL OF LIVERPOOL [1796], and BARON HAWKESBURY [1786], also a Baronet [1661], br. (of the half blood) and h., being s. of the first Earl by his second wife; b. 29 May 1784, in St. Geo. Han. sq.; served in the Royal Navy at an early age; Page of Honour, 1794; mat. at Oxford (Ch. Ch.), 28 April 1801; Sec. of Legation at Vienna, 1804, serving in the Austrian army as a volunteer at Austerlitz; M.P. for Sandwich, 1807-12; for Bridgnorth, 1812-18, and for East Grinstead, 1818-28; Under Sec. for War, 1809-10; suc. to the peerage, 4 Dec. 1828; D.C.L. of Oxford, 15 June 1841; P.C., 1841: Lord Steward of the Household, 1841-46; G.C.B., 3 Jan. 1846. He m., 19 July 1810, Julia Evelyn Medley, da. and h. of Sir George Augustus William SHUCKBURGH-EVELYN, formerly SHUCKBURGH, 6th Bart., by his second wife, Julia Annabella, da. and h. of James EVELYN, of Felbridge, co. Surrey. She, who was b. 6 Oct. 1790, d. 8 April 1814. He d. s.p.m., 3 Oct. 1851, at Buxted Park, Sussex, aged 67, and was bur. at Buxted, when all his peerage dignities became extinct, tho' the Baronetcy devolved on his cousin and h. male. Will pr. Nov. 1851.

LIVINGSTON.

Barony [S.] I. 1453? 1. SIR JAMES LIVINGSTON, of Calendar,(b) co. Stirling, s. and h. of Sir Alexander L., of the same, Justiciary [S.], 1449, by (—), da. of (—) DUNDAS, of Dundas; suc. his father about 1450; was one of the Commissioners to treat with England, 3 Jan. 1453; P.C., Master of the Household, and Great Chamberlain [S.], 1453, in which year probably, but certainly before 30 Aug. 1458, he was cr. LORD LIVINGSTON [S.] He m. Marian. He d. about 1467. His widow was living 4 July 1478.

II. 1467? 2. JAMES (LIVINGSTON), LORD LIVINGSTON [S.], s. and h.; sat in Parl. [S.], 1 Oct. 1487, and 11 Jan. 1487/8.(c) He m. firstly about July 1445 Christian,(d) da. and coheir of Sir John ERSKINE, of Kinnoull. He m. secondly (—), da. of Sir Robert CRICHTON. He m. thirdly Agnes HOUSTON with whom he had (as "James, Lord Livingston"), a charter of lands 30 Jan. 1499/500. He d. s.p. about 1505.

(a) In this period of 15 years which "has only been exceeded by the Ministries of Walpole and Pitt," he "concluded successfully the French war, carried the country thro' the perils which followed upon the peace of 1815 and brought it to the eve of the great Reform period." "History has hardly done justice to Liverpool's solid tho' not shining talents." [Nat Biogr.]

(b) The Barony of Calendar was granted by King David II. [S.] in 1346 to Sir William Livingston, having been forfeited by Patrick Calendar, of Calendar, whose da. and h, the said Sir William, married, and was by her great grandfather of Sir Alexander L., of Calendar, mentioned in the text.

(c) Mr. Hewlett remarks that "on both occasions he was not ranked amongst the Lords of Parl. [sed quere?] but placed as Sir (Dominus) James Livingstone amongst the Territorial or Lesser Barons from which it might be inferred that he had not then acquired the dignity of a Lord of Parl."

(d) See Spalding Misc., v, 382.

III. 1505? 3. JOHN (LIVINGSTON), LORD LIVINGSTON [S.], nephew and h., being s. and h. of Alexander LIVINGSTON, next br. of the late Lord. He m. firstly Elizabeth, da. of Robert (FLEMING), 1st LORD FLEMING [S.], by Janet, da. of James (DOUGLAS), EARL DOUGLAS [S.] He m. secondly (—), da. of Sir John HOUSTON, of Houston. He d. before 3 Feb. 1509/10.

IV. 1510? 4. WILLIAM (LIVINGSTON), LORD LIVINGSTON [S.], s. and h. by first wife; suc. his father before 3 Feb. 1509/10, having, before that date, m. Agnes, 2d da. of Adam HEPBURN, the younger, of Hales, he and the said Agnes being then living. He d. before 21 April 1518.

V. 1518? 5. ALEXANDER (LIVINGSTON), LORD LIVINGSTON [S.], only s. and h., living 3 Feb. 1509/10; suc. his father before 21 April 1518, and sat as a Lord of Parl. [S.]; was an extraordinary Lord of Session, 5 March 1542; Joint Custodian of the person of the Queen [S.], 24 April 1545, whom in 1548 he accompanied to France. He m. firstly Janet STEWART who was living as his wife, 30 March 1511, and 14 Jan. 1512/3. She d. s.p. He m. secondly Agnes, da. of John (DOUGLAS), 2d EARL OF MORTON [S.], by Janet,* da. of (—) CRICHTON, of Cranston Riddell. He d. in France about 1554.

VI. 1554? 6. WILLIAM (LIVINGSTON), LORD LIVINGSTON [S.], 2d but 1st surv. s. and h.(a) by second wife. He adhered to Queen Mary [S.] on whose side he fought at Langside. He m. before 1 Oct. 1558, Agnes (then living), da. of Malcolm (FLEMING), 3d LORD FLEMING [S.], by Lady Janet STEWART, illegit. da. of King James IV. [S.] He d. before 24 Dec. 1580.

VII. 1580? 7. ALEXANDER (LIVINGSTON), LORD LIVINGSTON [S.], s. and h.; suc. his father before 24 Dec. 1580. He was cr., 15 Nov. or 25 Dec. 1600, EARL OF LINLITHGOW, LORD LIVINGSTON AND CALENDAR, with which Earldom this Barony continued united till both were forfeited in 1716. See "LINLITHGOW," Earldom [S.], cr. 1600, *forfeited* 1716.

LIVINGSTON AND CALENDAR.

i.e., "LIVINGSTON AND CALENDAR," Barony [S.] (*Livingston*), cr. 1600, with the EARLDOM OF LINLITHGOW [S.], which see; *forfeited* 1716.

LIVINGSTON OF ALMOND.

i.e., "LIVINGSTON OF ALMOND," Barony [S.] (*Livingston*), cr. 1633, and, again, in 1641 with the EARLDOM OF CALENDAR, which see; *forfeited* (with the Earldoms of Linlithgow and Calendar [S.]) 1716.

LIVINGSTON OF FLACRAIG.

i.e., "LIVINGSTON OF FLACRAIG," Barony (*Livingston*), cr. 1660, with the EARLDOM OF NEWBURGH [S.], which see.

LIVINGSTON OF PEEBLES, or LIVINGSTON OF HYNDFORD.

i.e., "LIVINGSTON OF PEEBLES," Barony [S.] (*Livingston*), cr. 1696, with the VISCOUNTCY OF TEVIOT [S.], which see; resigned(b) for "LIVINGSTON OF HYNDFOORD," Barony [S.], cr. 1698; ex. 1711.

(a) John Livingston, Master of Livingston, his elder br., was slain v.p. and s.p. 10 Sep. 1547, at the battle of Pinkie.

(b) A full account of this proceeding is in "*Riddell*," pp. 1,057—1,062, where it is remarked that the inscription on the monument to Viscount Teviot in Westm. Abbey describes him "under his original Lordly style of *Baron Livingstone of Peebles*, while there is no mention of the later," *i.e.*, *Livingston of Hyndfoord*.

LIXNAW.

See "Kerry and Lixnaw," Barony [I.] (*Fitzmaurice*), cr. 1223?

LLANDAFF, and LLANDAFF OF THOMASTOWN.

Barony [I.] I. 1783.
Viscountcy [I.] I. 1793.
Earldom [I.] I. 1797.

1. Francis Mathew, of Thomastown, co. Tipperary, s. and h. of Thomas M. of the same, by (—), da. of Richard Mathews, of Dublin, b. 1738; *suc.* his father in 1777 and, having been many years M.P. for co. Tipperary, was cr., 12 Oct. 1783,(a) BARON LLANDAFF OF THOMASTOWN, co. Tipperary [I.], taking his seat on the 14th inst. He m. firstly, 6 Sep. 1764, Ellis, sister of Sir Edward Skeffington Smyth, Bart. (so cr. 1776), da. of James Smyth, of Tinney park, co. Wicklow, by Mary, da. of James Agar, of Gowran. She d. (of dropsy) 9 Aug. 1781. He m. secondly, 7 June 1784, Catherine, da. of Clotworthy (Skeffington), 1st Earl of Massereene [I.], by his second wife, Elizabeth, da. of Henry Eyre. She, who was *bap.* 15 July 1752, at St. Ann's, Dublin, d. s.p. 9 Feb. 1796. He m. thirdly, 30 May 1799 (—), da. of Jeremiah Coghlan. He d. at Swansea, in Wales, 30 July 1806, aged 68. Admon. Sep. 1806. His widow was living 1828.

II. 1806, to 1833.

2. Francis James (Mathew), Earl of Llandaff [1797], Viscount Llandaff [1793], and Baron Llandaff of Thomastown [1783], in the peerage of Ireland, s. and h., b. 20 Jan. 1768; *styled* Viscount Mathew from 1797 till he *suc. to the peerage* [I.], 30 July 1806. K.P., 8 Sep. (inv. 24 Nov.) 1831.(b) He m., 10 July 1797, Gertrude, 2d da. of John La Touche, of Harristown, co. Kildare, by Gertrude, da. of Robert Uniacke Fitzgerald, of Corkbegg, co. Cork. She d. before 1828. He d. s.p., 12 March 1833, aged 65, in Merrion square, Dublin. Will pr. (in England) June 1847.

LLANDEGAI.

See "Penrhyn of Llandegai, co. Carnarvon," Barony (*Douglas-Pennant*), cr. 1866.

LLANGATTOCK OF THE HENDRE.

Barony. I. 1892.

1. John Allan Rolls, of the Hendre and of Llangattock manor, both co. Monmouth, s. and h. of John Etherington Welch Rolls, of the same, by Elizabeth Mary, da. of Walter Long, of Preshaw House, Herts, by Mary, da. of William (Carnegie), 7th Earl of Northesk [S.]; b. 19 Feb. 1837; ed. at Eton and at Ch. Ch., Oxford; sometime Capt. Royal Glouc. Hussars; *suc.* his father 27 May 1870; High Sheriff for Monmouthshire, 1875; M.P. for co. Monmouth, 1880-85; was cr., 30 Aug. 1892,(c) BARON LLANGATTOCK OF THE HENDRE, co. Monmouth. He m., 20 Oct. 1868, Georgiana Marcia, 4th da. of Col. Sir Charles Fitzroy Maclean, 9th Bart. [S.], by Emily Eleanor, da. of Rev. the Hon. Jacob Marsham, Canon of Windsor.

(a) One of the Irish Baronies cr. by Fox in 1783 when the King refused to add to the British peerage. See a list of these in vol. iii, p. 44, note "d," *sub* "Delaval."

(b) One of the four extra Knights made at the Coronation of William IV. See list of them in vol. ii, p. 209, note "d," *sub* "Charlemont."

(c) This was one of the eight Baronies conferred by the Salisbury Ministry on leaving office. These were Ashcombe of Dorking (*Cubitt*); Knightley (*Knightley*); Blythswood (*Campbell*); Crawshaw (*Brooks*); Amherst of Hackney (*Amherst*); Newton (*Legh*); Dunleath of Ballywalter Park (*Mulholland*), and Llangattock of the Hendre (*Rolls*.) At the same time two Earldoms (that of Cranbrook on Viscount Cranbrook and that of Ancaster on Lord Willoughby de Eresby) were bestowed as also one Marquessate (that of Zetland) on the Earl of Zetland.

LLANOVER OF LLANOVER AND ABERCARN.

Barony. I. 1859, to 1867.

The Rt. Hon. Sir Benjamin Hall, Bart., was *cr.*, 29 June 1859, BARON LLANOVER OF LLANOVER AND ABERCARN, co. Monmouth. He was s. and h. of Benjamin Hall, of Hensol Castle, co. Glamorgan, and of Abercarn, co. Monmouth (who *d.* 31 July 1817, aged 39), by Charlotte, da. of William Crawshaw, of Cyfarthfa, co. Glamorgan; was *b.* 8 Nov. 1802; entered Westm. school, 1814, and mat. at Oxford (Ch. Ch.), 24 May 1820; M.P. for Monmouth borough, 1832-37, and for Marylebone, 1837-59; was *cr. a Baronet* (as "of Llanover, co. Monmouth"), 16 July 1838; P.C., 1854; President of the Board of Health, 1854-55; First Commissioner of Public Works, 1855-58, *raised to the peerage* as above, 29 June, and took his seat, 4 July 1859; Lord Lieut. of co. Monmouth, 1861. He *m.*, 4 Dec. 1823, Augusta, da. and coheir of Benjamin Waddington, of Llanover afsd., by Georgina Mary Ann, da. of John Port, formerly Sparrow, of Ilam, co. Derby. He *d.* s.p.m.s., 27 April 1867 (after a long illness) aged 64, at 9 Great Stanhope street, Mayfair,(a) and was *bur.* at Llanover, when the *Barony* became *extinct.* M.I. there and in Llandaff cathedral.(b) His widow living 1892.(c)

Family Estates.—These, in 1883, consisted of 6,312 acres in Monmouthshire and 221 in Glamorganshire. *Total* 6,533 acres, worth £8,136 a year. *Principal Residence.* Llanover, near Abergavenny.

LLANTHONY.

i.e., "Ormonde of Llanthony, co. Monmouth," Barony (*Butler*), *cr.* 1821; see "Ormonde" Marquessate [I.], *cr.* 1825.

LOCHABER.

i.e., "Badenoch, Lochaber, Strathaven," &c., Barony [S.] (*Gordon*), *cr.* 1684 with the Dukedom of Gordon [S.], which see; *ex.* therewith, 1836.

LOCHINVAR.

i.e., "Lochinvar" Barony [S.] (*Gordon*), *cr.* 1633 with the Viscountcy of Kenmure [S.], which see; *dormant* 1847.

LOCHLEVEN.

i.e., "Douglas of Lochleven, co. Kinross," Barony (*Douglas*), *cr.* 1791; see "Morton" Earldom [S.], *cr.* 1458, under the 18th Earl; *ex.* 1827.

LOCHMABEN.

i.e., "Murray of Lochmaben," Barony [S.] (*Murray*), *cr.* about 1622 with the Viscountcy of Annand [S.]; see "Annandale" Earldom [S.], *cr.* 1625; *ex.* 1658.

---

i.e., "Johnston of Lochwood, Lochmaben, Moffatdale, and Evandale," Barony [S.] (*Johnston*), *cr.* 1661 with the Earldom of Annandale and Hartfell [S.], and again in 1701 with the Marquessate of Annandale [S.]; see those dignities; *dormant* 1792.

(a) The measures chiefly supported by him were the abolition of church rates, the reform of ecclesiastical abuses, and the establishing of the Metropolitan Board of Works.

(b) His grandfather, the Rev. Benjamin Hall, D.D., was Chancellor of the Diocese of Llandaff, and *d.* 2 Feb. 1825, aged 82, having survived his eldest son, Benjamin Hall, abovementioned.

(c) She was the editor of the "autobiography of Mary (Granville), Mrs. Delany."

LOCHOW.

i.e., "LOCHOW AND GLENILA," Viscountcy [S.] (*Campbell*), *cr.* 1701 with the DUKEDOM OF ARGYLL [S.], which see.

LOCHWOOD.

i.e., "JOHNSTON OF LOCHWOOD, LOCHMABEN, MOFFATDALE, AND EVANDALE," Barony [S.] (*Johnston*), *cr.* 1661 with the EARLDOM OF ANNANDALE AND HARTFELL [S.], and again in 1701 with the MARQUESSATE OF ANNANDALE [S.]; see those dignities; *dormant* 1792.

LOCKINGE.

See "WANTAGE OF LOCKINGE, co. Berks" (*Loyd-Lindsay*), *cr.* 1885.

LOFTUS.

i.e., "LOFTUS OF ELY, King's county," Viscountcy [I.] (*Loftus*), *cr.* 1622; *ex.* 1725; see under "ELY."

---

i.e., "LOFTUS OF LOFTUS HALL, co. Wexford," Barony [I.] (*Loftus*), *cr.* 1751; also "LOFTUS OF ELY," Viscountcy [I.], *cr.* 1756; both of which became *ex.* (with the Earldom of Ely [I.]) 1783. See under "ELY."

---

i.e., "LOFTUS OF LOFTUS HALL, co. Wexford," Barony [I.] (*Loftus, formerly Tottenham*), *cr.* 1785; also "LOFTUS OF ELY" Viscountcy [I.], *cr.* 1789; also "LOFTUS OF LONG LOFTUS, co. York," Barony [U.K.], *cr.* 1801; see "ELY" Marquessate [I.], *cr.* 1800.

LOFTUS HALL.

i.e., "LOFTUS OF LOFTUS HALL, co. Wexford," Barony [I.], *cr.* 1751 (*Loftus*); see "ELY" [*i.e.*, "Loftus of Ely"], Viscountcy [I.], *cr.* 1756; *ex.* (with the Earldom of Ely [I.]) 1783.

---

i.e., "LOFTUS OF LOFTUS HALL, co. Wexford," Barony [I.] (*Loftus, formerly Tottenham*), *cr.* 1785; see "ELY" Marquessate [I.], *cr.* 1800.

LOHORT CASTLE.

See "ARDEN OF LOHORT CASTLE, co. Cork," Barony [I.] (*Perceval*), *cr.* 1770.

LONDESBOROUGH.

Barony. I. 1850.

I. LORD ALBERT-DENISON DENISON, *formerly* CONYNGHAM, 4th but 2d surv. s. of Henry (CONYNGHAM), 1st MARQUESS CONYNGHAM [I.], by Elizabeth, 1st da. of Joseph DENISON, of Denbies, in Dorking, co. Surrey, Banker of London, was *b.* 21 Oct. 1805, in Stanhope street, and *bap.* at St. Geo. Han. sq.; sometime an officer in the Horse Guards Blue; Attaché at Berlin, 1824, and at Vienna, 1825; Sec. of Legation at Florence, 1828, and at Berlin, 1829-31; K.C.H. (Civil), 1829; M.P. for Canterbury, 1835-41, and 1847-50; took the name of *Denison* in lieu of that of *Conyngham* by Royal lic., 4 Sep. 1849, in compliance with the will of his maternal uncle, William Joseph DENISON, of Seamer, co. York (most of whose vast estates he inherited) and was *cr.*, 4 March 1850, BARON LONDESBOROUGH in the East Riding, co. York. He was Vice Admiral of the Yorkshire Coast; F.R.S., F.S.A., &c. He *m.* firstly

6 July 1833, at St. Geo. Han. sq., Henrietta Maria, 4th da. of Cecil (Weld-Forester), 1st Baron Forester of Willey Park, by Katharine Mary, 2d da. of Charles (Manners), 4th Duke of Rutland. She, who was *b.* 10 Dec. 1809, *d.* 22 April 1841, at Mickleham Hall, and was *bur.* at Mickleham, Surrey. He *m.* secondly, 21 Dec. 1847, at Weston Hall, in Shiffnal, co. Stafford, Ursula Lucy Grace, 1st da. of Vice Admiral the Hon. Charles Orlando Bridgeman (2d s. of George, 2d Baron Bradford), by Eliza Caroline, da. of Sir Henry Chamberlain, Bart. He *d.* 15 Jan. 1860, aged 54, at 8 Carlton house terrace. His widow, who was *b.* 22 May 1823, *m.* 14 Dec. 1861, the Rt. Hon. Lord Otho Augustus Fitzgerald, who *d.* 19 Nov. 1882, aged 55. She *d.* 12 Nov. 1883, aged 60.

II. 1860. Earldom. I. 1887. *2* and *1*. William Henry Forester (Denison), Baron Londesborough, s. and h. by first wife; *b.* 19 June 1834, and *bap.* at St. Geo. Han. sq.; ed. at Eton; M.P. for Beverley, 1857-59, and for Scarborough, 1859-60; *suc. to the peerage*, 15 Jan. 1860; Vice Admiral of the Yorkshire Coast. He was *cr.*, 1 July 1887,(a) VISCOUNT RAINCLIFFE of Raincliffe, in the North Riding of co. York, and EARL OF LONDESBOROUGH in the said county. He *m.*, 10 Sep. 1863, at St. Geo. Han. sq., Edith Frances Wilhelmina, yst. da. of Henry (Somerset), 7th Duke of Beaufort, by his second wife, Emily Frances, da. of Culling Charles Smith. She was *b.* 1 June 1838.

[William Francis Henry Denison, *styled* Viscount Raincliffe, s. and h. ap., *b.* 30 Dec. 1864, in Hill street, Berkeley square; sometime in the Royal Navy. He *m.*, 11 Aug. 1887, at St. Andrew's, Wells street, Marylebone, Grace Augusta, 1st da. of Francis William Henry (Fane), 12th Earl of Westmorland, by Adelaide Ida, 2d da. of Richard William (Howe, formerly Curzon), 1st Earl Howe. She was *b.* 3 Oct. 1860.]

Family Estates.—These, in 1883, consisted of 52,655 acres in the three several Ridings of Yorkshire, worth £67,876 a year. *Principal Residence.* Londesborough Park, near Market Weighton, Yorkshire.

LONDONDERRY.

Earldom [I.] I. 1622. Sir Thomas Ridgeway, of Tor Mohun,(b) co. Devon, s. and h. of Thomas R. of the same, by Mary, da. of Thomas Southcote, of Bovey Tracey, in the said county, was *b.* about 1565;(c) *suc.* his father, 27 June 1597, and, having served in Ireland, was *knighted* in 1600, in which year he was Sheriff of Devon; was M.P. for Devon *temp.* James I. and employed in the colonization of Ulster; P.C. [I.]; was *cr. a Baronet*, 25 Nov. 1611, and was *cr.*, 25 May 1616,(d) LORD RIDGEWAY, BARON OF GALLEN-RIDGEWAY [I.], and finally,(e) 23 Aug. 1623, EARL OF LONDONDERRY [I.] He *m.* Cicely (sometime Maid of Honour to Queen Elizabeth) sister and coheir of Henry Macwilliam. He *d.* in London 1631.

(a) This was one of the "*jubilee*" creations. See vol. ii, p. 238, note "a," *sub* "Cheylesmore," for a list of these.

(b) The site of Tor Abbey was purchased at a later date, about 1599, by the family of Ridgeway, from that of Seymour.

(c) The date of the marriage of his parents was 1562-63.

(d) Privy Seal dat. 19 Feb. 1615/6, at Newmarket, the King by his letters subsequently declaring that he should have the precedence of Barons Brabazon and Moore [I.], whose creations by the Privy Seal were dated 14th and 15th respectively of the said month of Feb. but whose patents were not signed till July 1616.

(e) "Sir James Erskine, of Tullibody (yr. br. of Thomas, 1st Earl of Kellie [S.]), was a reckless spendthrift, in consequence of which, being driven to Ireland *with a blank patent of the dignity of an Earl* from James VI. [S.] (of whom he and his kindred were favourites) thereby to recruit his bankrupt fortunes, he acquired *by its sale* to the highest bidder the estate of Agher." [*Riddell*, pp. 869—870, where the authority is given and it is added] "The patent in question was thus advantageously disposed of to Thomas, Lord Ridgeway, afterwards, in 1622, through this *honourable transaction*, *Earl* of Londonderry."

II. 1631. 2. ROBERT (RIDGEWAY), EARL OF LONDONDERRY, &c. [I.], s. and h.; *knighted*, 6 July 1608, near Dundalk, by the Lord Deputy of Ireland; *styled* LORD GALLEN-RIDGEWAY from 1622 till he *suc. to the peerage* [I.] in 1631. He *m.* Elizabeth, da. and h. of Sir Simon WESTON, of Lichfield, co. Stafford. He *d.* at Rosconnel 1640. His widow *d.* at Yoxall, co. Stafford. Her admon. 1 Nov. 1647.

III. 1640. 3. WESTON (RIDGEWAY), EARL OF LONDONDERRY, &c. [I.], s. and h., *bap.* 4 April 1620 [*Qy.* at Torr?]; *styled* LORD GALLEN-RIDGEWAY from 1631 till he *suc. to the peerage* in 1640. He *m.*, 20 Sep. 1650, at St. Anne's, Blackfriars, London, Frances, da. of Sir Peter TEMPLE, of Stowe, Bucks, by his second wife, Christian, da. and coheir of Sir John LEVESON, of Trentham, co. Stafford. She is said to have *d.* in 1688-89. He *d.* at Torwood, Devon. Admon. 7 Nov. 1672, to a creditor (Thomas Temple) no mention being made of any wife.(a)

IV. 1672, to 1714. 4. ROBERT (RIDGEWAY), EARL OF LONDONDERRY [1622], and LORD RIDGEWAY, BARON OF GALLEN-RIDGEWAY [1616], in the peerage of Ireland, also a *Baronet* [1611], s. and h., *styled* LORD GALLEN-RIDGEWAY till he *suc. to the peerage* [I.] in 1672. He *m.* Lucy, da. and h. of Sir William JOPSON,(b) Bart. [S.], of Cudworth, co. York, by Lucy, da. of Henry TINDALL, of Brotherton, in that county. He *d.* s.p.m.s., 7 and was *bur.* 19 March 1713/4, at Tor Mohun, when all his dignities became *extinct*. Will pr. Sep. 1714. His widow *d.* 4 and was *bur.* 23 Sep. 1724, at Tor Mohun. Will pr. 1727.

[HENRY RIDGEWAY, *styled* LORD GALLEN-RIDGEWAY, *b.* 6 and *bap.* 11 April, 1688, at St. Anne's, Soho; *d.* v.p. and s.p. and was *bur.*, from St. Giles in the fields, 10 April 1708, in the Temple church, London.]

Barony [I.] I. 1719. Earldom [I.] V. 1726. 1. THOMAS PITT, Col. in the army, having *m.*, 10 March 1716/7, at St. Geo. the Martyr, Midx., Frances, da. and coheir (only child that left issue) of Robert (RIDGEWAY), EARL OF LONDONDERRY [I.], by Lucy, his wife, both abovenamed, was, on 3 June 1719, *cr.* BARON OF LONDONDERRY [I.], and subsequently, 8 Oct. 1726, was *cr.* VISCOUNT GALLEN-RIDGEWAY of Queen's county, and EARL OF LONDONDERRY. He was 2d s. of Thomas PITT, of Blandford, Dorset, Gov. of Fort St. George in the East Indies, by Jane, da. of James INNES, being next br. to Robert Pitt, the father of the 1st Baron Camelford and of the (celebrated) 1st Earl of Chatham. He was sometime M.P. for Wilton, and was Governor of the Leeward Isles. He *d.* at St. Kitts, 12 Sep. 1729, and was *bur.* at Blandford afsd. Will pr. 1730. His widow, who inherited the estate of Cudworth, *m.* Dec. 1732 Robert GRAHAM, of South Warnborough, Hants, who *d.* 6 Dec. 1749. She *d.* "to the unspeakable loss of the poor" 18 May 1772. Will pr. May 1772.

Earldom [I.] VI. Barony [I.] II. 1729. 2. THOMAS (PITT), EARL OF LONDONDERRY, &c. [I.], s. and h. He *d.* unm. aged about 17 by a fall from his horse 25 Aug. 1735, and was *bur.* at Blandford. Admon. 13 May 1743.

(a) Among the burials at Upton Pyne, Devon, occurs the following on 13 Dec. 1703, "Mary Rudgway, relict of (—), Earl of Londonderry." It seems almost impossible that this can relate to the widow of any such Earl, and, probably, from its wording it relates to a Mrs. or Lady Ridgeway, widow of a *son* or *brother* of such Earl. Compare an entry of a burial of one of the same family at Nantwich, Cheshire, on 13 Sep. 1688, "Mr. Ridgway, brother to the Earl of Londonderry."

(b) This Sir William Jopson *suc.* his *grandmother*, Dame Mary Bolles, in the Baronetcy (*cr.* 1635) on the death of the said Lady, the grantee, 5 May 1662, aged 80,

Earldom [I.] VII. Barony [I.] III. 1735, to 1765. 3. RIDGEWAY (PITT), EARL OF LONDONDERRY [1726], VISCOUNT GALLEN-RIDGEWAY [1726], and BARON LONDONDERRY [1719], in Ireland, br. and h., b. 1722. He d. unm. at Knightsbridge, Midx., 8 Jan. 1765, aged 43, when all his honours became *extinct*.(a) Will pr. 1765.

Barony [I.] IV. 1789. Earldom [I.] VIII. 1796. Marquessate [I.] I. 1816. 1. The Right Hon. ROBERT STEWART was on 20 Sep. 1789, *cr.* BARON LONDONDERRY [I.]; on 1 Oct. 1795, *cr.* VISCOUNT CASTLEREAGH [I.]; on 8 Aug. 1796, *cr.* EARL OF LONDONDERRY [I.], and finally on 13 Jan. 1816, *cr.*(b) MARQUESS OF LONDONDERRY [I.] He was s. and h. of Alexander STEWART, of Ballylawn Castle, co. Donegal, and of Mount Stewart, co. Down, by Mary, sister and h. of Sir Robert Cowan, Gov. of Bombay, only da. of John COWAN, Alderman of Londonderry. He was *b.* 27 Sep. 1739; was M.P. for co. Down, 1771-83; *suc.* his father in the family estates, 2 April 1781, and was raised to the Peerage in 1789 as above mentioned. REP. PEER [I.] (being one of the 28 original Representatives) 1801-21. He *m.* firstly, 3 June 1766, Sarah Frances, 2d da. of Francis (SEYMOUR-CONWAY), 1st MARQUESS OF HERTFORD, by Isabella, da. of Charles (FITZROY), DUKE OF GRAFTON. She, who was *b.* 27 Sep. 1747, *d.* 18 July 1770, and was *bur.* the 30th at Newton afsd. He *m.* secondly, 7 June 1775, Frances, 1st da. of Charles (PRATT), 1st EARL CAMDEN, by Elizabeth, da. and h. of Nicholas JEFFREYS. He *d.* 8 April 1821, in his 83d year, at Mount Stewart. Will dat. 26 Jan. 1820, pr. 20 Jan. 1821. His widow *d.* at Hastings 18 Jan. 1833, aged 82. Will pr. March 1833.

Marquessate [I.] II. Earldom [I.] IX. Barony [I.] V. 1821. 2. ROBERT (STEWART), MARQUESS OF LONDONDERRY, &c. [I.], 2d but 1st surv. s. and h., being only surv. s. by 1st wife. He was *b.* 18 June 1769; was *styled* VISCOUNT CASTLEREAGH, 1796—1821; was M.P. for Tregony, 1794-96; for Orford, 1796-97; for Boroughbridge and for Plympton as also [I.] for co. Down, 1790—1800,(c) and again [U.K.], 1812-21, and for Orford again (as an Irish Marquess) 1821-22. He was made P.C. in 1798; Ch. Sec. for Ireland, 1798—1801; President of the India Board (with a seat in the Cabinet), 1802-06; Sec. of War, 1805-06 and 1807-09, and Foreign Secretary from March 1812 till his death. He was also, 27 Dec. 1813, Envoy on a spec. mission to Prussia and Russia, and having (tho' a commoner) been el. K.G. on the 9th (inst. on the 28) June 1814, was Ch. Commissioner(d) for investing with that Order the Prince of Orange, afterwards (1848) King of the Netherlands, and the Emperor Francis of Austria, which ceremonies took place respectively at Brussels, 22 Aug. and at Vienna, 21 Sep. 1814. He was also one of the Plenipotentiaries to the Congress at Vienna, 11 Aug. 1814 (together with his br., Lord Stewart, afterwards the 3d Marquess) and to the conference at Aix-la-Chapelle, 18 Aug. 1818. G.C.H. (Civil) 1816. He *m.*, 9 June 1794, at St. Geo. Han. sq., Amelia Anne, yst. da. and coheir of John (HOBART), 2d EARL OF BUCKINGHAMSHIRE, by his second wife, Caroline, da. of William CONOLLY. He *d.* s.p. at North Cray, co. Kent, 12 Aug. 1822, aged 53 (having, during temporary insanity, severed the carrotid

(a) His sister and heir, Lucy, who inherited the Cudworth estate (derived from the families of Ridgeway and Jobson), *m.* Pierce Meyrick, of Bodrugan, co. Anglesey, and had issue.

(b) Thus his rise from the *status* of a Commoner to that of a *Marquess* was effected in 27 years, no very long period, but considerably less that of his fellow Marquess, the Marquess of Ely [I.], who obtained that high dignity (and four other separate peerages) within the space of 16 years.

(c) He bore a prominent part in obtaining the consent of the Irish House of Commons to the act of Union.

(d) See vol. ii, p. 192, note "a," *sub* "Cathcart," for a list of these special missions.

artery), and was *bur.* the 20th (from his house in St. James sq.) in Westm. Abbey.([a]) Will dat. 14 Aug. 1818, to 20 Oct. 1820, pr. 10 May 1823. His widow, who was *b.* 20 Feb. 1772, *d.* at St. James' square 12 and was *bur.* 20 Feb. 1829, aged 56, at Westm. Abbey. Will dat. 5 Feb. 1823, pr. 18 April 1829.

Marquessate [I.] III. Earldom [I.] X. Barony [I.] VI. } 1822.

3. CHARLES WILLIAM (VANE, *formerly* 1788—1819, STEWART), MARQUESS OF LONDONDERRY, &c. [I.], also BARON STEWART OF STEWART'S COURT AND BALLYLAWN, br. (of the half blood) and h., being s. of the first Marquess by his second wife. He (the Hon. Charles Stewart) was *b.* 18 May 1778, in Mary street, Dublin; entered the army at the age of 14 in which finally (1837) he became General. He served in Flanders in 1794; was wounded at Donauwert; was, as Lieut. Col. 5th Dragoons (1797—99), in the Irish rebellion, and, as Lieut. Col. 18th Dragoons (1799), was again wounded, under Abercromby, near Schagenburg; distinguished himself greatly as Adjutant General (1809-12) under Sir John Moore in Portugal and in the Peninsular, more particularly at the Douro and Talavera, receiving the thanks of the House of Commons, 5 Feb. 1810. Col. of the 25th Light Dragoons, 1813; K.B., 1 Feb. 1813, becoming G.C.B. in Jan. 1815; Knight Commander of the Tower and Sword of Portugal, 27 March 1813; Envoy to Berlin and Military Commissioner with the allied armies, 1813-14; Knight 4th Class of St. George of Russia and Knight of the Black Eagle of Prussia both on 30 Sep. 1813; Knight Grand Cross of the Sword of Sweden, 25 Oct. 1813, and Knight of the Red Eagle of Prussia, 12 March 1814. He had been M.P. for Thomastown, 1798—1800 [I.], and for co. Derry, 1801-07 and 1812-14, having also been, 1807-08, Under Sec. for War, and in 1812 a Groom of the Bedchamber. He was *cr.*, 1 July 1814, BARON STEWART OF STEWART'S COURT AND BALLYLAWN, co. Donegal; D.C.L. of Oxford, 16 June 1814; LL.D. of Cambridge, July 1814; P.C., 1814; Lord of the Bedchamber, 1814-27, to King Geo. III. and Geo. IV.; Ambassador to Vienna, 1814-23, being in Aug. 1814 (together with his brother, Viscount Castlereagh, afterwards the 2d Marquess), one of the Plenipotentiaries to the Congress there. G.C.H., March 1815, receiving the Gold War Cross with one Clasp; Col. of the 10th Hussars, 1820; *suc. as Marquess of Londonderry,* &c. [I.], 12 Aug. 1822, and was *cr.*, 28 March 1823, VISCOUNT SEAHAM of Seaham, co. Durham, and EARL VANE, with rem. to the heirs male of his body on the body of his then wife, Frances Anne, taking his seat accordingly.([b]) Governor of co. Derry, 1823; Vice Admiral and Lord Lieut. of co. Durham, 1842; Col. of 2d Reg. of Life Guards (Gold Stick), 1843-54. K.G., 19 June 1853. He *m.* firstly, 8 Aug. 1804, at St. Geo. Han. sq., Catherine, 4th da. of John (BLIGH), 3d EARL OF DARNLEY [I.], by Mary, da. and h. of John STOYTE. She, who was *b.* 6 May 1774, *d.* 11 Feb. 1812. He *m.* secondly, 3 April 1819, on which occasion he took by Royal lic., 5 May

---

([a]) His "Tory" views and his support of the (unpopular) King, in the matter of Caroline, the Queen Consort, made him very unpopular at the time of his death, and the poets of the "Liberal" party lampooned him severely. Moore writes—

"Why is a pump like Viscount Castlereagh?
Because it is an empty thing of wood,
That up and down its awkward arm doth sway,
And coolly spouts, and spouts, and spouts away
In one weak, washy, everlasting flood."

while the savageness with which Lord Byron, again and again, attacks him (even after his death) is almost revolting; yet, with the exception of the unfortunate Walcheren expedition (1809) with the planning of which he is credited, the whole of his foreign policy, during the long and troublous time he administered it, seems unexceptionable.

([b]) No objection appears to have been raised to his sitting in the House of Lords tho' the dignity was less than, the usual one, to heirs male of the body of the grantee. See vol. ii, p. 279, note "a," *sub* "Clarendon," for a similar grant 3 June 1756 (and sitting thereunder) of the Barony of Hyde of Hindon. In the case of the Dukedom of Somerset, 1547, tho' the eldest son was postponed to the younger the *final rem.* was to the heirs male of the body of the grantee.

1829, the name of *Vane* in lieu of that of *Stewart*, Frances Anne Emily,(a) da. and h. of Sir Henry Vane-Tempest, 2d Bart., of Long Newton, co. Durham, by Anne Catharine, *suo jure* Countess of Antrim [I.] He *d.* of influenza, 6 March 1854, aged 75, at Holdernesse house, Park lane, and was *bur.* at Long Newton. Will pr. April 1854. His widow, who was *b.* in St. James' sq. 7 and *bap.* 14 Feb. 1800, at St. James' Westm., *d.* 20 Jan. 1865, aged 65,(b) at Seaham Hall, and was *bur.* at Long Newton. Will pr. June 1865. Personalty under £400,000.

Marquessate [I.] IV.
Earldom [I.] XI.
Barony [I.] VII.
1854.

4. Frederick William Robert (Stewart), Marquess of Londonderry, &c. [I.], also Baron Stewart of Stewart's Court and Ballylawn, s. and h., being only s. by first wife; *b.* 7 July 1805, in South street, Grosvenor sq.: *styled* Viscount Castlereagh, 1822—1854; M.P. for co. Down (26 years), 1826-52; a Lord of the Admiralty, 1828; Vice Chamberlain of the Household, 1834-35; P.C., 1835; Col. of the North Down Militia, 1837; Lord Lieut. of co. Down, 1845-64; *suc. to the peerage* [I. and U.K.], 6 March 1854; K.P., 28 Aug. 1856. He *m.*, 2 May 1846, Elizabeth Frances Charlotte, Dow. Viscountess Powerscourt [I.], 1st da. of Robert (Jocelyn), 3d Earl of Roden [I.], by Maria Frances Catherine, da. of Thomas (Stapleton), Lord Le Despencer. He *d.* s.p. "after long seclusion in consequence of mental disease,"(c) 25 Nov. 1872, aged 67. His widow, who was *b.* 18 Dec. 1813, *d.* 2 Sep. 1884, at 25 Upper Brook street. Will pr. 10 Oct. 1884, above £44,000.

Marquessate [I.] V.
Earldom [I.] XII.
Barony [I.] VIII.
1872.

5. George Henry Robert Charles William (Vane-Tempest, *formerly*, 1821-54, Vane), Marquess of Londonderry, &c. [I.], also Earl Vane, Viscount Seaham, and Baron Stewart of Stewart's Court and Ballylawn, br. (of the half blood) and h., being s. of the 3d Marquess by his second wife. He was *b.* 26 April 1821, at Vienna; *styled* Viscount Seaham, 1823-54; ed. at Eton and at Ball. Coll., Oxford; matric., 14 June 1839; B.A. and M.A., 1867; sometime, 1845-48, Lieut. in the 1st Life Guards; M.P. for North Durham, 1847-54; *suc.* his father, 6 March 1854, as Earl Vane and Viscount Seaham under the spec. rem. in the creation, 28 March 1823, of those dignities, and took by Royal lic., 28 June 1854, the name of *Tempest* after that of *Vane*; Col. of the 2d North Durham Militia, 1862; Chief Commissioner with the Garter(d) to the Emperor Alexander II. of Russia, who was invested therewith, 28 July 1867, at Tsarkoeselo, near St. Petersburgh; Knight Grand Cross of St. Alexander of Newski of Russia, 1867. By the death of his brother, 25 Nov. 1872, he *suc.* as Marquess of Londonderry, &c. [I.]; K.P., 31 Aug. 1874; Lord Lieut. of co. Durham, 1880; D.C.L. of Durham Univ., 27 June 1882. He *m.*, 3 Aug. 1846, at St. Geo. Han. sq., Mary Cornelia, da. and h. of Lieut.

(a) She was 22 years his junior. Of this match Moore writes—

"And 'tis plain when a wealthy young lady so mad is,
Or any young lady can go so astray
As to marry old dandies that might be their daddies,
The *stars* are in fault, my Lord Stewart, not they."

The "old dandy," however, made good use of the "young lady's" great wealth, by developing the coal mines on the vast estates in Durham and by the construction of the harbour at Seaham (finished in 1847) accounted amongst the wonders of engineering achievements.

(b) She was many years a leader of the fashion in London Society.

(c) See "*The Times*," 27 Nov. 1872.

(d) See vol. ii. p. 192, note "a," *sub* "Cathcart," for a list of these special Garter missions.

Col. Sir John EDWARDS, Bart. (so cr. 1838) of Garth, co. Montgomery, by his second wife, Harriet, da. of the Rev. Charles JOHNSON, Preb. of Wells. He d. of apoplexy at Plas Machynlleth, 5 Nov. 1884, aged 63, and was bur. at Machynlleth. His widow living 1892.

Marquessate [I.] VI. Earldom [I.] XIII. Barony [I.] IX.	1884.	6. CHARLES STEWART (VANE-TEMPEST, afterwards, 1885, VANE-TEMPEST-STEWART), MARQUESS OF LONDONDERRY [1816], EARL OF LONDONDERRY [1796], VISCOUNT CASTLEREAGH [1795], and BARON LONDONDERRY [1789], in the peerage of Ireland, also EARL VANE [1823], VISCOUNT SEAHAM [1823], and BARON STEWART OF STEWART'S COURT AND BALLYLAWN [1814], s. and h., b. 6 July 1852, in Holdernesse House, Park lane; styled VISCOUNT SEAHAM, 1854-72; ed. at Eton; styled VISCOUNT

CASTLEREAGH, 1872-84; Lieut. Col. of the Seaham Artillery Volunteers, 1876; M.P. for co. Down, 1878-84; suc. to the peerage [I. and U.K.], 5 Nov. 1884, and by Royal lic., 8 Aug. 1885, took the family patronymic of *Stewart* after the names of *Vane-Tempest*. VICEROY OF IRELAND (as Lord Lieut.), 1886-89. K.G., 7 May 1888. He m., 2 Oct. 1875, Theresa Susey Helen, 1st da. of Charles John Chetwynd (TALBOT), 19th EARL OF SHREWSBURY, by Anna Theresa, da. of Richard Howe COCKERELL, Commander R.N. She was b. 6 June 1856.

[CHARLES STEWART HENRY VANE-TEMPEST-STEWART, *styled* VISCOUNT CASTLEREAGH, b. 13 May 1878.

Family Estates.—These, in 1883, consisted of 12,823 acres in co. Durham, 7,399 in Montgomeryshire, and 2,685 in Merionethshire, besides 23,554 in co. Down, 2,159 in co. Londonderry, and 1,673 in co. Donegal. Total (22,907 acres in England and 27,416 in Ireland), 50,323 acres,(a) worth £100,118 a year. *Principal Residences.* Wynyard Park, near Stockton-on-Tees, and Seaham Hall, near Sunderland, both in co. Durham, and Mount Stewart, near Newtonards, co. Down.

LONG LOFTUS.

i.e., "LOFTUS OF LONG LOFTUS, co. York," Barony (*Loftus*), *cr.* 1801; see "ELY" Marquessate [I.], *cr.* 1800.

LONGFORD [England.]

i.e., "LONGFORD, co. Wilts," Barony (*Bouverie*), *cr.* 1747 with the VISCOUNTCY OF FOLKESTONE, which see.

LONGFORD [Ireland.]

Barony [I.] I. 1621. 1. SIR FRANCIS AUNGIER, s. of Richard AUNGIER, by Rose, da. of William STEWART, both of Cambridge, b. about 1562; was Barrister at Law; *knighted*, 28 May 1609, at Greenwich; was appointed, 5 Oct. 1609, Master of the Rolls [I.] at the suit of the late Master (St. Leger) and held that office till his death, having been P.C. [I.], and from 10 April to 13 May 1619, Joint Lord Keeper [I.], and having been *cr.*, 29 June 1621,(b) BARON AUNGIER OF LONGFORD, co. Longford [I.] He m. firstly, about 1596, Douglas, sister of Gerald, 16th EARL OF KILDARE [I.], da. of the Hon. Edward FITZ-GERALD, by Mabel, da. and h. of Sir John LEIGH. He m. secondly Anne, da. of Sir George BARNE. He m. thirdly Margaret, widow of Sir John WYNNE,

---

(a) Altho' Lord Londonderry is not one of the noblemen who (in 1883) possessed above 100,000 acres in the United Kingdom, his rental is larger than most of them. See vol. ii, p. 51, note "a" (*sub* "Buccleuch"), for a list of these, and see some notice of Lord Londonderry and others towards the end of that note.

(b) The preamble is in "Lodge," vol. iii, p. 376, note

da. of Sir Thomas CAVE, of Stanford, co. Northampton, by Eleanor, da. of Nicholas ST. JOHN, of Lydiard Tregoz, Wilts. He *d.* 8 Oct. 1632, aged 70, and was *bur.* 6 Nov. in St. Patrick's cathedral. *Inq. post mortem.* Fun. certif. Will dat. 28 Nov. 1628,(a) pr. 26 Feb. 1632/3. His widow *m.* Sir Thomas WENMAN, of Dublin.

II. 1632. *2.* GERALD (AUNGIER), BARON AUNGIER OF LONGFORD [I.], 1st *s.* and h. by first wife; *b.* about 1536; admitted to Gray's Inn, 9 March 1614/5; *suc. to the peerage* [I.], 8 Oct. 1662. He *m.*, 6 Feb. 1637/8, at Acton, Midx.(Lic. London; he a bachelor aged 38 and she 28), Jane, widow of Sir Edward CARR, of Hillingdon, Midx., 2d da. of Sir Edward ONSLOW, of West Clandon, co. Surrey, by Elizabeth, da. of Sir Thomas SHIRLEY, of Preston, Sussex. He *d.* s.p. 1655, His widow was *bur.* 19 April 1661, at West Clandon.

III. 1655. Viscountcy [I.] I. 1675. Earldom [I.] I. 1677.

3 and *1.* FRANCIS (AUNGIER), BARON AUNGIER OF LONGFORD [I.], nephew and h., being *s.* and h. of the Hon. Ambrose AUNGIER, D.D., by Grisel, yr. da. of the Rt. Rev. Lancelot BULKELEY, Archbishop of Dublin, which Ambrose was second *s.* of the 1st Baron. He *suc. to the peerage* [I.] in 1655; was Capt. of a troop of Horse as early as 1660; ed. at Trin. Coll., Cambridge; B.A., 1665; M.A., 1669; incorp. at Oxford, 23 June 1674, being *cr.* D.C.L., 6 Aug. 1677; admitted to Gray's Inn, 10 March 1673/4; effected the incorporation of Longford, 3 Dec. 1668, and was *cr.*, on 8 Nov. 1675,(b) VISCOUNT LONGFORD [I.] and on 18 Dec. 1677,(b) EARL OF LONGFORD [I.] with in each case a *spec. rem.* failing heirs male of his body, to his brothers. In 1682 he was Commissioner of the Revenue; P.C. [I.]; was from 17 Nov. 1693, to 31 Dec. 1696, Joint Keeper of the Seal [I.]; Gov. of Carrickfergus and Master of the Ordnance [I.] He *m.* after Aug. 1677, Anne, Dowager COUNTESS OF GOWRAN [I.], da. and coheir of Arthur (CHICHESTER), 1st EARL OF DONEGALL [I.], by his third wife, Letitia, da. of Sir William HICKS, Bart. She *d.* 14 Nov. 1697. Will dat. 9 June 1696, pr. at Dublin. He *d.* s.p., 22 Dec. 1700, and was *bur.* at St. Patrick's afsd.

Earldom and Viscountcy [I.] II. Barony [I.] IV. 1700, to 1704.

2 and *4.* AMBROSE (AUNGIER), EARL OF LONGFORD [1677], VISCOUNT LONGFORD [1675], and BARON AUNGIER OF LONGFORD [1621], in the peerage of Ireland, yst. and only surv. br. and h.; *suc. to the peerage* [I.] (the Viscountcy and Earldom devolving under the spec. rem. abovenamed) 22 Dec. 1700; was a Commissioner of the Revenue. He *d.* s.p., 23 Jan. 1704, and was *bur.* at St. Patrick's afsd., when *all his honours* became *extinct.* Will pr. Nov. 1706.

Viscountcy [I.] I. 1713, to 1726.

CHRISTOPHER (FLEMING), BARON OF SLANE [I.], *suc.* his father in that dignity in 1676, being then aged seven years; was *attainted* 1691 but restored in blood and honours in 1708 and is said to have been *cr.* by Royal letters dated 1713 VISCOUNT LONGFORD [I.] but no such patent is enrolled. He *d.* s.p., 14 July 1726, when any *dignity* so conferred became *extinct.* See fuller particulars under "SLANE" Barony [I.]

See "MICKLETHWAIT OF LONGFORD," Viscountcy [I.] (*Micklethwait*), *cr.* 1727; *ex.* 1733.

i.e., "POLLINGTON OF LONGFORD," Barony [I.] (*Savile*), *cr.* 1753; see "MEXBOROUGH" Earldom [I.], *cr.* 1766.

(a) In it he mentions his lands at Marsland, co. Cambridge, and his parsonage at "Owking" [*i.e.*, Woking], co. Surrey.

(b) The preamble is in "Lodge," vol. iii, p. 376, note

Barony [I.] V. 1756.
Earldom [I.] III. 1785.

1 and *1*. THOMAS PAKENHAM, of Pakenham Hall, co. Westmeath, s. and h. of Edward P., of the same (s. and h. of Sir Thomas Pakenham, Prime Serjeant at Law [I.]), by Margaret, da. and h. of John BRADESTAN; *b.* at Pakenham Hall, May 1713; *suc.* his father in 1721; mat. at Oxford (Queen's Coll.), 11 July 1729; M.P. for the borough of Longford, 1745-56. He, having *m.*, 5 March 1739/40, Elizabeth, da. and h. of Michael CUFFE, of Ballinrobe, co. Mayo, by Frances, da. of Henry SANDFORD, of Castlereagh, co. Roscommon, which Michael (who *d.* 24 July 1744, aged 50), was 4th but eventually sole surv. s. and h. of Francis Cuff, who was s. and h. of Sir James Cuffe, by Alice, sister (whose issue became coheir) to Francis (AUNGIER), 2d EARL OF LONGFORD, abovementioned, was, in consequence of that alliance, *cr.*, 7 May 1756, BARON LONGFORD, co. Longford [I.], and took his seat accordingly. He *d.* 30 March 1766, aged 53, and was *bur.* at Killucan, co. Westmeath. His widow, who was *bap.* 26 July 1719, was *cr.*, 20 June 1785,(a) COUNTESS OF LONGFORD [I.], and *d.* 27 Jan. 1794, aged 74. Will pr. July 1795.

Barony [I.] VI. 1766.

2. EDWARD MICHAEL (PAKENHAM), BARON LONGFORD [I.], s. and h.; *b.* 1 April 1743, at Pakenham Hall; sometime, 1761-66, in the Royal Navy, retiring as Post Captain; M.P. for co. Longford, 1765-66; *suc. to the Barony* [I.] on the death of his father, 30 March 1766; P.C. [I.], 1777. He *m.*, 25 June 1768, at St. Mary's, Dublin, Catherine, da. of the Rt. Hon. Hercules Langford ROWLEY, by Elizabeth, *suo jure* VISCOUNTESS LANGFORD [I.] He *d.* 3 June 1792, aged 49. Will pr. Oct. 1793. His widow, who was *b.* 1743, *d.* 12 March 1816.

Barony [I.] VII. 1792.
Earldom [I.] IV. 1794.

3 and *2*. THOMAS (PAKENHAM), BARON LONGFORD [I.], s. and h.(b) *b.* 14 May 1774, in Dublin; *suc. to the peerage* [I.] as Baron, on the death of his father, 3 June 1792, and as Earl, on the death of his grandmother, 27 Jan. 1794. K.P., 17 Dec. 1813. He was *cr.*, 17 July 1821,(c) BARON SILCHESTER, co. Southampton. He *m.*, 23 Jan. 1817, Georgiana Emma Charlotte, 5th da. of William (LYGON), 1st EARL BEAUCHAMP, by Catherine, da. of James DENN. He *d.* 28 May 1835, aged 61, in Portland Place. Will pr. Sep. 1847. His widow *d.* 12 Feb. 1880, aged 82, at 24 Bruton street, Berkeley square.

Earldom [I.] V. Barony [I.] VIII. 1835.

3 and *4*. EDWARD MICHAEL (PAKENHAM), EARL OF LONGFORD [I.], &c., also BARON SILCHESTER, s. and h., *b.* 30 Oct. 1817, at Pakenham Hall, *styled* LORD PAKENHAM till 1821 and LORD SILCHESTER from 1821 till he *suc. to the peerage* in 1835; sometime, 1848-59, in the 2d Life Guards, retiring as Major. He *d.* unm., 27 March 1860, aged 42, at Limmer's Hotel, St. Geo. Han. sq.

Earldom [I.] VI. Barony [I.] IX. 1860.

4 and *5*. WILLIAM LYGON (PAKENHAM), EARL OF LONGFORD, &c. [I.], also BARON SILCHESTER, br. and h., *b.* 31 Jan 1819, at Pakenham Hall; ed. at Winchester and at Oriel Coll., Oxford; matric., 4 May 1836; entered the army, being Adjutant Gen. to the Forces in Turkey, 1855; served in the Crimea, receiving the Medal and Clasp; Officer of the Legion of

(a) "Not only in consideration of her Ladyship being grand niece and heiress to the last Earl of Longford, but also in consideration of the professional services of her two sons, Edward Michael, Lord Longford, and the Hon. Thomas Pakenham, both in the Royal Navy." [*Lodge*, vol. iii, p. 382.] The latter of these who became G.C.B. and Admiral of the Red, *d.* 2 Feb. 1836, aged 78.

(b) Two of his brothers greatly distinguished themselves in the Peninsular war, *viz.* (1) Major Gen. the Hon. Sir Edward Michael Pakenham, G.C.B., who fell in action 8 Jan. 1815, and (2) Lieut. Gen. the Hon. Sir Hercules Robert Pakenham, K.C.B., who *d.* March 1850, aged 69. His second sister, Catherine, was wife of the celebrated Arthur (Wellesley), Duke of Wellington.

(c) This was one of the "Coronation Peerages" of George IV. for a list of which see vol. ii, p. 351, note "d," *sub* "Conyngham."

Honour of France, and Com. (2d Class) of the Sardinian Order of St. Maurice and St. Lazarus; Knight of the Medjidie of Turkey; Dep. Adjutant Gen. to the Forces in India, 1857; Adjutant General, 1858-60, becoming finally, 1879, General in the army, and being, 1878, Col. of the 5th Fusileers; retired 1881. He *suc. to the peerage*, 27 March 1860. K.C.B., 1861; Under Sec. of War, 1866-68; Lord Lieut. of co. Longford, 1874; G.C.B., 1881. He *m.*, 12 Nov. 1862, at All Saints, Knightsbridge, Selina, 3d da. and coheir of George (RICE-TREVOR), BARON DINEVOR, by Frances, da. of Gen. Lord Charles FITZROY. He *d.* 19 April 1887, aged 68, at 24 Bruton street afsd., and was *bur.* at Kensal Green cemetery. Will pr. at Mullingar but resealed in London, 11 May 1887, over £180,000. His widow, who was *b.* 11 Sep. 1836, living 1892.

[WILLIAM PAKENHAM, *styled* LORD SILCHESTER, *s.* and h. ap., *b.* 19 Oct. 1864, in Leinster street, Dublin; *d.* v.p., 16 Feb. 1876, in his 12th year, at Pakenham Hall.]

Earldom [I.] VII. Barony [I.] X.	1887.

5 and *6*. THOMAS (PAKENHAM), EARL OF LONGFORD [1785], and BARON LONGFORD [1756], in the peerage of Ireland, also BARON SILCHESTER [1821], 2d but 1st surv. s and h., being twin br. of William, *styled* Lord Silchester, next abovenamed; *b.* 19 Oct. 1864, in Leinster street, Dublin, as afsd.; *styled* LORD SILCHESTER from Feb. 1876 till he *suc. to the peerage* in March 1887; ed. at Winchester and at Ch. Ch., Oxford; matric., 14 Oct. 1881; B.A., 1885; M.A., 1889; Lieut. 2d Life Guards; Lord Lieut. of co. Longford.

Family Estates.—These, in 1883, consisted of 420 acres in co. Dublin (worth £31,718 a year), 15,015 in co. Westmeath, and 4,555 co. Longford. *Total* 19,989 acres worth £47,198 a year. *Principal Residence.* Pakenham Hall, near Castle Pollard, co. Westmeath.

LONG LOFTUS, see p. 134.

LONGNEWTON or LANGNEWTOUN.

i.e., "KER OF NISBET, LANGNEWTOUN AND DOLPHINSTOUN," Barony [S.] (*Ker*), *cr.* 1633 with the EARLDOM OF ANCRUM [S.], which see.

LONGUEUIL, or DE LONGUEUIL.

The title of BARON DE LONGUEUIL of Longueuil, in the province of Quebec, in Canada,(a) was granted (at the time when Canada formed part of the Dominion of France) by letters patent of Louis XIV., King of France, dated 26 Jan. 1700, to CHARLES LE MOYNE, a distinguished Military Commander, the estate of Longueuil being erected into a Barony with rem. to the heirs (male or female) of his body so that, accordingly, his great granddaughter (the posthumous da. and h. of his grandson, the 3d Baron), Marie Charles Joseph, *suo jure* Baroness de Longueuil, inherited the same from her father (who *d.* 27 Sep. 1755), and was succeeded (at her death 17 Jan. 1841, aged 85), by her s. and h., Charles William GRANT, the 5th possessor of this Barony, who *d.* 5 July 1848, aged 66. To his grandson, Charles Colmore Grant, the 7th inheritor (*b.* 13 April 1844, and *suc.* his father, 26 Feb. 1879), the Royal recognition of the dignity was granted 4 Dec. 1880.(b)

(a) This dignity does not properly come within the scope of this work. It was undoubtedly a French dignity at its creation in 1700. By the treaty of Paris, however, 10 Feb. 1763 (after the conquest by the English of Quebec in 1759) all rights and privileges "of what kind soever" were reserved to all of French descent who were entitled thereto under the former [*i.e.*, the French] government.

(b) This appears to be the only Canadian hereditary title existing; its holder, tho' a Colonial Peer, has not, apparently, any *precedence* in right of that position.

LONGUEVILLE.

GASTON DE FOIX, Captain of Buche, yr. br. of John, COUNT OF FOIX, was by Henry V. *cr.*, 11 June 1419, COUNT OF LONGUEVILLE in Normandy.(a) He was about 1438 made K.G. and *d.* about 1458, being ancestor (by his wife, Margaret of Albret, whom he *m.* April 1410) of the Captains of Buche, the Counts of Candale, Gurson, and Fleix, and the Dukes of Rendan.]

LONGUEVILLE,(b), or DE LONGUEVILLE [England].

Viscountcy I. 1690. HENRY (YELVERTON), LORD GREY DE RUTHYN, who, in 1679, had *suc.* his br. Charles in that dignity, was *cr.* 21 April 1690, VISCOUNT DE LONGUEVILLE. He *d.* 13 May 1704. See fuller particulars under "GREY DE RUTHYN."

II. 1704. TALBOT (YELVERTON), VISCOUNT DE LONGUEVILLE, s. and h., was *cr.* 26 Sep. 1717, EARL OF SUSSEX. See that dignity, *extinct*, together with this Viscountcy, 1799.

LONGUEVILLE [Ireland].

Barony [I.] I. 1795. Viscountcy [I.] I. 1800, to 1811. RICHARD LONGFIELD, of Longueville [near Mallow] and of Castle Mary, both in co. Cork, 2d s. of Robert L. of the same by (—) da. of (—) GEARING was *b.* 1734; High Sheriff for co. Cork, 1758; M.P., for Charleville in 1761, and afterwards for co. Cork, and, having *suc.* to the family estate, on the death s.p., of his nephew, Robert Longfield, in 1775, was *cr.* 1 Oct. 1795, BARON LONGUEVILLE, of co. Cork [I.], and subsequently, 29 Dec. 1800,(c) VISCOUNT LONGUEVILLE, of co. Cork [I.]; REP. PEER [I.], 1801-11, being one of the 28 original representatives. He *m.* Margaret, da. of Richard WHITE, of Bantry, co. Cork, by Martha, da. of the Rev. Rowland DAVIS, Dean of Cork and Ross. He *d.* s.p. 23 May 1811, aged 77, when all his *honours* became *extinct*. Will pr. 1811.

LONGVILLIERS.

THOMAS DE LONGVILLIERS, was summoned by writ 25 Feb. (1341/2). 16 Ed. III, "to attend a great council at Westm., but never after, tho' he lived very many years; this solitary summons cannot be considered a call to Parl."(d) He *d.* s.p. 1374.

LONSDALE.

Viscountcy. I. 1696. *1.* SIR JOHN LOWTHER, Bart.,(e) [S.] of Lowther, co. Westmorland, s. and h. of Col. John LOWTHER, by his first wife, Elizabeth, da. and (1650) coheir of Sir Henry BELLINGHAM, 1st Bart., of Hilsington in that county, which John last named (who *d.* v.p. about 1665) was s. and h. ap. of Sir John LOWTHER, 1st Bart.(e) [S.], was *b.* 25

(a) This was one of the Norman Earldoms conferred by Henry V. as to which see vol. iii, p. 292, note "a," *sub* "Eu."

(b) See vol. iv, p. 107, note "e," *sub* "Grey de Ruthyn," as to the variation of the style from "De Longueville" to "Longueville."

(c) See vol. i, p. 208, note "c," *sub* "Avonmore," for a list of the 18 Irish Peerages *cr.* this day—the last batch before the Union.

(d) Banks's *Bar. Angl. conc.*

(e) There is, however, no mention of this Baronetcy of Nova Scotia, supposed to have been *cr.* 1630-41, in Milne's [well known] list, preserved in the Advocates' library at Edinburgh. If the remainder was to the heirs male *of the body* of the grantee, these, apparently, became extinct in 1802 on the death of James, Earl of Lonsdale.

April 1655 at Hackthorp Hall in Lowther; ed. at Kendal and Jedburgh; mat. at Oxford (Queen's Coll.) 12 July 1670; *suc.* his grandfather as 2nd Bart.(a) [S.] 30 Nov. 1675; Barrister (Inner Temple) 1677; M.P. for Westmorland (in seven parls.) 1675-96; a zealous promoter of the Revolution; P.C. 1689; Vice Chamberlain of the household, 1689-94; Lord Lieut. of Cumberland and Westmorland, 1689-94; First Lord of the Treasury, March to Nov. 1691, being *cr.* 28 May 1696, BARON LOWTHER of Lowther, co. Westmorland and VISCOUNT LONSDALE, co. Westmorland; LORD PRIVY SEAL, 28 May 1699 till his death; one of the "LORDS JUSTICES" [Regents] during the King's absence(b) 30 May to 18 Oct. 1699, and 27 June 1700; F.R.S. 1699. He *m.* 3 Dec. 1674, at Westm. Abbey, Katherine, 2d and yst. da. of Sir Henry Frederick THYNNE, 1st Bart, of Kempsford, by Mary, da. of Thomas (COVENTRY), 1st BARON COVENTRY OF AYLESBOROUGH. He *d.* 10 July 1700 aged 45 and was *bur.* at Lowther. Will pr. 18 Oct. 1700 and 2 April 1714.(c) His widow,(d) who was *b.* 21 Sep 1653 at Caus Castle, Salop, was *bur.* at Lowther 1713. Her will dat. 30 Sep. 1711, pr. 25 June 1713 and 19 July 1723.

II. 1700. *2.* RICHARD (LOWTHER), VISCOUNT LONSDALE, &c., s. and h., *b.* 1692, *suc to the peerage* in 1700. He *d.* (of the small pox) unm. 1 Dec. 1713 and was *bur.* at Lowther. Will pr. March 1714.

III. 1713 to 1751. *3.* HENRY (LOWTHER), VISCOUNT LONSDALE and BARON LOWTHER [1696], also a Baronet(a) [S.], br. and h.; *b.* 1694; *suc. to the peerage* 1713; distinguished himself in raising 10,000 men to oppose the Jacobite rising in 1715; a Lord of the Bedchamber 1717; LL.D. of Cambridge, 7 Oct. 1717; Constable of the Tower of London, 1726-31; P.C. 1726; a Commissioner of Claims at the Coron. of George II, 12 Aug. 1727; LORD PRIVY SEAL, 1733-35; Lord Lieut. of Cumberland and Westmorland, 1740; F.R.S., 1742. He *d.* unm., 12 March 1750/1, at Byram, co. York, when his *peerage dignities* became *extinct*. Will dat. 27 May 1747, pr. 1751, in which he devised his estates to his heir male (and, *ex sorore*, great nephew) as under.

Viscountcy. IV. 1784. Earldom. I. 1784, to 1802. *1.* SIR JAMES LOWTHER, Bart.(a) [S.], cousin and heir male, being 2d but 1st surv. s. and h. of Robert LOWTHER, of Mauds Meaburn, co. Westmorland, Gov. of Barbadoes, by Catherine, da. of Sir Joseph PENNINGTON, 2d Bart., of Muncaster (by Margaret, sister to Henry, Viscount Lonsdale, abovenamed), which Robert (who *d.* 1745, aged 63), was s. and h. of Richard LOWTHER, of Mauds Meaburn afsd. (*b.* 1638), who was 2d surv. s. of Sir John LOWTHER, 1st Bart.(a) [S.], the grandfather of the 1st Viscount. He was *b.* 5 Aug. and *bap.* 6 Sep. 1736, at St. George's Bloomsbury, and *suc.*, 12 March 1750/1, as 5th *Baronet*(a) [S.] on the death of his cousin [and great uncle] Henry, Viscount Lonsdale, abovenamed, whose estates he also inherited, as he did subsequently the estate of Whitehaven, and near £2,000,000, on the death, 2 Jan. 1755, of his cousin, Sir James Lowther, 4th Bart., of Whitehaven.(e) He was ed. at Cambridge; was M.P. for Cumberland, 1757-61; for Westmorland, 1761-63; for Cumberland (again), 1762-68; for Cockermouth, 1769-74, and for Cumberland (the 3d time), 1774-84, and was *cr.*, 24 May 1784,(f) BARON LOWTHER, of Lowther, co. Westmorland, BARON OF THE BARONY OF KENDAL in the said county and BARON OF THE BARONY OF BURGH, co. Cumberland. also VISCOUNT

(a) *Vide* p. 138, note "e."

(b) See vol. iii, p. 115, note "c," *sub.* "Devonshire" for a list of these Regents during the reign of William III.

(c) Extracts from an interesting memoir of him, which, "tho' printed is not published" is given in "Collins" vol. v, pp. 705-708.

(d) A second wife is sometimes attributed to him (see "Collins" edit. 1789) but manifestly in error.

(e) The Baronetcy of Lowther of Whitehaven (*cr.* 1642) became extinct on his death in 1755.

(f) The celebrated William Pitt owed his first seat (that of Appleby, 1781-84), to Sir James Lowther (thro' the request of the Duke of Rutland) and the shower of peerages rained upon him in 1784 was the result.

OF LONSDALE in the said co. of Westmorland and co. pal. of Lancaster and VISCOUNT OF LOWTHER in the said co. of Westmorland, and EARL OF LONSDALE in the said co. of Westmorland and co. pal. of Lancaster. Having been Col. of the Westmorland Militia (1759) and of the Cumberland Militia (1792) he was, in 1794, made Col. in the army during service. He was cr., 26 Oct. 1797, BARON AND VISCOUNT LOWTHER OF WHITEHAVEN, with a spec. rem. (he having no issue) to the heirs male of the body of Sir William Lowther, of Swillington, co. York. He m., 7 Sep. 1761, at St. Geo. Han. sq., Mary, 1st da. of John (STUART), 3d EARL OF BUTE [S.], by Mary, da. of Edward WORTLEY-MONTAGU. He d. s.p., 24 May 1802,([a]) aged 65, and was bur. 9 June, at Lowther, when the *Earldom and Viscountcy of Lonsdale* and the other honours cr. therewith in the patent of 1784 (as also presumably the Baronetcy([b]) [S.]) became *extinct*, but the Viscountcy and Barony of Lowther devolved (as below mentioned) on his cousin, afterwards [1807] cr. Earl of Lonsdale. His will dat. 18 Jan. 1798, pr. 1802.([c]) His widow, who was b. 20 Jan. 1768, at St. Geo. Han. sq., d. 5 April 1824. Will pr. 1824.

Earldom. II. 1807. *1.* WILLIAM (LOWTHER), VISCOUNT AND BARON LOWTHER OF WHITEHAVEN, s. and h. of the Rev. Sir William LOWTHER,([d]) Bart. (so cr. 22 Aug. 1764), of Swillington, co. York, by Anne, da. of the Rev. Charles ZOUCH, Vicar of Sandal, co. York, was b. 29 Dec. 1757; M.P. for Carlisle, 1780-84; for Cumberland, 1784-90, and for Rutland, 1796—1802, having *suc. his father*, 15 June 1788, as 2d *Baronet*; entered the army, 1794, in which finally, 1800, he became Lieut. Col.; *suc.* his cousin, the Earl of Lonsdale, 24 May 1802 *in the Viscountcy and Barony of Lowther of Whitehaven* (under the spec. limitation in the creation thereof, 26 Oct. 1797), as also in most of his estates;([e]) Lord Lieut. of Cumberland and Westmorland, 1802, and was cr., 7 April 1807, EARL OF LONSDALE, co. Westmorland; K.G., 18 July 1807; F.S.A., &c. He m., 12 July 1781, at St. James, Westm., Augusta, 1st da. of John (FANE), 9th EARL OF WESTMORLAND, by his first wife, Augusta, da. of Lord Montagu BERTIE, 2d s. of Robert, 1st DUKE OF ANCASTER. She, who was b. 18 Sep. 1761, d. 6 March 1838. He d. at York House, Twickenham, 19 March 1844, aged 86. Will pr. June 1844.

III. 1844. *2.* WILLIAM (LOWTHER), EARL OF LONSDALE, &c., s. and h., b. 30 July 1787, at Uffington, co. Lincoln; ed. at Harrow and at Trin. Coll., Cambridge; M.A., 1808; *styled* VISCOUNT LOWTHER, 1807-44; M.P. for Cockermouth, 1808-13, for Westmorland, 1813-31; for Dunwich, 1831, and again, for Westmorland, 1832-41; was a Lord of the Admiralty, 1809; a commiss. for Indian affairs, 1810-18; a Lord of the Treasury, 1813-27; Ch. Commiss. of Woods and

([a]) A good deal about him is to be found in Wraxall's "*Memoirs*," who mentions his great "eccentricities," his "fiery and overbearing temper"—"capricious, tyrannical," &c." The editor (Mr. H. B. Wheatley) of the edit. of 1884 adds this note (vol. iii, p. 358), "He was known throughout Westmorland and Cumberland as '*The bad Earl*' and '*Jimmy Grasp-all, Earl of Toadstool*,' was the sobriquet given him in the numerous election squibs. He frequently returned *nine* members who were known as his *ninepins*."

([b]) As to this Baronetcy, see p. 138, note "e."

([c]) An abstract of this will is in "Collins," vol. v, pp. 714-716; under it his wife had the house and furniture at Fulham, &c.; his sisters had above £60,000, besides the Barbadoes estate of £4,000 a year; while the estate in Yorkshire of £5,000 a year was devised to Mr. John Lowther, and those in Cumberland and Westmorland (supposed to be £40,000 a year) to Viscount Lowther on whom the Whitehaven estate was entailed and who received also near £100,000 in personalty.

([d]) This Rev. gentleman, whose services were rewarded with a Baronetcy, d. 1788, aged 81. He was only s. and h. of Christopher Lowther, of Little Preston, co. York (d. 1718), who was 8th son (but whose issue after 1763 were heirs male) of Sir William Lowther, of Swillington (d. 1705, aged 65), who was s. and h. of another Sir William L., of Swillington, yr. br. of Sir Christopher Lowther, 1st Bart., of Whitehaven (see p. 139, note "e"), and of Sir John Lowther, of Lowther, the grandfather the 1st Viscount Lonsdale and great grandfather of James, the 1st Earl of Lonsdale.

([e]) See note "c," next above.

Forests, 1828-30; P.C., 1828; Vice Pres. of the Board of Trade, 1834-35, and Treasurer of the Navy, 1834-35. He was sum. 8 Sep. 1841, to the House of Lords, v.p., in his fathers Barony as BARON LOWTHER OF WHITEHAVEN; Post Master Gen., 1841-45; *suc. to the Earldom of Lonsdale*, 19 March 1844; Lord Lieut. of Cumberland and Westmorland, 1844-68; LORD PRESIDENT OF THE COUNCIL, Feb. to Dec. 1852; F.R.S., &c. He *d.* unm. 4 March 1872, aged 84, at 14, Carlton House Terrace. Personalty under £700,000.

IV 1872. *3.* HENRY (LOWTHER), EARL OF LONSDALE, &c., nephew and h., being s. and h. of the Hon. Henry Cecil LOWTHER, by Lucy Eleanor, da. of Philip (SHERARD), 5th EARL OF HARBOROUGH, which Henry Cecil was next br. to the late Earl and *d.* 6 Dec. 1867, aged 77. He was *b.* 27 March 1818; ed. at Westminster and at Trin. Coll., Cambridge; M.A., 1838; sometime, 1841-52, an officer in the 1st Life Guards, retiring as Capt.; was M.P. for West Cumberland, 1847, till *he suc. to the peerage*, in 1872. Lord Lieut. of Cumberland and Westmorland, 1868; Lieut. Col. of the Westmorland Yeomanry, 1872-76. He *m.*, 31 July 1852, Emily Susan, da. of St. George Francis CAULFEILD, of Donamon Castle, co. Roscommon, by Susannah Anne, sister of Edward, BARON CROFTON OF MOTE [I.], 1st da. of Sir Edward CROFTON, 3d Bart. [I.], by Charlotte, da. of John (STEWART), 7th EARL OF GALLOWAY [S.] He *d.* 15 Aug. 1876, aged 58, at Whitehaven Castle. His widow living 1892.

V. 1876. *4.* ST. GEORGE HENRY (LOWTHER), EARL OF LONSDALE, &c., s. and h., *b.* 4 Oct. 1855, at Wilton Crescent; ed. at Eton; *styled* VISCOUNT LOWTHER, from 1872 till he *suc. to the peerage* in 1876. Hon. Col. of the Cumberland Militia, 1877. He *m.* 6 July 1878, at St. Paul's, Knightsbridge, Constance Gladys, sister to George Robert Charles, 13th EARL OF PEMBROKE, 3d and yst. da. of Sidney (HERBERT) 1st BARON HERBERT OF LEA, by Mary Elizabeth, da. of Lieut.-Gen. Charles Ashe A'COURT-REPINGTON. He *d.* s.p.m. at 14, Carlton House Terrace, 8 Feb. 1882 aged 26. His widow, who was *b.* 24 April 1859 and who had royal warrant, 30 May 1862 of the precedency of the da. of an Earl, *m.* 7 May 1885, at St. Martins in the fields, Frederick Oliver ROBINSON, *styled* EARL DE GREY and was living 1892.

VI. 1882. *5.* HUGH CECIL (LOWTHER), EARL OF LONSDALE [1807], VISCOUNT AND BARON LOWTHER OF WHITEHAVEN [1797] also a *Baronet* [1764] br. and h. male; *b.* 25 Jan. 1857, at Donamon Castle afsd.; ed. at Eton; *suc. to the peerage*, 8 Feb. 1882; Hon. Col. 3d. batt. Border Reg. of Militia. He *m.* 27 June 1878, at Orton Longueville, co. Huntingdon, Grace Cecilia, 3d da. of Charles (GORDON), 10th MARQUESS OF HUNTLY [S], by Elizabeth Henrietta, da. of Henry (CONYNGHAM), 1st MARQUESS CONYNGHAM [I.]. She was *b.* 15 Oct. 1854.

Family Estates.—These, in 1883, consisted of 39,229 acres in Westmorland, 28,228 in Cumberland, 493 in Rutland and 115 in Lancashire. *Total* 68,065 acres, worth £71,333 a year. *Principal Residences*; Lowther Castle, near Penrith, co. Westmorland, and Whitehaven Castle, co. Cumberland.

LORN, *afterwards* INNERMEATH.

Barony [S.]
I. 1439?

1. SIR ROBERT STEWART, of Lorn and Innermeath, 1st s. and h.(a) of Sir John STEWART, of Innermeath, *suc.* his father between 1412 and 1420, who had acquired the great Barony of Lorn in Argyllshire, by the surrender, in April 1388, of his brother

(a) His yr. br. Sir James Stewart, "the Black Knight of Lorn," was (by Joanna, the Queen Dowager [S.]) father of John Stewart, *cr.* Earl of Athole [S.] about 1457, a dignity which became extinct in 1595 (on the death of his descendant, the 5th Earl) but which was regranted in 1596 to John (Stewart), Lord Innermeath [S.], as mentioned in the text.

Robert Stewart and Janet "of Lorn" his wife,(a) the heiress of John of Lorn.(b) He was one of the Commissioners to England for the release of King James I. [S.] and, being in 1424 one of the hostages for his ransom, remained there till 1429. He was *cr.* a Baron and Lord of Parl. as LORD LORN [S.] before 5 Sep. 1439, at which date he is witness (as *Robertus, Dominus Lorn*), to a charter. He *m.* Margaret, da. of Robert (STEWART), 1st DUKE OF ALBANY [S.], the Regent [S.], by, probably, his first wife, Margaret, *suo jure* COUNTESS OF MENTEITH [S.] He *d.* before 1449.

II. 1449? 2. JOHN (STEWART), LORD LORN [S.], s. and h. He had, 20 June 1452, charter of the Lordships of Lorn, Innermeath, &c., to himself in tail male, with rem. to his four brothers, his uncle and cousins in like manner. He sat in Parl. [S.] as "Lord Lorn" 1449, 1452, and 1455. He *d.* s.p.m. legit. between 1455 and 1464.

III. 1460? 3. WALTER (STEWART), LORD LORN [S.], br. and h. male. He sat in Parl. [S.] as Lord Lorn in 1464 and 1469, but on 6 May 1471 (when he is the first named among the Barons) as LORD INNERMEATH [S.], he having resigned (with consent of the Crown, 14 April 1470), the Lordship of Lorn to Colin (Campbell), 1st Earl of Argyll [S.](c) (the husband of his niece, Isabel, 1st da. and heir of line of his elder br., John, Lord Lorn, next abovenamed), and receiving in exchange the *title of Innermeath*, as the style of his peerage [S.](d) He is said to have *m.* Margaret, da. of John (LINDSAY), 1st LORD LINDSAY OF THE BYRES [S.](e) He was living 12 July 1481, but *d.* before 25 Jan. 1498/9. His widow *m.* Henry WARDLAW, of Torry.

IV. 1490? 4. THOMAS (STEWART), 2d LORD INNERMEATH [S.], s. and h.; had charters of divers lands, 25 Jan. 1498/9. He *m.* Janet, widow of John LESLIE, Master of Rothes (who *m.* in 1478 but *d.* before 1488), 1st da. of William (KEITH), 1st EARL MARISCHAL [S.], by Mary, da. of Sir James HAMILTON. He was killed at the battle of Flodden,(f) 9 Sep. 1513.

V. 1513. 5. RICHARD (STEWART), 3d LORD INNERMEATH [S.], s. and h. He *m.* Margaret, 1st da. and coheir of John (LINDSAY), 3d LORD LINDSAY OF THE BYRES [S.], by Margaret, da. of Sir William BAILLIE. He *d.* 1528. His widow *m.* Sir James STEWART, of Beath, who was slain 1547 and on whose death she had a letter directed to her, as Lady Innermeath, from Mary, the Queen Regent [S.]

(a) Robert Stewart and Janet of Lorn were "ancestors of the respectable family [of Stewart] of Rosyth, which had the *blood* of Lorn without the Lordship" while the Lords Innermeath and the Campbells of Argyll (who derived from those Lords) "were Lords of Lorn *territorially*, but without a drop of blood of the old Highland family." [Sinclair's "*Filii Carnales*" (under "*the Lords of Lorn*") in the "*Her. and Gen.*," vol. vi.]

(b) Mr. J. Horace Round (to whom the Editor owes several valuable notices in this article) writes (Oct. 1892) "I have ascertained that *John of Lorne* was contumaciously absent from Parl. in 1366 but sat on a committee in Parl. 1368."

(c) The said Earl of Argyll and his successors, from this date, used the style of Lord Lorn in addition to their own peerage titles.

(d) Indre, 30 Nov. 1469, "the said Lord Erle [of Argyll] sal causs our Sovrane Lord to *continew* the said Walter, *Lord of Parliament*, and *his stile to be of Innermeath* or any other honorable place that pleisses him and to have sate in Parl., generale counsalis and other worschipful places as he now has." [Duke of Argyll's MSS. 4th Rep., Hist. MSS. comm. I. 474.] The bond of "Walter, Lord Innermeath," to the Earl of Argyll, *Lord Lorn*, is dated 13, and his resignation into the King's hands of the Lordship of Lorn is dated 14 April 1470.

(e) In that case, if her mother was a da. of Robert (Stewart), 1st Lord Lorn [S.] (which lady is said to have *m.* the 1st Lord Lindsay of the Byres [S.]) she would be niece to her husband.

(f) See p. 63, note "b," *sub* "Lennox," for a list of the Scotch nobles who were there slain.

VI. 1528. 6. JOHN (STEWART), 4th LORD INNERMEATH [S.], probably br. but possibly s. and h. of the above ;(a) Sheriff of co. Forfar, 1541 ; one of the extra. Lords of Session [S.], 1542. He m. before 1540 Elisabeth (one of the Mistresses of James V. [S.]), da. of Sir John BETHUNE, of Creich. He was living 16 Jan. 1561/2.

VII. 1565? 7. JAMES (STEWART), 5th LORD INNERMEATH [S.], s. and h. ; was one of the hostages(b) in 1569 for Mary, Queen of Scots. He m. before 7 July 1554, Helen, 4th da. of James (OGILVY), 4th LORD OGILVY OF AIRLIE [S.], by Helen, da. of Henry (SINCLAIR), 1st LORD SINCLAIR [S.] He d. before 17 May 1579.(c)

VIII. 1579? 8. JOHN (STEWART), 6th LORD INNERMEATH [S.], only s. and h. He was cr., 6 March 1595/6, EARL OF ATHOLE [S.], the Earldom of that name (cr. about 1457), having become extinct by the death (28 Aug. 1595), of his cousin, John (Stewart), 5th Earl of Athole [S.];(d) He d. 13 April 1605.

IX. 1605, to 1625. 9. JOHN (STEWART), EARL OF ATHOLE [1596], and LORD INNERMEATH [1439?], in the peerage of Scotland, only s. and h. He d. s.p. 1625 when the *Earldom of Athole* became *extinct*, and the *Barony of Innermeath* probably *extinct*, but certainly *dormant*.

See fuller particulars under "ATHOLE" Earldom [S.], cr. 1596; ex. 1625.

---

i.e., "LORN" Barony [S.] The Lordship of Lorn, co. Argyll, was resigned in 1470 by Walter Stewart (afterwards Lord Innermeath [S.]) to Colin (Campbell), 1st Earl of Argyll, who obtained, 17 April 1470, a crown charter (*Mag. Sig.* Lib. vii, No. 189), of the "*dominium de Lorne*," and who from that date (as were his successors) was usually designated "Earl of Argyll, Lord Campbell and *Lorn*."(e) See "Argyll" Earldom [S.], cr. 1457.

---

i.e., "KINTYRE AND LORN," Marquessate [S.] (*Campbell*),(e) cr. 1701 with the DUKEDOM OF ARGYLL [S.], which see.

L'ORTI, or DE URTIACO.

Barony by Writ.

I. 1299. 1. HENRY DE L'ORTI, OF DE URTIACO, of Curry-Revell, Somerset, and Esseleigh, Wilts, s. and h. of Henry DE URTIACO, or L'ORTRAI, or DE L'ORTI, by Sabina, da. and h. of Richard REVELL, of Curry Revell afsd., Sheriff of Cornwall and Devon, and Mabel, sister and heir of Walter DE ESSELEIGH, of Esseleigh afsd. ; suc. his father in 1241 and his mother after 1251, and, having served in the wars in Wales and

---

(a) "There seems some doubt whether John was son or brother of Richard. Nisbet says his son, on the authority of a *gift of the ward of Richard, Lord Innermeath, and of the marriage of John, Lord Innermeath, to the Laird of Lundie, in the register*. It appears extraordinary that the same person should have both the ward of the father and the marriage of the son." [Wood's "Douglas."] The note (as given in italics above) in Nisbet's Heraldry (vol. ii, appendix, p. 182, edit. 1816), refers to "1528" the date of Richard's *death*. It does not seem to refer to the relationship (which, probably, was that of brother) of the parties.

(b) Of these, three were to be Earls and the rest "Lords of Parl." [Hist. MSS. Com. 1st Rep. of Lord Salisbury's MSS., p. 420.]

(c) At that date the King directs an inventory to be taken of his goods "now pertaining to his faderless bairns." [5th Rep. Hist. MSS. Com. I, 640.]

(d) See p 141, note "a."

(e) The family of Campbell do not, however, descend from the old Lords of Lorn. See p. 142, note "a."

France, was sum. 8 June (1294), 22 Ed. I.,(a) with about 60 other persons to attend the King wherever he might be to advise on the affairs of the realm and was again so sum. 26 Jan. (1296/7), 25 Ed. I.,(a) being finally sum. to Parl. as a Baron (LORD L'ORTI or LORD DE URTIACO) by writ 6 Feb. (1298/9), 27 Ed. I., directed "*Henrico de Urtiaco.*" He *d.* (1321-22), 15 Ed. II.

II. 1322. 2. HENRY (DE L'ORTI), LORD L'ORTI, s. and h. He was sum. to Parl. as a Baron by writ 10 Oct. (1325), 19 Ed. II., directed "*Henrico de L'Orty.*" He *m.* Sybil who survived him. He *d.* (1341), 15 Ed. III.

III. 1341. 3. JOHN (DE L'ORTI), LORD L'ORTI, s. and h., was never sum. to Parl.(b) He *d.* s.p.m. when the *Barony* fell into *abeyance.*(c)

LORTON OF BOYLE.

Viscountcy [I.] I. 1806. 1. THE HON. ROBERT EDWARD KING, 2d s. of Robert Henry (KING), 2d EARL OF KINGSTON [I.], by Caroline, da. and h. of Richard FITZGERALD, of Mount Ophaly, co. Kildare, was *b.* 12 Aug. 1773 in Hill street, Berkeley Sq.; was an officer in the army, distinguishing himself at the taking of Martinique, St. Lucia and Guadaloupe, being wounded at Point-a-Petre, and becoming, finally, Lieut.-Gen.; was M.P. for Boyle, 1793-1800, and was, at the date of the union, *cr.* 29 Dec., 1800(d) BARON ERRIS OF BOYLE, co. Roscommon [I.] being, on 28 May 1806, *cr.* VISCOUNT LORTON OF BOYLE, co. Roscommon [I.]; REP. PEER [I.], 1822-54; Lord Lieut. of co. Roscommon and Col. of the Roscommon Militia. He *m.* 9 Dec. 1799, his cousin, Frances, da. and h. of Laurence (PARSONS), 1st EARL OF ROSSE [I.], by Jane, da. of Edward (KING), 1st EARL OF KINGSTON [I.]. She, who was *b.* 31 March 1775, *d.* 7 Oct. 1841 at Rockingham Castle, co. Roscommon. He *d.* there 20 Nov. 1854 in his 82d year.

II. 1854. 2. ROBERT (KING), VISCOUNT LORTON OF BOYLE and BARON ERRIS OF BOYLE [I.], s. and h., *b.* 17 July 1804; *suc.* his father, 20 Nov. 1854, in the peerage [I.] abovenamed, and *suc.* his cousin, 8 Sep. 1869, as EARL OF KINGSTON, &c. [I.] See "KINGSTON" Earldom [I.], *cr.* 1768, *sub* the 6th and succeeding Earls.

LOTHIAN.

[Lothian is that part of the country south of the Forth which is not comprehended in Galloway and Strathclyde. Patrick, Earl of Dunbar [S.], was called "Conte de Laonois" [*Lothian*] at the siege of Carlaverock in 1300. See vol. iii, p. 198, note "c," *sub* "Dunbar."]

Earldom [S.] I. 1606. 1. MARK KERR, s. and h. of Mark KERR,(e) Commendator [1567], of Newbottle (of which he formerly had been Abbot), by Helen, 2d da. of George (LESLIE), 4th EARL OF ROTHES [S.], was Vicar of Linton (on his father's presentation), 1567; Master of the Requests, 1577—1606; *suc.* his father in 1581(e) as Commendator of Newbottle; was

(a) See vol. i, p. 259, note "c," *sub* "Basset de Sapcote," as to the summons of 1294 and see vol. i, p. 111, note "b," *sub* "Ap Adam," as to that of 1295, neither of them constituting a regular writ of summons to Parl.

(b) In Collinson's "*Somerset*" (vol. iii, pp. 50 and 138), he is said to have *m.* "Elizabeth Child, of Stanford," but no issue is attributed to him.

(c) The coheirs were his two daughters, *viz.* (1) Sybil who *m.* Sir Lawrence de St. Martin and (2) Margaret, *m.* Henry de Esturmie.

(d) He was the last *commoner* raised to the peerage of Ireland on the eve of the Union. See vol. i, p. 166, note "a," *sub* "Ashtown."

(e) See "notes on the family of Kerr," by "S." [*i.e.* the well known Mr. Stodart] in the "Her. and Gen.," vol. vii, p. 418, &c., where several corrections of facts, dates, &c. to the usual account thereof are given.

an extra. Lord of Session [S.], 1584, and, having had his lands of Newbottle erected into a Barony,(a) was *cr.* a Lord of Parl., as LORD NEWBOTTLE [S.], 28 Oct. 1587(b), or 15 Oct. 1591,(c) with rem. to his heirs male and assignees. He was *cr.*, 10 July 1606, EARL OF LOTHIAN [S.], with rem. to his heirs male. He *m.* Margaret, da. of John (MAXWELL), LORD HERRIES [S.], by Agnes, *suo jure* BARONESS HERRIES OF TERREGLES [S.] He *d.* 8 April 1609. His widow, by whom he is said to have had 31 children,(d) *d.* at Preston Grange, 8 Jan. 1617.(e) Will dat. 7 Jan. 1617, confirmed at Edinburgh, 18 May 1619.

II. 1609, to 1624. 2. ROBERT (KERR), EARL OF LOTHIAN and LORD NEWBOTTLE [S.], s. and h.; was appointed (v.p.) Master of the Requests, 1606; *suc. to the peerage* [S.], 1609. Having no male issue, he is said to have surrendered his dignities to the Crown and to have received a new grant thereof to the heirs general of his body.(f) He *m.* Annabella, 2d da. of Archibald (CAMPBELL), 7th EARL OF ARGYLL [S.], by his first wife, Anne, da. of William (DOUGLAS), EARL OF MORTON [S.] He *d.* s.p.m., 15 July 1624, being found dead in his bed with his throat cut. His widow living in 1628, retired to France.

* * * * * * *

(a) See vol. iv, p. 247, note "a," *sub* "Holyroodhouse," and p. 408, note "b," *sub* "Kinloss," as to the grants of religious houses with a peerage [S].

(b) In the creations given in Wood's "Douglas" (vol. ii, p. 672), the date is given as 28 July 1587, and reference made to "Mag. Sig. L. xxxvii, No. 92," but in the account by Mr. Stodart (see p. 144, note "e") the date is given (as also elsewhere) as 15 Oct. 1591, it being added that this is "the first peerage conferred on the family of Kerr."

(c) See p. 144, note "e."

(d) Of these children but five sons reached maturity, all of whom *d.* s.p.m. James (the 4th) is named in the charter of novodamus, 1621, and John (the 5th and yst.), was alive in 1627. The eldest son was Earl Robert as mentioned in the text; the 2d son, Sir William Ker, assumed the Earldom in 1624. (See p. 144, note "e"), but *d.* before 1650; while the 3d son (the survivor), Sir Mark Kerr, of Mauldsie, became in 1650 (on the death of the Earl of Roxburghe [S.]) the head of the family of Kerr, of Cessford, being also heir *male* to the Earldoms of Roxburgh and Lothian, a position, which on his death s.p.m. before 1663, devolved on Sir Walter Kerr, of Fawdonside. At that date (1663) the *heirs male of the body* of the 1st Earl of Lothian (who, presumably, were the heirs indicated in the patent of 1606) became *extinct*.

(e) She is accused, by Scotstarvet, of witchcraft and even of having caused the death of her husband.

(f) If the resignation was a valid one it would have carried the Earldom (together with its old precedence) to the da. and heir of line of the resigner, and there would have been no occasion for the *new* grant of the Earldom in 1631 to her husband. The matter is fully discussed in "Riddell," pp. 73-79. See also p. 146, note "a" for some implied doubt of its validity in the letter of Charles I. of 1631. In this letter, the King expressly states that he has seen the "*patent*" of "the Earldom of Lothian and Lordship of Newbottle" granted by King James to Earl Robert "*and the act of Parl.* [no dates are mentioned] confirming the same." No such patent or act are, however, known of, while, on the contrary, there *is* a *charter* under the great seal, 29 March 1621, limiting (on the resignation of Earl Robert) the Lordship of Newbottle and family *estates* "*precisely* as by the deeds in Charles the First's letter *but without carrying the honours*," and this charter *is* confirmed by *act of Parl.* 4 Aug. following. The Lothian patent of 1678 which ratifies the grant [the date being still unsupplied] speaks of it not as a "*patent*" (as called by Charles I.) but as a "*charter* under the great seal," which (says Riddell) "identifies it with the preceding grant of 1621," and (he adds), "the only subjects, therefore, I conceive that went to heirs female were the *lands*, the *honours* still continuing in their former state." Mr. Stodart, in one of his many excellent articles on the families of "Kerr" [Marshall's "*Genealogist*, vol. ii, p. 380," &c.], puts the matter very plainly as under; "The second Earl of Lothian held both his *titles* and *estates* under a destination to heirs male till 1621 when he executed a resignation and obtained a charter of *novodamus* 29 March, ratified by act of Parl. following, conveying the *estates* (composing the Lordship of Newbottle) to himself and the heirs male of his body [with rem. to] his eldest heir female without division, and [to] his brother, James, [his cousins] Robert, Earl of Roxburghe [and] Sir Walter of Fawdonside, and their heirs male. It is

[From 1624 to 1631 the peerage was assumed by the 2d but 1st surv. s. and heir male of the body of the grantee, *viz.*, SIR WILLIAM KERR, of Blackhope, next br. to Earl Robert. He, however, was interdicted by the Lords of Council, 8 March 1632, from using it,(a) the title having been claimed the previous year by the heir of line as under.]

III. 1631. *1.* ANNE, eldest da. and heir of line, having, before July 1631, complied with the conditions in the regrant (1621) of the estates, by marrying a person of the name of Kerr, inherited the same accordingly, and under the alleged regrant (above alluded to) of her father's peerage dignities (to which the same condition is said to have been attached) became (if the same was valid) *suo jure* COUNTESS OF LOTHIAN(b) and BARONESS NEWBOTTLE [S.] However this may have been, the King *cr.* SIR WILLIAM KERR, her husband (whom she *m.* before 31 July 1631, probably in Jan. 1630/1), *Earl of Lothian, &c.* [S.], as under.

SIR WILLIAM KERR, who was thus *cr.*, 31 Oct. 1631,(c) EARL OF LOTHIAN and LORD NEWBOTTLE [S.], was s. and h. ap. of Sir Robert KER, of Ancrum, co. Roxburgh (afterwards, 1633, 1st EARL OF ANCRAM [S.]), by his first wife, Elizabeth, da. of Sir John MURRAY, of Blackbarony; was *b.* about 1605; ed. at Cambridge; was in the expedition to the Isle of Rhé in 1627, &c., returning to Scotland about 1630 where he *m.* as afsd. and was raised to the peerage accordingly. In 1638 on the breaking out of the rebellion against the King he took a decided part with the Covenanters; joined Leslie's army in England in 1640; was at the defeat of the Royalists at Newbury and was sometime Gov. of Newcastle for the Scotch; was in 1641 one of the four Commissioners of the Treasury. He protested against the "engagement" of 1648; was soon afterwards Sec. of State till 1652; was one of the Commissioners to England (to protest against proceeding to extremities against the King), as, also, in 1650 to Breda,

to be remarked that only one of Lord Lothian's brothers (of whom at least four were then alive) is included in this destination, and, also, that if the da. and heir female shall be married at the time of the decease of the preceding heir she is absolutely excluded from the succession, but if she be unmarried and thereafter marry a gentleman of the name of Kerr, of lawful blood and honourably descended (who shall assume and wear the arms of the Earldom of Lothian and house of Newbotle) she shall succeed. *This is the only charter or patent* before the death of this Earl *on which any claim to his title* can be grounded."

(a) This was in consequence of a somewhat "arbitrary" letter dated 31 Oct. 1631, of Charles I. (in favour of Sir William Ker, of Ancrum, the husband of the heiress), "easily reconcilable with the circumstances of the Kers of Ancrum [whom "he wished to prefer"], being Court favourites." This letter recites the intention of Earl Robert "so far as in him laye" to settle the dignities thus and seems to imply that he did not validly do so, inasmuch as it goes on to say that "*therefore* His Majesty has thoght fitt to *creat* the said Sir William Ker, of Ancrum, and his aires male ERLIS OF LOTHIAN AND LORDS OF NEWBOTTLE." See "*Riddell*," p. 74, note "1." See p. 145, note "d," as to the extinction of the male issue of the first Earl.

(b) In 1628 she is spoken of merely as "*Anna Ker*;" her mother "Annabel, Countess of Lothian," being her curatrix. See Mr. Stodart's article as on p. 145, note "f."

(c) He "naturally took his place [in Parl.] as junior Earl. It would almost appear as if there had been some irregularity in this creation; the patent dat. 31 Oct. 1631, was not recorded in the great Seal Register [S.], and the King in his letter of the same date, mentioning the creation, only says that the late Earl had intended to convey '*his whole estate and honor as far as in him lay*' to his heir female. On 1 March 1634, another charter was granted, to Lord Lothian, of the Earldom of Lothian and Lordship of Newbotle with all the honours and dignities of Earldom and Lordship competent according to the former diploma *by which he was cr. Earl of Lothian and Lord Ker of Newbotle*; the limitation is to himself and his heirs male whom failing to the lawful and nearest heirs and assignees of the said William, Earl of Lothian." See Mr. Stodart's article as on p. 145, note "f." See also "Riddell," p. 101, note 3.

in which year he attended on the King in Scotland. In 1655 he endeavoured to obtain recompense for his expences in the cause of the Covenant. At the Restoration he went to London to justify his conduct, but refused to take the abjuration oath in 1662 and was fined £6,000 Scots, to pay which he alienated his paternal estate of Ancrum. He d. at Newbottle, Oct. 1675, aged about 70.

IV. 1675.
Marquessate [S.]
I. 1701.

2 and 1. ROBERT (KERR), EARL OF LOTHIAN and LORD NEWBOTTLE [S.], s. and h., b. 1636; styled LORD KERR OF NEWBOTTLE till he suc. to the peerage [S.] in 1675, having in 1673 served as a volunteer in the Dutch war. At the Parl. [S.] of 26 June 1678, he protested against the precedency over him of the Earl of Roxburghe and certain other Earls (cr. between 1606 and 1631) obtaining from the King a patent under the great seal, 23 Oct. 1673, "that he should take place and precedency conform to the orig. patent of creation of 1606, but this seems to have been entirely disregarded and not ratified,"(a) for tho' the Earl "protested" in 1685, 1687, and 1690, and obtained on 14 May 1690, a decision in his favour ("and had his name inserted in the Rolls accordingly") yet (in consequence of counter-protests) a decreet of 1 July 1695, ranked the Earls of Roxburghe, &c., above him, thus disallowing his claim to the Earldom of Lothian as a creation of 1606.(b) He repeated his protest in 1696, 1698, and 1700, but the matter was ended(c) the next year by his being raised to a Marquessate [S.] as below stated. Meantime the Earl had been P.C. (Jan. to Sep. 1686) to James II. as also (being a supporter of the Revolution) to William III. by whom he was made Justice Gen., and in 1692 Commissioner to the Kirk. By the death, on Sep. 1690, of his uncle, Charles, 2d Earl of Ancram [S.], he had become EARL OF ANCRAM, LORD KER OF NISBET, LANGNEWTOUN, AND DOLPHINSTOUN [S.], according to the limitation in the creation of that title, 24 June 1633. He was cr., 23 June 1701, MARQUESS OF LOTHIAN, EARL OF ANCRAM, VISCOUNT OF BRIENE, LORD KER OF NEWBOTTLE, OXNAM, JEDBURGH, DOLPHINSTOUN AND NISBET [S.], with rem. to the heirs male of his body, which failing to the other heirs of entail succeeding to him in his estate in all time to come. He m. Jean, 2d da. of Archibald (CAMPBELL), the well known MARQUESS OF ARGYLL [S.], by Margaret, da. of William (DOUGLAS), 9th EARL OF MORTON [S.] He d. in London, 15 Feb. 1703. Fun. entry in Lyon office. His widow was bur. at Newbottle, 18 May 1700. Fun. entry in Lyon office.

Marquessate [S.]
II.
Earldom [S.]
V.
1703.

2 and 3. WILLIAM (KERR), MARQUESS OF LOTHIAN, EARL OF LOTHIAN, EARL OF ANCRAM, VISCOUNT BRIENE, LORD JEDBURGH, &c. [S.], s. and h. He was b. 1661 and was a zealous promoter of the Revolution. He suc. as LORD JEDBURGH [S.] on the death, 4 Aug. 1692, of his cousin, Robert (Kerr), 4th Lord Jedburgh [S.], according to the novodamus obtained, 11 July 1670, for that peerage, which was cr., 2 Feb. 1621/2;

(a) See Mr. Stodart's article (as on p. 145, note "f"), it being added, "this patent refers to the resignation and confirms the regrant as if they had really been complete." Mr. Riddell ("Riddell," p. 78), remarks, "whether the Lothian patent in 1673 alone could have caused the precedence in [sic, sed quere "of"] 1606 is a question that may be raised. Such a power, after all, is but analogous to the privilege of elevating in the peerage by a higher title which has not been denied the Crown, and, if we hold that the patent of the Barony of Sinclair in 1677 did not proceed on a resignation, that may be a parallel case."

(b) The final decision being thus against him, the Earldom of Lothian, as cr. in 1606, as well as the Barony of Newbottle [1587 or 1591] to which his right of inheritance is similar, are henceforth omitted. As to the extinction (before 1667) of the heirs male of the body of the grantee of both these dignities see p. 145, note "d."

(c) The victory in the end was, however, with his opponent who on 25 April 1707, obtained a Dukedom [Roxburghe] with rem. to his heirs in the Earldom of Roxburghe [S.]

was Lieut. Col. of the 7th Dragoons, 1696; of the 3d Foot Guards, 1707 to 1713, ranking as Lieut. Gen. in the army, 1708, and being finally Major Gen. on the staff in Scotland. He *suc.* his father as *Marquess of Lothian*, &c. [S.], 15 Feb. 1703; K.T., 30 Oct. 1705; a zealous supporter of the Union; Rep. Peer [S.], 1715, having also been so chosen in 1708 tho' informally, his name being erased in 1709. He *m.* his first cousin, Jean, sister of Archibald, 1st Duke of Argyll [S.], da. of Archibald (Campbell), 9th Earl of Argyll [S.], by his first wife, Mary, da. of James (Stuart), Earl of Moray [S.] She *d.* 31 July and was *bur.* 4 Aug. 1712, at Newbottle. Fun. entry in Lyon office. He *d.* 28 Feb. and was *bur.* 6 March 1721/2, at Westm. Abbey, aged 61.(a) Will dat. 14 Oct. 1719, pr. 29 March 1722.

Marquessate [S.] III. Earldom [S.] VI. 1722.

3 and *4*. William (Kerr), Marquess of Lothian, Earl of Lothian, Earl of Ancram, Viscount Briene, Lord Jedburgh, &c. [S.], only s. and h., *b.* about 1690; was not only *styled* but appears *actually to have been* Lord Jedburgh in his father's lifetime, voting, as such, at the election of Scotch Rep. Peers in 1712.(b) He *suc. to the Marquessate, &c.* [S.], 28 Feb. 1721/2, and was Rep. Peer [S.] in five Parls. for 30 years, 1731-61. K.T., 1734; Lord High Commissioner to the Kirk, 1732-38; Lord Clerk Register, 1739-56. He *m.* firstly, about 1710, Margaret, da. of Sir Thomas Nicolson, Bart. [S.], of Kemnay, co. Aberdeen. She *d.* 30 Sep. 1759, at Newbottle Abbey, and was *bur.* in a vault there. Fun. entry at Lyon office. He *m.* secondly, 1 Oct. 1760, his cousin, Jean Janet, 1st da. of Lord Charles Kerr (2d s. of the 1st Marquess of Lothian [S.]), by Janet, da. of Sir David Murray, Bart. [S.], of Stanhope, co. Peebles. He *d.* at Lothian House, Canongate, Edinburgh, 28 July 1767, and was *bur.* at Newbottle Abbey. His widow, by whom he had no issue, *d.* there 26 Dec. 1787, in her 76th year.

Marquessate [S.] IV. Earldom [S.] VII. 1767.

4 and *5*. William Henry (Kerr), Marquess of Lothian, Earl of Lothian, Earl of Ancram, Viscount Briene, Lord Jedburgh, &c., s. and h., by first wife; *b.* 1710; *styled*, at first, Lord Jedburgh, but afterwards, 1735-67, Earl of Ancram; entered the army, 1735; was wounded at the battle of Fontenoy, 30 April 1735; commanded the Cavalry (11th Dragoons) on the left wing at Culloden, 16 April 1746,(c) attaining, finally, 1770, the rank of full General, and being Col. of the 25th Foot, 1747, and of the 11th Dragoons (in succession to his grand uncle, Lord Mark Kerr), 1752-75. He was M.P. for Richmond, co. York, in three Parls., 1747-63; *suc. to the Marquessate, &c.* [S.], 28 July 1767. Rep. Peer [S.], 1768; K.T., 26 Oct. 1768. He *m.*, 6 Nov. 1735, at St. James Westm., Caroline, da. of Robert (Darcy), 3d Earl of Holdernesse, by Frederica, da. and coheir of Meinhart (Schomberg), 3d Duke of Schomberg. He *d.* at Bath, 12 April 1775, aged 65. Will pr. April 1765. His widow *d.* Oct. 1778. Her will pr. 1778.

(a) Macky says of him when he was aged 45, "active in the Revolution against King James; he hath abundance of fire and may prove a man of business when he applies himself that way; laughs at all revealed religion, yet sets up for a pillar of Presbytery and proves the surest card in their pack, being very zealous tho' not very devout; is brave in his person; loves his country and his bottle; a thorough Libertine; very handsome; black, with a fine eye."

(b) See vol. iv, p. 326, note "b," *sub* "*Jedburgh*," for some remarks respecting a possible limitation of the Jedburgh peerage, different from that recorded. It is also to be noted that, according to some authorities, the s. and h. *apparent* of a Scotch nobleman is himself (v.p.) an actual Peer [S.]

(c) At Culloden was slain (at the head of his company) his only br., Lord Robert Kerr, a Capt. of Grenadiers, in the "bloom of his youth and extremely handsome."

Marquessate [S.] V. Earldom [S.] VIII. } 1775.

5 and *6*. WILLIAM JOHN (KERR), MARQUESS OF LOTHIAN, EARL OF LOTHIAN, EARL OF ANCRAM, &c. [S.], only s. and h., *b.* 13 March 1737; entered the army, 1754, becoming finally, 1796, full General, and being Col. of the 1st Horse Guards (afterwards, 1788, Life Guards), 1777-89, and Col. of the 11th Dragoons, 1798; *styled* EARL OF ANCRAM from 1767 until he *suc. to the Marquessate*, &c. [S.], 12 April 1775; K.T., 11 Oct. 1776; REP. PEER [S.], 1778, 1780, and 1784-90. He *m.* in Ireland, 9 June 1763, Elizabeth, da. of Chichester FORTESCUE, of Dromisken, co. Louth, by Elizabeth, da. of Richard (WELLESLEY, *formerly* COLLEY), 1st BARON MORNINGTON [I.] She, who was *b.* 3 April 1745, *d.* 30 Sep. 1780, in Portland Place, Marylebone, aged 35. He *d.* 4 Jan. 1815, aged 77. Will pr. 1815.

Marquessate [S.] VI. Earldom [S.] IX. } 1815.

6 and *7*. WILLIAM (KERR), MARQUESS OF LOTHIAN, EARL OF LOTHIAN, EARL OF ANCRAM, &c. [S.], s. and h., *b.* 4 Oct. 1763; *styled* EARL OF ANCRAM, 1775—1815; was an officer in the army and was, as Col. of the Midlothian Cavalry, active in suppressing the Irish rebellion of 1798; *suc. to the Marquessate*, &c. [S.], 4 Jan. 1815; Lord Lieut. of Midlothian and Roxburghshire; K.T., 26 April 1820; was *cr.* a Peer [U.K.], 17 April 1821,(a) as BARON KER OF KERSHEUGH, co. Roxburgh. He *m.* firstly, 14 April 1793, at St. Marylebone, Henrietta, the divorced (1793) wife of the 1st EARL OF BELMORE [I.], 1st da. and coheir of John (HOBART), 2d EARL OF BUCKINGHAMSHIRE, by his first wife, Mary Anne, da. and coheir of Sir Thomas DRURY, Bart. She, who was *b.* 7 April 1762, *d.* in New Norfolk street, Grosvenor square, 14 July, and was *bur.* 13 Aug. 1805, at Newbottle Abbey, aged 43. He *m.* secondly, 1 Dec. 1806, at Dalkeith House, Harriet, 4th and yst. da. of Henry (SCOTT), 3d DUKE OF BUCCLEUCH [S.], by Elizabeth, only da. and h. of George (MONTAGU, *formerly* BRUDENELL), 1st DUKE OF MONTAGU, and 4th EARL OF CARDIGAN. He *d.* 27 April 1824, aged 60. Admon. July 1824. His widow, who was *b.* 1 Dec. 1780, *d.* 18, and was *bur.* 26 April 1833, aged 52, at Petersham, Surrey. Will pr. May 1833.

Marquessate [S.] VII. Earldom [S.] X. } 1824.

7 and *8*. JOHN WILLIAM ROBERT (KERR), MARQUESS OF LOTHIAN, EARL OF LOTHIAN, EARL OF ANCRAM, &c. [S.], also BARON KER OF KERSHEUGH, s. and h., by first wife, *b.* 1 Feb. 1794; *styled* EARL OF ANCRAM, 1815-24; M.P. for Huntingdon, 1820-24; *suc. to the peerage*, 27 April 1824; Capt. of the Yeomen of the Guard; Lord Lieut. of Roxburghshire and Col. of the Edinburgh Militia. He *m.*, 19 July 1831, Cecil Chetwynd, da. of Charles (TALBOT), 2d EARL TALBOT, by Frances Thomasine, da. of Charles LAMBART. He *d.* 14 Nov. 1841, aged 47, at Blickling House, Norfolk. Will pr. Jan. 1842. His widow, who was *b.* 17 April 1808, at Ingestre Hall, co. Stafford, *d.* 13 May 1877, at the Hotel de Rome, in Rome.

Marquessate [S.] VIII. Earldom [S.] XI. } 1841.

8 and *9*, WILLIAM SCHOMBERG ROBERT (KERR), MARQUESS OF LOTHIAN, EARL OF LOTHIAN, EARL OF ANCRAM, &c. [S.], also BARON KER OF KERSHEUGH, s. and h., *b.* 12 Aug. 1832, at Newbottle Abbey; styled EARL OF ANCRAM till he *suc. to the peerage*, 14 Nov. 1841; ed. at Eton and at Ch. Ch., Oxford; 1st Class in Classics, 1853; B.A. and first Class in Jurisprudence and Mod. History, 1854. He *m.*, 12 Aug. 1857, at Ingestre, co. Stafford, Constance Harriet Mahonese, 2d da. of his maternal uncle,

(a) This was one of the "Coronation" peerages of George IV. for a list of which see vol. ii, p. 351, note "d," *sub* "Conyngham."

Henry John (TALBOT), 18th EARL OF SHREWSBURY and 3d EARL TALBOT, by Sarah Elizabeth, da. of Henry (DE-LA-POER-BERESFORD), 2d MARQUESS OF WATERFORD [I.] He *d.* s.p., 4 July 1870, aged 31, at Clapham, Surrey. His widow, who was *b.* 15 June 1836, living 1892.

Marquessate [S.] IX. Earldom [S.] XII.	1870.	*9 and 10.* SCHOMBERG HENRY (KERR), MARQUESS OF LOTHIAN [1701], EARL OF LOTHIAN [1631], EARL OF ANCRAM [1633 and 1701], VISCOUNT BRIENE [1701], LORD JEDBURGH [1622], LORD NEWBOTTLE [1631], LORD KER OF NISBET, LANGNEWTOUN, AND DOLPHINSTOUN [1633], and LORD KER OF NEWBOTTLE, OXNAM, JEDBURGH, DOLPHINSTOUN AND

NISBET [1701], in the peerage of Scotland, also BARON KER OF KERSHEUGH [1821], in the peerage of the United Kingdom, br. and h. He was *b.* 2 Dec. 1833; ed. at Glenalmond, Eton, and (1851) at New Coll., Oxford; was in the Diplomatic service, being Attaché at Frankfort and Teheran; *suc. to the peerage,* 4 July 1870; Lord Keeper of the Privy Seal [S.], 1874; K.T., 1878; LL.D. of Edinburgh, 1882; P.C., 1886; Sec. of State and Keeper of the Great Seal [S.], 1887; Lord Rector of Edinburgh Univ., 1887-88; Capt. Gen. of the Royal comp. of Archers. He *m.*, 28 Feb. 1865, Victoria Alexandrina, 1st da. of Walter Francis (MONTAGU-DOUGLAS-SCOTT), 5th DUKE OF BUCCLEUCH [S.], by Charlotte Anne, yst. da. of Thomas (THYNNE), 2d MARQUESS OF BATH. She was *b.* 20 Nov. 1844.

[WILLIAM WALTER SCHOMBERG KERR, *styled* EARL OF ANCRAM, s. and h. ap., *b.* 29 March 1867; ed. at Eton and (1886) at New Coll., Oxford; was aide de camp to the Gov. of New South Wales, where he *d.* v.p. and unm., 15 June 1892, aged 24, being accidentally shot at Quideng, near Bombala, co. Wellesley; *bur.* at Sydney.]

[ROBERT SCHOMBERG KERR, *styled* EARL OF ANCRAM, 3d and yst. but only surv. s. and h. ap., *b.* 22 March 1874.]

Family Estates.—These, in 1883, consisted of 8,073 acres in Norfolk (worth £9,107 a year), besides 19,740 in Roxburghshire and 4,548 in Midlothian. *Total* 32,361 acres, worth £45,203 a year "exclusive of £6,296 for mines, and inclusive of £8,986 in Norfolk, owned by the Mchss. Dow." *Principal Residences.* Newbattle (formerly Newbottle) Abbey, near Dalkeith, Mount Teviot Lodge, near Jedburgh, and Blickling Hall, near Aylsham, co. Norfolk.

LOUDOUN.

Barony [S.] I. 1601. *1.* SIR HUGH CAMPBELL, of Loudoun, co. Ayr, s. and h. of Sir Matthew CAMPBELL,(a) of the same, by Isabel, da. of Sir John DRUMMOND, of Innerpeffry, *suc.* his father about 1572; was Sheriff of Ayr; P.C. [S.], and, having sat as a minor Baron [S.], 1597 and 1599, was *cr.* a Lord of Parl., 30 June 1601, as LORD CAMPBELL(b) OF LOUDOUN [S.] He *m.* firstly in 1572 Margaret, da. of Sir John GORDON, of Lochinvar. He *m.* secondly Isabel, the divorced wife of Sir Robert GORDON, of Lochinvar, da. of William (RUTHVEN), 1st EARL OF GOWRIE [S.], by Dorothea, da. of Henry (STEWART), 2d LORD METHVEN [S.] She *d.* s.p.m. He *m.* thirdly Margaret, da. of Sir David HOME, of Wedderburn, but by her had no issue. He *d.* s.p.m.s., 15 Dec. 1622.

(a) This Matthew was 9th in descent from Sir Duncan Campbell, of Loudoun, who acquired that estate, about 1318, by marriage with Susanna Crawford, the heiress thereof, the said Susanna being 5th in descent from Sir Reginald Crawford who *m.* (about 1200) Margaret, da. and h. of James Loudoun, of Loudoun.

(b) The title is given as "*Campbell* of Loudoun" in the appendix to Wood's Douglas" containing the patents, but there is no reference to the "*Mag. Sig.*" or any other authority. It seems generally to have been called "*Loudoun*" only.

II. 1622. Earldom [S.] I. 1633.

2 and 1. MARGARET [*suo jure?*] BARONESS CAMPBELL OF LOUDOUN [S.], grandaughter and heir of line, being eldest da. and coheir([a]) of George CAMPBELL, Master of Loudoun, by Jean, da. of John (FLEMING), 1st EARL OF WIGTOUN [S.], which George was only s. and h. ap. of the 1st Baron (by his first wife) but *d.* v.p. in 1612. She, who was *b.* about 1605, and *m.* before 8 March 1620, appears to have inherited the peerage under a resignation by her grandfather (shortly before his death) in favour of her husband, Sir John CAMPBELL, who was recognised as LORD LOUDOUN [S.] accordingly.([b])

SIR JOHN CAMPBELL, of Lawers, the husband of the above Margaret, who, on the death of her father, in Dec. 1622, *suc.* as LORD CAMPBELL OF LOUDOUN [S.] as abovementioned, was eldest son of Sir James CAMPBELL, of Lawers, by Jean, da. of James (COLVILL), 1st LORD COLVILL OF CULROSS [S.] He was *b.* 1598 and was (as "*Lord Loudoun*") *cr.*, 12 May 1633, EARL OF LOUDOUN, LORD TARRINZEAN([c]) AND MAUCHLINE [S.], with rem. to his heirs male; but, as he immediately took part against the Crown, the patent was superseded and continued so till in 1641 it was allowed to pass (as mentioned below) with the precedency attached thereto. Meanwhile he took a prominent part with the Covenanters; was one of their Commissioners at the pacification of Berwick in June 1639, at Whitehall in March 1640 (where he was imprisoned on suspicion of treason) and at Ripon in Oct. 1640. In Aug. 1641 the King opened the Scotch Parl. "and offices and titles of honour were conferred on the *prime Covenanters who were thought most capable to do him service.* Accordingly Loudoun '*the principal manager of the rebellion,*' (as Clarendon calls him), was appointed LORD CHANCELLOR of Scotland on 30 Sep. 1641,"([d]) taking his oath 2 Oct., the patent of his Earldom [S.], granted in 1633, being allowed to pass as above mentioned and a pension of £1,000 a year being granted. First Commiss. of the Treasury [S.], 1641; was sent to treat with the King at York, at Oxford, at Uxbridge (in 1645) at Newcastle, and (1647) at Carisbrooke; was President of the Parl. [S.] which met on 2 March 1648, where the proclamation of the new King was ordered but, quickly changing sides, did public penance for his conduct. He was, however, present at the coronation at Scone of Charles II. on 1 Jan. 1650, and at the battle of Dunbar. He joined in 1653 the Royalists in the Highlands, but surrendered to Gen. Monck and was excepted out of Cromwell's act of indemnity. At the Restoration he was deprived of the Chancellorship, and, tho' his pension was continued, was fined £12,000 Scots. He *d.* at Edinburgh, 15 March 1662/3, and was *bur.* at Loudoun. His wife survived him.

Earldom [S.] II. Barony [S.] III. 1663.

2 and 3. JAMES (CAMPBELL), EARL OF LOUDOUN, &c. [S.], who v.p. was *styled* LORD MAUCHLINE, and who, as such, was, with his father, excepted out of Cromwell's act of indemnity. He *suc. to the peerage* [S.], 15 March 1662/3.([e]) Being opposed to the Court measures he resided abroad. He *m.* Margaret, da. of Hugh (MONTGOMERY), 2d EARL OF EGLINTON [S.], by his second wife, Mary, da. of John (LESLIE), EARL OF ROTHES [S.] He *d.* at Leyden in Germany, 1684.

(a) Elizabeth, the 2d and yst. da. and coheir, *m.* Sir Hugh Campbell, of Cessnock.

(b) Special retour, 22 Nov. 1627, of "Domina Margareta Campbell, sponsa Johannis, *Domini Loudoun*;" again the patent, 12 May 1633, creating "Johannem, *Dominum Loudoun*," as Earl of Loudoun, &c. See "*Riddell*," p. 54, note 1. It was also recognised during the period (1633-41) when the *Earldom* (*cr.* 1633) was superseded, there being, 15 March 1634, a charter granted to John, *Lord Loudoun*, &c." See Wood's "Douglas."

(c) Sometimes given as "*Farrinyean.*"

(d) *Nat. Biogr.*

(e) If it be considered that his mother was a *suo jure* Baroness [S.] his inheritance of that dignity would not be till her death.

Earldom [S.] III. Barony [S.] IV. } 1684.

3 and *4*. HUGH (CAMPBELL), EARL OF LOUDOUN, &c. [S.], s. and h., *styled* LORD MAUCHLINE till he *suc. to the peerage* [S.] in 1684, taking his seat, 8 Sep. 1696; P.C. [S.], 1697 and 1708, and [E.], 1708; an extra. Lord of Session [S.], 1699—1731; a Commissioner of the Treasury [S.], 1702-04; Sec. of State [S.], 1705-07; K.T., 10 Aug. 1706; one of the Commissioners for the Union [S.] He resigned *his peerage dignities* and obtained a *novodamus* thereof, 7 Feb. 1707, with rem. to the heirs male of his body, rem. to heirs gen. of the body of the 1st Earl, rem. to the heirs male whatsoever of the 1st Earl. He was REP. PEER [S.] in seven success. Parls., 1707-31, being one of the original sixteen. LORD KEEPER [S.] (being the first since the Union), 1708-13; served as a volunteer at the battle of Sheriffmuir in 1715; High Commiss. to the gen. assembly of the Kirk during six years, *viz.*, 1722, 1725, 1726, 1728, 1730, and 1731, having a pension of £2,000 a year settled on him in 1727; Lord Lieut. of Ayrshire. He *m.*, 6 April 1700, at Kirkliston, Margaret, da. of John (DALRYMPLE), 1st EARL OF STAIR [S.], by Elizabeth, da. and h. of Sir John DUNDAS. He *d.* 20 Nov. 1731, at Loudoun. Will pr. 1732. His widow, who was *b.* 4 Sep. 1677, at Kirkliston, *d.* 3 April 1777, in her 100th year, having lived, during her widowhood, at Lorn Castle, co. Argyll.

Earldom [S.] IV. Barony [S.] V. } 1731.

4 and *5*. JOHN (CAMPBELL), EARL OF LOUDOUN, &c. [S.], only s. and h., *b.* 5 May 1705, and *styled* LORD MAUCHLINE till he *suc. to the peerage* [S.] in 1731. REP. PEER [S.] in eight Parls. for 48 years, 1734-82. Having entered the army in 1727, he was aide-de-camp to the King, 1743; raised in 1745 (as Colonel) a regiment of Highlanders of which nearly all were killed at Preston by the Jacobite insurgents, tho' shortly afterwards he effected the capture of Lord Lovat. Early in 1756 he was made Gov. Gen. of Virginia and Commander in Chief of the Forces in America (where the French had taken Ontario and Oswego) and prepared for making siege to Louisbourg. His measures were, however, unpopular and dilatory(a) and he was recalled in 1757. In 1762 he was second in command of the troops sent to Portugal against Spain. He had become Major Gen. in 1755; Lieut. Gen. in 1758, and full General in 1770, being at his death the third Field officer in the army. He was Col. of the 30th Foot, 1749-70; Col. of the 60th (Royal American), 1755-57, and Col. of the 3d Foot Guards, 1770-82; was Gov. of Stirling Castle, 1741; P.C., F.S.A., &c. He *d.* unm., 27 April 1782, in his 77th year, at Loudoun Castle.(b) Admon. July 1782.

Earldom [S.] V. Barony [S.] VI. } 1782.

5 and *6*. JAMES (MURE-CAMPBELL), EARL OF LOUDOUN, &c. [S.], nephew and h., being s. and h. of Lieut. Gen. the Hon. Sir James CAMPBELL, K.B. (Col. of the Scots Guards), by Jean, da. of David (BOYLE), 1st EARL OF GLASGOW [S.], eventually sole heir of her mother (the Earl's second wife), Jane, da. and h. of William MURE, of Rowallan, co. Ayr, which James Campbell was 3d and yst. son of James, 2d Earl of Loudoun, abovenamed. He was *b.* 11 Feb. 1726; *suc.* his father (who was slain at Fontenoy) 30 April 1745, in the family estate of Lawers; assumed the name of *Mure* before that of *Campbell*, having *suc.* (by the death of his mother) in Dec. 1729, to the estate of his maternal grandmother abovenamed; was Capt. of the Scots Greys (his father's regiment), 1745; Lieut. Col. of 2d Dragoon Guards and then of the 21st Dragoons, 1757 to 1763, becoming finally, 1781, Major Gen. in the army; was M.P. for Ayrshire, 1754-61. He *suc. to the peerage* [S.], 27 April 1782. He *m.*, 30 April 1777, Flora, 1st da. of John MACLEOD, of Rasay, co. Inverness. She *d.* 2 Sep. 1780, at Hope Park, near Edinburgh. He *d.* s.p.m., 28 April 1786, in his 61st year.

(a) "It was said of him by a Philadelphian that he was *like King George upon the signposts, always on horseback, but never advancing.*" [*Nat. Biogr.*]

(b) Under the act of 1747 for abolishing hereitable jurisdictions he received £2,675 (in full of his claim of £11,000) for the Sheriffship of Air and the regalities of Maucline and Loudoun.

Earldom [S.] VI. **Barony [S.]** VII. } 1786. **Viscountcy [U.K.]** I. 1817.

6, 7, and *1.* FLORA, *suo jure* COUNTESS OF LOUDOUN, BARONESS CAMPBELL OF LOUDOUN, &c. [S.], only da. and h., *b.* Aug. 1780; *m.* 12 July 1804, Francis (RAWDON-HASTINGS), 2d EARL OF MOIRA, &c. [I.], and BARON RAWDON, who was *cr.*, 13 Feb. 1817, VISCOUNT LOUDOUN, EARL OF RAWDON, and MARQUESS OF HASTINGS [U.K.], and who *d.* 28 Nov. 1826, aged 71. She *d.* 8 Jan. 1840, aged 59, and was *bur.* at Loudoun.

[FRANCIS-GEORGE-AUGUSTUS RAWDON-HASTINGS, *styled* LORD MAUCHLINE AND RAWDON, 1st s. and h. ap., *b.* in St. James sq., 22 Jan., and *d.* 13 Feb. 1807, an infant and v.p.]

Viscountcy [U.K.] II. 1826. **Earldom [S.]** VII. **Barony [S.]** VIII. } 1840.

2, 7, and *8.* GEORGE AUGUSTUS FRANCIS (RAWDON-HASTINGS), MARQUESS OF HASTINGS, EARL OF RAWDON, VISCOUNT LOUDOUN [U.K.], &c., also EARL OF LOUDOUN, LORD CAMPBELL OF LOUDOUN, &c. [S.], also EARL OF MOIRA &c. [I.], 2d but only surv. s. and h., *b.* 4 Feb. 1808, in St. James' place; *styled* LORD MAUCHLINE AND RAWDON till 1817, and *styled* EARL OF RAWDON from 1817 till he *suc. to the peerage* (on the death of his father), 28 Nov. 1826, as *Marquess of Hastings, Earl of Rawdon, Viscount Loudoun,* &c. By the death of his mother, 8 Jan. 1840, he became also a Peer of Scotland as *Earl of Loudoun,* &c. He *d.* 13 Jan. 1844, aged 35.

Earldom [S.] VIII. **Viscountcy [U.K.]** III. **Barony [S.]** IX. } 1844.

8, 3, and *9.* PAULYN REGINALD SERLO (RAWDON-HASTINGS), MARQUESS OF HASTINGS, EARL OF RAWDON, VISCOUNT LOUDOUN [U.K.], &c., also EARL OF LOUDOUN, &c. [S.], also EARL OF MOIRA, &c. [I.], s. and h., *b.* 2 June 1833, being *styled* EARL OF RAWDON till he *suc. to the peerage,* 13 Jan. 1844. He *d.* unm., 17 Jan. 1851, aged 18.

Earldom [S.] IX. **Viscountcy [U.K.]** IV. **Barony [S.]** X. } 1851.

9, 4, and *10.* HENRY WEYSFORD CHARLES PLANTAGENET (RAWDON-HASTINGS), MARQUESS OF HASTINGS, EARL OF RAWDON, VISCOUNT LOUDOUN [U.K.], &c., also EARL OF LOUDOUN, LORD CAMPBELL OF LOUDOUN, &c. [S.], also EARL OF MOIRA, &c. [I.], br. and h., *b.* 22 July 1842, *suc. to the peerage,* 17 Jan. 1851, and *d.* s.p., 10 Nov. 1868, aged 26, when of the titles abovenamed the *Marquessate of Hastings,* the *Earldom of Rawdon,* and the *Viscountcy of Loudoun* became *extinct,* as did also the *Earldom of Moira,* &c. [I.], but the *Earldom of Loudoun* and the other Scotch dignities devolved as under.

For fuller particulars see "HASTINGS" Marquessate, *cr.* 1817; *ex.* 1868.

Earldom [S.] X. **Barony [S.]** XI. } 1868.

10 and *11.* Edith Mary, *suo jure* COUNTESS OF LOUDOUN, BARONESS CAMPBELL OF LOUDOUN and BARONESS TARRINZEAN AND MAUCHLINE [S.], eldest sister and h. of line, *b.* 10 Dec. 1833, and *bap.* 4 Jan. 1834, at Castle Donington; *m.* 30 April 1853, at St. Geo. Han. sq., Charles Frederick CLIFTON, *afterwards* (1858), ABNEY-HASTINGS, who, after her death, was *cr.*, 4 May 1880, BARON DONINGTON of Donington Park, co. Leicester. See that title.

She, on 6 Nov. 1871, became *suo jure* BARONESS BORTREAUX, BARONESS HUNGERFORD, BARONESS DE MOLEYNS, and BARONESS HASTINGS DE HASTINGS, the abeyance of those Baronies, to which she was the senior coheir (heir to a fourth part) having been terminated at that date by letters patent in her favour. She *d.* at Ventnor in the Isle of Wight, 28 Jan. 1874, aged 40, and was *bur.* at Donington. Her husband living 1892.

Earldom [S.] XI. Barony [S.] XII. } 1874. *11* and *12*. CHARLES EDWARD (ABNEY-HASTINGS, *afterwards* RAWDON-HASTINGS), EARL OF LOUDOUN [1633], LORD CAMPBELL(a) OF LOUDOUN [1601] and LORD TARRINZEAN AND MAUCHLINE [1633], in the peerage of Scotland, also LORD BOTREAUX [1368], LORD HUNGERFORD [1426], LORD DE MOLEYNS [1445], and LORD HASTINGS DE HASTINGS [1461], s. and h., *b.* 5 Jan. and *bap.* 20 June 1855, at Grosvenor chapel, St. Geo. Han. sq.; *suc.* his mother *in the peerage*, 28 Jan. 1874, took his seat as Lord Hastings on 8 May 1876, and on 20 May 1880, as Lord Botreaux; took (together with his father) the name of *Rawdon-Hastings*(b) in lieu of that of *Abney-Hastings*, by Royal licence 8 April 1887. He *m.*, 4 Feb. 1880, at St. Mary's Roman Catholic church, Cadogan street, Chelsea, Alice Mary Elizabeth, 3d da. of Edward George (FITZALAN-HOWARD), 1st BARON HOWARD OF GLOSSOP, by his first wife, Augusta, da. and h. of the Hon. George Henry TALBOT, br. to John, 16th EARL OF SHREWSBURY. She was *b.* 20 June 1856.

Family Estates.—These, in 1883 (*including* that of his father, Lord Donington, "which is hopelessly mixed up therewith in the return," but "*excluding* £2,259 mine rent in Ayrshire") consisted of 18,638 acres in Ayrshire, 10,174 in Leicestershire, 2,750 in Derbyshire, and 1,348 in the West Riding of Yorkshire. *Total*, 32,910 acres, worth £39,977 a year. *Principal Residences.* Rowallan Castle and Loudoun Castle both in co. Ayr, Willesley Hall, co. Derby, Donington Park, co. Leicester, and Rawdon Hall, Yorkshire.

Barony. **LOUGHBOROUGH** (co. Leicester.)

I. 1558, to 1572. See "HASTINGS OF LOUGHBOROUGH, co. Leicester," Barony (*Hastings*), *cr.* 1558; *ex.* 1572.

II. 1643, to 1666. *1.* The HON. HENRY HASTINGS, 2d s. of Henry, 5th EARL OF HUNTINGDON, by Elizabeth, da. and coheir of Ferdinando (STANLEY), 5th EARL OF DERBY, was *b.* 28 Sep. 1610; distinguished himself in the Royal cause; Sheriff of Leicestershire, 1643, and Colonel General of that county; was *cr.*; 23 Oct. 1643,(c) BARON LOUGHBOROUGH, co. Leicester. Early in 1645 he was made Gov. of Leicester, which, however, he surrendered to Fairfax in June 1645, but retained Ashby till Feb. 1645/6. He was voted by the Commons one of the seven great delinquents in Nov. 1648, but the vote was revoked next month. He escaped to Holland in 1649. In 1661 he was Lord Lieut. of Leicestershire. He *d.* in London unm., 10 Jan. 1666, when his *peerage* became *extinct*. He was *bur.* (with his great uncle and predecessor in the title) at St. George's chapel, Windsor. Will dat. 28 Aug. 1665, pr. 15 May 1667.

III. 1780, to 1785. *i.e.*, "LOUGHBOROUGH, CO. LEICESTER," Barony (*Wedderburn*), *cr.* 1780; *ex.* 1805; see "ROSSLYN" Earldom, *cr.* 1801.

(a) See p. 150, note "b."

(b) The object of this taking the name of *Rawdon* is not very clear as he possessed none of the titles granted to (and under 1,400 acres of the estates of) the *Rawdon* family; while his principal estate (Rowallan) came from the family of *Mure*, his Scotch Earldom, &c., from the family of *Campbell* and his English Barony of Hastings (thro' which comes the other Baronies) from the family of *Hastings*. The name of *Abney* (thus relinquished) had been taken by Act of Parl. in 1859, on inheriting the Abney estates at Willesden, &c., co. Derby, by settlement dat. 1844, on the Rawdon-Hastings family, of Sir Charles *Abney*-Hastings, Bart., then decd.

(c) Black's "*Docquets*" as quoted in "Creations, 1483—1646, in ap. 47th Rep. D.K. Pub. Records."

LOUGHBOROUGH (co. Surrey).

i.e., "LOUGHBOROUGH of Loughborough, co. Surrey," Barony (*Wedderburn*, afterwards, 1805, *Erskine*), *cr.* 1795; see "ROSSLYN" Earldom, *cr.* 1801.

LOUGHGUYRE.

i.e., "LOUGHGUYRE, co. Limerick," Barony [I.] (*Fane*) *cr.* 1718 with the VISCOUNTCY OF FANE [I.], which see; *ex.* 1766.

LOUGHMORE.

NICHOLAS PURCELL, of Loughmore, co. Tipperary, Col. of a Reg. of Horse in 1689 in Ireland, in the service of King James II., is said to have been *cr.* by that King, when in exile, BARON LOUGHMORE [I.] See vol. i, p. 59, note "b" (*sub* "Albemarle") for a list of the "*Jacobite Peerages*."

LOUGHNEAGH.

i.e., "LOUGHNEAGH, co. Antrim," Barony [I.] (*Clotworthy*, afterwards, 1665, *Skeffington*) *cr.* 1660.

LOUR.

i.e., "LOUR," Barony [S.] (*Carnegy*) *cr.* 1639; exchanged for the BARONY OF ROSEHILL [S.] in 1662; see "NORTHESK" Earldom [S.], that title having been substituted (in 1662) for the EARLDOM OF ETHIE [S.], *cr.* 1647.

LOUTH.

Earldom [I.]
I. 1319, to 1329.

SIR JOHN DE BERMINGHAM, of Thetmoy, s. and h. of Peter Fitz James Mac Phioris DE BERMINGHAM,(a) of Thetmoy afsd., by Ela, sister and coheir of Edmund, and da. of William DE ODINGSELLS, of co. Warwick; *suc.* his father in 1308; *knighted* by the Lord Deputy [I.] in 1312; Commander of the English forces in Ireland, 1318; defeated the army of Edward Bruce, who had been crowned King of Ireland, and was, in reward, *cr.* 12 May (1319), 12 Ed. II,(b) EARL OF LOUTH [I.] (with the fee of £20 issuing out of that county), with rem. to heirs male of his body. In 1321 he was Chief Governor (as Lord Justice) of Ireland. He *m.* Catharine, 4th da. of Richard (DE BURGH), 2d EARL OF ULSTER [I.], by Margaret, da. of Sir John DE BURGH, of Lanvalley. He *d.* s.p.m.s.(c) 10 June 1329, being (with his brothers, Robert and Peter, and many of his race) treacherously slain at Ballybraggan by the rebellious Irish. At his death *the Earldom* became *extinct.*

[RICHARD DE BERMINGHAM, *styled* apparently(d) LORD ATHERDEE, only s. and h. ap.; he *d.* unm. and v.p.]

(a) See tabular pedigree in vol. i, p. 176, note "b," *sub* "Athenry."

(b) "Patent dat. in full Parl. at York 12 May (not 7 June as some write) 1319 (12 Ed. II), which was exemplified at Kilkenny, 1 Nov. 1375 (49 Ed. III), and is among the patent rolls of that year in the Birmingham tower. No. 156, F." [*Lodge* vol. iii, p. 34.] This is one of the six Irish Earldoms *cr.* before 1330, for a list of which see *sub* "ORMONDE."

(c) He had three daughters and coheirs, *viz.* (1) Matilda *m.* Sir Eustace Le Poer, ancestor to the Earls of Tyrone [I.] (2) Bartholomea *m.* John, son of Richard Fitz Richer, and had issue, and (3) Catharine, *m.* Edmund Lacy.

(d) "*Lodge*," vol. iii, p. 36 [last line of note] the Lordship of Atherdee (often confused with Athenry, *alias* Athenree) having been conferred on the Earl of Louth.

Barony [I.] I. 1541. 1. SIR OLIVER PLUNKETT, of Kilsaran, co. Louth, 2d s. but eventually h. male of Sir John (or Sir Patrick) PLUNKETT, of Bewley, Kilsaran, and Talanston, in that co., by Catharine, da. of Thomas NANGLE, of Navan, was, by Henry VIII., cr., 15 June 1541,(a) BARON LOUTH, co. Louth [I.] He m. firstly Catharine, da. and h. of John ROCHFORT, of Carrick, co. Kildare. He m. secondly Maud, widow of Walter GOLDING, da. and coheir of Walter BATH, of Rathfeigh. She survived him and m. (thirdly) Richard BELLEW.

II. 1555? 2. THOMAS (PLUNKETT), BARON LOUTH [I.], s. and h., by first wife; was in the Parl. [I.] of 1559, &c., *knighted* by the Lord Deputy in 1566. He m. Margaret, da. and h. of Nicholas BARNEWALL, of Dromnah, by Catharine, da. of Richard LUTTRELL, of Luttrellstown. He *d.* 1 May 1571. Will dat. 26 April 1571. His wife survived him.

III. 1571. 3. PATRICK (PLUNKETT), BARON LOUTH [I,], s. and h., aged 23 when he *suc. to the peerage* [I.] in 1571. He m. before 1571 Maude, 1st da. and coheir(b) of Christopher (PLUNKETT), 7th LORD KILLEEN [I.], by Ellice, da. of Sir Christopher BARNEWALL. He *d.* s.p.m., being slain in 1575 in a raid at Essexford, co. Monaghan. His widow m. (—) SHERGOLD.

IV. 1575. 4. OLIVER (PLUNKETT), BARON LOUTH [I.], br. and h. male; *suc. to the peerage* [I.], 1575; was present at the Parl. [I.], 26 April 1585, and also at the hosting at Tara, 24 Sep. 1593, with six mounted archers where he was made Leader of the county of Louth. He m. firstly Frances, da. of Sir Nicholas BAGNALL, Knight Marshal of Ireland, by whom he had eight children. He m. secondly Genet, widow of John BATH, Ch. Justice of the Common Pleas [I.], 1556-59, da. of Patrick DOWDALL, of Termonfeighan. He *d.* 5 March 1607, and was *bur.* at Tallanston. His widow, by whom he had no issue, *d.* 8 July 1617.

V. 1607. 5. MATTHEW (PLUNKETT), BARON LOUTH [I.], s. and h. by first wife; *suc. to the peerage* [I.] 5 March 1607, and was present at the Parls [I.] of 1613 and 1615. He m. Mary, sister of Thomas, 1st VISCOUNT FITZWILLIAM OF MERYON [I], da. of Sir Richard FITZWILLIAM, of Mount Meryon, co. Dublin, by Jane, da. of (—) PRESTON. He *d.* 19 July 1629. Will dat. 4 Dec. 1625. *Inq. post mortem.* His widow m. Gerald AYLMER.

VI. 1629. 6. OLIVER (PLUNKETT), BARON LOUTH [I.], s. and h., aged 21 years and 4 months and unm. when he *suc. to the peerage* [I.], 19 July 1629; lived chiefly at Carrick; had spec. livery of his estate, 1 April 1631; was present in Parl. [I.] 14 July and 4 Nov. 1634, being, 24 March 1639, on the Committee for Privileges. He, however, joined the rebels in Nov. 1639, and was at the siege of Drogheda, being named Col. Gen. of the forces to be raised in the county of Louth. He was taken prisoner in 1642 and outlawed,(c) in the county of Meath, 17 Nov. 1642. He was also excepted from pardon of life and estate by Cromwell's Act, 12 July 1652. He was among the remonstrant Roman Catholic nobility [I.] in 1662.(d) He m., after 1629, Mary, Dow. VISCOUNTESS DILLON [I.], da. of Randal (MACDONNELL), 1st EARL OF ANTRIM [I.], by Alice, da. or sister of Hugh (O'NEILL), EARL OF TYRONE [I.] He *d.* about 1679.

VII. 1679? 7. MATTHEW (PLUNKETT), BARON LOUTH [I.], only surv. s. and h. He served Charles II. when in exile, from whom (after 1660) he (as well as his Father) received several grants of lands, &c. He was

---

(a) The preamble is given in "*Lodge*," vol. vi, p. 164, note.
(b) See vol. iv, p. 377, note "b," *sub* "Killeen."
(c) This outlawry was by a resolution of the House of Lords [I.] in 1698, but apparently not previously, held to have deprived the family of their privilege of peerage. The retrospective effect of this resolution would be to deprive the 7th Baron of his peerage, but (tho' he never sat in the House of Lords) he appears to have been repeatedly recognised as a Peer both by the Crown and others.
(d) See vol. ii, p. 149, note "d," *sub* "Carlingford" for a list of these.

P.C. to James II., Col. of a Reg. of Foot in his army (1687), and Lord Lieut. of the Counties of Louth and Drogheda. He *m.* firstly (Articles 4 Feb. 1664) Jane, da. of Sir Luke FITZGERALD, of Tecroghan, co. Kildare. He *m.* secondly, Anne, widow of George HOLMES, da. of William HAMILTON, of Lisclony, Kings County. He was outlawed in 1689 by the Government very shortly before his death, which was in Sept. (before 8 Oct.) 1691, at which date his estate in land was £2,000 a year and his personalty £10,900. His widow *m.* (thirdly) John EYRE, of Eyre Court, co. Galway.

VIII. 1689. *8.* OLIVER (PLUNKETT), BARON LOUTH [I.], s. and h. by first wife; *b.* 1668. He delivered his writ of summons to the House of Lords [I.] on 29 Oct. 1692 (the first Parl. after the revolution) and again 12 Oct. 1695, but was informed, (a) 19 Oct. 1698, that the outlawry [1642] of his grandfather (the 6th Lord) was not reversed, and "that such Lords who stand outlawed on record shall not have privilege to sit in this House, but ought to be struck out of the rolls of the House."(b) He *m.* Mabella, da. of Henry (BARNEWALL), 2d VISCOUNT BARNEWALL OF KINGSLAND [I.], by his second wife Mary, da. of Richard (NUGENT), 1st EARL OF WESTMEATH [I.] He *d.* (of consumption) 1707, aged 38. His widow *m.* (as his second wife) Stephen TAAFFE, and *d.* Oct. 1710, aged 37.

IX.(b) *1707.* *9.*(b) MATTHEW (PLUNKETT), BARON LOUTH [I.], only s. and h.,(b) *b.* 1698. He *m.* in 1716, Susanna, sister of Christopher MASON, of Blackheath, co. Kent. He *d.* 20 June 1754, aged 56. His widow *d.* 21 Feb. 1767.

X.(b) *1754.* *10.*(b) OLIVER (PLUNKETT), BARON LOUTH [I.], s. and h.;(b) *bap.* 2 April 1727. He *m.* about 1750, Margaret, da. of the Hon. Luke NETTERVILLE (3d s. of Nicholas, 3d VISCOUNT NETTERVILLE OF DOUTH [I.]), by Anne, da. of (—) STANLEY, of Drogheda. He *d.* 4 March 1763. His widow *d.* 1787.

* * * * * *

Earldom [I.]
II. 1759, to 1799.

1. THOMAS (BERMINGHAM), LORD ATHENRY [I.], who *suc.* to his father in that dignity, 4 March 1749, was *cr.*, 23 April 1759, EARL OF LOUTH, (c) co. Louth [I.], taking his seat, as such, 28 Nov. following. He *d.* s.p.m.s., 11 Jan. 1799, aged 81, when the *Earldom of Louth* [I.] became *extinct*. See fuller particulars under "ATHENRY" Barony [I.], *cr.* 1172, *sub* the 18th holder.

* * * * * * * *

Barony [I.]
XI. *1763, and* 1798.

11. THOMAS OLIVER (PLUNKETT), BARON LOUTH [I.], s. and h., *b.* 28 Aug. 1757 at Louth Hall, co. Louth; *suc his father*, 4 March 1763,(b) *in the peerage* [I.], but owing to the resolution of the House of Lords [I.] in 1698, whereby it was held that the peerage had been forfeited in 1642, made formal claim to the same in 1798,(d) which was allowed the same year. He *m.*, 7 July 1808, Margaret, 1st da. of Randall (PLUNKETT), 13th LORD DUNSANY [I.], by his first wife

(a) Lords Jour. [I.], I, 690, as quoted in "Lodge," vol. vi, p. 178.

(b) It is by no means clear that their Lordships' decision in 1698, as to the outlawry of 1642 causing a forfeiture of the peerage (see p. 156, note "c") was the correct view. The peerage was, at all events, allowed in 1798 to the heir.

(c) His ancestor, Richard, Lord Athenry [I.], was second cousin of John Bermingham, *cr.* Earl of Louth [I.], in 1319. See tab. ped. in vol. i, p. 176, note "b."

(d) The claim of this Barony in 1798 is among the claims to Irish Peerages (preserved in the Record office in Dublin Castle) of which a list is given in "Lynch," p. 277. They are, chronologically, as under.

1709, Barony of Slane; 1717, Earldom of Tyrone; 1721, Barony of Kingsale; 1749, Barony of Upper Ossory; 1767, Barony of Le Poer; 1771-72, Viscountcy of Valentia, &c.; 1772, Viscountcy of Boyne, &c.; 1774, Barony of Castlestewart; 1782, Barony of Dunsany; 1788, Viscountcy of Costellogallen [*i.e.*, *Dillon* of Costello-gallen]; 1791, Earldom of Ormond and Ossory with the Viscountcy of Thurles and the Baronies of Butler and Arklow; 1792, Earldom of Roscommon, &c.; 1795, Barony of Trimblestown; 1795, Earldom of Fingall, &c.; 1798, Barony of Louth; 1800, Viscountcy of Gormanstown.

Margaret, widow of Edward MANDEVILLE, da. of Edward ARCHDEKIN, of co. Kilkenny. He d. 25 June 1823, aged 65. Admon. Feb. 1824. His widow, who was b. 4 June 1778, m. 1 April 1827, Lieut.-Col. Thomas TISDALL, of Charleville, co. Louth, and d. 28 July 1831.

XII. 1823. 12. THOMAS OLIVER (PLUNKETT), BARON LOUTH [I.], s. and h., b. 5 Aug. 1809; suc. to the peerage [I.] 25 June 1823. He m. 29 Nov. 1830, at St. Geo. Han. Sq., his cousin, Anna Maria, yst. da. of Philip ROCHE, of Donore, co. Kildare, by Anna Maria, da. of Randal (PLUNKETT), 13th LORD DUNSANY [I.], abovenamed. He d. 26 June 1849, aged 39, at Brighton. Will pr. July 1849. His widow d. 18 Jan. 1878, at Louth Hall, co. Louth.

XIII. 1849. 13. RANDAL PERCY OTWAY (PLUNKETT), BARON LOUTH [I.], s. and h.; b. 28 Aug 1832, at Worton Hall in Isleworth, Midx.; suc. to the peerage [I.] 26 June 1849. Was sometime, 1851-54 and 1855-60, an officer in the army. He m. firstly, 4 Oct. 1867, in Dublin (spec. lic.), Anne Maria MacGeough, 2d da. of Walter MacGeough BOND, of Drumsill and the Argosy, co. Armagh. She d. 27 Oct. 1869, aged 24, at Dieppe in France. He m. secondly, 14 July 1877, at St. Anne's, Tollington Park, Elizabeth Lily, divorced wife(a) of Capt. Hugh Hackett GIBSONE, 73d Foot, 1st da. of John BLACK, of Ceylon. He d. 19 July 1883, aged 50, at Louth Hall afsd. His widow m. (thirdly), 12 Aug. 1886, at Trinity, Cleygate, Surrey, Richard MULDOWNEY, of Clondalkin, co. Kildare, and was living 1892.

XIV. 1883. 14. RANDAL PILGRIM RALPH (PLUNKETT), BARON LOUTH [I.], only s. and h., by first wife; b. 24 Sep. 1868, on board the yacht "Pilgrim," off Dieppe; suc. to the peerage [I.] 19 July 1883. He m. 18 March 1890 at the British Consulate, Biarritz, Eugénie de Miaritze, da. of Edmund Hooke Wilson BELLAIRS, British Vice-Consul at Biarritz.

Family Estates.—These, in 1883, consisted of 3,578 acres in co. Louth, 178 in Monaghan, 161 in co. Meath and 4 in co. Galway; besides 178 acres in Somersetshire. *Total*, 4,099 acres, worth £4,604 a year. *Principal Residence.*—Louth Hall, near Ardee, co. Louth.

LOVAINE.

MATTHEW DE LOVAINE, of Estaines-ad-turrim, co. Essex, s. and h. of Matthew DE LOVAINE, of the same (said to be of the same family as the Dukes of Brabant) suc. his father in 1261, being then 24, and was sum. (with about 60 others) 8 June (1294), 22 Ed. I., to attend the King to advise on the affairs of the Realm, but this did not constitute a regular writ of summons to Parl.(b) He d. 1301, leaving Thomas his s. and h. then aged 12, who proved his age in 1314 and was sum. to be at Newcastle-upon-Tyne, 1317, but never sum. to Parl. His s. and h., John de Lovaine, d. s.p.m. in 1347.(c)

(a) The decree "nisi" for her divorce from Capt. Gibsone (for *crim. con.* with Lord Louth) was obtained 2 Dec. 1876.

(b) See vol. i, p. 259, note "c," *sub* "Basset de Sapcote."

(c) He left two daughters and coheirs, of whom the younger, Isabel, d. s.p., leaving Alianor, her eldest sister, sole heir. She m. Sir William Bourchier. Her descendants, the Lords Bourchier (see vol. i, p. 395, note "a"), and the Lords Ferrers are frequently (tho' erroneously) described as "Lords Lovaine." George (Townshend), Lord de Ferrers and Lord Compton (who suc. to those Baronies on the death of his mother, Viscountess Townshend, 14 Sep. 1770), was (v.p.) cr., 18 May 1784, Earl of Leicester, being in that patent (*inaccurately*) styled "Baron de Ferrers of Chartley, Baron Bouchier, *Lovaine*, Basset, and Compton." See also in vol. iii, p. 333, note "d," *sub* "Ferrers," as to the title of Lovaine being (*wrongly*) attributed to the 1st Earl Ferrers on a Mon. Inscr. in 1717 and in vol. i, p. 257, note "f" (*circa finem*), *sub* "Basset de Drayton," as to the three titles, Bourchier, Lovaine, and Bassett, thus (*wrongly*) assigned to the Earl of Leicester abovementioned.

LOVAINE OF ALNWICK.

Barony. I. 1784. 1. HUGH (PERCY *formerly* SMITHSON), 1st DUKE OF NORTHUMBERLAND (so cr. 1766); was cr., 28 Jan. 1784, LORD LOVAINE,(a) BARON OF ALNWICK, co. Northumberland, with *spec. rem.* to his second son, Lord Algernon Percy, and the heirs male of his body. He d. 6 June 1786, aged 74.

II. 1786. 2. ALGERNON (PERCY), LORD LOVAINE, BARON OF ALNWICK, second son but heir to the abovenamed dignity, according to the *spec. rem.* in its creation; b. 21 Jan. 1750, was cr., 2 Nov. 1790, EARL OF BEVERLEY, co. York. See that title.

LOVAT, or FRASER OF LOVAT.

Barony [S.] I. 1460? 1. HUGH FRASER,(b) of Lovat,(c) s. and h. of Thomas FRASER,(d) of the same; *suc.* his father about 1456 and was made a Lord of Parl. [S.] between 1458 and 1464(e) as LORD LOVAT or LORD FRASER OF LOVAT [S.] He was living 3 March 1472 16 Dec. 1494, and 1 Nov. 1499, but d. before 30 April 1501.

II. 1500? 2. THOMAS (FRASER), LORD LOVAT [S.], s. and h., being infeft, as such, on 30 April 1501; Justiciary of the north of Scotland during the reign of James IV. [S.] He m. firstly, before Oct. 1501 (at which date she was living) Janet, da. of Sir Alexander GORDON, of Midmar. He m. secondly, before 6 May 1509, Joneta, widow of Alexander BLAIR, da. of Andrew (GRAY), LORD GRAY [S.], by his second wife, Elisabeth, da. of John (STEWART), EARL OF ATHOLE [S.] He d. 21 Oct. 1524. His widow m. (thirdly) as his first wife David (LINDSAY), 9th EARL OF CRAWFORD [S.], who d. Sep. 1558. Her will is dat. 5 Feb. 1549.

III. 1524. 3. HUGH (FRASER), LORD LOVAT [S.], 1st surv. s. and h(f), by first wife, served heir 10 Jan. 1524/5. He resigned his estates, which were incorporated into a Barony and regranted to him 26 March 1539, with rem. to his heirs *male* whatsoever, whom failing to his heirs whatsoever. He was

(a) The grantee was, thro' the families of Smithson, Seymour, and Percy, descended from the house of *Lovaine*, Dukes of Brabant.

(b) The account of the earlier Lords as given in Burke's "Peerage" for 1884 (*et post*) which was corrected by George Burnett, Lyon, is here followed. This differs a good deal from that in Wood's "*Douglas*."

(c) The tower and fort of Lovat, near the Beauly in Inverness-shire, was possessed by Simon Fraser who was slain at Halidon hill in 1338.

(d) He was s. and h. of Hugh Fraser, of Lovat, who on 13 Dec. 1423, had safe conduct to meet King James I. [S.] at Durham, and who (having m. in 1416 Janet, sister and coheir of William Fenton), d. before 1440.

(e) The precedence assigned to Lovat in the decreet of ranking, 1606, was, however, a somewhat low one, viz., the 18th out of the 37 Baronies therein mentioned, being between Lord Oliphant and Lord Ogilvy. Simon, the 6th Lord Lovat, protested 9 Jan. 1630, before the Court of Session against the precedence of 12 (Saltoun, Ochiltree, Gray, Carleill, Yester, Forbes, Cathcart, Sempill, Herries, Elphinstone, Oliphant, and Sinclair), of the 17 Barons thus placed above him, while of the remaining five, four (Glamis, Fleming, Crichton of Sanquhar, and Maxwell), were merged at that date in a higher peerage dignity, leaving but one (Lindsay of the Byres) whose precedency over him he acknowledged. The Barony of Lovat is placed eleventh on the Union Roll of 1 May 1707, Forbes, Saltoun, Gray, Ochiltree, Cathcart, Sinclair, Mordington, Sempill, Elphinstone, and Oliphant, being ranked above it.

(f) His elder br., Thomas Fraser, Master of Lovat, d. unm. v.p., being (as also his uncle, Hugh Fraser, s. of the first Lord) killed at Flodden field, 9 Sep. 1513. See p. 63, note "b," *sub* "Lennox" for a list of the Scotch nobles and their eldest sons there slain.

Justiciary of the North of Scotland. He *m.* firstly Anne or Catharine,(a) widow of John HALLYBURTON, of Pitour, da. of John GRANT, of Grant and Frewchie. He *m.* secondly, before 19 June 1536, Jonet, da. of Walter Ross, of Balnagowan. He *d.* 2 June 1544, being slain (with his eldest son) in a bloody engagement with the Macdonalds, at Lochlochy, co. Inverness.

IV. 1544. 4. ALEXANDER (FRASER), LORD LOVAT [S.], 2d(b) but 1st surv. s. and h., by second wife. He *m.* Jonet, da. of Sir John CAMPBELL, of Cawdor. She was living 10 March 1554/5. He *d.* 1558.

V. 1558. 5. HUGH (FRASER), LORD LOVAT [S.], 1st s. and h.,(c) served heir of his father 1560; had a grant of lands, 6 Nov. 1571, from the Prior of Beaulieu. He *m.*, about 1570, Elizabeth, 1st da. of John (STEWART), 4th EARL OF ATHOLL [S.], by his first wife Elizabeth, da. of George (GORDON), 4th EARL OF HUNTLY [S.] He *d.* 1 Jan. 1576/7. His widow *m.* before 1579 Robert, (STUART), EARL OF LENNOX [S.], subsequently (1580) EARL OF MARCH [S.], from whom she obtained a divorce for impotency in or before 1581. She *m.* (thirdly), 6 July 1581, James (STEWART), EARL OF ARRAN [S.] (*attainted* in Nov. 1585), and *d.* April 1596.

VI. 1577. 6. SIMON (FRASER), LORD LOVAT [S.], only s. and h., *b.* about 1572; served heir to his father 20 June 1578. He *m.* firstly Margaret, sister of Kenneth, LORD MACKENZIE, OF KINTAIL [S.], 1st da. of Sir Colin MACKENZIE, of Kintail, by Barbara, da. of John GRANT, of Grant. He *m.* secondly (contract 1590) Jean, sister of James, EARL OF MORAY [S.], da. of James (STEWART), 1st LORD DOUNE [S], by Margaret, da. of Archibald (CAMPBELL), 4th EARL OF ARGYLL [S.] She was living 20 Dec. 1616. He *d.* 3 April 1633.(d)

VII. 1633. 7. HUGH (FRASER), LORD LOVAT [S.], 2d. but 1st surv. s. and h.(e) by first wife; served heir to his father 10 May 1633. He *m.* in 1614, Isabel, sister of John, 1st EARL OF WEMYSS [S.], da. of Sir John WEMYSS, of Wemyss, by his second wife Anne, da. of James (STEWART), 1st LORD DOUNE [S.] above named. He *d.* 16 Feb. 1646.

VIII. 1646. 8. HUGH (FRASER), LORD LOVAT [S.], grandson and heir, being s. and h. of HUGH FRASER, Master of Lovat, by Anne, 1st da. of Alexander (LESLIE), 1st EARL OF LEVEN [S.], which Hugh was 2d but 1st surv. son(f) and h. ap. of the late Lord, but *d.* v.p. March 1640 or May 1643.(g) He was *b.* 1643; *suc.* his grandfather in the *peerage* [S.] 16 Feb. 1646, and was served heir to his father (the Master of Lovat) 30 March 1647 and 18 May 1655. He *m.* (when at College and aged 16) July 1659, at Tarbat, Anne, sister of George, 1st EARL OF CROMARTY [S.], 2d da. of Sir John MACKENZIE, 1st Bart. [S.], of Tarbat, by Margaret, da. and coheir of Sir George ERSKINE. He *d.* 27 April 1672, aged 29.

(a) In Douglas' "*Baronage*," p. 343, she is called "Catherine," and her first husband is given as above.

(b) Hugh Fraser, Master of Lovat, his eldest br. (of the half blood) was slain (as abovementioned) with his father, 2 June 1544.

(c) Thomas Fraser, of Knockie and Strichen, co. Aberdeen, the second son, was the lineal ancestor of Thomas Alexander Fraser, of Strichen, who in 1837 was *cr.* Baron Lovat [U.K.], and who in 1857 became (on the reversal of the attainder) Lord Lovat [S.]

(d) See p. 159, note "e," as to his protest, 9 Jan. 1630, for the precedency of the Barony of Lovat over all (but one) of the then (separately) existing Baronies.

(e) His elder br., Simon Fraser, Master of Lovat, had a charter of the Barony of Kinkell Fraser, 20 June 1611. He *m.* Jean Moncreiff before 20 Dec. 1616, but *d.* v.p. and s.p.

(f) His elder br. Simon Fraser, Master of Lovat (to whom he was served heir 26 July 1642), *d.* unm. and v.p. in March 1640.

(g) *Both* these dates are given in Milne's Genealogical Notes, a manuscript "now (1884) at Dupplin Castle," but formerly at the Lyon office. *Ex inform.* R. R. Stodart.

IX. 1672, to 1696. 9. HUGH (FRASER), LORD LOVAT [S.], only s. and h., *suc. to the peerage* [S.] 27 April 1672, when a minor. He *m.* about 1683, Amelia, da. of John (MURRAY), 1st MARQUESS OF ATHOLE [S.] by Amelia Sophia, da. of James (STANLEY), 7th EARL OF DERBY. He *d.* s.p.m. 1696, having settled his estates, 20 March of that year, on his cousin and heir male, Thomas Fraser, of Beaufort, the *de jure* 10th Lord. His widow was "seized on" by Simon Fraser (afterwards, *i.e.*, in 1730, confirmed as Lord Lovat [S.]), who "got the marriage ceremony performed by a Minister, and forcibly consummated the nuptials,"(a) for which he was condemned 6 Sept. 1698, and was, subsequently, 17 Feb. 1701, outlawed in the Court of Justiciary. This marriage, however, appears to have been considered invalid. She *d.* at Perth, 6 May 1743, aged above 80.

On the death of the above Lord the question of succession arose between the heir *general* and the heir *male*, which was not finally settled till nearly 60 years later, the matter being complicated by two contradictory decisions (1702 and 1730) of the Court of Session.

X. *1696.* 10. Amelia, 1st da. and heir of line, was considered at her father's death *suo jure* BARONESS LOVAT [S.], and obtained a decision of the Court of Session, 2 Dec. 1702, that she was entitled to that dignity as also to the Lovat estates; but the decision was reduced, 8 July 1730, by a decision in favour of the heir *male*. She *m.* in 1702, Alexander MACKENZIE, of Preston Hall, who assumed the name of FRASER. He engaged in the rising of 1715 and was accordingly attainted, whereby his life interest in the Lovat estates was forfeited. He *d.* at Leith 3 June 1755, aged 72. She was living 1730, and probably much later. Their s. and h., Hugh Fraser, assumed (on his mother's death) the title of LORD LOVAT and *d.* at Edinburgh 9 Nov. 1770, aged 67. He had in 1733 sold his reversion (on the death of his parents) to any claim on the Lovat inheritance to Simon (Fraser), Lord Lovat (the heir *male*) below mentioned.

X. 1696. 10. THOMAS FRASER, *de jure* LORD LOVAT [S.], great uncle and h. male, being 3d and yst. s. of Hugh, 7th Lord. He was of Beaufort (Castle Downie), co. Inverness, which he inherited from the late Lord. His right to the peerage, tho' contrary to the decision of 2 Dec. 1702 (in favour of the heir *general*), was conformable to the final decision of 8 July 1730. He was a supporter of James II., serving under Dundee in 1689 and attempting to surprise Edinburgh Castle in 1696, and was (with his son) found guilty of high treason, 6 Sep. 1698. He *m.* Sibylla, 4th da. of John MACLEOD, of Macleod, by Sibylla, sister of Colin, 1st EARL OF SEAFORTH [S.], da. of Kenneth (MACKENZIE), 1st LORD KINTAIL [S.] He *d.* in May 1699, at Dungervan Castle, Isle of Skye, aged 63.

XI. *1699, and* 1730 to 1747. 11. SIMON (FRASER), LORD LOVAT [S.], 2d but 1st surv. s. and h.,(b) was *b.* about 1667,(c) probably at Tanich, in Rosshire; was ed. at the College of Aberdeen, being M.A. 1683.(c) On the death of his cousin, the 9th Lord, in 1696, he endeavoured to secure his da. and heir of line (Amelia, then considered as *suo jure* Baroness Lovat) in

(a) Wood's "Douglas."

(b) His elder br., Alexander Fraser (matric. at Aberdeen Univ. 1678), is said to have *d.* 1689 at Wardlaw, unm. and v.p. in his 25th year. He (the birth of Simon, his yr. br., being in 1667) could not have been born later than 1666. The claim of John Fraser, of Mount Pleasant, in Carnarvon, mining engineer (disallowed by the Committee for Privileges, 23 June 1885) for the Barony of Lovat was as great great grandson and heir male of this Alexander, he being s. of John, s. of another John, s. of a third John, said to be s. of the said Alexander, all four being miners in co. Carnarvon. The story runs that this Alexander, having killed a man in a brawl, escaped to the estate of the Marquess of Powis (a fellow Jacobite), in North Wales, and remained there concealed, working as a common miner. It is also stated that this Alexander *m.* at Llandulas in 1738 (when he would have been above 70), and *d.* in 1776 aged, apparently, 110 or upwards.

(c) These dates are taken from the "*Nat. Biog.*" (where is an able account of his career), but the age of 15 seems an early one to take the degree of M.A. His birth

marriage; but, having failed therein, compelled her mother (the Dowager Baroness) to marry him, tho' subsequently, apparently, that proceeding was held to be invalid. He was (with his father) found guilty of high treason, 1698, and outlawed 17 Feb. 1701. After intriguing heavily with the exiled Stuart family, he suddenly changed sides, and so valuable was his assistance to the Government in 1715, that, on 10 March 1716, he received a full pardon and a grant of the Lovat estates during the life of Alexander Mackenzie, *alias* Fraser abovenamed (the husband of the heir of line), who had forfeited his interest therein.(a) He now tendered his vote at the election of Scotch Peers in 1721, 1722 and 1727, which was objected to, on the ground that the Barony of Lovat was, by decree of the Court of Session on 2 Dec. 1702, vested in his cousin, the heir general; on which refusal he, in 1730, brought an action for "reducing" the said decree, which was accordingly done, and on 30 July 1730 he was declared to be *entitled to the Lovat peerage.*(b) He was one of the first to join the association (about 1737) for the landing of Prince Charles Edward in Scotland, receiving as a reward, about 1740 or 1743, the promise of a Dukedom (DUKE OF FRASER [S.]) from the *titular* King James III.(c) He began now to be suspected by the Government, and was deprived of the Sheriffalty of Inverness and of the command of his Highland regiment. After the battle of Prestonpans, 21 Sep. 1745, he sent round the fiery cross to summon his followers; was taken prisoner 11 Dec. 1745, but escaped 2 Jan. following, and having vainly exhorted the Prince, after his defeat, 10 April 1746, at Culloden, to make one more effort, was finally captured on Lake Morar, brought to the Tower of London; found guilty of high treason by the House of Lords, 18 March 1746/7, whereby *his honours* and estates were *forfeited.*(d) He *m.* (besides the connection with the Dow. Baroness Lovat above alluded to) firstly in 1717 Margaret, *da.* of Ludovick GRANT, of Grant, by his first wife, Janet, da. of Alexander BRODIE, of Lethen. She was living 1729. He *m.* secondly, 1 July 1733, Primrose, sister of John, 4th DUKE OF ARGYLL [S.], 5th da. of the Hon. John CAMPBELL, of Mamore, by Elizabeth, da. of John (ELPHINSTONE), 8th LORD ELPHINSTONE [S.] He was beheaded, 9 April 1747, in his 80th year, on Tower hill, and *bur.* in St. Peter's ad Vincula in the Tower.(e) His widow *d.* at Edinburgh, 23 May 1796, aged 86.

* * * * * * *

---

date is "according to his age at his death printed on his coffin and to several statements made by himself."

(a) This life rent he, by purchase from the reversioners, turned subsequently (about 1733) into an inheritance in fee simple.

(b) "Exclusively on this ground—that in virtue of the latest valid and effective charter (Great Seal Register) and effective charter and investiture of the Baronial fief, Lordship or superiority of Lovat, dat. 26 March 1539, both direct heirs male and even heirs male collateral, bearing *arma insigniaque et cognomen de Fraser*, were preferred to heirs whatsoever." See "*Riddell*," p. 371, where it is also stated that "Lord Hailes, a contemporary, explicitly states that the Lovat charter in 1539 was the grant upon which the Court of Session rightly adjudged the honours of Lovat to Simon Fraser." The decision, even then appears to have been arrived at by a narrow majority, *viz.*, but 8 out of 15 Judges. The case is quoted in Bankton's "*Institutes of the Law of Scotland*" (1751) as illustrating the law, that "If there is *no* patent, but only possession, *which is the case of our ancient Lords*, the *title of honour* must go *to the heir at law*, who inherits *all* hereditary rights *where a provision in favour of other heirs* does *not* appear; but if the old rights of the Barony and Lordship belonging to the family have *always gone* in a perpetual channel to *heirs male*, then all titles thereon founded will be understood to go in the same manner to the heirs male, tho' the rights of the estate came afterwards to be destined to heirs whatever." See the decision of 1633 in the case of the Barony of Oliphant [S.], as to the title of the heir *general* being preferable to that of the heir *male*.

(c) See vol. i, p. 59, note "b," *sub* "Albemarle" for a list of "the Jacobite peerages" so conferred. On or after 2 Jan 1746/7 he writes to his son "to take measures *to secure the patent of the Dukedom*, stating that if it was refused he must keep to his oath that he would never draw sword till that was done" [*Nat. Biogr.*]

(d) This was one of the seven Scotch peerages *forfeited* in the insurrection of 1745 which has, with two others (Strathallan and Wemyss) been restored. See fuller particulars in vol. iii, p. 393, note "a," *sub* "Forbes of Pitsligo."

(e) He had three sons, all of whom *d.* without surv. male issue, *viz.* (1) Simon

Barony [U.K.] I. 1837.
Barony [S.] XII. 1854.

1 and *12*. THOMAS ALEXANDER FRASER, of Strichen, co. Aberdeen, cousin and heir male, being s. and h. of Capt. Alexander Fraser, 1st Dragoon Guards (by Amelia Mary, da. of John LESLIE, of Balquhain), who was s. and h. of Alexander F., s. and h. of Alexander F. (a Lord of Session, 1730-75), yr. br. of James F. (who *d.* s.p.), both being sons of Alexander F., s. and h. of Thomas F., s. and h. of Thomas F. (who *d.* v.p.), s. and h. ap. of Thomas F. (*d.* 1645), s. and h. of the Hon. Thomas F. (*d.* 1612), all being of Strichen afsd., which Thomas was next br. of Hugh, the 5th Lord, being yr. son of Alexander, 4th Lord Lovat. He was *b.* 17 June 1802, at Strichen; *suc.* his father in 1803, and was *cr.*, 28 Jan. 1837,(a)BARON LOVAT of Lovat, co. Inverness. By act of Parl. (17 laters later), 10 July 1854, the attainder of the 11th Lord Lovat was removed and he became, accordingly, the 12th (he would have been 14th(b) but for the attainder) LORD LOVAT [S.] He was made K.T., 1865. He *m.*, 6 Aug. 1823, Charlotte Georgina, 1st da. of George William (JERNINGHAM), BARON STAFFORD, by Frances Henrietta, da. and coheir of Edward SULYARDE. He *d.* at Beaufort Castle, co. Inverness, 28 June 1875, aged 73. His widow, who was *b.* 8 Oct. 1800, *d.* 28 May 1876, aged 75, at Beaufort Castle.

Barony [S.] XIII.
Barony [U.K.] II.
1875.

13 and *2*. SIMON (FRASER), LORD LOVAT [S.], also BARON LOVAT [U.K.], s. and h.; *b.* 21 Dec. 1828, at Beaufort Castle afsd.; Lieut. Col. of the 2d Batt. Queen's Own Cameron Highlanders and Aide-de-Camp to the Queen; *suc. to the peerage*, 28 June 1875. He *m.*, 14 Nov. 1866, at the chapel in Ince Blundell Hall, co. Lanc., Alice Mary, da. of Thomas WELD-BLUNDELL, of Ince Blundell, by Teresa Mary Eleanora, da. of William Michael Thomas John VAUGHAN, of Courtfield. He *d.* suddenly on Moy Hall Moor, co. Inverness, 6 Sep. 1887, aged 60, and was *bur.* in Eskadale chapel. His widow living 1892.

Barony [S.] XIV.
Barony [U.K.] III.
1887.

14 and *3*. SIMON JOSEPH (FRASER), LORD LOVAT [S.], also BARON LOVAT [U.K.], 2d but 1st surv. s. and h.; *b.* 25 Nov. 1871; *suc. to the peerage* 6 Sep. 1887.

Family Estates.—These, in 1883, consisted of 181,791 acres in Inverness-shire, worth £30,300 a year. *Principal Residence.*—Beaufort Castle, near Beauly, Inverness-shire. Lord Lovat is one of the 28 noblemen who, in 1883 possessed above 100,000 acres in the United Kingdom and stands 10th in order of acreage, tho' but 25th in order of income. See a list of these in vol. ii, p. 51, note "a," *sub* "Buccleuch."

Fraser, Master of Lovat, *b.* 19 and *bap.* 30 Oct. 1726, at Kiltarity; attainted 4 June 1746, but obtained a free pardon in 1750. He became finally Lieut. Gen. in the army, in which he much distinguished himself and obtained (by act of Parl., 24 Geo. III.), subject to a payment of £20,983 restoration of all the family estates. He (who, but for the attainder would have been the 12th Lord Lovat), *d.* s.p., 8 Feb. 1782, in Downing street; (2) Hon. Alexander Fraser, *b.* 1729 at Kiltarity, *d.* unm. 7 Aug. 1762; (3) Hon. Archibald Campbell Fraser, *b.* 16 Aug. 1736, who in 1782 inherited the Lovat estates and who would, but for the attainder, have been the 13th Lord Lovat. He (having had no less than six sons) *d.* s.p.s., 8 Dec. 1815, when the issue male (not only of his father, but) of his father's great grandfather, Hugh, the 5th Lord, became *extinct* and the representation of the Barony devolved on Thomas Alexander Fraser, who in 1854 was restored thereto.

(a) Doubtless the advisers of the Crown were at that date satisfied that he was (as he afterwards was proved to be) the heir to the *Scotch* Barony of Lovat. A similar case is the creation of the Barony of Wemyss in 1821 and of the Earldom of Winton in 1859, both being conferred on persons presumed to be (subject to the reversal of an attainder) entitled to Scotch peerages of the same designation.

(b) See p. 162, note "a."

LOVEL, or LOVEL DE TICHMERSH.

Barony by Writ.

I. 1299. 1. SIR JOHN LOVEL, of Tichmersh, co. Northampton, Minster Lovel, Oxon, and Docking, co. Norfolk, s. and h. of John LOVEL, of Minster Lovel, by Maud, said to be da. and h. of (—) SYDENHAM, of Tichmersh, *suc.* his father in 1286, being then aged 32; was sum. 26 Jan. (1296/7), 25 Ed. I.,[a] to attend the King at Salisbury, and was sum. to Parl. as a Baron (LORD LOVEL or LORD LOVEL DE TICHMERSH) by writs directed "*Johanni Lovel*," and afterwards "*Johanni Lovel de Tichmersh*," from 6 Feb. (1298/9), 27 Ed. I., to 26 July (1311), 2 Ed. II. He had served in the wars in Gascony and in Scotland; was (as "*Johannes Lovel, Dominus de Dakking*") one of the signatories of the letter to the Pope in 1301,[b] and was sum. to the coronation of Edward II. He *m.* firstly, about 1280, Isabel, sister and heir of William, da. of Arnold DE BOIS, of Thorpe Arnold, Notts. She *d.* s.p.m.[c] before 1290. He *m.*, secondly, Joan, said to be da. of Robert (DE ROOS), LORD ROOS, by Isabel, da. and h. of William DE ALBINI. He *d.* (1310-11) 4 Ed. II.; Esch. 4 Ed. II.

II. 1311. 2. JOHN (LOVEL), LORD LOVEL DE TICHMERSH, s. and h., aged 22 when he *suc.* to his father in 1311. He was sum. to Parl. by writs, directed "*Johanni Lovel de Tichmersh*," from 8 Jan. (1312/3), 6 Ed. II., to 29 July (1314), 8 Ed. II. He *m.* Maud, sister and heir of Edward, LORD BURNELL (so *cr.* 1311), da. of Sir Philip BURNELL, of Acton Burnell, Salop, by Maud, da. of Richard (FITZALAN), EARL OF ARUNDEL. He *d.* (1314-15) 8 Ed. II; Esch. 8 Ed. II. His widow *m.* John DE HANDLO, who *d.* 1346. Esch. 20 Ed. III.

III. 1315. 3. JOHN (LOVEL), LORD LOVEL DE TICHMERSH, posthumous[d] s. and h., by second wife. He, who was never sum. to Parl. served in the wars of Scotland and France. He *m.* Isabella, said to be sister of William (ZOUCHE), LORD ZOUCHE DE HARYNGWORTH. He *d.* Nov. (1347), 21 Ed. III., Esch., 21 Ed. III. His widow *d.* (1351), 25 Ed. III.[d]

IV. 1347. 4. JOHN (LOVEL), LORD LOVEL DE TICHMERSH, 1st s. and h., aged 11 at the death of his mother in 1351.[d] He *d.* unm. and under age in Dec. 1361.

V. 1361. 5. JOHN (LOVEL), LORD LOVEL DE TICHMERSH, br. and h., being second s. of the 3d Lord, aged 19 when he *suc.* to (John) his brother in 1361, and came of full age in (1362), 37 Ed. III. He was in the wars with France, 1368, where he was made Gov. of the Castle of Banelyngham. He was sum. to Parl.[e] by writs directed "*Johanni Lovel de Tichmersh*" from 28 Dec. (1375), 49 Ed. III., to 26 Aug. (1407), 8 Hen. IV. In the reign of Ric. II. he at first took the popular side as against De Vere, the King's favourite, but afterwards changed sides and was one of those who were expelled from Court. K.G. [1405?] He *m.* in 1378 Maud (then aged 17) *suo jure* BARONESS HOLAND (see that dignity *cr.* 1314) granddaughter and heir of Robert (DE HOLAND), LORD HOLAND. He *d.* 1408, *styling* himself in his will, dat. 26 July and pr. 12 Sep. 1408, "*Lord Lovel and Holand.*" His widow was living (1420), 8 Hen. V., but was dead (1423), 1 Hen. VI.

VI. 1408. 6. JOHN (LOVEL), LORD LOVEL DE TICHMERSH, only s. and h. *Knighted* before 1408; had livery of his lands 1409. He was sum. to Parl. by writs directed "*Johanni Lovel de Tichmersh*" from 20 Oct. (1409),

---

(a) See vol. i, p. 111, note "b," *sub* "Ap. Adam," as to this not constituting a regular writ of summons to Parl.

(b) See "Nicolas," 761-809, for a full description of this letter.

(c) By her marriage settlement her only child, Maude (aged 30 at her father's death in 1311) inherited the Manor of Docking, co. Norfolk, which, thro' her, passed from the family of Lovel to that of Zouche of Harringworth.

(d) *Coll. Top et Gen.*," vol. vii, pp. 387—388.

(e) There is proof in the rolls of Parl. of his sitting.

11 Hen. IV., to 26 Sep. (1414), 2 Hen. V. He is said to have *m.* Alianore, da. of William (ZOUCHE), LORD ZOUCHE DE HARYNGWORTH. He *d.* 19 Oct. (1414), 2 Hen. V.

VII. 1414. 7. WILLIAM (LOVEL), LORD LOVEL DE TICHMERSH, s. and h., aged 17 when he *suc.* his father. He served in the French wars, temp. Hen. V. and Hen. VI. On the death [1420-23] of his paternal grandmother abovenamed, he became *de jure* LORD HOLAND. He was sum. to Parl. by writs directed "*Willielmo Lovel, Chl'r,*" [no further description been given] from 24 Feb. (1424/5), 3 Hen. VI., to 20 Jan. (1452/3), 31 Hen. VI.;(a) Constable of Wallingford Castle, 1450. He *m.* Alice, who in 1423 was aged 18, sister and coheir of William, LORD DEINCOURT, being 1st da. of John (DEINCOURT), LORD DEINCOURT, by Johanna, apparently da. and h.(b) of Robert (DE GREY), 4th LORD GREY DE ROTHERFIELD. He *d.* 13 June (1455), 33 Hen. VI. Will pr. at Lincoln, 1 Sep. 1455. His widow who (a few months later) by the death of her sister (15 Sep. 1455) became sole heir of her parents and consequently *de jure suo jure* BARONESS DEINCOURT and, apparently, BARONESS GREY DE ROTHERFIELD, *d.* 1475.

VIII. 1455. 8. JOHN (LOVEL), LORD LOVEL DE TICHMERSH, and *de jure* LORD HOLAND, 1st s. and h.,(c) aged 22 at his father's death. He was sum. to Parl. by writs directed "*Johanni Lovel, Chl'r,*" from 9 Oct. (1459), 38 Hen. VI., to 28 Feb. (1462/3), 2 Ed. IV. He was in 1460 made Forester of Whichwood forest, co. Northampton, by Henry VI., against whom, however, he, that same year, took part. He *m.* Joan, da. of William (BEAUMONT), 1st VISCOUNT BEAUMONT [6th *Lord Beaumont*], by Elizabeth, da. and h. of Sir William PHELIP, K.G., generally considered LORD BARDOLF. He *d.* 9 Jan. (1464/5), 4 Ed. IV., Esch., 1 Hen. VIII.

IX. 1465. Viscountcy. I. 1483, to 1485. 9 and 1. FRANCIS (LOVEL), LORD LOVEL DE TICHMERSH, and *de jure* LORD HOLAND, only s. and h.; aged nine years at his father's death. By the death of his paternal grandmother abovenamed in 1475 he became (also) *de jure* LORD DEINCOURT and, apparently, LORD GREY DE ROTHERFIELD.(d) He was *knighted* (by the Duke of Gloucester), 22 Aug. 1480. He was sum. to Parl. by writ directed "*Francisco Lovel de Lovel, Chl'r,*" 15 Nov. (1482), 22 Ed. IV., and was *cr.*, 4 Jan. 1482/3, VISCOUNT LOVEL. Having espoused the cause of Richard III.(e) he was in May 1483 made Chief Butler of England, and, on Richard's accession to the Crown in June following, Lord Chamberlain of the Household; P.C. and K.G., being bearer of the third sword

---

(a) Tho' sum. to Parl. as late as 1452, he, seven years previously, had obtained a patent in the 24 Hen. VI. stating that he was bound to come by the King's command to Parliament, "but, being infirm, it was provided that he should not be summoned during his life, with a *salvo* that this grant should not be prejudicial to him or his heirs, but that they might at any time have and enjoy the ancient place and seat of their ancestors in Parliaments and Councils." Pat. 24 Hen. VI., m. 19.

(b) But as to this see vol. iv. p. 104, note "f," *sub* "Grey."

(c) The second son, William Lovel, having *m.* the heiress of the Lords Morley, was sum. to Parl. in that Barony (*cr.* 1299) in 1469, being ancestor of the Lords Morley and Monteagle, which Baronies fell into abeyance about 1686.

(d) His arms on his Garter plate display the four coats (quarterly) of (1) Lovel; (2) Deincourt; (3) Holand; and (4) Grey de Rotherfield, which marshalling certainly favours the idea that he considered these Baronies vested in him.

(e) He, *Catesby*, and *Ratcliffe*, were the three principal councellors during that reign. They are thus alluded to in Fabyan's "Chronicle," in a rhyme made by one William Colinbourne "in derisyon of the Kyng and his councell as followeth—

The catte, the ratte, and Lovel, our dogge
Ruleth all Englande under a hogge.

The whyche was mente that (*Catysby*, *Ratclyffe*, and the Lord Lovell, ruled the lande under the Kynge, whyche bare *the whyte bore* for his conysaunce." To which remark may be added that the supporters to the arms of this King were two white boars.

at the Coronation, 7 July 1483.([a]) He *m.* before 14 Feb. 1467, Anne, da. of Henry (FITZHUGH), 5th LORD FITZHUGH, by Alice, da. of Richard (NEVILLE), EARL OF SALISBURY. He fought at Bosworth on behalf of King Richard and escaped thence into Burgundy. He was *attainted* by the new King (1 Hen. VII.) in 1485 whereby all his honours, *viz.*, the *Viscountcy of Lovel* (1483), the *Barony of Lovel of Tichmersh* (1299), as also his right to the *Barony of Holand* (1314), the *Barony of Deincourt* (1332), and the *Barony of Grey de Rotherfield* (1338) were forfeited.([b]) He *d.* s.p. at or soon after the battle of Stoke, at which he fought (on behalf of Lambert Simnel) 16 June 1487.([c])

LOVEL [of Castle Cary.]

Barony by Writ.

I. 1348, to 1351.

1. SIR RICHARD LOVEL, of Castle Cary, co. Somerset, s. and h. of Hugh LOVEL, of the same, *suc.* his father 1303, being then a minor, and having *m.* before (1310-11), 4 Ed. II., Muriel,([d]) da. and h. of (his guardian) John SOULIS, of Old Rokesburgh, had (with her) the custody of the Castles of Corfe and Purbeck committed to him in 1335 He was sum. to Parl. as a Baron [LORD LOVEL] by writs from 20 Nov. (1348), 22 Ed. III., to 25 Nov. (1350), 24 Ed. III., directed "*Richardo Lovell.*" He *d.* s.p.m.s. in 1351 when Muriel, his grandaughter (only surv. child and heir of James Lovel, his only s. and h. ap., who *d.* v.p. 1342), became his heir and possibly *suo jure* BARONESS LOVEL, being then aged 19 and the wife of Nicholas ST. MAUR, who was sum. to Parl, by writ, 15 Nov. 1351, as LORD ST. MAUR. See that dignity, which (together with the representation of this Barony) became united about 1420 with the *Barony of Zouche de Haryngworth.*

LOVEL DE MORLEY, *rectius* MORLEY.

WILLIAM LOVEL having *m.* Alianor, *suo jure* BARONESS MORLEY, was sum. to Parl. by writs from 10 Aug. 1469, to 15 Oct. 1471, directed "*Willielmo Lovel de Morley, Chl'r.*" See "MORLEY" Barony, *cr.* 1299, under the 7th holder of that dignity; *in abeyance* about 1686.

LOVEL OF MINSTER LOVEL.

i.e., "LOVEL OF MINSTER LOVEL, co. Oxford," Barony (*Coke*), *cr.* 1728; see "LEICESTER" Earldom, *cr.* 1744; *ex.* 1759.

([a]) See vol. iii, p. 8, note "c," *sub* "Dacre," for a list of the nobles there present.

([b]) His representatives were his two sisters, among whose descendants these Baronies are (subject to the attainder) in abeyance, as also was the Barony of Beaumont after the death of their maternal uncle, William (Beaumont), 2d Viscount Beaumont, which death not occuring till 1507, that Barony was free from the attainder of 1485. The abeyance of this last named Barony was terminated in 1840 in favour of the heir of the eldest coheir. See tabular pedigree in vol. i, p. 287, note "a," *sub* "Beaumont," shewing the representation of both of these ladies.

([c]) It is not very clear what was the end of this unfortunate nobleman. He is said to have been last seen on horseback, after the battle of Stoke, endeavouring to swim the river Trent, and (according to Bacon's "*Henry VII.*") was there drowned, but there is a tradition that he escaped, and hiding in a secret place was therein starved to death by treachery or negligence. In 1708 a skeleton (very probably his) was discovered in a vault at Minster Lovel, being that of a man sitting at a table with book, paper, pen, &c., before him. See full account in Banks' "*Baronage.*"

([d]) *Coll. Top. et Gen.*, vol. vii, p. 387 It appears (Pat. 4 Ed. II., m. 3), that the King granted to him the manor of Winford Eagle, Dorset, in exchange for that of Old Rokesburgh, "quod fuit Muriellæ, uxoris ejus, filiæ et hæredis Johannis Soules."

LOVEL AND HOLLAND OF ENMORE.

i.e., "LOVEL AND HOLLAND OF ENMORE, co. Somerset," Barony (*Perceval*), conferred 7 May 1762, on John, 2d EARL OF EGMONT [I.] See "EGMONT" Earldom [I.], *cr.* 1733, *sub* the second Earl.(a)

LOVELACE.

Earldom. I. 1838. 1. WILLIAM (KING, *afterwards* KING-NOEL), LORD KING, BARON OF OCKHAM, co. Surrey, s. and h. of Peter, 7th LORD KING, BARON OF OCKHAM, by Hester, 1st da. of Hugh (FORTESCUE), 1st EARL FORTESCUE, was *b.* 21 Feb. 1805, in Great George street, and *bap.* at St. Margaret's Westm.; ed. at Eton and at Trin. Coll., Cambridge; *suc. to the peerage* on the death of his father, 4 June 1833. He was *cr.*, 30 June 1838,(b) VISCOUNT OCKHAM of Ockham, co. Surrey, and EARL OF LOVELACE;(c) Lord Lieut. of co. Surrey, 1840. Took the name of *Noel* after that of *King* by Royal lic., 29 Sep. 1860.(d) He *m.* firstly (by spec. lic.) 8 July 1835, at Fordbrooke in Ealing, Midx. (the residence of her mother) Augusta Ada, only da. and h. of George Gordon (BYRON, *afterwards* NOEL), 6th BARON BYRON OF ROCHDALE (the famous poet), by Anne Isabella, afterwards (1856), *suo jure* BARONESS WENTWORTH. She, who was *b.* in Piccadilly terrace, Midx., 10 and *bap.* 20 Dec. 1815, at St. Geo. Han. sq., *d.* 27 Nov. 1852, aged 36, at 6 Great Cumberland Place, Marylebone, and was *bur.* (with her father) at Hucknall, Notts. He *m.* secondly, 29 March 1865, at St. James' Paddington, Jane Crawford, widow of Edward JENKINS, of the Bengal Civil Service.

[BYRON-NOEL KING, *afterwards* (1860), KING-NOEL, *styled* VISCOUNT OCKHAM (1838-62), 1st s. and h. ap. by first wife; *b.* 12 May and *bap.* 25 June 1836, at Ockham; was in the Royal Navy; *suc. to the peerage* as LORD WENTWORTH [1529], on the death, 16 May 1860, of his maternal grandmother, Anne Isabella, *suo jure*, BARONESS WENTWORTH abovenamed, and (together with his father) took the name of NOEL, after that of *King*, by Royal lic., 29 Sep. 1860. He *d.* unm., 1 Sep. 1862, aged 26.]

[RALPH-GORDON KING, afterwards (1860), KING-NOEL, and finally (1861) KING-MILBANKE, *styled* VISCOUNT OCKHAM since 1862. He was 2d s. by the first wife, of the 1st Earl and was *b.* in St. James square, 2 July 1839, and *bap.* at St. James Westm. He (together with his father) took the name of *Noel*, after that of *King*, by Royal lic., 29 Sep. 1860, and, subsequently, the name of *Milbanke* in lieu of that of *Noel*, by Royal lic., 6 Nov. 1861. By the death of his elder br. next abovenamed, 1 Sep. 1862, by became, by *courtesy*, VISCOUNT OCKHAM, and *suc. to the peerage* as LORD WENTWORTH [1524], which title was confirmed to him by the Committee for Privileges, 15 March 1864. He *m.* firstly, 25 Aug. 1869, Fannie, 2d da. of the Rev. George HERIOT, of Fellows Hills, co. Berwick, Vicar of St. Anne's, Newcastle upon Tyne. She *d.* 13 July 1878. He *m.* secondly, 30 Dec. 1880, Mary Caroline, 1st da. of the Rt. Hon. James STUART-WORTLEY, (s. of the 1st BARON WHARNCLIFFE) by Jane, da. of Paul Beilby (LAWLEY-THOMPSON), 1st BARON WENLOCK. She was *b.* 10 May 1848.]

Family Estates.—These, in 1883, consisted of 10,214 acres in Surrey; 4,568 (worth

(a) See vol. ii, p. 245, note "c," *sub* "Egmont," as to his Lordship's *non* representation of either of the Baronies of Lovel or Holand.

(b) This was one of the Coronation peerages of Queen Victoria, for a list of which see vol. ii, p. 145, note "b," *sub* "Carew."

(c) This title was chosen inasmuch as his then wife was, thro' the families of Byron, Milbanke, Noel, and Lovelace, a descendant (her mother being the representative) of the family of Lovelace, Barons Lovelace of Hurley.

(d) This was in consequence of the death (16 May 1860) of the *suo jure* Baroness Wentworth, his late wife's mother, who was heiress of the Noel estates in Leicestershire.

about £8,000 a year) in Leicestershire; 3,008 in Somersetshire; 668 in Warwickshire and 28 in Devonshire. *Total* 18,481 acres, worth £22,815 a year, of which the Leicestershire property was inherited from the Noel family. *Principal Residences.* Horsley Towers, near Leatherhead, and Ockham Park, near Ripley, both in co. Surrey.

LOVELACE OF HURLEY.

Barony. I. 1627. *1.* SIR RICHARD LOVELACE, of Hurley, Berks, s. and h. of Richard LOVELACE,(a) of the same, by (—), da. of (—); mat. at Oxford (Merton Coll.), 7 Feb. 1583/4, and then aged 16; appears to have been in the Irish wars and to have been *knighted*, 5 Aug. 1599, at Dublin; was M.P. for Berks, 1601; for Abingdon, 1604-11; for Windsor, 1614, and for Berks (again) 1621-22, and was *cr.*, 31 May 1627, BARON LOVELACE OF HURLEY, co. Berks. He *m.* firstly Katharine, widow of William HIDE, of Denchworth, Berks (who *d.* 1598), da. of George GYLL, of Wydial, Herts, by Gertrude, da. of Sir John PERYENT, also of Herts.(b) By her he had no issue. He *m.* secondly, about 1615, Margaret, da. and h. of William DODSWORTH, citizen of London. He *d.* 22 April 1634, and was *bur.* at Hurley. Will pr. 1634. His widow's will pr. 1652.

II. 1634. *2.* JOHN (LOVELACE), BARON LOVELACE OF HURLEY, s. and h., by second wife; mat. at Oxford (Ch. Ch.), 15 June 1632, and then aged 16; *suc. to the peerage*, 22 April 1634; was a Royalist and lived at Water Eaton, Oxon, in 1644. He *m.*, 11 July 1638, at St. Giles in the fields (lic. London, he aged 22 and she 15), Anne, da. of Thomas (WENTWORTH), EARL OF CLEVELAND, by his first wife, Anne, da. of Sir John CROFTS. He *d.* 25 Nov. 1670, much impoverished, at the Gate House of Woodstock manor, Oxon, and was *bur.* at Hurley. Will pr. Nov. 1670. His widow, who became in May 1686, *suo jure* BARONESS WENTWORTH,(c) *d.* 7 May 1697. Her admon. 26 April 1697, to a creditor.

III. 1670. *3.* JOHN (LOVELACE), BARON LOVELACE OF HURLEY, only s. and h., *b.* about 1640; mat. at Oxford (Wadham Coll.), 25 July 1655; M.A., 9 Sep. 1661; was M.P. for Berks, 1661, till he *suc. to the peerage* in 1670. He was a violent Whig and he took a prominent part in effecting the Revolution.(d) He was Capt. of the Band of Pensioners, 1689; Ch. Justice in Eyre south of Trent. By his extravagance great portion of his property had to be sold by decree of the Court of Chancery. He *m.* (lic. fac., 20 July 1662, Martha (then aged 20), da. and coheir of Sir Edmund PYE, Bart. (so *cr.* 1641) of Lekhampsted and Bradenham, Bucks, by Catharine, sister of John, 1st BARON LUCAS OF SHENFIELD, da. of Thomas LUCAS, of Colchester. He *d.* s.p.m.,(e) 27 Sep. 1693. His widow *d.* about 1704. Her admon. 1 June 1704.

IV. 1693. *4.* JOHN (LOVELACE), BARON LOVELACE OF HURLEY, cousin and h. male, being s. and h. of William LOVELACE, of Hurst, Berks, by Mary, sister and coheir of Sir Edward NEVILL, Bart., of Grove, Notts, which William Lovelace (who *d.* 1676) was s. of the Hon. Francis Lovelace (living 1672, aged 48), who was 2d s. of the first Baron. He *suc. to the peerage* in 1693. He was Governor of New York till his death in 1709. He *m.* Charlotte, da. of Sir John

(a) He was s. and h. of John Lovelace who *d.* 1558, possessed of Hurley, whose parentage appears to be unknown but who probably is the John Lovelace who *m.* Elizabeth, sister of William Frere (*m.* 1560; *d.* 1611), of Water Eaton, Oxon.

(b) See Gyll's "*Wraysbury*," p. 82.

(c) She was *suc.* in the Barony of Wentworth by Martha, her grandaughter and heir, da. and h. of John, the 3d Baron, her s. and h. ap., who had *d.* before her.

(d) See vol. i, p. 28, note "b," *sub* "Abingdon," for a list of the nobles and gentry (among whom he was) in arms in 1688 for the Prince of Orange.

(e) Martha, his only da. and h., *suc.* his mother (her grandmother) in 1697 as Baroness Wentworth. See note "c" next above.

CLAYTON. He *d.* at New York, 6 May 1709.(a) Admon. 1 Feb. 1713/4. His widow living 1736 *d.* about 1742. Her admon. as "of Hurley" 1 Dec. 1749.

V. 1709. 5. JOHN (LOVELACE), BARON LOVELACE OF HURLEY, s. and h., Ensign in Brigadier Munden's Regiment. He *d.* unm., 2 weeks after his father, in May 1709, at New York afsd. Admon. 21 Jan. 1718/9.

V. 1709, to 1736. 6. NEVILL (LOVELACE), BARON LOVELACE OF HURLEY, only br. and h., aged 2 years in 1710, *suc. to the peerage,* 1709, Gent. of the Bedchamber, 1735. He *d.* unm. at St. James, Westm., in 1736.(b)

LOWER CONNELLO.

i.e., "FITZGIBBON OF LOWER CONNELLO, co. Limerick, "Barony [I]. (*FitzGibbon*), *cr.* 1789; see "CLARE" Earldom [I.], *cr.* 1795; *ex.* 1864.

LOWTHER and LOWTHER OF WHITEHAVEN.

i.e., "LOWTHER of Lowther, co. Westmorland," Barony (*Lowther*), *cr.* 1696, with the VISCOUNTCY OF LONSDALE, which see; *ex.* 1751.

---

i.e., "LOWTHER of Lowther, co. Westmorland," Viscountcy and Barony (*Lowther*), *cr.* 1784 with the EARLDOM OF LONSDALE, which see; *ex.* 1802.

---

i.e., "LOWTHER OF WHITEHAVEN, co. Cumberland," Viscountcy and Barony (*Lowther*), *cr.* 1797, with a *spec. rem.*; see LONSDALE, Earldom, *cr.* 1784, and *ex.* 1802, as also "LONSDALE, Earldom, *cr.* 1807.

LUCAN.

PATRICK SARSFIELD, of Lucan, co. Dublin, 2d s. of Patrick S. of the same, *suc.* his elder br. William in that estate, served in France; was afterwards Lieut. of the Guards in England, raised a troop of horse in 1688 in Ireland for the service of King James II., of which he was Colonel, having the rank of Brigadier General, and distinguished himself greatly at the first siege of Limerick. In reward he was *cr.* by that King,(c) when in exile, BARON ROSBERRY, VISCOUNT OF TULLY and EARL OF LUCAN, co. Dublin [I.] in Jan. 1690/1, by a patent brought over from St. Germains by the Lord Deputy Tyrconnell [I.], and was constituted a Col. of Life Guards and Com.-in-Chief of the forces in Ireland, in which last post, however, he was from May to July 1691, superseded by the Marquis de St. Ruth. The favourable terms of the capitulation of Limerick, 3 Oct. 1691 were mainly owing to his skill.(d) After this he retired to France, where he was in command of the second troop of Irish Horse Guards. He was killed, at the head of a French division, at the battle of Landen in Flanders, 29 July 1693.(e) He *m.* Honora, 2d da. of William (DE BURGH), EARL OF CLANRICARDE [I.], by his second wife, Helen, da. of Donough (MAC CARTY), EARL OF CLANCARTY [I.] She *m.* secondly (as his first wife), 26 March 1675, James (FITZ JAMES), DUKE OF BERWICK-UPON-TWEED, who *d.* 12 June 1734, aged 63. She *d.* 16 Jan. 1698 in her 23d year(f) at Languedoc.

Earl Patrick is said(e) to have had one son, who *d.* unm. in Flanders, and one da. who *m.* "the well known Baron Theodore de Newburgh, King of Corsica."

(a) Macky in his "*Characters*" [circa 1705] writes of him (for the notice tho' headed "*Nevil*, Lord Lovelace [who was not *b.* till 1708] must refer to this Lord) that he "is Lieut Col. of the Horse Guards; a very pretty gentleman of good sense and well at Court; a short, fat, brown man, not 40 years old."

(b) Martha, his only sister and h. (one of the Maids of Honour in 1732) *m.* in 1738 Lord Henry Beauclerk (4th s. of the 1st Duke of St Albans) and had issue.

(c) See vol. i, p. 59, note "b," *sub* "Albemarle" for a list of the "*Jacobite Peerages.*"

(d) In these articles he is called Lord Lucan, thus *recognising* his creation as such.

(e) See Dalton's "King James' Irish army list" where is a good account of him.

(f) "*Her and Gen.*" vol. iii, pp. 57 and 64.

LUCAN, and LUCAN OF CASTLEBAR.

Barony [I.] I. 1776. Earldom [I.] I. 1795.

1. SIR CHARLES BINGHAM, BART. [S.] of Castlebar, co. Mayo, 2d son of Sir John BINGHAM, 5th Bart. [S.] by Anne, 1st da. and coheir of Agmondesham VESEY, of Lucan, co. Dublin (by Charlotte, only da. & h. of William SARSFIELD, elder br. of the famous Gen. Patrick SARSFIELD, who was cr. EARL OF LUCAN [I.] by King James II., when in exile) was b. 22 Sep. 1730; suc. as 7th Baronet [S.] on the death, in 1751, of his elder br. the 6th Baronet; was M.P. for co. Mayo from 1761 until he was cr., 24 July 1776, BARON LUCAN OF CASTLEBAR, co. Mayo [I], taking his seat 20 June 1778: was M.P. for Northamptonshire, 1782-84, and was cr. 1 Oct. 1795, EARL OF LUCAN [I.] He m. 25 Aug. 1760, at Bath, Margaret, da. and coheir of James SMITH, of Canons Leigh, Devon, and of St. Andries, Somerset, by Grace his wife. He d. 29 March 1799, aged 68, in Charles Street, Berkeley Square. Will pr. April 1799. His widow d. 27 Feb. 1814, Admon. March 1814 and Aug. 1842.

II. 1799. 2. RICHARD (BINGHAM), EARL OF LUCAN, &c., [I.], s. and heir., b. 4 Dec. 1764; M.P. for St. Albans, 1790-1800, styled LORD BINGHAM, 1795-99; suc. to the peerage [I.], 29 March 1799. REP. PEER [I.], 1801-39, being one of the 28 original representatives. He m., 26 May 1794, at St. Marylebone, Elizabeth, the divorced wife (May 1794) of Bernard Edward HOWARD (afterwards, 1815, DUKE OF NORFOLK), 3d da. and coheir of Henry (BELASYSE), 3d EARL FAUCONBERG OF NEWBOROUGH, by his first wife, Charlotte, da. of Sir Matthew LAMB, 1st Bart. She, who was b. Jan. 1770, d. 24 March 1819. He d. (suddenly) at Serpentine terrace, Knightsbridge, 30 June 1839, in his 74th year. Will pr. Sep. 1839.

III. 1839. 3. GEORGE CHARLES (BINGHAM), EARL OF LUCAN, &c. [I.], s. and h., b. 16 April 1800, in St. Geo. Han.-sq.; styled LORD BINGHAM till 1839; ed. at Westm.-school; entered the army in 1816, serving on the staff of the Russian army in Bulgaria in 1828; Knight of St. Anne of Russia, 2nd class; M.P. for co. Mayo, 1826-30; suc. to the peerage [I.], 30 June, 1839, and was a REP. PEER [I] 1840-88; Lord Lieut. of Mayo, 1845; was in command of a division of Cavalry (as Lieut.-Gen.) in the Crimean war of 1854, being wounded at Balaklava; received the Crimean Medal and 4 clasps; Knight of the legion of honour of France and Knight (1st class) of the Medjidie of Turkey; Col. of the 1st Life Guards and full General, 1865; G.C.B., 1869; Gold Stick in waiting, 1886; FIELD MARSHAL, 1887. He m. 20 Feb. or 29 June 1829, at St. Mary's, Bryanston square, Marylebone, Anne, 7th da. (and in 1868 coheir) of Robert (BRUDENELL), 6th EARL OF CARDIGAN, by Penelope Anne, da. of George John COOKE. She, who was b. 29 June 1809, d. 2 April 1877 at Richmond, co. Surrey. He d. 10 Nov. 1888, aged 88, at 12 South Street, Park lane and was bur. at Laleham, Midx. Will pr. at £44,669.

IV. 1888. 4. GEORGE (BINGHAM), EARL OF LUCAN [1795] AND BARON LUCAN OF CASTLEBAR [1776] in the peerage of Ireland, also a Baronet [S., 1634], s. and h., b. 8 May 1830; ed at Rugby; aide-de-camp to his Father in the Crimean war, 1854; Brevet Major, 1855; Knight of the legion of honour of France and of the Medjidie of Turkey, 1857; Lieut.-Col. Coldstream Guards, 1859 to 1860. He was M.P. for Mayo, 1865-74; suc. to the peerage [I], 10 Nov. 1888; REP. PEER [I] since 1890. He m. 17 Nov. 1859, at St. Geo. Han.-sq., Cecilia Catherine, 3d and yst. da. of Charles (GORDON-LENNOX), 5th DUKE OF RICHMOND, by Caroline, da. of Henry William (PAGET), 1st MARQUESS OF ANGLESEY. She was b. 13 April 1838.

[GEORGE CHARLES BINGHAM, styled LORD BINGHAM, 1st s. and h. ap.; b. 13 Dec. 1860; ed. at Harrow; Capt. 4th batt. Rifle Brigade.]

Family Estates.—These, in 1883, consisted of 60,570 acres in co. Mayo and 32 in co. Dublin, besides 1,191 in Cheshire, 984 in Middlesex and 159 in Surrey. *Total* 62,936 acres, worth £17,423 a year. Principal Residence. Laleham House, near Staines, Middlesex, and Castlebar, co. Mayo.

LUCAS OF SHENFIELD.

Barony. I. 1645. 1. SIR JOHN LUCAS, of Colchester, 1st (legit.) s. and h. of Sir Thomas LUCAS, of the same (Sheriff for Essex, 1617), by Elizabeth, da. and coheir of John LEIGHTON, of London, was b. 1606; suc. his father 25 Sep. 1625; and, having early espoused the Royalist cause, was imprisoned (his stately house at St. John's Colchester being plundered by the rabble in Aug. 1642), but escaped and fought at Newbury &c. He was cr. 3 Jan. 1644/5,(a) BARON LUCAS OF SHENFIELD, co. Essex with rem., in default of heirs male of his body, to Charles Lucas,(b) Knt., his brother, rem. to Thomas Lucas,(c) Knt., a bastard br., in like manner.(d) Some 20 years later he, having no male issue, procured another peerage for his da.; see "LUCAS OF CRUDWELL." He m. before 1633 Anne, da. of Sir Christopher NEVILL, K.B. (son of Edward, LORD ABERGAVENNY), by Mary, da. and coheir of Thomas DARCY of Tolleshunt, Darcy, co. Essex. She d. 22 Aug. 1660. He s.p.m.s. 2 July 1671, aged 65.(e) Both bur. at St. Giles, Colchester. His will pr. 1672.

II. 1671. 2. CHARLES (LUCAS), BARON LUCAS OF SHENFIELD, nephew, suc. to the peerage in 1671, according to the spec. rem. in its creation, he being s. and h. of Sir Thomas LUCAS (of Lexden, within Colchester), by Anne(f) da. of Sir John BYRON, K.B., which Thomas, was eldest, but illegit., br. of the late Lord. He lived at the Tenter House in Lexden parish. He m. Penelope, da. of Francis (LEKE), 1st EARL OF SCARSDALE, by Anne, da. of Sir Edward CARYE, of Aldenham, Herts. He d. s.p.m. 1688.(g) Admon. 19 Dec. 1688 to his widow, who was living 1705.

III. 1688, to 1705. 3. ROBERT (LUCAS), BARON LUCAS OF SHENFIELD, br. and h., male, b. in Ireland;(h) entered the army and, being the senior "protestant" officer in command at the Tower of London at the revolution, had the Government thereof accordingly and was afterwards confirmed as Lieut. of the Tower,(h) retaining that post during

(a) The last three peerages cr. by Charles I., that are entered on the patent rolls are (1.) *Lucas of Shenfield*, 3 Jan. 1644/5, (2) *Belasyse of Worlaby*, 27 Jan. 1644/5, and (3) *Rockingham*, 29 Jan. 1644/5. Since Dec. 1641, but 12 (in all) including the above three are so entered, tho' for three others (*the Earldom of Sunderland*, the *Barony of Hatton of Kirby* and the *Barony of Widdrington of Blankney*) there are signet bills.

(b) This Sir Charles Lucas, *knighted* 27 July 1629, was the yr. br. of the grantee and was a distinguished Royalist. He d. unm., being shot 28 Aug. 1648, together with Sir George Lisle, after the surrender of Colchester, by order of Fairfax, the Parl. General. His admon. 6 July 1652.

(c) This Sir Thomas Lucas, *knighted* 14 April 1628, was elder brother by the same mother, of the grantee but was born before marriage. His father settled upon him the estate of Lexden in Essex. He was sequestered by Parl. and d. in Ireland in or shortly before 1650. Will dat. 18 March 1648/9, pr. 26 Aug. 1650, admon. 5 April 1650. His widow "*Ann*" living Aug. 1650.

(d) Among "the Cavaliers imprisoned in 1655," were the Lords Byron, Coventry, Lucas, Maynard, Petre, St. John, with Sir Frederick (afterwards Lord) Cornwallis. Some rather witty verses were written upon them. See "*N. and Q.*, 7th S., x. 41.

(e) His only son John Lucas b. 1633, d. young, and his only da. Mary, was in 1663 cr. Baroness Lucas of Crudwell.

(f) The lic. for their marriage (London) is dat. 27 Jan. 1628/9, she being then 16 and he 31.

(g) Of his two daughters and coheirs (1) Anne (living Nov. 1704), m. Edward Carye and was mother of Lucius Henry, who in 1694 suc. as 6th Viscount Falkland [S.], and (2) Penelope, m. 17 July 1690, Isaac Selfe and d. 10 Feb. 1701/2, aged 38, leaving issue. It is to be noted that the Viscounts Falkland use the arms of Lucas as a quartering notwithstanding the illegitimacy of the second Lord's father.

(h) So stated in Macky's "Characters," where, in error, he is called "Charles" instead of "Robert." Macky adds that "it was great chance that made him a Lord and Governor of the most considerable garrison in the nation, both at the same time, to neither of which he could have aspired, if they had not dropt upon him,

the reign of William III., but not subsequently;[1] Col. of a Reg. of foot. He *d.* unm. 31 Jan. 1704/5, aged about 55, when the *Peerage* became *extinct*. Will dat. 30 Nov. 1704/5 to 31 Jan. 1704/5, pr. 12 March 1704/5.

LUCAS OF CRUDWELL.

[For fuller account see "KENT" Earldom, *cr.* 1465, *sub* the 11th and 12th Earls.]

Barony. I. 1663. *1.* Mary, wife of Anthony (GREY), 11th EARL OF KENT (whom she had *m.* 2 March 1662/3) only surv. child of John (LUCAS), 1st BARON LUCAS OF SHENFIELD, by Anne. his wife, both above named, was at her father's request *cr.* (v.p.), 7 May 1663, BARONESS LUCAS OF CRUDWELL, co. Wilts, with remainder of that peerage to her heirs male by the said Earl of Kent, and with a special and singular proviso (one that is probably unique) "that if at any time or times after the death of the said Mary, Countess of Kent, and in default of issue male of her body by the said Earl begotten, there shall be more persons than one who shall be coheirs of her body by the said Earl, so that the King or his heirs might declare which of them should have the dignity, or otherwise the dignity should be suspended or extinguished, then, nevertheless, the dignity should not be suspended or extinguished, but should go and be held and enjoyed from time to time by such of the said coheirs as by course of descent and the common law of the realm should be inheritable in other entire and indivisible inheritancy, as namely,—an office of honour and public trust, or a castle for the necessary defence of the realm, and the like, in case such inheritance had been given and limited to the said Countess and the heirs of her body by the said Earl begotten." The Earl *d.* 19 Aug. 1702 aged 57. His widow, the *suo jure* Baroness, *d.* (three months later) 1 Nov 1702.

II. 1702-18, and 1723-40. *2.* HENRY (GREY), EARL OF KENT and BARON LUCAS OF CRUDWELL, only s. and h., *bap.* 28 Sep. 1651; *suc. to the Earldom*, 19 Aug., and *to the Barony*, 1 Nov. 1702; *cr.* on 14 Nov. 1706, MARQUESS OF KENT, &c., on 28 April 1710, DUKE OF KENT, and on 19 May 1740, MARQUESS GREY, the said Marquessate of Grey being with a *spec. rem.* in favour of his grandaughter below mentioned. He *d.* s.p.m.s., 5 June 1740, aged 68.

III. 1718-23. *3.* ANTHONY GREY, *styled* (since 1706) EARL OF HAROLD, 1st s. and h. ap., was by writ 8 Nov. 1718 sum., v.p., in his father's Barony as LORD LUCAS OF CRUDWELL. He *d.* s.p. and v.p. 21 July, 1723, aged 27, when that Barony (so evoked) *reverted to his father*.

IV. 1740. *4.* JEMIMA, *suo jure* MARCHIONESS GREY and BARONESS LUCAS OF CRUDWELL, niece to Anthony, and grandaughter and eldest coheir of Henry, both next abovenamed; *suc. to the peerage*, on the death of her said grandfather, 5 June 1740, under the *spec. rems.* in the creations of the abovenamed dignities. She was 1st da. of John (CAMPBELL) 3rd EARL OF BREADALBANE [S.], and only surv. child of his first wife, Amabella, eldest of the four daughters and coheirs of Henry (GREY), DUKE, MARQUESS, and EARL OF KENT, &c., MARQUESS GREY and BARON LUCAS OF CRUDWELL abovementioned. She was *b.* 9 Oct. 1722; *m.* 22 May 1740, Philip (YORKE), 2d EARL OF HARWICKE, who *suc.* to that Earldom in May 1764, and who *d.* 16 May 1790, in his 70th year. See fuller particulars under "HARDWICKE" Earldom, *cr.* 1754, *sub* the 2d Earl. The *suo jure* Marchioness and

---

whether he would or not. He made his court very assiduously to the King and by this means he got his Majesty to excuse several slips that happened in his Government."

[1] Bishop Burnet's character of him, when aged 50 and upwards, with Dean Swift's additions thereto, placed *in italics*, is as under. "He is every way a plain man, yet took a great deal of pains to seem knowing and wise; everybody pitied him, when the Queen turned him out, for his seeming good nature and real poverty. He is very fat, very expensive, and very poor.—*A good plain humdrum.*"

Baroness (his widow), *d.* s.p.m., 10 Jan. 1797, aged 74, in St. James' square, when the *Marquessate of Grey* became *extinct*, but the Barony of Lucas of Crudwell devolved as below. Will pr. Jan. 1797.

V. 1797. 5. AMABEL, *suo jure* BARONESS LUCAS OF CRUDWELL, 1st da. and h.: *suc. to the peerage* on the death of her mother abovenamed, 10 Jan. 1797, under the *spec. rem.* in the creation of that dignity. She, who was *b.* 22 Jan. 1751, *m.* 16 July 1772, Alexander HUME-CAMPBELL, *styled* LORD POLWARTH, who *d.* 2 March 1781, aged 31. She was *cr.* 25 Oct. 1816, COUNTESS DE GREY OF WREST, co. Bedford, with a *spec. rem.* of that dignity. She *d. s.p.*, 4 May 1833, aged 82.

VI. 1833. 6. THOMAS PHILIP (WEDDELL, *afterwards* DE GREY *and formerly* ROBINSON) EARL DE GREY OF WREST, BARON LUCAS OF CRUDWELL and BARON GRANTHAM, nephew and h., being s. and h. of Thomas (ROBINSON), 2d BARON GRANTHAM, by Mary Jemima, only sister of Amabel, *suo jure* COUNTESS DE GREY OF WREST and BARONESS LUCAS OF CRUDWELL, abovenamed. He was *b.* 8 Dec. 1781; *suc.* his father, 20 July 1786, as BARON GRANTHAM; took the name of *Weddell* in lieu of his patronymic of *Robinson*, by Royal lic.. 7 May 1803; *suc.* his aunt abovenamed in the peerages or De Grey and Lucas, 4 May 1833, and took the name of *De Grey* in lieu of that of *Weddell* by Royal lic., 24 June 1833. He *d.*, s.p.m., 14 Nov. 1859, aged 77, when the Earldom of De Grey of Wrest, &c., devolved on his nephew and heir male, but the Barony of Lucas of Crudwell, as below.

For fuller particulars see "DE GREY OF WREST," Earldom, *cr.* 1816.

VII. 1859. 7. ANNE FLORENCE, DOW. COUNTESS COWPER, &c., and *suo jure*, BARONESS LUCAS OF CRUDWELL, 1st da. and h., *suc. to that Barony*, 14 Nov. 1859, under the *spec. rem.* in the creation thereof. She was *b.* 8 June 1806; *m.* 7 Oct. 1833, George Augustus Frederick (COWPER), 6th EARL COWPER, who had *suc. to that dignity*, 21 July 1837, and who *d.* 15 April 1856 in his 50th year. The *suo jure* Baroness (his widow) *d.* 23 July 1880, aged 74.

VIII. 1880. 8. FRANCIS THOMAS DE GREY (COWPER), EARL COWPER, &c., and BARON LUCAS OF CRUDWELL, s. and h.; *b.* 11 June 1834; *suc. to the Earldom of Cowper*, &c., 15 April 1856 on the death of his father, and *suc. to the Barony of Luca of Crudwell*, 23 July 1880 on the death of his mother abovenamed.

For fuller particulars see "Cowper" Earldom, *cr.* 1718, *sub* the 6th and 7th Earls.

LUCY.

GEOFFREY DE LUCY(a) was sum. to [*Montfort's*] Parl. 14 Dec. (1264), 49 Hen. III. Such summons, however, does not originate a hereditary Barony.(b) He *d.* in or before (1284), 12 Ed. I.

GEOFFREY DE LUCY, s. and h., aged 18 at his father's death, whose lands in Northumberland were in ward from (1284). 12 Ed. I., till he proved his age in (1288), 16 Ed. I. He was sum. to attend the King at Salisbury 26 Jan. (1296/7), 25 Ed. I., but such summons does not originate a hereditary Barony.(c) He *d.* 1304, leaving Geoffrey his s. and h., aged 16.(d)

(a) He is called by Mr. Courthope "s. and h. of Geoffrey de Lucy, Lord of Newington, co. Kent, and nearly allied to Richard de Lucy, Justice of England," which Geoffrey is said to have *d.* in 1252. Geoffrey de Lucy (possibly *this* Geoffrey) bore the Cap of State at the Coronation of Richard I.

(b) See as to this writ vol. iv. p. 365, note "d," *sub* "Fitz John," where also is given a list of those so summoned.

(c) See vol. i, p. 111. note "b," *sub* "Ap Adam."

(d) Courthope adds, "neither this Baron nor any of his posterity were ever afterwards sum. to Parl., but his descendants continued in the male line at Dallington, co.

Barony by Writ.

I. 1320.

1. Anthony de Lucy, 2d s. of Thomas de Lucy, formerly de Multon, by Isabel, da. and coheir of Adam de Boltesby, of Langley, co. Northumberland (which Thomas was s. of Alan de Multon, by Alice, da. and coheir of Richard de Lucy, of Egremont, co. Cumberland), *suc.* his elder br. Thomas de Lucy in the family estates, co. Cumberland, &c., in 1308, being then aged 25; served in the wars with Scotland; was several times Sheriff of Cumberland and was sum. to Parl. as a Baron (LORD LUCY) by writs from 15 May (1320), 14 Ed. II. to 24 Feb. (1342/3), 14 Edward III.(a) In (1322-23) 16 Ed. II., he obtained a grant of the Castle and Honour of Cockermouth. He assisted at the capture of Andrew (de Harcla) the rebel Earl of Carlisle; was Gov. of Berwick-upon-Tweed and was Ch. Gov. (as Lord Lieut.) of Ireland in 1331. He is said to have *m.* Elizabeth, da. of Robert Tilliolf, of Scaleby. He was dead in (1343) 17 Ed. III.

II. 1342.

2. Thomas (de Lucy), Lord Lucy, only s. and h. He was sum. to Parl. (v.p. ?) 25 Feb (1341/2), 16 Ed. III, as also from 20 April (1344), 18 Ed. III to 4 Dec. (1364), 38 Ed. III. He distinguished himself in the wars in Flanders, as also in Scotland at the siege, 1343, of Lochmaban Castle and at the battle of Durham. He *m.* before 1334 Margaret (then aged 24), sister and coheir of John, Lord Multon, she being 3d and yst. da. of Thomas (de Multon), 1st Lord Multon, both of Egremont, in Cumberland. With her he acquired very considerable property. He *d.* 5 Dec. (1365), 39 Ed. III.

III. 1365.

3. Anthony (de Lucy), Lord Lucy, only s. and h., aged 24 at his father's death. He was never sum. to Parl. He was joint Guardian of the marches towards Cumberland and Westmorland in 1366. He *m.* on or before 1366, Joane, widow of William, Lord Greystock, da. of Henry (Fitz Hugh), Lord Fitz Hugh. He *d.* s.p.m., Sep. 1368. His widow *m.* (thirdly) Sir Matthew Redman, and *d.* 1 Sep. 1404, being *bur.* at Clerkenwell.

IV. 1368.

4. Joane, *de jure, suo jure* Baroness Lucy, only da. and h., then aged 2 years and 3 months. She *d.* Oct. 1369, aged about 3 years.

V. 1369. to 1398.

5. Maud, Countess of Angus [S.], and *de jure, suo jure* Baroness Lucy, aunt and heir, being only da. of Thomas, the 2d Lord Lucy. She *m.* firstly (as his second wife), after Aug. 1350, but before 1369, Gilbert (de Umfravill), Earl of Angus [S.], who *d.* s.p., 7 Jan. 1380/1. She *m.* secondly (also as his second wife) about 1384, Henry (Percy), 1st. Earl of Northumberland, who was slain (leaving issue by his first wife), 29 Feb. 1407/8. She, however, *d.* s.p., previously, 24 Dec. 1398, leaving to him Prudhoe Castle (which she had inherited from her first husband), and her vast paternal estates, comprising the Honours of Egremont, Cockermouth, &c.(b) These

---

Northampton, till the reign of Henry VI., when, upon the death of Sir William Lucy, 1460, the representation vested in his sisters and coheirs—Eleanor, wife of Thomas Hopton, of Hopton, co. Salop, and Matilda, wife of Sir William Vaux, of Harrowden; the Earl of Portsmouth represents the former of these ladies, and the Lord Vaux of Harrowden the present Earl of Pembroke, and Edward Bourchier Hartop, Esq., represent the latter."

(a) There is proof in the rolls of Parl. of his sitting.

(b) Sir H. Nicolas (slightly altered by Courthope) remarks hereon that "In consequence of the marriage of Maud, the daughter of Thomas, and sister and eventually sole heir of Anthony, last Baron Lucy, with Henry [Percy], 1st Earl of Northumberland, it was stipulated that the Castle and honour of Cockermouth, part of the inheritance of the said Maud, should be settled upon himself and her and the heirs male of their two bodies, failing which, upon the heirs of her body, and in case she should die without issue, then upon Henry, Lord Percy, his s. and h. [ap.], begotten on his *first* wife, and the heirs male of his body, upon condition that the said Henry and his heirs male should bear the arms of Percy quarterly with the arms of Lucy (*viz.*), *Gules*, three Lucies, *argent*, in all shields, banners, ensigns, &c. Notwithstand-

being thus diverted from the heir of the Lucy family, the *Barony of Lucy* was never assumed by such heir, (a) but remained *dormant*.

LUDLOW [Salop.]

i.e., "LUDLOW, co. Salop," Viscountcy (*Herbert*), *cr.* 1748 with the EARLDOM OF POWIS, which see; *ex.* 1801.

---

i.e., "CLIVE OF LUDLOW," Viscountcy (*Clive*), *cr.* 1804 with the EARLDOM OF POWIS, which see.

LUDLOW, and LUDLOW OF ARDSALLAGH.

Barony [I.] I. 1755. Earldom [I.] I. 1760. *1.* PETER LUDLOW, of Ardsallagh, co. Meath, and Great Stoughton, co. Huntingdon, only surv. s. and h. of Peter LUDLOW, of Ardsallagh, by Mary, da. and h. of John PRESTON, also of Ardsallagh afsd., was *b.* 21 April 1730; *suc.* his father, 19 June 1750; was M.P. for co. Huntingdon; was *cr.*, 19 Dec. 1755, BARON LUDLOW OF ARDSALLAGH, co. Meath [I.], and subsequently was *cr.*, 3 Oct. 1760, VISCOUNT PRESTON OF ARDSALLAGH, co. Meath, and EARL LUDLOW [I.], taking his seat, 18 June 1776; P.C., 1782; Comptroller of the Household, 1782-84. He *m.*, 26 June 1753, at St. Geo. Han. sq., Frances, 1st da. of Thomas (LUMLEY-SAUNDERSON), 3d EARL OF SCARBROUGH, by Frances, da. of George (HAMILTON), EARL OF ORKNEY [S.] She *d.* 20 March 1796. He *d.* 26 Oct. 1803, aged 73.

II. 1803. *2.* AUGUSTUS (LUDLOW), EARL LUDLOW, &c., [I.] s. and h., *b.* 1 Jan. 1755; *styled* VISCOUNT PRESTON, 1760-1803; *suc. to the peerage* [I.] 26 Oct. 1803. He *d.* unm. 7 Nov. 1811, aged 56. Will pr. 1811.

III. 1811. Barony [U.K.] I. 1831, to 1842. *3.* and *1.* GEORGE JAMES (LUDLOW), EARL LUDLOW [1760], VISCOUNT PRESTON OF ARDSALLAGH [1760] and BARON LUDLOW OF ARDSALLAGH [1755], in the peerage of Ireland; only br. and h., *b.* 12 Dec. 1758; entered the army in 1778; served in the American war; was taken prisoner at York town and escaped hanging, only by having drawn the fortunate lot; served in Flanders in 1793, losing an arm at Roubain; was in command at Aboukir in 1801; served at the surrender of Alexandria, also in Hanover, 1805, and in the expedition to Copenhagen in 1807: becoming finally, in 1814, a full General; sometime Col. of the 38th Foot, and subsequently Col. of the Scots Fusileer Guards. K.B., 1804, becoming, consequently, in Jan. 1815, G.C.B.; Lieut. Gov. of Berwick. He *suc. to the peerage* [I.], 7 Nov. 1811, and was *cr.* 10 Sep. 1831(b) BARON

---

ing that the said Maud died *without issue* the descendants of the said Earl were often styled *Barons Lucy*, their pretensions to that Barony being manifestly without even the slightest foundation."

Thomas Percy (afterwards Earl of Northumberland) is often said to have been *cr.* (probably from the said assumption by his ancestors) on 1 May 1557, Baron "Percy, Poynings, *Lucy*, Bryan, and Fitz Payne," but in reality the sole dignity then conferred on him was that of "*Percy*" [alone.] See "*Creations*, 1483—1646," in ap. 47th Rep. D.K. Pub. Records.

(a) This heir was her first cousin, Sir William Melton, s. and h. of William Melton, by Joane, da. of Anthony, 1st Lord Lucy. His will was dat. 1398. The heirship continued in his issue male for five generations (see Banks' "*Bar. Angl. Conc.*"), when the heir general became Dorothy (da. and h. of Sir John Melton) aged 38 in Sep. 1546, and then wife of George (Darcy), Lord Darcy (who acquired with her the manor of Aston, co. York), as to whose descendants and representatives see vol. iii, p. 22, note "a," *sub* "Darcy."

(b) This was one of the Coronation peerages of William IV., for a list of which see vol. ii, p. 312, note "a," *sub* "Cloncurry."

LUDLOW [U.K.] He *d.* unm. at his residence, Cople House, Beds., in his 83d year, when *all his titles* became *extinct.*(a) Will pr. May 1842.

LUGTOUN.

i.e., "LUGTOUN," Viscountcy [S.] (*Leslie*), *cr.* 1680 with the DUKEDOM OF ROTHES [S.], which see; *ex.* 1681.

LUMLEY.

Barony by Writ.

I. 1384, to 1400.

1. SIR RALPH DE LUMLEY, of Lumley, co. Durham, Kilton, co. York, &c., 2d s. of Sir Marmaduke DE LUMLEY,(b) of the same, by Margaret, da. and h. of (—) HOLAND, *suc.* his elder br., Robert, in the family estates in 1375, being then aged 13 years, was *Knighted* about 1384, and was sum. to Parl. as a Baron (LORD LUMLEY) from 28 Sep. (1384), 8 Ric. II. to 30 Sep. (1399), 1 Hen. IV.(c) He was Gov. of Berwick-upon-Tweed, 1387. He *m.* about 1380, Eleanor, sister of Ralph, 1st EARL OF WESTMORLAND, da. of John (NEVILL), 3d LORD NEVILL DE RABY, by his first wife, Maud, da. of Henry PERCY, *styled* LORD PERCY. Having taken part in the insurrection to restore the deposed King Richard II., he was slain in a skirmish at Cirencester and having been attainted, 5 Jan. (1399/400) 1 Hen. IV., his *peerage* became *forfeited.*

* * * * * *

II. 1461. *2.* SIR THOMAS DE LUMLEY, of Lumley afsd., only s. and h., of Sir John DE LUMLEY, of the same by Felicia, da. of Sir Matthew REDMAN, Gov. of Berwick, which John, was 2d but 1st sur. s.(d) and eventually (1404) heir of Ralph, 1st LORD LUMLEY above named, was *b.* at Morpeth 29 Sep. 1408; *suc.* his father (who having been restored in blood by act of parl. 1412, was slain at Beaugé), 18 April 1421; was several times employed in divers treaties with the Scots; was by Henry VI. made Gov. (for life) of Scarborough Castle, in 1455; obtained at the accession of Ed. IV. in 1461, the reversal of the attainder of his grandfather abovementioned becoming thus LORD LUMLEY [1384] and was sum. to Parl. accordingly, from 26 July (1461) 1 Ed. IV. to 16 Jan. (1496/7) 12 Hen. VII. He was one of the nobles who attended at the coronation (6 July 1483) of Ric. III.(e) He *m.* Margaret da. of Sir James HARINGTON. He *d.* probably before 1480, tho' according to the writs of summons to Parl. not till in or after 1497,(f) in which year, however, he would have been in his 90th year.

(a) Having no very near relations, he devised his estates to the well known statesman, Lord John Russell (from admiration of his political character) who consequently, when some 20 years later he was raised to the peerage as Earl Russell, was at the same time *cr.* Viscount Amberley of Amberley, co. Gloucester, and of *Ardsalla*, co. Meath.

(b) This Marmaduke was s. and h. of Sir Robert de Lumley, by Lucy 3d da. (whose issue in 1374, became coheir) of Marmaduke (de Thweng), Lord Thweng, by which match the estate of Kilton and other considerable estates in Yorkshire, &c., devolved on the Lumley family. The arms of Thweng (*Arg.* a fess, *gules*, between three parrots, *vert*) were thenceforth adopted by the Lumley family.

(c) There is proof in the rolls of Parl. of his sitting.

(d) Marmaduke Lumley, the yst. son, was Bishop of Carlisle 1430, and Bishop of Lincoln 1451, having been Treasurer of England 1446.

(e) See vol. iii, p. 8, note "c," for a list of these.

(f) "Dugdale does not state in what year he died. Surtees, in his valuable History of Durham, says he died in 1485; if so, he was regularly sum. to Parl. until 1497, *twelve years* subsequent to his decease." [*Courthope.*] Considering, however, how frequently the christian name remains (in error) unchanged in the writs of Parl. as also the great age that this *Thomas* would be, if living as late as 1497, it seems more probable that the later writs (tho' directed to *Thomas*) refer to *George* his successor, who, says Collins, "I find *bearing the title of Lord Lumley* in 20 Ed. I.," *i.e.*, 1480.

III. 1480? 3. GEORGE (DE LUMLEY), LORD LUMLEY, only s. and h. He was *knighted* before 1462, being then, as also in 1463 and 1468-72, Sheriff of Northumberland; was M.P. for that county in 1466. In 1480 "bearing the title of Lord Lumley,"(a) he was in command, at the taking of Berwick from the Scots, and was made a Banneret in Hooton field, 22 Aug. 1480. He waited on Henry VII. in his northern progress in 1486; was in the Scotch expedition 1498, and accompanied the Princess Margaret as far as Berwick on her espousal to King James IV. [S.] in 1503. He *m.* Elizabeth, da. and h. of Roger THORNTON, of Newcastle-upon-Tyne, merchant, by Elizabeth, da. of John (DE GREYSTOCK), LORD GREYSTOCK. With her he acquired the estate of Witton, in Northumberland, besides others in Durham.(b) He *d.* 1508.

IV. 1508. 4. RICHARD (DE LUMLEY), LORD LUMLEY, grandson and h., being 1st s. and h., of Thomas LUMLEY (by Elizabeth his wife, formerly Elizabeth PLANTAGENET, spinster, illegit da. of **King Edward IV.**) which Thomas (living 27 Oct. 1495) was s. and h. ap. of the 3d Lord but *d.* v.p. He was sum. to Parl. from 12 Oct. (1509) 1 Hen. VIII. to 28 Nov. (1511) 3 Hen. VIII.(c) He *m.* (by dispensation, they being related in 4th degree, dat. at Rome, 28 Jan. 1488/9) Ann(d) sister of William, 1st LORD CONYERS, da. of Sir John CONYERS, K.G., of Hornby Castle, co. York, by Alice, da. and coheir of William (NEVILL), EARL OF KENT. He *d.* on Trinity Sunday, 26 May (1510) 2 Hen. VIII.

V. 1510, to 1544. 5. JOHN (DE LUMLEY), LORD LUMLEY, 1st s.(e) and h., aged 18 at his father's death in 1510. He distinguished himself at the battle of Flodden, 1513. He was sum. to Parl. from 23 Nov. (1514) 6 Hen. VIII. to 4 June (1543) 35 Hen. VIII. In 1520 he was with the King at his interview with the Emperor Charles V. and the King of France; was among those who signed the letter to the Pope, in 1531, urging the sanction to the King's proposed divorce; yet in 1537 was one of the leaders in the insurrection, on behalf of the *old faith*, called the "Pilgrimage of Grace," being one of the three nobles deputed to treat with the King's forces,(f) which resulted in a general pardon. He *m.* Joane, da. of Henry (SCROPE), 7th LORD SCROPE DE BOLTON, by his second wife Margaret, da. of Thomas (DACRE), 2nd LORD DACRE DE GILLESLAND. He *d.* 1544.

On his death *the Barony*, devolving on GEORGE LUMLEY his only s. and h., who had been executed for high treason, v.p., 20 June 1538,(g) and consequently *attainted*, became *forfeited*.

Barony. I. 1547, to 1609. 1. JOHN LUMLEY, grandson and h. of John, LORD LUMLEY abovenamed, being s. and h. of his only s. and h. ap. George Lumley (*attainted* v.p. as afsd.) by Jane, 2d da. and coheir of Sir Richard KNIGHTLEY, of Upton, co. Northampton, was *b.* about 1533. He, having set forth in a petition to King Ed. VI. that he was an infant at the death of his grandfather in 1544, to whose honours, &c. in consequence of his father's attainder, he did not succeed, obtained in 1547 an Act

(a) See p. 176, note "f," *circa finem.*

(b) The right to these lands was disputed by Giles Thornton, her bastard brother who was slain by Lord Lumley in a quarrel.

(c) To the last writ the following addition is made on the Roll "*Mortuus est ut dicitur.*" He had apparently been dead some 18 months.

(d) "On the monument at Cheam, for John, Lord Lumley [*d.* 1609] she is [erroneously] called Ann, da. of William, Lord Coigniers." [*Collins.*] The dispensation was issued at York, 10 Sep. 1489. See "*Test Ebor*" (Surtees Soc.) vol. iii, p. 355.

(e) The second son, Anthony Lumley, was grandfather of Richard, 1st Viscount Lumley of Waterford [I.], who was grandfather of Richard, 1st Earl of Scarbrough.

(f) See p. 25 note "g," *sub* "Latimer."

(g) See vol. iii, p. 20 *sub* "Darcy de Temple Hirst," Lord Darcy and Sir Thomas Percy being fellow sufferers with him.

of Parl. restoring him in *blood*, and enacting "that the said John Lumley and the heirs male of his body should have hold, enjoy and bear the name, dignity, state and pre-eminence of a *Baron of the realm*," whereby he became BARON LUMLEY (a new Barony of that name, in tail *male*, being thus created) and he was sum. to Parl. accordingly from 5 Oct 1553 to 5 Nov. 1605. K.B., 29 Nov. 1553; attending at the subsequent coronation of Queen Mary, being also a commissioner of claims at the coronations of Queen Elizabeth and of James I. He was suspected of treasonable dealings with Mary, Queen of Scots, and was, in 1570 (as also was the Earl of Arundel, his father-in-law) imprisoned; in Oct. 1586 he was one of the triers(a) of that Queen, as also in 1602 of the Earl of Essex. He *m.* firstly, before 4 March 1552, Joan, eldest(b) of the two daughters and coheirs of Henry (FITZALAN), EARL OF ARUNDEL, by his first wife Catharine, da. of Thomas (GREY), MARQUESS OF DORSET. She was one of the six principal ladies, that sat in the third chariot of state at the cornation of Queen Mary, in 1553. She was *bur.* (with her infant children), 9 March 1576/7, at Cheam, co. Surrey. He *m.* secondly, Elizabeth, da of Thomas (DARCY), 2d BARON DARCY OF CHICHE, by Frances, da. of Richard (RICH), 1st BARON RICH. He *d.*, s.p.s., 11 April 1609, aged 76, and was buried at Cheam afsd(c) M.I.(d) At his death the *Barony of Lumley* (*cr.* in 1547) became *extinct*(e). *Inq. post mortem* at Southwark, 30 May 1609. Will (whereby, as also by settlement, he had settled the bulk of his estates on his distant kinsman and heir *male*) dated 28 Jan. 1605/6, pr. 1609. His widow was *bur.* from St. Olive Hart street, London, 4 Feb. 1616/7, at Cheam afsd., M.I.(d) Will dated 6 Nov. 1616, pr. 1617.

(a) See vol. iii, p. 72, note "a," *sub* Derby, for the names of the 24 noblemen thus appointed.

(b) Mary the second da. (the only child of her father who had issue) *m.* Thomas (Howard), Duke of Norfolk, and was ancestress of the succeeding Dukes of Norfolk and Earls of Arundel.

(c) In Camden's "*Elizabeth*" his zeal, (which apparently exceeded his discretion) for his ancestry is thus alluded to "Had so great a veneration for the memory of his ancestors that he caused monuments to be erected for them in the collegiate church of Chester-on-the-street (opposite to Lumley Castle), in order as they succeeded one another, from Liulphus down to his own time; which he had either picked out of the demolished monasteries, or *made new*."

(d) This monument is engraved in "Sandford," p. 423.

(e) Splandian Lloyd, then aged 40 and upwards, was found to be his heir, being s. and h. of his only sister Barbara Williams deceased, which Barbara had *m.* firstly, Humphrey Lloyd, of Denbigh (who *d.* Aug. 1568, aged 41), and secondly, William Williams, of Cochwillan, co. Carnarvon. This Splandian was consequently the heir in 1609 to the Barony of Lumley as *cr.* by the writ of 1384, subject to the reversal of the attainder thereof. This Splandian *d.* s.p., but his great-grand-nephew and heir, Robert Lumley Lloyd, D.D., Rector of St. Paul's, Covent Garden (who had inherited from his ancestor, Lord Lumley, the estate of Cheam, in Surrey) laid claim to the Barony, as heir general, to whose petition the committee for privileges replied, 28 March 1723, "That the petitioner had no right to a writ of summons in parl. as prayed by his petition." This resolution was founded upon the previous report. (1) "That by the Act of parl. of 1 Ed. VI. [1547] a *new* Barony of Lumley was created and limited by express words to John, Lord Lumley, in tail male, and that upon his death without issue male, the said Barony became extinct. (2) That the attainder [1538] of George Lumley is not reversed by the said Act, but remains yet in force, and that the restitution of John, Lord Lumley, in *blood* only, while the attainder remains unreversed, could not possibly revive the ancient Barony, which was before merged in the crown in consequence of that attainder." The petition of 1723 is given in full in Collins' "*Baronies by writ*" pp. 373-377. The claim was opposed by the Earl of Scarbrough, the heir *male*, to whom (on account of this groundless and apparently wanton opposition) Dr. Lloyd, by his will dated 29 Dec. 1729, leaves the body of Richard "late Viscount Waterford" now in the vault belonging "to our family" at Cheam, with liberty (as he sarcastically adds) "to make such use thereof as he shall think fit." Dr. Lloyd *d.* Nov. 1730, apparently s.p. His numerous relatives are set forth in Burke's "*Extinct Peerage*," (*sub.* "Lumley") but he appears to have left the (Lumley) estate of Cheam (away from them) to the Duke of Bedford.

LUMLEY OF WATERFORD and LUMLEY OF LUMLEY CASTLE.

Viscountcy [I.] I. 1628. 1. SIR RICHARD LUMLEY, of Lumley Castle, co. Durham, s. and h. of Roger LUMLEY by Anne, da. of (—) KURTWICH, which Roger (who was living 1606), was s. and h. of Anthony LUMLEY, 2d s. of Richard, 4th LORD LUMLEY abovenamed, inherited, in 1609, Lumley Castle and other considerable estates,(a) under the will of his cousin, John, BARON LUMLEY above mentioned; was *Knighted* at Theobalds, 19 July 1616, and was *cr.* 12 July 1628, VISCOUNT LUMLEY OF WATERFORD [I.], taking his seat 4 Nov. 1634. Adhering faithfully to his King, he made Lumley Castle a garrison, and was in command in the west, when Bristol was surrendered to the Parl. 10 Sep. 1645. He was among the "Compounders" of 1655, being fined £1,955. He also signed the declaration before the meeting of the Restoration Parl. He *m.* firstly, Frances, widow of William HOLLAND (whom she *m.* 17 Aug. 1614), da. of Henry SHELLEY, of Worminghurst, co. Sussex, by his first wife, Barbara, da. of Sir William CROMER. He *m.* secondly, 11 May 1630, at St. Bride's, London, Elizabeth, widow of Sir William SANDYS, 2d da. of Sir William CORNWALLIS, of Brome, co. Suffolk, by his first wife Lucy, da. and coheir of John (NEVILL) LORD LATIMER. She *d.* s.p., and was *bur.* 2 Feb. 1657/8, in Westm. Abbey. Will dat. 18 Sep. 1641 to 26 July 1652, pr. 29 June 1659. He was *bur.* at Cheam, co. Surrey. Will dat. 18 April 1661, pr. 12 March 1662/3.

II. 1663. Barony [E.] I. 1681. Viscountcy [E.] I. 1689. 2 and 1. RICHARD (LUMLEY), VISCOUNT LUMLEY OF WATERFORD [I.], grandson and h., being s. and h. of the Hon. John LUMLEY, by Mary da. and eventually coheir of Sir Henry COMPTON, K.B., of Brambleteigh, co. Sussex, which John, was only s. and h. ap. of the 1st Viscount and *d.* v.p., being *bur.* 10 Oct. 1658, at St. Martin's in the fields. He *suc. to the peerage* [I.] in 1663, and was *cr.* 31 May 1681, BARON LUMLEY OF LUMLEY CASTLE, co. Durham (with a *spec. rem.* in favour of his br. Henry Lumley) and subsequently, 10 April 1689, VISCOUNT LUMLEY OF LUMLEY CASTLE, being finally *cr.* 15 April 1690, EARL OF SCARBROUGH; see that dignity.

LUNDIE.

i.e., "LUNDIE," Barony [S.] (*Campbell*), *cr.* 1642 with the EARLDOM OF IRVINE [S.], which see; *ex.* before 1660.

---

i.e., "DUNCAN OF LUNDIE, co. Perth," Barony (*Duncan*), *cr.* 1797 with the VISCOUNTCY OF DUNCAN OF CAMPERDOWN, which see, *sub* "CAMPERDOWN."

See "CAMPERDOWN OF LUNDIE, co. Forfar, AND GLENEAGLES, co. Perth," Earldom (*Duncan*), *cr.* 1831.

LUNEDALE.

i.e., "BOWES OF STREATLAM CASTLE, co. Durham, AND OF LUNEDALE, co. York," Barony (*Bowes*), *cr.* 1815; *ex.* 1820; also, Barony (*Bowes-Lyon*), *cr.* 1887; see (in both cases) under "STRATHMORE" Earldom [S.]

LUPTON.

See "CHURSTON OF CHURSTON FERRERS AND LUPTON, co. Devon," Barony (*Yarde-Buller*), *cr.* 1858.

(a) See Nichols' "*Leicestershire*," vol. iii, for a curious anecdote as to this his adoption by his said cousin.

LURGAN.

Barony. I. 1839. 1. The Rt. Hon. CHARLES BROWNLOW, of Lurgan, co. Armagh, 2d but 1st surv. s. and h. of Charles BROWNLOW,(a) of the same, Lieut. Col. 57th Foot, by Caroline, da. and coheir of Benjamin ASHE, of Bath, b. 17 April 1795, suc. his father, 11 Sep. 1822; was M.P. for co. Armagh in five Parls., 1818-32; P.C. [I.], 1837, and was cr., 14 May 1839, BARON LURGAN of Lurgan, co. Armagh. He m. firstly, 1 June 1822, his cousin, Mary, 2d da. of John (BLIGH), 4th EARL OF DARNLEY [I.], by Elizabeth, da. of the Rt. Hon. William BROWNLOW, of Lurgan afsd. She, who was b. 1 June 1796 d. s.p.m., 18 June 1828. He m. secondly, 15 July 1828, Jane, 4th da. of Roderick MACNEILL, of Barra, co. Inverness, by Jane, da. of Sir Evan CAMERON, 1st Bart. of Fassifern, co. Argyle. He d. at Lurgan Castle, co. Armagh, 30 April 1847, in his 52d year. Will pr. June 1849. His widow d. 6 Jan. 1878, aged 75, at Ridghill, Torquay, Devon.

II. 1847. 2. CHARLES (BROWNLOW), BARON LURGAN, s. and h., by second wife, b. 10 April 1831 in Eaton place; suc. to the peerage, 30 April 1847; sometime 1849-52, an officer in the 76th foot; K.P., 31 March 1864; a Lord in waiting, 1869-74. He m. 20 June 1853, at St. Geo. Han. sq. Emily Anne, 4th da. of John Cavendish (BROWNE), 3d BARON KILMAINE [I.], by his first wife, Eliza, da. of David LYON. He d. 16 Jan. 1882, at Brighton, aged 50, after seven years of paralysis. His widow, who was b. 14 March 1833, living 1893.

III. 1882. 3. WILLIAM (BROWNLOW), BARON LURGAN, 2d, but 1st, surv. s. and h.; b. 11 Jan. 1858, in Leinster street, Dublin; ed. at Eton; suc. to the peerage, 16 Jan. 1882; sometime in 86th foot, and subsequently Lieut. in the Grenadier Guards. He m., 7 Feb. 1893, at Trinity church, Sloane street, Emily Julia, 1st da. of George Henry (CADOGAN), 5th EARL CADOGAN, by Beatrix Jane, da. of William (CRAVEN), 2d EARL OF CRAVEN. She was b. 11 April 1871.

Family Estates.—These, in 1883, consisted of 15,166 acres in co. Armagh and 110 in co. Down. *Total* 15,276 acres, worth £20,589 a year. *Principal Residence.* Brownlow House, near Lurgan, co. Armagh.

LUTEREL, or LUTTRELL

Barony by Writ. I. 1295. 1. SIR ROBERT DE LUTEREL, of Irnham, co. Lincoln and Hoton Paganel, co. York, successor to, and said(b) to be, br. of Geoffrey, who was aged 30, and a lunatic in 1264, when he suc. his father, Sir Andrew DE LUTEREL, of Irnham afsd. This Robert, who was in the Welsh wars, was, with about 60 others, sum. 8 June (1294), 22 Ed. I. to attend the King to advise on the affairs of the realm,(c) and was sum. to Parl. as a Baron (LORD LUTEREL), by writs 24 June, 30 Sep. and 2 Nov. (1295), 23 Ed. I., but never afterwards. He d. (1297), 25 Ed. I., leaving Joane his widow and Geoffrey, his s. and h., aged 21; but "of this Geffrey" writes Dugdale, "in regard he never had summons to Parl. nor any of his descendants, I shall not speak any farther than to take notice that his posterity had fair possessions in Somersetshire, amongst which Cantokeshehed (situate upon the point of Quantok-hills) and Dunster Castle (whereof they are still owners) are part."(d)

(a) This Charles was next br. and h. to William Brownlow, M.P. for co. Armagh, 1795—1815, both being sons of the Rt. Hon. William Brownlow, also M.P. for the same, 1753-94, who was s. and h. of Arthur Brownlow, *formerly* Chamberlain, all of Lurgan afsd., which Arthur was s. and h. of Patrick Chamberlain, by Lettice, 1st da. and coheir of Sir William Brownlow, of Doughcoron, co. Armagh.

(b) [*Courthope.*]

(c) See vol. i, p. 259, note "c," *sub* "Basset de Sapcote" as to this not constituting a regular writ of summons to Parl.

(d) This Geoffrey Luttrell (aged 21 in 1297, as afsd.), was father of Sir Andrew Luttrell, of Irnham and Hoton Paganel, father of Sir Andrew L. (d. 1397), father of

LUTTRELSTOWN.

i.e., "IRNHAM OF LUTTRELLSTOWN, co. Dublin," Barony [I.] (*Luttrell*), *cr.* 1768; see "CARHAMPTON" Earldom [I.], *cr.* 1785; both dignities *ex.* 1829.

LUXBOROUGH.

i.e., "LUXBOROUGH OF SHANNON," Barony [I.] (*Knight*), *cr.* 1745; see "CATHERLOUGH," Earldom [I.], *cr.* 1763; both dignities *ex.* 1772.

LYDIARD TREGOZE.

i.e., "ST. JOHN OF LYDIARD TREGOZE, co. Wilts," Barony (*St. John*), *cr.* 1712, with the VISCOUNTCY OF BOLINGBROKE, which see.

LYLE.

Barony [S.]
I. 1446?

1. SIR ROBERT LYLE,(a) of Duchal, co. Renfrew, s. and h. of Sir Robert LYLE,(b) of the same, by Elizabeth, da. of Sir John STEWART, of Castlemilk, was *cr.* a Lord of Parl. (LORD LYLE [S.]) by King James II. [S.] apparently as early as 1446, and sat in Parl. 14 Oct. 1467. He *m.* firstly, in or before 1445, Margaret, 1st da. of Andrew (GRAY), LORD GRAY [S.] by Elizabeth, da. of Sir John WEMYSS. She *d.* s.p.m. He *m.* secondly, before 13 April 1466,(c) Margaret WALLACE. He was living 22 July 1468 but probably *d.* about 1470.

II. 1470.?

2. ROBERT (LYLE) LORD LYLE [S.], s. and h., by second wife; was P.C. to King James III. [S.] and Ambassador to England in 1472 and several times subsequently. He was tried for treason in Parl. [S.] 22 March 1481/2, but acquitted; was Great Justiciary and was a commissioner for opening the Parl. [S.] 8 Oct. 1488; was forfeited in June 1489, for having taken up arms to revenge the murder of the King, but was restored, 5 Feb. 1489/90. He *m.* firstly (—), da. of John SETON, Master of Seton, by Christian, da. of John (LINDSAY), 1st LORD LINDSAY OF BYRES [S.] She *d.* s.p. He *m.* secondly, Elizabeth, 2nd da. of Archibald (DOUGLAS), 5th EARL OF ANGUS [S.], by his first wife Elizabeth, da. of Robert (BOYD), LORD BOYD [S]. He appears to have *m.* thirdly Margaret HOUSTON, who as "*relicta quondam dni de Lyle*" was living 16 March 1506.(d) He was living 18 Sep. 1497, *d.* probably about 1500.

Sir Andrew L. (*d.* 1400), father of Sir Geoffrey L., who *d.* s.p. in 1417, on whose death the estate of Irnham devolved on his sister Hawise, or her descendants by her 2d husband, Sir Godfrey de Hilton. From the family of Hilton it descended, thro' that of Thimbleby, Conquest and Arundell, to the Clifford family. There is, however, not much reliance to be placed on the above pedigree, and a somewhat different one is given by Banks, in his "*Bar. Angl. conc.*"

(a) The name appears to be the same as L'Isle. It is stated in Wood's "*Douglas*" that "the surname of *L'Isle* or *Lyle*, was first assumed by the proprietors of some of the western isles, in the reign [1058-93] of Malcolm Canmore" and that "they had also possessions in the county of Renfrew, where Duchal Castle was their principal seat."

(b) This Robert was s. and h. of Sir John Lyle, of Duchal, by (it is said) one of the coheirs of the great family of Mar, and accordingly, on the death 1435 of Alexander (Stewart) Earl of Mar [S.], he put in a claim to that Earldom.

(c) There is a charter of that date entailing the Baronial fief of Lyle in what Riddell [p. 1082 "*index*"] calls a "strange limitation," as is fully set out in Wood's "*Douglas*," p. 163. The first limitation was to heirs male begotten by the said Robert, and Margaret, whom failing "heredibus inter Robertum et Margaretam *qualitercunque* genitis, assignandis tamen per dictum Robertum, et heredibus masculis legitime procreandis ex eisdem."

(d) See "*Reg. dioc. Glasgow*," II, 160. George Crawfurd suggests that she was "far rather" wife of the first Lord Lyle and adds that she remarried Andrew, Lord Gray. *Ex inform.*, M. J. Shaw-Stewart.

III. 1500.? 3. ROBERT (LYLE), LORD LYLE [S.], s. and h. He m. before 18 Sep. 1497, Mariot LINDSAY, of the house of Dunrod. He d. 1511.

IV. 1511, to 1545. 4. JOHN (LYLE), LORD LYLE [S.], only s. and h., under age at his father's death in 1511 and in ward to James Betoun, Archbishop of Glasgow, whose niece, Grisel, da. of David BETOUN, of Creech, he m., the settl. being dat. 9 May 1513. He was living 16 Oct. 1545, but d. s.p.m.,(a) apparently in the same year.(b) After his death *the title became dormant.*(c)

LYMINGTON.

i.e., "LYMINGTON, co. Southampton," Viscountcy (*Wallop*), *cr.* 1720; see "PORTSMOUTH" Earldom, *cr.* 1743.

LYNDHURST.

Barony. I. 1827, to 1863. 1. The Rt. Hon. SIR JOHN-SINGLETON COPLEY, Lord Chancellor of Great Britain, was *cr.*, 25 April 1827, BARON LYNDHURST, of Lyndhurst, co. Southampton. He was s. of John Singleton COPLEY, a member of the Royal Academy of Painters, by Mary Susannah Farnum, da. of Richard CLARKE, merchant, of Boston, in America, in which city he was *b.* 21 May 1772, tho', three years later, he and his parents removed to England. He was ed. at Dr. Horne's school at Chiswick; was a pensioner of Trin. Coll., Cambridge, 1790; B.A., 2d Wrangler, and Smith's prizeman, 1794; M.A., 1797, and Fellow, 1797—1804; entered Lincoln's Inn, 1794, studying as a special Pleader;(d) Barrister, 1804, going the Midland circuit; Serjeant at Law, 1813; King's Serjeant and Ch. Justice of Chester, 1818; Solicitor Gen., 1819-24, being *knighted*, Oct. 1819, and being one of the eleven Counsel(e) engaged at the trial of the Queen Consort Caroline; Attorney Gen., 1824-26, and, for eight months, Sep. 1826 to April 1827, Master of the Rolls as also Recorder of Bristol; P.C., 1826. He had been M.P. for Yarmouth (Isle of Wight), 1818; for Ashburton, 1818-26, and for some months in 1826 for Cambridge University, In April 1827 he was *raised to the peerage* as abovementioned, having been that month made LORD CHANCELLOR which office he held during three successive Ministries (those of Canning, Goderich, and Wellington), till the accession of the Whigs in Nov. 1830.

(a) His only son John Lyle had a charter from his father 29 Aug. 1541, of the manor of Lyle but *d.* s.p. and v.p.

(b) Milne (in his notes in the Lyon office), ascribes "1545" as the date of his death.

(c) Jean his only da. and h. (the heir of line of the Barony) *m.* Sir Niel Montgomery of Lainshaw (s. of Sir Niel M., the 3rd s. of Hugh, 1st Earl of Eglintoun [S.]) and her heirs existed in the male line down to David Montgomery of Lainshaw whose da. and h. of line, Elizabeth, wife of Alexander Cuninghame (who *d.* 1770) conveyed the representation to her s. and h. Sir Walter Montgomery-Campbell, Bart, who *suc.* his grandfather as Baronet in 1770. As to the right of these heirs to the Barony, Mr. Riddell writes as follows:—"The exclusive assumption of the title of Lord Lyle by James Montgomery of Lainshaw and his family, the undoubted heirs-female, and repeated protests by them in support of their right at elections in 1721, 1722 and afterwards, would also indicate the understanding of the same honours being decendible to heirs *general.*" It appears from Robertson's "Peerage Proceedings" [S.], that the claims of James Montgomery of Langshaw, "as representing the Lord Lyle" were, at the election of Scotch Peers on the 1st of June 1721, 21 April and 15 Aug. 1722, protested against "in regard that it did not appear by any writ that Langshaw is the representative of the family," and also because the peerage was not on the roll at the time of the Union [S.] Sixty years later a like protest was made by "Walter, Lord Lyle" (*i.e.* Sir Walter Montgomery-Campbell, Bart. abovementioned) at the election of 8 May 1784. This was followed by a petition to the House of Lords, presented and read 22 Dec. 1790, which however did not elicit any further proceedings.

(d) See vol. ii, p. 130, note "a," *sub* "Campbell."

(e) See vol. iii, p. 62, note "b," *sub* "Denman," for their names and some account of them.

He accepted the office of Lord Chief Baron of the Exchequer in Jan. 1831 which he held till Dec. 1834 a month after he had been for the second time made (Nov. 1834) LORD CHANCELLOR, which office he held but five months (till April 1835), being the total of the existence of the (first) Peel Ministry, resuming it, for the third and last time, under the (second) Peel Ministry from Sep. 1841 to July 1846. He was High Steward of the Univ. of Cambridge from 1840 to his death. F.R.S., &c. During almost all (1856-61) of the last 17 years of his life he, in spite of his great age, took an active part in the debates of the House of Lords.(a) He m. firstly, 13 March 1819, Sarah Garey, widow of Lieut. Col. Charles THOMAS (slain at Waterloo), da. of Charles BRUNSDEN. She, who was b. 1795, d. 15 Jan. 1834. Admon. Feb. 1834 He m. secondly, 5 Aug. 1837, at the British Embassy, Paris, Georgiana, da. of Lewis GOLDSMITH. He d. s.p.m., 12 Oct. 1863, in his 92d year, at 25 George street, Hanover square, and was bur. the 17th at Highgate cemetery, when the *peerage* became *extinct*. His widow living 1892.

LYNE.

i.e., "DOUGLAS OF NIELPATH, LYNE, AND MUNARD," Barony [S.] (*Douglas*), *cr.* 1697, with the EARLDOM OF MARCH [S.], which see.

LYNEDOCH OF BALGOWAN.

Barony. I. 1814, to 1843.

1. THOMAS GRAHAM, of Balgowan, co. Perth, 3d but only surv. s. and h. of Thomas G. of the same, by Christian, 6th da. of Charles (HOPE), 1st EARL OF HOPETOUN [S.], was b. 19 Oct. 1748, and is said to have entered Ch. Ch. Oxford (as a Gent. Comm.) in Nov. 1766,(b) leaving 1768. He *suc.* his father, 6 Dec. 1766, and purchased the estate of Lynedoch (or Lednoch) in Methven, co Perth, in 1787. He m. 26 June 1792, at her father's house in Grosvenor place, St. Geo. Han. sq., Mary, 2d da. of Charles (CATHCART), 9th LORD CATHCART [S.], by Jane, da. of Lord Archibald HAMILTON. She, who was b. 1 March 1757, d. 26 June 1792 (or 26 July 1791) on shipboard off Hyères. After her death he took to an active life; was M.P. (in the whig interest) for co. Perth. 1794-1806; raised the Perthshire volunteers (90th Foot), of which he became Lieut. Col. in 1794, was at the capture of Minorca, in 1798, and served with great distinction in the Peninsular war, obtaining a glorious victory at Barossa, 5 March 1811. K.B. (being invested at Elvas, near Badajos), 12 March 1812, becoming consequently G.C.B., in Jan. 1815, being also Knight of the Tower and Sword of Portugal, of San Fernando of Spain, and of Wilhelm the Lion of the Netherlands. He returned home at the peace, received the thanks of Parl. and was *cr.* 17 May 1814, BARON LYNEDOCH OF BALGOWAN, co. Perth, refusing a pension of £2,000 a year offered therewith. He became full General, 1821; was Col. of the 58th Foot, 1823; of the 14th 1826, and of the 1st Royals, 1834; Gov. of Dumbarton Castle, 1829; G.C.M.G., 19 May 1837. He *d.* s.p., 18 Dec. 1843, aged 95, at Stratton street, Piccadilly, when his *peerage* became *extinct*.(c) Will pr. March 1844.

LYNN REGIS.

i.e., TOWNSHEND OF LYNN REGIS, co. Norfolk," Barony (*Townshend*), *cr.* 1661; see "TOWNSHEND OF RAYNHAM," Viscountcy, *cr.* 1682.

THE HON. CHARLES TOWNSHEND, s. and h. ap. of Charles, 2d VISCOUNT TOWNSHEND OF RAYNHAM,(d) was sum. to Parl. v.p. by writ, 22 May 1723, directed to

(a) "No statesman maintained for so long a succession of years a name so unsullied as Lord Lyndhurst, and few have died in possession of more veneration and regard," writes Foss, who speaks, also, of "the beautiful simplicity of his style, the logical arrangement of his arguments, and the aptness of his illustrations."

(b) "*Nat. Biogr.*" No such matriculation however seems to be recorded.

(c) He started the project in 1815 of a General Military and Naval Club, which in 1817, was carried out, being the present Senior United Club, in Pall Mall, where his portrait (by Sir Thomas Lawrence) is preserved.

(d) A like instance of the eldest son of a Viscount being sum. v.p. in his father's Barony occurred in 1628, when Edward Conway, s. and h. ap. of Edward, Viscount

"*Charles Townshend de Lynn Regis, co. Norfolk, Chr.*," taking his seat in his father's Barony of *Townshend of Lynn Regis* (*cr.* 1661), but being in the journals of the House of Lords (erroneously) *styled* "LORD LYNN,"(a) such designation being, it is presumed, for the purpose of distinguishing him from his father, Viscount *Townshend* of Raynham, to whose peerage he *suc.* in 1738; see that dignity.

LYON.

i.e., "LYON AND GLAMIS," Barony [S.] (*Lyon*), *cr.* 1606 with the EARLDOM OF KINGHORN [S.], which see. After 1677, however, the designation of "Kinghorn" was changed to STRATHMORE AND KINGHORN.

LYONS OF CHRISTCHURCH.

Barony.
I. 1856.

1. EDMUND LYONS, 4th s. of John LYONS, of Lyons in Antigua and St. Austins, Hants, by Catharine, da. of Main Swete WALROND, of Antigua and of Montrath House, Devon, was *b.* 21 Nov. 1790, at Whites Hayes in Burton, near Christchurch, co. Southampton; ed. at Hyde Abbey school, Winchester; entered the Navy, June 1801; was in several actions during the French war; was in command at the taking of Morea Castle from the Turks in 1828; was from 1853 to 1855 second, and from 1855 first in command of the Mediterranean Fleet, giving (as such) most effective assistance to the Crimean Expedition, and becoming finally, Oct. 1857, Vice Admiral of the White. He had meanwhile been made a Knight of St. Louis of France, 1828; Knight Com. of the Redeemer of Greece in or soon after 1833, and K.C.H., 13 Jan. 1834. He was *Knighted* at the Pavilion in Brighton, 23 Jan. 1835; was Minister to Athens, July 1835; *cr. a Baronet* (as "Captain in the Navy") 29 July 1840; G.C.B. (civil) 10 July 1844; was Minister to Berne, 1850; Minister to Stockholm, 1851; Knight of the Medjidie of Turkey, 1st class, 17 May 1855; G.C.B. (Military), 5 July 1855;(b) Grand Cross of the Military Order of Savoy, 14 Feb. 1856; D.C.L. of Oxford, 4 June 1856, being *cr.* (on account of his services in the Crimea), 25 June 1856 (at which date he was Rear Admiral of the Red), BARON LYONS OF CHRISTCHURCH, co. Southampton; Grand Cross of the legion of honour of France, 6 Aug. 1856. He *m.* 18 July 1814, at Southwick, Hants, Augusta Louisa, 2d da. and coheir of Josiah ROGERS, of Lymington, Hants, Captain R.N. She *d.* 10 March 1852, at Stockholm. He *d.* 23 Nov. 1858, at Arundel Castle, Sussex (the seat of his son in law, the Duke of Norfolk), aged 68.

II. 1858,
Viscountcy.
I. 1881,
to
1887.

2 and *1.* RICHARD BICKERTON(c) PEMELL (LYONS), BARON LYONS OF CHRISTCHURCH, also *a Baronet*, 1st and only surv. s. and h.,(d) *b.* 26 April 1817, at Lymington; ed. at Winchester and at Ch. Ch., Oxford; B.A. and Hon. 4th in classics, 1838; M.A., 1845; Attaché at Athens (unpaid) 1839 and (paid) 1844; at Dresden, 1852; at Florence, 1853; Sec. of legation at Florence, 1856, and Chargé D'affaires, there, 1857; Spec. Envoy to Naples, March to July 1858; Minister to Florence, June 1858; *suc. to the peerage*, 23 Nov. 1858; Minister to Washington, 1858-64; K.C.B., 11 Dec. 1860;

Conway of Conway Castle, was sum. as Baron Conway of Ragley. He *suc.* to his father's peerage in 1631. In 1680 the s. and h. ap. of a Baron, possessing two Baronies (Conyers and Darcy) was so summoned.

(a) "The same erroneous course was pursued," says Courthope, when John Poulett, s. and h. ap. of the 1st Earl *Poulett*, was placed in 1733, in his father's Barony of *Poulett of Hinton St. George* (*cr.* 1627), tho' his name appears in the list of Peers as *Lord Hinton*. On the other hand, George Stevens Byng (s. and h. ap. of the 1st Earl of *Strafford*), who was sum. in 1853, in his father's Barony of *Strafford of Harmondsworth* (*cr.* 1835), took his seat "by his proper designation of *Lord Strafford*."

(b) He thus possessed the rare distinction of holding the highest grade in *both* of the classes (Military and Civil) of the order of the Bath.

(c) Admiral Sir Richard *Bickerton* was one of his godfathers.

(d) His yr. br. Edmund Mowbray Lyons, Capt. R.N., *d.* unm. and v.p. being killed in the Crimean campaign.

G.C.B., 21 Jan. 1862; P.C., 1865; D.C.L. of Oxford, 21 Jan. 1865; Ambassador to Constantinople, 1865-67, and (for 20 years) Ambassador to Paris (both to the Emperor and the Republic) from July 1867 till (a short time before his death) Oct. 1887. G.C.M.G., 24 May 1879. He was *cr.*, 24 Nov. 1881, VISCOUNT LYONS OF CHRISTCHURCH, co. Southampton. He, who was received into the Roman Catholic church, Nov. 1887, *d.* unm., 5 Dec. 1887, at Norfolk House, St. James' square (the residence of his nephew, the Duke of Norfolk), aged 70, when *all his honours* became *extinct*. Will dat. 28 May 1886, pr. March 1888, under £115,000.

LYSLE or LYSLEY, see LISLE.

LYTTELTON OF FRANKLEY.

Barony. I. 1756. *1.* The Rt. Hon. SIR GEORGE LYTTELTON, Bart., of Frankley, co. Worcester, s. and h. of Sir Thomas LYTTELTON, 4th Bart., by Christian, sister of Richard (TEMPLE), VISCOUNT COBHAM (so *cr.* 23 May 1718, with a *spec. rem.* in his said sister's favour), da. of Sir Richard TEMPLE, Bart., of Stowe, was *bap.* 17 Jan. 1708/9, at St. James' Westm.; mat. at Oxford (Ch. Ch.), 11 Feb. 1725/6; M.P. for Okehampton, 1735-56; Prin. Sec. to the Prince of Wales, 1737; a Lord of the Treasury, 1744-54; *suc. to the Baronetcy* (*cr.* 25 July 1618), on the death of his father (aged 65) 14 Sep. 1751; P.C., 1754; Cofferer of the Household, 1754-5; Chancellor of the Exchequer and one of the Commissioners of the Treasury, Nov. 1755 to Nov. 1756, being *cr.*, 18 Nov. 1756, BARON LYTTELTON OF FRANKLEY, co. Worcester; F.S.A. He *m.* firstly, June 1742, at St. Geo. Han. sq.,(a) Lucy, sister of Matthew, 2d BARON FORTESCUE OF CASTLE HILL, da. of Hugh FORTESCUE, of Filleigh, co. Devon, by his second wife, Lucy, da. of Matthew (AYLMER), 1st BARON AYLMER OF BALRATH [I.] She *d.* 19 Jan. 1746/7, aged 29, and was *bur.* at Over Arley, co. Stafford, but her M.I. is at Hagley, co. Worcester. He *m.* secondly, 10 Aug. 1749, in her father's house at Windsor, Elizabeth (then aged 38), da. of Field Marshal Sir Robert RICH, 4th Bart., of Rosehall, Suffolk, by (—), da. and coheir of Col. (—) GRIFFIN, Clerk to the Board of Green Cloth. He *d.* 22 Aug. 1773,(b) aged 64, at Hagley, and was *bur.* there. M.I. Will pr. Nov. 1773. His widow *d.* s.p., 17 Sep. 1795.(c) Will pr. Sep. 1795.

II. 1773, to 1779. *2.* THOMAS (LYTTELTON), BARON LYTTELTON OF FRANKLEY, and also a *Baronet*, only s. and h., by first wife, *b.* 30 Jan. 1743/4, and *bap.* at St. James' Westm.; mat. at Oxford (Ch. Ch.), 7 Nov. 1761; M.P. for Bewdley, 1768, till unseated in 1769; *suc. to the peerage*, 22 Aug. 1773; P.C., 1775; Chief Justice of Eyre north of Trent. He *m.*, 26 June 1772, at Hales Owen, co. Stafford, Apphia, widow of Joseph PEACH, Governor of Calcutta, 2d da. of Broome WITTS, of Chipping Norton, Oxon. He *d.* s.p., 27 Nov. 1779, aged 35, at Pitt Place, Epsom, Surrey.(d) Will pr. Jan. 1780. His widow who was *bap.* 15 May 1743, at Chipping Norton, Oxon, and who was well known for her many charities, *d.* (60 years later) 9 April 1840, at Great Malvern, aged 96. Will pr. May 1840.

(a) The marriage is stated to have taken place in that parish, but no entry thereof appears in the parish register.

(b) A long account of him and especially of his illness is in "*Collins*," vol. viii, pp. 352—357. He was an author of some note, his "*Reign of Henry II.*" being the best known of his many publications.

(c) "Her indiscretion made an unhappy household and she soon separated from her husband." "With good talents [she] was, I fear, little esteemed by any one tho' had been pretty," writes Mrs. Piozzi. See notes to Wraxall's "*Memoirs*" (edit. 1884), vol. i, p. 228.

(d) He had supported the North Ministry till April 1779 (a few months before his death) when he seceded on the petition for removing Lord Sandwich from the Admiralty. His life appears to have been one that alternated between "the most extravagant gaiety and the deepest despair" [" *Collins*," vol. viii, pp. 352—357] and the vision, which he had the day before his death, of a lady who warned him of his own death, forms one of the most famous of all "*Ghost-stories*." See full account of this story in Wraxall's "*Memoirs*" (edit. 1884), vol. i, pp. 226—230.

III. 1794. 1. WILLIAM HENRY LYTTELTON, yr. br. of Thomas, 1st BARON LYTTELTON OF FRANKLEY, being 6th s. of Sir Thomas LYTTELTON, 4th Bart. of Frankley, co. Worcester, by Christian, sister of Richard (TEMPLE) VISCOUNT COBHAM (so cr. 23 May 1718, with a *spec. rem.* in his said sister's favour), da. of Sir Richard TEMPLE, Bart., of Stowe, was *b.* 24 Dec. 1724, at St. Martin's in the fields; mat. at Oxford (St. Mary Hall) 22 June 1742; entered the Middle Temple, 1 Nov. 1743; Barrister, 1748; M.P. for Bewdley, 1748-55; Gov. of South Carolina, 1755-60; Gov. of Jamaica, 1760-66; Envoy to Lisbon, 1766-71; and was *cr.* 29 April or July 1776, BARON WESTCOTE(a) OF BALLYMORE, co. Longford [I.]; was one of the Lords of the Treasury, 1777-82.(b) He *suc. to the Baronetcy* (cr. 25 July 1618), on the death, 27 Nov. 1779, of his nephew, Thomas, 2d Baron Lyttelton of Frankley abovenamed; was D.C.L., of Oxford, 23 Nov. 1781, and was *cr.* 13 Aug. 1794, LORD LYTTELTON, BARON OF FRANKLEY, co. Worcester. He *m.* firstly, 2 June 1761, at St. Geo. Han. sq., Mary, 1st da. and coheir of James MACARTNEY, of Longford, co. Longford. She *d.* 28 May 1765, at Bath, in Jamaica and was *bur.*, at St. Thomas in the East, there. He *m.* secondly, 19 Feb. 1774, at St. James' Westm., Caroline, da. of John BRISTOW, of Quiddenham, Norfolk, by Anne Judith, da. of Paul FAISIN, of Paris, Merchant. He *d.* at Hagley, 14 Sep. 1808, aged 83. Will pr. 1809. His widow *d.* 19 Sep. 1809. Will pr. 1810.

IV. 1808. 2. GEORGE FULKE (LYTTELTON), LORD LYTTELTON, BARON OF FRANKLEY, also BARON WESTCOTE OF BALLYMORE [I.], s. and h. by first wife, *b.* 27 Oct. 1763, at Spanish town in Jamaica; mat. at Oxford (Ball. Coll.), 24 April 1781; M.P. for Bewdley, 1790-96; for Granard, 1798—1800; *suc. to the peerage*, 14 Sep. 1808. He *d.* unm. at Hagley, 12 Nov. 1828, aged 65. Will pr. March 1829.

V. 1828. 3. WILLIAM HENRY (LYTTELTON), LORD LYTTELTON, BARON OF FRANKLEY, also BARON WESTCOTE OF BALLYMORE [I.], br. of the half-blood and h., being 6th and yst. s. of the 1st Lord, by his second wife; *b.* 3 April 1782 in Berners street, Marylebone; mat. at Oxford (Ch. Ch.), 24 Oct. 1798;(c) B.A., 1802; M.A., 1805; *cr.* D.C.L., 5 July 1810; Student of his College till 1812; M.P. for Worcestershire, 1806-20; *suc. to the peerage*, 12 Nov. 1828; Lord Lieut. of Worcestershire. He *m.* 4 March 1813, Sarah, 1st da. of George John (SPENCER), 2d EARL SPENCER, by Lavinia, 1st da. of Charles (BINGHAM), 1st EARL OF

(a) The family of Lyttelton is paternally descended from Thomas *Westcote*, of Westcote, co. Devon, who having *m.* Elizabeth, da. and h. of Thomas Lyttelton, of South Lyttelton, co. Worcester, assumed her name, and was father of the celebrated Sir Thomas Lyttelton, K.B., one of the Justices of the Common Pleas, 1475-81, author of "*The Treatise on tenures*," whose three sons were ancestors respectively (1) of the Lytteltons of Frankley, Baronets (1618), Barons Lyttelton of Frankley (1756-79 and, again, 1794), Barons Westcote in Ireland (1776), who, in 1889, inherited the Viscountcy of Cobham; (2) of the Littletons of Pillaton Hall, co. Stafford, Baronets (1627 to 1812) now represented, in the female line, by the Barons Hatherton, and (3) of the Lytteltons of Spetchley, of whom was the Lord Keeper, Baron Lyttelton of Mounslow (1640 to 1645), and the Baronets (1642 to 1710) of Stoke Milburgh, co. Salop.

(b) In the debate of 12 June 1781, when "Fox, strenuously supported by Pitt, made an ineffectual effort for compelling the administration to abandon the further prosecution of the American war and to conclude peace with the Colonies," to which many of Lord North's supporters and even he himself made but a feeble opposition, "one noble individual only, then an Irish Peer [*i.e.*, Lord Westcote] was found sufficiently enthusiastic to avow that he considered the struggle as a *Holy War*, a declaration which he made from the Treasury bench." This was ridiculed very aptly by Townshend, who compared the war with the "Crusades," both of them having "originated in folly, madness or delusion," while "both conduced to slaughter or to ruin."—Wraxall's "*Memoirs*" (edit. 1884), vol. ii, p. 120.

(c) "His academical learning and knowledge of Greek were considered to be superior to most of his contemporaries." [*Annual Reg.* 1837.]

LUCAN [I.]. He *d.* 30 April 1837, aged 56, at Spencer House, in the Green Park, Midx. Will pr. May 1837. His widow, who was *b.* 29 July 1787, and who was for many years Governess to the children of Queen Victoria, *d.* 13 April 1870, aged 82, at Hagley. Will pr. 1870 under £10,000.

VI. 1837. *4.* GEORGE WILLIAM (LYTTELTON), LORD LYTTELTON, BARON OF FRANKLEY also BARON WESTCOTE OF BALLYMORE [I.], s. and h., *b.* 31 March 1817 in Saville Row, Piccadilly; ed. at Trin. Coll., Cambridge; B.A. and M.A., Chancellor's Medallist and Senior Classic, 1838,(a) having *suc. to the peerage*, 30 April 1837. Fellow of Eton College; Lord Lieut. of Worcestershire, 1839; Principal of Queen's Coll., Birmingham, 1845; Under Sec. for the Colonies, Feb. to July 1846; LL.D., Cambridge, 1862; P.C., 1869; K.C.M.G., 1869; D.C.L., Oxford, 22 June 1870; Chief Commissioner of endowed schools; F.R.S., &c. He *m.* firstly, 25 July 1839(b) Mary, 2d and yst. da. of Sir Stephen Richard GLYNNE, 8th Bart., of Hawarden, co. Flint, by Mary, da. of Richard (ALDWORTH-NEVILLE, *afterwards* GRIFFIN), 2d BARON BRAYBROOKE. She, who was *b.* 1813, and who was a Lady of the Bedchamber (and whose issue, in 1874, became coheir to her br. the 9th and last Baronet), *d.* 17 Aug. 1857, at Hagley Park. He *m.* secondly, 10 June 1869, at Foy, co. Hereford, Sybella Harriet, widow of Humphrey Francis MILDMAY, da. of George CLIVE, of Perrystone Court, co. Hereford, by Anne Sybella Martha, da. of Sir Thomas Harvie FARQUHAR, Bart. He *d.* 18 April 1876, at 18 Park crescent, Regent's park, aged 59,(c) and was *bur.* the 22d at Hagley. His widow, who was *b.* 20 June 1836, living 1892.

VII. 1876. *5.* CHARLES GEORGE (LYTTELTON), LORD LYTTELTON, BARON OF FRANKLEY [1794] also BARON WESTCOTE OF BALLYMORE in the peerage of Ireland [1776] also *a Baronet* [1618], s. and h., by 1st wife, *b.* 27 Oct. 1842; ed. at Eton and at Trin. Coll., Cambridge; M.P. for East Worcestershire, 1868-74; *suc. to the peerage*, 18 April 1876; Land Commr., 1881-89; *suc.* as VISCOUNT COBHAM AND BARON COBHAM, on the death, 26 March 1889, of his distant cousin (the Duke of Buckingham and Chandos, Viscount Cobham, &c.), under the *spec. rem.* in the creation of that dignity, 23 May 1718. He *m.* 19 Oct. 1878, Mary Susan Caroline, 2d da. of William George (CAVENDISH), 2d BARON CHESHAM, by Henrietta Frances, da. of the Rt. Hon. William Saunders Sebright LASCELLES. She was *b.* 19 March 1853.

Family Estates.—These, in 1883, consisted of 5,907 acres in Worcestershire and 1,032 in Herefordshire. *Total* 6,939 acres, worth £10,263 a year. *Principal Residence.* Hagley Park,(d) near Stourbridge, Worcestershire.

LYTTELTON OF MOUNSLOW.

Barony. I. 1641, to 1645. *1.* The Rt. Hon. SIR EDWARD LITTLETON, Keeper of the Great Seal of England, was *cr.*, 18 Feb. 1640/1, BARON LYTTELTON OF MOUNSLOW, co. Salop.(e) He was s. and h. of Sir Edward LITTLETON, of Henley, co. Salop, Ch. Justice of North Wales, by Mary, da. of Edmund WALTER, Ch. Justice of South Wales; was *b.* in 1589 at Mounslow afsd.; mat. at Oxford (Ch. Ch.), 28 Nov. 1606; B.A., 1609, being subsequently, 31 Jan. 1642/3, *cr.* D.C.L. He was M.P. for Bishop's Castle, 1614; for Leominster, 1625 and 1626, and for Carnarvon, 1628-29. He was Barrister, 1617, and Treasurer, 1624-28, of the Inner Temple; Ch. Justice of North Wales (in succession to his father), 1621; Recorder of London,

(a) He contributed several pieces to the well-known "*Arundines Cami*," of which his translation of Tennyson's "Oh mother Ida," is perhaps the best known.

(b) At the same time her eldest sister, Catherine *m.* the well known statesman, William Ewart Gladstone, who in 1874, *suc.* to the estate of Hawarden.

(c) The cause of his death was his having flung himself down stairs; the verdict being "suicide while of unsound mind."

(d) Frankley, the ancient seat of the family, was destroyed in the civil war.

(e) A full account of this patent, now in Lord Lyttelton's possession at Hagley Park, is given in "*the Her. and Gen.*," vol. i, pp. 435—438.

1631; Solicitor Gen., 1634-40, being *knighted*, 6 June 163[illegible]; Ch. Justice of the Common Pleas, Jan. 1639/40 to Jan. 1640/41; Lord Keeper, Jan. 1640/1, being *raised to the peerage*, as above, the next month, and (tho' the Houses of Parl. voted, 10 Nov. 1643, for a new Great Seal), holding office for the King (whom he followed to York and subsequently to Oxford) till his death in 1645. He was First Commissioner of the Treasury in 1641 and again in March 1643. He, in May 1644, raised a regiment from the Inns of Court of which he was Colonel. He *m.* firstly Anne, 4th da. of John Littleton, of Frankley, co. Worcester, by Muriel, da. of Sir Thomas Bromley. She *d.* 6 Feb. 1623, and was *bur.* in the church of the Inner Temple, London. He *m.* secondly Elizabeth, widow of Sir George Calverley, da. of Sir William Jones, one of the Justices of the King's Bench, 1624-40. He *d.* s.p.m., 27, and was *bur.* 28 Aug. 1645,(a) in Christ Church Cathedral, Oxford, aged 56, when his *peerage* became *extinct*.(b) Will pr. 1649.

LYTTLETON, see Lyttelton.

LYTTON and LYTTON OF KNEBWORTH.

Barony. I. 1866. *1.* The Rt. Hon. Sir Edward-George-Earle-Lytton Bulwer-Lytton, Bart. (formerly Edward George Earle Lytton Bulwer), was *cr.*, 14 July 1866, BARON LYTTON OF KNEBWORTH, co. Hertford. He was 3d(c) and yst. s. of William Earle Bulwer, *formerly* Wiggett,(d) of Heydon Hall and Wood Dalling, co. Norfolk, by Elizabeth Barbara, da. and h. of Richard Lytton, formerly Warburton, of Knebworth, Herts;(e) was *b.* 25 May 1803, at No. 31, Baker street, Marylebone, tho' not *bap.* till many (7?) years later; ed. at Trin. Hall, Cambridge; B.A., 1826; M.A., 1835; was M.P. for St. Ives, 1831-32; for Lincoln, 1832-41, and for Herts, 1852-66, having been *cr. a Baronet*, 18 July 1838, as "of Knebworth, Herts," to which estate he *suc.* on his mother's death, six years later, when by Royal lic., 20 Feb. 1844, he took the name of *Lytton* after that of *Bulwer*; D.C.L. of Oxford, 9 June 1853; Rector of Glasgow Univ., 1856 and 1858; P.C., 1858; Sec. of State for the Colonies, 1858-59; LL.D. of

(a) His integrity and his talents were undoubted. He is spoken of by Whitelocke (who was of the opposite side) as "a man of courage and of excellent parts and learning," but his endeavours "to be the friend of all parties," as also "to resist the encroachments on the Constitution" and "to support the Sovereign when his power was threatened" made his career somewhat weak and incongruous. See Foss's "*Judges*."

(b) Anne, his only da. and h., *m.* her cousin, Sir Thomas Littleton, 2d Bart., of Stoke Milburgh, and was *bur.* (as his widow) at North Ockendon, Essex, 4 Dec. 1705, leaving issue, Sir Thomas Littleton, 3d Bart., Speaker of the House of Commons, who *d.* s.p., Jan. 1710.

(c) His eldest br. inherited Heydon Hall and is ancestor of the Bulwer family there settled, while the second br. was *cr.* Baron Dalling and Bulwer in 1871 and *d.* s.p. the next year.

(d) He was s. and h. of William Wiggett, of Guestwich, co. Norfolk (who was s. and h. of Rice Wiggett, by Sarah, sister and coheir of William Bulwer, of West Dalling), which William took the name of *Bulwer* in lieu of *Wiggett* by act of Parl. 1756.

(e) This Richard (who *d.* s.p.m. in 1810, aged 55), assumed the name of Lytton (in lieu of Warburton) on inheriting the estate of Knebworth by the death (in 1762) of his maternal uncle, John Robinson-Lytton, s. and h. (in 1732) of William Robinson-Lytton (formerly Robinson) of the same. None of the abovenamed parties have *any* descent from the old family of Lytton, of Knebworth, which estate was devised in 1710 to the said William Robinson by the will of Lytton Lytton, formerly Lytton Strode, whose *mother*, Margaret (wife of Sir George Strode), was sister of another William Robinson, the father of the abovenamed William Robinson, afterwards William Robinson-Lytton. The *paternal grandmother* of the testator (Lytton Lytton, *formerly*, Lytton Strode) Judith, wife of Sir Nicholas Strode, was one of the sisters of Sir William Lytton, of Knebworth, who *d.* 1705, aged 61, being the last heir male of his race. The descendants of the other sister, Dame Anne Russell, of Strensham (the heirs at law and representatives of the race of Lytton) were passed over by the testator in favour of his *maternal* relatives, the abovementioned family of Robinson.

Cambridge, 3 June 1864, and was *raised to the peerage*, 14 July 1866, as afsd. G.C.M.G., 30 June 1869. He *m.*, 29 Aug. 1827, at St. James' Westm., Rosina Doyle, da. of Francis Massy WHEELER, of Lizzard Connell, co. Limerick, by Anne, da. of the Rev. Nicholas Milley DOYLE, of Clonmell. He *d.* (of inflammation of the brain) at Torquay, Devon, on 18, and was *bur.* 25 Jan. 1873, at Westm. Abbey,(a) aged 69. His widow (from whom he had been long separated) *d.* at Glenômera, Upper Sydenham, 12, and was *bur.* 18 March 1882, in her 79th year, at Shirley, co. Surrey.

II. 1873. **Earldom.** I. 1880. *2* an *1*. EDWARD ROBERT LYTTON (BULWER-LYTTON), BARON LYTTON OF KNEBWORTH, only s. and h., *b.* 8 Nov. 1831; ed. at Harrow and at the Univ. of Bonn; entered early into the Diplomatic Service, being attached to the Legation at Washington, 1849; at Florence, 1852, and at Paris, 1854; paid Attaché at the Hague, 1856; at St. Petersburg, 1858; at Constantinople, 1858, and at Vienna, 1859; Consul at Belgrade, 1860; Sec. of Leg. at Copenhagen, 1863; at Athens, 1864; at Lisbon, 1865, and at Madrid, 1868; Sec. of Embassy to Vienna, 1868, and to Paris, 1872-74; *suc. to the peerage*, 25 Jan. 1873; Minister to Lisbon, 1874-76; VICEROY AND GOV. GEN. OF INDIA, 1876-80; G.C.B. (Civil), 1 Jan. 1878. He was *cr.*, 28 April 1880, VISCOUNT KNEBWORTH, of Knebworth, co. Hertford, and EARL OF LYTTON, in the county of Derby. G.C.S.I., 8 June 1880, and C.I.E. AMBASSADOR TO PARIS, 1887, till his death in 1891; Rector of Glasgow Univ., 1887; P.C., 1888. He *m.*, 4 Oct. 1864, Edith, da. of the Hon. Edward Ernest VILLIERS (br. of George William Frederick. 4th EARL OF CLARENDON), by Elisabeth Charlotte, da. of Thomas Henry (LIDDELL), 1st BARON RAVENSWORTH. He *d.* (suddenly), 24 Nov. 1891, at the British Embassy, Paris, aged 60. Will pr. at £75,270. His widow *b.* 15 Sep. 1841, and C.I., living 1892.

Earldom. II. **Barony.** III. } 1891. *2* and *3*. VICTOR ALEXANDER GEORGE ROBERT (BULWER-LYTTON), EARL OF LYTTON [1880], VISCOUNT KNEBWORTH [1880], and BARON LYTTON OF KNEBWORTH [1866], also *a Baronet* [1838], 3d but 1st surv. s. and h.,(b) *b.* 10 Aug. 1876, at Simla, in India, being godson to Queen Victoria; ed. at Eton; *styled* VISCOUNT KNEBWORTH from 1880 till he *suc. to the peerage*, 24 Nov. 1891.

Family Estates.—These, in 1883, consisted of 4,863 acres in Herts, worth £5,366 a year. *Principal Residence.* Knebworth Park, near Stevenage, Herts.

LYVEDEN.

Barony. I. 1859. *1*. The Rt. Hon. ROBERT-VERNON SMITH was *cr.* 28 June 1859, BARON LYVEDEN of Lyveden, co. Northampton. He was s. of Robert Percy SMITH, of Cheam, co. Surrey, Judge Advocate Gen. in India, by Caroline Maria, 2d da. and coheir of Richard VERNON, and Evelyn, his wife, Dow. COUNTESS OF UPPER OSSORY [I.] He was *b.* 23 Feb. 1800, in Guildford street, and *bap.* at S. Pancras, Midx.; ed. at Eton and at Ch. Ch., Oxford; mat. 2 Feb. 1819; B.A, and 2d class in Classics, 1822; M.P. for Tralee, 1829-31; for Northampton 1831-59; a Lord of the Treasury, 1830-34; Sec. to Board of Control, 1835-39; Under Sec. for the Colonies, 1839-41; P.C., 1841; Sec. at War, 6 to 28 Feb. 1852; President of the Board of Control, 1855-58, being *raised to the peerage* as above 28 June 1859, and taking by Royal Lic. (a few weeks later). 14 July 1859 the name of *Vernon* in lieu of that of *Smith*. G.C.B. (civil) 1872. He *m.* 15 July 1823, at St. Geo. Han. sq., Emma Mary, illegit. da.(c) of John

(a) As a writer of fiction he has seldom (perhaps never, save, probably, in the case of Sir Walter Scott) been surpassed. Among his earlier works are "Rienzi," "The last days of Pompeii," "Ernest Maltravers," &c., while among the later are "The Caxtons," "My Novel," &c.

(b) His elder br. (the 2d but then only surv. s. of his father) *d.* in Paris, 1 March 1874, aged 1 year and 11 months.

(c) Her br. the Rt. Hon. John Wilson Fitzpatrick, *b.* 1811, was in 1869 *cr.* Baron Castletown of Upper Ossory.

(FITZPATRICK), 2d EARL OF UPPER OSSORY [I.] He d. 10 Nov. 1873, at Farming Woods, co. Northampton, aged 73. His widow (from whom he derived the estate of Lyveden, Farming Woods, &c., in Northamptonshire), d. 22 Sep. 1882, at Sunnyside, Buxton.

II. 1873. 2. FITZPATRICK HENRY (VERNON, *formerly* SMITH), BARON LYVEDEN, s. and h., b. 27 April 1824, and bap. at St. James' Westm.; ed. at Eton and at Durham; authorised by Royal Lic., 5 Aug. 1845 to take the name of *Vernon* in lieu of that of *Smith*; Attaché at Madrid, 1846-48; at Hanover, 1848-49, and at Berlin, 1849. Private Sec. to the head of the Woods and Forest department, 1840; to his father when at the War office, 1852, and when at the Board of Control, 1855-58. He m. 21 June 1853, at St. Geo. Han. sq., Albreda Elizabeth, 7th and yst. da. of Charles William (WENTWORTH-FITZWILLIAM), 5th EARL FITZWILLIAM, by Mary, da. of Thomas (DUNDAS), 1st BARON DUNDAS OF ASKE. She, who was b. 3 Sep. 1829, d. 11 Nov. 1891, at 4 Belgrave place.

Family Estates.—These, in 1883, consisted of 4,138 acres in Northamptonshire, worth £5,529 a year. *Principal Residence.* Farming Woods, near Thrapstone, co. Northampton.

M.

MACARTNEY, MACARTNEY OF LISSANOURE, MACARTNEY OF DERVOCK and MACARTNEY OF PARKHURST AND AUCHINLECK.

Barony [I.] 1. 1776. Viscountcy [I.] I. 1792. Earldom [I.] I. 1794. Barony [G.B.] I. 1796, to 1806.

1. GEORGE MACARTNEY, of Lissanoure, co. Antrim, only s. and h. of George MACARTNEY, of the same, by Elizabeth, yst. da. of the Rev. John WINDER, Rector of Carmony and Preb. of Kilroot, was b. 4 June 1737; was Envoy to Russia, 1764-66, and Ambassador there, 1767-68, having been *knighted*, 13 Oct. 1764, and made a Knight of the White Eagle of Poland, June 1766; M.P. for Cockermouth, April 1768; for Armagh [I.], July 1768; for the Ayr Boroughs, 1774, and for Beeralston, 1780: Ch. Sec. for Ireland, 1768-72; P.C. [I.], 1769; K.B., 29 May 1772; Gov. of the Caribbean Islands, 1776-84, and was cr., 19 July 1776, LORD MACARTNEY, BARON OF LISSANOURE, co. Antrim [I.], taking his seat, 12 March 1788. He was Gov. of Madras, 1784-85, and was, in Feb. 1785, appointed Gov. GEN. OF INDIA, but declined the post. From 1792 to 1794 he was Ambassador to China, being cr., 19 July 1792, VISCOUNT MACARTNEY OF DERVOCK, co. Antrim [I.]; P.C., 1792, and, on his return home, being cr., 1 March 1794, EARL MACARTNEY [I.] In 1795 he was on a mission to Italy, and was on his return cr. BARON MACARTNEY OF PARKHURST, co. Surrey, AND OF AUCHINLECK,(a) in the Stewartry of Kircudbright [G.B.] He was Gov. of the Cape of Good Hope, 1796-98. He m., 1 Feb. 1768, at St. Geo. Han. sq., Jane, 2d da. of John (STUART), 3d EARL OF BUTE [S.], the celebrated Minister, by Mary, *suo jure* BARONESS MOUNT STUART OF WORTLEY. He d. s.p., 31 March 1806, aged 68, at Corney House, Chiswick, and was *bur.* 9 April at Chiswick when *all his honours* became *extinct*.(b) M.I. at Lissanoure, co. Antrim. Will pr. 1806. His widow, who was b. April 1742, d. 28 Feb. 1828. Will pr. 1828.

(a) His grandfather, George Macartney, of Lissanoure afsd., was a younger son of George Macartney, of *Auchinleck*, near Kircudbright, in Scotland.

(b) He left the estate of Lissanoure, after the death of his widow, to his niece, Elizabeth, wife of the Rev. Travers Hume, the only child of his sister, Elizabeth, by John Balaquier, Major 13th Dragoons. Her descendants took the name of Macartney after that of Hume.

MACAULAY OF ROTHLEY.

Barony.
I. 1857,
to
1859.

1. THOMAS BABINGTON MACAULAY, 1st s. of Zachary MACAULAY,(a) a Merchant of Sierra Leone, by Selina (formerly Selina MILLS, spinster), a Quakeress of Bristol, was b. 25 Oct. 1800, at Rothley Temple,(b) co. Leicester; ed. at Trin. Coll., Cambridge; gaining twice (for poems on "*Pompeii*" and on "*Evening*") the Chancellor's medal; second Craven Scholar; B.A., 1822; M.A., 1825, and for many years Fellow of his College; Barrister (Linc. Inn), 1826, becoming Bencher in 1849. M.P. for Calne, 1830; for Leeds, 1832; for Edinburgh, 1840-47, and again, 1852-56; a Commissioner of Bankrupts; a Commissioner and subsequently (1832) Sec. to the Board of Control; 5th member of and Legal Adviser to the Supreme Council of India; P.C., 1839; Sec. at War, 1839-41; Paymaster Gen. of the Forces with a seat in the Cabinet, 1846-48; Lord Rector of the Univ. of Glasgow, 1848; Professor of ancient history in the Royal Academy, 1850; member of the Prussian Order of Merit, 1853; High Steward of Cambridge, 1857. He was *cr.*, 16 Sep. 1857, BARON MACAULAY OF ROTHLEY,(b) co. Leicester. Well known as a Whig statesman he was far more famous as a writer,(c) both of (most exquisitely expressed) prose and of several spirited ballads. He *d.* unm., 28 Dec. 1859, aged 59, at Holly Lodge, Campden hill, Kensington, when the *peerage* became *extinct.* He was *bur.* 9 Jan. 1860, in *Poets' Corner*, Westm. Abbey.

MACCLESFIELD.

Earldom.
I. 1679.

1. CHARLES GERARD, s. and h. of Sir Charles GERARD, of Halsall, co. Lancaster, by Penelope, sister and coheir of Sir Edward FITTON, 2d Bart., and da. of Sir Edward FITTON, 1st Bart. of Gawsworth, co. Chester, was *b.* about 1618, entered at Leyden Univ., 23 March 1633, and, having been trained in the discipline of war in the united provinces, joined the Royal army in defence of his King, being Col. of a Reg. of Horse, 1643, and Comm. in Chief in South Wales, 1644, wherein having greatly distinguished himself,(d) he was made Lieut.-Gen. of the King's horse and was *cr.* 8 Nov. 1645,(e) BARON GERARD OF BRANDON,(f) co. Suffolk. In April 1649, as also in June 1660, he was a Gent. of the Bedchamber; P.C., 1650-81; Capt. of the Life Guards, 1660-68, riding at the head thereof at the King's restoration; Envoy to Paris, 1662; Lieut. Gen. of all the forces, 1678-79. He was *cr.* 23 July 1679, VISCOUNT BRANDON,(f) co. Suffolk, and EARL OF MACCLESFIELD,(g) co Chester, but shortly afterwards intrigued with the Duke of Monmouth whom he entertained, 5 Sept. 1682. On

(a) He was a member of the so called "*Clapham set*" well known for their evangelical doctrines, &c. He *d.* 13 May 1838, and like the rest "of the heroes of the abolition of the slave trade" has a monument ("in the Whigs' corner of the nave") in Westm. Abbey. [Stanley's "*Westm. Abbey.*"]

(b) Rothley Temple was the seat of Thomas Babington, the husband of his father's sister, Jean, da. of the Rev. John Macaulay, Presbyterian Minister of Cardross.

(c) His "History of England from the accession of James II." is (says the "*Annual Reg.*" for 1859), "despite of any amount of criticism, a very great work, and Macaulay will be read, *whatever his deviations from strict accuracy.*"

(d) Dugdale points out that two of his brothers, *viz.* (1) Edward Gerard, a Col. of Foot, wounded in the first battle of Newbury and (2) Sir Gilbert Gerard slain near Ludlow, were sufferers in the Royal cause, as also two uncles, *viz.* (1) Sir Gilbert Gerard, Gov. of Worcester, and (2) Ratcliffe Gerard, Lieut. Col. to his said brother; and that three sons of the said Ratcliffe, *viz.* Ratcliffe, John and Gilbert (*cr.* a Baronet, 1666), were in the battle of Kiveton, of whom John was beheaded for a plot to assassinate the Protector Cromwell.

(e) Black's "docquets" as quoted in "*Creations*, 1483—1646," in 47th Rep. D.K. Pub. Records.

(f) Lord Clarendon says (tho' it seems hardly probable) that he chose this designation for no better reason than "there was once an eminent person called Charles *Brandon*, who was afterwards made a Duke."

(g) It is said that the title first chosen was EARL OF NEWBURY (Banks's *Baronage*, vol. iii, p. 305), in allusion to the first battle of Newbury (20 Sep. 1643), where he fought with great distinction.

7 Sep. 1685, a warrant was issued for his apprehension and he fled to the continent, and was outlawed, which sentence was reversed April 1689. He returned to England in 1688, and was one of those in arms(a) for the Prince of Orange, at whose landing, he was in command of his body guard.(b) P.C., 1689; Lord Lieut. of North and South Wales, and of the counties of Monmouth, Gloucester, and Hereford, and of the city of Bristol, 1689. He *m.* before 1 Dec 1656, Jane, da. of Pierre DE CIVELLE, Equerry to the Queen Consort, Henrietta Maria. She was living in 1663, being then dismissed from court, but *d.* before her husband. He *d.* (of vomiting), 7 Jan. 1693/4, and was *bur.* the 18th in Westm. Abbey. Admon. 26 April 1694, 2 Dec. 1701, and 5 Jan. 1702/3.

II. 1694. *2.* CHARLES (GERARD), EARL OF MACCLESFIELD, &c., s. and h., *b.* in Paris, about 1659; nat. by Act of Parl. 1676/7; *styled* VISCOUNT BRANDON, 1679-94; M.P. for Lancashire, 1679-85, and 1689-94; was convicted Nov. 1685 of high treason (Rye House plot), but released Jan. 1686/7, the attainder being reversed Nov. 1687; Lord Lieut. of Lancashire, 1689; *suc. to the peerage*, 7 Jan. 1693/4, taking his seat on the 24th; Major Gen. in the army and Col. of a Reg. of Carabiniers, 1694, taking part in the unsuccessful attack on Brest in June 1694; Lord Lieut. of North Wales, 1695/6. First Commissioner(c) for the investiture of the Elector of Hanover (afterwards King George I.), with the Garter, which took place at Hanover, 4 Aug. 1701, on which occasion he presented the Dow. Electress (Sophia) with a copy of the Act of succession. He *m.* 18 June 1683, at St. Lawrence Jewry (Lic. Fac.) Anne (then aged about 15), da. of Sir Richard MASON, of Bishops Castle, Salop, and of Sutton, Surrey, Comptroller of the Household, by Anna Margaretta, da. of James LONG, of Draycott, Wilts. She was divorced by Act of Parl.(d) 2 April 1698, and her two children declared illegitimate.(e) He is sometimes said to have *m.* secondly (—) da. of (—) HARBORD, but his will dat. 2 July, and pr. 17 Dec. 1701, and again 3 Feb. 1725/6, makes no allusion thereto.(f) He *d.*, s.p. legit., 5 and was *bur.* 14 Nov. 1701, aged 42, in Westm. Abbey.

III. 1701, to 1702. *3.* FITTON (GERARD), EARL OF MACCLESFIELD [1679], VISCOUNT BRANDON [1679], and BARON GERARD OF BRANDON [1645], br. and h.; *b.* about 1665; M.P. for Yarmouth (Isle of Wight), 1689-90; for Clitheroe, 1693-95; for Lancaster, 1697-98, and for Lancashire, 1698—1700; *suc. to the peerage*, 4 Nov. 1701. He *d.* unm., 26 Dec. 1702, aged about 37, when *all his honours* became *extinct*. Will dat. 23 Dec. 1702, pr. 9 Jan. 1702/3, and 3 Dec. 1707.

Barony. I. 1716. Earldom. IV. 1721. *1.* THOMAS PARKER, s. of Thomas PARKER, of Leek, co. Stafford, an Attorney, by Anne, da. and coheir of Robert VENABLES, of Nuneham, Cheshire, was *b.* 23 July 1666, at Leek; ed. at Newport, Salop, at Derby, and (1685) at Trin. Coll., Cambridge; Student of the Inner Temple, 1683/4; Barrister, 1691; M.P. for Derby, 1705-10; Serjeant at Law and Queen's Serjeant, 1705; *knighted*, 8 July 1705; was attached to the Whig party; took a leading part in the impeachment of Dr. Sacheverell, was made P.C. and

---

(a) See vol. i, p. 28, note "b," *sub* "Abingdon" for a list of these.

(b) He was witness to three of the most striking epochs in English history, *viz.* (1) the beheading and deposing of Charles I. (2) the restoration of the monarchy under Charles II., and (3) the revolution, and the expulsion of the race of Stuart.

(c) See vol. ii, p. 192, note "a," *sub* "CATHCART," for a list of these special missions.

(d) No *previous* decree had (as had hitherto always been the case) been given by the Spiritual Court for a divorce "*a mensâ et thoro*," tho' a suit begun in 1697 was still pending.

(e) These were Anne Savage, *b.* 1695, who *d.* an infant at Chelsea, and Richard Savage, *b.* in Fox Court, Gray's Inn lane, 16 Jan. 1696/7, whose history, after 1698, is unauthentic, but with whom Richard Savage, the Poet, claimed to be identical. Their father was Richard (Savage), Earl Rivers, who *d.* 1712. The divorced Countess (whose large fortune was returned to her) *m.* about 1700 Lieut. Col. Henry Brett (who *d.* 1724), and *d.* in Old Bond street, 11 Oct. 1753, aged 85. Their da., Anna Margaretta Brett, was the Mistress of George I. when in his 65th year.

(f) In it, however, he leaves a great diamond to "Mrs. Letitia Harbord."

LORD CH. JUSTICE OF THE QUEEN'S BENCH in 1710, which office he held 8 years, having been meanwhile one of the seven Regents of the Realm,(a) 1 Aug. to 18 Sep. 1714, on the demise of Queen Anne, and being (consequently?) *cr.* by her successor (George I.), 10 March 1716, BARON PARKER OF MACCLESFIELD, co. Chester. He was made, 12 May 1718, LORD CHANCELLOR OF GREAT BRITAIN; was Lord Lieut. of Warwickshire, 1719; one of the Lord Justices (Regents) of the Realm, during the King's absence therefrom in 1719, 1720 and 1723; and was *cr.* 15 Nov. 1721, VISCOUNT PARKER OF EWELM, co. Oxford, and EARL OF MACCLESFIELD, with a *spec.* rem of those dignities, failing heirs male of his body, to his only da. Elizabeth, wife of William HEATHCOTE, of Hursley, co. Southampton (afterwards, 1733, *cr.* a Baronet), in like manner.(b) He resigned the office of Lord Chancellor, 4 Jan. 1725 (owing to heavy losses by the South Sea bubble, &c.), and was three weeks later impeached for corruption, being in May 1725 found guilty and fined £30,000.(c) He *m.* his second cousin, Janet, da. and h. of Robert CARRIER,(d) of Wirksworth, co. Derby, and Elizabeth his wife. He *d.* 28 April 1732, aged 65, at Soho square, and was *bur.* at Shirburn, Oxon. Will pr. 1732. His widow *d.* 23 Aug. 1733, at Shirburn Castle, and was *bur.* at Shirburn afsd. Admon. 16 May 1735.

Earldom. V. Barony. II. } 1732.

2. GEORGE (PARKER), EARL OF MACCLESFIELD, &c., 1st and only surv. s. and h.; *b.* about 1697; one of the Tellers of the Exchequer, 1719-64; *styled* VISCOUNT PARKER 1721-32; M.P. for Wallingford, 1722-27; F.R.S., 1722; *suc. to the peerage*, 28 April 1732; was one of the pall bearers at the funeral of the Prince of Wales, 13 April 1751; F.S.A., 1752; President of the Royal Society, 1752-64; took a great part in the act for the adoption of the "*new style*" in 1751; D.C.L. (Oxford), 7 July 1759. He *m.* firstly,(e) 18 Sep. 1722, Mary, 1st da. and coheir of Ralph LANE,(f) a Turkey merchant, by Anne, da. and h. of John ISHAM, of Pytchley, co. Northampton. She *d.* 4 June 1753, and was *bur.* at Shirburn. Admon. 22 Nov. 1753. He *m.* secondly, 20 Dec. 1757, at the house of Mrs. Catherine Rogers, Poland street, St. James' Westm., Dorothy NESBITT, Spinster. He *d.* 17 March 1764, aged 67, and was *bur.* at Shirburn. Will pr. 1764. His widow *d.* s.p., 14 July 1779. Will pr. Sep. 1779.

Earldom. VI. Barony. III. } 1764.

3. THOMAS (PARKER), EARL OF MACCLESFIELD, &c., 1st s. and h., by first wife; *b.* 12 and *bap.* 19 Dec. 1723, at his grandfather's (the Lord Chancellor's) house in Linc. Inn fields, and *bap.* at St. Giles in the fields; *styled* VISCOUNT PARKER, 1732-64; mat. at Oxford (Hertford Coll.), 10 May 1740; M.A., 1743. He was M.P. for Newcastle-under-Lyne, 1747-54; for Oxfordshire, 1754-61, and for Rochester, 1761-64; *suc. to the peerage*, 17 March 1764; High Steward of Henley; F.R.S.; D.C.L. of Oxford, 7 July 1773. He *m.*, 12 Dec. 1749, at St. James' Westm., his cousin, Mary, 1st da. of Sir William HEATHCOTE, 1st Bart., by Elizabeth, only da. of Thomas (PARKER), 1st EARL OF MACCLESFIELD abovenamed.

(a) See a list of these vol. iii, p. 116, note "b," *sub* "Devonshire."

(b) The Lord Chancellor had but one son, then unm. and abroad; but that fact does not seem sufficient reason for the unusual favour of so extended a limitation of the peerage. There is this curious note in Le Neve's "Knights" about this son. "It was commonly discoursed that he was married beyond sea to a French woman in his travels who came after him but the matter was hushed up A.D. 1723."

(c) His great predecessor, Francis Bacon, Viscount St. Albans, was in 1621, similarly found guilty and fined £40,000.

(d) This Robert was s. of Richard Carrier (sometime Fellow of St. John's Coll., Cambridge), of Wirksworth afsd. by Janet, da. of Thomas Parker, of Browsholme in Bolland, co. York, whose yr. s., George Parker, of Parkhall, co. Stafford, was grandfather of the 1st Earl.

(e) See note "b," next above, as to a reputed previous marriage.

(f) His descent from the family of Lane of Glendon, co. Northampton, is given in "Collins," vol. iv, p. 194.

He *d.* 9 Feb. 1795, aged 71, and was *bur.* at Shirburn. Will pr. Feb. 1795. His widow, who was *b.* 1726, *d.* 20 May 1812. Will pr. 1813.

Earldom. VII. Barony. IV. } 1795.

4. GEORGE (PARKER), EARL OF MACCLESFIELD &c., 1st s. and h.; *b.* 24 Feb., and *bap.* 21 March 1755, at St. James', Westm.; *styled* VISCOUNT PARKER, 1764-95; ed. at Eton; mat. at Oxford (Ex. Coll.), 2 July 1773; M.P. for Woodstock, 1777-84, and for Minehead 1790-95; Lieut. Col. of the Oxon Militia, 1778; Lord of the Bedchamber to the Prince of Wales, 1780; P.C., 1791; Comptroller of the Household, 1791-97; *suc. to the peerage*, 9 Feb. 1795; High Steward of Henley; Lord of the Bedchamber, 1797; D.C.L., of Oxford, 28 June 1797; Pres. of the Board of Agriculture, 1816-18; Lord Lieut. of Oxon, 1817. Councillor (as *Custos personæ*) to the Queen Consort, 1818. He *m.* 25 May 1780 at St. Marylebone, Mary Frances, 2d da. and coheir of Rev. Thomas DRAKE, D.D., Rector of Amersham, Bucks, by Elizabeth, da. of Isaac WHITTINGTON, of Orford, co. Suffolk. She, who was *b.* 1761, *d.* 1 Jan. 1823, at Sherborne Castle. He *d.* s.p.m. 20 March 1842, aged 87, at 9, Conduit street, St. Geo. Han. sq. Will pr. May 1842.

Earldom. VIII. Barony. V. } 1842.

5. THOMAS (PARKER), EARL OF MACCLESFIELD, &c., br. and h. male, *b.* 9 June and *bap.* 8 July 1768, at St. Marylebone; sometime (1780-82), an officer in the Coldstream Guards; High Sheriff of Oxfordshire, 1808; Col. of the North Oxon Militia, 1810; D.C.L., of Oxford, 11 June 1834; *suc. to the peerage*, 10 March 1842; High Steward of Henley, 1842. He *m.* firstly, 16 March 1796 (—) 1st da. of Lewis EDWARDS, of Talgarth, co. Merioneth. She, who was *b.* 1779, *d.* s.p.m. 9 April 1803. He *m.* secondly, 19 March 1807, Eliza, yst. da. of William BRETON-WOLSTENHOLME, of Holyhill, Sussex. He *d.* 31 March 1850, in his 87th year, at Ensham Hall, Oxon. Will pr. April 1850. His widow *d.* 1 Jan. 1862.

Earldom. IX. Barony. VI. } 1850.

6. THOMAS AUGUSTUS WOLSTENHOLME (PARKER), EARL OF MACCLESFIELD [1721], VISCOUNT PARKER OF EWELM [1721] and BARON OF MACCLESFIELD [1716], only s. and h. by second wife, *b.* 17 March 1811, at Marylebone; ed. at Eton; matric. at Oxford (Ch. Ch.), 24 June 1829; M.P. for Oxfordshire, 1837-41; *styled* VISCOUNT PARKER, 1842-50; *suc. to the peerage*, 31 March 1850; High Steward of Henley, 1850. He *m.* firstly, 11 July 1839, Henrietta, yst. da. of Edmund TURNOR, of Stoke Rochford, co. Lincoln, by his second wife, Dorothea, da. of Lieut. Col. TUCKER. She *d.* a few months later, 19 Nov. 1839. He *m.* secondly, 25 Aug. 1842, at St. Geo. Han. sq., Mary Frances, 2d da. of Richard (GROSVENOR), 2d MARQUESS OF WESTMINSTER, by Elizabeth Mary, da. of George Granville (LEVESON-GOWER), 1st Duke of Sutherland. She was *b.* 2 Dec. 1821, and was, in 1863, Lady of the Bedchamber to the Princess of Wales.

[GEORGE AUGUSTUS PARKER, *styled* VISCOUNT PARKER, s. and h. ap., *b.* 19 Oct. 1843, in Conduct street, St. Geo. Han. sq.; ed. at Eton; mat. at Oxford (Ch. Ch.), 25 Jan. 1862; Lieut. 1st Life Guards, 1867-68. He *m.* firstly, 14 March 1878, at St. Geo. Han. sq., Edith, widow of Thomas Rumbold RICHARDSON, 1st Life Guards, da. of Frederick Henry HARFORD, of Down Place, Berks. She *d.* s.p., 4 April 1885, on board ship. He *m.* secondly, 26 Jan. 1887, at St. Paul's, Knightsbridge, Caroline Agnes, sister of Sir Pryse Pryse, 1st Bart., da. of Pryse LOVEDEN of Gogerddan, co. Cardigan, by Margaretta Jane, da. of Walter RICE.]

Family Estates.—These, in 1883, consisted of 5,518 acres in Oxfordshire, 5,947 in Staffordshire, and 3,088 in Devonshire. *Total* 14,453 acres, worth £17,937 a year. *Principal Residence.* Shirburn Castle, near Tetsworth, Oxon, which estate was bought by the Lord Chancellor, the 1st Earl.

MACDONALD, or MACDONNELL.

No less than four persons of this name were raised to the Peerage (3 as BARONS and one as a BARONESS) in 1716 by the *titular* King James III.([a]) the designation of whose peerages [MACDONALD?] have not been ascertained. These were (1) PENELOPE MACDONALD, da. of Col. MACKENZIE, Gov. of Tangier, widow of Alan Macdonald, of Clanranald, who, having joined the rising of 1715 on behalf of the Stuart dynasty, was slain s.p. at Sheriffmuir (2) RANALD MACDONALD, of Clanranald (br. to Alan abovenamed) who *d.* unm. at St. Germains in 1725 (3) ALISTAIR MACDONALD, or MACDONNELL, of Glengarry, bearer of the Royal standard at Killiecrankie, who *d.* 1724, being ancestor of the present race of Macdonnell, of Glengarry, and (4) SIR DONALD MACDONALD, 2d Bart. [S.], of Slate, *attainted* 1718, whose only s., Donald, *d.* unm. in 1720.

MACDONALD OF EARNSCLIFFE.

Barony. I. 1891.

1. DAME SUSAN-AGNES MACDONALD, widow of the Rt. Hon. SIR JOHN ALEXANDER MACDONALD, G.C.B., Prime Minister of the Dominion of Canada, was in consideration of her late husband's services *cr.* (within three months of his death), 14 Aug. 1891, BARONESS MACDONALD OF EARNSCLIFFE, in the Province of Ontario and Dominion of Canada. He was 1st s. of Hugh MACDONALD, of Kingston in Canada west, was *b.* 1815; ed. at the Grammar School at Kingston afsd.; was Barrister, 1836; Queen's Counsel, 1846; Attorney Gen., 1854-62, 1864-67, and Prime Minister of Canada, 1867-73, and 1875-91, being the first Premier of the United Provinces. P.C., 1879. He was K.C.B. (Civil Extra), 1867, and G.C.B. 1884; Knight Grand Cross of Isabella the Catholic of Spain; D.C.L. (Oxford), 21 June 1865; LL.D. Queen's Univ., Canada, &c. He *m.* firstly Isabella, da. of Alexander CLARK, of Dalnavert, co. Inverness. He *m.* secondly, 3 Sep. 1867, the abovenamed Susan Agnes, who was da. of T. J. BERNARD, a member of the Privy Council of Jamaica. He *d.* s.p., 6 June 1891, in his 87th year, at Ottawa, Canada, and was *bur.* at Kingston. His widow, the *suo jure* Baroness, living 1893.

MACDONALD OF SLATE.

Barony. I 1776.

1. SIR ALEXANDER MACDONALD,([b]) Bart.([c]) [S.], of Slate, in the isle of Skye, co. Inverness, 3d s. of Sir Alexander MACDONALD, 7th Bart.([b]) [S.], by his second wife, Margaret, da. of Alexander (MONTGOMERY), 9th EARL OF EGLINTON [S.], was *b.* about 1745; was sometime (1761-66), an officer in the Coldstream Guards; *suc.* his elder br. James (who *d.* unm. at Rome, aged 24), 26 July 1766 as *9th Baronet*([c]) [S.], and was *cr.* 17 July 1776, BARON MACDONALD OF SLATE, co. Antrim [I.]([d]) He *m.* 3 May 1768, at St. Giles in the fields, Elizabeth Diana, 1st da. of (whose issue in 1813 became coheir to) Godfrey BOSVILE, of Gunthwaite, co. York, by Diana, da. of Sir

([a]) See vol. i, p. 59, note "b," *sub* "Albemarle," for a list of "Jacobite Peerages."

([b]) This family descend from Hugh Macdonald, an illegit. br. of John, Earl of Ross [S.] (who *d.* 1498), thro' Donald Macdonald of Slate, who claimed to be "*Lord of the Isles*," and who was attainted and executed in 1587. See vol. iv, p. 324, note "c." *sub* "Isles."

([c]) The second Baronet is said to have been attainted in 1716, and it is not very clear how the forfeiture of the dignity (thereby presumably occasioned), is explained away. It is, however, recognised, as existing, in the docquet of the creation of the peerage in 1776.

([d]) "Slate, co. Antrim" is non existant, the place alluded to being Slate or Sleat in Scotland. Such fictions were not unfrequently used when Scotchmen were (after the union with Scotland) raised to the peerage; *e.g.*, a Barony of Kilbryde, co. *Cavan*, and an Earldom called *Fife* in *Ireland*, conferred (1735 and 1759), on William DUFF, &c. Similar instances are also to be found in England as "Mansfield, co *Middlesex*," 1792; &c.

William Wentworth, 4th Bart. of Bretton. She, who was bap. at Denby chapel, 25 July 1748, d. 18, and was bur. 22 Oct. 1789, at St. Margaret's, Westm. He d. 12, and was bur. 23 Sep. 1795, at St. Margaret's afsd. Will pr. Jan. 1796.

II. 1795. 2. Alexander Wentworth (Macdonald), Baron Macdonald of Slate [I.], s. and h., b. 9 Dec. 1773; sometime an officer in the 10th Light Dragoons; suc. to the peerage [I.], 12 Sept. 1795; was M.P. for Saltash, 1798—1806. He d. unm. in Welbeck street, Marylebone, 19, and was bur. 25 June 1824, aged 51, at St. Margaret's, Westm. Admon. May 1825.

III. 1824. 3. Godfrey (Bosville-Macdonald, formerly Bosville and, theretofore, Macdonald), Baron Macdonald of Slate [I.], br. and h., b. 14 Oct. 1775; was an officer in the army serving in Holland (1799), in the West Indies, and at the reduction of the Cape of Good Hope, becoming finally, 1830, Lieut. Gen. in the army. By the death of his maternal uncle, William Bosville, he suc. to the estate of Gunthwaite afsd., and took by Royal lic., 11 April 1814, the name of Bosville only; but having suc. to the peerage [I.], 9 June 1824, he by another Royal lic., 20 July 1824, resumed his patronymic of Macdonald after that of Bosville. He m. 15 Dec. 1803, Louisa Maria, da. of Farley Edsir. He d. 13 Oct. 1832, aged 57. Will pr March 1833. His widow d. 10 Feb. 1835.

IV. 1832. 4. Godfrey William Wentworth (Bosville-Macdonald), Baron Macdonald of Slate [I.], eldest legit. s. and h.,(a) b. 16 March 1809, in London; suc. to the peerage [I.], 13 Oct. 1832. He m. 21 Aug. 1845, at St. Geo. Han. sq., Maria Anne, 1st da. and coheir of George Thomas Wyndham, of Cromar Hall, Norfolk, by Marie Augusta, Dow. Countess of Listowell [I.], da. of William Windham, formerly Lukin, of Felbrigg, Norfolk. He d. 25 July 1863, aged 54, at Bessingby Hall, co. York. His widow d. at Folkestone (26 Clifton Gardens), 21 April 1892, aged 64, and was bur. there.

V. 1863. 5. Somerled James Brudenell (Bosville-Macdonald), Baron Macdonald of Slate [I.], s. and h., b. 2 Oct. 1849, in Edinburgh; suc. to the peerage [I.], 25 July 1863. He d. unm. in Edinburgh, 25 Dec. 1874, aged 25.

VI. 1874. 6. Ronald Archibald (Bosville-Macdonald), Baron Macdonald of Slate [I.], also a Baronet [S. 1625], b. 9 June 1853, in Edinburgh; ed. at Eton; suc. to the peerage [I.], 25 Dec. 1874. He m., 1 Oct. 1875, at the Cathedral, Inverness, his cousin, Louisa Jane Hamilton, 2d da. of George William Holmes Ross, of Cromarty house, co. Cromarty, by Adelaide Lucy, da. of Duncan Davidson, of Tulloch, co. Ross, and his first wife, Elizabeth Diana, da. of Godfrey (Bosville-Macdonald), 3d Baron Macdonald of Slate [I.]

Family Estates.—These, in 1883, consisted of 129,919 acres in Invernessshire besides 2,500 (valued at £5,000 a year) in Bucks. Total 132,419 acres, valued at £16,613 a year. *Principal Residence.* Armadale Castle, Isle of Skye.

Lord Macdonald is one of the 28 noblemen who, in 1883, possessed above 100,000 acres in the United Kingdom and stands 16th in order of acreage tho' 28th and last in order of income. See a list of these vol. ii, p. 51, note "a," sub "Buccleuch."

(a) His elder br., Alexander William Bosville, by the same parents, born (12 Sep. 1803) before their marriage, inherited the estates of Gunthwaite and Thorpe, and is ancestor of the family of Bosville there located.

MACDONNELL AND ARRASS.

Barony [S.] I. 1660, to 1680.

1. ÆNEAS MACDONNELL, of Glengarry, s. and h. of Alexander MACDONNELL, of the same, by Jean, da. of Allan CAMERON, of Locheil, having distinguished himself for his loyalty, for which he was "*forfeited*" in 1651, by Cromwell, was in reward, at the Restoration, *cr.* 20 Dec. 1660,(a) LORD MACDONNEL AND ARRAS [S.](b) He *m.* Margaret, 1st da. of Sir Donald MACDONALD, 1st Bart. [S.], by Janet, da. of Kenneth (MACKENZIE), 1st LORD MACKENZIE OF KINTAIL [S.] He *d.* s.p.m. 1680,(c) when *the peerage* became *extinct.*

MACDUFF.

i.e., "MACDUFF," Viscountcy [I.] (*Duff*), *cr.* 1759, with the EARLDOM OF FIFE [I.], which see.

---

i.e., "MACDUFF," Marquessate (*Duff*), *cr.* 1889, with the DUKEDOM OF FIFE, which see.

MACGILL OF COUSLAND.

i.e., "MACGILL OF COUSLAND," Barony [S.] (*Macgill*), *cr.* 1651, with the VISCOUNTCY OF OXFURD [S.], which see; *dormant* 1706.

MACHANSYRE or MACHANSHIRE.

i.e., "MACHANSYRE AND POLMONT," Barony [S.] (*Hamilton*), *cr.* 1639, with the EARLDOM OF LANARK [S.]; see "HAMILTON" Dukedom [S.], *cr.* 1643, under the 2d Duke.

MACINTOSH or MACKINTOSH.

LAUCHLAN MACINTOSH, of that ilk, was in 1716 *cr.* a BARON (the designation of the peerage being unknown) by the *titular* King James III.(d) He *d.* s.p. 1731.

MACKENZIE OF KINTAIL.

Barony [S.] I. 1609.

1. KENNETH MACKENZIE, of Kintail, co. Ross, s. and h. of Colin MACKENZIE, of the same, by his first wife, Barbara, da. of John GRANT, of Grant, *suc.* his father, 14 June 1594, and was *cr.*, 19 Nov. 1609, LORD MACKENZIE OF KINTAIL [S.] He *m.* firstly Anne, da. of George ROSS, of Balnagowan. He *m.* secondly, before 12 March 1607, Isabel, da. of Sir Gilbert OGILVY, of Pourie. He *d.* March 1611.

II. 1611. *2.* COLIN (MACKENZIE), LORD MACKENZIE OF KINTAIL [S.], s. and h. by first wife; *suc. to the peerage* [S.], March 1611, and was *cr.*, 3 Dec. 1623, EARL OF SEAFORTH [S.], with rem. to heirs male whatsoever; see that dignity, *forfeited*, with this Barony, 1715.

(a) The preamble to the patent is given in Wood's "*Douglas*," vol. ii, p. 100.

(b) He was commanded by the Privy Council, 18 July 1672, "*as chief of the name and clan of Macdonald*" to find caution for several of that name to keep the peace.

(c) It is stated in Wood's "Douglas" [vol. i, p. 508, and vol. ii, p. 166], that his "only da. *m.* the Hon. James Montgomery, of Coylsfield, 4th s. of Alexander, 6th Earl of Eglintoun, and had issue." The late Mr. Stodart however (Lyon Clerk Depute) writes (doubtless correctly) "it is *not* the case that Lord Macdonnell had a da. who *m.* Hon. James Montgomery."

(d) See vol. i, p. 59, note "b," *sub* "Albemarle," for a list of "Jacobite Peerages."

i.e., "MACKENZIE OF KINTAIL, co. Ross," Barony (*Mackenzie*), *cr.* 1797, with the BARONY OF SEAFORTH [G.B.], which see; *extinct* 1815.

MACKINTOSH, see MACINTOSH.

MACLEAN.

SIR JOHN MACLEAN was *cr.* a BARON (the designation of the peerage being unknown) in 1716 by the *titular* King James III.([a])

MACLEOD.

i.e., "MACLEOD AND CASTLEHAVEN," Barony [S.] (*Mackenzie*), *cr.* 1685, with the VISCOUNTCY OF TARBAT [S.], and again 1703 with the EARLDOM OF CROMARTY [S.], which see; *forfeited* therewith, 1746.

NORMAN MACLEOD, of that ilk, who *suc.* his br. therein in Aug. 1699 was in 1716 *cr.* a BARON (the designation of the peerage being unknown) by the *titular* King James III.([a]) He *d.* before 1731 leaving male issue who succeeded him.

MACLEOD OF CASTLE LEOD.

i.e., "MACLEOD OF CASTLE LEOD, co. Cromartie," Barony (*Sutherland-Leveson-Gower*), *cr.* 1861 with the EARLDOM OF CROMARTIE, which see.

MAC MAHON.

Colonel DONALD MAC MAHON was in 1722 *cr.* a VISCOUNT (the designation of the peerage being unknown) by the *titular* King James III.([a])

MACNAGHTEN OF RUNKERRY.

Barony for life.
I. 1887.

1. THE RT. HON. EDWARD MACNAGHTEN was, on 25 Jan. 1887, appointed a LORD OF APPEAL IN ORDINARY (under "the Appellate Jurisdiction Act, 1876"), and was granted "the dignity of a *Baron for life* ([b]) by the style and title of BARON MACNAGHTEN OF RUNKERRY, co. Antrim." He was 2d s. of Sir Edmund Charles WORKMAN-MACNAGHTEN, 2d Bart., of Dundarave, co. Antrim, by Mary Anne, only child of Edward GWATKIN; *b.* 3 Feb. 1830; ed. at Trin. Coll., Cambridge; B.A. and Fellow, 1852; M.A., 1856; Barrister (Linc. Inn), 1857; Queen's Counsel, 1880; M.P. for co. Antrim, 1880-85, and for North Antrim, 1885-87, being *appointed* in 1887 *a Lord of Appeal with a life peerage* as abovestated. He *m.*, 18 Dec. 1858, at St. Peter's, Eaton square, Frances Arabella, da. of the Rt. Hon. Sir Samuel MARTIN, of Orindle, co. Londonderry, one of the Barons of the Exchequer, 1850-74, by Frances Homera, 1st da. of the Rt. Hon. Sir Frederick POLLOCK, Lord Ch. Baron of the Exchequer, 1844-66.

MADERTY.

Barony [S.]
I. 1609.

1. THE HON. JAMES DRUMMOND, 2d s. of David, 2d LORD DRUMMOND [S.], by his second wife, Lilian, da. William (RUTHVEN), 2d LORD RUTHVEN [S.], was ed. with King James VI. [S.], to whom he was Gent. of the Bedchamber 1585, being in attendance on him at the time (5 Aug. 1600) of the (so called) Gowrie-conspiracy;

([a]) See vol. i. p. 59, note "b," *sub* "Albemarle," for a list of "Jacobite Peerages.

([b]) See vol. iv, p. 157, note "a," *sub* "Hannen."

was M.P. for Perth, 1585, 1592, 1593, 1597 and 1600, and having inherited from his father the lands of the Abbey of Inchaffray in Strathern (of which he was Commendator), obtained the erection of the same into a temporal Lordship, and was *cr.* 31 Jan. 1608/9, LORD MADERTY [S.] He *m.* Jean, da. of Sir James CHISHOLM, of Cromlix (by Jean, da. of Sir John Drummond, of Innerpeffry), with whom he obtained the Barony of Innerpeffry, being her mother's portion. He *d.* Sep. 1623.

II. 1623. 2. JOHN (DRUMMOND), LORD MADERTY [S.], s. and h., *suc. to the peerage* [S.] in Sep. 1623. He joined Montrose after the battle of Kilsyth in 1645, for which he was imprisoned, but in 1649, bound himself not to oppose the Parl. He *m.* (contract 30 April 1622) Helen, da. of Patrick LESLIE, 1st LORD LINDORES [S.], by Jean, da. of Robert (STEWART), EARL OF ORKNEY [S.]

III. 1650? 3. DAVID (DRUMMOND), LORD MADERTY [S.], s. and h. He was imprisoned (v.p.) with other friends of Montrose in 1644. He *m.* firstly, Alison, da. and h. of John (CREIGHTON, of Haltoun and Luncardine. She *d.* s.p.m. March 1639. He *m.* secondly, Beatrix, sister to James, 1st MARQUESS OF MONTROSE [S.], 4th da. of John (GRAHAM), 4th EARL OF MONTROSE [S.], by Margaret, da. of William (RUTHVEN), 1st EARL OF GOWRIE [S.] He is said(a), when lying sick, to have resigned his honours, 11 April 1684, in favour of his br. and h. presumptive. He *d.* s.p.m.s.

IV. 1684? 4. WILLIAM (DRUMMOND), LORD MADERTY [S.], br. and h. male who was *cr.* 16 Aug. 1686,(b) VISCOUNT OF STRATHALLAN and LORD DRUMMOND OF CROMLIX [S.], with rem. to heirs male whatsoever. See "STRATHALLAN," Viscountcy [S.], *cr.* 1686.

MAGDALA.

See "NAPIER OF MAGDALA in Abyssinia AND OF CARYNGTON in co. Chester," Barony (*Napier*), *cr.* 1868.

MAGENNIS OF IVEAGH.(c)

Viscountcy [I.] I. 1623. 1. SIR ARTHUR MAGENNIS, of Rathfrilan, co. Down, having been *knighted*, 1 Nov. 1604, by the Lord Deputy [I.], and having released, before 1613, all his territorial claim to the district of Iveagh, received several extensive grants and was *cr.*, 18 July 1623, VISCOUNT MAGENNIS OF IVEAGH, co. Down [I.] He was attainted in 1642 which was apparently reversed after 1660. He *m.*, before 1599, Sarah, da. of Hugh (O'NEILL), EARL OF TYRONE [I.], by his second wife, Judith, da. of Manus O'DONNELL. He *d.* 7 May and was *bur.* 15 June 1629, at Drumbalong.

II. 1629. 2. HUGH (MAGENNIS), VISCOUNT MAGENNIS OF IVEAGH [I.], s. and h., *b.* 1599. He *m.* Mary, da. of Sir John BELLEW, of Castleton. He *d.* April 1630. His widow living 1641.

(a) "Fountainhall" i, 295, as quoted in Wood's "Douglas."

(b) In this creation he is called (Wood's "Douglas" vol. ii, p. 690) "Hon. General William Drummond, 5th s. of John, Lord Maderty," which would seem as if his elder brother David, the 3d Lord Maderty, was still living.

(c) "*Magh-inis* was, according to Joyce, the ancient name of Lecale, a Barony in Down, and signifies *level island*, part of Lecale being a peninsula." See "*N. and Q.*," 7th s., xi, 250, in which vol. (*passim*, under "Iveagh, Lords of"), are several notices of the family, as also in Dalton's "Irish Army List, 1689" (p. 908), where it is stated that they were "from very ancient times the territorial *Lords of Iveagh* in Delaradia (county of Down) ranking as the head of the Clanna Rory."

III. 1630. 3. ARTHUR (MAGENNIS), VISCOUNT MAGENNIS OF IVEAGH [I.], s. and h. He was excepted from pardon in Cromwell's act of 1652 and was one of the Roman Catholic nobility [I.] who "remonstrated" in 1663.[a] He *d.* s.p. and was *bur.* 1 May 1683, in St. Catherine's church, Dublin.

IV. 1683. 4. HUGH (MAGENNIS), VISCOUNT MAGENNIS OF IVEAGH [I.], br. and h. He *d.* s.p. and was *bur.* 5 Dec. 1684, at St. Catherine's afsd.

V. 1684, to 1691. 5. BRYAN (MAGENNIS), VISCOUNT MAGENNIS OF IVEAGH [I.], br. and h., who, in 1689, sat in the Parl. [I.] of King James II. for whom he raised a regiment of Dragoons and one of Infantry and by whom he was nom. Lord Lieut. of co. Down. He *m.* in 1689 Margaret, da. of William (DE BURGH), 7th EARL OF CLANRICARDE [I.], by Lettice, da. of Sir Henry SHIRLEY, Bart. By his attainder in 1691 the *peerage* became *forfeited.* He, at the close of the Irish campaign on behalf of James II., entered the Austrian service with a battalion of 500 men, whom he landed (from Cork) at Hamburgh in June 1692. He *d.* s.p. 1693. His widow, who was *b.* 1673, *m.* in 1696 Thomas BUTLER, of Kilcash, co. Tipperary, and *d.* there (a widow) 19 July 1744.[b]

MAGHERAMORNE.[c]

Barony. I. 1887. 1. SIR JAMES MACNAGHTEN MACGAREL-HOGG, Bart., was *cr.* 5 July 1887,[d] BARON MAGHERAMORNE of Magheramorne, co. Antrim. He was s. and h. of the Rt. Hon. Sir James Weir HOGG, Bart. (so *cr.* 20 July 1846), Administrator Gen. of Bengal, and sometime Chairman of the East India Company, by Mary Claudine, da. of Samuel SWINTON, of Swinton, co. Berwick, and was *b.* 3 May 1823, at Calcutta; ed. at Eton and at Ch. Ch. Oxford; matric. 12 May 1842; entered the army 1843; Lieut. Col. 1st Life Guards, 1855-59; M.P. for Bath, 1865-68; for Truro, 1871-75, and for the Hornsey division, 1885-87; Chairman of the Metrop. Board of Works, 1870-89; K.C.B. (civil) 1874; *suc.* his father *as second Baronet,* 27 May 1876; *suc.* to the estate of Magheramorne, by the death of Charles MACGAREL (his uncle by marriage) in compliance with whose will he took by Royal lic., 8 Feb. 1877, the name of *MacGarel,* before that of *Hogg,* being 10 years afterwards *raised to the peerage,* in 1877, as aforesaid. He *m.* 31 Aug. 1857, at Llandegai, co. Carnarvon, Caroline Elizabeth Emma, 1st da. of Edward Gordon (DOUGLAS-PENNANT), 1st BARON PENRHYN OF LLANDEGAI, by his first wife, Julianna Isabella Mary da. and coheir of George Hay DAWKINS-PENNANT. He *d.* 27 June 1890, aged 67, at 17 Grosvenor gardens, and was *bur.* in Brompton cemetery. Will pr. at £159,718. His widow who was *b.* 20 May 1834, living 1893.

II. 1890. 2. JAMES DOUGLAS (MACGAREL-HOGG), BARON MAGHERAMORNE, also a Baronet [1846], s. and h., *b.* 16 Jan. 1861, at Prince's terrace, Hyde Park; sometime Capt. in the 1st Life Guards; *suc. to the*

(a) See vol. ii, p. 149, note "d," *sub* "Carlingford," for a list of these. See also Burke's "Extinct Peerage," edit. 1883, p. 611, for a curious account of the state of this family soon after the Restoration.

(b) The title seems to have been assumed by various parties even as late as 1783, in which year was hung for murder Daniel Magennis, M.D., whose nephew thus styled himself. See "*N. and Q.*," 7th s., xi, 398. It is stated in Burke's "Extinct Peerage" (edit. 1883, p. 611), that "Magennis, styling himself Viscount Iveagh, was Col. of the Irish Brigade in Spain at or shortly before the breaking out of the great French Revolution. Documents signed by him as *Viscount Iveagh* are in existence."

(c) The name is that of the settlement of the ancient tribe of Morne. The estate was acquired in 1842, by Charles MacGarel, who *m.* in 1856, Mary Rosina, sister of Sir James Weir Hogg, Bart., to whose son (the 1st Baron Magheramorne) he left it on his death s.p. in 1876.

(d) This (was one of the eight "Jubilee" Baronies *cr.* in July 1887, for a list of which see vol. ii, p. 238, note "a," *sub* "Cheylesmore."

peerage, 27 June 1890. He *m.* 23 Oct. 1889, at St. Paul's, Knightsbridge, Evelyn Harriet, 2d da. of Anthony (ASHLEY-COOPER), 8th EARL OF SHAFTESBURY, by Harriet Augusta Anne Seymourina, da. of George Hamilton (CHICHESTER), 3d MARQUESS OF DONEGALL [I.] She was *b.* 27 June 1865.

Family Estates.—These, in 1883, consisted of 3,541 acres in co. Antrim, valued at £4,083 a year. *Principal Residence.* Magheramorne, near Larne, co. Antrim.

MAGUIRE OF ENNISKILLEN.

Barony [I.] I. 1628. *1.* SIR BRYAN MAGUIRE was *cr.*, 3 March 1627/8, LORD MAGUIRE, BARON OF ENNISKILLEN, co. Fermanagh [I.] He *m.* Rose, da. of Art Mac Avernan O'NEILL, of Carrickoalikin, co. Armagh. He *d.* 15 Dec. 1633, and was *bur.* at Auchive, co. Fermanagh.

II. 1633, to 1644. *2.* CONNOR (MAGUIRE), LORD MAGUIRE, BARON OF ENNISKILLEN [I.], s. and h.; was *knighted* (v.p.) 20 June 1616, at Whitehall. He *m.* Mary, da. of Thomas FLEMING, of Castle Fleming. He was one of the native Irish who took a principal lead in the great Irish rebellion of 1641; was tried in London and found guilty of high treason, being hung at Tyburn, 10 Feb. 1644, when the *peerage* became *forfeited.*(a)

MAHARAJPORE.

See "GOUGH OF CHIN-KANG-FOO in China AND OF MAHARAJPORE AND THE SUTLEJ in the East Indies," Barony (*Gough*), *cr.* 1846.

MAHON.

See "STANHOPE OF MAHON in the island of Minorca," Viscountcy (*Stanhope*), *cr.* 1717.

MAIDSTONE.

i.e., "MAIDSTONE, co. Kent," Viscountcy (*Finch*), *cr.* 1623; see "WINCHILSEA" Earldom, *cr.* 1628.

MAITLAND and MAITLAND OF THIRLESTANE.

Barony [S.] I. 1590. *1.* SIR JOHN MAITLAND, of Leithington, 2d son(b) of Sir Richard MAITLAND, of Thirlestane and Leithington, sometime Keeper of the Privy Seal [S.], by Mary, da. of Sir Thomas CRANSTOUN, of Corsbie; *b.* 1545; was Commendator of Coldingham priory, 8 March 1565/6; Keeper of the Privy Seal [S.], 26 Aug. 1567, and a Lord of Session in Ordinary, 2 June 1568; was *forfeited* for adherence to the Queen's party, 1570, but *restored*, 17 Feb. 1580/1; was (again) a Lord of Session, 1581; *knighted* and made Sec. of State [S.] for life, 18 May 1584, an office he resigned in 1591; KEEPER OF THE GREAT SEAL [S.], 31 May 1586, and soon afterwards LORD CHANCELLOR [S.] He accompanied King James VI. [S.] to Denmark, in Dec. 1589, and on his return was *cr.*, 18 May 1590, LORD MAITLAND OF THIRLESTANE [S.] He *m.* Jean, only

(a) He left a son. The first Lord had four sons, of whom the second, Col. Rory Maguire, had male issue. Several of the family served in foreign service and assumed the style of "LORD MAGUIRE." See O'Callaghan's "*Irish Brigades*" and Dalton's "*Army List of James II.*"

(b) His elder br. was Sir William Maitland, well known as Secretary and one of the most attached adherents to Mary, Queen of Scots. He *d.* by his own hand, 9 June 1573, leaving one son, James, who sold the estate of Leithington to his uncle, Sir John. This James was living 1620 but *d.* s.p. when his sister, Margaret, Countess of Roxburgh [S.], or her issue, became his heir.

da. and h. of James (FLEMING), 4th LORD FLEMING [S.], by Barbara, da. of James (HAMILTON), EARL OF ARRAN [S.], Regent of Scotland. He *d.* at Thirlestane,(a) 3 Oct. 1595, aged 50, and was *bur.* at Haddington. M.I.(b) His widow *m.* Nov. 1597 John (KENNEDY), 5th EARL OF CASSILLIS [S.], who *d.* s.p. Oct. 1615. She *d.* 28 June 1609, aged 55, and was *bur.* at Haddington afsd.

II. 1595. Viscountcy [S.] I. 1624. Earldom [S.], *cr.* 1624.

2 and *1.* JOHN (MAITLAND), LORD MAITLAND OF THIRLESTANE [S.], only s. and h., *suc. to the peerage* [S.], 3 Oct. 1595; was *cr.* on 2 April 1616, VISCOUNT OF LAUDERDALE [S.], and on 11 March 1624, EARL OF LAUDERDALE, VISCOUNT MAITLAND, &c. [S.] See "LAUDERDALE"

MALAHIDE.

See "TALBOT OF MALAHIDE, AND MALAHIDE OF MALAHIDE, co. Dublin," Barony [I.] (*Talbot*), *cr.* 1831.

---

i.e., FURNIVAL OF MALAHIDE IN IRELAND," Barony [U.K.] (*Talbot*), *cr.* 1839; *ex.* 1849; see "TALBOT OF MALAHIDE," Barony [I.], *cr.* 1831, under the second holder thereof.

---

i.e., "TALBOT DE MALAHIDE, co. Dublin, Barony [U.K.] (*Talbot*), *cr.* 1856; see "TALBOT OF MALAHIDE," Barony [I.], *cr.* 1831, under the fourth holder thereof.

MALDEN.

i.e., "MALDEN, co. Essex," Viscountcy (*Capell*), *cr.* 1661, with the EARLDOM OF ESSEX, which see.

MALLOW.

See "GLENTWORTH OF MALLOW," Barony [I.] (*Pery*), *cr.* 1790.

MALMESBURY.

i.e., "MALMESBURY, co. Wilts," Marquessate (*Wharton*), *cr.* 1715, with the MARQUESSATE OF WHARTON, which see; *ex.* (together with the DUKEDOM OF WHARTON) 1731.

Barony. I. 1788. Earldom. I. 1800.

1. The Rt. Hon. SIR JAMES HARRIS, K.B., only surv. s. and h. of James HARRIS, of Salisbury, sometime (1763-65), one of the Lords of the Treasury, by Elizabeth, da. and eventually h. of John CLARKE, of Sandford, co. Somerset, was *b.* 9 April 1746, in the Close, at Salisbury; ed. at the Grammar School there, at Winchester College, and (as a Gent. Commoner) at Merton Coll., Oxford (matric. 13 June 1763) and finally, 1765-66, at Leyden; was M.P. for Christchurch, 1770-74 and 1784-88; Sec. of Embassy at Madrid, 1768; Chargé D'Affaires, 1769, and Minister there, 1771-72, where his spirited conduct gained him great credit;

(a) He appears to have acquired the estate of Thirlestane from his nephew, as, undoubtedly, he did that of Leithington. He re-built the family mansion of Thirlestane.

(b) This is said to have been written by the King. It is printed in Crawford's '*Peerage*.' A long character of him (in Latin) written by Robert Johnston, is given in Wood's "Douglas." He was an author.

Envoy to Berlin, 1772-76; Ambassador to St. Petersburgh, 1776-83; K.B., Dec. 1778, receiving the insignia thereof, from the Russian Empress, 21 March 1779. P.C., 1784; Envoy (1784-88), and Ambassador (1788-89) to the Hague, and, having carried out the treaty of alliance between England, Holland and Russia, was *cr.* 19 Sep. 1788, BARON MALMESBURY of Malmesbury, co. Wilts; D.C.L., of Oxford, 3 July 1793; Envoy to Berlin, Nov. 1793; Envoy to Brunswick, Nov. 1794, acting as proxy for the Prince of Wales's marriage with the Princess Charlotte of Brunswick.(a) Ambassador to the Republic at Paris, 1796-97, endeavouring to negotiate a treaty of peace at Lisle.(b) He was *cr.* 29 Dec. 1800, VISCOUNT FITZ-HARRIS OF HURN COURT, co. Southampton, and EARL OF MALMESBURY; Lord Lieut. of Hants, 1807. He *m.* 28 July 1777, in Lincoln's Inn fields, Harriet Maria, yst. da. of Sir George AMYAND, 1st Bart., by Maria, da. of John Abraham KORTEEN, a Merchant of Hamburgh. He *d.* in Hill street, Mayfair, 21 Nov. 1820, aged 74, and was *bur.* in Salisbury Cathedral. M.I. Will pr. 1820. His widow *d.* 20 Aug. 1830, in Charles street, Berkeley square, in her 70th year, and was *bur.* 25th in Grosvenor chapel, South Audley street. Will pr. Aug. 1830.

II. 1820. *2.* JAMES EDWARD (HARRIS), EARL OF MALMESBURY, &c., s. and h., *b.* 19, and *bap.* 23 Aug. 1778, at St. Petersburg; ed. at Eton; mat. at Oxford (Ch. Ch.), 16 Jan. 1796; M.A., 20 June 1798; *styled* VISCOUNT FITZ-HARRIS, 1800-20; Sec. to Board of Trade, 1801; M.P. for Helston, 1802-04; for Horsham, 1804-07; for Heytesbury, 1807-12, and for Wilton, 1816-20; a Lord of the Treasury, 1804-06; Under Sec. for Foreign Affairs, March to Aug. 1807; Vice Admiral of the Isle of Wight, 1807; *suc. to the peerage*, 12 Nov. 1820. He *m.* 17 June 1806, at St. Martin's in the fields, Harriet Susan, da. of Francis Bateman DASHWOOD, of Well Vale, co. Lincoln, by Teresa, da. and coheir of John MARCH, of Willesley Park, co. Cambridge. She, who was *b.* 29 Oct. 1783, *d.* 4 Sep. 1815, aged 32, and was *bur.* in the Priory church, Christchurch, Hants. He *d.* 10 Sep. 1841, aged 63, at Earl de Grey's villa, on Putney Heath, and was *bur.* in the Priory church afsd. Will pr. Oct. 1841.

III. 1841. *3.* JAMES HOWARD (HARRIS), EARL OF MALMESBURY, &c., s. and h., *b.* in Spring Gardens, 25 March, and *bap.* 1 May 1807, at St. Martin's in the fields; ed. at Eton; *styled* VISCOUNT FITZ-HARRIS, 1820-41; mat. at Oxford (Oriel Coll.), 23 March 1825; B.A., 1828; M.P. for Wilton, 1841, in which year, 10 Sep., he *suc. to the peerage*; P.C., 1852; Foreign Sec., Feb. to Dec. 1852, and again, Feb. 1858 to June 1859; D.C.L. of Oxford, 7 June 1853; Col. of the Hants Militia Artillery, 1854-74; G.C.B. (Civil), 15 June 1859; LORD PRIVY SEAL, July 1866 to Dec. 1868, and again, Feb. 1874 to Aug. 1876. He *m.* firstly, 13 April 1830, at her father's house, 26 Grosvenor square, Corisande Emma, da. of Charles Augustus (BENNET), 5th EARL OF TANKERVILLE, by Corisande, da. of Antoine, DUKE DE GRAMONT in France. She, who was *b.* 10 Aug. 1807, *d.* 17 May 1876, in Stratford place, Marylebone, and was *bur.* in the Priory church afsd. He *m.* secondly, 1 Nov. 1880, at St. Marylebone, Susan, da. of John HAMILTON, of Fyne Court, co. Somerset. He *d.* s.p., 17 May 1889, aged 82, at Heron Court, Hants, and was *bur.* in the Priory church of Christchurch afsd. His widow, who was *b.* 1854, living 1893.

IV. 1889. *4.* EDWARD JAMES (HARRIS), EARL OF MALMESBURY [1800], VISCOUNT FITZ HARRIS OF HURN COURT [1800], and BARON MALMESBURY [1788], nephew and h., being s. and h. of Admiral Sir Edward Alfred John HARRIS, K.C.B., by Emma Wylie, yst. da. of Samuel CHAMBERS, Capt. R.N., which Edward was 2d s. of the second Earl and *d.* 17 July 1788, aged 80. He was *b.*

(a) "The Prince [afterwards George IV] never forgave him even this official share in bringing about the match." [*Nat. Biogr.*]

(b) "With this mission his public life closed. At that time he was undoubtedly at the head of the diplomatic service. He continued in close intimacy with Canning and Pitt and was frequently consulted on questions of foreign policy. In July 1803, he was sounded about entering the cabinet, but he refused to join Addington." [*Nat. Biogr.*]

12 April 1842; *suc. to the peerage*, 17 May 1889; was sometime Hon. Lieut. Col. of the Royal Irish Rifles. He *m.*, 16 Nov. 1870, Sylvia Georgiana, da. of Alexander STEWART, of Ballyedmond, co. Down, by Elizabeth, da. of James DOUGLAS.

[JAMES EDWARD HARRIS *styled* (since 1889) VISCOUNT FITZ HARRIS, 1st s. and h. ap., *b.* 18 Dec. 1872.]

Family Estates.—These, in 1883, consisted of 4,165 acres in Hants; 1,079 in Wilts, and 212 in Dorset. *Total* 5,446 acres worth £6,304 a year. *Principal Residence* Heron Court, near Christchurch, Hants.

MALPAS.

i.e., "MALPAS, co. Chester," Viscountcy (*Cholmondeley*), *cr.* 1706 with the EARLDOM OF CHOLMONDELEY, which see.

MALTON.

i.e., "MALTON, co. York," Barony, *cr.* 1728; also "MALTON, co. York," Earldom, *cr.* 1733; (*Watson-Wentworth*, afterwards *Wentworth*); see "ROCKINGHAM," Marquessate, *cr.* 1746; *ex.* 1782.

MALTRAVERS.

Barony by Writ.

I. 1330, to 1364.

1. SIR JOHN MALTRAVERS, *junior*, eldest son of Sir John MALTRAVERS,(a) of Lytchett Maltravers, Dorset, was, with his father, sum. to attend the King, *cum equis et armis*" at Newcastle-upon-Tyne, 5 April (1326), 1 Ed. III.(b) He(c) was sum. to Parl. as a Baron (LORD MALTRAVERS) by writ, 25 Jan. (1329/30), 4 Ed. III. directed "Johanni *Mautravers, Juniori*," as also by writ, 5 June following, where the word, "*juniori*" is omitted. In that Parl. he was found guilty of the death(d) of Edmond, Earl of Kent, and sentenced to be hung. He fled abroad, but having surrendered himself to the King at Flanders, received from him a safe convoy to England, 5 Aug. (1345), 19 Ed. III., and was *again sum. to Parl.* 18 Nov. (1351), 25 Ed. III., but never afterwards, tho' he was fully restored by Parl.(e) He was at the battle of Cressy (1346) and Poitiers (1356), having under him 20 archers on horseback, 19 Esquires, &c.; was Gov. of the Isles of Guernsey, Jersey, &c. He *m.* firstly, Eva, 1st da. of Maurice (BERKELEY), LORD BERKELEY, by his first wife, Eva, da. of Eudo LA ZOUCHE. He *m.* secondly, about 1330, Agnes, widow of Sir John DE NERFORD (who *d.* 1329), relict formerly of Sir John DE ARGENTINE (who *d.* 1318), da. of William BEREFORD. He *d.* 16 Feb. (1363/4), 38 Ed. III. s.p.m.s., when the *Barony* fell into *abeyance*. He was *bur.* at Lytchett Maltravers. *Esch.*, 38 Ed. III. The will of his widow is dat. 18 Feb. 1374/5.(f)

(a) A "carefully considered" pedigree of Maltravers by "G.S.S." [Mr. G. S. Steinman] is in "*Coll. Top. et Gen.*" iii, pp. 77-79; who states that "the genealogical information" given in "Dugdale" is "very imperfect and erroneous."

(b) The elder John is said by Mr. Townsend (whose account has been followed in the text) to have been sum. to the great Council in (1330), 4 Ed. III., and to have been alive in (1335), 9 Ed. III., but dead in (1345), 19 Ed. III. ["*Coll. Top. et Gen.*" V, 150—154], where the "confusion and error" in the text of Dugdale, is corrected; but in Mr. Steinman's account (see note "a" next above), he, who is stated to have been aged 30 in 1296, is said to have died (1316-17), 9 Ed. II.

(c) Either he or (more probably) his father was the custodian of King Edward II. at the time (21 Sep. 1327) of that king's murder.

(d) "Inasmuch as he, well knowing that King Edward II. was really dead, falsely and wickedly induced the said Earl to believe that he was alive and *so* eventually was the cause of the Earl's death." See Townsend's account as in note "b" next above.

(e) He was, however, sum. 15 March (1360/1), 35 Ed. III. "de concilio quorundam Magnatum tenendo apud Westm.," but "that writ" says Nicolas "was evidently not a summons to Parl."

(f) Her son, Sir John Maltravers (living Feb. 1374/5) was of Hooke, co. Dorset and

The coheirs to the Barony on the death of Lord Maltravers (16 Feb. 1363/4), were his two granddaughters, the sisters and coheirs of Henry MALTRAVERS, (*b.* 1359 and *d.* young between 1360 and 1363), all three being children of SIR JOHN MALTRAVERS, by Wensiliana, his wife, which John was s. and h. ap. (by the first wife) of Lord Maltravers, but *d.* v.p., 13 Oct. 1360. These coheirs were (1) Joan, aged 22 in 1364 (relict of Thomas Roos), but then wife of Sir John KYMES. She *d.* s.p. when the right devolved to her sister (2) Alianore, aged 19 in 1364, who eventually became heir to her grandfather, as below.

II. 1377? *2.* ALIANORE (*de jure*) *suo jure* BARONESS MALTRAVERS, on the death of her sister, Joan abovenamed, when she became the sole representative of her grandfather, John, LORD MALTRAVERS, at whose death, 16 Feb. 1363/4, she was aged 19. She *m.* firstly John ARUNDEL, *alias* FITZALAN, yr. s. of Richard, EARL OF ARUNDEL, who, in consequence probably of such alliance, was sum. to Parl as a Baron from 4 Aug. (1377), 1 Ric. II., to 20 Oct. (1379), 3 Ric. II. (*not*, however, *as Lord Maltravers*, but) as LORD ARUNDEL, the writs being directed "*Johanni de Arundel.*"(a) He *d.* 15 Dec. 1379, being drowned in the Irish sea and was *bur.* in Lewes priory. His widow *m.* about 1380(b), as his second wife, Reginald (COBHAM), LORD COBHAM [of Sterborough], who *d.* 6 July 1403. See that dignity, *cr.* 1342, under the second holder thereof. She *d.* 10 Jan. 1404/5, aged 60. Will in which she directs to be *bur.* in Lewes priory dat. at Lytchett Maltravers, 26 Sep. (1404), 5 Hen. IV., pr. at Maidstone, 16 Jan. 1404/5.(c) *Esch.*, 6 Hen. IV.

III. 1405. *3.* JOHN FITZALAN, *alias* ARUNDEL, LORD MALTRAVERS, grandson and h., being s. and h. of John, LORD ARUNDEL (never, however, sum. to Parl.), who was s. and h. ap. of the said Alianore, by her first husband, John, LORD ARUNDEL abovementioned, who died before her in 1391. He was *b.* 1387, but tho' in Jan. 1404/5, he became, by his abovenamed grandmother's death, *entitled to the Barony of Maltravers*, he was never sum. to Parl. in that Barony. In 1415 he *suc.* to the Castle and *Earldom of Arundel* and in Sep. 1416 was sum. to Parl. as EARL OF ARUNDEL. See "ARUNDEL," Earldom, with which dignity the Barony of Maltravers was (with others) entailed by act of Parl. in 1627 on the family of Howard.(d)

See fuller particulars under "ARUNDEL" Barony 1377.

Crowell, Oxon, being father of two sons, each named John, of whom (1) Sir John M. of Hooke and Crowell, *d.* s.p.m., 13 June 1386 and (2) Sir John M. of Melbury Sampford (*jure uxoris*) also *d.* s.p.m., when the male line of the family appears to have become extinct.

(a) There is proof in the rolls of Parl. of his sitting.

(b) The marriage was within the third degree (the lady's paternal grandmother, Lady Maltravers, being Eva, sister to Thomas, Lord Berkeley, the maternal grandfather of her spouse, Lord Cobham), but absolution for it was given by the Pope, 11 Nov. 1384, and the issue legitimatised.

(c) In it she (curiously enough) ignores her second marriage and styles herself "*Alianor Arundell.*" See further particulars in vol. ii, p. 322, *sub* "Cobham."

(d) The title of *Lord Maltravers* was used by the s. and h. ap. of the successive Earls of Arundel, and three such sons have been sum. v.p. to Parl. in that Barony, *viz.* (1) Thomas Fitzalan, *alias* Arundel, (s. and h. ap. of William, Earl of Arundel), who was so sum. by writs addressed "*Th. Arundell de Maltravers*" from 15 Nov. (1482), 22 Ed. IV., till he *suc.* to the Earldom in 1487, being the first instance of any eldest son of a Peer so sum. See vol. i, p. 149, note "f," *sub* "Arundel." He, indeed, seems to have *sat* in Parl. as Lord Maltravers, or Lord Arundel de Maltravers, as early as (1471), 11 Ed. IV., tho' no writ (those from 13 to 24 Ed. IV. being lost) is extant of his summons (2) Henry Fitzalan, grandson of the above, (being s. and h. ap. of William, Earl of Arundel), who was so sum. by writ addressed "*Henrico Fitzalan de Maltravers, Chl'r.*," to the Parl. commencing 5 Jan. (1533/4), 25 Hen. VIII., till he *suc.* to the Earldom in 1544 (3) Henry Charles Howard, *styled* Earl of Surrey (s. and h. ap. of Bernard, Duke of Norfolk, Earl of Arundel, Surrey, &c.), who was so sum. by writ, 16 Aug. 1841, directed "*Henry Charles Howard de Maltravers, Chevalier*," and placed in his father's Barony of Maltravers till he *suc.* in 1842 to his father's Dukedom, &c.

MAN, Isle of.

The Isle of Man, formerly a parcel of Scotland, was, 20 Dec. 1324, granted by King Robert I. [S.] to his nephew, Thomas (Randolph), Earl of Moray [S.], who is described as "*Dominus Mannia*" in a charter 26 March 1325. This has been considered as a "*Scottish Barony* constituted in 1324 with a Regality and duty of attendance on Parl. as a condition of tenure."(a)

MANCHESTER.

Earldom. I. 1626. *I.* The Rt. Hon. Sir Henry Montagu, yr. br. of Edward, 1st Baron Montagu of Boughton,(b) and elder br. to Sir Sydney Montagu (ancestor of the Earls of Sandwich), all three being sons(c) of Sir Edward Montagu,(d) of Boughton, co. Northampton, by Elizabeth, da. of Sir James Harington, of Exton, co. Rutland, was *b.* about 1563; ed. at Christ's Coll., Cambridge; Barrister, Middle Temple; was M.P. for Higham Ferrers, 1591-93, 1597-98, and 1601-03; for London, 1604-11 and 1614-16; Recorder of London, 1603-15, being *knighted*, 23 July 1603, at the Coronation; King's Counsel, 1607; Serjeant at law and King's Serjeant, 1611; Ch. Justice of the King's Bench, 1616-21; P.C.; Lord High Treasurer, Dec. 1620 to Sep. 1621, being *cr.* 19 Dec. 1620,(e) BARON MONTAGU OF KIMBOLTON, co. Huntingdon and VISCOUNT MANDEVILLE.(f) First Commissioner of the Great Seal, May to July 1621; Lord President of the Council, Sep. 1621 to June 1628; a Commissioner for claims at the Coronation, 23 Jan. 1626, being *cr.* 5 Feb. 1625/6,(g) EARL OF MANCHESTER, co. Lancaster. Lord Privy Seal, June 1628-42, being Speaker of the House of Lords, Feb. 1630 and May 1642; a Commissioner of Treasury, 1635-42, and a Commissioner

(a) "Riddell," [1842] p. 1,083 (*i.e.*, in the index), see also (the text), pp. 102—103. In Riddell's "*Remarks*" [1833], p. 56, it is stated (after quoting the grant wherein are the words "*faciendo personalem appresentiam ad parliamenta nostra tenenda per rationabiles et durum summonitiones*") that "this is clearly a hereditary parliamentary honour from the heritible service of attending Parliament in virtue of the summons," while in "Riddell" [1842], p. 103, it is added that "it is the earliest instance preserved of the kind, there being no corresponding constitution extant until the ensuing century, in 1445, in the case of the hereditary Lordship of Hamilton, which was far less explicit and not accompanied with such Regal and important privileges."

(b) Ancestor of the Dukes of Montagu (so *cr.* 1705, and again 1766); *ex.* in the *male* line, 1749, and in the second race, (represented by the Dukes of Buccleuch [S.]) 1790.

(c) The yst. son was James Montagu, Bishop of Bath and Wells, 1608-16, and Bishop of Winchester, 1616-18.

(d) This Sir Edward, who *d.* 26 Jan. 1601/2, was s. and h. of Sir Edward Montagu, Ch. Justice of the Common Pleas, 1545-54, the son of Thomas Montagu, of Hemington, co. Northampton "Gentleman," who *d.* 5 Sep. 1517. The parentage of this Thomas is not proved, tho' a fabulous descent from Simon, stated to have been a br. of John (Montacute), 3d Earl of Salisbury is generally attributed to him. It is stated (1812), by Sir Egerton Brydges, in "*Collins*" vol. ii, p. 12 "that the late Mr. Thorpe (and it seems Mr. Anstis concurred in this opinion) suspected this family to be descended from James Montagu, a *natural* son of Thomas the [4th and] last Earl of Salisbury. This James lies *bur.* in the church of Ludsdowne in Kent, of which place he derived the manor from his father. The *bordure* round the arms of the present family favours the idea."

(e) Lord Clarendon, in his very interesting notice of him, says that the peerage was given him "to allay the sense of the dishonour" of his having been "reduced to the almost empty title of President of the Council" in lieu of that of Lord Treasurer. The dates, however, do not tally herewith.

(f) This title was "chose by him as he was in possession of the Lordship and Castle of Kimbolton, which many years since, belonged to the family of Mandevil." ["*Collins*," vol. ii, p. 52.]

(g) He was one of eight noblemen *cr.* at that date, for a list of whom, see vol. ii, p. 283, note "c," *sub* "Cleveland."

of Regency, March 1639 and Aug. to Nov. 1641; Lord Lieut. of co. Huntingdon, 1636-42; High Steward of the Univ. of Cambridge, 1640. He *m.* firstly, 1 June 1601, Catharine, da. of Sir William SPENCER, of Yarnton, Oxon, by Margaret, da. of Francis BOWYER, of Middlesex. She *d.* 7 Dec. 1612, and was *bur.* at St. Botolph's, Aldersgate.(a) He *m.* secondly, Anne, widow of Sir Leonard HALLIDAY, Lord Mayor of London 1605-06 (who *d.* 9 Jan. 1611/2), da. of William WINCOLL, of Langham, co. Suffolk, by (—) da. of (—) VAUGHAN. She was *bur.* at St. Botolph's, Aldersgate, Nov. (—). Fun. certif. at Coll. Arms.(b) He *m.* thirdly, 26 April 1620, at Totteridge, Herts, Margaret, widow of John HARE, da. of John CROUCH, of Cornbury, Herts. He *d.* 7 Nov. 1642, aged about 80, and was *bur.* at Kimbolton. M.I. Will pr. March 1645. His widow was *bur.* 29 Dec. 1653, at Totteridge. Her will pr. 31 Jan. 1653/4.

II. 1642. 2. EDWARD (MONTAGU), EARL OF MANCHESTER, &c., s. and h.,(c) by first wife; *b.* 1602; ed. at Sidney Sussex Coll., Cambridge, M.A.; was M.P. for co. Huntingdon, 1624-26; K.B. at the Coronation of Charles I., 1 Feb. 1626; *styled* (indifferently), from 1626 to 1642 VISCOUNT MANDEVILLE (which he was by courtesy) or LORD KIMBOLTON (which he was by right) inasmuch as he was sum. to Parl. v.p. in his father's Barony as LORD MONTAGU OF KIMBOLTON and took his seat, 22 May 1626. He, being a zealous Parliamentarian, was one of the 16 "*popular*" noblemen(d) named Sep. 1640 to treat with the Scots; P.C., 1641, and a Commissioner of Regency, Aug. to Nov. 1641, but was, in Jan. 1641/2, accused by the King (with five members of the House of Commons) of high treason.(e) He was by the Parl. made Lord Lieut. of co. Huntingdon, 1642, and Col. of a Reg. of Foot, which he commanded at the battle of Edgehill, 12 Oct. 1642. He *suc. to the Earldom of Manchester*, 7 Nov. 1642; was member of the Assembly of Divines, 1643; Lord Lieut. of Northamptonshire, 1643; Gen. of the Horse (Parl. army), 1643-45; Serjeant-Major-General of the counties of Essex, Herts, Cambridge, Norfolk, Suffolk, Huntingdon, and Lincoln, 1643-45; captured the town of Lynn and (May 1644) the city of Lincoln; was in chief command at the battle of Marston Moor, 2 July 1644,(f) but resigned all his military posts in April 1645. He was Speaker of the House of Lords and (with the Speaker of the Commons) Joint Comm. of the Great Seal, 1646-48. He was one of the few Peers among the 237 "commanders" for the Commonwealth(g) and was one of the nine Peers(h) who in 1657 were members of Cromwell's "*Upper House.*"(i) He had been Chancellor of the Univ. of Cambridge, 1649-51, and was re-appointed in 1660 when (for the second time) he was Speaker of the House of Lords, having taken an active part in bringing about the Restoration. Lord Chamberlain of the Household, 1660-71; Joint Lord Lieut. of co. Huntingdon, 1660; Chamberlain of South Wales, 1660; el. and inv. K.G., 1, and inst., 15 April 1661; Bearer of the Sword of State at the Coronation, 23 April 1661; Joint Commissioner for the office of Earl Marshal, 26 May 1662; *cr.* M.A. of Oxford, 8 Sep. 1665; entertained the King at his house at Waltham, 28 July 1668. He *m.* no less than five times,(k) *viz.*,

(a) "*Collins*," vol. ii, p. 55, but *query* if not an error for the second wife?

(b) The date of the year is unfortunately omitted; but there is no doubt of the entry referring to *her* (and not to her predecessor) as she is fully described.

(c) His yr. br. (s. of the 1st Earl by his third wife), was the Hon. George Montagu, of Horton, co. Northampton, father of Charles, 1st Earl of Halifax, a dignity which became extinct in 1772.

(d) See their names in vol. iii, p. 286, note "b," *sub* "Essex."

(e) This accusation and the King's appearance in the House of Commons, with intent to seize the said five members, are said by Clarendon to have been "among the signal causes of the Civil war."

(f) After this success Cromwell is said to have quarrelled with him and to have, ever since that date, held him in hatred.

(g) It is stated in "Whitlock's "*Memorials*" (p. 188), that it was voted in Parl., 1 Dec. 1645, that the Earls of Northumberland, Essex, Warwick and Pembroke, should be made Dukes, and that the Earls of Salisbury and Manchester should be made Marquesses.

(h) See vol. i, p. 299, note "d," *sub* "Bedford" for a list of these.

(i) See vol. ii, p. 84, note "c," *sub* "Burnell" for a list of Cromwell's "House of Lords."

(k) See "*Her. and Gen.*" vol. v, p. 448, for an account of these five marriages.

firstly, 6 Feb. 1623, Susanna, da. of John HILL, of Honiley, by Dorothy, sister of Mary, *suo jure* COUNTESS OF BUCKINGHAM, da. of Anthony BEAUMONT. She *d.* s.p. He *m.* secondly, 1 July 1625, at Stoke Newington, Midx., Anne, da. of Robert (RICH), 2d EARL OF WARWICK, by his first wife, Frances, da. of Sir William HATTON, *alias* NEWPORT. She *d.* 14 Feb. 1641. M.I. (as "*Lady Mandeville*") at Kimbolton. He *m.* thirdly, 20 Dec. 1642, at St. Mary's Aldermanbury, London, Essex, widow of Sir Robert BEVILL, K.B., da. of Sir Thomas CHEKE, of Pirgo, co. Essex, by Essex, da. of Robert (RICH), 1st EARL OF WARWICK. She *d.* at Twickenham, Midx., 28 Sep., and was *bur.* 13 Oct. 1658, at Kimbolton. M.I. He *m.* fourthly, July 1649, Eleanor, Dow. COUNTESS OF WARWICK, relict (1) of Sir Henry LEE, Bart., of Quarendon (2) of Edward (RATCLIFFE), 6th EARL OF SUSSEX, who *d.* 1641 and (3) of Robert (RICH), 2d EARL OF WARWICK, she being 4th da. of Sir Richard WORTLEY, co. York, by Elizabeth, da. of Edward BOUGHTON, of Cawston, co. Warwick. She was *bur.* 31 Jan. 1666. at Kimbolton. Will pr. 1667. He *m.* fifthly and lastly (Lic. Vic. Gen., 31 July 1667), Margaret, Dow. Countess of Carlisle, da. of Francis (RUSSELL), 4th EARL OF BEDFORD, by Katharine, da. and h. of Giles (BRYDGES), 3d BARON CHANDOS OF SUDELEY. He *d.*, somewhat suddenly of "cholic," 5 May 1671, in his 69th year, at Whitehall, and was *bur.* at Kimbolton. M.I. Will pr. June 1671. His widow was *bur.* 1 Dec. 1676 (in the Russell vault) at Chenies, Bucks. Will pr. 1676.

III. 1671. 3. ROBERT (MONTAGU), EARL OF MANCHESTER, &c., s. and h. by second wife; *b.* and *bap.* 25 April 1634, at St. Margaret's, Westm.; *styled* VISCOUNT MANDEVILLE, 1642-71; M.P. for Huntingdonshire, 1660-71; was one of the six (by courtesy *styled*) Lords, part of 12 Commoners deputed to the Hague, 7 May 1660, to invite the return of the King; Train Bearer at the Coronation, 13 April 1661; Gent. of the Bedchamber, 1666-81; Capt. of a Reg. of Horse, 1666; *suc. to the peerage*, 5 May 1671, taking his seat, 4 Feb. 1672; Joint Lord Lieut. of co. Huntingdon, 1671-81. He *m.* 27 June 1655, at St. Gile's in the fields, Anne, da. of Sir Christopher YELVERTON, 1st Bart., of Easton Manduit, co. Northampton, by Anne, da. of Sir Thomas TWISDEN, Bart. He *d.* at Montpelier, in France, 14 March 1682/3, aged 48, and was *bur.* at Kimbolton. Will pr. 1684. His widow *m.* Charles MONTAGU, afterwards 1st EARL OF HALIFAX (who *d.* 19 May 1715, aged 54), and was *bur.* 28 July 1698,[a] at St. James', Westm.

IV. 1683. Dukedom. I. 1719. 4 and 1. CHARLES MONTAGU), EARL OF MANCHESTER, &c., 3d but 1st surv. s. and h., *b.* about 1662, *styled* VISCOUNT MANDEVILLE, 1671-83; ed. at Trin. Coll., Cambridge; M.A., 1680; *suc. to the peerage*, 14 March 1682/3; Carver to the Queen Consort at the Coron. of James II., 23 April 1685; Capt. of a Troop of Horse, 1685; was a vehement supporter of the revolution;[b] bearer of St. Edward's staff at the Coron. 11 April 1689, of William and Mary; was at the battle of the Boyne, 1690; Capt. of the Yeoman of the Guard, 1689—1702; Lord Lieut. of Huntingdon, 1689, and again 1714. P.C., 1698; 1702 and 1714. Ambassador to Venice, 1697-98; to Paris, 1699—1701, and to Vienna, 1706-08. High Steward of the Univ. of Cambridge, 1697; Sec. of State for the North, Jan. to May, 1702;[c] a Lord of the Bedchamber, 1714; Carver at the Coron. of George I., 20 Oct. 1714, by whom he was *cr.* 28 April 1719, DUKE OF MANCHESTER. He *m.* (Lic. at Fac. office, 19 Feb. 1690/1, to marry at Bremar, Hants), Dodington, 2d da. and coheir of Robert (GREVILLE), 2d BARON BROOKE OF BEAUCHAMPS COURT, by Anne, da. and at length heir of John DODINGTON, of Bremer. She *d.* 6 Feb. 1720/1. He *d.* 20 Jan. 1721/2, aged about 60. Will pr. 1722.

(a) See as to her, vol. iv, p. 135, note "g" *sub* "Halifax."

(b) He was one of the nobility "in arms" for the Prince of Orange, 1688, for a list of whom see, vol. i, p. 28, note "b," *sub* "Abingdon."

(c) Macky in his "*Characters*," says of him, "when about 40" that "he is a gentleman of greater application than capacity; of good address, but no elocution; is very honest; a lover of the constitution of his country, which he takes pains to understand and serve; is of a middle stature, well shaped, with a very beautiful countenance; fair complexion."

Dukedom. II. Earldom. V. } 1722.

2 and 5. WILLIAM (MONTAGU), DUKE OF MANCHESTER, EARL OF MANCHESTER, &c., s. and h.; b. April 1700, in France; *styled* VISCOUNT MANDEVILLE till 1722; one of the Pages at the Coron. of Geo. I., 20 Oct. 1714; ed. at Cambridge; a Lord of the Bedchamber to Geo. I. and Geo. II., 1722 and 1727; *suc. to the peerage*, 20 Jan., and took his seat, 1 Feb. 1721/2; Lord Lieut. of co. Huntingdon, 1722; K.B., 27 May 1725; Bearer of the Spurs at the Coron. of Geo. II., 11 Oct. 1727; *cr.* LL.D. of Cambridge, 25 April 1728; Capt. of the Yeomen of the Guard, 1737. He *m.*, 16 April 1723, Isabella, 1st da. and coheir of John (MONTAGU), 2d DUKE OF MONTAGU, by Mary, da. and coheir of the celebrated John (CHURCHILL), 1st DUKE OF MARLBOROUGH. He *d.* s.p., 21 Oct. 1739, aged 39, at Bath. Will pr. 1739. His widow *m.* 1743 Edward HUSSEY, afterwards (1749) HUSSEY-MONTAGU, who was *cr.*, in 1784, EARL OF BEAULIEU, and who *d.* s.p., 25 Nov. 1802, in his 82d year. Her Grace (for she retained the style of her former husband), *d.* 20 Dec. 1786.

Dukedom. III. Earldom. VI. } 1739.

3 and 6. ROBERT (MONTAGU), DUKE OF MANCHESTER, EARL OF MANCHESTER, &c., only br. and h., *b.* about 1710; M.P. for co. Huntingdon, 1734-39; Vice Chamberlain to the Queen Consort, 1735-37; *suc. to the peerage*, 21 Oct. 1739; Lord Lieut. of co. Huntingdon, 1739; a Lord of the Bedchamber, 1739; Lord Chamberlain to the Queen Consort, 1761. He *m.*, 3 April 1735, Harriett, da. and coheir of Edmund DUNCH, of Little Wittenham, Berks, by Elizabeth, da. of Col. Charles GODFREY, and Arabella, his wife, sister to John (CHURCHILL), 1st DUKE OF MARLBOROUGH abovenamed. She *d.* 25 Feb. 1755. Admon. Feb. 1803. He *d.* 10 May 1762, aged about 52. Will pr. 1762.

Dukedom. IV. Earldom. VII. } 1762.

4 and 7. GEORGE (MONTAGU), DUKE OF MANCHESTER, EARL OF MANCHESTER, &c., s. and h.; *b.* 6 April 1737; *styled* VISCOUNT MANDEVILLE, 1739—1762; entered the army, 1757, in which, in 1779, he became a Colonel during service; M.P. for Huntingdonshire, 1761, till he *suc. to the peerage*, 10 May 1762; Collector of Subsidies in the port of London,(a) 1762; a Lord of the Bedchamber, 1762-70; Lord Lieut. of Huntingdonshire, 1763; *cr.* D.C.L. of Oxford, 6 July 1763; P.C., 1782; Lord Chamberlain of the Household, 1782-83; Ambassador to Paris, 1783. He *m.*, 23 Oct. 1762, at St. Geo. Han. sq., Elizabeth, 1st da. of Sir James DASHWOOD, 2d Bart., of Northbrook, Oxon, by Elizabeth, da. of Edward SPENCER, of Rendlesham, co. Suffolk. He *d.* 2 Sep. 1788, aged 51. Admon. April 1789, July 1832, and April 1845. His widow *d.* 26 June 1832, in her 92d year, in Berkeley square.

[GEORGE MONTAGU, *styled* VISCOUNT MANDEVILLE, 1st s. and h. ap., *b.* 11 Nov. 1763; *d.* young and v.p., 24 Feb. 1772.]

Dukedom. V. Earldom. VIII. } 1788.

5 and 8. WILLIAM (MONTAGU), DUKE OF MANCHESTER, EARL OF MANCHESTER, &c., 3d but 1st surv. s. and h., *b.* and *bap.* 21 Oct. 1771, at St. Marylebone; *styled* VISCOUNT MANDEVILLE, 1772—1788; ed. at Harrow; entered the army, 1787, in which, in 1794, he became a Col. during service; *suc. to the peerage*, 2 Sep. 1788; Lord Lieut. of co. Huntingdon, 1793; Gov. of Jamaica, 1808—1827; Postmaster General, 1827—1830. He *m.*, 7 Oct. 1793, Susan, sister and coheir of George (GORDON), 5th DUKE OF GORDON [S.], 3d da. of Alexander, the 4th

(a) In 1830 the Dow. Duchess received an annuity of £2,928 for compensation for the loss of the office of Collector of Customs outwards, formerly held by the late Duke. This pension ceased on the death of the 5th Duke (her son) in 1843.

Duke, by Jane, da. of Sir William MAXWELL, 3d Bart. [S.] She, who was b. 2 Feb. 1774, d. 26 Aug. 1828. He d.([a]) at Rome, 18 March 1843, aged 71.([b]) Will pr. June 1843.

Dukedom. VI. Earldom. IX. } 1843. *6* and *9*. GEORGE (MONTAGU), DUKE OF MANCHESTER, EARL OF MANCHESTER, &c., s. and h., b. 9 July 1799, at Kimbolton Castle; *styled* VISCOUNT MANDEVILLE, till 1843; entered the Navy, 1812, in which, in 1822, he became Commander; M.P. for co. Huntingdon, 1826-37; *suc. to the peerage*, 18 March 1843. He m. firstly, 8 Oct. 1822, at St. James', Westm., Millicent, da. and h. of Robert Bernard SPARROW, of Brampton Park, co. Huntingden, Brig. Gen. in the army, by Olivia, 1st da. of Arthur (ACHESON), 1st EARL OF GOSFORD [I.]. She, who was b. 25 Jan. 1798, d. 21 Nov. 1848, at Kimbolton Castle, aged 50. Will pr. Feb. 1849. He m. secondly, 29 Aug. 1850, at Kilroot, Temple Corran, Harriet Sydney, 5th da. of Conway Richard DOBBS, of Castle Dobbs, co. Antrim, by Charlotte Maria, da. and coheir of William SINCLAIR, of Fort William, co. Antrim. He d. 18 Aug. 1855, at Tunbridge Wells, aged 56. Will pr. Sep. 1855. His widow, who was b. 1834, m. 16 Dec. 1858, at St. Geo. Han. sq., Sir Stevenson Arthur BLACKWOOD, K.C.B., Sec. to the Gen. Post office, and was living 1893.

Dukedom. VII. Earldom. X. } 1855. *7* and *10*. WILLIAM DROGO (MONTAGU), DUKE OF MANCHESTER, EARL OF MANCHESTER, &c., s. and h., by first wife, b. 15 Oct. 1823, at Kimbolton Castle, and was generally known (during the life of his grandfather), as LORD KIMBOLTON till 1843; ed. at Sandhurst; entered the the army, 1841; *styled* VISCOUNT MANDEVILLE, 1843—1844; Aide-de-camp at Cape of Good Hope, 1843-44; Capt. Grenadier Foot Guards, 1846-50; M.P. for Bewdley, 1847-52, and for Huntingdon, 1852-55; a Lord of the Bedchamber to Prince Albert (Prince Consort), March to Dec. 1852; *suc. to the peerage*, 18 Aug. 1855; LL.D. of Cambridge, 8 June 1874; K.P., 8 March 1877. He m., 22 July 1852, Louisa Frederica Augusta, COUNTESS VON ALTEN, da. of Charles Francis Victor, COUNT VON ALTEN, of Hanover. He d. 22 March 1890, at Naples, aged 56, and was bur. at Kimbolton. Personalty sworn at £76,600. His widow, who was b. Dec. 1832, and who was Mistress of the Robes, 1858—1859,([c])

([a]) The cause was a violent fever of three days. See Wraxall's "*Memoirs*" (edit. 1884, p. 172), who adds, "the opposition lost in him a steady adherent. His person and manners were most dignified, but neither his abilities nor his fortune corresponded with his figure;" again (*ib.* ii, p. 59), on his having been appointed by Fox to the French Embassy, "his figure was noble, his manners affable and corresponding with his high rank, but his fortune bore no proportion to his dignity. Tho' a man of very dissipated habits and unaccustomed to diplomatic business, he did not want talents."

([b]) It appears that in his youth he was "distinguished as a first rate waterman on the Thames," also that he was "a staunch Conservative in politics." See "*Annual Register*" for 1843.

([c]) The following is a list of the Mistresses of the Robes to Queen Victoria (an office which, when the Queen is a Queen *Regnant*, is an important one and changes with the Government) by which it will be seen that none, during that reign, was under the rank of a Duchess (1) the Duchess of Sutherland [wife of the 2d Duke], 1837-41, 1846-52, 1853-58, and 1859-61; (2) The Duchess of Buccleuch [wife of the 5th Duke] 1841-46; (3) the Duchess of Athole, 1852-53, and as joint "acting-mistress" since 1892; (4) the Duchess of Manchester, 1858-59; (5) the Duchess of Wellington, 1861-68, and 1874-80; (6) the Duchess of Argyll, 1868-70; (7) the Duchess of Sutherland [wife of the 3d Duke] 1870-74; (8) the Duchess of Bedford, 1880-83, and, as "acting-mistress," Feb. to Aug. 1886; (9) the Duchess of Roxburghe, 1883-85, and as joint "acting-mistress" since 1892; (10) the Duchess of Buccleuch [wife of the 6th Duke] 1885 to Feb. 1886, and again, Aug. 1886 to 1892.

The post (then a *non* political one) was held by the Dow. Duchess of Leeds, during the whole reign of William IV., to the Queen Consort Adelaide, and by Mary, Duchess of Ancaster, 1761-93, and by Elizabeth, Marchioness of Bath, 1793—1819 during the reign of George III., to the Queen Consort Charlotte.

m., 16 Aug. 1892,(a) at Christ Church, Mayfair, Spencer Compton (CAVENDISH), 8th DUKE OF DEVONSHIRE, and was living 1893.

Dukedom. VIII. Earldom. XI. } 1890. *8* and *11*. GEORGE VICTOR DROGO (MONTAGU), DUKE OF MANCHESTER, EARL OF MANCHESTER, &c., only s. and h., *b.* 17 June 1853, King *George* of Hanover being one of his Sponsors; *styled* VISCOUNT MANDEVILLE, 1855—1890; sometime Capt. 3d Batt. Royal Irish Fusileers; M.P. for co. Huntingdon, 1877-80; *suc. to the peerage*, 22 March 1890. He *m.* 22 May 1876, Consuelo, *da.* of Antonio Ysnaga DEL VALLE, of Ravenswood, Louisiana, U.S.A., and of Cuba. He *d.* at Tanderagee Castle, co. Armagh, 18 Aug. 1892, aged 39, and was *bur.* at Tanderagee. Will dat. 30 Jan. 1891, pr. 24 Oct. 1892, at £25,190 gross value. His widow living 1893.

Dukedom. IX. Earldom. XII. } 1892. *9* and *12*. WILLIAM ANGUS DROGO (MONTAGU), DUKE OF MANCHESTER [1719], EARL OF MANCHESTER [1626], VISCOUNT MANDEVILLE and BARON MONTAGU OF KIMBOLTON [1620], only s. and h.; *b.* 3 March 1877.

Family Estates.—These, in 1883, consisted of 13,835 acres in co. Huntingdon; 1,124 in co. Cambridge, and 55 in co. Bedford, besides 12,298 in co. Armagh (said to be worth £17,842 a year). *Total* 27,312 acres, worth £40,360 a year. *Principal Residences.* Kimbolton Castle, co. Huntingdon, and Tanderagee Castle, co. Armagh.

MANDEVILLE.

i.e., "MANDEVILLE," VISCOUNTCY (*Montagu*), *cr.* 1620; see "MANCHESTER," EARLDOM, *cr.* 1626.

MANNERS.

Barony by Writ. I. 1309. *1*. BALDWIN DE MANNERS(b) was sum. to Parl. as a Baron (LORD MANNERS) by writ 26 Oct. (1309), 3 Ed. II., directed "*Baldewyno de Man'iis*," but never afterwards, "and on his death the *dignity* is presumed to have become *extinct*." [*Courthope.*]

MANNERS DE ROSSE.

The summons to Parl. of THOMAS MANNERS by writ 12 Nov. (1515), 7 Hen. VII., directed "*Thomæ Manners de Rosse, Chev'r,*" was (in reality) a summons in the old *Barony of Roos* of which his grandmother was a coheir.(c) He was *cr.*, 15 April 1523, EARL OF RUTLAND; see that dignity.

MANNERS DE HADDON.

Barony by Writ. I. 1679. *1*. JOHN MANNERS, s. and h. ap. of John, 8th EARL OF RUTLAND, was sum. to Parl. v.p. as a Baron, LORD MANNERS DE HADDON by writ 30 April (1679), 31 Car. II.,(d) directed "*Johanni Manners de Haddon.*" By this title (tho' by the death of his father, 29 Sep. 1679, he became EARL OF RUTLAND), he appears in the Parl. begun 17 Oct. (1679), 31 Car. II., and in that begun 21 March (1680/1), 32 Car. II. He was *cr.* 29 March 1703, DUKE OF RUTLAND; see that dignity.

(a) This marriage was 40 years after her previous one and was but two days before the death of her eldest son, the eight Duke.

(b) There is no account of him in Dugdale's Baronage.

(c) See vol. ii, p. 302, note "b," *sub* "Clifton," as to this (apparently the first) instance of a Barony by writ being transmitted thro' female heirs.

(d) This summons is so stated by "Nicolas" followed by "Courthope." According to Dugdale's "*summons*" his name is *not* in the Parl., begun 6 March (1678/9), 30 Car. II., tho' it occurs in that begun 17 Oct. (1679), 31 Car. II.

MANNERS OF FOSTON.

Barony. I. 1807. 1. THE RT. HON. SIR THOMAS MANNERS-SUTTON, 5th s.(a) of Lord George MANNERS-SUTTON (3d s. of John, 3d DUKE OF RUTLAND), by his first wife, Diana, da. of Thomas CHAPLIN, of Blankney, co. Lincoln, was b. 24 Feb. 1756; ed. at Charter House and at Eman. Coll., Cambridge; B.A. and 5th Wrangler, 1777; Barrister (Linc. Inn), 1780; M.P. for Newark, 1796—1805; one of the Welsh Judges, 1797; King's Counsel, 1800; Solicitor Gen. to the Prince of Wales, 1800; Solicitor Gen., 1802-05, being *knighted*, 19 May 1802; one of the Barons of the Exchequer, 1805-07; P.C., 1807; was *cr.*, 20 April 1807, BARON MANNERS OF FOSTON, co. Lincoln, and made, 1 May 1807, LORD CHANCELLOR OF IRELAND, which office he held more than 20 years till Nov. 1827 (b) being then in his 72d year. He *m.* firstly, 4 Nov. 1803, Anne, da. of Sir Joseph COPLEY, Bart. (so *cr.* 1778), by Mary, da. of John BULLER, of Morvall, co. Cornwall. She *d.* s.p., 5 Aug. 1814. He *m.* secondly, 28 Oct. 1815, Jane, sister of Richard, 1st EARL OF GLENGALL [I.], da. of James (BUTLER), 9th BARON CAHER [I.], by Sarah, formerly Sarah NICHOLA. He *d.* 31 May 1842, in his 87th year, in Brook street. Will pr. July 1842. His widow, who was *b.* 1 Aug. 1779, *d.* 2 Nov. 1846, aged 67, at Fornham Hall, near Bury, Suffolk. Admon. March 1847.

II. 1842. JOHN THOMAS (MANNERS-SUTTON), BARON MANNERS OF FOSTON, 2d but only surv. s. and h., by second wife; *b.* 17 Aug. 1818, at St. Stephen's green, Dublin; *suc. to the peerage*, 31 May 1842. He *m.* 28 Sep. 1848, Lydia Sophia, 3d da. of Vice Admiral William Bateman DASHWOOD. He *d.* 14 Nov. 1864, aged 46, at 12, Robertson terrace, Hastings. His widow living 1893.

III. 1864. 3. JOHN THOMAS MANNERS-SUTTON), BARON MANNERS OF FOSTON, s. and h., *b.* 15 May 1852; *suc. to the peerage*, 14 Nov. 1864; ed. at Trin. Coll., Cambridge; M.A., 1880; Lieut. Gren. Guards, 1875-83.(c) He *m.* 12 Aug. 1885, at Clovelly, Devon, Constance Edwina Adelaide, 4th da. of Col. Henry Edward HAMLYN-FANE, by Susan Hester, 1st da. and coheir of Sir James HAMLYN-WILLIAMS, 3d Bart., of Clovelly Court. She was *b.* 28 Sep. 1861.

Family Estates.—These, in 1883, seem to have been under 2.000 acres. *Principal Residence.* (1891) Cold Overton Hall, near Oakham, co. Rutland.

MANNY.

Barony by Writ. I. 1347. 1. SIR WALTER MANNY,(d) s. of "Le Borgne" MANNY, a Knight of Hainault, came into England, in 1327, in the suite of Philippa of Hainault on her marriage to King Edward III; was *knighted* (K.B.), 1331; was one of the most eminent Commanders of

(a) His next elder br., Charles, Archbishop of Canterbury, 1805-28, was father of Charles, 1st Viscount Canterbury.

(b) "His decisions as an Equity Judge were held in high estimation." [Foss's *Judges*.]

(c) Lord Manners, "who in the Spring of 1882, won the Liverpool steeplechase with his own horse, Seaman," is the 20th master of "the Quorn Hunt," one of the oldest and most celebrated in this kingdom. It was started by Mr. Hugo MEYNELL in 1758, who remained master for 47 years! After him came (2) the EARL OF SEFTON [I.], 1800-05; (3) LORD FOLEY, 1805-07; (4) the celebrated Mr. ASSHETON-SMITH, "*the first master of Hounds in the Shires, who hunted them himself*" 1807-17; (5 and 6) Mr. OSBALDESTON and Sir Bellingham GRAHAM, 1817-27; (7) LORD SOUTHAMPTON, 1827-31; (8) Sir Harry GOODRICHE, 1831-33; (9) Mr. Francis HOLYOAKE, 1833-35; (10) Mr. Rowland ERRINGTON, 1835, who sold the pack by auction. After a lapse of time came (11) LORD SUFFIELD, for one season (1838 ?); then (12) Mr. Thomas HODGSON (from 1838 ?) for two seasons; (13) Mr. Henry GREENE, and a committee, 1841-47; "then came the magnificent reign of (14) Sir Richard SUTTON, [1847-55], who is said to have spent £10,000 a year in the Quorn Hunt, and who just before his death in 1855, divided it into two parts," of which, the "Quorn proper" was purchased by (15) the EARL OF STAMFORD, 1855-63; (16) Col. CLOWES, 1863-66; (17) the MARQUESS OF HASTINGS, 1866-68; (18) Mr. CHAWORTH-MASTERS, 1868-70; (19) Mr. John COUPLAND, 1870—1884; (20) LORD MANNERS. See "the Times" newspaper, 11 Nov. 1884.

(d) A full and accurate account of him (whose name is "associated with all that is bright and pleasing in the Knightly character") is given in Beltz's "*Knights of the Garter.*"

the age in the Scotch wars, 1334-36, and more particularly in the French wars at the battle of Cressy and at the taking of Calais where the King and Prince fought under his banner. He was sum. to Parl. as a Baron (LORD MANNY) by writs from 12 Nov. (1347), 21 Ed. III., to 8 Jan. (1370/1), 44 Ed. III.(a) K.G., 1359. He m. about 1335 Margaret, *suo jure* COUNTESS OF NORFOLK, widow of John (SEGRAVE), LORD SEGRAVE, da. and h. of Thomas (PLANTAGENET, *styled* "of Brotherton"), EARL OF NORFOLK, who was 2d s. of **King Edward I.** He *d.* s.p.m. in London, 13 Jan. 1371/2, and was *bur.* in the Charter house, of which he was joint Founder. Will dat. 30 Nov. 1371, pr. at Lambeth, 13 April 1372. His widow, who was *b.* about 1320, and who was *cr.*, 19 Sep. 1397, DUCHESS OF NORFOLK (see that dignity) was ancestress (by her first husband) of the succeeding Dukes of Norfolk. She *d.* 24 May 1399.

II. 1372. 2. ANNE, COUNTESS OF PEMBROKE, and *suo jure* BARONESS MANNY, only da. and h.(b) of her father, at whose death, in 1372, she was aged 16, having *m.* in 1368, as his second wife, John (HASTINGS), 2d EARL OF PEMBROKE, who *d.* 16 April 1375, aged 28. She *d.* 2 April 1384.

III. 1384, to 1389. 3. JOHN (HASTINGS), EARL OF PEMBROKE [1339], LORD HASTINGS [1295], and LORD MANNY [1347], only child and h. He *suc.* his father in 1375 in the Earldom of Pembroke, &c., and his mother, in 1384, in the *Barony of Manny*. He *d.* unm., 30 Dec. 1389, aged 17, when the *Earldom of Pembroke* and the *Barony of Manny* became *extinct*.

See fuller particulars under "Pembroke" Earldom, *cr.* 1339; *ex.* 1389.

MANOR GORE.

i.e., "GORE OF MANOR GORE, co. Donegal," Barony [I.] (*Gore*), *cr.* 1764; see "ROSS" Earldom [I.], *cr.* 1772; *ex.* 1802.

MANOR HAMILTON.

i.e., "LEITRIM OF MANOR HAMILTON, co. Leitrim," Barony [I.] (*Clements*), *cr.* 1783; see "LEITRIM" Earldom [I.], *cr.* 1795.

MANSELL OF MARGAM.

Barony. I. 1712. 1. SIR THOMAS MANSELL, Bart., of Margam, co. Glamorgan, 2d but 1st surv. s. of Sir Edward MANSELL, 3d Bart. [a dignity *cr.* 22 Nov. 1611], by Martha, da. of Edward CARNE, of Ewenny, co. Glamorgan, was *b.* about 1668; matric. at Oxford (Jesus Coll.), 7 March 1684/5, being then aged 17; B.A. (Trin. Coll.) 1686; M.A. (New Inn Hall) 1699; was M.P. for Brecon, 1678 till void 1 April 1679; for Cardiff, 1689-98, and for co. Glamorgan (in six Parls.) 1699—1712; Sheriff of co. Glamorgan, 1701; P.C., 1704; Comptroller of the Household, 1704-08; *suc. his father as 4th Bart.*, 17 Nov. 1706; a Commissioner of the Treasury, 1710; a Teller of the Exchequer; Vice Admiral of South Wales and Gov. of Milford Haven, and was *cr.* 1 Jan. 1711/2,(c) BARON MANSELL OF MARGAM, co. Glamorgan, taking his seat the next day. He *m.* 18 May 1686, at Westm. Abbey (Lic. Vic. Gen., she being about 17), Martha, da. and h. of Francis MILLINGTON, of London, Merchant, and of Newick place, near Lewes, Sussex, by Martha, da. of Samuel VYNER, of London. She *d.* 10, and was *bur.* 17 June 1718, aged 49, in Westm. Abbey. Will dat. 16 Aug. 1717, pr. 17 May 1719. He *d.* 10 Dec. 1723, aged about 55,(d) at Margam, and was *bur.* there. Will pr. March 1724.

(a) There is proof in the rolls of Parl. of his sitting.

(b) Thomas Manny, her only br., *d.* v.p., being drowned in a well at Deptford.

(c) He was one of the 12 Peers *cr.* within five days to give a majority in the House of Lords to the Tory ministry. See vol. i, p. 209, note "d," *sub* "Bathurst" for a list of them.

(d) It appears from Macky's '*Characters*" (about 1705), that "he always made an agreeable figure in the House of Commons" and "was generally [an] opposer of the

II. 1723. 2. THOMAS (MANSELL), BARON MANSELL OF MARGAM, grandson and h., being s. and h. of the Hon. Robert MANSELL, by Anne, da. and coheir of Admiral Sir Cloudesley SHOVEL, of May place, in Crayford, co. Kent, which Robert, was s. and h. ap. of the late Lord, but *d.* v.p., 29 April 1723, and was *bur.* at Crayford. He *suc.* to the peerage, 10 Dec. 1723, but *d.* unm. 29 Jan. and was *bur.* 8 Feb. 1743/4, at Crayford.(a) Admon. 2 March 1743/4.

III. 1743/4. 3. CHRISTOPHER (MANSELL), BARON MANSELL OF MARGAM, uncle and h., *suc. to the peerage*, Feb. 1743/4, but *d.* unm. the same year, 26 Nov. 1744, at Newick place afsd. Will pr. 1745.(b)

IV. 1744, to 1750. 4. BUSSY (MANSELL), BARON MANSELL OF MARGAM [1712] also a *Baronet* [1611], br. and h. He inherited (in fee) Breton ferry, and other estates in Glamorganshire, from his distant kinsman, Thomas Mansell, and (for life) St. Donat's, and other estates in that county from Sir Thomas Stradling. He was M.P. for Cardiff, 1722, 1727, 1734 and 1741, and *suc. to the peerage*, in Feb. 1743/4. He *m.* firstly, 17 May 1724, Elizabeth, 1st da. of John (HERVEY), 1st EARL OF BRISTOL, by Elizabeth, da. and h. of Thomas FELTON, Bart. She *d.* s.p. 23 Dec. 1727, in her 29th year. He *m.* secondly, 13 March 1728/9, Barbara, widow of Sir William BLACKETT, Bart., da. of William (VILLIERS), 2d EARL OF JERSEY, by Judith, da. of Frederick HERNE. He *d.* s.p.m.(c) "immensely rich" in Upper Grosvenor street, 29 Nov., and was *bur.* 1 Dec. 1750, at St. James' Westm., when *all his honours* became *extinct*. Will pr. 1750. His widow *d* 11 June 1761, and was *bur.* at Newick, Sussex. Will pr. 1761.

MANSFIELD.

i.e., "MANSFIELD, co. Nottingham," Viscountcy (*Cavendish*), *cr.* 1620; see "NEWCASTLE" Dukedom, *cr.* 1664; *ex.* 1691.

MANSFIELD [co. Nottingham], and MANSFIELD [co. Middlesex.]

Barony. I. 1756, to 1793.
Earldom. I. 1776.
Earldom. I. 1792.

1. THE HON. WILLIAM MURRAY, 4th s. (one of 14 children) of David (MURRAY), 5th VISCOUNT STORMONT [S.], by Marjory, da. of David SCOTT, of Scotstarvet, co. Fife, was *b.* 2 March 1704/5, at Scone palace, co. Perth; ed. at Perth grammar School; at Westm. as King's Scholar (1719), and at Ch. Ch., Oxford; B.A., 1727; M.A., 1730; Barrister (Linc. Inn), 1730; M.P. for Boroughbridge, 1742-56; Solicitor Gen., 1742-54; Attorney Gen., 1754-56, being made(d) Lord Chief Justice of the King's Bench and *cr.* (the same day), 8 Nov. 1756, LORD MANSFIELD, BARON OF MANSFIELD, co. Nottingham; P.C., 1756; was twice, April to June 1757, and Sep. to Oct. 1767, *ex officio*, Chancellor of the Exchequer (refusing the post of Lord Chancellor) and twice, Oct. 1760, and Jan. 1770 to Jan. 1771, Speaker of the House of Lords. He was *cr.*, 31 Oct. 1776, EARL

measures of King William's reign," also that "he is a gent. of a great deal of wit and good nature, a lover of the ladies, and a pleasant companion; is very thin, of a fair complexion, noble stature and turned of 30 years old"; to which Dean Swift adds "of a very good nature, but a very moderate capacity.

(a) The entry there is by mistake recorded as "*Robert*, Lord Mansell, from London."

(b) His sister Mary (whose issue, in 1786, represented this family), *m.* John Ivory Talbot, of Lacock Abbey, Wilts, and is ancestress of the family of Mansell-Talbot of Margam, as well as of the family of Talbot of Lacock.

(c) His only da. and h. (by his second wife) Louisa Barbara, was first wife of George (Venables Vernon), 2d Baron Vernon of Kinderton and *d.* Jan. 1786, leaving a da. and only surv. child, Louisa Barberina, who *d.* unm. the same year, when the estate of Breton ferry, &c., which she had inherited from the family of Mansell, devolved on the family of Villiers, Earls of Jersey.

(d) In vain was every effort made by the Prime Minister, the Duke of Newcastle, "in the shape of Tellerships, Reversions, and a large pension, to induce him to forego his acknowledged right to the office" and so continue in the House of Commons; at last, however, "the Duke was obliged to submit, but with the loss of his able *Lieutenant* was soon forced to resign his command." [Foss's "*Judges*."]

OF MANSFIELD, co. Nottingham, with a *spec. rem.* of that dignity,(a) failing heirs male of his body to LOUISA, VISCOUNTESS STORMONT, wife of [his nephew and heir presumptive] David (MURRAY), VISCOUNT STORMONT [S.], and the heirs male of her body by her said husband. He retired from the Chief Justiceship, 4 June 1788, after holding it 32 years, and was *cr.*, 1 Aug. 1792, EARL OF MANSFIELD, co. Middlesex,(b) with a *spec. rem.* of that dignity,(a) failing heirs male of his body to his nephew the said DAVID (MURRAY), VISCOUNT STORMONT [S.] He *m.*, 20 Sep. 1738, at Raby Castle, co. Durham, Elizabeth, 6th da. of Daniel (FINCH), 6th EARL OF WINCHILSEA, by his 2d wife, Anne, da. of Christopher (HATTON), 1st VISCOUNT HATTON OF GRENDON. She *d.* 10 and was *bur.* 20 April 1784, aged 79, in Westm. Abbey. He, who lived the last four years of his life in retirement at Kenwood, in Highgate, Midx., *d.* there 20, and was *bur.* 28 March 1793, at Westm Abbey, aged 88.(c) Will dat. 17 April 1782 (with 19 codicils) to 19 Oct. 1791, pr. 28 March 1793.

Earldom. II. 1793. 2. LOUISA, *suo jure*, COUNTESS OF MANSFIELD, co. Nottingham, *suc. to that dignity*, 20 March 1793, under the spec. lim. in the creation [1776] thereof, being then wife of David (MURRAY) 2d EARL OF MANSFIELD, co. Middlesex, who on the same day, had *suc.* to *that* dignity under the spec. lim. in the creation (1792) thereof. She was 3d da. of Charles (CATHART), 9th LORD CATHCART [S.], by Jane, da. of Lord Archibald HAMILTON; *b.* 1 July 1758; *m.* (as his second wife), 5 May 1776, at St. Geo. Han. sq. the abovementioned David, then VISCOUNT STORMONT [S.], but subsequently EARL OF MANSFIELD, co. Middlesex as abovestated, who *d.* 1 Sep. 1796, as below mentioned. She *m.* secondly, 19 Oct. 1797, the Hon. Robert Fulke GREVILLE, who *d.* 27 April 1824, aged 72. She *d.* 11 July 1843, at Richmond Hill, Surrey, aged 85. Will pr. March 1844.

II. 1793. 2. DAVID (MURRAY), EARL OF MANSFIELD, co. Middlesex, *suc. to that dignity*, 20 March 1793, under the spec. rem. in the creation [1792] thereof, being also Viscount STORMONT [1621], LORD SCONE [1608], and LORD BALVAIRD [1641], in the peerage of Scotland. He was nephew and h. of the late Earl, being s. and h. of David, 6th VISCOUNT STORMONT, &c. [S.], by Anne, da. and h. of John STEWART, which David, was elder br. of William, 1st EARL OF MANSFIELD abovenamed. He was *b.* 9 Oct. 1727, ed. at Westm. school, and at Ch. Ch., Oxford; matric. 28 May 1744; B.A., 1748; *suc. to the peerage*, [S.], as VISCOUNT

(a) The strange limitation of the Earldom in 1776 was doubtless owing to a notion then prevalent that no British peerage granted *even in remainder* to a Scotch Peer would enable such Peer to sit in Parl., &c. This was founded on the absurd resolution passed by the House of Lords in 1711 as to the like impotency of a British peerage granted to a Peer of Scotland (see vol iii, p. 164, note "d," *sub* "Dover"), which resolution was rescinded in 1782. Accordingly, in 1792, the limitation of the Earldom was made with a *direct* remainder to the grantee's nephew, tho' a Peer of Scotland.

(b) "Mansfield, *co. Middlesex*," is, of course, non existant, and was merely invented to distinguish it from the Earldom of "Mansfield, *co. Nottingham*," *cr.* 16 years previously. See p. 195, note "d," *sub* "Macdonald."

(c) As an Advocate "the silver-tongued Murray" (as he was called by Pope) was probably unrivalled: within 18 months of his call to the Bar he was in three Appeal cases to the House of Lords (one being "on the all absorbing subject of the South Sea bubble"), while "his success in the House of Commons was as brilliant," he being, during the Ministry of the Duke of Newcastle "the trusted leader and almost the entire prop of the Government." As a Judge he is spoken of "as the great oracle of law and the founder of commercial jurisprudence." [Foss's "*Judges*."] *Per contra*, however, Wraxall ["*Hist. Memoirs*," edit. 1884, vol. ii, p. 53], alludes to his "constitutional and characteristic timidity in his *political* capacity," adding, also, that "in his *judicial* character he manifested a devotion to the wishes of the Court scarcely exceeded by any example to be adduced even under the Stuart reigns. He was, adds Wraxall, compared, by *Junius*, "to the most prostitute Judges of the most arbitrary reigns." His decisions as to the law of succession in the cases of the Scotch peerage shew an ignorance of the laws of his native country that is freely commented upon (*passim*) in "Riddell."

STORMONT, on the death of his father, 23 July 1748; REP. PEER [S.], from May 1754, till his death in 1796.([a]) Envoy to Warsaw, 1756-61; P.C., 1763; Ambassador to Vienna, 1763-72; K.T., 30 Nov. 1768; Ambassador to Paris,([b]) 1772-78; Lord Justice Gen. [S.], 1778-94; Sec. of State for the South, 1779-82; Lord President of the Council, April to Dec. 1783, and again, Dec. 1794 till his death in 1769; *suc. to the peerage*, [G.B.] in 1793, as EARL OF MANSFIELD as abovestated; D.C.L., of Oxford, 3 July 1793; Chancellor of Marischal College, Aberdeen, 1793; Joint Chief Clerk of the Pleas in the court of King's Bench, &c. He *m.* firstly, 16 Aug. 1759, at Warsaw, Henrietta Frederica, da. of Henry, COUNT BUNAU, of Saxony, by (—), da. of Gustavus, BARON RAGNITZ. She *d.* s.p.m. at Vienna, 16 March 1766, as VISCOUNTESS STORMONT, her heart being *bur.* at Scone. M.I. He *m.* secondly, 5 May 1776, at St. Geo. Han. sq., Louisa, who became 20 March 1793, *suo jure*, COUNTESS OF MANSFIELD, co Nottingham as abovestated. He *d.* at Brighton 1 and was *bur.* 9 Sep. 1796, at Westm. Abbey, aged 69. Will pr. 1796. See as to his widow (who survived him till 1843), the paragraph next above.

III. 1796. *3.* DAVID WILLIAM (MURRAY), EARL OF MANSFIELD, co. Middlesex [1792], also VISCOUNT STORMONT, &c. [S.], s. and h., by second wife; *b.* in Paris, 7 March 1777; ed. at Westm. School and at Leipsic; *styled* VISCOUNT STORMONT, 1793-96; mat. at Oxford (Ch. Ch.), 2 June 1794; *suc. to the peerage*, 1 Sep. 1796; Lieut. 7th Foot, 1798; Lord Lieut. of Clackmannanshire, 1803; K.T., 4 March 1835; F.R.S., F.S.A., &c. He *m.*, 16 Sep. 1797, at Bishopthorpe, co. York, Frederica, da. of the most Rev. William MARKHAM, Archbishop of York [1776—1807], by Sarah, da. of John GODDARD, of Cork and Rotterdam. He *d.* at Leamington, 18 Feb. 1840, aged 62. Will pr. March 1840. His widow *d.* 29 April 1860, aged 86, in Langham place, Marylebone.

IV. 1840. / III. 1843. *4* and *3.* WILLIAM DAVID (MURRAY), EARL OF MANSFIELD, co. Middlesex [1792], also VISCOUNT STORMONT, &c. [S.], s. and h., *b.* 21 Feb. 1806, in Portland place, Marylebone; *styled* VISCOUNT STORMONT till 1840; ed. at Westm. School and at Ch. Ch., Oxford; mat. 14 April 1823; Lieut. Col. Stirlingshire Militia, 1828-35; M.P. for Aldborough, 1830-31; for Woodstock, 1831-32; for Norwich, 1832-37, and for Perthshire, 1837-40; a Lord of the Treasury, 1834-35; *suc. to the peerage* (as Earl of Mansfield, co. *Middlesex*, &c., as above) 18 Feb. 1840, and *suc.* (by the death of his grandmother abovementioned), 11 July 1843, as EARL OF MANSFIELD, co. *Nottingham*, a dignity of an earlier (1776) creation. K.T., 18 June 1843. Lord High Commissioner to the Church [S.], 1852, 1858, and 1859. Lord Lieut. of Clackmannanshire, 1852. He *m.*, 8 April 1829, at the Chapel Royal (reg. at St. Margaret's, Westm.), Louisa, 3d da. and coheir of Cuthbert ELLISON, of Hebburn, co. Durham, by Isabella Grace, da. and coheir of Henry IBBETSON, of St. Anthony's, co. Northumberland. She *d.* (as Viscountess Stormont) 24 Nov. 1837, at Scone palace.

[WILLIAM DAVID MURRAY, *styled* VISCOUNT STORMONT, s. and h. ap., *b.* 22 July 1835, in Jermyn street, St. James' Westm.; an officer in the Gren. Guards, 1854-56, serving in the Crimean war; Col. 3d Bn. Royal Highlanders (M) and A.D.C. to the Queen. He *m.*, 6 Aug. 1857, at St. James', Emily Louisa, 1st da. of Sir John Atholl Bannatyne MAC GREGOR, 3d Bart., by Mary Charlotte, da. of Rear Admiral Sir Thomas Masterman HARDY, Bart.]

Family Estates.—These, in 1883, consisted of 31,197 acres in Perthshire, 14,342 in Dumfriesshire, 1,705 in Clackmannanshire, and 795 in Fifeshire, besides 539 in

([a]) There being no election between 1790 and 1796, he continued to sit as a Rep. Peer [S.] for three years after he had *suc.* to an Earldom of Great Britain.

([b]) He had there "manifested no great vigilance, nor displayed any superior penetration" and it was "commonly believed he had been deceived, previous to the open interference of France in the affairs of America." So says Wraxall (*Hist. Memoirs*), who adds that "Decorated with the insignia of the order of the Thistle, his person, noble and imposing, presented the appearance of a man of quality; but his manners, destitute of amenity, stiff and constrained, were not calculated to ingratiate. His enemies accused him of parsimony."

Middlesex, 250 in Derbyshire,(a) 224 in Cheshire (worth £3,110 a year) (a) and 22 in Cumberland. *Total* 49,074 acres, worth £42,968 a year, " exclusive of coals rented at £1,886." *Principal Residences*. Scone Palace, co. Perth; Cumlongan Castle, Dumfriesshire and Caen Wood (formerly Kenwood) in Hampstead, Middlesex.

MANVERS.

I. 1806. *1*. CHARLES PIERREPONT, formerly MEDOWS, 2d s.(b) of Philip MEDOWS, Dep. Ranger of Richmond Park, by Frances,(c) only sister of Evelyn (PIERREPONT), 2d and last DUKE OF KINGSTON-UPON-HULL, was *b*. 14 Nov. 1737; entered the Navy, becoming, in 1757, Post Captain, R.N.; was M.P. for Notts, 1778-96, having by Royal lic., 17 Sep. 1788, taken the name of *Pierrepont* instead of that of *Medows* on inheriting the estates of the former family under the will of his maternal uncle, the Duke of Kingston-upon-Hull abovenamed, at the death (16 Aug. 1788), of his Grace's widow. D.C.L. of Oxford, 4 July 1793; was *cr*., 23 July 1796, BARON PIERREPONT of Holme Pierrepont,(d) and VISCOUNT NEWARK of Newark-on-Trent,(d) both in co. Nottingham, and was *cr*., ten years later, 9 April 1806, EARL MANVERS.(e) He *m*., 14 March 1774, at Richmond, Surrey, Anne ORTON, yst. da. of William(f) MILLS, of Petersham, she being then a minor. He *d*. 17 June 1816, in his 69th year. Will pr. 1816. His widow, who was *b*. 14 Sep. 1756, *d*. 24 Aug. 1832, aged 76, at Holme Pierrepont. Will pr. Oct. 1832.

II. 1816. *2*. CHARLES HERBERT (PIERREPONT), EARL MANVERS, &c., 3d(g) but 1st surv. s. and h., *b*. 11 Aug. 1778, at the Ranger's Lodge, Richmond Park, and *bap*. 8 Sep. at Great Gaddesden, Herts; entered the Navy, becoming, in 1798, Post Captain, R.N.; M.P. for Notts, 1801-16; *styled* VISCOUNT NEWARK from 1806 till he *suc. to the peerage* in 1816. He *m*., 23 Aug. 1804, at the Grove, Notts, Mary Letitia, da. of Anthony Hardolph EYRE, of Grove Park, Notts, by Frances Alicia, sister of Edward, 1st BARON SKELMERSDALE, da. of Richard WILBRAHAM-BOOTLE. She, who was *b*. 11 Oct. 1784, at Marylebone, *d*. 7 Sep. 1860, aged 75, at Thoresby Park. He *d*. there, a few weeks later, 27 Oct. 1860, aged 82.

[CHARLES-EVELYN PIERREPONT, *styled* (since 1816) VISCOUNT NEWARK, *b*. 2 Sep. 1805, at Holme Pierrepont; mat. at Oxford (Ch. Ch.), 21 Oct. 1823; B.A., and 1st Class Classics, 1826; M.P. for East Retford, 1830-35. He *m*. 16 Aug. 1832, Emily, 1st da. of Edward John (LITTLETON), 1st BARON HATHERTON, by Hyacinthe

(a) The 500 acres or so in the counties of Derby and Chester were devised to the first Earl, on his entrance into public life, by Mr. Vernon, a mercer on Ludgate hill, whose only son (who predeceased him) had been a great friend of the future Earl when at Westminster school.

(b) See vol. iv, p. 407, note "c," *sub* "Kingston-upon-Hull."

(c) This appears to have been a love match, the gentleman having not above £900 while the lady had £20,000 a year; she had refused, also, a settlement of £16,000 a year and a sum of £100,000 offered by the old Duchess of Marlborough, provided she would marry "Jack Spencer," her Grace's grandson. See a contemporary letter in the (—) report of the Hist. MSS.

(d) The Viscountcy of Newark and Barony of Pierrepont had been previously conferred in 1627 on the Pierrepont family but became extinct (with the Dukedom of Kingston, &c.), in 1773.

(e) It is not clear *what* this word (*Manvers*) signifies, whether it is the name of a place or of a family, or why it was adopted, instead of the well known title of "*Kingston-upon-Hull*" to which the grantee had equal claims as to the title of "*Newark*," &c. See vol. ii, p. 102, note "a," *sub* "Cadogan," as to this species of Earldom.

(f) His name is generally called "John" but his will and his M.I. at Petersham proves it to have been "William."

(g) The eldest son, the Hon. Evelyn Henry Frederick Pierrepont (M.P. for Notts, 1796), *d*. unm. and v.p., 22 Oct. 1801, aged 26, having survived his next yr. br.

Mary, his first wife. He *d.* s.p. and v.p., 28 Aug. 1850, in his 45th year at Torquay. His widow, who was *b.* 16 Nov. 1814, *d.* co. March 1851, at Braddon Tor, Torquay.]

III. 1860. 3. SYDNEY WILLIAM HERBERT (PIERREPONT), EARL MANVERS [1806], VISCOUNT NEWARK [1796], and BARON PIERREPONT, 2d and yst., but only surv s. and h.; *b.* 12 March 1825, at Holme Pierrepont; ed. at Eton, and at Ch. Ch., Oxford; matric. 9 June 1843; B.A., 1846; *styled* VISCOUNT NEWARK, 1850-60; M.P. for South Notts, 1852-60; *suc. to the peerage*, 27 Oct. 1860; Lieut. Col. 1868-79, and Hon. Col. 1879, South Notts Yeomanry. He *m.* 15 June 1852, Georgiana Jane Elizabeth Fanny, 2d da. and coheir of Augustin Louis Joseph Cassimir Gustave (DE FRANQUETOT), DUC DE COIGNY in France, by Henrietta Dundas, only da. and h. of Sir Hew DALRYMPLE-HAMILTON, 4th Bart. [S.] She was *b.* 4 Aug. 1826.

[CHARLES-WILLIAM-SYDNEY PIERREPONT, *styled* (since 1860) VISCOUNT NEWARK, 1st s. and h. ap.; *b.* 2 Aug. 1854 in Tilney street, Mayfair; ed. at Eton; sometime, 1872-80, in the Gren. Guards; M.P. for Notts (Newark div.) 1885. He *m.* 26 Sep. 1880, at Ardgowan chapel, Helen, 1st surv. da. of Sir Michael Robert SHAW-STEWART, 7th Bart. [S.], by Octavia, da. of Richard (GROSVENOR), 2d MARQUESS OF WESTMINSTER.]

Family Estates.—These, in 1883, consisted of 26,771 acres in Notts; 5,019 in Lincolnshire; 3,729 in Derbyshire; 1,500 in Wilts and 1,026 in the west riding of Yorkshire. *Total* 38,036 acres, worth £51,649 a year. "The value does not include mines or tithe" and the "Wilts figures are only approximate." *Principal Residence.* Thoresby Park,(a) near Ollerton, Notts.

MAR, or MARR.(b)

[MAR with BUCHAN (the territory comprising that now occupied by the counties of Aberdeen and Banff) formed one of the *seven original Earldoms* (Mormaerships) of Scotland,(c) the holders of which, tho' in the 10th century styled *Mormaers*,(d) were in the 12th century more generally known as *Earls*. Before, however, the 12th century "Buchan" had become separated from "Mar."]

Earldom [S.] I. 1115. 1. RODERICK, RUADRI, or ROTHRI, MORMAER OF MAR, was witness, in 1115, to the charter of Scone as "*Rothri, Comes*," (*Earl* Rothri) equivalent to Rothri, EARL OF MAR [S.] He appears, however, again as "*Mormaer*" in 1132 (*viz.* as "*Ruadri, Mormaer of Mar*") in a charter to the monastery of Deer, of that date.

(a) Thoresby, formerly belonging to the *Dukes* of Kingston; Worksop to the *Dukes* of Norfolk; Clumber to the *Dukes* of Newcastle, and Welbeck to the *Dukes* of Portland (all four being in Sherwood forest, Notts), constitute what is called "*the Dukeries*."

(b) The following publications will be referred to, in this account of the Mar peerage, under the letters, "A," "B," "C," and "D" *viz.* (1) "A." The masterly work of the Earl of Crawford entitled "*The Earldom of Mar in sunshine and shade*," two vols., 8vo, 1882; (2) "B." Skene's "*Celtic Scotland*," three vols., 8vo, 1880; (3) "C." An article on "*The early Earls of Mar*," by G. Burnett, Lyon King of Arms, in "*The Genealogist, N.S.*," vol. iv, pp. 177—193; (4) "D." Another article in the same work, vol. iii, pp. 1-24 (which, doubtless, tho' unsigned, is by the same hand) entitled "*The Earldom of Mar*," at the end of which last named article is printed the act, 6 Aug. 1885, for the restitution of that dignity.

(c) See vol. i, p. 68, *sub* "Angus," for a fuller account of these seven Earldoms.

(d) Donald, an early *Mormaer of Mar*, is said to have been one of the 10 Mormaers [S.] who crossed over to Ireland to assist Brien Boroihme against the Danes, by whom both were slain at the battle of Clontarf in 1014. The names of Donald's successors are unknown until the time of Roderick, early in the 12th century, who, accordingly, is in the text numbered as the *first* Earl of Mar.

II. 1140? 2. MORGUND, EARL OF MAR [S.] He is stated (which is doubtful) to have been son(a) of Gillocher,(b) a previous MORMAER OF MAR. "His legitimacy was challenged, but appears to have stood its ground."(c) He and his wife, "Agnes, Countess of Mar," grant jointly several charters between 1141 and 1178, his said wife, in some cases, granting charters alone."(d) He possibly m. (as a second wife) Orabilis,(e) da. of one Ness, a foreign settler in Fifeshire. He d. before 1183, probably about 1178, leaving male issue, by none of which, however, he was immediately succeeded.

III. 1178? 3. GILCHRIST, EARL OF MAR [S.], appears in charters, 1178—1244.(f) "His filiation is unknown; he represented apparently the succession opposed in hereditary claim to that of Earl Morgund."(c) He was a great benefactor to the church. "He seems, along with a son Malcolm, to have been witness [1208-14] to a charter(g) to the monastery of Cupar.

IV. 1220? 4. DUNCAN, EARL OF MAR [S.], one of the four sons of EARL MORGUND and the COUNTESS AGNES, both abovenamed. He "was Earl of Mar, early in the reign [1214-19] of Alexander II." being "Gilchrist's successor in the Earldom,"(h) by whose heirs, probably, it was that his legitimacy was disputed before 1233. He was living 1239, but d. before Sep. 1244.

V. 1240? 5. WILLIAM, EARL OF MAR [S.], s. and h. His right to the succession was unsuccessfully contested, on the ground of the illegitimacy(i) of his father Duncan) and grandfather (Morgund), by Alan Doorward,(k)

(a) His relation to his predecessor is unknown, beyond that (as was the rule in all the Celtic tribes) each was descended in the *male* line from the common founder of the race. It was not till after the introduction of the *feudal* system into Scotland, in the 12th century, that "the Celtic Earldoms, originally descendible to *male agnates* only, became thenceforward descendible to *heirs general*, like every other description of hereditary office and dignity as amply proved by Lord Hailes." [See "A" (vol. i, p. 168), as in note "b" on p. 218.]

(b) In a document purporting to be a grant, 16 Kalends of June 1171, from King William the Lion, of the Earldom of Mar to this Morgund, the grantee is styled "*filium Gillocheri, quondam Comitis de Marre.*" This deed was possessed by Selden and was printed by him in his "*Titles of Honour.*" There are, however, great doubts of its authenticity. [See "A" (vol. i, p. 168), and "B" (vol. iii, pp. 441—447), as in note "b" on p. 218.]

(c) See "A" (vol. i, p. 167), as in note "b" on p. 218.]

(d) "These charters are undoubtedly suggestive of Morgund having been Earl *in right of his wife*, and such the late Joseph Robertson believed to have been the case; but it is, on the other hand, difficult to recognise this supposition with the importance afterwards attached to the question of Morgund's legitimacy, and it would rather seem that some other explanation must be sought of Agnes thus dealing with the Earldom in her own name." [See "C" as in note "b" on p. 218.]

(e) See "C" as in note "b" on p. 218, for a contradiction of Dr. Skene's hypothesis [in "B" as in said note "b"] that this Orabilis was the wife of Earl Gilchrist.

(f) "The contemporary charter evidence to support the surmise that Gilchrist had superseded Morgund in the Earldom, *circa* 1170, is worthless." [See "C" is in note "b," on p. 218.]

(g) See "C" as in note "b" on p. 218, where it is added that in "the abbreviate" of this chartulary the words "*G. de Mar*" have been wrongly extended to "*Gratney, Comes,*" but that "there is no where else a trace of any *Gratney*, Earl of Mar, at that date."

(h) See "C" as in note "b" on p. 218.

(i) This alleged illegitimacy was certainly never established; indeed, since the succession of Earl Donald, "no other Earl of Mar appears except as his *direct* descendant." [See "A" as in note "b" on p. 218.]

(k) Alan was s. and h. of Thomas Durward, who [1140-80?] had contested the succession of Earl Morgund. This Thomas, formerly Thomas de Lundin, was the King's "Hostiarius" or "Doorward," which name of Durward he assumed. It has been

who, in such case, claimed to be the rightful heir.(a) He was one of the nobles at the treaty of Newcastle, 1244; was Great Chamberlain [S.], 1252-55, and again from 1262, or earlier, to 1267, having in 1270 been sent to England to recover the Earldom of Huntingdon for the Crown [S.] He m. firstly, Elizabeth, da. of William (COMYN), EARL OF BUCHAN [S.], by Marjory, *suo jure*, COUNTESS OF BUCHAN [S.] She d. 1267. He m. secondly, Muriel, da. of Malise, EARL OF STRATHERN [S.], by Marjory, da. of Robert DE MUSCHAMP, to whom she was coheir. He d. about 1281.(b) His widow, who, only a few months before her death, did homage to King Edward I., d. s.p., before 12 Nov. 1491.

VI. 1281? 6. DONALD, EARL OF MAR [S.], s. and h., by first wife. He had been *Knighted* at Scone, 29 Sep. 1270; was a party to the marriage contract, 15 July 1281 of the Princess Margaret [S.] also to the convention at Brigham, 17 March 1289/90; and, as one of the "*Septem Comites regni Scotiæ*"(c) protested against the choice of Balliol and in favour of Bruce as King of Scotland. He swore fealty to King Edward I., 13 June 1291, and again, 10 July and 28 Aug. 1276, having been in arms against him at Dunbar in April 1296. He m. Helen, widow of Malcolm, EARL OF FIFE [S.] (who d. 1266), da. of Llewellyn, PRINCE OF NORTH WALES. He was living, 25 July 1291, but d. very soon afterwards.

VII. 1292? 7. GRATNEY, EARL OF MAR [S.], s. and h. He was thanked by King Edward I., on 11 June 1297, for his seal. He m. Christiana, sister of Robert, King of Scotland [1306-29], da. of Robert (BRUCE), EARL OF CARRICK [S.], by Margaret, *suo jure*, COUNTESS OF CARRICK [S.] With her he obtained the castle of Kildrummie and *the Lordship* (sometimes called Earldom) *of Garioch*.(d) He d. before the end of 1305. His widow m. Sir Christopher SETON. She m. (thirdly), Sir Andrew MORAY, of Bothwell (b. 1298) before 22 July 1326, for which (they being related in the 4th degree) dispensation was granted 20 Sep. following.(e) She d. at a great age in 1357.

VIII. 1305? 8. DONALD, EARL OF MAR [S.], s. and h., who *suc.* to the Earldom when a child. He was brought up in England, whose cause he at first favoured till 1327, when he opposed the same. He m. Isabel STEWART,(f) who, thro' maternal descent, inherited from the Baliol family part of the lands of Cavers. He was chosen REGENT [S.] in July 1332, "and to his incompetency and imprudence has been ascribed the disastrous defeat at Dupplin in Aug. following,"(g) where he was slain. His widow m. before 13 Sep. 1344, Geoffrey MOUBRAY.

---

suggested that his mother was da. and h. of Earl Gilchrist. It is manifest that his claim shews that at this period the Earldom was *feudalised*, so as to descend to the heir *general*, for the family of Lundin could have descended from that of Mar only thro' *female* descent.

(a) Alan had obtained a commission from the Pope to the Prior of Aberdeen, Oct. 1257, for investigating the legitimacy of Morgund, having alleged that "William of Mar withheld the Earldom of Mar, of right belonging to the aforesaid Alan," and "it seems," says Burnett, "to have been in compromise of this claim that the Doorwards [Durwards] acquired the district between Don and Dee, known as Coull and Oneil."

(b) "He was dead before 1281," say Burnett [see "C" as in note "b" on p. 218] who adds, that Earl *Donald* (his s. and h.) was living "*as Earl of Mar*" 15 July 1281, tho', in another place, he states that Earl William "was alive as late as Michaelmas, 1281," for which the (unimpeachable) authority of *Bain's Calendar*, ii, 202" is given.

(c) The names of the other Earldoms, excepting only that of Fife, do not appear in this protest which was edited by Palgrave, for the Record Commissioners.

(d) See vol. iv, p. 14, note "d," *sub* "Garioch," for Mr. Burnett's remarks "as to *the Garioch dignity*."

(e) See Mr. Bain's note on this marriage in "*the Genealogist*," N.S. vi. p. 63.

(f) "There is" writes Mr. Burnett "record evidence that she was a Stewart [Fœd. ii, p. 1019]" but not that she was (as commonly asserted), da. of Sir Alexander Stewart of Bonkyl." "If so she must have been by a different mother from the Earl of Angus and [have] inherited [Cavers], thro' her mother." [See "C," as in note "b," p. 218.]

(g) See "C" as in note "b" on p. 218.

She m. thirdly before 23 March 1346/7, William Carswell and d. before 15 Jan. 1347/8, leaving him surviving.

"Sir Richard Talbot, of Goderich, one of the *disinherited Barons*, who, in right of his wife, a Comyn, claimed large possessions in Scotland, had, on 17 Feb. 1333/4, a grant of Kildrummy Castle from Edward Baliol and for a short time designed himself LORD OF MAR [S.], and on one occasion (according to the chronicle of Lanercost) EARL OF MAR [S.] But Christian Bruce, mother of the late Earl, retained possession of Kildrummy, and Talbot was before long glad to escape out of Scotland."(a)

IX. 1332. 9. Thomas, Earl of Mar [S.], only s. and h. of Earl Donald, and Isabel, his wife, both abovenamed; b. about 1330, being a minor in 1348. He was a hostage in 1357 for the ransom of King David II. [S.] from whom he obtained confirmation of the lands and Lordship of Garioch(b) in 1358, late held by his grandmother, Christian Bruce, deceased, becoming thus (according to some) Earl of Mar and Garioch [S.]; Great Chamberlain [S.], 1358 and 1359. In 1360 he was in the service of England, save only as against Scotland, with whose King, however, he was frequently in disgrace. He m. firstly (dispensations 15 Aug. 1352, and again in 1354), Margaret, *suo jure* Countess of Menteith [S.] (see that dignity), widow of John Moray, of Bothwell. She was divorced before 9 Sep. 1361.(c) He m. secondly Margaret, *suo jure* Countess of Angus [S.] (see that dignity.) He d. s.p. between 20 June 1376, and 22 July 1377. His profligate widow (who, in his lifetime or very shortly afterwards, was mother of a bastard son, George Douglas, afterwards [1389] Earl of Angus [S.]) was living (being styled "*Countess of Angus and Mar*") as late as 23 March 1417/8.

X. 1376-77. 10. Margaret, *suo jure* Countess of Mar or Countess of Mar and Garioch [S.], only sister and heir, m. probably about Nov. 1357 William (Douglas), 1st Earl of Douglas [S.], who appears accordingly as "*Earl of Douglas and Mar*" in 1377 and 1380. He d. May 1384. She m. secondly (as his first wife) Sir John Swinton, of Swinton (slain at Homelden 14 Sep. 1402), by whom she had no issue, but who, after the death of her son, Earl James, in 1388, is styled "*Lord of Mar*."(d) She was alive 5 Dec. 1389, and apparently 18 March 1390/1, but d. s.p.m.s. before 22 Nov. 1395.

[James (Douglas), Earl of Douglas [S.], only s. and h. ap. of the above Countess Margaret (by her first husband), b. about 1358; *suc.* his father, as Earl of Douglas, in May 1384. He is once (23 July 1388) described as "*Earl of Douglas and Mar*" (probably by a mistake of the scribe) but, even to that charter, his *seal* is as "*Douglas*" alone.(e) He d. s.p. legit. in his mother's lifetime, 19 Aug. 1388.]

For fuller particulars see "Douglas" Earldom [S.], cr. 1358.

XI. 1395? 11. Isabel, *suo jure* Countess of Mar, or Countess of Mar and Garioch [S.], only da. and h. by first husband; b. about 1360,

(a) See "C" as in note "b," p. 218.

(b) In his charters "in and about 1359 he generally designs himself *Earl of Mar and Lord of Cavers and of the Garioch*." See "C" as in note "b" on p. 218.

(c) Date of dispensation for her marriage with the Regent-Duke of Albany. See letter by "Sigma" in "*N. and Q.*" (7th S., x. 164), as to a marriage in 1360 with Sir John Drummond, probably referring to her mother, not to herself.

(d) Having had no issue by the Countess he would not be entitled to be designated (by courtesy) Earl of Mar.

(e) It, indeed, is possible that the comitatus of Mar might have been surrendered to him by his mother to whom (in that case) at his death it would again revert. The seal of his father, to whom unquestionably it *had* been so surrendered, is inscribed "*Sigillum Willelmi, Comitis de Douglas et Mar*," and he is so described "in every one of the numerous charters granted to him and by him subsequently to 1377." [See "D" (p. 17) as in note "b," p. 218.]

and *suc. to the peerage dignity*, on the death before 22 Nov. 1395(a) of her mother the Countess Margaret, having previously, on the death (1388) of her brother, Earl Douglas, abovenamed, *suc.* to the unintailed estates of the house of Douglas. She *m.* firstly, Sir Malcolm DRUMMOND, of Drummond (br. of Annabella, the Queen Consort [S.], who in her right is styled (1398), Lord of Mar,(b) and who *d. s.p.* before 27 May 1403.(c) She *m.* secondly, Sir Alexander STEWART, who had besieged her castle of Kildrummie, and forced her to make a charter, 12 Aug. 1404, settling the Earldom, failing the heirs of her body, on him and his heirs. This charter (which was extorted by violence, and which would in any case have been invalid till it had the Royal sanction), he surrendered five weeks later, 19 Sep. 1404,(d) when (at her age of, probably, 40 or upwards) she chose him in free marriage, and on 9 Dec. 1404 (when the marriage took place) by a new charter in which she styles herself "*Isabel de Douglas, Comitissa de Mar et de Garviach*" settled the *Earldom of Mar*, the castle of Kildrummie, the forest of Jedburgh, the Lordship of Garviach or Garioch, the Barony of Strathelvech in Banffshire, the Barony of Crichmond in Buchan, &c. to the said Alexander, who became thenceforth EARL OF MAR [S.], with rem. to the heirs to be begotten between them, whom failing, with rem. to her right heirs "*ex utraque parte.*"(e) The charter of 9 Dec. 1404, was confirmed by Royal charter, 21 Jan. 1404/5.(f) The Countess *d. s.p.* previous to 10 Feb. 1407/8.

(a) An obligation of King Robert III. [S.], not to accept any resignation, which "Isabel, *Countess of Mar and Garioch*" may make of those Earldoms, in prejudice of the Erskine family, the heirs thereof, is dat. 22 Nov. 1395. This important document was produced at the decreet of ranking in 1606, and is printed in Lord Hailes's *Sutherland Case.*

(b) See p. 221, note "d."

(c) It is probable (and such is Mr. Tytler's opinion) that Alex. Stewart, who *m.* his widow, was the virtual author of his death.

(d) The charter of 12 Aug. 1404 (notwithstanding its resignation) was registered more than 70 years later, ! ! by the special command of King James III. [S.], 26 April 1476, for the purpose of supporting the Crown in its claim to dispose of this important Earldom. The instrument, 19 Sep. 1404, of the *renunciation of the August charter* (a charter extorted but a few weeks previously) "altho' not produced from the Mar chest in 1875, was there in 1764, when the article "*Mar*" in Douglas's peerage was written, where it is described at length. It was produced and founded on in the processes instituted before the Court of Session by the Treasurer-Earl of Mar where, we have minute description of the instrument; and in one of these processes a special interlocutor was pronounced affirming its authenticity. It is hardly necessary to say *if no sasine had passed* on the charter of 12 Aug., it was so completely *extinguished by the renunciation* [made a few weeks later] that *no sasine* could *afterwards* have been taken on it, and it *could not* [consequently, 72 years *after such extinction*] have been *validated* by the Royal confirmation." [See "A" (vol. i, p. 206) as in note "b," on p. 218.]

(e) The doctrine of *materna maternis*, by which, according to English law, "a subject derived from a mother does not go to the children's *paternal* heirs (supposing the children to have succeeded and died without issue) but to the heirs of the mother" does not prevail in Scotland; hence "if the Earldom had still been descendible to heirs at law there might in 1435 have been an opening for the Douglas representative," but the Supreme Civil Court decided, in 1624, that as the charter of 1404 contained lands that had descended to the Countess from the families *both* of her father (Douglas) and her mother (Mar), the words (which by accident or otherwise are *omitted* in the royal confirmation, 21 Jan. 1404/5), should be interpreted as "paterna paternis, materna maternis." [See Riddell's "*Remarks*" (1833), pp. 45-55. It is certain, however, that Janet, wife of Sir Thomas Erskine, the great granddaughter (thro' her mother's mother) of Earl Gratney, was looked upon as the heir presumptive to the Countess Isabel, as early as 22 Nov. 1393, when King Robert III. [S.] declared, under the great seal, that he would not accept any resignation of the Countess Isabel to their prejudice. This promise, indeed, he retracted, 24 May 1397, so far as any such resignation made, or to be made, in favour of George Douglas, afterwards Earl of Angus, but finally (practically) substantiated, when confirming (21 Jan. 1404/5,) the settlement made by the Countess Isabel, dated 9 Dec. 1404.

(f) It is either from this date or from 1395 that the Earldom of Mar takes its precedence on the Union Roll, these being the oldest vouchers produced by the then Earl of Mar at the decreet of ranking in 1606. The charters of 12 Aug. 1404, and 9 Dec. 1404, and the Royal confirmation of the latter, 21 Jan. 1404/5, are printed in "A," (vol. i, p. 207), as in note "b" on p. 218.

XII. 1426 to 1435. *1.* ALEXANDER (STEWART), EARL OF MAR, or EARL OF MAR AND GARIOCH [S.], by virtue of the charter of 9 Dec. 1404, above mentioned, made by his wife, the Countess Isabel, in favour of him and their common issue, was a bastard son of Robert (STEWART), EARL OF BUCHAN [S.], who was 4th s. of **King Robert II.** [S.] He was several times (1406, 1407, and again 1416), Ambassador to England; assisted the Duke of Burgundy in 1408 in quelling an insurrection at Liege; was in command of the Royal forces at the battle of Hawlaw, against the Lord of the Isles, 1411, and was, about 1418, Warden of the Marches. Tho' by the death s.p. of his wife, the Countess Isabel, above mentioned, and the consequent failure of any of *his* heirs being in succession to the Earldom he had become but a *life* tenant thereof, he obtained from his Crown on his resignation (just as if such resignation had been that of a dignity to which he was *absolutely* entitled) a regrant thereof, and was *cr.*, 28 May 1426, EARL OF MAR [S.] for his life, with rem. to his bastard son, Sir Thomas STEWART, and the heirs male of his body with rem. to the Crown. He *m.*, secondly, Marie, widow of Thierry DE LIENDEN (who *d.* 1408), da. and h. of Willem VAN HOORN, of Duffel in Brabant, by his wife, Marie VAN RANDERODE. The will of this lady ("*Dame de Duffel*") is dat. April 1433, and she was dead before 28 June 1436.(a) The Earl *d.* s.p. legit. 1435, when (his bastard son, who was in rem. to the dignity, having *d.* s.p. and v.p.), *the Earldom cr. by the charter of* 1426, *reverted to the Crown.*

[SIR THOMAS STEWART, Master of Mar, bastard s. of the above, was, by the charter of 28 May 1426, in remainder to the Earldom of Mar [S.] thereby created. He *m.* about 1425, Elizabeth, widow of John (STEWART), EARL OF BUCHAN [S.], who *d.* 17 Aug. 1424. He *d.* s.p. and v.p. His widow, who retained the lands of Garioch in dower, *m.* thirdly, as his first wife, William (SINCLAIR), EARL OF ORKNEY, *afterwards* EARL OF CAITHNESS [S.], (who *d.* before 1476) and *d.* before 1456.]

XIII. 1435. *12.* ROBERT (ERSKINE), EARL OF MAR [S.], cousin and heir, *ex parte maternâ*, to Isabel, *suo jure* Countess of Mar, being great grandson of Elyne,(b) 1st or only(c) da. of Earl Gratney abovenamed, the said

---

(a) Her nephew and heir, "Johan Van Hoorn, Sire de Perwes," speaks of her at that date as deceased. He styles her "*Countesse de Marr et de Garriach, Dame de pays de Duffel et de Gheel*" [*Scot. Antiquary or northern N. and Q.*," vol. vii, p. 1.] The Earl is spoken of, on 13 March 1410 [*Reg. Mag. Sig.*, p. 250], as "*Alexr. Senes-chall, Comes de Mar et de Garviach ac Dnus de Duffle in Brabancia.*"

(b) In the retours before the Court of Session in 1628 (relative to the claim of the then Earl of Mar to the alienated estates of his ancestors) this Elyne is expressly called "*Great grandmother of Robert*, who was grandfather of Alexander, who was great grandfather of John [the then] Earl of Mar."

(c) It seems not improbable that there was another (a younger) da. of Earl Gratney thro' whom it was that the Lords Lyle [S.] claimed a moiety of the Mar estates. No such da. is, however, assigned to him by Burnett (see "C" as in note "b," on p. 218), nor in Wood's "*Douglas*" (under "Marr") tho' she exists in the *old* edition of 1764. Sir John Lyle (father of Sir Robert Lyle and grandfather of the 1st Lord Lyle [S.]), is stated by Crawford (Peerage [S.], 1716, p. 291), to have "married a lady who was one of the coheirs of the Earldom of Mar, tho' I know not precisely who she was, but in her right the Lord Lyle in the time of King James II. laid claim to a part of that estate and from thenceforth added the coat of Mar to his paternal arms." The continuator of Fordun alludes to this claim of the Lyle family, stating, under 1438, "Obiit Alexander Stewart, Comes de Marr, et, quia bastardus erat, Rex illi successit, quamvis jure hereditario *Domini Erskine et Lyle* successisse debuissent." This agrees well with the fact that in *April* 1438 Lord Erskine was served heir to [but] half of the Comitatus of Mar, tho' only six months later he was served heir to the other half, indicating, perhaps, that in the meanwhile the Lyle family had compromised for or given up their claim; at all events such claim was never afterwards urged to the estates of *Mar*, tho' as to those of *Garioch* it appears to have been continued somewhat longer. The petition of Sir Thomas Erskine, 13 March 1390/1, stating that his wife is heir presumptive to *half* the Earldom, favours also the idea of the Lyle family being such

Robert being 1st, or 1st surv.(a) s. and h. of Sir Thomas Erskine, of Alloa and Dun, by his second wife, Janet, widow of Sir David Barclay, da. and h. of Sir Edward Keith, of Synton(b) and Christian his wife, sister and h. of Sir John Menteith, of Strathgartney, da. of Sir John Menteith, of Arran, by Elyne, da. of Gratney, Earl of Mar abovenamed, which Elyne was sister of Donald, Earl of Mar, the grandfather of the abovenamed (*suo jure*) Countess Isabel.(c) This Robert Erskine,

---

heir to the other half, but is (doubtless) capable of being otherwise explained, *e.g.*, by supposing there to have been a younger sister to (Janet) Erskine's wife or to (Christian) her mother. There does not, however, appear to be any document whereby the Erskine family recognise the claim of the Lyle or any other rival family to a moiety. The ground of the claim is very obscure and might possibly be as representatives or co-representatives of some of the earlier Earls of Mar.

(a) "Alexander Erskyn de eadem" was not improbably his elder brother. He was one of the hostages for James I. [S.] and is alluded to in a letter from Henry II., 20 June 1432 (*Rot. Scot.*, ii, 276.) He must have *d.* s.p. soon afterwards. [*Ex. inform.* M. J. Shaw-Stewart.]

(b) The estate of Synton, which was acquired by the marriage of Isabella of Synton with Sir Edward Keith, was (or at all events the superiority of it was) in possession of the Earls of Mar as late as 1620.

(c) The following pedigree illustrates the relationship of the various parties—

Donald, Earl of Mar., [S.], *d.* 1294. ═ | Robert Bruce, Earl of Carrick [S.] grandson of Robert Bruce and **Isabel of Scotland.** ═

Gratney, Earl of Mar., *d.* 1300. ═ Christian Bruce, heiress of Garioch, *d.* 1305. | Isabel of Mar, 1st wife. ═ **King Robert I.** [S.] 1306-1329. ═ Elizabeth de Burgh, 2nd wife.

Donald, Earl of Mar, the Regent, *d.* 1332. ═ | Sir John Menteith, of Arran, *d.* before 1359. ═ Elyn "of Mar," *b.* about 1297, "niece to King Robert." | Margory, *m.* Walter the High Steward. ═ | **King David II.** [S.] 1331-1371, *d.* s.p.

Sir John Menteith, of Strathgartney, *d.* s.p | Sir Edward Keith, of Synton, *d.* 1347. ═ Christian [*Query* if not the same who *m.*, 1355, Sir Robert Erskine.] ∷ Sir Robert Erskine of Alloa and Dun. ═ Beatrix Lindsay.

Sir David Barclay, *d.* s.p.m., 1st husb. ═ Janet, living 1412, *d.* before 1416. ═ Sir Thomas Erskine, a hostage in 1357, *d.* about 1419. ═ Mary Douglas, *d.* s.p. about 1366, 1st wife.

Robert, Lord Erskine, 1st son and heir of his mother (as well as of his father) retoured in 1438 as Earl of Mar. ═ → Earls of Mar. | John Erskine of Dun. ═ → Erskine of Dun.

Thomas, Earl of Mar, *d.* s.p. 1377. | William (Douglas), Earl of Douglas and Mar. ═ Margaret, *suo jure* Countess of Mar, *d.* 1390. | **King Robert II.** [S.] 1371-1390. ═

James (Douglas) Earl of Douglas, *d.* s.p. 1388. | Sir Malcolm Drummond, *m.* before 1390, *d.* s.p. 1402, 1st husb. ═ Isabel, *suo jure* Countess of Mar, d. s.p. 1407. ═ Alexander (Stewart) Earl of Mar, *d.* s.p. 1435.

The above pedigree is confirmed in all substantial points by "*A genealogicall history of the family of Mar by Mr. George Erskyn, Bailie of Alloa* [so appointed in 1701] *in the year 1709*," which, having been produced from the Mar charter chest, was in the

who was taken prisoner in 1402, at the battle of Homildon), *suc.* his father about

opinion of the Committee for Privileges (23 May 1870) "admissible in evidence *quantum valeat.*" The following are extracts therefrom [*Mar Evidence*, 1868-75, pp. 514—515.]

"Helen of Mar, da. to the last Gratnay, Earle of Mar, *m.* Sir John Monteith, Dominus de Arran, Scipinco, Strathgartney and Knapdale, who had to him two daughters [1] Christian and [2] (—) the younger [who] died without issue. Dame Christian Monteith *m.* Sir Edward Keith, of Syntoun, who had to him Joanetta. He was killed at the battle of Durham in the year 1347. She [*i.e.*, Dame Christian] *m.* Sir Robert of Erskine, of whom no issue. Dame Jannet Keith *m.* first Sir David Barclay, who they alleadge was murthered by the Douglas's, by whom no issue [*i.e.*, none that was *her* heir, she having, subsequently, *male* issue by her second husband] and after her death *m.* Sir Thomas of Erskine [being by him mother of Robert Erskine *her son and heir*], by which marriage the two families of Mar and Erskine were joyned in one."

Again, "Sir Robert of Erskine of that ilk, Baron of the Baronies of Strathgartney, Alloa, Dun, Kinnoul, Nisbet, Edenham, Crawboth, and Malherb," &c., "*m.* Beatrix Lindsay, da. to Sir David Lindsay, who had to him [1] Thomas [2] Sir Nicoll Erskine of Kinnoul and [3] Isobell, Lady Olyphant; after her death he *m.* the above designed Dame Christian Monteith (da. to Dame Helen of Mar) who had no issue by him."

"Sir Thomas of Erskine, of that ilk, *m.* the above Dame Jannet Keith, relict of Sir David Barclay. She had to him [1] Robert, afterwards Earle of Mar, in her right [2] Sir John Erskine, who gott the lands of Dun to him and the heirs male of his body."

"The said Thomas gave in [1] a petition to K. Rob. in full Parl. in 1390, craving that the King might not receive any resignations or confirmations of lands and others which did belong to Isobell, Countes of Mar, in prejudice of his wife, *who was her next heir*, which the King promised not only not to do, but declared, in case he had already granted any, the same to be null. The said Sir Thomas also made [2] another protest in Parl. in 1390, mentioning he heard there was a contract made betwixt the above Sir Malcolm of Drummond and Sir John Swintoun *anent the Earldom of Mar*, therefor beseeching his Majestie not to grant resignation or confirmation of the same *in prejudice* of his wife, which the King promised not to do. *Both said petitions are in the Earle of Mar's charter chest* with the King's declaration, under the quarter seall upon the first dated 22 Nov. [1393], and of the King's reign the 4th year."

The proofs of the heirship of Robert, Lord Erskine, to the Earldom of Mar, which had to be established in proving the preamble of the Mar restitution act of 1885, were most ably set forth by Mr. W. A. Lindsay, the Counsel for the heir general, and are summarised in "*the Genealogist*" N.S., vol. iii, pp. 16-19, to the following effect.

The tenure of the Earldom, as *in their own right*, by the Countess Margaret and (her da.) the Countess Isabel, was fully demonstrated, as also was the heirship of John, Lord Erskine, in 1565, to the Countess Isabel, involving the validity of the charter of 9 Dec. 1404, the *heirship*, under it, *of Robert, Lord Erskine* [in 1435] to the lands and title, &c. To establish this heirship, the documentary evidence included (1) A grant of Strathgartney, 1359, to Sir John Menteith, called son of Ellen of Mar, Ellen herself being styled niece of King Robert (Acts Parl. [S.], I., p. 524); (2) A crown charter, 1368 to Sir Robert Erskine† and Christian Keith, his wife (the King's cousin), of Alloa in exchange for Strathgartney (*ibid.* p 534; *Mar minutes*, p. 381); (3) a deliverance by King Robert III. on a petition, 18 March 1390/1, of Sir Thomas Erskine, stating that Janet, his wife, was, failing Isabel, wife of Sir Malcolm Drummond, heir "by right of inheritance" to half of the said Earldom of Mar, and the Lordship of Garioch; (4) the obligation by the same King, 22 Nov. 1395, not to sanction any alienation by Isabel Douglas, Countess of Mar and Garioch in prejudice of the heirs of Sir Thomas Erskine, as *veri hæredes* of these Earldoms; (5) "a series of entries in the Exchequer Rolls (*Scottish Record Series*) regarding a certain annuity

† See vol. iv. Appendix, pp. i and ii (Nos. 19 and 23) for the Papal dispensation for the marriage of "*Robertus Erskine, Miles et Christiana de Beth*" [*i.e.*, Keth] in 1355, and for that of "*Thomas Erskine et Maria de Douglas*," in 1366. It is possible that this Christian, was *da.* of Sir Edward Keith and Christian, his wife (as acutely suggested by Mr. Hallen, *vide infra*) and not (as in the above pedigrees) Christian, *née* Menteith, the *widow* of the said Sir Edward Keith.

1419; was one of the hostages for the ransom of King James [S.] in 1424, (his revenue

---

from the fishings of Aberdeen taken in connexion with the proof (by means of a charter of 1357; *Reg. Mag. Sig.*, p. 33, No. 86), that the island of *Arran* then *belonged to Sir John Monteith*." The payment of this annuity was as under; 1373-84, to Robert Erskine, husband of Christian Keith; 1386, to Christian Keith, widow of Robert Erskine; 1389—1404, to Sir Thomas Erskine, husband of Janet Barclay; 1405, to Janet Barclay, widow of Sir Thomas Erskine; 1416, &c., to Sir Robert Erskine, son and heir of the said Janet. In the entries of 1428 this annuity is expressly stated "to have been granted by a charter of Robert II. *in excambium terrarum de Arane*. The chain of proof was completed by the retours of 1438; the charters granted by Robert, Lord Erskine, *as Earl of Mar*; the service of John, Lord Erskine, in 1565; the charter of 23 June 1565, with its ratification [by act of Parl. 19 April 1567], and the act [of Parl.] of 1587." The evidence of the heirship of the said Robert Erskine to the Countess Isabel was thus held to be proved (his mother, Janet, to whom he was heir, being shewn to be da. and heir of Christian who was da. and eventually heir to Sir John Monteith and to Ellen of Mar, his wife), and the Royal assent to the bill was given 6 Aug. 1885, whereby, in consequence of the above descent, the heir general of the (then) late Earl of Mar was restored to the peerage which "descended" to the said Countess Isabel.

It will be observed that in these proofs the *paternal* descent of the said Janet, wife of Sir Thomas Erskine, is not mentioned, and that inasmuch as she is always styled "Janet Barclay," while (in like manner) Christian, the sometime wife of Sir Robert Erskine, is similarly styled "Christian Keith," it would be a natural inference that (according to the present usage of Scotland) the father of Janet was a Barclay, and that the father of Christian was a Keith. An ingenious article in "*The Genealogist*," N.S., vol. ix, pp. 4-6 (by the Rev. A. W. Cornelius Hallen) assumes that such *was* the case, and, indeed, that (*more Scotico*) it could not be otherwise. It accordingly deduces the descent of Janet from her maternal grandmother, Ellen of Mar, thro' the same *mother*, indeed, as in the tabular pedigree above, but in lieu of Sir Edward Keith) gives her Sir David Barclay for a *father*, as in the pedigree next below.

Sir John Monteith.=Elyne of Mar, da. of Gratney, Earl of Mar. *b.* circa 1297.

Sir Edward Keith, killed 1346, 1st husband.=Christian Monteith.=Sir David Barclay of Brechin and Dun, killed 1353, 2nd husband.=Margaret de Brechin, *m.* 1325, 1st wife.

Beatrice Lindsay, 1st wife.=Sir Robert Erskine, *d.* circa 1384.=Christian Keith, *d.* s.p., circ. 1389. | Sir David Barclay of Brechin, *d.* 1373. | Janet Barclay from whom the Maules descend.

Mary Douglas, d. s.p., 1st wife.=Sir Thomas Erskine.=Janet Barclay, heiress of Dun, *m.* ante 1368. | Margaret Barclay, heiress of Brechin, *m.* 1378 Walter (Stewart) Earl of Athole: line failed.

Sir Robert Erskine from whom the Earls of Mar. | John Erskine from whom the house of Dun.

The author of the above cleverly constructed pedigree states in its support [1] that "the evidence produced during the Mar case brought out *the fact* that the wife of Sir Thomas Erskine was Janet Barclay, *daughter of Sir David Barclay*, of Brechin, by his wife, Christian Monteith, da. of Elyne of Mar." This, however, is clearly an error for (so far from *any descent from Barclay* having been therein established) the pedigrees, brought from the Mar charter chest (which were received and acquiesced in by the Committee) accounted for the heirship of the Erskines to Mar thro' *descent from Keith* (whose lands at Synton they inherited) which descent is *incompatible* with a descent from Barclay. [2] That the estate of Dun was brought by the said Janet to the Erskine family, she having inherited it from her father, Sir David Barclay. But that estate (*ex inform.* Joseph Bain, F.S.A.), was, before 1375, in possession of Sir Robert Erskine, the *father of Thomas*, who married the said Janet. Presumably,

being then estimated at 1,000 marks,) and was set at liberty 19 June 1425. He was cr.

also, as Janet is credited (not only with a sister, also named Janet, but) with a brother, *he*, and not *she*, would have inherited any estate vested in their common father. The chief point however, in support of this pedigree, is [3] that the appellation of "Janet Barclay" and "Christian Keith" must *of necessity* indicate the *maiden* name of these ladies and not the name of a previous husband, and that such paternity can only thus be accounted for. On this point Mr. W. A. Lindsay writes (24 Jan. 1893), as under, "Now, as regards women's names; Egidia, half sister of Robert II., married Sir James Lindsay in 1351 and was thrice re-married. All thro' her career, as wife of Eglintoun and of Douglas, she is called *Lindsay* [not *Stewart*.] Stewart was, perhaps, not then a surname. Of course women were always called by their *maiden* names [in] later [times] but *query* when did this become the established rule? In very early times, I doubt, if they bore any surnames at all. It appears to me that we know too little of this [subject] to argue from Janet being called Barclay that she was *born* Barclay. It really comes, I think, to no more than this [that] because Barclay must have been her maiden name had she lived in the 16th century, it was, therefore, her name in the 14th."

The matter, however, of "Janet Barclay" whether "widow" or "spinster" is likely to be thrashed out in the current vol. (vol. ix) of "*The Genealogist*," N.S., in which one article on the subject, by Mr. J. Horace Round, has already (Jan. 1893) appeared.

Without in any way attempting to *disprove* the Barclay descent, the following objections to it, of a negative as well as a positive kind, may be considered (1) the absence of any proof of the marriage of Christian, *neé* Menteith, with Sir David (or any other) Barclay by whom she could be mother of Janet. (2) the attestation (*Registrum de Panmure*, vol. ii, p. 230) of Thomas Bisset in 1437, sometime servitor to Sir Thomas Erskine and Dame Janet his wife, to the effect that he had frequently heard that the said Janet was the mother (by a former husband "the last Sir David Barclay, of Brechin"), of [Margaret] the Countess of Atholo [heiress of Brechin] the mother of David Stewart. This important testimony, given by one likely to be well acquainted with the facts of the case (which makes it impossible that Janet should be the da. of Sir David Barclay the elder, who in the pedigree next above is made her *husband's* father) is rejected altogether by Mr. Hallen, chiefly, apparently, on the ground that as Janet was the wife of Sir Thomas de Erskine in 1369 (*Reg. Mag. Sig.*, p. 64), she could not have been the relict of *the last* Sir David Barclay of Brechin, who was alive in 1371 (*Exch. Rolls*, ii, 394), tho' dead in 1373 (*Ib.* 433). The identity, however of the "David Barclay," Deputy of the Sheriff of Fife, to whom a payment is made in 1371, with "*Sir* David Barclay" [of Brechin], the wardship of whose da. and h. was in 1373 granted to Sir Thomas Erskine, is, tho' very probable, not conclusive, when opposed to contradictory evidence. The pedigree of Barclay is very hazy. The last Sir David of Brechin is generally made *son* of the Sir David, who *m.* the heiress of Brechin, yet he mention Sir David Barclay and Sir Alexander Lindsay, as his *uncles*, so that it seems more probable, that his mother was a sister to the said Alexander and his father a brother of the said David, he himself being (consequently) *grandson* (not son) of the Sir David who *m.* the heiress of Brechin [*Ex inform*, W. A. Lindsay]. Another David Barclay is alluded to ["*Athenæum*," 3 July 1886, *sub* "The Exch. Rolls of Scotland] as existing in 1378 (*rectius*, 1358), and as being "the representative of a collateral line then rising into importance"; (3) the descent of the estate of Synton from the family of Keith (who acquired it by marriage with Isabella of Synton) to that of Erskine (by whom it, or, at all events, the superiority of it) was held as late as 1620, indicates a descent from Keith, which (as before stated) is incompatible with one from Barclay; (4) That Christian Keith, stated in the old family pedigrees to have been da. of Helen of Mar, married Sir Robert de Erskine is proved by a charter of Robert II. [Mar evidence, 1875, p. 381]; (5) That Janet, called Janet Barclay, da. of Christian Keith, married Sir Thomas Erskine and was mother of Robert, retoured Earl of Mar, is asserted by the old [rival] pedigrees [Mar evidence, 1885, No. 3]. Mr. W. A. Lindsay adds (letter 24 Jan. 1893). "I cannot prove the parentage of Christian and Janet as independent facts, outside their being links in the course of heirship. The line stated in the old pedigree exactly accounts for the heirship to the [Countess] Isabella. It has not been denied or disproved and it is corroborated by the new Monteith-evidence which Burnett found in the Exchequer Rolls [See Mar minutes, 1885, part 3]. It satisfied the committee; and the Preamble [to the [Mar restitution

Q[2]

about that date, probably before 1426, but certainly before 24 May 1429, a Lord of Parl.([a]) as LORD ERSKINE [S.] On the death, 1 Aug. 1435, of Alexander, Earl of Mar (who was entitled to that dignity for his life, not only by the creation of 28 May 1426, but also under the ratified charter([b]) of 9 Dec. 1404) he became (under the said charter) EARL OF MAR [S.] By special([c]) service,

---

bill of 1885], was held to be proved." The well-known Mr. Riddell ["*Riddell*," pp. 1039—1040], while disbelieving the marriage of any Sir Robert Erskine† with any Christian Keith, *widow*, and holding (as does Mr. Hallen) that Sir Robert's wife was Christian Keith, *spinster* (both which points, however, are immaterial in the descent of the dignity of the Earldom of Mar) asserts positively that "Sir Thomas Erskine, married Janet, da. of Sir Edward Keith, by his wife, Christian, da. of Sir John Menteith, by Elene, da. of Gratney, Earl of Marr, in virtue of which marriage the Earldom of Marr, came into the Erskine family, *as is proved by irrefragable evidence I have seen* in the Marr charter-chest and, thro' means of the same, especially, by Lord Hailes in the Sutherland case. See chap. v., sect. ii, pp. 43-44 *et seq.*" The same pedigree, from Helen of Mar downwards, is given by Sir William Fraser (adviser of the opposing party *i.e.* the heir *male*) in his "*Red Book of Menteith*," (1881), and has in fact, been generally received, and in no point *disproved*, and tho' (as has before been remarked) the paternity of Dame Janet Erskine (thro' whom the Eardom descends) has never been strictly proved, it may very fairly and most probably be attributed to Sir Edward Keith, of Synton, as stated in the text.

This long note should not be concluded without acknowledging the kind assistance thereto given (extending in some instances to many pages of writing), by Mr. Joseph Bain, F.S.A., Mr. W. A. Lindsay, Mr. M. J. Shaw-Stewart and the Rev. A. W. Cornelius Hallen (himself) the author of the article, which upsets (what Mr. Round [*Genealogist*, N.S., ix, 129] calls, with, perhaps, a slight touch of sarcasm) "*The orthodox pedigree*," a pedigee which these remarks are intended in some measure to justify.

([a]) See vol. iii, p. 275, note "a," *sub* "Erskine," as to the probability of this Barony belonging to the heir *general* and not to the heir *male*.

([b]) The charters of 12 Aug. 1404, and 9 Dec. 1404, and the consequences attending upon them are thus spoken of by Lord Crawford [See "A" (vol. i, p. 209), as in note "b," p. 218], "The last (the *legal* and *confirmed*) charter of 9 Dec. 1404, was in full recognition during the remaining years of the Countess Isabel's life, and was, after the death of her husband, Alexander, Earl of Mar, the basis of the right of Sir Robert Erskine, Earl of Mar, to the fief and dignity to which he succeeded under a retour of 1438 by legal right, as finally determined in 1626. The first (the *extorted*, *nonconfirmed*, *renounced* and *rejected*) charter of 12 August 1404, rules from 1457 to 1565 but was *formally condemned* as *null*, *void*, and *of no effect* by the final judgment of 1626 which, at the same time, *recognised* and *enforced* the charter 9 December 1404, as confirmed by the Royal charter 21 Jan. 1404/5."

([c]) "In contradistinction from a *general* service. The retour of a general service only established propinquity without giving right to a special service." ["A" (vol. i, p. 261, note "i"), as in note "b," p. 218.]

† Mr. Riddell, after quoting a Royal charter, 18 Jan. 1365/61, of the lands of Kinnoull in favour of Nicholas de Erskine, son of "*Roberti de Erskine, militis et Christiane de Keth, sponse sue*" adds that the latter "was *not* a Menteith and had married *a separate* and earlier [Sir Robert] Erskine." He, however, gives no authority for either of these *positive* statements and the identity of the Sir Robert Erskine who *m.* Christian Keith, with that of Sir Robert Erskine of Alloa and Dun (the father of Sir Thomas) seems more than probable. With respect, however, to the Lady (Christian), Mr. Hallen mentions a charter of 1361 [Chartulary of Cambus kenneth, p. 255] which was granted by Janet (*née* Menteith) Countess of Strathern (a yr. sister of Christian, who *m.* Sir Edward Keith) "*Domino Roberto de Erskine, militi et Domine Christiane de Keith sponse sue, consanguinee nostre carissime.*" In this the word "*consanguinea*" certainly seems to indicate a more distant connection than that of "*sister*," and tends to support the theory that the wife of Sir Robert was *née* Keith, and a *daughter* (*not* the widow) of Sir Edward Keith the husband of Christian, *née* Menteith, sister to the said Countess. This Sir Edward Keith is stated (by Sir Henry Barkly, in "*The Genealogist*," N.S., vol. ix, p. 198, note 2), to have *d.* in 1350, *not* in 1346 (at the battle of Durham) as is generally stated.

22 April 1438, he was returned heir in half([a]) of the lands of Mar, &c., and by another such service, 16 Oct. following, in the other half. Seisin([b]) thereof was given on 21 Nov. 1438, which completed the legality of his possession of the said dignity and fief. Various agreements between him and the Crown, as to the surrender of castles, &c., were entered into, and a final adjustment of the Crown's rights was postponed by the Council till King James II. [S.], attained his full age, but nothing was finally settled till 1457, six years after that period([c]) and five after the Earls death. He appears to have *m.*, soon after Dec. 1400,([d]) a da. of David (LINDSAY), 1st EARL OF CRAWFORD [S.] He *d.* between 26 Aug. 1452, and 21 March 1452/3.

[The Earldom of Mar "the succession and inheritance to which was" during the interval between the death (1407) of the Countess Isabella and the year 1565 "treated by successive Kings of Scotland as if the same had been by some means extinguished"([e]) was, on the death of Earl Alexander in 1435, claimed by King James I. [S.] by reason of the bastardy of the last possessor, who was thus held (under the *renounced* and *nonconfirmed* charter of *August* 1404) to have been the *absolute* owner thereof and, as such, entitled to resign it and obtain the regrant of 1426. The King accordingly in 1435 seems to have possessed himself of some or possibly the greater part of the lands thereof, but shortly afterwards, 20 Feb. 1437, was murdered, when (in the following year) 1438, the heir of line (under the *confirmed* charter of *Dec.* 1404) Robert, Lord Erskine, was enfeoffed thereof, as abovestated. His s. and h., Thomas, Lord Erskine, was, however, unable to obtain such enfeoffment on his father's death in 1452, and, five years later, the King, James II. [S.], obtained at a Justiciary Court at Aberdeen, 15 May 1457, a (posthumous) *reduction* of the retour in 1438 in right of Robert, Lord Erskine, and a statement that the Earldom had devolved on the late King in 1435, on the grounds abovenamed. James II. [S.] *d.* but three years later 3 Aug. 1460, tho' not before he had dealt with the Earldom as under.]

XIV. 1458? to 1479. *1.* The Lord JOHN STEWART, 3d and yst. s. of the reigning **King James II.** [S.], by Mary, da. of Arnold, DUKE OF GUELDRES, was *b.* (after Oct. 1456) about 1457 and was *cr.* between 21 June 1458, and 23 June 1459, EARL OF MAR AND GARIOCH [S.] He signs as "*Jhonne Erll of Mar and Gerwyacht*" two deeds 18 Nov. 1475, and 1 March 1477/8.([f]) He *d.* unm. in 1479 at Canongate, Edinburgh, where he was apparently murdered by the orders of his br., the then King James III. [S.] whom he had offended. His *honours* became *extinct* at his death.

ROBERT COCHRANE (whose parentage is unknown) an Architect, one of the King's "favourites" (as early as 1476) took a great part in fomenting the King's displeasure against his brothers and was, on the murder of the yst. thereof (as above mentioned) rewarded with his estate, being said to have been *cr.* EARL

([a]) See p. 223, note "c."

([b]) "To the uther half of the said Earldome of Mar and Lordschipe of Garrioche." See the schedule of these deeds in 1626 which were at that date (but are not now) in existence. ["A" vol. i, pp. 264—265), as in note "b," p. 218.]

([c]) The King had meanwhile, by charter 26 Aug. 1452, made a grant as to the "*terras Comitatus nostri de Garioch*" to Mary, the Queen Consort, for her life.

([d]) See "*Lives of the Lindsays*" (edit. 1849), vol. i, p. 105, note

([e]) "Earldom of Mar Restitution Bill," 1885.

([f]) Between these dates, *viz.* on 26 April 1476, the unconfirmed and superseded charter of 12 Aug. 1404 (which according to the decreet of 1626 was the sole foundation of the King's "*pretendit*" right of possession of the Earldom) was [more than *seventy* years after its date] inscribed on the Great Seal Register by special mandate of the King "irregularly and illegally introduced, no confirmation of the charter having passed the Great Seal, and *no private charter*, such as this of the 12th Aug., much less an unconfirmed charter having a right to insertion thereon." ["A," (vol. i, p. 299) as in note "b," p. 218.]

OF MAR [S.] in 1479 or 1480.(a) He was hung (with six others) in sight of the King, over the bridge of Lauder, in July 1482, by several of the Scotch nobles whom his sudden rise had disgusted. At his death his *peerage dignity* (if, indeed, any such legally existed) *lapsed to the Crown.*

XV. 1483. *1.* ALEXANDER (STEWART), DUKE OF ALBANY [S.], elder br. of John (STEWART), EARL OF MAR [S.], abovenamed, being 2d s. of the late King James II. [S.], was, about Jan. 1482/3 *cr.* EARL OF MAR AND GARIOCH, but was "*forfeited*" a few months later and is said to have *d.* in 1485. See fuller particulars under "ALBANY" Dukedom [S.] *cr.* 1456; *forfeited* 1483.

XVI. 1486, to 1502. *1.* The LORD JOHN STEWART, 3d and yst. s. of the reigning King James III. [S.], by Margaret, da. of Christian I., KING OF DENMARK, was *b.* 1479 or 1480, and was *cr.* 2 March 1485/6, EARL OF MAR AND GARIOCH [S.] He *d.* unm., 11 March 1502/3,(b) when *all his honours* became *extinct.*(c)

XVII. 1562. *1.* JAMES (STEWART), EARL OF MORAY [S.] (who had been so *cr.* 30 Jan. 1561/2,) was (a week later), *cr.* 7 Feb. 1561/2, EARL OF MAR(d) [S.], with a clause that he and his heirs male should be called by that title. He, however resigned the same, a few months later, sitting in Parl. [S.], on 10 Sep. 1562, as EARL OF MAR, and on 15 Oct. following as EARL OF MORAY. See "MORAY" Earldom [S.], *cr.* 1562.

[During the interval of rather more than a century that elapsed between 15 May 1457, and 23 June 1565, when the Earldom was, under the retour of the former date (subsequently found to be "utterly(e) erroneous") held by the Crown, the *de jure* heirs thereof under the (royally confirmed) charter of Dec. 1404 (by which the descent of the Earldom has ever since 1565 been regulated) were as follows.]

(a) "It is probable that only the revenues of the Earldom were assigned to him without the title, which, however, his flatterers or his own vanity might use." Wood's "*Douglas.*"

(b) See Exchequer accounts [S.] In Wood's "Douglas" it is stated that "an act of Parl. 15 Feb. 1489, contains a provision of the Duke of Ross and Earl of Marr."

(c) The two immediate successors (1488—1542) of James III. [S.], made no grant of the dignity of Mar, retaining "the territorial comitatus in their own hands," tho' bestowing "various portions and dependencies" to their favourites but "to none on the same scale" as the grants (1507-10), by James IV. to Alexander Elphinstone (afterwards Lord Elphinstone [S.]), which comprised "the Castle of Kildrummie the chief messuage of the Earldom of Mar." [See "A," (vol. i, pp. 299—300) as in note "b," p. 218.

(d) He was a bastard of King James V. [S.], by Margaret, da. of John (Erskine, *de jure* Earl of Mar. Hence his choice of the title of Mar and his readiness to surrender it to, its right heir, his first cousin, John, 6th Lord Erskine, who was restored thereto in 1565.

(e) The four points on which it rested are given in Wood's *Douglas*," vol. ii, p. 205, and their refutation on p. 206. One of them was that the King was himself heir to Isabel, Countess of Mar, as descended from Isabel de Mar, wife of King Robert I. [S.], whereas in point of fact Isabel was *sister* while Elyn, (ancestress of the Erskine family,) was *daughter* of Gratney, Earl of Mar, the great grandfather of the said Countess Isabel. See p. 231, note "d."

XIV.(bis) 1452. *13.* THOMAS (ERSKINE), LORD ERSKINE [S.], who may be considered as *de jure*(a) EARL OF MAR [S.], only s. and h. of Robert, 1st LORD ERSKINE, who in 1435, became EARL OF MAR [S.], as beforestated, *suc.* his father in 1452, but, being unable to obtain seisin of that Earldom, never assumed the title thereof, the said Earldom, being subsequently, 15 May 1457, declared to have reverted in 1435 to the Crown whereby his father's retour (in 1438) as heir thereto was reduced. He *d.* between Aug. 1489, and 6 Dec. 1494.

XV.(bis) 1490? *14.* ALEXANDER (ERSKINE), LORD ERSKINE [S.], who may be considered as *de jure*(a) EARL OF MAR [S.], only s. and h. He *d.* between 29 Jan. 1506/7, and 17 June 1510.

XVI.(bis) 1510? *15.* ROBERT (ERSKINE), LORD ERSKINE [S.], who may be considered as *de jure* EARL OF MAR [S.], He was slain at Flodden,(b) 9 Sep. 1513.

XVII.(bis) 1513. *16.* JOHN (ERSKINE), LORD ERSKINE [S.], who may be considered as *de jure*(a) EARL OF MAR [S.], 2d but 1st surv. s. and h. He *d.* 1552.

See fuller particular under "ERSKINE" Barony [S.], *cr.* about 1426.

XVIII. *1552,* *17* and *1.* JOHN (ERSKINE), LORD ERSKINE [S.], who *recognised* in 1565.

I. 1565.

may be considered as *de jure*(a) EARL OF MAR [S.], 3d but 1st surv. s. and h.;(c) *suc.* his father in 1552 both *in the peerage* [S.] as also as Keeper of Edinburgh Castle, which important post he held with great impartiality as between the party of the Court and of the People. Though one of the Reformers he refused to sign the Book of Discipline in 1560; P.C. [S.], 1561. As the first step towards obtaining the restitution of the Earldom, he was by a general service, 5 May 1565, found heir to Robert "late Earl of Mar and Garioch and Lord Erskine," the grandfather of his great grandfather;(d) after which finding, the Queen [S.] by charter, 23 June 1565, restored to him "*his heirs and assigns heredit*ally *all and hail the said Earldom of Mar,*"(e) together with all the lands thereof which yet remained in the Crown and all

(a) Having regard to the Act of Parl., 29 July 1587, ratifying the restoration (1565) of the Earldom of Mar to John (Erskine), Earl of Mar, "as if the said Earl were immediate heir to the said Dame Issobell Dowglas, or to the deceased Robert, Earl of Mar, Lord Erskine, her heir"; and having regard to the "*Earldom of Mar restitution act,*" 1885, which was (in the words of Lord Selborne, the Chairman of the Select Committee) "intended to relieve against forfeiture and surrender, *if there was one,* without absolutely deciding that there was" [Minutes of Evidence, p. 24.]

(b) See p. 63, note "b," *sub* "Lennox" for a list of the Scotch nobles there slain.

(c) Of his two elder brothers (1) Robert Erskine, Master of Erskine, *d.* v.p. and s.p. legit., being slain at the battle of Pinkie, 10 Sep. 1547 (2) Thomas Erskine, Master of Erskine, sometime Ambassador to England, *d.* v.p. and s.p. legit. 1551. His next yr. brother was Sir Alexander Erskine, of Gogar, father of Thomas, *cr.* Earl of Kellie [S.], in 1619, with rem. to his heirs male, in consequence of which that Earldom was inherited in 1829 (on failure of the heirs male of the grantee's body) by John Francis Miller (Erskine), Earl of Mar, as below stated.

(d) "It is not impossible that the issue of this service of 1565 may have been proceeded by an assize of error and inquiry into and reversal of the proceedings of 1457. A document existed formerly in the Mar charter chest and is quoted by Sir Robert Douglas in which reasons are assigned (according to Sir Robert's report) why the grounds of these proceedings were erroneous [see p. 230, note "e"], but the document, whatever was its character, does not now, it would appear, exist, and consequently has not been available as evidence. The invalidity, however, of the service negative, of 1457, based on the charter of 12 *August* 1404, is in no need of any independent vindication." ["A" (vol. i, p. 333), as in note "b," p. 218].

(e) "The grant of the *Comitatus* is precisely in the same form as similar grants innumerable, which, up to that date and later still, carried the dignity or title of honour without special mention of it, as shadow follows substance. It did so necessarily in

right over such as had been alienated, as also the lands of the Lordship of "Gareach," provision being made that forasmuch as Kildrummie, the ancient chief messuage of the Earldom had been alienated by the Crown, the manor of Migvie should serve for the seisin of Mar and the Castle of Dunnydeer for that of Garioch. The warrant for seisin was dated 24 June 1565, and when (but not before) that was accomplished (which was in about three weeks[a]) time) he became *legally* entitled to the dignity, and, accordingly, appeared at Council, 1 Aug. 1565, as EARL OF MAR [S.] It is at this period, or a few days sooner, that according to the remarkable decision of the House of Lords (26 Feb. 1875) an *Earldom of Mar* [S.] is held to have been created *de novo*[b]) with a

---

the present instance. The hypothesis of a *lost charter* conferring a personal peerage, apart from the fief, is purely gratuitous and unwarrantable; it was stated [*i.e.*, such a supposition was advanced] by Sir Robert Gordon in 1771 in order to disprove the hereditary transmission of the Earldom of Sutherland but rejected by the House of Lords." ["A" as in note "b," p. 218 (vol. i, p. 338.)] Again, "of the multitudes of existing charters of Earldoms, original and on a resignation, *from the earliest date down to 1578* only five can be pointed out in which *the dignity* of Earl is directly mentioned, and in four out of these five there is an obvious reason for its specification. In 1578 the practise began to vary and from that date down to 1600 *half* the recorded charters of Earldoms (they were 10 in all) *did* and *half did not* specify the dignity. Yet *in every case* the grantee was recognised as Earl and the line of heirs in the charters enjoyed *the dignity* as well as the lands. Moreover *no one* professes to have seen in either record or charter chest a patent or charter of the title of Earl *earlier* than [that of Winton in] 1600." See "D" (p. 11, note 2), as in note "b," p. 218.]

"Before that time [*i.e.*, the time of James VI. [S.]], titles of honour and dignity were created *by erecting lands* into Earldoms and Lordships and probably by some other method that cannot now [1740] in matters so ancient be with any certainty discovered." Report of the Court of Session (of which the celebrated Duncan Forbes was then President) relating to the Peerage of Scotland, 27 Feb. 1740, iii, p. 6, which Court also reports (*ib.*) "That they cannot discover, in any records, *any patent* of honour creating a peerage *earlier* than the reign of James VI."

([a]) The instrument of infeftment for Mar is missing, but that for Garioch, which is preserved, is dated 24 July 1565.

([b]) As to this supposed new creation, those who believe in it must also believe (1) that it was cr. with a *different* limitation to that of the *Earldom restored at the same date*, which, having been inherited by the Erskine family from heirs *general*, was restored (with the lands appertaining thereto) to such heirs; (2) that the patent or charter supposed to have effected such creation is not only non-registered and non-apparent (there being also not the *slightest* documentary evidence in proof of its existence) but is actually of a date some 40 years previous (see p. 231, note "e"), to any similar patents of Scotch Earldoms; (3) that such supposed *new* Earldom was ignored by its (supposed) grantee, who, on 6 July 1565 (some 3 weeks before its presumed creation) granted an obligation (evidently considering himself as restored to the *old* title) on the narration that the Queen had given him the "*Earldom of Mar and lands pertaining thereto*" [*Mar minutes*, p. 61]; (4) that such new creation was unknown (*only* 40 *years* after its presumed birth), in 1606, at *the decreet of ranking*," when the Earldom of Mar was ranked according to the charters of 1395 or 1404 therein produced, between the Earldom of Sutherland (for which the most ancient date then produced was 1347) and (1459) the Earldom of Rothes; (5) that some 100 years later its existence had *still* remained undiscovered, the only Earldom of Mar that figures in 1707 on the Union Roll [S.], being one that ranks next immediately under the said Earldom of Sutherland; (6) that the House of Lords shared such ignorance when in four successive Parliaments, 1707—1715, the holder of Earldom of Mar was placed above all Scotch Earldoms save that of Sutherland; (7) that the Act of Parl., 17 June 1824, has (to use Lord Redesdale's words as applied to the places assigned to the Earldom of Sutherland† and Mar at the decreet of ranking in 1606) "OF COURSE, been

† In neither case, however, *was* such ruling wrong. The peerages were in 1606 ranked (*only*) according to the documents produced and approved. At a future period (1771) the Earldom of Sutherland shewed grounds for an earlier date of creation (on fresh evidence produced) but that did not make it wrong to have already allowed it a precedence not exceeding such earlier date.

rem. (not to heirs *general* as above, but) to heirs male of the body. The Royal charter of 23 June 1565, was ratified in Parl. [S.] 19 April 1567, reciting that the dignity of Mar was "*disponit*" to him on the ground that he was "lauchfullie discendit" of the ancient heretouris of the said Erledom and had the *undoubtit right thereof*." The said charter was also 'proceeded upon' in an act (20 years later) 1587. The restored Earl received the custody of the newly born Prince (afterwards James VI. [S.]) in June 1566, whom he removed to the Castle of Stirling, giving up at the same time the custody of Edinburgh Castle to the Earl of Bothwell [S.], for which act he was exonerated by Parl. 16 April 1567. He took part against the Queen [S.], signing 16 June 1567, the order for her committal to Loch Leven Castle, and being, in July following, one of the Government Council. On the death of the Regent Earl of Lennox [S.] he was made **Regent of Scotland**, 6 Sep. 1571, and so continued (being also Custodian of the young King) till his death a year later, tho' the *virtual* direction of the affairs of the Realm was with (his Lieut. Gen. of the Forces) the Earl of Morton [S.] He *m.* before 29 Jan. 1556/7, Annabella, da. of Sir William MURRAY, of Tullibardine, by Catharine, da. of Sir David CAMPBELL, of Glenurchy. He *d.* 29 Oct. 1572. His will dat. 9 Aug. 1568, at Stirling, directs his burial to be at Alloa.(a) His widow was living 1602.(b)

XIX, and II, } 1572. *18* and *2*. JOHN (ERSKINE), EARL OF MAR, &c. [S.], only s. and h., *b.* about 1558; *styled* LORD ERSKINE since 1565; was served heir, 3 March 1572/3, "*in toto et integro Comitatu de Mar*. He was educated together with the King (of whom his mother and his uncle, Sir Alexander Erskine, of Gogar, had the charge) at Stirling Castle. On 26 April 1578, he possessed himself of that fortress and of the King's person, and in 1582 joined in the raid of Ruthven, for which he was pardoned, 29 Nov. 1583. He was, however, attainted, 22 Aug. 1584, but restored Dec. 1585 to his honours and estates as also to the command of Stirling Castle. Here, in 1595, he had the custody of Prince Henry [S.] till 1603, receiving, meanwhile, several grants of Abbey lands, &c. He accompanied the King to England in 1603; was P.C. and was el. 25 June 1603, K.G., being inst. 9 July. HIGH TREASURER [S.], Dec 1615 to April 1630, entertaining the King in Scotland in 1617 with great magnificence. He had devoted himself for nearly 50 years but more especially during the last 15 years thereof (1620-35) to the recovery (under the service to his father of 5 May 1565) of such of the family estates as had been alienated by the Crown (1435—1565) for which recovery the reduction by the Court of Session of the several charters so granting them was

found wrong" inasmuch as such act restored the Earldom of Mar to John Francis Erskine, as "*grandson and lineal representative* [which, *thro' his mother*, he was] of the said John, Earl of Mar" (who was attainted in 1716), when (in Lord Redesdale's opinion) "OF COURSE" such restoration was made to him only because he was [which, indeed he also happened to be] *great-nephew and collateral heir male* of the said Earl, tho' such fact [being immaterial, inasmuch as his *representation* of the dignity *was* (not as great-nephew, but) *as grandson* as recited in the act] was not even alluded to in the act; (8) that the limitation of the Earldom was unknown to the trustees of 1725, who were authorised to repurchase the forfeited estates and entail them on the heirs of the Earldom, which they entailed accordingly on heirs *general*, tho' one of the two trustees Lord Grange, a Judge of the Court of Session), was himself at that time the *nearest collateral male heir* and had a direct interest to maintain a contrary view.

By the "Earldom of Mar restitution act, 1885," the *ancient* Earldom thereby restored is placed "at all elections of Rep. Peers for Scotland next after the Earldom of Sutherland" (such being its position both at the decreet of ranking in 1606, and on the Union Roll in 1707), while *that* Earldom of Mar, of which a creation *in tail male* was assumed (by the House of Lords, in 1875) to have been in 1565, and which (according to such presumption), vested in Walter Henry (Erskine), Earl of Mar and Kellie [S.], was relegated to the place of "an Earldom created in 1565, anything in the decreet of ranking (made 5 March 1606, under the commission issued by James VI. then King of the Scots) to the contrary thereof notwithstanding."

(a) Printed in "*N. and Q.*," 4th S, viii, 321, where, however, no account of its whereabouts is given, it being said to have "recently turned up."

(b) She was, according to Knox the Reformer, "a verray Jesabell."

necessary, the Earl's right of *regress* being protected by an act of Parl. 29 July 1587.(a) His efforts were successful, the vast estate of Kildrummie, which had been alienated to the family of Elphinstone, being among the lands so recovered. In the course of these proceedings "the Court of Session affirmed in the most solemn manner the validity of the charter of 9 Dec. 1404, and of the retours of 1438."(b) The "ranking" of the Earldom of Mar was settled (during his lifetime) at the "*decreet of ranking*" in 1606.(c) He was cr., 10 June 1610, LORD OF CARDROSS [S.] with power

(a) "This remarkable document" is given "at very full length" in "A" (vol. i, p. 380, as in note "b," p. 218), as also are the proceedings for the various recoveries. The act (which was long before the act of 1617 as to *forty* years being the period of prescription) did away with any right of prescription.

(b) See "D" as in note "b," p. 218.

(c) *The decreet* of the Royal Commissioners in 1606, as to the precedence of Mar, which has never been over ruled by the Court of Session (the only place at which such award was liable to be challenged) is, according to the edict of James VI. [S.] respecting such decreets, "*not to be contravened.*" A constitutional attempt to upset it was once made but failed. Out of the ten Earls placed *under* "Mar" (who, had the creation been one of 1565, would have been *above* him) no less than six protested against the precedency assigned to him as holding his Earldom "by services of heirs," but this protest was *not* confirmed by the Court of Session. In the article "D" as in note "b," p. 218, it is stated that "except in the case of the five Earls at the head of the list [Angus, Argyle, Crawford, Erroll, and Marischal], who owed their place to office or privilege, the precedence awarded was in strict correspondence with the antiquity of the writs produced. The Earl of Sutherland [the 6th Earldom of this ranking] produced a charter of 1347; Mar [the 7th of such Earldoms] one of 1404 [Countess Isabel's charter of *December* that year], Rothes [the 8th such Earldom], one of 1459, &c., and they were ranked accordingly." The date of 1457 often assigned† as being that of the Earldom (a date which would be sufficiently early to place "Mar" before "Rothes" was [erroneously] supposed by the present writer (see "Remarks on the Earl of Redesdale's letter, of 1883, on the Earldom of Mar" in Marshall's "*Genealogist*," vol. vii, pp. 145—156), to have been the date acted upon at the decreet of 1606. Mr. Burnett, late Lyon King of Arms (in a letter, 9 July 1883, to G. W. Marshall, the then Editor of the Genealogist) points out two serious errors in this article of which he otherwise speaks most favourable, viz. (1) the assumption that the rank of *any* of the five Earls, who head the list, was due to anything else but *privilege* or *office*, remarking of "Crawford" (the only one of the five to whom such remark might seem to be inapplicable) that "I think there are sufficient grounds, not exactly those adduced by the late Earl of Crawford, for holding *Crawford's position* to have been also *connected with privilege*. In the 15th century the Earls of Douglas and Crawford wielded an authority which often overshadowed the Crown and no other Earl could possibly have taken precedence of them *on the plea of greater antiquity*. The right of *Angus* (who came in place of Douglas) to bias the Crown and precede all Earls, if not Dukes, was, as your contributor shews, fully recognised by the Crown only a few years before the decreet; *Argyll*, he also allows to rank where he does from privilege or office; the official precedence of [*Erroll* the] Constable and [of *Marischal*, the] Marischal is often alluded to in the records, tho' sometimes called in question, but as both were Commissioners, under the remit, it would have been strange if it had been wholly unrecognised. It seems to me evident, in the light of subsequent Court-of-Session proceeding that the *ranking by seniority* began with *Sutherland*, whom the Commissioners meant to rank from 1347, and *Mar* from 1395 or 1404, I would say 1395." (2) as to the assumption (above alluded to) that 1457 (not 1395 or 1404) was the date acted upon in the decreet of 1606. On this, Mr. Burnett remarks (as above) "the position of Menteith furnishes one of the many disproofs of this [1457] date. Menteith was ranked as of 1466, by the Commissioners, on the strength of

† On 15 May 1457, the retour of Robert (Erskine), Earl of Mar, in 1438, as heir to Isabel, *suo jure* Countess of Mar, was *reduced* at the instigation of the Crown confirmed by act of Parl. *5 Nov.* following, but (on the other hand) by charter 23 June 1565 (confirmed, also, by act of Parl. 19 April 1567), the Queen declared the then Lord Erskine to be "*as if he stood in the place of his predecessor, Robert, Earl of Mar.*" The date therefore, of *5 Nov. 1457* (when the above cited act of Parl. was passed) was [erroneously] considered by some as the date of the peerage itself.

of nomination of that dignity, which power he exercised in favour of his 3d son, Henry Erskine. (See "Cardross" Barony [S.]) He *m.* firstly Anne, da. of David (DRUMMOND), 2d LORD DRUMMOND [S.], by his second wife, Lilias, da. of William (RUTHVEN), 2d LORD RUTHVEN [S.] He *m.* secondly, before 29 May 1593, Mary, 2d da. of Esme (STUART), 1st DUKE OF LENNOX [S.], by Katharine, da. of Guillaume DE BALSAC, SEIGNEUR D'ENTRAGUES. He *d.* at Stirling, 14 Dec. 1634, aged 77, and was *bur.* 7 April 1635, at Alloa. He was *suc.* in the BARONY OF CARDROSS [S.] according to his nomination (see that dignity) but in the rest of his honours as below.

XX, and III. 1634. *19* and *3.* JOHN (ERSKINE), EARL OF MAR, &c. [S.], s. and h., by first wife, being only child of his mother,(a) *b.* about 1585; *styled* LORD ERSKINE till 1634; was, with many others,(b) *cr.* M.A. at Oxford, 30 Aug. 1605; K.B., 30 May 1610, at the creation of the Prince of Wales; P.C. [S.]; Gov. of Edinburgh Castle, 1615-38; an extraordinary Lord of Session [S.], 1620-26 and 1628-30; *suc. to the peerage* [S.], 1634. In 1638, he sold to the King the heritable Sheriffdom of Stirlingshire, &c., for £8,000; P.C., by the Parl., 1641, but joined the King's party in that year. His estates were sequestrated, and having purchased estates in Ireland (from the sale

the oldest document produced by the Earl. But, in 1639 (to make up in a measure for his arbitrary treatment, as to the Earldom of Strathern) he got a charter of the Earldom of Airth, with the old precedence of Menteith which was defined as 1428. In accordance with this charter the ranking of Menteith on the roll of Peers was rectified, when he was placed, *not* before Mar, as would have been the case had your contributors view [as to the date of 1457 being that of Mar], been right but *between* Mar (1395 or 1404) and Rothes (1459) as appears by the records of Parl. in 1639, and following years, and from the Union Roll. The supposed date of 1457, Lord Redesdale can trace only to the Royal Calendar of 1825. I can trace its history into last century and explain its original so as a combined blunder and misprint."

The following extract from "A," as in note "b," on p. 218, (vol. ii, p. xii in the "Analysis of Contents") elucidates "the ranking of the first seven Earls [which] proceeded on well-ascertained principles; the first five on grounds *independent of antiquity*; and Sutherland and Mar *in accordance with antiquity produced.*"

"1. *Angus.* Proof from 1398 only (while Sutherland went back to 1347) but he had by special grant *the first place* and vote in Parl. and it became a question whether he validly resigned it on being made Marquess of Douglas. *He bore the Crown.*"

"2. *Argyle.* Created 1457; would by date of creation have been postponed to [1347], Sutherland and [1398] Crawford; but he was Justiciary-General and *bore the Sceptre.*"

"3. *Crawford.* Proof from 1398; would by antiquity have been postponed to [1347] Sutherland; had no great hereditary office. Preference could not be from exceptional influence exerted by the then Earl (*the prodigal Earl*) but placed here from usuage of Crawford *carrying the Sword*, the third of the honours. Sutherland had never attended Parl. from time of Robert I. till late in the 15th century. Perhaps the belief that Crawford was entitled to the Dukedom of Montrose led him to be placed as high as possible among the Earls. Sir David Lindsay's Armorial."

"4. *Erroll.* Creation 1452; had his precedence over Sutherland and Mar as *Constable.*"

"5. *Marischal.* Also ranked before Sutherland and Mar in virtue of office" [of Marshal.]

"6. *Sutherland.* His charter of 1347 would have given him the *first* place but for causes stated."

"7. *Mar.* Ranked second to Sutherland in consideration of earlier date [1347] proved by Sutherland. Sutherland's supposed ranking in virtue of new creation, 1518, negatived by the fact that the precedency awarded [was that of] a date avowedly long before 1518."

(a) Of his seven yr. brothers, all of whom were by his father's *second* wife (1) James became Earl of Buchan [S.] in right of his wife and was ancestor of the two succeeding Earls (2) Henry, was ancestor of the Lords Cardross [S.], and since 1695 of the Earls of Buchan [S.] (3) Col. Sir Alexander Erskine, *d.* 1640 (4) Sir Charles Erskine, of Alva, was ancestor of the Erskines, Baronets [S.], and, since 1805, of the Earls of Rosslyn.

(b) See vol. iii, p. 236, note "a," *sub* "Effingham," for their names.

of lands in Scotland), he lost that property also in the Irish rebellion. He *m.* Christian, da. of Francis (HAY), EARL OF ERROLL [S.], by his third wife Elizabeth, da. of William (DOUGLAS), EARL OF MORTON [S.]. He *d.* 1654.

XXI, and IV. 1654. *20* and *4*. JOHN (ERSKINE), EARL OF MAR, &c. [S.], s. and h.; *styled* LORD ERSKINE, 1634-54; was in command of the Scotch army in 1640, but joined the King's side in 1641, was at the rout at Philiphaugh, 13 Sep. 1645, and was fined 24,000 marks; *suc. to the peerage* [S.], 1654, tho' his estates continued sequestrated till the restoration.(a) He *m.* firstly (contract 1641), his first cousin, Mary, 1st da. of Walter (SCOTT), 1st EARL OF BUCCLEUCH [S.], by Mary, da. of Francis (HAY), EARL OF ERROLL [S.] abovenamed. She, who was *b.* Nov. and *bap.* 8 Dec. 1621, *d.* s.p., before 28 July 1647. He *m.* secondly, before 1650, Mary, 1st da. of George (MACKENZIE), 2d EARL OF SEAFORTH [S.], by Barbara, da. of Arthur (FORBES), 9th LORD FORBES [S.] She *d.* in May and he in Sep. 1668.

XXII, and V. 1668. *21* and *5*. CHARLES (ERSKINE), EARL OF MAR, &c. [S.], s. and h., *b.* 19 Oct. 1650; *styled* LORD ERSKINE from 1654, till he *suc. to the peerage* [S.], in Sep. 1668. The debts and fines of his father and grandfather compelled him to alienate great part of his estates, including the Barony of Erskine in Renfrewshire, the original possession of his family. He raised and was, 1679-86, Col. of the 21st foot, known as the Scots Fusileers; P.C., 1682. He *m.* Mary, da. of George (MAULE), 2d EARL OF PANMURE [S.], by Jean, da. of John (CAMPBELL), EARL OF LOUDOUN [S.] Having joined the disaffected party, he was arrested in March, and *d.* 23 April 1689, aged 38, being *bur.* at Alloa. His widow *m.*(b) 29 April 1697, at Alloa, Col. John ERSKINE, 2d s. of the Hon. Sir Charles Erskine, of Alva.

XXIII, and VI. 1689, to 1716. *22* and *6*. JOHN (ERSKINE), EARL OF MAR and LORD ERSKINE [S.], s. and h., *b.* at Alloa, Feb. 1675, and *styled* LORD ERSKINE, till he *suc. to the peerage* [S.], in April 1689, being left heir to "more debt than estate."(c) He took his seat in Parl. [S.], 8 Sep. 1696, "protesting against the calling of any Earl before him in the Roll."(d) P.C. [S.], 1697; was in command of a Reg. of Foot; one of the Commissioners, 1705, for the Union [S.]; K.T., 1706; Sec. of State [S.], 1706-07; being, after the Union, made Keeper of the Signet [S.], with a pension; REP. PEER [S.], 13 Feb. 1707, being re-elected, 1708, 1710 and 1713.(e) P.C. [G.B.] 1708, and one of Secretaries of State, 1713. He signed the proclamation of King George I., for whom he procured a loyal address from the Highland clans, but by whom he was dismissed from office. He then joined the Stuart cause and proclaimed "*King James*," at Braemar, 6 Sep. 1715, for whom he was Commander in Chief. At the head of about 12,000 men he was, "thro' the entire absence of common precaution or even any definite arrangements defeated"(f) by about 4,000 and forced to return to Perth, where he attended the Chevalier, at his public entry, 2 Jan. 1715/6. With that

(a) He lived in a small cottage at the gates of Alloa house till the Restoration (before which event he had become blind) when he was one of the three Earls (Crawford, Sutherland, and Mar), who bore respectively the Crown, Sceptre, and Sword (lately recovered from their hiding place at Dunottar) at the State opening of the Scotch Parl. 1 Jan. 1660/1.

(b) "*Northern N. and Q.*," I. and II., p. 188, footnote.

(c) "Memoirs of the Master of Sinclair" (p. 59), as quoted in the "Nat. Biogr.," *sub* "Erskine."

(d) Wood's "Douglas." He thus disputed the precedence allotted, *by virtue of office*, to four (Argyll, Crawford, Erroll, and Marischal), of the five Earls who were *on that ground* placed, in the "*ranking*" of 1606, before him (Angus, the remaining one of the five, having obtained a Marquessate) as also the precedence, *by virtue of antiquity*, allotted therein to Sutherland.

(e) His place in the House of Lords was in accordance with that assigned to the Earldom of Mar at the ranking of 1606 and on the Union Roll and not (it is almost needless to state) that of the one (evolved by the House of Lords in 1875) as having been created *de novo* in 1565.

(f) "Nat. Biogr.," *sub* "Erskine."

Prince he fled the country, 4 Feb. following and was *attainted* by Act of Parl. 17 Feb. 1715/6, as from 19 Jan., whereby *all his honours* (and his estate valued at £1,679 per annum) became *forfeited*.(a) He accompanied his Chief (the titular King. James III.) to Rome, by whom he was in 1715,(b) *cr.* DUKE OF MAR [S.], and in 1716, K.G., and to whom he was a chief adviser till 1724, when, after a long series of intrigues,(c) he finally abandoned his cause. He *m.* firstly, 6 April 1703 (lic. Bp. of London), at Twickenham, Midx., Margaret, 1st da. of Thomas (Hay), 6th Earl of Kinnoul [S.], by Elisabeth, da. of William (Drummond), 1st Viscount Strathallan [S.] She, who was *b.* 30 Sep. 1686, *d.* at Dupplin, 25 April 1707, in her 21st year and was *bur.* 3 May at Alloa. Fun. entry at Lyon office. He *m.* secondly, 26 July 1714, at Acton, Midx., Frances, da. of Evelyn (Pierrepont), 1st Duke of Kingston-upon-Hull, by his first wife, Mary, da. of William (Feilding), Earl of Denbigh. He *d.* May 1732, at Aix-la-Chapelle, aged 57. His widow, who had been declared a lunatic in March 1730, *d.* 4 and was *bur.* 9 March 1761, at Marylebone, aged above 80.

[Thomas Erskine, *styled* Lord Erskine, 1st and only surv. s. and h., by first wife, *b.* about 1705; M.P. for Stirling Burghs, 1728-34; for co. Stirling, 1747, and for co. Clackmannan, 1747-54; Commissary of Stores at Gibraltar, 1729. Owing to the *attainder* of 1716 he *did not suc. to the peerage* at his father's death, in May 1732, but in 1739 the family estate of Alloa, which had been forfeited, was conveyed to him.(d) He *m.*, 1 Oct. 1741, at Hopetoun house, Charlotte, 8th da. of Charles (Hope), 1st Earl of Hopetoun [S.] He *d.* s.p., 16 March 1766, aged about 60, at Gayfield. Will pr. 8 Sep. 1766. His widow, who was *b.* 4 March 1720, *d.* 24 Nov. 1788, at Edinburgh.]

* * * *

XXIV, and VII. 1824. 23 and 7. John Francis Erskine, of Alloa, co. Clackmannan, s. and h. of James Erskine, Knight Marischal [S.] (*d.* Feb. 1785, aged 71), by (his first cousin) Frances, only da. and (since 1766) heir of line of John, the attainted Earl of Mar abovenamed (being only child of her mother, the Earl's second wife), which James Erskine was 3d but (since 1774) eldest surv. s. and h. of the Hon. James Erskine, of Grange, next br. to the said John, Earl of Mar above-

(a) See vol. iii, p. 192, note "a," *sub* "Duffus," for a list of the peerages forfeited by the insurrection of 1715.

(b) See vol. i, p. 59, note "b," *sub* "Albemarle," for a list of "Jacobite Peerages."

(c) The following is the character given of him by Macky when "30 years old" (1705) "He is a very good manager in his private affairs which were in disorder when his father died and is a staunch countryman; fair complexioned, low stature," to which Dean Swift adds, "He is crooked; he seems to be a gentleman of good sense and good nature." Both these characters, however, seem too favourable. The Master of Sinclair (*Memoirs*, 59), says that he inherited from his mother the "hump he has got on his back and his dissolute, malicious, meddling spirit," while Bishop Atterbury says that "It was impossible for him ever to play a fair game or to mean but one thing at a time." He was in fact equally distrusted by the Jacobite party and the Government, and was popularly known as "Bobbing John."

(d) The friends of the family were permitted to re-purchase from the Government certain of the forfeited estates including Alloa for the heir of the house. This was completed in 1725 "by terms of this entail (1) the destination is to *heirs general* in preference to heirs *male* collateral of whom the nearest was Lord Grange [*i.e.*, the Hon. Thomas Erskine, a Lord of Session, next br. to the attainted Earl], himself the principal trustee. The attainted Earl's daughter succeeded under the entail, and, on her death, her son, the afterwards restored Earl (2) it was obligatory on *heirs general*, being strangers to the house of Erskine to adopt the name and arms of the Erskines, Earls of Mar (3) should the attainder be reversed the same class of heirs had to adopt the title dignity and honours of the family. The opinion of Lord Grange, as heir male, a trustee and a Lord of Session, was thus that the dignity was descendible to *heirs general*." [See "A" as in note "b," p. 218 (vol. ii, p. xvi)] and it is also evident that the clause as to adopting "*the name and arms* of Erskine" would not apply to the heirs *male*.

named. He, who was *b.* 1741, was thus grandson and *heir general*, as well as great nephew and *heir male* collateral, to the said Earl; was an officer in the army, 1757-70 (retiring as Capt. 1st Horse) and *suc.* to the family estate of Alloa, on the death of his mother, Lady Frances Erskine (on whom(a) they had been entailed) 20 June 1776. He *m.*, 17 March 1770, at Upway, Dorset, Frances, da. of Charles FLOYER, Gov. of Madras, by Mary, da. of (—) BERRIMAN. She *d.* 20 Dec. 1798, at Alloa. At length, in his 83d year, he was as "*grandson and lineal representative*"(b) of John, the forfeited Earl of Mar, restored(c) by act of Parl. 17 June 1824 (being therein styled "John Francis Erskine of Mar") "*to the dignity and title of Earl of Mar*" (no other peerage dignity that was forfeited(d) therewith being mentioned) and became thus EARL OF MAR [S.] He *d.* 20 Aug. 1825, aged 84. Will pr. Jan. 1853.

XXV, and VIII. 1825. *24* and *8.* JOHN THOMAS (ERSKINE), EARL OF MAR [S.], s. and h., *b.* 1772; *styled* LORD ERSKINE from 1824 till he *suc. to the peerage* [S.], 20 Aug. 1825. He *m.* 17 Jan. 1795, at Dalswinton, co. Dumfries, Janet, da. of Patrick MILLER, of Dalswinton afsd., br. of Sir Thomas Miller, Bart., so *cr.* in 1788 She *d.* 25 Aug. 1825. He *d.* 20 Sep. 1828, at Alloa House, aged 56.

XXVI, and IX. 1828. *25* and *9.* JOHN FRANCIS MILLER (ERSKINE). EARL OF MAR [S.], only s. and h., *b.* 28 Dec. 1795; was many years in the army, serving at Quatre Bras and Waterloo; *styled* LORD ERSKINE from 1825 till he *suc. to the peerage* [S.], 20 Sep. 1828. He *suc.* on the death of his distant cousin, Methven (ERSKINE), EARL OF KELLIE, &c. [S.], in 1828 or 1829 to the dignities of EARL OF KELLIE [1619], VISCOUNT FENTOUN [1606 and 1619], and LORD ERSKINE OF DIRLETOUN [1604]. in the peerage of Scotland, decision in favour of his right thereto being given 3 Sep. 1835. He *m.*, 24 April 1827, Philadelphia Stuart, 1st da. of Sir Charles Granville STUART-MENTETH, 1st Bart., of Closeburn, co. Dumfries, by Ludivina, da. of Thomas LOUGHNAN. She *d.* 15 Feb. 1853, at Alloa House. He *d.* there s.p., 19 June 1866, in his 71st year. At his death, the *Earldom of Kellie* and the honours inherited therewith devolved on his cousin and heir male (see "KELLIE" Earldom [S.], *cr.* 1619, *sub* the 12th Earl) as also did *that Earldom of Mar*, which, according to the decision of the House of Lords on 25 Feb. 1875, was supposed to have been *cr.* (*de novo*) by patent in 1565 in tail *male*, while the right to the *Earldom of Mar*, which, before 9 Dec. 1404, had "descended to Isabella, Countess of Mar,"(e) devolved as under.

XXVII. 1866; *confirmed* in 1885. *26.* JOHN FRANCIS ERSKINE (GOODEVE-ERSKINE, *formerly* GOODEVE), EARL OF MAR [1395 or 1404] in the peerage of Scotland, nephew and heir of line, being s. and h. of William James GOODEVE, of Clifton, co. Somerset (*d.* 1861), by Frances Jemima (*d.* 20 June 1842), 1st sister of John Francis Miller (ERSKINE), late EARL OF MAR. He was *b.* 29 March 1836, at Clifton; ed. at Queen's Coll., Cambridge; M.A., 1860, and

(a) See p. 237, note "d."

(b) The act proceeded upon a report to the Crown, drawn up by the Attorney Gen. [Copley] and the Lord Advocate [Rae] tracing his decent, *thro' his mother* from the attainted Earl, without alluding to the fact of his also being (thro' his father) the great nephew and collateral heir male of the said Earl, in which latter capacity (only) he could have inherited the Earldom under the supposed limitation thereof held (in 1875) by the House of Lords. It appears to be assumed (and is accordingly so treated in the text) that this last mentioned Earldom or supposed Earldom (to which, as before mentioned, his heirship was not set forth) was by this act also restored to the restored Earl.

(c) This was one of the ten Scotch peerages restored by acts of Parl. (in 1824, 1826, and subsequently), out of 19 which had been forfeited for the insurrection of 1715. See vol. iii, p. 192, note "a," *sub* "Duffus."

(d) The Barony of Erskine [S.] was undoubtedly so forfeited as also was any right to any other dignity, *e.g.*, that of the Earldom or Barony of Garioch [S.] which may have been vested in the attainted Earl.

(e) Earldom of Mar restitution act, 1885.

"comitatis causa," at Oxford, 19 June 1862; in Holy Orders and sometime Curate of Teastone Wafer, co. Hereford; *suc. to the peerage* [S.] (tho' not to the family estates) on the death of his maternal uncle, 19 June 1866, when he assumed the name of *Erskine*, after that of *Goodeve*; but inasmuch as, owing (in a great measure) to the strange judgment of the House of Lords, 25 Feb. 1875 (whereby an Earldom of Mar [S.], hitherto unheard of, was supposed to have been *cr.* in 1565, with a rem. to heirs male of the body), "doubts" might "exist whether the ancient honour, dignity and title of peerage of Earl of Mar, which descended to Isabella, Countess of Mar, *was*, or *was not*,(a) previously to 1565 by any lawful means surrendered or merged in the Crown," tho' (as it was also recited) "until the decision" of 1875, the same "was commonly reputed to be still subsisting, and to have been enjoyed and possessed by John, Lord Erskine, his heirs and successors"(b) an act was passed, 6 Aug. 1885 (which practically(c) overruled the finding of 1875), whereby, in case of the former contingency, "THE SAID J. F. E. GOODEVE-ERSKINE AND ALL OTHER PERSONS, who would be entitled after him to succeed to the honours, dignities and titles of peerage anciently belonging to or enjoyed and held with the territorial Earldom of Mar, which descended to Isabella, Countess of Mar, as afsd., in case the honours, dignities and titles had never been by an lawful means forfeited or surrendered, or in case (being so forfeited or surrendered) they had been expressly and effectually restored to the said John, Lord Erskine, and his lawful heirs general, by the hereinbefore recited charter [1565], of Mary, Queen of Scots, SHALL BE AND THEY ARE HEREBY RESTORED TO THE SAID ANCIENT HONOURS, DIGNITIES AND TITLES OF PEERAGE, as fully and effectually to all intents and purposes as if the same had without any impediment descended to the said John, Lord Erskine, or had been duly and effectualy restored to the said John and his lawful heirs general by the said charter or by other means effectual in law."(b) The said Earldom was, accordingly, ordered to be called at the election of Scotch Rep. Peers [in its old place] next after that of Sutherland.(d) He *m.* 12 Sep. 1866, at St. Maughans, Llangattock-Vibon-Avel, co. Monmouth, Alice Mary Sinclair, 1st da. of John HAMILTON, of Hilston Park, co. Monmouth, by Anne, da. of Pryce JONES, of Cyfronydd, co. Montgomery.

(a) The Royal warrant, 15 Oct. 1885, granting to the sisters of the Earl of Mar, the precedence that would have been due to them if their *mother* had lived to succeed her brother (who died in 1866) as [*suo jure*] Countess of Mar, indicates that the then advisers of the Crown did *not* consider the mediæval Earldom (the only one which could thus have passed to a female heir of line) to have been surrendered or forfeited.

(b) Earldom of Mar restitution Act, 1885.

(c) "The relation of the Act [of 1885] and the judgment of 1875, to each other suggests some curious considerations. While the preamble of the act assumes that the judgment of 1875, must be upheld, as giving Lord Kellie *an* Earldom [of Mar] of 1565, it also unequivocally affirms that the *rationes decidendi* of the Lords, who pronounced it, were wrong. It *affirms*, in opposition to Lord Redesdale, *that the old Earldom had been inherited* by Countess Isabel, and had therefore *not* been extinguished in 1377; and it affirms, in opposition to Lord Chelmsford, *that the regulating charter was* (not that of 12 Aug. 1404, which diverted the succession to Alexander Stewart's heirs), but *that of* 9 *Dec.* 1404, which brought in Isabel's heirs. * * * The continued existence of the old dignity is left an open question. On the alternative of the doubts being well founded [*i.e.*, doubts as to whether it had not been at some date *forfeited* or *surrendered*] the effect of the act is to restore the representative of the Earldom of Mar to the rights of which the proceedings of 1875, had (technically) deprived him. If again the doubts are *not* well founded,—and this is the view of most Scotch lawyers and probably that of the noble Earl, who benefits by the Act—what the Act has done is to place the right of that Earl, which was previously good in law, wholly beyond challenge." ["D" as in note "b," p. 218.] See also note "a" next above.

(d) As to "the Earldom of Mar" evolved by the decision of 1875 [which declares it to be "now vested in Walter Henry, Earl of Mar and Kellie"], this act decrees that it shall be called in the place of "an Earldom *created* in 1565." Thus the Earldom of Mar on the Union Roll [S.] is the mediæval dignity and the one which is enjoyed by the heir general, while the Earldom brought into existence in 1875 as a *creation* of 1565 and then assigned to the Earl of Kellie is as Lord Crawford observes ["A," as in note "b," p. 218], "a phantom which has no backbone of its own and exists only through the force of illegal strain."

[John Francis Hamilton Sinclair Cunliffe Brooks Forbes GOODEVE-ERSKINE, *styled* LORD GARIOCH,(a) only s. and h. ap., b. 27 Feb. 1868, at Bournemouth, Hants; ed. at Eton and at Mag. Coll., Cambridge.]

Family Estates.—These were left by the late Earl (who d. in 1866) to his distant cousin and heir *male*, the Earl of Kellie [S.], to the exclusion of his nephew and heir of line. The Restitution Act of 1885 expressly declares that nothing therein contained "shall affect or in any manner prejudice the right or title" thereto of any the heirs "in the direct male line of the said John, Lord Erskine."

MAR.

i.e., "MAR" Earldom [S.] (*Erskine*), *cr.* (according to a judgment of the House of Lords in 1875, previous to which date its existence was unknown) in 1565. See "MAR" Earldom [S.], *sub* (the 18th holder of that dignity) 1565.

MARCH

[in Scotland], *i.e.*, the Scotch Marches.

Earldom [S.] I. 1289. *1.* PATRICK (DE DUNBAR), EARL OF DUNBAR [S.], s. and h. of Patrick, EARL OF DUNBAR [S.], b. about 1242, *suc.* his father in 1289 and was the *first of his race who called himself* EARL OF MARCH(b) [S.] He d. 1309.

II. 1309. *2.* PATRICK (DE DUNBAR), EARL OF MARCH or DUNBAR [S.], s. and h. Resigned his title in 1368 and d. 1369, aged 84.

III. 1368. *3.* GEORGE (DE DUNBAR), EARL OF MARCH or DUNBAR [S.] He d. 1420, aged 82.

IV. 1420, to 1435. *4.* GEORGE (DE DUNBAR), EARL OF MARCH or DUNBAR [S.], s. and h., b. about 1370; *forfeited* 1435; living 1454, d. before 1457.

[PATRICK DUNBAR, of Kilconquhar, co. Fife, *styled* (even after his father's attainder) "MAISTER OF THE MARCH," s. and h., living 1457.]

See fuller particulars under "DUNBAR" Earldom of [S.], cr. 1130, under the 8th to the 11th holders thereof.

V. 1455, to 1483. ALEXANDER STEWART, 2d s. of King James II. [S.], b. about 1454, was EARL OF MARCH [S.] before 8 July 1455, and was styled "*Lord of Annandale and Earl of March*" in(c) an act of Parl., 4 Aug. 1455, and was soon afterwards (certainly before 8 July 1458), cr. DUKE OF ALBANY [S.] See that title, *forfeited* (with this) in 1483; soon after

(a) "Garioch" whether as an Earldom or Barony, was unquestionably a dignity anciently held with the territorial Earldom of Mar and, as such, may be considered as having been restored under the act of 1885 to the then Earl. See, however, vol. iv p. 14, note "d," *sub* "Garioch," as to this Barony having, probably, never been a Lordship of Parl.

(b) *The Merse*, or March, was part of the land in Berwickshire granted in 1072 by Malcolm III. [S.] to Earl Cospatrick, the ancestor of this Earl. It was not till the Parl. at Brigham in March 1290 that these Earls of Dunbar appear to have had the designation of Earls of March [*Comes de Marchia*] since which period they were generally so known.

(c) "He carried the armorial insignia of the Earldom as is shewn by his seal in 1473 exhibiting the lion and roses of *Dunbar*; the three legs of *Man*, and the saltire and chief of *Annandale* (Laing's catalogue, No. 790.") See "Her. and Gen.," vol. vii, p. 89. This Earl appears to have had the Castle of Dunbar and the Lordship of Dunbar possessed formerly by th Earls of March of the Dunbar family.

which, by act of Parl., 1 Oct. 1487, the Earldom of March, the Baronies of Dunbar and Coldbrandspath and the Lordship of Annandale, with the Castles of Dunbar, Coldbrandspath, and Lochmaben, were annexed to the Crown.

VI. 1580, to 1586. ROBERT (STUART), EARL OF LENNOX [S.], was, on resigning that Earldom (to which he had been advanced 16 June 1578), cr., 5 March 1579/80, EARL OF MARCH and LORD OF DUNBAR [S.], which creation was confirmed by Royal charter, 5 Oct. 1582. He was 2d s. of John, 2d EARL OF LENNOX [S.], by Anne, da. of John (STEWART), EARL OF ATHOLE [S.]; was Provost of the Collegiate Church of Dumbarton, and was in 1542 Bishop of Caithness but was kept out of that See by the Regent Arran [S.] against whom he had joined with his brother, the then Earl of Lennox. Taking part with the Reformation he had the Priory of St. Andrew's conferred on him by the Crown. In 1567 the Earldom of Lennox [S.] which had vested in the Crown (by the accession thereto of his great nephew James VI. [S.]), was conferred on him by charter, 16 June 1578, but (the King being anxious to dispose of this Earldom elsewhere) he shortly afterwards resigned the same for the *Earldom of March*, &c. [S.], as above stated. He m. Elizabeth, widow of Hugh (FRASER), LORD LOVAT [S.] (who d. 1 Jan. 1576), 1st da. of John (STEWART), 4th EARL OF ATHOLE [S.], by his 1st wife, Elizabeth, da. of George (GORDON), 4th EARL OF HUNTLY [S.] She obtained a divorce from him for impotency.(a) He d. s.p. at St. Andrew's, 29 March 1586, in his 70th year, when all his *honours* became *extinct*.(b)

Marquessate [S.] I. 1672, to 1682. JOHN (MAITLAND), EARL OF LAUDERDALE [S.], was cr. 1 May 1672, DUKE OF LAUDERDALE and MARQUESS OF MARCH(c) [S.] He d. s.p.m., 24 Aug. 1682, in his 67th year, when the *dignities* thus conferred, became *extinct*. See "LAUDERDADE," Earldom [S.], cr. 1624, under the 2d Earl.

Earldom [S.] VII. 1697. *1.* LORD WILLIAM DOUGLAS, 2d s. of William (DOUGLAS), 1st DUKE OF QUEENSBERRY [S.], by Isabel, 6th da. of William (DOUGLAS), 1st MARQUESS OF DOUGLAS [S.], was b. about 1665; was Lieut. Col. of a Reg. of Horse to James II.; obtained (on his marriage) from his father, 12 Oct. 1693, the Castle of Niedpath and a considerable estate in co. Peebles, in tail, and, tho' a non-juror during the greater part of King William's reign, was, having at last taken the oaths, cr. 20 April 1697, EARL OF MARCH (d) VISCOUNT OF PEEBLES, LORD DOUGLAS OF NIEDPATH, LYNE AND MUNARD, with a rem. to the heirs male of his body, with (*if genuine*), a further limitation, *viz.*, "to the other heirs male and of entail contained in the infeofment of the land and Lordship of Niedpath," under the entail of 1693 above alluded to.(e) He took his seat in Parl., 21 July 1698; was Gov. of the Castle of

---

(a) She m. (as her 3d husband) 6 July 1581, the notorious James (STEWART), EARL OF ARRAN [S.], who was *attainted* in 1585.

(b) *The Earldom of March* conferred 7 June 1619, on his great nephew, Esme (Stuart), Duke of Lennox [S.], was unquestionably an *English dignity*. See p. 245 and note "a" thereto.

(c) This title was selected to commemorate his descent from Patrick (Dunbar), Earl of March, or Dunbar [S.], 1309-68, whose da., Elizabeth, m. his ancestor, John Maitland.

(d) The Douglas family having in the 15th century been gorged with the estates of the family of Dunbar, Earls of March [S.], whose ruin they chiefly accomplished, apparently felt, in the 17th century, a predilection towards their ancient peerage, tho' not in possession of any of the lands, from which the title of *March* was taken.

(e) The limitation is to him "et hæredes masculos de ejus corpore, *quibus deficientibus, alios ejus hæredes masculos et talliæ contentos in ejus infeofamentis terrarum et Dominii de Niedpath.*" Mag. Sig. M. lxxiv., No. 98. Mr. Foster, however in his Peerage (1883), p. 724, states that "the words *in italics*, are not to be found in the

Edinburgh, Dec. 1702 to Oct. 1704. He m. (contract 12 Oct. 1693), Jane, 2d da. of John (HAY), 1st MARQUESS OF TWEEDALE [S.], by Jean, da. of Walter (SCOTT), EARL OF BUCCLEUCH [S.] He d. at Edinburgh, 2 Sep. 1705, and was bur. at Peebles.(a) His widow d. at Edinburgh, July 1729, and was bur. with him. Fun. entry at Lyon office.

II. 1705. 2. WILLIAM (DOUGLAS), EARL OF MARCH, &c. [S.], 1st s. and h., b. about 1696. He m. Ann, 1st da. of John (HAMILTON), EARL OF RUGLEN [S.], afterwards [1739] EARL OF SELKIRK [S.], by his first wife, Anne, da. of John (KENNEDY), 7th EARL OF CASSILLIS [S.] He d. at Barnton, co. Edinburgh, 7 March 1731, in his 35th year. His widow, who was b. 5 April 1698, became, on the death of her father, suo jure COUNTESS OF RUGLEN [S.] She m. secondly, Jan. 1747, Anthony SAWYER, Paymaster of the Forces [S.] She d. at York, 21 April 1748, in her 51st year.

III. 1731. 3. WILLIAM (DOUGLAS), EARL OF MARCH, &c. [S.], only s. and h., b. 16 Dec. 1725. He suc. his mother, on her death, 21 April 1748, as EARL OF RUGLEN, &c. [S.], a peerage cr. 14 April 1697, six days before that of the Earldom of March. He suc. his cousin, 22 Oct. 1778, as DUKE OF QUEENSBERRY, &c. [S.] For fuller particulars see "QUEENSBERRY," Earldom of [S.], cr. 1633, under the 6th Earl and 4th Duke. His Grace d. unm. 23 Dec. 1810, in his 86th year, when such of his dignities as did not become extinct devolved in three separate ways, of which one, viz., *the Earldom of March and the titles cr. therewith* (20 April 1697), devolved (unless, indeed, they be considered as having become *extinct* by the failure of heirs male of the body of the grantee) as under.

IV. 1810. 4. FRANCIS CHARTERIS-WEMYSS, afterwards CHARTERIS-WEMYSS-DOUGLAS, styling himself, EARL OF WEMYSS [S.], cousin and h., according to the spec. lim. in the patent of 1697, being grandson and h. of Francis Charteris-Wemyss, also styling himself EARL OF WEMYSS (who d. 1808), 2d but 1st surv. s. and h. of James, EARL OF WEMYSS (who d. 1756), s. and h. of David, EARL OF WEMYSS, by his first wife, Ann, da. of William (DOUGLAS), 1st DUKE OF QUEENSBERRY [S.], sister of William, 1st EARL OF MARCH, she being the person on whose heir male of the body the Earldom of March, &c., together with the castle and estate of Niedpath, devolved. He was, on 17 July 1821, cr. a Peer [U.K.] as BARON WEMYSS of Wemyss, co. Fife, and on 1826, by the reversal of the attainder in 1746, of his ancestor) became EARL OF WEMYSS, &c. [S.] See "WEMYSS" Earldom of [S.], cr. 1633, *attainted* 1746, but *restored* 1826; with which Earldom, the Earldom of March, &c. (if, indeed, the extended remainder thereof be considered *genuine*) continues united.

MARCH [in England].

i.e., the English Marches towards Wales.

---

original signed patent, having been inserted in Scotland subsequently." The settlement of the lands and lordship of Niedpath, 12 Oct. 1693, is fully set out in Wood's "Douglas," vol. ii, p. 691, and, by it, the peerage would be unquestionably vested (as those lands are), in the Earl of Wemyss. It is stated in "Riddell" (p. 208) "that in the docquet of the March signature in 1697, the solitary word '*which*' prefaces the blank that has been noticed [*i.e.*, one immediately following the grant to heirs male of the body] and seems to evince that an ulterior limitation had been in view." See "Riddell" pp. 207-8, 1052-3 *et seq.* and 1065, note 3.

(a) His elevation to a peerage by King William seems extraordinary, considering his Jacobitish antecedents; Macky, in his "Characters," writes of him that "he hath no great genius, but is a good-natured gentleman, handsome in his person." He adds, however that he is "turned of 50 years old," which seems as if there is some confusion, as the Earl could not have been much more than 40, even at his death in 1705, his *elder* br. being b. in 1662.

Earldom. I. 1328, to 1330.

1. ROGER (MORTIMER), LORD MORTIMER DE WIGMORE, s. and h. of Edmund, LORD MORTIMER (so *cr.* by writ 23 June 1295), was *b.* about 29 April 1286; *suc.* his father (who was slain at Builth, co. Brecon), in 1303; *knighted*, 22 May 1306; Bearer of the vestments at the Coronation of Edward II., 25 Feb. 1308; was in the Scotch wars; Ch. Gov. of Ireland, 1316-19; and became notorious as the paramour of Isabel, the Queen Consort, to whose Household in 1325 he was Steward. He was *cr.*, 9 Nov. 1328,(a) EARL OF MARCH [" *Comitem de Marchiâ Walliæ*"(b)] with £10 annual rent issuing out of the counties of Salop and, Stafford and, together with the Queen Dowager, had the chief control of the Kingdom. He *m.* before 1308, Joan, da. and h. of Peter DE GENEVILL, of Trim, in Ireland. He was taken prisoner at Nottingham, convicted of treason, and was hung at Smithfield in London 26 or 29 Nov. 1330, when, having been attainted, *all his honours* were *forfeited*. He was *bur.* at Grey Friars but afterwards removed to Wigmore. His widow *d.* 1356.

II. 1354. 2. ROGER (MORTIMER), LORD MORTIMER DE WIGMORE, grandson of the above, being s. and h. of his eldest son, Edmund, LORD MORTIMER (so *cr.* by writ 20 Nov. 1331), by Elizabeth, 3d da. and coheir of Bartholomew (BADLESMERE), LORD BADLESMERE, was *b.* about 1327; *suc.* his father in 1331; was in the war with France and was *knighted* by the Black Prince, 13 July 1346, having already been elected, 23 April 1344, K.G., as one of the Founders of that Order.(c) He was sum. to Parl. as a Baron from 20 Nov. (1348), 22 Ed. III., to 15 March (1353/4), 28 Ed. III., by writs sometime addressed "*Rogero de Mortuomari*" [only] and sometimes (24, 25, and 27 Ed. III.), with the addition of the words "*de Wigmore.*" The attainder of his grandfather abovenamed having been reversed in the Parl. of 27 Ed. III. (about 26 April 1354), he thus became EARL OF MARCH, and, as such, was sum. to Parl. 20 Sep. (1355), 29 Ed. III. He was Warden of the Cinque Ports, 1355; Constable of the army in France, 1359. He *m.* Philippa, da. of William (MONTACUTE), 1st EARL OF SALISBURY, by Catherine, da. of William (GRANDISON), LORD GRANDISON. He *d.* 26 Feb. 1359/60, at Romera, in Burgundy, while in command of the forces there, and was *bur.* at Wigmore.

III. 1360. 3. EDMUND (MORTIMER), EARL OF MARCH, &c., 2d but only surv. s. and h., *b.* 1 Feb. 1351, and *suc.* his father, at his age of nine, in Feb. 1360. Having *m.* (shortly after her father's death, 17 Oct. 1368), the Lady Philippa PLANTAGENET,(d) *suo jure* COUNTESS OF ULSTER [I.],(e) only child of

---

(a) In Courthope's "Observations on dignities," *sub* "Earldoms," after stating that from the time of Richard I. "the girding on of the sword [of the county] became the common form of investiture for an Earl whether Palatine or otherwise," it is added that for a long time "the titles of these Earldoms continued to be derived *from counties*, but, when in 1328, Roger Mortimer was girded with a sword, according to custom, and had given to him the title of Earl of March (a name derived neither from county nor city) we may consider that no vestige than remained of the significant meaning that had once attached to the ceremony of creating Earls" [Mr. C. adding in MS.] "altho' investiture was still thought necessary for the perfecting the dignity."]

(b) This is the form given in Baker's [contemporary] chronicle, where he is given as the second of three Earls made in the Parl. of Salisbury, 16 to 31 Oct. 1328, the first of whom was the King's brother, *cr.* Earl of Cornwall, while the third was the "Pincerna Hiberniæ," *cr.* Earl of Ormonde.

(c) See vol. i, p. 276, note "a," *sub* "Beauchamp," for a list of these Founders.

(d) Her issue became, on the death of King Richard II. (14 Feb. 1399/400), the heirs of line to the Crown, in which right her great-great-grandson, King Edward IV. (the grandson of her grandaughter, Lady Anne Mortimer, Countess of Cambridge), ascended the Throne in 1460.

(e) Of "the six Irish Earldoms *cr.* before 1330" the first was Ulster, *cr.* (1205-06), 7 John, with a rem. to heirs general which passed accordingly "thro' females from Lacy to De Burgh, from De Burgh to Plantagenet, &c." See [" *The Earldoms of Ormond*" [I.], by J. H. Round, in Foster's "*Coll. Gen.*," p. 84.] See vol. vi, *sub* "Ormond," as to these six Earldoms.

Lionel, DUKE OF CLARENCE (2d surv. s. of **King Edward III.**), by his first wife, Elizabeth, also *suo jure* COUNTESS OF ULSTER [I.], he became (in right of the said Philippa, his wife), EARL OF ULSTER [I.], and acquired, also, the vast Lordship of Clare in Suffolk. He was MARSHAL OF ENGLAND, 1369-72; Ambassador to France, 1378; Bearer of the second sword and the spurs at the Coron., 16 July 1377, of Ric. II., being also one of the Councillors of the Regency; CH. GOV. OF IRELAND, as Lieutenant, 1379-81. He *d.* at Cork, 27 Dec. 1381, aged 30, and was *bur.* at Wigmore. His widow, who was *b.* 16 Aug. 1355, survived him but a few days, and *d.* also at Cork, 5 Jan. 1381/2.

IV. 1381. 4. ROGER (MORTIMER), EARL OF MARCH, &c., also EARL OF ULSTER [I.], s. and h., *b.* 11 April 1374, and *suc.* his father, at the age of seven, in Dec. 1381, the Lieutenancy of Ireland, being conformed to him, 24 Jan. 1381/2, which he appears to have held till 1383. In 1387, he was declared by King Ric. II., *heir presumptive* to the *throne of England* and was *Knighted* (by him), 23 April 1390; CH. GOV. OF IRELAND, as Lieutenant, 1395-98. He *m.* Eleanor, 1st da. (whose issue became coheir) of Thomas (HOLAND), EARL OF KENT, by Alice, da. of Richard (FITZALAN), EARL OF ARUNDEL. He was slain at Kenlis, by the Irish of Leinster, 20 July (St. Margaret's day) 1398, aged 24. His widow *m.* (as his first wife) Edward (CHERLETON), LORD CHERLETON DE POWYS, who *d.* s.p.m., 14 March 1420/1. She *d.* 23 Oct. 1405.

V. 1398. 5. EDMOND (MORTIMER), EARL OF MARCH and LORD MORTIMER DE WIGMORE, also EARL OF ULSTER [I.], s. and h., *b.* 6 Nov. 1391; *suc.* his father (also) at the age of seven, in July 1398; was kept in prison at Trim. Castle (owing to his claim to the throne), by Henry IV. till 1413, but was, by the new King, made K.B., 8 April 1413, and was bearer of the first sceptre at the Coronation of Katherine, the Queen Consort, 21 Feb. 1421, and one of the Councillors of Regency, 5 Dec. 1422. CH. GOV. OF IRELAND, as Lieutenant, 1423-25. He *m.* Anne, da. of Edmund (STAFFORD, 5th EARL OF STAFFORD, by Anne, da. of Thomas (PLANTAGENET), DUKE OF GLOUCESTER. He *d.* sp., 19 Jan. 1424/5, aged 33, in Ireland and was *bur.* at Stoke, near Clare, co. Suffolk. His widow *m.* (as his first wife) before 1427, John (HOLAND), 1st DUKE OF EXETER, who *d.* 5 Aug. 1447. She was *bur.* at St. Katherine's by the Tower of London (11 Hen. VI.), 1422-23. Earl Edmund appears to have been *suc.* in his peerage dignities (they being at all events, whether rightly or wrongly, so assumed) by his nephew (*ex sorore*) and heir, as under.

VI. 1425. 6. RICHARD (PLANTAGENET), EARL OF MARCH and LORD MORTIMER DE WIGMORE, also EARL OF ULSTER [I.], nephew and h., being only s. and h. of Richard (PLANTAGENET), EARL OF CAMBRIDGE, by his first wife, Anne, eldest of the two sisters[a] of Edmond (MORTIMER), EARL OF MARCH, &c., next abovenamed. He was *b.* 1412, and in right of his mother, who had *d.* before 1415, appears to have inherited the honours of her family. The attainder of his father was not reversed till 1461, but he was restored as DUKE OF YORK, on Whit-Sunday, 1426. He was, by Henry VI., *declared heir to the Crown*, 25 Oct. 1460, but was slain two months later, 30 Dec. 1460, aged 58.

VII. 1460, to 1461. 7. EDWARD (PLANTAGENET), DUKE OF YORK, EARL OF MARCH, and LORD MORTIMER DE WIGMORE, also EARL OF ULSTER [I.], s. and h., *b.* 28 April 1442; *styled* EARL OF MARCH till he *suc.* his father as DUKE OF YORK, 30 Dec. 1460. He was proclaimed **King of England**, 4 March 1460/1, as **Edward IV.** (*post conquestum*) when *all his honours merged in the Crown.*

For fuller particulars see "YORK," Dukedom, *cr.* 1385, *sub* the third and fourth Dukes.

(a) The yst. sister, Lady Eleanor Mortimer, *m.* Sir Edward Courtenay, K.B. (s. and h. ap. of Edward, the blind Earl of Devon), and *d.* s.p. before 1418.

VIII. 1479, to 1483. *1.* EDWARD (PLANTAGENET), DUKE OF CORNWALL at his birth, 2 Nov. 1470, being s. and h. ap. of **King Edward IV.** next abovenamed, was *cr.* **Prince of Wales** and EARL OF CHESTER, 26 June 1471; *cr.* DUKE OF CORNWALL, in Parl., 17 July 1471, and finally was *cr.* 18 July 1479, EARL OF MARCH and EARL OF PEMBROKE to hold the same during the King's pleasure. On 9 April 1483, he ascended the throne as **Edward V.** (*post conquestum*) when *all his honours merged in the Crown.* See fuller particulars under "CORNWALL" Dukedom, 1470 to 1483.

IX. 1619. *1.* LORD ESME STUART, 2d s. of Esme, 1st DUKE OF LENNOX [S.], *b.* 1579, was *cr.* 7 June 1619, BARON STUART OF LEIGHTON BROMSWOLD, co. Huntingdon, and EARL OF MARCH.(a) He *suc.* 16 Feb. 1623/4, as DUKE OF LENNOX, and *d.* 30 July 1624. See fuller particulars under "LENNOX," Dukedom [S.], *cr.* 1581, under the 3d Duke.

X. 1624. *2.* JAMES (STUART), DUKE OF LENNOX, &c. [S.], also EARL OF MARCH, &c. [E.], s. and h.; *b.* 6 April 1612; *suc. to the peerage,* 30 July 1642. He was *cr.*, 8 Aug. 1641, DUKE OF RICHMOND, with a spec. rem. He *d.* 30 March 1655.

XI. 1655. *3.* ESME (STUART), DUKE OF RICHMOND, EARL OF MARCH, &c. [E.], also DUKE OF LENNOX, &c. [S.], only s. and h.; *b.* 2 Nov. 1649; *suc. to the peerage,* 20 March 1655. He *d.* unm., 10 Aug. 1660.

XII. 1660, to 1672. *4.* CHARLES (STUART), DUKE OF RICHMOND, EARL OF MARCH, EARL OF LICHFIELD, &c. [E.], also DUKE OF LENNOX, &c. [S.], cousin and heir male; *b.* 7 March 1670. He was *cr.*, 10 Dec. 1645, EARL OF LICHFIELD, &c., and *suc.* to the two Dukedoms [E. and S.], the Earldom of March, &c., 10 Aug. 1660, but *d.* s.p.s., 12 Dec. 1672, when *all his honours* save the Barony of Clifton of Leighton Bromswold, became *extinct* or *merged* in the Crown.

[X.–XII.: See fuller particulars under "Richmond" Dukedom, *cr.* 1641; *ex.* 1672.]

XIII. 1675. *1.* CHARLES LENNOX, illegit. s. of **King Charles II.**, *b.* 29 July 1672; was (when three years old) *cr.*, 9 Aug. 1675, BARON OF SETRINGTON, co. York, EARL OF MARCH, and DUKE OF RICHMOND. See "Richmond" Dukedom, *cr.* 1675.

MARCHMONT.

Earldom [S.] I. 1697. *1.* SIR PATRICK HUME, 2d Bart. [S.], of Polwarth, co. Berwick, s. and h. of Sir Patrick HUME, 1st Bart.(b) [S.], of Polwarth afsd., by Christian, da. of Sir Alexander HAMILTON, of Innerwick, was *b.* 13 Jan. 1641; *suc.* his father in the Baronetcy in April 1648; was M.P. for Berwickshire, 1669-74 and 1689-90. He had distinguished himself for his opposition to the Government and, being suspected of complicity with "*Shaftesbury's plot,*" was imprisoned, accordingly, 1675-79. He took part in 1685 in the rebellion of the Earl of Argyll (on behalf of the Duke of Monmouth) whereby he was "*forfeited*" and escaped to Holland, returning thence, in 1688, when he became a great favourite of the new King; was P.C. [S.] and was *cr.*, 26 Dec. 1690, LORD

(a) See p. 67, note "a," *sub* "Lennox," as to his great uncle Robert (Stuart), Earl of Lennox [S.], having been *cr.* in 1580, EARL OF MARCH *in Scotland,* which dignity became *extinct* at his death in 1586.

(b) The Baronetcy was *cr.*, 19 Dec. 1637, to heirs male. See "*Riddell,*" p. 673, where it is added "that the date of creation assigned to this Baronetcy in 1625 [*Qy.* 28 Dec. 1625], is not correct.'

POLWARTH [S.], with rem. to the heirs male of his body and the heirs of the said heirs. Sheriff of Berwickshire, 1692—1702, and again 1714-24; one of the extraordinary Lords of Session [S.], 1693; HIGH CHANCELLOR [S.], 2 May 1696, to June 1702, being *cr.*, 23 May 1697, EARL OF MARCHMONT, VISCOUNT OF BLASONBERRIE, LORD POLWARTH OF POLWARTH, REDBRAES AND GREENLAW [S.], with rem. to heirs male whatsoever; was Commissioner to the Parl. [S.], 19 July 1698, and to the Gen. Assembly [S.], 1702, after which date he held no office till made one of the Lords of Police [S.] by George I.(a) He *m.*, in or before 1665, Grizel, da. of Sir Thomas KER, of Cavers. She *d.* at Edinburgh, 11 Oct. 1703, and was *bur.* in the Canongate. He *d.* at Berwick, 2 Aug. 1724, in his 84th year, and was *bur.* with her. Fun. entry in Lyon office. Admon. 10 Dec. 1724.

[PATRICK HUME, *styled* LORD POLWARTH, 1st s. and h. ap.; was in the service of the Prince of Orange, in Holland with whom in 1688, he came over; was HIGH TREASURER [S.] in the Parl of 1698; Col of the 7th Dragoons. 1700. He *m.* firstly, 2 Dec. 1697, Elizabeth, da. of James HUME, of Hume Castle in Ireland. He *m.* secondly, Jane, da. of Charles (HOME), 6th EARL OF HOME [S.] He *d.* v.p. and s.p. in 1710.]

II. 1724. 2. ALEXANDER (HUME-CAMPBELL), EARL OF MARCHMONT, &c. [S.] 2d but 1st surv. s. and h., *b.* 1676; was a member of the Faculty of Advocates, 1696; M.P. for Kirkwall, 1698—1702, and for Berwickshire, 1706-07. He, having *m.* 29 July 1697, Margaret, da. and h. of Sir George CAMPBELL, of Cessnock, co. Ayr, assumed the name of *Campbell*, was *knighted* and (as Sir A. C.) was a Lord of Session, 1704-14; was *styled* LORD POLWARTH, from 1710 to 1724; was a Commissioner of the Exchequer; P.C. [S.]; supported the Union in Parl.; Envoy to Denmark and to Prussia, 1715; LORD CLERK REGISTER [S.], 1716-33. Ambassador to the Congress at Cambray, 1721; *suc. to the peerage* [S.], 2 Aug. 1724; K.T., 7 March 1725; P.C., 1726; REP. PEER [S.] 1727-34, being dismissed from all office in May 1733, owing to his opposition to the Prime Minister Walpole. His wife abovenamed was living in 1710. He *d.* in London, 27 Feb. 1740, in his 65th year. Funeral entry in Lyon office.

[GEORGE HUME-CAMPBELL, *styled* LORD POLWARTH, 1st s. and h. ap., *b.* 17 Jan. 1704. He *d.* unm. and v.p., 18 Oct. 1724, in his 21st year, at Montpelier, in France.]

III. 1740, to 1794. 3. HUGH (CAMPBELL), EARL OF MARCHMONT [1697], VISCOUNT OF BLASONBERRIE [1697], LORD POLWARTH [1690], and LORD POLWARTH OF POLWARTH, REDBRAES AND GREENLAW [1697] in the peerage of Scotland, 3d but 1st surv. s. and h.; *b.* 15 Feb. 1708, at Edinburgh, *styled* LORD POLWARTH from 1724 to 1740; M.P. for Berwick, 1734-40; first Lord of Police [S.] 1747; REP. PEER [S.], 1750-84; Keeper of the Great Seal [S.], 1764-94. He *m.* firstly, 1 May 1731, at St. James', Westm., Anne, 3d da. and coheir of Robert WESTERN, of St. Peter's Cornhill, London, by Anne, 1st sister and coheir of Sir Richard SHIRLEY, Bart., of Preston, Sussex. She *d.* 9 May 1747, at Redbraes. He *m.* secondly, 30 Jan. 1748, in London, Elizabeth, da. of Windmill CROMPTON, of Hatton Garden, a linen draper in Cheapside. He *d.* s.p.m.s., 10 Jan. 1794, in his 86th year, at Hemel Hempstead, Herts, when the *Earldom of Marchmont*, and the honours *cr.* therewith in 1697 became *dormant*,(b) but the right to the *Barony*

(a) Macky says of him when "towards 70 years old" that "he hath been a fine gentleman of clear parts, but always a lover of set long speeches, and could hardly give advice to a private friend without them; zealous for the *Presbyterian government* in the church and *its divine rights*, which was the great motive that encouraged him against the Crown. Business and years have now almost wore him out; he hath been handsome and lovely and was so since King William came to the Throne; on the Queen's accession he was discharged from all his employments."

(b) The dignity [1697] was claimed in 1804 and 1822, by Alexander Home, heir male of the body of George Home of Wedderburn, elder br. of Sir Patrick Home of Polwarth, ancestor of the Earls of Marchmont, both being sons of David Home, s. and h. ap. of Sir David Home of Wedderburn (1413-50), second son of Sir Thomas Home, of Home. This Alexander was, 2 Aug. 1799, served heir male of the said Sir

of Polwarth [*cr.* in 1690] devolved on the heir general.(a) See that dignity. His will was pr. March 1794. His widow *d.* 12 Feb. 1797, at Hemel Hempstead afsd. Her will pr. March 1797.

[PATRICK HUME-CAMPBELL, *styled* LORD POLWARTH, 1st s. and h. ap., by first wife. He *d.* young and v.p.]

[ALEXANDER HUME-CAMPBELL, *styled* LORD POLWARTH, 2d but 1st surv. s. and h. ap. by second wife, *b.* 1750; was *cr.* v.p. 20 May 1776, BARON HUME OF BERWICK. He *d.* s.p. and v.p., 9 March 1781, aged 30, at Wrest park, Beds. See fuller particulars under "HUME OF BERWICK," Barony, *cr.* 1776; *ex.* 1781.]

MARE or DE LA MARE.

See "DE LA MARE, Barony (*Delamare*), *cr.* 1299; *ex.* 1316.

MARGAM.

See "MANSELL OF MARGAM, co. Glamorgan," Barony (*Mansell*), *cr.* 1712.

MARISCHAL.

Earldom [S.] I. 1458? *1.* SIR WILLIAM KEITH, GREAT MARISCHAL OF SCOTLAND,(b) s. and h. of Sir Robert Keith, also GREAT MARISCHAL [S.], by his first wife, the heiress of TROUP, co. Banff, *suc.* his father between 1421 and 1442, and is stated(c) to have *cr.* in 1430, LORD KEITH [S.] He is described in a charter, dat. 20 May 1443, confirmed by the King, 28 Oct. 1444, as *William, Lord Keith, Marischal of Scotland*, and he sat in Parl. 26 Oct. 1451, as William, Lord Keith, the King's Marischal. He was *cr.* EARL MARISCHAL [S.] before 4 July 1458, as he is described by that title in an Exchequer roll relating to the shire of Kincardine, under that date, and the acts of Parl. [S.], also, shew that he sat in Parl. as *Earl Marischal*, 14 Oct. 1467."(d) He *m.* Mary, da. of Sir James HAMILTON, of Cadyow. He *d.* before 1476.

David Home (the first of Wedderburn) therein called "*pater atavi tritavi.*" He *d.* 1828, and the claim was continued (1838-48), by Capt. Francis Douglas Home, his s. and h. The evidence established his descent, altho' it did not prove the extinction of other lines from whom, if existing in the male line, a nearer heir male could be deduced.

(a) His grandson and h. general, Hugh Scott, of Harden, was allowed that Barony in 1835.

(b) "The office of *Marshal* was even of still higher antiquity [then that of *the Constable*], but the original grant is nowhere extant. The oldest conveyance respecting it is a charter by Robert Bruce in favour of Sir Robert Keith, proceeding upon his resignation *in pleno consilio nostro*, whereby he confirms to him (*inter alia*) *terras de Keith cum officio Mareschalli, eidem terræ pertinenti.* From this it would appear that the office was *not personal*, but *annexed to land* and held by grand serjeantry as was frequent in England in the case of high hereditary offices. When the family had been raised to the dignity of *Earl* Marshal, the office still continued as before under its ancient denomination. [See 'Retour 10 Oct. 1637, of George, Earl Marshal, in various lands among others in *Keith Marshall cum officio Mariscallatus Scotiæ, &c.*'] As the greater part of Keith or Keith Marshal, if not the whole, had been alienated previous to the forfeiture of George, Earl Marshal in 1715, a question might possibly arise as to its present situation." ["*Riddell*," 1833, p. 119.] "The Court of Session, 2 Feb. 1682, decided that the hereditary office of Marshal in Scotland, so long in the noble house of Keith was of the nature of a Peerage, and not *in commercio.*" ["*Riddell*," p. 24.] At the decreet of ranking in 1606, the Earldom was given "official precedence" over some of more ancient creation. See p. 284, note "c," *sub* "Mar."

(c) Douglas peerage, 1st edit., 1760.

(d) "Hewlett," p. 156.

II. 1475? 2. WILLIAM (KEITH), EARL MARISCHAL, &c. [S.], 2d but 1st surv. s. and h. male ;(a) sat in Parl. [S.] *as Earl Marischal*, 1 July 1476, and, having joined the party of the Prince, sat there again on his accession (as King James IV. [S.]) in 1488. He *m.* Mariota, 3d da. of Thomas (ERSKINE), 2d LORD ERSKINE [S.] (dispossessed EARL OF MAR [S.]), by Janet DOUGLAS, his wife. He was living 10 Dec. 1482, but *d.* soon afterwards.

III. 1485? 3. WILLIAM (KEITH), EARL MARISCHAL, &c. [S.], s. and h., *suc.* his father about 1485 and sat in Parl. [S.], 28 April 1491. In 1519 he was custodian of the young King James V. [S.] at Edinburgh Castle. He *m.* (contract 1482) Elizabeth, 5th da. of George (GORDON), 2d EARL OF HUNTLY [S.] by his first wife, the Lady Annabella STEWART, da. of King James I. [S.] He *d.* about 1530.

[ROBERT KEITH, *styled* LORD KEITH, 1st s. and h. ap. ;(b) *m.* before 8 Jan. 1505/6, Beatrix or Elizabeth, da. of John (DOUGLAS), 2d EARL OF MORTON [S.] He *d.* v.p., 9 Sep. 1513, being slain (together with his br., William Keith, of Troup), at the battle of Flodden.(c)]

IV. 1530? 4. WILLIAM (KEITH), EARL MARISCHAL &c. [S.], grandson and h., being s. and h.(d) of Robert KEITH, *styled* LORD KEITH, and Beatrix or Elizabeth, his wife, both abovenamed ; *suc.* his grandfather about 1530; accompanied King James V. [S.] to France in 1536; was an extraordinary Lord of Session [S.], 1541, and again, 1561 to 1573 ; was at the battle of Pinkie in 1547 ; a supporter of the Reformation, 1560, and was possessed of property worth 270,000 marks of yearly rent. He *m.* before 30 June 1538(e) Margaret, 1st da. and heir of line of Sir William KEITH, of Innerugie, co. Banff, by whom he had nine children. He *d.* 7 Oct. 1581.

[WILLIAM KEITH, *styled* LORD KEITH, 1st s. and h. ap. ;(f) was taken prisoner by the English in 1558 and ransomed next year for £2,000. He *m.* Elizabeth, 1st da. of George (HAY), 7th EARL OF ERROLL [S.] He *d.* v.p., 10 Aug. 1580.]

V. 1581. 5. GEORGE (KEITH), EARL MARISCHAL, &c. [S.], grandson and h., being s. and h. of William KEITH, *styled* LORD KEITH, and Elizabeth, his wife, both abovenamed. He, who was *b.* 1554 , *suc.* his grandfather in Oct. 1581 ; studied at several of the Universities abroad ; P.C. [S.], 1589, being sent as Ambassador to Denmark to arrange the marriage of the King [S.] with the Princess of Denmark. He *suc.* his uncle between 1589, and 26 Sep. 1592, as LORD ALTRIE [S.], under the spec. rem. in the creation, 29 July 1587, of that dignity. In 1593, he *founded the Marischal College at Aberdeen*, containing a Principal and four Professors

(a) His elder br., Robert Keith, to whom his father had resigned the estates and offices, *d.* v.p. and s.p.m., leaving a da. and h., Jean (the heir of line to the 1st Earl) who *m.* as his first wife Andrew (GRAY), 2d LORD GRAY [S.], who *d.* 1513/4. The date of this resignation is given as 1442 and that of Robert's death as 1446 (Wood's "*Douglas*"), but these dates seem hardly probable.

(b) From Alexander, the 4th and yst. son, descend the family of Keith of Ravelstoun, afterwards (1766) of Dunottar, who, since 1778, appear to represent the male line of heirs of the 1st Earl.

(c) See p. 63, note "b," *sub* "Lennox," for a list of the Scotch nobles and their elder sons slain at Flodden field.

(d) Robert Keith, Abbot of Deer, his next br., was father of a bastard son, Andrew Keith, *cr.* LORD DINGWALL [S.], in 1584, a dignity which appears to have ceased before 1606.

(e) Her marriage, worth £10,000, was sold by the Duke of Albany as early as 1521.

(f) Robert Keith, Commendator of Deer Abbey, his next br., was *cr.*, 29 July 1587, LORD ALTRIE [S.] for life, with a spec. rem. to his nephew, George, Earl Marischall [S.] He was of great age in 1589 and *d.* s.p. before 1592.

of Philosophy. This was ratified by Act of Parl. He was High Commissioner to the Parl. [S.], 6 June 1609. He m. firstly, Margaret (b. before 5 Dec. 1565), da. of Alexander (HOME), 5th LORD HOME [S.], by his first wife, Margaret, da. of Sir Walter KER, of Cessford. He m. secondly, Margaret, da. of James (OGILVY), LORD OGILVY OF AIRLIE [S.], by Jean, da. of William (FORBES), 7th LORD FORBES [S.] He d. 2 April 1623, in his 70th year, at Dunottar Castle and was bur. in St. Bride's, Dunottar. His widow m.(a) Sir Alexander STRACHAN, of Thornton.

VI. 1623. 6. WILLIAM (KEITH), EARL MARISCHAL, LORD KEITH, and LORD ALTRIE [S.], s. and h., by first wife; had charters, v.p., 21 Oct. 1612, as "LORD KEITH, Master of Marischal"; suc. to the peerage, [S.], in 1623, and had charter 28 May 1625, of the Barony of Keith Marischal in Nova Scotia. P.C. to King Charles I.; fitted out a fleet in 1634, for the service of Poland. He m. Mary, da. of John (ERSKINE), EARL OF MAR [S.], by his second wife, Mary, da. of Esme (STUART), 1st DUKE OF LENNOX [S.] He d. 28 Oct. 1635. His widow m., as his third wife, Patrick (MAULE), 1st EARL OF PANMURE [S.], who d. 22 Dec. 1661.

VII. 1635. 7. WILLIAM (KEITH), EARL MARISCHAL, &c. [S.], s. and h., suc. to the peerage [S.], in 1635; joined the association at Cumbernauld, Jan. 1641 in favour of the King, raising a troop of horse for his rescue in 1648. He escaped from the rout at Preston; received Charles II. in 1650, at Dunottar Castle; was imprisoned in the Tower of London, 1651-60, being excepted from Cromwell's act of grace, in 1654. P.C. and PRIVY SEAL [S.], 1660-61. He m. firstly in 1637, Elizabeth, da. of George (SETON), 3d EARL OF WINTOUN [S]., by his first wife, Anne, da. of Francis (HAY), EARL OF ERROLL [S.] She d. in child bed, 1650, aged 28. He m. secondly, April 1654, in London, Anne, da. of Robert (DOUGLAS), 8th EARL OF MORTON [S.], by Elizabeth, da. of Sir Edward VILLIERS. He d. s.p.m.s. in 1661.(b) His widow d. s.p. about 1689. Will dat. 27 Feb 1686/7, pr. 8 Feb. 1688/9.

[WILLIAM KEITH, styled LORD KEITH, s. and h. ap., by first wife, b. 11 Aug. 1638, at Tranent; d. an infant and v.p.]

VIII. 1661. 8. GEORGE (KEITH), EARL MARISCHAL, &c. [S.], br.(c) and h. male; served in the French army where he became Colonel; was in command ex parte Regis at the battle of Preston, 1648, and of Worcester, 1650; suc. to the peerage [S.] in 1661. He m. Mary, 1st da. of George (HAY), 2d EARL OF KINNOULL [S.], by Anne, da. of William (DOUGLAS), 2d EARL OF MORTON [S.] He d. 1694.

IX. 1694. 9. WILLIAM (KEITH), EARL MARISCHAL, &c. [S.], only s. and h., b. about 1660; suc. to the peerage [S.] in 1694 and took the oaths and his seat in Parl. 19 July 1698, opposing the Union [S.] and entering a protest, as heritable Keeper of the Regalia, against their removal without his sanction. He appears to have favoured the Stuart cause and is said to have been made K.T. in 1705 by the titular King James III. He was, however, REP. PEER [S.], 1710-12. He m. about 1690, Mary, 1st da. of James (DRUMMOND), 4th EARL OF PERTH [S.], by his first wife, Jane, da. of William (DOUGLAS), 1st MARQUESS OF DOUGLAS [S.] He d. in London, 27 May 1712, aged about 52.(d) Fun. entry in Lyon office. His widow d. at

(a) Ex inform. R. R. Stodart (late) Lyon Depute.

(b) He left four daughters (1) Mary, Lady Hope of Hopetoun; (2) Elizabeth Viscountess Arbuthnot [S.]; (3) Jean, Baroness Banff [S.], and (5) Isabel, Lady Turner, all of whom had issue.

(c) Of the two other brothers (1) Sir Robert Keith d. unm. and (2) John Keith, of Inverurie, was cr., 20 June 1677, Earl of Kintore, Lord Keith of Inverurie and Keith Hall [S.], the rem. of which dignities was extended, 22 Feb. 1694, so as to include the heirs male of the body of his elder br., George, Earl Marischal, whom failing to the heirs general of his own body, which heirs general, on the death of George's grandson (the attainted Earl), in 1778, became entitled to the Kintore peerage. See sub "Kintore."

(d) His character, by "Macky," when "45 years old" is as follows, "He always opposed the measures of King William's reign, but waited on the Queen at her accession to the Throne and acknowledged her Government. He is very wild, incon-

Edinburgh, 7 March 1729, and was *bur.* in the Abbey church there. Fun. entry in Lyon office.

X. 1712, to 1716. 10. GEORGE (KEITH), EARL MARISCHAL, LORD KEITH, and LORD ALTRIE [S.], s. and h.,(a) *b.* about 1692; *suc. to the peerage* [S.] in May 1712; was Capt. of the Scotch troop of Horse Gren. Guards, 3 Feb. 1714; signed the proclamation of George I. on 1 Aug. 1714, but, being deprived of his command, joined the Jacobite rising in 1715, receiving the Chevalier at his house at Newburgh, 22 Dec. 1715. He was attainted accordingly whereby *all his honours were forfeited.*(b) In 1719 he again landed in Scotland with some Spanish troops but was defeated at Glenshiel and again escaped abroad. He is said to have been made K.T. in 1725 by the *titular* King James III. by whom he was sent on an embassy to Spain. He, however, took no part in the Jacobite rising of 1745, at which date he entered the service of Frederick, King of Prussia. In 1751 he was Prussian Ambassador at Paris, receiving the Prussian Order of the Black Eagle in 1752, and being made Gov. of Neufchatel. In 1759 he was Prussian Ambassador to Spain, whence he sent intelligence of the Bourbon intrigues to England and was accordingly pardoned, 29 May 1759, by George II. and enabled to inherit any real estate. By the death, 22 Nov. 1761, of his second cousin, William (Keith), Earl of Kintore [S.], he became entitled to *the Earldom of Kintore*, &c. [S.] (under the *spec. rem.* in the *novodamus* of that dignity *cr.* 1677) which peerage, however, in consequence of his attainder, remained *dormant* till his death 16 years later (see "KINTORE" Earldom [S.], *cr.* 1677), tho', under the act of 1759, he *suc.*, in 1761, to the estate of Keith Hall for his life. In 1764 he re-purchased Dunottar and other family estates. He *d.* unm., 28 May 1778,(c) in his 86th year, at Potsdam, where for many years he had resided in close intimacy with the King of Prussia, having survived the forfeiture of his honours(d) 62 years.

---

stant and passionate; does everything by starts; hath abundance of flashy wit, and, by reason of his quality, hath good interest in the country; all Courts endeavour to have him at their side for he gives himself liberty of talking when he is not pleased with the Government. He is a thorough Libertine, yet sets up mightily for Episcopacy; a hard drinker; a thin body; a middle stature; ambitious of popularity."

(a) His only br., the Hon. James Francis Edward Keith, *b.* at Innerugie, 4 June 1696, was (likewise) attainted for the Jacobite rising of 1715. He became Field Marshal in the service of Frederick III., King of Prussia, and was slain 13 Oct. 1758, at the battle of Hoch Kirchen by the Austrians in his 63d year. He *d.* unm.

(b) See vol. iii, p. 192, note "a," *sub* "Duffus," for a list of the peerages forfeited by the insurrection of 1715.

(c) His two sisters (1) Mary, Countess of Wigtoun [S.], and (2) Anne, Countess of Galloway [S.], both left issue, of whom Lady Clementina Fleming, the only da. and heir of the elder one, *m.* in 1735, Charles, 10th Lord Elphinstone [S.], and became, on her uncle's death, *his* heir of line tho' not such heir to the *first* Earl Marischal. Her second son was *cr.* Viscount Keith in 1814.

(d) These honours were in tail *male*, the heir general having been twice (1475 and 1661) passed over. This heir male in 1778, was apparently Alexander Keith, of Ravelston, whom the attainted Earl acknowledged as such and to whom in 1766 he sold the lands at Dunottar accordingly. He, who was descended from Alexander Keith, of Pittendrum, 4th and yst. s. of William, 3d Earl Marischal, was *b.* 9 March 1705, and apparently, but for the attainder, would have been the 11th Earl, after his cousin's death in 1778 till his own death, 12 Sep. 1792. Of his four sons, Alexander, his s. and h. (12th Earl, apparently, but for the attainder) Knight Marshal of Scotland, and *knighted*, 20 July 1819, *d.* s.p.m. about 1833, leaving an only da. and h. whose s. and h. (Sir Patrick Keith Murray, 8th Bart. [S.], of Ochtertyre), sold the estates of Dunottar and of Ravelston. Of the three brothers of the said Alexander, Robert and George *d.* unm. but William Keith (*m.* 3 Nov. 1779), left at his death in 1803 four sons, *viz.*, Alexander, James, William, and John.

MARJORIBANKS OF LADYKIRK.

Barony. I. 1873, June, 12 to 19.

1. DAVID ROBERTSON of Ladykirk, co. Berwick, formerly DAVID MARJORIBANKS, 4th s. of Sir John MARJORIBANKS, Bart. (so cr. 1815), by Alison, da. of William RAMSAY, of Barnton in Midlothian, was b. 2 April 1797; ed. at Edinburgh Univ. He m. 10 Sep. 1834, Marianne Sarah, 1st da. and coheir of Sir Thomas HAGGERSTON, 6th Bart., by Margaret, only da. and h. of William ROBERTSON, of Ladykirk afsd., and, a few days previous, took by Royal lic., 2 Sep. 1834, the name of *Robertson* in lieu of his patronymic of *Marjoribanks*. He was a merchant in London, was M.P. for Berwickshire, 1859-73, and Lord Lieut. of that county. He was cr. 12 June 1873, BARON MARJORIBANKS OF LADYKIRK, co. Berwick, but s.p.m.s. (only seven days afterwards), 19 June 1873, aged 76, in Upper Brook street, Midx., when the *peerage* became *extinct*.(a) His widow d. 19 Aug. 1889, at Ripley Castle. Personalty sworn over £34,000.

Family Estates.—These, in 1883, consisted of 6,832 acres in Berwickshire, valued at £11,754 a year. *Principal Residence*; Ladykirk, near Berwick.

MARKENFIELD.

See "GRANTLEY OF MARKENFIELD, co. York," Barony (*Norton*), cr. 1782.

MARKETHILL.

See "GOSFORD OF MARKETHILL, co. Armagh," Barony [I.] (*Acheson*), cr. 1776; and Viscountcy [I.], cr. 1785.

MARLBOROUGH.

Earldom. I. 1626.

1. JAMES LEY, 6th and yst. s. of Henry LEY, of Teffont-Ewyas, Wilts, by Dyonisia DE ST. MAYNE, was b. there 1552; ed. at Brasenose Coll., Oxford; B.A., 3 Feb. 1573/4; Barrister (Linc. Inn), 1584; M.P. for Westbury, 1597-98, 1604-05, and 1609-11; for Bath, 1614, and for Westbury (again 1621); was Justice of Carmarthen, Pembroke and Cardigan, June 1603; *Knighted* 8 Oct. 1603, at Wilton, Wilts; Serjeant at Law, Nov. 1603; Ch. Justice of the King's Bench [I.] 1603-08, being from April to Nov. 1605, a Commissioner of the Great Seal [I.] Returning to England, he was made Attorney of the Court of Wards, Nov. 1608, and was cr. a *Baronet* (as "of Westbury, Wilts") 20 July 1619; Ch. Justice of the King's Bench [E.] 1621-24. Speaker of the House of Lords, and Joint Commissioner of the Great Seal, May to July 1621; P.C., 1624; LORD HIGH TREASURER, 1624-28, being cr. 31 Dec 1625, BARON LEY of Ley, co. Devon, and on 5 Feb. 1625/6,(b) EARL OF MARLBOROUGH, co. Wilts, with a *spec. rem.* to the heirs male of his body by Jane,(c) his then wife, whom failing to the heirs male of his body. He was Joint Commissioner for the claims at the Coronation of Charles I. in Jan. 1626, and was PRESIDENT OF THE Council, from July to Dec. 1628. He m. firstly, before 1595, Mary, 1st da. of John PETTIE, of Stoke Talmage, Oxon, by Elizabeth, da. and heir of Thomas, or Edward, SNAPE, of Fawler, near Witney. By her he had 11 children. He m. secondly (Lic. London, 13 Feb. 1617/8), Mary, widow of Sir William BOWYER, of Denham, Bucks, da. and coheir of Thomas PIERSON, Usher of the Court of the Star Chamber. By her he had no issue. He m. thirdly, 4 July 1621, Jane, 3d da. of John (BOTELER), 1st BARON BOTELER OF BRANTFIELD, by Elizabeth, sister (of the half blood) to George, DUKE OF BUCKINGHAM, da. of Sir George VILLIERS.(d) He d. in Lincoln Inn, 14

(a) The Barony of Farnborough (*May*), cr. 11 May 1886, lasted a still shorter time *viz.* only six days. See vol. iii, p. 318, note "b."

(b) See vol. ii. p. 282, note "c," *sub* "Cleveland" for a list of the eight noblemen cr. that day.

(c) This was by the influence of his said wife's uncle, the all-powerful Duke of Buckingham.

(d) See vol. i, p. 383, note "e," *sub* "Boteler."

March 1628/9, aged 77, and was *bur.* at Westbury, Wilts.(a) M.I. Will pr. 1629. His widow left "young, beautiful, childless, and rich," *m.* in 1629, William ASHBURNHAM, Cofferer to Charles I. and II., who was *bur.* at Ashburnham, Sussex, 16 Dec. 1679. She was *bur.* there 28 March 1672. M.I.

II. 1629. 2. HENRY (LEY), EARL OF MARLBOROUGH, &c., s. and h., by first wife, *b.* before 1595; M.P. for Westbury, 1614; for Devizes, 1621-22; for Wilts, 1625, and for Devizes, again, 1626-28; *knighted* at Vale Royal, Cheshire, 24 Aug. 1617; sum. to Parl. v.p. in his father's Barony, as LORD LEY, taking his seat, 2 March 1625/6, a month after his father's elevation to an Earldom *to which Earldom*, three years later, he *suc.*, 14 March 1628/9. He *m.*, 5 Nov. 1616, at Hadham Parva, Herts (lic. London, he about 21 and she about 18), Mary, 1st da. of Sir Arthur CAPELL, of Hadham afsd., by Margaret, da. of Lord John GREY. He *d.* 1 April 1638. Will pr. 1638. His widow, who was *bap.* 20 March 1596/7, at Hadham Parva, *m.*(b) Thomas WANKLYN (son of "a Smith") and *d.* 2 June 1670, being *bur.* in a garden privately but subsequently removed to Westbury, Wilts.

III. 1638. 3. JAMES (LEY), EARL OF MARLBOROUGH, &c., only s. and h., *b.* 1618; *styled* LORD LEY, 1629-38; *suc. to the peerage*, 1 April 1638; was distinguished as a mathematician and navigator; was Gen. of the Ordnance in the West (*ex parte Regis*) and Admiral in command at Dartmouth in 1643; took out a Colony to Santa Cruz in the West Indies, obtaining a grant of the Caribbee Islands, 1645; was in command of a squadron to the East Indies in 1662 to receive Bombay from the Portuguese, who, however, refused to deliver it up; was made Gov. of Jamaica in 1664 but was slain when in command of the "old James," 3 June 1665, in an action with the Dutch off Texel. He *d.* unm. and was *bur.* the 14th in Westm. Abbey. Will dat. 26 March to 25 May, pr. 22 June 1665.

IV. 1665, to 1679. 4. WILLIAM (LEY), EARL OF MARLBOROUGH [1626], and BARON LEY [1625], also a *Baronet* [1619], uncle and h. male, being 3d and yst. s. of the 1st Earl by his first wife; *b.* about 1599; *suc. to the peerage*, 3 June 1665. He *m.* Margaret, da. of Sir William HEWETT, of Beccles, Norfolk. He *d.* s.p. in 1679 when *all his honours* became *extinct*. Admon. 9 June 1680, to Margaret, his widow.

V. 1689. Dukedom. I. 1702. 1. JOHN CHURCHILL, 2d but 1st surv. s. and h. of Sir Winston CHURCHILL, Comptroller of the Board of Green Cloth, by Elizabeth, sister of Sir John DRAKE, 1st Bart., of Ashe, co. Devon, was *b.* there 24 and *bap.* 28 June 1650, at Axminster; ed. at St. Paul's school, London; entered the army (Foot Guards), 1667, serving at Tangiers in 1671, and being, during the reign of Charles II. in the Household of James, Duke of York,(c) to whom he was Page of Honour in 1667; Gent. of the Bed-

---

(a) "Ley tho' a feeble statesman was an able, erudite, and impartial Judge." He is described by Milton as—

"That Good Earl, once President
Of England's Council and her Treasury,
Who lived, in both, unstained with gold or fee,
And left them both, more in himself content."

But "on the other hand Sir James Whitelocke denounces him as *an old dissembler* who was wont to be called *Vulpone*, and says that he borrowed money of the Judges when Lord Chief Justice." [*Nat. Biogr.*] He was a good antiquary and author of several pamphlets on that subject, *e.g.*, "The antiquity of arms in England," "The office of Chancellor," &c.

(b) See "Anthony a Wood's life" for an account of this marriage, &c.

(c) "The Duke of York's love for [Arabella Churchill], his sister (by whom he was the father of the Duke of Berwick and other children) first brought him to Court, and the beauty of his own person and his good address so gained on the Duchess of Cleveland (then Mistress to King Charles II.) that she effectually established him there." [Macky's "*Characters*," 1705.] He is, indeed, said to have intrigued with the said Duchess and to have received large sums of money from her. His tall, handsome, noble, and

chamber in 1673 and (probably) M.P. for Newtown (Isle of Wight), 1678-79, being Master of the Wardrobe in 1679. He was cr., 21 Dec. 1682 (a Scotch Peer as) LORD CHURCHILL OF EYEMOUTH, co. Berwick [S.], and in Nov. 1683 was Col. of the Royal Regiment of Dragoons. At the accession of James II. he was (March to April 1685) Ambassador to Paris; was Gent. of the Bedchamber to that King during all his reign, being cr. by him, 14 May 1685,(a) BARON CHURCHILL OF SANDRIDGE, co. Hertford; Col. of the 3d troop of Horse Guards, 1685, and Lieut. Gen. in the army in 1688. He was, however (his hatred of Popery being set forth as his excuse) one of the first to desert the King (his benefactor) voting for the vacancy of the Throne and for the accession thereto of the Prince and Princess of Orange,(b) and was accordingly (two days before their Coronation) cr., 9 April 1689, EARL OF MARLBOROUGH,(c) co. Wilts. He assisted King William in the reduction of Ireland; was P.C. and a Gent. of the Bedchamber in 1689, and was, in 1690, Commander of the English forces in the Netherlands. He was dismissed from these posts in 1692 on suspicion (apparently very well grounded) of intrigues with the exiled King James II. In 1698, being restored to favour, he was again P.C. and a Cabinet Minister as also (till 1700) Master of the Horse and Governor to H.R.H. the young Duke of Gloucester. He was one of the Lords Justices (Regents) of England during the King's absence therefrom, 20 June to 3 Dec. 1698, 2 June to 18 Oct. 1699, and 5 July to 18 Sep. 1700,(d) being made, in June 1701, Com. in Chief of the British and Dutch forces in the Netherlands. At the accession of Queen Anne (over whom his wife exercised an all powerful influence) he was immediately el. K.G., 14 March 1701/2, and inst., 13 March 1702/3; Ambassador to the Hague, 1702, being also, in 1702 (war having been declared against France and Spain, 2 May 1702), Capt. Gen. of the English forces at home and abroad, Generalissimo of the allied forces, and Master Gen. of the Ordnance. In this year (from 5 Sep. to 29 Oct.) he took Venloo, Stevenswaert, Ruremonde, and finally Liege, thus commencing a successful campaign carried on for nine years. He was in reward cr., 14 Dec. 1702, MARQUESS OF BLANDFORD, co. Dorset, and DUKE OF MARLBOROUGH, with a grant of £5,000 a year during the Queen's life. Two years later, 2 July 1704, he defeated the Bavarians at Donauwerth, and a few weeks subsequently, 13 [2, *old style*] Aug. 1704, with a loss of 4,500 (besides 7,500 wounded) he obtained the crushing victory (40,000 slain and 11,000 taken prisoners) over the French at Blenheim "the greatest triumph achieved by an English General, since the middle ages."(e) The grant 28 Jan. 1704/5, of (about 22,000 acres) the manor of Woodstock and hundred of Wotton, in Oxfordshire, the site of the future "Blenheim Palace" was his reward.(f) He was Col. of the 1st Foot Guards, 1704-11; Lord Lieut. of Oxon. 1705. The Emperor (Leopold) cr. him a *Prince of the Empire* in 1704, and on 18 Nov. 1705, he received (from the Emperor Joseph) the *Principality of Mindelheim* in Suabia (of which he got investiture 24 May 1706) which in 1713 was exchanged (under the Emperor Charles VI.) for the county of Nellenburgh (then erected into a Principality) in Upper Austria. He continued a series of victories, the chief being that of Tirlemont, 18 July 1705; of Ramilies, 23 May 1706; of Oudenarde, 11 July 1708 and (with a loss of 18,000 men) of Malplaquet, 11

graceful appearance is spoken of by Burnet, Evelyn, and Lord Chesterfield, who adds that "his figure was beautiful but his manner was irresistible." A character of him by Bp. Burnet in which "his clever head and sound judgment" are set forth, is concluded by two words following, written by Dean Swift, "*detestably covetous*."

(a) See vol. iii, p. 78, note "a," *sub* "Derwentwater," for a list of the English peerages (but 10 in all), cr. by James II.

(b) "See vol. i, p. 28, note "b," *sub* "Abingdon," for a list of the "Nobility and Gentry in arms for the Prince of Orange," among whom he was.

(c) The title was probably chosen from a slight connection with the former Earls of that name; his mother, Elizabeth, being da. of Sir John Ashe, by Helena, da. of John (Boteler), 1st Lord Boteler of Brantfield, sister of Jane, the third (tho' childless) wife of James (Ley), 1st Earl of Marlborough. He appears to have had no property at Marlborough or its vicinity.

(d) See vol. iii, p. 115, note "c," *sub* "Devonshire," for a list of these important officers during the reign of William III.

(e) *Nat. Biogr.*

(f) "The whole sum spent" on the works at Blenheim "was according to Coxe, £300,000, of which £60,000 was spent by the Marlboroughs. The remainder was paid from the civil list." [*Nat. Biogr.*]

Sep. 1709, with the capture of Mons. He forced the French lines at Arleux, 5 Aug. and captured Bouchain, 13 Sep. 1711. Having no male issue surviving, he obtained 21 Dec. 1706, an act of Parl. (6 Anne, cap. vii) *whereby*, after reciting that John, Duke of Marlborough, had been created *Baron Churchill of Sandridge* and *Earl of Marlborough*, to him and the heirs male of his body, and that by letters patent dat. 14 Dec. [1702] 1 Anne, he had been created *Marquess of Blandford* and *Duke of Marlborough*, to him and the heirs male of his body, *the said honours* were limited, failing the heirs male of his body, to Lady Harriet, his eldest da., wife of Francis Godolphin. Esq. (s. and h. ap. of Sidney, Lord Godolphin), and the heirs male of her body begotten; in default of which, to Anne, Countess of Sunderland, his 2d da., wife of Charles, Earl of Sunderland, and the heirs male of her body begotten; in default of which, to Elizabeth, Countess of Bridgewater, his 3rd da., wife of Scroope, Earl of Bridgewater, and the heirs male of her body begotten; in default of which to Mary, his youngest da., wife of John Montagu (s. and h. ap. of Ralph, Duke of Montagu), and the heirs male of her body begotten; in default of which, to such other daughter or daughters of the said Duke to be begotten, severally and respectively according to priority of birth, and the heirs male of their bodies severally and respectively; in default of which, to the 1st da. of the aforesaid Lady Harriet Godolphin. and the heirs male of the body of such 1st da. begotten, failing which to every other da. of the said Lady Harriet, severally and respectively, and the heirs male of their bodies respectively; in default of which, to each of the daughters of the other daughters of the said Duke, according to to priority of birth (in the same manner as is limited to the daughters of Lady Harriet), and the heirs male of their bodies severally and respectively; and lastly, "to all and every other the issue male and female, lineally descending of or from the said Duke of Marlborough, in such manner and for such estate as the same are before limited to the before-mentioned issue of the said Duke, it being intended that the said honours shall continue, remain, and be invested in all the issue of the said Duke, so long as any such issue male or female shall continue, and be held and enjoyed by them severally and successively in manner and form aforesaid, the elder and the descendants of every elder issue to be preferred before the younger of such issue." By the next clause it is provided that all persons to whom the said honours shall descend shall have the same precedence as was then enjoyed by the said Duke in virtue of the said letters patent bearing date the 14 Dec. [1702] 1 Anne. The Duke was, however, *dismissed from all his offices*,(a) 30 Dec. 1711, tho' after the accession of George I., he was in 1714, restored to many of them, being made Capt. Gen. of the Forces, Master Gen. of the Ordnance, Col. of the 1st Foot Guards, Gov. of Chelsea Hospital and P.C.(b) He *m.* 1 Oct. 1678,(c) Sarah, 2d da. and coheir of Richard Jennings, of Sandridge, Herts, by Frances, da. and coheir of Sir Giffard Thornhurst, Bart. (so

(a) "The Duke had £7,000 as Plenipotentiary; £10,000 as General of the English forces; £3,000 as Master of the Ordnance; £2,000 as Col. of the Guards; £10,000 from the States General; £5,000 pension; £1,825 for travelling and £1,000 for a table; in all £39,825. He received also £15,000 as *per centage* (which, according to him, was spent on secret service) and handsome presents from foreign powers. The Duchess had £3,000 as Groom of the Stole, and £1,500 for each of her three offices as Ranger of Windsor park, Mistress of the Robes and Keeper of the Privy Purse, or in all £7,500. The united sums thus amount to £62,325. She ultimately received also the nine years pension at £2,000 a year. Besides this she had, after the death [1705] of the Queen Dowager, a lease '*for 50 years at first*' of the ground called the '*Friery*' in St. James' park, on which Marlborough house was built in 1709, at a cost, she says, of from £40,000 to £50,000." [*Nat. Biogr.*] "A commission, appointed to examine into the public accounts, reported that among other evidences of corruption and abuse, there was full proof of the Duke having received in the shape of a bribe an annual present of £5,000 or £6,000 from the contractors of bread for the army." Jesse's "*Court of England*, 1688-1760," vol. i, p. 400—where is quoted Evelyn's account of his dismissal for like "venality" in 1692, who states that such dismissal was "for his excessive taking of bribes, covetousness, and extortion on all occasions from his inferior officers."

(b) His character is ably compared with that of the great Duke of Wellington, by Earl Stanhope, in his "*History of England*, 1701-13" (edit. 1870) p. 67.

(c) The marriage (which was in the presence of Mary, Duchess of York) is sometimes said to have taken place when she was 15 (1675) and to have been declared "in the winter of 1677." See Miss Strickland's "*Queen Mary II.*"

cr. 1623) of Agnes Court, co. Kent. The Duke d. s.p.m.s.,(a) 16 June 1722, aged 72 at Cranbourne Lodge, near Windsor, and was bur. 9 Aug. in Westm. Abbey, being removed thence, in or before 1744, to the chapel of Blenheim palace. On his death the *Barony of Churchill of Eyemouth* [S.], became extinct; as also, probably, the Principality of the Holy Roman Empire.(b) Will dat. 19 March 1721/2, pr. 6 July 1722. His widow, who was b. at Holywell, near St. Albans, Herts, on (the restoration day), 29 May 1660, is well known for the influence she exercised over Queen Anne, to whom she was Groom of the Stole, Keeper of the Privy Purse, Mistress of Robes, being also Ranger of Windsor park, but was dismissed from all her offices in 1711.(c) She bought Wimbledon manor,(d) Surrey, and other large estates. In 1742, she published an account of her "*Conduct*" to the year 1710. She d. (probably at Marlborough House, Westm.), 18 Oct. 1744, aged 84, and was bur. in the chapel at Blenheim. Will dat. 11 to 15 Aug. 1744, pr. 1744.(e)

[JOHN CHURCHILL, *styled* 1689—1709, LORD CHURCHILL, and, since 1709, MARQUESS OF BLANDFORD, s. and h. ap., b. 13 Feb. 1689/90. He d. of the small pox, v.p. at King's Coll., Cambridge, 20 Feb. 1702/3, aged 13.]

II. 1722. 2. HENRIETTA, COUNTESS OF GODOLPHIN, and *suo jure* DUCHESS OF MARLBOROUGH, MARCHIONESS OF BLANDFORD, COUNTESS OF MARLBOROUGH, and BARONESS CHURCHILL OF SANDRIDGE, 1st da. and coheir, who, as *eldest* da., inherited the said honours under the act of Parl., 21 Dec. 1706. She was b. 20 and bap. 29 July 1681, at St. Martin in the fields. She m. (lic. fac., 23 April 1698), Francis (GODOLPHIN), 2d EARL OF GODOLPHIN (*styled* VISCOUNT RIALTON from 1706 to 1712) who d. 17 Jan. 1766, aged 87. See fuller particulars of him under "GODOLPHIN" Earldom, cr. 1684, *sub* the 2d Earl. Her Grace, who was patroness of William Congreve, the Dramatist, d. 24 Oct. and was bur. 9 Nov. 1733, s.p.m.s.(f) at Westm. Abbey, in her 53d year. Will dat. 11 July 1732 (in which she expresses her desire that her remains should never be removed to Blenheim) pr. 19 May 1736.

[WILLIAM GODOLPHIN, *styled* VISCOUNT RIALTON from 1712 to 1722, and MARQUESS OF BLANDFORD from 1722 till his death, only s. and h. ap.; b. about 1700; M.P. for Penrhyn, 1720-22, and for Woodstock, 1727-31; cr. D.C.L. of Oxford (Ball. Coll.), 30 Aug. 1730. He m., 25 April 1729, Maria Catherina,(g) da. of Peter DE JONGE, of Utrecht, in Holland. He d. s.p. of apoplexy, at Oxford, in the lifetime of both his parents, 24 Aug. 1731, aged about 31, and was bur. at Blenheim. Admon. 16 June 1731, to Cornelia Alletta de Jong, spinster, the principal creditor. His widow m. (as his 2d wife), 1 June 1734, at Harlington, Midx., Sir William WYNDHAM, 3d Bart., who d. 17 July 1740. She was bur. 13 Sep. 1779, at Mortlake, Surrey. Will pr. Sep. 1779.]

(a) Of his four daughters and coheirs (1) Henrietta, *suc.* as Duchess of Marlborough, and d. 1733; (2) Anne, Countess of Sunderland, was mother of Charles (Spencer), Duke of Marlborough after 1733, ancestor of the succeeding Dukes; (3) Elizabeth, Duchess of Bridgewater, d. 22 March 1712/3, whose male issue became extinct five years later, and (4) Mary, Duchess of Montagu, who d. without surviving male issue.

(b) The grant of that dignity is in the usual form, which it is considered entitles *all male descendants* to the dignity, as also *for their lives* (but *not* with right of transmission) *the daughters* of such male descendants.

(c) See p. 254. note "a."

(d) This she left to John Spencer (ancestor to the Earls Spencer) the 3d and yst. s. of her second da. Anne, Countess of Sunderland.

(e) An abstract thereof is in "*Gent Mag.*" 1744, p. 588.

(f) Of her two daughters and coheirs (1) Henrietta, Duchess of Newcastle, d. s.p. 1776, and (2) Mary, Duchess of Leeds, who d. 1764 (the only child that had issue) was mother of the 5th Duke and ancestress of the succeeding Dukes of Leeds, who, failing the Earls of Sunderland of the Spencer family (heirs *male* of the body of Anne, *second* da. of the great Duke of Marlborough), are next in rem. under the act of Parl. of 1706 (as heirs *male* of the body of the first *daughter* of the *first* da. of the great Duke) to the Marlborough peerage.

(g) She was sister to Isabella, Countess of Denbigh.

III. 1733. *3.* CHARLES (SPENCER), DUKE OF MARLBOROUGH [1702], MARQUESS OF BLANDFORD [1702], EARL OF SUNDERLAND [1643], EARL OF MARLBOROUGH [1689], BARON SPENCER OF WORMLEIGHTON [1603], and BARON CHURCHILL OF SANDRIDGE [1685], nephew of the *suo jure* Duchess, being 3d but 1st surv. s. and h. of Charles (SPENCER), 3d EARL OF SUNDERLAND, &c., by his second wife, Anne, (*d.* 15 April 1716), 2d da. and coheir of John (CHURCHILL), 1st DUKE OF MARLBOROUGH abovenamed. He was *b.* 22 Nov. 1706, and *suc.* his elder br., 27 Sep. 1729, as 5th *Earl of Sunderland* and 7th *Baron Spencer of Wormleighton* and *suc.* his maternal aunt, Henrietta, *suo jure* Duchess of Marlborough abovenamed, 24 Oct. 1733, as *Duke of Marlborough*, &c. He distinguished himself, 16 June 1743 (as Brig. Gen.) at the battle of Dettingen; was Com. in Chief in the Expedition, May to June 1758, against St. Malo, as also of the forces in Germany in July 1758, being at that date full General in the army; was Col. of the 38th Foot, 1738; of the 1st Dragoons 1739; of the 2d troop of Horse Guards, 1740, and of the Coldstream Foot Guards, 1742; was a Lord of the Bedchamber, 1738; Lord Lieut. of Oxon and Bucks, 1739; K.G., 20 March 1740/1, being inst., 21 April 1741; F.R.S., 1744; *cr.* D.C.L. of Oxford, 4 June 1746; P.C., 1749; Lord Steward of the Household, 1749-55; one of the LORDS JUSTICES (Regents) of the Realm, 1750, 1752, and 1755. PRIVY SEAL, Jan. to Dec. 1755; Master Gen. of the Ordnance, 1755-58. He *m.*, 23 May 1732, at East Barnet, Elizabeth, da. and h. of Thomas (TREVOR), 2d BARON TREVOR OF BROMHAM, by Elizabeth, da. of Timothy BURRELL, of Cuckfield, Sussex. He *d.* of a fever, 20 Oct. 1758, in his 52d year, at Munster in Westphalia, and was *bur.* in the chapel at Blenheim. Will pr. 1758. His widow *d.* 7 Oct. 1761. Will pr. 1761.

IV. 1758. *4.* GEORGE (SPENCER), DUKE OF MARLBOROUGH, &c., s. and h., *b.* 26 Jan. 1738/9, *styled* MARQUESS OF BLANDFORD, till 1758, was in the Coldstream Guards, 1755, and Capt. 20th Foot, 1756; *suc. to the peerage*, 20 Oct. 1758; Ranger of Wichwood forest, 1758; Lord Lieut. of Oxon, 1760; Bearer of the Sceptre with the Cross at the Coronation, 22 Sep. 1761; Lord Chamberlain of the Household, 1762-63; PRIVY SEAL, 1763-65; D.C.L., of Oxford, 6 July 1763; K.G., 12 Dec. 1768, being inst., 25 July 1771; F.R.S., 1786. He *m.* 23 Aug. 1762, in Bedford House, St. Geo., Bloomsbury, Caroline, da. of John (RUSSELL), 4th DUKE OF BEDFORD, by his second wife, Gertrude, da. of John (LEVESON-GOWER), 1st EARL GOWER. She was *b.* Jan. 1742/3, was one of the 10 train bearers of Queen Charlotte, at her marriage (8 Sep. 1761), and *d.* 26 Nov. 1811, at Blenheim, aged 68. He *d.* there 29 Jan. 1817, aged 78. Will pr. June 1817.

V. 1817. *5.* GEORGE (SPENCER, *afterwards* SPENCER-CHURCHILL), DUKE OF MARLBOROUGH, &c., s. and h.,(a) *b.* 6 March and *bap.* 3 April 1766, at St. Martin in the fields; *styled* MARQUESS OF BLANDFORD,(b) till 1817; ed. at Eton and at Ch. Ch., Oxford; M.A., 9 Dec. 1786, and D.C.L., 20 June 1792. M.P. for Oxon, 1790-96; for Tregony, 1802-04; a Lord of the Treasury, 1804-06, and was sum. to Parl. v.p., 12 March 1806, in his father's Barony, as BARON SPENCER OF WORMLEIGHTON [1603.] He *suc.* to the Dukedom, 29 Jan. 1817, and by Royal lic., 26 May following, took the name of *Churchill*, after that of *Spencer*. F.S.A., &c. He *m.* 15 Sep. 1791, at St. James', Westm., Susan, 2d da. of John (STEWART), 7th EARL OF GALLOWAY [S.], by Anne, da. of Sir James DASHWOOD, Bart. He *d.* at Blenheim, 5 March 1840, the day before his 74th birthday.(c) Will pr. Jan. 1841. His widow, who was *b.* 10 April 1767, *d.* 2 April 1841, in her 74th year in Park lane, Midx. Her will pr. May 1841.

(a) His yst. br., Lord Francis-Almeric Spencer, was *cr.* in 1815 Baron Churchill of Wychwood.

(b) Trial for adultery, 1801, Marquess of Blandford with Lady Sturt.

(c) His gardens and library at White Knights, near Reading, occasioned him great expence. For the latter he bought in 1812 a "Boccaccio," dated 1471, for £2,260, &c. Most of his collections were dispersed in his lifetime and during his latter years "he lived in utter retirement at one corner of his magnificent palace, a melancholy instance of the results of extravagance." [*Ann. Reg.*, 1840.]

VI. 1840. 6. GEORGE (SPENCER-CHURCHILL), DUKE OF MARLBOROUGH, &c., s. and h., *b.* 27 Dec. 1793, at Bill hill, in Sonning Berks; usually known as EARL OF SUNDERLAND till 1817; ed. at Eton and at Ch. Ch., Oxford; *styled* MARQUESS OF BLANDFORD, 1817-40; was M.P. for Chippenham, 1818-20; for Woodstock, 1826-31, 1832-35, and 1838-40; *suc. to the peerage,* 5 March 1840; D.C.L., of Oxford, 15 June 1841; Lord. Lieut. of Oxon, 1842-57; Lieut. Col. Comm., Oxon Yeomanry Cavalry, 1845. He *m.* firstly, 11 Jan. 1819, his cousin, Jane, 1st da. of his maternal uncle, George (STEWART), 8th EARL OF GALLOWAY [S.], by Jane, da. of Henry (PAGET), 1st EARL OF UXBRIDGE. She, who was *b.* 29 March 1798, *d.* 12 Oct. 1844, at Blenheim. He *m.* secondly, 10 June 1846, at the chapel of Lambeth palace, Charlotte Augusta, da. of Henry Jeffery (FLOWER), 4th VISCOUNT ASHBROOK [I.], by his second wife, Emily Theophila, da. of Sir Thomas Theophilus METCALFE, 1st Bart. She, who was *b.* 25 Nov. 1818, *d.* 20 April 1850, at Mivart's hotel, St. Geo. Han. sq., and was *bur.* in Blenheim chapel. M.I. at Yarnton, Oxon. Admon. Dec. 1850. He *m.* thirdly, 18 Oct. 1851, at Blenheim palace, his cousin Jane Frances Clinton, da. of the Hon. Edward Richard STEWART (yr. br. of George, 8th EARL OF GALLOWAY [S.] abovenamed), by Katherine, da. of Francis WEMYSS, CHARTERIS, *styled* LORD ELCHO. He *d.* 1 July 1857, at Blenheim, aged 63. Will pr. Sep. 1857, under £200,000. His widow, who was *b.* 27 May 1817, living 1893. (a)

VII. 1857. 7. JOHN WINSTON (SPENCER-CHURCHILL), DUKE OF MARLBOROUGH, &c., s. and h. by first wife; *b.* 2 June 1822, at Garboldisham Hall, Norfolk; usually known as EARL OF SUNDERLAND till 1840; ed. at Eton and at Oriel Coll., Oxford; *styled* MARQUESS OF BLANDFORD, 1840-57; M.P. for Woodstock, 1840-45 and 1847-57;(b) D.C.L. of Oxford, 7 June 1853; *suc. to the peerage,* 1 July 1857; Lord Lieut. of Oxon, 1857-83; P.C., 1866; Lord Steward of the Household, 1866-67; Lord President of the Council, 1867-68; K.G., 23 May 1868; VICEROY OF IRELAND (as Lord Lieut.), 1876-80.(c) He *m.*, 12 July 1843, Frances Anne Emily, da. of Charles William (VANE-STEWART), 3d MARQUESS OF LONDONDERRY [I.], by his second wife, Frances Anne Emily, da. and h. of Sir Harry VANE-TEMPEST, Bart. He *d.* 5 July 1883, aged 62, at 29 Berkeley square, and was *bur.* in the chapel at Blenheim.(d) Will pr. 15 Sep. 1883, above £146,000. His widow, who was *b.* 15 April 1822, living 1893.(a)

VIII. 1883. 8. GEORGE CHARLES (SPENCER-CHURCHILL), DUKE OF MARLBOROUGH, &c., s. and h., *b.* 15 May 1844, in Wilmington crescent; usually known as EARL OF SUNDERLAND till 1857; *styled* MARQUESS OF BLANDFORD, 1857-83; ed. at Eton; an officer in the Horse Guards, 1863-69; *suc. to the peerage,* 5 July 1883. He *m.*, 8 Nov. 1869, at Westm. Abbey, Albertha Frances Anne, 6th da. of James (HAMILTON), 1st DUKE OF ABERCORN [I.], by Louisa Jane, da. of John (RUSSELL), 6th DUKE OF BEDFORD She, who was *b.* 29 July 1847, was divorced(e) (on her own petition) in 1883 by decree "*nisi,*" 10 Feb., which was made

---

(a) She is one of *three* Dowager Duchesses living in 1893 besides the mother (who does not so style herself) of the present (1893) Duke. See p. 258, note "a." Similarly from Oct. 1886 to Oct. 1891 there were three Dowager Marchionesses of Ailesbury living, besides the mother of the [then] Marquess, whose father had died when a Commoner.

(b) He was the author of "the Blandford Act, 1856," to enable the division of extensive parishes.

(c) "His administration of Ireland was popular, and he endeavoured to benefit the trade of the country." His wife "instituted a famine relief fund by which she collected £112,484 which was spent in seed-potatoes, food, and clothing." [*Nat. Biogr.*, under "Churchill."]

(d) He began a series of sales of the family collections which was carried on by his successor. In 1875 "*the Marlborough Gems*" were sold (in one lot at Christie's) for £10,000; in 1882-83 "*the Sunderland Library*" realised nearly £60,000; in 1883 "*the Blenheim enamels*" fetched above £73,000; while in 1884-85 eleven pictures were sold of which nine went abroad, but two (Raphael's "*Madonna degli Ansidei*" for £70,000! ! and Vandyke's "*Equestrian portrait of Charles I.*" for £17,500) were purchased for the nation.

(e) Her husband's *crim. con.* with the Countess of Aylesford was proved.

absolute, 20 Nov. 1883.(a) He m. secondly, 29 June 1888, in the City Hall, New York,(b) Lily Warren, widow of Lewis Hammersley, of New York afsd., da. of Cicero Price, Commodore of the U.S.A. Navy. He d. somewhat suddenly, at Blenheim palace, 9 Nov. 1892, aged 48, and was *bur.* at Woodstock. Will pr. above £350,000 gross. His widow living 1893.(c)

IX. 1892. 9. Charles Richard John (Spencer-Churchill), Duke of Marlborough [1702], Marquess of Blandford (1702), Earl of Sunderland [1643], Earl of Marlborough (1689), Baron Spencer of Wormleighton [1603] and Baron Churchill of Sandridge [1685], only s. and h., by first wife, *b.* 13 Nov. 1871, at Simla, in India; usually known as Earl of Sunderland till 1883; *styled* Marquess of Blandford, 1883-92; ed. at Trin. Coll., Cambridge; *suc. to the peerage*, 9 Nov. 1892.

Family Estates.—These, in 1883, consisted of 21,944 acres in Oxon; 1,584 in Wilts and 83 in Berks. Total 23,511 acres, worth £36,557 a year. *Principal Residence*; Blenheim palace, near Woodstock, Oxon.

MARLEY.

See "Wotton of Marley, co. Kent," Barony (*Wotton*), *cr.* 1603; *ex.* 1630.

MARMION.

William Marmion, yr. s. of Robert Marmion, Sheriff of Worcestershire, *temp.* Hen. II. and Ric. I., was sum. to [*Montfort's*] Parl. 14 Dec. (1264), 49 Hen. III., but such summons does not originate a hereditary Barony.(d) He appears to have *d.* s.p.

Barony. I. 1313. 1. John Marmion, of Witringham, co. Lincoln and of the Hermitage, in West Tanfield, co. York, s. and h. of William Marmion,(e) of Witringham afsd. by Lora, da. of Roese de Dovor, of Loddington, co. Northampton, was sum. (with about 60 other persons), 8 June (1294), 22 Ed. I.(f) to attend the King whenever he might be, and was also so sum. on 26 Jan. (1296/7), 25 Ed. I.(g) He was in the Scotch war, 1310, and was finally sum. as a Baron (LORD MARMION), by writs, 26 July (1313), 7 Ed. II. to 14 March (1321/2), 15 Ed. II. He *d.* (1322-23), 16 Ed. II.

(a) She was living 1893 retaining (oddly enough) the style of Marchioness of Blandford tho' her husband had *suc.* to the Dukedom of Marlborough more than four months before her divorce was made absolute. See also p. 257, note "a."

(b) The Mayor of that city officiated; the religious ceremony that followed was at the Tabernacle Baptist Church, Second Avenue, near St. Mark's place.

(c) See p. 257, note "a."

(d) See vol. iii, p. 365, note "d," *sub* "Fitz-John" where, also a list of those, so sum. is given.

(e) This William was s. and h. of Robert Marmion (*junior*), of Witringham and Coningsby, co. Lincoln, who was a *younger* son of Robert Marmion, of Tamworth, co. Warwick and of Scrivelsby, co. Lincoln, who (by his *eldest* s. and h. Robert Marmion, *Senior*), was grandfather of Philip Marmion, whose two daughters and coheirs (Mazera Cromwell, and Joane Ludlow) were the respective ancestors of the families of Freville of Tamworth afsd., and of Dymoke of Scrivelsby afsd., which last (in right of that tenure) exercised the office of "*Champion*" at the Coronations.

(f) See vol. i, p. 259, note "c," *sub* Basset de Sapcote" as to the writ of 1294, not constituting a regular writ of summons.

(g) See vol. i, p. 111, note "b," *sub* "Ap. Adam" as to the writ of 1297, not constituting a regular writ of summons.

I. 1323. 2. JOHN (MARMION), LORD MARMION, s. and h., aged 30 in 1323 when he *suc.* his father. He was sum. to Parl. by writs 3 Dec. 1326), 20 Ed. II., to 1 April (1335), 9 Ed. III. He served in the Scotch wars in 1327. He *m.* Maud, said to have been a da. of LORD FURNIVALL. He *d.* (1335), 9 Ed. III. His widow, who founded a chantry at West Tanfield, long survived him.

III. 1335. 3. ROBERT MARMION, only s. and h., was never sum. to Parl. as a Baron. He was of an infirm constitution and *d.* s.p. when the *Barony* fell into abeyance.(a)

MARNHULL.

i.e., "MARNHULL, co. Dorset," Barony (*Howard*), *cr.* 1604 with the EARLDOM OF NORTHAMPTON, which see; *ex.* 1614.

MARNY or DE MARNY.

Barony. I. 1523. 1. SIR HENRY MARNY, of Layer-Marney, co. Essex, s. and h. of Sir John MARNY, of the same, by Joan, da. of John THROCKMORTON, of co. Glouc.; was P.C. to Henry VII., 1485, for whom he fought at the battle of Stoke in 1487 and of Blackheath in 1497; P.C. to Henry VIII., 1509; K.G., 23 April 1510, being inst. the 27th; Capt. of the Guard; received considerable portions of the estates of the attainted Duke of Buckingham; PRIVY SEAL, 4 Feb. (1522/3), 14 Hen. VIII., being *cr.*, 9 April 1523 ("*Baro de Marny*") BARON MARNY(b) but a month before his death. He *m.* firstly Thomasine, da. of Sir John ARUNDEL, of Lanherne, co. Cornwall, by his second wife, Katherine, da. of Sir John CHIDIOCKE. He *m.* secondly Elizabeth, da. of Sir Nicholas WYFOLD or WILFORD, sometime (1450-51) Lord Mayor of London. He *d.* 24 May 1523, at his house in St. Swithins, London, and was *bur.* at Layer-Marney. Will dat. 22 May, pr. 15 June 1523. Fun. certif. at Coll. of Arms.

II. 1523, to 1525. 2. JOHN (MARNY), BARON MARNY, only s. and h., by first wife. He was (v.p.) one of the Esquires of the body to Hen. VIII. and Gov. of Rochester Castle, 1509; *suc. to the peerage*, 24 May 1523. He *m.* firstly Christian, da. and h. of Sir Roger NEWBURGH. He *m.* secondly Bridget, widow of Thomas FINDERN, of Little Horkesley, Essex, da. of Sir William WALDEGRAVE. He *d.* s.p.m., 27 April 1525, when *the Barony became extinct*.(c) He was *bur.* at Layer-Marney. Will dat. 10 March 1524/5, pr. 28 June 1525. His widow, by whom he had no issue, was *bur.* at Little Horkesley, 20 Sep. 1549. Will dat. 16 Sep. 1549, pr. 29 April 1550.

MARR, see MAR.

(a) The coheirs were his two sisters of whom (1) Joan *m.* Sir John Bernack and (2) Avice who *m.* after 1335 (as 2d wife) John (Grey), 1st Lord Grey de Rotherfield, who *d.* 1 Sep. 1359, leaving her surviving. She had two sons, both of whom took the name of Marmion; the elder *d.* s.p. but the yr. s., Robert, had a da. and h., Elizabeth, who *m.* Henry (Fitzhugh), Lord Fitzhugh, and *d.* 1427, being ancestress of the succeeding Lords Fitzhugh, who and whose heirs represent the moiety of this Barony that was vested in the said Avice.

(b) See "*Creations*, 1483—1646," in ap. 47th Rep. D.K. Pub. Records.

(c) He had two daughters and coheirs by his first wife, *viz.* (1) Katherine who *m.* firstly George Ratcliffe, and secondly Thomas (Poynings), Baron Poynings, who *d.* s.p. in 1545 (2) Elizabeth who *m.* Thomas (Howard), 1st Viscount Bindon.

MARSHAL.

[*Remarks.*—The office of "*Marshal of England*"(a) (8th in rank of the great offices(b) of State) is not, of itself, a peerage dignity, tho' it might (not improperly) be held to have been so in, and after, 1397, when it was conferred as "*Earl Marshal.*" A brief notice of some of its earlier holders is here subjoined. This high office is, apparently, quite distinct from the office of "*Marshal of the King's Household,*"(c) which, *temp.* Hen. I., was held (apparently with the name of Hempsted Marshall,(d) Berks), by Gilbert Marshall,(e) and transmitted by him to his son, John Mar-

(a) See "*The Book of the Court*" by William J. Thoms, F.S.A., for a good account of the office of "*The Earl Marshal of England.*"

(b) The great officers of state are as under, *viz.* (1) the LORD HIGH STEWARD (*Magnus Angliæ Seneschallus*) a hereditary office, long enjoyed by the Earls of Leicester but which merged in the Crown at the accession (1399) of Henry IV. and has never since been regranted save *pro hâc vice* (2) the LORD HIGH CHANCELLOR, or Keeper of the Great Seal, of which the first *lay* holder was Sir Thomas More, *temp.* Hen. VIII. (3) the LORD HIGH TREASURER, of which the first *lay* holder was Richard, Lord Scrope de Bolton, in 1371. This great office has for more than 200 years been in commission, being executed by five persons of whom the chief, who is styled *First Lord of the Treasury*, is usually the Prime Minister (4) the LORD PRESIDENT OF THE COUNCIL, an office held (by statute 21 Hen. VIII.) *durante bene placito* (5) the LORD PRIVY SEAL, of whom the first *lay* holder was Henry, Lord Marny, *temp.* Hen. VIII. (6) the LORD GREAT CHAMBERLAIN OF ENGLAND, a hereditary office long enjoyed by the family of *De Vere*, Earls of Oxford, from whom it passed to the family of *Bertie*, Lords Willoughby de Eresby, Earls of Lindsey, and Dukes of Ancaster. See vol. i, p. 207, note "d," *sub* "Aveland," for some account thereof (7) the LORD HIGH CONSTABLE, a hereditary office formerly held by the family of *Bohun*, Earls of Hereford, and that of *Stafford*, Dukes of Buckingham; but which since the attainder of Duke Edward, in 1521, has never been granted save *pro hâc vice* (8) the EARL MARSHAL OF ENGLAND, as in the text (9) the LORD HIGH ADMIRAL, which office (save when from 2 May 1827 to 12 Aug. 1828 it was held by H.R.H. the Duke of Clarence afterwards King William IV.) has been in commission since 1709 (10) the LORD STEWARD OF THE HOUSEHOLD (*Seneschallus Hospitii*) and (11) the LORD CHAMBERLAIN OF THE HOUSEHOLD (*Camerarius Hospitii*) the appointment to both of which offices has for some time been in the hands of the Prime Minister for the time being. Of these eleven offices the rank of all but that of the first (the High Stewardship) which had previously (1399) lapsed to the Crown, was settled (in the above order among themselves) by statute 31 Hen. VIII. under which the High Chancellor, the High Treasurer,* the President of the Privy Council, and the Privy Seal, take rank (if Barons) above all Dukes, save those of the blood Royal, while the Great Chamberlain, the High Constable,* the Earl Marshal, the High Admiral,* the Steward of the Household, and the Chamberlain of the Household, *if of Ducal rank*, next follow, but, if of a lower grade, take precedence above all Peers of their own degree. See Sir C. G. Young's "*Order of Precedence,*" and see also note "a" next above.

(c) So also the office of "*Steward of the Household*" is totally distinct from that of the "*High Steward of England,*" as also is the office of "*Chamberlain of the Household*" from that of the "*Great Chamberlain of England.*"

(d) Which manor, the "old records state, the Marshals held *in marescagiâ et per virgam Mareschilliæ,*" whereas the office of *Marshal of England* was never "holden by tenure or serjeantry, as the offices of Lord High Steward and High Constable were." See note "a" next above. Hempsted (or Hampsted) Marshall appears to have passed to the Crown in 1806 and was, in 1333, given by Thomas (Plantagenet), Earl of Norfolk, to his da., Alice, wife of Edward (de Montacute), Lord Montacute, after which it was held by the family of Hankford and (*temp.* Eliz.) by that of Parry, till in 1620 it was purchased by the Craven family, who still hold it.

(e) Gilbert Mareschal and John, his son, were *temp.* Hen. I. impleaded but without success (by Robert de Venois and William de Hastings) "for the office of Mareschall to the King," which John was "the King's Marshal" in 1163-64 upon the difference of King Henry II. with Archbishop à Becket. "According to Camden, this office of

* The three offices so marked (*viz.*, the High Treasurer, the High Constable, and High Admiral), do not at present exist.

shall,([a]) whose s. and h., another John Marshall, *d.* s.p. 1199, leaving William Marshall, his br. and h., who (oddly enough) became *jure uxoris* (as stated below) *Marshal of England* and Earl of Pembroke, and who is stated to have been confirmed, 20 April 1200, as "Chief Marshal of the King's Court."([b]) "Thus the *two offices* of Marshal of the King's house and Marshal of England *became united* and inheritable in the same family."([c])

The first "*Marshal of England*" is generally considered to have ROGER DE MONTGOMERY, who was Marshal of the Norman army at the Conquest, but the first on record is GILBERT DE CLARE, who acquired that office in 1135, and who in 1138 was *cr.* EARL OF PEMBROKE. He *d.* 1148 and was *suc.* by his s. Richard (called "Strongbow,") who was "Marshal of England," at the Coronation of Henry II. in 1154. He *d.* s.p.m. 1176, leaving a da. and h., Isabel, who *m.* WILLIAM MARSHALL, *Marshal of the Household* (see above) who, in *her* right, became *Marshal of England* and EARL OF PEMBROKE. He *d.* 1219, leaving William, his s. and h., who having been, v.p. one of the 25 Barons to enforce (1215) the *Magna Charta*, was then styled "*Comes Mareschal, junior.*" He *d.* 1231, being *suc.* by his four younger brothers successively, on the death of the last of whom, in 1245, King Henry III., in 1248-49, "gave the Marshal's Rod" into the hands of Maud,([d]) Countess of Norfolk, eldest of the five sisters and coheirs of the last five Earls of Pembroke, which she thereupon delivered to ROGER (BIGOD), EARL OF NORFOLK, her s. and h. ap. "whose homage the King received for the same."([c]) He *d.* s.p. 1270, and was *suc.* by his nephew and h. Roger, Earl of Norfolk, who surrendered the reversion (on his death) of his Earldom and the Marshal's Rod to the King, 12 April 1302, and *d.* s.p., 11 Dec. 1306, when the *office* became *vested in the Crown.*

King Edward II. (after some grants "*durante bene placito*") conferred the office of "*Marshal of England,*" 10 Feb. 1316, on his br. THOMAS (PLANTAGENET), EARL OF NORFOLK, who *d.* s.p.m. in 1338, whose da. and h. Margaret, *suo jure* Countess and afterwards (1397) Duchess of Norfolk, was often styled Countess or Lady Marshal.([e]) The office was however frequently disposed of during her life, until her grandson and h. ap., Thomas (Mowbray), Earl of Nottingham (afterwards Duke of Norfolk) was, 10 Feb. 1397, made "*Earl* Marshal of England." See below.

The office of "*Marshal*" or "*Great Marischall*" *of Scotland* was held in that kingdom from a very early period (1010, by tradition) by the family of KEITH, of whom Sir William Keith was *cr.* in or before July 1458, EARL MARISHAL [S.] See full particulars under that dignity, *cr.* 1458; *forfeited* 1716.

As to the office of *Marshal of Ireland*, see vol. i, p. xvii., for (a somewhat hazy) notice of the same, taken from the "*Lib. Hib.*" Walter DEVEREUX), 1st EARL OF ESSEX, was, 9 May 1576, made *Earl Marshal of Ireland.* He *d.* 22 Sep. 1576, aged 35, at Dublin.

MARSHAL, *i.e.*, EARLS MARSHAL([f]) OF ENGLAND.

A list of these is as under.

I. 1397, to 1398. 1. THOMAS (MOWBRAY), EARL OF NOTTINGHAM, s. of John (MOWBRAY), LORD MOWBRAY, by Elizabeth, da. and h. of John (SEGRAVE), LORD SEGRAVE by Margaret, his wife, *suo jure* DUCHESS AND COUNTESS OF NORFOLK, who was da. and h. of Thomas (PLANTAGENET), EARL OF NORFOLK and *Marshal of England* abovenamed, was *b.* 1367, and having *suc.* his br. (John, Earl of Nottingham), [See fuller account under his Peerage dignity.]

Mareschall, here set forth, appears to mean the office of *Marshal of the King's House*, an office distinct from that afterwards known by the name of *Earl Marshal of England.*" See note "a" next above.

([a]) To this John "King Henry II. confirmed his office of Marshal, which John at the Coronation of Richard I. bore the great gilt spurs." See p. 260, note "a."

([b]) Doyle's "*Official Baronage*" under "Pembroke."

([c]) *Vide* p. 260, note "a."

([d]) To her also was assigned the manor of Hempsted Marshall (see p. 260, note "d"), whereby it would seem that she and her heirs would have right to the office of Marshal of the Household.

([e]) "Nobilis Dña, *Dna Margareta Marshall, Comitissa Northfolk et Dña de Segrave*, quæ obiit 24° die Maii, anno dñi 1389." M.I. at Greyfriars, London.

([f]) This office alone of all the great offices of England (see p. 260, note "b"), has the

as LORD MOWBRAY and SEGRAVE in 1383, was *cr.* in that year, EARL OF NOTTINGHAM, and was, 10 Feb. 1397 (in his said grandmother's lifetime) constituted "EARL MARSHAL OF ENGLAND," being *cr.* (in the same year), 29 Sep. 1397, DUKE OF NORFOLK, but was banished and apparently deprived of his dignities in 1398.(a) He *d.* 27 Sep. 1400, aged 39.

II. 1398. *1.* THOMAS (DE HOLAND), DUKE OF SURREY, EARL OF KENT, &c., made "MARSHAL OF ENGLAND," 30 Jan. 1398 and 17 Sep. 1398.(a) *Beheaded* 6 Jan. 1400.

III. 1399. *1.* RALPH (NEVILL), EARL OF WESTMORLAND, was made "EARL MARSHAL OF ENGLAND," 30 Sep. 1399. He *d.* 25 Oct. 1425.

IV. 1413. *2.* JOHN MOWBRAY, 2d but 1st surv. s. and h.(b) of Thomas, DUKE OF NORFOLK, and *Earl Marshal* above-named, *b.* 1390; was sum. to Parl., 22 March 1412/3, as EARL MARSHAL,(c) and was *restored* 14 July 1424 as DUKE OF NORFOLK, &c. He acted as *Earl Marshal*, at the Coronation, 6 Nov. 1429, of Henry VI. He *d.* 19 Oct. 1432.

V. 1432. *3.* JOHN (MOWBRAY), DUKE OF NORFOLK, &c., and EARL MARSHAL,(c) s. and h. He acted as *Earl Marshal*, at the Coronation, 28 June 1461, of Edward IV. He *d.* 6 Nov. 1461, aged 46.

VI. 1461. *4.* JOHN (MOWBRAY), DUKE OF NORFOLK, [1397], EARL OF NORFOLK [1312], EARL OF NOTTINGHAM [1383], EARL OF SURREY AND WARENNE [1451], LORD MOWBRAY, LORD SEGRAVE, and EARL MARSHAL,(c) only s. and h.; *b.* 1444; was *cr.* v.p. in 1451, EARL OF SURREY AND WARENNE, and *suc.* to the other dignities in Nov. 1461. He, who appears never to have exercised the office of *Earl Marshal*, *d.* s.p.m., 17 Jan. 1475/6, aged 31, when the *Dukedom of Norfolk, and the Earldoms of Nottingham, Surrey and Warenne* became *extinct*.

VII. 1476,(d) 7. ANNE, *suo jure* COUNTESS OF NORFOLK, BARONESS MOWBRAY, BARONESS SEGRAVE and (presumably) COUNTESS MARSHAL,(c) only da. and h. She at her age of seven, *m.* 15 Jan. 1477/8, RICHARD (PLANTAGENET), DUKE OF YORK (second s. of King Edward IV.) who, in contemplation of such marriage, was *cr.* on 12 June 1476, EARL OF NOTTINGHAM, and on 7 Feb. 1477, EARL WARENNE and DUKE OF NORFOLK. She appears to have *d.* s.p. (an infant) in the lifetime of her

See fuller account under their respective Peerage dignities.

---

prefix of "*Earl.*" It is not, however, contended that such prefix would of itself indicate a peerage dignity, tho' it is difficult not to allow such dignity to John Mowbray after his summons to Parl., 22 March 1412/3, by writ directed "*Comiti Mareschallo*" more especially as he had *inherited no peerage*, his father having been *attainted*. In any case, however, a list of the various "Earls Marshals" (each of whom is more fully described under his peerage dignity) is given in the text.

(a) John (Montagu), Earl of Salisbury, was on 23 Sep. 1398, made *Deputy* Earl Marshal of England for three years. He was beheaded 7 Jan. 1400.

(b) Thomas Mowbray, his elder br., *styled* himself EARL MARSHAL. He *d.* s.p., being beheaded 1405.

(c) The writ of summons to Parl. 22 March 1412/3 (1 Hen. V.), directed "*Comiti Mareschallo*" would appear to have *cr.* a *Peerage dignity* (similar to the "Earl Marischal" in Scotland) as *Earl Marshal*. See p. 261, note "f."

(d) Between 1476 and 1483 "SIR THOMAS GREY, Knt.," is said by Camden to have held the office. The only Thomas Grey likely to have obtained such a post was the Marquess of Dorset (so *cr.* 1475) who in 1483 was made Constable of the Tower of London, &c. His son and successor (in 1501) another Thomas Grey, *b.* in 1477, would not be likely, when a mere child, to have been *cr.* Earl Marshal, especially as the family of Grey had not any hereditary claim to that office.

husband who was (together with his br. **King Edward V.**) murdered (in his 10th or 11th year), 23 June 1483. Neither of them exercised the office of *Earl Marshal*. At her death *all her dignities* fell into *abeyance*.[a]

* * * * *

VIII. 1483, to 1485. *1.* JOHN (HOWARD), LORD HOWARD, s. and h. of Sir Robert HOWARD, by Margaret, da. (whose issue became coheir) of Thomas (MOWBRAY), DUKE OF NORFOLK, EARL OF NORFOLK, EARL OF NOTTINGHAM, LORD MOWBRAY, LORD SEGRAVE, and EARL MARSHAL was *b.* before 1435; sum. to Parl. as a Baron (LORD HOWARD), 15 Oct. 1470, and was *cr.* 28 June 1483, DUKE OF NORFOLK and EARL MARSHAL OF ENGLAND, *with rem. to heirs male of his body*.[b] He was slain 22 Aug. 1485, fighting for his King, Richard III., and was accordingly *attainted* 7 Nov. following (under the new dynasty) when *all his honours* became *forfeited*.

* * * * *

IX. 1486, to 1492. *1.* WILLIAM (BERKELEY), EARL OF NOTTINGHAM [1483], VISCOUNT BERKELEY [1481], and LORD BERKELEY, s. and h. of James, LORD BERKELEY, by Isabel, da. (whose issue became coheir) of Thomas (MOWBRAY), DUKE OF NORFOLK, EARL OF NORFOLK, EARL OF NOTTINGHAM, LORD MOWBRAY, LORD SEGRAVE, and *Earl Marshal*; was *b.* 1426; *suc.* his father in 1463 as LORD BERKELEY; was *cr.* in 1481 VISCOUNT BERKELEY and, having *suc.* to a moiety of the vast estates of the Mowbray family, was *cr.*, 28 June 1483, EARL OF NOTTINGHAM. At the Coronation, 30 Oct. 1485, he was Joint Lord High Steward and *Earl Marshal for the occasion*,[c] having been so *cr.* by letters patent (now lost) 26 Oct., 1 Hen. VII.,[b] and was *cr.*, 19 Feb. 1485/6, "EARL MARSHAL OF ENGLAND, *with rem. to heirs male of his body*."[c] He was *cr.* 28 Jan. 1488/9 MARQUESS OF BERKELEY. He *d.* s.p., 14 Feb. 1491/2, in his 67th year, when *all his honours*, save the Barony of Berkeley, became *extinct*.

X. 1493? to 1509. *1.* HENRY [TUDOR], 2d s. of **King Henry VII.**, *b.* 1491; was on or before 15 Oct. 1495, "EARL MARSHAL OF ENGLAND," he being at that date so styled, when *cr.* DUKE OF YORK, on 31 Oct. 1494.[b] He became DUKE OF CORNWALL in 1502 and was *cr.* in 1503 **Prince of Wales**, and EARL OF CHESTER. He ascended the throne, 21 April 1509 as **King Henry VIII.**, when *all his honours merged in the Crown*.

XI. 1510, to 1524. *2.* THOMAS (HOWARD), EARL OF SURREY (so *cr.* 1483), s. and h. of John, DUKE OF NORFOLK, *Earl Marshal of England* abovenamed (*attainted* 1485), was *cr.* 10 July 1510, EARL MARSHAL OF ENGLAND," *for life*.[c] He was *cr.* 1 Feb. 1513/4, DUKE OF NORFOLK. He *d.* 21 May 1524, aged 81, when the office of Earl Marshal (granted him for life) reverted to the Crown.

See fuller account under their respective Peerage dignities.

(a) The coheirs were the descendants of the two daughters (who had issue) of Thomas (Mowbray), Duke of Norfolk, so *cr.* in 1397. These were (1) William (BERKELEY), VISCOUNT BERKELEY, s. and h. of James, Lord Berkeley, and Lady Isabel Mowbray (*d.* 1452) his wife. He was *cr.*, 28 June 1483, EARL OF NOTTINGHAM on the same day that the other coheir (Lord Howard) was *cr.* Duke Norfolk and Earl Marshal. The Earl of Nottingham was *cr.* subsequently *Earl Marshal* in 1485/6 (as mentioned in the text) and finally in 1489 MARQUESS OF BERKELEY; On his death s.p. 1491/2 the representation of his mother devolved on his br., Maurice, Lord Berkeley, in whose issue it still remains (2) John (HOWARD), LORD HOWARD, s. and h. of Sir Robert Howard and Lady Margaret Mowbray, his wife. He was *cr.*, 28 June 1483, DUKE OF NORFOLK and *Earl Marshal* as mentioned in the text.

(b) See "*Creations*, 1483—1646," in ap. 47th Rep. D.K. Pub. Records.

(c) See vol. i, p. 331, note "a," *sub* "Berkeley."

XI. 1524, to 1534. *1.* CHARLES (BRANDON), DUKE OF SUFFOLK (so *cr.* 1514) is said(a) to have been, "EARL MARSHAL OF ENGLAND," from 21 May 1524 to 20 May 1534.(b) He *d.* 14 Aug. 1545, aged 61.

XII. 1534, to 1547; and 1553, to 1554. *3.* THOMAS (HOWARD), DUKE OF NORFOLK, s. and h. of Thomas, DUKE OF NORFOLK, *Earl Marshal of England* (for life) abovenamed, was *b.* 1473; *cr.* EARL OF SURREY, 1514; *suc.* his father in the Dukedom, 21 May 1524, and was *cr.*(a) 28 May 1534,(b) EARL MARSHAL OF ENGLAND, with (presumably) rem. to the heirs male of his body. He was *attainted* 20 Jan. 1546/7, whereby *all his honours became forfeited*, but was *restored* 3 Aug. 1553. He *d.* 25 Aug. 1554, aged 80.

XIII. 1547, to 1551. *1.* EDWARD (SEYMOUR), DUKE OF SOMERSET (so *cr.* 16 Feb. 1546/7), was *cr.* (the next day) 17 Feb. 1546/7, EARL MARSHAL OF ENGLAND," for life"(c) but appears to have resigned or forfeited the same before April 1551. He was beheaded 22 Jan. 1552, aged about 52, when, having been *attainted*, all his *honours became forfeited.*

XIV. 1551, to 1553. *1.* JOHN (DUDLEY), EARL OF WARWICK (so *cr.* 1547), was *cr.* 20 April 1551, "EARL MARSHAL OF ENGLAND," for life.(c) He was beheaded, 22 Aug. 1553, aged about 52, when, having been *attainted*, all his *honours became forfeited.*

XV. 1554, to 1572. *4.* THOMAS (HOWARD), DUKE OF NORFOLK, EARL MARSHAL OF ENGLAND, &c., grandson and h. of Thomas, DUKE OF NORFOLK, *Earl Marshal of England* abovenamed, *suc.* to the honours of his grandfather on his death, 25 Aug. 1554. He was beheaded, 2 June 1572, aged 36, when, having been *attainted*, all his *honours became forfeited.*

XVI. 1573, to 1590. *1.* GEORGE (TALBOT), EARL OF SHREWSBURY, who *suc.* to that peerage on 21 Sep. 1560, was *cr.* 2 Jan. 1572/3, "EARL MARSHAL OF ENGLAND," for life.(c) He *d.* 18 Nov. 1590, aged above 62.

In 1590, the office was exercised by commissioners, whose description at that period was [1] William (Cecil), Baron Burleigh, *Lord Treasurer* [2] Charles (Howard), Baron Howard of Effingham, *Lord High Admiral*, and [3] Henry (Carey), Baron Hunsdon, *Lord Chamberlain of the Household.*

XVI. 1597, to 1601. *1.* ROBERT (DEVEREUX), EARL OF ESSEX, who *suc.* to that peerage on 22 Sep. 1576, was *cr.*(a) 28 Dec. 1597,(b) EARL MARSHAL OF ENGLAND, presumably, for life. He was beheaded, 25 Feb. 1601, aged 33, when, having been attainted, all his *honours became forfeited.*

[Side note to all entries above: See fuller account under their respective Peerage dignities.]

(a) No such creation, however, appears among the "*Creations* 1483—1646" in ap. 47th Rep. D.K. Pub. Records.
(b) The date is thus given in Doyle's "Official Baronage."
(c) See "*Creations*, 1483—1646," as in note "a" next above.

In 1602 the office was exercised by Commissioners whose description at that period was [1] Thomas (Sackville), Baron Buckhurst, *Lord Treasurer* [2] Charles (Howard), Earl of Nottingham, *Lord High Admiral*, and [3] Edward (Somerset), Earl of Worcester, *Master of the Horse*.

XVII. 1603, 1604, 1605, and 1610, *1.* EDWARD (SOMERSET), EARL OF WORCESTER, who *suc.* to the peerage, 22 Feb. 1589, was *cr.* [—] 1603([a]) EARL MARSHAL OF ENGLAND to hold that dignity from 20 to 28 July, *i.e.*, for the Coronation of King James I. He was also so *cr.*, 10 March 1603/4,([a]) to hold the same from sunrise to sunset on the 15th inst. (on the occasion of a Royal procession thro' the city); also on 3 May 1605,([a]) to hold the same from that day to the 6th inst. (on the occasion of the christening of the Princess Mary) and also on 1 June 1610 (on the occasion of the creation of Prince Henry as Prince of Wales) to hold the same from that day to the 8th inst.([a]) He *d.* 3 March 1628, aged 75.

Between these dates, however, *viz.*, in 1604 and 1616 the office was twice exercised by Commissioners, whose description, at those respective periods, was as follows, *viz.*, in 1604 [1] Thomas (Sackville), Earl of Dorset, *Lord Treasurer* [2] Ludovic (Stuart), Duke of Lennox in Scotland [3] Charles (Howard), Earl of Nottingham, *Lord High Admiral* [4] Thomas (Howard), Earl of Suffolk, *Lord Chamberlain of the Household* [5] Edward (Somerset), Earl of Worcester, *Master of the Horse* [6] Charles (Blount), Earl of Devonshire, *Master of the Ordnance*, and [7] Henry (Howard), Earl of Northampton, *Lord Warden of the Cinque Ports*. On 25 Sep. 1616, the Commissioners were [1] Edward (Somerset), Earl of Worcester, *Lord Privy Seal* [2] Ludovic (Stuart), Duke of Richmond, *Lord Steward of the Household* [3] George (Villiers), Marquess of Buckingham, *Master of the Horse* [4] Charles (Howard), Earl of Nottingham, *Lord High Admiral* [5] William (Herbert), Earl of Pembroke, *Lord Chamberlain of the Household*, and [6] Thomas (Howard), Earl of Arundel and Surrey.

XVIII. 1621, to 1646. *5.* THOMAS (HOWARD), "EARL OF ARUNDEL AND SURREY,"([a]) who was restored as such in 1604, being s. and h. of Philip, EARL OF ARUNDEL (*attainted* 1589) who was s. and h. of Thomas, DUKE OF NORFOLK, *Earl Marshal of England*, abovenamed (*attainted* 1572), was *cr.*, 29 Aug. 1621, EARL MARSHAL OF ENGLAND for life.([a]) He was *cr.*, 6 June 1644, EARL OF NORFOLK. He *d.* 4 Oct. 1646, aged 60.

* * * * * *

XIX. 1661. *6.* JAMES (HOWARD), EARL OF SUFFOLK, who *suc.* to that dignity 8 June 1640, being s. and h. of Theophilus, 2d EARL OF SUFFOLK (*d.* 1640), s. and h. of Thomas, 1st EARL OF SUFFOLK (*d.* 1626), yr. s. of Thomas, DUKE OF NORFOLK, *Earl Marshal of England*, abovenamed (*attainted* 1572) was *cr.* EARL MARSHAL OF ENGLAND from 18 to 24 April 1661, for the Coronation of King Charles II. He *d.* 7 Jan. 1688/9.

On 26 May 1662, the office was (for the last time) exercised by Commissioners whose description at that period was [1] Thomas (Wriothesley), Earl of Southampton, *Lord High Treasurer* [2] John (Robartes), Baron Robartes of Truro, *Lord Privy Seal* [3] Henry (Pierrepont), Marquess of Dorchester [4] Montagu (Bertie), Earl of Lindsey, *Lord Great Chamberlain of England* [5] Edward (Montagu), Earl of Manchester, *Lord Chamberlain of the Household*, and [6] Algernon (Percy), Earl of Northumberland.

See fuller account under their respective Peerage dignities.

XX. 1672. *7.* HENRY (HOWARD), BARON HOWARD OF CASTLE RISING (so *cr.* 1669), yr. br. of Thomas, DUKE OF NORFOLK (so *restored* 1660), both being sons of Henry Frederick, EARL OF ARUNDEL (*d.* 1652), the 2d but

([a]) See "*Creations*, 1483—1646," in ap. 47th Rep. D.K. Pub. Records.

1st surv. s. and h. of Thomas, EARL OF ARUNDEL, SURREY, and NORFOLK, *Earl Marshal of England* for life, abovenamed (*d.* 1646), was *cr.* EARL OF NORWICH, 19 Oct. 1672, being on the same day *cr.* EARL MARSHAL OF ENGLAND with rem. to the heirs male of his body whom failing(1) to those of his grandfather, Thomas (Howard), Earl of Arundel, Surrey, and Norfolk (2) to those of Thomas (Howard), Earl of Suffolk (3) to those of Lord William Howard, of Naworth (yst. s. of Thomas, 4th Duke of Norfolk), and (4) to those of Charles (Howard), 3d Earl of Nottingham. He *suc.* (his brother) 1 Dec. 1677, as DUKE OF NORFOLK, with which title this dignity has continued united. See "NORFOLK" Dukedom, *cr.* 1483, under the 6th and subsequent Dukes.

MARSHAL.

Barony by Writ.

I. 1309.

1. WILLIAM MARSHAL, of Hingham,(a) co. Norfolk, s. and h. of John M. of the same, *suc.* his father in 1283, being then five years of age; was one of the Barons whose signature (as "*Willus Mareschall, Dominus de Hengham*") appears on the letter to the Pope dat. 1301;(b) was in the wars with Scotland in 1305-06, and was sum. to Parl. as a Baron (LORD MARSHAL) by writs dat. from 9 Jan. (1308/9), 2 Ed. II., to 26 Nov. (1313), 7 Ed. II. He *d.* 1314.

II. 1314, to 1317.

2. JOHN (MARSHAL), LORD MARSHAL, s. and h., aged 22, at the death of his father. He accompanied the Queen Consort to Scotland about that date. He was never sum. to Parl. and *d.* unm. (1316-17) 10 Ed. II. since which date the *Barony has remained dormant*, but the representation thereof devolved on his sister.(c)

MARSHAM OF THE MOTE.

i.e., "MARSHAM OF THE MOTE, co. Kent," Viscountcy (*Marsham*), *cr.* 1801, with the EARLDOM OF ROMNEY, which see.

MARSTON.

i.e., "BOYLE OF MARSTON, co. Somerset," Barony (*Boyle*), *cr.* 1711. See "ORRERY" Earldom [I.], *cr.* 1660, under the 4th Earl.

MARTIN.

Barony by Writ.

I. 1295.

1. WILLIAM MARTIN, of Kemeys, co. Pembroke, and of Barnstaple, co. Devon, s. and h. of Nicholas M. (who *d.* v.p.) and grandson and h. of Nicholas MARTIN, of Kemeys, by Maud, da. and h. of Guy DE BRYAN, of Barnstaple, *suc.* his said grandfather, 10 Ed. I. (1282) doing homage for his lands in Devon and Somerset that same year; was sum. to Parl. as a Baron (LORD MARTIN), from 23 June (1295) 23 Ed. I. to 6 May (1325) 18 Ed. II.;(d) his name appearing (as "*Willelmus Martin, Dominus de Camesio*") in the letter to the Pope, dat. 1301.(e) He *m.* Eleanor, da. of William DE MOHUN. He *d.* 1325.

(a) Aliva, 1st da. and coheir of Hubert de Rye, of Hingham, brought that estate to this family. She *m.* Sir John Marshall, said to have been Marshal of Ireland *temp.* John. He *d.* 1234, being grandfather of William Marshal who joined the Barons against King Henry III. and *d.* 1264, being father of John, the father of William, the 1st Baron.

(b) See full account of this letter in "*Nicolas,*" pp. 761—809, where there is a note to this Baron stating that "his seal contains two batons one on each side of his arms which [batons] were probably indicative of his hereditary office of Marshall of Ireland, which was granted in fee to John Marshall, his great great grandfather by King John."

(c) Her name was Hawyse, and she was aged 15, at his death. She *m.* Robert (Morley), Lord Morley, who *d.* 1360, with which dignity this Barony continued united, till its abeyance in 1686.

(d) There is proof in the rolls of Parl. of his sitting.

(e) See "*Nicolas,*" pp. 761—809 for a full account of this letter.

II. 1325, to 1326. 2. WILLIAM (MARTIN), LORD MARTIN, 1st surv. s. and h.,(a) then aged 30. He was sum. to Parl., 10 Oct. (1325) 19 Ed. II. He *d.* unm. 1326, when the *Barony* fell into *abeyance*.(b)

MARYBOROUGH.

See "MOLYNEUX OF MARYBOROUGH, in the Queen's county," Viscountcy [I.] (*Molyneux*), *cr.* 1628.

---

i.e., "MARYBOROUGH OF MARYBOROUGH, in the Queen's county," Barony (WESLEY-POLE, *formerly* WESLEY), *cr.* 1821; see "MORNINGTON" Earldom [I.], *cr.* 1760, under the 3d, 4th and 5th Earls; *ex.* 1863.

MASHAM.

i.e., "SCROPE DE MASHAM," see "SCROPE" Barony (*Scrope*), *cr.* 1350 and (in 1403) as "SCROPE DE MASHAM;" *in abeyance* since 1517.

MASHAM OF OTES.

Barony. I. 1712. 1. SAMUEL MASHAM, Cofferer of the Household, 8th but 1st surv. s. and h. of Sir Francis MASHAM, 3d Bart., of Otes in High Laver, co. Essex, by his first wife, Mary, da. of Sir William SCOTT, Bart., of Rouen, Marquis de la Mezansene in France, was Page of Honour to the Princess Anne, and, after her accession to the Throne, was Gent. of the Chamber to her Consort, Prince George of Denmark, and having *m.* in 1707 a lady whose influence over the Queen was at that time paramount, obtained a Reg. of Foot (with the rank of Brig. General); was Cofferer of the Household (1711-14) and was *cr.*, 1 Jan. 1711/2,(c) BARON MASHAM OF OTES, co. Essex; Remembrancer of the Exchequer, 1716; *suc. to the Baronetcy* (*cr.* 20 Dec. 1621), on the death of his father, 7 Feb. 1723. He *m.* privately, in or shortly before June 1707, in Dr. Arbuthnot's apartments (the Queen, however, being present) the lady above alluded to (one of the Queen's "*dressers*"), Abigail, da. of Francis HILL, of London, Turkey merchant, by (—), one of the 23 children of Sir John JENNINGS, K.B., sister of Richard JENNINGS, father of Sarah, the celebrated DUCHESS OF MARLBOROUGH, to whose influence, over Queen Anne, the said Abigail succeeded. She *d.* 6 Dec. 1734.(d) He *d.* 16 Oct. 1758. Both were *bur.* at High Laver. His will pr. 1758.

(a) He appears to have had an elder br. Edward, for whom (as "s. and h. of William Marshal, Lord of Kemeys") was made (1296-97), 25 Ed. I., a treaty for marriage, with Janetta, da. of John, Lord Hastings; another treaty being also made at the same time for the marriage of William, s. and h. of the said Lord Hastings with Alianore, da. of the said William, Lord Marshall. (See pat. roll, 25 Ed. I., m. i., part 2, as quoted in Banks's "*Bar. Angl.*")

(b) The coheirs were his two sisters or their issue *viz.* (1) Eleanor, aged 40, relict of William Hastings, but then (1326) *wife* of Philip (Columbers), Lord Columbers, who *d.* 1342. She *d.* s.p.; and (2) James, Lord Audley, then aged 14, s. and h. of Joane, Dow. Countess of Lincoln (the other sister) by Nicholas (Audley) Lord Audley, her second husband. This James, Lord Audley, appears to have been entitled to the Barony of Martin on the death s.p. of his maternal aunt, Eleanor Columbers. So also would have been his s. and h., Nicholas, Lord Audley, on whose death s.p. in 1391, his Baronies fell into abeyance between his three sisters (Joane Tuchet, Margaret Hilary and Margaret Fitzwarine) or their descendants, in which state the Barony of MARTIN still continues, tho' the abeyance of the Barony of Audley was terminated in 1405, in favour of the Touchet family.

(c) "*Horâ secundâ post meridiem.*" He was one of the 12 Peers *cr.* in five days to secure a majority for the Tory administration. See a list of them in vol. i, p. 209, note "d," *sub* "Bathurst."

(d) Her character is given (1) by Lord Dartmouth, who says "she was exceedingly mean and vulgar in her manners; of a very unequal temper; childishly exceptious and passionate," while (2) Swift says, "she was of a plain sound understanding, of great

II. 1758, to 1776. 2. SAMUEL (MASHAM), BARON MASHAM OF OTES [1712], also a *Baronet* [1621], 2d but 1st surv. s. and h., *b.* 1712; was v.p. a Lord of the Bedchamber to King Geo. II.; *suc. to the peerage* as also to the Remembrancership of the Exchequer, 16 Oct. 1758; Groom of the Bedchamber to the Prince of Wales, 1758. He *m.* firstly, 16 Oct. 1736, at St. Geo. Han. sq., Henrietta ("worth £20,000"), da. of Salway WINNINGTON, of Stanford Court, co. Worcester, by Ann, da. of Thomas FOLEY, of Whitley, in that county. She *d.* 1761 and was *bur.* at High Laver. He *m.* secondly Charlotte (one of the Maids of Honour to the Princess of Wales), da. of John DIVE, by Dorothy, da. and h. of Walter ASTON, of Millwich, co. Stafford. She *d.* 21 May 1773, aged 61, and was *bur.* at High Laver. He *d.* s.p., 14 June 1776, aged 64, when *all his honours became extinct*. Will pr. June 1776.

MASHAM OF SWINTON.

Barony. I. 1891. 1. SAMUEL CUNLIFFE-LISTER, of Swinton Park, in Masham, co. York, 4th s. of Ellis CUNLIFFE-LISTER-KAY(a) (formerly Ellis CUNLIFFE), of Manningham, co. York, by his second wife, Mary, da. of William KAY, of Cottingham, in that county, was *b.* 1 Jan. 1815; High Sheriff for Yorkshire, 1887; sometime Col. of the West Riding Volunteers and was *cr.* 15 July 1891, BARON MASHAM OF SWINTON,(b) co. York. He *m.* 6 Sep. 1854, Anne, 1st da. of John DEARDEN, of Hollins Hall, near Halifax. She *d.* 1875.

Family Estates.—These, in 1883, consisted of 24,240 acres in the North Riding and 329 in the West Riding of Yorkshire. *Total.* 24,569 acres, worth £17,253 a year. *Principal Residence.* Swinton Park, near Bedale, Yorkshire.

MASSEREENE.

Viscountcy [I.] I. 1660. 1. SIR JOHN CLOTWORTHY, of Antrim, co. Antrim, s. and h. of Sir Hugh CLOTWORTHY, Sheriff of co. Antrim, by Mary, da. of Roger LANGFORD, of Muckmaire, in that county, *suc.* his father, 12 Feb. 1630; was M.P. in the English Parl. *temp.* Car. I.; M.P. for co. Antrim, 1634; was greatly instrumental in forwarding the Restoration and, in reward thereof, having been made P.C., was *cr.*, 21 Nov. 1660,(c) BARON OF LOUGHNEAGH and VISCOUNT MASSEREENE, both in co. Antrim [I.], with (in an Irish peerage a *very* unusual) *spec. rem.*, failing heirs male of his body, to Sir John SKEFFINGTON (his son in law) and the issue male of the said John by Mary, his wife [only child of the grantee], whom failing to *the heirs general of his own body*.(d) He took his seat, 8 May 1661. He was Col. of a Reg. of Foot and a Commissioner for the Court of Claims; *Custos Rot.*, co. Derry, 1663 [I.] He *m.* Margaret, 1st da. of Roger (JONES), 1st VISCOUNT RANELAGH [I.], by his first wife, Frances, da. of Gerald (MOORE), 1st VISCOUNT DROGHEDA [I.] He *d.* s.p.m. Sep. 1665.

---

truth and sincerity, without the least mixture of falsehood or disguise; of an honest boldness and courage, firm and disinterested in her friendship, and full of love, duty, and veneration for the Queen, her mistress."

(a) He took the name of *Lister* under the will of Samuel Lister, of Manningham, and the name of *Kay* on the death of William Kay, of Cottingham. He was descended from the family of Lister, being s. and h. of John Cunliffe, of Ilkley, who was s. and h. of Ellis Cunliffe, of the same, by Elizabeth, 1st da. and coheir of Thomas Lister, of Manningham.

(b) See p. 82, note "b," *sub* "Leicester of Holkham," as to this class of peerage, where the greater is subordinated to the less; so also "Truro of Bowes," "Halifax of Monk Bretton," &c., the title being (by the addition) thus explained away as *not* having reference to the *place of note* (town, city, or country), whose name it bears.

(c) The preamble of the patent is in "*Lodge*," vol. ii, p. 378.

(d) *The* ancient Eardoms [I.], of Ulster, Carrick, and Ormond, were to "heirs *general*," but since the creation of the last (1328), it is believed that no patent (save this one of 1661) has conferred an Irish dignity to such heirs. In none of the three kingdoms have a greater number of *ladies* been raised to the dignity of peerage, but the rem. (when any existed) has been always to the heirs *male* of the body of the grantee or of her husband or, in the case of a *male* grantee, to the issue male of a da. or daughters.

II. 1665. 2. JOHN (SKEFFINGTON), VISCOUNT MASSEREENE, &c. [I.], son in law and heir, according to the *spec. rem.* in the creation of the dignity. He was s. and h. of Sir Richard SKEFFINGTON,(a) by Anne, da. of Sir John NEWDIGATE, of Arbury, co. Warwick. He *suc. to the Baronetcy* (*cr.* 8 May 1627) on the death of his nephew the 3d Bart., 1 April 1652. He was M.P. for co. Antrim from 1661 till he *suc. to the peerage* [I.], in Sep. 1665. P.C. to Charles II. and James II.; *Custos Rot.* of co. Derry, 1666, and Governor of co. Derry and Coleraine, 1685, but, taking part against the then Government (bring a zealous supporter of the Protestant interest) was *attainted* by King James' Parl., 7 May 1689,(b) tho' restored by King William in Oct. 1692, taking his seat in Parl. on the 17th of that month. He *m.* 20 July, 1654, at St. Paul's Covent garden, Mary, only da. and h. of John (CLOTWORTHY), 1st VISCOUNT MASSEREENE [I.], by Margaret his wife both abovenamed. She *d.* 20 Sep. 1686. He *d.* 21 June 1695, and was *bur.* at Antrim. Will pr. in Ireland.

III. 1695. 3. CLOTWORTHY (SKEFFINGTON), VISCOUNT MASSEREENE, &c. [I.], 2d and yst., but only surv. s. and h.; *b.* after 1666; took part with his father in the Protestant cause in Ulster, being Col. of Reg. of Foot, and joint Com. in Chief of co. Antrim, and consequently attainted by King James' Parl. in 1689, tho' restored by King William. He *suc. to the peerage* [I.], 21 June, and took his seat, 27 Aug. 1695, signing the declaration, 2 Dec. 1697, in favour of King William and the Protestant succession.(c) He *m.* (Lic. Vic. Gen., 7 Jan. and 9 March 1679/80, he "of Fisherwick, co. Stafford" about 20, and she about 18), Rachel, 1st da. of Sir Edward HUNGERFORD, K.B.,(d) probably by his first wife, Jane, da. of Sir John HELE.(e) He *d.* at Antrim, March 1713/4. Will pr. Feb. 1717. His widow *d.* there Feb. 1731. Her will dat. 5 Sep. 1730, pr. 26 Oct. 1731,(f) at Dublin. Both *bur.* at Antrim.

IV. 1714. 4. CLOTWORTHY (SKEFFINGTON), VISCOUNT MASSEREENE, &c. [I.], s. and h. He was M.P. for co. Antrim, 1703-14, till he *suc. to the peerage* [I.], March 1713/4, taking his seat accordingly, 2 Dec. 1715. He *m.*, 9 Sep. 1713, Catharine, 1st da. of Arthur (CHICHESTER), 3d EARL OF DONEGALL [I.], by his second wife, Catharine, da. of Arthur (FORBES), EARL OF GRANARD [I.] He *d.* at Antrim, 11 Feb. 1738. His widow, who was *bap.* at St. Peter's, Dublin, 9 Sep. 1687, *d.* 1 July 1749. Both *bur.* at Antrim.

V. 1738. Earldom [I.] I. 1756. 5 and 1. CLOTWORTHY (SKEFFINGTON), VISCOUNT MASSEREENE, &c. [I.], s. and h., *suc. to the peerage* [I.], 11 Feb. 1738, and took his seat, 9 Oct. 1739; P.C. [I.], 1746; D.C.L. of Dublin, 22 Oct. 1751, and was *cr.*, 28 July 1756, EARL OF MASSEREENE [I.] He *m.* firstly, 10 March 1738, Anne, 1st da. of Rev. Richard DANIEL, D.D, Dean of Down, 1731-39. She, who was *bap.* 2 Nov. 1719, *d.* s.p., 24 March 1740, and was *bur.* at St. Michan's, Dublin. He *m.* secondly,

---

(a) Altho' this Sir Richard is called "*Baronet*" on his monument at Broxbourne, Herts, he never succeeded to that dignity, dying June 1647 in the lifetime of his nephew, Sir William Skeffington, 3d Bart., who *d.* (5 months after his father the 2d Bart.), 1 April 1652.

(b) His estate, then valued at £4,340 a year, was sequestrated for that period.

(c) His estates (probably inherited from his mother) were then valued at £800 a year in England and £600 in Ireland.

(d) "The Spendthrift" who sold Farleigh Castle in 1686, and *d.* in poverty in Spring Gardens, being *bur.* 8 July 1711, at St. Martin's in the fields.

(e) Lady Massereene's second son was named "Hele." In Le Neve's "*Knights*" this Jane is called the second wife and the first wife is said to be "widow of Collomb" and "d. and h. of Cullumb" and to be the mother of Lady Massereene and of Edward Hungerford, who *d.* v.p. Lady M. in her will mentions the picture of her *grandfather*, "Sir John Lacy," which, possibly, might elucidate matters.

(f) See "*Lodge*," vol. ii, p. 384, for a very interesting abstract thereof, illustrating the (intricate tho' illustrious) Hungerford pedigree, &c.

25 Nov. 1741, Anne, da. and h. of Henry Eyre, of Rowter, co. Derby, by his first wife, Elizabeth, da. of Sir Willoughby Hickman, Bart. He d. suddenly (when out "fowling"), near Antrim, 17 Sep. 1757, and was bur. there. His widow d. 29 May 1805, in her 89th year.(a) at Merrion square, Dublin. Will dat. 31 Jan. to 19 Feb. 1800, pr. 22 May 1812.

Earldom [I.] II. Viscountcy [I.] VI. 1757.

2 and 6. Clotworthy (Skeffington), Earl of Massereene, Viscount Massereene, &c. [I.], s. and h.; b. 28 Jan. 1742; styled Lord Loughneagh from 1756 till he suc. to the peerage [I.], 17 Sep. 1757: was ed at Benet's Coll., Cambridge; "in his early days figured very considerably in the walks of fashion,"(b) but, having contracted large debts in France, was imprisoned at Paris, about 20 years, escaping in May 1789. He m. firstly, 19 Aug. 1789, at St. Peter's, Cornhill, London (altho' said to have been "twice" married previously in France to the same lady), Marie Anne, da. of Mons. (—) Barcier, Gov. of the Chatelet in Paris, where he was imprisoned. She "the once celebrated and beautiful Countess," d. at Greenwich, in Oct. 1800, aged 38.(b) He m. secondly, Elizabeth Lane. He d. s.p. 28 Feb. 1805, aged 62, at Antrim Castle. His widow m. George Doran, who was living 1828, and thirdly (as second wife) the Hon. George Massy, who d. 13 Aug. 1834, aged 70. She d. 19 March 1838, at Gloucester, aged 65. Will pr. April 1838.

Earldom [I.] III. Viscountcy [I.] VII. 1805.

3 and 7. Henry (Skeffington), Earl of Massereene, Viscount Massereene, &c. [I.], next br. and h.; b. about 1744, sometime Lieut. Col. 2d Reg. of Horse; M.P. for Belfast and Gov. of Cork; suc. to the peerage [I.], 28 Feb. 1805. He d. unm. 12 June 1811, aged 66. Will pr. 1811.

Earldom [I.] IV. Viscountcy [I.] VIII. 1811.

4 and 8. Chichester (Skeffington), Earl of Massereene [1756], and Viscount Massereene and Baron Loughneagh [1660] in the peerage of Ireland, also a Baronet [1627], only surv. br. and h., being 5th s. of the 1st Earl; b. about 1750; sometime M.P. for Antrim. He m. in 1780, Harriett, 1st da. of Robert (Jocelyn), 1st Earl of Roden [I.], by Anne, da. and h. of James (Hamilton), Earl of Clanbrassill [I.] He d., s.p.m., in Dublin, 25 Feb. 1816, in his 67th year, when the Earldom of Massereene (as also the Baronetcy) became extinct, but (the issue male of the 2d Viscount having failed) the Viscountcy devolved as below. His widow d. 7 July 1831.

Viscountcy [I.] IX. 1816.

9. Harriet, suo jure, Viscountess Massereene and Baroness Loughneagh [I.], only da. and h., being also heir general of the body of John (Clotworthy), 1st Viscount Massereene [I.], and, as such, entitled to the peerage dignity to which she suc. 25 Feb. 1816. She m. 20 Nov. 1810, the Hon. Thomas Foster, who, consequently, by Royal lic., 8 Jan. 1817, took the name of Skeffington in lieu of that of Foster. He, on the death of his mother, 20 Jan. 1824, became VISCOUNT FERRARD and BARON ORIEL OF COLLON [I.], becoming, also, on the death of his father, 16 Aug. 1828, BARON ORIEL OF FERRARD [U.K.] He d. 18 Jan. 1843. See fuller particulars of him under "Ferrard" Viscountcy [I.], cr. 1797, sub the second holder of that dignity. His wife, the suo jure Viscountess d. before him, 2 Jan. 1831.

(a) She "had been a most beautiful woman and retained her vivacity and accomplishments to the last." [Ann. Reg., 1809.] She is (wrongly) called Elizabeth in "Lodge" (1789) and succeeding peerages.

(b) Annual Reg. for 1800 (p. 65), and for 1805 (p. 469) where is a long account of the Earl's romantic career, and of the Countess' curious death.

X. 1831. *10.* JOHN (FOSTER-SKEFFINGTON, *formerly* FOSTER), VISCOUNT MASSERRENE and BARON LOUGHNEA, s. and h., *b.* 30 Nov. 1812, in Dublin; *suc. to the abovenamed peerage* [I.] on the death of his mother, 2 Jan. 1831, and *suc.* as VISCOUNT FERRARD, &c. [I.], and BARON ORIEL OF FERRARD [U.K.], on the death of his father, 18 June 1843; assumed the name of *Skeffington* in addition to that of *Foster* in 1843; sometime Lieut. Col. of the Louth Militia; K.P., 3 July 1851. He *m.*, 1 Aug. 1835, Olivia, 4th da. of Henry Deane GRADY, of Stillorgan, co. Dublin, by Dorcas, da. of Thomas SPREAD, of Ballycorn, co. Cork. He *d.* 28 April 1863, at Antrim Castle, aged 50.[a] His widow *d.* 10 May 1874, aged 67, at Massereene lodge, Torquay, Devon.

XI. 1863. *11.* CLOTWORTHY JOHN EYRE (FOSTER-SKEFFINGTON), VISCOUNT MASSERENE [1660], VISCOUNT FERRARD [1797], BARON LOUGHNEAGH [1660], and BARON ORIEL OF COLLON [1790], in the peerage of Ireland, also BARON ORIEL OF FERRARD [1821, U.K.], s and h., *b.* 9 Oct. 1842, in Dublin; *suc. to the peerage* [I. and U.K.], 28 April 1863; Lieut. Col. of the Antrim Artillery Militia, 1872-84; Lord Lieut. of co. Louth. He *m.*, 4 Oct. 1870, at St. Peter's, Onslow Gardens, Florence Elizabeth, only child of George John WHYTE-MELVILLE, of Bennochy, co. Fife, sometime Major in the Coldstream Guards, by Charlotte, da. of William (HANBURY, *afterwards* BATEMAN-HANBURY), 1st BARON BATEMAN OF SHOBDON COURT.

Family Estates.—These, in 1883, consisted of 11,777 acres in co. Antrim; 7,193 in co. Louth; 2,045 in co. Meath, and 9 in co. Monaghan. Total 21,024 acres, worth £15,018 a year. *Principal Residences.* Antrim Castle, co. Antrim, and Oriel Temple, near Collon, co. Louth.

MASSY OF DUNTRILEAGUE.

Barony [I.] I. 1776. *1.* HUGH MASSY, of Duntrileague, co. Limerick, 1st s. and h.[b] of Col. Hugh MASSY, of the same, by Elizabeth, sister of George, 1st BARON CARBERY [I.], da. of the Rt. Hon. George EVANS, was *b.* 1700;[c] was M.P. for co. Limerick, 1759-76, and for Old Leighlin, 1776, and was *cr.*, 4 Aug. 1776, BARON MASSY OF DUNTRILEAGUE, co. Limerick [I.], taking his seat, 18 Dec. 1777. He *m.* firstly, before 1733, Mary, da. and h. of Col. James DAWSON, of Newforest, co. Tipperary. He *m.* secondly, 16 March 1754, Rebecca, one of the two daughters and coheirs of Francis DELAP, of the Isle of Antigua. He *d.* 30 Jan. 1788, aged 88.

II. 1788. *2.* HUGH (MASSY), BARON MASSY OF DUNTRILEAGUE [I.], s. and h. by first wife; *b.* 14 April 1733; M.P. for Askeaton, 1776-83, and for co. Limerick, 1783-88; *suc. to the peerage* [I.], 30 Jan. 1788. He *m.* Sep. 1760 Catharine, 1st da. and coheir[d] of Edward TAYLOR, of Askeaton, co. Limerick, by Anne, da. of Richard MAUNSELL, of Limerick. He *d.* 10 May 1790, aged 57. His widow *d.* 16 Aug. 1791

III. 1790. *3.* HUGH (MASSY), BARON MASSY OF DUNTRILEAGUE [I.], s. and h., *b.* 24 Oct. 1761; *suc. to the peerage* [I.], 10 May 1790. He *m.*, 12 March 1792, Margaret Everina, yst. da. of William BARTON, of the Grove, co. Tipperary, by Grace, da. of the Very Rev. Charles MASSY, Dean of Limerick. He *d.* 20 June 1812, aged 50, at the Hermitage, co. Limerick. His widow *d.* 14 Sep. 1820, in Montagu Place, Midx.

(a) From the effects of a fall from a terrace in his garden while uprooting a shrub, which gave way, too suddenly, with him.

(b) The 6th and yst. son, Eyre Massy, was *cr.* in 1800 Baron Clarina of Elm Park [I.]

(c) So stated in "Lodge," vol. iv, where also his age is given as 88, in 1788, but where, however, his father is said to have been born [but 15 years before him] in 1685.

(d) The other coheir *m.* Henry Thomas (Butler), 2d Earl of Carrick [I.]

IV. 1812. 4. HUGH HAMON (MASSY), BARON MASSY OF DUNTRILEAGUE [I.], s. and h., b. 13 Feb. 1793; *suc. to the peerage* [I.], 20 June 1812. He m., 22 June 1826, Matilda, sister of Henry, 1st BARON ANNALY, da. of Luke WHITE, of Woodlands, co. Dublin, by his first wife, Eliza, da. of Andrew MAZIERE, of Dublin. He d. 27 Sep 1836. aged 43. His widow d. 27 Feb. 1883, aged 84, at Milford house, Limerick.

V. 1836. 5. HUGH HAMON INGOLDSBY (MASSY), BARON MASSY OF DUNTRILEAGUE [I.], 1st s. and h., b. 14 April 1827, at the Hermitage afsd.; *suc. to the peerage* [I.], 27 Sep. 1836. He m., 4 Jan. 1855, in Charlotte square, Edinburgh, Isabella, 1st da. of George More Nisbet, of Cairnhill, co. Lanark. He d. s.p., 27 Feb. 1874, aged 46, at 12 Atholl crescent, Edinburgh. His widow living 1893.

VI. 1874. 6. JOHN THOMAS WILLIAM (MASSY), BARON MASSY OF DUNTRILEAGUE [I.], only br. and h.; b. 30 Aug. 1835; *suc. to the peerage* [I.], 27 Feb. 1874. REP. PEER [I.], 14 March 1876. He m., 19 March 1863 (by spec. lic.) at Mount Juliet, co. Kilkenny, Lucy Maria, da. of Somerset Richard (BUTLER), 3d EARL OF CARRICK [I.], by his second wife, Lucy, da. of Arthur FRENCH. She was b. 9 Nov. 1837.

Family Estates.—These, in 1883, consisted of 24,671 acres in co. Leitrim and 8,432 in co. Limerick. *Total* 33,003 acres, valued at £12,101 a year. *Principal Residences.* The Hermitage, near Castle Connell, co. Limerick, and Larsheen house, near Kinlough, co. Leitrim.

MAUCHLINE.

i.e., "TARRINZEAN AND MAUCHLINE," Barony [S.] (*Campbell*), *cr.* 1633, with the EARLDOM OF LOUDOUN [S.], which see.

MAUDUIT.

JOHN MAUDUIT, of Somerford Mauduit, Wilts, served in the Scotch wars and was sum. to Parl. as a Baron (LORD MAUDUIT) by writ 12 Sep. (1342), 16 Ed. III., but never afterwards, neither were any of his posterity so summoned.(a) He d. (1347), 21 Ed. III., leaving Agnes, his widow, and John, his son and heir, then aged 15.(b)

MAULE.

i.e., "MAULE, BRECHIN AND NAVAR," Barony [S.] (*Maule*), *cr.* 1646, with the EARLDOM OF PANMURE [S.], which see; *forfeited* 1716.

MAULE OF WHITECHURCH.

i.e., "MAULE OF WHITECHURCH, co. Waterford," Viscountcy and Barony [I.] (*Maule*), *cr.* 1743, with the EARLDOM OF PANMURE OF FORTH [I.], which see; *ex.* 1782.

(a) This solitary summons, there being also no proof of any sitting under it, cannot be held to constitute a peerage dignity.

(b) Nothing more seems known of this John. Dugdale suggests that he may be the same as John Mauduit who died 1 April 1364, seized of the manor of Wermenstre, Wilts, and lands in Dorset, Gloucestershire, &c., leaving Maud, da. of his son, Thomas (who d. v.p.), his heir, and then aged nine.

MAULEY, or DE MAULEY.

Barony by Writ. I. 1295. 1. PETER DE MAULEY,(a) of Mulgrave and Doncaster, co. York, s. and h. of Peter DE MAULEY, of the same, by Nichola, sister and coheir of Gilbert (DE GANT), LORD GANT, had livery of his lands (1279), 7 Ed. I.; served in the Welsh, Scotch, and French wars, and was sum. to Parl. as a Baron (LORD MAULEY, or LORD DE MAULEY) by writs directed "*Petro de Malalacu*" from 23 June (1295), 23 Ed. I., to 12 Dec. (1309), 3 Ed. II. Though not sum. to the Parl. at Lincoln he was one of the Barons whose signature as ("*Petrus de Malolacu de Mulgrave*") is affixed to the famous letter of the Barons to the Pope in 1301.(b) He was one of the Barons sum. to attend the coronation of King Edward II. He *m.* Eleanor, da. of Thomas (FURNIVALL), LORD FURNIVALL. He *d.* 1310.

II. 1310. 2. PETER (DE MAULEY), LORD MAULEY, or LORD DE MAULEY, aged 28 at the death of his father, having v.p. been made, in 1306, K.B. He had livery of his lands (1310), 9 Ed. II. He was sum. to Parl. from 19 Dec. (1311), 5 Ed. II. to 22 Jan. (1335/6), 9 Ed. III. by writs directed "*Petro Malolacu,*" and from 24 Aug. (1336), 9 Ed. III., to 15 March (1353/4), 28 Ed. III, by writs directed "*Petro de Malolacu, le Quint.*"(a) He was in the Scotch wars and was in command at the battle of Durham in 1346. He *m.* Margaret, da. of Robert (CLIFFORD), LORD DE CLIFFORD. He *d.* 31 July (1355), 29 Ed. III. His wife survived him.

III. 1355. 3. PETER (DE MAULEY), LORD MAULEY, or LORD DE MAULEY, s. and h., aged 24, at his father's death. He served in the wars in France, being at the battle of Poitiers, 19 Sep. 1356; was Gov. of Berwick, 1368. He was sum. to Parl. from 20 Sep. (1355), 29 Ed. III. to 7 Jan. (1382/3), 6 Ric. II. by writs directed "*Petro de Malolacu, le Sisme,*"(a) tho' in the last few writs the words "*Le Sisme*" are omitted. He *m.* firstly in 1357, Elizabeth, Dow. BARONESS DARCY DE KNAITH, *de jure* apparently, *suo jure* BARONESS MEINILL, being da. and h. of Nicholas (DE MEINILL), LORD MEINILL, by Alice, da. of William (DE ROOS), LORD ROOS. She *d.* 1368. He *m.* secondly, Matilda, da. and coheir of Sir Thomas SUTTON,(c) of Holdernesse, co. York, probably, *de jure* LORD SUTTON DE HOLDERNESSE, but by her had no male issue. He *d.* 19 March (1382/3), 6 Ric. II. Will, as "*Petrus de malo lacu, sextus,*"(a) dat. 8 March 1381, at Bergh near Watton (directing his burial to be at the church of the Brother's Minor at Doncaster), pr. at York.(d) His widow is said to have *m.* Sir John GODARD, Sheriff of York, 1389.(e)

IV. 1383, to 1415. 4. PETER (DE MAULEY), LORD MAULEY, or LORD DE MAULEY, grandson and heir, being s. and h. of Peter DE MAULEY (*Septimus*),(a) by Margery, da. and coheir of Thomas SUTTON(c) abovenamed, which Peter, who was s. and h. ap. of the last Lord (by his first wife), *d.* v.p. He was aged five, at his grandfather's death in 1383, and had livery

(a) Each Baron of this race was named Peter; hence they are usually spoken of as "Peter, *the first,*" "Peter, *the second,*" &c. The first of these Lords was "*Petrus de Malolacu,*" a native of Poitiers, who for the murder of Prince Arthur, the rightful heir (*jure hereditario*) to the Crown was rewarded, by John the *de facto* King, by obtaining in marriage the heiress of the lands of Mulgrave and Doncaster, co. York. He (by his son, Peter the second, and grandson, Peter the third), was great grandfather of Peter the fourth, sum. to Parl. as a Baron in 1295. This Peter was father of Peter "*Le Quint,*" and grandfather of Peter "*Le Sisme,*" the succeeding Barons.

(b) See full particulars thereof in "*Nicolas,*" pp. 761—809.

(c) This Thomas was br. and h. of John, Lord Sutton de Holderness, who *d.* s.p. (1361), 35 Ed. III., leaving him his heir and then aged 40. They were both sons of John, Lord Sutton de Holdernesse, who was sum. to Parl. as such in 1332. Thomas, however, seems never to have been so sum. and dying s.p.m. before July (1401), 2 Hen. IV., any right to this Barony fell into abeyance.

(d) Printed in extenso in the "*Test. Ebor.*" pub. by the Surtees society.

(e) Banks's "*Bar. Angl.*" vol. ii, p. 140, *sub* "Sutton."

of his lands (1398-99), 22 Ric. II.; being sum. to Parl.(a) from 18 Aug. (1399), 23 Ric. II. to 12 Aug. (1415), 3 Hen. V., by writs directed "*Petro de Malo lacu*"; was K.B. at the Coronation (13 Oct. 1399) of Henry IV. He m. Matilda, da. of Ralph (NEVILL), 1st EARL OF WESTMORLAND, by his first wife, Margaret, da. of Hugh (STAFFORD), EARL OF STAFFORD. He *d.*, s.p. (1415), 3 Hen. V., when the *Barony* fell into *abeyance*.(b) His will as "*Petrus de Maulay, Octavus,*(c) *Dominus de Mulgreve,*" directing his burial to be at St. John's, Bridlington, dat. at Mulgrave, 5 Sep. 1415, pr. at York, 24 April 1416.(d) The will of his widow, as "*Matildis, Domina de Mauley,*" dat. 1 and pr. 8 Oct. 1428, at York,(d) directs her burial to be at the Friars Preachers at Scardeburgh.

MAXWELL.(e)

Barony [S.] I. 1445? 1. SIR HERBERT MAXWELL, of Maxwell, co. Roxburgh, Caerlaverock, co. Dumfries, &c., s. and h. of Herbert MAXWELL, of the same by his first wife (dispens. 1386), Katherine, da. of John STEWART, of Dalswinton; had a safe conduct, 3 Nov. 1413 as one of the "obsides pro solutione redemptionis"; was *knighted*, 21 May 1424; one of the guarrantees of a treaty with the English, 15 Dec. 1430, and was *cr.* a Lord of Parl., LORD MAXWELL [S.], prior to 3 July 1445.(f) He was subsequently (14 Aug. 1451, and 23 May 1453), a Conservator (1451, &c.), of a truce with England. He *m.* firstly (—), da. of Sir Robert HERRIES, of Terregles. He *m.* secondly Catharine, widow of Sir Alan STUART, of Darnley (who *d.* 1439), da. of Sir William SETON, of Seton. He *d.* before 14 Feb. 1453/4. His widow living 20 March 1475/6.

II. 1452? 2. ROBERT (MAXWELL), LORD MAXWELL [S.], s. and h., by first wife, was served heir, 4 Feb. 1453; was present in Parl. [S.], 9 June 1455, 14 Oct. 1467, 6 April 1478, &c.; was a guarrantee of a truce with England, 11 June 1457, and 12 Sep. 1459. He *m.* Janet, da. of Sir John FORRESTER, of Corstorphin, by Jean, da. of Henry (SINCLAIR), EARL OF ORKNEY [S.] He was living 22 April 1485.

III. 1485? 3. JOHN (MAXWELL), LORD MAXWELL [S.], grandson and h., being s. and h. of John MAXWELL, Master of Maxwell, by Janet, da. of George (CRICHTON), EARL OF CAITHNESS [S.], which John was s. and h. ap. of

(a) There is proof in the rolls of Parl. of his sitting.

(b) The coheirs were his sisters of whom, apparently, one, Isabel, wife of Richard Lindsey *d.* before him and s.p. As to the other two (1) Constance was in 1415, aged 30, and wife of her 2d husband, Sir John Bigot, by whom she was mother of Ralph Bigot, who inherited Mulgrave, and who was succeeded therein by six generations in the male line. By her first husband, William Fairfax, of Walton, she also left issue; (2) Elizabeth, was in 1415 aged 25, and wife of George Salvaine, whose s. and h. Sir John Salvaine inherited Doncaster, and whose posterity, in the male line, long continued so possessed. The representation of this coheir passed thro' Mary, sister and eventually sole heir of Thomas Salvaine, to Barbara, her da. and h. by Sir John Webb, Bart., which Barbara was wife of Anthony (Ashley-Cooper), 5th Earl of Shaftesbury, whose da. and h., Lady Barbara Ashley-Cooper m. the Hon. William Francis Spencer-Ponsonby, who in consequence of such alliance was *cr.* in 1838, Baron *de Mauley of Canford* co. Dorset.

(c) *Vide* p. 273, note "a."

(d) *Vide* p. 273, note "d."

(e) The Editor is much indebted to Mr. M. J. Shaw-Stewart, for his careful revision of this article.

(f) "The dignity of Lord Maxwell appears to be as ancient as the introduction of Lords of Parl. into the Parl. of Scotland, and the Baron of Maxwell and Caerlaverock was probably one of the Barons on whom the honour of a *Lord of Parl.* was first conferred. Herbert, the 1st Lord Maxwell, witnessed in Parl. the charter creating James Hamilton a Peer, on 3 July 1445, and he and four other Peers were specially described *as Lords of Parliament.*" ["*Hewlett,*" p. 168.] See also vol. iv, p. 138, note "d," *sub* "Hamilton."

the late Lord, but *d.* v.p. 22 July 1484,(a) being slain at the battle of Kirtle. He was infefted 8 May 1485 as heir to his grandfather; was a Conservator of a truce for the West Marches, 3 July 1486, and a Commissioner to treat with England, 29 July 1494. He *m.* Agnes, da. of Sir Alexander STEWART, of Garlies, by Elizabeth, da. of Sir Archibald DOUGLAS, of Cavers. He *d.* 9 Sep. 1513, being slain at the battle of Flodden (b)

IV. 1513. 4. ROBERT (MAXWELL), LORD MAXWELL [S.], s. and h.; was *knighted* v.p. before 10 June 1513; was an extraordinary Lord of Session, 2 July 1541; was taken prisoner at Solway in Nov. 1542 but ransomed in July 1543 for 1,000 marks; was one of the English party in Scotland and was a great supporter of the reformed religion. He was hereditary Sheriff of Kirkcudbright and Warden of the West Marches. He *m.* firstly in 1509, Janet, da. of Sir William Douglas, of Drumlanrig, by Elizabeth, da. of Sir John GORDON, of Lochinvar. He *m.* secondly, between Sep. 1513 and Sep. 1529, Agnes, Dow. COUNTESS OF BOTHWELL [S.], illegit. da. of James (STEWART), EARL OF BUCHAN [S.], by Margaret MURRAY, of the house of Philiphaugh. He *d.* at Logan 9 July 1546. His widow obtained letters of legitimation under the Great Seal [S.], 31 Oct. 1552.

V. 1546. 5. ROBERT (MAXWELL), LORD MAXWELL [S.], 1st s.(c) and h. by first wife, served heir 1 Aug. 1550; Warden of the West Marches; a Commissioner to England, 8 May 1551. He *m.* (lic. for marriage contract dat. 25 July 1530),(d) Beatrix, yst. da. and coheir of James (DOUGLAS), 3d EARL OF MORTON [S.], by Lady Katherine STEWART, illegit. da. of **King James IV. [S.]** He *d.* 14 Sep. 1552.

VI. 1552. 6. ROBERT (MAXWELL), LORD MAXWELL [S.], s. and h. He *d.* at Hills, in childhood before Aug. 1553.

VII. 1553. 7. JOHN (MAXWELL), LORD MAXWELL [S.], br. and h., being posthumous s. of the 6th Lord; *b.* 1552; was served heir to his father, 24 May 1569. On the attainder and execution of his uncle (the husband of his mother's sister), James (DOUGLAS), 4th EARL OF MORTON [S.] (the Regent) in June 1581, he was *cr.* (his mother being one of the daughters and coheir of the 3d Earl), by Royal charter, 5 June,(e) ratified by Parl. 19 Nov. 1581, EARL OF MORTON [S.] He sat in Parl. as such, 30 Oct. 1581, and subsequently, but the attainder being reversed 29 Jan. 1585/6, and the Earldom, consequently reverting to the heir of entail, he was thereafter known [only] as Lord Maxwell. In 1588, he assisted the Spaniards in their proposed invasion: but was taken prisoner at Dumfries and was (for some time) deprived of his office of Guardian of the West Marches. He

(a) Sir William Fraser (in his "*Book of Carlaverock*") numbers him as the *third* Baron on the ground that "having been put into possession of the Barony in the lifetime of his father," he "was thereafter *occasionally* styled Lord Maxwell."

(b) See p. 63, note "b." *sub* "Lennox," for a list of the Scotch nobility slain at Flodden field.

(c) The second son, Sir John Maxwell, *m.* Agnes, *suo jure* Baroness Herries of Terregles [S.], and was great grandfather of John, Lord Herries of Terregles, who, as heir male of the Maxwell family, *suc.* in Oct. 1667, as Earl of Nithsdale, *Lord Maxwell*, &c. [S.]

(d) This date (considering the age of the sons who suc. him) seems somewhat early. The parties were possibly very young. See, however, Fraser's "*Carlaverock*," I, 210.

(e) "The only contemporary evidence of the creation is an entry in the Books of Record of the Lyon King at Arms, of which a certified copy was produced, from the muniments of Lord Herries, in the Herries peerage claim (Herries minutes of evidence, p. 487). The entry merely states that at Holyroodhouse, on 29 April 1581, John, Lord Maxwell, was *cr.* Earl of Morton, Lord Carleill and Eskdaill, &c. In the Nithsdale letters-patent the creation is stated to have taken place in Oct. 1581, but probably the creation was held not to have been completed until Lord Maxwell took his seat in Parl. under it, and he did not sit as Earl of Morton till 30 Oct. 1581." [*Hewlett*," p. 169]. Sir W. Fraser suggests ("*Carlaverock*," I, 253), that 29 *April* is a mistake for 29 *October*. The creation was ratified by act of Parl. 29 Nov. 1581.

m. (settl. 4 or 6 Feb. 1571/2), Elizabeth, da. of David (DOUGLAS), EARL OF ANGUS [S.], by Margaret, da. of Sir John HAMILTON. He was slain by the Laird of Johnstone and his retainers, 7 Dec. 1593. His widow m. (as his 2d wife) Sir Alexander STEWART, of Garlies. She m. subsequently John WALLACE, of Craigie, before 5 Aug. 1598. She d. at Edinburgh, Feb. 1637, and was bur. at Lincluden.

VIII. 1593. 8. JOHN (MAXWELL), LORD MAXWELL [S.], s. and h., served heir 11 April 1601, &c. He m. Margaret, da. of John (HAMILTON), 1st MARQUESS OF HAMILTON [S.], by Margaret, da. of John (LYON), LORD GLAMIS [S.] He slew Sir James Johnston (the murderer of his father) on 6 April 1608, and tho' he escaped from Scotland, returned there in 1612, when he was beheaded at Edinburgh, 21 May 1613. He d. s.p.

IX. 1613. 9. ROBERT (MAXWELL), LORD MAXWELL [S.], br. and h. was not recognised as a Peer till restored, by letters under the great seal, 13 Oct. 1618, to the title and estate of the family and served heir of his brother, 18 July 1619. He was cr. 20 Aug. 1620, EARL OF NITHSDALE, LORD MAXWELL, ESKDALE AND CARLEILL [S.], with precedency from 29 Oct. 1581, the date his father's creation as Earl of Morton [S.] See "NITHSDALE" Earldom [S.] with which dignity the Barony of Maxwell continued united, till both were *forfeited* in 1716.

MAYNARD,

i.e., "MAYNARD OF WICKLOW, MAYNARD OF ESTAINES-AD-TURRIM *alias* LITTLE EASTON, MAYNARD OF EASTON-AD-MONTEM *alias* MUCH EASTON, and MAYNARD OF EASTON LODGE.

Barony [I.] I. 1620.
Barony [E.] I. 1628.

1. SIR WILLIAM MAYNARD, of Estaines Parva, or Little Easton, co. Essex, 1st s. and h.(a) of Sir Henry MAYNARD, of the same (Sec. to the Lord Treasurer Burleigh), by Susan, da. and coheir of Thomas PIERSON, was b. before 1589 ; ed. at St. John's Coll., Cambridge ; was Gent. of the Privy Chamber about 1608 ; *knighted*, 7 March 1608/9 ; M.P. for Penrhyn, 1609-11, and for Chippenham, 1614 ; *suc.* his father in the family estates, 11 May 1610 ; was *cr.* a *Baronet* (as "of Estaines Parva, co. Essex "), 29 June 1611. He was, nine years later, *cr.* an Irish Peer, 30 May 1620, as BARON MAYNARD OF WICKLOW [I.] ; was Lord Lieut. of Cambridgeshire, 1620, and was *cr.* a Peer of England, 14 March 1627/8, as BARON MAYNARD OF ESTAINES-AD-TURRIM, *alias* LITTLE EASTON. He was Joint Lord Lieut. of Essex, 1635. He m. firstly Frances, da. of William (CAVENDISH), 1st BARON CAVENDISH OF HARDWICK (afterwards, 1618, 1st EARL OF DEVONSHIRE), by his first wife, Anne, da. and coheir of Henry KEIGHLEY. She d. s.p.m., 1 Sep. 1613, aged 20, and was bur. at Little Easton. He m. secondly Anne, da. and h. of Sir Anthony EVERARD, of Great Waltham, Essex, by his first wife, Anne, da. of Sir Thomas BARNADISTON, of Kedington, Suffolk. He d. 17 Dec. 1640. Fun. certif. in Pub. Record office ; bur. at Little Easton. Will dat. 20 Aug. 1638, pr. 22 Feb. 1641. His widow, who was b. at Much Waltham, d. 5 Aug. 1647, and was bur. at Little Easton. Her will dat. 3 Dec. 1646, pr. 29 Nov. 1647.

II. 1640. 2. WILLIAM (MAYNARD), BARON MAYNARD OF ESTAINES, &c., also BARON MAYNARD OF WICKLOW [I.], and a Baronet, only surv. s. and h. by second wife ; b. 1623 ; *suc. to the peerage* [E. and I.], 18 Dec. 1639 ; Joint Lord Lieut. of Cambridgeshire, 1640-42 ; was impeached by the Commons of high treason, 8 Sep. 1647, but discharged by the Lords, 6 June 1648 ; was one of the

(a) The second son was Sir John Maynard, K.B., whose only son, another Sir John Maynard, K.B., d. s.p. in 1604 ; the third son, Charles Maynard, Auditor of the Exchequer (who d. 1665, aged 66), was father of Sir William Maynard, *cr. a Baronet* (as "of Walthamstow, co. Essex "), 1 Feb. 1681/2, whose grandson, William, the 4th Bart., *suc.* in 1775 as 2d Viscount Maynard.

few Peers who rejected the ordinance for the trial of King Charles I.;(a) was Chief Larderer(b) at the Coronation of Charles II, 23 April 1661; Capt. of a reg. of Horse, 1666; P.C., 1672, and Comptroller of the Household, 1672-87. He *m.* firstly Dorothy, only da. of Sir Robert BANASTRE,(c) of Passenham, co. Northampton, by his third wife, Margaret. She *d.* v.p., 30 Oct. 1649. and was *bur.* at Little Easton. He *m.* secondly Margaret, 2d da. and coheir of William (MURRAY), 1st EARL OF DYSART [S.], by Catharine BRUCE, his wife. She *d.* 4 and was *bur.* 30 June 1682, at Little Easton. He *d.* 3 Feb. 1698/9, in his 76th year, and was *bur.* there. Will dat. 31 May 1698, pr. 22 May 1699.(d)

III. 1699. *3.* BANASTRE (MAYNARD), BARON MAYNARD OF ESTAINES, &c., also BARON MAYNARD OF WICKLOW [I.], and a Baronet, s. and h., by first wife; *b.* 1642; M.P. for Essex, 1663-78; *suc. to the peerage* [E. and I.], 3 Feb. 1698/9. He *m.* 9 Nov. 1665, at Flitton, Beds, Elizabeth, da. of Henry (GREY), EARL OF KENT, by his second wife Amabel, da. of Sir Anthony BENN. She *d.* 24 March 1714. He d. 4 March 1717/8, in his 76th year, both being *bur.* at Little Easton. His will pr. April 1718.

IV. 1718. *4.* HENRY (MAYNARD), BARON MAYNARD OF ESTAINES, &c., also BARON MAYNARD OF WICKLOW [I.], and a Baronet, 3d but 1st surv. s. and h.,(e) *b.* about 1673; was Capt. in the Royal Navy, 1701; *cr.* D.C.L., of Oxford, 16 July 1718; *suc. to the peerage* [E. and I.], 4 March 1717/8. He *d.* unm. 7 Dec. 1742, in his 70th year and was *bur.* at Little Easton. Will pr. 1743.

V. 1742. *5.* GREY (MAYNARD), BARON MAYNARD OF ESTAINES, &c., also BARON MAYNARD OF WICKLOW [I.], and a Baronet, br. and h., *b.* about 1680; Yeoman of the Standing Wardrobe, 1710; *suc. to the peerage* [E. and I.], 9 Dec. 1742. He *d.* unm. in Grosvenor square, 27 April 1745, aged 65, and was *bur.* at Little Easton. Will pr. 1745.

VI. 1745. *6* and *1.* CHARLES (MAYNARD), BARON MAYNARD OF ESTAINES AD TURRIM, also BARON MAYNARD OF WICKLOW [I.], and a Baronet, br. and h., being 8th and yst. s. of the 3d Baron; *b.* about 1690; sometime Fellow of Christ's Coll., Cambridge; M.A., 1711; *suc. to the peerage* [E. and I.] 27 April 1745, taking his seat [E.], 28 Jan. 1748/9. Recorder of Saffron Walden, 1749. Lord Lieut. of Suffolk, 1762-69. Having no issue and no very near male relatives he was *cr.* 28 Oct. 1766, BARON MAYNARD OF MUCH EASTON *alias* EASTON AD MONTEM, and VISCOUNT MAYNARD OF EASTON LODGE, both co. Essex, with a *spec. rem.*, failing heirs male of his body, to [his third cousin] Sir William Maynard [4th] Bart., of Walthamstow, Essex. He *d.* unm. 30 June 1775, aged 85, and was *bur.* at Little Easton, when the English Barony of *Maynard of Estaines* [*cr.* 1628] the Irish Barony of *Maynard of Wicklow* [*cr.* 1620], and the *Baronetcy* [*cr.* 1611] became *extinct*, but the Viscountcy and Barony [*cr.* 1766] devolved as below.

Viscountcy. and Barony. [G.B.] I. 1766.

(a) He was one of the Cavaliers imprisoned in 1655. See p. 171, note "d," *sub* "Lucas."

(b) The claim of "Chief Lardiner" is fully discussed in Taylor's "*Glory of Regality*" (pp. 128—131) but among the "manors held by Coronation service" in that work (p. 157) "Easton" which claims the office of "Caterer and Lardiner" is marked as one of those manors of which the services are extinct or not allowed.

(c) The two grandaughters (children of his only son who *d.* v.p.) were the heirs in blood of this Sir Robert, who *d.* 15 Dec. 1649, æt. 80. See Baker's "Northamptonshire," vol. ii, p. 190. His widow, Margaret (mother of Lady Maynard) was living in 1662.

(d) In it he styled himself "Baron of Estaines ad Turrim," tho' the creation of the dignity was Baron *Maynard* of Estaines ad Turrin."

(e) His elder br. the Hon. William Maynard, *d.* unm. and v.p. 8 March 1716/7, in his 50th year.

II. 1775. 2. CHARLES (MAYNARD), VISCOUNT MAYNARD OF EASTON LODGE, &c., third cousin; inherited the peerage according to the *spec. rem.* in the creation thereof [1776], being s. and h. of Sir William MAYNARD, 4th Bart., of Walthamstow, Essex (on whom the peerage was entailed), by Charlotte, da. of Sir Cecil BISSHOPP, 5th Bart., which William (who *d.* 1772, aged 51), was only s. and h. of Sir Henry Maynard, 3d Bart., (who *suc.* to that dignity on the death of his br. in 1715, and *d.* 1738), who was 4th and yst. s. of Sir William Maynard, of Walthamstow, 1st Bart. (so *cr.* 1661/2), who was s. of Charles Maynard (*d.* 1665, aged 66), yr. br. of William, 1st Baron Maynard. He was *b.* 9 Aug. 1751, at Walton in Ashdon, co. Essex; ed. at Eton and at Sidney Sussex Coll., Cambridge; M.A., 1772; *suc.* his father as 5th Baronet, 18 Jan. 1772, and *suc. to the peerage*, as afsd., 30 June 1775. He *m.* 12 June or July 1776, Anne PARSONS *alias* HORTON,(a) Spinster. She is said(b) to have *d.* about 1808. He *d.* s.p. at Easton Lodge, 10 March 1824, in his 73d year.(c) Will pr. 1824.

III. 1824, to 1865. 3. HENRY (MAYNARD), VISCOUNT MAYNARD OF EASTON LODGE, and BARON MAYNARD OF MUCH EASTON *alias* EASTON AD MONTEM [1766], also a Baronet [1681], nephew and h., being only s. and h. of the Rev. Henry MAYNARD, Rector of Radwinter, Essex, by Susan, da. of the Rev. Francis BARNARD, Rector of Caxton, co. Cambridge, which Henry (who *d.* May 1806, aged 48), was br. to the last Peer. He was *b.* 13 March 1788; *suc. to the peerage*, 10 March 1824; Lord Lieut. and Vice Admiral of Essex, 1825. He *m.*, 28 Dec. 1810, Mary, da. of Reginald RABETT, of Bramfield hall, Suffolk, by Mary, sister of Sir Edward KERRISON, Bart., da. of Matthias K., of Bungay. She, who was *b.* at Bramfield hall, 14 Dec. 1794, *d.* at 38 Grosvenor square, 22 Oct. 1857, aged 62. He *d.* s.p.m.s.,(d) 19 May 1865, aged 77, at Easton lodge, when *all his honours* became *extinct.* Will dat. 29 April 1843, to 13 June 1861, pr. 17 July 1865, under £50,000.

MAYO.

Viscountcy [I.] I. 1627. 1. SIR THEOBALD BOURKE,(e) of Mayo, s. and h. of Sir Richard BOURKE, "*the Mac William Eighter,*"(f) by Grace, or Grany, da. of Owen O'MALLEY, of the Owles, was *b.* at sea (being thence called "Tibbot-my-Lung" or "Tibbot of the ships") took part sometime against the Crown, but supported it, in 1599, against the

(a) "*Nancy Parsons*" whose features are well known from Gainsborough's portrait of her (belonging to the Marquess of Lansdowne) under that name and who was "endowed with rare powers of attraction. This woman was the da. of a tailor in Bond street and she first lived with *Hoghton* or *Horton*, a West-India-captive merchant, with whom she went to Jamaica, but from whom she fled to England." [*Nat. Biogr.* under "Fitzroy, A. H.," 3d Duke of Grafton.] She is described by Horace Walpole in 1764 (12 years before this marriage) as "one of the commonest creatures in London; now out of date," and is called "the Duke of Grafton's *Mrs. Horton*, the Duke of Dorset's *Mrs. Horton*, everybody's *Mrs. Horton*."

(b) Baker's "Northamptonshire," vol. ii, p. 190.

(c) Forty-five years earlier, in Jan. 1779, a report reached London that "poor simple Lord Maynard had shot himself at Naples."

(d) His only s. and h. ap., Col. the Hon. Charles Henry Maynard, *d.* (a few months before him) 2 Jan. 1865, s.p.m., in his 51st year, at 15a Hill street, Berkeley square, leaving two daughters and coheirs, of whom the eldest, Frances Evelyn, *b.* 10 Dec. 1861, inherited the whole of the family estates. (See vol. ii, p. 35, *sub* "Brooke"), and the youngest, Blanche, *b.* 14 Feb. 1864, *m.* Lord Agernon Gordon-Lennox.

(e) Another Theobald Bourke, of Mayo, was made the "Mac William" (see note "f" next below) in 1595, fled to Spain soon afterwards, and was *cr. Marquis of Mayo*, by Philip II., King of Spain, who "settled a pension upon him and his posterity suitable to that dignity which he and his son, Walter, enjoyed, who dying s.p. left it in the custody of his half br., Col. Plunkett, until it should be claimed by some of his heirs general." ["*Lodge*," vol. iv, p. 229—230.]

(f) The head of the Bourke family *in Galway* was styled "Mac William *Oughter*"

Spaniards at Kingsale; was *knighted* at Dublin, 4 Jan. 1602/3; surrendered his estates and obtained a regrant thereof under English tenure, 25 Sep. 1603; was M.P. for co. Mayo, 1613, and was *cr.*, 21 June 1627, VISCOUNT MAYO or VISCOUNT BOURKE OF MAYO [I.].(a) He *m.* Maud, da. of Charles O'CONOR, of Sligo. He *d.* 18 June 1629, and was *bur.* at Ballintober.

II. 1629. 2. MILES (BOURKE), VISCOUNT MAYO [I.], s. and h., said to have been (as well as his s. and h. ap.) *cr.* a Baronet [S.], about 1633;(b) *suc. to the peerage* [I.], 18 June 1629, took his seat, 4 Nov. 1634, and, being a Protestant, was made Joint Gov. of co. Mayo. He *m.* firstly, Honora, da. of Sir John BOURKE, of Derrymaclaghtny, co. Galway, by Margaret, da. of Ulick (BOURKE, or DE BURGH), 3d EARL OF CLANRICARDE [I.] He *m.* secondly, Elizabeth (Ellis or Isabella), widow of (—) BENBOW and da. of (—) FREKE. He *d.* 1649, being (after death) excepted from pardon by Cromwell's Act, 12 Aug. 1652, in consequence of his conduct at the massacre (13 Feb. 1641) of the English after the capture of Castlebar.(c) His widow, who was allowed a small pension by Government in 1654, was *bur.* (with her first(d) husband) 25 April 1665 (at a great age), at St. Martin's in the fields. Will dat. 28 Feb. 1664, pr. 3 May 1666.

III. 1649. 3. THEOBALD (BOURKE), VISCOUNT MAYO [I.], s. and h. by first wife; said to have ed. *at Oxford* in the protestant religion. He is also said to have been (as well his father), *cr.* a Baronet [S.], about 1638; (b) was M.P. for co. Mayo, 1639, and distinguished himself in the Royal cause; *suc. to the peerage* [I.], in 1649. He *m.* firstly, Elinor, da. of (—) TALBOT, of co. York. He *m.* secondly, Eleanor, da. of Sir Luke FITZ-GERALD, of Tecroghan, co. Meath. He was in Dec. 1652 found guilty by Cromwell's High Court of Justice, at Connaught, of murders committed in the late rebellion, and was "shot to death" 12 Jan. 1652/3, at Galway and *bur.* there. His widow, who in 1656 was allowed 40s. a week, *d.* 1693.

IV. 1663. 4. THEOBALD (BOURKE), VISCOUNT MAYO [I.], s. and h., by first wife was a minor when he *suc. to the peerage* [I.] in 1653; ed. at Dublin Free school, 1653-56; took his seat in parl. [I.] 14 May 1661, and was restored to his estate (50,000 acres in co. Mayo) in 1666. He *m.* firstly, Ellen, sister of Adam, VISCOUNT LISBURNE [I.], da. of Sir Adam LOFTUS, of Rathfarnham, by Dorothy, da. of Richard (BOYLE), EARL OF CORK [I.] He *m.* secondly, shortly before 1576, Lady OWENS. He *d.* s.p. (accidentally, from an over dose of laudanum), 5 and was *bur.* 8 June 1676, at Patrick's, Dublin.

V. 1676. 5. MILES (BOURKE), VISCOUNT MAYO [I.], br. and h., *suc. to the peerage* [I.] in June 1676. He alienated a considerable part of the family estates. He *m.* Jane, da. of Francis (BERMINGHAM), LORD ATHENRY [I.], by Bridget, da. of Sir Lucas DILLON. He *d.* at Castle Bourke, March 1681, and was *bur.* at Ballintober. His widow *d.* 6 June 1687, at (her father's seat) Turlovaughan.

VI. 1681. 6. THEOBALD (BOURKE), VISCOUNT MAYO [I.], only s. and h., *b.* 6 Jan. 1681, and *suc. to the peerage* [I.] in March following. He conformed to the established church 19, and took his seat, in Parl., 21 June 1709. He *m.* firstly, 8 July 1702, his cousin, Mary, yst. da. of John BROWNE, of Westport, co.

(or Upper) while the head thereof *in Mayo* was styled "Mac William *Eighter*" (or Lower) inasmuch as *Galway* was the *Upper* while *Mayo* was the *lower* part of the province of Connaught.

(a) The preamble is in "Lodge," vol. iv, p. 236. It speaks of the grantee as "ex illustrissimâ, *olim in Angliâ*, prosapiâ oriundus."

(b) The creation, however, is not in the Great Seal Register.

(c) A very long account of this proceeding is given in a note to "*Lodge*" vol. iv, pp. 239-243.

(d) *Query* "John Benbow, Esq." *bur.* at St. Martin's in the fields, 8 Oct. 1625; brought from Eltham.

Mayo, by Maud, da. of Theobald (BOURKE), 3d VISCOUNT MAYO [I.], abovenamed. He *m.* secondly, June 1731, Margaret, widow of Francis HOUSTON, of Ashgrove, co. Roscommon, relict of William LYSTER, of Athleague, and (previously) of John EDWARDS, of Dublin, da. of Bryan GUNNING, of Castle Coote, co. Roscommon. By her he had no issue. He *d.* in Dublin, 25 June 1741. His widow *d.* 1771 and was *bur.* at Ballintober.

VII. 1741. 7. THEOBALD (BOURKE), VISCOUNT MAYO [I.], s. and h. by first wife; *suc. to the peerage* [I.], 25 June 1741, and took his seat, 6 Oct. following. He *m.* in March 1726, Ellis, da. of James AGAR, of Gowran, co. Kilkenny, by his second wife, Mary, da. of Sir Henry WEMYSS. He *d.* s.p.s. in London, 7 Jan. 1741/2, in his 36th year, and was *bur.* at Ballintober. M.I. His widow was *cr.*, 1 Aug. 1781, COUNTESS OF BRANDON [I.] (see that dignity) and *d.* s.p., 11 March 1789, in her 81st year.

VIII. 1742, to 1767. 8. JOHN (BOURKE), VISCOUNT MAYO [I.], only br. (of the full blood) and h.; *suc. to the peerage* [I.], 7 Jan. 1741/2, and took his seat, 10 Nov. 1743. He *m.* in or before 1743, Catharine, widow of (—) HAMILTON, of co. Galway, da. of Whitgift AYLMER, of the West Indies, a Major in the army. He *d.* s.p.m.s.(a) in Pall Mall, 12 Jan., and was *bur.* 5 Feb. 1767, at St. James' Westm., when the *title became extinct or dormant.*(b) Will pr. Jan. 1767. His widow *m.*, in July 1770, Edmond JORDAN, of Legan, co. Mayo, and *d.* Jan. 1776.

MAYO, and MAYO OF MONYCROWER.

Viscountcy [I.] I. 1781. Earldom [I.] I. 1785. 1. The Rt. Hon. JOHN BOURKE, of Monycrower, co. Mayo and of Palmerston and Kill, co. Kildare, only surv. s. and h. of Rickard BOURKE, LL.D. (who *d.* 1727), of Dublin, by Catharine, da. of Charles MINCHIN, of Ballynakill, co. Tipperary; was *b.* about 1705; *suc.* to the family estates on the death (1751) of his cousin, Theobald Bourke, of Monycrower; was M.P. for Naas, 1727-60; for Old Leighlin, 1761-68, and for Naas (again), 1769-76, until *cr.*, 1 Aug. 1776, BARON NAAS of Naas, co. Kildare [I.], taking his seat, 14 Oct. 1777; was P.C. [I.] and First Commissioner of the Revenue [I.] till 20 Dec. 1780, obtaining, on his resignation, a pension of £1,033. He was *cr.*, 13 Jan. 1781, VISCOUNT MAYO OF MONYCROWER, co. Mayo [I.], taking his seat, 4 Dec. 1781, and finally was *cr.*, 24 June 1785, EARL OF THE COUNTY OF MAYO [I.] He *m.* in 1725, Mary, 3d da. and coheir of the Rt. Hon. Joseph DEANE, Ch. Baron of the Court of Exchequer [I.], by Margaret, sister of Henry, 1st EARL OF SHANNON [I.], da. of Henry BOYLE, of Castle Martyr, co. Cork. She (by whom he had six sons and seven daughters) *d.* 21 July 1774. He *d.* 2 Dec. 1790, aged about 85.

II. 1790. 2. JOHN (BOURKE), EARL OF MAYO, &c. [I.], 2d but 1st surv. s. and h.; *b.* about 1735; M.P. for Naas (in five Parls.), 1763-90, being *styled* LORD NAAS from 1785 till he *suc. to the peerage* [I.], 2 Dec. 1790. He *m.* in Feb. 1764 Margaret, 1st da. of Joseph (LEESON), 1st EARL OF MILLTOWN [I.], by his first wife, Cecilia, da. of Francis LEIGH. He *d.* s.p., 20 April 1792. His widow, who was *b.* 12 Nov. 1734, *d.* April 1809.

(a) Bridget, his da. and h., *m.*, 11 May 1758, Edmund Lambert, of Boyton, Wilts, and *d.* May 1773, leaving a s. and h., Aylmer Bourke Lambert. "*Lord Mayo's son*" is *bur.* 23 July 1748, at Donnybrook, co. Dublin. He is called in "Lodge" (where it is stated that he was *b.* 17 Nov. 1743) "*Sir* Aylmer Bourke," and it is there remarked (vol. iv, p. 236), that "certain it is that the eldest son of the Viscount Mayo enjoys the title of Baronet and is styled *Sir* during his father's lifetime." See vol. iv. of this work, p. 245, note "c," *sub* "Holles."

(b) It seems extremely probable that issue male may exist from the 1st Viscount, thro' his 4th and yst. son Richard ("*Iron-Dick*") who had four sons of whom, tho' the eldest, Col. Miles Bourke, *d.* s.p. in 1715, two of the other three had numerous sons.

III. 1792. 3. JOSEPH DEANE (BOURKE), EARL OF MAYO, &c. [I.], ARCHBISHOP OF TUAM, br. and h.; *b.* about 1740; was Bishop of Leiglin and Ferns, 1772-82, and Archbishop of Tuam, 1782-94. He *m.* in 1760, Elizabeth, sister of John, 1st EARL OF CLANWILLIAM [I.], da. of Sir Richard MEADE, 3d Bart. [I.], by Catharine, da. of Henry PRITTIE. His Grace *d.* 20 Aug. 1794. His widow *d.* 18 March 1807.

IV. 1794. 4. JOHN (BOURKE), EARL OF MAYO, &c. [I.], s. and h.; *b.* 18 June 1766; mat. at Oxford (Ch. Ch.), 12 Jan. 1784; *cr.* D.C.L., 18 July 1793, having been *styled* LORD NAAS, since 1792, till he *suc. to the peerage*, 20 Aug. 1794; Col. of the Kilkenny Militia; P.C. [I.], 1810; REP. PEER [I.], 1816-49; G.C.H. (Civil), 1819. He *m.*, 24 April 1792, Arabella, 4th da. of William Mackworth PRAED, of Bitton house, Devon, by Susanna, da. and coheir of John STOKES, of Rill, in Aylesbeare, in that co. She, who was *b.* Nov. 1766, and was Lady of the Bedchamber to Adelaide, the Queen Consort, *d.* 19 Nov. 1843, at Bersted lodge, in Bognor, Sussex. He *d.* there s.p., 23 May 1849, aged 82. Will pr. Sep. 1849.

V. 1849. 5. ROBERT (BOURKE), EARL OF MAYO, &c. [I.], nephew and h., being only s. and h. of the Hon. Richard BOURKE, BISHOP OF WATERFORD AND LISMORE [1813-32], by Frances, da. of Robert FOWLER, ARCHBISHOP OF DUBLIN, which Richard was next br. to the last Earl. He was *b.* 12 Jan. 1797, at the Archbishop's palace, Dublin; *suc. to the peerage* [I.], 23 May 1849; REP. PEER [I.], 1852-67. He *m.*, 3 Aug. 1820, in Dublin, Anne Charlotte, only da. and h. of the Hon. John JOCELYN, of Fair Hill, co. Louth (4th s. of Robert, 1st EARL OF RODEN [I.]), by Margaret, da. of the Rt. Hon. Richard FITZGERALD, of Mount Ophaley. She (by whom he had seven sons) *d.* 26 Jan. 1867, at Sydenham. He *d.* (a few months later), 12 Aug. 1867, at 18 Cleveland square, Paddington, aged 70.

VI. 1867. 6. RICHARD SOUTHWELL (BOURKE), EARL OF MAYO, &c. [I.], s. and h.; *b.* 21 Feb. 1822, in Dublin; *styled* LORD NAAS, 1849-67; ed at Trin. Coll., Dublin; B.A., 1844; M.A., 1851, and LL.D., 1852; was M.P. for co. Kildare, 1847-52; for Coleraine, 1852-57; for Cockermouth, 1857-68; P.C. [G.B. and I.], 1852; Ch. Sec. for Ireland, March to Dec. 1852, Feb. 1858 to June 1859, and June 1866 to Sep. 1868. VICEROY AND GOV. GEN. OF INDIA, 1868-72; K.P.,(a) 1868; G.C.S.I. He *m.*, 31 Oct. 1848, Blanche Julia, 4th da. of George (WYNDHAM), 1st BARON LECONFIELD, by Mary Fanny, da. of the Rev. William BLUNT. He *d.* 8 Feb. 1872, in his 50th year, being assassinated at Port Blair, in the Andaman islands (while on a tour of inspection) by an Afghan convict, named Shere Ali. He was *bur.* (in state) at Johnston church, near Naas, 26 April following.(b) His widow, who was *b.* 21 Nov. 1826, was Lady of the Bedchamber, 1872, and an extra Lady, 1874; V.A. (3rd class) and C.I., living 1893.(c)

VII. 1872. 7. DERMOT ROBERT WYNDHAM (BOURKE), EARL OF MAYO [1785], VISCOUNT MAYO OF MONYCROWER [1781], and BARON NAAS [1776], in the peerage of Ireland, s. and h.; *b.* 2 July 1851; *styled* LORD NAAS till he *suc. to the peerage* [I.], 8 Feb. 1872; ed. at Eton; an officer in the 10th Hussars and Gren. Guards, 1870-76; REP. PEER [I.], 1890. He *m.*, 8 Nov. 1885, at St. Mark's, North Audley street, Geraldine, 1st da. of the Hon. Gerald Henry Brabazon PONSONBY (7th s. of John William, 4th EARL OF BESSBOROUGH [I.]), by Maria Emma Catherine, sister of George William (COVENTRY), 9th EARL OF COVENTRY. She was *b.* 7 March 1863.

Family Estates.—These, in 1883, consisted of 4,915 acres in co. Kildare; 2,360 in co. Meath, and 559 in co. Mayo. *Total* 7,834 acres, worth £7,690 a year. *Principal Residence.* Palmerston House, near Straffan, co. Kildare.

(a) He was *cr.* a Knight Extraordinary, 11 Nov. 1868, becoming a Knight in Ordinary, 2 March 1869, by the death of Viscount Gough. He was invested at Calcutta.

(b) His untiring energy and profound good sense made the three years of his rule most beneficial and it is spoken of by the Queen as "the able, vigilant, and impartial rule of one who so faithfully represented her as Viceroy of her Eastern Empire."

(c) She received from Parl. an annuity of £1,000 and from the Council of India a like pension, together with (from the latter) a sum of £20,000.

MEAFORD.

i.e., "JERVIS OF MEAFORD, co. Stafford," Barony (*Jervis*), *cr.* 1797, with the EARLDOM OF ST. VINCENT, which see; *ex.* 1823.

See "ST. VINCENT OF MEAFORD, co. Stafford," Viscountcy (*Jervis*), *cr.* (with a *spec. rem.*) 1801.

MEATH.

[See vol. i, p. xi, for some remarks on the great Lordship of Meath from 1172 to 1460.]

Earldom [I.] I. 1627. *1.* WILLIAM (BRABAZON), LORD BRABAZON, BARON OF ARDEE [I.], s. and h. of Edward, LORD BRABAZON, BARON OF ARDEE, co. Louth [I.] (so *cr.* 19 July 1616), by Mary, da. of Edward SMITH, of Mitcham, Surrey; was *b.* about 1580; was *knighted* (v.p.) 22 Feb. 1603/4, by the Lord Deputy [I.] at Ruban Castle; *suc.* his father *in the peerage* [I.] in 1625, having livery of his estate, 28 Jan. 1625/6, being then aged 46, and was *cr.*, 16 April 1627,(a) EARL OF MEATH [I.] with *spec. rem.* failing heirs male of his body, to his br., Sir Anthony Brabazon; was *Custos Rot.* of co. Dublin; was present in the Parl. [I.] of 1634 and of 1642, being a great sufferer by the troubles of those times; was in 1644 one of those sent to consult with the King at Oxford and was taken prisoner by the Parl. and confined 11 months in the Tower of London. He *m.* Feb. 1607, Jane, 1st da. of the Rt. Hon. Sir John BINGLEY, Comptroller of the Musters. She was *bur.* at St. Catharine's, Dublin, 19 Dec. 1644. He was *bur.* there (also on) 19 Dec. 1651. Admon. 28 May 1652.

II. 1651. *2.* EDWARD (BRABAZON), EARL OF MEATH, &c. [I.], s. and h., *b.* about 1610; *styled* LORD BRABAZON, 1627-52; said to have been *knighted* v.p.; M.P. for Athlone, 1634; Capt. of a troop of horse (*ex parte Regis*) 1645, and again in 1661; *suc. to the peerage* [I.] in Dec. 1651, taking his seat, 25 June 1661; P.C. [I.], 1662. He *m.* in 1632, Mary, yr. da. of Calcot CHAMBRE, of Denbigh in Wales and of Carnowe, co. Wicklow. He *d.* 25 March 1675, being drowned, off Holyhead, in his passage to England. Will dat. 27 July 1674, pr. 27 April 1675. His widow was *bur.* at St. Catherine's, Dublin, 14 Sep. 1685.

III. 1675. *3.* WILLIAM (BRABAZON), EARL OF MEATH, &c. [I.], s. and h., *b.* about 1635; *styled* LORD BRABAZON,(b) 1651-75; *Cust. Rot.* of co. Dublin, 1662, and again 1671. He was sum. to the House of Lords [I.], v.p.(c) in his father's Barony, by writ 30 Oct. 1665.(d) He *suc. to the Earldom* (10 years later), 25 March 1675. He *m.* before 1671, Elizabeth, sister of Thomas (LENNARD), 1st EARL OF SUSSEX, da. of Francis, LORD DACRE, by Elizabeth, da. of Paul (BAYNING), 1st VISCOUNT BAYNING OF SUDBURY. He *d.* s.p.m.s., and was *bur.* 1 March 1684/5, at St. Paul's Covent Garden. Will dat. 22 Feb. 1684, pr. April and Aug. 1685. His widow, who *m.* before Oct. 1686, the Hon. William MOORE, *d.* 28 and was *bur.* at St. Paul's afsd., 31 Dec. 1701. Her will pr. 16 Feb. 1709, by her said husband.

(a) The preamble (declaring a descent of the grantee "ex oppido de Brabazon in Normandia") is in "Lodge," vol. i, p. 275.

(b) He is called "*Lord Brabazon*" (*not* "Lord Ardee") in his father's will, dat. 1674.

(c) In consequence of this summons his great grandson & (eventually) heir general Chidley Coote, of Mount Coote, co. Limerick laid claim in 1762 to a Barony of Ardee [I.], as having been *cr.* in fee by this summons. See vol. i, p. 116, note "c," *sub* "Ardee."

(d) The date of the privy seal was 28 June previous. See vol. i, p. 2, note "a," *sub* "Abercorn," for a list of the nine cases in which eldest sons of Irish Peers have been sum. to parl. in their father's lifetime of which cases the writ of summons in 1665, and that in 1714 to the s. and h. ap. of the (then) Earl of Meath constitute two.

[EDWARD BRABAZON, *styled* LORD BRABAZON, only s. and h. ap. He *d.* an infant and v.p., and was *bur.* 1 July 1677, at St. Catherine's, Dublin.]

IV. 1685. 4. EDWARD (BRABAZON), EARL OF MEATH, &c. [I.], next br. and h. male; *b.* about 1638; Capt. of Foot, 1661, and subsequently of Horse; M.P. for co. Wicklow, 1666; Ranger of Phœnix Park and of all the Royal Parks in Ireland, 1675; *suc. to the peerage* [I.] Feb. 1684/5; *Custos Rot.* of co. Dublin and co. Kildare, 1685; was attainted by King James' Parl., 7 May 1689, his estate of £2,000 a year being sequestrated: was in command against that King at Carrickfurgus in Aug. 1689; at the Boyne and at Limerick in 1690 where he was wounded; was P.C. to King William and Queen Anne; a Commissioner of the Great Seal [I.], 31 Oct. and 17 Nov. 1693, and 21 Dec. 1697. He *m.* firstly Cecilia, da. of Sir William BRERETON, 1st Bart., of Honford, Cheshire, by his second wife, Cecilia, da. of Sir William SKEFFINGTON, Bart. She *d.* 12 July 1704. He *m.* secondly, 22 Sep. following, Dorothea, da. of James STOPFORD, of Tara Hill, co. Meath, by his second wife, Mary, da. of the Rt. Hon. Sir Robert FORTH. He *d.* s.p., 22, and was *bur.* 26 Feb. 1707, at St. Catharine's afsd. His widow *m.* (as second wife), Dec. 1716, Lieut. Gen. Richard GORGES, of Kilbrew, and *d.* there, 10 April 1728.(a)

V. 1707. 5. CHAMBRE (BRABAZON), EARL OF MEATH, &c. [I.], br. and h.; *b.* about 1645; was in commission for a troop of horse and was Pay Master of Ireland in 1675; *suc. to the peerage* [I.], Feb. 1707, and took his seat, 8 Aug. 1709; *Custos Rot.* of co. Dublin, 1709; P.C. to Queen Anne and to George I. He *m.* in or before 1682, Juliana, only da. and h. of Patrick (CHAWORTH), 2d VISCOUNT CHAWORTH OF ARMAGH [I.], by Grace, da. of John (MANNERS), 8th EARL OF RUTLAND. She was *bur.* 12 Nov. 1692 (as "Madam Brabazon") at St. Mary's, Nottingham. He *d.* suddenly at Nottingham, 1, and was *bur.* 2 April 1715, at St. Mary's afsd. Will dat. July 1713, pr. May 1715.

VI. 1715. 6. CHAWORTH (BRABAZON), EARL OF MEATH, &c. [I.], 1st surv. s. and h.;(b) *b.* 1686; *styled* LORD BRABAZON, 1707-15; M.P. for co. Dublin, 1713-14, being sum. to the House of Lords [I.] v.p.(c) in his father's Barony, by writ 9 March 1714; *suc. to the Earldom* [I.] in April 1715, taking his seat, as such, 17 Dec. following; P.C. [I.], Lord Lieut. of co. Dublin and co. Wicklow. He *m.*, 11 Dec. 1731, Juliana, da. of Sir Thomas PRENDERGAST, 1st Bart. [I.], of Gort, co. Galway, by Penelope, da. of Henry CADOGAN, of Lismullen. He *d.* s.p. at Calais, 14 May 1763, aged 77, and was *bur.* at Canterbury. His widow *d.* at Bath, 12, and was *bur.* 30 Dec. 1758, in Bath Abbey.

VII. 1763. 7. EDWARD (BRABAZON), EARL OF MEATH, &c. [I.], only surv. br. and h.; *bap.* 24 Nov. 1691, at St. Mary's, Nottingham; M.P. for co. Dublin, 1715-58; *suc. to the peerage* [I.], 14 May 1763, taking his seat, 29 Nov. following. He *m.* about 1720, Martha, da. of the Rev. William COLLINS, of Warwick. She *d.* 24 April 1762. He *d.* 24 Nov. 1772, aged 81.

VIII. 1772. 8. ANTHONY (BRABAZON), EARL OF MEATH, &c. [I.], s. and h.; *bap.* 17 Feb. 1721; *styled* LORD BRABAZON, 1763-72; M.P. for co. Wicklow, 1745-60, and for co. Dublin, 1761-72; *suc. to the peerage* [I.], 24 Nov. 1772, taking his seat, 24 Oct. 1773. He *m.* 20 May 1758, Grace, da. of John LEIGH, of Ross Garland, co. Wicklow, by Mary, da. of John CLIFFE, of New Ross in that county. He *d.* 4 Jan. 1790, aged 69. His widow *d.* 23 Oct. 1812.

(a) She is the "Countess Doll" alluded to by Dean Swift, who wrote a humorous epitaph on her and her second husband (Richard Gorges) entitled "Doll and Dicky."

(b) "Chambrey, s. of Chambrey Brabazon, Esq.," (another son) was *bur.* 7 Dec. 1691, at St. Mary's, Nottingham.

(c) *Vide* p. 282, note "d."

[CHAWORTH BRABAZON, *styled* LORD BRABAZON, 1st s. and h. ap.; *b.* 18 Aug. 1760; *d.* v.p. and unm. Dec. 1779.]

IX. 1790. *9.* WILLIAM (BRABAZON), EARL OF MEATH, &c., 3d but 1st surv. s. and h.; *b.* 6 July 1769; *styled* LORD BRABAZON, from Dec. 1779 to Jan. 1790; sometime M.P. for co. Dublin; *suc. to the peerage* [I.], 4 Jan. 1790. He *d.* unm. 26 May 1797, being killed in a duel.

X. 1797. *10.* JOHN CHAMBRE (BRABAZON), EARL OF MEATH, &c. [I.], next br. and h., being yst. s. of the 8th Earl; *b.* 9 April 1772; *suc. to the peerage* [I.], 26 May 1797; Lord Lieut. of co. Dublin and *Custos Rot* of co. Wicklow. K.P., 19 July 1821([a]); P.C., 1831. He was *cr.* 10 Sep. 1831,([b]) BARON CHAWORTH OF EATON HALL, co. Hereford.([c]) He *m.* 31 Dec. 1801, Melosina Adelaide, 4th da. of John (MEADE), 1st EARL OF CLANWILLIAM [I.], by Theodosia, da. and h. of Robert HAWKINS-MAGILL. He *d.* 15 March 1851, aged 78, at Great Malvern. His widow *d.* 26 March 1866, at 27 Pembridge square, Bayswater.

[ANTHONY BRABAZON, *styled* LORD ARDEE *or* LORD BRABAZON, 1st s. and h. ap.; *b.* 10 Nov. 1802; *d.* v.p. and unm. 9 Feb. 1826.]

XI. 1851. *11.* WILLIAM (BRABAZON), EARL OF MEATH, &c. [I.], also BARON CHAWORTH OF EATON HALL [U.K.], 2d but 1st surv. s. and h.; *b.* 25 Oct. 1803, in Merrion square, Dublin; *styled* LORD ARDEE, or LORD BRABAZON, 1826-51; M.P. for co. Dublin, 1830-32 and 1837-41; High Sheriff for co. Wicklow, 1848; Col. 5th Batt. Dublin Fusileers (Militia) 1847-81, *suc. to the peerage* [I. and U.K.] 15 March 1851; Lord Lieut. for co. Wicklow, 1871-87. He *m.* 28 Nov. 1837, at Halton chapel, Cheshire, Harriot, da. of Sir Richard BROOKE, 6th Bart., of Norton, by Harriot, da. of Sir Foster CUNLIFFE, Bart. He *d.* 26 May 1887, at Kilruddery house, co. Wicklow, aged 84, and was *bur.* at Bray. Will pr. Aug. 1887 above £25,000. His widow, who was *b.* 1811, living 1893.

XII. 1887. *12.* REGINALD (BRABAZON), EARL OF MEATH [1627], and LORD BRABAZON, BARON OF ARDEE [1616] in the peerage of Ireland, also BARON CHAWORTH OF EATON HALL [1831], 2d and yst. but only surv. s. and h.; *b.* 31 July 1841; *styled* LORD BRABAZON, 1851-87; ed. at Eton; Sec. to the Legation at Athens, 1873; an Alderman of the London County Council; *suc. to the peerage* [I. and U.K.], 26 May 1887. He *m.*, 7 Jan. 1868, at St. Geo. Han. sq., Mary Jane, da. and eventually (1854) sole heir of Thomas (MAITLAND), 11th EARL OF LAUDERDALE [S.], by Amelia, da. of William YOUNG. She was *b.* 15 March 1847.

REGINALD-LE-NORMAND BRABAZON, *styled* LORD ARDEE, 1st s. and h. ap., *b.* 24 Nov. 1869; ed. at Wellington College; Lieut. Gren. Guards, 1889.]

Family Estates.—These, in 1883, consisted of 14,717 acres in co. Wicklow and 36 in co. Dublin, besides 695 (worth £1,453 a year) in Herefordshire. *Total* 15,448 acres, worth £9,398 a year. *Principal Residences*, Kilruddery Castle, near Bray, co. Wicklow, and Eaton Court, Herefordshire.

MEDWAY.

i.e., "MEDWAY OF HEMSTED, co. Kent," Barony (*Gathorne-Hardy*), *cr.* 1892 with the EARLDOM OF CRANBROOK, which see.

([a]) One of the six Knights Extraordinary at the Coronation of Geo. IV. He became a Knight in Ordinary (on the death of the Earl of Carysfort) 7 April 1828.

([b]) This was one of "*the Coronation Peerages*" of William IV. for a list of which see vol. ii, p. 312, note "a," *sub* "Cloncurry."

([c]) See vol. iii, p. 267, note "a," as to titles [U.K.] selected by Scotch and Irish Peers.

MEINILL, or MEYNILL.

Barony by Writ.

I. 1295.

1. NICHOLAS MEINILL, of Whorlton, co. York, said to be s. and h. of Stephen, who was s. and h. ap. of Robert MEINILL, whom (probably) he *suc.*; served in the Welsh and Scotch wars; received in 1285 a grant, from the Crown, of Castle Levinton, co. York, and was sum., 8 June (1294), 22 Ed. I., with about 60 other persons, to advise on the affairs of the Realm,(a) being afterwards sum. to Parl. as a Baron (LORD MEINILL) from 23 June (1295), 23 Ed. I., to 6 Feb. (1298/9), 27 Ed. I. He *m.* Christian whom, in 1290, he accused of endeavouring to poison him but who manifested her innocence.(b) He *d.* (1298-99), 27 Ed. I. His wife survived him.

II. 1299, to 1322.

2. NICHOLAS (MEINILL), LORD MEINILL, s. and h., aged 23 years old in 1299. His name appears as "*Nicholas de Meynhyl, Dominus de Wherleton*" to the letter to the Pope from the Barons in 1301.(c) He was sum. to Parl. as a Baron from 22 May (1313) to 14 March (1321/2), 15 Ed. II. He *d.* s.p. legit. 1322. Esch. 15 Ed. II. After his death the *Barony* became *dormant*, tho' John MEINILL,(d) his br. and h. then aged 40, was heir to the first Lord, and, as such, *suc.* to Castle Levington afsd. &c.

III. 1336.

1. WILLIAM DE MEINILL,(e) bastard son of the above Nicholas, LORD MEINILL, by Lucy, wife of William, LORD LATIMER, da. and h. of Robert DE THWENG,(f) inherited Whorlton and a considerable portion of his father's estates in Yorkshire, and was sum. to Parl. as a Baron (LORD MEINILL), from 22 Jan. (1335/6), 9 Ed. III. to 25 Feb. (1341/2), 16 Ed. III. He *m.* Alice, da. of William (DE ROOS), LORD ROOS. He *d.* s.p.m. 1342. Esch. 16 Ed. III.

IV. 1342.

2. ELIZABETH, *suo jure*, apparently, BARONESS MEINILL, da. and h. She proved her age in 1348, about which date she *m.* John (DARCY), LORD DARCY DE KNAYTH, who *d.* March 1355/6, aged about 39. See fuller particulars under that title. She *m.* secondly (as his first wife) about 1357, Peter (DE MAULEY), LORD MAULEY, who *d.* 19 March 1382/3. See fuller particulars under that title. She *d.* 1368.

(a) See vol. i, p. 259, note "c," *sub* "Basset de Sapcote," as to this not being a regular summons to Parl.

(b) *Esch.* 28 Ed. I., n. 28, *De dote assignanda.*

(c) See "*Nicolas,*" pp. 761—809, for a full account thereof, there being a note to this Baron (p. 774) to the effect that tho' he was in the Scotch wars in 1300 he was not sum. to Parl. until 1313, and consequently "no cause presents itself to which his being present as a Baron in this [1301] Parl. can be attributed."

(d) This John, says Dugdale, left by John, his s. and h. ap., a grandson and h., John Meinill, who *d.* (1349), 23 Ed. III., seized of Castle Levinton, &c., leaving Alice his sister and heir, then aged 22, and wife of John de Boulton. The pedigree is, however, more accurately set forth in Banks's "*Bar. Angl.,*" by which it appears that this Alice had three husbands, *viz.* (1) Robert (not John) de Boulton who *d.* s.p. (2) Walter Boynton, by whom a son, Walter, and (3) William Percy, by whom William and Margaret. Of her three children the eldest, Walter Boynton, inherited Castle Levington, but *d.* s.p. (1391-92), 15 Ric. II., being *suc.* by his brother (ex parte maternâ) William Percy, who also *d* s.p. and was suc. by his sister, Margaret, wife of Thomas, and mother of John Blanfront 1399.

(e) Dugdale mentions a Sir Hugh de Meinill, K.B., who "in 1 Ed. III. [1327] had summons to Parl. amongst the Barons of this Realm but not after." This supposed summons to parl. is erroneous, tho' his name appears in the writ of summons "*equis et armis*" to Newcastle upon Tyne. The person indicated was Sir Hugh de Meignill, of Langley Meinill, co. Derby, of whom and whose descendants there is a good pedigree in "the Top. and Gen.," vol. i, p. 357.

(f) See p. 22, note "g," *sub* "Latimer," as to this lady, who was *b.* in 1279 at Bylton. In the "Ingleby MSS." (app. 6th Rep. Hist. MSS. Comm.) is an account of this scandal.

V. 1368. 3. PHILIP (DARCY), LORD DARCY DE KNAYTH, and, apparently, *de jure* LORD MEINILL, 2d but 1st surv. s. and h. of his mother; aged 11 in 1362 when he *suc.* his eldest br. as LORD DARCY, under which title (only) he was sum. to Parl. 1377 to 1397. He *suc.* on the death of his mother in 1368 to Whorlton and her vast estates, co. York, as well as to the representation of the Barony of Meinill, which continued united with the Barony of Darcy de Knayth till both fell into *abeyance* in 1414. See "DARCY DE KNAYTH" Barony, *cr.* 1332, and see also tabular pedigree in vol. iii, p. 28, note "a."

See "DARCY" and "DARCY AND MEINILL," Barony (*Darcy*), *cr.* 1641, *sub* the second Baron, who was sum. as "*Conyers de Darcie et Meynill*" from 1678 to 1680; *ex.* (together with the Earldom of Holdernesse) 1778.

MELBOURNE and MELBOURNE OF KILMORE.

Barony [I.] I. 1770. Viscountcy [I.] I. 1781. Barony [U.K.] I. 1815.

1. SIR PENISTON LAMB, Bart., of Brocket Hall, Herts, only s. and h. of Sir Matthew LAMB, Bart. (so *cr.* 17 Jan. 1755), by Charlotte, sister and h. of George Lewis COKE, of Melbourne,(a) co. Derby, da. of the Rt. Hon. Thomas Coke, Vice Chamberlain to Queen Anne; was *b.* 29 Jan. 1740 or 1748; *suc.* his father as second Baronet, 6 Nov. 1768; was M.P. for Ludgershall, 1768, 1774, and 1780; for Malmesbury in 1784 and for Newport (Isle of Wight), 1793-96, having been (as a follower of Lord North) *cr.*, 8 June 1770, LORD MELBOURE, BARON OF KILMORE, co. Cavan [I.], and subsequently, 16 Dec. 1780, VISCOUNT MELBOURNE OF KILMORE, co. Cavan [I.] He was a Gent. of the Bedchamber to the Prince of Wales in 1783 and a Lord of the Bedchamber (to the King) in 1812. He was *cr.*, 11 Aug. 1815, BARON MELBOURNE of Melbourne, co. Derby [U.K.] He *m.*, 13 April 1769, at the Bishop of Peterborough's house in Great George street, St. Geo. Han. sq., Elizabeth, da. of Sir Ralph MILBANKE, 5th Bart., of Halnaby, co. York, by Elizabeth, da. of John HEDWORTH, of Chester-le-Street. She *d.* 6 April 1818, aged 65,(b) at Melbourne house, Whitehall.(c) He *d.* there, 22 July 1828, aged 80 or 88.(d) Will pr. Nov. 1828.

II. 1828. 2. WILLIAM (LAMB), VISCOUNT MELBOURNE OF KILMORE, &c. [I.], also BARON MELBOURNE [U.K.], 2d but 1st surv. s. and h.;(e) *b.* 15 March at Melbourne house, Piccadilly,(c) and *bap.* 11 April 1779, at St. James' Westm.; ed. at Eton and (as a Fellow Commoner in 1796) at Trin. Coll., Cambridge,

---

(a) The manor of Melbourne was held by the Bishops of Carlisle from 1133 till 1704 when the then Bishop by act of Parl. conveyed the fee to Thomas Coke, the lessee. It is described in 1873 as being of 2,787 acres worth £6,670 a year, and now (1893) belongs, by descent, to Earl Cowper.

(b) "The rise of the family was due to her brilliant qualities." [*Nat. Biogr.*, *sub.* "Lamb, William."] She appears to have been "when no longer in her first youth" one of the numerous objects of admiration of the Prince of Wales. ["*Wraxall*," edit. 1884, vol. v, p. 370]. Her graceful figure is well depicted by Reynolds.

(c) Melbourne house, *Whitehall*, formerly known as "York house" (and subsequently as "Dover house") was acquired by him from the Duke of York and *Albany* in exchange for "Melbourne house, *Piccadilly*," which latter (afterwards, from its new owner, called "*The Albany*") he had previously acquired from Lord Holland in 1770 and had built at a vast expence on the site of the old "Piccadilly house"

(d) He was "principally known by the distinguished place that he occupies in the annals of meretricious pleasure, the memoirs of Mrs. Bellamy or Mrs. Baddeley, the syrens and courtesans of a former age." He appears in a great measure to have squandered the "splendid fortune" which his father "from an inferior situation of life" had attained. See "Wraxall" as in note "b" next above.

(e) See p. 287, note "a."

and at Glasgow Univ.; M.A. (Cambridge), 1799; Barrister (Linc. Inn), 1804, but gave up practise next year on the death of his eldest br.;(a) M.P. for Leominster, 1806; for Portarlington, 1807-16; for Peterborough, 1816-19; for Herts, 1819-26; for Newport (Isle of Wight), 1827, and for Blechingley, 1727-28; P.C., 1827; was Ch. Sec. for Ireland, 1827-28. He *suc. to the peerage* [I. and U.K.], 22 July, 1828, taking his seat 1 Feb. 1829; was Home Secretary, 1830-34, under the Grey Ministry and was FIRST LORD OF THE TREASURY (*Prime Minister*) from July to Nov. 1834 and again from April 1835 to Sep. 1841, both to King William IV. and Queen Victoria.(b) He *m.* 3 June 1805 in Great George street, St. George Han. sq., Caroline, da. of Frederick (PONSONBY), 3d EARL OF BESSBOROUGH [I.], by Henrietta Frances, da. of John (SPENCER), 1st EARL SPENCER. She, who was *b.* 13 Nov. 1785, and *bap.* at St. Marylebone, and who was well known from her infatuated admiration of Byron, *d.* (as "*Lady Caroline Lamb*"), at Melbourne house, Whitehall, 26 Jan. 1828, aged 42, and was *bur.* at Hatfield, Herts. He *d.* s.p.s.,(c) 24 Nov. 1848, in his 70th year, at Melbourne, co. Derby.(d) Will pr. March 1849.

III. 1848, to 1853. 3. FREDERICK JAMES (LAMB), VISCOUNT MELBOURNE OF KILMORE [1781], and LORD MELBOURNE, BARON OF KILMORE [1770], in the peerage of Ireland, and also BARON MELBOURNE [1815] and BARON BEAUVALE [1839] also *a Baronet* [1755], next and only surv. br. and h. He was *b.* at Melbourne house, Piccadilly,(e) 17 April, and *bap.* 14 May 1782, at St. James' Westm.; ed. at Eton, at Glasgow Univ., and at Trin. Coll., Cambridge; M.A., 1803; Sec. of Legation, &c., to Naples, 1811-13; to Vienna, 1813-15; Minister to Munich, 1815-20; P.C., 1822; G.C.B. (Civil), 1827; Minister to Madrid, 1825-27; Ambassador to Lisbon, 1827, and to Vienna, 1831-41. He was *cr.*, 20 April 1839, BARON BEAUVALE of Beauvale, Notts, and, eight years later, *suc.* his brother as VISCOUNT MELBOURNE OF KILMORE, &c [I.] and BARON MELBOURNE [U.K.] He *m.*, 25 Feb. 1841, at Vienna, Alexandrina Julia Theresa Wilhelmina Sophia, COUNTESS VON-MALTZAN, da. of Joachim Charles Louis Mortimer, COUNT VON-MALTZAN, the Prussian Envoy to the Court of Vienna. He *d.* s.p., 29 Jan. 1853, in his 71st year, at Brocket hall, Herts, when *all his honours* became *extinct*.(f) Will pr. Feb. 1853. His widow (who was *b.* 5 Jan. 1818, being 36 years his junior), *m.*, 10 June 1856, at St. John's, Paddington, John George Weld (WELD-FORESTER), 2d BARON FORESTER OF WILLEY PARK, who *d.* s.p., 10 Oct. 1874, aged 73. She was living 1893.

(a) The Hon. Peniston Lamb, the 1st son of the 1st Viscount, *b.* 3 May 1773, M.P. for Herts, &c., *d.* unm. and v.p, 24 Jan. 1805.

(b) On two occasions he was a co-respondent in actions for divorce, *viz.*, one in Michaelmas, 1829, on behalf of William (Crosbie), 4th Baron Brandon [I.], which was withdrawn, and another, in June 1836, on behalf of the Hon. George Chapple Norton, husband of the well known poetess, "The Hon. Caroline Norton," *neé* Sheridan.

(c) His only child that survived infancy was a hopeless invalid, George Augustus Frederick (to whom King George IV. stood sponsor) who *d.* unm. and v.p., 27 Nov. 1836, aged 29.

(d) In the *Annual Reg.* for 1848, is a very good account of his political career. The latter part, however, of his ministry was "divided and discredited and the Premier himself was involved in the *Lady Flora Hastings* affair. Before the meeting of Parl., 16 Jan. 1840, the Government has committed itself to wars with Persia, Afghanistan and China, while the discontent of the working classes had found vent in the Chartist riots at Newport and Birmingham." (*Nat. Biogr.*)

(e) See p. 286, note "c."

(f) His only surv. sister, Emily Mary, was his sole heir. She, who was *b.* 21 April 1787, *m.* firstly, 20 July 1805, the 5th Earl Cowper, who *d.* 21 July 1837, aged 59, and *m.* secondly, 16 Dec. 1839, Henry John (Temple), 3d Viscount Palmerston [I.], who *d.* s.p., 18 Oct. 1865, aged 81. She *d.* 11 Sep. 1869, in her 83d year, at Brocket hall, Herts, being *suc.* in that and her other estates by her s. and h., the 6th Earl Cowper.

MELCOMBE.

Barony I. 1761, to 1762.

1. GEORGE BUBB, afterwards (1717) BUBB-DODINGTON, was s. of Jeremiah BUBB,(a) by (—), sister of George DODINGTON, of Eastbury, Dorset, only da. of John DODINGTON, of Lexton (d. 1663), by (according to some) Hester, da. of Sir Peter TEMPLE, 2d Bart., of Stowe, or (according to others) "Ann, relict of (—) BOREMAN, da. of (—) HOPKINS."(b) He was b. about 1691; matric. at Oxford (Ex. Coll.), 10 July 1707, aged 16; Student of Lincoln's Inn, 1711; M.P. for Winchelsea, 1715; for Bridgewater, 1722-54; for Weymouth, 1755-61. He was Envoy to Spain, 1715-17. In compliance with the wish of his maternal uncle abovenamed, he, by act of Parl., 1717, took the name of *Dodington*, and on his uncle's death, shortly afterwards, *suc.* to his estates in Dorset and elsewhere and to considerable Parliamentary influence;(c) Lord Lieut. of Somersetshire, 1721; a Lord of the Treasury, 1724-40; Treasurer of the Chamber to the Prince of Wales, 1749-51; P.C., 1745; Treasurer of the Navy, 1744-49, Dec. 1755, to Nov. 1756, and from April to June 1757. In 1761 he "reached the summit of his ambition,"(d) and obtained a peerage from the Bute Ministry, being *cr.*, 6 April 1761, LORD MELCOMBE, BARON OF MELCOMBE-REGIS, co. Dorset. He *m.* in 1725 (such marriage being acknowledged in 1742) Katharine "Mrs. BEHAN, who had been regarded as his mistress."(e) She was *bur.* 28 Dec. 1756, at St. James' Westm.(e) He *d. s.p.* at his villa called "La Trappe" in Hammersmith, 28 July 1762, aged 71, when the *peerage* became *extinct*. He was *bur.* at Fulham. M.I. at Hammersmith. Will pr. 1762.(f)

MELDRUM OF MORVEN.

i.e., "MELDRUM OF MORVEN, co. Aberdeen," Barony (*Gordon*), *cr.* 1815; see "HUNTLY" MARQUESSATE [S.], *cr.* 1599, *sub* the 9th Marquess, who, when EARL OF ABOYNE [S.], obtained, in 1815, this Barony.

(a) In his son's matriculation this Jeremiah is called "of London, Esq.," but he is "variously described as an Irish fortune-hunter and an Apothecary at Weymouth or Carlisle." [*Nat. Biogr.*]

(b) Pedigree subscribed by "George Dodington" entered in "5 D xiv" in the Coll. of Arms.

(c) He could command the representation of Winchelsea, Weymouth, Melcombe Regis (which returned four members) and (generally) of Bridgewater; hence he mainly derived his political importance.

(d) "*Nat. Biogr.*" where his character is ably depicted, and see also Jesse's "Court of England, 1688 to 1762." His unblushing self-seeking, shewn by his frequent alternations between the King's party (the Ministry of Walpole, &c.), and that of the opposition (the Prince of Wales, &c.), occasioned much ridicule even in that venal age. These changes since 1749 (when his well known "*Diary*" begins) are set forth without any sense of shame *by himself*. He also affected to be the "Mæcenas" of the period and was the last of the "Patrons" of the Poets (Young, Thomson, &c.) He himself was well versed in ancient and in modern literature. He was also one of the 12 members of the notorious "*Hell fire Club.*" See vol. iii., p. 95, note "f," *sub* "Despencer."

(e) There can be little doubt that the entry "Mrs. Katharine Dodington, w" [*i.e.*, "woman"] refers to her. Horace Walpole says she died late in 1756, and Dodington's house was in Pall Mall *in St. James' parish*.

(f) The family estate of Eastbury (on which he had spent £140,000) went to Richard (Grenville), Earl Temple, whose mother (Hester, *suo jure* Countess Temple), was da. of Sir Richard Temple, 3d Bart., brother (apparently) of Lord Melcombe's maternal grandmother abovenamed; but the personalty, including the famous diary, was left to another cousin, Thomas Wyndham.

MELFORT.

Viscountcy [S.] I. 1685. Earldom [S.] I. 1686. 1. The Hon. JOHN DRUMMOND, 2d s. of James, 3d EARL OF PERTH [S.], by Anne, 1st da. of George (GORDON), 2d MARQUESS OF HUNTLY [S.], was b. about 1650; was Capt. of the Scotch Foot Guards, 1673; Master of the Ordnance, 1680; Sec. of State [S.], 1684, and was cr. 14 April 1685,(a) VISCOUNT OF MELFORT and LORD DRUMMOND OF GILLESTOUN [S.], with a spec. rem. to the heirs male of his body by his second(b) marriage, failing whom, to heirs male of his body whatsoever(c); being, also, cr. on 12 Aug. 1686, EARL OF MELFORT, VISCOUNT OF FORTH, LORD DRUMMOND OF RICCARTOUN CASTLEMAINS AND GILSTOUN [S.], with a like spec. rem. He was K.T., 6 June 1687, being one of the eight orig. knights of that order,(d) as also was his br. the Earl of Perth [S.], indeed the "two brothers ruled Scotland" during the three years of the reign of James II. On the landing of the Prince of Orange he escaped to France, 16 Dec. 1688, whence he accompanied King James to Ireland in 1689; was sent by him on an embassy to Rome and was, by him (after his dethronement) made K.G. in 1692, and cr. 17 April 1694, DUKE OF MELFORT, MARQUESS OF FORTH, EARL OF ISLA AND BURNTIZLAND VISCOUNT OF RICKERTON, LORD CASTLEMAINS AND GALSTON [S.], with the like spec. rem. as in the previous creations.(e) He was outlawed 23 July 1694, and *attainted* by act of Parl., 2 July 1695, whereby *all his honours* became *forfeited.* After the death of James II. in 1701, he was recognised as a *French* Peer by Louis XIV. as DUC DE MELFORT, holding the same spec. rem. of that dignity as afsd. He m. firstly, 30 Sep. 1670, Sophia da. and eventually h. of line of Robert MAITLAND, of Lundin, co. Fife (yr. s. of John, 1st EARL OF LAUDERDALE [S.]) by Margaret, da. and h. of John LUNDIN, of Lundin afsd. By her he had male issue whose right of succession to his peerage dignities was postponed to that of their brethren of the half blood. He m. secondly before 1682, Euphemia, da. of Sir Thomas WALLACE, of Craigie, a Lord of Session (1671-80), by Euphemia, da. and h. of William GEMMILL, of Templelands, co. Ayr. He d. 25 Jan. 1714/5,(f) after a long illness, and was bur. at St. Sulpice, Paris. His widow who was "a great beauty in her time"(g) and who was latterly "supported by keeping one of the two faro tables authorised by Louis XIV,"(h) d. in 1743, at St. Germains, aged 90.

(a) This was one of the six hereditary Scotch Peerages cr. by James II., for a list of which see vol. iii, p. 208, note "a," *sub* "Dundee."

(b) His children by his first wife, who bore the name of Lundin, having inherited their mother's estate of Lundin, were protestants. James Lundin (afterwards Drummond) of Lundin, b. 1707, became, 7 Feb. 1760, the representature of the Earls of Perth, and styled himself accordingly Earl of Perth, notwithstanding the attainder of that dignity. His only surv. s. and h., obtained in 1785 possession of the Perth estates and was cr. a Peer [G.B.] as Lord Perth in 1797. He d. s.p.m. 2 July 1800 when the issue male, by the *first* wife, of the 1st Earl of Melfort became extinct.

(c) The creation of the Dukedom of Somerset in 1547 was a similar case, *i.e.* one in which the children of the existing wife were preferred to that of the previous one.

(d) See vol. i, p. 187, note "d," *sub* "Athole."

(e) See "*Riddell*," pp. 963, 965, as to this particular creation, and see vol. i. (of this work), p. 59, note "d," *sub* "Albemarle" as to the "Jacobite creations" in general.

(f) Macky, in his "*Characters*" [1705?] says of him, when past 50," he is very ambitious, hath abundance of lively sense, will stick at nothing to gain his end; a well-bred gentleman; understands the *belles lettres*, is very proud, cannot bear a rival in business, nor is he much to be trusted himself, but where his ambition can be fed. He is tall, black, stoops in the shoulders, thin." He states also that "being very handsome and a fine dancer" he had obtained the favour of the Duchess of York (afterwards Queen Consort), and became afterwards "one of the chief favourites of the Court."

(g) *Nat. Biogr.*

(h) Wood's "*Douglas.*"

The heirs to the Earldom of Melfort, had it not been for the attainder, were as under.

II. *1715.* 2. JOHN DRUMMOND, *titular* DUKE OF MELFORT, &c., yr. s. but heir under the *spec. rem.* in the creations of 1685 and 1686, to the various dignites therein specified, being the first son of the *second* wife. He was *b.* 26 May 1682 in Scotland; *styled* VISCOUNT FORTH, 1686 to 1715, when, at his father's death, he assumed his peerage titles; was Major-Gen. in the rising in Scotland in 1715, whence he escaped 4 Feb. 1715/6. He *m.* 25 May 1707, at St. Eustache in Paris, Marie Gabrielle D'Audibert, widow of Henry FITZ JAMES, *titular* DUKE OF ALBEMARLE, COUNTESS DE LUSSAN in France. He *d.* 29 Jan. 1754, and was *bur.* at St. Nicholas-des-Champs, Paris.

III. *1754.* 3. JAMES DRUMMOND, *titular* DUKE OF MELFORT, &c., also DUC DE MELFORT and COMTE DE LUSSAN in France, s. and h., *b.* 13 May 1708, at St. Germains, in France. He *m.* 26 July 1755, at Lussan, Marie DE BERENGER. He possessed a considerable estate in Lower Languedoc. He *d.* 25 Dec. 1766.

IV. *1766.* 4. JAMES LEWIS DRUMMOND, *titular* DUKE OF MELFORT, &c., s. and h.(a); was a General in the French Service. He *m.* 30 April 1788, Aglae Elizabeth Jacqueline, da. of VICOMTE d'Alaix. By the death, July 1800, of James (Drummond) Lord Perth, Baron Drummond of Stobhall (titular Duke and Earl of Perth), he became head of the Drummond family and the heir male of the *Earldom of Perth*(b) and, but for the attainder, would have been EARL OF PERTH, &c. [S.] He *d.* s.p. at Lepus island, in Spain, in Sep. 1800.

V. *1800.* 5. CHARLES EDWARD DRUMMOND, *titular* DUKE OF MELFORT, EARL OF PERTH, EARL OF MELFORT, &c., next br. and h.; *b.* 1 Jan. 1752,(a) was a Roman Catholic Prelate. He entered a clam in 1803, for the Perth estates in the Court of Session, which was dismissed in 1808. He *d.* unm. at Rome, 9 April 1840.

VI. *1840.* 6. GEORGE DRUMMOND, *titular* DUKE OF MELFORT, EARL OF PERTH, EARL OF MELFORT, &c., nephew and h., being only surv. s. and h. of Leon Maurice DRUMMOND (*b.* 12 April 1761; (c) *d.* 26 April 1826), by Marie Elizabeth Luce DE LONGUEMARRE, his wife, which Leon was yst. s. of James, 3d (titular) Duke of Melfort abovenamed. The attainder of his ancestors was reversed 28 June 1853, whereby he became *de facto* Earl of Perth Earl of Melfort, &c. [S.] as stated below.

II. 1853. 2. GEORGE DRUMMOND, *titular* DUKE AND EARL OF MELFORT, &c., great great grandson (as above shewn), and heir male of the 1st Earl of Melfort [S,] was *b.* 6 May 1807. In 1841 he established in France before the *Conseil d'Etat* and the *Tribunal de la Seine* his right to the French titles of DUC DE MELFORT, COMTE DE LUSSAN, and BARON DE VALROSE, while, in England, (12 years later) the attainder of his ancestors having been reversed he was 19 July 1853, declared to be entitled to the dignities of EARL OF PERTH [1605], EARL OF MELFORT [1686], VISCOUNT FORTH [1686], LORD DRUMMOND [1488], and LORD DRUMMOND OF RICCARTOUN, CASTLEMAINS AND GILSTOUN [1686], in the peerage of Scotland. See "PERTH" Earldom of [S.], *cr.* 1605, *sub* the 5th Earl.

(a) The three elder sons of James, the 3d (titular) Duke were apparently born before their parents marriage as the yst. son, Leon Maurice, petitioned for the Perth estates on the ground that he (only) was born after his parents marriage. This, however, would not (according to Scotch law) make them illegitimate.

(b) See p. 289, note "b" and see also tabular pedigree, *sub* "Perth" (vol. vi.) in which this representation is depicted.

(c) Being accordingly born *after* his parents marriage; see note "a" next above.

MELGUM.

Viscountcy [S.] I. 1627, to 1630.

I. LORD JOHN GORDON, 2d s. of George, 1st MARQUESS OF HUNTLY [S.], by Henrietta, da. of Esme (STUART), 1st DUKE OF LENNOX [S.], was cr., 20 Oct. 1627,(a) VISCOUNT OF MELGUM and LORD ABOYNE [S.], with rem. "*suis heredibus masculis, cognomen et insignia de Gordon, gerentibus.*" He m. Sophia, 5th da. of William (HAY), 9th EARL OF ERROLL [S.], by his third wife, Elizabeth, da. of William (DOUGLAS), EARL OF MORTON [S.] He d. s.p. Oct. 1630 (being burnt to death at Frendraught with his host, Sir James Crichton, of Frendraught afsd.), when the *peerage* became *extinct*.(b) His widow d. 12 March 1642.(c)

MELGUND.

i.e., "MELGUND, of Melgund, co. Forfar," Viscountcy (*Elliot-Murray-Kynynmond*), cr. 1813 with the EARLDOM OF MINTO, which see.

MELLEFONT.

i.e., "MOORE OF MELLEFONT, co. Louth," Barony [I.] (*Moore*); see "MOORE OF DROGHEDA," Viscountcy [I.], cr. 1622, *sub* "Drogheda."

MELROS, or MELROSE.

i.e., "RAMSAY OF MELROSE," Barony [S.] (*Ramsay*), *conferred* 1615 on VISCOUNT HADDINGTON [S.], but *resigned* in 1618; see "HOLDERNESSE" Earldom, cr. 1621; ex. 1626.

---

i.e., "RAMSAY OF MELROSE," Barony [S.] (*Ramsay*), cr. 1618, but changed next year (1619) for the title of "RAMSAY OF DALHOUSIE," which see, *sub* "Dalhousie."

---

i.e., "MELROSE," Earldom [S.] (*Hamilton*), cr. 1619, but changed eight years subsequently (1627) for the title of "HADDINGTON," which see.

MELROS OF TYNINGHAME.

i.e., "MELROS OF TYNINGHAME, co. Haddington," Barony (*Hamilton*) cr. 1827; ex. 1858; see "HADDINGTON" Earldom [S.], *sub* the ninth Earl.

MELROSE, see MELROS.

(a) The original charter is in the "Aboyne or rather Huntly charter chest." ["*Riddell*," p. 624.]

(b) See "*Riddell*," pp. 624-6, and pp. 1,020-1; also Riddell's "*Remarks*" [1833], p. 26, as to the meaning of "*heirs male*" (even when accompanied with the name and arms clause) being no more than heirs male of *the body* in direct contradiction to Lord Mansfield's ruling in the case of Kirkcudbright. In the patent of the Viscountcy of Aboyne, conferred 20 April 1632, on the brother of Viscount Melgum, it is recited that the Viscountcy of Melgum was conferred on John Gordon "*et hæredes suos masculos, nomen et insignia de Gordon gerentes*," and expressly stated that the said Viscount had died "*absque hæredibus masculis* DE CORPORE SUO *legitime procreatis, in quos* [be it observed the patent adds] *dictus titulus conferendus fuit*," so that the meaning of the words is expressly declared to extend no further than to *heirs of the body*.

(c) Her "*genus, mens, et forma*," are extolled in some Latin verses by Arthur Johnston. [Wood's "*Douglas*," *sub* "Erroll."]

MELVILLE and MELVILLE OF MONYMAILL [Scotland].

Barony [S.] I. 1616. 1. SIR ROBERT MELVILLE, of Murdocarny, 2d s. of Sir John MELVILLE, of Raith, by Helen, da. of Sir Alexander NAPIER, of Murchistoun, was sometime in the court of Henry II., King of France, but returning to Scotland became P.C., was Ambassador to England in 1562, and again in 1587 endeavouring to save the execution of Queen Mary [S.]; was made Hereditary Keeper of Linlithgow palace 1567; *knighted* Oct. 1582; Vice Chancellor and Treasurer Depute [S.], 1589; an extra. Lord of Session [S.], 1594—1601, under the style of *Lord Murdocarny* and was *cr.* a Lord of Parl., 30 April 1616, as LORD MELVILLE OF MONYMAILL [S.], with *spec. rem.*, failing heirs male of his body, to those of his elder brother John. He *m.* firstly, before 14 Feb. 1563/4 (when she was living), Catharine, da. of William ADAMSON, of Craigcrook, co. Edinburgh. He *m.* secondly, Mary, da. of Andrew (LESLIE), 4th EARL OF ROTHES [S.], by his second wife, Jean, da. of Patrick (RUTHVEN), 3d LORD RUTHVEN [S.] She *d.* s.p. He *m.* thirdly, Jean, widow of Patrick (LESLIE), 1st LORD LINDORES [S.] (who *d.* 1606-09), da. of Robert (STEWART), EARL OF ORKNEY [S.], by Janet, da. of Gilbert (KENNEDY), 3d EARL OF CASSILLIS [S.] He *d.* Dec. 1621, aged 94. His widow was living 1642.

II. 1621. 2. ROBERT (MELVILLE), LORD MELVILLE OF MONYMAILL [S.], only s. and h., by first wife; was *knighted* v.p.; P.C. [S.] and an extra Lord of Session (on the resignation of his father), 1601 to 1608, and again 1610, under the style of *Lord Burntisland*. He *suc. to the peerage* [S.], Dec. 1621 obtaining a *novodamus* thereof, dat. 10 Aug. 1627, at Bagshot, with rem. to the heirs of his body whatsoever, whom failing "to his heirs male, general or of conquest or either of them, bearing the name and arms of Melville, as it should please him to designate at any time during his life and his assignees whatsoever." He *m.* firstly, Margaret, da. of Thomas KER, of Fernyhirst, by his first wife, Janet, da. and h. of William KIRKALDY, of Grange. He *m.* secondly before 14 Aug. 1613, Jean, widow of Robert (ROSS), LORD ROSS [S.] (who *d.* Oct. 1595), da. of Gavin HAMILTON, of Raploch. She *d.* May 1631. He *d.* s.p. at Edinburgh, 9 March and was *bur.* 15 April 1635, at Monymail.

III. 1635. 3. JOHN (MELVILLE), LORD MELVILLE OF MONYMAILL [S.], cousin and h. male, being s. and h. of John MELVILLE, of Raith (*d.* 17 Jan. 1626), by Margaret, da. of Sir William SCOTT, of Balwearie, which John, was s. and h. of John MELVILLE, of Raith (*d.* 13 Jan. 1603), who was elder br. of Robert, the 1st Lord. He *suc.* his father in the estate of Raith in 1626, and *suc. to the peerage* [S.], on the death, in 1635, of his cousin afsd., to whom he was served "heir of conquest and provision." He *m.* before 1636, Anne, 1st da. and coheir of Sir George ERSKINE, of Innerliel, a Lord of Session, 1617-46. He *d.* 1643.

IV. 1643. Earldom [S.] I. 1690. 4 and 1. GEORGE (MELVILLE), LORD MELVILLE OF MONYMAILL [S.], s. and h. *b.* 1636; *suc. to the peerage* [S.], 1643; was a zealous Presbyterian; entered into the conspiracy of the Duke of Monmouth, and was consequently "*forfeited*" and fled to Holland, but coming back with the Prince of Orange in 1688, was *restored* in 1689, and was *cr.* 8 April 1690, EARL OF MELVILLE, VISCOUNT OF KIRKCALDY, LORD RAITH, MONYMAILL AND BALWEARIE [S.]; Sec. of State [S.], 1690-91; High Commissioner to Parl. [S.] 1690; Privy Seal [S.], 1691-96, and President of the Council [S.], 1666—1702. He *m.* 18 Jan. 1655, Catharine, sister of Alexander, 2d EARL OF LEVEN [S.], only da. of Alexander LESLIE, *styled* LORD BALGONIE, by Margaret, da. of John (LESLIE), EARL OF ROTHES [S.] He *d.* 20 May 1707, aged 71.(a) His widow *d.* 2 April 1713.

(a) Macky in his "Characters" [1705?] says of him.—"At the revolution he came over with King William; was made Sec. of State; created from *Lord* to *Earl;* Commissioner to the first Parl. His *eldest* son [Alexander] had the management of the Revenue and his second son, the Earl of Leven, was made Gov. of Edinburgh Castle and had a regiment; and indeed the administration of the whole affairs of

[ALEXANDER MELVILLE, *styled* LORD RAITH, 1st s. and h. ap., *b.* about 1658; was Treasurer Depute [S.], 1689-98, having, as such, the chief management of the public revenue. He *m.* in or before 1692, Barbara, 3d da. of Walter DUNDAS, of Dundas. He *d.* s.p.s. 27 March 1698. His widow *d.* 23 Feb. 1719.

Earldom [S.] II. Barony [S.] V. 1707. 2. and 5. DAVID (MELVILLE, *afterwards* LESLIE), EARL OF MELVILLE, VISCOUNT KIRKCALDY, LORD MELVILLE OF MONYMAILL and LORD RAITH, MONYMAILL AND BALWEARIE [S.], 2d but 1st surv. s. and h.; *b.* 5 May 1660; *assumed* the title of EARL OF LEVEN and LORD BALGONIE [S.], on the death, 21 Jan. 1676, of his cousin, Catherine, *suo jure* COUNTESS OF LEVEN, &c. [S.], but was not *recognised* therein, till the death, s.p.m., 27 July 1681, of the Duke of Rothes [S.], some of whose (possible) issue male had a prior right thereto. By the death of his father, 20 May 1707, he *suc.* to his paternal dignities, as EARL OF MELVILLE, &c. [S.] See "LEVEN" Earldom [S.], *cr.* 1641, *sub* the 5th holder of that peerage, with which dignity the Earldom and Barony of Melville continues united.(a)

MELVILLE [U.K.]

Viscountcy. I. 1802. 1. THE RT. HON. HENRY DUNDAS, was 4th s. of Robert DUNDAS, of Arniston, co. Edinburgh, President of the Court of Session [S.], 1748-53, by his second wife, Anne, sister and coheir of Sir John, da. of Sir (William?) Gordon,(b) Bart., of Invergordon. He was *b.* 28 April 1742; ed. at the High School and the Univ. of Edinburgh; Advocate, 1763; Solicitor Gen. [S.], 1766-75; M.P. for Midlothian, 1774-82; for Newtown, Isle of Wight, 1782; for Midlothian (again), 1783-90, and for Edinburgh (city), 1790—1802; Lord Advocate [S.], 1775-83; Joint Keeper, 1777-79, and Keeper, 1779—1800, of the Signet [S.]; Rector of the Univ. of Glasgow, 1781-83; Chairman of the newly-established Board for Indian affairs,(c) 1781; Treasurer of the Navy

---

Scotland were in his family for some years. On the Queen's accession [1702], he and his son were dismissed from all their employments. He hath neither learning, wit, nor common conversation; but a steadiness of principle and a firm boldness for Presbyterian Government in all reigns hath carried him thro' all these great employments, and his weakness made him the fitter tool, for my Lord Portland and Mr. Carstairs supported him. He makes a very mean figure in his person, being low, thin, with a great head, a long chin and little eyes; is 70 years old."

(a) "In the Leven charter of 1664," the dignities are limited to the second son of George, Lord Melvill and Catherine his spouse and the heirs male of his body with this qualification—that if he or they shall "succeed also to be Lord Melvil, in that case the said Countesse of Levin's honour and dignitie, &c., shall *ipso facto* pertene to the next air of taillie, in whose favor the person succeeding shall be holden to denude themselfis, *omni habili modo* of the said Countess of Leven's Dignitie ["*Riddell*" p. 69]. "This is from the signature under the Caschet of which the Charter is a literal extension in Latin." Mr. Riddell adds, "Can this union [of the Earldom of Melville with that of Leven] continue in the face of the above prohibition or should not the latter rather diverge and separate accordingly?" The question, however of "*jumping*" or "*revolving*," peerages (*i.e.* such as should, according to their limitation, leave the person in whom they have once *vested*) is a difficult one. See vol. ii, p. 59, note "b," *sub* "Buckhurst" for some remarks thereon.

(b) She was probably sister of Isabel who *m.* 23 Sep. 1724, George (Mackenzie), 3d Earl of Cromarty [S.] The christian name of her father is given as "William," "Robert," or "John." A Sir *John* Gordon, Bart., of Invergordon, died 25 May 1783 [Ann. Reg.], and it appears that the mother of a certain Niel Douglas, who was tried at Edinburgh, 12 July 1816, was niece by her mother of Lord Melville's mother, both being, as the prisoner stated, daughters of a Sir *John* Gordon. [*Ex inform.* M. J. Shaw-Stewart.]

(c) "As the practical head of the Board of Control, the management of Indian affairs was in his hands for more than 16 years. For nearly 30 years he was the most powerful man in Scotland, and, as the election agent for the Government, controlled the elections of the Scotch Rep. Peers as well as of the Scotch members of the House of Commons." [*Nat. Biogr.*]

1782—1801; P.C., 1782—1805, and again (his name having been erased) from 1807 till his death; one of the Lords of Trade, 1784-86; Chancellor of the Univ. St. Andrew's, 1788; LL.D. Edinburgh, 11 Nov. 1789; Home Secretary, 1791-94; President of the Board of Control for India, 1793—1801; Secretary for War and the Colonies, 1794—1801; Privy Seal [S.], 1800, and was *cr.*, 24 Dec. 1802,(a) BARON OF DUNIRA, co. Perth, and VISCOUNT MELVILLE of Melville, co. Edinburgh. He was first Lord of the Admiralty from May 1804 to April 1805, when he resigned that post on being impeached of malversation when Treasurer of the Navy. He was tried by the House of Lords on 10 charges but acquitted, 12 June 1806, on all, tho' it was but by a small majority (27 and 31) on that of having permitted his Paymaster (Trotter) to withdraw public money and to employ it for his [Melville's] use.(b) He *m.* firstly, 16 Aug. 1765, Elizabeth, da. of David Rennie, of Melville Castle, co. Edinburgh. She was, however, divorced [1775?] probably about ten years later.(c) He *m.*, secondly, 2 April 1793, at St. Marylebone, Jane, da. of John (Hope), 2d Earl of Hopetoun [S.], by his second wife, Jane, da. of Robert Oliphant. He *d.* at Edinburgh (at the house his nephew and son in law, the Lord Chief Baron [S.]), 29 May 1811, in his 70th year, and was *bur.* in Lasswade church, Midlothian. Will pr. 1811. His widow, who was *b.* 12 Nov. 1766, *m.*, 16 Feb. 1814, Thomas (Wallace), Baron Wallace of Knaresdale (so *cr.* 1828) who *d.* 23 Feb. 1844. She *d. s.p.*, 9 June 1829, aged 62.

II. 1811. 2. Robert (Saunders-Dundas, *formerly* Dundas). Viscount Melville, &c., only s. and h. by first wife; *b.* 14 March 1771; ed. at the High School, Edinburgh, and at Eman. Coll., Cambridge; M.P. for Hastings, 1794-96; for Rye, 1796—1801, and for Midlothian (in four Parls.), 1801-11; Private Sec. to his father, 1794—1801; Joint Clerk Register of Seisins [S.], 1799; Keeper of the Signet [S.], 1800; P.C., 1807; President of the [Indian] Board of Control, 1807-09, and 1809-12; Ch. Sec. to the Viceroy of Ireland, April to Oct. 1809; *suc. to the peerage*, 29 May 1811; Lord Privy Seal [S.], 1811-51; First Lord of the Admiralty, 1812-27, and 1828-30;(d) Chancellor of the Univ. of St. Andrew's, 1814; K.T., 17 July 1821; one of the "Lord Guardians" of the realm, 18 Sep. 1821; Gen. of the Royal Scottish Archers; F.R.S., &c. He *m.* 29 Aug. 1796, Anne, 1st da. and coheir(e) of Richard Huck-Saunders, *formerly* Huck, M.D., by Jane, da. of Peter Kinsey, and Anne his wife, sister of Admiral Sir Charles Saunders, K.B. Having suc. to the Saunders property he took the name of *Saunders* before that of *Dundas* in compliance with the will of the said Sir Charles Saunders, proved 14 Dec. 1775. His wife *d.* 10 Sep. 1841, at Melville Castle. He *d.* there 10 June 1851, aged 80.

III. 1851. 3. Henry (Dundas), Viscount Melville, &c., s. and h., *b.* 25 Feb. 1801, at Melville Castle; entered the army in 1819, becoming finally, 1868, full General. He distinguished himself in Canada during the

(a) He had resigned his office of Sec. of War in 1801 on the resignation of the Ministry of Pitt, whose peculiar friend and coadjutor he had been and to whose great surprise he accepted a peerage from the Addington Ministry.

(b) He is said to have borrowed £10,000 and £20,000 at a time of Trotter who had "so far as could be ascertained advanced to him £46,000 and purchased stock on his account, but all was greatly complicated by their having, on the appointment of the enquiry, burnt "their accounts for £134,000,000 of public money which had passed through their hands," which certainly (as Mr. Howard Evans remarks in "*Our Old Nobility*") is "the very last thing which an honest man, an inquiry pending over his head, would have done." On the other hand this prosecution, which certainly failed of conviction, was not unfrequently considered to have been a malignant trick of the Whig party to destroy "Lord Melville's utility as a statesman" and to deprive Pitt "of an able coadjutor." [Edinb. Review, clx, p. 441.]

(c) She re-married Everard Fawkner (*Qy.* if he did not *d.* 1803) and *d.* his widow at a great age.

(d) Taking great interest in the Arctic Expedition, "the Melville Sound" was named after him.

(e) The 2d and yst. da. and coheir became Countess of Westmorland.

rebellion, 1837-38; C.B., 30 March 1839; Aide-de-camp to the Queen, 1841-42; was in command in India in the second Sikh war, 1849, and took a leading part at the battles of Moultan and Goojerat, receiving the thanks of Parl.; K.C.B., 5 June 1849; *suc. to the peerage*, 10 June 1851; Gov. of Edinburgh Castle, &c., 1855-60; Gen. of the Royal Scottish Archers; G.C.B., 28 March 1865. He *d.* unm. at Melville Castle, 1 Feb. 1876, in his 75th year.

IV. 1876. *4.* Robert (Dundas), Viscount Melville, &c., br. and h.; *b.* 14 Sep. 1803, at Melville Castle; Deputy Comptroller of the Navy, 1830; Store Keeper Gen., 1832-69; *suc. to the peerage*, 1 Feb. 1876. He *d.* unm., 18 Feb. 1886, at Southwood house, Ramsgate, Kent, and was *bur.* (from Melville Castle) at Lasswade. Will pr. June 1886, over £71,000.

V. 1886. *5.* Robert (Dundas), Viscount Melville and Baron Duneira, nephew and h., being s. and h. of Rev. the Hon. Charles Dundas, Rector of Epworth, co. Lincoln, by Louisa Maria, 1st da. of Sir William Boothby, 9th Bart., which Charles was 4th and yst. s. of the 2d Viscount, and *d.* 24 Feb. 1883, aged 76. He was *b.* 8 March 1835, and *suc. to the peerage*, 18 Feb. 1886. He *m.* 18 June 1891, at St. Paul's, Knightsbridge, Violet, 3d and yst. da. of Alexander Dundas Ross (Cochrane-Wishart-Baillie), 1st Baron Lamington, by Annabella Mary Elizabeth, da. of Andrew Robert Drummond. She was *b.* 20 Nov. 1856.

Family Estates.—These, in 1883, were under 2,000 acres. *Principal Residence.* Melville Castle, near Lasswade, co. Edinburgh.

MEMBLAND.

See "Revelstoke of Membland, co. Devon," Barony (*Baring*), *cr.* 1885.

MENDIP.

Barony. I. 1794. *1.* The Rt. Hon. Welbore Ellis, 6th and yst. but only surv. s. of the Rt. Rev. Welbore Ellis, Bishop of Meath, 1731-33, by Diana, da. of Sir John Briscoe, of Amberley Castle, Sussex, was *b.* at Kildare, 15 Dec. 1713; ed. at Westm., 1728-32, whence he obtained a Studentship at Ch. Ch., Oxford in 1732; B.A., 1736. He was M.P. for Cricklade, 1741-47; for Weymouth, 1747-54; for Aylesbury, 1761-68; for Petersfield, 1768-74; for Weymouth (again) 1774-90, and for Petersfield (again), 1791-94. Meanwhile he was a Lord of the Admiralty, 1747-55; Joint Vice Treasurer of Ireland, 1756-61, again 1765-66, and thirdly 1770-77; P.C., 20 March 1760; Sec. at War, 1762-65, and Treasurer of the Navy, 1777-82. D.C.L., Oxford, 7 July 1773. From Feb. to March 1782, he held the (then very critical) post of Sec. of State for America and the Colonies. In 1793 he joined the Ministerial side in politics([a]) and was (at the

([a]) An opponent to any concessions to America, as also to the liberty of the Press, he is depicted by "*Junius*" (where he is nicknamed "Grildrig") with the utmost contempt, and is spoken of by Lord Stanhope as "ridiculed for his diminutive stature, not redeemed by any loftiness of mind." There are many interesting notices of him in Wraxall's "*Memoirs*" where his character is thus summed up "After occupying during several years a distinguished place in the ranks of opposition under Lord North and Fox [he was] raised, in the winter of life, by Pitt (like so many other individuals) to the dignity a British Peer. He might be considered as the *Nestor* of the Ministry and of the House of Commons. In his figure, manner, and deportment, the very essence of form, he regularly took his place on the Treasury bench dressed in all points as if he had been going to the drawing room at St. James's. His eloquence was precise, grave, and constrained, unilluminated by taste, and calculated to convince, more than to exhilirate or electrify, his audience. The respect due to his age, character and employment, rather than the force of his arguments commonly secured him a patient hearing, but he was neither listened to with enthusiasm, nor regretted when he ceased actively to exert his abilities in support of the measures of the administration.

age of 80), *cr.* 13 Aug. 1794, BARON MENDIP of Mendip, co. Somerset with *spec. rem.* (failing heirs male of his body) in favour of the three elder sons(a) (or their issue male) of his sister, Anne, by her husband Henry AGAR, of Gowran. He was F.R.S., &c. He *m.* firstly 18 Nov. 1747, Elizabeth, only da. and h. of the Hon. Sir William STANHOPE, K.B., by his first wife, Margaret, da. of John RUDGE, of Wheatfield, Oxon. She *d.* Tylney hall, Hants, 1 Aug. 1761,(b) and was *bur.* at Shelford, Notts. He *m.* secondly, 20 July 1765, at St. Geo. Han. sq. (Lic. Fac.) Anne, sister and h. of the Rt. Hon. Hans. STANLEY, 1st da. of Hans STANLEY, of Poulton's park in the New Forest, Hants. He *d.* s.p. in Brook street, 2 and was *bur.* 7 Feb. 1802, at Westm. Abbey, aged 88. Will pr. 1802. His widow *d.* at Twickenham, Midx., 7 and was *bur.* 12 Dec. 1803, at Westm. Abbey, aged 88. Will dat. 5 March 1799, pr. Jan. 1804.

II. 1802. *2.* HENRY WELBORE (ELLIS *formerly* AGAR), VISCOUNT CLIFDEN, &c. [I.], also BARON MENDIP, great nephew and h., being s. and h. of James, 1st VISCOUNT CLIFDEN OF GOWRAN [I.], who was s. and h. of Henry AGAR. of Gowran, co. Kilkenny, by Anne, sister of Welbore (ELLIS), 1st BARON MENDIP abovenamed. He was *b.* 22 Jan. 1761; *suc. his Father in the peerage* [I.], 1 Jan. 1789, and *suc. his Great Uncle* in the peerage [G.B.], 7 Feb. 1802. See "CLIFDEN OF GOWRAN," Viscountcy [I.], *cr.* 1781, *sub* the second Viscount.

MENTEITH,(c) or MONTEITH.(d)

[STRATHERNE, with MENTEITH(e) (now, together, forming the southern part of Perthshire, was one of the *seven original Earldoms* [Mormaerships] of Scotland,(f) the holders of which, who in the 10th century were styled "MORMAERS," were in the 12th century known as "EARLS." Before, however, the 12th century, "MENTEITH" had become separate from "STRATHERNE," tho' (unlike the case of "Buchan," which, in a somewhat similar manner, had become separate from "MAR") Menteith was not one of "*the seven Earldoms*" [S.] in 1115.]

Earldom [S.] I. 1160? *1.* GILCHRIST, EARL OF MENTEITH [S.], was apparently one of the Earls *cr.* [1153—1165], by King Malcolm IV. [S.]. He was witness to a charter 1164, and was living 1175-1178 but *d.* between 1180 and 1199.

II. 1190? *2.* MURDOCH, EARL OF MENTEITH [S.], probably s. and h.; living 1199; *d.* before 1213.

(a) The 4th and yst. son was alone omitted. This was the Rev. Henry Agar, Rector of Inniscarra, co. Cork, who *d.* 14 May 1798, leaving three sons. The eldest son of Henry Agar (*the Father*) by Anne (Ellis) was James, 1st Viscount Clifden [I.], who had *d.* before the grantee) in 1798, leaving (also) three sons all mentioned, *nominatum*, in that patent) of whom the eldest (the 2d Viscount) suc. to the Mendip peerage.

(b) Through her he inherited Pope's villa, at Twickenham, which had been bought in 1744, by her father.

(c) Sir William Fraser has dealt with this family in one of his sumptuous works, entitled "*The Red Book of Menteith*," 2 vols., 4to., 1880.

(d) There are a few exceptional examples, in the seventeenth century, of the orthography of "MONTEITH," which is that adopted by Sir N. H. Nicolas in his "*Earldoms of Strathern, Monteith, and Airth.*" They are, however, *very* few. In the charter of 1631, in the proceedings for cancelling the retour, in the Acts of Parl. *passim*, &c., the spelling is Menteith.

(e) A considerable district, thro' which the river *Teith* runs, is called the Stewartry of Menteith, Meneteth, Maneth, or Monteith.

(f) See fuller account of these seven Earldoms in the remarks under "ANGUS," vol. i, p. 88

III. 1210? 3. MAURICE, THE ELDER, EARL OF MENTEITH [S.], probably s. and h. He, by agreement dat. at Edinburgh, 1213, *resigned the Earldom* with consent of King William [S.] to his brother, Maurice, retaining certain lands for his life.(a) He d. s.p.m.(b)

IV. 1213. 4. MAURICE, THE YOUNGER, EARL OF MENTEITH [S.], br. and (according to the abovenamed resignation) heir. He was one of the seven Earls present at the enthronement of King Alexander II. [S.]; was living, as Sheriff of Sterling, 27 March 1226, but d. before 1231.

V. 1230, to 1258? 5. ISABELLA, *suo jure* COUNTESS OF MENTEITH [S.], da. and heir of line. She m. before 3 Feb. 1231, WALTER COMYN, who in her right became EARL OF MENTEITH [S.] He was second s. (by his first wife) of William COMYN, who afterwards, in right of his *second* wife, became EARL OF BUCHAN [S.] He, with his father, was present at York in 1221 at the marriage of King Alexander II. [S.] from whom he obtained a grant of the extensive country of Badenoch before 1230. In 1234 he is described as *Earl of Menteith*;(c) in Sep. 1237 he was one of the jurors to the treaty between England and Scotland. He took an active part at the coronation, 13 July 1249, of Alexander III. [S.], and in the struggles during that King's minority. He d. s.p. in 1258. His widow immediately afterwards m. Sir John RUSSELL, an English Knight. She was accused of the murder of her first husband and appears to have been *deprived of the Earldom* by Parl.(d) She quitted Scotland and applied to the Pope for remedy who summoned (tho' the summons was of no effect) the Scotch nobles to York in 1262 to try the cause. She appears to have d. s.p.m. apparently between 1262 and 1272.

VI. 1258. 6. WALTER le STEWART called "BAILLOCH" (*i.e.*, "the Freckled,") 3d s. of Walter, HIGH STEWARD OF SCOTLAND (1204—1246) by Beatrix, da. of Gilchrist, EARL OF ANGUS [S.], having m. Mary, the younger sister of Isabella, *suo jure* COUNTESS OF MENTEITH [S.], next abovenamed, had the title of EARL OF MENTEITH [S.] "adjudged to him by the Scottish nobles, in 1258,"(e) in right of his said wife (after the deposition therefrom of her said sister) and under that title confirmed a grant to the Abbey of Paisley, 1262. He was at the battle of Largs, 1263; he accompanied (with his wife) the Princess Margaret [S.] to Norway in 1281; was *confirmed in the Earldom*,(f) by Parl. in 1285; was one of the nominees of

---

(a) See "*Riddell*," p. 172, note 1 (where it is suggested that "there was probably some impediment in the way of the legitimacy of Maurice, *senior*, at the time of his birth which did not apply to Maurice, *junior*." See also Riddell's "*Scotch Peerage Law*" [1833], pp. 149—152.

(b) Provision for his daughters were made in the deed of resignation.

(c) There is a statement by Riddell ["*Riddell*," p. 172, note 1, as also "*Scotch Peerage Law*" (1833), p. 151], that there appears to have been a contemporary Earl of Menteith named Malcolm "perhaps the representative of Maurice, senior," for, in a treaty of peace between England and Scotland, 1237, King Alexander [S.] "fecit jurare *Walterum* Comyn, *Comitem de Meneteth*, et præterea Comitem *Maucolmum*, *Comitem de Meneteth*." This, however is "a slip. *Earl Malcolm* is the Earl of *Fife*; Walter Comyn, Earl of *Menteith*, had been previously mentioned, so his *title* only is repeated when he is again named in the treaty. Lord Hailes [*Annals*] took, I think, this view." [*Ex inform*. Joseph Bain, F.S.A., to whom the Editor is indebted for kindly revising this article.]

(d) "Walter Stewart laid claim to the Earldom and *by the favour of Parl.* obtained it. The elder Countess insulted, disgraced, and despoiled of her fortune, retired out of Scotland with her husband." [Wood's "*Douglas*."]

(e) Wood's "*Douglas*."

(f) The Earldom was claimed by William Comyn, in 1273, s. and h. of John Comyn, the Red, who was nephew and h. (being s. and h. of Richard, eldest br.) of Walter (Comyn), Earl of Menteith, *jure uxoris*, as abovementioned. This William claimed it in right of his wife, Isabella, da. and h. of Isabella, the dispossessed (*suo jure*) Countess of

Bruce in the competition for the Crown [S.], in 1292; swore fealty to King Edward I. [E.], 13 June 1292, by whom he was sum. to attend him into France, 1 Sep. 1294, but appears to have *d.* soon after that date,(a) his wife having *d.* before him probably before 1286.

VII. 1295? 7. ALEXANDER (DE MENTEITH, or STEWART), EARL OF MENTEITH [S.], 1st s. and h.,(b) was v.p. under the designation of "*Alisandre de Meneteth*" one of the nobles who (5 Feb. 1283/4) supported the right of succession of "Margaret of Norway" to the Crown [S.] He was taken prisoner by the English at Dunbar, 28 April 1296. He *m.* Matilda. He *d.* soon after 1296, certainly before 1306.

VIII. 1300? 8. ALAN (DE MENTEITH, or STEWART), EARL OF MENTEITH [S.], s. and h. He supported Robert Bruce in his claim to the throne in 1306 in which year he was taken prisoner by the English. He *m.* Margery.(c) He *d.* s.p.m. (d) before 18 March 1308/9, in England.

IX. 1308? 9. MURDOCH (DE MENTEITH, or STEWART), EARL OF MENTEITH, [S.], br. and h. male.(e) He in 1330 made an agreement with Mary, da. and h. of Earl Alan, for the possession of the Earldom.(f) He, probably, *m.* Alice.(g) He was killed at the battle of Halidon Hill, 19 July 1333.

X. 1333. 10. MARY, *suo jure* COUNTESS OF MENTEITH, da. and sole heir of Earl Alan abovenamed, appears, after the death of Earl Murdoch, to have been recognised in that dignity, being then wife of SIR JOHN GRAHAM, who in her right became EARL OF MENTEITH [S.], and who (as such) resigned the Barony of Barnbougle to the Crown, 2 May 1346. He was taken prisoner by the English at the battle of Durham, 17 Oct. 1346, when, having previously

---

Menteith, by her second husband (see "*Close Rolls*," 19 Ed. I., m. 10), Sir John Russell. Nothing, however, was done in the matter till the Parl. at Scone in 1285 decreed that half the lands should be erected into a Barony for this William, but that the Earldom of Menteith should remain with Walter Stewart. William Comyn *d.* s.p. between the feast of St. Gregory, 1290. and 3 Aug. 1291. His widow *m.* about 1293 Edmund (Hastings), Lord Hastings. See "Hastings" [of Inchmahome in Menteith, Scotland]. Barony (*Hastings*), *cr.* 1299; *ex.* 1314.

(a) "That he was taken at Dunbar, 28 April 1296, in his 76th year, and put to death by Edward I., has been disproved by Lord Hailes, *Annals*, iii, 43." [Wood's "*Douglas.*"]

(b) His yr. br., Sir John Menteith, was ancestor of a numerous race of that name, among whom was Sir John Menteith, of Strathgartney, co. Perth, who by his wife, Lady Elyne of Mar, da. of Gratney, Earl of Mar [S.], was great grandfather of Robert (Erskine), Earl of Mar [S.] See tabular pedigree, p. 224, note "c," *sub* "Mar."

(c) Patent Rolls.

(d) His da. and h. *suc.* to the Earldom in 1333: her claim thereto, owing probably to her minority in 1309, being postponed to that of her uncle the heir male.

(e) His relationship (previously unknown) to his predecessor is settled by a charter (quoted in Fraser's "*Red Book of Menteith*," vol. i., p. 95) where he describes himself as Earl of Menteith, son of Sir Alexander, formerly Earl of Menteith.

(f) Giving divers lands to her as "consanguinese suæ, Marie de Menteth, filiæ unicæ quondam Alani, Comitis de Menteth." [Wood's "*Douglas.*"]

(g) Alice, "Countess of Meneteth," to whom King Edward III. granted sums of money from 24 Sep. 1335, to 20 Feb. 1340 (reciting that she "infra regnum nostrum ad fidem nostram moratur") was probably his widow.

sworn fealty to King Edward III. he suffered death as a traitor in Feb. 1346/7. He *d.* s.p.m. The Countess was living 15 Aug. 1352,(a) and not improbably as late 1360,(b) tho' dead before 1361.

XI. 1360? *11.* MARGARET, *suo jure* COUNTESS OF MENTEITH [S.], only da. and h. She *m.* firstly (dispensation 21 Nov. 1348), John MORAY, of Bothwell, who *d.* s.p. 1352. She *m.* secondly (disp. 15 Aug. 1352, and again 1354), Thomas, EARL OF MAR [S.] from whom she was divorced in or before 1360 or 1361. She, or possibly her mother(c) had dispensation 18 April 1360 to marry (and pardon for having "*olim*" contracted marriage with) John DRUMMOND. Finally(d) she had dispensation 9 Sep. 1361 to marry Robert STEWART, afterwards EARL OF FIFE and DUKE OF ALBANY [S.], and sometime **Regent of Scotland**. To him who *d.* 3 Sep. 1419, she was first wife.

XII. 1390? to 1425. *12.* MURDOCH (STEWART), EARL OF MENTEITH, s. and h.; *suc.* his mother in that dignity. He, subsequently, 3 Sep. 1419, *suc.* his father as DUKE OF ALBANY, &c. [S.], and as **Regent of Scotland**. He was *beheaded* 24 May 1425, when, having been attainted, *all his honours* were *forfeited.*

For fuller particulars see "ALBANY" Dukedom [S.], *cr.* 1398; *forfeited* 1425.

XIII. 1425, or 1427. *1.* MALISE (GRAHAM), EARL OF STRATHERN [S.], only s. and h. of Euphemia, *suo jure* COUNTESS OF STRATHERN [S.], by Sir Patrick GRAHAM,(e) who *jure uxoris* was (1406), EARL OF STRATHERN, which Euphemia, was da. and h. of David (STEWART), EARL OF STRATHERN [S.], the elder of the two sons by the *second* wife(f) of **King Robert II.** [S.] He *suc.* his father 10 Aug. 1418, but was a minor as late as 1425, about which time he was *divested*(g) of the *Earldom of Strathern* [S.], by King James I. [S.] (on the ground that it was a male fee) and, was *cr.* EARL OF MENTEITH [S.], obtaining

---

(a) See note "d," next following.

(b) The arguments that it was she (and not her da., *Margaret*), who *m.* (dispensation and pardon for having formerly ["*olim*"] contracted marriage, dated 18 April 1360), John Drummond (the word "Margaret" being conjectured to be a misprint for "Mary") are very ably put forward by "*Sigma*" in "N. and Q.," 7th s. X, 163, where is quoted a charter, 30 March 1372, of King Robert II. [S.] confirming (*Reg. Mag. Sig.*, 113, 3), the donation which "*Maria*, Comitissa de Menteth, fecit et concessit Joh'ni de Dromond;" a donation more likely to be made on her *own* marriage than on the third re-marriage of her daughter.

(c) See note "b" next above.

(d) In the four dispensations the lady is thus (severally) described, *viz.*, (1) In 1348 as Margaret, da. of John Graham, Earl of Menteith. (2) In 1352 as Margaret, widow of John de Moravia, while (3 and 4) in 1360 and 1361, she is called Margaret, Countess of Menteith. Mr. Burnett (Exch. Rolls [S.], vol. iv. clxxv-clxxvii), argues, therefrom, her succession to her mother Mary, in that Earldom as being between 1352 and 1360.

(e) He was yr. br. of the half blood of Sir William Graham, of Kincardine, *cr.* about 1415, Lord Graham who was ancestor of the Earls and Dukes of Montrose [S.]

(f) The questionable legitimacy of that King's children by his *first* wife, gave the heir of line of the *second* marriage a not unplausible pretext for a claim to the throne and was the cause of constant jealousy between them and the reigning family, the issue of the *first* marriage. See p. 301, note "a."

(g) This unjust deprivation is usually said to have been one of the causes of the assassination of King James I. [S.], and it is said that when King James VI. [S.], was solicited to bestow the Earldom of Strathern he replied "that he had nothing else for the murder of King James I." See some interesting remarks thereon in appendix vi. (pp. xiv-xv.) of Sir Harris Nicolas's "Earldoms of Strathern, Monteith and Airth."

charter thereof, 6 Sep. 1427,(a) with rem. to heirs male of his body. Under that designation he went to England as a hostage, 9 Dec. 1427, whence he was not released till 17 June 1453. He *m.*(b) Marion. He *d.* between Dec. 1485 and May 1491. His widow *m.* John DRUMMOND.

XIV. 1490? 2. ALEXANDER (GRAHAM), EARL OF MENTEITH [S.], grandson and h., being s. and h. of Patrick GRAHAM, by Isobel, da. of Thomas (ERSKINE), LORD ERSKINE, which Patrick, who was 3d but (after 19 Oct. 1478) 1st surv. s, & h. ap. of Earl Malise, *d.* v.p.(c) He was served heir to his grandfather, 6 July 1493, and was present in Parl. 10 July 1525. He *m.* Margaret, da, of Walter BUCHANAN, of Buchanan. He *d.* between 1531 and 1540.

XV. 1535? 3. WILLIAM (GRAHAM), EARL OF MENTEITH [S.], s. and h.,(d) was present in Parl., 10 Dec. 1540, and probably 14 March 1541, and 4 and 15 Dec. 1543.(e) He *m.* Margaret, da. of John MOUBRAY, of Barnbougal. "Little is known of this 3d Earl: he met a tragical death in 1543"(g) traditionally in a clan fight in 1543 or 1544 (before 7 April 1544) with the Tutor of Appin, whose men had carried off the dinner just cooked for him.

XVI. 1544? 4. JOHN (GRAHAM), EARL OF MENTEITH [S.], s. and h.,(f) who possibly was present in Parl., 14 March 1541, and 4 and 15 Dec. 1543,(e) and certainly from 26 June 1545, to Aug. 1560.(h) He was taken prisoner at the rout of the Solway in Nov. 1542 but ransomed in July 1543. He *m.* Marion, 1st da. of George (SETON), 4th LORD SETON [S.], by his first wife, Elizabeth, da. of John (HAY), LORD HAY OF YESTER [S.] He *d.* 1564. His widow *m.* soon afterwards (as his third wife) John (GORDON), EARL OF SUTHERLAND [S.], and *d.* (as did her then husband) from poison in July 1567.

XVII. 1564. 5. WILLIAM (GRAHAM), EARL OF MENTEITH [S.], only s. and h., was present in Parl. from July 1567 to March 1574.(i) He *m.* about May 1571, when he was under age, Margaret, Dow. BARONESS CRICHTON

(a) The earliest proof of the creation of the Earldom that was produced at "the decreet of ranking" (1606) was a charter, 8 Feb. 1466, "*Comiti de Monteith*" erecting the town and port of that name into a free town.

(b) His marriage with "Lady Anne Vere, da. of Henry, Earl of Oxford" (as given in Wood's "Douglas") or with "Jane Rochford" (as elsewhere stated) rests on no proof whatever; neither indeed was there *any* Earl of Oxford named "Henry" at that date.

(c) Earl Malise had 5 sons, *viz.* (1) Alexander, a hostage in England, June 1413, who *d.* v.p. and s.p. before 7 April 1469, when (2) John is called the 1st s. and received the lands of Kilbryde. He *d.* v.p. and s.p.m. (3) Patrick, mentioned in the text; (4) John, the younger, living 1485-94, of whom (says Fraser) "nothing is known," and (5) Walter, living 1485-94, said to be ancestor of the Grahams of Boquhaple. Sir William Fraser ("*Red Book of Menteith*" I. 299) evidently discredits the alleged descent of the family of Graham of Netherby, Preston, &c., from one of these sons.

(d) From his yr. br., Walter, the Grahams of Gartur (extinct in the male line in 1818) claim descent.

(e) "The Earl of Monteith" was present in Parl. on those dates (1541 and 1543), but no christian name being given, it is not clear whether Earl William is meant, or Earl John his s. and h.

(f) From his yr. br., Gilbert, the Grahams of Gartmore claim descent. Those in 1644 sold that estate to William Graham of Polder, afterwards Sir William Graham of Gartmore.

(g) Fraser's "*Red Book of Menteith*," I. p. 310. See also Scott's "*Tales of a Grandfather.*"

(h) *John*, Earl of Monteith, was present in Parl. in Aug. 1560; but it is stated in Wood's "*Douglas*" that he was killed Oct. 1547. This, more probably, refers to his father, Earl William, tho', if so, it should, apparently, be Oct. 1543.

(i) In Nicolas's "*Earldoms of Strathern*," &c., it is said that he was in Parl. on "23 March 1578" (when a resolution concerning him was passed) but "was certainly dead in Oct. 1587."

of Sanquhar [S.], da. of Sir James Douglas, of Drumlanrig, by his second wife, Christian, da. of John Montgomery, Master of Eglintoun. He *d.* probably in 1579 but certainly before Oct. 1587. His widow *m.* thirdly (—) Wauchope, of Niddry.

XVIII. 1580? 6. John (Graham), Earl of Menteith [S.], only s. and h.; served heir of his father, 29 Oct. 1587, being then a minor. He *m.* (contract 22 Oct. 1587) Mary, 3d da. of Sir Colin Campbell, of Glenorchy, by Catharine, da. of William (Ruthven), Lord Ruthven [S.] He *d.* Dec. 1598.

XIX. 1598. 7. William (Graham), Earl of Menteith [S.], s. and h.; *b.* 1589; served heir to his father, 7 Aug. 1610, being then of full age; P.C. [S.], and, having ingratiated himself at Court, Lord Justice General [S.], 1628-33; an extra. Lord of Session, 1628-32, and President of the Privy Council [S.], 1629-33. Being anxious to assert his hereditary right to the *Earldom of Strathern* [S.] as heir of line(a) to Prince David, son of King Robert II. [S.], he was on 25 May 1630, served heir of line to the said David, Earl of Strathern. Having renounced all claim to the lands belonging thereto, save the lands of Kilbride, he was on 31 July 1631, confirmed in that dignity by Royal charter "to him and his heirs male and of entail, directing that he and they should thereafter be styled Earls of Strathern and Menteith" [S.](b) He is accordingly designed "EARL OF STRATHERN AND MENTEITH, LORD KINPONT AND KILBRYDE"(c) [S.], in a charter of the lands and Barony of Airth, co. Stirling, dated 21 July 1632. This right, however, to the peerage of Strathern was very shortly afterwards taken from him by the Court of Session, which, on 22 March 1633, set aside the retour of 25 Aug. 1630, on the [erroneous] ground that David, Earl of Strathern (to whom that retour has served him heir as "*abavus atavi*") had died without issue. The King accordingly revoked the Royal charter, 31 July 1631, which confirmed the said Earldom of Strathern) and by patent 28 March 1633 (the warrant being dat. at Whitehall 21 Jan. preceding) erected the lands and Barony of Airth into an Earldom and united it with the Earldom of Menteith, declaring its precedency to be that which was due to that Earldom, therein defined as having been *cr.*, 6 Sept. 1428,(d) and

---

(a) As such heir of line it was considered that a claim to the Crown was foreshadowed, and, indeed, he was accused of having said that he had "the reddest blood in Scotland." It, also, is to be observed that in his renunciation of right to such ancestral lands as the Crown had appropriated he reserved "the right and dignity of *blood* pertaining to him as the heir of David, Earl of Strathern." The facts of the case were these:—By the death s.p.m. of King James V. [S.] on 14 Dec 1542, the issue male of King Robert II. [S.] became extinct. That King had procured an act of Parl. in 1373 entailing the Crown on his five surviving sons (the three elder by Elizabeth Mure and the two younger by Euphemia Ross) *nominatim* (so that no question as the legitimacy of the elder sons would have any effect) and to their issue in tail male, failing which the remainder was *to his heirs whomsoever*. Mary, Queen of Scots accordingly succeeded in 1542 to the Crown as *such* heir. Had her cousin, John (Stewart), Duke of Albany [S.], lived but six or seven years longer (he *d.* in 1536) *he*, who was paternal grandson of King James II. [S.] (and *not* Mary) would have succeeded to the Scotch Crown. The question of the legitimacy of the issue of King Robert by Elizabeth Mure became of vital importance, only when his heir *general* had been to be ascertained. If the three elder sons were illegitimate, Queen Mary's claim, which was thro' one of them, was nowhere, and the *heir of line of David, Earl of Strathern* [S.] (the eldest son of King Robert, by Euphemia Ross), *was entitled to the throne*. The then Earl of Menteith, who, in Dec 1542 was *this* heir, was, however, at that time (1542-43) a prisoner in England and did not on his return, as neither did his son or grandson, take any steps to urge such claim, which was put forward by his great grandson, in 1630, nearly 90 years after it had accrued.

(b) "*Hewlett*," p. 71, &c., and Riddell's "*Scotch Peerage Law*" (1833), p. [illegible]

(c) Kinpont is in co. Linlithgow and Kilbryde is in co. Perth.

(d) This date is, oddly enough, in error as to a year; it should be 6 Sep. 1427. In right of this clause of precedency the Earl of Menteith (who in the "Decreet of Ranking" had been ranked under the date of 1466) was (subsequently) placed next *below* "Mar" and next *above* "Rothes" (*cr.* 1457) as appears in the records of Parl. 1639.

"ordained the said Earl and his heirs to be called in all time coming EARLS OF AIRTH [S.] and to bruik and enjoy the honours, dignity, and precedence due to them by virtue of the said charter granted to the said Malise, Earl of Menteith, before all others."(a) After this date he was styled EARL OF AIRTH AND MENTEITH [S.], obtaining a new investiture of the lands of the Earldom which by charter, 11 Jan. 1644, was confirmed to himself in life rent, with rem. to John, his s. and h. ap. and his heirs male whatever.(b) He m. (settl. 30 Jan. 1610/1), Agnes, da. of Patrick (GRAY), LORD GRAY [S.] She was living Jan. 1644. He d. between Jan. 1661 and 14 July, 1662.(c)

[JOHN GRAHAM, *styled* LORD KINPONT, or LORD GRAHAM OF KINPONT, s. and h. ap. He m. April 1632 Mary, 1st da. of William (KEITH), 6th EARL MARISCHAL. He joined (with 400 Royalists) Montrose, at whose victory, 1 Sep. 1644, at Tippermuir, he was present, and in whose camp at Collace, co. Perth, he was basely murdered.(d) He *d.* v.p.]

XX. 1660? to 1694. 8. WILLIAM (GRAHAM), EARL OF AIRTH AND MENTEITH [S.], grandson and h., being s. and h. of John GRAHAM, *styled* LORD KINPONT, and Mary, his wife, both abovenamed He *suc. to the peerage* [S.] before Oct. 1662(c) and sat in Parl. as "*Earl of Airth*" from July 1670 to April 1685, but in April 1693 as "*Earl of Monteith*," having, after the expulsion of the Stuart Kings, so styled himself. Being greatly in debt and having no issue, he was desirous of resigning his peerage dignities as well as his estates in favour of the Marquess of Montrose [S.] (the chief of the house of Graham) and his issue, and obtained a Royal warrant in May 1680 to that effect, but it was ratified by Parl., 6 Sep. 1681, only so far as concerned the *territorial* Earldom of Menteith, the Crown being "unwilling to alter the settled course of succession of the *titles* of honour of the Earl of Monteith and Airth and others contained in his [the Earl's] patent." He m. firstly Anne HEWES, from whom, on 2 Jan. 1683/4, he obtained a divorce for her adultery.(e) He m. secondly (whilst this cause was pending) Catherine, da. of Thomas BRUCE, of Blairhall, co. Perth. She d. before him. He d. s.p., 12 Sep. 1694, and was *bur.* with his ancestors in the Isle of Inchmahome in the loch of Monteith. After his death *all his honours* became *dormant* or *extinct.*

(a) Possibly this was for the purpose of getting rid of the title of Menteith as being one which in some measure (tho' of course not so much as in the case of Strathern) was connected with Royal descent.

(b) He sat in Parl. in Jan. 1621, April 1629, and Aug. 1631, as Earl of *Monteith*; in Sep. 1631, April and Sep. 1632, as *Earl of Strathern*, and in Aug. 1639 and possibly May 1662 as *Earl of Airth*. "After his creation to the Earldom of Airth he never used the title of Monteith except in conjunction with the title of Airth." [Nicolas's "*Earldoms of Strathern*," &c.]

(c) The death of the 7th Earl "must have taken place before, possibly many years before, 1663, for his grandaughter, Lady Mary Graham, when she was m. to Sir John Allardice in Oct. 1662 was certainly *sister* to the then Earl of Airth. See the contract of marriage in the *Evidence in the Airth case*, p. 32, and the entry of the marriage in the parish register of Arbuthnot, *ibid*, p. 68," as quoted in Craik's "*Romance of the Peerage*," vol. iii, where is an interesting account of the Earldom of Menteith and where (p. 388, *note*), Nicolas's blunder of assuming that the 7th Earl lived till 1670 is commented upon.

(d) The perpetrator was James Stewart, of Ardvoirlich, whose pardon for the same was ratified Jan. 1645 and who became a Major in Argyll's Foot in 1648. See Scott's "*Legend of Montrose*" (who, erroneously, represents Lord Kilpont *as* Earl of Monteith) and the notes thereto, including one from Robert Stewart, of Ardvoirlich.

(e) The evidence against her was by *women* witnesses only, and "this judgment appears to have been opposed to the almost uniform tenor of precedent." See Craik's "*Romance*" as in note "c" next above.

[The question of heirship is in this case a difficult matter. The issue *male* of the 3d Earl and subsequent Earls appears to be extinct, but male descendants of the 1st and possibly of the 2d Earl not improbably exist. With respect to the heir *general*, the seniority of the two elder([a]) sisters of the 8th Earl was doubtful, but the issue of one (Lady Elizabeth Graham) became extinct in 1803, so that the heir of line of the other sister (Lady Mary Allardice) would be such heir. The dignity was, however, assumed as below.]

XXI. *1744,* *to* *1783.* 9. WILLIAM GRAHAM, younger of the two sons of William GRAHAM, of Edinburgh, Writer to the Signet, by Mary, only da. and h. of James HODGE, of Gladsmuir, by Mary, sister of Sir John GRAHAM, Bart. (who was cognosced insane in 1696, and who *d.* July 1708), and the only child that had issue of Sir William GRAHAM, Bart., of Gartmore, by Elizabeth, one of the two elder sisters of William (GRAHAM), 8th EARL OF MENTEITH [S.], abovenamed, was *b.* about 1715; *suc.* his elder br. (James Graham) before May 1740; assumed the title of EARL OF MENTEITH [S.], on the presumption (1) that his maternal great grandmother, the abovenamed Elizabeth, was *eldest* of the sisters of William, EARL OF AIRTH AND MENTEITH [S.], and (2) that the *Earldom of Menteith* was destined to the heir of line. He *voted as such Earl* at the election of Peers [S.], in Oct. 1744, Aug. 1747, March 1749, July and Nov. 1752, and May 1761, but his assumption of that dignity was prohibited by an order of the House of Lords, 2 March 1762, tho' he, notwithstanding, continued to make use of the same. He, who was called "the beggar Earl," and who subsisted by charity, *d.* unm., 30 June 1783,([b]) a wanderer by the way-side at Bonhill, and was *bur.* there,([c]) aged about 70.

([a]) There was a third sister, Catherine, who *m.* (—) Sellick and had two daughters both living in 1717, and one as late as 1783.

([b]) He had three sisters all of whom *d.* before him, two of them dying s.p., but one, Mary, wife of John Bogle (who *d.* 1 May 1787, at a great age), left one son and two daughters. Of these three children, Grisell *d.* unm. before 1802, but John Bogle, the son, who was a miniature portrait painter in Edinburgh and London, represented his maternal great-great grandmother (his mother's mother's mother) Elizabeth, one of the two sisters of the last Earl of Airth and Menteith, and any claim accruing thro' her to the Menteith Earldom. He *d.* s.p. in Edinburgh in 1803, when Mary (who styled herself "Lady Mary Bogle") his only surv. sister, became such representative. She *d.* unm. 12 Nov. 1821, when the issue of the said Lady Elizabeth Graham became extinct.

([c]) In 1834, the Earldom of Airth, and in 1840, the Earldoms of Strathern and Menteith were claimed by Robert Barclay-Allardice, s. and h. of Robert Barclay-Allardice (formerly Barclay) of Urie. co. Kincardine, by Sarah Ann (*d.* 1833, aged 76) da. and h. of James Allardice, of Allardice (*d.* 1765, aged 38), s. and and h. of another James A. (*d.* 1728, aged 35), s. and h. of Sir George Allardice (*d.* 1709, aged 37), the only s. that had issue of Sir John Allardice (*d.* 1676), by Mary (formerly Lady Mary Graham, Spinster) one of the sisters of the last Earl of Airth and Menteith. The said lady Mary Allardice (who *d.* in 1720, having survived both her sons) always asserted her right to be Countess of Menteith, as *eldest* of the sisters and coheirs of the late Earl. Her issue since the extinction of the issue of her sister (Lady Elizabeth Graham), in 1821 are, since that date, the undoubted *heir of line*, even if not the *sole* heir to the said Earl. Her great-great-great grandson, Robert Barclay-Allardice abovenamed, the claimant in 1834 and 1840 to the Earldoms as above stated, *d.* in 1854, but the claim was continued by Margaret his only da. and h. (Mrs. Barclay-Allardice) and was heard in 1870 and 1871, tho' no decision thereon was made. The claim was opposed by William Cunninghame Bontine, formerly Graham, of Ardoch and Gartmore as heir male of the body of the 1st Earl of Menteith, thro' Sir John Graham of Kilbryde, the second son of that Earl.

MERCHISTOUN.

See "NAPIER OF MERCHISTOUN," Barony [S.] (*Napier*), *cr.* 1627.

MEREDYTH OF DOLLARDSTOWN.

i.e., "MEREDYTH OF DOLLARDSTOWN, co. Meath," Barony (*Somerville*), *cr.* 1866; see "ATHLUMNEY OF SOMERVILLE AND DOLLARDSTOWN," Barony [I.], *cr.* 1863.

MERYON.

See "FITZWILLIAM OF MERYON," Viscountcy [I.], (*Fitzwilliam*) *cr.* 1629; *ex.* 1833.

MERTON.

i.e., "MERTON OF TRAFALGAR AND OF MERTON, co. Surrey," Viscountcy; also "NELSON OF TRAFALGAR AND OF MERTON, co. Surrey," Earldom (*Nelson*), both *cr.* 1805.

METCALFE OF FERN HILL.

Barony. I. 1845 to 1846.

1. THE RT. HON. SIR CHARLES-THEOPHILUS METCALFE, Bart., G.C.B., 2d s. of Sir Thomas METCALFE, 1st Bart. (so *cr.* 21 Dec. 1802), of Fern Hill, in Winkfield, Berks, by Susanna Selina Sophia, da. and coheir of John DEBONNAIRE, of the Cape of Good Hope, was *b.* 30 Jan. 1785; went to India as "writer" in 1800; first Assistant to the Resident at Delhi, 1806; Dep. Sec. to the Gov. Gen., 1809; Resident at Delhi, 1811; at Hyderabad, 1820; *suc. to the Baronetcy* on the death, 15 Aug. 1822, of his br., the 2d Bart.; Member of the Council, 1827; President of the Board of Revenue, 1828; Gov. of the Presidency of Agra, 1834; Gov. GEN. OF INDIA (provisionally), 1835; G.C.B., 14 March 1835; Lieut. Gov. of the North Western Provinces, 1836-38; P.C., 1839; Gov. of Jamaica, 1839, and Gov. GEN. OF CANADA, New Brunswick, &c., 1843-45. He was *cr.*, 25 Jan. 1845, BARON METCALFE OF FERN HILL, co. Berks. He *d.* unm., 12 Sep. 1846, aged 61, at Malshanger, near Basingstoke, Hants, when the *peerage* became *extinct*, but the Baronetcy devolved on his br. and h. Will pr. Sep. 1846.

METHELL.

i.e., "ELCHO AND METHELL," Barony [S.] (*Wemyss*), *cr.* 1633, with the EARLDOM OF WEMYSS [S.], which see.

METHLICK.

i.e., "HADDO, METHLICK TARVES AND KELLIE," Barony [S.] (*Gordon*), *cr.* 1682, with the EARLDOM OF ABERDEEN [S.], which see.

METHUEN OF CORSHAM.

Barony. I. 1838.

1. PAUL METHUEN, of Corsham Court, Wilts, s. and h. of Paul Cobb METHUEN,(a) of the same by Matilda, da. of Sir Thomas GOOCH, 3d Bart. of Benacre, Suffolk, was *b.* 21 June and *bap.* 17 July 1779, at St. Marylebone; mat. at Oxford (Ch. Ch.), 26 Jan. 1797; *suc.* his father, Sep. 1816; was M.P. for Wilts (in the Tory interest), 1812-19, and (in the Whig interest) for North Wilts from 1833 to 1837, when, having lost his

(a) His father, Paul Methuen, inherited Corsham from his cousin the Rt. Hon. Sir Paul Methuen (who *d.* unm. in 1757), who was s. and h. of John Methuen (Lord Chancellor of Ireland, 1697—1703). well known as the author of the Methuen treaty with Portugal. The said Paul (first above named) received Royal lic., 11 May 1775, for himself and his heirs to bear the arms of Methuen "on the breast of an eagle with two heads displayed, *sable*."

re-election, he was *cr.* 13 July 1838,(a) BARON METHUEN OF CORSHAM, co. Wilts. He *m.* 3 July 1810, Jane Dorothea, da. of Sir Henry Paulet St. John Mildmay, *formerly* St. John, 3d Bart., by Jane, 1st da. and coheir of Carew Mildmay, of Shawford, Hants. She *d.* 15 March 1846, aged 58, at 128 Park street, Grosvenor square. He *d.* there, 14 Sep. 1849, aged 70. Will pr. Nov. 1849.

II. 1849. 2. Frederick Henry Paul (Methuen), Baron Methuen of Corsham, 2d but 1st surv. s. and h.; *b.* 23 Feb. and *bap.* 16 Nov. 1818, at Corsham; sometime an officer in the army, but retired in 1842; *suc. to the peerage*, 14 Sep. 1849; Militia Aide-de-Camp to the Queen with rank of Colonel, 1860; a Lord in Waiting, 1859-66, 1868-74, 1880-85, and from Feb. to Aug. 1886. He *m.*, 14 Oct. 1844, at St. Geo. Han. sq., Anna Horatia Caroline, da. of the Rev. John Sanford, of Nynehead, Somerset. He *d.* 26 Sep. 1891, aged 73, at Corsham Court. His widow living 1893.

III. 1891. 3. Paul Sanford (Methuen), Baron Methuen of Corsham, s. and h., *b.* 1 Sep. 1845; entered the army (Scots Fusileer Guards, of which he was Lieut. Col., 1876-81), becoming, in 1890, Major General; Military Attaché at Berlin, 1877-80; Quarter Master Gen. for the Home district, 1881-84; Commandant in the Egypt expedition, 1882; C.B., 1882; in command of the Bechuanaland field force, 1885; C.M.G., 1886; Dep. Adj. Gen. in South Africa, 1888-91; *suc. to the peerage*, 26 Sep. 1891; in command of the Home district, 1892. He *m.* firstly, 18 June 1878, at Alderbury, Wilts, Evelyn, da. of Sir Frederick Hutchinson Hervey-Bathurst, 3d Bart., by his second wife, Clare Emily, da. of Sir Richard Brooke, 6th Bart., of Norton. She *d.* s.p., 2 June 1879, at Cannes, in France. He *m.* secondly, 9 Jan. 1884, Mary Ethel, 2d da. of William Ayshford Sanford, of Nynehead, Somerset, by Sarah Elizabeth Harriet, 1st da. of Lord Arthur Charles Hervey, Bishop of Bath and Wells.

Family Estates.—These, in 1883, consisted of 5,542 acres in Wiltshire, worth £10,208 a year. *Principal Residence.* Corsham Court, near Chippenham, Wilts.

METHVEN.

Barony [S.] I. 1528. 1. Henry Stewart, 2d s. of Andrew, Lord Avondale [S.], by Margaret, da. of Sir John Kennedy, of Blairquhan, was *b.* about 1495. He *m.* firstly "the Lady Leslie,"(b) who *d.* or was divorced before March 1527/8, in which month he *m.* Margaret, **Queen Dowager**, and sometime **Queen Regent of Scotland**, the divorced(c) wife of Archibald (Douglas), Earl of Angus [S.], formerly Lady Margaret Tudor, 1st da. of **King Henry VII.**, by Elizabeth ("*of York*"), his Queen. By her, who was *b.* 29 and *bap.* 30 Nov. 1489, at Westm. Abbey, he had previously in 1524 been appointed Treasurer and Lord Chancellor [S.], and with her he acquired the lands of Methven, and Balquhidder, co. Perth, being *cr.* (by her son, the young King James V. [S.]), 17 July 1528,(d) LORD METHVEN [S.] She, by whom he had no child

(a) This was one of the coronation peerages of Queen Victoria, for a list of which see vol ii, p. 145, note "b," *sub* "Carew."

(b) See the "*Stuarts of Castle Stewart,*" p. 136, where it is added that by her "he had a son killed at Pinkie." This doubtless was "John Stewart, son of Lord Methven, recorded as receiving a pardon for holding heretical opinions in March 1540," and who as "*Master of Methven*" was slain v.p. at the battle of Pinkie, 10 Sep. 1547. [Green's "*Princesses,*" vol. iv, p. 505, note 3.]

(c) The sentence from Rome was dat. 11 March 1526/7, but its arrival in Scotland was not till late in 1527. The ground was that Angus had plighted his troth to another woman (Jane Douglas, of Traquair), and, therefore, that the marriage was invalid, tho' the issue legitimate.

(d) Methven was the only peerage conferred during the reign (1513—1542) of James V. [S.] It is remarkable that there were but four peerages—(1) the Earldom of Moray, (2) the Barony of Torpichen, (3) the Dukedom of Albany (including the Earldom of Ross, bestowed on the same person a few days previous), and (4) the

that survived infancy, *d.* at Methven, 18 Oct. 1541, in her 53d year, and was *bur.* in state at the Carthusian Monastery of St. John, in Perth. He *m.* thirdly, before 5 June 1545, Jonet,(a) widow, or divorced wife, of Sir Hugh KENNEDY, relict (1529) of Alexander GORDON, Master of Sutherland, 1st da. of John (STEWART), 2d EARL OF ATHOLE [S.], by Mary, da. of Archibald (CAMPBELL), 2d EARL OF ARGYLL [S.] He was living, 10 Oct. 1551, but *d.* soon afterwards. His widow *m.* (as her 4th husband) contract, 9 April 1557, Patrick (RUTHVEN), 3d LORD RUTHVEN [S.], who *d.* 13 June 1566, aged about 46.

II. 1555? 2. HENRY (METHVEN), LORD METHVEN [S.], only surv. s. and h., by third wife; *b.* before his parent's marriage but subsequently in 1551 (Privy Seal Record) legitimated; *suc. to the peerage* [S.] about 1555. He *m.* Jean, 1st da. of (his step father) Patrick (RUTHVEN), 3d LORD RUTHVEN [S.], by his first wife, Janet DOUGLAS, illegit. da. of Archibald, EARL OF ANGUS [S.] He *d.* 3 March 1571/2, being killed by a cannon-shot from Edinburgh Castle. His widow *m.* (as second of his three wives) Andrew (LESLIE), 5th EARL OF ROTHES [S.], who *d.* 1611.

III. 1572, to 1580? 3. HENRY (METHVEN), LORD METHVEN [S.], only s. and h., *suc. to the peerage* [S.], 3 March 1571/2. He *m.* (—), da. of Henry STEWART, 2d s. of James STEWART, *cr.* EARL OF ARRAN [S.], in 1581. He *d.* s.p. probably about 1580(b) when the *peerage* became *extinct.*

---

i.e., "METHVEN(b) OF TORBOLTON" [or "TORBOLTON"], Barony [S.] (*Lennox*), *cr.* with the DUKEDOM OF LENNOX [S.], 1675; see "RICHMOND" Dukedom, *cr.* 1675.

MEXBOROUGH OF LIFFORD.

Earldom [I.] I. 1766. 1. SIR JOHN SAVILE, K.B., only s. and h. of Charles SAVILE, of Methley Hall, co. York, by Alathea, 2d and yst. da. and coheir of Gilbert MILLINGTON, of Felley Priory, Notts, was *b.* at Thrybergh, co. York, Dec. 1719; *suc.* his father, 5 June 1741; M.P. for Heydon, co. York, 1747-54, and for Shoreham, 1761-68; K.B., 23 June 1749; LL.D. Cambridge (King's Coll.), 1749; was *cr.*, 8 Nov. 1753, BARON POLLINGTON, co. Longford [I.], and subsequently, 11 Feb. 1766, VISCOUNT POLLINGTON OF FERNS and EARL MEXBOROUGH OF LIFFORD, co. Donegal [I.], taking his seat, 17 Oct. 1769. He *m.*, 20 Jan. 1760, at the house of Lady Milbank, in Argyle street, St. James' Westm., Sarah, sister of John Hussey, 1st BARON DELAVAL OF SEATON DELAVAL, yst. da. of Francis Blake DELAVAL, by Rhoda, da. of Robert APREECE, of Washingley, co. Huntingdon. He *d.* 17 and was *bur.* 27 Feb. 1778, at Methley, aged 58. Will pr. 1778. His widow, who was *b.* 14 March 1742 (being 22 years his junior) *m.*, 4 May 1780, Rev. Sandford HARDCASTLE, who *d.* 24 Oct. 1788. She *d.* 9 Aug. 1821, in Dover street. Will dat. 11 Feb. 1815, to 27 June 1821, pr. 22 Sep. 1821.

Dukedom of Orkney (of which the last two were conferred respectively on the Queen's then Consort), granted (1542—1567) during the succeeding reign of Queen Mary. In fact, for a period of above sixty years (1510—1572), only *five* persons received peerage dignities, of whom only *three* (Methven, Moray, and Torpichen) were first raised to peerage rank.

(a) She, who was often called "Countess [*i.e.*, *Domina*], of Sutherland" (in right of her first husband, "the Master of Sutherland"), was celebrated for her beauty and (like other members of her race) profligacy. Her four "adulterous" children (one son and three daughters) by Lord Methven were all born before their marriage. ["Riddell," p. 582, note 1.]

(b) "The Lordship of Methven and Barony of Balquhidder were granted to Ludovick, Duke of Lennox, in 1584." [Wood's "Douglas."]

II. 1778. 2. JOHN (SAVILE), EARL MEXBOROUGH OF LIFFORD, &c. [I.], s. and h., b. 8 April 1761; *styled* VISCOUNT POLLINGTON, 1766-78; *suc. to the peerage* [I.], 12 Feb. 1778; M.P. for Lincoln, 1808-12. He *m.*, 30 Sep. 1782, at St. Geo. Han. sq., Elizabeth (then a minor) only da. and h. of Henry STEPHENSON, of East Burnham, Bucks, and of Cox Lodge, near Newcastle-on-Tyne, by Sarah, his wife. She, who was *b.* 25 April 1762, *d.* in Piccadilly 7 and was *bur.* 18 June 1821, in Westm. Abbey, aged 59. Admon. (under £1,500) 5 July 1821, and April 1830. He *d.* 3 Feb. 1830, at Methley Park, aged 68. Will pr. March 1830.

III. 1830. 3. JOHN (SAVILE), EARL MEXBOROUGH OF LIFFORD, &c. [I.], only s. and h., *b.* [illegible] July 1783, in Dover street; *styled* VISCOUNT POLLINGTON till 1830; ed. at Trin. Coll. Cambridge; M.A., 1803; M.P. for Pontefract, 1807-26, and 1831-32; *suc. to the peerage* [I.], 3 Feb. 1830. He *m.*, 29 Aug. 1807, at St. James' Westm., Anne, 1st da. of Philip (YORKE), 3d EARL OF HARDWICKE, by Elizabeth, da. of James (LINDSAY), 5th EARL OF BALCARRES [S.] He *d.* in Portman square, 25 Dec. 1860, aged 77. His widow, who was *b.* 13 April 1783, *d.* 17 July 1870, at Brighton, aged 87. Will pr. under £25,000.

IV. 1860. 4. JOHN CHARLES GEORGE [illegible]), EARL MEXBOROUGH OF LIFFORD [1766], VISCOUNT [illegible] FERNS [1766], and BARON POLLINGTON [1753], in the peerage of Ireland, [illegible], *b.* 4 June 1810, in Dover street afsd.; *styled* VISCOUNT POLLINGTON, 1830-[illegible]; ed. at Eton and at Trin. Coll., Cambridge; M.A., 1830; M.P. for Gatton, 1831-[illegible] Pontefract, 1835-37, and 1841-47; *suc. to the peerage* [I.], 2 Dec. 1860. He *m.* firstly, 24 Feb. 1842, Rachael Katherine, 1st da. of Horatio (WALPOLE), 3d EARL OF ORFORD, by Mary, da. of William Augustus FAWKENER. She, who was *b.* [illegible] Feb. 1824, *d.* (as Viscountess Pollington) 21 June 1854, in Eaton terrace, aged 30.[a] He *m.* secondly, 27 July 1861, at St. Mary's, Bryanston square, Agnes Louise Elizabeth, yst. da. of John RAPHAEL.

[JOHN HORACE SAVILE, *styled* VISCOUNT POLLINGTON, 1st s. and h. ap., by first wife, *b.* 17 June 1843, in Dover street afsd.; ed. at [illegible] and at Trin. Coll., Cambridge; High Sheriff for the West Riding, 1877. He *m.* 27 (or 24) April 1867, at St. Geo. Han. sq., Venetia, 2d surv. da. and coheir [illegible] STANLEY, *afterwards* ERRINGTON, 11th Bart., by Julia, 1st da. of [illegible] Sir John MACDONALD, K.C.B.]

Family Estates.—These, in 1883, consisted of 6,969 acres in the West Riding of Yorkshire; 1,769 in Herts; 527 in Notts, and 269 in Kent. *Total* 9,534 acres, worth £34,565 a year. *Principal Residence.* Methley Park, near Leeds, Yorkshire.

MEYNILL, see "MEINILL."

MICKLETHWAITE OF PORTARLINGTON, and MICKLETHWAITE OF LONGFORD.

Barony [I.] I. 1724. Viscountcy [I.] I. 1727, to 1734.

1. JOSEPH MICKLETHWAITE, of Swine, in Holderness, co. York, 2d s. of Joseph MICKLETHWAITE, of the same, by Constance, da. of Sir Thomas MIDDLETON, of Stansted Montfitchet, co. Essex, *b.* about 1680; sometime Secretary to Earl Stanhope (with whom he was taken prisoner) in Spain; M.P. for Arundel and for Hull; *suc.* his eldest br., the Rt. Hon. Thomas Micklethwaite, in the family estates, 4 April 1718, and was *cr.*, 14 Aug. 1724, BARON MICKLETHWAITE OF PORTARLINGTON, in Queen's county [I.], and subsequently, 6 June 1727, VISCOUNT MICKLETHWAITE OF LONGFORD [I.] He *d.* unm., 16 Jan. 1733/4, and was *bur.* the 26th at Hadley, Midx. M.I. At his death the *title* became *extinct.* Will pr. (by Anne Ewer, spinster, the executrix) March 1734.

(a) He and his first wife are the "Lord and Lady Gaverstock" in Disraeli's "*Coningsby*" (1844.) See "*N. and Q.*" 8th S. iii. 363, where the key to sixty-one of the characters there personated is given.

MIDDLEBIE.

i.e., "DOUGLAS OF KINMONT, MIDDLEBIE AND DORNOCK," Barony [S.] *Douglas*), *cr.* 1682, with the Marquessate, and, again, 1684, with the DUKEDOM OF QUEENSBERRY [S.], which see.(a)

MIDDLESEX (county of.)

Earldom. I. 1622. 1. THE RT. HON. SIR LIONEL CRANFIELD, yr. s. of Thomas CRANFIELD, of London, Citizen and Mercer, by Martha, da. of Vincent RANDILL, also of London, Citizen and Mercer, was *bap.* 13 March 1574/5, at St. Michael's, Bassishaw; became free of the Mercers Company and of the Merchant Adventurers, trading, as such, with considerable success; Receiver of Customs for the counties of Dorset and Somerset, 1605; Lieut. of Dover Castle, 1613; *knighted* at Oatlands, 4 July 1613; Surveyor Gen. of the Customs, 1613-24; was nominated Sheriff of London both in July 1614 and June 1615, but excused from serving; M.P. for Hythe, 1614, and for Arundel, 1621-22; one of the Masters of Request, 1616; Keeper of the Great Wardrobe, 1618-22; Master of the Court of Wards and Liveries, 1619-24; Ch. Commissioner of the Navy, 1619-24; P.C., 1620-25; a Commissioner of the Treasury, Jan. to Dec. 1620. In all these departments he effected great reforms(b) and was accordingly *cr.*, 9 July 1621,(c) BARON CRANFIELD of Cranfield, co. Bedford. He was from Sep. 1621 to May 1624 LORD HIGH TREASURER, being *cr.*, 16 Sep. 1622, EARL OF MIDDLESEX, but, two years later, he was found guilty of mismanagement of the offices of (1) the Wardrobe (2) the Customs (3) the Ordnance, and (4) the Court of Wards, being sentenced, 13 May 1624, to lose all his offices, &c., fined £50,000, and (for two weeks) imprisoned in the Tower.(d) He was, however, restored to his seat in the House of Lords, 4 May 1640. He *m.* firstly, about 1596, Elizabeth, da. of Richard SHEPHERD, of London, Citizen and Grocer, to whom he had been apprenticed. She *d.* s.p.m. before 1619. He *m.* secondly about 1620 Anne, da. of James BRETT, of Hoby, co. Leicester, by Anne (sister of Mary, *suo jure* COUNTESS OF BUCKINGHAM), da. of Anthony BEAUMONT, of Glenfield, co. Leicester. He *d.* 6 and was *bur.* 13 Aug. 1645, in Westm. Abbey. Will dat. 21 Aug. 1642, pr. 4 Oct. 1645. Funeral certificate in Public Record office. His widow possibly re-married Sir (—) ANDERSON.(e) She *d.* 8 and was *bur.* 12 Feb. 1669/70, in Westm. Abbey. Her nunc. will (within a year of her death) as of St. Giles in the fields, pr. 12 June 1670, and 4 Nov. 1674.

II. 1645. 2. JAMES (CRANFIELD), EARL OF MIDDLESEX, &c., s. and h., by second wife; *bap.* 27 Dec. 1621, at Chelsea; *styled* LORD CRANFIELD, 1622-45; M.P. for Liverpool, April to May 1640; *suc. to the peerage*, 6 Aug. 1645. He took the part of the Parl. by whom in 1646, he was made Lord Lieut. of Staffordshire, and in 1647, Keeper of Kingswood forest; was imprisoned in 1647, for acting against the army; Commissioner from the Lords to the King, 1 Aug. 1648, and Joint Commissioner at the Conference of Newport, Sep. to Nov. 1648. He

---

(a) See also vol. iii, p. 160, note "b," *sub* "Douglas."

(b) "In the Household alone he effected an annual saving of £23,000; in the Wardrobe he saved the King at least £14,000 a year." [*Nat. Biog.*]

(c) It was supposed that he would have been appointed Lord Chancellor, in succession to Bacon, against whose abuses he (in 1621) had taken a prominent part.

(d) "The belief that he had been hardly treated was very general," and the impeachment of the Duke of Buckingham, two years later, was unfavourably compared with this one. By that Duke "he complained in his letters, Chelsea House was forced from him, like Naboth's vineyard, and £5,000 in addition demanded." [*Nat. Biog.*] Fuller in his "*Worthies*" calls him, "A proper person, of comely presence, cheerful, yet grave countenance, and surely a solid and wise man."

(e) Among the entries of burials at St. Martin's in the fields occurs on 28 Feb. 1669/70, "*Comitissa Middx et D'na Anderson*," which, however, possibly refers to two distinct persons. This is one of many instances where baptisms, marriages, and burials, are recorded in a parish with which the parties were connected, such record not necessarily implying that the event took place in that parish.

m. 3 March 1645/6, at St. Barth. the Great, London, Anne, 3d da. and coheir of Edward (BOURCHIER), 4th EARL OF BATH, by his first wife, Dorothy, da. of Oliver (ST. JOHN), 3d LORD ST. JOHN. He d. s.p.m.,(a) and was bur. 13 Sep. 1651, in Westm. Abbey. Will dat. 7, and pr. 16 Sep. 1651. His widow m. Sir Chichester WREY, 3d Bart., of Trebitch, to whom she brought the estate of Tawstock, Devon, and who was bur. 17 May, 1668, at St. Giles in the fields. She was bur. at St. Giles afsd., 9 Sep. 1662.

III. 1651, to 1674, 3. LIONEL (CRANFIELD), EARL OF MIDDLESEX [1622], and BARON CRANFIELD [1621], br. and h. male; b. about 1625; suc. to the peerage, 13 Sep. 1651; was one of the six peers sent to Charles II. to invite his return; a Gent. of the Bedchamber, 1673. He m. 1 May 1657, at St. Bride's, London (publication at St. Giles in the fields), Rachael, Dow. COUNTESS OF BATH, da. of Francis (FANE), 1st EARL OF WESTMORLAND, by Mary, da. and h. of Sir Anthony MILDMAY. He d. s.p., 26 Oct. 1674, aged about 50, and was bur. 6 Nov. in Westm. Abbey, when all his honours became extinct. Will dat. 30 March, and pr. 2 Nov. 1674. His widow, who was b. at Mereworth, Kent, and who had obtained a Royal warrant, 19 March 1660, to retain her precedency as "Countess of Bath" (the Earldom of Middlesex being a more recent creation), d. 11 Nov. 1680, at St. Giles in the fields, aged 67, and was bur. (with her first husband), at Tawstock, Devon. M.I. Will dat. 8 Dec. 1679, pr. 17 Nov. 1680.

IV. 1675. 1. CHARLES SACKVILLE, styled LORD BUCKHURST, s. and h. ap. of Richard (SACKVILLE), 5th EARL OF DORSET, by Frances, sister (of the whole blood), and coheir of Lionel (CRANFIELD), 3d and last EARL OF MIDDLESEX, b. 24 Jan. 1638; was cr. 4 April 1675, BARON CRANFIELD of Cranfield, co. Bedford and EARL OF MIDDLESEX. By the death of his father, 27 Aug. 1677, he became EARL OF DORSET and BARON BUCKHURST. See "DORSET" Earldom, cr. 1604, sub the 6th Earl. All the abovementioned titles became extinct together with the Dukedom of Dorset) in 1843.

MIDDLETON [Scotland.]

Earldom [S.] I. 1660, with the precedency of 1656. 1. JOHN MIDDLETON, s. and h. of John MIDDLETON, of Caldhame, by Helen, da. of John STRACHAN, b. about 1617, having served in France with the Scotch army; entered the service of the Parl. of England in 1642; became Lieut. Gen.; contributed to the defeat of the Royalists at Philiphaugh in 1645. He subsequently, however, joined the party for the rescue of King Charles I., and was made prisoner in 1648 at the battle of Preston. Later on he took an active part in favour of King Charles II. for whom he was Major Gen. at the battle of Worcester, 1651, where he was again taken prisoner. He, however, contrived to escape, and was in command of the Royalists in the Highlands, but being defeated by Gen. Monck at Lochgeary, 26 July 1654, he joined the King at Cologne, by whom in Sep. 1656 he was cr. an Earl. This creation is recited in the patent,(b) 1 Oct. 1660 (in which, however, he is spoken of not as an Earl but merely as Lieut. Gen. John Middleton) whereby he was cr. EARL OF MIDDLETON, LORD OF CLAIRMONT [CLERMONT] AND FETTERCAIRN [S.], with rem. to his heirs(c) bearing the surname and arms of Middleton and with the precedency of Sep. 1656.(d) He was appointed Commander in

(a) Of his two daughters (1) Anne, who was under 16 in 1651, d. unm., and was bur. 22 March 1652/3, in Westm. Abbey; (2) Elizabeth, m. 17 Nov. 1664, John Egerton, styled Viscount Brackley (afterwards, 1686, 3d Earl of Bridgwater) and d. s.p.s. 3 March 1669/70, aged 22.

(b) See "The Earls of Middleton and the Middleton Family," by A. C. Biscoe, London, 1876, in which there is a copy of this patent.

(c) This presumably is equivalent to "heirs male," but it is open to a possible interpretation of "heirs general" provided such take the name and arms of Middleton.

(d) See "Riddell," pp. 47-48, and 59-60, for remarks on the regrants in 1660 of the Marquessate of Montrose and the Earldom of Middleton, reintegrating the inchoate signatures of 1644 and 1656.

Chief [S.], Gov. of Edinburgh Castle, and Commissioner to the Parl. [S.], which met, 1 Jan. 1660/1,(a) and again, 8 May 1662; was one of the extra. Lords of Session 1662. His intemperate habits and (what was considered) abuse of power made him very unpopular,(b) and he was dismissed from office in 1663. He was, however, in command of Rochester when the Dutch burnt the English ships at Chatham, and was made, 15 April 1667, Governor of Tangiers. He m. firstly, July 1639, Grizel, widow of Sir Gilbert Ramsay, of Balmain (whom she m. in 1630) and relict formerly of Sir Alexander Fotheringham, da. of James (and sister of Sir Alexander) Durham, of Pitkerrow. She d. at Cranstoun, Sep. 1666. He m. secondly, 16 Dec. 1667, at St. Andrew's, Holborn (lic. Vic. Gen.) Martha, da. and coheir of Henry (Carey), 2d Earl of Monmouth, by Martha, da. of Lionel (Cranfield), 1st Earl of Middlesex. He d. at Tangiers in 1673,(c) aged about 56, leaving his estate much in debt. Admon. 25 Nov. 1674. His widow d. s.p.m.s., 28 Jan. 1705/6, aged 71, in the precincts of Worcester cathedral, and was bur. there.(d) M.I. Will dat. 4 Jan. and pr. 12 March 1705/6.

II. 1673, to 1695. 2. Charles (Middleton), Earl of Middleton, Lord Clermont and Fettercairn [S.], s. and h., by first wife; b. about 1640; was with his father in Scotland in 1654, and then (tho' hardly 14), a Captain; escaped to France and returned at the restoration in 1660, being *styled* Lord Clermont, from 1660, till he *suc. to the peerage* [S.], in 1673; Envoy to Vienna till 1682; Sec. of State [S.], 1682; an extra. Lord of Session, 1681; P.C. [E.], 1684; one of the Princ. Secretaries of State [E.], from Aug. 1684, having during the reign of James II. (together with Lord Preston, another Scotch Peer) the chief management of the House of Commons. To that King he remained faithful and, having joined him in France, was tried for high treason and outlawed by the Court of Justiciary, 23 July 1694 and "forfeited" by Act of Parl., 2 July 1695, whereby *all his honours became forfeited*. From 1692 to 1702, and from 1703 to 1713, he had the chief control of affairs at the exiled Court of St. Germains, his conversion to the Roman Catholic faith (which was the cause of his retirement, 1702-03), not being till *after* the death of King James, under whose will he was made one of the Council to assist the young Prince [*the titular King*] and the Queen Dowager, his mother. He is said (immediately after the death, 16 Sep. 1701, of the exiled King James II.) to have been *cr.* by the *titular* King James III., in 1701, EARL OF MONMOUTH in England.(e) From 1714 till his death he was

(a) It was opened in unwonted state, the Crown, Sceptre, and Sword, being carried respectively by the Earls of Crawford, Sutherland, and Mar.

(b) *E.g.*, the annulling of all acts of Parl. passed since 1633 and the re-establishment of Episcopacy in Scotland.

(c) "In a fit of intoxication he fell down a staircase and broke his arm so badly that the bone protruded thro' the flesh; it mortified and caused his death." See p. 309, note "d."

(d) No notice is given of her children in Wood's "Douglas." It is, however, certain that she had (1) a son, John, who d. before her, 28 Feb. 1696, and is *bur.* in Worcester cathedral; M.I.; and (2) a daughter, Elizabeth, who m. William Spelman, of Wickmer, co. Norfolk (by whom she had Mary, living 1705, and then under 14, who d. before her), which Lady Elizabeth Spelman d. s.p.s., 11 Jan. 1747/8. See as to her, in "Her. and Gen.," iv, pp. 45 and 142.

(e) Macky in his "characters," writes of him [1702 ?] when towards 60 years old, "He was against the violent measures of King James' reign and for that reason made no great figure at Court, while that Prince was upon the throne; yet was proof against all the offers made him by King William and, after being frequently imprisoned in England, followed King James to France when he had the chief administration given him. He is one of the politest gentlemen in Europe, has a great deal of wit, mixed with a sound judgment and a very clear understanding; of an easy indifferent address, but a careless way of living. He is a black man, of a middle stature, with a sanguine complexion, and one of the pleasantest companions in the world." To which Dean Swift adds, "*Sir William Temple told me he was a very valuable man and a good scholar. I once saw him.*"

Great Chamberlain to the Dowager Queen. He *m.* about 1670, Catharine, da. of Robert (BRUDENELL), 2d EARL OF CARDIGAN, by his second wife, Anne, da. Thomas (SAVAGE), VISCOUNT SAVAGE. He *d.* at St. Germain-en-laye 1719, aged about 79. Will dat. 7 July 1719 [N.S.], pr. 4 March 1726/7, and again 3 March 1812. His widow, who was Governess to the Princess Louise (1692-1712), at St. Germain, *d.* there, 11 March 1743 in her 95 year.([a]) Her will dat. 26 Oct. 1740, pr. 25 May 1749.

III. 1719, to 1746? 3. JOHN MIDDLETON, *styled* VISCOUNT CLERMONT, who, but for the attainder would have been EARL OF MIDDLETON, &c. [S.], s. and h. He, being then a Colonel, and his br. Capt. Charles Middleton taking part in the attempted invasion of Scotland in 1708 were captured by Admiral Byng; sent prisoners to the Tower of London but were released in 1711. At his father's death in 1719 *he assumed the title* of EARL OF MIDDLETON, &c. [S.], and was known as such. He who survived his mother appears to have *d.* unm. in or shortly before Feb. 1746/7, when the *issue male of*([b]) *the grantee* became *extinct.*([c]) Will dat. 14 Feb. 1740/1, pr. 25 Feb. 1746/7.

MIDDLETON [Great Britain.]

Barony. I. 1712. 1. SIR THOMAS WILLOUGHBY, Bart., of Wollaton, co. Nottingham, 2d and yst. s. of Francis WILLOUGHBY,([d]) of Wollaton afsd., and of Middleton, co. Warwick (a celebrated ornithologist), by Emma, da. and coheir([e]) of Sir Henry BERNARD, of Bridgenorth; was *b.* about 1670; *suc.* his brother as *second Baronet* (a dignity *cr.* with a *spec. rem.* 7 April 1677) in Sep. 1688; was M.P. for Notts (in five Parls.), 1698—1710, and for Newark, 1710-12, being *cr.*, 1 Jan. 1711/2,([f]) BARON MIDDLETON of Middleton, co. Warwick. He *m.*, about 1690, Elizabeth, da. and coheir([g]) of Sir Richard ROTHWELL, Bart., of Ewerby and Stapleford, co. Lincoln. He *d.* 2 and was *bur.* 17 April 1729, at Middleton. Will pr. 13 May 1729. His widow *d.* at Tong Castle, Salop. Admon. 25 Feb. 1735/6.

([a]) Miss Strickland, in her life of "Queen Mary Beatrice," says she lived till 1745, and having heard of the triumphant entrance of Prince Charles Edward into Edinburgh, "died in the fond delusion that a new restoration of the Stuarts was about to take place." This "fond delusion," however, appears to be one of the *authoress*, for the death of the Countess "at St. Germains, aged upwards of 90" appears in the "London Mag." for March 1743.

([b]) His only brother Charles, is presumed to have *d.* before him without issue, no mention being made of him in his will or in that of their mother, dated Oct. 1740. Of his sisters (1) Elizabeth, titular Duchess of Perth (his residuary legatee) *d.* s.p. at Paris, at a great age (2) Catherine who *m.* firstly in or shortly after June 1706, "the Chevalier [*Query* Sir John ?] Gifford" (by whom she had a child, Mary, living 1740), and secondly Michael, Comte de Rothe, *d.* at Paris, 10 July 1763, aged 78.

([c]) The heirs *male* to the Earldom are to be looked for among the numerous descendants of the first Earl's younger brother, Alexander Middleton, D.D., Principal of King's College, Aberdeen, who *d.* 28 May 1726, in his 82d year. It is said (N. and Q., 8th s., ii, 335), that the eldest of his 12 [should be 13] children had 18 children, of whom "the eldest (omitted by *Douglas* altogether) had eleven at least." See also "*the Earls of Middleton*" as on p. 309, note "d."

([d]) He was descended in the male line from William, 5th Lord Willoughby de Eresby (*d.* 1409), but the whole of his estates (Wollaton, Cossall, &c.), were derived from a totally distinct family of Willoughby, formerly Bugge, whose arms (instead of being "*Or, fretty azure,*" like that of the old line) were "*Or*, on two bars, *gules*, three water bougets, *argent.*" The heiress of this last named family, Dorothy, da. of Sir Edward Willoughby, of Wollaton, *m.* Robert Willoughby, of Bore Place, Kent, by whom she was great great grandmother of Francis, the father of the 1st Baron.

([e]) Her eldest sister, Elizabeth, *m.* James (Brydges), 8th Baron Chandos of Sudeley.

([f]) "*Horâ decimâ ante meridiem.*" See vol. i, p. 269, note "d," *sub* "Bathurst."

([g]) The other coheir *m.* Sir Thomas Barnadiston, of Ketton.

II. 1729. 2. FRANCIS (WILLOUGHBY), BARON MIDDLETON, s. and h., *b.* 23 Sep. 1693; M.P. for Notts, 1710-15, and for Tamworth, 1722-27; *suc. to the peerage*, 2 April 1729. He *m.*, 25 July 1723, at Westm. Abbey (lic. fac.), Mary, da. and coheir of Thomas EDWARDS, of the Middle Temple, London, and of Filkins, Oxon, by Mary, his wife. He *d.* 31 July 1758, at Bath, aged about 65, and was *bur.* at Wollaton. Will dat. 26 July and pr. 7 Sep. 1758. His widow *d.* in St. James' street, 12 March 1762, aged 59, and was *bur.* at Wollaton. Will dat. 13 Aug. 1759, pr. 1 April 1762.

III. 1758. 3. FRANCIS (WILLOUGHBY), BARON MIDDLETON, s. and h., *b.* 25 Jan. and *bap.* 20 Feb. 1725/6, at St. Anne's, Soho; *suc. to the peerage*, 31 July 1758. He *d.* unm., 16 Dec. 1774, and was *bur.* the 20th at Wollaton. Will dat. 18 Aug. 1774, pr. 3 March 1775.

IV. 1774. 4. THOMAS (WILLOUGHBY), BARON MIDDLETON, br. and h., *b.* 19 Dec. 1728, and *bap.* 10 Jan. following at St. Peter's, Nottingham; *suc. to the peerage*, 16 Dec. 1774. He *m.*, 7 April 1770, in the house of "John Sutton, Esq., St. James' Place, St. James' Westm.," Georgiana, da. of Evelyn CHADWICK, of West Leake, Notts. He *d.* s.p., 19 Jan. 1781, aged 52, and was *bur.* at Wollaton. Will dat. 28 June 1775, pr. 22 Feb. 1781. His widow, who was *b.* 27 April 1746, at Stroxton, co. Lincoln, and who became coheir of her br., James CHADWICK, *m.*, 14 Jan. 1783, Edward Miller MUNDY, of Shipley, co. Derby, and *d.* 29 June 1789. Will pr. 1789.

V. 1781. 5. HENRY (WILLOUGHBY), BARON MIDDLETON, cousin and h. male, being 2d but 1st surv. s. and h. of the Hon. Thomas WILLOUGHBY, by Elizabeth, da. and h. of Thomas SOUTHBY, of Birdsall, co. York, which Thomas Willoughby, who *d.* 2 Dec. 1742, aged 48, was second s. of the 1st Baron. He was *b.* at York, 19 Dec. 1726, and *bap.* at the Minster there 4 Jan. following; was High Sheriff of Yorkshire, 1757, and *suc. to the peerage*, 19 Jan. 1781. He *m.*, 25 Dec. 1756, at Garton, co. York, Dorothy, da. and coheir of George CARTWRIGHT, of Ossington, Notts, by Mary, sister and coheir of John DIGBY, of Mansfield Woodhouse, in that county. He *d.* 14 June 1800, aged 73. Will pr. June 1814. His widow *d.* 19 July 1808. Will pr. 1808.

VI. 1800. 6. HENRY (WILLOUGHBY), BARON MIDDLETON, only s. and h., *b.* 24 April 1761, and *bap.* at the Minster, York, 28 May following; sometime (1783), Col. of the Notts Militia; *suc. to the peerage*, 14 June 1800; High Steward of Sutton Coldfield. He *m.* 21 Aug. 1793 at Mayfair chapel, St. Geo. Han. sq., Jane, sister of Robert, 1st BARON WENLOCK, da. of Sir Robert LAWLEY, 5th Bart., by Jane, da. of Beilby THOMPSON, of Escrick, co. York. He *d.* s.p. 19 June 1835, aged 74. Will pr. Aug. 1835. His widow *d.* 17 Dec. 1852, aged 83, at Escrick villa, near York. Will pr. Jan. 1853.

VII. 1835. 7. DIGBY (WILLOUGHBY), BARON MIDDLETON, cousin and h. male, being s. and h. of Francis WILLOUGHBY, of Hesley Hall, Notts, by Octavia, da. and coheir of Francis FISHER of the Grange, in Grantham, co. Lincoln, which Francis (*b.* 1727) was yr. br. to Henry the 5th Baron. He was *b.* at Hesley Hall, and *bap.* 29 Nov. 1769, at Harworth, Notts; entered the Royal Navy, 1782, serving as Lieut. in Earl Howe's victory (1794), and becoming a retired Capt. in 1840. He *suc. to the peerage*, 19 June 1835, and *d.* unm. at Wollaton Hall, 5 Nov. 1856, aged 87. Will pr. March 1857, under £25,000.

VIII. 1856. 8. HENRY (WILLOUGHBY), BARON MIDDLETON, cousin and h. male, being s. and h. of Henry WILLOUGHBY, of Birdsall and Settrington, co. York, by Charlotte, da. of the Ven. John EYRE, Rector of Babworth, Notts, Archdeacon of Nottingham, which Henry last named (who *d.* 20 Nov. 1849, aged 68), was only s. and h. of the Rev. James WILLOUGHBY, Rector of Guiseley, co. York (*d.* 16 Feb. 1816, aged 84), yst. br. to Henry, the 5th Baron. He was *b.* at Apsley Hall, 28 Aug. and *bap.* 10 Sep. 1817, at Radford, Notts; *suc. to the peerage*,

5 Nov. 1856; was Hon. Col., 1st Brig. East Riding Artillery Volunteers, 1862. He *m* 3 Aug. 1843, at St. Geo. Han. sq., Julia Louisa, da. of Alexander William Robert BOSVILE, formerly MACDONALD,(a) of Thorpe Hall and Gunthwayte, co. York, by (—), da. of (—). He *d.* 20 Dec. 1877, aged 60, at Birdsall House, afsd., from the effects of a fall from his horse ten months before. His widow, who was *b.* 5 April 1824, at York, living 1893.

IX. 1877. *9.* DIGBY WENTWORTH BAYARD (WILLOUGHBY), BARON MIDDLETON [1712], also a Baronet [1677], s. and h.; *b.* 24 Aug. 1844, at Thorpe House, near Bridlington, co. York; ed. at Eton; sometime (1867-69), Lieut. Scots Fusileer Guards; *suc. to the peerage,* 20 Dec. 1877. He *m.* 24 Aug. 1844, Eliza Maria, da. of Sir Alexander Penrose GORDON-CUMMING, 3d Bart., by Anne Pitcairn, da. of the Rev. Augustus CAMPBELL, Rector of Liverpool.

Family Estates.—These, in 1883, consisted of 14,045 acres in the north and east Ridings in Yorkshire; 15,015 in Notts; 3,809 in Lincolnshire; 3,641 in Warwickshire, 50 in Staffordshire, and 16 in Derbyshire, besides 63,000 acres (worth but £1,957 a year) in Ross-shire in Scotland. *Total* 99,576 acres, worth £54,014 a year. *Principal Residences.* Wollaton Hall, Notts; Birdsall Hall and Settrington House, Yorkshire; Middleton Hall, Warwickshire and Appleton House (near Loch Carron) Ross-shire.

Lord Middleton's acreage is just *under* 200,000 acres. See a list of holders of *above* that acreage in vol. ii, p. 51, note "a," *sub* "Buccleuch."

MIDHURST.

See "BOHUN DE MIDHURST," Barony (*Bohun*), *cr.* 1363; *dormant* 1367.

MIDLETON, and BRODRICK OF MIDLETON.

Barony [I.] I. 1715. Viscountcy [I.] I. 1717.

1. ALAN BRODRICK,(b) 2d s. of St. John BRODRICK, of Midleton,(c) co. Cork, by Alice, da. of Randall CLAYTON, of Thelwall, co. Chester, was *b.* about 1656; admitted to the Inner Temple, London, 7 Jan. 1669/70; matric. at Oxford (Mag. Coll.), 3 May 1672, being then aged 16; took an active part in favour of the revolution and was, consequently, *attainted* by King James' Parl. in 1689, tho' appointed by William III., 19 Feb. 1690/1, Serjeant at Law. He was M.P. for Cork, 1692—1713, and for co. Cork, 1713-14, being Speaker of the House of Commons [I.], 1713. Meanwhile he had been Solicitor Gen. [I.], 1695—1704, and Attorney Gen. [I.], 1707-10, and Ch. Justice of the Queen's Bench [I.], 1710-11. By George I., whose succession he had favoured, he was made, 1 Oct. 1714, LORD HIGH CHANCELLOR [I.], a post which he resigned in 1725. He was *cr.* 13 April 1715, BARON BRODRICK OF MIDLETON,(c) co. Cork [I.], taking his seat 12 Nov. following, and was *cr.* 15 Aug. 1717, VISCOUNT MIDLETON(c) of Midleton, co. Cork [I.], taking his seat on the 27th.(d) He was one of the Lords Justices (Regents) of Ireland, 1716, 1717, 1719, 1723 and 1724. He was also M.P. [E.] for Midhurst, 1717-28. He *m.* firstly, Catharine, 2d da. of Redmond BARRY, of Rathcormick, co. Cork, by Mary, da. of John Boyle, of Castle Lyons. He *m.* secondly in 1695, Alice, sister and coheir of Col. John COURTHOPE, da. of Sir Peter COURTHOPE,

(a) He was elder br. (by the same parents) of Godfrey William Wentworth (Bosville-Macdonald), 4th Baron Macdonald of Slate [I.], but was *b.* (12 Sep. 1803), three months prior to the marriage of his parents.

(b) There is a good pedigree of this family in Howard's "*Mis. Gen. et Her,*" 1st series, vol. ii, pp. 359-370.

(c) "In 1653, a large grant of lands in the Barony of Barrymore, [co.] Cork," was granted to St. John Brodrick ("who had taken an active part in the civil wars beginning in 1641") and this "was supplemented under the act of settlement in 1670, by an additional grant of lands in the Baronies of Barrymore, Fermoy and Orrery, the whole being erected into the manor of *Midleton.*" [*Nat. Biogr.*]

(d) The preamble of both patents is in "Lodge," vol. v, pp. 166-167.

of Little Island, co. Cork, by his second wife, Elizabeth, da. of Sir John GIFFARD. She was *bur.* 30 June 1703, at St. Michan's, Dublin. He *m.* thirdly, 1 Dec. 1716, Anne widow of the Rt. Hon. Michael HILL, of Hillsborough, co. Down, da. and finally h. of Sir John TREVOR, Master of the Rolls, by Jane, da. of Sir Roger MOSTYN, Bart. He *d.* at Ballyanan, co. Cork and was *bur.* 29 Aug. 1728, at Midleton, aged about 72. Will dat. 19 April 1726, pr. 2 Aug. 1731. His widow (by whom he had no issue), *d.* 5 Jan. 1747, and was *bur.* (with her first husband), at Hillsborough.

II 1728. 2. ALAN (BRODRICK), VISCOUNT MIDLETON, &c. [I.], 3d([a]) but 1st surv. s. and h. male, by 2d wife, *bap.* 31 Jan. 1701/2, at St. Michan's, Dublin; admitted to the Middle Temple, London, 1 Nov. 1721; one of the Commissioners of the Custom, 1727-30; *suc. to the peerage* [I.], 29 Aug. 1728, taking his seat, 26 Nov. 1733; Joint Comptroller of the Army, Aug. 1730. In Oct. 1730 he *suc.* his uncle, the Rt. Hon. Thomas Brodrick, in the family estates, of Midleton, co. Cork, Wandsworth, co. Surrey, &c., and in the representation of the family. He *m.*, 7 May 1729, Mary, 2d and yst. da. of Algernon (CAPELL), 2d EARL OF ESSEX, by Mary, da. of William (BENTINCK), 1st EARL OF PORTLAND. He *d.* 8 and was *bur.* 13 June 1747, aged 45, at Wandsworth. Will dat. 1 Feb. 1744, pr. 10 June 1747. His widow, who was *bap.* 19 Oct. 1700, at Watford, Herts, *d.* 3 May 1756.([b]) Will dat. 13 Feb. 1755, pr. 22 May 1756.

III. 1747. 3. GEORGE (BRODRICK), VISCOUNT MIDLETON, &c. [I.], 1st and only surv. s. and h., *b.* 3 Oct. 1730, the King (*George* II.), standing in person as one of his sponsors; *suc. to the peerage* [I.], 8 June 1747, taking his seat, 29 Oct. 1751; M.P. [E.] for Ashburton, 1754-61, and for Shoreham, 1761-65. He *m.*, 1 May 1752, at Mr. Selwyn's house in Cleveland Court, St. James' Westm., Albinia, sister of Thomas, 1st VISCOUNT SYDNEY, 1st da. of the Hon. Thomas TOWNSHEND, by Albinia, da. of John SELWYN, of Matson, co. Gloucester. He *d.* 22 and was *bur.* 28 Aug. 1765. at Wandsworth, in his 35th year. Will dat. 17 Aug. 1761, pr. 30 Sep. 1765. His widow *d.* 18 and was *bur.* 24 Sep. 1808, at Wandsworth, aged 77. Will dat. 18 Sep. 1800, to 3 Aug. 1808, pr. 14 Nov. 1808.

IV. 1765. 4. GEORGE (BRODRICK), VISCOUNT MIDLETON, &c. [I.], 1st s. and h., *b.* 1 and *bap.* 21 Nov. 1754, at St. James' Westm.; *suc. to the peerage* [I.], 22 Aug. 1765; M.P. [E.] for Whitchurch, 1774-96. He was *cr.* a Peer [G.B.], 11 June 1796, as BARON BRODRICK OF PEPER HAROW, co. Surrey, with a *spec. rem.* failing heirs male of his own body to those of his father. He *m.* firstly, 4 Dec. 1778, at her father's house, Stratton street, St. Geo. Han. sq., Frances, 2d da. of Thomas (PELHAM), 1st EARL OF CHICHESTER, by Anne, only da. and h. of Frederick Meinhart FRANKLAND. She, who was *b.* 4 Dec. 1760, and *bap.* 1 Jan. 1761, at St. George's afsd., *d.* s.p.m., 23 June, and was *bur.* 4 July 1783, at Wandsworth, aged 22. He *m.* secondly, 13 June 1797, at Englefield, Berks, Maria, 2d da. of Richard BENYON, of Englefield House (formerly of Gidea Hall in Romford), by Lavinia, da. and coheir of James SMYTH, of St. Audries, Somerset. He *d.* at Peper Harow, co. Surrey, 12, and was *bur.* 19 Aug. 1836, at Wandsworth, aged 81. Will pr. Nov. 1836. His widow, who was *bap.* 1772, at St. Geo Han. sq., *d.* at Bath, 14, and was *bur.* 22 Jan. 1852, at Wandsworth, aged 79. Will pr. May 1852.

V. 1836. 5. GEORGE ALAN (BRODRICK), VISCOUNT MIDLETON, &c. [I.], also BARON BRODRICK OF PEPER HAROW, only s. and h., by second wife; *b.* 10 June and *bap.* 9 July 1806, at Peper Harow. He *m.*, 14 May 1833, at St. Geo. Han. sq., Ellen GRIFFITH, of Peper Harow afsd., spinster. He *d.* s.p., 1, and was *bur.* 9 Nov. 1848, at Peper Harow, aged 42. Will pr Nov. 1850. His widow *m.*, 28 April 1859, at St. John's, Paddington, Richard QUAIN, F.R.S., Surgeon

---

([a]) His eldest br. (by his father's *first* wife) the Rt. Hon. St. John Brodrick, *d.* v.p., 29 Feb. 1727/8, leaving five daughters and coheirs.

([b]) Mary, Dow. Baroness Middleton (*née* Edwards), who *d.* 12 March 1762, is often confused with this lady.

Extraordinary to the Queen (who *d.* 15 Sep. 1887, aged 87), and *d.* (10 months before him) 13 Nov. 1886, at 32 Cavendish square. Will dat. 4 Sep. to 27 Oct. 1886, pr. 11 Dec. 1886, above £23,000.

VI. 1848. 6. CHARLES (BRODRICK), VISCOUNT MIDLETON, &c. [I.], also BARON BRODRICK OF PEPER HAROW, cousin and h. male, being s and h. of the Hon. Charles BRODRICK, Archbishop of Cashel, by Mary, da. of Richard WOODWARD, Bishop of Cloyne, which Archbishop was 4th s. of the 3d Viscount, and *d.* 6 May 1822, aged 62. He was *b.* at Cahirmore, 14, and *bap.* 18 Oct. 1791, at Midleton; *ed.* at St. John's Coll., Cambridge; M.A., 1812; Barrister (Linc. Inn), 1819. He *suc. to the peerage*, 1 Nov. 1848, inheriting the Barony [G.B.] under the *spec. rem.* which extended it to the heirs male of the body of the 3d Viscount. He *m.*, 5 May 1825, at Cheltenham, Emma, da. of Thomas (STAPLETON), LORD LE DESPENCER, by Elizabeth, da. of Samuel ELIOT, of Antigua. He *d.* s.p.m., 2, and was *bur.* 8 Dec. 1863, at Peper Harow, aged 72. His widow, who was *b.* 7 Feb. 1796 and *bap.* at St. Marylebone, *d.* 29 Dec. 1879, at the Longhills, Lincoln, in her 84th year.

VII. 1863. 7. WILLIAM JOHN (BRODRICK), VISCOUNT MIDLETON, &c. [I.], also BARON BRODRICK OF PEPER HAROW, br. and h. male; *b.* 8 July 1798, and *bap.* at St. Geo. Han. sq., mat. at Oxford (Ball. Coll.), 21 June 1816; B.A., 1820; M.A., 1823; in Holy Orders; Curate of Ashtead, Surrey, 1822-25; Rector of Castle Rising, Norfolk, 1825-39; Rector of Bath, 1839-54; Chaplain to the Queen, 1847; had Royal warrant, 2 April 1849, of precedence as the son of a Viscount; Canon of Wells, 1856; Dean of Exeter, 1863-67; *suc. to the peerage*, 2 Dec. 1863, inheriting the Barony [G.B.], under the *spec. rem.* which extended it to the heirs male of the body of the 3d Viscount. He *m.* firstly, 16 March 1824, in Portman square, Marylebone, Elizabeth Anne, widow of the Hon. John PERCEVAL, 1st da. of Robert (BRUDENELL), 6th EARL OF CARDIGAN, by Penelope Anne, da. of George John COOKE. She, who was *b.* 6 March 1795, *d.* s.p., 24 Nov., and was *bur.* 1 Dec. 1824, at Wandsworth. He *m.* secondly at her father's house in Upper Brook street, St. Geo. Han. sq., 31 March 1829, his cousin Harriet, sister and coheir of George Alan (BRODRICK), 5th VISCOUNT MIDLETON [I.], 5th da. of the 4th Viscount, being his 4th da. by his second wife, Maria, da. of Richard BENYON. He *d.* at Peper Harow, 29 Aug., and was *bur.* there 3 Sep. 1870, aged 72. His widow, who was *b.* 10 Aug., and *bap.* 9 Sep. 1804, at Peper Harow, living 1893.

VIII. 1870. 8. WILLIAM (BRODRICK), VISCOUNT MIDLETON [1717], and BARON BRODRICK OF MIDLETON [1715], in the peerage of Ireland, also BARON BRODRICK OF PEPER HAROW [1796], s. and h.; *b.* 6 Jan. 1830, and *bap.* at Castle Rising, Norfolk; *ed.* at Eton and at Ball. Coll., Oxford; B.A., 1851; M.A., 1861; Barrister (Linc. Inn), 1855; M.P. for Mid Surrey, 1868-70; *suc. to the peerage*, 29 Aug. 1870; High Steward of Kingston-on-Thames, 1875. He *m.*, 25 Oct. 1853, at St. Peter's, Eaton square, Augusta Mary, 3d da. of Thomas Francis (FREMANTLE), 1st BARON COTTESLOE, by Louisa Elizabeth, da. of Field Marshal Sir George NUGENT, Bart. She was *b.* 6 June 1828.

Family Estates.—These, in 1883, consisted of 6,475 acres (worth £8,018 a year) co. Cork, besides 3,105 in co. Surrey. *Total* 9,580 acres, worth £10,752 a year. *Principal Residences* Peper Harow Park, near Godalming, co. Surrey, and Cahirmone, near Midleton, co. Cork.

MILBROKE.

Barony. I. 1442, to 1443. 1. JOHN (CORNWALL), BARON FANHOPE, was *cr.* in Parl., 30 Jan. 1442,(a) BARON OF MILBROKE, co. Bedford, but *d.* s.p. legit in 1443 when *all his honours* became *extinct*. See fuller account under "FANHOPE" Barony, *cr.* 1433; *ex.* 1443.

(a) This was the fourth of the sixteen Baronies which were *cr.* by patent before the 16th century. See vol. iii, p. 316, note "c," *sub* "Fanhope."

MILFORD.

Barony [I.]
I. 1776, to 1823.

1. Sir Richard Philipps, Bart., of Picton Castle, co. Pembroke, only s. and h. of Sir John Philipps, 6th Bart., of the same, by Elizabeth, da. of Henry Shepherd, of London, was *b.* 1744; *suc.* his father as 7th Baronet (a dignity *cr.* 9 Nov. 1621), 23 June 1764; was M.P. for co. Pembroke in several Parls.; Lord Lieut. of Haverfordwest, 1770—1824, and was *cr.*, 22 July 1776, BARON MILFORD[a] in Ireland [I.]; Lord Lieut. of co. Pembroke, 1780—1824. He *m.*, 2 June 1764, Mary, da. of (—) Philips, of Pontypark. co. Pembroke. She *d.* before him. Her admon. April 1817. He *d.* s.p., 28 Nov. 1823, in his 85th year, at Picton Castle, afsd., when *the peerage became extinct*, but the Baronetage devolved on his distant cousin and heir male. Will dat. 21 Jan. 1820, pr. 3 Feb. 1824.

MILFORD OF PICTON CASTLE.

Barony.
I. 1847, to 1856.

1. Sir Richard-Bulkeley-Philipps Philipps, Bart., formerly Richard Bulkeley Philipps Grant, 1st s. and h. of John Grant, of Nolton, co. Pembroke, by Mary Philippa Artemesia, who was da. of James Child, of Bigelly House, in that county, and only surv. issue and h. of his first wife, Maria Philippa Artemesia, only surv. issue of Bulkeley Philipps, of Abercover, co. Carmarthen (which Bulkeley was 2d s. of Sir John Philipps, 4th Bart., of Picton Castle, co. Pembroke), was *b.* at Narbeth, 7 June 1801 and *bap.* there (baptism reg. at Nolton) and, having inherited Picton Castle and other estates from his distant cousin, Richard (Philipps), Baron Milford [I.], took by Royal lic., 10 Feb. 1824, the name of *Philipps* in lieu of that of *Grant*; was Lord Lieut. of Haverfordwest, 1824-57; M.P. for Haverfordwest, 1826-35, and 1837-47; was *cr. a Baronet*, 13 Feb. 1828, and was *cr.*, 21 Sep. 1847, BARON MILFORD OF PICTON CASTLE, co. Pembroke. He *m.* firstly, 14 Oct. 1824, at Hanwell, Midx., Eliza, da. of John Gordon, of Hanwell. She *d.* 24 March 1852, at Picton Castle, aged 49. He *m.* secondly, 3 June 1854, at St. James' Westm., Anne Jane, 4th da. and coheir of William (Howard), Earl of Wicklow [I.], by Cecil Frances, da. of John James (Hamilton), 1st Marquess of Abercorn. He *d.* s.p., 3 Jan. 1857, aged 56, at Picton Castle afsd., when *all his honours became extinct.* Admon. (13 months later) 25 Feb. 1858, under £50,000. His widow, who was *b.* 10 Dec. 1824, *m.*, 4 June 1861, at Ingatestone Hall, Essex, Thomas Joseph Eyre, of Upper Court, co. Kilkenny (*b.* 11 June 1821), and was living 1893.

MILFORD-HAVEN.

i.e., "Milford-Haven" Earldom, *cr.* 1706, with the Dukedom of Cambridge, which see; *merged* therewith in the Crown, 1727.

MILLTOWN.

Earldom.
I. 1763.

1. Joseph Leeson, of Russborough, co. Wicklow, only s. and h. of Joseph Leeson, of Dublin, Brewer, by Margaret, da. and coheir of Andrew Brice, Alderman, and sometime Sheriff of Dublin, was *b.* 11 March 1722; *suc.* his father in 1741; was M.P. for Rathcormick, 1743-56, and was *cr.* 5 May 1756, BARON OF RUSSBOROUGH, co. Wicklow [I.], taking his seat two days later. He was *cr.* 8 Sep. 1760, VISCOUNT RUSSBOROUGH OF RUSSELLSTOWN, co. Wicklow [I.], taking his seat, 22 Oct. 1761, and finally was *cr.* 10 May 1763, EARL OF MILLTOWN, co. Dublin [I.], taking his seat, 11 Oct. following. He was P.C. [I.], 1763. He *m.* firstly, Jan. 1729, Cecilia, 1st da. of Francis Leigh, of Rathlagan, co. Kildare. She *d.* 29 Nov. 1737. He *m.* secondly, 20 Oct. 1738, Anne, da. of Nathaniel Preston, of Swainstown, co. Meath, by Anne, da. of Baron Dawson. She *d.* 17 Jan. 1766. He *m.* thirdly, 10

(a) "Milford *in Ireland*" is not existant, the place alluded to being in Pembrokeshire. See p. 195, note "d," *sub* "Macdonald."

Feb. 1768, Elizabeth, yst. da. of the Very Rev. William FRENCH, Dean of Ardagh, by Arabella Frances, da. of the Very Rev. Jeremy MARSH, Dean of Kilmore. He d. 2 Oct. 1783, aged 61. His widow survived him more than 58 years and d. 23 Jan. 1842, at the age (it is said) of 100.

II. 1783. 2. JOSEPH (LEESON), EARL OF MILLTOWN, &c. [I.], s. and h., by first wife, b. 1730; M.P. for Thomastown, 1757-60; styled VISCOUNT RUSSBOROUGH, 1763-83; suc. to the peerage [I.], 2 Oct. 1783. He d. unm. 27 Nov., and was bur. 5 Dec. 1801, at St. James', Westm.

III. 1801. 3. BRICE (LEESON), EARL OF MILLTOWN, &c. [I.], br. (of the whole blood) and h., b. 20 Dec. 1735; suc. to the peerage [I.], 27 Nov. 1801. He m. 25 Oct. 1765, Maria, da. of John GRAYDON, of Dublin, by Cassandra, da. of Gabriel TAHOURDIN, of Wanstead, Essex. She d. 25 July 1772. He d. 10 Jan. 1807, aged 72.

IV. 1807. 4. JOSEPH (LEESON), EARL OF MILLTOWN, &c. [I.], grandson and h., being s. and of Joseph LEESON, by Emily, 3d da. of Archibald DOUGLAS, of Darnock, which Joseph was 1st s. and h. ap. of Bryce (afterwards) 3d Earl, but d. v.p. 1800, aged 34, before his father had suc. to the peerage. He was b. 11 Feb. 1799; was styled VISCOUNT RUSSBOROUGH, 1800-07; suc. to the peerage [I.], 10 Jan. 1807. K.P., 13 March 1841. He m. July 1828, Barbara, Dow. BARONESS CASTLECOOTE [I.], 2d da. and coheir of Sir Joshua Colles MEREDYTH, Bart. [I.], of Greenhills, co. Kildare, by his first wife, Maria, da. and h. of Laurence Coyne NUGENT, of co. Westmeath. He d. of bronchitis, 31 Jan. 1866, aged 66, at Bray Strand. His widow d. 14 Feb. 1874, at DE Vesci terrace, Kensington.

V. 1866. 5. JOSEPH HENRY (LEESON), EARL OF MILLTOWN, &c. [I.], s. and h., b. 10 May 1829, in Dublin; styled VISCOUNT RUSSBOROUGH till 1866; Ensign 68th Foot, 1848-51; sometime Aide-de-Camp to the Viceroy of Ireland; suc. to the peerage [I.], 31 Jan. 1866. He d. unm. (of congestion of the lungs) 3 April 1871, at Russborough house, co. Wicklow, in his 41st year.

VI. 1871. 6. EDWARD NUGENT (LEESON), EARL OF MILLTOWN, &c. [I.], br. and h., b. 9 Oct. 1835; ed. at the Univ. of Dublin; B.A., 1856; Barrister (Inner Temple), 1862, practising as a special pleader; suc. to the peerage [I.], 3 April 1871; REP. PEER [I.], 1881-90; Lord Lieut. of co. Wicklow; P.C. [I.], 1888; Hon. Commissr. in Lunacy, 1889; K.P., 7 Feb. 1890. He m., 19 Oct. 1871, at St. Stephen's, Kensington, Geraldine Evelyn, sister and coheir (22 Feb. 1866) of the 6th Earl, being 2d and yst. da. of Leicester Fitz Gerald Charles (STANHOPE), 5th EARL OF HARRINGTON, by Elizabeth Williams, da. and h. of William GREEN. He d. s.p. (somewhat suddenly) 30 May 1890, aged 54, at Russborough House, and was bur. at Russborough. Will pr. at £25,811. His widow, who was b. 26 Jan. 1841, living 1893.

VII. 1890. 7. HENRY (LEESON), EARL OF MILLTOWN, &c. [I.], only surv. br. and h., b. 22 Jan. 1837; ed. at the Univ. of Dublin; B.A., 1858; Barrister (Dublin). 1860; Vice Chamberlain, 1859-62, and Chamberlain, 1862-74, to the Viceroy of Ireland; suc. to the peerage [I.], 30 May 1890. He d. unm. 24 March 1791, aged 53, at the Imperial hotel, Torquay, Devon. Personalty £26,816.

* * * * * *

[Since 1891 the title has remained dormant, tho' an heir obviously exists to the same; the two younger sons, Hon. John Leeson, (b. 1767), and the Hon. Robert Leeson, (b. 1772), of the 2d Earl having left numerous issue, and the youngest son Hon. Robert Leeson, (b. 1773), of the 1st Earl having done so likewise.]

Family Estates.—These, in 1883, consisted of 5,042 acres in the counties of Wicklow, Dublin, and Tipperary, worth £2,597 a year. *Principal Residence.* Russborough House, near Blessington, co. Wicklow.

MILSINGTON.

i.e., "MILSINGTON," Viscountcy [S.] (*Colyear*), *cr.* 1703 with the EARLDOM OF PORTMORE [S.], which see; *ex.* 1835.

MILTON, or MILTOWN.

i.e., "MILTON, co. Kent," Barony (*Sydney*), *cr.* 1689 with the VISCOUNTCY OF SYDNEY OF SHEPEY, co. Kent; see "ROMNEY" Earldom, *cr.* 1694; all which titles became *ex.* 1704.

---

i.e., "MILTON [or "MILTOWN"] co. Westmeath" Viscountcy [I.] (*Fitzwilliam*) *cr.* 1716 with the EARLDOM OF FITZWILLIAM [I.], which see.

---

i.e., "FITZWILLIAM OF MILTON, co. Northampton, Barony" (*Fitzwilliam*), *cr.* 1742; also "MILTON, co. Northampton," Viscountcy, *cr.* 1746 with the EARLDOM OF FITZWILLIAM OF NORBOROUGH, which see.

MILTON OF SHRONEHILL, and MILTON OF MILTON ABBEY.

i.e., "MILTON OF SHRONEHILL, co. Tipperary," Barony [I.] (*Damer*), *cr.* 1753; also "MILTON OF MILTON ABBEY, co. Dorset," Barony *cr.* 1762; also Viscountcy, *cr.* 1792 with the EARLDOM OF DORCHESTER, which see; all which titles became *ex.* 1808.

MILTOWN, see MILLTOWN and MILTON.

MINSHULL.

The following notice is given by Courthope, slightly altering the one previously given by Sir Harris Nicolas. "JOHN MINSHULL is said by some writers to have been *cr.* BARON MINSHULL of Minshull, co. Chester, in 1642, and it is stated that the title became *extinct* on his death. Dugdale, however, takes no notice of such a Peer. No notice of such a patent is to be found enrolled, and the probability is that it was never regularly executed; Banks, in his 'Dormant and Extinct Peerage,' asserts that the said John Minshull left issue male, whose descendants in the male line are still existing, and who, it may be presumed, would assert their claim to the dignity if a patent could be produced."

MINSTER.

i.e., "MINSTER OF MINSTER ABBEY, co. Kent," Barony (*Conyngham*), *cr.* 1821; see "CONYNGHAM" Marquessate [I.], *cr.* 1816.

MINSTER-LOVEL.

i.e., "LOVEL OF MINSTER LOVEL, co. Oxford," Barony (*Coke*), *cr.* 1728; see "LEICESTER," Earldom, *cr.* 1744; *ex.* 1759.

MINTO.

Barony. I. 1797. Earldom. I. 1813.

1. The Rt. Hon. SIR GILBERT ELLIOT MURRAY-KYNYNMOUND, *formerly* ELLIOT, Bart. [S.], of Minto, s. and h. of Sir Gilbert ELLIOT, 3d Bart. [S.], by Agnes, da. and h. of Hugh DALRYMPLE-MURRAY-KYNYNMOUND (*formerly* DALRYMPLE), of Melgund, co. Forfar, and of Lochgelly and Kynynmound, co. Fife, was *b.* 23 April 1751, at Grey Friars, Edinburgh; ed. at Paris and at Ch. Ch., Oxford; M.A., 1772; Barrister of Linc. Inn; *suc. as 4th Baronet* (a dignity cr. 19 April 1700), 11 Jan. 1777; M.P. for Morpeth, 1776-77; for co. Roxburgh, 1777-84; for Berwick, 1786-90, and for Helston, 1790-95;(a) D.C.L. (Oxford), 4 July 1793; P.C., 1793; Minister to the Italian States, March to May, 1794; Viceroy of Corsica, June 1795 to Oct. 1796, on return from which, he had confirmed to him by Royal lic., 2 Oct. 1797, the names of *Murray-Kynynmound* after that of *Elliot* (which names he had so assumed since the death of his mother in 1778) and was cr. (a few days later) 20 Oct. 1797, BARON MINTO of Minto, co. Roxburgh. He was Envoy to Vienna, 1799—1801, obtaining in 1800 a treaty of alliance with the Emperor of Germany, which, however, was broken by the treaty of Luneville next year. F.R.S., 1803; President of the Board of Control for India, Feb. to July 1806; GOVERNOR GENERAL OF INDIA, 1806-13, being (consequently) cr., 24 Feb. 1813, VISCOUNT MELGUND of Melgund, co. Forfar, and EARL OF MINTO, co. Roxburgh. He m., 3 Jan. 1777, at St. Geo. Han. sq., Anna Maria, 1st da. of Sir George AMYAND, 1st Bart., by Maria, da. of John Abraham KORTEEN, of Hamburgh, merchant. He d. at Stevenage, Herts, 21 June 1814, and was bur. from 4 Burlington street, on the 29th in Westm. Abbey, aged 63. Will pr. 1815. His widow, who was b. 26 March 1752, at St. Mary Abchurch, London, d. 8 March 1829, at Brighton. Will pr. Jan. 1830.

II. 1814. 2. GILBERT (ELLIOT-MURRAY-KYNYNMOUND), EARL OF MINTO, &c., s. and h., b. 16 June 1782, at Lyons in France; ed. at Eton and at Edinburgh Univ.; M.P. for Ashburton, 1806-07; and for Roxburghshire, 1812-14; *styled* VISCOUNT MELGUND from 1813 till (next year) he *suc. to the peerage*, 21 June 1814; P.C., 1832; Ambassador to Berlin, 1832-34; G.C.B., 20 Dec. 1834; First Lord of the Admiralty,(b) 1835-41; F.R.S., 1836; LORD PRIVY SEAL, 1846-52; Envoy to Sardinia, Tuscany, &c., 1847-48. He m., 4 Sep. 1806, Mary, 1st da. of Patrick BRYDONE, of Lennuel House, co. Berwick, by Mary, da. of William ROBERTSON, of Edinburgh, M.D. She d. 21 July 1853, aged 67, at Nervi, near Genoa. He d. 31 July 1859,(c) after a long illness, aged 76, at 48 Eaton square

[GILBERT ELLIOTT-MURRAY-KYNYNMOUND, *styled* (1807-17) VISCOUNT MELGUND, b. 3 Oct. 1807; d. v.p. in infancy, 26 Sep. 1817.]

III. 1859. 3. WILLIAM HUGH (ELLIOT-MURRAY-KYNYNMOUND), EARL OF MINTO, &c., 5th but 1st surv. s. and h., b. 19 March 1814, at Minto Castle; *styled* VISCOUNT MELGUND, 1817-59; ed. at Trin. Coll., Cambridge; M.P. for Hythe, 1837-41; for Greenock, 1847-52, and for Clackmannan, 1857-59; Chairman of the Survey Commission [S.] 1857; *suc. to the peerage*, 31 July 1859. K.T., 13 May 1870. He m. 20 May 1844, at St. Geo. Han. sq., Emma Eleanor Elizabeth, da. and h. of Gen. Sir Thomas HISLOP, 1st Bart., G.C.B., by Emma, da. of the Rt. Hon. Hugh ELLIOT, yr. br. to the 1st EARL OF MINTO. She d. 21 April 1882, at Eaglescliff, in Bournemouth, aged 58. He d. 17 March 1891, in his 77th year, at 2 Portman square.

IV. 1891. 4. GILBERT JOHN (ELLIOT-MURRAY-KYNYNMOUND), EARL OF MINTO [1813] VISCOUNT MELGUND [1813], and BARON MINTO [1797], also a *Baronet* [S. 1700], s. and h., b. 9 July 1845, in Wilton Crescent; *styled* VISCOUNT MELGUND, 1859-91; ed. at Trin. Coll., Cambridge; B.A., 1866; Lieut.

(a) His Parliamentary career was marked by the part he took in impugning the conduct in India of Warren Hastings (the Gov. Gen.) and Sir Elijah Impey (the chief Justice) an attack which (tho' it has now been "conclusively proved that there was not a tittle of evidence to support the charges insinuated rather than alleged" therein) raised his estimation with his party so much so that he was twice (in Jan. and in June 1789) a candidate for the Speakership. [See "*Nat. Biogr.*"]

(b) "It was said, at the time, that his period of office was *distinguished only by the* outcry raised at the *number of Elliots* who found places in the Naval service." [*Nat. Biogr.*] See vol. iv, p. 95, note "e," *sub* "Grey," for a somewhat similar benevolence to his own kindred by Earl Grey, also a Whig Minister, tho' one of much higher mark.

(c) Though "an indifferent speaker and undistinguished by administrative capacity he possessed considerable influence in affairs of State" [*Nat. Biogr.*] a fact perhaps to be explained by his daughter having m., in 1841, Lord John Russell (afterwards Earl Russell) who was Prime Minister, 1846-52, as well as 1865-66.

Scots Fusileer Guards, 1867-70, serving as a volunteer, in the Egyptian campaign, 1882, and in Afghanistan, &c.; *suc. to the peerage*, 17 March 1891: Col. of the South of Scotland Volunteer Brigade. He *m.* 28 July 1883, at St. Margaret's, Westm., Mary Caroline, 4th and yst. da. of Gen. the Hon. Charles Grey (2d s. of Charles, 2d EARL GREY), by Caroline Eliza, da. of Sir Thomas Harvie FARQUHAR, 2d Bart. She was *b.* 13 Nov. 1858.

[VICTOR GILBERT LARISTON GARNET ELLIOT-MURRAY-KYNYNMOUND, *styled* VISCOUNT MELGOUND, *b.* 12 Feb. and *bap.* 25 March 1891, at the Chapel Royal, St. James Palace, the Queen being (by proxy) one of the Sponsors.]

Family Estates.—These, in 1883, consisted of 8,663 acres in Roxburghshire; 3,446 in Forfarshire; 2,930 in Fifeshire and 1,032 in Selkirkshire. *Total*, 16,071 acres, worth £13,056 a year; exclusive of minerals, rented at £2,804.

MISORE, see MYSORE.

MITCHELSTOWN.

i.e., "KINGSTON OF MITCHELSTOWN, co. Cork," Barony [U.K.] (*King*), *cr.* 1821; *ex.* 1869; see "KINGSTON" Earldom [I.], *cr.* 1768, *sub* the 3rd, 4th, and 5th Earls.

MOATE.

See "ASHTOWN OF MOATE, co. Galway," Barony [I.] (TRENCH), *cr.* 1800.

MOELS.

Barony by Writ.

I. 1299. *1.* JOHN DE MOELS, of NORTH CADBURY, co. Somerset, &c., s. and h. of Roger DE MOELS, of the same, by Alice, da. and h. of William DE PREUX, *suc.* his father in 1294, being then aged 26; served in the Scotch wars and was sum. to Parl. as a Baron (LORD MOELS) from 6 Feb. (1298/9). 27 Ed. I. to 16 June (1311), 4 Ed. II.(a) He was previously sum. 26 Jan. (1296/7). 25 Ed. I. to attend the King at Salisbury, but such summons cannot be considered in the right of *regular* writ of summons to Parl.(b) Altho he was not at the Parl. at Lincoln in (1301), 29 Ed. I., his name as "*Johannes de Moels, de Cadbury*," appears to the letter to the Pope, sent by the Barons in that year.(c) He is said(d) to have *m.* a da. of the LORD GREY DE RUTHIN. He *d.* about 1309. *Esch.* 3 Ed. II.

II. 1309? *2.* NICHOLAS (DE MOELS), LORD MOELS, s. and h., aged 20, at his father's death in 1309-10; did homage the next year; was in the Scotch wars and was sum. to Parl. from 19 Oct. (1311), 5 Ed. II. to 6 Oct. (1315). He *m.* Margaret, sister of Hugh EARL OF DEVON, da. of Sir Hugh COURTENAY, of Okehampton. He *d.* s.p. 1315-16. Esch. 9 Ed. II. His wife survived him

III. 1315? *3.* ROGER DE MOELS, br. and h., aged 20 at his brother's death, when he had livery of his lands of inheritance. He was never sum. to Parl. as a Baron. He *d.* s.p. (1325-26), 19 Ed. II.

(a) Two years or so after his death; no very unusual occurrence.
(b) See vol. i, p. 111, note "b," *sub* "Ap. Adam."
(c) See "*Nicolas*," pp. 761-809, for a full account of that letter.
(d) "Dugdale," quoting the collections of R. Glover, Somerset Herald

IV. 1325. to 1337. 4. SIR JOHN DE MOELS, br. and h., who in 1326-27, had been made K.B. He, likewise, was never sum. to Parl. as a Baron, tho' he served in the Expedition to Scotland in 1333. He m. Joane, da. of Sir Richard LOVEL, of Castle Cary, co. Somerset. He d. s.p.m. 1337, when the right to the *Barony* fell into *abeyance*.(a) Esch. 11 Ed. III.

MOFFATDALE.

i.e., "JOHNSTON OF LOCHWOOD, LOCHMABEN, MOFFATDALE AND EVANDALE," Barony [S.] (*Johnston*), *cr.* 1681 with the EARLDOM OF ANNANDALE AND HARTFELL [S.], and again in 1701 with the MARQUESSATE OF ANNANDALE [S.]; see those dignities; *dormant* 1792.

MOHUN, or MOHUN DE DUNSTER.

Barony by Writ.

I. 1299. 1. JOHN DE MOHUN, of Dunster, co. Somerset, s. and h. of John DE MOHUN, of the same, by his first wife, Joan,(b) widow of William AGUILLON, da. of William (DE FERRERS), EARL OF DERBY, by his first wife (to whom she was coheir) Sibel, da. and coheir of William (MARSHALL), EARL OF PEMBROKE; *suc.* his father, 11 June 1279, being then aged 10 years. He served in the wars in Gascony and in Scotland. He surrendered, 1298-99, lands in Ireland to the King, receiving in exchange the manor of Long Compton, co. Warwick. He was sum. to Parl. as a Baron (LORD MOHUN) from 6 Feb. (1298/9), 27 Ed. I., to 23 Oct. (1330), 4 Ed. III., being one of those Barons whose name (as "*Johes de Mohun, Dominus de Dunsterre*"), appears in the famous letter sent by them in 1301 to the Pope.(c) He was at the Coronation of Edward II. He *m.* before 1299 Auda, da. of Sir John DE TIBETOT. He *d.* about 1330. *Esch.*, 4 Ed. III.

II. 1330, to 1376. 2. JOHN (DE MOHUN), LORD MOHUN, grandson and h., being s. and h. of John DE MOHUN, s. and h. ap. of the last Baron, by Sibylla, da. of John DE SEGRAVE, which John de Mohun *d.* v.p. He was aged 10 at the death of his grandfather in 1330. He was sum. to a Council (which was not a Parl.) as early as 25 Feb. (1341/2), 16 Ed. III., and subsequently was sum. to Parl. 20 Nov. (1348), 22 Ed. III., to 4 Oct. (1373), 47 Ed. III., as LORD MOHUN DE DUNSTER, the writs being directed "*Johi Mohun de Dunsterre.*" He distinguished himself in the French wars under the Black Prince

---

(a) The coheirs were his two daughters, of whom [I.] Muriel, aged 15 in 1337, *m.* Sir Thomas Courtenay, and had (besides a son Hugh who *d.* s.p.) two daughters, *viz.* (1) Margaret, who *m.* Sir Thomas Peverell, whose da. and heir, Catherine *m.*, Walter (Hungerford), 1st Lord Hungerford and was ancestress of the succeeding Lords Hungerford (2) Joan, who *m.* Sir John Dynham, of Hartland, Devon, and who is represented by the descendants of the four sisters and coheirs (see "*Coll. Top. et Gen.*," vol. iv., p. 361), of her great grandson, John, Lord Dynham. [II.] Isabel, aged 12 in 1337, *m.* William (Botreaux), 1st Lord Botreaux and was ancestress of the succeeding Lords Botreaux; so that the representation of one moiety and of half of the other moiety of the Barony of Moels vested in the family of Hastings (who had inherited both the Barony of Botreaux and the Barony of Hungerford) till the death s.p. in 1868, of the 4th Marquess of Hastings. The representation, however of the other fourth thereof, *not* being so vested, made it an *assumption* on the part of the Hastings family to style themselves (as they sometimes did) as Lords Moels, the abeyance of that Barony having never been determined in their favour. See vol. iv, p. 186, note "b," *sub* "Hastings."

(b) Her parentage is wrongly stated in "*Dugdale.*" See "*Coll. Top. et Gen.*," iv p. 354.

(c) See "*Nicolas*," pp. 761-809, for a full account of that letter.

and was (with him) made K.G. on the institution of that Order, 23 April 1344.(a) He m. Joane, da. of Bartholomew (Burghersh), Lord Burghersh, by Elizabeth, da. and coheir of Theobald (de Verdon), Lord Verdon. He d. s.p.m. between 14 April 1375, and 4 April 1376,(b) when the *Barony* fell into *abeyance*.(c) His widow who in 1384 and 1386 had, from the Wardrobe, robes of the Order of the Garter, d in 1404(d) and in her will directs her burial to be in Canterbury cathedral.

* * * * * * *

III. 1431. *3.* Richard (le Strange), Lord Strange de Knokin, and Lord Mohun, grandson and heir, being s. and h. of John, Lord Strange de Knokin, by Maud, 3d and yst. da. of John (Mohun), Lord Mohun de Dunster, abovenamed; *suc.* his father in 1397 (being then aged 15) as Lord Strange de Knokin, and became by the death s.p. of his mother's sisters(c) in 1431 Lord Mohun. See "Strange de Knokin" Barony, *cr.* 1299, with which dignity the *Barony of Mohun* continued united from 1431 till 1594 when *both* [on the death of Thomas (Stanley), 2d Earl of Derby], fell into *abeyance*.

MOHUN OF OKEHAMPTON.

Barony. I. 1628. *1.* "John Mohun, of Boconnock, co. Cornwall, Esq."(e) 2d but 1st surv. s. and h. ap. of Sir Reginald Mohun, Bart. (so *cr.* 25 Nov. 1611), by his second wife, Philippa, da. of John Hele, was *b.* 1595; M.P. for Grampound 1624-25, and was *cr.* (v.p.), 15 April 1628, BARON MOHUN OF OKEHAMPTON,(f) co. Devon. He *suc.* his father, 26 Dec. 1639, as 2d Baronet, and took a leading part in the west of England on behalf of the King in the civil wars. He *m.* Cordelia, widow of Sir Roger Aston, of Cranford, Midx. (who *d.* 1612), da. of Sir John Stanhope, of Shelford, Notts, by his second(g) wife, Catherine, da. of Thomas Trentham. She is probably the "*Dna Mohun*," who was *bur.* 2 Oct. 1639, at St. Martin's in the fields. He *d.* 28 Nov. 1640, aged about 45. *Inq. post mortem* (1641-42), 17 Car. I.

(a) See vol. i, p. 276, note "a," *sub* "Beauchamp," for a list of the Founders of the Order of the Garter, among whom was his wife's brother, Bartholomew (Burghersh), Lord Burghersh.

(b) On the first date robes of the Order of the Garter were directed to be issued to him, and on the last date his stall was in possession of Sir Thomas Holand. See Beltz's "*Knights of the Order.*" Mr. Courthope remarks that "No inquisition appears to have been taken after his decease, and although in two out of the six inquisitions taken on the death of his widow in 1404, his 2d daughter, Philippa, is made to be born in 1378 and 1380 (subsequent to the date of death assigned to her father), there are others making her to be born in 1370 and 1376; there is likewise a variation of ten years in the age assigned by these inquisitions to her elder sister, Elizabeth. Philippa must, in fact, have been born as early as 1376 inasmuch as her nephew, Richard le Strange (the son of her *younger* sister) was of full age in 1404 and she herself was first married to Walter, Lord Fitzwalter (who died 1386), and secondly to Sir John Golafre, Lord of Langley, co. Oxon (who died 1396)."

(c) The coheirs were (1) Elizabeth, his 1st da., who *m.* (as second wife) William (Montacute), Earl of Salisbury, and *d.* a widow and s.p. 14 Jan. 1415 (2) Philippa his 2d da., *m.* (for her third husband) Edward (Plantagenet), Duke of York, but *d.* s.p. 1431 when the abeyance terminated in favour of (3) Richard (Le Strange), Lord Strange de Knokin, s. and h. of Maud, 3d and yst. da. of the said Lord Mohun.

(d) In Collinson's "*Somerset*" it is stated that she sold in (1376), 50 Ed. III. the reversion of the manor of Dunster, &c., to Dame Elizabeth Luttrell.

(e) See "*Creations*, 1483—1646" in ap. 47th Rep. D.K. Pub. Records.

(f) He is called "*the Lord Okehampton*" when sponsor to Francis Annesley in Jan. 1628. See baptisms of the children of the 1st Viscount Valentia [I.] as from copies of entries from family bibles, *penes* A. Scott-Gatty, York Herald.

(g) Her mother is called the *second* wife in all the Stanhope pedigrees; the *first* wife (the mother of the 1st Earl of Chesterfield) was *Cordelia* Allington.

II. 1640. 2. WARWICK (MOHUN), BARON MOHUN OF OKEHAMPTON, 2d([a]) but 1st surv. s. and h.; M.P. for Grampound in April 1640, till "void" on 20th of that month; aged 20 years and 11 months when he *suc. to the peerage*, 28 Nov. 1640. He *m.* Catherine, da. of (—) WELLS, of Brember, Hants. His burial reg. 12 May 1665, at St. Martin's in the fields. Will dat. 30 April and pr. 28 July 1665. The admon. of his widow granted 23 Dec. 1710 to George CUSACK, husband of Catherine da. of the deceased.

III. 1665. 3. CHARLES (MOHUN), BARON MOHUN OF OKEHAMPTON, s. and h.; under age when he *suc. to the peerage* in 1665. He *m.* Philippa, 4th da. of Arthur (ANNESLEY), 1st EARL OF ANGLESEY, by Elizabeth, da. and coheir of Sir James ALTHAM. He was *bur.* at St. Giles in the fields, 7 Oct. 1677, entry reg. at St. Martin's in the fields on the 2d. Admon. 8 May 1688, 26 June and 10 July 1693, and 7 Nov. 1724. His widow *m.* before July 1693, William COWARD, Serjeant at Law, by whom she had issue. She *d.* a widow and was *bur.* 2 March 1714/5, at Lee, co. Kent. Will dat. 21 June 1714, pr. 18 Jan. 1715/6.

IV. 1677, to 1712. 4. CHARLES (MOHUN), BARON MOHUN OF OKEHAMPTON [1628], also a *Baronet* [1611], only s. and h.; *b.* about 1675; *suc. to the peerage* in Oct. 1677; was twice tried for murder by the House of Peers, before he was 20 years old;"([b]) served as a volunteer in the expedition to Brest in 1694; was Col. of a Reg. of Foot. He *m.* firstly, Charlotte, da. and h. of Thomas MANWARING, by Charlotte, da. (whose issue in 1702, became coheir) of Charles (GERARD), 1st EARL OF MACCLESFIELD. He *m.* secondly before March 1710, Elizabeth, widow of Col. Edward GRIFFITH, da. of Thomas LAWRENCE, M.D., Physician to Queen Anne. The well known duel between him and the Duke of Hamilton, wherein both combatants perished, took place at Hyde park, 15 Nov. 1712. He *d.* s.p.m. and was *bur.* the 25th at St. Martin's in the fields when *all his honours* became *extinct*. Will dat. 23 March 1710, pr. 6 March 1712/3 and 8 Nov. 1725, leaving all to his then wife, she paying £100 to Elizabeth "my pretended da. by my first wife." His widow *m.* Col. Charles MORDAUNT, who survived her.([c]) She was *bur.* 21 May 1725, at Fulham, co. Midx. Admon. July 1725.

MOIRA, and RAWDON OF MOIRA.

Barony [I.] I. 1750. Earldom [I.] I. 1762. 1. SIR JOHN RAWDON, Bart., of Rawdon Hall, co. York, and of Moira, co. Down, 2d but 1st surv. s. and h. of Sir John RAWDON, 3d Bart., of the same. by Dorothy, da. of the Rt. Hon. Sir Richard LEVINGE, Bart. [I.], Chief Justice of the Common Pleas [I.], was *b.* 17 March 1719-20; *suc.* his father, 1 Feb. 1723; was ed. at Trin. Coll., Dublin, where he was *cr.* LL.D., 1753; F.R.S., London. On 9 April 1750, he was *cr.* BARON RAWDON OF MOIRA, co. Down [I.], taking his seat the next day, and on 30 Jan. 1762, he was *cr.* EARL OF MOIRA [I.], taking his seat 9 Feb. following. He *m.* firstly, 10 Nov. 1741, Helena, yst. da. of John (PERCEVAL), 1st EARL OF EGMONT [I.], by Catharine, 1st da. of Sir Philip PARKER A MORLEY, Bart. She *d.* s.p.m. at the Hot Wells, Bristol, 11 June 1746. He *m.* secondly, 23 Dec. 1746, Anne, sister to Wills, 1st MARQUESS OF DOWNSHIRE [I.], da. of Trevor (HILL), 1st VISCOUNT HILLSBOROUGH [I.], by Mary, da. and coheir of Anthony ROWE. She *d.* s.p., 1 Aug. 1751, and was *bur.* at Moira. He *m.* thirdly,

([a]) John Mohun, his elder br. (aged 5 in 1620), who is often considered to have *suc.* to the title, *d.* unm. and v.p. being *bur.* at Kensington, 31 Oct. 1639 as "John Mohuen, Esq., son of the Rt. Hon. John, Lord Mohuen, Baron of Ochamton."

([b]) Macky's "*Characters*" written when he was "not 30 years old, of a middle stature inclining to fat." Macky adds that tho' in his youth "a scandal to the Peerage" he now "rectifies as fast as he can his former slips." Dean Swift, however, says of him. "He was little better than a conceited talker in company." His trial for the murder of William Mountford, an actor, in 1692, is fully set forth by Macaulay in his history of that period.

([c]) Probably the "Charles Mordaunt, Esq." who was *bur.* at Fulham, 8 May 1762.

26 Feb. 1752, his cousin, Elizabeth, 1st and only surv. da. of Theophilus (HASTINGS), 9th EARL OF HUNTINGDON, by Selina, da. and coheir of Washington (SHIRLEY), 2d EARL FERRERS, and Mary, his wife, da. of the abovenamed Sir Richard LEVINGE, Bart. [I.] He *d.* 20 June 1793, at Moira, in his 73d year. His widow who was *b.* 23 March 1731, and who was well known both for her literary talents and as a leader of the Dublin society,(a) became (by the death, 2 Oct. 1789, of her br. Francis (Hastings, 10th EARL OF HUNTINGDON), *suo jure* BARONESS BOTREAUX, HUNGERFORD, DE MOLEYNS HASTINGS DE HASTINGS, AND HASTINGS DE HUNGERFORD. She *d.* 11 April 1808, at Moira House, where, or in Dublin, she had (excepting one year's absence in France) resided 56 years, and was *bur.* at Moira. Admon. Nov. 1825.

II 1793. 2. FRANCIS (RAWDON-HASTINGS), EARL OF MOIRA, and BARON RAWDON OF MOIRA [I.], also BARON RAWDON [G.B.], s. and h. He had previously (v.p.) been *cr.* 5 March 1783, BARON RAWDON, of Rawdon co. York. In 1809 his claim to the BARONY OF HASTINGS *of Hastings* (in right of his mother) was allowed, and on 13 Feb. 1817, he was *cr.* MARQUESS OF HASTINGS, &c. With this title the *Earldom of Moira* and *Barony of Rawdon of Moira* continued united until, on the death of the 4th and last Marquess, on 10 Nov. 1868, they became *extinct*. See "HASTINGS" Marquessate, *cr.* 1817; *ex.* 1868.

MOLESWORTH OF SWORDS and MOLESWORTH OF PHILLIPSTON.

Viscountcy and Barony. [I.]

I. 1716. 1. ROBERT MOLESWORTH, of Brackanstown, co. Dublin, posthumous s. and h. of Robert MOLESWORTH [who had obtained large grants of land (2,500 acres) in the Baronies of Moghergallin and Lune, co. Meath, from the Parl. of England, whose cause he had greatly assisted and who became subsequently a merchant at Dublin], by Judith, 1st da. and coheir of John BYSSE, afterwards (1660) Chief Baron of the Exchequer [I.], was *b.* 7 Sep. 1656, in Dublin and ed. at that University. He took a strong part in promoting the accession of King William III. to the throne; was *attainted*, 7 May 1689, by the Parl. [I.] of James II. (his estate of £2,825 a year being sequestrated) but shortly afterwards was *restored*; P.C. to William III., Queen Anne, and George I.; Envoy to the Court of Denmark, 1692; M.P. for Dublin [I.], 1695-99; for Swords [I.], 1703-15; for Lostwithiel [E.], 1705-06; for East Retford [E.], 1706-08, and for St. Michael [G.B.], 1715-22. In reward for his stedfast adherence to the House of Hanover he was by George I. made a Commissioner of Trade and Plantations, Nov. 1714 to Dec. 1715, and on 16 July 1716, was *cr.* LORD MOLESWORTH, BARON OF PHILLIPSTOWN, in King's county, and VISCOUNT MOLESWORTH OF SWORDS, co. Dublin(b) [I.], taking his seat, 1 July 1719; F.S.A., &c. He *m.* Lætitia, sister to Richard, EARL OF BELLOMONT [I.], 3d da. of Richard (COOTE), BARON COOTE OF COLOONY [I.], by Mary, 2d da. of Sir George ST. GEORGE, Bart. [I.] He *d.* 22 May 1725, and was *bur.* at Swords, co. Dublin.(c) Will dat. 30 April 1725, pr. Nov. 1726. His widow *d.* 18 March 1729, and was *bur.* the 20th at St. Audoen's, Dublin.

II. 1725. 2. JOHN (MOLESWORTH), VISCOUNT MOLESWORTH OF SWORDS, &c. [I.], s. and h., *bap.* 4 Dec. 1679; Commissioner of the Stamp Office, May 1710; Envoy to Tuscany, 1711; *suc.* his father as a Commissioner of Trade and Plantation, Dec. 1715; Envoy to Turin, 1720-25, having been Minister at Florence, Venice, and Geneva; *suc. to the peerage* [I.], 22 May, and took his seat, 7 Sep. 1725. He *m.* Mary, da. and coheir of Thomas MIDDLETON, of Stansted Montfitchet, Essex, by Elizabeth, 1st da. of Richard (ONSLOW), BARON ONSLOW. He *d.* s.p.m. in London, 17 Feb. 1725/6. Will pr. 1726. His widow *d.* in Hill street, St. Geo. Han. Sq., 12 Aug. 1766 and was *bur.* in the family vault at Edlington, co. York. Will pr. 18 Aug. 1766.

(a) There is a most eulogistic account of her in the "Annual Register" for 1808, p. 150.

(b) See the patent fully set out in the claim of this Peerage 1821. The preamble is in "Lodge," vol. v, p. 135.

(c) In his will he directs his burial to be at Edlington, co. York, and he therein styles himself "Lord Molesworth, Baron of Philipstowne, and *Viscount Swords*."

III. 1726. 3. RICHARD (MOLESWORTH), VISCOUNT MOLESWORTH OF SWORDS, &c. [I.], br. and h. male; Student at Law of the Temple, London. A volunteer in the army in Flanders; and afterwards (1702) an officer. Capt. of Horse and Aide-de-Camp to the Duke of Marlborough (whose life he is said to have saved) at Ramilies (a) Was wounded at the battle of Preston. Lieut of the Ordnance, 1714. Col. of a Regiment of Foot, 1724, &c. Master Gen. of the Ordnance, 1739. Gen. of Horse, 1741. Commander in Chief [I.] 1751, and finally FIELD MARSHAL. He was also M.P. for Swords, 1715-26. He *suc. to the peerage* [I.], 17 Feb. 1725/6, and took his seat, 5 Oct. 1731. P.C., 1733; one of the Deputy Keepers of the Great Seal [I.], 1736. He *m.* firstly, Jane, da. of (—) LUCAS, of Dublin. She *d.* s.p.m.s., 1 April 1742, and was *bur.* at Swords. He *m.* secondly, 7 Feb. 1743, Mary, da. of the Ven. William USHER, Archdeacon of Clonfert. He *d.* 12 Oct. 1758, aged 78, and was *bur.* the 16th at Kensington. Will pr. 1758. His widow (to whom a pension of £500 a year after her husband's death had been granted in 1755), *d.* 6 May 1763, being (with two of her daughters and five others) burnt to death in her house,(b) at Upper Brook street. St. Geo. Han. sq.

IV. 1758. 4. RICHARD-NASSAU (MOLESWORTH), VISCOUNT MOLESWORTH OF SWORDS, &c. [I.], only s. and h. by 2d wife, *b.* 4 Nov. 1748; *suc. to the peerage* [I.], 12 Oct. 1758, and took his seat 5 Dec. 1769. He *d.* unm. 23 June 1793, and was *bur.* 9 July, at Kensington. Admon. July 1793.

V. 1793. 5. ROBERT (MOLESWORTH), VISCOUNT MOLESWORTH OF SWORDS, &c. [I.], cousin and h. male, being s. and h. of Capt. the Hon. William MOLESWORTH, by Anne, 1st da. of Robert ADAIR, of Hollybrook, co. Wicklow, which William (who *d.* 6 March 1770), was 2d s. of the 1st Viscount. He was *bap.* 22 Dec. 1729; Cornet, 1745 and Lieut. 1753 in his uncle's (the third Viscount's) Regiment of Dragoons. He *suc. to the peerage* [I.], 23 June 1793, and took his seat 23 Jan. 1795. He *m.* 18 Aug. 1761, Mary Anne, da. of Israel ALLEYNE, of Cork. He *d.* 29 Jan. 1813. Will dat. 7 Sep. 1805, pr. 15 Feb. 1813. His widow *d.* 2 Aug. 1819. Will pr. 1819.

VI. 1813. 6. WILLIAM JOHN (MOLESWORTH), VISCOUNT MOLESWORTH OF SWORDS. &c. [I.], only surv. s. and h., *b.* 18 Aug. 1763; was a Major-Gen. in the army, being Lieut. Col. of the 95th Foot. He *m.* (—) da. of (—.) Both he and his wife were lost at sea (in the "Arniston" transport) on Lagullas reef, off the Cape of Good Hope, on their passage from Ceylon, 30 May 1815. He *d.* s.p. Admon. as "a widower" (c) 26 April 1816, to his mother.

VII. 1815. 7. RICHARD PIGOTT (MOLESWORTH), VISCOUNT MOLESWORTH OF SWORDS, &c. [I.], first cousin and h. male, being s. and h. of Richard M., by Katherine, da. of Francis Thomas COBB, of Twickenham, Midx., which Richard was next br. of the 5th Viscount, and *d.* 29 Sep. 1799. He was *b.* 23 July 1786, and *bap.* 17 Aug. at St. Giles, Camberwell, Surrey; entered the East Indian Military Service, 1802, retiring as Captain in 1826; *suc. to the peerage* [I.], 30 May 1815. He *d.* unm., 20 June 1875, aged 88, at 43 Grand Parade, Brighton.

VIII. 1875. 8. SAMUEL (MOLESWORTH), VISCOUNT MOLESWORTH OF SWORDS, &c. [I.], nephew and h., being only s. and h. of John MOLESWORTH, Capt. R.N., by Louisa, da. of Rev. (—) TOMKYNS, D.D., which John (who *d.* 14 Aug. 1858) was next surv. br. to the 7th Viscount. He was *b.* 19 Dec. 1829; ed. at St. John's Coll., Cambridge; B.A., 1853; M.A., 1856; took Holy Orders, 1865; *suc. to the peerage* [I.], 20 June 1875; Rector of St. Petrock Minor,

---

(a) See "Lodge," vol. v, p. 142, note

(b) See "Lodge," vol. v, p. 146, and see also the Annual Reg. for 1763.

(c) The law in these cases presumes the survival of the husband, as being the stronger of the two parties, failing any evidence to prove the contrary.

Cornwall, 1876. He *m.* firstly, at the British Embassy, Paris, 6 May 1862, Georgina Charlotte Cecil, yst. da. and coheir of George Bagot Gossett, 4th Dragoon Guards, by Charlotte, his wife, formerly Charlotte Douglas, spinster.[a] She *d.* 22 Jan. 1879, at Bournemouth. He *m.* secondly, 23 Jan. 1883, at St. Mary Abbots, Kensington, Agnes, 1st da. of Dugald Dove, of Nutshill, co. Renfrew, and of Palace Gate, Kensington.

Family Estates.—These, in 1883, appear to have been under 2,000 acres.

MOLEYNS, MOLINES, MOLYNS, or DE MOLEYNS.

[Sir John de Molyns, of Stoke Pogis, Bucks, was sum. to a Council,[b] 18 Feb. (1346/7), 21 Ed. III, by writ directed "*Joki de Molyns;*" this summons was clearly not such as to entitle him to a hereditary Barony tho' he is generally spoken of as such. Neither his son, grandson, or great grandson were so summoned.[c] This great-grandson (Sir William de Moleyns, also of Stoke Pogis) was slain at Orleans in 1428, aged 22, leaving a da. and h. who *m.* Robert Hungerford, as under.]

Barony by Writ.

I. 1445.

1. Robert Hungerford, s. and h. ap. of Robert, Lord Hungerford, by Margaret, *suo jure* Baroness Botreaux, was *b.* about 1420, and having *m.* in or before 1441 (when she was aged 13), Eleanor da. and h. of Sir William de Moleyns abovenamed (slain 1428) was sum. (v.p.) to Parl. as a Baron (LORD DE MOLEYNS) from 13 Jan. (1444/5), 23 Hen. VI., to 20 Jan. (1451/2), 30 Hen. VI. He *suc.* on the death of his father, 14 May 1459, to the *Barony of Hungerford*, with which dignity this Barony ever after continued united, falling into *abeyance* therewith in 1668, and being revived therewith in 1871. See "Hungerford" Barony, *cr.* 1426, *sub* the third and subsequent holders thereof.

MOLTON.

i.e., "Boringdon of North Molton, co. Devon," Viscountcy (*Parker*), *cr.* 1815 with the Earldom of Morley, which see.

MOLYNEUX OF MARYBOROUGH.

Viscountcy [I.]

I. 1628.

1. Sir Richard Molyneux, Bart., of Sefton, co. Lancaster, s. and h. of Sir Richard Molyneux, Bart. of the same (who was *cr.* a Baronet, 22 May 1611, being the second person so advanced) by Frances, da. of Sir Gilbert Gerard, Master of the Rolls, was *b.* about 1594; mat. at Oxford (Brasenose Coll.), 24 Nov. 1609, being then aged 15; *knighted* 27 March 1613; M.P. for Wigan, 1614; for Lancashire, 1625 and 1628-29; *suc.* his father *as second Baronet* in or before 1623, and was *cr.* 22 Dec. 1628, VISCOUNT MOLYNEUX OF MARYBOROUGH, in the Queen's county [I.], taking his seat 4 Nov. 1634. He *m.* Mary, 1st da. and coheir (whose issue, in 1655, became sole heir) of Sir Thomas Caryll, of Bentons in Shipley, co. Sussex, by Mary, da. of Sir John Tufton, Bart. He *d.* 8 May 1636, and was *bur.* at Sefton. Fun. certif. at Pub. Record office. Will pr. 1637. His widow, who was *bap.* 12 Aug. 1596, at Harting, co Sussex, *m.* Raphael Tartereau, Carver to the Queen Consort, who survived her. She *d.* before 21 June 1639. Admon. as of St. Martin's in the fields, 18 July 1639. Fun. certif. in Pub. Record office.

(a) She *m.* secondly, 30 July 1840, the Marquis de Vinchiaturo.

(b) The writ is headed "*D' Veniendo ad cons.*" He was one of (but) 16 Laymen who were so summoned.

(c) See vol. iii, p. 276, *sub* "Hungerford," for some account of the De Moleyns family in which notice (on line 3), the words "*William* de Moleyns, sum. to *Parl.*," are inadvertently put for "*John* de Moleyns, sum. to a *Council*." See also Lipscomb's "Bucks," vol. iv, 544—547, *sub* "Stoke Poges."

II. 1636. 2. RICHARD (MOLYNEUX), VISCOUNT MOLYNEUX OF MARYBOROUGH [I.], s. and h., b. about 1620. He (with his br. Caryll), took an active part in the civil war, on behalf of the King, raising two regiments of horse and foot, both being at the surrender of Oxford and, in 1651, at the battle of Worcester. He m. Frances, da. of William (SEYMOUR), 2d DUKE OF SOMERSET, by his second wife, Frances, da. of Robert (DEVEREUX), 2d EARL OF ESSEX. He d. s.p. at Croxteth, co. Lancaster about 1653. Fun. certif. at Pub. Record office. Admon. (to a creditor), 28 Nov. 1654. His widow m. (as his 3d wife), Thomas (WRIOTHESLEY), 4th EARL OF SOUTHAMPTON, who d. 16 May 1667, aged 60. She m. thirdly (as the third of his four wives) Conyers (DARCY), 2d EARL OF HOLDERNESSE, who d. 13 Dec. 1692). She was bur. 5 Jan. 1680/1, in Westm. Abbey. Admon 11 Feb, 1680/1.

III. 1653? 3. CARYLL (MOLYNEUX), VISCOUNT MOLYNEUX OF MARYBOROUGH [I.], br. and h., b. 1622; suc. to the peerage [I.], about 1653. Having taken part with his brother (as beforestated) on behalf of the King, he was accordingly outlawed by the Parl., but finally obtained. possession of his estates on payment of a large fine. By James II. he was made Lord Lieut. of Lancashire and Admiral of the narrow seas, He m. about 1650, Mary, da. of Sir Alexander BARLOW, of Barlow, co. Lancaster, by his second wife, Dorothy, da. of Sir Thomas GRESLEY, Bart. She d. 6 Feb. 1691,(a) and was bur. at Sefton. M.I. He d. at Croxteth, co. Lanc. 2 Feb. 1698/9, aged 77, and was bur. at Sefton.

IV. 1699. 4. WILLIAM (MOLYNEUX), VISCOUNT MOLYNEUX OF MARYBOROUGH [I.], 3d and yst. but only surv. s. and h.;(b) b. about 1655; suc. to the peerage [I.], 9 Feb. 1698/9. He m. firstly, about 1675, Bridget, da. and h. of Robert LUCY, of Charlecote, co. Warwick, by Margaret, da. of Thomas SPENCER, of Upton. She d. 23 April 1713, aged 58, and was bur. 5 May at Sefton. He m. secondly, 22 July 1716, at Warrington, Mary, da. of Lieut. Gen. (—) SKELTON.(c) He d. 8 and was bur. 12 March 1717, at Sefton, aged 62. She d. s.p. at Woolton, near Liverpool, 20 Feb. 1766.

V. 1717. 5. RICHARD (MOLYNEUX), VISCOUNT MOLYNEUX OF MARYBOROUGH [I.], s. and h. by 1st wife, b. about 1678; suc. to the peerage [I.], 8 March 1717.(d) He m. before 1706 Mary, 1st da. of Francis BRUDENELL, styled LORD BRUDENELL (s. and h. ap. of Robert, 2d EARL OF CARDIGAN), by Frances, da. of James (SAVILE), EARL OF SUSSEX. He d. s.p.m.s.,(e) 12 Dec. 1738, aged 60, at Little Oulton, Cheshire, and was bur. the 15th at Sefton. His widow m. Capt. Peter OSBORNE (who d. before her) and d. 2 April 1765, at Hoxton square, Midx. Will dat. 30 Nov. 1761, to 27 April 1764, pr. 28 June 1765.

(a) The date is given as "1691" in the pedigree entered at the College of Arms ("Howard" 152), but the date "1661" is given in the copy of the M.I. in "Lodge" (vol. iii, 256) thus "obiit 8 idus Februarii, Sanctæ Dorotheæ sacro, Anno Dni M.D.C.LXI."

(b) His eldest br., the Hon. Richard Molyneux, m. Mary, da. of William (Herbert), 1st Marquess of Powis, but d. s.p. and v.p. at Powis Castle, co. Montgomery.

(c) The following is taken from the Non Parochial Registers, Somerset House (237, Lib. 1), "1716, mense Julii. die 22. Denunciationibus omnibus omissis, nullo legitimo impedimento detecto, in oppido dicto, Warrington, ego infrascriptus [Thomas Worthington, O.P.], Gulielmum, Ld Molineux et filiam Mariam Skelton interrogavi, eorumque mutuo consensu habito, solemniter per verba de præsenti, matrimonio conjunxi; præsentibus testibus notis (——) Skelton, Roberto Molyneux, Jacobo Leyburn." See Estcourt and Payne's "English Catholic Nonjurors of 1715" where a list of the Viscount's lands are added, viz., "Manors of Sefton, Netherton, &c., entailed to his son, Richard and sons of Richard, by Mary, his wife, and failing issue to his younger sons, Caryl, William, Thomas and Edward. £2,351 19s. 1½d."

(d) The Hon. Richard Molyneux was one of "English Catholic Nonjurors of 1715," having "rent charge out of the estate of his father, William, Lord Molyneux, and a house at Much Woolton [Lancashire] £1,100."

(e) William, his only son, d. 15 Feb. 1706.

VI. 1738. 6. CARYLL (MOLYNEUX), VISCOUNT MOLYNEUX OF MARYBOROUGH [I.], br. and h. male; *b.* about 1680; *suc. to the peerage* [I.], 12 Dec. 1738. He *d.* unm. at Croxteth, 11, and was *bur.* 13 Nov. 1745, at Sefton.

VII. 1745. 8. WILLIAM (MOLYNEUX), VISCOUNT MOLYNEUX OF MARYBOROUGH [I.], br. and h. He was a Priest of the Society of Jesus. He *suc. to the peerage* [I.] in Nov. 1745, but being "old and not having any intention to marry "released his estate to his br. Thomas, who, however *d.* before him, 3 Dec. 1756. He *d.* unm. at Scoles, 30 March and was *bur.* 2 April 1759, at Sefton.

VIII. 1759. 9. CHARLES WILLIAM (MOLYNEUX), VISCOUNT MOLYNEUX OF MARYBOROUGH [I.], *also a Baronet* [1611], nephew and h. being only s. and h. of the Hon. Thomas MOLYNEUX, of Croxteth Hall, co. Lancaster, by Maria, widow of Joseph GRIFFIN, da. of James LEVESY, of London. He was *b.* 30 Sep. 1748; *suc.* his father in the family estates, 3 Dec. 1756, and *suc.* his uncle *in the peerage* [I.], 30 March 1759. Having conformed to the established religion, 5 March 1769, he was, two years later, *cr.* 30 Nov. 1771, EARL OF SEFTON in Ireland;[a] see that title.

MONAGHAN.

i.e., "BLAYNEY OF MONAGHAN[b] co. Monaghan," Barony [I.], (*Blayney*), *cr.* 1621; *ex.* 1874.

See "ROSSMORE OF MONAGHAN, co. Monaghan," Barony [I.] (*Cuninghame, afterwards Westenra*), *cr.* 1796; and "ROSSMORE OF MONAGHAN, co. Monaghan," Barony [U.K.] (*Westenra*), *cr.* 1838.

MONCHENSI, see MUNCHENSI.

MONCK.

i.e., "MONCK OF POTHERIDGE, BEAUCHAMP AND TEYES," Barony (*Monck*), *cr.* 1660 with the DUKEDOM OF ALBEMARLE, which see; *ex.* 1688.

MONCK OF BALLYTRAMMON.

Barony [I.] I 1797. Viscountcy [I.] I. 1801.

1. CHARLES-STANLEY MONCK, of Charleville co. Wicklow and Grange Gorman, co. Dublin, 1st s. of Thomas MONCK, Barrister at Law, by Judith, da. of Robert MASON, of Mason Brook; *suc.* on the death s.p.m. in 1787 of his uncle Henry MONCK, of Charleville and Grange Gorman afsd., to those estates; was M.P. for Newborough *alias* Gorey, 1790-97, and was *cr.* 23 Nov. 1797, BARON MONCK OF BALLYTRAMMON, co. Wexford [I.], and, three years later, was *cr.* 5 Jan. 1801, VISCOUNT MONCK OF BALLYTRAMMON, co. Wexford [I.] He *m.* in 1784, his cousin, Anne, da. of Henry QUIN, M.D., of Dublin, by Anne, da. of (his grandfather) Charles MONCK, of Grange Gorman. He *d.* 9 June 1802. His widow *m.* (as his fourth wife), Sir John Craven CARDEN, 1st Bart. [I.], who *d.* 21 Nov. 1820. She *d.* 20 Dec. 1823.

(a) "*Sefton in Ireland*" is, of course, a fiction. See p. 195, note "d," *sub* "Macdonald."

(b) The creation however is "Lord BLAYNEY, Baron of Monaghan, co. Monaghan."

II. 1802. 2. HENRY STANLEY (MONCK), VISCOUNT MONCK OF BALLYTRAMMON, &c. [I.], s. and h., b. 26 July 1785; suc. to the peerage [I.], 9 June 1802. He was cr. 12 Jan. 1822, EARL OF RATHDOWNE [I.] He m. 28 July 1806, Frances, 5th da. of William Power Keating (TRENCH), 1st EARL OF CLANCARTY [I.], by Anne, da. of the Rt. Hon. Charles GARDINER. She who was b. Oct. 1787, d. 22 Nov. 1843 in her 56th year at Charleville, co. Wicklow. He d. there, s.p.m.s.,(a) 20 Sep. 1848, in his 64th year when the Earldom of Rathdowne [I.] became extinct.

III. 1848. 3. CHARLES JOSEPH KELLY (MONCK), VISCOUNT MONCK OF BALLYTRAMMON [I.], br. and h. male; b. 12 July 1791; ed. at Rugby, 1799; Lieut. 43d Light Infantry, being present at the battles of Vittoria, Nive, Nivelle, Pyrenees and Tolouse, gaining a medal of five clasps. He suc. to the peerage [I.], 20 Sep. 1848. He m. 29 Nov. 1817, Bridget, da. of John WILLINGTON, of Killoskenane, co. Tipperary, by his second wife, Bridget, da. of Theobald BUTLER, of Knocke Castle, in that county. She d. 22 Jan. 1843. He d. in Merrion square, Dublin, 20 April 1849, in his 58th year.

IV. 1849. Barony [U.K.] I. 1866. 4. CHARLES STANLEY (MONCK), VISCOUNT MONCK OF BALLYTRAMMON, &c. [I.], s. and h.; b. 10 Oct. 1819, at Templemore, co. Tipperary; ed. at Trin. Coll., Dublin; Barrister (Dublin), 1841; suc. to the peerage [I.], 20 April 1849; M.P. for Portsmouth, 1852-57; a Lord of the Treasury, 1855-58; GOVERNOR GEN. OF CANADA, 1861, becoming, in 1867, Gov. GEN. OF BRITISH AMERICA, but resigned office in 1868. He was cr., 12 July 1866, BARON MONCK OF BALLYTRAMMON, co. Wexford [U.K.]; P.C., 1869; G.C.M.G., 1869; one of the Lord Justices of Ireland, 1873; Lord Lieut. of co. Dublin, 1874-92. He m., 23 June 1844, his cousin, Elizabeth Louisa Mary, 4th da. and coheir of Henry Stanley (MONCK), EARL OF RATHDOWNE [I.] and Frances, his wife, both abovenamed. She, who was b. 1 March 1814, d. at Charleville, 16 June 1892, aged 78, and was bur. at Powerscourt.

Family Estates.—These, in 1883, consisted of 5,717 acres in co. Wexford; 5,544 in co. Kilkenny; 2,478 in co. Wicklow; 212 in co. Westmeath, and 193 (valued at £2,237 a year) in co. Dublin. *Total* 14,144 acres worth £10,466 a year. *Principal Residence*; Charleville, near Bray.

MONCKTON OF SERLBY.

i.e., "MONCKTON OF SERLBY, co. Nottingham," Barony (*Monckton-Arundell*), cr. 1887;(b) see "GALWAY" Viscountcy [I.], cr. 1727, sub the 7th Viscount.

MONCREIFF OF TULLIEBOLE.

Barony. I. 1874. 1. "THE RT. HON. SIR JAMES MONCREIFF, Bart., Her Majesty's Justice Clerk, and President of the second division of the Court of Session in Scotland, and also one of the Senators of the College of Justice there;" was 2d s. of Sir James Wellwood MONCREIFF, 9th Bart.; one of the Lords of Session and Justiciary [S.], by Anne, da. of George ROBERTSON, Lieut. R.N.; was b. 29 Nov. 1811, in Edinburgh; ed. at the High School and at the University there; Advocate, 1833; Solicitor Gen. [S.], 1850-51; M.P. for Leith, 1851-59; for Edinburgh, 1859-68, and for the Universities of Glasgow and Aberdeen, 1868-69; was four times (April 1851 to March 1852, Dec. 1852 to March 1858, June 1859 to July 1866, and Dec. 1868 to Nov. 1869), Lord Advocate [S.]; Dean of the Faculty of Advocates [S.], 1858-69; Lord Rector of Edinburgh University, 1868-71; P.C., 1869; Lord Justice Clerk and President of the

(a) Besides two sons (who d. young and before he was advanced to an Earldom) he had no less than *eleven* daughters.

(b) This was one of the "Jubilee" peerages, for a list of which see vol. ii, p. 238, note "a," sub "Cheylesmore."

second division of the Court of Session [S.], 1869-88; *cr.* a *Baronet* (as "of Kilduff, co. Kinross"), 28 May 1871, being *cr.*, 9 Jan. 1874, BARON MONCREIFF OF TULLIEBOLE, co. Kinross. By the death s.p.m. of his eldest br., the Rev. Sir Henry Wellwood MONCREIFFE, 10th Bart. [S.], 3 Nov. 1883, aged 74, he *suc.* to the *Baronetcy* [S.], *cr.* 22 April 1626.(a) He *m.*, 12 Sep. 1834, Isabella, da. of Robert BELL, of Edinburgh, Procurator of the church of Scotland. She *d.* at 15 Great Stuart street, Edinburgh, 19 Dec. 1881.

Family Estates.—These, in 1883, were under 2,000 acres.

MONCY, see MUNCY.

MONEYDIE.

i.e., "MONEYDIE" Viscountcy [S.] (*Davia*), *cr.* 1698 by James II., when in exile, together with the EARLDOM OF ALMOND [S.], which see.

MONK, see MONCK.

MONK-BRETTON.(b)

See "HALIFAX OF MONK-BRETTON in the West Riding of the county of York," Viscountcy (*Wood*), *cr.* 1866.

MONK-BRETTON(b) OF CONYBORO AND HURSTPIERPOINT.

Barony. I. 1884. 1. THE RT. HON. JOHN GEORGE DODSON, of Conyboro, co. Sussex, only s. and h. of the Rt. Hon. Sir John DODSON, of the same, Judge of the Prerog. Court of Canterbury (1852-58), by Frances Priscilla, da. of George PEARSON, M.D., was *b.* 18 Oct. 1825; ed. at Eton and at Ch. Ch., Oxford; B.A. (1st Class Classics), 1847; M.A., 1850; Barrister (Linc. Inn), 1851; M.P. for East Sussex, 1857-74; for Chester, 1874-80, and for Scarborough, 1880-84; Dep. Speaker of the House of Commons, 1865-72; P.C., 1872; Financial Sec. to the Treasury, 1873-74; President of the Local Government Board, 1880-82, and Chancellor of the Duchy of Lancaster, 1882-84, being *cr.*, 4 Nov. 1884, BARON MONK-BRETTON(b) OF CONYBORO AND HURSTPIERPOINT, co. Sussex. He *m.*, 3 Jan. 1846, Florence, 2d da. of William John CAMPION, of Danny, co. Sussex, by Harriet, da. of Thomas Read KEMP, of Kemp-town, Brighton.

Family Estates.—These, in 1883, consisted of 2,916 acres in Sussex and 181 in the West Riding of Yorkshire. *Total* 3,097 worth £8,467 a year. *Principal Residence.* Conyboro, near Lewes, co. Sussex.

MONKSWELL.

Barony. I. 1885. 1. THE RT. HON. SIR ROBERT-PORRETT COLLIER, one of the Judges of the Judicial Committee of the Privy Council, eldest son of John COLLIER, of Grimstone and Monkswell, Devon, sometime (1832-41), M.P. for Plymouth, by Emma, da. of John PORRETT, of North Hill, Devon, was *b.* 21 June 1817, at Mount Tamar, near Plymouth; ed. at Trin. Coll., Cambridge; B.A., 1841; Barrister (Inner Temple) 1843; Recorder of Penzance; M.P. for Plymouth (in the Liberal interest), 1852-71; Queen's Counsel, 1854; Judge Advocate of the Fleet and Counsel to the Admiralty, 1859-63; Solicitor Gen. 1863-66, being *knighted*, 23 Nov. 1863; Attorney Gen. 1868-71; P.C. 1871; made

(a) The right of succession to this Baronetcy, after 1744, is somewhat doubtful.

(b) Monk Bretton, a town near Barnsley, in Yorkshire, with about 4,000 population, has been very hardly used as a peerage title. "Halifax of Monk Bretton" seems as absurd as "Manchester of Liverpool," while as to "Monk Bretton of Conyboro and Hurstpierpoint *in Sussex*" we must go to "Truro [in *Cornwall*] of Bowes," a hamlet in Southgate, co. *Middlesex*, and to "Leicester of Holkham" for a parallel.

a Justice of the Common Pleas on the 7th, and (two weeks later) made on the 22d Nov. 1871 (the former appointment being necessary to qualify for the latter one) one of the Judges of the Judicial Committee of the Privy Council.(a) He was (15 years later), *cr.* 1 July 1885,(b) BARON MONKSWELL of Monkswell, co. Devon. He *m.* 14 April 1844, Isabella Rose, da. of William Rose Rose, *formerly* HOLDEN, of Wolston Heath, co. Warwick, and of Daventry, co. Northampton, by Maria Isabella, da. and coheir of the Rev. George STRAHAN, D.D., Canon Res. of Rochester. She, who was *b.* 8 March 1815, *d.* 11 April 1886, at 7 Chelsea Embankment, and was *bur.* in Brompton cemetery. He *d.* six months later, 27 Oct. 1886, aged 69, at Grasse, near Cannes, in France, and was *bur.* with her. Will pr. 10 Dec. 1886 at above £82,000.

II. 1886. 2. ROBERT (COLLIER), BARON MONKSWELL, s. and h., *b.* 26 March 1845; ed. at Eton and at Trin. Coll., Cambridge; B.A. (1st Class, Law), 1866; Barrister (Inner Temple), 1869; sometime Conveyancing Counsel to the Treasury and an Examiner of the High Court of Justice; *suc. to the peerage*, 27 Oct. 1886; a Lord-in-Waiting, 1892. He *m.*, 21 Aug. 1873, Mary Josephine, da. of Joseph Alfred HARDCASTLE, of Holt, co. Norfolk.

Family Estates.—These, in 1883, were under 2,000 acres.

MONMOUTH.

Earldom. I. 1622. 1. "SIR ROBERT CARY, Knt., Chamberlain of the Household of Charles, Prince of Wales,"(c) 9th and yst. s. of Henry (CAREY), 1st BARON HUNSDON, by Anne, da. of Sir Thomas MORGAN, was *b.* 1560; M.P. for Morpeth, 1586-89; for Callington, 1593; for Northumberland, 1597-98, and 1601; and for Grampound, 1621-22; served as a volunteer against the Spanish Armada in 1588, and was in command in Normandy in 1591, being *knighted* (by the Earl of Essex) in Oct. 1591; sometime Deputy Warden of the West and East Marches, and afterwards Warden of the East and Middle Marches; was the first to announce the death of Queen Elizabeth to King James in Scotland, with whom he had previously ingratiated himself, and to whom he was a Gent. of the Bedchamber, from March to May 1603, when he was made a Gent. of the Privy Chamber; was, in 1605, Master of the Household to Prince

(a) This appointment which lasted but a few days (7 to 22 Nov. 1871), was practically an illusory one, and was in direct contravention of the act which, *but a few months before*, had established the Judicial Committee of the Privy Council as a body that should consist of none save those who had previously been Judges, either in India or in the superior courts at Westminster. "*The Collier Juggle*" (as it was generally called) created great scandal. It was marvellously well hit off by a cartoon in "Punch" of that date, representing Sir Robert (with his legal robes well held up), jumping from the back of a horse, as a performer in an equestrian circus, through a series of hoops *at once*, held up for him by Mr. Gladstone as "the clown." The manner in which the Prime Minister (Gladstone) tried to throw the blame on the (not-over-strong-minded) Chancellor, Lord Hatherley, is well depicted in the "Personal Remembrances of Sir Frederick Pollock" under an account of a dinner party, 1 Feb. 1872, more than two months after this stroke of legerdemain, which was still, aparently, uppermost, in conversation. "The Lord Chancellor seemed very happy, notwithstanding *the Collier affair*, in which the course taken by the Government is almost universally condemned. Frank Doyle, the other day, said that the division of responsibility between the Chancellor and Mr. Gladstone in the recent appointment of Collier to the Judgeship-in-the-Privy Council, so as to make *each* individually innocent, reminded him of Sterne's story of the Abbess of Andouillet and the Novice, when dividing between them the pronunciation of the *naughty words* used to make the obstinate mule go on." Both the Chief Justices (Cockburn and Bovill) protested against this fraud on an act so recently passed, and a vote of censure on the Ministry was moved in 1872, in both houses, being lost in the Commons by 268 to 241, and in the Lords by only two votes, *viz.* 89 to 87.

(b) See vol. iv, p. 235, note "a," *sub* "Hobhouse" for a batch of a dozen Baronies, of which this was one, *cr.* in June and July 1885.

(c) So described when *cr.* a Baron (1622) in the "*Creations*, 1483—1646," in ap. 47th Rep. D.K. Pub. Records.

Charles, to whom in 1611, he was Master of the Robes, and from 1617 to 1625 Chamberlain, and was *cr.* 6 Feb. 1621/2, BARON CAREY OF LEPPINGTON, co. York. He was Gent. of the Bedchamber to King Charles, 1625, and was by him *cr.* 7 Feb. 1625/6,(a) EARL OF MONMOUTH. Lord Lieut. of Staffordshire, 1627-28; Councellor of the North, 1628. He *m.* 20 Aug. 1593, at Berwick upon Tweed, Elizabeth, widow of Sir Henry WIDDRINGTON (whose will was pr. at Durham, 15 Feb. 1592/3), da. of Sir Hugh TREVANION, of Caerhayes, co. Cornwall, by Sybilla, sister of Anne, BARONESS HUNSDON, da. of Sir Thomas MORGAN, abovenamed. He *d.* at Moor Park, Herts, 12 April 1639, and was *bur.* at Rickmansworth.(b) Will (in which he desires to be *bur.* with his parents in Westm. Abbey), dat. 3 Sep. 1635, pr. 20 June 1639.(c) Funeral certif. at Pub. Record. His widow *d.* three years later, and was *bur.* at Rickmansworth. Will pr. July 1641.

II. 1639, to 1661. 2. HENRY (CAREY), EARL OF MONMOUTH [1626], and BARON CAREY OF LEPPINGTON [1622], s. and h., *bap.* 27 Jan. 1595/6, at Denham, Bucks; mat. at Oxford (Ex. Coll.), 7 June 1611; B.A. (by disp.), 17 Feb. 1613/4; K.B. at the creation of the Prince of Wales, 3 Nov. 1616; M.P. for Camelford, 1621-22; for Beverley, 1624-25; for Tregony, 1625; for St. Mawes, 1626, and for Grampound, 1628-29; *styled* LORD LEPPINGTON from 1626 till he *suc. to the peerage*, 12 April 1639; Keeper of Kenilworth Castle, &c. 1660. He *m.* (settl. 16 Feb. 1619/20), Martha, 1st da. of Lionel (CRANFIELD), 1st EARL OF MIDDLESEX, by his first wife, Elizabeth, da. of Richard SHEPHERD, of London, Merchant. He *d.* s.p.m.s., 13 June 1661, aged 65, and was *bur.* at Rickmansworth, when *all his honours* became *extinct*.(d) His will dat. 31 July 1659, pr. 20 June 1661. His widow who was *bap.* 12 July 1601, at St. Michael's Bassishaw, *d.* in St. James square, 10 April 1677. Will dat. 26 March, pr. 12 June 1677.

[LIONEL CAREY, *styled* LORD LEPPINGTON, s. and h. ap. He *d.* unm. and v.p., being slain *ex parte Regis* at the battle of Marston Moor, 4 July 1644.]

[HENRY CAREY, *styled*, since 1644, LORD LEPPINGTON, 2d but 1st surv. s. and h. ap. He *m.* Mary, illegit. da. of Emanuel (SCROPE), EARL OF SUNDERLAND, by Martha JEANES, spinster. He *d.* v.p. of the small pox, 1649, and was *bur.* in the Savoy chapel. Admon. 5 May 1649. His widow *m.*, 12 Feb. 1654/5, at St. Dionis, Backchurch, Charles (POWLETT), 1st DUKE OF BOLTON, who *d.* 27 Feb. 1698/9. She *d.* 1 Nov. 1680, at Moulins, in France, and was *bur.* the 12th at Wensley, co. York.]

[HENRY CAREY, *styled* LORD LEPPINGTON, grandson and h. ap, being only child and h. of Henry CAREY, *styled* LORD LEPPINGTON, and Mary, his wife, both abovenamed. He *d.* very young and before his grandfather and was *bur.* 24 May 1653, in Westm. Abbey.]

Dukedom. I. 1663, to 1685. 1. SIR JAMES SCOTT, *formerly* CROFTS, illegit. s. of King Charles II.(e), by Lucy WALTERS, *alias* BARLOW, spinster,(f) was *b.* 9 April 1649, at Rotterdam, and being placed, about 1657, under the charge of William (Crofts), Baron Crofts of Saxham, was thenceforth known by the surname of *Crofts*; ed. at Port Royal, Paris; came over to England at the Restoration in 1660 as "Capt. Crofts;" was *knighted*, and, having assumed the name of *Scott* (in anticipation of his marriage which

---

(a) See list of the six Earls (of which he was one), *cr.* that day, in vol. ii, p. 283, note "c," *sub* "Cleveland."

(b) See "*Her. and Gen.*" vol. iv, p. 45, &c., for a good account of his family, &c.

(c) His "*Memoirs*" first published in 1759, greatly illustrate the history of the Court transactions of that period.

(d) He is said to have been a voluminous author, tho' Walpole remarks that "we have scarce anything of his own composition."

(e) His great beauty, so unlike that of the King his reputed father, makes it more than probable that he was (as often considered) a son of Algernon Sydney, one of a handsome race, noted for gallantry to the fair sex. The Duke is also said to have had a mole on the upper lip which was a characteristic feature of that family.

(f) See "*N. and Q.*," 2d s. II, 375, as to her descent, where one correspondent (who

took place two months later) was as "Sir James Scott" *cr.*, 14 Feb. 1662/3, BARON SCOTT OF TINDALL,[a] co. Northumberland, EARL OF DONCASTER, co. York, and DUKE OF MONMOUTH;[b] M.A. of Cambridge (*per lit. reg.*), 16 March 1662/3, being incorp. at Oxford, 28 Sep. following; K.G., 28 March, being inst., 22 April 1663. Having *m.*, 20 April 1663, at the house of her stepfather, the Earl of Wemyss [S.], in London, Anne, *suo jure* COUNTESS OF BUCCLEUCH [S.] (who was *b.* 11 Feb. 1651, at Dundee, and who *suc.* to that dignity 12 March 1660/1), he and she were *cr.*, on the day of their marriage, LORD AND LADY SCOTT OF WHITCHESTER AND ESKDALE, EARL AND COUNTESS OF DALKEITH, and DUKE AND DUCHESS OF BUCCLEUCH [S.]; P.C., 1670.[c] In 1672-73 he was in command of the British Auxiliaries sent to France, and was Lieut. Gen. in the French army, distinguishing himself at the capture of Maestricht from the Dutch. He was also in 1672 Ambassador to Paris and Utrecht, Chief Justice in Eyre, south of Trent, 1673-79; Great Chamberlain [S.] for life, 1673; Lord Lieut. of the East Riding, 1673-79; Master of the Horse, 1674-79; Chancellor of the Univ. of Cambridge, 1674-82; Lord Lieut. of Staffordshire, 1677-79; was in command of the British Auxiliaries sent to Flanders, in 1678, and of the forces sent to Scotland in 1679 where, 22 July 1679, he defeated the Covenanters at Bothwell bridge. P.C. [S.], 1679. In that year, however, he was deprived of all his offices (other than those for life), and ordered to leave the kingdom. Soon after the accession of James II., he landed, 11 June 1685, at Lyme, in Dorset, and assumed the title of King. His forces were routed, 5 July following, at Sedgemore,[d] and he was captured three days afterwards when, having been attainted on the 15 June of high treason, he was executed 15 July 1685, in his 37th year, on Tower Hill, and *bur.* in the chapel of St. Peter's ad vincula.[e] His English honours, *the Dukedom of Monmouth*, *the Earldom of Doncaster* and the *Barony of Scott of Tindall became* accordingly *forfeited*, but the Scotch peerages enjoyed, *suo jure*, by his widow, were not affected. This lady long survived him. See under "BUCCLEUCH" Dukedom [S.], *cr.* 1663.

[CHARLES SCOTT, *styled* EARL OF DONCASTER, s. and h. ap.; *b.* 24 Aug. 1672, and *d.* 9 Feb. 1673/4.]

[JAMES SCOTT, *styled* EARL OF DONCASTER till (the forfeiture of his father), 1685, being subsequently *styled* EARL OF DALKEITH, 2d but 1st surv. s. and h.; *b.* 23 May 1674; *d.* before his mother, 14 March 1704/5.]

See fuller particulars under "Buccleuch," Dukedom [S.]

ignores her mother) makes her the da. of Richard Walter, said to have assumed the name of Barlow, who was said to be son of [an undoubted] Roger Walter, of Haverfordwest, living with issue in 1609, tho', at that date, he had no son named Richard; while another makes her "*b.* at Ros Market, about five miles from Haverfordwest," being da. of "Richard Walter, Esq., of Roch and Trefran, co. Pembroke," by "Bridget, da. of Henry Midleton, of Midleton Hall, co. Carmarthen, Esq.;" but see also Howard's "*Mis. Gen. et Her.*," 2d s., vol. iv, p. 264, where a nearly contemporary (1684) pedigree by J. F. Van Bassen, goes fully into her ancestry, making her da. of *William* Walters, of Roche Castell, co. Pembroke, by Elizabeth, da. of John Protheroe, of Hawkesbrook, co. Carmarthen, Master of the Requests. It is not very clear why she was generally known as "Mrs. Barlow." She was living in Paris in July 1656, and is believed to have died soon afterwards.

(a) In Sir William Fraser's "*Scotts of Buccleuch*" it is stated that in the original warrant, 10 Nov. 1662, the designation of this Barony was "of Fotheringay."

(b) Pepys, in his diary, 2 Feb. 1662/3, says that the Duke of Monmouth was to have precedence of the Duke of Buckingham and all other Dukes. He speaks of him in 1665 as "the most skittish, leaping gallant that ever I saw."

(c) At some date between 1674 and 1686 the King gave licence to all his natural sons to be called "*Fitz Roy*," a privilege of which apparently the Duke of Monmouth, the Duke of Richmond, and the Earl of Plymouth, did not avail themselves. See vol. ii, p. 285, note "d," *sub* "Cleveland."

(d) See "*N. & Q.*," 1st S, I, 427, as to the possible whereabouts of some of the Monmouth correspondence.

(e) He had six children all born between 1672 and 1678, but subsequently he deserted his wife for Henrietta, *suo jure* Baroness Wentworth, to whom he considered himself as lawfully married before God and who survived him but a few months.

[FRANCIS (SCOTT), DUKE OF BUCCLEUCH, &c. [S.], grandson and h., being s. and h. of James SCOTT, *styled* EARL OF DALKEITH, next abovenamed; *b.* 11 Jan. 1694/5; *suc.* his grandmother, 6 Feb. 1732, as DUKE OF BUCCLEUCH, &c. [S.], and was *restored*, by Act of Parl., 23 March 1743 *to the English Peerages* of BARON SCOTT OF TINDAL and EARL OF DONCASTER (but *not*(a) however to the *Dukedom of Monmouth*) forfeited by the attainder of his grandfather, James, Duke of Monmouth, abovenamed. See "*Buccleuch*," Dukedom [S.], *cr.* 1663, *sub* the second Duke.

---

i.e., "MONMOUTH" Earldom (*Mordaunt*), *cr.* 1689; see "PETERBOROUGH" Earldom, *cr.* 1628, *sub* the 3d Earl, with which Earldom this dignity became united in 1697 till both became *extinct* in 1814.

CHARLES (MIDDLETON), 2d EARL OF MIDDLETON [S.], who was *attainted* in 1689 was *cr.* by the *titular* King James III. soon after the death (16 Sep. 1701), of the exiled King James II., EARL OF MONMOUTH.(b) His issue male became extinct on the death of his son, John, in or shortly before Feb. 1746/7.

MONSON OF CASTLEMAINE.

Viscountcy [I.]
I. 1628,
to
1661.

1. SIR WILLIAM MONSON, 2d s. of Sir Thomas MONSON, 1st Bart., of Carleton, co. Lincoln, by Margaret, da. of Sir Edmund ANDERSON, Lord Ch. Justice of the Common Pleas; was *b.* 1607; was twice tried but both times acquitted of being concerned in the poisoning of Sir Thomas Overbury; was *knighted* at Theobalds, 12 Feb. 1622/3, and was *cr.*, 23 Aug. 1628, BARON BELLINGNARD, co. Limerick, and VISCOUNT MONSON OF CASTLEMAINE, co. Kerry [I.] Tho' concerned as late as 1646 on behalf of the King at Oxford, he about that time in the House of Commons took the side of the rebels; was a "committee man" for the county of Surrey and finally (8 to 23 Jan. 1648/9), one of the Regicide Judges tho' not one who actually signed the death warrant of the King. After the restoration he was *degraded from all his honours*, 12 July 1661, and sentenced to be drawn in a sledge, with a rope round his neck, to Tyburn) which was done, 30 Jan. 1662/3, on the anniversary of the King's murder) and to remain a prisoner in London for life. He *m.* firstly Margaret, widow of Charles (HOWARD), 1st EARL OF NOTTINGHAM (who *d.* 14 Dec. 1624), da. of James (STEWART), EARL OF MORAY [S.], by Margaret, da. and h. of James (STEWART), also EARL OF MORAY [S.], sometime Regent of Scotland. She *d.* 4 Aug. 1639, at Covent Garden, and was *bur.* the 19th (with her first husband) at Chelsea. Fun. certif. in Pub. Record office. He *m.* secondly Frances, da. of Thomas ALSTON, of Polstead, co. Suffolk, by Frances, da. of Simon BLOMFIELD. She *d.* before 25 Feb. 1650/1 (being then late of St. Martin's in the fields) when admon. was granted to her husband, Viscount Monson. He *m.* thirdly Elizabeth, widow of Edward HORNER, of Mells, co. Somerset, relict formerly of Sir Francis FOLJAMBE, Bart. (who *d.* 17 Dec. 1640), da. of Sir George REREBY, of Thribergh, co. York, by Elizabeth, da. and coheir of John TAMWORTH. He *d.* s.p.m.s. in 1678. His widow *m.* (for her 4th husband) Sir Adam FELTON, 3d Bart., who *d.* Feb. 1696/7, and *d.*, before him, 26 Dec. 1695, at Bury St. Edmund's, Suffolk. Admon. 24 July 1696.

MONSON OF BURTON.

Barony.
I. 1728.

1. SIR JOHN MONSON, Bart., K.B., s. and h. of George MONSON, of Broxbourne, Herts (who *d.* 16 Oct. 1726, aged 67), by Anne, da. and h. of Charles WREN, of the isle of Ely, was *b.* about 1693; mat. at Oxford (Ch. Ch.), 26 Jan. 1707/8, aged 15; was M.P.

(a) See vol. ii, p. 48, note "b," *sub* "Buccleuch" as to the probable reason for such omission which reason however ceased in 1814, on the extinction of the Earldom of Monmouth.

(b) See vol. i, p. 59, note "b," *sub* "Albemarle," for a list of "Jacobite Peerages."

for Lincoln, 1722-28; inv. K.B., 27 May and inst. 17 June 1725, being one of the orig. knights at the restoration of that order; *suc.* as *Baronet* and to the family estates of Carlton and Burton, co. Lincoln, on the death, 7 March 1726/7, of his uncle, Sir William Monson, 4th Bart. (a dignity *cr.* 29 June 1611), and was 28 May *cr.* 1728, BARON MONSON OF BURTON, co. Lincoln. He was Capt. of the Gent. Pensioners, 1733; P.C., 1737; first Commission of Trade, 1737-48. He *m.* 8 April 1725, at St. Geo. the Martyr, Queen square, Margaret, 4th and yst. da. of Lewis (WATSON), 1st EARL OF ROCKINGHAM, by Catherine, da. and coheir of George (SONDES), EARL OF FEVERSHAM. He *d.* in Piccadilly, 18 July 1748, aged 55, and was *bur.* at South Carlton, co. Lincoln. Will pr. 1748. His widow, who was *bap.* 22 March 1695/6, at ROCKINGHAM, *d.* in South Audley street, 24 Feb. 1751/2, and was *bur.* at South Carlton. Her admon. 9 March 1752.

II. 1748. 2. JOHN (MONSON), BARON MONSON OF BURTON, 1st s. and h.,(a) *b.* 23 July 1727, *suc. to the peerage*, 18 July 1748; *cr.* LL.D. of Cambridge, 1749; Ch. Justice in Eyre, south of Trent, 1765-66. He *m.* 23 June 1752, at Harpswell, co. Lincoln, Theodosia, da. of John MADDISON, of Stamford, in that county, by Catherine, da. of George WHICHCOTE, of Harpswell afsd. He *d.* in Albemarle street,(b) 23 July 1774, aged 47, and was *bur.* at South Carlton. Will pr. July 1774. His widow, who was *b.* 15 June, 1725, at Ketton, co. Rutland, *d.* (nearly 50 years after her husband), 20 Feb. 1821, at Tunbridge Wells, in her 96th year, having outlived by 12 years the accession of her *great grandson* to the title. She was *bur.* at Eltham, co. Kent. Will pr. 1821.

III. 1774. 3. JOHN (MONSON), BARON MONSON OF BURTON, s. and h., *b.* 25 May, and *bap.* 22 June 1753, at St. James' Westm.; *suc. to the peerage*, 23 July 1774; was Recorder of the city of Lincoln. He *m.* 18 July 1777, at Cashiobury, in Watford, Herts, Elizabeth, da. of William Anne Holles (CAPEL), 4th EARL OF ESSEX, by his first wife, Frances, da. and coheir of Sir Charles HANBURY-WILLIAMS, K.B. He *d.* in Seymour place, Paddington, 20 May 1806, in his 53d year, and was *bur.* at South Carlton. Will dat. 11 June 1791, pr. 6 Feb. 1806. His widow, who was *b.* 10 Aug. 1755, *d.* 23 Feb. 1834, near St. Albans, Herts, aged 78, and was *bur.* at St. Peter's, in St. Albans afsd. Will pr. June 1834.

IV. 1806. 4. JOHN GEORGE (MONSON), BARON MONSON OF BURTON, only s. and h., *b.* 1 Sep. 1785, at Burton afsd.; ed. at Harrow; mat. at Oxford (Ch. Ch.), 19 April 1804; *suc. to the peerage*, 20 May 1806. He *m.* 30 Oct. 1807, at St. Geo. Han. sq., Sarah Elizabeth, da. of John (SAVILE), 2d EARL MEXBOROUGH OF LIFFORD [I.], by Elizabeth, da. and h. of John STEPHENSON. He *d.* in Seymour place afsd., 14 Nov. 1809, aged 24, and was *bur.* at South Carlton. Will pr. 1810. His widow, who was *b.* 4 Feb. 1786, *m.* 21 Oct. 1816, at St. James' Westm., Henry Richard (GREVILLE), 3d EARL BROOKE OF WARWICK CASTLE and EARL OF WARWICK, who *d.* 10 Aug. 1853, aged 74. She *d.* 30 Jan. 1851, in Carlton gardens, Midx., aged 64, and was *bur.* at Gatton, co. Surrey Will pr. April 1851.

V. 1809. 5. FREDERICK JOHN (MONSON), BARON MONSON OF BURTON, only s. and h., *b.* 3 Feb. 1809 in Seymour place afsd., and *suc. to the peerage* 14 Nov. following; mat. at Oxford (Ch. Ch.), 31 March 1827; *cr.* D.C.L., 11 June 1834. He *m.*, 21 June 1832, at St. James' Westm., Theodocia, yst. da. of Latham BLACKER, of Newent, co. Gloucester, sometime Major in the 65th Foot. He *d.* s.p. at Brighton, 7 Oct. 1841, aged 32, and was *bur* at Gatton afsd. Will pr. Dec. 1841. His widow, who was *b.* and *bap.* at Warkworth, co. Northumberland *d.* at Malvern Wells, 8 July 1891, aged 88. Will pr. at £65,220.

(a) Lewis Monson, his next brother, took the name of Watson, on inheriting, in 1746, the estates of that (his maternal family), and was *cr.* in 1760, Baron Sondes of Lees Court, co. Kent.

(b) So says the "*Annual Reg.*" but elsewhere it is said that he died at Scarborough co. York.

VI. 1841. 6. WILLIAM JOHN (MONSON), BARON MONSON OF BURTON, cousin and h. male, being only s. and h. of Col. the Hon. William MONSON, by Anne, yst. da. and coheir of John DEBONNAIRE, of Lisbon, Merchant, which William (who *d.* 26 Dec. 1807, aged 47), was 4th s. of John, the 2d Baron. He was *b.* 14 May 1796, at Negapatam, in the East Indies; mat. at Oxford (Ch. Ch.), 27 Jan. 1814; B.A., 1817; M.A., 1820; Student of Lincoln's Inn, 1817; *suc. to the peerage*, 7 Oct. 1841; F.R.S., F.S.A., &c. He *m.*, 8 May 1828, at St. Giles in the fields, Eliza, da. of Edmund LARKEN, of Bedford square, Midx., by Anne, da. of John GREAVES, of Mark Lane, London. He *d.* at the Great Western hotel, Paddington, 17 Dec. 1862, in his 67th year, and was *bur.* at South Carlton. His widow, who was *b.* 24 Oct. and *bap.* 24 Nov. 1803, at St. Botolphs, Bishopsgate, *d.* (a month later) 22 Jan. 1863, aged 60, at Norwood, co. Surrey, and was *bur.* at South Carlton.

VII. 1862. 7. WILLIAM JOHN (MONSON), BARON MONSON OF BURTON [1728], also a *Baronet* [1611], s. and h., *b.* 18 Feb. 1829, in Queen Anne street, Marylebone; *bap.* there 19 March; ed. at Eton and at Ch. Ch.), Oxford; B.A., 1849; M.P. for Reigate, 1858-62; *suc. to the peerage*, 17 Dec. 1862; Treasurer of the Household, 1873-74; Capt. of the Yeomen of the Guard, 1880-85; one of the Speakers of the House of Lords, 1882. He was *cr.*, 13 Aug. 1886, VISCOUNT OXENBRIDGE OF BURTON, co. Lincoln; Master of the Horse, 1892. He *m.*, 7 Aug. 1869, at St. Peter's, Eaton square, Maria Adelaide, Dow. COUNTESS OF YARBOROUGH, 2d da. of Cornwallis (MAUDE), 3d VISCOUNT HAWARDEN [I.], by Jane Crawfurd, da. of Patrick Crawfurd BRUCE. She was *b.* Dec. 1814.

Family Estates.—These, in 1883, consisted of 8,100 acres in Lincolnshire, and 2,034 co. Surrey. *Total* 4,743 acres worth £7,247 "gross annual value." *Principal Residence.* Burton Hall, co. Lincoln, the estate of Gatton Park, near Reigate, Surrey, having been sold since 1883.

MONT, see (also) under MOUNT.(a)

MONTACUTE, or MONTAGU.

Barony by Writ.

I. 1299. 1. SIMON DE MONTACUTE, of Shipton-Montacute, co. Somerset, s. and h. of William DE MONTACUTE (living 1257), was in 1282 in the expedition against Wales, and in 1294 in the French and subsequently in the Scotch wars; Gov. of Corfe Castle, 1298, and was sum. 8 June (1294), 22 Ed. I., with about 60 others, to advise on the affairs of the Realm,(b) being afterwards sum. to Parl. as a Baron (LORD MONTACUTE) by writs directed "*Simoni de Monte acuto*" from 29 Dec. (1299), 28 Ed. I., to 6 Oct. (1315), 9 Ed. II. His name appears as "*Simon, Dominus de Monte acuto,*" to the famous letter of the Barons in 1301 to the Pope.(c) He is said to have *m.* Aufrica, da. of Fergus, and sister of Orray, KING OF MAN. He *d.* about 1316.

II. 1316? 2. WILLIAM (DE MONTACUTE), LORD MONTACUTE, s. and h., who had v.p. distinguished himself in the French and Scotch wars and been made K.B. in 1306. He was sum. to Parl. from 20 Nov. (1317), 11 Ed. II., to 25 Aug. (1318), 12 Ed. II.; was Steward of the Household, 1317, and Seneschal of Aquitaine. He *m.* Elizabeth, da. of Sir Peter DE MONTFORT, of Beaudesert Castle, co. Warwick. He *d.* in Gascony, 6 Nov. 1319, and was *bur.* at St. Frideswide's Monastery, Oxford. His widow *m.* (as his second wife) Thomas (DE FURNIVALL), 1st LORD FURNIVALL, who *d.* 3 Feb. 1331/2. She *d.* March 1354 and was *bur.* at St. Frideswide's afsd. M.I.

(a) Many of the titles now spelt "*Mont*" were formerly spelt "*Mount*," but the converse does not hold good. Accordingly *all* such titles under either spelling, are *noticed* under the latter (tho' in some cases they are described under the former) spelling.

(b) See vol. i, p. 259, note "c," *sub* "Basset de Sapcote," as to this not constituting a regular writ of summons to Parl.

(c) See "*Nicolas*," pp. 761—809, for a full account of this letter.

III. 1319. 3. WILLIAM (DE MONTACUTE), LORD MONTACUTE, s. and h., aged 18 at his father's death in 1319; was sum. to Parl. from 5 June (1331), 5 Ed. III., to 29 Nov. (1336), 10 Ed. III., being *cr.*, 16 March 1337, EARL OF SALISBURY. He *d.* 30 Jan. 1344.

IV. 1344. 4. WILLIAM (DE MONTACUTE), EARL OF SALISBURY, and LORD MONTACUTE, s. and h., *b.* 25 June 1328; K.G., 1348. He *d.* s.p.s., 3 June 1397.

V. 1397, to 1400. 5. JOHN (DE MONTACUTE), EARL OF SALISBURY [1337], LORD MONTACUTE [1299], LORD MONTHERMER [1309], and LORD MONTACUTE [1357], nephew and h., being s. and h. of John, LORD MONTACUTE (so sum. in 1357) by Margaret, *de jure suo jure* BARONESS MONTHERMER, which John was next br. to William, Earl of Salisbury, and Lord Montacute, next abovenamed. K.G., 1397. He was *beheaded* 7 Jan. 1400, when, being considered attainted, *all his honours were forfeited.*

* * * * * *

VI. 1421. 6. THOMAS DE MONTACUTE, s. and h., *b.* 1388; sum. to Parl. as EARL OF SALISBURY, 26 Oct. 1409; K.G., 1414; was *restored*(a) to the dignities held by his father in (1421), 9 Hen. V., becoming thereby LORD MONTACUTE, &c. He *d.* s.p.m., 3 Nov. 1428, aged 40.

VII. 1428. 7. ALICE, *suo jure* COUNTESS OF SALISBURY, BARONESS MONTACUTE, &c., only da. and h., *suc.* in 1428, being then wife of SIR RICHARD NEVILL, who accordingly was recognised, 12 July 1429,(b) as EARL OF SALISBURY, and was confirmed in that Earldom " by patent 4 May 1442,"(c) K.G., about 1438. He was *attainted* Nov. 1459, but *restored in blood and honours*, 7 Oct. 1460. He was beheaded, 31 Dec. 1460, aged 60.

VIII. 1460, to 1471. 8. RICHARD (NEVILL), EARL OF WARWICK, EARL OF SALISBURY, LORD MONTACUTE, &c., s. and h., *b.* 22 Nov. 1428, who, having *m.* before 23 July 1449, Anne, *suo jure* COUNTESS OF WARWICK, was confirmed in the Earldom of Warwick, 23 July 1449. He *suc.* as EARL OF SALISBURY, &c., 31 Dec. 1460; K.G. 1460/1. This famous Earl ("the Kingmaker") *d.* s.p.m. (being slain at Barnet), 15 April 1471, when *all his honours* became *dormant*, or fell into *abeyance.*(d)

* * * * *

IX. 1485, to 1499. 9. EDWARD (PLANTAGENET), EARL OF WARWICK, EARL OF SALISBURY, &c., s. and h. of George, DUKE of Clarence, by Isabel, 1st da. and coheir of Richard (NEVILL), EARL OF WARWICK AND SALISBURY, LORD MONTACUTE, &c., next abovenamed; *b.* 21 Feb. 1474; was, on the death of his mother's sister, 16 March 1485, the representative of the said Earl Richard, his maternal grandfather and as such(e) (being heir to his Baronies) became LORD MONTACUTE [1299], LORD MONTHERMER [1309], and LORD MONTACUTE [1357]. He *d.* unm. being beheaded 24 Nov. 1499, aged 25, when *all his honours* became *forfeited.*

* * * *

For fuller particulars see "SALISBURY," Earldom, cr. 1337

(a) The attainder of his father was not however reversed till (1461), 1 Ed. I.

(b) In Doyle's "*official Baronage*," it is stated that he was "*cr.* Earl of Salisbury, 12 July 1429."

(c) "*Courthope*," *sub* "Salisbury" and " Warwick."

(d) The coheirs were his two daughters of whom (1) Isabel, *b.* 5 Sep. 1451, *m.* 11 July 1469, George (Plantagenet) Duke of Clarence (who was attainted and executed, 18 Feb. 1477/8), and *d.* 22 Dec. 1476, leaving issue, as in the text. (2) Anne, Queen Consort to Richard III. She *d.* s.p. (a few months before that King), 16 March 1485; when the abeyance terminated.

(e) Notwithstanding the attainder of his father, the dignities he inherited thro' his mother appear to have been allowed to him.

X. 1513. *10.* MARGARET, *suo jure* COUNTESS OF SALISBURY, wife of Sir Richard POLE, K.G., only sister and h., was *b.* about 1476; and was *restored* by act of Parl. (1513), 5 Hen. VIII. to the dignity of COUNTESS OF SALISBURY(a) as "sister and heir of blood of Edward [PLANTAGENET], late EARL OF SALISBURY AND WARWICK, son of Isabel, da. and h.(b) of Richard [NEVILL], EARL OF SALISBURY, son and heir of Alice, COUNTESS OF SALISBURY." It is presumed that she would thereby be entitled to inherit *the Baronies of Montacute and Monthermer.* She was *attainted* in 1539, whereby *all her honours* were *forfeited* and was *beheaded*, 27 May 1541.

For fuller particulars see "SALISBURY," Earldom, cr. 1337.

XI. 1529, to 1539. *11.* SIR HENRY POLE, s. and h. ap. of the abovenamed Margaret, by Sir Richard POLE, K.G., *b.* about 1492; *suc.* his father Nov. 1504; was *knighted*, 25 Dec. 1513, at Touraine;(c) had livery of his lands, 1513; was "restored to the King's favour by the title of LORD MOUNTAGUE in [1521-22], 13 Hen. VIII.,"(d) and sat (1 Dec. 1529), in the Parl. that was sum., 3 Nov. 1529, in the Barony of Montacute, then vested in his mother, being also sum. to Parl. 5 Jan. (1533/4), 25 Hen. VIII., and 8 June (1536), 28 Hen. VIII., by writs directed "*Henrico Pole de Montagu*" [LORD MONTAGU] and sitting in the precedency belonging to the said Barony of Montacute. He was one of the signatories "rankt the first in number"(e) of the letter to the Pope concerning the proposed divorce of the King, whom he accompanied to France, Oct. to Nov. 1532. He *m.* before May 1520, Jane, da. of George (NEVILL), LORD ABERGAVENNY, by his second wife, Mary, da. of Edward (STAFFORD), DUKE OF BUCKINGHAM. He *d.* s.p.m., being *beheaded* on Tower Hill, 9 Jan. 1539, when, having been *attainted*, all his honours became *forfeited*.(f)

I.(*bis*) 1342. *1.* SIR EDWARD DE MONTACUTE, br. of William, 1st EARL OF SALISBURY, being 3d and yst. s.(g) of William (DE MONTACUTE), 2d LORD MONTACUTE, by Elizabeth, da. of Sir Peter DE MONTFORT, having distinguished himself in the wars with Scotland and France, was sum. to Parl. as a Baron (LORD MONTACUTE) by writs directed "*Edwardo de Monte acuto*" from 25 Feb. (1341/2), 16 Ed. III., to 20 Nov. (1360), 34 Ed. III. He *m.* Alice, 2d da. and coheir of Thomas (PLANTAGENET, styled "*of Brotherton*"), EARL OF NORFOLK (yr. s. of King Edward I.), by Alice, da. of Sir Roger HALYS. He *d.* s.p.m. 1361.

II.(*bis*) 1361, to 1375. *2.* Joan, *de jure suo jure* BARONESS MONTACUTE, only da. and h., *b.* at Bungay, in Norfolk, and *bap.* there (1349), 23 Ed. III., *m.* (as his first wife) William (DE UFFORD), 2d EARL OF SUFFOLK, who *d.* 15 Feb. 1382. She *d.* s.p. 1375, when the *Barony* became *extinct.* Esch. (1381), 5 Ric. II.

(a) "*Courthope*," *sub* "Salisbury" and "Warwick."

(b) She, however, was never more than a *coheir* in her lifetime, tho' her issue in 1485 became the sole heir.

(c) See his coat of arms (8 quarterings) in Metcalfe's "*Knights*," p. 49. He is said to have been made a K.B., 30 May 1533, at the coronation of Anne Boleyn, but his name does not appear among the 17 Knights so made.

(d) Stow's "Annals."

(e) Dugdale.

(f) The coheirs, subject to the attainder, were his two daughters, *viz.* (1) Katharine who *m.* (settl. 24 June 1532), Francis (Hastings), 3d Earl of Huntingdon, and is represented by the coheirs of the 4th Marquess of Hastings, who *d.* s.p. in 1868 (2), Winifred, whose only issue was by her second husband, Sir Thomas Barrington, and who is represented by the family of Lowndes, of co. Buckingham. These two ladies were restored in blood and honours by act of Parl. (1554-55), 1 Philip and Mary.

(g) Simon de Montacute, the 2d son, was Bishop of Ely, 1336 to 1345.

I.(*ter*) 1357. *1.* SIR JOHN DE MONTACUTE, 2d s. of William (DE MONTACUTE), 1st EARL OF SALISBURY, by Catharine, da. of William (DE GRANDISON), LORD GRANDISON; served in the French wars, being present (26 Aug. 1346), at the battle of Cressy, and was sum. to Parl. as a Baron (LORD MONTACUTE) by writs from 15 Feb. (1356/7), 31 Ed. III., to 6 Dec. (1389), 20 Ric. II.(a) He *m.* before 1349 (she being then aged 21) Margaret, *de jure suo jure* BARONESS MONTHERMER (see that dignity) in consequence of which alliance he not improbably received his writ of summons as a Baron. He *d.* 25 Feb. (1389/90), 13 Ric. II. Will dat. 20 March 1388/9.(b)

II.(*ter*) 1390. *2.* JOHN (DE MONTACUTE), LORD MONTHERMER [1309] and LORD MONTACUTE [1357], s. and h. By the death, 3 June 1397, of his paternal uncle, he became EARL OF SALISBURY and LORD MONTACUTE [1299], with which last named Barony, this Barony and that of Monthermer, ever afterwards continued united. See "MONTACUTE," Barony, *cr.* 1299, under the 5th Lord.

MONTAGU, and NEVILL DE MONTAGU.

Barony by Writ.

I. 1461.

Marquessate.

I. 1470, to 1471.

1. SIR JOHN NEVILL, 3d s. of Richard (NEVILL), EARL OF SALISBURY, was *b.* about 1430; *knighted* 25 Dec. 1449; attainted Nov. 1459, but restored Oct. 1460; P.C., 1461; Lord Chamberlain of the Household, 1461, and was sum. to Parl.(a) as a Baron (LORD MONTAGU, or LORD NEVILL DE MONTAGU), by writ, 23 May (1461), 1 Ed. I., directed "*Johanni Nevyll, Domino de Montagu, Chl'r*" and by writs, 22 Dec. (1462), 1 Ed. IV. to 28 Feb. (1462/3), 2 Ed. IV., directed "*Johanni Nevyll de Montagu*"; K.G., 21 March 1461/2; Warden of the East Marches, 1463-70; *cr.* 27 May 1464 or 1465, EARL OF NORTHUMBERLAND, which creation was brought into chancery and cancelled (1468-69), 8 Ed. IV., he being *cr.* 25 March 1470, MARQUESS OF MONTAGU.(c) He *m.* 25 April 1456, Isabel, da. and h. of Sir Edmund INGOLDSTHORPE, of Borough Green, co. Cambridge, by Joane, da. and coheir of John (TIPTOFT), LORD TIPTOFT. Together with his br., the Earl of Warwick (the King-Maker), he took part in the restoration of King Henry VI. in 1470, and was slain at the battle of Barnet, 14 April 1471,(d) when, having been attainted, *all his honours* became *forfeited*.(e) His body was exposed three days in St Paul's Cathedral, London, and was *bur.* at Bisham, Berks. His widow *m.* Sir William NORRIS.

Viscountcy.

I. 1554.

1. SIR ANTHONY BROWNE, of Battle Abbey and Cowdray Park,(f) co. Sussex, s. and h. of Sir Anthony BROWNE, K.G., by Alice, da. of Sir John GAGE, K.G., which last named Anthony, was s. and h. of Sir Anthony BROWNE, Standard Bearer of England, by

---

(a) There is proof in the rolls of Parl. of his sitting.

(b) See Nicolas's "*Test. Vet.*"

(c) This was the *fifth* Marqessate that was created. See vol. iii, p. 146, note "g," *sub* "Dorset" for a list of the first eleven. A facsimile of his signature, as "J. MOUNTAGU" is given in Doyle's "*Official Baronage.*"

(d) According to Leland (as quoted by Dugdale), "Though he outwardly made shew of joining the Lancastrians at Barnet, he privately got on King Edward's livery, with purpose to take his part; which being discerned by some of his brother's servants, they forthwith fell upon him and killed him."

(e) His sons both *d.* s.p. (the eldest, George, who had been v.p. *cr.* Duke of Bedford, was *degraded* by Parl. in 1477), but his five daughters all married, and their issue represents the Barony of 1461.

(f) William (Fitzwilliam), Earl of Southampton (who *d.* 1542), and who was his father's elder br. (of the half blood, *ex parte maternâ*), had purchased that estate, which he left to his said br., Sir Anthony Browne, who finished the building of that magnificent house, which was destroyed by fire in 1793. There is an interesting history of "Cowdray," by Mrs. C. Roundell. The estate was sold in 1843 by the da. of Mrs. Poynts (sister and heir to the last Viscount), to the 6th Earl of Egmont [I.]

Lucy, 4th da. and eventually coheir of John (NEVILL), MARQUESS OF MONTAGU abovenamed, was *b.* about 1528; was one of the 40 knights (made as K.B's.), 20 Feb. 1546/7, at the coronation of Ed. VI.,(a) *suc.* his father, 6 May 1548; was M.P. for Guildford, 1547-52; for Petersfield, March and Oct. 1553, and for Surrey, 1554; Sheriff for Surrey and Sussex, 1553; Master of the Horse to King Philip, April to Sep. 1554, and was *cr.* 2 Sep. 1554, VISCOUNT MONTAGU;(b) el. K.G., 23 April and inst. 17 Oct. 1555; Ambassador to the Pope and to Venice, 1555; P.C., 1557; Lord Lieut. of Sussex, March to Oct, 1558; was one of the two Peers who opposed the separation of England from the Roman Catholic Church; Ambassador to Madrid, Jan. to July 1560; to Flanders, 1564; one of the 24 noblemen(c) for the trial of the Queen of Scots at Fotheringay in Oct. 1586; took an active part in the repelling of the threatened Spanish invasion, and entertained the Queen most sumptuously at Cowdray for six days in 1591. He *m.* firstly, Jane, da of Robert (RATCLIFFE), 1st EARL OF SUSSEX, by his second wife, Margaret, da. of Thomas (STANLEY), EARL OF DERBY. She *d.* 22 July 1552. He *m.* secondly, Magdalen, da. of William (DACRE), LORD DACRE OF GILLESLAND, by Elizabeth, da. of George (TALBOT), 4th EARL OF SHREWSBURY. He *d.* at Horsley, co. Surrey, 19 Oct. 1592, and was *bur.* at Cowdray. Will dat. 19 July 1592, pr. 14 March 1592/3. *Inq. post mortem*, at Midhurst, 19 April 1593. His widow, who was *b.* in 1538, at Naworth Castle, Cumberland, *d.* 21 Jan. 1608.(d) Will pr. 1608.

II. 1592. 2. ANTHONY MARIA (BROWNE), VISCOUNT MONTAGU, grandson and h., being s. and h. of the Hon. Anthony BROWNE, by Mary, da. of Sir William DORMER, of Ethorp, Bucks, which Anthony was s. and h. ap. of the 1st Viscount by his first wife, but *d.* six months before his father, 29 June 1592. He was *b.* 1 Feb. 1573/4, and *suc. to the peerage*, 19 Oct. 1592; was *cr.* M.A. of Oxford, 30 Aug. 1605. In 1605 he was accused of being privy to the "Gunpowder Plot" and was imprisoned for 40 weeks in the Tower. He *m.*, 3 Feb. 1591, Jane, da. of Thomas (SACKVILLE), 1st EARL OF DORSET, by Cicely, da. of Sir John BAKER. He *d.* 23 Oct. 1629, aged 55, and was *bur.* the 27th at Midhurst.(e) Fun. certificate. Admon. 30 April 1630, and 9 Feb. 1630/1. *Inq. post mortem* at Southwark, 1 Feb. 1629/30. His widow's will dat. 29 July 1651, pr. 8 Jan. 1651/2.

III. 1629. 3. FRANCIS (BROWNE), VISCOUNT MONTAGU, only s. and h., *b.* 1610; *suc. to the peerage*, 23 Oct. 1629, and became of full age, 9 Feb. 1630/1. He was a great sufferer in the Royal cause during the Civil wars; was assistant Cupbearer at the coronation, 23 April 1661, of Charles II. He *m.* (lic. London, 6 July 1637), Elizabeth, yst. da. of Henry (SOMERSET), 1st MARQUESS OF WORCESTER, by Anne, da. and h. of John RUSSELL, *styled* LORD RUSSELL, s. and h. ap. of Francis, EARL OF BEDFORD. He *d.* 2 Nov. 1682, aged 72, and was *bur.* at Midhurst. Will dat. 15 May 1677, pr. 29 Nov. 1682. His widow's will pr. 8 Dec. 1684.

IV. 1682. 4. FRANCIS (BROWNE), VISCOUNT MONTAGU, 1st surv. s. and h.; *b.* 1638; *suc. to the peerage*, 2 Nov. 1682; was assistant Cupbearer at the coronation, 23 April 1685, of James II.; Lord Lieut. of Sussex, Jan. to Dec. 1688. He *m* Mary,(f) widow of the Hon. Richard MOLYNEUX, 1st da.

(a) See vol. iii, p. 71, note "c," *sub* "Derby."

(b) A facsimile of his signature as "ANTHONY MOUNTAGUE," is given in Doyle's "*Official Baronage.*" It does not appear that he represented his grandmother, Lucy, one of the younger daughters and coheirs of John (Nevill) Marquess of Montagu, and *Lord Montagu*, as she, by her *first* husband (Fitzwilliam), had male issue, of which Thomas Fitzwilliam left daughters, among whose issue, her heir general would be found.

(c) See vol. iii, p. 72, note "a," *sub* "Derby" for a list of them.

(d) Her life is written in Latin by Richard Smith, Bishop of Chalcedon and was translated into English in 1627.

(e) At the age of 23 he compiled a book (which was held in some repute) of regulations for the Government of his family and household.

(f) With this lady, when Mary Molyneux, lived Edward Turbervill, of Skerr, co. Glamorgan, author of a tract called "*Information of E. Turbervill*" folio, 1680 touching Welsh Papists and Recusants.

of William (HERBERT), 1st MARQUESS OF POWIS, by Elizabeth, da. of Edward (SOMERSET), 2d MARQUESS OF WORCESTER. He *d.* s.p. June 1708 and was *bur.* at Midhurst. Will dat. 1686 to 12 Feb. 1707/8, pr. 12 July 1708. His widow *d.* 30 Oct. 1744,(a) and was *bur.* in the church of the English Augustine Nuns at Bruges. M.I. Will dat. 23 May 1738, pr. 31 Oct. 1745.

V. 1708. 5. HENRY (BROWNE), VISCOUNT MONTAGU, only br. and h.; *b.* before 1641; was Sec. of State to King James II. when in exile, 1691; *suc. to the peerage*, June 1708. He *m.* before 1685 Barbara, sister of James, da. of Thomas WALSINGHAM,(b) of Chesterford, co. Essex, by Anne, da. of Theophilus (HOWARD), EARL OF SUFFOLK. He *d.* 25 June 1717, at Epsom, co. Surrey, and was *bur.* at Bath.(c) His widow *d.* 23 Nov. 1723.

VI. 1717. 6. ANTHONY (BROWNE), VISCOUNT MONTAGU, only s. and h.; *b.* 1686; *suc. to the peerage*, 25 June 1717; sold Battle Abbey, 1719; was elected "Grand Master of the Free and Accepted Masons" in April 1732.(d) He *m.*, 28 July 1720, Barbara, 3d da. of Sir John WEBB, 3d Bart., by Barbara, da. and coheir of John (BELASYSE), BARON BELASYSE OF WORLABY. He *d.* 23 April 1767, aged 81, and was *bur.* at Eastbourne, Sussex. Will pr. 19 May 1767. His widow *d.* 7 April 1779, aged 80. Will pr. April 1779.

VII. 1767. 7. ANTHONY JOSEPH (BROWNE), VISCOUNT MONTAGU, 2d and yst. but only surv. s. and h.(e); *b.* in Stratton street, Westminster, 11 April 1728; *suc. to the peerage*, 23 April 1767. He conformed to the established religion of England. He *m.*, 22 July 1767, at St. Geo. Han. sq., Frances, Dow. BARONESS FALCONER OF HALKERTOUN [S.], da. of Herbert MACKWORTH, of the Gnoll, co. Glamorgan, by Jane, da. of Edward (NOEL), EARL OF GAINSBOROUGH. He *d.* 9 April 1787, aged 59. Will pr. 1788. His widow *d.* 3 March 1814, in her 83d year. Admon. 20 April 1814, under £1,000.

VIII. 1787. 8. GEORGE SAMUEL (BROWNE), VISCOUNT MONTAGU, only s. and h.; *b.* 26 June 1769, and *bap.* at St. Marylebone; *suc. to the peerage*, 9 April 1787. He *d.* unm., aged 24, being drowned(f) Oct. 1793 in a mad attempt to shoot the falls of Schauffhausen on the Rhine. By his death the male issue of the 2d Viscount became apparently extinct, but the peerage (presumably) devolved as under.

IX. 1793, to 1797. 9. MARK ANTHONY (BROWNE), VISCOUNT MONTAGU, cousin and h. male, being s. and h. of Mark BROWNE, of Eastbourne, co. Sussex, by his second wife, Anastasia, da. of Sir Richard MOORE, Bart., of Fawley, Berks, which Mark (who *d.* 7 Feb. 1755), was s. of Stainslaus BROWNE, s. and h. of another Stainslaus Browne (living 1687), who was s. and h. of John BROWNE, all three of Eastbourne afsd., which John was yr. br. to the second Viscount. He was *b.* 2 and *bap.* 10 March 1744/5, at Eastbourne; was a Monk at Fontainebleau in France, but, having *suc. to the peerage* in Oct. 1793, he

(a) 30 Oct. 1745, according to "*Top. and Gen.*," ii, 535.
(b) See Walsingham pedigree in Manning and Bray's "*Surrey*," ii, 540.
(c) According to Mrs. Roundell's "*Cowdray*," he was profligate and superstitious, and having shot a Priest, who had refused him absolution, lived in hiding ever since.
(d) "Collins," edit. 1779, vol. vi, p. 22.
(e) His elder br. *d.* at Rouen, in Normandy, aged one year.
(f) There is said to have been a curse on the race (which, tho' professing the old faith, scrupled not to be enriched with the spoils of the church) as to its perishing by "fire and water." In this same year, 1793, was the fire by which Cowdray house was destroyed, while not only did the young Viscount perish by water but (22 years later) the two only sons of his only sister (Mrs. Poyntz) were also drowned (in sight of their parents) in July 1815.

obtained a dispensation to marry,(a) and *m.* 11 Feb. 1797, at Little Burstead, co. Essex, Frances, 2d da. of Thomas MANBY, of Downsell Hall, in that county. He *d.* s.p., 27 Nov. 1797, when the *title* is presumed to have become *extinct.*(b) He was *bur.* 7 Dec. following in the family vault at Midhurst. Will dat. 13 Nov. 1797, pr. 26 Feb. 1798. His widow *m.* 21 May 1800, at St. Geo. Han. sq., Henry SLAUGHTER, M.D., who survived her (his will dat. 7 Aug. 1819, was pr. 3 May 1823), and *d.* at Phillimore place, Kensington, 7 Jan. 1823. Admon. 3 May 1825, under £20.

MONTAGU and MONTAGU OF BOUGHTON.

Barony. I. 1621.

1. SIR EDWARD MONTAGU, of Boughton in Weekley, co. Northampton, s. and h.(c) of Sir Edward MONTAGU, of the same, by Elizabeth, da. of Sir James HARINGTON, of Exton, co. Rutland, was *b.* about 1562; M.P. for Beeralston, 1584-86; for Brackley, 1601, and for Northamptonshire, 1604-11, 1614 and 1621, being, in 1605, the mover of the resolution to keep, as a festival, the anniversary of the gunpowder plot. He *suc.* his father, in the family estates, 26 Jan. 1601/2; was K.B., at the Coronation, 23 July 1603. Lord-Lieut. of Northamptonshire, 1642, exerting himself, tho' of great age, on behalf of the King. He *m.* firstly, Elizabeth, da. and h. of Sir John JEFFREY, of Chiddingley, co. Sussex, Chief Baron of the Exchequer (1577-78), by his first wife, Elizabeth da. and h. of John ANSLEY, of London. She *d.* s.p.m. and was *bur.* at Chiddingley afsd. He *m.* secondly, before 1613, Frances, da. of Thomas COTTON, of Conington, co. Huntingdon, by his second wife, Dorothy, da. of John TAMWORTH, of Hawsted, co. Lincoln. She *d.* 15 June 1620, and was *bur.* at Weekley. M.I. He *m.* thirdly, 16 Feb. 1624/5, at St. Michael's Cornhill, London, Anne, widow of Sir Ralph HARE, relict formerly of Richard CHAMBERLAIN, and previously of Robert WYNCOLL, da. of John CROUCH, of Corneybury, in Layston, Herts, by Joan, da. and h. of John SCOTT, of London. He *d.* while a prisoner (on account of his loyalty) in the Savoy, Westminster, 15 June 1644, in his 82d year, and was *bur.* at Weekley.(d) M.I. Will pr. 1646. His widow *d.* 11 July 1648, aged 75, and was *bur.* at Weekley. M.I. Will dat. 10 Oct. 1646, to 6 Jan. 1647/8, pr. 19 Jan. 1663/4.

II. 1644.

2. EDWARD (MONTAGU), BARON MONTAGU OF BOUGHTON, 2d but 1st surv. s. and h., by second wife;(e) *b.* 1617; ed. at Sidney Sussex Coll., Cambridge; M.P. for Huntingdon, 1640-44; *suc. to the peerage*, 15 June 1644; Joint Commissioner from the Parl. to the King, 1647. He *m.* (settlement 1633) Anne, da. of Sir Ralph WINWOOD,(f) of Ditton, Bucks, Sec. of State (1614-17), by Elizabeth, da. and coheir of (—) BALL, of Totness. She *d.* 1648 and was *bur.* in London. He *d.* 10 Jan. 1683. Will pr. Jan. 1685.

(a) Mrs. Roundell's "*Cowdray.*"

(b) The issue male of the 1st s. and h. ap. of the 1st Viscount (by his first wife) is, in all probability, extinct, but, by his second wife (Magdalen Dacre), he had no less than six sons some of whom left numerous issue. The title has frequently been claimed. Nicolas alludes (1825) to the claim "by a Mr. John Browne, of Storington, as the descendant of George, the 2d son of John Browne, 2d son of Anthony, the 1st Viscount Montagu" having been lately referred by the crown to the Attorney-General. Courthope alludes to one "now [1856] before the House."

(c) Of his younger brothers (1) Henry Montagu, was *cr.* Earl of Manchester, in 1626, being ancestor of the Dukes of Manchester while (2) Sydney Montagu is ancestor of the Earls of Sandwich. As to the conjectured descent of this family from that of Montacute, Earls of Salisbury, see p. 206, note "d," *sub* "Manchester."

(d) A fac-simile of his signature as "EDWARD MOUNTAGU" is given in "Doyle's "*Official Baronage.*"

(e) His eldest br., the Hon. Edward Montagu, *d.* unm. and v.p., being slain at Bergen, 1665.

(f) A good account of him is in Bloxam's "*Mag. Coll. Reg.*," iv, 211—221. His quarrel with the Lord Keeper Bacon, in July 1617, was only three months before his death, in his 36th year. He was *bur.* 30 Sep. 1617, at St. Barth. the Less, London, where also were *bur.* some of his children, and on 28 Sep. 1659, his widow, "the Lady Winwood." All of his three surviving sons *d.* s.p., the survivor (his heir) Richard Winwood, of Quainton, Bucks, *d.* 28 June 1688, in his 80th year, after the death of whose widow (1 May 1691), the Winwood property devolved on the Montagu family.

III. 1680. Earldom. I. 1680. Dukedom. I. 1705.

3 and 1. RALPH (MONTAGU), BARON MONTAGU OF BOUGHTON, 2d but 1st surv. s. and h.; b. at his grandmother's (Lady Winwood's) house in London, and bap. 29 Dec. 1638, at St. Bartholomew's the Less; Master of the Horse to the Queen Consort, 1665-88; Ambassador to Paris where he affected the greatest splendor, 1666, 1669, 1676, and 1677-78; P.C., 1672-78, and again, 1689; Master of the Wardrobe, 1671-85, and again, 1689-95; M.P. for Northampton, 1678; for Huntingdonshire, 1678-79, and for Northampton (again), 1679-83, supporting the Bill of Exclusion in the House of Commons. He suc. to the peerage, 10 Jan. 1683; took a most active part in the House of Lords in promoting the Revolution, and was, by the new Sovereigns, restored to his office in the Wardrobe, and cr., 9 April 1689, VISCOUNT MONTHERMER,(a) of Monthermer, co. Essex, and EARL OF MONTAGU. In 1695 he entertained King William III. with great splendour at Boughton house, co. Northampton. He was cr. (by Queen Anne), 14 April 1705, MARQUESS OF MONTHERMER(a) and DUKE OF MONTAGU.(b) He m. firstly in 1671 at Titchfield, Hants, Elizabeth, Dow. COUNTESS OF NORTHUMBERLAND, da. and coheir of Thomas (WRIOTHESLEY), 4th EARL OF SOUTHAMPTON, by his second wife, Elizabeth, da. and coheir of Francis (LEIGH), 1st EARL OF CHICHESTER. She was bur. 26 Sep. 1690, at Warkton, co. Northampton. He m. secondly, 8 Sep. 1692, Elizabeth, Dow. DUCHESS OF ALBEMARLE, 1st da. and coheir of Henry (CAVENDISH), 2d DUKE OF NEWCASTLE, by Frances, da. of the Hon. William PIERREPONT. He d. suddenly at Montagu house, Bloomsbury, 9, and was bur. 16 March 1708/9, at Warkton.(c) Will pr. Dec. 1709. His widow, who was well known as "the mad Duchess" d. s.p.s. at Newcastle house, Clerkenwell, Midx., 28 Aug., and was bur. 11 Sep. 1734, in Westm. Abbey, aged 80, or, according to the journals of the day, 96. Admon. 4 Nov. 1734.

[WINWOOD MONTAGU, styled LORD MONTHERMER, 2d(d) but 1st surv. s. and h. ap., by first wife. He d. v.p. and unm. at Flanders,(e) aged about 20, and was bur. 28 June 1702, at Warkton.]

(a) The Barony of Monthermer devolved soon after 1340 on the family of Montacute from whom the grantee assumed himself to be descended. See p. 206, note "d," sub "Manchester."

(b) That this distinction was beyond what was merited may be inferred from the following lines "written by Mr. Gwinnett" alluding to this creation together with the Knighthood of Sir Edward Hannes, one of the Queen's physicians (who "having been for some time mad, died July 1710") and of Sir William Read, an occulist, ("a mountebank formerly" and a "barber at Ashdon, in Essex," who "can neither write nor read") at the same date.

"The Queen, like Heaven, shines equally on all,
Her favours now *without distinction* fall,
Great READ and slender HANNES, both *knighted*, show
That none their honours shall to merit owe,
That popish doctrine is exploded quite,
Or RALPH had been no *Duke*, and READ no *Knight*;
That none may virtue or their learning plead,
This has no GRACE, and *that* can hardly READ."

See "*Top. and Gen.*," iii, 153 and 379.

(c) Macky in his "*Characters*" says of him, "he is a great supporter of the French and other Protestants who are drove into England by the tyranny of their Princes; an admirer of learning and learned men, especially the *Beaux Esprits* and the *Belles Lettres*; a good judge of architecture and painting as his fine pictures at his houses in Northamptonshire [Boughton house] and London [Montagu house, Bloomsbury], do show; he hath one of the best estates in England which he knows very well how to improve; is of a middle stature, inclining to fat, of a coarse, dark, complexion, and is near 60 [in 1705, however, he was nearer 70] years old."

(d) Ralph Montagu, his eldest br. b. 8 Aug. 1679, d. at the age of about 12, before his father had attained the Earldom.

(e) He died, "coming from Hanover [being] said to be killed with drinking too much in that Court." *Le Neve's memoranda* as in *Top. and Gen.* iii., 41.

Dukedom and Earldom. II. Barony. IV. 1709, to 1749.

2 and *4*. JOHN (MONTAGU), DUKE OF MONTAGU [1705], MARQUESS OF MONTHERMER [1705], EARL OF MONTAGU [1689], VISCOUNT MONTHERMER [1689], and BARON MONTAGU OF BOUGHTON [1621], 3d and yst. but only surv. s. and h. by first wife; *b.* 1689; *styled* LORD MONTHERMER from his brother's death in 1702, till he *suc. to the peerage*, 9 March 1708/9; was an officer in the army, serving in Flanders and becoming finally, in 1739, Lieut. General, and in 1746, General of Horse; Col. of 1st troop of Horse Guards, 1715-21 and 1737, and Col. 2d Reg. of Horse, 1740. LORD HIGH CONSTABLE for the Coronation of George I., 20 Oct. 1714; Lord Lieut. of Northamptonshire and of Warwickshire, 1715; *cr.* M.D. of Cambridge, 7 Oct. 1717; Fellow of the Coll. of Physicians, 1717; el. **K.G.**, 31 March and inst., 30 April 1718; **K.B.**, 27 May 1725, being Grand Master of that order, on its reconstruction at that date; Bearer of the Sceptre with the Cross at the Coronation of George II., 11 Oct. 1727; Gov. of the Isle of Wight, 1733-34; Capt. of the Gent. Pensioners, 1734-40; P.C., 1736; Master Gen. of the Ordnance, 1742-49; one of the Lords Justices [Regents] of the Realm, May to Aug. 1745, and May to Nov. 1748; F.R.S., &c. He *m.* 17 March 1704/5,(a) Mary, 4th and yst. da. and coheir of the celebrated John (CHURCHILL), 1st DUKE OF MARLBOROUGH, by Sarah, da. and coheir of Richard JENNINGS. He *d.* s.p.m.s. (of a violent fever), 16 July 1749, aged 59,(b) at his house in Privy Gardens, and was *bur.* at Warkton. M.I., when *all his honours* became *extinct*. Will pr. 1749. His widow *d.* 14 May 1751, aged 61, and was *bur.* at Warkton. M.I.(c) Will pr. 1751.

[JOHN MONTAGU, *styled* MARQUESS OF MONTHERMER, 1st but only surv. s. and h. ap., *b.* 1 Nov. 1706. He *d.* v.p. in his 5th year and was *bur.* 7 Sep. 1711, at Warkton afsd.]

Barony. V. 1762, to 1770.

1. JOHN MONTAGU, *formerly* [1735-89], BRUDENELL, *styled* LORD BRUDENELL, s. and h. ap. of George BRUDENELL, *afterwards* MONTAGU), 3d EARL OF CARDIGAN (who on 5 Nov. 1766, was *cr.* MARQUESS OF MONTHERMER and DUKE OF MONTAGU), by Mary, 3d da. and coheir of John (MONTAGU), 2d DUKE OF MONTAGU above described, was *b.* 18 March 1734/5, in Albemarle street, St. Geo. Han. sq., and was *cr.* 8 May 1762, BARON MONTAGU OF BOUGHTON, co. Northampton. He, in consequence of his father's elevation to the said Dukedom and Marquessate (see next below), was since 5 Nov. 1766, *styled* MARQUESS OF MONTHERMER. He *d.* unm. and v.p. on 11 and was *bur.* 23 April 1770, at Walton, co. Northampton, aged 35, when the *Barony of Montagu of Boughton* became *extinct*. Admon. 26 May 1770, and July 1798.

Dukedom. III. 1766-90. Barony. VI. 1786.

1. GEORGE (BRUDENELL, *afterwards* MONTAGU), 4th EARL OF CARDIGAN, who *suc.* to that dignity, 5 July 1732, having *m.*, 7 July 1730, Mary, da. and coheir (only child that issue) of John (MONTAGU), 2d DUKE OF MONTAGU above described, assumed the name of *Montagu* on the death s.p.m.s., 16 July 1749 of the said Duke, and was *cr.* 5 Nov. 1766, MARQUESS OF MONTHERMER and DUKE OF MONTAGU. Having no male issue surviving he was *cr.* 21 Aug. 1786, BARON MONTAGU

For fuller particulars see "CARDIGAN" Earldom, *cr.* 1661, *sub* the 4th Earl.

(a) "The marriage consummated at St. James on or about Thursday, 17 Jan. 1705 [1705/6], being then married at St. James." [*Le Neve's Memoranda* as in Top. and Gen. iii, 154.]

(b) "He was very tall in stature, of a good shape and symmetry. His aspect was grand, manly and full of dignity; his carriage genteel [and] polite. He appeared very gracefully on horseback. ["*Family memoirs*" by the Rev. W. Stukeley, M.D., I. p. 115.]

(c) The monuments of the 2d Duke and his Duchess at Warkton by Roubiliac command much space and some admiration.

OF BOUGHTON, co. Northampton for life with a *spec. rem.* of that dignity to the 2d and every other yr. s. of his da. Elizabeth, DUCHESS OF BUCCLEUCH [S.], and their issue in tail male successively. His wife *d.* 1 May 1775, aged 64, and was *bur.* the 16th, at Walton afsd. Will pr. May 1775. His Grace *d.* s.p.m.s., 23 May 1790, aged 77, when the *Marquessate of Monthermer* and the *Dukedom of Montagu* became *extinct*, the Earldom of Cardigan, &c., devolving on his br. and h. male, while the Barony of Montagu of Boughton devolved as below. His will pr. June 1790. For fuller particulars see "CARDIGAN" Earldom, *cr.* 1661, *sub* the 4th Earl.

Barony. VII. 1790, to 1845.

2. HENRY JAMES (MONTAGU-SCOTT), BARON MONTAGU OF BOUGHTON, formerly Lord Henry James SCOTT, maternal grandson of the above, being 2d s. of Henry (SCOTT), 3d DUKE OF BUCCLEUCH [S.], by Elizabeth, da. and h. of the said George (MONTAGU *formerly* BRUDENELL), DUKE OF MONTAGU; *b.* 16 Dec. 1776 in London; *suc. to the peerage* on the death of his maternal grandfather, 23 May 1790, under the *spec. rem.* in the creation of that dignity; ed. at St. John's Coll., Cambridge; M.A., 1797; Lieut. Col. of the Dumfries Militia, 1802; Lord Lieut. of Selkirkshire, 1823; *cr.* D.C.L., of Oxford, 11 June 1834. He *m.* 22 Nov. 1804, at Dalkeith House, Jane Margaret, da. of Archibald James Edward (DOUGLAS, *formerly* STEWART), 1st BARON DOUGLAS, by his first wife, Lucy, da. of William (GRAHAM), 2d DUKE OF MONTROSE [S.] He *d.* s.p.m.,(a) 30 Oct. 1845, aged 68, at 6 Hamilton place, Midx., when the *Barony* became *extinct*. Will pr. Nov. 1845. His widow, who was *b.* 21 Dec. 1779, *d.* 8 Jan. 1859, at Ditton park, Bucks, in her 80th year.

MONTAGU OF BEAULIEU.

Barony. I. 1885.

1. LORD HENRY-JOHN MONTAGU-DOUGLAS-SCOTT, of Beaulieu, co. Southampton, 2d s. of Walter Francis (MONTAGU-DOUGLAS-SCOTT), 5th DUKE OF BUCCLEUCH [S.], by Charlotte Anne, da. of Thomas (THYNNE), 2d MARQUESS OF BATH, was *b.* 5 Nov. 1832; ed. at Eton; M.P. for Selkirkshire, 1861-68, and for South Hants, 1868-84, and was *cr.*, 29 Dec. 1885, BARON MONTAGU OF BEAULIEU,(b) co. Southampton; Verderer of the New Forest, 1890-92. By Royal lic., 6 May 1886, he took the name of *Montagu* in addition to and after those of *Douglas-Scott*. He *m.*, 1 Aug. 1865, at Westm. Abbey, Cicely Susan, yst. da. of John (STUART-WORTLEY), 2d BARON WHARNCLIFFE OF WORTLEY, by Georgiana Elizabeth, da. of Dudley (RYDER), 1st EARL OF HARROWBY. She was *b.* 14 Oct. 1835.

Family Estates.—These, in 1883, consisted of 8,922 acres in Hants, besides 24 acres in Peebleshire. Total 8,946 acres, worth £7,386 a year. *Principal Residence.* Palace House, Beaulieu, Hants.

MONTAGU OF BOUGHTON.

i.e., "MONTAGU OF BOUGHTON, co. Northampton," Barony (*Montagu*), *cr.* 1621 and *ex.* 1749; *cr.* 1762 and *ex.* 1786, and *cr.* 1786 and *ex.* 1845. See above, under "MONTAGU and MONTAGU OF BOUGHTON."

MONTAGU OF KIMBOLTON.

i.e., "MONTAGU OF KIMBOLTON, co. Huntingdon," Barony (*Montagu*), *cr.* 1620 with the VISCOUNTCY OF MANDEVILLE. See "MANCHESTER" Earldom, *cr.* 1626.

(a) Had he died without issue male in the lifetime of his mother (who *d.* in 1827), the peerage would have been *in suspense* until her death, as she herself was not (tho' her issue was) in remainder thereto.

(b) He was paternal great-grandson of Henry (Scott), 3d Duke of Buccleuch [S.], by Elizabeth, da. and h. of George (Montagu *formerly* Brudenell), Duke of Montagu.

MONTAGU OF SAINT NEOTS.

i.e., "MONTAGU OF ST. NEOTS, co. Huntingdon," Barony (*Montagu*), *cr.* 1660 with the EARLDOM OF SANDWICH, which see.

MONTALT or DE MONTALT.

Barony by Writ. I. 1295, to 1297. *1.* ROGER DE MONTALT,[a] s. and h. of Robert DE MONTALT,[b] of Hawarden, co. Flint (a manor "held[c] by the service of Steward"); *suc.* to the family estates on the death of his father in 1278, being then aged 18; was in the wars in Gascony and was sum. to Parl. as a Baron (LORD MONTALT) 23 June (1295), 23 Ed. I.[d] He *m.* Julian, da. of Roger DE CLIFFORD. He *d.* s.p. (1297), 25 Ed I., when the *Barony* became *extinct.*

II. 1299. to 1329. *1.* ROBERT DE MONTALT br. and h. of the above, and then aged 27. He served in the Scotch and French wars and was sum. to Parl. as a Baron (LORD MONTALT) by writs from 6 Feb. (1298/9) 27 Ed. I. to 13 June (1329) 3 Ed. III. He was one of the Barons whose name (as "*Rob'tus de Monte Alto, Dominus Hawardyn*") appears to the famous letter[e] sent by them in 1301 to the Pope. He *m.* Emma who was living (1237) 1 Ed. III. in which year he, having no issue, granted the reversion (on his death) of his great estates[f] to the Queen Mother for life and to her son John, afterwards Earl of Cornwall, in fee. He *d.* s.p. (1329) 3 Ed. III. and was *bur.* at Shouldham, co. Norfolk, when the *Barony* became *extinct.*

See "DE MONTALT OF HAWARDEN, co. Tipperary," Barony [I.] (*Maude*) *cr.* 1776; *ex.* 1777.

i.e. "DE MONTALT OF HAWARDEN, co. Tipperary," Barony [I] (*Maude*) *cr.* 1785; see "HAWARDEN" Viscountcy [I.], *cr.* 1791.

i.e. "DE MONTALT OF DUNDRUM, co. Tipperary," Earldom [I] (*Maude*) *cr.* 1886; see "HAWARDEN," Viscountcy [I.], *cr.* 1791, under the 4th Viscount.

MONTEAGLE or MOUNTEAGLE.

Barony by Writ. I. 1514. *1.* SIR EDWARD STANLEY, of Hornby Castle, co. Lancaster, 5th s. of Thomas (STANLEY), 1st EARL OF DERBY, by his first wife, Eleanor, da. of Richard (NEVILL) EARL OF SALISBURY, having greatly distinguished himself when in command of the rear of the English army at the victory of Floddon,[g] 9 Sep. 1513, was el. K.G.,

(a) The chief place of the residence of this family was "at a little hill in Flintshire then called *Montalt*, but of late time (vulgarly) *Moulde*." ["*Dugdale.*"]

(b) This Robert was 2d son but eventually (on the death of his br., John), heir to Roger de Montalt (*d.* 1260) one of the most powerful of the Barons *temp.* Henry III., by Cicely, sister and coheir of Hugh (de Albini), Earl of Arundel, which Cicely brought considerable estates to the Montalt family.

(c) "Dugdale."

(d) His name occurs in the rolls of Parl. before the record of writs of summons commenced.

(e) See "*Nicolas,*" pp. 751-809 for a full account of that letter.

(f) Besides the Lordships of Montalt, of Hawarden with the Stewardship of Chester, of Walton upon Trent, co. Derby, of Cheylesmore by Coventry, co. Warwick, these included the Manor of Kenninghall, the Castle of Rising, &c. and other estates in Norfolk and Suffolk derived from the family of Albini, Earls of Arundel.

(g) "As a reward for which service King Henry commanded [at Whitsuntide 1514] that in consideration of those his valiant acts against the Scots done in that battel, where he won the *Hill*, as also for that his ancestors bore the *eagle* in their crest he should be proclaimed *Lord of Montaygle*" [*Dugdale*]. Hence he was sum. as a Baron by that title a few months later.

28 April, and inst., 8 May 1514; attended the Princess Mary into France on her marriage, 9 Oct. 1514, with King Louis XII., and was sum. to Parl. as LORD MONTEAGLE, by writs from 23 Nov. (1514), 6 Hen. VIII., to 12 Nov. (1515), 7 Hen. VIII., directed "*Edwardo Stanley de Mount Egell, Chl'r.*" He *m.*(a) firstly Anne, da. and coheir of Sir John HARINGTON, of Hornby afsd., by Maud, da. of Thomas (CLIFFORD), LORD CLIFFORD. She who was aged five in 1460 (at the death of her father) *d.* s.p., 5 Aug. 1489. He *m.* secondly, Elizabeth, widow of (—), LORD GREY DE WILTON, da. of Sir Thomas VAUGHAN, of Tretower, co. Brecon.(b) by Cissil, da. of Morgan ap Jenkin PHILIP, of Gwent Ischoed. He *d.* 6 April 1523, and was *bur.* at Hornby. Will dat. 5 April 1523, pr. 25 Aug. 1524.

II. 1523. 2. THOMAS (STANLEY), LORD MONTEAGLE, s. and h. by second wife; a minor at his father's death; attended Cardinal Wolsey on his Embassy to France in 1528; had livery of his lands, 1529-30; and was made K.B., 30 May 1533, at the Coronation of Queen Anne Boleyn. He *m.* before 1529, Mary, da. of Charles (BRANDON), DUKE OF SUFFOLK, by his first wife, Anne, da. of Sir Anthony BROWNE, of Cowdray, Sussex. She who was *b.* about 1510 (by whom he had six children), *d.* between 1540 and 1544.(c) He *m.* secondly, Helen, widow of Sir James LEYBOURNE, da. of Thomas PRESTON, of Levens, co. Westmorland. He *d.* 25 Aug. 1560, at Hornby Castle, and was *bur.* at Melling. Will dat. 28 July to 29 Dec. 1558, pr. at Richmond, co. York, 29 Aug. 1564. Fun. certif. 1560. The admon. of his widow was granted, 14 Nov. 1571 to William (Stanley), Lord Monteagle, and his wife, Anne, who was a da. of the deceased.

III. 1560. 3. WILLIAM (STANLEY), LORD MONTEAGLE; only s. and h. by first wife, was under age in 1560; was sum. to Parl. from 11 Jan. (1562/3), 5 Eliz. to 6 Jan. (1580/1), 23 Eliz. He *m.* firstly Anne, da. of Sir James LEYBOURNE, of Conswyke, co. Westmorland, by Helen his wife, both abovenamed. She was living Nov. 1571. He *m.* secondly, Anne, 5th da. of Sir John SPENCER, of Althorpe, co. Northampton, by Katherine, da. of Sir Thomas KITSON. He d. s.p.m. 1581. His widow *m* (as 2d wife) Henry (COMPTON), 1st LORD COMPTON, who *d.* Dec. 1589. She *m.* thirdly (as 2d wife) Robert (SACKVILLE), 2d EARL OF DORSET (who *d.* 27 Feb. 1608/9), and *d.* 22 Sep. 1618. Will pr. 1618.

IV. 1581. 4. Elizabeth, *de jure, suo jure* BARONESS MONTEAGLE, only da. and h. by first wife, wife of Edward (PARKER), LORD MORLEY, who was sum. in that last named Barony to Parl. from 1581 to 1614, and who *d.* 1 April 1618.

V. 1604. 5. WILLIAM (PARKER), LORD MONTEAGLE, s. and h., who was sum. v.p. from 19 March 1603/4 to 5 April 1614, in his *mother's* Barony as *Lord Monteagle*, but who after the death (1618) of his father, was sum. 30 Jan. 1620/1 to 4 Nov. 1621 as LORD MORLEY AND MONTEAGLE. He *d.* 1 July 1622.

VI. 1622. 6. HENRY (PARKER), LORD MORLEY AND MONTEAGLE, s. and h. was sum. to Parl. in these dignities, 12 Feb. 1623/4 to 8 Nov. 1639. He *d.* June 1655.

VII. 1655, to 1686? 7. THOMAS (PARKER), LORD MORLEY AND MONTEAGLE, only s. and h. was sum to Parl. in these dignities from 8 May 1661 to 19 May 1685. He *d.* s.p. about 1686, when these *Baronies* fell into *abeyance*.

[For fuller particulars see "MORLEY" Barony, cr. 1299.]

(a) Tho' he had no issue by this marriage the Hornby estate was thereby acquired by the Stanley family.

(b) At the funeral of his son (see fun. cert. 1560) a banner was born which contained the arms of "Edwarde, Lord Mounteagle, and of Elizabeth, Ladye Grey of Wylton, da. of Sir Thomas Vawghan, of Tretower, Knt., in pale." No match with Grey (prior to that with Stanley) is indicated to this Lady Monteagle in the ped. of Vaughan in Jones' "*Breconshire*," ii, 507. In some pedigrees, however, she is made to be relict of Sir Thomas Cokesey (*Query* of him who *d.* in 1498) as also of John, Lord Grey de Wilton.

(c) See *Historical appendix* to Miss Holt's "*Harvest of yesterday.*"

MONTEAGLE OF BRANDON.

Barony I. 1839. 1. THE RT. HON. THOMAS-SPRING RICE, only s. and h. of Stephen Edward RICE, of Mount Trenchard, co. Limerick, by Catherine, da. and h. of Thomas SPRING, of Bally Crispin, co. Kerry, was b. 8 Feb. 1790, in S. Michael's parish, Limerick: Barrister at Law; M.P. for Limerick, 1820-39; for Cambridge, 1832-39, being cr. M.A. of that Univ. in 1833; Under Secretary for Home, 1827-30; Sec. to the Treasury, 1830-36; P.C. [E, and I,] 1834: Colonial Sec. July to Nov. 1834, and Chancellor of the Exchequer, 1835-39, being cr. 5 Sep. 1839, BARON MONTEAGLE(a) OF BRANDON, co. Kerry. He was Comptroller Gen. of the Exchequer (£2,000 a year) 1839; F.R.S., F.S.A., &c. He m. firstly, 11 July 1811, Theodosia, 2d da. of Edmond Henry (PERY), 1st EARL OF LIMERICK [I.], by Alice Mary, da. and h. of Henry ORMSBY. She, who was b. 15 Jan. 1787, d. 11 Dec. 1839. He m. secondly, 13 April 1841, Mary Anne, 1st da. of John MARSHALL, of Headingley, co. York, sometime M.P. for that county, by Jane, da. of William POLLARD, of Halifax. He d. 7 Feb. 1866, aged 76, at Mount Trenchard, and was bur. at Shanagolden, co. Limerick. Will pr. 18 May 1866, under £10,000 [E.] His widow d. s.p., 11 April 1889, aged 89, at Onslow Gardens, Brompton.

II. 1866. 2. THOMAS SPRING (RICE), BARON MONTEAGLE OF BRANDON, grandson and h., being s. and h. of the Hon. Stephen Edmond Spring RICE, by Ellen Mary, da. of William FRERE, Serjeant at Law, which Stephen was 1st s. and h. ap. of the 1st Baron by his first wife and d. v.p. 9 May 1865, aged 50. He was b. 31 May 1849; suc. to the peerage, 7 Feb. 1866; was ed. at Harrow and at Trin. Coll., Cambridge; B.A. and Senior Opt. in Mathematics, 1872. He m., 26 Oct. 1875, at Ardbraccan, co. Meath, Elizabeth, 1st da. of the Rt. Rev. Samuel BUTLER, Bishop of Meath (1866), by Mary, da. of John LEAHY, of Killarney.

Family Estates.—These, in 1883, consisted of 6,445 acres in co. Limerick and 2,310 in co. Kerry. *Total* 8,755 acres, worth £6,137 a year. *Residence.* Mount Trenchard, near Foynes, co. Limerick.

MONTEAGLE OF WESTPORT.

i.e., "MONTEAGLE OF WESTPORT, co. Mayo," Barony [I.] (*Browne*), cr. 1760; see "ALTAMONT" Earldom [I.], cr. 1771; also "MONTEAGLE OF WESTPORT, co. Mayo," Barony [U.K.] (*Browne*), cr. 1806; see "Sligo"(b) Marquessate [I.]; cr. 1800.

MONTEITH see MENTEITH.

(a) It is not known why the title of "*Monteagle*" was selected by two Irish families, *viz.*, (1) that of Browne in 1760, and (2) that of Rice in 1839, neither of whom pretended to any the smallest connection with the illustrious family of Stanley, on whom the Barony of that name had, in 1514, been, *honoris causâ*, conferred, and between whose numerous coheirs (amongst whom most certainly Messrs. Browne and Rice were *not*) it was *still in abeyance*. "Monteagle" may possibly be the name of some hill (in one case) in co. Westport, and (in the other) in co. Kerry. The first of these creations, however, has the excuse of originating in an *Irish* Barony long before the Union, and being *subsequently* (1806) granted as a Barony of the United Kingdom; but no such excuse applies to the second, which, originating as a Barony [U.K.], interfered with a Barony [U.K.] that was then in existence (and had been for above 30 years) while, to add to the absurdity thereof, the grantee was actually in possession of *one* mountain, "*Mount* Trenchard," to which lofty designation (in spite of his ambition "*imponere Pelion Ossæ*") he might very properly have been restricted.

(b) The 3d Earl of Altamont and Baron Monteagle of Westport [I.] was, in 1800, cr. Marquess of Sligo [I.], being, in 1806, cr. Baron Monteagle of Westport [U.K.]

MONTFORT.

Barony by Writ.

I. 1295.

1. JOHN DE MONTFORT, of Beaudesert, co. Warwick, s. and h. of Peter DE MONTFORT, of the same, *suc.* his father in 1287, and, having distinguished himself in the French wars, was sum. to Parl. as a Baron (LORD MONTFORT), by writs dat. 23 June, 1 Oct. and 2 Nov. (1295), 23 Ed. I. He *m.* Alice, da. of William DE LA PLAUNCHE. He *d.* (1295-96), 24 Ed. I. *Esch.*, 24 Ed. I.

II. 1296.

2. JOHN (DE MONTFORT), LORD MONTFORT, s. and h., aged 5 years at the death of his father. He was sum. to Parl., 26 July (1313), 7 Ed. II., in which year he was pardoned for his share in the murder of Piers de Gaveston. He *d.* s.p. being slain by the Scots in the battle of Stryvelin 1314.

III. 1314, to 1367.

3. PETER (DE MONTFORT), LORD MONTFORT, br. and h. He was formerly a Priest, but obtaining dispensation was *knighted*, made Gov. of Warwick Castle, and was sum. to Parl. as a Baron from 22 Jan. (1335/6), 9 Ed. III. to 10 March (1348/9), 23 Ed. III. He *m.* Margaret, da. of "the LORD FURNIVAL." He *d.* s.p.m.s.(a) in 1367, when the *Barony* became *extinct* or in *abeyance*.(b) Will directing his burial to be at the Friars Preachers, Warwick, dat. 12 Dec. 1367.

MONTFORT OF HORSEHEATH.

Barony.

I. 1741.

1. HENRY BROMLEY, of Horseheath, co. Cambridge and Holt Castle,(c) co. Worcester, only s. and h. of John BROMLEY,(d) of Horseheath afsd., by Mercy, da. and eventually sole h. of William BROMLEY, of Holt Castle afsd., was *b.* 20 Aug. 1705; *suc.* his father, 1 Nov. 1718; ed. at Eton, and, as a Fellow Commoner, at Clare Hall, Cambridge; M.A. (per lit. reg.) 1726; M.P. for Cambridgeshire, 1727-41, being *cr.* 9 May 1741, LORD MONTFORT, BARON OF HORSEHEATH, co. Cambridge. High Steward of the town of Cambridge. He *m.* 18 March 1726, Frances, sister and h. of Sir Francis WYNDHAM, Bart., da. of Thomas WYNDHAM, of Trent, co. Somerset, by Lucy, da. of Richard MEAD, of Westminster. She *d.* in childbed, and was *bur.* at St. Margaret's Westm., 1 Feb. 1732/3. He *d.* 1 Jan. 1755, in his 50th year, and was *bur.* in Trinity chapel, South Audley street, St. Geo. Han. sq. Will pr. 1755.

II. 1755.

2. THOMAS (BROMLEY), LORD MONTFORT, BARON OF HORSEHEATH, only s. and h. *b.* Jan. 1732/3; ed. at Eton; sometime M.P. for Cambridgeshire; *suc. to the peerage*, 1 Jan. 1755; Col. of the Cambridgeshire Militia. He *m.* 1 March 1772, at St. Marylebone, Mary Anne, sister of Sir Patrick BLAKE, Bart., of Langham, da. of Andrew BLAKE, by Marcella, da. of (--), FRENCH, of Ireland. He sold the estate of Horseheath. He *d.* 24 Oct. 1799, aged 65.(e) Will pr. 1808. His widow *d.* about 1830. Will pr. Aug. 1830.

(a) The only *legit* s. (who also was h. ap.), Grey de Montfort *m.* Margaret, da. of Thomas (Beauchamp), Earl of Warwick and *d.* s.p. and v.p., leaving, however, a bastard son, ancestor of the family of Montfort, long settled at Coleshill, co. Warwick.

(b) The coheirs to the Barony *cr.* by the writs of 1295, if such writs were sufficient to create a hereditary dignity (for any Barony *cr.* by writs to the 2d or 3d Barony was *extinct*) were the sisters (or their issue) of the 2d and 3d Barons, *viz.* (1) Elizabeth who *m.* Sir Baldwin de Freville and (2) Maud who *m.* Bartholomew de Sudeley.

(c) "Holt Castle and its appendant estates were sold by the late [1812] Peer or his father to Lord Foley for less than £20,000." [*Collins.*]

(d) See "*Coll. Top. et Gen.*" vol. iv. pp. 47—48, for some account of the coffins at Horseheath of this family, as also a notice as to the arms of this branch thereof, implying a bastard descent.

(e) As to his taste for "*Menageries*" see vol. i, p. 352, note "a," *sub* "Bessborough," relating to the amusements of "Men of Fashion" in 1782.

III. 1799, to 1851. 3. HENRY (BROMLEY), LORD MONTFORT, BARON OF HORSEHEATH, only s. and h., b. 14 May and bap. 12 June 1773; suc. to the peerage, 14 Oct. 1799, and (the estates having been alienated) received a pension of £300 a year from 8 Oct. 1800. He m., 5 Sep. 1793, Elizabeth, alias Betty WATTS, spinster.(a) She, who resided at Monks Grove, St. Ann's Hill, in Chertsey, d. in Eaton street, 10 Dec. 1847. Her will pr. Nov. 1848 and March 1849. He m. secondly (within two weeks of his first wife's death), 23 Dec. 1847, at St. Mary's, Bryanstone square, Marylebone, Anne, da. of William BURGHAM, of Upton Bishop, co. Hereford. He d. s.p., 30 April 1851, in his 78th year, at 24 Upper Montagu street, Marylebone, when the peerage became extinct. Will pr. June 1851. His widow d. 27 Dec 1878, in her 78th year, at 6 Milton street, Dorset sq., Marylebone.

MONTGOMERIE.

Barony [S.] I. 1448? 1. SIR ALEXANDER MONTGOMERIE, of Ardrossan, s. and h. of Sir John M., of the same, by Margaret, da. of Sir Robert MAXWELL, of Caerlaverock; suc. his father between 1425 and 1430; was several times (1438–1460) employed in negotiations with England; was P.C. to Kings James I. and II. [S.], and was cr. a Peer of Parl. as LORD MONTGOMERIE [S.] before 31 Jan. 1448/9. He m. Margaret, sister of Robert, 1st LORD BOYD [S.], 2d da. of Sir Thomas BOYD, of Kilmarnock. He d. soon after June 1461.

II. 1461? 2. ALEXANDER (MONTGOMERIE), LORD MONTGOMERIE [S.], grandson and heir, being s. and h. of Alexander MONTGOMERIE, Master of Montgomerie, by Elizabeth, 1st da. of Sir Adam HEPBURN, of Hales, which Alexander last named d. v.p. in 1452. He suc. to the peerage [S.] about 1461. He m. before 1459 Catharine, da. of Gilbert (KENNEDY), 1st LORD KENNEDY [S.], by his first wife, Catharine, da. of Herbert (MAXWELL), LORD MAXWELL [S.] He d. between 1465 and 1480.

III. 1475? 3. HUGH (MONTGOMERIE), LORD MONTGOMERIE [S.], s. and h., was b. about 1460, and suc. to the peerage [S.], when under age. He was cr. in Jan. 1507/8, EARL OF EGLINTON [S.], see that dignity.

MONTGOMERY.

SIR JOHN DE MONTGOMERY was sum. to a Council, which was not a Parl., on 25 Feb. (1361/2), 16 Ed. III., but never afterwards. He, who was Admiral of the King's Fleet, appears to have d. s.p.

MONTGOMERY [county or town.]

i.e., "MONTGOMERY, in Wales," Earldom (Herbert), cr. 1605; see "PEMBROKE" Earldom, cr. 1551, under the 4th Earl.(b)

i.e., "MONTGOMERY," Viscountcy (Herbert), cr. 1687 with the MARQUESSATE OF POWIS, which see; ex. 1748.

i.e., "MONTGOMERY," Marquessate (Herbert), cr. 1689 or 1690 by King James II.(c) when in exile with the DUKEDOM OF POWIS, which see.

(a) She was said to have been possessed of some fortune and to have been the da. of the owner of "a sponging house" where he was confined for debt.

(b) There is an (inexplicable) administration dated 18 Dec. 1574, of "Sir Gabriel Montgomery, Knt., Earl of Montgomery," granted to the Lady Elizabeth Touche, "Countess," relict of the same.

(c) See vol. i, p. 59, note "b," sub "Albemarle," for a list of "Jacobite Peerages."

MONTGOMERY OF THE GREAT ARDS.

Viscountcy [I.] I. 1622. 1. SIR HUGH MONTGOMERY, of Braidstane, in Scotland, s. and h.[a] of Adam M., of the same, by (—), da. of John MONTGOMERY, of Haselheads, emigrated to Ireland and was *cr.*, 3 May 1622, VISCOUNT MONTGOMERY OF THE GREAT ARDS, co. Down [I.] He *m.* firstly, in 1587, Elizabeth, 2d da. of John SHAW, of Greenock. He *m.* secondly Sarah, widow of John (FLEMING), EARL OF WIGTON [S.] (who *d.* April 1619) relict formerly of Sir James JOHNSTON, da. of William (MAXWELL), LORD HERRIES OF TERREGLES [S.], by Catharine, da. of Mark KERR, of Newbottle. She, by whom he had no issue, was *bur.* 29 March 1636, at Edinburgh. He *d.* about 1637. Will dat. 20 May 1636.

II. 1637? 2. HUGH (MONTGOMERY), VISCOUNT MONTGOMERY OF GREAT ARDS [I.], s. and h.; *suc. to the peerage* [I.] about 1637; was Col. of a Regiment during the rebellion in Ireland in 1641. He *m.*, 3 Aug. 1620, at Kensington, Jean, 1st da. of William (ALEXANDER), 1st EARL OF STIRLING [S.], by Janet, da. and coheir of Sir William ERSKINE. He *d.* in 1642. His widow *m.* Major Gen. MONROE.

III. 1642. 3. HUGH (MONTGOMERY), VISCOUNT MONTGOMERY OF GREAT ARDS [I.], s. and h. *suc. to the peerage* [I.] in 1642. Having distinguished himself on behalf of his King, he was *cr.*, 18 July 1661, EARL OF MOUNT ALEXANDER [I.] See that dignity, which, together with this Viscountcy, became *extinct* in 1757.

MONTHERMER.

Barony by Writ. I. 1309. 1. RALPH DE MONTHERMER, whose parentage is unknown, one of the Esquires in the household of Gilbert (de Clare), Earl of Gloucester and Hertford, having *m.* clandestinely (as her second husband) about Jan. 1296/7, JOAN, COUNTESS OF GLOUCESTER AND HERTFORD, widow of the said Earl, formerly Lady Joan PLANTAGENET, (called "*Joan of Acres*"), 3d but 2d. surv. da. of **King Edward I.**, by his first wife, Eleanor, da. of FERDINAND III., KING OF CASTILE, and having obtained the King's pardon for such marriage, 2 Aug. 1297, on which day he did homage at Eltham palace, as (*jure uxoris*), EARL OF GLOUCESTER AND HERTFORD,[b] was sum. to Parl. as such Earl by writs directed "*Comiti Gloucestr et. Hertf.*" from 6 Feb. (1298/9), 27 Ed. I. to 3 Nov. (1306), 34 Ed. I. He was at the siege of Carlaverock in 1300, in the Scotch wars, under his (father in law) Edward I., who, about 1306, conferred on him the whole of Annandale with the title of EARL OF ATHOLE [S.], which dignity, however, he for 5,000 marks, resigned in (1307) 35 Ed. I., in favour of David de Strabolgi, the s. and h. of the late possessor thereof. His wife (the Princess Joan), *d.* 23 April 1307, aged 35, and was *bur.* in the priory of Stoke Clare, co. Suffolk, and, tho' after her death he continued to be constantly styled (as indeed was his second wife) by the title of the said Earldom, he was sum. to Parl. as a *Baron* (only) by writs directed *Radulpho de Monthermer* [LORD MONTHERMER] from 4 March (1308/9), 2 Ed. II., to 30 Oct. (1324), 18 Ed. II. He *m.* secondly (also clandestinely) about 1313, Isabel, widow of John (DE HASTINGS), LORD HASTINGS, da. of Hugh (LE DESPENCER), EARL OF WINCHESTER. By her he had no issue. He *d.* in or before 1325. Will enrolled at the court of Hustings, London, 20 July 1325. His widow *d.* 1336.

II. 1325? 2. THOMAS (DE MONTHERMER), LORD MONTHERMER, s. and h. by first wife. He was never sum. to Parl. He *m.* Margaret. He *d.*, s.p.m., in 1340, being slain in a sea fight against the French. *Esch.* 23 Ed. III. His widow *d.* in or shortly before 1349.

(a) His next br., George Montgomery, was Bishop of Meath, 1610-21.

(b) Possibly because the lady was considered *suo jure* Countess thereof, as being entitled to a life interest therein. See vol. iv, p. 41, note "c," *sub* "Gloucester."

III. 1340. *3.* Margaret, *suo jure* BARONESS MONTHERMER, da. and h., aged 10 at the death of her father. She *m.* before 1349, Sir John DE MONTACUTE (2d *s.* of William, EARL OF SALISBURY), who distinguished himself in the French wars, and was present at the battle (26 Aug. 1346) of Cressy, and who, most probably owing to such alliance, was sum. to Parl. as a Baron, LORD MONTACUTE, from 15 Feb. (1356/7), 31 Ed. III., to 6 Dec. (1389), 20 Ric. II.,(a) the writs being directed to him (*not* under the name of Monthermer, but) under that of Montacute. He *d.* 25 Feb. (1389/90), 13 Ric. II. Will dat. 20 March 1388/9.(b)

IV. 1390. *4.* JOHN (DE MONTACUTE), LORD MONTHERMER [1309], and LORD MONTACUTE [1357], s. and h. By the death, 3 June 1397, of his paternal uncle, he became EARL OF SALISBURY and Lord Montacute [1299], with which last named Barony the *Barony of Monthermer* (as well as the Barony of Montacute, *cr.* in 1357), ever afterwards continued united. See "MONTACUTE," Barony, *cr.* 1299, under the 5th Lord.

I.(*bis*) 1337. *1.* EDWARD DE MONTHERMER, a younger son of Ralph, LORD MONTHERMER, by the Princess Joan, both abovenamed, was sum. to Parl. as a Baron (LORD MONTHERMER) by writs 23 April and 21 June (1337), 11 Ed. III., but never afterwards. Nothing further is known of him, save that he was *bur.* (with his mother) in the priory of Stoke Clare, co. Suffolk. His *honours* are presumed to have become *extinct* on his death.

MONTJOY, or MOUNTJOY; see MOUNTJOY.

MONTRATH, see MOUNTRATH.

MONTREAL.

See "AMHERST OF MONTREAL, co. Kent," Barony (*Amherst*), *cr.* 1788.

MONTROSE.

Dukedom [S.] I. 1488, and 1489, to 1495. *1.* DAVID (LINDSAY), EARL OF CRAWFORD [S.], who was *b.* 1440 and who *suc.* his father in that peerage [S.], Sep. 1453, was *cr.*, 18 May 1488, DUKE OF MONTROSE [S.], with rem. to his heirs, but was deprived of that dignity under the act recissory of Oct. 1488, being, however, on 19 Sep. 1489, restored to the same, but only for his life. He *d.* Christmas 1495, in his 55th year, when the *Dukedom*, as conferred in 1489, became extinct. See fuller account under "CRAWFORD" Earldom [S.], *cr.* 1398, *sub* the 5th Earl.

Earldom [S.] I. 1505. *1.* WILLIAM (GRAHAM), LORD GRAHAM [S.], s. and h. of William, 3d LORD GRAHAM [S.], by Anne [Christian ?], da. of George (DOUGLAS), 4th EARL OF ANGUS [S.]; *suc.* his father *in the peerage* [S.], 1472; sat in the first Parl. of King James IV. [S.], 7 Oct. 1488, and was *cr.*, 3 March 1504/5, EARL OF MONTROSE [S.] He *m.* firstly, 25 Nov. 1479, at the parish church of Muthyll, co. Perth, Annabella,(c) 4th da. of John (DRUMMOND), LORD DRUMMOND [S.], by Elisabeth, sister of David, DUKE OF MONTROSE [S.], abovenamed, da. of Alexander (LINDSAY), 4th EARL OF CRAWFORD [S.] He *m.* secondly, Janet, da. of Sir Archibald EDMONSTONE, of Duntreath. She *d.* s.p.m. He *m.* thirdly Christian, widow of Patrick (HALYBURTON), LORD DIRLETOUN [S.] (who *d.* 1506), da. of Thomas WAWANE, of Stevenstoun, co. Haddington. He was slain at the battle of Flodden, 9 Sep. 1513.(d)

(a) There is proof in the rolls of Parl. of his sitting.
(b) See Nicolas's "*Test Vet.*"
(c) See vol. iii, p. 174, note "e," as to her and her five sisters.
(d) See p. 63, note "b," *sub* "Lennox," for a list of Scotch nobles slain at Flodden.

II. 1513. 2. WILLIAM (GRAHAM), EARL OF MONTROSE, &c. [S.] s. and h., by first wife; *styled* LORD GRAHAM from 1505 till he *suc. to the peerage* [S.], 9 Sep. 1513; was, in 1514, one of the custodians of the young King James V. [S.] for whom (many years later) in 1536 he was a Commissioner of Regency; was joint Keeper of Stirling Castle and of the person of Mary, Queen of Scots, in 1543. He m. probably before 1520, Janet, 1st da. of William (KEITH), 3d EARL MARISCHAL [S.], by Elizabeth, da. of George (GORDON), 2d EARL OF HUNTLY [S.] She was living 24 April 1538. He d. 24 May 1571.

[ROBERT GRAHAM, *styled* LORD GRAHAM, s. and h. ap. He m. Margaret, 3d da. of Malcolm (FLEMING), 3d LORD FLEMING [S.] He d. v.p., being slain at the battle of Pinkie, 10 Sep. 1547. His widow m. Thomas ERSKINE, Master of Erskine (who d. 1551), and thirdly John (STEWART), EARL OF ATHOLE [S.], who d. 24 April 1579, leaving her surviving.]

III. 1571. 3. JOHN (GRAHAM), EARL OF MONTROSE, &c. [S.], grandson and h., being posthumous s. and h. of Robert GRAHAM, *styled* LORD GRAHAM, and Margaret, his wife, both abovenamed. He was b. 1548 and was *styled* LORD GRAHAM till he *suc. to the peerage* [S.], 24 May 1571, having meanwhile (24 July 1567), been one of the Commissioners to receive Queen Mary's resignation of the Crown [S.] at Lochleven. He was Chancellor of the jury at the trial of the Earl of Morton [S.] in 1581; was an Extra. Lord of Session [S.], 1584-85, and 1591-96; High Treasurer [S.], 1584; High Chancellor [S.], 1599—1604; Viceroy ("*Supremus regni Scotiæ procurator*") of Scotland, 1604, supporting the re-establishment of Episcopacy. He m. in 1569 Jean, da. of David (DRUMMOND), 2d LORD DRUMMOND [S.], by his second wife, Lilias, da. of William (RUTHVEN), 2d LORD RUTHVEN [S.] He d. 9 Nov. 1608, aged 60.

IV. 1608. 4. JOHN (GRAHAM), EARL OF MONTROSE, &c. [S.], s. and h., *styled* LORD GRAHAM till he *suc. to the peerage* [S.], 9 Nov. 1608; was President of the Council [S.] from July to Nov. 1626. He m. Margaret, 1st da. of William (RUTHVEN), 1st EARL OF GOWRIE [S.], by Dorothea, da. of Henry (STEWART), 1st LORD METHVEN [S.] He d. 24 Nov. 1626.

V. 1626.
Marquessate [S.]
I. 1644.

5 and 1. JAMES (GRAHAM), EARL OF MONTROSE, &c. [S.], only s. and h., b. 1612; *styled* LORD GRAHAM till he *suc. to the peerage* [S.], 24 Nov. 1626. He, at first, took part with the Covenanters but after the treaty of Ripon, 1640, espoused the Royal cause and was by warrant under sign manual, dat. at Oxford, 6 May 1644, *cr.* MARQUESS OF MONTROSE, EARL OF KINCARDINE, LORD GRAHAM AND MUGDOCK [S.], which creation was confirmed after his death by patent, 12 Dec. 1660, with the original precedence.([a]) He, as Commander in Chief of the King's forces [S.] obtained a series of victories, 1644-45, with a greatly inferior force, over the party of the Covenanters; at Tippermuir and Aberdeen in Sep. 1644, at Inverlochy in Feb., at Aldern in May, at Alfurd in July, and at Kilsyth (with the slaughter of above 5,000 men) in Aug. 1645, soon after which Edinburgh and Glasgow submitted to him. He was, however, totally defeated by General Leslie at Philiphaugh on 13 Sep. following, and, being commanded by the King to disband his forces, retired to the Continent. He declined the appointment of Lieut. Gen. in the French army but was made Field Marshal by the Emperor Ferdinand III. He joined Charles II. at the Hague, by whom he was made K.G. (being el. at Jersey, 12 Jan. 1649/50, tho' never installed), the insignia being sent to him in Norway, where he was preparing for the invasion of Scotland. Having landed at Orkney, he was defeated at Invercharron, in Caithness-shire, and tho' he himself escaped, was delivered up (by the treachery of Macleod of Assynt) and was hung, drawn, and quartered, at Edinburgh, 21 May 1650, aged 38, his remains being

---

([a]) See p. 309, note "d," *sub* "Middleton," as to this re-integration of the inchoate signature of 1644.

subsequently *bur.* in Holyroodhouse church and finally in St. Giles cathedral, Edinburgh. He *m.* (contract, 10 Nov. 1629), Magdalen, 6th da. of David (Carnegie), 1st Earl of Southesk [S.], by Margaret, da. of Sir David Lindsay, of Edzell.

[(—) Graham, *styled* Earl of Kincardine, 1st s. and h. ap. He accompanied his father in his campaign in 1645, and *d.* v.p. and unm. at the Bog of Gicht, in March 1645, in his 16th year, being *bur.* at Bellie church.]

Marquessate [S.] II. Earldom [S.] VI. 1650.

2 and *6.* James (Graham), Marquess of Montrose, &c. [S.] (generally known as "*The good Marquess*") 2d but only surv. s. and h.; *b.* about 1631; *styled* Earl of Kincardine from 1645 till *he suc. to the peerage* [S.], his father's Marquessate, &c. [S.], being confirmed (as before stated) to him with the precedency of 6 May 1644, by a patent of *novodamus*, 12 Dec. 1660, when the estates, which had been forfeited in 1650, were restored. He declined, in 1661, to vote at the trial of (his father's great enemy) the Marquess of Argyll [S.]; was P.C. [S.], and one of the extra. Lords of Session, 1668-69. He *m.* Isabel, widow of Robert (Kerr), 1st Earl of Roxburghe [S.] (who *d.* 18 Jan. 1650), 5th da. of William (Douglas), Earl of Morton [S.], by Anne, da. of George (Keith), 5th Earl Marischal [S.] He was *bur.* 23 Feb. 1669, aged about 38, in the chapel of Aberruthven, co. Perth.

Marquessate [S.] III. Earldom [S.] VII. 1669.

3 and *7.* James (Graham), Marquess of Montrose, &c. [S.], s. and h., *styled* Earl of Kincardine till he *suc. to the peerage* [S.], in Feb. 1669, at which date he was very young. He was subsequently appointed (by King Charles II.), Capt. of the Guards and in 1682, President of the Council [S.] He *m.* Christian, 2d da. and coheir of John (Leslie), Duke of Rothes [S.], by Anne, da. of John (Lindsay), Earl of Crawford and Lindsay [S.] He *d.* 25 April 1684. Fun. entry at Lyon office. His widow *m.* May 1687, Sir John Bruce, 2d Bart. [S.], of Balcaskie and Kinross, who *d.* s.p.m. She *d.* at Edinburgh, 21 April and was *bur.* 4 May 1710 in the Abbey church there. Fun. entry at Lyon office.

Marquessate [S.] IV. Earldom [S.] VIII. Dukedom [S.] II. 1707. 1684

4, *8*, and *1.* James (Graham), Marquess of Montrose, &c. [S.], only s. and h., *b.* about 1680; *styled* Earl of Kincardine till he *suc. to the peerage* [S.], 25 April 1684, at which date he was very young; was a Commissioner of the Treasury [S.], 1705-07; High Admiral [S.], 1705-06; President of the Council [S.], 1704, and again, 1706. He obtained, 5 Sep. 1706, on resignation, a new charter of the *Marquessate of Montrose* [S.], ratified by act of Parl. with extended limitation to heirs female and heirs of nomination. Being a zealous supporter of the Protestant succession and of the act of union, he was *cr.*, 24 April 1707, DUKE OF MONTROSE, MARQUESS OF GRAHAM AND BUCHANAN, EARL OF KINCARDINE, VISCOUNT OF DUNDAFF, and LORD ABERRUTHVEN, MUGDOCK, AND FINTRIE [S.], with a similar rem. as that of the Marquessate.(a) He was Rep. Peer [S.] in six Parls., *viz.*, 1707-10, and 1715-34; P.C., 1708; Lord

---

(a) The words of the patent, which extends the limitation, run "to the other heirs provided to succeed to the title and dignity of Marquis of Montrose by the former patents of honour made and granted to the said James, Marquis of Montrose, *his predecessours.*" It is pointed out in "Riddell" (pp. 200—202), that the only patent of that Marquessate to *the predecessors* of the grantee was that of 1660 which was to "heirs male of the body," all of which, save the grantee, had failed, but that probably the words refer to the patent of the previous year (1706) granted to the grantee *himself* whereby the limitation of the Marquessate was extended.

Privy Seal [S.], 1709-13; one of the LORDS REGENT OF THE KINGDOM, 1 Aug. to 18 Sep. 1714,(a) on the death of Queen Anne; Princ. Secretary of State [S.], 1714-15; Lord Clerk Register [S.], 1716; Keeper of the Great Seal [S.], 1716-33; P.C., 1717. He m. Christian, 2d da. of David (CARNEGIE), 3d EARL OF NORTHESK [S.], by Elizabeth, da. of John (LINDSAY), EARL OF CRAWFORD AND LINDSAY [S.] He d. in London, 7 Jan. 1742, aged about 62. Fun. entry at Lyon office.(b) His widow d. at Edinburgh, 25 May 1744.

[JAMES GRAHAM, *styled* EARL OF KINCARDINE, 1st s. and h. ap., *d.* young and v.p.]

[DAVID GRAHAM, *styled* MARQUESS OF GRAHAM, 2d but 1st surv. s. and h. ap., *b.* about 1705; was v.p. raised to the peerage of Great Britain,(c) being *cr.*, 23 May 1722, BARON GRAHAM OF BELFORD, co. Northumberland, and EARL GRAHAM,(d) with a *spec. rem.* of that dignity, failing heirs male of his body to his brothers, William Graham and George Graham, in like manner. He took his seat, 19 Jan. 1727. He *d.* v.p. and unm., 30 Sep. 1731, at Cleay, co. Norfolk.]

Dukedom [S.] III. Marquessate [S.] V. Earldom [S.] IX. 1742.

2, 5, and *9.* WILLIAM (GRAHAM), DUKE OF MONTROSE, &c. [S.], also EARL GRAHAM, &c. [G.B.], 3d but 1st surv. s. and h., *b.* about 1710; Ensign, 3d Foot Guards, 1730; *suc.* his br., 30 Sep. 1731, *in the peerage* [G.B.] (as EARL GRAHAM, &c.), and *suc.* his grandfather in the peerage [S.], 4 Jan. 1742; was Chancellor of the Univ. of Glasgow, 1743-81.(e) He *m.*, 28 Oct. 1742 in London, Lucy, yst. da. of John (MANNERS), 2d DUKE OF RUTLAND, by his second wife, Lucy, da. of Bennet (SHERARD), 2d BARON SHERARD OF LEITRIM [I.] She *d.* in London, 18 June 1788, aged 71. He *d.* at Twickenham, Midx., 23 Sep. 1790, aged about 80. Both were *bur.* at Aberruthven, co. Perth. Will pr. Dec. 1790.

Dukedom [S.] IV. Marquessate [S.] VI. Earldom [S.] X. 1790.

3, 6, and *10.* JAMES (GRAHAM), DUKE OF MONTROSE, &c. [S.], also EARL GRAHAM, &c. [G.B.], only surv. s. and h.,(f) *b.* 8 Feb. 1755; *styled* MARQUESS OF GRAHAM till 1790; ed. at Trin. Coll., Cambridge; M.A., 1775; M.P. for Richmond, 1780-84, and for Great Bedwyn, 1784-90; Chancellor of the Univ. of Glasgow, 1781—1836; a Lord of the Treasury, 1783-89; Joint Paymaster, 1789-91; Vice President of the Board of Trade, and P.C., 1789; Lord Lieut. of Huntingdonshire, 1790-93; *suc. to the*

(a) See vol. iii, p. 116, note "b," *sub* "Devonshire," for a list of these Regents.

(b) Macky in his "*Characters*" says of him when "about 25" [in 1705] "he inherits all the great qualities of those two families [*i.e.*, Graham and Leslie], with a sweetness of behaviour which charms all those who know him; hath improved himself in most foreign courts; is very beautiful in his person;" to which Dean Swift adds, "*now very homely and makes a sorry appearance*," and Lockhart states that he was "led by the nose" and "governed by his mother and her relations."

(c) See vol. iii, p. 164, note "d," *sub* "Dover," also vol. iv, p. 147, note "b," and p. 148, note "a," *sub* "Hamilton," as to the strange resolution of the House of Lords, 14 Jan. 1720, which continued in force till 11 June 1782. It was, doubtless, in consequence of this resolution that the peerage of Great Britain was not conferred on the Duke himself but on his son.

(d) See vol. ii, p. 102, note "a," for instances of Earldoms where the family name serves for the title of peerage.

(e) He, under the Jurisdiction Act of 1747, obtained £3,000 for the Sheriffship of Dumbartonshire and £2,578 for the regalities of Montrose, Menteith, Lennox, and Darnley, being in all £5,578 in lieu of his claim of £15,000.

(f) An elder br. was *b.* and *d.* 20 Jan. 1746.

peerage [S., and G.B.], 23 Sep. 1790; Master of the Horse, 1790-95, and again 1807; a Commissioner for Indian affairs, 1791—1803; K.T., 14 June, 1793, which honor he resigned when in 1812 he acquired the Garter;([a]) Lord Lieut. of Stirlingshire, 1795; Lord Justice General [S.], 1795—1836; President of the Board of Trade and Joint Postmaster Gen., 1804-06; Master of the Horse (for the second time), 1807-30; K.G., 31 March 1812;([a]) Lord Lieut. of Dumbartonshire, 1813; Lord Chamberlain of the Household, 1821-27 and 1828-30.([b]) He *m.* 3 March 1785, at his father's house, Grosvenor street, St. Geo. Han. sq., Jemima Elizabeth, 1st da. of John (ASHBURNHAM), 2d EARL OF ASHBURNHAM, by Elizabeth, da. and coheir of John CROWLEY. She who was *b.* 1 Jan. 1762 died (as *Marchioness of Graham*) in childbed, 18 Sep. 1786, aged 24, in Grosvenor square, and was *bur.* at Aberruthven. He *m.* secondly, 24 July 1790, at Kensington palace, St. Margaret's Westm., Caroline Maria, 1st da. of George (MONTAGU), 4th DUKE OF MANCHESTER, by Elizabeth, da. of Sir James DASHWOOD, Bart. He *d.* 30 Dec. 1836, aged 81, and was *bur.* at Aberruthven. Will pr. Feb. 1837. His widow, who was *b.* 10 Aug. 1770 and *bap.* at St. Marylebone, *d.* at Petersham, Surrey, 24 March and was *bur.* there 1 April 1847, aged 76. Will pr. April 1847.

[WILLIAM GRAHAM, *generally known* as EARL OF KINCARDINE, 1st s. and h. ap., by the first wife; *b.* 4 Sep. 1786, *d.* v.p. an infant 23 April 1787, before his father had *suc.* to the peerage; and was *bur.* at Aberruthven.]

Dukedom [S.] V. Marquessate [S.] VII. Earldom [S.] XI. — 1836.

4, 7, and *11.* JAMES (GRAHAM), DUKE OF MONTROSE, &c. [S.], also EARL GRAHAM, &c. [G.B.], 2d but 1st surv. s. and h., being eldest son by the second wife; *b.* 16 July 1799; *styled* MARQUESS OF GRAHAM till 1836; ed. at Trin. Coll., Cambridge; M.A., 1819; P.C., 1821; Vice Chamberlain of the Household, 1821-27; M.P. for Cambridge, 1825-32; Commissioner for Indian affairs, 1828-30; *suc. to the peerage* [S. and G.B.], 30 Dec. 1836; Chancellor of the Univ. of Glasgow, 1837; Lord Lieut. of Stirlingshire, 1843; K.T., 12 March 1845; Lord Steward of the Household, 1852-53; Chancellor of the Duchy of Lancaster, 1858-59; Postmaster General, 1866-68; Major Gen. of the Royal body guard of Scotch Archers. He *m.* 15 Oct. 1836, at St. Geo. Han. sq., Caroline Agnes, 3d da. of John (HORSLEY-BERESFORD), 3d BARON DECIES [I.], by Charlotte Philadelphia, da. and h. of Robert HORSLEY. He *d.* at Cannes, in France, 30 Dec. 1874 (exactly 38 years after his predecessor), aged 75. His widow, who was *b.* 1818, *m.* 22 Jan. 1876, at Trinity church, Sloane street, Chelsea, William Stuart STIRLING-CRAWFORD, of Milton, co. Lanark (well known in the sporting world), who *d.*, also at Cannes. on 23 Feb. 1883, aged 63, his will being proved under £154,000. She *m.* thirdly, 26 July 1888, at St. Andrews, Fulham, Marcus Henry MILNER, who is said to have been *b.* 16 April 1864. If so, he was 46 years her junior.

[JAMES GRAHAM, *styled* MARQUESS OF GRAHAM, 1st s. and h. ap.; *b.* 7 Feb. 1845; *d.* an infant and v.p. 31 Jan. 1846.]

[JAMES GRAHAM, *styled* MARQUESS OF GRAHAM, 2d but 1st surv. s. and h. ap.; *b.* 22 June 1847, in Belgrave square; an officer in the Life Guards; Capt. 1869. He *d.* in London, unm. and v.p. from typhoid fever, 8, and was *bur.* 11 April 1872, aged 24, in Buchanan church, Loch Lomond.]

([a]) See vol. i, p. ii, note "b," *sub* "Aberdeen," for a list of the knights of the Thistle (12 in all), who subsequently obtained the Garter.

([b]) In the Greville memoirs he is spoken of very disparagingly, but Wraxall (vol. iii, pp. 385—387. Edit. 1884), after stating that "few individuals, however distinguished by birth, talents, interests, or public services, arrived at greater honours under the reign of Geo. III." than did he, states that "he possessed a ready elocution, sustained by all the confidence in himself necessary for addressing the House," while his "devotion" to the cause of George III., was only equalled by that of his ancestor to the cause of Charles I., he being "also in his person, elegant and pleasing" and not deficient "in the accomplishments befitting his illustrious descent."

Dukedom [S.] VI. Marquessate [S.] VIII. Earldom [S.] XII.	1874.	*5, 8,* and *12.* DOUGLAS-BERESFORD-MALISE-RONALD (GRAHAM), DUKE OF MONTROSE [1707], MARQUESS OF MONTROSE [1644, confirmed 1660], MARQUESS OF GRAHAM AND BUCHANAN [1707], EARL OF MONTROSE [1505], EARL OF KINCARDINE [1644 and 1660], VISCOUNT OF DUNDAFF [1707], LORD GRAHAM [1415 ?], LORD GRAHAM AND MUGDOCK [1644 and 1660], LORD ABERRUTHVEN, MUGDOCK AND FINTRIE [1707], in the peerage of Scotland; also EARL GRAHAM and BARON GRAHAM OF BELFORD [1722], in the peerage of Great

Britain, 3d but only surv. s. and h., *b.* 7 Nov, 1852; ed. at Eton; *styled* MARQUESS OF BUCHANAN, after his brother's death in April 1872 till he *suc. to the peerage* [S. and G.B.], 30 Dec. 1874; was sometime, 1872-77, an officer in the Coldstream Guards and the 5th Lancers; Gen. of the Royal Body Guard of Scotch Archers. K.T., 29 Nov. 1879; Lord Lieut. of Stirlingshire, 1885; Lord Clerk Register [S.] 1890. He *m.* 24 July 1876, Violet Hermione, 2d da. of Sir Frederick Ulric GRAHAM, 3d Bart., of Netherby, by Jane Hermione, 1st da. of Edward Adolphus (SEYMOUR), 12th DUKE OF SOMERSET.

[JAMES GRAHAM, *styled* MARQUESS OF GRAHAM, *b.* 1 May 1878, at 35 Chester square, Pimlico.]

Family Estates.—These, in 1883, consisted of 68,565 acres in Stirlingshire; 32,294 in Perthshire, and 2,588 in Dumbartonshire. *Total* 103,447 acres, worth £24,872 a year. *Principal Residence*; Buchanan Castle, co. Stirling.

The Duke of Montrose is one of the 28 noblemen who, in 1883, possessed above 100,000 acres in the United Kingdom (none of his property being in England) and stands 27th in point of acreage and 26th in point of income. See a list of these in vol. ii, p. 51, note "a," *sub* "Buccleuch."

MONYCROWER.

See "MAYO OF MONYCROWER," Viscountcy [I.] (*Bourke*), *cr.* 1781 see "MAYO" Earldom [I.], *cr.* 1785.

MONYMAIL.

See "MELVILLE OF MONYMAIL," Barony [S.] (*Melville*), *cr.* 1627, and again 1627.

---

i.e., "RAITH, MONYMAIL AND BALWEARIE," Barony [S.] (*Melville*), *cr.* 1690 with the EARLDOM OF MELVILLE [S.], which see.

MONYPENNY.

Barony [S.] I. 1460? *1.* SIR WILLIAM MONYPENNY, of Monypenny, formerly Halliserth, co. Stirling, s. and h. of Sir William M., of the same, by Margaret, da. of Philip ARBUTHNOTT, of Arbuthnott, acquired not only the lands of Conquirsall, in France, but also many estates in Scotland forfeited by the family of Douglas, and was *cr.* a Peer of Parl., LORD MONYPENNY [S.], at some date between 9 Nov. 1458, and 17 July 1464. He was Ambassador from France to England, 16 Feb. 1471.(a) He was living 20 March 1483/4.

II. 1485? to 1500. *2.* ALEXANDER (MONYPENNY), LORD MONYPENNY [S.], s. and h. He exchanged in 1495 his Barony of Earlshall, co. Fife, for lands called Escariot in France. He *d.* s.p.m. when the *peerage* became *dormant*, or, more probably, *extinct.*

(a) *Styled* "Guillaume, Seigneur et Baron Banneret de Monypenny *et de Congressault*" [Wood's "*Douglas*."]

MOORE OF DROGHEDA.

i.e., "MOORE OF DROGHEDA," Viscountcy [I.] (*Moore*), *cr.* 1622; see under "DROGHEDA."

MOORE OF MELLEFONT.

i.e., "MOORE OF MELLEFONT, co. Louth," Barony [I.] (*Moore*), *cr.* 1616; see "Drogheda" Viscountcy [I.], *cr.* 1622.

MOORE OF TULLAMORE.

Barony [I.] I. 1715. 1. THE RT. HON. JOHN MOORE, of Croghan, s. and h. of Thomas MOORE,(a) of the same, by Ellen, da. of Dudley COLLEY, of Castle Carbery, co. Kildare, was many years M.P. for King's county; P.C.; 1714, and was for his services for the protestant religion and the Hanoverian succession, *cr.* 22 Oct. 1715, BARON MOORE OF TULLAMORE [I.] He *m.* firstly, 15 Sep. 1697, Mary, da. of Elnathan LUM, of Dublin, Banker. She, who was *bap.* 7 Nov. 1681, *d.* 7 Nov. 1722. He *m.* secondly, Elizabeth, widow of Sir John KING, Bart. [I.], 1st da. and coheir of John SANKEY, of Tenelick, co. Longford. He *d.* 8 Sep. 1725, and was *bur.* at Tullamore. His widow *m.* (as his second wife), Brabazon (PONSONBY), 1st EARL OF BESSBOROUGH [I.], (who *d.* 4 July 1758), and *d.* 17 July 1738, aged 58, being *bur.* at Fidowne.

II. 1725, to 1764. 2. CHARLES (MOORE), BARON MOORE OF TULLAMORE [I.], only s. and h. by first wife, *b.* 1712; *suc. to the peerage* [I.], 8 Sep. 1725, and took his seat 16 Oct. 1729. He was *cr.* 16 Sep. 1758, EARL OF CHARLEVILLE, in the Kings County [I.] He *d.* s.p. 17 Feb. 1764, when all his *honours* became *extinct*. See fuller particulars under "CHARLEVILLE" Earldom [I.], *cr.* 1758; *ex.* 1764.

MOORE PARK.

See "BUTLER OF MOORE PARK, co. Hertford," Barony (*Butler*), *cr.* 1666; *attainted with the Dukedom of Ormonde*, 1715.

MORAY.

[MORAY with Ross (the territory comprising that now occupied by the counties of Inverness and Ross) was one of the *seven original Earldoms* (Mormaerships) of Scotland,(c) of which the holders originally bore the title of "*Ri*" (*i.e.*, KING), tho' in the 10th century (with, perhaps, the exception of Moray), each such ruler was styled *Mormaer*, while early in the 12th century he was more generally known as *Earl*. Of these twelve districts MORAY was the first to break up,(d) the *male* line of its Celtic rulers terminating apparently with Maelsnechtan,(e) who was *Ri* (or *Mormaer*) *of Moray* in 1086, tho' possibly others (apparently connected with the earlier Lords) held it somewhat later.]

Earldom [S.] I. 1115. 1. BETH, who under the designation of "*Beth, Comes*," was witness to the charter of Scone in 1115, was possibly EARL OF MORAY [S.] tho' more probably EARL OF FIFE [S.] He may (not improbably) have acquired some right to the Earldom of Moray by marriage with a sister of Maelsnectan, Mormaer of Moray, abovenamed.

(a) His descent from the same stock as that of the Moores of Drogheda is set out in "Lodge," vol. ii, pp. 84—92.
(b) The preamble to the patent in given in "Lodge" vol. ii, p. 89.
(c) See vol. i, p. 68, *sub* "Angus," for a fuller account of these seven Earldoms.
(d) See Skene's "*Celtic Scotland*" (1880), vol. iii, p. 287.
(e) He was s. of Lulach Mac Gilcomgar, who was s. of Gilcomgar, sometime Mormaer of Moray, which Lulach was, for a few months in 1057, successor to Macbeth as King of Scotland.

II. 1120? 1. ANGUS, EARL OF MORAY [S.], was nephew (by the sister) of Maelsnectan, Mormaer of Moray, abovenamed, his mother being a da. of Lulach, who (for a few months) was **King of Scotland**, in 1057. He was slain in rebellion against King David I. [S.] in 1130 at Strickathrow, co. Fife.

[The family of *Mac Heth*, whose founder, Wymund, asserted himself to be a son of this Angus, claimed the EARLDOM OF MORAY [S.], so also did the family of *Mac William*, who in addition "claimed to be the nearer line of the Royal family to the throne of Scotland, and it was not till the year 1222 that the pretensions of these two families were finally extinguished by Alexander II."(a) [S.] MORGUND, EARL OF MAR [S.], claimed, according to a grant of 1171,(b) to be also EARL OF MORAY [S.], asserting that his father, Gillocher, had died seized of both these Earldoms.]

III. 1314? 1. SIR THOMAS RANDOLPH, only s. and h. of Thomas RANDOLPH, of Strathdon, sometime Chamberlain of Scotland, by Isabel, sister of **King Robert I.** [S.], da. of Robert (BRUCE), EARL OF CARRICK [S.], *suc.* his father soon after 1294, distinguished himself in behalf of Bruce's claim to the Crown [S.], and was in command of the left wing at the battle of Bannockburn, 24 June 1314. He was *cr.* by the said King, his uncle, probably in 1314, but perhaps as early as 1312, EARL OF MORAY [S.], receiving the extensive district of that name, with rem. to the heirs male of his body.(c) He distinguished himself in Ireland, under Edward Bruce; at Mitton, at the defeat of the English, in 1319, signed the letter to the Pope in 1320, as to the indepency of Scotland and was REGENT OF SCOTLAND from 1329 till his death. He *m.* (probably) Isabel, only da. of Sir John STEWART, of Bonkyl, with whom he is said to have acquired the Barony of Garlies. He *d.* 20 July 1332, at Musselburgh.

IV. 1332. 2. THOMAS (RANDOLPH), EARL OF MORAY [S.], s. and h., who survived his father but 23 days, being slain 12 Aug. 1332, at the battle of Dupplin against the English. He *d.* unm.

V. 1332, to 1346. 3. JOHN (RANDOLPH), EARL OF MORAY [S.], only br. and h. He was in command at the defeat of Balliol, at Annan, in Dec. 1332, and at the battle of Hallidon hill, 19 July 1333. In 1334, he was JOINT REGENT OF SCOTLAND. He *m.* his cousin, Isabel, da. of Sir Alexander STEWART, of Bonkyll. He *d.* s.p. being slain by the English at the battle of Durham, 17 Oct. 1346, when, the issue male of his father having failed, the *Earldom*, according to the charter [1314 ?] became *extinct.*

VI. 1359, to 1361. 1. HENRY (PLANTAGENET), DUKE OF LANCASTER, was *cr.* (by King David II. [S.]), 5 April 1359,(d) EARL OF MORAY [S.] He *d.* s.p.m. 13 March 1360/1, aged about 60, when that *dignity* is presumed to have *reverted to the Crown* [S.] See fuller particulars under "LANCASTER," Dukedom, *cr.* 1351; *ex.* 1361.

(a) See Skene's *Celtic Scotland* " (1880), vol. iii, p. 287.

(b) See p. 219, note "b," *sub* "Mar," as to this document, of the authenticity of which, however, there are great doubts.

(c) This was the first Earldom (*Douglas*, in 1357, being the second and *Crawford*, in 1398, the third), *cr.* after the extinction (1290) of the Celtic dynasty." See vol. ii, p. 408, note "d," *sub* "Crawford." "From the tenor of this charter it appears that the lands ["omnes terras nostras in Moravia, sicut fuerunt in manibus Domini Alexandri, Regis Scotiæ"] were not formerly an Earldom for in the beginning they are called the King's lands in Moray," tho' "immediately after the clause of erection, the lands are called *Comitatus*, and Thomas Randolph is called *Comes*." [Suth. Add. Case, iv. 48.]

(d) See as to "the unaccountable grant [by King David II.] of the Earldom of Moray in favour of Henry, Duke of Lancaster and the heirs male of his body," &c., in Bain's "Calendar of documents" [S.] (Vol. iv, p. x) a work which is simply *invaluable* with reference to Scottish dignities.

VII. 1372, *1.* JOHN DUNBAR, yr. br. of George, EARL OF MARCH or DUNBAR [S.], being 2d s. of Sir Patrick DUNBAR, by Isabel, yst. of the two daughters and coheirs (her issue before Nov. 1368 becoming sole heir) of Thomas (RANDOLPH), 1st EARL OF MORAY [S.], abovenamed, having m. (dispensation, 11 July 1370), the Lady Marjory STEWART, da. of **King Robert II.** [S.], by his first wife, Elizabeth, da. of Sir Adam MURE, obtained a charter of the Earldom of Moray from the King, his father in law, 9 March 1371/2, to himself and his said wife for life, they becoming thereby EARL AND COUNTESS OF MORAY [S.] with rem. failing the heirs procreated between them, to his heirs whatsoever. He, who fought 10 Aug. 1388, at the battle of Otterburn, *d.* at York 1391.

VIII. 1391. *2.* THOMAS (DUNBAR), EARL OF MORAY [S.], s. and h. He was taken prisoner at the battle of Homildon, 14 Sep. 1402.

IX. 1410? *3.* THOMAS (DUNBAR), EARL OF MORAY [S.], only s. and h. He was one of the hostages for King James I. [S.], 31 May 1421, and 13 Dec. 1423, being released, 16 July 1425. He *m.* Marion SETON. He *d.* s.p. 1427 ?(a) His widow *m.* Sir John OGILVY, of Lintrathen.

X. 1427? *4.* JAMES (DUNBAR), EARL OF MORAY [S.], cousin and h., being s. and h. of Alexander DUNBAR, of Frendraught, by Mauld, da. and h. of (—) FRASER, of Frendraught. He was a hostage for James I., 28 March 1424, but liberated, 9 Nov. 1427. He is said(b) to have *m.* Janet, 1st da. of Alexander (GORDON), 1st EARL OF HUNTLY [S.], by his third wife, Elizabeth, da. of William (CRICHTON), 1st LORD CRICHTON [S.] He *d.* s.p.m. legit.,(c) being murdered at Frendraught, 10 Aug. 1429.]

XI. 1429, to 1445. *5.* ELIZABETH,(d) *suo jure* COUNTESS OF MORAY [S.], youngest of the two daughters and coheirs, having *m.* Archibald DOUGLAS, yr. s. of James, EARL OF DOUGLAS [S.], obtained for her husband and herself (1443), 6 Jac. II. [S.], thro' the influence of the Douglas family, the *Earldom of Moray* (to the detriment of her elder sister) the said Archibald Douglas becoming consequently by such right EARL OF MORAY [S.] He, as such, was one of the conservators of a truce with England 1449, 1451, and 1453. He joined his br. James, Earl of Douglas [S.], in the rising against the King, by whose forces he was slain, 1 May 1455, at Arkinholm, in Dumfries-shire, and being afterwards (12 June 1455), attainted as "*Archibaldus, pretensus Comes Moraviæ*" the *Earldom was forfeited.* His widow (who 20 days after his death contracted to marry George Gordon, Master of Huntly, a marriage which did not take place), *m.* Sir John COLQUHOUN of Luss, being then called "*olim Comitissa Moraviæ.*"(e)

[Notwithstanding the apparent forfeiture of the Earldom, Janet, sister of the Countess Elizabeth, and eldest da. of James (DUNBAR), EARL OF MORAY [S.], assumed the title of COUNTESS OF MORAY [S.], being styled in 1454 "*Janeta,*

(a) "It is said [*Lovat case*, 21], he had a da., Lady Janet Dunbar, *m.* (contract dat. 9 Aug. 1422), Hugh, Lord Fraser of Lovat, but this seems doubtful as the title devolved on the son of his uncle." [Wood's "*Douglas.*"]

(b) There is, however, good reason to doubt this match. See "*Exch. Rolls*" [S.], vi, preface, p. cxxxvi.

(c) "Sir Alexander Dunbar, of Westfield, Sheriff of Moray, was son of James, Earl of Moray, by Isabel, da. of Sir Walter Innes, of Innes, her second cousin, who *d.* before a papal dispensation for their marriage could be obtained." [Wood's "*Douglas.*"]

(d) She is erroneously called by "Riddell" (and others) da. of Earl *Thomas* (the penultimate Earl) but this is refuted by a deed quoted by Mr. A. Sinclair in his article on "The Earldom of March" [*Her. and Gen.*, vi, 306], in which deed "when Earl James had been some years dead the Earldom was settled upon Archibald Douglas and Elizabeth Dunbar, one of the two daughters of James, Earl of Moray."

(e) Mr. Sinclair's article in the "*Her. and Gen.*," vi, 307.

Comitissa Moraviæ, Domina Frendraught et Crichton." She, however, "did not bear the title many years, tho' it seems not known how it came to be dropped."(a) She had inherited the estate of Frendraught from her father and had *m.* (firstly) James (CRICHTON), 2d LORD CRICHTON [S.], who is said in a contemporary chronicle (generally very accurate) to have been belted "EARL OF MORAY" [S.] in 1452,(b) being so called in the Exch. Accounts [S.] both in his lifetime, July 1454, and after his death in 1456, but he appears never to have been in the actual possession of that Earldom, or, if so, not improbably resigned it to the Crown. He *d.* probably about 1455. The lady *m.* secondly, before 17 Jan. 1458/9, John SUTHERLAND, who was living at that date. She was alive in 1493, when, under the name of Janet Dunbar, Lady of Frendraught, she resigned that estate to her grandson, James Crichton. See "CRICHTON" Barony [S.], *cr.* 1443 ? *sub* the 2d Lord.]

XII. 1501 to 1544. *1.* JAMES STEWART, illegit. *s.* of **King James IV.** [S.], by Janet, da. of John (KENNEDY), LORD KENNEDY [S.], was *b.* about 1499, and was *cr.* by his father (with grant of the lands of the Earldom) EARL OF MORAY, LORD ABERNETHY AND STRATHEARN [S.],(c) with rem. to heirs male of his body. He was Lieut. Gen. of the Realm [S.], 1532. He *m.* before 24 Aug. 1529, Elizabeth, da. of Colin (CAMPBELL), 3d EARL OF ARGYLL [S.], by Jane, da. of Alexander (GORDON), 3d EARL OF HUNTLY [S.] He *d.* s.p.m., 12 June 1544, aged about 45, when all *his honours* became *extinct.* His widow *m.* before 6 Aug. 1546 (as his first wife) John (GORDON), EARL OF SUTHERLAND [S.], who *d.* July 1568, aged 41.

XIII. 1549 to 1562. *1.* GEORGE (GORDON), EARL OF HUNTLY [S.], who had *suc.* to that dignity in 1524; had a grant of the lands of the *Earldom of Moray*, 13 Feb. 1548/9, becoming, apparently, thereby, EARL OF MORAY [S.] Having, however, lost the confidence of Queen Mary [S.], that Earldom was bestowed by her, 30 Jan. 1561/2, on her bastard brother (as under) by whom this Earl himself was slain, 28 Oct. 1562. See "HUNTLY" Earldom [S.], *cr.* 1445 ? under the 4th Earl.

XIV. 1562, or 1564. *1.* JAMES STEWART, Commendator of St. Andrew's and Pittenweem, illegit. *s.* of **King James V.** [S.], by Margaret, da. of John (ERSKINE), LORD ERSKINE, *de jure* EARL OF MAR [S.]; was *b.* 1534; made Prior of St. Andrew's, 1538; joined the reformed religion and Lords of the Congregation in 1559; P.C., 1561, and having the power of Prime Minister, was *cr.* (by the Queen, his sister), 30 Jan. 1561/2,(d) EARL OF MORAY, LORD ABERNETHY AND STRATHEARN [S.],(c) with rem. to heirs male of his body.(e) About a week later he was *cr.* 7 Feb. 1561/2, EARL OF MAR

(a) Mr. Sinclair's article in the "*Her. and Gen.*, vi, 307.

(b) "If the standing investiture of that Earldom was still that of 1371-72 his wife was *de jure* Countess of Moray, tho' supplanted by her younger sister, but there may have been an intervening resignation and regrant, not now on record, in favour of heirs male. Crichton is supposed to have made a compulsory resignation of the Earldom into the King's hands." *Ex. inform.* [1886] G. Burnett, Lyon.

(c) *i.e.*, "Strathdearn" in Moray.

(d) See p. 305, note "d," *sub* "Methven."

(e) "The following appears to be the position of the Moray titles. A charter of the Earldom of Moray was granted, 30 Jan. 1561/2, in favour of the future Regent and the heirs male of his body, but as Huntly, who was then in disgrace (tho' not yet attainted) had had a prior grant of the same subject, the writ was for a time kept *in retentis* and the 'belting' of Stewart, as Earl of Moray, only took place on 10 Feb. 1562/3. Then, lest exception should be taken to the date of the charter as being *before* Huntly's forfeiture, the Earl deemed it expedient to have a second and corroborative charter, with the same limitation, which bore date 22 Jan. 1563/4. A third charter was granted him on his resignation, 1 June 1566, bringing in heirs female. The Regent was assassinated, in 1569/70, leaving no male issue; his da., Countess Elizabeth, *d.* in 1591, and her husband met soon afterwards his well known

[S.],(a) with a clause that he and his heirs male should be called by that title. He however *resigned that Earldom* a few months later(b) for tho' he sat in Parl. [S.], on 10 Sep. 1562, as *Earl of Mar*, he sat there on 15 Oct. following as *Earl of Moray*. He opposed the Queen's marriage with Darnley and was outlawed in 1565, but pardoned in 1566. He became (till his death three years later) REGENT OF SCOTLAND, 22 Aug. 1567 (being known as "*the good Regent*") taking active measures against the Queen's party, by one of whom (Hamilton of Bothwellhaugh), he was assassinated at Linlithgow, 21 Jan. 1569/70, in his 37th year. He *d.* s.p.m., and was *bur.* at St. Giles,' Edinburgh. M.I. He *m.* 8 Feb. 1561, Anne, 1st da. of William (KEITH) 1st EARL MARISCHAL [S.], by Margaret, da. and coheir of Sir William KEITH His widow *m.* (as his second wife), Colin (CAMPBELL), 6th EARL OF ARGYLL [S.], who *d.* Oct. 1584. She *d.* July 1588; funeral entry at Lyon office.

XV. 1570. 2. ELIZABETH, *suo jure*, COUNTESS OF MORAY [S.], 1st da. and coheir, and heir of line. She *m.* in 1580, James STEWART who, at that time, was s. and h. ap. of James, 1st LORD DOUNE [S.], by Margaret, da. of Archibald (CAMPBELL), 4th EARL OF ARGYLL [S.], and he, on such marriage assumed *jure uxoris*, the title of EARL OF MORAY [S.], being so styled in the acts of Parl. 1581.(c) He is well known as "*the bonny Earl of Moray*," having been of great beauty and accomplishments and high in the favour of Anne, the Queen Consort [S.] He *suc.* his father as LORD DOUNE [S.], on 20 July 1590. His wife *d.* (three months before him,) 18 Nov. 1591, he being slain 7 Feb. 1591/2, by his hereditary enemy, the Earl [afterwards Marquess] of Huntly [S.], in a raid at Dunibirsil.

---

tragic fate. The 3d Earl (grandson of the Regent) had, in 1592, a Parliamentary ratification of the charter of 1 June 1566, and all other charters granted to the Regent, and, in 1611, a *new charter* of the Earldom of Moray, on his resignation, with an *altered limitation* to heirs male. The circumstances connected with this last named charter shew that it included dignity as well as lands, and it was so construed on Earl Alexander's death in 1700 when the Earl's second but eldest surv. son *suc.* in preference to the daughter of his eldest son. It seems, therefore, to follow that the Earl of Moray's creation must date either from 30 Jan. 1561/2, or (if the charter bearing that date be liable to exception) from 22 Jan. 1563/4, a date in exact correspondence with the place of Moray in the decreet of ranking [1606], namely, immediately before the Earl of Orkney (Stewart) who was certainly Earl on 28th Oct. 1581, and almost certainly so before 7 July 1576." See "*Earldom of Mar*" (doubtless) by G. Burnett, Lyon, in "Genealogist," vol. iii, N.S., pp. 1-24.

(a) His mother was da. of John (Erskine), Lord Erskine, the *de jure*, Earl of Mar [S.]

(b) The Earldom of Mar was in 1565 restored to its right heir, his cousin, John (Erskine), Lord Erskine [S.]

(c) From some MS. notes (to which Mr. Riddell had access) of a speech of Lord Loughborough, respecting the sustaining of the votes of the Earl of Moray on the election of Rep. Peers [S.], 6 June 1793, it may be gathered (1) that Lord L. "ignored the fact, vouched for by the clearest record evidence, that on her father's death, Elizabeth, da. of the Regent Moray, became Countess of Moray in her own right" and (2) that his opinion was that in 1584 [*rectius* 1581] the *Bonny Earl* had a new charter of the dignity. This has been sometimes construed as a *decision* of the Lords that the 1st creation and consequent precedence of the Earldom of Moray was in 1581, and the Lord Clerk Register (if truly reported) is said to have so stated it in an election on 10 Dec. 1884. But "during the whole discussion [in 1793] the bearing of the question on *precedency* seems never to have been thought of, and, if we suppose with Lord Loughborough, that the *Bonny Earl* had in 1584, or at any other date, a new charter with rem. to heirs male, we now known that that charter could only have proceeded on his wife's resignation and must therefore have *left untouched the original precedence*; for there is no more firmly established principle in Scottish peerage law than that a charter of resignation bringing in new heirs (nay even strangers in blood) did not derogate from the precedence of the resigner." See "*Earldom of Mar*" as alluded to on p. 361, note "e" next above, and see also said note "e" *circa finem*.

XVI. 1592. *3*. JAMES (STEWART), EARL OF MORAY, &c. [S.], s. and h., who by the King's special mediation was reconciled to his father's murderer, whose da. *viz.* Anne, 1st da. of George (GORDON), 1st MARQUESS OF HUNTLY [S.], by Henrietta, da. of Esme (STUART), 1st DUKE OF LENNOX [S.], he married in 1601. He had in 1592 a ratification in Parl. of the charter of 1 June 1566, and all other charters granted to the Regent Earl, and finally (after resignation) obtained, 17 April 1611, a new grant of the Earldom with rem. to heirs male of his body, whom failing, to his brother Francis in like manner.(a) He appears at some date between 27 Oct. 1612,(b) and 1620 to have *suc.* as LORD ST. COLME [S.], on the death s.p.m. of his cousin James (STEWART), 2d LORD ST. COLME [S.], having, at the latter date, charters of the Lordship of St. Colme.(c) He *d.* at Darnaway 6, and was *bur.* 7 Aug. 1638, at the church of Dyke, without any pomp.

XVII. 1638. *4*. JAMES (STEWART), EARL OF MORAY, &c. [S.], only s. and h.; *styled* LORD DOUNE till he *suc. to the peerage* [S.], 6 Aug. 1638; had a grant of the castle of Spynie, 12 Nov. 1641; was a royalist but took no active part in the civil war. He *m.* Margaret, 1st da. of Alexander (HOME), 1st EARL OF HOME, by his second wife, Mary, da. of Edward (SUTTON *alias* DUDLEY), LORD DUDLEY), she being eldest of the two sisters and coheirs of James, 2d EARL OF HOME [S.] He *d.* 4 March 1653.

[JAMES STEWART, *styled* LORD DOUNE, 1st s. and h. ap. He *d.* unm. and v.p.]

XVIII. 1653. *5*. ALEXANDER (STEWART, *or* STUART), EARL OF MORAY, &c. [S.], 2d but 1st surv. s. and h.; *styled* LORD DOUNE after the death of his elder br. till he *suc. to the peerage* [S.], on 4 March 1653; was fined £3,500 under Cromwell's act of Grace, 1654; Justice Gen. [S.], 1675; one of the Lords of the Treasury [S.], 1678; Sec. of State [S.], and an extra. Lord of Session, 1680; Commissioner to the Parl. [S.], 1686; K.T. (being one of the eight orig. knights at the revival of that order), 29 May 1687.(d) He was deprived of all his offices at the revolution in 1689.(e) He *m.* Emilia, da. of Sir William BALFOUR, of Pitcullo, Lieut. of the Tower of London. He *d.* at his residence, Dunibirsel, 1 Nov. 1701, and was carried to Darnaway and *bur.* in the church of Dyke, 24 Jan. 1701/2. Fun. entry at Lyon office.

[JAMES STUART, *styled* LORD DOUNE, 1st s. and h. ap. He *m.* Katharine (step da. of John, DUKE OF LAUDERDALE [S.]), da. of Elizabeth, *suo jure* COUNTESS OF DYSART [S.], by Sir Lionel TOLLEMACHE, 3d Bart. He *d.* v.p. and s.p.m.(f) 1685. His widow *m.* (as second of his three wives), John (GORDON), EARL OF SUTHERLAND [S.], who *d.* 27 June 1733. She *d.* before Feb. 1703.]

(a) See p. 361, note "e."

(b) The date in Wood's "*Douglas*" (vol. ii, p. 466), of "1642" is an *erratum* for "1612," as has been verified.

(c) Henry Stewart, yr. br. of his father, was *cr.* 7 March 1611, Lord St. Colme [S.], with rem to heirs male.

(d) See vol. i, p. 87, note "a," *sub* "Athole."

(e) Macky in his "characters," says of him, about 1700, that after having been made "Commissioner [S.] to take off the penal laws which his great ancestor [the Regent Moray] laid on" in which he did not succeed, "he turned Roman Catholick, and at the Revolution retired to his country seat. He is a very good natured man and was wrought upon by the court to do whatever they pleased; he is very fat and fair near 70 years old.

(f) Of his two daughters (1) Elizabeth, *m.* Alexander Grant and *d.* s.p. (2) Emilia, *m.* firstly Thomas Fraser, and secondly John (Lindsay), Earl of Crawford [S.], and had issue by both husbands, her descendant (by first marriage) being Lord Lovat [S.], who is heir of line to the 5th and preceding Earls of Moray.

XIX. 1701. 6. CHARLES (STUART), EARL OF MORAY, &c. [S.], 2d but 1st surv. s. and h. male. He was v.p. *cr.* a Baronet [S.], 23 Sep. 1681,(a) with rem. to heirs male of his body. He was *styled* LORD DOUNE after the death of his elder br. in 1685, till he *suc. to the peerage* [S.], 1 Nov. 1701. He *m.* his cousin, Anne, widow of Richard (MAITLAND), 4th EARL OF LAUDERDALE [S.] (who *d.* 1695), 2d da. of Archibald (CAMPBELL), 9th EARL OF ARGYLL [S.], by his first wife Mary, da. of James (STEWART), 4th EARL OF MORAY [S.] She *d.* at Dunibirsil, 18 Sep. or Dec. 1734, in her 76th year. Funeral entry at Lyon office. He *d.* there, s.p. 7 Oct. 1735, also in his 76th year, when the *Baronetcy* [S.], became *extinct*.

XX. 1735. 7. FRANCIS (STUART), EARL OF MORAY, &c., br. and h. male; *b.* about 1673; was sum. to surrender in 1715 on suspicion of being disaffected to the Government; *suc. to the peerage* [S.], 7 Oct. 1735. He *m.* firstly Elizabeth, only child of the Hon. Sir John MURRAY, of Drumcairn, a Lord of Session, 1681-89. She *d.* s.p.s. He *m.* secondly, about 1707, Jean, 2d da. of John (ELPHINSTONE), 4th LORD BALMERINOCH [S.], by Christian, da. of Hugh (MONTGOMERY), EARL OF EGLINTON [S.] She *d.* at Dunibirsel, 14 May 1739. Funeral entry in Lyon office. He *d.* there (a few months later), 11 Dec. 1739, in his 66th year.

XXI. 1739. 8. JAMES (STUART), EARL OF MORAY, &c. [S.], s. and h., by second wife; *b.* about 1708; *styled* LORD DOUNE from 1735 till he *suc. to the peerage* [S.], 11 Dec. 1739; K.T., 23 Feb. 1741; REP. PEER [S.], 1741-67.(b) He *m.* firstly, Dec. 1734, Grace, Dow. COUNTESS OF ABOYNE [S.], da. of George LOCKHART, of Carnwath, by Euphemia, da. of Alexander (MONTGOMERY), EARL OF EGLINTON [S.] She *d.* at Darnaway, 17 Nov. 1738. He *m.* secondly, 24 April 1740, Margaret, da. of David (WEMYSS), EARL OF WEMYSS [S.], by his second wife, Mary, da. and coheir of Sir John ROBINSON, Bart. He *d.* at Dunibirsel, 5 July 1767, in his 59th year.

XXII. 1767. 9. FRANCIS (STUART), EARL OF MORAY, &c. [S.], s. and h., by first wife; *b.* 11 Jan. 1737, N.S.; *styled* LORD DOUNE, 1739-67; completed his education abroad.(c) He *suc. to the peerage* [S.], 5 July 1767. He is said to have planted above thirteen million trees on his estates of Darnaway, Doune, and Dunibirsel. REP. PEER [S.], 1784-96,(d) being *cr.*, 4 June 1796, BARON STUART OF CASTLE STUART, co. Inverness [G.B.]; Lord Lieut. of the county of Moray or Elgin. He *m.*, 28 June 1763, at Gray, co. Forfar, Jean, 1st da. of John (GRAY), LORD GRAY [S.], by Margaret BLAIR, his wife, heiress of Kinfauns, co. Perth. She *d.* 19 Feb. 1786. He *d.* at Drumsheugh, 28 Aug. 1810, aged 73, and was *bur.* at Dunibirsel.

(a) "Mr. Charles Steuart, second son to the Earle of Murray."

(b) He obtained under the act (1747) for abolishing heritable jurisdiction £3,000 for the Sheriffship of Moray or Elgin, and £1,200 for the Stewartry of Menteith; in all £4,200 in full of his claim of £14,000.

(c) He was one of the few English at Turin in 1759 who "were remarkable for their diligent attention to their studies," having "masters for dancing, music, Italian, French, and for the Civil law." [Wood's "*Douglas.*"]

(d) His vote was objected to at the Gen. Election of Rep. Peers [S.] in 1790 on the ground that the dignity was one to the heir general and as such would be in the descendants of the da. of James Stuart, styled Lord Doune, eldest son of Alexander, 5th Earl of Moray. The House of Lords, however, on 6 June 1793, came to the resolution "that the votes given by the Earl of Moray at the said election were good." This, says the article in "the Genealogist," (vol. iii, N.S., pp. 1-24) above alluded to "is absolutely all we learn on the subject from the proper official source—the House of Lords journals." See, however, p. 362, note "c," as to how Lord Loughborough's notes thereon have been wrongfully construed to indicate the declaration of their Lordships of a *new* creation in 1581 or 1584, with, consequently, no earlier precedency than that date. In "Riddell" (p. 984) the finality of the resolution of 1793 is questioned as having been made in the absence of (the opposing party) the heir general.

[JAMES STUART, *styled* LORD DOUN, 1st s. and h. He *d.* v.p. at Bath, 11 July 1776, aged about 12.]

[JOHN STUART, *b.* at Edinburgh, 11 Feb. 1768; *styled* LORD DOUN after the death, 1776, of his elder br. abovenamed; was M.P. for Great Bedwyn, 1790-91. He *d.* unm. and v.p., 6 July 1791, aged 23, and was *bur.* at Dunibirsel.]

XXIII. 1810. *10.* FRANCIS (STUART), EARL OF MORAY, &c. [S.], also BARON STUART OF CASTLE STUART [G.B.], 3d but 1st surv. s. and h., *b.* at Edinburgh, 2 Feb. 1771; *styled* LORD DOUNE, after the death (1791) of his elder br. till he *suc. to the peerage* [S. and G. B.], 28 Aug. 1810. He, who had raised (v.p.), a company of foot, (disbanded in 1791), was K.T., 3 Sep. 1827; Lord Lieut. of Elginshire. He *m.* firstly at Bellevue, 26 Jan. 1795, Lucy, 2d da. and coheir(a) of John SCOTT, of Balcomie, co. Fife (Major Gen. in the army), by Margaret, yst da. of Robert DUNDAS, Lord President of the Court of Session [S.] She *d.* at Tidwell House, Devon, 3 Aug. 1798. He *m.* secondly, at Edinburgh, 7 Jan. 1801, his cousin, Margaret Jane, 1st da. of Sir Philip AINSLIE, of Pilton, co. Edinburgh, by Elizabeth, 5th da. of John (Gray), LORD GRAY [S.], abovementioned. She *d.* 3 April 1837. He *d.* 12 Jan. 1848, at Darnaway Castle, in his 77th year. Will pr. March 1848.

XXIV. 1848. *11.* FRANCIS (STUART), EARL OF MORAY, &c. [S.], also BARON STUART OF CASTLE STUART [G.B.], 1st s. and h. by first wife; *b.* 7 Nov. 1795, at Valleyfield, co. Perth, *styled* LORD DOUNE from 1810 till he *suc. to the peerage* [S. and G.B.], 12 Jan. 1848. He *d.* unm. 6 May 1859, aged 63, at Hayes Park, Midx.

XXV. 1859. *12.* JOHN (STUART), EARL OF MORAY, &c. [S.], also BARON STUART OF CASTLE STUART [G.B.], br. of the whole blood and h.; *b.* 25 Jan. 1797, at Bruntsfield House, Edinburgh; entered the army, 1815, becoming a Captain in 1825; *suc. to the peerage* [S. and G.B.], 6 May 1859. He *d.* unm., 8 Nov. 1867, aged 70, at Doune Lodge, Perthshire.

XXVI. 1867. *13.* ARCHIBALD GEORGE (STUART), EARL OF MORAY, &c. [S.], also BARON STUART OF CASTLE STUART [G.B.], br. of the half blood and h., being s. of the 10th Earl by his second wife; *b.* 3 March 1810; entered the army 1829; Capt. 6th West India Reg., 1839; retired as Lieut. Col. in 1861; *suc. to the peerage* [S. and G.B.], 8 Nov. 1867. He *d.* unm., 12 Feb. 1872, aged 61, at Darnaway Castle, co. Elgin.

XXVII. 1872. *14.* GEORGE (STUART), EARL OF MORAY, LORD ABERNETHY AND STRATHEARN [1562], LORD DOUNE [1581], and LORD ST. COLME [1611], in the peerage of Scotland, also BARON STUART OF CASTLE STUART [1796], in the peerage of Great Britain, only surv. br. and h.; *b.* 14 Aug. 1816; *suc. to the peerage* [S. and G.B.], 12 Feb. 1872. By the death, 27 May 1878 of his kinswoman, Margaret, *suo jure* Baroness Gray [S.], he became LORD GRAY [S.], a dignity *cr.* about 1445.

Family Estates.—These, in 1883, consisted of 40,553 acres in Perthshire; 21,669 in Elginshire; 7,463 in Fifeshire; 7,035 in Inverness-shire; 339 in Kirkcudbrightshire; 238 in Midlothian; 315 in Nairnshire, besides, in Lady Gray's name, 2,478 acres in Perthshire (worth £7,873 a year), and 1,539 in Forfarshire. *Total* 81,629 acres, worth £46,863 a year), "inc. of £3,000 for salmon fisheries but exc. of £2,350 for mines." *Principal Residences.* Doune Lodge, Perthshire; Darnaway Castle, Elginshire; Dombristle, Fifeshire, and Castle Stuart, Inverness-shire.

(a) See vol. ii, p. 134, note "a," *sub* "Canning."

MORDAUNT.

Barony by Writ.

I. 1529.

1. Sir John Mordaunt, of Turvey, Beds, 2d s. of Sir John Mordaunt, of the same, sometime Chancellor of the Duchy of Lancaster, by Edith, da. and coheir of Sir Nicholas Latimer, of Dantish, co. Dorset, *suc.* his elder br. William M., in the family estate about 1505; was Sheriff for Beds and Bucks (1509-10), 1 Hen. VIII., was *knighted* before 4 June 1520, and was sum. to Parl as a Baron (LORD MORDAUNT), from 4 May (1529), 21 Hen. VIII. to 5 Nov. (1558), 5 and 6 Ph. and Mary. He accompanied the King to France, at his interview with the King thereof, in 1532. He *m.* about 1507, Elizabeth, da. and coheir of Sir Henry Vere, of Drayton, co. Northampton, by Isabella, da. of Thomas Tresham, of Sywell, co. Northampton. She *d.* before him and was *bur.* at Turvey. His will dat. 1 Aug. 1560, pr. 1 Sep. 1561, directs his burial to be there.

II. 1561. *2.* John (Mordaunt), Lord Mordaunt, s. and h., *b.* 1508; K.B. at the Coronation of Queen Anne Boleyn, 1 June 1533; Sheriff of Essex and Herts, 1540; M.P. for Beds, 1553-55; was one of the first who were in arms for the succession of Queen Mary, to whom he was P.C. He was sum. to Parl. from 11 Jan. (1562/3), 5 Eliz. to 8 May (1572), 14 Eliz. He *m.* firstly, Elizabeth, sister and heir of John, being only da. of Sir Richard Fitz Lewis, of West Thorndon, Essex, by Mary, or Alice, da. and coheir of John Harleston. She, who was a great heiress, *d.* 2 June 1543. *Inq. post mortem* 8 Nov., 35 Hen. VIII. He *m.* secondly (Lic. Fac. 3 Dec. 1545), Joanna Wilford, widow of St. Martin's Bishopsgate. His will, directing his burial to be at Turvey, dat. 16 April, and pr. 19 Oct. 1571. The will of his widow, by whom he had no issue was pr. 1592.

III. 1571. *3.* Lewis (Mordaunt), Lord Mordaunt, only s. and h. by first wife, at whose death, June 1543, he was aged five years. He was M.P. for Beds, 1563-67; was *knighted*, 1568; was sum. to Parl. from 8 Feb. (1575/6), 18 Eliz., to 24 Oct. (1597), 39 Eliz. He was one of the 24 noblemen[a] who were in Oct. 1586 the triers of the Queen of Scots at Fotheringay. He *m.* Elizabeth, da. of the Hon. Sir Arthur Darcy, by Mary, da. and coheir of Sir Nicholas Carew, K.G. He *d.* 16 June 1601, at Drayton Manor house, co. Northampton, and was *bur.* 29 July at Turvey.

IV. 1601. *4.* Henry (Mordaunt), Lord Mordaunt, only s. and h. He was sum. to Parl. from 27 Oct. (1601), 43 Eliz., to 5 Nov. (1605), 3 Jac. He was suspected of complicity in the gunpowder plot and was fined and imprisoned in 1605 but released, 3 June 1606. He *m.* Margaret, sister of William, 1st Earl of Northampton, da. of Henry (Compton), 1st Lord Compton, by his first wife, Frances, da. of Francis (Hastings), 2d Earl of Huntingdon. He *d.* about 1608. Admon. of "Lady Margaret Mordaunt, of Turvey, Beds," 18 Feb. 1644/5, granted to a creditor.

V. 1608. *5.* John (Mordaunt), Lord Mordaunt, s. and h., *b.* before 1600; *suc. to the peerage* about 1608; K.B., 3 Nov. 1616; sum. to Parl. from 30 Jan. (1619/20), 18 Jac. I., to 17 May (1625), 23 Jac. I. He was *cr.*, 9 March 1627/8, EARL OF PETERBOROUGH, co. Northampton. He *d.* 18 June 1644.

VI. 1644. *6.* Henry (Mordaunt), 2d Earl of Peterborough, and Lord Mordaunt, *b.* 16 Nov. 1621; styled Lord Mordaunt from 1628 till he *suc. to the peerage* in 1644. He *d.* s.p.m., 19 June 1697.

See fuller account under "Peterborough" Earldom, *cr.* 1628, *sub* the 1st and 2d Earls.

(a) See a list of these in vol. iii, p. 72, note "a," *sub* "Derby."

VII. 1697. 7. MARY, DUCHESS OF NORFOLK, and *suo jure* BARONESS MORDAUNT, only surv. da. and heir([a]) of the abovenamed Earl Henry, by Penelope, da. of Barnabas (O'BRIEN), 6th EARL OF THOMOND [I.] She m. firstly, 8 Aug. 1677, Henry (HOWARD), 7th DUKE OF NORFOLK (who d. 2 April 1701, in his 47th year), but was separated([b]) from him in Michaelmas 1685 and *divorced* by act of Parl., 11 April 1700. She m. secondly (lic. fac.,([c]) 15 Sep. 1701) as his first wife, Sir John GERMAINE, Bart. (so cr. 25 March 1698), who d. s.p., 11 Dec. 1718. She d. s.p., 16 Nov. 1705, and was *bur.* at Lufwick, St. Peter's, co. Northampton, having settled Drayton Manor, and other the family estates on her said second husband.([d]) To him was granted admon. of her goods, 14 March 1705/6, she being therein styled *Duchess "Dowager of Norfolk."*([e])

VIII. 1705. 8. CHARLES (MORDAUNT), 3d EARL OF PETERBOROUGH [1628], EARL OF MONMOUTH [1689], VISCOUNT MORDAUNT OF AVALON, &c. [1659], and LORD MORDAUNT [1529], cousin and heir, being s. and h. of John, 1st VISCOUNT MORDAUNT OF AVALON, &c., next br. to Henry, 2d EARL OF PETERBOROUGH abovenamed; was *b.* about 1658; *suc.* his father in the peerage, 5 June 1675 as VISCOUNT MORDAUNT OF AVALON, &c.; was *cr.* 9 April 1689, EARL OF MONMOUTH; *suc.* his uncle, 19 June 1697, as EARL OF PETERBOROUGH, and suc. his cousin (the Duchess Mary) abovenamed, 16 Nov. 1705, as LORD MORDAUNT. He *d.* 25 Oct. 1735.

[JOHN MORDAUNT, *styled* VISCOUNT MORDAUNT, 1st s. and h. ap. who *d.* v.p. 6 April 1710.]

IX. 1735. 9. CHARLES (MORDAUNT), 4th EARL OF PETERBOROUGH, &c., and LORD MORDAUNT, grandson and h., being s. and h. of Charles MORDAUNT, *styled* VISCOUNT MORDAUNT abovenamed; *b.* 1706; was *styled* VISCOUNT MORDAUNT till he *suc. to the peerage*, 25 Oct. 1735. He *d.* 1 Aug. 1779.

X. 1779. 10. CHARLES HENRY (MORDAUNT), 5th EARL OF PETERBOROUGH, &c., and LORD MORDAUNT, 1st and only surv. s. and h. by second wife; *b.* 10 May 1758; *styled* VISCOUNT MORDAUNT till he *suc. to the peerage*, 1 Aug. 1779. He *d.* unm., 16 June 1814, in his 57th year, when *all his honours* became *extinct*, save the *Barony of Mordaunt* which devolved as under.

For fuller particulars see "Peterborough" Earldom, cr. 1628; *sub* the 3d, 4th and 5th Earls.

XI. 1814. 11. MARY ANASTASIA GRACE, *suo jure* BARONESS MORDAUNT, sister (of the half blood) and heir, being only surv. da. of Charles, 4th EARL OF PETERBOROUGH, by his first wife, Mary, da. of John Cox. She was *b.* 5 June 1738, and *d.* unm., June 1819. Will pr. 1819.

([a]) Elizabeth, her elder and only sister, *d.* unm., and was *bur.* 18 June 1676, at Turvey.

([b]) The Duke on 24 Nov. 1698, "recovered 100 marks damages in the King's Bench against Mr. Jermain [Germain] for lying with the Dutchess." [Salmon's "*Chronol. Historian.*"]

([c]) He of St. James, Westm., about 47, Bach., she as "the *Lady Mary Mordaunt*" about 40, "spinster."

([d]) He left them to his second wife by whom they were devised to Lord George Sackville, afterwards *Sackville-Germaine*, who was *cr.*, in 1782, Viscount Sackville of Drayton, co. Northampton.

([e]) Notwithstanding her legal divorce and re-marriage in her first husband's lifetime. See also note "c" next above, where her description is different, and more correct.

XII. 1819. *12.* Alexander (Gordon), Duke of Gordon, Marquess of Huntly, &c. [S.], also Earl of Norwich, &c. [G.B.], and Lord Mordaunt, cousin and h., being s. and h. of Cosmo George, 3d Duke of Gordon [S.], who was s. and h. of Alexander, 2d Duke of Gordon [S.], by Henrietta, da. of Charles (Mordaunt), 3d Earl of Peterborough, and Lord Mordaunt abovenamed. He *suc. to the peerage* [S.], 5 Aug. 1752; was *cr.* Earl of Norwich, &c., 2 July 1784, and *suc.* his cousin abovenamed as Lord Mordaunt in June 1819. He *d.* 17 June 1827, in his 84th year.

XIII. 1827, to 1836. *13.* George (Gordon), Duke of Gordon, Marquess of Huntly, &c. [S.], also Earl of Norwich, Lord Mordaunt, &c., s. and h., *b.* 2 Feb. 1770; *suc. to the peerage* [S., E., and G.B.], 17 June 1827. He *d.* s.p., 28 May 1836, when the *Dukedom of Gordon* and certain other of his Scotch titles as also the *Earldom of Norwich*, &c. [G.B.] became *extinct* but the *Barony of Mordaunt*, as, possibly, the *Barony of Beauchamp*,(a) fell into *abeyance* between his sisters and coheirs or their descendants.(b)

For fuller particulars see "Gordon" Dukedom [S.], cr. 1684; *sub* the 4th and 5th Dukes.

MORDAUNT OF AVALON, and MORDAUNT OF RYEGATE.

Viscountcy and Barony. I. 1659. *1.* The Hon. John Mordaunt, 2d s. of John, 1st Earl of Peterborough, by Elizabeth, da. and h. of William (Howard,) Lord Howard of Effingham, s. and h. ap. of Charles, 1st Earl of Nottingham, was *b.* 18 June 1626; is said(c) to have been ed. at Brasenose College, Oxford; joined in the attempt of the Earl of Holland for the rescue of King Charles I., and, subsequently, in several abortive schemes for the restoration of Charles II., being tried for his life in 1658, by the High Court of Justice, and escaping only thro' the casting vote of (John Lisle) its President.(d) He joined the young King at Brussels, whence he was, 11 March 1659 sent to England to effect a rising in his favour, and by whom he was *cr.* 10 July 1659,(e) BARON MORDAUNT OF RYEGATE co. Surrey and VISCOUNT MORDAUNT OF AVALON, co. Somerset. He took a principal part in effecting the Restoration in 1660, in which year (26 May) he was *knighted* by the King; was Capt. of a troop of horse; Col. of a Reg. of Foot; High Steward of Windsor; Constable of Windsor Castle, Warden of Windsor forest and Keeper of the Great Park. He was Lord Lieut. of Surrey, 1660 and 1662. He *m.* probably about 1650, Elizabeth, da. and eventually sole h. of the Hon. Thomas Carey, Groom of the Bedchamber (2d s. of Robert, 1st Earl of Monmouth), by Margaret, da. and h. of Sir Thomas Smith, of Parsons green, co. Midx., Master of the Requests. He *d.* 5 June 1675, in his 48th year, and was *bur.* the 14th at Fulham, Midx. M.I. Will pr. 11 June 1675. His widow, who was aged 1½ years in 1634 was *bur.* there 1 May 1679. Her will dat. 1 Nov. 1677 to 22 Jan. 1677/8, pr. 20 May 1679.

(a) See vol. iv. p. 52, note "d," *sub* "Gordon."

(b) These were (1) Charlotte, Duchess of Richmond, who *d.* 5 May 1842, and whose descendant and heir the present Duke is the senior coheir (2) Lady Madelina Palmer, who *d.* in June 1847, leaving issue male by her first husband, Sir Robert Sinclair, 7th Bart. [S.], of Stevenson; (3) William (Montagu), Duke of Manchester, s. and h. of Susan, Duchess of Manchester, who *d.* 20 Aug. 1828. He is represented by his descendant, the present Duke; (4) Louisa, Marchioness Cornwallis, who *d.* s.p.m., 5 Dec. 1850; (5) Georgiana, Duchess of Bedford (2d wife of the 6th Duke), who *d.* 28 Feb. 1853, leaving numerous issue.

(c) Doyle's "*Official Baronage*."

(d) A full account of this proceeding is given in Clarendon's "*Rebellion*."

(e) See p. 14, note "b," *sub* "Langdale of Holme" for a list of Peerages, *cr.* by Charles II., during his exile.

II. 1675. 2. CHARLES (MORDAUNT), VISCOUNT MORDAUNT OF AVALON, AND BARON MORDAUNT OF RYEGATE, s. and h., b. about 1658; *suc. to the peerage*, 5 June 1675. He was *cr.* 9 April 1689, EARL OF MONMOUTH; *suc.* 19 June 1697, as 3d EARL OF PETERBOROUGH, on the death of his cousin the 2d Earl, and *suc.* 16 Nov. 1705 as LORD MORDAUNT (a Barony *cr.* 1529), on the death of his cousin, the Duchess of Norfolk. See "PETERBOROUGH" Earldom, *cr.* 1628 (*sub* the 3d Earl), with which Earldom *all his dignities* (save the Barony of Mordaunt of 1529) became *extinct* in 1814.

MORDEN.

The patent for the creation of the HON. CHARLES YORKE, Lord Chancellor (for three days) as BARON MORDEN (Royal warrant, 18 Jan. 1770), was awaiting his signature on the table before which he was found dead.[a]

MORDINGTON.

Barony [S.] I. 1641, with the precedency of 1456? 1. SIR WILLIAM DOUGLAS, of Mordington, co. Berwick, 2d s. of William, EARL OF ANGUS [S.], by Elizabeth, 1st da. of Laurence (OLIPHANT), LORD OLIPHANT [S.], having *m.* his cousin, Anne, only da. and h. of Laurence (OLIPHANT), LORD OLIPHANT [S.] (grandson and h. of the abovenamed Laurence), by Lilias, da. of James (DRUMMOND), 1st LORD MADERTY [S.], claimed in right of his said wife (as heir *general* of her father who had *d.* in or before 1631) the *Barony of Oliphant* [S.] as against the heir *male*. It was, however, found by the Court of Session, 11 July 1633, that the late Lord having resigned his peerage (so as to favour the collateral heir male) and no regrant thereof having been made "had denuded himself and his descendants of the dignities" till the King should declare his pleasure therein.[b] The King accordingly *cr.* the heir male a Baron, by the title of Lord Oliphant, and by Royal letters, 10 March 1640 (which appear to have been acted upon, 14 Nov. 1641), in which he recited the lady's "rycht of blood flowing from the first Lord Oliphant" decreed that "the said stile and title of Lord Oliphant[c] shall be established" in her person and in that of her spouse and the

---

(a) See vol. iv, p. 165, note "c," *sub* "Hardwicke."

(b) See the matter fully set out in "*Riddell*," pp. 17-20, where it is pointed out that the King himself being present as a spectator the decision hence obtains the utmost force and effect. The "*material points regarding dignities*" which were so decided were [1] "that *use* and *solemn recognitions* were enough by the law of the Realm to constitute and transmit them when the patent did not exist;" [2] "that they were descendible to *heirs female* if not specially barred;" [3] "that they were not *in commercio* or required infeftment," and [4] "that the late Lord Oliphant, by his procuratory of resignation, had denuded himself of the dignities ay and while [*i.e.*, always and until] the Prince should declare his pleasure and either confer the honour on the pursuer or defender."

It is to be observed that clause No. 2, of the above, gives the judgment of the highest court of Scotland (in 1633) that *the descent of the early Scotch dignities* is to be presumed as being to *heirs general*, such judgment being in flat opposition to Lord Mansfield's theory (some 150 years later) as to the presumption being in favour of *heirs male*. The words of the King [" *Riddell*," p. 180], are "*Yat ye title and honour*, quich he [the late Lord] could not dispone and transmitt to any other *not* being ye true and lineal heir of blood without his Majesties consent, *is due and proper to ye said Dame Anna* as lineally descended of umquhile Laurence, Lord Oliphant, her grandchir, who was immediately last Lord before her said umquhile father." See also p. 162, note "b," *sub* "Lovat," as to the preferable title of the heir *general* to that of the heir *male*.

(c) It is there called the "Lordschip of Oliphant, Aberdalgy, and Duplin," which says Riddell (p. 180, note 1), "were the old titles of the Lords Oliphant. Aberdalgy, and Duplin, were noted designations."

heirs "procreate betwixt yame," which failing, to the heirs of her body, but that the designation thereof be changed to Mordington. They were thus *created* LORD AND LADY MORDINGTON [S.] (tho' with the precedency of the Barony of Oliphant) and he is alluded to as Lord Mordington in Parl., 30 May 1651. He *d.* 11 Feb. 1656.

II. 1656. *2.* WILLIAM (DOUGLAS), LORD MORDINGTON [S.], s. and h. He sat in Parl., 1 Feb. 1661 and subsequently, in the precedency of the ancient Lords Oliphant [S.] He *m.* Elizabeth, da. of Hugh (SEMPILL), LORD SEMPILL [S.], by his second wife, Elizabeth, da. of Francis (HAY), EARL OF ERROLL [S.] He was living, 2 Aug. 1662.

III. 1700? *3.* JAMES (DOUGLAS), LORD MORDINGTON [S.], 1st s. and h.(a) He voted at the election of Rep. Peers [S.], 10 Nov. 1710. He *m.* Jean, 1st da. of Alexander (SETON), 1st VISCOUNT OF KINGSTON [S.], by his first wife, Jean, da. of Sir George FLETCHER.

IV. 1720? *4.* GEORGE (DOUGLAS), LORD MORDINGTON [S.], only s. and h. He voted at several elections of Rep. Peers [S.] He *m.* Catharine, da. of the Rev. Robert LAUNDER, M.A., Rector of Shenley, Herts. He *d.* in Covent Garden, Midx., 10 June 1741.(b) His wife survived him but *d.* before 18 Dec. 1741, when admon. of his goods was granted.(c)

V. 1741? to 1791. *5.* MARY, *suo jure* BARONESS MORDINGTON [S.], da. and heir of line. She, who was unm. in Dec. 1741, *m.* William WEAVER, an officer in the Horse Guards who fought at Dettingen and Fontenoy, and who *d.* 28 April 1796, aged above 80, at Hallow park, co. Worcester. The Baroness *d.* s.p., 22 July 1791.

[Since 1791 the title has never been assumed or claimed, but, if, as seems to be the case, the issue of the second Lord became at that date extinct, the heir of line of the Barony is the descendant and heir of line of the only da. of the first Lord, *viz.* Anne, who *m.* Robert, Lord Sempill [S.], and who is ancestress of the succeeding Lords of that name with which Barony that of Mordington is presumed, since 1791, to have become united.]

MORETON.

See "DUCIE OF MORETON, co. Stafford," Barony (*Moreton*), *cr.* 1720; *ex.* 1770.

---

i.e., "MORETON OF TORTWORTH, co. Gloucester," Barony. *Reynolds-Moreton*), *cr.* 1837, with the EARLDOM OF DUCIE, which see.

MORLEY.

Barony by Writ.

I. 1299. *1.* WILLIAM DE MORLEY, of Morley, co. Norfolk, having served in the Scotch wars, was sum. to Parl. as a Baron (LORD MORLEY), by writs from 29 Dec. (1299), 28 Ed. I. to 3 Nov. (1306), 34 Ed .I.

(a) The second son, the Hon. Lewis Douglas, was *bur.* at Kensington, 7 July 1682.

(b) He was author of some pamphlets against Popery, &c. In a copy of the "*Scotch Compendium*" of 1725 (belonging to the writer) is written, in old hand-writing, "The present Ld. Mordington keeps a gaming table in London, 1738." See vol. ii, p. 175, note "d," *sub* "Cassillis," where however the remark would seem to refer to 1745, *i.e.*, to the *suo jure* Baroness.

(c) Charles Douglas, having joined in the rising of 1745, was taken prisoner and arraigned at Carlisle, as a Commoner, 11 Sep. 1746. He pleaded his peerage as heir *male* of the body of the 2d Lord Mordington, and, having proved his descent accordingly, the plea appears to have been allowed, without any proof having been required as to the limitation of the dignity being, as he alleged, to the *male* heir. See "*Riddell.*" He appears to have *d.* s.p. before 1791.

II. 1310? 2. ROBERT (DE MORLEY), LORD MORLEY, s. and h. was sum. to Parl.(a) from 20 Nov. (1317), 11 Ed. II. to 15 Feb. (1356/7), 31 Ed. III. He was one of the most famous warriors of the period both in the Scotch and French wars; was Admiral of the Northern Fleet, and, as such, achieved (at Sluys in Flanders) the greatest naval victory hitherto obtained over the French; was present at Cressy, and was Constable of the tower of London. He m. Hawyse, who apparently was *suo jure* BARONESS MARSHAL, being sister and heir of John, LORD MARSHAL, at whose death in 1316-17, she was aged 15, and being da. of William (MARSHAL), LORD MARSHAL so cr. 1309. With her he acquired Hingham, co. Norfolk, Hallingbury, co. Essex, and other considerable estates elsewhere, beside a claim to the hereditary Marshalship of Ireland.(b) He m. secondly, Joane, da. of Sir Peter DE TYES, which Joan died the same year that he did.(c) He d. in France, about Mid Lent (1359/60), 34 Ed. III.

III. 1360. 3. WILLIAM (DE MORLEY), LORD MORLEY, s. and h. by first wife; was in the French wars and was *knighted* v.p. in 1356; was 30 (or, according to another inquisition, 40) years old at his father's death. He was sum. to Parl. from 4 Dec. (1364), 38 Ed. III., to 3 Dec. (1378), 2 Ric. II. In 1364 his tenure of the office of Marshal of Ireland (b) was recognised. He m. Cecily, da. of Thomas (BARDOLPH), LORD BARDOLPH. He d. 30 April 1379. Will dat. 15th, at Halingbury, directing his burial to be at the Austin Friars, Norwich. His widow d. Dec. (1386), 10 Ric. II. Will directing her burial to be with her husband.

IV. 1379. 4. THOMAS (DE MORLEY), LORD MORLEY, s. and h.; aged 25 at the death of his father in 1379. He was sum. to Parl.(e) from 16 July (1381), 5 Ric. II., to 3 Sep. (1417), 4 Hen. V.; was Marshal of Ireland, petitioning(d) to execute that office by deputy. He was K.G. about 1411. He distinguished himself in the wars with France, being in (1416), 4 Hen. V., Capt. Gen. of all the Forces there. He m. firstly Joan. He m. secondly Anne, (sometimes called Joan) widow of Sir Hugh HASTINGS, of Elsing, da. of Edward (DESPENCER), LORD LE DESPENCER, by Elizabeth, *suo jure* BARONESS BURGHERSH. He d. at Calais, 24 Sep. (1416), 4 Hen. V. Admon. at Lambeth, 3 March 1416/7.

V. 1416. 5. THOMAS (DE MORLEY), LORD MORLEY, grandson and h., being s. and h. of Sir Robert (or Thomas) MORLEY, by Isabel, da. of John (DE MOLINES), LORD MOLINES, which Robert (or Thomas) was s. and h. ap. of the late Lord but d. v.p. He was aged 23 at the death of his grandfather in 1417. He (who was Marshal of Ireland) was sum. to Parl.(a) from 15 July (1427), 5 Hen. VI., to 5 July (1435), 13 Hen. VI.(e) He m. Isabel, da. of Michael (DE LA POLE), 2d EARL OF SUFFOLK, by Catharine, da. of Hugh (STAFFORD), 2d EARL OF STAFFORD. He d. Dec. 1435 and was *bur.* at Hingham afsd. His widow, whose will dat. 1464 was pr. 1466, is also *bur.* there.

VI. 1435. 6. ROBERT (DE MORLEY), LORD MORLEY, only s. and h., aged 17 at the death of his father in 1435. He was sum. to Parl.,(a) 3 Dec. (1441), 20 Hen. VI. He m. Elizabeth, da. of William (DE ROOS), LORD ROOS. He d. s.p.m. (1442-43), 21 Hen. VI.

(a) There is proof in the rolls of Parl. of his sitting.

(b) As to this office see p. 266, note "b," *sub* "Marshal."

(c) Her son, Sir Robert Morley, attended the Black Prince into Aquitaine and distinguished himself in the French wars. His male issue appears to have become extinct with his grandson, Sir Thomas Morley, whose da. and h. m. Sir Geoffrey Ratcliffe.

(d) *Rot. Parl.*, vol. iii, p. 130, no. 16; as quoted in Banks's "*Bar. Angl.*"

(e) In Dugdale's list of summons a "*John* de Morley" is said to have been sum. to Parl. 24 May (1433), 11 Hen. VI. This is unquestionably a mistake for "*Thomas*" whose name appears in the summons of 5, 6, and 13 Hen. VI. Moreover "*Thomas* de Morley, Chivaler," was present in the Parl. 11 Hen. VI. (Rot. Parl., vol. iv, p. 422), the very year in which the writ (as afsd.) summons "*John*." [See "*Nicolas*."]

VII. 1443. 7. ALIANORE, *suo jure*, BARONESS MORLEY, da. and h., aged six months at her father's death in 1443. She was aged 23 in 1466, and then the wife of WILLIAM LOVEL, a yr. s. of William, 7th LORD LOVEL DE TICHMERSH, by Alice, *de jure, suo jure* BARONESS DEINCOURT. He was sum. to Parl. in her right (as LORD MORLEY) by writs from 10 Aug (1469), 9 Ed. IV. to 15 Oct. (1471), 10 Ed. IV. directed "*Willielmo Lovel de Morley, Chl'r.*" He *d.* July 1476. His wife survived him.

VIII. 1480? 8. HENRY (LOVEL), LORD MORLEY, only s. and h., a minor at his father's death in 1476. He was one of the 45 nobles present, 6 July 1483, at the Coronation of Richard III.(a) He had livery of all his lands in 1489, being then of full age. He *m.* Elizabeth, da. of John (DE LA POLE), DUKE OF SUFFOLK, by Elizabeth, sister of the **Kings Edward IV. and Richard III.**, da. of Richard (PLANTAGENET), DUKE OF YORK. He *d.* s.p. being slain at Dixmude in Flanders (1488-89), 4 Hen. VII.

IX. 1489. 9. ALICE, *suo jure* BARONESS MORLEY, sister and heir, then (1489), wife of SIR WILLIAM PARKER, who had been Standard Bearer and Privy Councillor to King Richard III. He *d.* 1510, not having been sum. to Parl. in her right. She *m.* secondly, Sir Edward HOWARD, K.G., Admiral of the Fleet, 2d s. of Thomas, 2d DUKE OF NORFOLK. He, who, likewise, was not so sum. to Parl., *d.* s.p. legit. His will dat. 1512, pr. 18 July 1513.(b) Her will directing her burial to be at Hingham afsd., dat. 9 April 1518, pr. 22 Feb. 1518/9.

X. 1519. 10. HENRY (PARKER), LORD MORLEY, s. and h. He was sum. to Parl. (as LORD MORLEY), from 15 April (1523), 14 Hen. VIII. to 28 Oct. (1555), 2 and 3 Ph. and Mary, by writs directed "*Henrico Parker de Morley, Chl'r.*" He was one of the peers who signed the letter to the Pope, urging his consent to a divorce of King Henry VIII. from his first Queen. He obtained judgment by Parl. (1533-34). 25 Hen. VIII., in favour of his precedence over the Lord Dacre of Gillesland.(c) He *m.* Alice, da. of Sir John ST. JOHN, of Bletso, Beds. He *d.* at Hallingbury 1555.(d) Admon., 24 Jan. 1561/2.

XI. 1555. 11. HENRY (PARKER), LORD MORLEY, grandson and h., being 1st s. and h.(e) of Sir Henry PARKER, K.B., by his first wife, Grace, da. of John NEWPORT, of Brent Pelham, Herts, which Henry was only s. and h. ap. of the late Lord, but *d.* v.p. (1551), 5 Ed. VI. He was sum. to Parl. from 20 Jan. (1557/8), 4 and 5 Ph. and Mary, to 8 May (1572), 14 Eliz. He *m.* about 1550 Elizabeth, da. of Edward (STANLEY), 3d EARL OF DERBY, by his first wife, Dorothy, da. of Thomas (HOWARD), DUKE OF NORFOLK. He *d.* 22 Oct. 1577. The admon. of Elizabeth, Lady Morley, (probably) his widow was granted, 5 Feb. 1590/1.(f)

XII. 1577. 12. EDWARD (PARKER), LORD MORLEY, s. and h., *b.* about 1551, being admitted to Gonville and Caius Coll., Cambridge, 10 Feb. 1561/2, and then aged 11. He was sum. to Parl. from 26 Jan. (1580/1), 23 Eliz., to 5 April (1614), 12 Jac. I. He was one of the triers of Mary, Queen of Scots,

---

(a) See vol. iii, p. 8, note "c," *sub* "Dacre," for a list of these.

(b) In it he mentions his wife as "Alice, Lady Morley," thus showing that the Barony was recognised as existing in her, tho' neither he nor her former husband were sum. therein. He was nominated K.G., 23 April 1513, but is said to have died before he received notification thereof. [*Test. Vet.*]

(c) See vol. iii, p. 9, note "a," *sub* "Dacre."

(d) He is said to have been a voluminous writer in Walpole's "Noble Authors."

(e) The second son of this Sir Henry Parker, being the 1st. s. by his *second* wife, Elizabeth, da. and h. of Sir Philip Calthorpe, of Erwarton, co. Suffolk, was Sir Philip Parker, of Erwarton, ancestor of the Parker, Baronets, of that place, *cr.* 1661; *extinct* 1740/1.

(f) The admon. of "Domina Elizabetha Morley" (who *d.* abroad), was granted to Anne Bruncker, the da. of the decd.

in 1586,(a) and subsequently (1509) of Philip, Earl of Arundel, and (1601) of Robert, Earl of Essex. He m. Elizabeth, *de jure, suo jure* BARONESS MONTEAGLE; see that Barony cr. 1514. She appears to have d. in or before 1603. He d. 1 April 1618, at Mile End, in Stepney, Midx., and was *bur.* in Stepney church. Admon.(b) 20 June 1618, to a creditor.

XIII. 1618. *13.* WILLIAM (PARKER), LORD MORLEY AND MONTEAGLE, s. and h. He, in right of his mother, was sum. to Parl. v.p. as LORD MONTEAGLE from 19 March 1603/4, to 5 April 1614, by writs directed "*Willielmo Parker de Monteagle, Chl'r.*" He was the person to whom as "Lord Monteagle" the letter was written by which the Gunpowder Plot of 1605 was discovered. After, however, his father's death, in 1618, when he had *suc.* to the *Barony of Morley*, he was sum. to Parl. by writs, 30 Jan. 1620/1, to 4 Nov. 1621, directed "*Willielmo Parker de Morley et Monteagle.*" He m. Elizabeth, sister of Sir Lewis TRESHAM, 1st Bart., da. of Sir Thomas TRESHAM, of Rushton, co. Northampton, by Muriel, da. of Sir Robert THROKMORTON, of Coughton, co. Warwick. He d. 1 July 1622, at Hallingbury afsd. and was *bur.* in the church there. Will in which he is styled "Lord Morley, Baron of Rye," dat. 19 June and pr. 8 July 1622.

XIV. 1622. *14.* HENRY (PARKER), LORD MORLEY AND MONTEAGLE, s. and h. He had v.p. been cr. K.B., 3 Nov. 1616. He was sum. to Parl. from 12 Feb. (1623/4), 21 Jac. I. to 3 Nov. (1639), 15 Car. I., by writs directed "*Henrico Parker de Morley et Monteagle.*" He m. before June 1622, Philippa, 2d and yst. da. and coheir of Sir Thomas CARYLL, of Bentons in Shipley, co. Sussex, by Mary, da. of Sir John TUFTON, Bart. He d. 10 May 1655, and was *bur.* at Hallingbury afsd. Will pr. 1659. His widow, who was *bap.* 5 Oct. 1600, at Harting, Sussex, d. about 1660. Her will, in which directs her burial to be at Shipley, dat. 11 Dec. 1660, pr. 1 March 1660/1.

XV. 1655, to 1686? *15.* THOMAS (PARKER), LORD MORLEY AND MONTEAGLE, only s. and h. He was sum. to Parl. from 8 May (1661), 13 Car. II., to 19 May (1685), 1 Jac. II. He m. Mary, da. of Henry MARTIN, of Langworth, Berks, s. and h. of Sir Henry MARTIN, Judge of the Admiralty Court. He d. s.p.s. about 1686, when the *Baronies of Morley* [1299], *and Monteagle* [1514] as also, apparently, the right to that of *Marshal* [1309] *fell into abeyance.*(c)

Earldom. I. 1815. *1.* JOHN (PARKER), BARON BORINGDON, only s. and h. of John, 1st BARON BORINGDON (so cr. 1784), by his second wife, Theresa, da. of Thomas (ROBINSON), 1st BARON GRANTHAM, was b. 3 May 1772; *suc. to the peerage*, 27 April 1788; matric. at Oxford (Ch. Ch.), 7 April 1789, being cr. D.C.L., 18 June 1799; F.R.S., 26 Feb. 1795; Col. of the North Devon Militia, 1790, and, being a frequent speaker in the House of Lords in support of the Tory ministry, was cr. VISCOUNT BORINGDON OF NORTH MOLTON, and

---

(a) See vol. iii, p. 72, note "a," *sub* "Derby," for a list of the 24 noblemen who were on that commission.

(b) He is therein called "Baron of Rye."

(c) The representatives are among the issue of his aunt or aunts, *viz* (1) Elizabeth who m. Edward Cranfield of whose issue (if any) nothing is known; and (2) Katharine (the 1st da.), who m. as his first wife John (Savage), Earl of Rivers, who d. 10 Oct. 1654, leaving, by her 3 sons and five daughters. The issue of all the sons became extinct (with the Earldom of Rivers), in 1728, while two of the daughters d. s.p. Of the three other daughters of the Countess Rivers (1) Lady Jane Savage, is represented by her issue by her third husband George Pitt, of whom were the Barons Rivers, extinct 1880, (2) Lady Catherine, by her second husband, was represented by the Earls of Portmore [S.], extinct 1835; and (3) Lady Mary m. (as his first wife), Henry Killigrew, Groom of the Bedchamber, by whom she had a son, James, living March 1682/3, who is said to have d. s.p.

EARL OF MORLEY,(a) both in co. Devon. He *m.* firstly, 20 June 1804, at her father's house in Berkeley square, St. Geo. Han. sq., Augusta, 2d da. of John (FANE), 10th EARL OF WESTMORLAND, by his first wife, Sarah Anne, da. and h. of Robert CHILD, of Osterley Park, Midx. She, who was *b.* 17 March 1786, was *divorced* 14 Feb. 1809.(b) He *m.* secondly, 23 Aug. 1809, Frances, da. of Thomas TALBOT, of Gonville, co. Norfolk. He *d.* 14 March 1840, in his 68th year, at Saltram, near Plymouth. Will pr. April 1840. His widow *d.* at Saltram, 7 Dec. 1857, aged 76.

[HENRY VILLIERS PARKER, *styled* (since 1815), VISCOUNT BORINGDON, 1st s. and h. ap., being only child by first wife; *b.* 28 May 1806; *d.* v.p., near Paris, 1 Nov. 1817,(c) aged 11.]

II. 1840. 2. EDMUND (PARKER), EARL OF MORLEY,(a) &c., 2d but only surv. s. and h., being 1st s. by the second wife; *b.* 10 June 1810, in London; *styled* VISCOUNT BORINGDON, 1817-40; mat. at Oxford (Ch. Ch.), 21 Jan. 1828; B.A., 1830; Lord of the Bedchamber to H.R.H. Prince Albert, 1840; *suc. to the peerage*, 15 March 1840; Col. South Devon Militia, 1845; a Lord in Waiting, 1846-52; Spec. Dep. Warden of the Stannaries, 1852-64. He *m.*, 1 March 1842, his cousin, Harriet Sophia, widow of William CORYTON, da. of Montagu Edmund PARKER, of Whiteway, Devon, by Harriet, da. and coheir of John NEWCOMBE, of Starcross, Devon. He *d.* 28 Aug. 1864, aged 54, at Whiteway afsd. Will pr. at Exeter, Feb. 1865, under £80,000. His widow living 1893.

III. 1864. 3. ALBERT EDMUND (PARKER), EARL OF MORLEY [1815], VISCOUNT BORINGDON OF NORTH MOLTON [1815], and BARON BORINGDON [1784], only s. and h.; *b.* 11 June 1843, at Kent House; *styled* VISCOUNT BORINGDON till 1864; ed. at Eton and at Balliol Coll., Oxford; matric., 19 Oct. 1861; 1st Class (Classics), 1865; B.A., 1866, having *suc. to the peerage*, 28 Aug. 1864; a Lord in Waiting, 1868-74; Sec. to the Local Government Board, 1873-74; Under Sec. of State for War, 1880-85; First Commr. of Works, Feb. to April 1886; Chairman of Committees and Dep. Speaker of the House of Lords, 1889. He *m.*, 17 June 1876, at St. Geo. Han. sq., Margaret, 1st da. of Robert Stanyer HOLFORD, of

---

(a) The estate at Moreleigh, or Morley, a small village, near Totnes, co. Devon, was sold in 1778 to the family of Seale, from whom it was purchased by Lord Boringdon, just in time to enable its possessor to make use of its name as the title of his Earldom. It is impossible to speak too strongly of the contemptible and vulgar vanity and want of all right feeling which induced the grantee of 1815 to select his title from this newly acquired and unimportant property, such selection being doubtless (as was, in all probability the purchase itself) in the hope of [fraudulently], palming himself off as being of the ancient stock of the family of *Parker*, who for many generations (in the 15th, 16th, and 17th centuries) were *Lords Morley*. There was not however the *slightest* connection between these families, whose armorial bearings are totally distinct; the one family (of historic note) springing from a Standard bearer to one of the Plantagenet Kings, and having its chief possessions in East Anglia, while the other family (which has the very different origin of being first known as the tenants of a monastery at North Molton, Devon), acquired early in the 17th century the position of Gentry in Devonshire, out of which county they have never (at any period) held any lands or position.

(b) She *m.* (two days subsequently), 16 Feb. 1809, at Heckfield, Hants, Sir Arthur Paget, from whom damages of £10,000 had been awarded to Lord Boringdon, in an action (1808) of *crim. con.*

(c) His recent death is thus recorded in the Scots Mag. lxxix, ii, 502 (Dec. 1817). "At St. Maude near Paris, aged 11 years, Lord Boringdon, eldest son of the Earl of Morley. A stalk of rye which he had inadvertently swallowed the latter end of July, was the cause of his sufferings; it was found, after his death, three inches in length, in its original state, lodged in the intestines."

Westonbirt, co. Gloucester, by Mary Anne, 2d da. of Lieut. Gen. James LINDSAY, of Balcarres.

[EDMUND ROBERT PARKER, *styled* VISCOUNT BORINGDON, 1st s. and h. ap., *b.* 19 April 1877.]

Family Estates.—These, in 1883, consisted of 4,238 acres in Devonshire, worth £8,209 a year. The property of the Dowager Countess was 10,540 acres in co. Cavan, worth £2,734 a year, and 1,924 acres in Devon, worth £2,465 a year.

MORNE.

i.e., "NEWRY AND MORNE, co. Down," Viscountcy [I.] (*Needham*), *cr.* 1822, with the EARLDOM OF KILMOREY [I.], which see.

MORNINGTON.[a]

Barony [I.] I. 1746. *1.* RICHARD COLLEY, *afterwards* (1728), WESLEY, of Dangan Castle, co. Meath, 6th and yst. s. but eventually (1723), heir *male*[b] of Henry COLLEY, of Castle Carbery, co. Kildare, by Mary, da. of Sir William USHER, of Dublin, was *b.* about 1690; was sometime Auditor and Register of the Royal Hospital, near Dublin; second Chamberlain of the Court of Exchequer [I.], 1713; inherited (by devise) the estates of Dangan and Mornington, co. Meath, on the death s.p. of his cousin, Garret Wesley,[c] 18 March 1727, and took accordingly (pat. roll., 2 Geo. II.), the surname of *Wesley*; was High Sheriff of co. Meath, 1734, being M.P. for Trim from 1729 till he was *cr.* 9 July 1746, BARON OF MORNINGTON, co. Meath [I.], taking his seat 6 Oct. 1747. He *m.* 23 Dec. 1719, Elizabeth, 1st da. of John SALE, LL.D., Register of the diocese of Dublin and M.P. for Carysfort. She *d.* 17, and was *bur.* 20 June 1738, at St. Andrews, Dublin. He *d.* 31 Jan. 1758.

II. 1758. Earldom [I.] I. 1760. *2* and *1.* GARRET (WESLEY *alias* WELLESLEY), BARON MORNINGTON [I.], only surv. s. and h.; *b.* 19 July and *bap.* 10 Aug. 1735, at St. Andrews, Dublin; M.P. for co. Meath, 1757, till he *suc.* *to the peerage* [I.], 31 Jan. 1758, taking his seat 13 Feb. following; *Custos Rot.* for co. Meath, 1759. He was *cr.* 2 Oct. 1760, VISCOUNT WELLESLEY OF DANGAN CASTLE and EARL OF MORNINGTON, co. Meath [I.], taking his seat 19 Nov. 1761. He *m.* 6 Feb. 1759, Anne, da. of Arthur (HILL, *afterwards* HILL-TREVOR), 1st VISCOUNT DUNGANNON [I.], by his second wife Anne, da. of Edmund Francis STAFFORD. He *d.* at Kensington, 22 May 1784, in his 50th year,[d] and was *bur.* in Grosvenor chapel, South Audley street. His widow, who was *b.* 23 June 1742, *d.* 10 Sep. 1831, in her 90th year, and was *bur.* as afsd. Will pr. Sep. 1831.

---

[a] Mornington, or Mariner's town, styled in charters about 1200 "*Villa Marinarii*," belonged anciently to the family of Martin, of Castle Martin, whose heir, Joan, *m.* Sir Richard Wellesley, Sheriff of Kildare, 1415.

[b] The Viscounts Harberton [I.] are the heirs *general* of the family of Colley, thro' Mary, the only child that had issue of Henry Colley, of Castle Carbery (who *d.* 1723), the 5th, but 1st surv. s. of Henry Colley abovenamed. This Mary *m.* 20 Oct. 1747, Arthur (Pomeroy), 1st Viscount and Baron Harberton of Carbery afsd. [I.]

[c] He was son of another Garret Wesley, of Dangan, by Elizabeth da. of Dudley Colley, one of the seven paternal aunts of the said Richard Colley, his testamentary heir. This Richard Colley had in him (thro' the family of Cusack) a slight strain of Wesley blood (tho' of course, no representation of that family) he being a yr. s. of Henry, s. and h. of Dudley, s. and h. of Sir Henry, s. and h. of another Sir Henry, who was s. and h. of a third Sir Henry Colley or Cowley (all of Castle Carbery, co. Kildare), by Catharine, da. of Sir Thomas *Cusack*, Lord Chancellor [I.], and Alison, da. of William *Wesley*, of Dangan, which lady was, accordingly, great-great-great-great-grandmother to the said Richard Colley. See also vol. ii, p. 392, note "a," *sub* "Cowley."

[d] He was well known for his musical talents.

Earldom [I.] II. Barony [I.] III. — 1784.

2 and 3. RICHARD (WELLESLEY), EARL OF MORNINGTON, &c. [I.], 1st s. and h., b. 20 June 1760, at Dangan Castle; *styled* VISCOUNT WELLESLEY, till 1784: ed. at Harrow, Eton and Oxford, where he matric. (Ch. Ch.), 24 Dec. 1778;(a) *suc. to the peerage* [I.], 22 May 1781; K.P. (one of the 15 original(b) knights), 5 Feb. 1783, being inst. 17 March following, but resigning the order in 1810, when he obtained the Garter;(c) M.P. for Trim, 1780-81; for Beeralston, 1784-86; for Saltash, 1786-87; for Windsor, 1787-96, and for old Sarum, 1796-97. P.C. [I.], 1784; a Lord of the Treasury, 1786-97; a Commissioner for Indian affairs, 1793-97; Governor of Madras, May 1797, and GOVERNOR GENERAL OF BENGAL, 1797—1805 (being Commander in Chief, 1800-05), during which period he effected the capture of Seringapatam and the complete destruction of the empire of the Mysore. He was *cr.* 20 Oct. 1797, BARON WELLESLEY of Wellesley, co. Somerset [G.B.], being, two years later, *cr.*, 2 Dec. 1799,(d) MARQUESS WELLESLEY OF NORRAGH [I.] He had been made Chief Remembrancer of the Court of Exchequer [I.] in 1798; Knight of the Crescent of Turkey, 19 Nov. 1805; Ambassador to the Central Junta of Spain, 1809; Sec. of State for the Foreign Department, 1809-12; K.G., 3 March 1810, being inst., 31 March 1812, when he resigned the Order of St. Patrick;(c) Knight of the Lion and Sun of Persia, 29 July 1812; Bearer of the Sceptre with the Cross at the Coronation of George IV., 19 July 1821. VICEROY OF IRELAND (as Lord Lieut.), 1821-28. and again, 1833-34, having meanwhile (1830-33) been Lord Steward of the Household. Lord Chamberlain of the Household, April to May 1835. He *m.*, 29 Nov. 1794, at St. Geo. Han. sq., Hyacinthe Gabrielle,(e) da. of Pierre ROLAND, of Paris. She *d.* 5 Nov. 1816. Will pr. Jan. 1817. He *m.* secondly, 29 Oct. 1825, at the Vice Regal Lodge, Dublin, Marianne,(f) widow of Robert PATTERSON, da. of Richard CATON, of Maryland, in America, by (—), da. of Charles CARROLL, of Carrollstown, in Maryland. He *d.* s.p. legit., 26 Sep. 1842, aged 82, at Kingston House, Knightsbridge, Midx., when the *Marquessate of Wellesley of Norragh* [I.] and the *Barony of Wellesley* [G.B.] became *extinct*.(g) He was *bur.* in the chapel of Eton College, Bucks. M.I. Will pr. Feb. 1843. His widow, who was a Lady of the Bedchamber to the Queen' Dowager Adelaide, *d.* at Hampton Court Palace, 17 Dec. 1853. Will pr. May 1854.

Earldom [I.] III. Barony [I.] IV. — 1842.

3 and 4. WILLIAM (WELLESLEY-POLE, *formerly* WELLESLEY), EARL OF MORNINGTON, &c. [I.], also BARON MARYBOROUGH [U.K.], next surv. br. and h.(g); *b.* 20 May 1763, at Dangan Castle; ed. at Eton; entered the Royal Navy; assumed the additional surname of *Pole* in 1778 on succeeding to the estates of his cousin, William POLE,(h) of Ballyfin, in Queen's county; was M.P. for Trim, 1783-90; for East Looe, 1790-94; for Queen's county, 1801-21; Clerk of the Ordnance, 1802-06, and again, March to July 1807; Chief Sec. [I.], 1809-12; P.C., 1809; Chanc. Exch. [I.], 1811-12; Master of the Mint, 1815-23,

---

(a) His exquisite Latin poems are well known. Some are given in the "*Anthologia Oxoniensis.*"

(b) See vol. i, p. 186, note "d," *sub* "Arran" for a list of them.

(c) A like resignation was made by Earl Talbot in 1844.

(d) He was greatly vexed at not obtaining a Marquessate of Great Britain, but it was pointed out to him that tho' his predecessor, Lord Cornwallis, had obtained it, it was because he already enjoyed an Earldom *of Great Britain*, while in his own case the Earldom enjoyed was of *Ireland*.

(e) "They had had several children but separated very soon after marriage without any further issue and were not afterwards reconciled." [*Annual Reg.*, 1842.]

(f) One of her sisters was Duchess of Leeds and another Baroness Stafford.

(g) He was one of five brothers, of whom no less than four were Peers. See vol. ii, p. 393, note "a," *sub* "Cowley."

(h) This gentleman's mother, Anne, da. of Henry Colley, of Castle Carbery, was only sister to Richard, 1st Baron Mornington [I.] He was accordingly first cousin to the first Earl, the father of the legatee.

being *cr.*, 17 July 1821, BARON MARYBOROUGH of Maryborough, Queen's county; Master of the Buckhounds, 1828-30; G.C.H. (Civil), 1830; Postmaster General, 1834-35; Captain of Deal Castle, 1838-43. He *suc. to the Earldom*, &c. [I.], on the death of his said br. Marquess Wellesley, 26 Sep. 1842. He *m.*(a) 17 May 1784, in Savile Row, St. James' Westm., Katharine Elizabeth, 1st da. and coheir of Admiral the Hon. John FORBES (2d s. of George, 3d EARL OF GRANARD [I.]), by Mary, da. of William (CAPELL), 3d EARL OF ESSEX. He *d.* 22 Feb. 1845, in his 82d year, in Grosvenor square, and was *bur.* (with his parents) in Grosvenor chapel afsd. Will pr. March 1845. His widow *d.* in Grosvenor square, 23 Oct. 1851, aged 91, and was *bur.* as afsd. Will pr. Nov. 1851.

Earldom [I.] IV. Barony [I.] V. — 1845.

4 and 5. WILLIAM (POLE-TYLNEY-LONG-WELLESLEY, *formerly* WELLESLEY-POLE), EARL OF MORNINGTON, &c. [I.], also BARON MARYBOROUGH, only s. and h.; *b.* 22 May 1788; Sec. of Embassy and Minister at Constantinople and subsequently at Copenhagen. He *m.* firstly, 14 March 1812, at St. James' Westm., Catherine, 1st sister and coheir(b) of Sir James TYLNEY-LONG, 8th and last Bart., of Draycot, Wilts (who *d.* 14 Sep. 1805, aged 11), da. of Sir James TYLNEY-LONG, 7th Bart., by his second wife, Catherine Sidney, da. of Other Lewis (WINDSOR), 4th EARL OF PLYMOUTH.(c) In contemplation of this marriage, he, by royal lic., 14 Jan. 1812, took the additional surnames of *Tylney-Long* between those of *Pole* and *Wellesley*. She, who was *b.* 2 Oct. 1789, *d.* at Richmond, Surrey, 12 Sep. 1825, aged 35, and was *bur.* at Draycot. He *m.* secondly, 10 Nov. 1828, Helena, widow of Thomas BLIGH, Capt. Coldstream Guards, da. of Col. Thomas PATERSON, by Anne, da. and coheir of Boyd PORTERFIELD, of Porterfield, co. Renfrew. He was *styled* VISCOUNT WELLESLEY, since his father's accession to the Earldom, 26 Sep. 1842, till he *suc. to the peerage* [I. and U.K.], 22 Feb. 1845. He *d.* in poverty, 1 July 1857, aged 69, at lodgings in Thayer street, Marylebone. Will pr. Oct. 1857. His widow, by whom he had no issue, *d.* 7 April 1869, aged 75, at West Cowes, Isle of Wight.

Earldom [I.] V. Barony [I.] VI. — 1857.

5 and 6. WILLIAM RICHARD ARTHUR (POLE-TYLNEY-LONG-WELLESLEY), EARL OF MORNINGTON [1760], VISCOUNT WELLESLEY OF DANGAN CASTLE [1760], and BARON MORNINGTON [1746], in the peerage of Ireland, also BARON MARYBOROUGH [1821], 1st s. and h. by first wife; *b.* 7 Oct. 1813, at Wanstead House, Essex. He was *styled* VISCOUNT WELLESLEY from 1845 till he *suc. to the peerage* [I. and U.K.] 1 July 1857. He *d.* unm. at Paris, 25 July 1863, aged 49, and was

---

(a) His signature thereto is "William Wesley Pole," shewing that as late as 1784 the spelling of "*Wellesley*" was not universally adopted by the family.

(b) The estates she inherited amounted to £25,000 a year; besides £300,000 personalty. The estate of Wanstead, co. Essex and of Tylney, Hants, came from her paternal grandmother, Emma, da. of Richard (Child), Earl Tilney of Wanstead [I.], which Emma was heir to her brother the 2d Earl.

(c) "Of the miseries which followed this marriage and of the subsequent scandals of the deceased's career it is better to say nothing. The vast property he had acquired by marriage and all that came from his own family he squandered; and, after many years of poverty and profligacy, he subsisted on a weekly pension from his relatives, the late and present Dukes of Wellington." [*Annual Reg.*, 1857]. Among other estates thus sold was Wanstead House, Essex, the erection of which had cost more than £360,000, which (in 1823) fetched but £10,000, the materials being cleared by Lady-day, 1825; also Tylney Park, near Rotherfield, Hants, &c. His career and his "long" name (but slightly altered) are alluded to (as early as 1812) in the brother Smith's inimitable "*Rejected Addresses.*" (See "*Loyal effusion,*" by W. T. F.[itzgerald]) as under—

"Bless every man possess'd of aught to give,—
Long may *Long-Tilney-Wellesley-Long-Pole* live;—
* * * * *
And, oh! in Downing street should Old Nick revel
England's prime minister, then bless the Devil!"

bur. at Draycot afsd.; when the *Barony of Maryborough* [U.K.] became *extinct*. Will dat. 27 June to 13 July 1863, pr. 20 Aug. 1863 under £80,000, and again (1865) under £90,000.(a)

Earldom [I.] VI. Barony [I.] VII. 1863. 6 and 7. ARTHUR RICHARD (WELLESLEY), DUKE OF WELLINGTON, MARQUESS OF WELLINGTON MARQUESS OF DOURO, &c., also EARL OF MORNINGTON, &c. [I.], cousin and h., being s. and h. of Arthur, 1st DUKE OF WELLINGTON, by Catherine, da. of Edward Michael (PAKENHAM), 2d BARON LONGFORD [I.], which Arthur was yr. br. to the 2d and 3d Earls of Mornington, being 3d surv. s. of the 1st Earl and 2d Baron. He, who was *b.* 3 Feb. 1807, and *styled* LORD DOURO, 1812-14, and MARQUESS OF DOURO, 1814-52, *suc.* his father *in the peerage* [U.K.], 14 Sep. 1852, and *suc.* his cousin in *the Irish peerage*, 25 July 1863, as afsd. See "WELLINGTON" Dukedom, *cr.* 1815, under the second Duke.

MORPETH.

i.e., "HOWARD OF MORPETH," Viscountcy (*Howard*), *cr.* 20 July 1657, by the "Lord Protector;" see "CARLISLE" Earldom, *cr.* (by the King) 1661.

i.e., "HOWARD OF MORPETH, co. Northumberland," Viscountcy (*Howard*), *cr.* 1661, with the EARLDOM OF CARLISLE, which see.

MORRIS OF SPIDDAL.

Barony for life. I. 1889. THE RT. HON. SIR MICHAEL MORRIS, Bart., Lord Chief Justice of Ireland, was, on 5 Dec. 1889, appointed a LORD OF APPEAL IN ORDINARY (under "*the appellate Jurisdiction Act, 1876*"), being granted the dignity of a Baron for life(b) by the style or title of BARON MORRIS OF SPIDDAL, co. Galway. He was 1st s. and h. of Martin MORRIS, of Spiddal afsd. (who *d.* 27 June 1862, aged 77), by Julia, da. of Charles BLAKE, M.D., of Galway; was *b.* 14 Nov. 1827, at Galway; ed. at Galway College and at Trin. Coll., Dublin; B.A., 1817, being First Senior Moderator and Gold Medallist; Barrister [I.], 1849; Q.C. [I.], 1863; M.P. for Galway, 1865-67; P.C. [I.], 1866; Solicitor Gen. [I.], July to Nov. 1866; Attorney Gen. [I.], 1866-67; third Justice of the Common Pleas [I.], 1867-76; Chief Justice of that Court, 1876-87, having being *cr. a Baronet*, 14 Sep 1885; Hon. LL.D. of Dublin, 1887; Lord Chief Justice [I.], 1887-89, when he was appointed a Lord of Appeal and *cr. a life Peer* as abovestated; P.C. [G.B.], 1889. He *m.*, 18 Sep. 1860, Anna, da. of George Henry HUGHES, one of the Judges of the Court of Exchequer [I.]

MORTAIGNE.

JOHN (PLANTAGENET), EARL OF GLOUCESTER, *jure uxoris*, was more generally known as COUNT OF MORTAIGNE(c) in Normandy and is *styled* in several charters "*Comes Moritonie.*" He ascended the throne as **King John**, 6 April 1199. See vol. iv, p. 39, *sub* "Gloucester."

(a) By it he left the estate of Draycot, Wilts (derived from his *mother*) to his *paternal* cousin Earl Cowley and his sons in tail.

(b) See vol. i, p. 357, note "a," *sub* "Blackburn," as to the nature and extent of these creations.

(c) William, yst. s. of **King Stephen**, had also been Count of Mortaigne in Normandy. He suc. his elder br. in 1152 as Count of Boulogne and *d.* s.p. 1159.

MORTIMER.

WILLIAM DE MORTIMER, of Attleborough, co. Norfolk, was, with about 60 other persons, sum., 8 June (1294), 22 Ed. I., to attend the King to advise on the affairs of the Realm, and was again sum. 26 Jan. (1296/7), 25 Ed. I., but neither of these writs constituted a regular summons to Parl.(a) He d. 1297 leaving CONSTANTINE DE MORTIMER, then aged 10, as his s. and h., who was sum. to a Council (which was not a Parl.), 25 Feb. (1341/2), 16 Ed. III.

MORTIMER, or MORTIMER DE WIGMORE.

Barony by Writ.

I. 1295.

1. SIR EDMUND DE MORTIMER, of Wigmore, co. Hereford, 2d but 1st surv. s. and h. of Sir Roger DE MORTIMER, of the same, by Maud, da. and coheir of William DE BRAOSE, of Brecknock; *suc.* his father in 1282, being then aged 21; served with distinction in the Welsh wars; was sum., with about 60 other persons, 8 June (1294), 22 Ed. I., to attend the King to advise on the affairs of the Realm(a) and was sum. to Parl. as a Baron (LORD MORTIMER) from 23 June (1295), 23 Ed. I., to 2 June (1302), 30 Ed. I. His name appears as "*Edmundus de Mortuo Mari, Dominus de Wigemor,*" to the famous letter of the Barons to the Pope in 1301.(b) He *m* about 1280, Margaret, da. of Sir William DE FIENNES, kinswoman to the Queen Consort, Eleanor of Castile. He was mortally wounded at the battle of Builth against the Welsh, 1304, and *d.* at his Castle of Wigmore, being *bur.* in the Abbey there. His widow was living (1317-18), 11 Ed. II.

II. 1304. *2.* ROGER (DE MORTIMER), LORD MORTIMER, or LORD MORTIMER DE WIGMORE, s. and h., aged 17 at the death of his father in 1304, being *b.* about 12 April 1286. He was sum. to Parl. from 22 Feb. (1305/6), 22 Ed. I., to 3 Dec. (1326), 20 Ed. II., the writs having the addition of the words "*de Wigmore.*" He was *cr.*, 9 Nov. 1328, EARL OF MARCH (see fuller particulars under that dignity) but was hung, 26 or 29 Nov. 1330, when, having been attainted, *all his honours* were *forfeited.*

* * * * * *

III. 1331. *1.* SIR EDMUND DE MORTIMER, s. and h., did not, in consequence of the attainder of his father, succeed to his honours. He was *knighted*, 1 Feb. 1328, at the Coronation of King Edward III. and was sum. to Parl. as a Baron (LORD MORTIMER) by writ 20 Nov. (1331), 5 Ed. III. He *m.* about 1328, Elizabeth, 3d da. and coheir of Bartholomew (DE BADLESMERE), LORD BADLESMERE, by Margaret, da. and coheir of Thomas DE CLARE. He *d.* "in the flower of his youth," 17 Dec. (1331), 5 Ed. III. at Stanton Lacy. His widow *m.* in 1338, William (DE BOHUN), 1st EARL OF NORTHAMPTON (who *d.* 16 Sep. 1360), and *d.* (1356), 30 Ed. III.

IV. 1331. *2* and *4.* ROGER (DE MORTIMER), LORD MORTIMER, or LORD MORTIMER DE WIGMORE, s. and h., was *b.* about 1327; *suc.* his father in 1331; was in the war with France and was *knighted* by the Black Prince, 13 July 1346, having already been elected, 23 April 1344, K.G., as one of the Founders of that Order.(c) He was sum. to Parl. as a Baron from 20 Nov. (1348), 22 Ed. III., to 15 March (1353/4), 28 Ed. III., by writs sometime addressed "*Rogero de Mortuomari*" [only] and sometimes (24, 25, and 27 Ed. III.), with the addition of the words "*de Wigmore.*" The attainder of his grandfather abovenamed having been reversed in the Parl. of 27 Ed. III. (about 26 April 1354), he thus became EARL OF MARCH, and, as such, was sum. to Parl. 20 Sep. (1335), 29 Ed. III. By this reversal, also, he became entitled to the *Barony of Mortimer*, as *cr.* in 1295. See "*March*" Earldom, which, together with these Baronies (1295 and 1331) of Mortimer (and the Dukedom of York) became *merged in the Crown*, 4 March 1460/1, on the accession of **King Edward IV.**

(a) See vol. i, p. 259, note "c," *sub* "Basset de Sapcote," as to the writ of summons of 1294, and vol. i, p. 111, note "b," *sub* "Ap Adam," as to that of 1297.
(b) See "*Nicolas,*" pp. 761—809, for a full account of that letter.
(c) See vol. i, p. 276, note "a," *sub* "Beauchamp" for a list of these Founders.

MORTIMER.

Barony by Writ.

I. 1296.

1. SIMON DE MORTIMER (possibly a yr. br. of Edmund, 1st LORD MORTIMER) was sum. to Parl. as a Baron (LORD MORTIMER), 26 Aug. (1296), 24 Ed. I, but never afterwards. There is no acount of him in "*Dugdale*," or, apparently, elsewhere.

MORTIMER, or MORTIMER DE CHIRCKE.

Barony by Writ.

I. 1299.

1. ROGER DE MORTIMER, br. to Edmund, 1st LORD MORTIMER (being a yr. s. of Sir Roger DE MORTIMER, of Wigmore, co. Hereford, by Maud, da. and coheir of William DE BRAOSE, of Brecknock), having acquired,(a) the Lordship of Chirk, co. Denbigh, was sum. to Parl. as a Baron (LORD MORTIMER) from 6 Feb. (1298/9), 27 Ed. I., to 3 Nov. (1306), 34 Ed. I. by writs directed "*Rogero de Mortuo Mari*" and (as LORD MORTIMER DE CHIRCKE), by writs from 26 Aug. (1307), 1 Ed. II., to 15 May (1321), 14 Ed. II.,(b) with the addition of the words "*de Chircke*."(c) His name appears as "*Rogerus de Mortuo Mari, Dominus de Pentkellyn*," in the famous letter of the Barons to the Pope, 1301 (d) He served in the wars with France, Scotland and Wales, being the King's Lieutenant in Wales and subsequently (1322) Justice of all Wales. Taking part against the Despencers he was (with his nephew, Lord Mortimer de Wigmore) imprisoned in 1322. He *m.* Lucy, da. of Sir Robert DE WAFRE. He *d.* after 4½ years imprisonment in the Tower of London, 3 Aug. 1336, and was *bur.* in the Abbey of Wigmore.

II. 1336. *2.* ROGER DE MORTIMER, of Chirk, s. and h., was never sum. to Parl. as a Baron. He *m.* Joane DE TURBERVILLE and was *suc.* by JOHN DE MORTIMER, his s. and h., who sold the estate of Chirk to Richard (Fitzalan), Earl of Arundel, and who was never summoned as a Baron, nor any of his posterity tho' the Barony is presumably *in abeyance* among them.

MORTIMER [of Richards Castle.]

Barony by Writ.

I. 1299, to 1304.

1. HUGH DE MORTIMER, of Richards Castle, co. Hereford, s. and h. of Robert DE MORTIMER,(e) of the same, by Joyce, da. and h. of William ZOUCHE, *suc.* his father in 1287 and became of full age about 1295; was sum., 26 Jan. (1296/7), 25 Ed. I., to a meeting at Salisbury, such summons, however, not being a regular summons to Parl.,(f) and was sum. to Parl. as a Baron (LORD MORTIMER) on 6 Feb. (1298/9) and 10 April (1299), 27 Ed. I. He *m.* about 1290 Maud. He *d.* s.p.m. (1303-04), 32 Ed. I., when the *Barony* fell into *abeyance*.(g)

(a) It is stated by Powel, the Welsh historian, that he was guardian to the younger of the two sons of Griffith ap Madoc, who took the part of the English; John (de Warenne), Earl of Surrey, being guardian to the elder son, whose portion was the Lordship of Bromfield, while the Lordship of Chirk, was that of the younger. Both these guardians, however "so guarded these, their wards, that they never returned to their possessions and, shortly after, obtained these lands to themselves by charter."

(b) His name occurs in the rolls of Parl. before the record of writs of summons commenced.

(c) "In 1307, his nephew Roger de Mortimer of Wigmore became of age and the addition of *de Chircke* was adopted to distinguish them." [*Courthope.*]

(d) See full account of this letter in "*Nicolas*," pp. 761—809.

(e) This Robert, who was aged 22 in 1275, when he *suc.* his father, was s. and h. of Hugh de Mortimer (*d.* 1275), who was s. and h. of Robert de Mortimer (dead in 1219), by Margaret, da. and h. of Hugh de Ferrers, by Mabel, da. and h. of Hugh de Say, of Richards Castle abovenamed.

(f) See vol. i, p. 111, note "b," *sub* "Ap Adam," as to this not constituting a regular writ of summons to Parl.

(g) The coheirs were his two daughters of whom (1) Joan, aged 12, in 1304, was wife of Sir Thomas de Bikenor in 1315-16, by whom she had no issue. She *m.*

MORTIMER.

See "ZOUCHE DE MORTIMER," Barony (*Zouche*, formerly *Mortimer*) *cr.* 1323, in *abeyance* 1406.

---

i.e., "MORTIMER" Earldom (*Harley*), *cr.* 1711 with the EARLDOM OF OXFORD, which see; *ex.* 1853.

MORTON.[a]

Earldom [S.] I. 1458. *1.* JAMES (DOUGLAS), LORD DALKEITH [S.], s. and h. of James, 2d LORD DALKEITH [S.], by his 2d wife, Elizabeth, sister of James GIFFORD, *suc.* his father *in that peerage* [S.] (a dignity *cr.* 1430?) about 1456, and, having *m.* or being about to marry the LADY JOAN STEWART, da. of **King James I.** [S.], by Joan, da. of John (BEAUFORT), EARL OF SOMERSET, was *cr.* 14 March 1457/8,[b] EARL OF MORTON [S.] He was one of the Ambassadors to England, 14 June 1491 and 28 July 1494, but *d.* before 13 May 1504.

II. 1500? *2.* JOHN (DOUGLAS), EARL OF MORTON, &c. [S.], only s. and h., was present in Parl. [S.], 13 May 1504. He *m.* Janet, da. of (—) CRICHTON, of Cranston-Riddel, both being living, 22 Feb. 1506/7. He *d.* before 6 Feb. 1516.

III. 1515? *3.* JAMES (DOUGLAS), EARL OF MORTON, and LORD DALKEITH [S.], s. and h., who on 6 Feb. 1516, had safe conduct to go to England. He *m.* Catharine STEWART, illegit. da. of **King James IV.** [S.], by Mary BOYD, spinster. She was living in 1540, in which year he was induced by the King to resign his estates and honours (subject to his own life rent and his wife's "tierce") in favour of a distant cousin[c] (his nearer relative, the heir male presump-

---

secondly Sir Richard Talbot, who became in her right of Richards Castle, which continued in their descendants in the male line till the death of their great grandson, John Talbot, in 1388 (2) Margaret, aged 10, in 1304, wife of Sir Geoffrey Cornwall, in 1315-16, who in her right was of Burford, Oxon, being, by her, ancestor of the family of Cornwall, who styled themselves "Barons of Burford."

(a) The Editor is indebted to Mr. M. J. Shaw-Stewart for his kind assistance in this article.

(b) It was, as a protest against this creation, asserted that the lands of Morton belonged heritably to his step-grandmother, Janet, Lady Dalkeith (widow of the 1st Lord) and to her son, William Douglas, to which the Chancellor answered that "Lord Dalkeith was not to receive his title in the Earldom for the lands of Morton lying in the Lordship of Niddisdale but for the lands of Mortoun in the territory of Calder-cleir." The Earldom is elsewhere called that of "Morton in Dumfries-shire."

(c) *Tabular Pedigree shewing the relationship of the earlier Earls of Morton* [S.] *to each other and to the house of Douglas, of Douglas.*

Archibald Douglas, of Douglas, 1213-1240.

Sir William Douglas, of Douglas, 1240-1271; ancestor of the Earls of Douglas and (by bastard descent) of the Earls of Angus, Queensberry, &c. [S.]

See vol. iii, p. 154, note "a."

Andrew Douglas, 2d son, living 1248.

William D. of Midlothian, s. & h., living 1296.

Sir James D. of Laudon, s. & h., ancestor of the houses of Douglas of Dalkeith, Aberdour, Morton and Lochleven; *d.* 1320.

A

tive being passed over) Sir Robert Douglas, of Lochleven, with whom the King had apparently made terms. This Robert accordingly had a charter, 17 Oct. 1540, of the

A

Sir William D. of Liddesdale, Eskdale, Dalkeith, Aberdour, &c., all which lands he acquired; sometime Earl of Athole [S.] He d. s.p.m. 1353.

Sir John D., 2d son; d. 1350.

Sir James D. of Dalkeith and Aberdour, Knight, Banneret, 1st son; suc. his uncle 1353; d. 1420.

Sir Henry D. of Lochleven, 2d son, living 1390.

Sir James D. of Dalkeith, Aberdour, Morton-in-Nithsdale, &c., s. & h., cr. Lord Dalkeith [S.] about 1430; d. 1440.

Sir William D. of Lochleven, s. & h.

James, 2nd Lord Dalkeith [S.], s. & h.; d. 1456.

Sir Henry Douglas of Borg, co. Galloway.

Sir William Douglas of Whittingham in East Lothian, whose descendants *in the male line* are said to be still (1893) in existence.

Sir Henry D. of Lochleven, s. & h. 1427-1464

I. James, 3rd Lord of Dalkeith [S.], s. & h., cr. *Earl of Morton* [S.] 1458; living 1494.

Robert D. of Lochleven, s. & h., slain at Flodden 1513.

II. John, *Earl of Morton* [S.], only s. & h. 1504-1507.

Sir Robert D. of Lochleven, only s. & h.; suc. in 1513.

III. James, *Earl of Morton* [S.], s. & h.; d. s.p.m. 1553.

Sir George Douglas, of Pittendriech, br. to Archibald, 6th Earl of Angus [S.]

Thomas D., only s. & h. ap., d. v.p.

James (Hamilton), Earl of Arran [S.], **Regent of Scotland,** 1543; d. 1575.

Margaret, 1st da.

Robert (Maxwell) Lord Maxwell, [S.]

Beatrix, yst. da.

Elizabeth, 2d da.

IV. James Douglas *suc.* as *Earl of Morton* [S.] in 1553, **Regent of Scotland,** 1572. He d. s.p., being beheaded 1581.

David, 7th Earl of Angus [S.], s. & h., d. 1558.

Dukes of Hamilton [S.] descendants.

V. John, Lord Maxwell [S.], cr. 1581 *Earl of Morton* [S.]; deprived 1585; d. 1593.

VI. Archibald, 8th Earl of Angus [S.], only s. & h. He *suc.* as *Earl of Morton* [S.] in 1585. He d. s.p.m. 1588, when the *Earldom of Morton* reverted to the family of Douglas of Dalkeith & Lochleven.

Sir Robert D. of Lochleven, only s. & h., slain 1547.

John, Lord Maxwell [S.], s. & h., d. s.p. 1613.

Robert, Lord Maxwell [S.], cr. Earl of Nithsdale [S.] *with the precedency of 1581*, the date of *the Earldom of Morton* [S.], conferred on his late Father.

Earls of Nithsdale [S.] descendants.

VII. Sir William Douglas of Lochleven, s. & h., who, in 1588, *suc.* as *Earl of Morton* [S.]

Sir Robert Douglas, 2d son, who *jure uxoris* became Earl of Buchan [S.]

Earls of Morton [S.] descendants in the *male* line.

Earls of Buchan [S.] descendants in the *female* line.

Lordship of Dalkeith,(a) the Earldom of Morton in Dumfries-shire, &c., but the Earl (after the King's death in Dec. 1542) obtained an annullment thereof (as having been extorted from him) from the Court of Session, 29 March 1542,(b) and executed a regrant confirmed the same day by Royal charter, 22 April 1543, in favour of James Douglas, husband of Elizabeth, his second da., and the longest liver of them and their issue male, with rem. to David Douglas, br. of the said James,(c) and divers other remainders. The Earl *d.* s.p.m. in 1553.

IV. 1553, to 1581. *4.* JAMES (DOUGLAS), EARL OF MORTON, and LORD DALKEITH(d) [S.], husband (before 1543) of Elizabeth, second of the three daughters and coheirs of the last named Earl, which lady, who had long been insane, *d.* (seven years before him) Sep. 1574. He was yr. br. to David, EARL OF ANGUS [S.] (who *suc.* to that dignity in 1556), being s. of Sir George DOUGLAS, of Pittendriech, by Elizabeth, da. and h. of David DOUGLAS, of Pittendriech *afsd.* Since 1543 he was called "Master of Morton" till in 1553 he *suc. to that Earldom*, &c. [S.], his right thereto being confirmed by a grant of the "*Comitatus*," 2 June 1564, with divers *spec.* remainders, confirmed by act of Parl. 19 April 1567. His career, in which he took the side of the reformed religion and the English party, is a matter of Scotch history.(e) He was Lord Chancellor [S.], 1562-67, but, having taken a principal part in the murder of Rizzio (9 March 1566), was obliged to leave the Kingdom. He was, however, re-instated as Chancellor [S.] in the same year (1567), holding that office till 1572; was in command at the battle of Langside (13 May 1568), on the part of the infant King [S.]; was **Regent of Scotland**, 1572-78; Lord High Admiral [S.], 1578-81. His firm administration, however, had made him unpopular and (notwithstanding that he had obtained, 25 July 1578, the approbation of Parl. of all his acts) he was found guilty of high treason (*i.e.*, implication in the murder of Darnley, the King Consort), and was executed in the Grassmarket, Edinburgh, 2 June 1581, when his estates and *honors* became *forfeited*. He *d.* s.p. legit., and was *bur.* in the Grey Friars churchyard.

V. 1581, to 1585. *1.* JOHN (MAXWELL), LORD MAXWELL [S.], posthumous s. of Robert, LORD MAXWELL [S.], by Beatrix, yst. da. and coheir of James (DOUGLAS), 3d EARL OF MORTON [S.], *suc.* his elder br. as LORD MAXWELL [S.], between Sep. 1552 and Aug. 1553, and was, on the attainder and execution of his uncle (the husband of his mother's sister) James (DOUGLAS), 4th EARL OF MORTON next abovenamed, *cr.* by Royal charter, 5 June 1581(f) (ratified by Parl., 19 Nov. following), EARL OF MORTON

(a) Since that date (1540) the Barony of Dalkeith appears to have followed the Earldom of Morton.

(b) "Riddell, 1833," p. 122, note, and also "Riddell" [1842], pp. 6 and 44-46, where the power of the Court of Session and the territorial nature of the dignity are duly dwelt upon.

(c) Wood's "Douglas," vol. ii, p. 270, where, however, the order of the remainders differs somewhat from that in the Appendix of that work p. 667.

(d) See note "a" next above.

(e) Above 12 double columned and closely printed pages are devoted to it in the "*Nat. Biography*."

(f) See p. 275, note "e," *sub* "Maxwell," as to this creation. The date 1692 (which seems an error) is ascribed in "*Riddell*," p. 44, both to the creation and to the act of Privy Council, but Sir William Fraser (following Crawfurd) gives, 29 Jan. 1585/6, as the date of reversing the attainder of the Regent Earl, and adds, "neither by this act nor by any other was John, Lord Maxwell, deprived of the title of Earl of Morton." Accordingly Fraser speaks of his successor, John, Lord Maxwell, as the *2d Earl of Morton* (of the creation of 1581) saying, also, of Robert, Lord Maxwell, br. and h. of the last named John, that he had a restoration of all lands, dignities, &c., 5 Oct. 1618 (his br. having been attainted in 1613) and so "became Lord Maxwell and *3d Earl of Morton*," till *cr.* in substitution Earl of Nithsdale, quoting as authority the terms of the patent of 29 Aug. 1620, which conferred that Earldom [Fraser's "*Carlaverock*," I, 327.] This would entail two concurrent sets of Earls of Morton from 1585 to 1620, a theory which, tho' not impossible, is not very probable.

[S.], and sat in Parl. as such 30 Oct. 1581, to Dec. 1585, notwithstanding an act of Privy Council of that last named year, revoking the grant of 1581. The attainder of the late Earl was, however, formally reversed 29 Jan. 1585/6, when the *Earldom of Morton* reverted to the heir of entail, this grantee([a]) being thereafter known [only] as LORD MAXWELL [S.] See "MAXWELL" Barony [S.], *cr.* 1445 ? under the 7th Baron.

VI. 1586. 5. ARCHIBALD (DOUGLAS), EARL OF ANGUS, EARL OF MORTON, and LORD DALKEITH [S.], only s. and h. of David, EARL OF ANGUS [S.], by Margaret, or Elizabeth, da. of Sir John HAMILTON, which Earl David was elder br. of James (DOUGLAS), 4th EARL OF MORTON [S.], *suc.* his father in 1558 (when but 2 years old) as *Earl of Angus*, and by the act of indemnity of 1585, and letters of rehabilitation, 29 Jan. 1585/6, *suc.* his paternal uncle, the said Earl James, as *Earl of Morton*, &c., under the spec. rem. in the regrant (June 1564), of that dignity, which had been under attainder since 1581. He *d.* 1588, s.p.m.,([b]) when the *Earldom of Angus* devolved on his cousin and h. male. See fuller particulars under "ANGUS," Earldom [S.] The Earldom of Morton, however, devolved as below.

VII. 1588. 6. WILLIAM (DOUGLAS), EARL OF MORTON and LORD DALKEITH [S.], a distant cousin([c]) in the male line of the first three Earls, being first([d]) s. and h. of Sir Robert DOUGLAS, by Margaret, da. of John (ERSKINE), LORD ERSKINE [S.], which Robert, was only s. and h. of Thomas D. (who *d.* v.p.), only s. and h. of Sir Robert D. s. and h. of (another) Robert D. (slain at Flodden, 1513), 1st s. and h. of Sir Henry D. (living 1464), 1st s. and h. of Sir William D., 1st s. and h. of Sir Henry D. (living 1390), all being of Lochleven, which Sir Henry was yr. br. of Sir James Douglas, of Dalkeith and Aberdour, father of the 1st LORD DALKEITH [S.], and great grandfather of the 1st EARL OF MORTON [S.] He *suc.* his father (who was slain at the battle of Pinkie), 10 Sep. 1547, in the estate of Lochleven, being served heir in 1555. He was custodian of Queen Mary at Lochleven Castle in 1566. He, with his son Robert, was engaged in the raid of Ruthven, Aug. 1582, both obtaining remission of treason, 27 Dec. 1583. He *suc.* to the peerage [S.], in 1588, under the *spec. rem.* in the regrant, 2 June 1564, made to the 4th Earl, and the letters of rehabilitation, 29 Jan. 1585/6, which reversed the attainder of that Earl. His title was confirmed by act of Privy Council, 12 July 1592.([e]) He *m.* before 1565, Agnes, 1st da. of George (LESLIE), 4th EARL OF ROTHES [S.], by Margaret (one of his numerous wives), illegit. da. of William (CRICHTON), 3d LORD CRICHTON [S.] She was living 20 July 1589. He *d.* 24 Sep. 1606.

VIII. 1606. 7. WILLIAM (DOUGLAS), EARL OF MORTON, &c. [S.], grandson and h., being s. and h. of Robert DOUGLAS (sometimes([f]) called Master of Morton), by Jean, da. of John (LYON), LORD GLAMIS [S.], which Robert was s. and h. ap. of the late Earl, but *d.* v.p. March 1584 (being drowned off Holland) before his father had *suc.* to the peerage. He was *b.* 1582 ; was served heir

---

([a]) Robert, Lord Maxwell [S.], his son, was *cr.*, 20 Aug. 1620, Earl of Nithsdale, &c [S.], with the precedency of 29 Oct. 1581, *viz.*, the date of the creation of this Earldom of Morton.

([b]) In Burke's peerage for 1887 (downwards) it is stated that this Earl was *suc.* by an infant son, Earl of Angus and Morton, who *d.* 1588.

([c]) See tabular pedigree on p. 381, note "c."

([d]) The second son, Sir Robert Douglas, became *jure uxoris* Earl of Buchan [S.], being ancestor (in the female line) of the existing Earls of Buchan. The third son was the well known Sir George Douglas, who aided the escape of Queen Mary from Lochleven in 1567, and who was *by her* (according to Bishop Burnet in the MS. of his history) father of another George Douglas. See also "*N. and Q.*," 2d s., xi, 51.

([e]) Foster's peerage, 1883.

([f]) See a letter by "*Sigma*" in "*N. & Q.*" shewing that he was called "*Master of Morton*" as early as 1582 (when taken captive at Algiers) as well as at his death in 1584. It is possible that his father (tho' he did not legally succeed thereto till 1588) may have styled himself *Earl of Morton* soon after the death (1581) of the 4th Earl, there being then but one person (and he childless and an Earl of a more ancient creation) between him and the right of succession to that dignity.

of his father, 3 July 1605, and of his grandfather, 4 Nov. 1606. P.C. [S.]; a Gent. of the Bedchamber to James VI. [S.], and to Charles I.; High Treasurer [S.], 1630-35; Capt. of the Yeomen of the Guard, 1635; P.C. [E.]; el. K.G., 9 Nov. 1633, and inst. 21 April 1634; nom. in 1641 (but never elected), High Chancellor [S.] In his zeal for the Royal cause he, who before that time had been one of the richest and greatest nobles, alienated the family estate of Dalkeith and other lands of the annual value of £100,000 Scots, receiving in reward, the islands of Orkney and Zetland, 15 June 1643, subject to their redemption for £30,000 by the Crown. He was one of those who waited on the King at Newcastle in 1646. He *m.* Anne, 1st da. of George (KEITH), 5th EARL MARISCHAL [S.], by his first wife, Margaret, da. of Alexander (HOME) 5th LORD HOME [S.] He *d.* at Orkney, 7 Aug. 1648, in his 66th year.

IX. 1648. *8.* ROBERT (DOUGLAS), EARL OF MORTON, &c. [S.], *b.* before 1616; s. and h., *styled* LORD DALKEITH[a] till he *suc. to the peerage* [S.], 7 Aug. 1648; being served heir to his father, 29 March 1649. He *m.* Elizabeth, sister of William, 2d VISCOUNT GRANDISON [I.], da. of Sir Edward VILLIERS, by Barbara, da. of Sir John ST. JOHN. He *d.* in Orkney, late in 1649. His widow *d.* Dec. 1654.

X. 1649. *9.* WILLIAM (DOUGLAS), EARL OF MORTON, &c. [S.], s. and h., *suc. to the peerage* [S.], in 1649. He, in 1662, procured a new grant of the islands of Orkney and Zetland in trust for his family, but this and the former grant were afterwards held to be invalid and the islands were, by act of Parl., 27 Dec. 1669, annexed to the Crown. He *m.* 12 June 1662, at Holyrood House, Grizel, 1st da. of John (MIDDLETON), 1st EARL OF MIDDLETON [S.], by his first wife, Grizel, da. of Sir James DURHAM. She *d.* March 1666. He *d.* s.p.s. 1681.

[CHARLES DOUGLAS, *styled* LORD DALKEITH, s. and h. ap. He *d.* v.p. and unm.]

XI. 1681. *10.* JAMES (DOUGLAS), EARL OF MORTON, &c. [S.], uncle and h. He was *knighted*, 23 Sep. 1635 (by the Earl of Lindsey) on board the Royal ship "Marie Honor;" was a Gent. of the Privy Chamber to Charles I. He *suc. to the peerage* [S.] in 1681. He *m.* Anne, da. and coheir of Sir James HAY, 3d Bart. [S.], of Smithfield, by Grace, da. of the Rev. Thomas CLAVERING. He *d.* 1686. His widow was *bur.* 17 Feb. 1700. Funeral entry in Lyon office.

[CHARLES DOUGLAS, 1st s. and h. ap., *styled* "LORD ABERDOUR,[b] who perished at sea on his passage to Holland unmarried."[c]

XII. 1686. *11.* JAMES (DOUGLAS), EARL OF MORTON, &c. [S.], 2d but 1st surv. s. and h., *b.* about 1650; *suc. to the peerage* [S.] in 1686; was a supporter of the Revolution; P.C. to Queen Anne and one of the Commissioners for the Union [S.] which he vigorously supported. He obtained in 1707 an act of Parl. granting him the islands of Orkney and Zetland (formerly granted to his grandfather as afsd.), redeemable on payment of £30,000. He *d.* unm., 10 Dec. 1715. Funeral entry in Lyon office.

(a) In a charter of 9 Oct. 1616, he is called "Lord of Dalkeith, Master of Morton," and in a charter of 3 Nov. 1632, "Lord Dalkeith."

(b) It appears that soon after the alienation of the Dalkeith estate the designation of "Aberdour" (tho' not apparently a title of peerage) was adopted as the style of the heir apparent of this house (it being one of the estates held by them) in lieu of "Dalkeith."

(c) Wood's "Douglas."

XIII. 1715. *12.* ROBERT (DOUGLAS), EARL OF MORTON, &c. [S.], br. and h.; *suc. to the peerage* [S.], 10 Dec. 1715. He is said to have been "a man of parts, honour, and probity, peculiarly well versed in the knowledge of the antiquities of his country."(a) He *d.* unm. at Edinburgh, 22 Jan. 1730, and was *bur.* in the Abbey church there. Funeral entry in Lyon office.

XIV. 1730. *13.* GEORGE (DOUGLAS), EARL OF MORTON, &c. [S.], yst. and only surv. br. and h., *b.* 1662; was sometime in the army, rising to the rank of Colonel. He was M.P. for Kirkwall in the last Parl. of Scotland, 1702-07, supporting the Union [S.] and being subsequently M.P. [G.B.] for Wick Burghs, 1708-10; for Linlithgow Burghs (in two Parls.), 1708-13, and again, 1715-22, and for Orkney and Shetland, 1713-15, and again (in two Parls.), 1722, till he *suc. to the peerage* [S.] on 22 Jan. 1730. REP. PEER [S.], 1730-34; Vice Admiral [S.], 1733-38. He *m.* firstly (—), da. of (—) MUIRHEAD, of Linhouse, co. Edinburgh. He *m.* secondly, before 1702, Frances, da. of William ADDERLEY, of Halstow, co. Kent. He *d.* at Edinburgh, 4 Jan. 1738, in his 77th year, and was *bur.* in the Greyfriars there.

XV. 1738. *14.* JAMES (DOUGLAS), EARL OF MORTON, 1st surv. s. and h., by second wife; *b.* 1702 or 1703, was, apparently, *styled* LORD ABERDOUR,(b) 1730-38; *suc. to the peerage* [S.], 4 Jan. 1738, being "a nobleman of distinguished abilities as well as of eminent learning,"(c) K.T., 1738; REP. PEER [S.], 12 May 1739 till his death, some 30 years later. Being in France in 1746, he (with his wife and child) were (for some unavowed cause) imprisoned 3 months in the Bastile, but allowed to return to England, 3 May 1747. Lord Clerk Register [S.], 1760-67; a Trustee of the British Museum, and President of the Royal Society, 1764-68. By act of Parl, 1742, he obtained the absolute Lordship of Orkney and Zetland, but disposed of the same in 1766, for £63,000 to the Dundas family.(d) He *m.* firstly, before 1731, Agatha, da. and h. of James HALYBURTON, of Pitcur, co. Forfar. She *d.* in the Canongate Edinburgh, 11 Dec. 1748, and was *bur.* the 17th at the Abbey church, Holyrood. Funeral entry in Lyon office. He *m.* secondly, 31 July 1755, at her father's house, St. James' square, St. James' Westm., Bridget, 1st da. of Sir John HEATHCOTE, 2d Bart., of Normanton, co. Rutland, by Bridget, da. of John WHITE, of Wallingwells, Notts. He *d.* at Chiswick, Midx., 12 Oct. 1768, in his 66th year. Will pr. 1769. His widow, who survived him 37 years, *d.* 2 March 1805, aged 82, in Lower Brook street. Will pr. 1805.

XVI. 1768. *15.* SHOLTO CHARLES (DOUGLAS), EARL OF MORTON, &c. [S.], 2d(e) but 1st surv. s. and h., *b.* 1732; was, apparently, *styled* LORD ABERDOUR, 1738-68; raised a corps of Light Dragoons in 1759, of which he was Capt. Commandant; was one of the Lords of Police from 1760 till his death; *suc. to the peerage* [S.], 12 Oct. 1768. He *m.* 19 Nov. 1758, at Edinburgh, Katherine, 4th da. and coheir of the Hon. John HAMILTON (2d s. of Thomas, 6th EARL OF HADDINGTON [S.]), by Margaret, da. of Sir John HOME, Bart. [S.], of Blackadder. He *d.* 25 Sep. 1774, aged 42, at Taormina, in Sicily. Will pr. July 1775. His widow, who was *b.* Dec. 1736, *d.* 25 April 1823. Will pr. 1823.

(a) Wood's "Douglas." Macky, in his "*Characters*," says of him, when 55 years old, that he "is very fair, sanguine complexioned, well shaped, taller than the ordinary size; was zealous for the Revolution and always a follower of the Duke of Queensberry, of no great capacity but for the ladies, and hath been famous that way." With respect to this way (in which he was thus famous) see Luttrell's "*Diary*" (vol. v, 431), as to his trial in June 1704 "at the Old Bailey for a rape," of which, however, he was acquitted, "the prosecution being looked on as malicious."

(b) See p. 385, note "b."

(c) Wallace, 375, as quoted in Wood's "Douglas."

(d) Under the act for abolishing heritable jurisdictions in 1747 he obtained £7,147 for the office of Steward and Justiciar of Orkney and Zetland, besides £93 for the regality of Aberdour.

(e) Charles, his elder br., who was *b.* 7 April 1731, *d.* young, apparently before 1738 at which date his father *suc.* to the peerage.

XVII. 1774. *16.* GEORGE (DOUGLAS), EARL OF MORTON, &c. [S.], only s. and h., *b.* 3 April 1761; was, apparently *styled* LORD ABERDOUR,(a) 1768-74; *suc. to the peerage* [S.], 25 Sep. 1774. REP. PEER [S.], 1784-90, being *cr.* 11 Aug. 1791, BARON DOUGLAS OF LOCHLEVEN, co. Kinross [G.B.]; Chamberlain of the Household to the Queen Consort, 1792—1818; K.T., being invested (at St. James), 26 July 1797. Lord High Commissioner to the Kirk [S.], 1820-24; Lord Lieut. of Fifeshire, 1808-24, and of Midlothian 1824 till his death in 1827. Vice President of the Royal Society, F.S.A., &c. He *m.* 13 Aug. 1814, Susan Elizabeth, sister of John, 1st BARON CHURSTON, 1st da. of Sir Francis YARDE-BULLER, 2d Bart., by Elizabeth Lydia, da. and h. of John HOLLIDAY. He *d.* s.p., 17 July 1827, at Dalmahoy near Edinburgh, aged 66, when the *Barony of Douglas of Lochleven* became *extinct*. Will pr. Oct. 1827. His widow *m.* 17 Sep. 1831, at St. Geo. Han. sq., Edward GODFREY, of Old Hall, near East Bergholt, Suffolk, where she *d.* 23 July 1849, aged 56. Will pr. Dec. 1849.

XVIII. 1827. *17.* GEORGE SHOLTO (DOUGLAS), EARL OF MORTON, &c. [S.], cousin and h. being s. and h. of Lieut. Col. the Hon. John DOUGLAS, by Frances, 1st da of Edward (LASCELLES), 1st EARL OF HAREWOOD, which John (who *d.* 1 May 1818, in his 52d year), was second s. of James the (XVth), 14th Earl, being his only s. by Bridget, his second wife. He was *b.* 23 Dec. 1789, in London; ed. at Trin. Coll., Cambridge; M.A., 1810; Attaché at Madrid, 1811; Sec. of legations at Stockholm, 1812; at Florence, 1814; at Berlin, 1816-25; *suc. to the peerage* [S.], 17 July 1827; REP. PEER [S.], 1830-58; a Lord-in-Waiting, 1841-49, and from Feb. to Dec. 1852; Lieut. Col. of Midlothian Yeomanry Cavalry, 1843-44. He *m.* 3 July 1817, Frances Theodora, sister of Hugh Henry, BARON STRATHNAIRN, 1st da. of the Rt. Hon. Sir George Henry ROSE, G.C.H., by Frances, da. and coheir of Thomas DUNCOMBE, of Duncombe Park, co. York. He *d.* 31 March 1858, aged 68, at 47, Brook street, London. His widow, who was *b.* 31 Aug. 1798, *d.* 12 July 1879, at 45, Brook street, in her 81st year.

XIX. 1858. *18.* SHOLTO JOHN (DOUGLAS), EARL OF MORTON, &c. [S.], s. and h., *b.* 13 April 1818, at Berlin; *styled* LORD ABERDOUR,(a) 1827-58; sometime (1843-44) Lieut. 11th Hussars; Lieut. Col. of the Midlothian Yeomanry Cavalry, 1844-53, and Lieut. Col. Commandant, 1853-72; *suc. to the peerage* [S.], 31 March 1858; REP. PEER [S.], 1859-84. He *m.* firstly, 24 Jan. 1844, at Barnes, Helen, da. of James WATSON, of Saughton, co. Midlothian. She *d.* (as "*Lady Aberdour*"), 17 Dec. 1850, at Saughton afsd. He *m.* secondly, 7 July 1853, at St. James' Westm., Alice Anne Caroline, da. of John George (LAMBTON), 1st EARL OF DURHAM, by his second wife, Louisa Elizabeth, da. of Charles (GREY), 2d EARL GREY. He *d.* 24 Dec. 1884, aged 66, at Dalmahoy afsd. His widow, who was *b.* 16 April 1831, and who was Lady of the Bedchamber to the Princess of Wales, 1863, living 1893.

XX. 1884. *19.* SHOLTO GEORGE WATSON (DOUGLAS), EARL OF MORTON [1458] and LORD DALKEITH [1430 ?] in the peerage of Scotland, only s. and h.; *b.* 5 Nov. 1844 at Dalmahoy afsd.; *styled* LORD ABERDOUR,(a) 1858-84; ed. at Trin. Coll. Cambridge; *suc. to the peerage* [S.], 24 Dec. 1884; REP PEER [S.], since 1886. He *m.* 25 July 1877, at St. Mark's, North Audley Street, Helen Geraldine Maria, 4th da. of Charles Frederick Ashley Cooper (PONSONBY) 2d BARON DE MAULEY OF CANFORD, by Maria Jane Elizabeth, da. of John William (PONSONBY), 4th EARL OF BESSBOROUGH [I]. She was *b.* 12 Dec. 1852.

[SHOLTO CHARLES DOUGLAS, *styled* LORD ABERDOUR,(a) 1st s. and h. ap.; *b.* 4 Dec. 1878.]

Family Estates.—These, in 1883, consisted of 49,214 acres in Argyllshire (worth but £1,870 a year); 10,411 in Midlothian (worth £14,763 a year); 2,551 in Berwickshire; 1,644 in Fifeshire and 91 in Linlithgowshire; besides 650 (worth £1,080 a year) in Leicestershire. *Total* 65,161 acres, worth £22,288 a year. *Principal Residences.* Dalmahoy, near Wilkieston, co. Midlothian; Aberdour Castle, co. Fife; Conaglen House, near Ardour, co. Argyll, and Loddington Hall, co. Leicester.

(a) See p. 385, note "b."

MORVEN.

i.e., "INVERARY, MULL, MORVEN AND TIRIE," Barony [S.] (*Campbell*), *cr.* 1701 with the DUKEDOM OF ARGYLL [S.], which see.

---

i.e., "MELDRUM OF MORVEN, co. Aberdeen," Barony (*Gordon*), *cr.* 1815; see "HUNTLY" Marquessate (S.), *cr.* 1599, *sub* the 9th Marquess, who, when EARL OF ABOYNE [S.], obtained, in 1815, this Barony.

MORVILL.

Barony by Writ.

I. 1319, to 1320.

1. NICHOLAS DE MORVILL (of whom Dugdale gives no account) was sum. to parl. as a Baron (LORD MORVILL) by writs dat. 6 Nov. (1319) 13 Ed. II. and 5 Aug. (1320) 14 Ed. II. but never after. Nothing more is known of him.

MOSSTOWN.

i.e., "NEWCOMEN OF MOSSTOWN," Barony [I.] (*Newcomen*), *cr.* 1800; see "NEWCOMEN" Viscountcy [I.], *cr.* 1803; both *ex.* 1825.

MOSTYN.

Barony.

I. 1831.

1. SIR EDWARD-PRYCE LLOYD, Bart., s. and h. of Bell LLOYD, of Bodfach, co. Montgomery, by Anne, da. and h. of Edward PRYCE, of Bodfach afsd., which Bell (who *d.* 6 May 1793, aged 63) was only s. and h. of William LLOYD, of Pontryffwyd, co. Flint (who *d.* 1730) elder br. of Sir Edward Lloyd, 1st Bart. (so *cr.* May 1778 with *a spec. rem.* in favour of his said brother's issue) was *b.* 17 Sep. 1768 and *suc.* his said great uncle as second Baronet, 26 May 1795; was M.P. for the Flint burghs, 1806 to 1831, save when he was (1808-12) M.P. for Beaumaris, and was sometime Sheriff for the counties of Flint, Carnarvon and Merioneth. Having *m.* 11 Feb. 1794, Elizabeth, sister and coheir of Sir Thomas MOSTYN, 6th Bart. of Mostyn, co. Flint (at whose death, 7 April 1831, aged 44 that Baronetcy (*cr.* 1660), became *extinct*) da. of Sir Roger MOSTYN, 5th Bart. by Margaret, da. and h. of the Rev. Hugh WYNNE, LL.D., Prebendary of Salisbury, he was *cr.* 10 Sep. 1831[a] BARON MOSTYN of Mostyn, co. Flint. His wife *d.* 26 Nov. 1842. Admon. May 1856. He *d.* at Pengwern, near St. Asaph, 3 April 1854 in his 86th year. Admon. Nov. 1854.

II. 1854. *2.* EDWARD MOSTYN (LORD MOSTYN, *formerly* LLOYD), BARON MOSTYN, s. and h.; *b.* at Mostyn afsd., 13 Jan. 1795; took by Royal lic., 9 May 1831, for himself and issue the name of *Mostyn*, after that of *Lloyd*, in compliance with the will of his maternal uncle, Sir Thomas MOSTYN, Bart., abovenamed, whose estate of Mostyn he inherited; was M.P. for Flintshire, 1831-37, and 1841-42; for Lichfield, 1846-47, and for Flintshire (again) 1847-54; Lord Lieut. of Merionethshire, 1840-84; *suc. to the peerage*, 3 April 1854; Vice Admiral of North Wales, 1854-84. He *m.* 20 June 1827, at St. Geo. Han. sq., Harriet Margaret, 1st da. of Thomas (SCOTT), 2d EARL OF CLONMELL [I.], by Henrietta Louisa, da. of George (GREVILLE), 2d EARL BROOKE and EARL OF WARWICK. He *d.* at Mostyn afsd., 17 March 1884, aged 89. His widow, who was *b.* 2 Dec. 1805, *d.* 27 May (or 3 June), 1891, at Richmond, Surrey, and was *bur.* at Llanrhos.

III. 1884. *3.* LLEWELYN NEVILL VAUGHAN (LLOYD-MOSTYN), BARON MOSTYN [1831], and a Baronet [1778], grandson and h., being s. and h. of the Hon. Thomas Edward LLOYD-MOSTYN, by Henrietta Augusta, 2d da. of

(a) This was one of the coronation peerages of William IV., for a list of which see vol. ii, p. 312, note "a," *sub* "Cloncurry."

William (NEVILL), 4th EARL OF ABERGAVENNY, which Thomas Edward, who was s. and h. ap. of the 2d Baron, *d.* v.p. 8 May 1861, aged 31. He was *b.* 7 April 1856; ed. at Eton; was sometime Lieut. 3d Norfolk Regiment; *suc. to the peerage,* 17 March 1884. He *m.* 1 May 1879, Mary Florence Edith, sister of Robert Bermingham (CLEMENTS), 4th EARL OF LEITRIM [I.], 7th and yst. da. of Rev. the Hon. Francis Nathaniel CLEMENTS, by Charlotte, da. of the Rev. Gilbert KING. She was *b.* 1 May 1857.

Family Estates—These, in 1883, were under 2,000 acres. *Principal Residence,* Mostyn, near Holywell, co. Flint, and Gloddaeth Hall, near Llandudno.

MOTE.

See "CROFTON OF MOTE, co. Roscommon," Barony [I.], *cr.* 1797.

---

i.e., "MARSHAM OF THE MOTE, co. Kent," Viscountcy (*Marsham*), *cr.* 1801 with the EARLDOM OF ROMNEY, which see.

MOUNSLOW.

See "LYTTELTON OF MOUNSLOW, co. Salop," Barony (*Lyttelton*), *cr.* 1641; *ex.* 1645.

MOUNTAGU, see MONTAGU.

MOUNT-ALEXANDER.

Earldom [I.]
I. 1661.

1. HUGH (MONTGOMERY), VISCOUNT MONTGOMERY OF GREAT ARDS, co. Down [I.], s. and h. of Hugh, 2d VISCOUNT MONTGOMERY OF GREAT ARDS [I.], by Jean, da. of William (ALEXANDER), 1st EARL OF STIRLING [S.], was *b.* about 1622; *suc. to the said peerage* [I.] (a dignity *cr.* 3 May 1622), in 1642, and, having been a great sufferer in the Royal cause during the Civil wars, was at the Restoration *cr.*, 18 July 1661, EARL OF MOUNT-ALEXANDER [I.].[a] He *m.* firstly in Dec. 1648 Mary, sister of Henry (MOORE), 1st EARL OF DROGHEDA [I.], first da. of Charles, 3d VISCOUNT MOORE OF DROGHEDA [I.], by Alice, da. of Adam (LOFTUS), 1st VISCOUNT LOFTUS OF ELY [I.] She was *b.* 1631 and was living 1650. He *m.* secondly Catharine, widow of Sir William PARSONS, Bart., da. of Arthur (JONES), 2d VISCOUNT RANELAGH [I.], by Catharine, da. of Richard (BOYLE), 1st EARL OF CORK [I.]

II. 1680? *2.* HUGH (MONTGOMERY), EARL OF MOUNT-ALEXANDER, &c. [I.], s. and h. by first wife; *b.* 1650; *suc. to the peerage* [I.] about 1680, having been since 1661 *styled* VISCOUNT MONTGOMERY. He was Master of the Ordnance and a Brigadier General; one of the Chief Governors of Ireland (as Lords Justices) 1702-04. He *m.* firstly in 1672 Catharine, 1st da. of Carey (DILLON), 6th EARL OF ROSCOMMON [I.], by Catharine, da. of John WERDEN. She *d.* 26 and was *bur.* 27 Jan. 1674, at St. Michan's, Dublin. He *m.* secondly Eleanor, da. of Maurice (BERKELEY), 3d VISCOUNT FITZHARDINGE [I.], by Anne, da. of Sir Henry LEE, 1st Bart. He *d.* s.p.s. before Sep. 1714.

III. 1710? *3.* HENRY (MONTGOMERY), EARL OF MOUNT-ALEXANDER, &c. [I.], br. of the whole blood and h.; *suc. to the peerage* [I.] before Sep. 1714, at which date he was made P.C. [I.] He *m.* in 1672 Mary, da. of William (ST. LAWRENCE), 12th LORD HOWTH [I.], by Elizabeth, da. and coheir of Nicholas (ST. LAWRENCE), 11th LORD HOWTH [I.] She *d.* suddenly, 26 Aug. 1705. He *d.* 12 Feb. 1716/7.

(a) The title seems to have been chosen in compliment to his maternal family of Alexander.

IV. 1717. 4. HUGH (MONTGOMERY), EARL OF MOUNT-ALEXANDER, &c. [I.], s. and h.; *suc. to the peerage* [I.] in Feb. 1716/7, having formerly been *styled* VISCOUNT MONTGOMERY. He *m.* in 1703 Elinor, da. of Sir Patrick BARNEWALL, 3d Bart. [I.], of Crickstown, co. Meath, by Frances, da. of Richard BUTLER, of Kilcash. He *d.* s.p., 27 Feb. 1744/5, in Ireland.

V. 1745, to 1757. 5. THOMAS (MONTGOMERY), EARL OF MOUNT ALEXANDER [1661] and VISCOUNT MONTGOMERY OF GREAT ARDS [1622] in the peerage of Ireland, br. and h. *suc to the peerage* [I.] 27 Feb. 1744/5. He *m.* Mary Angelica, da. of (—) DELACHEROIS, of Lisburn. He *d.* s.p. 7 April 1757 in Ireland, when *all his honours* became *extinct.* The Dow. Countess (probably his but possibly his brother's widow) *m.* 5 Oct. 1759 ([a]) Richard MOUNTENEY, second Baron of the Court of Exchequer [I.], and *d.* July 1771 in Ireland.

MOUNTALT, see MONTALT.

MOUNTCASHELL.

THE HON. JUSTIN MACCARTY, 3d and yst. s. of Donough, 1st EARL OF CLANCARTY [I.] by Eleanor, sister of James, DUKE OF ORMONDE, da. of Thomas BUTLER, *styled* VISCOUNT THURLES, served in the French army, but was recalled to England in 1678: was in high command in Ireland under James II., by whom he was *cr.* 23 May 1689 ([b]) (after that King's exclusion from the throne of *England* [11 Dec. 1688] but when he was in full possession of all his Royal rights as King of *Ireland*) BARON CASTLEINCH, and VISCOUNT MOUNTCASHELL, both in the co. of Tipperary [I.] ([c]). He was however defeated and taken prisoner 31 July 1689 at Newtown Butler, but escaped in Dec. following, and was afterwards in command of an Irish regiment in France. He *m.* Arabella 2d and yst. da. of Thomas (WENTWORTH), 1st EARL OF STAFFORD, by his 2d wife Arabella, da. of John (HOLLES), EARL OF CLARE. He *d.* s.p. 21 July 1694 at the baths at Barèges, when *all his honours* became *extinct.*

MOUNTCASHELL.

Viscountcy and Barony [I.] I. 1706. 1. SIR PAUL DAVYS, of St. Catherine's, co. Dublin, s. and h. of Sir John DAVYS, of Thomastown, in that county, Clerk of the Privy Council [I.], *suc.* his father about 1684; was High Sheriff for co. Dublin, 1700, and, having *m.* Catherine, da. of Callaghan (MACCARTY), 3d EARL OF CLANCARTY [I.], by Elizabeth, da. of George (FITZGERALD), EARL OF KILDARE [I.] (which Callaghan, was elder br. of Justin MACCARTY, *cr.* VISCOUNT MOUNTCASHELL [I.], by James II. in 1689 [after his dethronement] as abovestated) was himself *cr.*, 31 Jan. 1705/6, VISCOUNT and BARON MOUNTCASHELL, co. Tipperary [I.] He *d.* 5 Aug. 1716. His widow was *bur.* 19 April 1738, at St. Audoen's, Dublin.

([a]) See "*N. and Q.*" 2[d] S. xii, 254. Mounteney's first wife was *bur.* 8 April 1756 at Donnybrook.

([b]) This is one of the seven Irish peerages so created, all of which were duly inserted on the patent rolls [I.], from which they have never been erased. See vol. i, p. 59, note "b," *sub* "Albemarle" for an account of these and other *Jacobite* creations.

([c]) "Early in May 1689 he was *cr.* Lord Viscount Mountcashel and Baron of Castleinchy and was introduced with that title on the second day of the meeting of of the Parl. of Dublin, to the House of Peers." See Dalton's "*King James's Irish Army List*, 1689," where there is a good account of this "*Colonel Justin Macarty*" and his Regiment of Infantry.

II. 1716. 2. JAMES (DAVYS), VISCOUNT AND BARON MOUNTCASHELL [I.], s. and h.; *suc. to the peerage* [I.], 5 Aug. 1716. He died aged 9 years, 10 March 1718/9, and was *bur.* at St. Audoen's afsd.

III. 1719, to 1736. 3. EDWARD (DAVYS), VISCOUNT AND BARON MOUNTCASHELL [I.], br. and h., *b.* 1711, at St. Catherine's afsd.; ed. at Trin. Coll., Dublin; B.A., 1730. He *d.* unm. at St. Catherine's, 30 July 1736, aged 25, and was *bur.* 1 Aug. at St. Audoen's, when *all his honours* became *extinct.*

Viscountcy [I.] IV. 1766. 1. STEPHEN MOORE, of Kilworth, co. Cork, only s. and h. of Richard MOORE, sometime M.P. for Clonmel, by Elizabeth, first da. of William (Ponsonby), 1st VISCOUNT DUNCANNON [I.], was *b.* about 1695; *suc.* his father (who *d.* v.p.) in 1701, and his grandfather, Stephen MOORE, of Kilworth afsd., a few years later; was M.P. for Tipperary, 1738-60, and was *cr.* 14 July 1764, BARON KILWORTH OF MOORE PARK, co. Cork [I.], being subsequently *cr.* 22 Jan. 1766, VISCOUNT MOUNTCASHELL of the city of Cashell, co. Tipperary [I.] He *m.* in or before 1725, Alicia, sister and heir of Robert COLVILL, da. of Hugh COLVILL, who was s. and h. of the Rt. Hon. Robert COLVILL, of Newtown, co. Down. She *d.* (before her husband's elevation to the peerage), 10 Aug. 1762, aged 62, at Moore Park, co. Cork. He *d.* 1 March, 1766, aged about 70, at Moore Park afsd., a few months after his creation as a Viscount.

V. 1766. Earldom [I.] I 1781. 2 and 1. STEPHEN (MOORE), VISCOUNT MOUNTCASHELL, &c. [I.], 2d but 1st surv. s. and h.(a) *b.* 25 July 1730; M.P. for Lismore, 1761-66; *suc. to the peerage* [I.], 1 March 1766, taking his seat 1 May following. He was *cr.* 5 Jan. 1781, EARL(b) MOUNTCASHELL [I.] He *m.* 8 June 1769, Helena, 2d da. of John (RAWDON), 1st EARL OF MOIRA [I.], by Helena, da. of John (PERCEVAL), 1st EARL OF EGMONT [I.] He *d.* 14 May 1790, in his 60th year. His widow, who was *b.* in London, 27 March 1744, *d.* 3 June 1792.

Earldom [I.] II. Viscountcy [I.] VI. 1790. 2 and 3. STEPHEN (MOORE), EARL MOUNTCASHELL, &c. [I.], s. and h., *b.* 19 March 1770; *styled* LORD KILWORTH, 1781-90; M.P. for Clonmel till he *suc.* to the peerage [I.], 14 May 1790; REP. PEER [I.], 1815-22. He *m.* 12 Sep. 1791, Margaret Jane, 1st da. of Robert (KING), 2d EARL OF KINGSTON [I.], by Caroline, da. of Richard FITZ GERALD. He *d.* 27 Oct. 1822, aged 52, at Moore Park afsd. His widow, *m.* George William TIGHE, and *d.* abroad 29 Jan. 1835. Will pr. April 1835.

Earldom [I.] III. Viscountcy [I.] VII. 1822. 3 and 4. STEPHEN (MOORE), EARL MOUNTCASHELL, &c. [I.], s. and h., *b* 20 May 1792 in St. Stephen's Green, Dublin; *styled* LORD KILWORTH till 1822; ed. at Trin. Coll., Cambridge; M.A., 1812; *suc. to the peerage* [I.], 27 Oct. 1822; REP. PEER [I.], 1826-83; F.R.S., &c. He *m.* 31 May 1819, at St. Marylebone (this marriage being recited in another marriage of the same parties, 20 April 1823 by spec. lic. at 8 Duke street, in the parish of St. James' Westm.), Anna Maria, da. of Samuel WYSS, of the Canton of Berne, Switzerland. She *d.* at Moore Park afsd., 4 July 1876, in her 84th year. He *d.* in Oxford terrace, Paddington, 10 Oct. 1883, aged 91, having had a seat in the House of Lords for 57 years.(c) Will pr. at Cork, and in London at £30 6s. 6d.

(a) His elder br. Richard Moore (*b.* 15 Dec. 1725), was M.P. for Clonmel in 1761 but *d.* unm. 29 Sep. in that year, at Moore Park afsd.

(b) See vol. ii, p. 102, note "a," *sub* "Cadogan."

(c) In point of age, if not in point of standing (the Earl of Chichester, who *d.* March 1886, aged 81, *suc.* to his peerage in July 1826), he was probably its oldest member. He is said (when between 84 and 90) to have been engaged to marry a Miss Kennedy.

Earldom [I.] IV. Viscountcy [I]. VIII. 1883.

4 and 5. STEPHEN (MOORE), EARL MOUNT-CASHELL, &c. [I.], s. and h., b. 11 March 1826, at Moore Park afsd.; *styled* LORD KILWORTH till 1883; ed. at Eton; sometime Lieut. in the Rifle Brigade; High Sheriff for co. Cork, 1849; *suc. to the peerage* [I.], 10 Oct. 1883. Having long been a lunatic (an inmate of the Brislington Asylum, near Bristol), he *d.* unm., 9 Nov. 1889, aged 64, at Moore Park afsd., and was *bur.* at Kilworth.

Earldom [I] V. Viscountcy [I.] IX. 1889.

5 and 6. CHARLES WILLIAM (MORE, *formerly* MORE-SMYTH and *previously* MOORE), EARL MOUNTCASHELL [1781], VISCOUNT MOUNTCASHELL [1766], and BARON KILWORTH [1764], in the peerage of Ireland, br. and h.; *b.* 17 Oct. 1826; ed. at Eton. Having *m.* firstly, 18 Jan. 1848, Charlotte Mary, only child of Richard SMYTH, of Ballynatray, co. Waterford, by Harriet, da. of Hayes (ST. LEGER), 2d VISCOUNT DONERAILE [I.], he by Royal lic., 7 July 1858, took the name of *Smyth* after his patronymic of *Moore* but relinquished it in 1889 and assumed the name of *More*. He was High Sheriff of co. Waterford (as "More-Smyth") in 1862. His said wife *d.* 17 Jan. 1892. He *m.* secondly, 25 Oct. 1892, at Dublin, Agnes, widow of Sir Edward Porter COWAN, da. of Andrew COWAN, of Glenghana, co. Down.

[CLAUDE-STEPHEN-WILLIAM-RICHARD MOORE-SMYTH, *styled* LORD KILWORTH, grandson and h. ap., being only s. and h. of Richard Charles MOORE-SMYTH, by Helen Stirling, da. of the Rev. William MAKELLAR, of Edinburgh, which Richard Charles was only s. and h. ap. of the above Earl (by his first wife) but *d.* v.p. 3 Jan. 1888, aged 28, before his father's succession to the peerage, and but 16 days after the birth of his said son. He was *b.* 19 Dec. 1887, but *d.* an infant, 1 Oct. 1890, in his 3d year, at 8 Charlotte street, Edinburgh.]

Family Estates.—These, in 1883, consisted of 5,961 acres in co. Cork and 6,383 in co. Tipperary, of which latter the value of 6,000 acres thereof (being set down in the tenant's name and the rental not mentioned) was unstated. Total 12,344 acres, of which the value of 6,344 (part thereof) was £3,725 a year. *Principal Residence*; Moore Park, near Kilworth, co. Cork.

MOUNTCASTLE or MOUNTCASTELL.

i.e., "PAISLEY, HAMILTON, MOUNTCASTELL AND KILPATRICK" Barony [S.] (*Hamilton*), *cr.* 1606 with the EARLDOM OF ABERCORN [S.], which see.

i.e., MOUNTCASTLE, co. Tyrone," Barony [I.], (*Hamilton*), *cr.* 1701 with the VISCOUNTCY OF STRABANE [I.]; see "ABERCORN" Earldom [S.], *cr.* 1606, *sub* the 6th Earl.

MOUNT-CHARLES.

See "CONYNGHAM OF MOUNT-CHARLES, co. Donegal," Barony [I.], (*Conyngham*), *cr.* 1753; *ex.* 1781; also Viscountcy [I.], *cr.* 1756; *ex.* 1781; also Earldom [I.], *cr.* and *ex.* in 1781; and also Barony [I.], *cr.* 1781 with a *spec. rem.*; also Viscountcy [I.], *cr.* 1789.

i.e., "MOUNT-CHARLES," Viscountcy [I.], (*Conyngham*), *cr.* 1797 with the EARLDOM OF CONYNGHAM [I.]; also Earldom [I.], *cr.* 1816 with the MARQUESSATE OF CONYNGHAM [I., under which last creation see.

MOUNT-CRAWFORD.

i.e., "MOUNT-CRAWFORD," Viscountcy [S.], (*Crawford*, alias *Lindsay-Crawford*), *cr.* 1703, the designation being however changed in the same year to that of "GARNOCK," which see.

MOUNTEAGLE, see MONTEAGLE.

MOUNT-EARL.

i.e., "MOUNT-EARL," Viscountcy [I.], (*Quin*), *cr.* 1816: also "DUNRAVEN AND MOUNT-EARL" Earldom [I.], *cr.* 1822: under which last creation see.

MOUNT EDGCUMBE, MOUNT EDGCUMBE AND VALLETORT, and EDGCUMBE OF MOUNT EDGCUMBE.

Barony. I. 1742.

1. RICHARD EDGCUMBE, of Mount Edgcumbe, co. Devon, and of Cotele, co. Cornwall, 3d and yst., but eventually only surv. s. and h. of Sir Richard EDGCUMBE K.B., of the same, by Anne, da. of Edward (MONTAGU), 1st EARL OF SANDWICH, was *b.* at Mount Edgcumbe, and *bap.* 23 April 1680; *suc.* his elder br. Piers EDGCUMBE, in the family estates in 1694; was ed. at Trin. Coll., Cambridge; M.A., 1698; was M.P. for St. Germans, 1701-02, and for Plympton, 1702-42; was a Lord of the Treasury, 1716-17, and 1720-24; Paymaster General [I.], 1724-42; P.C. [I.], 1734, and, having had the management of the Cornish Boroughs for the Prime Minister Walpole, was (on Walpole's fall), *cr.* 20 April 1742, BARON EDGCUMBE OF MOUNT EDGCUMBE, co. Devon; Lord Lieut. of Cornwall, 1742; Chancellor of the Duchy of Lancaster, 1743-58; P.C., 1744; was one of the 12 noblemen commissioned to raise a regiment in 1745 (during the insurrection) of which he was consequently Colonel; Major Gen., 1755; Chief Justice in Eyre, North of Trent, 1758. He *m.* 12 March 1715, Matilda, da. of Sir Henry FURNESE, 1st Bart., of Waldershare, co. Kent, Alderman of London, by his second wife, Matilda, da. of Sir Robert VERNON. She *d.* 9 March 1721, and was *bur.* at Waldershare, He *d.* 22. Nov. 1758, aged 78. Will dat. 11 Sep. 1756, pr. 28 Dec. 1758.

II. 1758.

2. RICHARD (EDGCUMBE), BARON EDGCUMBE OF MOUNT EDGCUMBE, 1st s. and h.; *b.* 2 and *bap.* 12 Aug. 1716, at St. Martins in the fields; entered the army, becoming finally, 1755, Major General; was M.P. for Plympton, 1742-47; for Lostwithiel, 1747-54; and for Penrhyn, 1754-58; a Lord of Trade, 1754-55; a Lord of the Admiralty, 1755-56; Comptroller of the Household, 1756-61; P.C., 1756; *suc. to the peerage.* 22 Nov. 1758; Lord Lieut. of Cornwall, 1759. He *d.* unm. 10 May 1761,(a) and was *bur.* at Maker, co. Devon.

III. 1761. Viscountcy. I. 1781. Earldom. I. 1789.

3 and *1.* GEORGE (EDGCUMBE), BARON EDGCUMBE OF MOUNT EDGCUMBE br. and h.; *b.* 3 March 1720, and *bap.* 5 May 1721 at St. Martins afsd.; entered the Navy (serving under Hawke and Boscawen) in which he finally, 1782, became Admiral of the White; Clerk of the Council of the Duchy of Lancaster, 1747-62; *suc. to the peerage* 10 May 1761. Lord Lieut. of Cornwall, 1761; Treasurer of the Household, 1765-66; P.C., 1765; Commander in Chief at Plymouth, 1765-71; Joint Vice Treasurer [I.], 1770-72 and 1784-93; Capt. of the Gent. Pensioners, 1772-82; D.C.L., Oxford, 2 July 1773. He was *cr.* 5 March 1781,(b) VISCOUNT MOUNT EDGCUMBE AND VALLETORT, co. Devon, being *cr.* 31 Aug. 1789, EARL OF MOUNT EDGCUMBE, co. Devon. Vice Admiral of Cornwall, 1782; F.R.S., F.S.A., &c. He *m.* 16 Aug. 1761, at her Father's house at Twickenham, Midx., Emma, only child of John GILBERT, Archbishop of York (who *d.* but 3 days afterwards), by Margaret, sister of Philip, 2d EARL OF HARBOROUGH, da. of the Hon. Philip SHERARD. He *d.* 4 Feb. 1795 in his 74th year. Will pr. March 1795. His widow, who was *b.* 28 July 1729, *d.* 26 Dec. 1807 in Upper Grosvenor street.

(a) There is a good account of his career in the "*Nat. Biogr.*" where it is said that "Dick Edgcumbe, for so he was invariably called, was one of the choicest spirits of his time. He was the close friend of Horace Walpole, George Selwyn, &c., but he threw away his life at the gambling table." Reynolds painted in 1760 the portrait of his mistress, afterwards Lady Fenouilhet.

(b) This is said to have been in compensation of damage done to his woods at Mount Edgcumbe, by the repairing of the fortifications at Plymouth.

Earldom, &c., II. Barony, IV. } 1795. *2 and 4.* RICHARD (EDGCUMBE), EARL OF MOUNT EDGCUMBE, &c., only s. and h.; *b.* 13 and *bap.* 14 Sep. 1764 at Putney, Surrey; baptism reg. at St. Geo., Han. Sq.; ed. at Harrow and at Ch. Ch., Oxford: *styled* VISCOUNT VALLETORT, 1789-95; M.P. for Lostwithiel, 1790-91; for Fowey, 1791-95; D.C.L. of Oxford, 4 July 1793; *suc. to the peerage* 4 Feb. 1795; Lord Lieut. and Vice Admiral of Cornwall, 1795; Capt. of the Gent-Pensioners, 1808-12; P.C., 1808; Sewer at the coronation, 19 July 1821; F.R.S., &c. He *m.* 21 Feb. 1789,[a] at St. Geo., Han. sq., Sophia, 3d da. and coheir of John (HOBART), 2d EARL OF BUCKINGHAMSHIRE, by his first wife Mary Anne, da. and coheir of Sir Thomas DRURY, Bart. She, who was *b.* 5 April 1768, *d.* 17 Aug. 1806 at Tunbridge Wells.[b]. He *d.* 26 Sep. 1839 aged 75 at Richmond Hill and was *bur.* 3 Oct. at Petersham, Surrey. Will pr. Oct. 1840.

[WILLIAM RICHARD EDGCUMBE, *styled* VISCOUNT VALLETORT, 1st s. and h. ap., *b.* 19 Nov. 1794. He *d.* unm. and v.p., 29 Oct. 1818 at Mount Edgcumbe.]

Earldom, &c., III. Barony, V. } 1839. *3 and 5.* ERNEST AUGUSTUS (EDGCUMBE), EARL OF MOUNT EDGCUMBE, &c., 2d but 1st surviv. s. and h.; *b.* 23 March 1797, at Richmond Hill; sometime, 1814-19, an officer in the 1st Reg. of Foot guards receiving the Waterloo medal in 1816: *styled* VISCOUNT VALLETORT, 1818-39; M.P. for Fowey, 1819-26 and for Lostwithiel, 1826-32; Militia aide-de-camp to King William IV., with rank of Colonel, 1830; Vice Chamberlain to the Queen Consort, Adelaide, at her coronation, 8 Sep. 1831; Militia aide de camp to Queen Victoria, 1837; *suc. to the peerage*, 26 Sep. 1839. Spec. Dep. Warden of the Stannaries, 1852. He *m.* 3 Dec. 1831, at Bowood, Carolina Augusta, 1st da. and coheir of Rear Admiral Charles FEILDING, by Elizabeth Theresa, da. of Henry Thomas (FOX-STRANGWAYS), 2nd EARL OF ILCHESTER. He *d.* 3 Sep. 1861 aged 64, in his yacht off Erith. His widow was sometime a Lady of the bedchamber, and, from 1854 an extra Lady thereof. She, was V.A. (2d class), and *d.* 2 Nov. 1881 aged 73, at Saltram, near Plymouth.

Earldom, &c. IV. Barony. VI. } 1861. *4 and 6.* WILLIAM HENRY (EDGCUMBE), EARL OF MOUNT EDGCUMBE [1789], VISCOUNT MOUNT EDGCUMBE AND VALLETORT [1781], and BARON EDGCUMBE OF MOUNT EDGCUMBE [1742], 1st s. and h.; *b.* 5 Nov. 1832, in Sackville street; *styled* VISCOUNT VALLETORT, 1839-61; ed. at Harrow and at Ch. Ch., Oxford; extra Equerry to the Prince of Wales, 1858; M.P. for Plymouth, 1859-61; *suc. to the peerage*, 3 Sep. 1861; a Lord of the Bedchamber to the Prince of Wales, 1862 to 1866 when he became an extra Lord thereof to 1879; *cr.* D.C.L. of Oxford, 16 June 1863; Lord Lieut. of Cornwall, 1877; P.C., 1879; Lord Chamberlain of the Household, 1879-80; a Councillor of the Duchy of Cornwall, 1882; Lord Steward of the Household, June 1885 to Feb. 1886, and Aug. 1886 to 1892; A.D.C. to the Queen, 1887. He *m.* 26 Oct. 1858, at St. James' place, Westm., Katherine Elizabeth, 4th da. of James (HAMILTON), 1st DUKE OF ABERCORN [I.], by Louisa Jane, da. of John (RUSSELL), 6th DUKE OF BEDFORD. She, who was *b.* 9 Jany. 1840, *d.* 3 Sep. 1874, at Mount Edgcumbe, aged 34.

(a) Madᵉ D'Arblay says of him in 1789 (*Diary* vol. v., p. 59), "He is a most neat little beau, and his face has the roses and lilies as finely blended as that of his pretty young wife."

(b) Lord Chief Justice Kenyon in 1796 alludes to the evil doings of three Peeresses of that date, *viz.*, (1) Albinia, Countess of Buckinghamshire; (2) the Countess of Mount Edgcumbe; and (3) the Lady Archer. They kept "*faro*" tables, at which the young men were (it was popularly supposed) very considerably fleeced. They were, accordingly, wittily caricatured as *Pharaoh's* daughters.

[PIERS-ALEXANDER-HAMILTON EDGCUMBE, *styled* VISCOUNT VALLETORT, only s. and h. ap.; *b.* 2 July 1865].

Family Estates.—These, in 1883, consisted of 13,288 acres in Cornwall, and 4,935 in Devon. *Total* 18,223 acres worth £24,181 a year. *Principal residence.* Mount Edgcumbe, near Devonport, Devon.

MOUNTFLORENCE, OF FLORENCE COURT.

Barony [I.]
I. 1760.

1. JOHN COLE, of Florence Court, co. Fermanagh, s. and h. of John COLE, of the same, many years M.P. for Enniskillen, by his first wife, Florence, da. of Sir Bourchier WREY, 3d Bart. of Trebitch, co. Cornwall, was *b.* 13 Oct. 1709; *suc. his father* July 1726; was sheriff of co. Fermanagh, 1732, being M.P. for Enniskillen from 1730 till he was *cr.* 8 Sep. 1760, BARON MOUNTFLORENCE OF FLORENCE COURT, co. Fermanagh [I.], being introduced 22 Oct. 1761. He *m.* in Oct. 1728, Elizabeth, 1st da. of Hugh Willoughby MONTGOMERY, of Carrow, co. Fermanagh. He *d.* in Ireland 30 Nov. 1767. His widow *d.* at Bath, April 1771.

II. 1767. *2.* WILLIAM WILLOUGHBY (COLE), BARON MOUNTFLORENCE OF FLORENCE COURT (I.), s. and h.; *b.* 1736. He was *cr.* 20 July 1776, VISCOUNT ENNISKILLEN, co. Fermanagh [I.], and subsequently, 18 Aug. 1789, EARL OF ENNISKILLEN [I.]; see that title.

MOUNTFORT, see MONTFORT.

MOUNTGARRET.(a)

Viscountcy [I.]
I. 1550.

1. THE HON. SIR RICHARD BUTLER, 2d s. of Pierce (BUTLER), EARL OF ORMONDE AND OSSORY [I.], by Margaret, da. of GERALD (FITZ GERALD), 8th EARL OF KILDARE [I.], having been *knighted*, was, for his "many great services to the crown of England," *cr.*(b) by King Edward VI., 23 Oct. 1550, VISCOUNT MOUNTGARRET,(a) co. Wexford [I.], and (according to some) BARON OF KELLS [I.] He was Keeper of Ferns Castle, and was present in Parl. [I.], 12 Jan. 1559/60. He *m.* firstly, Eleanor, da. of Theobald BUTLER, of Nechum, co. Kilkenny. He *m.* secondly, Catharine, da. and h. of Peter BARNEWALL, of Stackallan, co. Meath. He *m.* thirdly, in 1541, Anne, da. of John (PLUNKETT), 5th LORD KILLEEN [I.], by his first wife Margaret, da. of William (PRESTON), 2d VISCOUNT GORMANSTON [I.] She, however, was *divorced* that same year.(c) He *d.* 20 Dec. 1571, and was *bur.* at St. Canice, Kilkenny. M.I.

II. 1571. *2.* EDMUND (BUTLER), VISCOUNT MOUNTGARRET [I.], 1st s. and h., by first wife. He was M.P. for co. Carlow, 1559; *suc. to the peerage* [I.], 20 Dec. 1571, and sat in the Parl. [I.], of 1585. He distinguished himself against the rebel Irish of the Pale. He *m.* Grany, da. of Barnaby (Fitzpatrick), 1st BARON OF UPPER OSSORY [I.], by his first wife, Margaret, da. of Pierce (BUTLER), EARL OF ORMONDE AND OSSORY [I.] He *d.* 24 Nov. 1602, and was *bur.* at St. Canice afsd.

(a) "In the records this name is variously written, as *Monkegarret*, *Montegarrete*, and in the patent of creation *Montegarret*" [*Lodge*, vol. iv, p. 23]. It is possible that the name alludes to the grantee's maternal descent from the noble family of Fitz Gerald, Garret and Gerald being synonomous.

(b) The preamble is given in "Lodge," vol. iv, p. 23, in it he is described as "Richardus Butler, Miles, filius secundo genitus Petri Butler, Militis, nuper Comitis Ormond et Ossory defuncti."

(c) She *m.* William Fleming.

III. 1602. 3. RICHARD (BUTLER), VISCOUNT MOUNTGARRET [I.], 1st s. and h. He, in 1599, joined the rebellion of (his father in law), the Earl of Tyrone [I.] He *suc. to the peerage* [I.], 24 Nov. 1602, being then aged 24, and sat in the Parls. [I.], of 1613, 1615, and 1634. He was Gov. of co. Kilkenny during the Irish rebellion of 1641, which cause he favoured, but was defeated at Kilrush, 10 April 1642, by the Earl of Ormonde [I.] He was President of the Supreme Council formed in 1642, at Kilkenny, and continued to act as General of the Irish in the civil war. He *m.* firstly, before 1599, Margaret, da. of Hugh (O'NEILL), EARL OF TYRONE [I.], by his second wife, Judith, da. of Manus O'DONNELL. He *m.* secondly Thomazine (afterwards(a) Elizabeth), da. of Sir William ANDREWS, of Newport Pagnell, Bucks. She *d.* s.p. 1625. He *m.* thirdly Margaret, widow of Sir Thomas SPENCER, Bart., of Yarnton, Oxon, da. of Richard BRANTHWAITE, Serjeant at Law. He *d.* 1651, and was *bur.* at St. Canice afsd. M.I. By Cromwell's act, 12 Aug. 1652, he was (tho' dead) excepted from pardon. His widow *d.* at St. Giles in the fields, 16 and was *bur.* 21 Dec. 1656, at Yarnton afsd. Will pr. 1657.

IV. 1651. 4. EDMUND (BUTLER), VISCOUNT MOUNTGARRET [I.], called "*Roe*," 1st s. and h. by first wife. He lived at Bally Roe, co. Kilkenny, joined his Father in the proceedings of 1641 and was Gov. of Kilkenny in 1646. He *suc. to the peerage* [I.] in 1651. He was Capt. in the army of Charles II. when in exile, from whom he on 12 Dec. 1660, received pardon for all insurrections, &c. He was one of the Roman Catholic nobles(b) who in 1663 presented a remonstrance to the King. He *m.* firstly Dorothy, 2d da. of Mervyn (TOUCHET), 2d EARL OF CASTLEHAVEN [I.], by his first wife, Elizabeth, da. of Benedict BARNHAM. She *d.* at Park's Grove, near Ballyragget, 10 and was *bur.* 11 Feb. 1634 at St. Canice afsd. He *m.* secondly, in 1637, Elizabeth widow of William CONYERS, da. of Sir George SIMEON, of Brightwell, Oxon, by his first wife, Mary, sister and coheir of Henry (VAUX), 5th LORD VAUX OF HARROWDEN. She *d.* 18 Feb. 1673 and was *bur.* at St. Michan's, Dublin.(c) He *d.* "oppressed with age and infirmities," 1679. Will dat. 13 Oct. 1673 to 28 June 1678, pr. at Dublin 24 June 1679.

V. 1679. 5. RICHARD (BUTLER), VISCOUNT MOUNTGARRET [I.], s. and h., by first wife, served sometime as a Capt. in the French army; *suc. to the peerage* [I.] in 1679 and was Capt. of Horse in the Irish army of James II in 1689, leading the forlorn hope against Londonderry, where he was taken prisoner and outlawed. He claimed his seat in Parl. [I.], 29 Oct. 1692, but refusing to take the oath of supremacy was, under a resolution of the House of Lords [I.], of 19 Oct. 1698, struck out of the roll thereof. He *m.* firstly Emilia da. of William BLUNDELL, of Crosby, co. Lancaster by Anna, da. of Sir Thomas HAGGERSTON, 1st Bart. He *m.* secondly, Margaret, widow of Gilbert BUTLER, da. of Richard SHEE, of Shee's Court. He *d.* Feb. 1706.

VI. 1706. 6. EDMUND (BUTLER), VISCOUNT MOUNTGARRET [I.], s. and h. by first wife, *suc. to the peerage* [I.], Feb. 1706. By resolution of the House of Lords [I.], 16 Dec. 1715, his name was inserted among the list of Peers, the outlawries of 1641 being declared to have been reversed, &c. He accordingly on 9 Oct. 1721 took the oath of allegiance and his seat. He *m.* firstly (—) da. of (—) BUCHANAN, of Londonderry. He *m.* secondly Elizabeth, widow of Oliver GRACE (who *d.* 8 June 1708), da. of John BRYAN, of Bawnmore, co. Kilkenny, by his second wife Ursula, da. and coheir of Walter WALSH, of Castle Hoel in that county. He *d.* in Dublin 25 July 1735 and was *bur.* at St. Canice afsd. His widow *d.* in London, 18 June 1736, and was *bur.* at St. Giles in the fields.

(a) She, "at her confirmation took the name of Elizabeth and was so called in 1619." [*Ulsters office* as quoted in "Lodge" vol. iv, p. 66].

(b) See their names in vol. ii, p. 149, note "d," *sub* "Carlingford."

(c) In favour of her descendant and heir of line, George Charles Mostyn, (whose mother, Maria Lucinda, was da. and h. of George Butler, of Ballyragget) the abeyance of the Barony of Vaux of Harrowden was terminated in (the halcyon time, 1838-41, for such terminations) 1838. See vol. i, p. 288 note "b," *sub* "Beaumont."

VII. 1735. *7.* RICHARD (BUTLER), VISCOUNT MOUNTGARRET [I.], s. and h. by first wife; *suc. to the peerage* [I.], 25 July, and took his seat, 7 Oct. 1735. He *m.*, 19 Oct. 1711, Catherine, sister of Charles O'NEILL, of Edenduffecarrick or Shane's Castle, co. Antrim. He *d.* s.p. in Dublin, 14 May 1736, and was *bur.* at St. George's in that city. His widow *d.* 15 April 1739, and was *bur.* at St. Michan's, Dublin.

VIII. 1736. *8.* JAMES (BUTLER), VISCOUNT MOUNTGARRET [I.], br. and h. He served in the army of the Emperor of Germany and distinguished himself in the campaign on the Rhine in 1735. He *suc. to the peerage* [I.], 14 May 1736. He *m.*, Jan. 1736, Margaret, 2d da. of John (BARNEWALL), 11th BARON TRIMLESTOWN [I.], by Margaret, da. of Sir John BARNEWALL, of Crickston. He *d.* suddenly and s.p., 13 May 1742.

IX. 1742. *9.* EDMUND (BUTLER), VISCOUNT MOUNTGARRET [I.], only surv. br. and h., who conformed to the established church, 7 Nov. 1736; *suc. to the peerage* [I.], 13 May 1742. and took his seat, 10 Oct. 1749. He *m.* Anne, 1st da. of Major Toby PURCELL, of Ballymartin and Cloghpooke, co. Kilkenny. He *d.* 6 March 1750. His widow *d.* June 1764.

X. 1750. *10.* EDMUND (BUTLER), VISCOUNT MOUNTGARRET [I.], only s. and h.; Barrister at Law, 25 Nov. 1749; *suc. to the peerage* [I.], 6 March 1750, and took his seat, 11 Nov. 1751. He *m.* in 1744 Charlotte, 1st da. of Sir Simon BRADSTREET, 1st Bart. [I.], by (—), sister of Samuel BRADSTREET, of Tinnicully, co. Kilkenny. She *d.* in Paris, 27 March 1778, and was *bur.* at Barony church, near Ballyconra, co. Kilkenny. He *d.* 9 Feb. 1779, and was *bur.* there. Will pr. Feb. 1780.

XI. 1779. *11.* EDMUND (BUTLER), VISCOUNT MOUNTGARRET [I.], 1st s. and h.; *b.* 27 July 1745; M.P. for co. Kilkenny, 1776-79; *suc. to the peerage* [I.], 9 Feb., and took his seat, 26 Nov. 1779. He *m.*, 7 Oct. 1768, Henrietta, 2d and yst. da. of Somerset Hamilton (BUTLER), 1st EARL OF CARRICK [I.], by Juliana, da. of Henry (BOYLE), 1st EARL OF SHANNON [I.] She, who was *b.* 15 Aug. 1750, *d.* 20 June 1785. He *d.* 16 July 1793, in his 48th year.

XII. 1793. *12.* EDMUND (BUTLER), VISCOUNT MOUNTGARRET [I.], 1st s. and h.. *b.* 6 Jany. 1771 and bap. at St. Marylebone; *suc. to the peerage* [I.], 16 July 1793, being, a few months later, *cr.* 20 Dec. 1793, EARL OF KILKENNY [I.]. He *m.* 8 June 1793, Mildred, 1st da. of Robert FOWLER, Archbishop of Dublin (1779-1801), by Mildred, 1st da of William DEALTRY, of Gainsborough, co. Lincoln. She *d.* 30 Dec. 1830. He *d.* s.p. 16 July 1846 aged 75 at Ballyconra, co. Kilkenny when the *Earldom of Kilkenny* [I.], became *extinct.*

XIII. 1846. *13.* HENRY EDMUND (BUTLER), VISCOUNT MOUNTGARRET and (according to some) BARON OF KELLS [I. 1550], nephew and h., being only s. and h. of the Hon. Henry BUTLER, of Linton, co. York, by Anne, yst. da. and coheir of John HARRISON, of Newton House, co. York, which Henry (who *d.* 6 Dec. 1842 aged 69) was 3d s. of the 11th Viscount. He was *b.* 20 Feb. 1816 at Linton Spring, near Weatherby; mat. at Oxford (Worc. Coll.) 7 June 1834; B.A., 1839; *suc. to the peerage* [I.] 16 July 1846. He *m.* 11 March 1844, at St. Geo., Han. sq., Frances Penelope,(a) only child of Thomas RAWSON, of Nidd Hall, co. York, by Frances Penelope, 3rd da. of John PLUMBE-TEMPEST, of Tong Hall, in that county. She who was *b.* 1825 *d.* 19 Oct. 1866, at 77 South Audley street.

Family Estates. These, in 1883, consisted of 14,073 acres in co. Kilkenny, and 505 in co. Wexford, besides 120 in the West Riding of Yorkshire. *Total* 14,698 acres, worth £9,606 a year. *Principal Residence.* Ballyconra, near Kilkenny, co. Kilkenny.

The Estates of Miss Rawson (of Nidd Hall, near Ripley, co. York, in 1883), which, since 1891, have devolved on the family were, 7,604 acres in Yorkshire; 1,307 in Herefordshire and 160 in Lancashire. *Total* 9,071 acres worth £12,045 a year.

(a) On the death of her aunt, Miss Rawson of Nidd Hall, in 1891, Lord Mountgarret inherited personalty to the amount of £561,300, his son inheriting the large real estate of the Rawson family.

MOUNTGOMERY, see MONTGOMERY.

MOUNTHERMER, see MONTHERMER.

MOUNTJOY, or MONTJOY.

Barony. I. 1465. 1. SIR WALTER BLOUNT, of Elvaston, co. Derby (a family noted for its Lancastrian allegiance), was s. and h. of Sir Thomas BLOUNT,(a) of the same, Treasurer of Normandy, by his first wife, Margaret, da. of Sir Thomas GRESLEY; *suc.* his father in 1456; was Treasurer for Calais, 1460; K.B. at the Coronation of Edward IV., 27 Jan. 1461, and fought for that King at Towton, 29 March 1461. From King Edward he received many of the estates forfeited by the Earls of Devon and other Lancastrians. He was LORD HIGH TREASURER, 1465 to 1466, being *cr.* 20 June 1465,(b) BARON MOUNTJOY(c); el. K.G., 24 April 1472. He *m.* firstly about 1440, Helena, da.

(a) In a most accurate and erudite work, by F. M. Nichols, F.S.A., entitled "*The Hall of Lawford Hall*" will be found a good account of this branch of the Blount family, who inherited Lawford from the family of Saye.

(b) This was one of the 16 Baronies, which were granted *by patent* before the reign of Henry VIII. See a list thereof, vol. iii, p. 31, note "e," *sub* "Daubeny."

(c) The title is so spelt in the patent. There is no addition of the territorial designation "of Thurvaston co. Derby" (as is generally supposed) tho' an annuity of 20 marks, some of which were out of the manor of Thurvaston, was added.

Mr. J. Horace Round sends the following curious extract from a peerage claim in 1597. "Are not the Viscountcy of Montagu and the Eardom of Rivers *in France?* the Barony of Mountjoy *in Spain?* and yet all these Peers of *our* Parliament." According to the following statement, however, "Mountjoy" is more *French* than Spanish. "*Mont-joie St. Denis*," was "a famous French war cry in the middle ages, and *Montjoye* is the title of the chief Herald of France, corresponding to our *Garter*. Both the war cry and the heraldic title doubtless refer to some victory, which was commemorated by the casting up of a mound of earth or a great heap of stones [*Mont-joie*] a practise of the highest antiquity. In charters the name was written indifferently *De monte gaudii*, and *De monte Jovis*" [Lower's "*Family names*."]

"This creation" (remarks Mr. F. M. Nichols in his "*Lawford Hall*," see note "a" above) supplies one of the earliest examples of the grant of a Baronial title, not being of a territorial character, nor the title of a dignity before existing; the creation of a new Barony with a title distinct from the family name, having been itself an innovation of the 15th century. The first examples of a title so borne seems to have been Sir John Cornwall, *cr.* a Baron by pat. 10 Hen. VI. with the express addition of the name and title of Baron of Fanhope, and who tho' his summons was addressed *Johanni Cornewayll, Chivaler* is called in the rolls of Parl., *le Sir de Faunhope*. This was apparently a territorial title. The nearest precedents for the Mountjoy title were those of (1) Sir James Fenys *cr.* in Parl. 1447 *Baron Say of Seale*, being a descendant but not heir of the older Lords Say, and (2) Sir Richard Widevile *cr.* by patent in the following year *Lord Rivers*. This title was also assumed to be that of an ancient Barony, since among the seignories granted with the dignity were those of *the Baronies of Rivers and Ledet*, under the latter [of which] the ancient Barony of Widevile had been held."

"The name of *Montjoie* adopted by Sir Walter Blount from the surname of a maternal ancestor must have carried with it some chivalric associations to the ears of those who had taken part in the French wars, while the family name, both in its original form of *Le Blond* and in its English form of *Blunt*, may have appeared of a homely cast. The title of *Mountjoy* (so spelt in the patent of creation) appears to have been originally prounced in the French fashion the *t* not being heard. In later times the English pronunciation probably became more common. The seal of the first Lord bore this inscription, *Sigillum Walteri Domini Monjoy filii et heredis Thome Blount quondam thesurarii Normannie*."

It is however very possible that the name was in honour of the family of Mountjoy, in Derbyshire, the heiress of whom (Isolda, da. and h. of Sir Thomas de Mountjoy) *m.* the Great Grandfather of the grantee, who, tho' he did not descend from that match, is said to have inherited her estates.

of Sir John Byron, of Clayton, co. Lancaster, by Margaret, da. of John Booth, of Barton, in that county. She was *bur.* at Elvaston afsd. He *m.* secondly in 1467 Anne, Dow. Duchess of Buckingham, da. of Ralph (Nevill), 1st Earl of Westmorland, by his second wife, Lady Joane Beaufort, the legitimated da. of John (Plantagenet, styled "*of Gaunt*") Duke of Lancaster. He *d.* 1 Aug. 1474, and was *bur.* in the Grey Friars, London.(a) M.I. Will dat. 8 July 1474, pr. 10 Feb. 1474/5. His widow, by whom he had no issue, *d.* 20 Sep. 1480, and was *bur.* at Plesby, co. Essex. Her will, without date, pr. 31 Oct. 1480.

II. 1474. *2.* Edward (Blount), Baron Mountjoy, grandson and h., being 2d but only surv. s. and h. of Sir William Blount, by Margaret, da. and h. of Sir Thomas Echingham, of Midley, co. Kent, which William, was s. and h. ap. of the late Lord, but *d.* v.p., being slain at the battle of Barnet, 14 April 1471. He was aged but 7 when he *suc. to the peerage*, 1 Aug. 1474, and *d.* shortly afterwards, before 30 Oct. 1475, being *bur.* in the Grey Friars afsd.(b)

III. 1475. *3.* John (Blount), Baron Mountjoy, uncle and h. male, aged 30 when he *suc. to the peerage*. He was Governor of Guisnes and Hamme near Calais from 1476 to 1485; K.B., 17 Jan. 1478. He *m.* in or before 1477, Lora, da. of Sir Edward Berkeley, of Beverstone Castle, co. Glouc., by Christina, da. and h. of Richard Holt. He *d.* 12 and was *bur.* 14 Oct. 1485, at Grey Friars afsd. Will dat. 6 Oct., and pr. 22 Nov. 1485. *Inq. post mortem* (Wigorn), 20 April and (Leicester), 7 Aug. 1486. His widow *m.* Sir Thomas Montgomery, of Falkbourne, co. Essex, K.G., who *d.* 11 Jan. 1495. She *m.* thirdly before 9 March 1497, when she was aged 30 and upwards (as his second wife) Thomas (Butler), 7th Earl of Ormonde [I.], who *d.* s.p.m., 8 Aug. 1515, but she predeceased him and was *bur.* (with her second husband) in New Abbey.

IV. 1485. *4.* William (Blount), Baron Mountjoy, s. and h.; *b.* at Barton Blount, co. Derby, about 1478, being aged 7 when he *suc. to the peerage* in Oct. 1485. He was the pupil and friend of Erasmus, who calls him "*inter Nobiles doctissimus.*" He was P.C. to Henry VII.; K.B. at the coronation, 23 June 1509, of Henry VIII.; Master of the Mint, 1509-24; Chamberlain to Catherine, the Queen Consort, 1512-33, having, as such, to announce to her (in July 1533) the King's resolution to divorce her; Governor of Tournay, 1514-17; el. K.G., 24 April and inst. 6 May 1526; signed in 1533 the letter to the Pope, urging the divorce of the King.(c) He *m.* firstly about Easter 1497 Elizabeth, one of the two daughters and coheirs of Sir William Say, of Essendon, Herts, and Lawford, co. Essex by his second wife Elizabeth, widow of Sir Thomas Waldegrave, (who *d.* 28 April 1472), 1st da. and coheir of Sir John Fray, Chief Baron of the Exchequer, She *d.* s.p.m. before 21 July 1506 and was *bur.* at Essendon.(d) He *m.* secondly, before 30 July 1509, Agnes de Venegas, a Spanish Lady in the court of Katharine, the Queen Consort. She *d.* s.p. He *m.* thirdly before 5 Feb. 1515, Alice, widow of William Browne, Lord Mayor of London (who *d.* during office, 3 June 1513), da. of Henry Keble of St. Mary Aldermary, sometime (1510-11) Lord Mayor of London. She *d.* 7 June 1521 and was *bur.* at the Grey Friars. He *m.* fourthly before 4 Nov. 1523, Dorothy, Dow. Baroness Willoughby de Broke, da. of Thomas (Grey), 1st Marquess of Dorset by Cicely, *suo jure* Baroness Harington and Bonvile. He *d.*

(a) He received, in 1467, part of the forfeited lands of the Earl of Devon in Devonshire and Cornwall, which property (says Mr. F. M. Nichols), "appears to have reverted to the Courtenay family on the restoration of the Earldom of Devon in 1485." See p. 398, note "a."

(b) Anne, the eldest of his two sisters and coheirs, *m.* Andrews (Windsor), Lord Windsor, and was ancestress of Thomas (Hickman Windsor), 1st Viscount Windsor [I.], who was *cr.* in 1712 *Baron Mountjoy* of the Isle of Wight.

(c) In 1527 Lord Mountjoy was assessed, for the subsidy, at £1,000, a sum exceeded by only three or four other noblemen.

(d) Of her two daughters and coheirs (1) Gertrude, *m.* Henry (Courtenay), Marquess of Exeter, and (2) Mary, *m.* Henry (Bourchier), Earl of Essex.

at Sutton on the Hill, co. Derby, 8 Nov. 1534, and was *bur.* at Barton Blount. Will dat. 13 Oct. 1534, pr. 11 Feb. 1535/6, Dorothy, his widow, renouncing. Her will pr. 1553-54.

V. 1534. 5. CHARLES (BLOUNT), BARON MOUNTJOY, s. and h.; by third wife, *b.* at Tournay in France, 28 June 1516 and *suc. to the peerage* 8 Nov. 1534. He was in the expedition against the French in 1544. The magnificent style he affected at Court greatly diminished the family estates and resources. He *m.* about Aug. 1530, Anne, da. of Robert (WILLOUGHBY), 2d LORD WILLOUGHBY de BROKE, by his second wife (her husband's step mother abovenamed) Dorothy, da. of Thomas (GREY) 1st MARQUESS OF DORSET. He *d.* 14 Oct. 1544 and was *bur.* (with his maternal grandfather) at St. Mary Aldermary afsd. Will pr. 1544.

VI. 1544. 6. JAMES (BLOUNT), BARON MOUNTJOY, s. and h., *suc. to the peerage*, when a minor, 14 Oct. 1544. He was K.B. at the coronation of Queen Mary 28 Sep. 1553; was Lord Lieut. of Dorsetshire in 1559 and was one of the peers who sat on the trial (1572) of the Duke of Norfolk. He expended large sums of money in alchemical experiments. He *m.* about 1558, Catherine, da. of Sir Thomas LEIGH, D.C.L., of St. Oswald's, co. York. She was *bur.* 25 June 1576, from St. Leonard's, Shoreditch, at the Grey Friars. He *d.* about 1581. Admon. 9 Nov. 1581, to his son.

VII. 1581. 7. WILLIAM (BLOUNT), BARON MOUNTJOY, s. and h., *suc. to the peerage* in 1581 and, by his prodigality, much reduced the family property. He *d.* unm. in his 36th year at the Bishop of London's house by St. Paul's and was *bur.* thence, 23 July 1594, at St. Mary's, Aldermary.(a) Admon. as "late of Brooke, co. Wilts, but decd. at St. Botolph's, Aldersgate, London," 16 July 1594.

VIII. 1594, to 1606. 8. CHARLES (BLOUNT), BARON MOUNTJOY, br. and h., *b.* 1563; ed. at Oxford, where he was *cr.* M.A., 16 June 1589; M.P. for St. Ives, 1584-85; for Beeralston, 1586-87, and 1592-93; *knighted* (by the Earl of Leicester), 7 Dec. 1587, in Holland; *suc. to the peerage* in July 1594; el. K.G., 23 April, and inst., 24 May 1597. In 1599 he was made General of the army in Ireland and was VICEROY [I.] as "Lord Deputy" from 1600 to 1603, and as "Lord Lieutenant" from 1603, having during that period subjugated the great Irish rebellion under the Earl of Tyrone. He was (in reward thereof), *cr.*, 21 July 1603,(b) EARL OF DEVONSHIRE;(c) P.C., 1603; Master of the Ordnance, 1603; Capt. of the town of Portsmouth, 1604; Joint Lord Lieut. of Hants, 1604; Joint Commissioner for the office of Earl Marshal, 1604. He went thro' the ceremony of marriage, 26 Dec. 1605,(d) at Wanstead House, Essex, with

---

(a) Registers of St. Gregory's, London. He is elsewhere said to be *bur.* 27 July 1594, at Trinity Minories.

(b) One of three Earldoms which (with eight Baronies) were conferred that day. See list thereof in vol. iii, p. 113, note "c," *sub* "Devonshire."

(c) The words in the creation are "*Comes Devon.*" See vol. iii, p. 113, note "d," *sub* "Devonshire." The Earl mentions in his will his lands in the counties of Devon, Somerset, Dorset, Southampton, Worcester, Northampton, and Leicester.

(d) The officiating minister was his Chaplain, William Laud, afterwards Archbishop of Canterbury, who, however, "in his defence alledged that he was ignorant that the lady was the wife of Lord Rich" [Croke's "*Croke family originally Le Blount,*" vol. ii, p. 239], and repeatedly refers to it as "*my cross.*"

Penelope,[a] who had obtained an ecclesiastical divorce (*a mensa et thoro*) 15 Nov. 1605, from Robert (RICH), LORD RICH (afterwards, in 1618, *cr.* EARL OF WARWICK), da. of Walter (DEVEREUX), 1st EARL OF ESSEX, by Lettice, da. of Sir Francis KNOLLYS, K.G. He did not, however, long survive this incident, but *d.* s.p. legit.,[b] 3 April 1606, at Savoy House, in the Strand, of inflammation of the lungs, aged 43. At his death *all his honours* became *extinct.*[c] Will dat. 2 April and pr. 3 June 1606. The lady is said to have *d.* the next year.

MOUNTJOY OF MOUNTJOY FORT [*Ireland*] and MOUNTJOY OF THURVESTON [*England*].

Barony [I.], I. 1618. Barony [E.], I. 1627.

1. MOUNTJOY BLOUNT, eldest of the three illegit. sons[b] of CHARLES (BLOUNT), EARL OF DEVONSHIRE and BARON MOUNTJOY, by Penelope, da. of Walter (DEVEREUX), 1st EARL OF ESSEX, abovenamed, was *b.* about 1597; *suc.* to Wanstead, co. Essex and other portions of his Father's estates on his death (s.p. legit.) 3 April 1606 and was *cr.* 31 Jan. 1617/8, LORD MOUNTJOY, BARON OF MOUNTJOY FORT,[d] co. Tyrone (I.), being, some ten years later, *cr.* 5 June 1627, BARON MOUNTJOY OF THURVESTON, co. Derby, with a special clause of precedency[e] over all Barons (the *all* being, however, but *two, i.e.*, Fauconberg and Lovelace) *cr.* since 20 May last. This precedence however was on 24 April 1628 reported against by the Lords' committee for privileges.[f] Accordingly the King *cr.* the grantee, 3 Aug. 1628, EARL OF NEWPORT in the Isle of Wight. See that title, which, with this Barony, became *extinct* in 1681.

(a) This prolific lady, *b.* in 1560, was in 1580 *m.* "against her will to Lord Rich," and between that date "and the spring of 1583 when [Sir Philip] Sidney himself married, was guilty of a criminal intimacy with [him] her former lover. A few years after Sidney's death, in 1586, Mountjoy appears to have *suc.* to his place in Lady Rich's affections. By her husband she had seven children but after 1590 she became Mountjoy's mistress and bore him three sons and two daughters." [*Nat. Biog.*]

(b) The names of the (bastard) children of the Earl of Devonshire are given in his will dat. 2 April 1606 (in which is also mentioned the child his wife now "goeth with") in the following order (1) Mountjoy (2) St. Johns (3) Charles (4) Penelope and (5) Isabella. They are also mentioned in a scarce and frequently cancelled page (p. 493) in Milles's "*Catalogue of Honour*" (folio 1,610) where it is stated that the Earl *d.* 1606 "without any issue lawfully begotten. Naturall children which he had by Penelope, da. to Walter Devereux, Earle of Essex, and sister to Robert, Earle of Essex, she being wife to Robert, Baron Rich [1] Charles [2] Montjoy [3] Saint Johns [4] Elizabeth and [5] another daughter."

(c) A claim to the Barony of Mountjoy (presumably as heir male collateral) is said to have been made in 1606 by the family of Blount, of Mapledurham, Oxon, as descendants of Sir Thomas Blount, yr. br. of the 1st Baron Mountjoy.

(d) Mountjoy Fort had been erected by his Father when Chief Governor of Ireland.

(e) "Quod prædictus Baro Mountjoy et heredes sui masculi prædicti de cet'o impertuum habebunt capient et tenebunt in omnibus locis et omni de causa, locum et precedentiam præ omnibus aliis baronibus quibuscunque hujus regni [illegible] per nos post vicesimum diem Maii jam ultimum preteritum factis sive creatis aliquo in presentibus contento, aut aliqua alia re causa vel materia quacunque in contrarium in aliquo, non obstante." [See "*Creations*, 1483—1646" in ap. 47th Rep. D. K. Pub. Records].

(f) See account of this and similar proceedings, as to the precedency of Peers in Parl. by royal warrant, in vol. i, p. 229 note "a," *sub* "Banbury."

MOUNTJOY OF THE ISLE OF WIGHT.

Barony.
I. 1712.

1. THOMAS (HICKMAN-WINDSOR), VISCOUNT WINDSOR OF BLACKCASTLE [I.], who was so *cr.* 19 July 1699, was *cr.* 1 Jan. 1711/2(a) BARON MOUNTJOY(b) of the Isle of Wight. He *d.* 1738.

II. 1738, to 1758.

2. HERBERT (HICKMAN-WINDSOR), VISCOUNT WINDSOR OF BLACKCASTLE [I.], also BARON MOUNTJOY, of the Isle of Wight, only *s.* and h.; *b.* 1707; *d.* s.p. 1758.

For fuller particulars see "Windsor of Blackcastle," Viscountcy [I.], *cr.* 1699; *ex.* 1758.

Viscountcy.
I. 1796.

1. JOHN (STUART), EARL OF BUTE [S.], who *suc.* his father in that dignity, 10 March 1792, having *m.*, 1 Nov. 1766, Charlotte Jane, 1st da. and coheir (eventually sole heir) of Herbert (HICKMAN-WINDSOR), 2d VISCOUNT WINDSOR OF BLACKCASTLE [I.], and BARON MOUNTJOY abovenamed, was *cr.*, 21 March 1796, VISCOUNT MOUNTJOY of the Isle of Wight, EARL OF WINDSOR, and MARQUESS OF THE COUNTY OF BUTE. See "BUTE" Marquessate, *cr.* 1796.

MOUNTJOY, CO. TYRONE [*Ireland.*]

Viscountcy [I.]
I. 1683.

1. SIR WILLIAM STEWART, Bart. [I.], of Ramalton, co. Donegal, *s.* and h. of Sir Alexander STEWART, 2d Bart. [I.], by Catharine, da. of Sir Robert NEWCOMEN, Bart. [I.], *suc.* his father in the Baronetcy (*cr.* 2 May 1623), 3 Sep. 1653, and was *cr.*, 19 March 1682/3, BARON STEWART OF RAMALTON, co. Donegal, and VISCOUNT MOUNTJOY, of co. Tyrone [I.] He was at the same time made Master Gen. of the Ordnance and Col. of a Reg. of Foot. He served in Hungary; was at the siege of Buda in 1686, being on his return made Brig. General. Being in 1688 on a mission to the exiled King, James II. at Paris from the Lord Deputy [I.], he was imprisoned there at the Bastile till 1692, when he entered into the service of King William III. He *m.* Mary, 1st da. of Richard (COOTE), 1st BARON COOTE OF COLOONY [I.], by Mary, da. of Sir George ST. GEORGE, Bart. [I.] He was slain at the battle of Steinkirk, 24 Aug. 1692.

II. 1692. *2.* WILLIAM (STEWART), VISCOUNT MOUNTJOY, &c. [I.], *suc. to the peerage* [I.], 24 Aug. 1692. He also was in the army, becoming finally (1709), Lieut. General; Master Gen. of the Ordnance. He *m.* 23 Nov. 1696, Anne, yst. da. but eventually (2 June 1732), sole h. of Murrough (BOYLE), 1st VISCOUNT BLESINGTON [I.], by his second wife, Anne, da. of Charles (COOTE), 2d EARL OF MOUNTRATH [I.] He *d.* in London, 10 Jan. 1727/8. Will dat. 9 March to 10 Aug. 1726, pr. 7 June and 4 Nov. 1728. His widow *m.* John FARQUHARSON, and *d.* in Calais, 27 Oct. 1741. Will pr. 1741.

III. 1728, to 1769.

3. WILLIAM (STEWART), VISCOUNT MOUNTJOY, &c. [I.], also a Baronet [I.], only surv. *s.* and h.; *b.* 7 April 1709; *suc. to the peerage* [I.], 10 Jan. 1727/8, and, having also *suc.* to the estates of his maternal ancestors, was *cr*, 7 Dec. 1745, EARL OF BLESINGTON, co. Wicklow; P.C. [I.], 1748; Gov. of Tyrone. He *m.* 10 Jan. 1733, at Dublin, Eleanor, da. and h. of Robert FITZGERALD, of Castle Dod, co. Cork, Prime Serjeant at Law [I.] He *d.* s.p.s. in Charles street, Berkeley sq., 14 Aug. 1769,

(a) At seven o'clock, a.m. See vol. i, p. 269, note "d," *sub* "Bathurst."

(b) So spelt in the patent. The grantee was descended, thro' his paternal grandmother, Elizabeth (wife of Dixie Hickman, da. of Henry, 5th Lord Windsor), from Sir Andrews Windsor, K.B., who *m.* Elizabeth, sister and coheir of Edward (Blount), 2d Baron Mountjoy. He, however, did not represent that lady.

and was *bur.* at Silchester, Hants, when *all his peerage dignities* became *extinct*, tho' the Baronetcy [I.], devolved on a distant cousin and h. male. His widow *d.* 1 Oct. 1774, at an advanced age, in Berkeley sq., and was *bur.* at Silchester. Will dat. 24 Feb. to 19 July, and pr. 10 Oct. 1774.

[WILLIAM STEWART, 1st s. and h. ap., *styled* VISCOUNT MOUNTJOY, *b.* 14 March 1734, *d.* unm. and v.p., 2 Feb. 1754, at Paris, and was *bur.* at Silchester afsd.]

Barony [I.] I. 1789. **Viscountcy** [I.] I. 1795.

1. THE RT. HON. LUKE GARDINER, s. and h. of the Rt. Hon. Charles GARDINER, of Dublin, by Florinda, da. of Robert NORMAN, of Lagore, co. Meath, which Charles was s. and h. of the Rt. Hon. Hon. Luke GARDINER Vice Treasurer of Ireland, by Anne, da. and h. of the Hon. Alexander STEWART, 2d s. of William, 1st VISCOUNT MOUNTJOY [I.], was *b.* 7 Feb. 1745; *suc.* his father, 15 Nov. 1769, who, some three months before his death, had on the death of the 3d Viscount Mountjoy, inherited much of the property of that family; was M.P. for Dublin; P.C. [I.], and Col. of the Dublin Militia, and was *cr.* 19 Sep. 1789, BARON MOUNTJOY of Mountjoy, co. Tyrone [I.], being subsequently *cr.* 30 Sep. 1795, VISCOUNT MOUNTJOY of Mountjoy, co. Tyrone [I.] He *m.* firstly, 3 July 1773, Elizabeth, 1st da. of Sir William MONTGOMERY, 1st Bart., of Magbiehill, co. Peebles, by his first wife Hannah, da. and coheir of Alexander TOMKYNS, of Prehen, co. Londonderry. She *d.* 7 Nov. 1783. He *m.* secondly 20 Oct. 1793, Margaret, 1st da. of Hector WALLIS, of Spring Mount, Queen's county. He *d.* 5 June 1798, being slain at the head of his regiment at the battle of Ross in Ireland.

II. 1798, to 1829.

2. CHARLES JOHN (GARDINER), VISCOUNT MOUNTJOY and BARON MOUNTJOY [I.], 2d but only surv. s. and h.; *b.* 14 July 1782; *suc. to the peerage* [I.], 5 June 1798; was Gov. of co. Tyrone; REP. PEER [I.], 1809-29 and was *cr.* 12 Jan. 1816 EARL OF BLESINGTON [I.]; see that creation. He who was *m.* twice, *d.* s.p.m.s. 25 May 1829 aged 46 when *all his honours* became *extinct*.

[LUKE WELLINGTON GARDINER, *styled* (1816-23) VISCOUNT MOUNTJOY, 1st s. and h. ap., by first wife: *b.* 11 Sep. 1818; *d.* unm. and v.p. 26 March 1823].

MOUNT-LEINSTER.

[*Memorandum.* This is one of the seven Irish peerages *cr.* by James II., after his exclusion from the throne of *England* (11 Dec. 1688), but when he was in full possession of all his royal rights as King of *Ireland*. All these creations were duly inscribed on the patent rolls [I.], from which they have never been erased. See vol. i, p. 59, note "b," *sub* "Albemarle" for an account of these and other *Jacobite* creations.]

Viscountcy [I.], I. 1689, to 1693.

1. EDWARD CHEEVERS,(a) of Macetown, s. and h. of John C. of the same, having *m.* Ann, sister to the gallant Patrick SARSFIELD, who was *cr.* EARL OF LUCAN [I.], by King James II. while in banishment, joined him and other his relatives in the support of that King, in Ireland, in 1688, being his aide-de-camp at the battle of the Boyne, and was *cr.* by him, by patent 23 Aug, 1689 BARON BANNOW, co. Wexford and VISCOUNT MOUNT-LEINSTER, co. Carlow [I.]. Tho' included in the articles of Limerick he accompanied King James into exile, and *d.* s.p. in France, 1693, when the *peerage* (so created) became *extinct*.

(a) There is a good account of this family in Burke's "extinct peerage."

MOUNTMORRES OF CASTLEMORRES.

Barony [I.] I. 1756.
Viscountcy [I.] I. 1763.

1. Hervey Morres, of Castle Morres, co. Kilkenny, s. and h. of Francis Morres, of the same, by Catherine, da. and h. of Sir William Evans, Bart. [I.], of Kilkreen, in that county, which Francis was only surv. s. of Hervey Morres, 2d s. of Sir Redmond Morres, 2d Bart. [I.], (a dignity *cr.* 28 March 1631) of Knockagh, co. Tipperary ; was M.P. for Irishtown, *alias* Canice, from 1734 until *cr.*, 4 May 1756, BARON MOUNTMORRES OF CASTLEMORRES, co. Kilkenny [I.], taking his seat on the 7th inst. He was *cr.* in the subsequent reign, 29 June 1763, VISCOUNT MOUNTMORRES OF CASTLEMORRES, co. Kilkenny [I.] taking his seat, 11 Oct. following. He *m.* firstly, 3 Nov. 1742, Letitia, yst. da. of Brabazon (Ponsonby), 1st Earl of Bessborough [I.], by his first wife, Sarah, da. of James Margetson. She *d.* 9 Feb. 1754, aged about 34. He *m.* secondly, July 1755, Mary, widow of John Baldwin, 2d da. of William Wall, of Coolnamucky Castle, co. Waterford. She, who was *b.* 9 Jan. 1713, *d.* Sep. 1779. He *d.* 6 April 1766.

II. 1766. *2.* Hervey Redmond (Morres), Viscount Mountmorres of Castlemorres, &c. [I.], s. and h. by first wife ; *suc. to the peerage* [I.], 6 April 1766, and took his seat, 4 Oct. 1777. He, however, abandoned Ireland for London in "the fallacious hope of acquiring a place in the English House of Commons "(a) to oppose the measures of the Coalition Ministry. He was *cr.* M.A. of Oxford, 3 July 1766, and D.C.L., 8 July 1773. He is said to have *suc.* in 1795 to *the* (family) *Baronetcy* [I.] by the death of his distant cousin.(b) He *d.* unm., 17 Aug. 1797, aged about 54, leaving all the estates(c) to his sisters (of the whole blood) to the exclusion of his br. (of the half blood) the heir male.(d) Will pr. June 1798, a prior admon. having issued in Jan.

III. 1797. *3.* Francis Hervey (Morres, *afterwards*, 1815, De Montmorency), Viscount Mountmorres of Castle Morres, &c. [I.], br. (of the half blood) and h., being s. of the 1st Viscount by the second wife. He was *b.* 31 Aug. 1756, and *suc. to the peerage* [I.] tho' to none of the estates, 17 Aug. 1797. He took by Royal lic., 17 June 1815, the name of *De Montmorency* in lieu of that of *Morres*.(e) He *m.*, 4 April 1794, Anne, da. of Joseph Reade, of Castle Hoyle, co. Kilkenny. She *d.* 21 July 1823, in her 48th year, at Plas Nevin, co. Dublin. He *d.* 23 March 1833, aged 86.

IV. 1833. *4.* Hervey (de Montmorency, *formerly* Morres), Viscount Mountmorres of Castle Morres, &c. [I]., only s. and h. ; *b.* 20 Aug. 1790, at Snugborough, co. Kilkenny ; was in Holy orders ; *suc. to the peerage* [I.], 23 March 1833 ; Dean of Cloyne, 1845-50 ; Dean of Achonry 1850-72 ; chaplain

(a) Wraxall's "Hist. Memoirs" where is a spirited description of his person and his restless enthusiasm. Two "*probationary odes*" are assigned to him in the "*Rolliad*," while "to all the other individuals selected for ridicule" therein, only *one* is given. Wraxall also alludes to a singular escapade of some one (whom he conjectures to have been Lord M., "then a very young man") who personated the executioner of the King at the time of the Wilkes riots in 1769.

(b) This cousin, according to Foster's peerage (1883), was "Sir Nicholas Morres, 8th Bart.," but according to Burke's (1893) was "Sir Simon Morres, 6th Bart."

(c) The annual rental of the estates of the second Viscount, as also that of other Irish noblemen then generally resident in England, is thus stated in the "*Annual Register*" for 1787 ; "Marquis Donegal, £48,000 ; Marquis Downshire, £24,000 ; Marquis Hertford, £15,000 ; Marquis Lansdowne, £13,000 ; Duke of Devonshire, £11,000 ; Earl Fitzwilliam, £9,000 ; Earl of Barrymore, £7,500 ; Viscount Mountmorres, £5,000 ; Viscount Downe, £7,000."

(d) These devolved principally on the yst. son of Sarah, the yst. sister, by the Rev. Joseph Pratt. He assumed the name of De Montmorency and is ancestor of the family of that name now of Castle Morres.

(e) See vol. iii, p. 401, note "c," *sub* "Frankfort de Montmorency."

to the Viceroy of Ireland, 1853. He *m.* 5 July 1831, Sarah, da. of William SHAW, of Temple Hill, co. Kildare. He *d.* 23 Jan. 1872 aged 75, at Killiney, co. Dublin. His widow *d.* 22 Feb. 1877 at her residence, Marino, co. Dublin.

V. 1872. *5.* WILLIAM BROWNE (DE MONTMORENCY), VISCOUNT MOUNTMORRES OF CASTLE MORRES &c. [I.], s. and h., *b.* 21 April 1832, at Kingstown, co. Dublin; *suc. to the peerage* [I.], 23 Jan. 1872. He *m.* 12 Nov. 1862, at South Kirkby, co. York, Harriet, 2d da. of George BROADRICK, of Hamphall Stubbs, by Jane Mudge, da. of Lieut. Col. Sir Richard FLETCHER, 1st Bart., of Carrow, co. Cork. He was murdered in cold blood at Rutheen near Ballinrobe, 25 Sep. 1880, aged 48, and was *bur.* from Ebor Hall, co. Galway, at Monkstown, co. Dublin. His widow, who had apartments in Hampton Court palace, living 1893.

VI. 1880. *6.* WILLIAM GEOFFREY BOUCHARD (DE MONTMORENCY), VISCOUNT MOUNTMORRES OF CASTLE MORRES [1763] and BARON MOUNTMORRES OF CASTLE MORRES [1756] in the peerage of Ireland, also a Baronet [I., 1631]; 2d but only surv. s. and h.; *b.* 23 Sep. 1872 at Ebor Hall afsd.; *suc. to the peerage* [I.], 25 Sep. 1880; *ed.* at Radley School (scholar 1886) and at Ball. Coll. Oxford (Science exhibitioner) 1889.

Family Estates.—These, in 1883, appear to have been under 2,000 acres. *Principal Residence.* Ebor Hall, near Clonbur, co. Galway.

MOUNTNORRIS.

Barony [I.], I. 1629. *1.* SIR FRANCIS ANNESLEY, Bart. [I.], s. and h. of Robert ANNESLEY, of Newport Pagnel, Bucks, by Beatrix, da. of John CORNWALL, of Moore Park, Herts, was *bap.* 2 Jan. 1585/6; and settling in Ireland, held for nearly 40 years several of the highest official appointments there; was *knighted* at Theobalds 16 July 1616 and was *cr. a Baronet* [I.], 7 Aug. 1620; receiving soon afterwards, 11 March 1620/1, a reversionary grant of the VISCOUNTCY OF VALENTIA [I.], on the death s.p.m. of its then holder Being Governor of the fort of Mountmorris he was *cr.* 8 Feb. 1628/9 BARON MOUNTNORRIS of Mountnorris, co. Armagh [I.]. He became, 14 years later, VISCOUNT VALENTIA, co. Kerry [I.], succeeding as such, on the death of the previous holder of that dignity, under the reversionary grant above mentioned. He was *bur.* 23 Nov. 1660 at Thorganby, co. York, aged 75. See fuller particulars of him under "VALENTIA" Viscountcy [I.], *sub* the second Viscount.

For fuller particulars see "ANGLESEY" Earldom, cr. 1661; ex. 1761.

II. 1660. *2.* ARTHUR (ANNESLEY), VISCOUNT VALENTIA and BARON MOUNTNORRIS [I.], s. and h.; *b.* 10 July 1614, was *cr.* 20 April 1661, BARON ANNESLEY OF NEWPORT PAGNEL, co. Bucks, and EARL OF ANGLESEY in Wales. He *d.* 6 April 1686.

III. 1686. *3.* JAMES (ANNESLEY), EARL OF ANGLESEY, &c. [E.], also VISCOUNT VALENTIA and BARON MOUNTNORRIS [I.], s. and h. He *d.* 1 April 1690.

IV. 1690. *4.* JAMES (ANNESLEY), EARL OF ANGLESEY, &c. [E.], also VISCOUNT VALENTIA and BARON MOUNTNORRIS [I.], s. and h.; *b.* about 1670. He *d.* s.p.m., 21 Jan. 1701/2.

V. 1702. *5.* JOHN (ANNESLEY), EARL OF ANGLESEY, &c. [E.], also VISCOUNT VALENTIA and BARON MOUNTNORRIS [I.] br. and h. male; *bap.* 18 Jan. 1676, at Farnborough, Hants. He *d.* s.p.s., 18 Sep. 1710.

VI. 1710. *6.* ARTHUR (ANNESLEY), EARL OF ANGLESEY, &c. [E.], also Viscount Valentia and Baron Mountnorris [I.], br. and h. male. He *d.* s.p. 1 April 1737.

VII. 1737. 7. RICHARD (ANNESLEY), EARL OF ANGLESEY and and BARON ANNESLEY OF NEWPORT PAGNEL [E.], also VISCOUNT VALENTIA, BARON MOUNTNORRIS and BARON ALTHAM [I.], cousin and h. male, being yr. s. of Richard, 3d BARON ALTHAM [I.], who was a yr. s. of Arthur, 1st EARL OF ANGLESEY, &c. [E.], 2d VISCOUNT VALENTIA and BARON MOUNTNORRIS [I.] He was *b.* about 1691; *suc.* his elder br., on 14 Nov. 1727, as BARON ALTHAM [I.], and suc. his cousin (ten years later), 1 April 1737 in the other titles. His marriage, 15 Sep. 1741 (again celebrated 8 Oct. 1754) with Juliana, da. of Richard DONOVAN, was disallowed 22 April 1771 by the *English* House of Lords, tho' allowed by the *Irish* House. He *d.* 14 Feb. 1761, aged about 70, when (in consequence of the *English* decision) the *Earldom of Anglesey* and the *Barony of Annesley of Newport Paynell* became *extinct*. The Irish honours however (in consequence of the *Irish* decision) passed to his son (by the said Juliana) as below.

For fuller particulars see "ANGLESEY," Earldom, cr. 1661, *ex.* 1761.

VIII. 1761. Earldom [I.], I. 1793. 8 and 1. ARTHUR (ANNESLEY), VISCOUNT VALENTIA, BARON MOUNTNORRIS and BARON ALTHAM [I.], *legit.* s. and h. (by Juliana afsd.) according to several decisions of the *Irish* House of Lords, was *b.* 7 Aug. 1744; matric. at Oxford (Ch. Ch.), 8 Sep. 1761; *cr.* M.A. 13 July 1763; *suc to the peerage* [I.], 14 Feb. 1761, taking his seat 6 Dec. 1765 and again 7 Nov. 1771; Gov. of co. Wexford; P.C. [I.]. His claim (1765) for a writ to the *English* House of Lords was disallowed by that house, 22 April 1771. He was *cr.* 20 Dec. 1793 EARL OF MOUNTNORRIS [I.]. He *m.* firstly, 10 May 1767, Lucy Fortescue, sister and h. of Thomas (LYTTELTON) 2d BARON LYTTELTON OF FRANCKLEY, only da. of George, the 1st Baron, by his first wife Lucy, da. of Hugh FORTESCUE. She *d.* (as Viscountess Valentia) 20 May 1783. He *m.* secondly, 20 Dec. 1783, Sarah, da. of Sarah, *suo jure* BARONESS WATERPARK [I.], and the Rt. Hon. Sir Henry CAVENDISH, 1st Bart. He *d.* at Paris, of apoplexy, 4 July 1816, aged 72. Will pr. 1816. His widow, who was *b.* 21 May 1763, *d.* 2 Jan. 1819 aged 85 at Chesham place. Will pr. May 1849.

Earldom [I.], I. Barony [I.], IX. 1816. 1 and 9. GEORGE (ANNESLEY), EARL OF MOUNTNORRIS [1793] VISCOUNT VALENTIA [1621], BARON MOUNTNORRIS [1628] and BARON ALTHAM [1681], in the peerage of Ireland, also a *Baronet* [I. 1620], s. and h. by first wife, *b.* 2 Nov. 1769 at Airly, co. Worcester; matric. at Oxford (Bras. Coll.), 17 Nov. 1787; *styled* VISCOUNT VALENTIA 1793-1816; M.P. for Yarmouth (Isle of Wight) 1808-10; *suc. to the peerage* [I.], 4 July 1816; Gov. of co. Wexford; F.R.S., F.S.A., F.L.S., &c. He *m.* 3 Sep. 1790, Anne, 8th da. of William (COURTENAY), 2d VISCOUNT COURTENAY OF POWDERHAM CASTLE, *de jure*(a) EARL OF DEVON, by Frances, da. of Thomas CLACK. She, who was *b.* 2 Feb. 1774, *d.* 6 Jan. 1835. He *d.* s.p.m.s., 23 July 1844, at Arley Castle, co. Stafford, aged 74, when the *Earldom of Mountnorris* and the *Barony of Altham* [I.], became *extinct*, but the *Viscountcy of Valentia* and the *Barony of Mountnorris* [I.] devolved on his distant cousin and h. male. His will was pr. Aug. 1844. See "VALENTIA," Viscountcy [I.], *cr.* 1621; *sub.* the 10th Viscount.

[GEORGE ARTHUR ANNESLEY, *styled* (1816-41) VISCOUNT VALENTIA, s. and h. ap., *b.* 20 Oct. 1793; matric. at Oxford (Ch. Ch.), 15 May 1812; M.P. for co. Wexford, 1830-31. He *m.* 21 Oct. 1837, Francis Cockburn, da. of Charles James SIMS, of Jamaica. He *d.* s.p. and v.p. 16 March 1841, at Brixton, aged 47. Admon. April 1841. His widow *d.* 22 Jan. 1856 at High Beech. Her admon. April 1856.]

MOUNTNORTH.

See "LISLE OF MOUNTNORTH, co. Cork," Barony [I.] (*Lysaght*), *cr.* 1758.

(a) According to the (extraordinary) decision of the House of Lords, 14 March 1831.

MOUNTRATH.

Earldom [I.]
I. 1660.

1. SIR CHARLES COOTE, Bart. [I.], of Castle Coote, co. Roscommon, s. and h. of the Rt. Hon. Sir Charles COOTE, 1st Bart. [I.] (a dignity *cr.* 2 April 1621), by Dorothea, yr. da. and coheir of Hugh CUFFE, of Cuffe's wood, co. Cork, was *b.* about 1610 ; was M.P. for co. Leitrim, 1639 ; *suc.* his father, 7 May 1642, *in the Baronetcy* [I.], and also as Provost Marshal of Connaught ; was very diligent in suppressing the Irish rebellion of that period ; was made Lord President of Connaught, 12 May 1645, which post he held (later on) for the Parl., being appointed 17 Dec. 1652, first Commissioner in that province, and being, in Jan. 1659, a Commissioner of the Government. About this time he took active measures in favour of the restoration of the King, by whom, 30 July 1660, he was made President of Connaught and Keeper of the Castle of Athlone ; was one of the Lords Justices (Regents) of Ireland (1660-61) and was *cr.*, 6 Sep. 1660, BARON COOTE OF CASTLE CUFFE in King's county, VISCOUNT COOTE OF CASTLE COOTE, co. Roscommon, and EARL OF MOUNTRATH(a) in Queens county [I.] He *m.* firstly Mary, 2d da. and coheir of the Rt. Hon. Sir Francis RUISH,(b) of Castle Jordan and of Ruish Hall, in Queens county. He *m.* secondly, before May 1645, Jane, da. of Sir Robert HANNAY,(c) Bart. [S.], of Mochrum, co. Kirkcudbright. He *d.* (of the small pox), 18 Dec. 1661, and was *bur.* 6 Feb. 1661/2, at Christ Church Cathedral, Dublin. Will dat. 2 Feb. 1658, pr. in Dublin. His widow, who *m.* Sir Robert READING, 1st Bart. [I.], of Dublin (who was *bur.* 25 March 1689, at Newark, Notts), was *bur.* 18 Nov. 1684, at Westm. Abbey.(d)

II. 1661.

2. CHARLES (COOTE), EARL OF MOUNTRATH, &c. [I.], s. and h., by first wife was *b.* about 1630 ; *styled* VISCOUNT CASTLECOOTE 1660-61 ; *suc. to the peerage* [I.], 18 Dec. 1661, and had a general pardon, 30 June 1662, of all offences committed during the rebellion. He *m.* (articles 23 June 1653), Alice, da. of Sir Robert MEREDYTH, of Greenhills, co Kildare, Chancellor of the Exchequer [I.], by Anne, 6th da. of Sir William USHER, Clerk of the Council [I.] He *d.* 30 Aug. 1672, at Dublin, and was *bur.* in Christ Church Cathedral afsd. Will dat. 23 Aug. 1672, pr. 10 April 1673, at Dublin. His widow was attainted in 1689, by King James' Parl., when her jointure (of £950 a year) was sequestrated.

III. 1672.

3. CHARLES (COOTE), EARL OF MOUNTRATH, &c., s. and h., *b.* about 1655 ; *styled* VISCOUNT CASTLECOOTE till he *suc. to the peerage* [I.], 30 Aug. 1672. His estate of £2,250 a year was sequestrated by King James' Parl. in 1689. He was P.C. to King William III. and Queen Anne ; took his seat in the House of Lords [I.], 10 Oct. 1692 ; carried the banner of Ireland at the funeral of Queen Mary II., 5 March 1694 ; one of the Lords Justices (Regents) of Ireland, 1696-97. He *m.* about 1675, Isabella, 2d da. (whose issue on 29 Nov. 1709, became coheir) to Charles (DORMER), 2d EARL OF CARNARVON, by his first wife, Elizabeth, da. of Arthur (CAPELL), 1st BARON CAPELL OF HADHAM. She *d.* before Oct. 1705. Admon. 13 Jan. 1709/10. He *d.* May 1709. Will dat. 14 Oct. 1705, pr. 12 Sep. 1709.

(a) "The surprising passage thro' Mountrath woods" effected by the grantees father (who continued almost 48 hours on horseback) in April 1642, for the relief of Birr "justly occasioned the entailing the title of *Earl of Mountrath* on his posterity." [*Lodge*, vol. ii, p. 66.] The preamble of the patent is given in "*Lodge*."

(b) He *d.* 18 Jan. or 17 June 1623, leaving issue Thomas who *d.* unm. 18 Nov. 1629, æt. 20, and was *bur.* at St. Andrew's, Dublin and (1) Eleanor, *m.* Sir Robert Loftus, 1st s. of Adam, Viscount Ely [I.] ; (2) Mary, Lady Coote above named and (3) Anne.

(c) He was *bur.* in St. Michan's church, Dublin, 30 April 1689.

(d) It is stated in Lodge that she *d.* 18, and was *bur.* 22 Nov. 1684, at St. Michan's, Dublin, but it can hardly be supposed that her remains were removed there two days after her burial in London. See Col. Chester's note on the entry in the "*Westm. Abbey Registers.*"

IV. 1709. 4. CHARLES (COOTE), EARL OF MOUNTRATH, &c. [I.], s. and h.; *b.* about 1680; *styled* VISCOUNT CASTLECOOTE till he *suc. to the peerage* [I.], May 1709; took his seat 10 Aug. 1711; was sometime M.P. for Knaresborough; P.C. to King George I, 1714. He d. unm. at Bourbon, in France, 14 Sep. and was *bur.* 27th Oct. 1715 in St. James', Westm. Will pr. Nov. 1715.

V. 1715. 5. HENRY (COOTE), EARL OF MOUNTRATH, &c. [I.], br. and h.; *b.* 4 and *bap.* 10 Jan. 1683/4 at St. Martins in the fields; was M.P. for Knaresborough 1714-20; *suc. to the peerage* [I.], 14 Sep. 1715. He *d.* unm. at Bath, 27 March 1720, aged 36. Burial registered (1 April 1720) at Bath Abbey and 7 April 1720 at St. James, Westm. Will pr. 1720.

VI. 1720. 6. ALGERNON (COOTE), EARL OF MOUNTRATH, &c., [I.], br. and h.; *bap.* 6 June 1689 at St. James, Westm. He *suc. to the peerage* [I.], 27 March 1720, and took his seat 29 March 1723. M.P. for Castle Rising, 1723 and for Heydon (co. York), 1741; P.C. [I.]; Gov. of Queens county. He *m.* 28 Nov. 1721, Diana, yst. da. of Richard (NEWPORT), 2d EARL OF BRADFORD, by Mary, da. of Sir Thomas WILBRAHAM, 3d Bart. He *d.* 27 Aug. and was *bur.* 7 Sep. 1744 in Westm. Abbey, aged 55. Will dat. 26 July and pr. 8 Sep. 1744. His widow *d.* 14 July 1766([a]), aged 70 and was *bur.* 25 in Westm. Abbey, "in a new vault made in Holles chapel for her and her late husband" whose remains were removed accordingly. Will (bequeathing £2,500 for such new vault and for a monument) dat. 9 June and pr. 27 Nov. 1766.

VII. 1744, to 1802. 7. CHARLES HENRY (COOTE), EARL OF MOUNTRATH, VISCOUNT COOTE OF CASTLE COOTE and BARON COOTE OF CASTLE CUFFE [I.], only s. and h., *b.* about 1725; *styled* VISCOUNT CASTLECOOTE, till he *suc. to the peerage* [I], 27 Aug. 1744, taking his seat 19 Dec. 1753; P.C. [I.]. Having no legitimate issue([b]), and there being no heir presumptive to his peerage dignities, he was *cr.* 31 July 1800([c]) BARON CASTLE COOTE [I.], with a spec. rem. of that dignity, failing the heirs male of his body to his kinsman (*not* however his heir male), the Rt. Hon. Charles Henry COOTE. He *d.* unm. 1 March 1802 aged about 77, at Strawberry hill, co. Devon.([d]) At his death the *Earldom of Mountrath, the Viscountcy of Coote of Castle Coote* and the *Barony of Coote of Castle Cuffe* [I.], became *extinct*; while the *Barony of Castle Coote* [I.] (*cr.* in 1800), devolved (according to the spec. rem. abovenamed) to his distant cousin, (but became *extinct* in 1827) and the *Baronetcy* [I. 1621] devolved on another distant cousin, his heir male collateral. Will pr. 1802, leaving his English estates (Dereham Abbey, co. Norfolk, &c.), to his maternal relations, but his Irish estates to the Coote family.

MOUNTREAL, see MONTREAL.

MOUNTROSE, see MONTROSE.

([a]) This is the Lady to whom Horace Walpole alludes, "The reverend head of the Law [Lord Hardwicke] is frequently shut up here [at Twickenham] with my Lady Mountrath, who is as rich and tipsy as *Cacafogo* in the comedy. What a jumble of avarice, lewdness, dignity and claret!"

([b]) On 6 Sep. 1761, "Charles, b.b. son of the Earl of Mountrath and Mary Preston, born 30 July," was *bap.* at St. James, Westm.

([c]) One of the 16 Irish Baronies *cr.* that day, for a list of which see vol. iv, p. 205, note "c," *sub* "Henniker."

([d]) There is a long and curious account of him in the *Annual Reg.* for 1802. His dread of small pox was so great "that he had relays at five houses between his seat in Norfolk and his house in Devonshire to prevent the chance of infection; and at these houses small establishments were kept, as he dared not sleep at an inn." He appears latterly to have lived "absolutely the life of a recluse."

MOUNT SANDFORD OF CASTLEREA.

Barony [I.] I. 1800. 1. HENRY MOORE SANDFORD, of Castlerea, co. Roscommon, s. and h. of Henry SANDFORD, of the same, by Sarah, da. of Stephen (MOORE), 1st VISCOUNT MOUNTCASHELL [I.], was b. 28 July 1751; suc. his Father 12 Feb. 1797, and was cr. 31 July 1800(a) BARON MOUNT SANDFORD OF CASTLEREA, co. Roscommon, with a spec. rem. of that dignity, failing heirs male of his body, to his brothers. He m. 13 June 1780, Katharine, 1st da. of the Rt. Hon. Silver OLIVER, of Castle Oliver, co. Limerick, by Isabella Sarah, da. and coheir of Richard NEWMAN, of Newbury, co. Cork. He d. s.p.s. 29 Dec. 1814, aged 63. His widow d. 19 Oct. 1818 in her 56th year, near Dublin.

II. 1814. 2. HENRY (SANDFORD), BARON MOUNT SANDFORD OF CASTLEREA [I.], nephew and h., being only s. and h. of the Rev. William SANDFORD, by Jane, da. of the Rt. Hon. Silver OLIVER abovenamed, which William was next br. to the last Baron and d. 17 Aug. 1809 aged 57. He was b. 10 March 1805 and suc. to the peerage [I.]. 29 Dec. 1814 under the spec. rem. abovementioned. He d. unm. 14 June 1828 aged 23, being killed in a riot at Windsor. Will pr. Aug. 1828.

III. 1828, to 1846. 3. GEORGE (SANDFORD), BARON MOUNT SANDFORD OF CASTLEREA [I.], uncle and heir, being yr. br. of the 1st Baron. He was b. 10 May 1756; was sometime Capt. in the 18th Dragoons; M.P. for co. Roscommon. He suc. to the peerage [I.], 14 June 1828, under the spec. rem. abovementioned. He d. unm. at Stowey, co. Somerset, 25 Sep. 1846 aged 90, when the title became extinct. Will pr. March 1847.

MOUNT STEPHEN OF MOUNT STEPHEN AND OF DUFFTOWN.

Barony. I. 1891. 1. SIR GEORGE STEPHEN, Bart., of Montreal, in Canada, s. of William STEPHEN, of Dufftown, co. Banff, by Elspet, da. of John SMITH, of Knockando, co. Elgin, was b. 5 June 1829, at Mortlach, co. Banff; was many years a woollen manufacturer in Aberdeen and London, but emigrated to Canada in 1851, where he was President of the Bank of Montreal as also of the Canadian Pacific Railway from its commencement to 1888; was cr. a Baronet, 3 March 1886, and was cr., 23 June 1891, BARON MOUNT STEPHEN OF MOUNT STEPHEN in the province of British Columbia and Dominion of Canada AND OF DUFFTOWN in the county of Banff. He m., 8 March 1853, Charlotte Annie, da. of Benjamin KANE.

Principal Residences.—La Fourche, Causapscal, and Grand Metis, in Canada; Faskally House, near Pitlochry, in Scotland.

MOUNT-STUART.

i.e., "MOUNT-STUART, CUMRA, AND INCHMARNOCK," Barony [S.] (*Stuart*), *cr.* 1703, with the EARLDOM OF BUTE [S.], which see.

MOUNT-STUART OF WORTLEY.

Barony. I. 1761. 1. MARY, COUNTESS OF BUTE [S.], wife of John (STUART), 3d EARL OF BUTE, VISCOUNT OF KINGARTH, LORD MOUNT-STUART, CUMRA AND INCHMARNOCK [S.], only da. (and in 1776 heir) of Edward WORTLEY-MONTAGU, of Wortley, co. York; b. Feb. 1718; m., 24 Aug. 1736; was cr., 3 April 1761, BARONESS MOUNT-STUART OF WORTLEY, co. York [G.B.], with rem. of that dignity to the heirs male of her body by her said husband. She d. 6 Nov. 1794. For fuller particulars see "BUTE" Earldom [S.], cr. 1703, sub the third Earl.

(a) See p. 408, note "c."

II. 1794. 2. JOHN (STUART), EARL OF BUTE, &c. [S.], also BARON MOUNT-STUART OF WORTLEY, and BARON CARDIFF [G.B.], s. and h., b. 30 June 1744; suc. his father in the Scotch Earldom and dignities, 10 March 1792, having v.p. been cr. (20 May 1766), Baron Cardiff, and having suc. his mother, 6 Nov. 1794, as BARON MOUNT-STUART OF WORTLEY. He was cr., 21 March 1796, MARQUESS OF BUTE; see that dignity.

MOUNT-TEMPLE.

i.e., "TEMPLE OF MOUNT-TEMPLE, co. Sligo," Barony [I.] (*Temple*), cr. 1723 with the VISCOUNTCY OF PALMERSTON [I.], which see; *extinct* 1865.

Barony. I. 1880, to 1888. 1. THE RT. HON. WILLIAM-FRANCIS COWPER-TEMPLE, *formerly* COWPER, 2d s. of Peter Leopold Louis Francis Nassau (COWPER), 5th EARL COWPER, by Emily Mary, 1st da. of Peniston (LAMB), 1st VISCOUNT MELBOURNE [I.], which lady m. secondly Henry John (TEMPLE), 3d VISCOUNT PALMERSTON and BARON TEMPLE OF MOUNT TEMPLE [I.], the celebrated Minister (who d. s.p. 18 Oct. 1865, aged 81), was b. 13 Dec. 1811, at Brocket Hall, Herts; ed. at Eton; sometime, 1830-35, an officer in the Royal Horse Guards, becoming Capt. (unattached) 1835, and Major, 1852; M.P. for Hertford, 1835-68, and for South Hants, 1868-80; a Lord of the Treasury, 1841; a Lord of the Admiralty, 1846-52, and again 1853-55; P.C., 1855; Under Home Sec. 1855; President of Board of Health, 1855-57 and 1857-58. Paymaster General, 1859-60; Chief Commissioner of Works, 1860-66. Took by Royal lic. 17 Nov. 1869, the name of *Temple*, after that of *Cowper*, on inheriting (at the death, 11 Sep. 1869 of his mother) the estates (Broadlands in Hampshire, &c., as also certain Irish estates) under the will of his stepfather, Viscount Palmerston abovenamed. He was cr. 25 May 1880, BARON MOUNT-TEMPLE of Mount Temple, co. Sligo. He m. firstly 27 June 1843, at St. James' Westm., Harriett, Alicia, da. of Daniel GURNEY, of North Runcton, co. Norfolk, by Harriett Jemima, da. of William (HAY), EARL OF ERROLL [S.] She d. 28 Aug. following in her 19th year, at North Runcton. He m. secondly 21 Nov. 1848, at St. Peters Pimlico, Georgiana, 9th da. of Vice Admiral John Richard Delap TOLLEMACHE, *formerly* HALLIDAY, by Elizabeth, da. of John (STRATFORD), 3d EARL OF ALDBOROUGH [I.] He d. s.p. (after a short illness), 17 Oct. 1888, in his 77th year, at Broadlands, and was bur. in the cemetery at Romsey, Hants, when *the Barony* became *extinct*.(a) Will pr. at £76,123. His widow living 1893.

Family Estates.—These, in 1883, consisted of 6,135 acres in Hampshire; 1,249 in the West Riding of Yorkshire, and 23 in Herts; besides 738 (worth as much as £6,738 a year) in co. Dublin. *Total* 8,145 acres, worth £16,270 a year.(b) *Principal Residence.* Broadlands, near Romsey, Hants.

MOWBRAY, or MOWBRAY DE AXILHOLM.

Barony by Writ. I. 1283, or 1295. 1. ROGER DE MOWBRAY, of the Isle of Axholme, co. Lincoln, one of the most considerable Barons of the north, s. and h. of Roger DE MOWBRAY of the same. by Maud, da. and coheir of William DE BEAUCHAMP, of Bedford, which Roger, last named, was s. of William DE MOWBRAY, one of the 25 Barons(c) appointed to enforce the *Magna Charta*, suc. his Father in (1266-67), 51 Hen. III.; served in the wars in Wales and France and was sum. by writ 28 June (1283), 11 Ed.

(a) He "had been till recently a consistent and zealous member of the Whig party and a supporter of Mr. Gladstone's policy. He took an active part in the work of endeavouring to ameliorate the condition of the poorer classes and was a prominent member of several charitable institutions." [*Morning Post*, 17 Oct. 1888.]

(b) His estates in Ireland were left to his widow absolutely, but his estates in Hampshire and Yorkshire, his pictures at Broadlands, &c., to his nephew, the Hon. Anthony E. M. Ashley, with a request that he should take the name of Temple.

(c) "ROGER DE MOWBRAY, a younger brother of this Baron, [William] ought, perhaps, to be ranked among the Barons of this period [1215], as he is generally considered to have been another of the celebrated 25 Barons appointed to enforce the observance of MAGNA CHARTA, though some writers call him Roger de Montbezon. This Roger de Mowbray died s.p." [*Nicolas*].

I.(a) to the meeting at Shrewsbury, which appears since 1877 to be held as constituting a regular summons to Parl.(b) He was also sum. 8 June (1294), 24 Ed. I. and 26 Aug. (1297), 25 Ed. I. to meetings which were not Parliaments.(c) He was, however, sum. to an undoubted parl., 24 June (1295), 23 Ed. I,(d) as also 26 Aug. (1296), 24 Ed. I. Accordingly he became in 1295, if not in 1283, LORD MOWBRAY. He *m.* Rose, da. of Richard (DE CLARE), EARL OF GLOUCESTER AND HERTFORD, by Maud, da. of John (DE LACY), EARL OF LINCOLN. He *d.* at Ghent, in Flanders (1296-97), 25 Ed. I., and was *bur.* at Fountain's Abbey, co. York. Esch. 26 Ed. I.

II. 1297. 2. JOHN (DE MOWBRAY), LORD MOWBRAY, s. and h., *b.* 2 Nov. 1286; *suc.* his father at the age of 11. and was, even during his minority, distinguished in the Scotch wars. He was sum. to parl. as a Baron from 26 Aug. (1307) 1 Ed. II. to 5 Aug. (1320) 14 Ed. II.; was Sheriff of Yorkshire (1312-13) and Governor of the city of York; Warden of the Scotch marches. He *m.* Aliva, da. and coheir of William (DE BRAOSE), LORD BRAOSE(e), by Elizabeth, da. and h. of Edmund DE SULLY. He joined in the insurrection of Thomas, Earl of Lancaster, with whom he was made prisoner at the battle of Boroughbridge, 16 March 1321/2, and was hung at York (no attainder taking place) soon afterwards. His widow who inherited the district of Bramber in Sussex and of Gower in South Wales, *m.* Sir Richard PESHALL and d. (1331) 5 Ed. III.

III. 1322. 3. JOHN (DE MOWBRAY), LORD MOWBRAY, s. and h.; received livery of his lands from King Edward III., in 1327 at his *age* of 21. He was sum. to parl. as a Baron from 10 Dec. (1327) 1 Ed. III. to 20

(a) "The House of Lords, 26 July 1877, resolved that it was proved by the writ of summons addressed to Roger de Mowbray in 11 Edward I., and the other evidence adduced on behalf of the petitioner [Lord Stourton], that the Barony of Mowbray was in the reign of Edward I. vested in Roger de Mowbray. The House came to a *similar resolution in regard to the Barony of Segrave*, and decided that the writs of summons of 49 Hen. III. could not create Peerages. [See as to this point vol. iii, p. 90, note "c," *sub* "Despencer;"] and, in consequence, that *the writ of* 11 *Ed. I.*, *is the earliest of record* to which the creation of a Peerage can be referred. Lord Segrave was sum. 49 Hen. III. and was found to be a rebel for his adherence to Simon de Montfort, but was afterwards pardoned. The House however referred the creation of his peerage to the writ of 11 Ed. I. It is, therefore, proved that Roger, Lord Mowbray, was sum. to Parl. by one of the earliest writs, which could create a Peerage, and as the Lords Mowbray have always claimed to be the *Premier Barons* of England and as their right was fully admitted by the Crown [*Query*, this admittance *of the Crown*] in the reign of Charles I. and Charles II., (on the election of the then Lords Mowbray as Knights of the Garter), Lord Mowbray, Segrave and Stourton insists that, as it has been decided that the writ of summons of 49 Hen. III. (under which Lord de Ros is placed in the House of Lords) could *not* create a peerage, he [Lord M.] is entitled to be placed as the Premier Baron of England." [Burke's "Peerage" edit. 1893].

(b) See note "a" next above. The writ is dat. 28 [not 23 as given in Burke's "Peerage" for 1893] June, "*apud Rochel*," and described in the app. to the Lords' report on the dignity of the Peerage" as "*de tractatu habendo de David fil Griffini.*" Besides 10 Earls, (including therein 2 Scotch Earls, and "William de Valence," who is placed below 4 and above 5 Earls) there are no less than 99 ! ! others so summoned. With respect to the writ of 1283, Mr. J. Horace Round states that Bishop 'Stubbs writing in 1875 declared there to be *no valid writs* between 1264 and 1295, so the production (in 1876) of 1283 [as a valid writ of summons] was a revolution."

(c) See vol. i, p. 259, note "c," *sub* "Basset de Sapcote" as to the summons of 1294 and vol. i, p. 8, note "b," *sub* "Ap. Adam" as to that of 1297.

(d) Mowbray is one (and Segrave is another) of the six Baronies still existing out of the 53 Barons summoned in 1295. See vol. iii, p. 90, note "c," *sub* "Despencer."

(e) See vol. ii, p. 7, note "d," *sub* "Braose," as to the coheirship of that Barony often (wrongfully) assumed by the Mowbray family.

Nov. (1360) 34 Ed. III.(a) He distinguished himself greatly in the wars with France, as also at the victory over the Scots at Durham, 17 Oct. 1346; was Governor of Berwick-upon-Tweed. He *m.* about 1325, Joan, da. of Henry (PLANTAGENET), EARL OF LANCASTER, by Maud, da. and h. of Sir Patrick CHAWORTH. He *d.* at York, of the pestilence, 4 Oct. (1361) 35 Ed. III., and was *bur.* in the Grey Friars, Bedford. Esch. 36 Ed. III.

IV. 1361. *4.* JOHN (DE MOWBRAY), LORD MOWBRAY, s. and h., *b.* 1326, at Epworth, co. Lincoln; served in the French wars both before (1355) and after (1367) his father's death. He was sum. to Parl. as a Baron (LORD MOWBRAY DE AXILHOLM) from 14 Aug. (1362), 36 Ed. III., to 20 Jan. (1365/6), 39 Ed. III., by writs directed "*Johanni de Mowbray de Axilholm.*"(a) He *m.* about 1363 Elizabeth (*de jure*) *suo jure* BARONESS SEGRAVE, da. and h. (1353) of John (DE SEGRAVE), LORD SEGRAVE, by Margaret, his wife, *suo jure* DUCHESS AND COUNTESS OF NORFOLK, who was da. and h. of Thomas (PLANTAGENET), EARL OF NORFOLK, and *Marshal of England*, yr. s. of King Edward I. Having joined the Crusades he was slain by the Turks near Constantinople, 9 Oct. (1368), 42 Ed. III. His widow, who was aged 13 in 1353, *d.* about 1375, Esch. 50 Ed. III.

V. 1368. *5.* JOHN (DE MOWBRAY), LORD MOWBRAY, s. and h., *b.* 1364; *suc.* his father at the age of four in that peerage. By the death of his mother, in or about 1375, he became also LORD SEGRAVE; was *knighted* by Edw. III., 23 April 1377, and was *cr.*, 16 July 1377 (at the coronation(b) of Ric. II.) EARL OF NOTTINGHAM, "*sibi et heredibus suis.*"(c) He *d.* in London unm. and under age, 10 Feb. (1381/2), 5 Ric. II.(d) and was *bur.* in the Friars Carmelites, Fleet street. *Inq.* 22 June (1382), 6 Ric. II.

VI. 1382. *6.* THOMAS (DE MOWBRAY), LORD MOWBRAY and LORD SEGRAVE, br. and h.; *b.* 1367; was *cr.*, 12 Feb. 1383, EARL OF NOTTINGHAM, and was, 10 Feb. 1397, constituted *Earl Marshal of England*. He was *cr.*, 29 Sep. 1397, DUKE OF NORFOLK, but was banished and apparently deprived of that dignity in 1398. By the death of his maternal grandmother abovementioned on 24 May 1398, he (apparently) *suc.* her as EARL OF NORFOLK.(e) He *d.* 27 Sep. 1400, aged 39. For fuller particulars of him see "NORFOLK" Dukedom, *cr.* 1397, *forfeited* 1398.

VII. 1400. *7.* THOMAS (DE MOWBRAY), EARL OF NORFOLK, EARL OF NOTTINGHAM, LORD MOWBRAY, and LORD SEGRAVE, *Earl Marshal of England*, s. and h. of the above, by his second wife, Elizabeth, sister and coheir of Thomas (FITZALAN), EARL OF ARUNDEL. He was *b.* about 1387; *suc.* his father at the age of 14 in (apparently) all his dignities save that of the DUKE OF NORFOLK,(f)

(a) There is proof in the rolls of Parl. of his sitting.

(b) "He and William de Latimer made claim to exercise on that day the office of Almoner which had belonged to their ancestor, William de Beauchamp of Bedford." [Burke's "*Peerage*," 1893.]

(c) One of the many cases in which these words of such wide import must be construed as relating only to heirs "of the body" of the grantee. See vol. iii, p. 107, note "c," *sub* "Devon."

(d) The date is wrongly given as "6 Ric. II." in Dugdale. See "*Coll. Top. et Gen.*," vol. vii, p. 138.

(e) That dignity had been granted to her Grace's father and "the heirs of his body," 16 Dec. 1312.

(f) "The title of Duke of Norfolk was withheld from him upon the erroneous plea that having been conferred upon him in the Parl. of 21 Richard II. the proceedings in which were avoided by an act of 1 Hen. IV. the dignity of Duke of Norfolk fell under that act." [Burke's "*Peerage*," 1893.]

being usually known under the style of "EARL MARSHALL." He m. Constance, da. of John (HOLAND), DUKE OF EXETER, by Elizabeth, da. of John (PLANTAGENET, *styled* "of Gaunt"), DUKE OF LANCASTER. He *d.* s.p., being beheaded (without any trial or attainder) at York, 10 June 1405, aged 18 (having joined in the Scrope conspiracy) and was *bur.* in York Minster. His widow *m.* Sir John GREY, K.G., s. and h. ap. of Reginald, 3d LORD GREY DE RUTHIN, by whom, who *d.* v.p. 27 Aug. 1439, she was mother of Edmund, 1st EARL OF KENT.

VIII. 1405. *8.* JOHN (DE MOWBRAY), EARL OF NORFOLK, EARL OF NOTTINGHAM, LORD MOWBRAY and LORD SEGRAVE, *Earl Marshal of England*, br. and h., *b.* 1390; was sum. to Parl. 22 March 1412/3, as EARL MARSHAL,(a) and was *restored* 14 July 1424, as DUKE OF NORFOLK, &c. He *d.* 19 Oct. 1433.

IX. 1432. *9.* JOHN (DE MOWBRAY), DUKE OF NORFOLK, EARL OF NORFOLK, EARL OF NOTTINGHAM, EARL MARSHAL,(a) LORD MOWBRAY and LORD SEGRAVE, &c., only s. and h.; *b.* 12 Sep. 1415. He *d.* 6 Nov. 1461, aged 46.

X. 1461. *10.* JOHN (DE MOWBRAY), DUKE OF NORFOLK [1397], EARL OF NORFOLK [1312], EARL OF NOTTINGHAM [1383], EARL MARSHAL(a) [1413], EARL OF SURREY AND WARENNE [1451], LORD MOWBRAY and LORD SEGRAVE, &c., only s. and h.; *b.* 18 Oct. 1544; *cr.* v.p. 24 March 1451, EARL OF SURREY AND WARENNE; *suc.* to the other dignities in Nov. 1461. He *d.* s.p.m., 17 Jan. 1475/6, aged 31, when the *Dukedom of Norfolk* and the *Earldoms of Nottingham, Surrey and Warenne* became *extinct.*

XI. 1476, to 1478.? *11.* ANNE, *suo jure* COUNTESS OF NORFOLK [1312], BARONESS MOWBRAY and BARONESS SEGRAVE and (presumably) COUNTESS MARSHAL,(a) only da. and h. She, at her age of seven, *m.* 15 Jan. 1477/8, Richard (PLANTAGENET), DUKE OF YORK (second s. of **King Edward IV.**), who, in contemplation of such marriage, was *cr.* on 12 June 1476, EARL OF NOTTINGHAM and, on 7 Feb. 1477, EARL WARENNE and DUKE OF NORFOLK. She appears to have *d.* an infant and s.p. [1478], in the lifetime of her husband, who (together with his br. **King Edward V.**) was murdered (in his 10th or 11th year), 23 June 1483. (See fuller particulars of him, under "YORK," Dukedom, *cr.* 1477; *ex.* 1483). At her death *all her peerage dignities* reverted to the Crown, or fell *into abeyance* (b)

* * * *

For fuller particulars, see "NORFOLK," Dukedom *cr.* 1397, and Earldom *cr.* 1312.

(a) See p. 262, note "c," *sub* "Marshal."

(b) The coheirs were the representatives of her great grand aunts, the two daughters of Thomas (Mowbray), 1st Duke of Norfolk, *viz.* (1) Isabel, who *m.* firstly Henry Ferrers who *d.* s.p.m. and secondly (1423-24) James (de Berkeley), Lord Berkeley. She *d.* 27 Sep. 1472 being ancestress of the succeeding Lords Berkeley, of whom William, her 1st s. and h. was, in 1483, *cr.* Earl of Nottingham (one of the Mowbray Earldoms), being afterwards *cr.* Marquess of Berkeley; (2) Margaret, who *m.* Sir Robert Howard (who *d.* 1436), by whom she was mother of John, Lord Howard, *cr.* in 1483, Duke of Norfolk, ancestor of the succeeding Dukes.

XII. 1484? to 1485. 12. SIR JOHN HOWARD, s. and h. of Sir Robert HOWARD by Margaret, one of the two daughters (whose issue, about 1478, became coheirs) to Thomas (MOWBRAY), 1st DUKE OF NORFOLK, EARL OF NORFOLK, EARL OF NOTTINGHAM, LORD MOWBRAY and LORD SEGRAVE, *suc.* his father (when an infant) in 1436, was *cr.* LORD HOWARD, 15 Oct. 1470 and subsequently, 28 June 1483, was *cr.* DUKE OF NORFOLK and Earl Marshal of England. The *abeyance of the Baronies of Mowbray and Seagrave* appears to have been *terminated in his favour*(a) by King Richard III. [1484?] who issued letters missive addressed to him as "DUKE OF NORFOLK, LORD MOBRAY AND SEGRAVE." He was slain at the battle of Bosworth 22 Aug. 1485, aged above 50, when, having been attainted, *all his honours* became *forfeited*.(b)

* * * * *

XIII. 1554, to 1572. 13. "SIR THOMAS HOWARD, Knt., *otherwise called* EARL OF SURREY," grandson and h. ap. of Thomas (HOWARD), DUKE OF NORFOLK, who was s. and h. of Thomas DUKE OF NORFOLK (so *cr.* 1514; *d.* 1524), who was s. and h. of John, 1st DUKE OF NORFOLK, next abovenamed, was restored in blood and honours, 2 Sep (1553) 1 Mary, whereby it is presumed, that (the next year) on the death of his said grandfather, 25 Aug. 1554, he inherited not only the *Dukedom of Norfolk* and *Earldom of Surrey* (enjoyed by his said grandfather), but also the *Baronies of Mowbray, Segrave* and *Howard*, which had been forfeited in 1485 by his said grandfather's grandfather (the 1st Duke) as above stated, thus becoming DUKE OF NORFOLK, EARL OF SURREY, LORD MOWBRAY, SEGRAVE and HOWARD.(c) He was beheaded 2 June 1572 aged 36, when, having been attainted, *all his honours* became *forfeited*.

For fuller particulars see "NORFOLK," Dukedom, *cr.* 1483.

* * * * *

XIV. 1604. 14. THOMAS HOWARD, s. and h. of Philip, sometime (1580-89) EARL OF ARUNDEL, who by attainder (1589) had forfeited that dignity and who was s. and h. of Thomas, DUKE OF NORFOLK, EARL OF SURREY, LORD MOWBRAY, SEGRAVE and HOWARD next abovenamed, was *b.* 7 July 1585; *suc.* his father 19 Oct. 1595 and was restored in blood by Act of Parl. 18 April 1604, as EARL OF ARUNDEL and EARL OF SURREY as also to such Baronies as had

(a) It should be noted, however, that, in the resolution of the House of Lords, 27 July 1877, on the claim to these Baronies, it is not expressly stated that the abeyance had been terminated *by Richard III.*, but only that it had been so terminated *subsequently to* 1481 [*sic.*, tho' (as it has never been suggested that the abeyance was terminated by Edward IV. or V.) one would have expected 1483], *but before Queen Elizabeth's time* [1558] in favour of the Howard family by whom the said Baronies had been forfeited in 1572 tho' restored in 1604. Their Lordships had taken into consideration (1) that Richard III. addressed like letters missive to the *other* coheir (William Berkeley) as "Earl of Nottingham and Lord Berkeley," of which titles Nottingham was one belonging to the Mowbray family; and (2) that there had been constant use of the titles of "Mowbray and Segrave," by the Dukes of Norfolk on funeral certificates, Garter plates, &c., *e.g.*, in 1563 at the funeral of Margaret, Duchess of Norfolk, in 1611 on the Garter plate of Thomas (Howard), Earl of Arundel afterwards Duke of Norfolk, &c.

(b) All the Howard titles were forfeited in Aug. 1485, on the death of the 1st Duke of Norfolk, which would include (besides the Dukedom) the Barony of Howard and apparently (as conjectured in the text) the Baronies of Mowbray and Segrave.

(c) Their Lordships in 1877 decided that these Baronies were in the Howard family *before* the time (1558) of Queen Elizabeth (and, consequently, were forfeited in 1572) and it is not seen how that fact can be accounted for otherwise than as indicated in the text.

been possessed by his Grandfather, the attainted Duke of Norfolk, becoming thereby LORD MOWBRAY, SEGRAVE and HOWARD. In 1627 he obtained an act of Parl. which annexed the *Baronies of Fitzalan of Clun and Oswaldestre* and *Maltravers* to the Earldom of Arundel. He was *cr.* 6 June 1644, EARL OF NORFOLK. He *d.* 26 Sep. 1646 aged 61.

XV. 1639. *15.* HENRY FREDERICK HOWARD, 2d but (since July 1624), 1st surv. s. and h. ap.; *b.* 15 Aug. 1608; *styled* LORD MALTRAVERS since 1624 till 13 April 1639, when he was sum. v.p. to Parl. in his father's Barony,(a) as LORD MOWBRAY and placed at the upper end(b) of the Barons bench on the 16th inst. He *suc.* his father, 26 Sep. 1646, as EARL OF ARUNDEL, SURREY and NORFOLK, &c. He *d.* 17 April 1652, aged 43.

See fuller particulars under "ARUNDEL," Earldom.

XVI. 1652. *16.* THOMAS (HOWARD), EARL OF ARUNDEL, SURREY and NORFOLK, LORD MOWBRAY,(c) SEGRAVE, &c., s. and h.; *b.* 12 July 1628. He was restored, 29 Dec. 1660, together with the heirs male of the body of the 1st Duke of Norfolk, to that Dukedom, becoming thereby DUKE OF NORFOLK [1483]. He *d.* unm. 13 Dec. 1677, aged 49.

XVII. 1677. *17.* HENRY (HOWARD), DUKE OF NORFOLK, &c., LORD MOWBRAY, SEGRAVE, &c., br. and h., who had previously been *cr.* BARON HOWARD OF CASTLE RISING in 1669, and EARL OF NORWICH in 1672. He *d.* 11 Jan. 1684, aged 55.

XVIII. 1679. *18.* HENRY HOWARD, s. and h. ap., *b.* 11 Jan. 1655, *styled* EARL OF ARUNDEL, 1677-84; being sum. v.p. to Parl. 14 Jan. 1678/9, in his father's Barony(d) as LORD MOWBRAY, and placed (as was his grandfather) at the upper end of the Baron's bench. He *suc.* his father as DUKE OF NORFOLK, &c., 11 Jan. 1684. He *d.* s.p. 2 April 1701, aged 46.

For fuller particulars see "NORFOLK," Dukedom, *cr.* 1483.

(a) See vol. i, p. 155, note "f," *sub* "Arundel," and see note "d" next below. Mr. Courthope, however, held the opinion (usually entertained till their Lordships decision in 1877) that the Barony of Mowbray (as also that of Segrave) was in abeyance between the original coheirs (Berkeley and Howard) till (at all events) 1639. He writes as under, "Henry Frederick Howard was not one of the coheirs of the Barony of Mowbray in 1639, nor did he become so until the death of his father in 1646, after which period he never sat in Parliament in the Barony of Mowbray, as he then succeeded to the Earldom of Arundel." *Since* the decision of 1877, however, it must (presumably) be held that he was s. and h. ap. of one who *had the* [whole of the] *Barony vested in him* and so was rightly sum. in his father's Barony.

(b) The three next immediately below him were Lord Clifford, Lord Abergavenny and Lord Audley.

(c) On 8 March 1669/70. His Grace *as Lord Mowbray* disputed the claim of Lord Fitzwalter for precedency over all other Barons. See vol. iii, p. 374, note "a," *sub* "Fitzwalter."

(d) "There being question whether he should sit in and enjoy the ancient place of the Lord Mowbray, the Journal Book of the House of Peers was produced, wherein it did appear that on the 16th April 1640, Henry, Lord Mowbray, was introduced and placed at the upper end of the Barons' Bench, and after a full consideration the House resolved that the said Lord Mowbray should be called in and introduced, and placed in the precedence of his grandfather, as Lord Mowbray, at the upper end of the Barons' Bench, which was done accordingly." Mr. Courthope, writing in 1857, adds, "It is thus certain that Henry Frederick Howard was considered to have been duly summoned in the ancient Barony of Mowbray in 1639, and, consequently, as Henry, Duke of Norfolk, his son, succeeded to whatever honours the said Henry Frederick possessed, the House was correct in allowing to the son of the said Duke when summoned in his father's Barony, the precedency which had been allowed to his grandfather. Notwithstanding which proceedings, it appears by no means certain

XIX. 1701. *19.* Thomas (Howard), DUKE OF NORFOLK, &c., LORD MOWBRAY, SEGRAVE, &c., nephew and h., being s. and h. of Thomas, next br. to the late Duke. He *d.* s.p. 23 Dec. 1732, aged 49.

XX. 1732, to 1777. *20.* EDWARD (HOWARD), DUKE OF NORFOLK, EARL OF ARUNDEL, SURREY, NORFOLK and NORWICH, LORD MOWBRAY, SEGRAVE, &c., br. and h. He *d.* s.p. 20 Sep. 1777, aged 91, when the *Earldom of Norwich* [1672], and the *Barony of Howard of Castle Rising* [1669], became *extinct*, while *the Dukedom of Norfolk, the Earldom of Arundel* (and the Baronies attached thereto by Act of Parl. 1627), the *Earldom of Surrey* and *the Earldom of Norfolk* devolved on his cousin and h. male, but the *Baronies of Mowbray, Segrave*, and any others held in fee *fell into abeyance.*(a)

For fuller particulars, see "NORFOLK" Dukedom cr. 1397, and Earldom cr. 1312.

* * * *

XXI. 1878. *21.* ALFRED JOSEPH (STOURTON), BARON STOURTON, 3d but 1st surv. s. and h. of Charles, 18th BARON STOURTON, by Mary Lucy, da. of Charles (CLIFFORD), 6th BARON CLIFFORD OF CHUDLEIGH, *b.* 28 Feb. 1829; Lieut. Yorkshire Yeomanry Cavalry, 1853; *suc. to the peerage*, 23 Dec. 1872. By a resolution of the House of Lords, 27 July 1877, he was found the senior of the two coheirs of the Baronies of Mowbray and Segrave, which their Lordships held had been terminated in favour of the Howard family(b) prior to the reign of Queen Elizabeth. The abeyance of these Baronies was accordingly terminated in his favour and he thus became LORD MOWBRAY and LORD SEGRAVE and was sum. by writ to Parl. in Jan. 1878.(c) He *m.*, 13 Sep. 1865, at Skyne, Mary Margaret, only child of Matthew Elias CORBALLY, of Corbalton Hall, co. Meath, by Matilda, da. of Jenico (PRESTON), 12th VISCOUNT GORMANSTON [I.] He *d.* (of influenza) 18 April 1893, aged 64, at the Hotel St. James, Paris. Will pr. 1893 at £27,971 gross but £8,034 net. His widow living 1893.

---

that the abeyance of the ancient Barony of Mowbray has ever [*i.e.* ever *before the date of* 1857, *when this was written*], been legally terminated, and if not, the Writ of Summons to Henry Frederick Howard in 1639 [see note "a" next above], created a *new* Barony of the same name, which is now in abeyance between his coheirs the Lords Petre and Stourton, who are also coheirs of one moiety [the Lords Berkeley representing the other moiety] of the original dignity."

(a) The coheirs were his two nieces (the daughters and coheirs of his br. Philip Howard), or their representatives. These, in 1777, were (1) Charles Philip Stourton, s. and h. of Winifred, the 1st da. (who *d.* 15 July 1754), by William, 15th Baron Stourton, which Charles, who was *b.* 22 Aug. 1752, *suc.* his father, 3 Oct. 1781, as 16th Baron Stourton and was great grandfather of the 19th Baron Stourton, in whose favour the abeyance of the Baronies of Mowbray and Segrave was terminated in 1878 (2) Anne, the 2d da., wife of Robert Edward (Petre), 9th Baron Petre of Writtle, ancestress of the succeeding Barons.

(b) See p. 414, notes "a" and "c."

(c) His Lordship claimed "that as it has been decided that the writ of summons of 49 Hen. III. under which Lord de Ros is placed in the House of Lords could not create a peerage he [Lord Mowbray] is entitled to be placed as the *Premier Baron of England*." [Burke's "*Peerage*," 1893.] See vol. iii, p. 90, note "c," *sub* "Despencer," as to the writ of 49 Hen. III. which the Barony of Despencer, as well as that of De Ros, claims for its origin. Both of these Baronies were in abeyance when, in 1639 and 1679, Mowbray was placed at the head of the Baronies, but, had they then been in existence, it seems not improbable that Mowbray (which was placed *above* the anomalously-venerated Barony of Abergavenny, usually allowed to head the list) would have been placed before them.

XXII. 1893. 22. CHARLES BOTOLPH JOSEPH (STOURTON), LORD MOWBRAY, LORD SEGRAVE and BARON STOURTON, s. and h.; b. 23 May 1867; sometime Lieut. 3d Batt. East Yorkshire Reg. Militia; *suc. to the peerage* 18 April 1893 and *m.* 26 July following at St. Mary's (Rom. Cath. church), Chelsea, Mary, da. and h. of Thomas CONSTABLE, of the manor house, Otley, co. York, by Elizabeth Ducarel, da. of Henry Pierre, COUNT DE LAPASTURE.

Family Estates. These, in 1883, consisted of 5,097 acres in the West Riding of Yorkshire, valued at £9,347 a year. *Principal Residence.* Stourton Towers, near Knaresborough, co. York.

MOYDRUM.

See "CASTLEMAINE OF MOYDRUM, co. Westmeath," Barony [I.], (*Handcock*); *cr.* 1812.

MOYARTA.

i.e., "MOYARTA," Barony [I.] (*O'Brien*); *cr.* 1662 with the VISCOUNTCY OF CLARE [I.]; which see; *forfeited* 1691, and *extinct* 1774.

MUCH EASTON.

i.e., "MAYNARD OF MUCH EASTON, *alias* EASTON AD MONTEM, co. Essex," Barony (*Maynard*); *cr.* 1766 with the VISCOUNTCY OF MAYNARD OF EASTON LODGE," which see; *extinct* 1865.

MUGDOCK.

i.e., "GRAHAM AND MUGDOCK," Barony [S.], (*Graham*); *cr.* 1644 with the MARQUESSATE OF MONTROSE [S.], which see.

---

i.e., "ABERRUTHVEN, MUGDOCK AND FINTRIE," Barony [S.], (*Graham*), *cr.* 1707 with the DUKEDOM OF MONTROSE [S.], which see

MULGRAVE.

Earldom. I. 1626. 1, EDMUND (SHEFFIELD), BARON SHEFFIELD OF BUTTERWICKE[a], only s. and h. of John, 2d BARON SHEFFIELD,[a] by Douglas, da. of William (HOWARD), 1st BARON HOWARD OF EFFINGHAM, was *b.* about 1564; *suc. to the peerage*, 10 Dec. 1568; mat. at Oxford (Ch. Ch.) 1574-79, when aged 12; was a volunteer in Holland, 1585; Capt. of a man of war, 1588, taking an active part in the measures to repel the Spanish armada; *Knighted* 25 June 1588 by the Lord High Admiral; el. K.G., 23 April and inst. 25 June 1593; Governor of Brill in Holland, 1598; Lord Lieut. of Yorkshire, 1603-19; Lord President of the north, 1603-19; Councillor of the north, 1625, being *cr.* 5 Feb. 1625/6.[b] EARL OF MULGRAVE, co. York. In July 1646 (at the age of 84) he was a commissioner for the Parl. to treat with Scotland. He *m.* before 1590, Ursula, da. of Sir Robert TYRWHITT, of Kettleby, co, Lincoln, by Elizabeth, da. and h. of Thomas OXENBRIDGE. He *m.* secondly, 4 March 1619, Mariana, da. of Sir William IRWIN *alias* ERWIN. He *d.* Oct. 1646 in his 83d year, at Butterwick House, in Hammersmith and was *bur.* at Fulham, M.I. Will pr. 1646. His widow *d.* at Kensington on or before 1676. Admon. 7 Oct. 1676.

(a) The title is usually considered to have been "Sheffield of Butterwicke, co. Lincoln," but the creation of 15 Feb. 1546/7 gives it as "*Baron Sheffield*" only. See "*Creations* 1483-1646" in app. 47th Rep. D.K. Pub. Records. It is however called "Baron Sheffield of Butterwicke" when the 3d Baron was *cr.* an Earl in 1626.

(b) See vol. ii, p. 282, note "c," *sub* "Cleveland" for a list of the 6 noblemen who were *cr.* Earls on that day.

2 D

II. 1646. 2. EDMUND (SHEFFIELD), EARL OF MULGRAVE, &c., grandson and h., being only s. and h. of Sir John SHEFFIELD, by Grizel da. of Sir Edmund ANDERSON, Chief Justice of the Court of Common Pleas, which John was 2d s. of the 1st Earl by his first wife, but d. v.p., being drowned in the Humber, Dec. 1614 with two of his brothers. He was b. about Dec. 1611; was *styled* LORD SHEFFIELD, 1626-46; and *suc. to the peerage* in Oct. 1646; was a commissioner of the navy and custom, 1647 and a Councillor of State, 1649 and again (to Cromwell) in or before 1654. He was one of the nine (lawful) Peers(a) who, 10 Dec. 1657, were among the (62) members of Cromwell's "*House of Lords.*" He m. (Lic. London, 13 April 1631, to marry at Waltham abbey, he aged 20 and she 23) Elizabeth, 2d da. of Lionel (CRANFIELD), 1st EARL OF MIDDLESEX by his first wife, Elizabeth, da. of Richard SHEPHERD. He d. on his way to London, 24 Aug. 1658. Will pr. 1658. His widow m. 28 Oct. 1661, at St. Andrew's Undershaft, London (Lic. Fac.), as his first wife, Sir John BENNET, K.B., afterwards, (24 Nov. 1682) cr. Baron Ossulton, (who d. 1688, in his 70th year) and d. before May 1768.

III. 1658. 3. JOHN (SHEFFIELD), EARL OF MULGRAVE, &c., only s. and h.; b. 8 Sep. 1647, *suc. to the peerage*, 24 Aug. 1658. He was cr. 10 May 1694, MARQUESS OF NORMANBY, co. Lincoln and on 23 March 1702/3, DUKE OF THE COUNTY OF BUCKINGHAM AND OF NORMANBY. He d. 24 Feb. 1720/1, in his 73d year.

IV. 1721, to 1735. 4. EDMUND (SHEFFIELD), DUKE OF BUCKINGHAM AND NORMANBY [1703], MARQUESS OF NORMANBY [1694], EARL OF MULGRAVE [1626], and BARON SHEFFIELD OF BUTTERWICKE [1547], 3d but only surv. s. and h.; b. 3 Jan. 1715/6. He d. unm. 30 Oct. 1735, when *all his honours* became *extinct*.

See fuller particulars under "BUCKINGHAM," Dukedom, cr. 1703; ex. 1735.

MULGRAVE, and MULGRAVE OF NEW ROSS.

Barony [I.] I. 1767. 1. CONSTANTINE PHIPPS, of Mulgrave Castle, co. York, s. and h. of William PHIPPS.(b) by Catharine, da. and h. of James (ANNESLEY), 3d EARL OF ANGLESEY, and Catharine his wife (illegit. da. of King James II.), which Catharine last named was, afterwards, wife of John (SHEFFIELD), 1st DUKE OF BUCKINGHAM AND NORMANBY, and 4th EARL OF MULGRAVE abovenamed (being by him mother of the last Duke, who devised to her the estates of the Sheffield family) was *bap.* at St. Andrew's Holborn, 22 Aug. 1722; *suc.* his father, 1 Feb. 1729/30; was admitted to the Middle Temple, London, 11 July 1739, and having on the death, 13 March 1742/3, of his grandmother, the Dow. Duchess of Buckingham abovenamed, *suc.* to the estate of Mulgrave, &c., co. York, was cr. 8 Sep. 1767, BARON MULGRAVE OF NEW ROSS, co. Wexford [I.] He m. 26 Feb. 1742/3, at St, James Westm., Lepell, 1st da. of John (HERVEY), LORD HERVEY (s. and h. ap. of John, 1st EARL OF BRISTOL), by Mary, da. of Brig. General Nicholas LEPELL. He d. 13 Sep. 1775, aged 53, at Spa in Germany, and was *bur.* at Croydon, Surrey. Admon. 13 Nov. 1775, and Aug. 1804. His widow, who was b. Jan. 1722/3, d. 11 and was *bur.* 13 March 1780, at Croydon, aged 57.

(a) See vol. i, p. 299, note "d." *sub* "Bedford" for a list of these. Among "the commanders in the armies of the Commonwealth" is "Capt. Sheffield eldest s. to the Earl of Mulgrave" which probably refers to the Hon. James Sheffield, 1st *surv.* s. of the *late* Earl (see Visit. of Middlesex, 1663), being his first son by his *second* wife. The six sons of the 1st Earl, by his *first* wife, all d. in his lifetime, and only one of them (John) left a child. The eldest, Charles, d. a natural death, but John, Edmund and Philip were drowned in the Humber, William being drowned in France, while George "broke his neck in a new riding house, which his father had made of an old consecrated chapel as I have heard." [*Dugdale*].

(b) He (who was *bap.* 11 Oct. 1698, at St. Andrew's, Holborn), was the only surv. s. of eleven children of Sir Constantine Phipps, Lord Chancellor [I.], 1710 to 1714 (who d. 9 Oct. 1723), by Catharine (mar. lic. at Vic. Gen. office, 10 Oct. 1684), da. of George Sawyer.

II. 1775. Barony [G.B.] I 1790, to 1792.

2 and *1*. CONSTANTINE JOHN (PHIPPS), BARON MULGRAVE OF NEW ROSS [I.], s. and h.; *b.* 30 May 1744; entered the Navy, 1757, and was Capt. R.N., 1765, making in April 1773, a voyage of discovery towards the north pole; *suc. to the peerage* [I.], 13 Sep. 1775; was M.P. for Lincoln, 1768-74; for Huntingdon, 1776-84; and for Newark, 1784-90, taking an active part in support of the Ministry;(a) a Lord of the Admiralty, 1777-82; P.C., 1784; a Commissioner of the Board of Trade, 1784-86, and of the Board of Control, 1784-91; Joint Paymaster General, 1784-89. He was *cr.* a Peer of Great Britain, 7 July 1790, as BARON MULGRAVE of Mulgrave, co. York; F.R.S. (1771), &c. He *m.* 20 June 1787, at St. James' Westm., Anne Elizabeth, yst. da. of Nathaniel CHOLMLEY, of Howsham and Whitby, co. York, by his second wife, Henrietta Catherine, da. of Stephen CROFT, of Stillington in that county. She, who was *b.* at Howsham, 7 Nov. 1769, *d.* 22 May 1788, and was *bur.* at Lyth, co. York. He *d.* s.p.m., 10 Oct. 1792, aged 48, when the *Barony of Mulgrave* [G.B.], became *extinct*. He was *bur.* at Lyth afsd. Will pr. Nov. 1792.

Barony [I.] III. 1792. Barony [G.B.] II. 1794. Earldom [U.K.] I. 1812.

3 and *1*. HENRY (PHIPPS), BARON MULGRAVE OF NEW ROSS [I.], next surv. br. and h., being 3d s. of the 1st Baron; *b.* 14 Feb. 1755; entered the 1st Foot Guards, 1775, becoming, in 1793, Col. of the 31st Foot and eventually (1809) General in the army; M.P. for Totnes, 1784-90, and for Scarborough, 1790-94, having *suc. to the peerage* [I.], 10 Oct. 1792. He was *cr.* a Peer of Great Britain, 13 Aug. 1794, as BARON MULGRAVE of Mulgrave, co. York; P.C., 1804; Chancellor of the Duchy of Lancaster, 1804-05; Foreign Secretary of State, 1805-06; First Lord of the Admiralty, 1807-10; Lord Lieut. of the East Riding of Yorkshire, 1807; Master Gen. of the Ordnance, 1810-18. He was *cr.*, 7 Sep. 1812, VISCOUNT NORMANBY of Normanby, co. York,(b) and EARL OF MULGRAVE, in the said county, being made G.C.B., 20 May, 1820; F.S.A. (1793), &c. He *m.*, 20 Oct. 1795, at Houghton le Spring, Martha Sophia, da. of Christopher Thompson MALING, of West Herrington, co Durham, by Martha, da. of John SHERIS, of Queen square, Middlesex. He *d.* 7 April 1831, aged 76. Will pr. Aug. 1831. His widow *d.* 17 March 1849, in Eaton square. Will pr. April 1849.

Earldom. II. Barony. III. Barony [I.] IV. } 1831.

2 and *4*. CONSTANTINE HENRY (PHIPPS), EARL OF MULGRAVE, VISCOUNT NORMANBY, and BARON MULGRAVE, also BARON MULGRAVE OF NEW ROSS [I.], 1st s. and h.; *b.* 15 May 1797; *styled* VISCOUNT NORMANBY, 1812-31; *suc. to the peerage* [U.K., G.B., and I.], 7 April 1831. He was *cr.*, 25 June 1838,(c) MARQUESS OF NORMANBY, co. York. See that dignity.

MULL.

i.e., "INVERARY, MULL, MORVEN, AND TIRIE," Barony [S.] (*Campbell*), *cr.* 1701 with the DUKEDOM OF ARGYLL [S.], which see.

(a) He is frequently alluded to in Wraxall's "*Memoirs*" where it is said that "being formed on rather a heavy colossal scale, the opposition [party in the House of Commons] denominated him *Ursa Major*. They likewise gave him the name of *Alphesibœus*." He possessed "two distant voices, the one strong and hoarse, the other shrill and querulous." This peculiarity is alluded to in "*the Rolliad*," in the following alliterative lines.

* * * * "within his lab'ring throat
The shrill shriek struggles with the harsh hoarse note."

(b) There is a village of Normanby, near Whitby, in co. York, as well as the one, near Market Raisin, in co. Lincoln.

(c) This was one of the "Coronation" peerages of Queen Victoria for a list of which see vol. ii, p. 145, note "b," *sub* "Carew."

MULLINGAR.

i.e., "VAUGHAN OF MULLINGAR, co. Westmeath," Barony [I.] (*Vaughan*), *cr.* 1621; see "CARBERY" Earldom [I.], *cr.* 1628, both becoming *extinct* 1712.

MULTON, or MULTON DE EGREMONT.

Barony by Writ.

I. 1299. *1.* THOMAS DE MULTON, of Multon, co. Lincoln and of Egremont and Cockermouth, co. Cumberland, s. and h. of Thomas DE MULTON of the same, who was s. and h. of Lambert DE MULTON, by Amabel, da. and coheir of Richard DE LUCY, of Egremont and Cockermouth afsd., *suc.* his father in 1294; served in the wars with Scotland; was sum. 26 Jan. (1296/7) 25 Ed. I.(a) to attend the King at Salisbury and was sum. to Parl. as a Baron (LORD MULTON or LORD MULTON DE EGREMONT) by writs, 6 Feb. (1298/9) 27 Ed. I. to 15 May (1320) 14 Ed. II., such writs having, after 1 Ed. II. (1307-08), the addition of the words "*de Egremund.*" He was one of the Barons whose name, as "*Thomas de Multon, Dominus de Egremon,*" appears to the letter in 1301 to the Pope.(b) He *m.* Alianore, who survived him, and *d.* 1321-22. Esch, 15 Ed. II.

II. 1322, to 1334. *2.* JOHN (DE MULTON, LORD MULTON or LORD MULTON DE EGREMONT, s. and h., who did homage (1329) 3 Ed. III., being then not of full age. He was sum. to Parl. from 27 Jan. (1331/2) 6 Ed. III. to 24 July (1334) 8 Ed. III. He *d.* s.p.(c) 23 Nov. 1334) 8 Ed. III., when the *Barony fell into abeyance.*(d)

MULTON DE GILLESLAND.

Barony by Writ.

I. 1307. *1.* THOMAS DE MULTON, of Gillesland, co. Cumberland, s. and h. of Thomas DE MULTON, of the same, by Isabel, his wife, which Thomas *suc.* his grandmother (Maud, widow of Thomas DE MULTON, da. and h. of Hubert DE VAUX, of Gillesland) in that estate shortly after 1293, *suc.* his father 1295 when he was aged 13; served in the Scotch wars, and was sum. to Parl. as a Baron (LORD MULTON DE GILLESLAND) from 26 Aug. (1307) 1 Ed. II. to 26 Nov. 1313) 7 Ed. II. He *d.* s.p.m. soon afterwards. Claus. 11 Ed. II.

II. 1313? *2.* MARGARET, *de jure*, *suo jure*, BARONESS MULTON DE GILLESLAND da. and h.; aged 13 at her Father's death. She, being then in ward to the King, was carried off from Warwick Castle and *m.* in 1317, by RALPH DACRE, who however obtained the royal pardon for his offence. In consequence, doubtless, of this alliance he was sum. to Parl. as a Baron (LORD DACRE) from 13 May 1321 to 15 Nov. 1338. See "DACRE" Barony, *cr.* 1321.(e)

(a) See vol. i, p. 111, note "b," *sub* "Ap. Adam" as to this not constituting a regular writ of summons to Parl.

(b) See "*Nicolas,*" pp. 761-809 for a full description of this letter.

(c) The marriage of Amabel de Holbech attributed to him by Dugdale, refers to some other John de Multon, one who was father of a Sir John Multon living (1367/88) 11 Rich. II. See "*Coll. Top. et Gen.,*" vol. vii, p. 389.

(d) The coheirs were his three sisters, of whom (1) Joan, then aged 30 was wife of Robert (Fitzwalter), Lord Fitzwalter, whose descendant and representative Robert (Radcliffe), 1st Earl of Sussex was incorrectly styled. (See vol. iii, p. 372, note "a") in 1542 "*Lord Egremond.*" (2) Elizabeth, then aged 28 and wife of Walter de Bermingham, whose representation devolved on her s. and h., by her first husband Sir Robert de Harington (*i.e.*, John, Lord Harington, 1347-63) and his issue (3) Margaret, then aged 24 and wife of Thomas de Lucy, afterwards (1342-65) Lord Lucy, whose issue became extinct, in 1348, on the death of her da. Maud, second wife to Henry (Percy), 1st Earl of Northumberland, to whom she left her considerable estates, still enjoyed by his descendants, who frequently, tho' incorrectly styled themselves "*Barons Lucy.*" See p. 174, note "b," *sub* "Lucy."

(e) See vol. ii, p. 2, note "e," *sub* "Dacre," as to the presumed merger (a theory held by Sir Harris Nicolas) of this Barony of Multon de Gillesland in that of Dacre.

MUNARD.

i.e., "DOUGLAS OF NIEDPATH, LYNE AND MUNARD," Barony [S.], (*Douglas*), *cr.* 1679 with the EARLDOM OF MARCH [S.], which see.

MUNCASTER.

Barony [I.]
I. 1783.

1. JOHN PENNINGTON, s. and h. ap. of Sir Joseph PENNINGTON, 4th Bart., of Muncaster, co. York, by Sarah, da. and h. of John MOORE, of co. Somerset, was *b.* about 1740; entered the army about 1760, becoming finally a Colonel; was M.P. for Melborne Port, 1781-96; for Colchester, 1796—1802, and for Westmorland, 1806-13, and was *cr.* v.p. 21 Oct. 1783,(a) BARON MUNCASTER [I.], with a spec. rem. of that dignity, failing heirs male of his body, to his brother Lowther Pennington. He *suc.* his father 3 Feb. 1793 as *Baronet*, a dignity *cr.* 21 June 1676. He *m.* 26 Sep. 1778, at St. James' Westm., Penelope da. and h. of James COMPTON (great grandson of Spencer, 2d EARL OF NORTHAMPTON) by Frances RIGGS, of New York in America,(b) presumably da. of Samuel RIGGS, of London, Merchant. She *d.* 13 Nov. 1806, and was *bur.* at Copgrove, co. York. He *d.* s.p.m.s., at Muncaster, 8, and was *bur.* there 15 Oct. 1813, aged about 73. Will pr. Jan. 1814.

II. 1813. *2.* LOWTHER (PENNINGTON), BARON MUNCASTER [I.], only surv. br. and h. male; *b.* 1745, entered the army in which he finally (1808) became General and Col. of the 4th Royal Veteran Battalion; *suc. to the peerage* [I.], 8 Oct. 1813, according to the spec. rem. in the creation of that dignity. He *m.* 13 Jan. 1802, Esther, widow of James MORRISON, Capt. 58th foot, 2d da. of Thomas BARRY, of Clapham, co. Surrey. He *d.* in Grosvenor place, 29 July 1818, aged 73, and was *bur.* in the vaults of St. Geo. Han. sq. Will pr. 1818. His widow *d.* 7 Oct. 1827. Admon. June 1838.

I. 1818. *3.* LOWTHER AUGUSTUS JOHN (PENNINGTON), BARON MUNCASTER [I.], only s. and h.; *b.* 14 Dec. 1802; *suc. to the peerage* [I.], ıly 1818. He *m.* 15 Dec. 1828, at Brotherton, Frances Catherine, yst. da. of Sir RAMSDEN, 4th Bart., of Byrom, co. York, by Louisa Susan, da. and coheir of (INGRAM), 10th VISCOUNT IRVINE [S.] He *d.* at the Green Park Hotel, r, 30 April, and was *bur.* 15 May 1838, at Warter, co. York, aged 35. M.I. June 1838. His widow, who was *b.* 1805, *d.* 30 Jan. 1853, aged 47, at place west, Hyde Park. Will pr. July 1854.

4. GAMEL AUGUSTUS (PENNINGTON), BARON MUNCASTER [I.], s. and h.; *b.* 3 Dec. 1831 at Warter Priory, and *bap.* 31 July ter; ed. at Trin. Coll., Cambridge; B.A., 1853; High Sheriff of 9. He *m.* 2 Aug. 1855, at St. Geo. Han. sq., Jane Louisa Octavia, l (GROSVENOR), 2d MARQUESS OF WESTMINSTER, by Elizabeth Mary, ge Granville (LEVESON-GOWER), 1st DUKE OF SUTHERLAND. He *d.* s.p.m. stric fever) at Castellamare, near Naples, 13 June 1862, aged 30, and was *bur.* 29 July at Muncaster. His widow, who was *b.* 29 Aug. 1834, *m.* 3 Oct. 1863, at the Episcopal chapel, Banchory, co. Aberdeen, Hugh Barlow LINDSAY, Bombay Civil Service, and was living 1893.

V. 1862. *5.* JOSSLYN FRANCIS (PENNINGTON), BARON MUNCASTER [I.], also a *Baronet* [1676], next surv. br. and h. male; *b.* 25 Dec. 1834, in Hamilton Place, Piccadilly, and *bap.* 17 June 1835, at Muncaster; entered the army, being, in 1856, Capt. of the 90th Foot and, in 1857, Capt. Rifle Brigade;

(a) This was one of nine *Irish* creations made, by Fox, at a time when the King refused to make any additions to the *British* peerage. See a list of them, vol. iii, p. 44, note "d," *sub* "Delaval."

(b) A certified copy of the marriage of this James Compton, 29 April 1736, at the chapel in Fort George in New York, is among the Compton papers of the Earl of Crawford at Haigh. *Ex. inform.* W. A. Lindsay.

suc. to the peerage [I.], 13 June 1862; was captured, with his wife and others, by Greek Brigands in 1870 when four of the party were put to death before the ransom arrived; was M.P. for West Cumberland, 1872-80, and for the Egremont division since 1885; Lord Lieut. of Cumberland. He *m.*, 9 April 1863, at Maltby, co. York, Constance, 2d da. of Edmund L'ESTRANGE, of Tynte Lodge, co. Leitrim, by Henrietta Susan Beresford, sister of Richard George (LUMLEY), 9th EARL OF SCARBROUGH.

Family Estates.—These, in 1883, consisted of 5,811 acres in the counties of Cumberland, Lancaster, and Westmorland, worth £2,629 a year. *Principal Residence.* Muncaster Castle, near Ravenglass, co. Cumberland.

MUNCHENSI.

WILLIAM DE MUNCHENSI, a powerful Baron of the county of Norfolk, &c., s. and h. of Warine DE MUNCHENSI; *suc.* his father in 1255; took a leading part with the Barons against King Henry III. and was sum. to [*Montfort's*] Parl. 24 Dec. (1264), 49 Hen. III. Such summons, however, does not originate a hereditary Barony.(a) He *d.* s.p.m. 1289, being slain in battle against the Welsh

MUNCY or MONCY.

Barony by Writ.

I. 1299, to 1308.

1. WALTER DE MUNCY,(b) of Thornton, near Skipton, co. York, was sum. to Parl. as a Baron (LORD MUNCY) from 6 Feb. (1298/9), 27 Ed. I., to 22 Feb. (1306/7), 35 Ed. I.(c) He was at the siege of Carlaverock(d); was present at the Parl. at Lincoln an' his name as "*Walterus de Moncy, Dominus de Thornton,*" apper among the signatories of the famous letter to the Pope in 130' He was Keeper of Framlingham Castle (1307/8), 1 Ed. II., b' before (1308/9), 2 Ed. II.(f)

MUNSTER.

i.e., "MUNSTER" Dukedom [I.] (*Von der Schulenberg*), *cr.* "KENDAL" Dukedom, *cr.* 1719, both being peerages for life; *extinct* 17

---

i.e., "MUNSTER" Earldom [I.] (*H.R.H. Prince Willi* 1789, with the DUKEDOM OF CLARENCE, which see; *merged* in the (

(a) See vol. iii, p. 365, note "d," *sub* "Fitz John," where also a list of those so sum. is given.

(b) There is no account of him in "Dugdale," but see Banks's "*Bar. Angl. Con.*" (vol. ii, p. 105), where, under the "*Barones Pretermissi*," many particulars of him and of the family of "De Monceaux" are given.

(c) There is proof in the rolls of Parl. of his sitting.

(d) The arms on his banner were "chequy, *arg.* and *gu.*"

(e) See "Nicolas," pp. 761--809, for a full account of that letter.

(f) "His heir was probably a female *m.* to Goushall who had two daughters, who were his coheirs, whereof (1) Margaret *m.* first (—) Despencer (and had a son, Philip Despencer), and secondly John de Roos, who *d.* without issue by her, 12 Ed. III., leaving her, the said Margaret, surviving, who deceased about 22 Ed. III. (2) Isabel, sister of Margaret, appears afterwards to have been found her heir and wife of Durand Bard." [Banks's "*Bar. Angl. Con.*," vol. ii, p. 105.]

Earldom. I. 1831. 1. GEORGE AUGUSTUS FREDERICK FITZ-CLARENCE, eldest of the five illegit sons of **King William IV.**, (sometime, 1789 to 1830) DUKE OF CLARENCE, &c, and also EARL OF MUNSTER [I.]), by Dora(a) (generally known as "*Mrs. Jordan*,") da. of Francis BLAND (apparently "a stage underling"(b) at Cork), was *b.* 16 Jan. 1794; ed. at the Military College at Harlow; entered the 10th Hussars (when 14) 1807, serving in the peninsular and being severely wounded at Toulouse; served subsequently (in the 24th Light Dragoons) in India, 1814-18; retired in 1878 as Lieut.-Col. becoming finally, 1841, Major General. On the accession of his Father to the throne, he was, 1830, made Aide-de-camp to the King; Dep. Adjutant General of the Forces, July to Dec. 1830 and was *cr.* 4 June 1831, BARON TEWKESBURY, co. Gloucester, VISCOUNT FITZ-CLARENCE and EARL OF MUNSTER, with a spec. rem. of those dignities, failing the heirs male of his body, to Frederick FITZ-CLARENCE, Adolphus FITZ-CLARENCE, and Augustus FITZ-CLARENCE.(c) He was Lieut. of the Tower of London, 1831-33; Col. of the 1st Tower hamlets militia, 1831-42; Constable of Windsor Castle, 1833-42; P.C. 1833; Knight Grand Cross of Ferdinand of Wurtemburg; Aide-de-camp to Queen Victoria, 1837. F.R.S., F.S.A., and, in 1841, President of the Royal Asiatic Society, of which he had been an original (1824) member.(d). He *m.* 18 Oct. 1819, Mary WYNDHAM(e), illegit. da. of George (WYNDHAM), 3d EARL OF EGREMONT, by (—) ILIFF, Spinster. He committed suicide by shooting himself, in Upper Belgrave street, 20 March 1842, aged 48, and was *bur.* in Hampton church, Midx. Will pr. Ap. 1842. His widow *d.* a few months later, 3 Dec. 1842, in Portland place.

II. 1842. 2. WILLIAM GEORGE (FITZ-CLARENCE), EARL OF MUNSTER, &c., s. and h., *b.* 19 May 1824; *styled* VISCOUNT FITZ-CLARENCE, from 1831 till he *suc. to the peerage* 20 March 1842; an officer in the Life Guards, 1842 to 1852, when he retired as Captain. He *m.* 17 April 1855, at All Saints, Knightsbridge, his first cousin, Wilhelmina, da. of the Hon. John KENNEDY-ERSKINE, of Dun, co. Forfar, by Augusta FITZ-CLARENCE, one of the sisters (by the same parents) of the 1st EARL OF MUNSTER. She was *b.* 27 June 1830.

[EDWARD FITZ-CLARENCE, *styled* VISCOUNT FITZ-CLARENCE, 1st s. and h.; *b.* 29 March 1856, at Rutland Gate, Hyde Park. He *d.* v.p. 20 Nov. 1870 in his 15th year.]

[GEOFFREY GEORGE GORDON FITZ-CLARENCE, *styled* LORD TEWKESBURY since 1870, 3d but 1st surv. s. and h. ap.; *b.* 18 July 1859; Capt. King's Royal rifle corps, 1888.]

Family Estates. These, in 1883, were under 2,000 acres.

MURRAY, see also MORAY.

[The Scotch Earldoms held by the families of Randolph, Dunbar and Stewart are entered under the spelling of *Moray*.]

(a) She was *b.* near Waterford, 1762, and *d.* at St. Cloud near Paris, 5 July 1816. As an actress of comedy (1782-1815) she is said to have been unrivalled for "perfect nature with arch simplicity." Besides her ten children by the Royal Duke, she had (previously) 5 daughters, viz., four by Sir Richard Ford, a police magistrate and one by Richard Daly, manager of the Cork theatre.

(b) "*Nat. Biog*," under "Jordan."

(c) These were his three surviving brothers—the other brother, Henry Fitz-Clarence, had *d.* unm. in India. They and three of their (five) sisters were granted, by royal warrant, 24 May 1831, the precedence of the children of a Marquess.

(d) He "had collected an immense mass of information from the great continental libraries and other sources for a *History of the art of war among Eastern nations*." His "*Journal of a Route across India*, &c., 1817-18," is "a work exhibiting much observation and containing some curious plates of Indian military costumes of the day, from sketches of the author." [*Nat. Biog.*, *sub* "*Fitz-Clarence*."]

(e) Her br. George Wyndham, was, in 1859, *cr.* Baron Leconfield.

MURRAY.

THE HON. ALEXANDER MURRAY, 4th s. of Alexander, 4th LORD ELIBANK [S.], having taken an active part, against the GOVERNMENT, in the Westminster election of 1750, fled the county and resided in France till 1777, where he was known as "COUNT MURRAY." He had been *cr.* an Earl in 1759, by the titular King James III., but *query* if the title was not EARL OF INVERNESS [S.] He *d.* unm. 1777.(a)

MURRAY.

i.e., MURRAY, BALVANY AND GASK," Barony [S.] (*Murray*), *cr.* 1676, with the MARQUESSATE OF ATHOLE [S.], which see.

---

i.e., "MURRAY, Barony [S.] (*Murray*), *cr.* 1696, with the EARLDOM OF TULLIBARDINE [S.], for life; *extinct* 1724, see "ATHOLE" Dukedom [S.], *cr.* 1703.

---

i.e., "MURRAY, BALVENIE AND GASK," Barony [S.], *cr.* 1703, with the DUKEDOM OF ATHOLE [S.], which see.

MURRAY OF BLAIR, MOULIN AND TILLEMONT.

i.e., "MURRAY OF BLAIR, MOULIN AND TILLEMONT, Barony [S.], (*Murray*), *cr.* 1686, with the EARLDOM OF DUNMORE [S.], which see.

MURRAY OF GASK.

i.e., "MURRAY OF GASK," Barony [S.] (*Murray*), *cr.* 1628, with the EARLDOM OF TULLIBARDINE [S.], which see.

MURRAY OF LOCHMABEN.

i.e., "MURRAY OF LOCHMABEN," Barony [S.] (*Murray*), *cr.* 1622, with the VISCOUNTCY OF ANNAND [S.]; see "ANNANDALE" Earldom [S.], *cr.* 1625; *extinct* 1658.

MURRAY OF STANLEY.

i.e., "MURRAY OF STANLEY, co. Gloucester," Barony (*Murray*), *cr* 1786, with the EARLDOM OF STRANGE. See "ATHOLE" Dukedom [S.], *cr.* 1703, *sub* the 4th Duke

MURRAY OF TULLIBARDINE.

i.e., "MURRAY OF TULLIBARDINE" Barony [S.] (*Murray*), *cr.* 1604; see 'TULLIBARDINE" Earldom [S.], *cr.* 1606.

MURROUGH.

See vol. iv, p. 321, note "c," as to this fictitious Viscountcy [I.] pretended to have been *cr.*, 1572-85, with the DUKEDOM OF IRELAND, by the Pope's Nuncio.

(a) See vol. i, p. 59, note "b," *sub* "Albemarle" for a list of the "*Jacobite Peerages.*"

MUSGRAVE.

Barony by Writ.

I. 1350.

1. SIR THOMAS MUSGRAVE, presumed (by Dugdale) to be a son of Thomas M. who obtained a charter (1277-78) 6 Ed. I. for a fair at Overton and who was in the Scotch wars, 1310-11, was in command at the victory over the Scotch at Durham, 18 Oct. 1346; was Gov. of Berwick and Justiciar of the English lands in Scotland, 1347, and was sum. to parl. as a Baron (LORD MUSGRAVE), from 25 Nov. (1350) 24 Ed. III. to 4 Oct. (1373) 47 Ed. III. He was subsequently Sheriff of Yorkshire, Gov. of York Castle and, in 1368, Eschaetor of the counties of York, Northumberland, Cumberland and Westmorland. He was, however, defeated by the Scots, and (with his son) taken prisoner (1378-79) 2 Ric. II., but was released, after having prevailed on John Nevill and others to become bound for his ransom, which he subsequently refused to discharge. For this disgraceful conduct he was imprisoned by the King (1381-82) 5 Ric. II., after which no more is heard of him. He appears to have *m.* three times, his third wife, whom he *m.* in (1370) 44 Ed. III., being Isabel, widow of Robert CLIFFORD, s. of Robert, LORD CLIFFORD. The Barony was possibly considered as forfeited; certainly none of his descendants were sum. to Parl. or advanced any claim so to be, tho' they, in the male line, being also "persons of great note in those parts continue there [says Dugdale] to this day."(a)

MUSGRAVE.

In 1650 King Charles II., then at Breda, signed a warrant for the creation of SIR PHILIP MUSGRAVE (b) 2d Bart., of Hartley Castle, to a Barony (BARON MUSGRAVE OF HARTLEY CASTLE?) but it never passed the seals.(c) He *d.* 1678, being ancestor of the succeeding Baronets.

MUSKERRY.

Viscountcy [I.]

I. 1628.

1. SIR CHARLES (*alias* CORMAC OGE) MACCARTY, of Blarney and Muskerry, co. Cork, s. and h. of Sir Cormac MACCARTY, of the same, by his first wife, Mary, da. of Theobald (BUTLER), 1st BARON CAHER [I.], *suc.* his father, 23 Feb. 1616, and was *cr.* 15 Nov. 1628,(d) BARON BLARNEY and VISCOUNT MUSKERRY, both of co. Cork [I.], for life, with rem. to his son Donough(e) and the heirs male of his body, with rem. to the heirs male of the body of the grantee. He *m.* firstly, about 1590, Margaret, da. of Donough (O'BRIEN), 4th EARL OF THOMOND [I.], by his first wife, Ellen, da. of Maurice (ROCHE), VISCOUNT FERMOY [I.] He *m.* secondly, Ellen, widow of Donell MACCARTHY REAGH, da. of David (ROCHE), VISCOUNT FERMOY [I.], by Joan, da. of James (BARRY), VISCOUNT BUTTEVANT [I.] He *d.* in London and was *bur.* 27 May 1640,(f) in Westm. Abbey. His widow *m.* (for her 3d husband) the Hon. Thomas FITZ MAURICE, 4th s. of Thomas, LORD KERRY [I.]

(a) Banks in his "*Bar. Angl. Conc.*" says the heir to the Barony is Thomas Davison Bland, of Kippax Park, co. York, whose ancestress, Mary, only da. and h. of Sir Richard Musgrave, 3d Bart., *m.* Thomas Davison. It, however, is not clear that this Sir Richard was the heir *general* of the Baron.

(b) This Sir Philip was father of Sir Richard, the 3d Bart. (alluded to in note "a" next above) as also of Sir Christopher, 4th Bart., ancestor of the present line of Baronets.

(c) The warrant is printed in Burton's "*Life of Sir Philip Musgrave*," 1840.

(d) There is an erroneous idea that this peerage was *cr.* earlier than 1628, and that it was conferred on one of Sir Charles's ancestors. This probably arises from the territorial Barony of Muskerry having been held by them for several generations.

(e) Donough was the second son, but his elder br., Cormac, is said to have *d.* young, tho' he might be living (possibly an idiot) at this time.

(f) His death is generally given as 20 *Feb.* 1640.

II. 1640. 2. DONOUGH (MACCARTY), VISCOUNT MUSKERRY, &c [I.], s. by first wife and heir (according to the spec. rem. in its creation) of that dignity. He was *b.* 1594; *suc. to the peerage* [I.], in May 1640. He was *cr.* 27 Nov. 1658, EARL OF CLANCARTY, co. Cork [I.] See that dignity, which together with this one, was *attainted* in 1691.

Barony [I.] I. 1781. 1. SIR ROBERT-TILSON DEANE, Bart. [I.], of Springfield, co. Limerick, 2d but 1st surv. s. and h. of the Rt. Hon. Sir Robert DEANE, 5th Bart. [I.], of Dromore, co. Cork, by Charlotte, 2d da. of Thomas TILSON, of Dublin, was *bap.* 29 Nov. 1745; *suc.* his father in the Baronetcy [I.] (a dignity *cr.* 10 March 1709), in Feb. 1770; was M.P. for Carysfort, 1771-76, and for co. Cork, 1776-80, and was *cr.* 5 Jan. 1781, BARON MUSKERRY, co. Cork [I.], taking his seat, 9 Oct. 1785. He was Gov. of co. Limerick and P.C. [I.] He *m.* May 1775, Anne, only child of John FITZMAURICE by (—), da. of (—), which John was s. and h. ap. of John FITZMAURICE, of Springfield Castle, co. Limerick, nephew to Thomas, 1st EARL OF KERRY [I.] He *d.* 25 June 1818, aged 72. His widow *d.* 30 July 1830.

II. 1818. 2. JOHN THOMAS FITZMAURICE (DEANE), BARON MUSKERRY [I.], 2d but 1st surv. s. and h.; *b.* 27 Sep. 1777; entered the army, in which he subsequently (1821) became Major General; C.B.; *suc. to the peerage* [I.], 25 June 1818. He *m.* 17 Jan. 1815, Sarah, 2d da. of M. HAYNES of Bishop's Castle, Salop. He *d.* s.p. at Caen, 24 Dec. 1824, aged 47, and was *bur.* in the Protestant burial ground there. M.I. Will pr. Feb. 1825. His widow *m.* in 1826, Frederick Dundas RADFORD,[a] who *d.* 30 Feb. 1837, and *d.* 2 Aug. 1852.

III. 1824. 3. MATTHEW FITZMAURICE (DEANE), BARON MUSKERRY [I.], only surv. br. and h., *b.* 29 March 1795, at Springfield Castle; *suc. to the peerage* [I.], 25 Dec. 1824. He *m.* firstly, 13 Aug. 1825, at Stillorgan, co. Dublin, Louisa Dorcas, 2d da. of Henry Deane GRADY, of Lodge, co. Limerick, by Dorcas, da. of Thomas SPREAD, of Ballycannon, co. Cork. She *d.* 25 Sep. 1846, in Merrion square, Dublin. He *m.* secondly, 13 April 1864, Lucy, widow of Col. ALDRICH, of the Royal Engineers. She *d.* 16 Jan. 1867, at 3 Upper Wimpole street, Marylebone. Will dat. 30 Dec. 1865, to 19 Nov. 1866, pr. 19 Feb. 1867. He *m.* thirdly Elizabeth (—). He *d.* in London, 19 May 1868, aged 73, at 14 Cranley Place, Brompton, Midx. Will pr. at Dublin. His widow *d.* 4 Dec. 1884, at Cranley Place afsd. Admon. 17 Jan. 1885.[b]

IV. 1868. 4. HAMILTON MATTHEW TILSON FITZMAURICE (DEANE-MORGAN), BARON MUSKERRY [I.], and also a *Baronet* [I. 1709], grandson and h., being only s. and h. of the Hon. Robert Tilson Fitzmaurice DEANE-MORGAN, *formerly* DEANE, by Elizabeth Geraldine, 1st da. and coheir of Hamilton Knox GROGAN-MORGAN, of Johnstown Castle, co. Wexford, which Robert (who took the additional name of *Morgan* by Royal lic., 14 Dec. 1854), was s. and h. ap. of the 3d Baron by his first wife and *d.* v.p., 28 Feb. 1857, aged 30. He was *b.* 18 May 1854; served in the Royal Navy, and *suc. to the peerage* [I.], 19 May 1868. He *m.*, 23 Nov. 1872, Flora Georgina, 3d da. of the Hon. Chichester Thomas FOSTER-SKEFFINGTON (2d s. of Harriet, *suo jure* VISCOUNTESS MASSEREENE [I.]), by Amelia, da. of Arthur BLENNERHASSET, of Ballyseedy, co. Kerry. She was *b.* 4 June 1852.

(a) See "Annual Register" of 1837. It is, however, otherwise said that the lady's husband was named James Dawson, who, possibly, was a *third* husband.

(b) It was granted to Belinda Anne Moore, of Widcombe, Bath, widow, sister and next of kin.

Family Estates.—These, in 1883, consisted of 10,824 acres in co. Wexford; 3,161 in co. Limerick; 742 in co. Tipperary; 419 in co. Carlow; 851 in co. Waterford; 252 in co. Kilkenny, and 28 co. Cork. *Total* 15,277 acres, worth £10,736 a year. *Principal Residence.* Springfield Castle, near Drumcollober, co. Limerick.

"Only £2,995 of these rents are his Lordship's, the rest being held by his mother the Hon. Mrs. Deane-Morgan, who also holds 541 acres in common with Lady Granard." [Bateman's "*Great Landowners*," 1883.]

MYSORE.

See "HARRIS OF SERINGAPATAM AND MYSORE in the East Indies AND OF BELMONT, co. Kent," Barony (*Harris*), *cr.* 1815

CORRIGENDA ET ADDENDA.

p. 3, note "a," line 2; *after* "Coningsby," *insert* "[see p. 307, note 'a,' *sub* '*Mexborough*.']"

p. 4, line 29; *after* "sometimes," *insert* "tho' probably erroneously."

p. 6, line 27; *for* "by this and other writs," *read* "and subsequently."

p. 7, line 12; *for* "is said to have been," *read* "was, on 5 April 1559."

p. 9, lines 1 and 21; *for* "Normandy," *read* "France."

p. 10, note "b," line 5; *after* "titles," *insert* "See also *addenda* to p. 31, line 28."

p 16. *after* p. 9, *insert* "LANGNEWTOUN, see LONGNEWTON."

p. 19, lines 26, 27, and 28; *after* "Lansladron," *insert* "or Nansladron."

p. 22, line 15; *after* "however," *insert* "(who was *b.* in the spring of 1279 at Bylton.)"

p. 23, line 16; *after* "1430," *insert* "Will, in which he makes no mention of his wife, dat. at Poppleton, near York, 8, and pr. 14 Dec. 1430, at York."

p. 24, note "b;" The dispensation for Edward Willoughby to marry Margaret Nevill, (they being related in the third degree) was issued 9 Oct. and recorded 22 Nov. 1505 at York. See *Test Ebor* (Surtees Soc.), vol. iii, p. 564.

p. 25, line 25; *for* "s. and h., *b.* 1493," *read* "1st s. and h., *b.* 17 Nov. 1493," *and add as a note thereto* "See *Coll. Top. et Gen.*, vol. ii, p. 174, for dates of birth [1493—1513] of the 15 children of Richard, Lord Latimer."

p. 31, line 28, *to* "LAUNCESTON," *add this as a note*, "See vol. ii, p. 375, note 'a,' *sub* 'Cornwall,' for a list of Royal or semi-Royal titles of peerage." To that note should be added a reference to an interesting letter of Garter Anstis, shortly before the creation of the Dukedoms granted to the two Princes, Frederick and William (grandsons of King George I.) in 1726. Anstis recommends the choice of "*Aberfrau* and *Snawdon*, which were the titles of the ancient Princes of Wales" and of "*Lanceston* and *Trematon* which are the chief honours of the Dutchy of Cornwall." Accordingly the young Prince Frederick (afterwards, 1729-51, Prince of Wales), was, when *cr.*, 26 July 1726, Duke of Edenburgh, made at the same time Baron of *Snawdon* and Viscount of *Launceston*. He was also made "Marquess of the Isle of *Ely*," as to which place there is in Anstis's letter the following paragraph, "All the cities of England give denominations to the nobility save London, Westminster, Canterbury (which may as well be granted as York), Durham, and *Ely* (which have not been granted, being Palatinates), Gloucester, Bath, and Wells." The *Dukedom of London*, the *Marquessate of Edinburgh*, and the *Earldom of Dublin or Ulster* in Ireland were also suggested, but the *Irish Earldom* was omitted as also was the title of "*London*," tho' that of "*Edinburgh*" was selected as a Dukedom, the title of "*Eltham*" (one of the ancient palaces of the Crown, some of which are also mentioned by Anstis) being taken as the Earldom. The suggested title of *Trematon* in Cornwall was conferred (as a Viscountcy) 27 July 1726, with the Dukedom of Cumberland on Prince William the younger of the two brothers. With respect to "Cumberland" and other counties, Anstis says that "all the counties of England and Wales give [in 1726] denominations save the [eight] following ones, *viz.* (1) *Brecknock*, void by the attainder of the late Duke of Ormond (2) *Cumberland* [vacant since 1708] (3) *Flint*, never a title, but esteemed an appendage to the Earldom of Chester (4) *Glamorgan* [as to which] the family of [Somerset, Dukes of], Beaufort allege they have some signet from Charles I., but no patent (5) *Gloucester* [which] hath been esteemed unfortunate (6) *Lancaster* [which] is of a particular nature. Without consulting two acts of Parliament, which have not hitherto been printed, I cannot determine whether by that in 1 Hen. IV., the Dukedom can be granted separate from the possessions, or whether by the method of entail in 1 Ed. IV., it can be granted. If this title should be pitched upon [*i.e.*, as one to be conferred on the

s. and h. ap. of the Prince of Wales] the matter should be stated for the opinion of the Judges (7) *Merioneth*, a word of that sound that no person ever took it (8) *Northumberland*; an Earldom for several descents in [the family of] Percy."

It is to be observed that Anstis reckons Gloucester *twice* over (as above quoted) once among the *cities* and once among the *counties*. One does not gather whether the peerages of York, Lincoln, Stafford, Worcester, &c., are considered by him as representing the cities or the counties of those names.

p. 40, note "h," line 3; *after* "attribute," *insert* "(as in the text of this article.)"

" note "g." *Commence this note as under.* Since this article was written there has appeared (July 1893) in *the Genealogist*, N.S. (vol. x, pp. 1-16), a masterly account of "*The ancient Earls of Leicester*, by G. W. Watson," containing "charters, many of which have been briefly referred to in the notes" to this article, which notes were, indeed, kindly supplied by him. Mr. Watson's excellent summing up of the vexed question as to whether "Robert, Count of Meulan in the Vexin Francais, Sire de Beaumont, Pont-Audemer, Brionne and other lands in Normandy," *should*, or *should not*, be held to be the first Earl of Leicester is, as follows. "There seems to be no doubt that he possessed the *comitatus* [of Leicester] which must be held to have comprehended the dignity of Earl. Yet it is equally certain that he never styled himself Earl of Leicester. It is not however to be expected that the Count of Meulan, already a *Comes*, would either have dropped his illustrious name to assume the title of Earl of Leicester, or else would have used both titles together; either course would have been without a parallel and indeed without a purpose, for at the commencement of the 12th century *the territorial designation* was held *of little account*. Hence it is not surprising that we find him styled Count of Meulan only, both in charters and in chronicles." Mr. Watson discredits the *inspeximus* by King Edward (alluded to below) in which his grant of the manor of Thoftes runs as being by "*Robertus, Comes de Mellento et Leicestrie*," tho' it was confirmed by Henry II. as having been "*ex dono Roberti, Comitis Mellenti*," without any mention of Leicester.

p. 41, lines 7 and 8; *dele* "(with his father)."

" note "f," line 3; *after* "Preaux," *insert* "leaving six sons, of whom Robert succeeded him."

" note "f," line 3 to 5; *dele* "Of the two daughters," &c., *down to* "Gloucester." [By an *unfortunate piece of carelessness* these two ladies were misplaced here, thus making them *sisters* instead of *daughters* of Earl Robert "*Le Bossu*." See (true) names and descriptions of the *sisters* of this Earl Robert in Mr. Watson's "*Earls of Leicester*," as quoted in the corrigenda to p. 40, note "g."]

p. 42, line 17; *to* "s. and h." *add this as a note.* "He appears to have been an only son and have had four sisters of whom (1) Isabel *m.* firstly Simon (Saint Liz), Earl of Northampton and Huntingdon, who *d.* Aug. 1153. She *m.* secondly Gervase Paynell, of Dudley (2) Hawise, *m.* William (Fitz Robert), Earl of Gloucester, who *d.* 23 Nov. 1183 (3) [—], *m.* Robert de Toeni, who *d.* 1162 (4) [—], a nun."

p. 44, *to note* "*a*," *add* "The Earl had another sister (besides Amicia de Montfort above-named). *viz.* Margaret, who *m.* Saher de Quincy, afterwards Earl of Winchester."

p. 50, line 16; *after* "coheir," *add this as a note* "Mary, the other coheir, *m.* the Hon. Thomas Sydney."

" line 16; *for* "REEVES, of Thwates co. Suffolk," *read* "REEVES, 2d Bart., of Thwaite, co. Suffolk, by Margaret, sister of Sir Richard ONSLOW, Bart."

" line 17: *after* "1705," *add* "His widow *m.* May 1709 John SHEPPARD, of Campsey Ash, co. Suffolk."

p. 68, line 2; *for* "VII. 1672," *read* "VII. 1675"; line 6; *for* "*cr.* 1673," *read* "*cr.* 1675."

p. 70, line 38; *for* "s.p.," *read* "s.p.m."

p. 71, last line; *after* "London," *insert* "Admon. Nov. 1857."

p. 75, line 31; *after* "1718," *insert* "and *bap.* 22 at St. Martin's in the fields."

p. 78, line 19; *after* "He *m.*," *insert* "15 Dec. 1766, at St. Giles in the fields."

p. 93, line 17; *for* "b. 1516," *read* "b. 11 March 1516, at Bath place."

" line 19; *for* "before 14 Aug. 1545," *read* "8 March 1534," *and add this as a note thereto* "Lisle Papers vii, 18, in a letter of John Rookwood 'from the Courte, the 8th day of Marche,' the internal evidence whereof shews the year to be 1534. See hist. appendix to Miss E. S. Holt's *Harvest of Yesterday*."

p. 94, line 18; *for* "(CLINTON)," *read* "(CLINTON, *alias* FIENNES)."
,, line 30; *after* "Sep. 1616," *insert* "and was *bur.* at Tattershall."
p. 95, note "a," *insert at end.* "The way in which the Clinton family clung to the name of Fiennes, or Fynes, is illustrated by the following burial entries at Tattershall (see "N. and Q.," 5th S., iv, 168), 1615 Sep. 20, "The Rt. Hon. Henry *Fynes*, Knt, Lord Clinton and Say, Earl of Lincoln"; 1618 Jan. 15, "The Right Hon. Thomas *Fynes*, Earl of Lincoln; " 1618 Jan. 7, Katharine *Fynes*, da. of Thomas, Earl of Lincoln."
p. 96. *Add this note to the 7th Earl.* "It appears from Oliphant's 'Jacobite Lairds of Gask' that Lord Lincoln, 'with only £500 per annum,' having been mentioned as one of 'the poor quality in England' to 'Lord Torrington.' [*Query* the Earl of Torrington ?], who hated his heir at law, that Lord (tho' he had never seen him) left him an estate of £6,000 a year."
p. 99, line 18; *for* "Sir Robert Stuart, of Lorn," *read* "Robert (STEWART), 1st LORD LORN [S.]"
p. 104, lines 3 and 4; *for* "JEFFERIES of Shillingley," *read* "Jeffrey of Chidingley."
,, lines 38 and 39; *dele* "widow of the Hon. George Berkeley"; *for* "da.," *read* "2d and yst. da.," *add to* "coheir," *this as a note* "Elizabeth, the eldest da. and coheir *m.* George, Earl Berkeley."
,, line 40; *for* "PELLIT," *read* "PETTIT."
p. 108, line 16; *to* "forfeited" *add this as a note* "See vol. iii, p. 192, note 'a,' *sub* 'Duffus,' for a list of the peerages forfeited in the rising of 1715."
p. 124, line 9; *after* "widow," *insert* "who was *bap.* 21 July 1777, at Chicheley, Bucks"; *for* "69, and was *bur.*," *read* "69, at Norbiton Hall, and was *bur.* 24."
p. 141, line 6; *to* "1872" *add this note.* He is the *Lord Eskdale* in Disraeli's novel of *Coningsby* [1844]. See p. 307, note "a," *sub* "Mexborough."
p. 149, line 22; *to* "firstly" *add this as a note* "See *N. and Q.* 3d S., viii. 48, as to a supposed first wife who *d.* at Farnham, 1792-93, leaving an infant, 'Mary Kerr Hart,' a Poetess."
p. 157, line 17; *for* "*Taaffe*, and *d.* Oct. 1710, aged 37," *read* "*Taaffe* (who *d.* 15 Oct. 1730, aged 60) and *d.* Oct. 1710, or 1711, aged 37; M.I. at Duleek." *Add as note thereto.* "See *N. and Q.*, 5th S, ii. 65."
p. 167, line 13; *for* "1840," *read* "1840-93."
,, line 22; *after* "service," *insert* "da. of John JENKINS."
p. 178, line 1; *after* "blood" *add this note.* "See '*Genealogist*' N.S., vol. ix. p. 203, *sub.* 'the Earldom of Kildare' for some able remarks of Mr. J. Horace Round, as to this 'restoration,' or rather new creation."
,, line 17; *after* "s.p.a." *add* "at his house in St. Olave's, Hart Street, London."
p. 187, note "a"; *insert at end.* "Either he, or George Smythe, afterwards the 7th Viscount Strangford [I.] is supposed to be *Coningsby* [himself] in Disraeli's novel of *Coningsby* [1844]. See p. 307, note 'a,' *sub.* 'Mexborough.'"
p. 192, note "e"; *insert at end.* "Dr. Doran, however, in '*Their Majesties' servants*' (vol. i, p. 345) rejects the theory that the poet, Savage, was son of this Countess." See *N. and Q.*, 8th S., iv, 111.
p. 193, *add this note to the second Earl.* "He is grouped with other dull sons of distinguished Sires (all these "Sires" being curiously enough, Lord Chancellors) by Pope (in the "Dunciad") as below.

* * * "Great C[owper], H[arcourt], P[arker], K[ing],
Why all your toils ? Your *sons* have learn'd to sing
How quick ambition hastes to ridicule—
The Sire is made a Peer, the Son a Fool." [See "*N. and Q.*," 8th S., iv. 24.]

p. 196, line 23; *for* "Cromar," *read* "Cromer."
p. 219, note "b," line 3. *After* "Marre" *insert.* "The Earldom of Moray [S] also was therein attributed to him as well as to his father, Gillocher."
p. 220, line 21; *for* "*m.*" read "*m.* not earlier than 1292."
p. 221, line 28; *to* "Earl of Douglas and Mar," *add this note,* "An article, by Mr. J. Horace Round, on *the Earldoms of Douglas and Mar*, is announced for the forthcoming number (Oct. 1893) of *the Genealogist.*"
p. 224, note "c." *In pedigree, under* "Sir Edward Keith, of Lynton," *for* "*d.* 1347," *read* "*d.* 1350."
p. 230, note "d"; line 1; *for* "John (Erskine," *read* "John (Erskine), Lord Erskine."

p. 245, line 2; *for* "1325," *read* "1295."
" line 4; *after* "1306," *insert.* "He was sum. to Parl. from 22 Feb. 1305/6 to 3 Dec. 1326, the writs having the addition of the words 'de Wigmore.'"
p. 245, line 26; *after* "Ed. III," *insert.* "By this reversal he became, also, entitled to the Barony of Mortimer, cr. by the writ of 1295."
p. 252, line 35; *to* "28 June 1650," *add this note.* "This baptism is also registered at Musbury, co. Devon, the date there given being 26 *May*, 1650. See *N. and Q.*, 8th S., iv, 62."
p. 275, line 27; *for* "6th," *read* "5th."
" line 34; *to* "Lord Maxwell," *add this note.* "See p. 383, note 'f,' *sub* 'Morton,' as to the right both of himself and his two sons (1581-1620) to be Earls of Morton under the creation of 1581, until the date of the creation (in substitution thereof) of the Earldom of Nithsdale in 1620."
p. 280, line 17; *for* "of (—) HAMILTON," *read* "of Mark HAMILTON."
" line 18; *after* "the army," *insert* "by Gertrude, his wife, a native of Holland," *and add this note.* "The admon. of this Gertrude (who *d.* 31 Dec. 1729) was granted to 'Stephen Browne, Esq.,' her husband, 10 Oct. 1732. Revocation thereof was demanded by her da., Lady Mayo, in Oct. 1752, on the ground that when Mr. Browne married the said Gertrude (in or soon after Nov. 1720, at Jamaica) he was already married to one Eleanor Cutts. Lady Mayo's legitimacy was questioned, but was established in 1757. Mr. Browne proved before the Court of Delegates, in 1760, that Lady Mayo had lived with him and her mother (acknowledging their marriage) till 4 March 1727, when she *m.* Mark Hamilton."
p. 315, line 33; for "living 1893," *read* "*d.* 13 Aug. 1893, aged 89, at Ely House, Richmond, Surrey." Will pr. at £67,979.
p. 318, line 21; *to* "Baron Minshull," *add this note.* "A Viscountcy, that of MINSHULL OF LEMPSTER [i.e., Leominster] co. Hereford, is also attributed to him. See Lipscomb's 'Bucks,' where 'the Viscount' is said to have *d* in 1673, and see also *N. and Q.*, 4th S., xi, 457. The pedigree, however, is somewhat confused."
p. 343, line 24; *after* "who was," *insert* "*b.* 22 Feb. 1654 and was."
p. 410, line 38; *to* "MOWBRAY," *add this note*;—The validity of the writ of 1283 (or indeed of any other writ before 1295) as the origin of an hereditary Barony (alluded to on p. 411, note "b") is a grave question. "*The determination of the Mowbray abeyance*" is fully dealt with in an article, of that name, about to appear from the pen of Mr. J. Horace Round, criticising the decision of the Committee for privileges.
p. 411, note "b"; *add thereto.* "See for fuller details an article on *The Peerage* in a forthcoming *Quarterly Review.*"

THE FOLLOWING PEERAGES

(in the earlier letters of the alphabet) having been created in or after July 1885, during the progress of this work and thus incapable of being inserted alphabetically therein, are relegated (excepting when otherwise stated) to the appendix in the 8th and last volume, *viz.*—

ADDINGTON of Addington, co. Buckingham, Barony (*Hubbard*), *cr.* 22 July 1887.
AMHERST OF HACKNEY, co. London, Barony (*Tyssen-Amherst*), *cr.* 26 Aug. 1892.
*ANCASTER, Earldom, *cr.* 1892, see WILLOUGHBY DE ERESBY, Barony.
ARMSTRONG OF CRAGSIDE, co. Northumberland, Barony (*Armstrong*), *cr.* 6 July 1887.
ASHBOURNE of Ashbourne, co. Meath, Barony (*Gibson*), *cr.* 4 July 1885.
ASHCOMBE OF DORKING, co. Surrey, AND OF BODIAM CASTLE, co. Sussex, Barony (*Cubitt*), *cr.* 22 Aug. 1892.
*ATHLONE, Earldom, *cr.* 1890, with the Dukedom of CLARENCE AND AVONDALE, which see.
BASING OF BASING BYFLETE AND OF HODINGTON, both in co. Southampton, Barony (SCLATER-BOOTH), *cr.* 7 July, 1887.
BATTERSEA of Battersea, co. London and of Overstrand, co. Norfolk, Barony (*Flower*), *cr.* 5 Sep. 1892.
BLYTHSWOOD of Blythswood, co. Renfrew, Barony (*Campbell*), *cr.* 24 Aug. 1892.
BOWEN OF COLWOOD, co. Sussex, Barony for life (*Bowen*), *cr.* Sep. 1893.
CLARENCE AND AVONDALE, Dukedom, as also the EARLDOM OF ATHLONE (H.R.H. Prince *Albert-Victor-Christian-Edward*), *cr.* 24 May 1890; *ex.* 14 Jan. 1892.

*CRANBROOK, Earldom, *cr.* 1892 ; see CRANBROOK, Viscountcy.
CRAWSHAW OF CRAWSHAW, co. Lancaster, AND OF WHATTON, co. Leicester, Barony (*Brooks*), *cr.* 25 Aug. 1892.
CROMER of Cromer, co. Norfolk, Barony (*Baring*), *cr.* 15 June 1892.
DUNLEATH OF BALLYWALTER PARK, co. Down, Barony (*Mulholland*), *cr.* 29 Aug. 1892.
FARRER OF ABINGER, co. Surrey, Barony (*Farrer*), *cr.* June 1893.
HAMBLEDEN of Hambleden, co. Buckingham, Viscountcy (*Smith*), *cr.* 11 Nov. 1891.
HAWKESBURY OF HASELBEACH, co. Northampton, AND OF OLLERTON, Sherwood forest, co. Nottingham, Barony (*Foljambe*), *cr.* June 1893.
HOOD OF AVALON, co. Somerset, Barony (*Hood*), *cr.* 23 Feb. 1892.
*INVERNESS, Earldom, *cr.* 1892, with the DUKEDOM OF YORK, which see.
*KELHEAD of Kelhead, co. Dumfries, Barony (*Douglas*), *cr.* June 1893 ; see under QUEENSBERRY, Marquessate [S.]
KELVIN OF LARGS, co. Ayr, Barony (*Thomson*), *cr.* 23 Feb. 1892.
*KILLARNEY, Barony, *cr.* 1892, with the DUKEDOM OF YORK, which see.
KNIGHTLEY OF FAWSLEY, co. Northampton, Barony (*Knightley*), *cr.* 23 Aug. 1892.

October, 1893.

---

* Described under another title.

APPENDIX TO VOLUME.

List of Subscribers to the Complete Peerage.

Allen, E. G., 28, Henrietta Street, London
Amphlett, John, Clent, Stonebridge
Annesley, Major-General, The New Club, Edinburgh
Antrobus, Rev. Fred., The Oratory, South Kensington, S.W.
Armytage, Geo. J., F.S.A., Clifton Woodhead, Brighouse
Arnold, C. T., 29, Whitehall Place, S.W.
Astley, John, 3, Queen's Road, Coventry
Assheton, Ralph, Downham Hall, Clitheroe (3)
Athill, Charles H., Richmond Herald, Coll. of Arms, E.C.
Bacchus, Mrs. Henry, The Manor House, Lillington, Leamington
Bain, James, 1, Haymarket, S.W.
Batten, John, Aldon, Yeovil
Bell, Geo. & Sons, Covent Garden, London
Bigge, Rev. H. J., Cottingham, near Uppingham
Birch, Rev. W. M., The Vicarage, Ashburton
Boase, Charles W., Exeter College, Oxford
Boase, Frederick, 36, James Street, Buckingham Gate
Bools, Wm. Edward, 7, Cornhill, E.C.
Bridgeman, Hon. and Rev. John, R.O., Frognal, Torquay
Brooking-Rowe, J., F.S.A., Clifton Woodhead, Brighouse
Carington, R. Smith, St. Cloud, near Worcester
Carmichael, Sir T. D. Gibson, Bart., Castlecraig, Dolphinston, N.B.
Chamberlaine, W. H. Keevil, Trowbridge, Wilts
Clements, H. J. B., Ashfield Lodge, Cootehill, Cavan
Colby, Rev. F. T., D.D., Litton Cheney, Dorchester, Dorset
Condor, Edward, jun., Langston House, Charlbury, Chadlington
Coote, C. John, 9, Marlborough Buildings, Bath
Cornish, J. E., 16, St. Ann's Square, Manchester
Crawford, The Earl of, 2, Cavendish Square, W.
Cust, Lady Elizabeth, 13, Eccleston Square, London
Davison, R. J. W., The Grammar School, Ilminster
Devon and Exeter Institution, The Close, Exeter
Duckett, Sir G. F. Bart., Newington, Wallingford
Farewell, W., Westwood, Lansdown, Bath

Foster, H., Tolworth Hall, Surrey
Foster, Joseph, 21, Boundary Road, N.W.
Fox, Charles Henry, The Beeches, Brislington, Bristol
Gatty, A. Scott, York Herald, College of Arms, E.C.
Gibbs, Antony, Tyntesfield, Bristol
Gibbs, Henry Hucks, St. Dunstan's, Regent's Park, London
Gibbs, H. Martin, Barrow Court, Flax Bourton, Somerset
Gibbs, Rev. J. Lomax, The Rectory, Clyst St. George, Devon
Gibbs, Rev. K. F., Aldenham Vicarage, Watford, Herts
Gough, H. S., Sandcroft, Redhill, Surrey
Graves, R. E., British Museum, W.C. (2)
Gray, H. L., Exeter
Grays Inn, Hon. Sec. of, Library, Grays Inn, London
Grazebrook, H. Sydney, Middleton Villa, Grove Park, Chiswick
Green and Sons, 18 and 20, St. Giles Street, Edinburgh
Greene, Major-General, 31, Boyken Street, Morristown, U.S.A.
Griffith, Rev. H. T., Smallburgh Rectory, Norwich
Hallen, Rev. R. W. Cornelius, Alloa, N.B.
Hardy, W. J., 21, Old Buildings, Lincolns Inn, W.C.
Harrison and Sons, 59, Pall Mall, London, S.W.
Haslewood, Rev. Dr., Chislet Vicarage, Canterbury
Hawkesbury, Lord, c/o Hatchard's, Piccadilly, W.
Head, Hugh Stanley, Buckingham, Old Shoreham, Sussex
Hibbert, Col. F. D., 4, Belgrave Place, Brighton
Hogg, S., 32, Charing Cross, S.W.
Holthouse, Edwin, 45, Weymouth Street, London, W.
Hovendon, R., F.S.A., Heathcote Park, Hill Road, Croydon
Howard, J. J., LL.D., Dartmouth Row, Blackheath
Hughes, H. R., Kinmel, Abergele, North Wales
Jewers, A. J., F.S.A., Wells, Somerset
Jessopp, Rev. A., D.D., Scarning, E. Dereham
Johnston, W. and A. K., London
Landon, Percival, Palheiro, Putney, S.W.
Law, Thos. G., Signet Library, Edinburgh
Layton, C. Miller, Shortlands, Castle Hill Avenue, Folkestone
Lea, J. Henry, 26, Gubyon Ave, Herne Hill, S.E.
Lindsay, Leonard C., Deer Park, Honiton
Lindsay, W.A., College of Arms, London, E.C.
Littledale, Mrs., 26, Cranley Gardens, South Kensington, S.W.
Long, Col. Wm., Woodlands, Congresbury, R.S.O.
Lyte, H. C. Maxwell, C.B., 3 Portman Square, W.
McGrath, Rev. J. R., Queen's College, Oxford
Maclean, Sir John, F.S.A., Glasbury House, Richmond Hill, Clifton, Bristol
Macray, Rev. W. D., Ducklington Rectory, Witney, Oxon.
Maddison, Rev. A. R., Vicar's Court, Lincoln.
Manning, Rev. C. R., Diss Rectory, Norfolk
Marshall, G. W., LL.D., Sarnesfield Court, Weobley, R.S.O.
Marsham, Hon. Robt., 5, Chesterfield Street, Mayfair, W.
Maskelyne, A. Story, Public Record Office, W.C., and 53, Rosetti Gardens Mansions, Chelsea (2)

Montgomerie, Fredk., 1, Cromwell Place, S.W.
Murray, Keith, 37, Cheniston Garden, Kensington, W.
New England Historic Genealogical Society, 18, Somerset Street, Boston, Mass., U.S.A.
Newman, S. A., Bridge Street, Walsall
Parker, Henry A., 1, Mercer Street, Cambridge, Massachussetts, U.S.A.
Penfold, Hugh, Rustington, Worthing
Pink, W. Duncombe, Leigh, Lancashire
Poynton, Rev. J. F., Kelston Rectory, Bath
Ramsay, Sir James H., Bart., Old House, Wimbledon
Reid, F. Nevile, Minori, Per Ravello, province of Salerno, Italy
Richardson, W. H., 2, Lansdowne Place, Russell Square, W.C.
Royce, Rev., David, Netherswell Vicarage, Stow-on-the-Wold, Gloucester
Rye, Walter, Frognal House, Hampstead, N.W.
Schomberg, Arthur, Seend, Melksham
Science and Art Department, London, S.W.
Seizco, L.D., 404, Willow Street, Syracuse, N.Y.U.S.A.
Shadwell, Walter H., 21, Nottingham Place, W.
Smith, J. Challoner, Probate Registry, Somerset House, London (2)
Smith, Mark, Alnwick
Southall, Miss, 73, Wellington Road, Edgbaston, Birmingham
Stevens, Henry and Son, 39, Great Russell Street, London, W.C.
Stoddart, A. R., Fishergate Villa, York
Strathmore, The Earl of, Glamis Castle, Glamis, N.B.
Stuart, G. B., Surgeon-Major, 7, Carlton Street, Edinburgh
Tempest, Sir Robert, Tong Hall, Drighlington, Bradford
Tenison, C. M., c/o Union Bank of Australia, Hobart, Tasmania
Thynne, F. J., 67, Eaton Place, London, S.W.
Trevanion, Hugh C., 3, Lowndes Square, London, S.W.
Trollope, Rev. Andrew, Edith Weston Rectory, Stamford
Verulam, The Earl of, Gorhambury, St. Albums
Vienna, I. H. Heraldic Society, c/o, J. Klemme, 1, Rosengasse, Vienna
Wade, Edward Fry, Axbridge, Somerset
Weldon, W. H., Windsor Herald, College of Arms, E.C.
Williams, Rev. Augustin, Todenham Rectory, Moulton-in-Marsh
Woods, Sir Albert W., K.C.M.G., Garter, College of Arms, E.C.
Woodward, Rev. John, F.S.A., Montrose, N.B.

October, 1893.

Notice as to the issue and price of the

Complete Peerage

OF

England, Scotland, Ireland, Great Britain

AND

The United Kingdom,

EXTANT, EXTINCT, OR DORMANT,

ALPHABETICALLY ARRANGED AND EDITED BY

G. E. C.

In 8 vols., 8vo.

Volumes I *to* V,

A. to **M.**

PRICE **(£7 7s. 0d,) 7 Guineas,**

Are now ready.

It is proposed to complete this work in three more volumes, to be issued annually at **£1 1s.** to Subscribers, which price will be raised to **£1 11s. 6d.** *after* publication. Vols. II, III, IV and V, can be had separately at **£1 11s. 6d.**; Vol. I. (of which only a few copies remain), at **£2 2s.**

Subscribers' names to be sent and all applications to be made to the Publishers,

WILLIAM POLLARD & CO., PRINTERS,

EXETER.

OCT., 1893.

The Episcopal Registers

OF THE

Diocese of Exeter,

BY THE

REV. F. C. HINGESTON-RANDOLPH, M.A.,

Of Exeter College, Oxford,

Prebendary of Exeter and Rector of Ringmore.

I.

The Registers of **Bishop Walter Bronescombe** (A.D. 1257—1280), and **Bishop Peter Quivil** (A.D. 1280—1291), with some Records of the Episcopate of **Bishop Thomas de Bytton** (A.D. 1292—1307), and the Taxation of Pope Nicholas IV. (Diocese of Exeter); with three *facsimiles;* pp. xxviii, 498. Price 15s.

II.

The Register of **Bishop Walter de Stapeldon** (A.D. 1307—1326), with a *facsimile;* pp. xxxiv, 584. Price (the Subscription List being now closed), 21s.

III.

The Register of **Bishop John de Grandisson** (A.D. 1327—1369), with some Records of Bishop James de Berkeley (A.D. 1327), and of the Administration of the Diocese *Sede Vacante* (A.D. 1326-7). Part I. (about 600 pages), with a *facsimile*, is in the Press. Price to Subscribers, 15s.; after publication, 21s.

IV.

The Registers of **Bishop Edmund de Stafford** (A.D. 1395—1419); pp. xvj., 485. This volume, the first published, was issued in 1886. Only a few copies remain unsold—price 21s.

SERIAL PUBLICATIONS.

THE ARCHÆOLOGICAL JOURNAL, published under the direction of the Council of the Royal Archæological Institute of Great Britain and Ireland, for the encouragement and prosecution of researches into the Arts and Monuments of the Early and Middle Ages. Published in March, June, September and December.

TRANSACTIONS of the Exeter Diocesan Architectural Society. Published in large 4to illustrated vols., at intervals. The late Canon Ellacombe's "Bells of the Church, and other important works on Campanology appeared in the first instance, in the publications of this Society.

THE VISITATIONS OF THE COUNTY OF DEVON. From the Harleian "MSS." never before published, and continued, where possible, to the present day. Price 5s. each part. Edited by LIEUTENANT-COLONEL VIVIAN. Demy 4to. Subscribers' names received by William Pollard & Co., Printers, Exeter.

GENEALOGY AND FAMILY HISTORY.

THE COMPLETE PEERAGE OF ENGLAND, SCOTLAND, IRELAND, Great Britain, and the United Kingdom, extant, extinct, and dormant; alphabetically arranged and edited by G.E.C. Vols. I. to V., A. to M., now ready. See two pages back.

ANTIQUARIAN WORKS.

THE STORY OF THE DRAMA IN EXETER during its best period, 1787 to 1823, with reminiscences of Edmund Kean, by WILLIAM COTTON, F.S.A., author of "An Elizabethan Guild," &c., with portrait and facsimiles. Handsomely bound, cloth; price 2s. 6d.

A CARTULARY OF WINCHCOMBE ABBEY, containing 840 Papal Bulls, Charters granting lands to the Abbey, and divers other records extending from the Charter of Knulf, the founder, to A.D. 1422, 2 vols., royal 8vo., half-bound Roxburgh. For Subscribers only. Edition limited to 250 small, and 20 large paper copies. Edited by the REV. DAVID ROYCE, M.A. Subscription per copy, large paper, 15s., small paper, 10s. (VOL. II. *in the Press.*)

This book is a preservation photocopy
produced on Weyerhaeuser acid free
Cougar Opaque 50# book weight paper,
which meets the requirements of
ANSI/NISO Z39.48-1992 (permanence of paper)

Preservation photocopying and binding
by
Acme Bookbinding
Charlestown, Massachusetts
1994

CPSIA information can be obtained
at www.ICGtesting.com
Printed in the USA
LVHW080147200221
679374LV00003B/42